Almanac of American Education

2013

Almanac of American Education 2013

Edited by Deirdre A. Gaquin
and Gwenavere W. Dunn

Lanham, MD

Published in the United States of America
by Bernan Press, a wholly owned subsidiary of
The Rowman & Littlefield Publishing Group, Inc.
4501 Forbes Boulevard, Suite 200
Lanham, Maryland 20706

Bernan Press
800-865-3457
customercare@bernan.com
www.bernan.com

ISBN: 978-1-59888-601-6
e-ISBN: 978-1-59888-602-3

∞™ The paper used in this publication meets the minimum requirements of American National Standard for Information Sciences—Permanence of Paper for Printed Library Materials, ANSI/NISO Z39.48-1992.
Manufactured in the United States of America.

Contents

Tables

PART A—NATIONAL EDUCATION STATISTICS

ENROLLMENT TABLES

HISTORICAL ENROLLMENT TABLES

ATTAINMENT TABLES

HISTORICAL ATTAINMENT TABLES

POSTSECONDARY EDUCATION TABLES

PART B—REGION AND STATE EDUCATION STATISTICS

PART C—COUNTY EDUCATION STATISTICS

Figures

PART A—NATIONAL EDUCATION STATISTICS

PART B—REGION AND STATE EDUCATION STATISTICS

PART C—COUNTY EDUCATION STATISTICS

Preface

The Almanac of American Education serves as a guide to understanding and comparing the quality of education at the national, state, and county levels. Compiled from sources such as the U.S. Census Bureau and the National Center for Education Statistics (NCES), *The Almanac* contains historical and current data, insightful analysis, and useful graphics that paint a compelling picture of the state of education in the United States.

The Almanac is organized into three sections: Part A—National Education Statistics; Part B—Region and State Education Statistics; and Part C—County Education Statistics. Most of the data presented in Part A are no longer available in print form from the Census Bureau. Additional tables in Part A are excerpted from the *Digest of Education Statistics* from the NCES, providing an overview of higher education in the United States. The data in Parts B and C have been specially tabulated for this publication from data obtained from the NCES, the Census Bureau, and other sources.

The Almanac's contents and coverage allow users to answer—and ask—important questions about education, including:

- What are the nationwide trends in earnings by educational attainment level?
- Is the earnings gap between high school graduates and college graduates growing or shrinking?
- Which states have the highest and lowest high school dropout rates?
- Which states have the largest county-to-county variation in student-teacher ratios?
- Is there a relationship between student poverty rates and county-level expenditures per student?

The data in this volume meet the publication standards of the federal statistical agencies and the few nongovernmental organizations from which they were obtained. Every effort has been made to select accurate, meaningful, and useful data. All statistical data are subject to error arising from sampling variability, reporting errors, incomplete coverage, imputation, and other causes. The responsibility of the editors and publisher of this volume is limited to reasonable care in the reproduction and presentation of data obtained from established sources.

Deirdre A. Gaquin edited this edition of *The Almanac of American Education*. Ms. Gaquin has been a data use consultant to private organizations, government agencies, and universities for more than 30 years. Before that, she was Director of Data Access Services at Data Use & Access Laboratories, a pioneer in private sector distribution of federal statistical data. A former President of the Association of Public Data Users, Ms. Gaquin has served on numerous boards, panels, and task forces concerned with federal statistical data and has worked on five decennial censuses. She holds a Master of Urban Planning (MUP) degree from Hunter College. Ms. Gaquin is also an editor of Bernan Press's *The Who, What, and Where of America: Understanding the American Community Survey*; *Places, Towns and Townships*; *County and City Extra*; and *Congressional District Atlas*.

Gwenavere W. Dunn is a research editor with Bernan Press. She holds a Master of Science degree in Human Resource Management from Trinity Washington University. She is a former senior editor with the Board of Governors of the Federal Reserve System and was managing editor of the Board's *Federal Reserve Bulletin*. She is the assistant editor of *The Who, What, and Where of America: Understanding the American Community Survey;* and editor of *Crime in the United States* and *Employment, Hours, and Earnings;* all published by Bernan Press.

Much appreciation is due to the federal agency personnel who prepared the original data and generously responded to our requests for assistance.

PART A

NATIONAL EDUCATION STATISTICS

PART A—NATIONAL EDUCATION STATISTICS

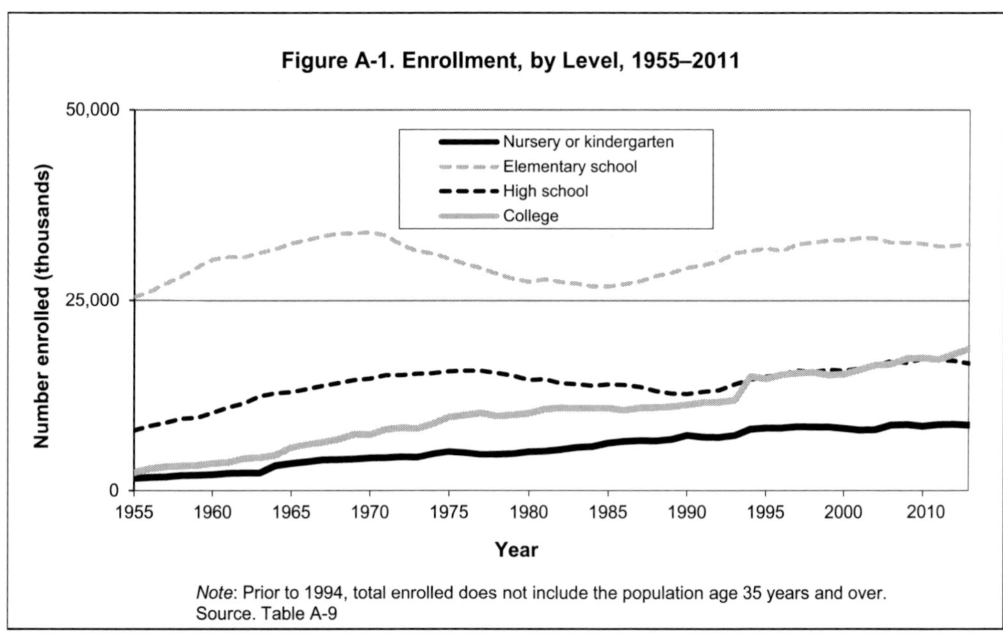

More than 79 million people were enrolled in school in 2011. This enrollment reflected steady increases of about one percent per year during the past decade, after even larger increases during the 1990s. Total enrollment had decreased in the 1980s but 1991 had the highest level yet measured for the nation, and it has continued to increase since then. Most of the increase in the twenty-first century has been in college enrollment. Elementary school enrollment has remained between 32 and 33 million through the decade, similar to the baby boom levels of the 1960s but never quite reaching the nearly 34 million elementary school enrollees of 1970. College enrollment in 2011, however, at a little more than 20 million, was more than double the levels of the 1970s. (Table A-9)

In 2011, 26.9 percent of people age 3 years and over were enrolled in school. For the population 3 to 34 years old, 6.9 percent were enrolled in nursery school or kindergarten, and 24.6 percent were enrolled in elementary school. Among the population 18 to 24 years old, 48.7 percent were enrolled in school, as were 14.8 percent of 25 to 29 year olds. The proportion of 35 to 44 year olds enrolled in school remained slightly above 4 percent, a level first reached in 2008. (Table A-1)

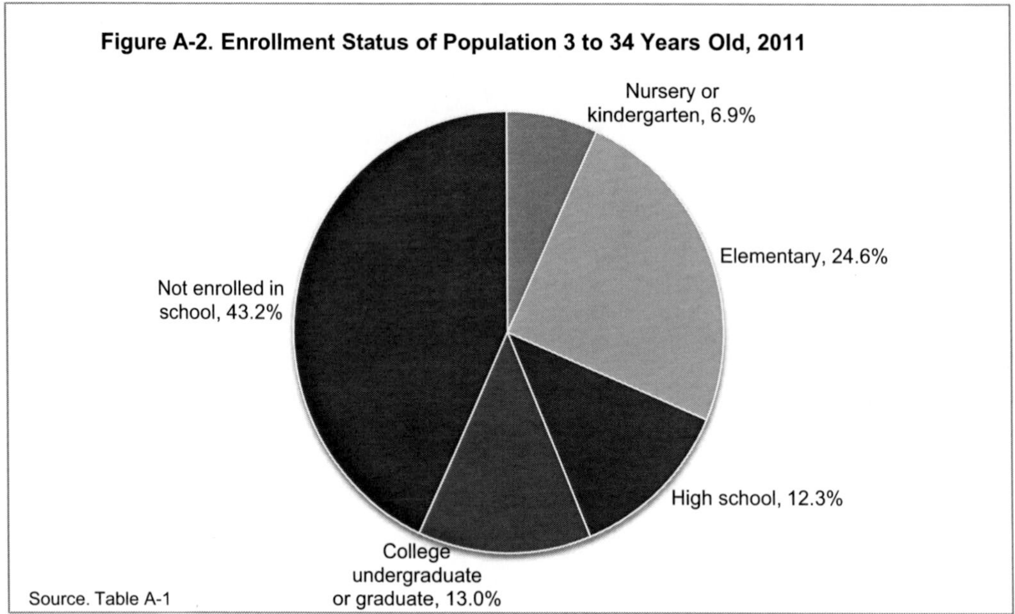

In 2011, 52.4 percent of all 3- and 4-year-olds were enrolled in nursery school or kindergarten, the lowest proportion since 2001. Approximately 66.3 percent of children from families with incomes of higher than $75,000 were enrolled in nursery school or kindergarten, while nearly 47 percent of 3- and 4-year-olds from families with incomes of lower than $20,000 attended school. Private school enrollment declined as grade level increased. Although 41 percent of all nursery school students were enrolled in private school in 2011, only 8.8 percent of elementary school students and 7.1 percent of high school students were enrolled in private schools that year. Nearly 21 percent of college students were enrolled in private institutions. (Tables A-3, A-9, and A-10)

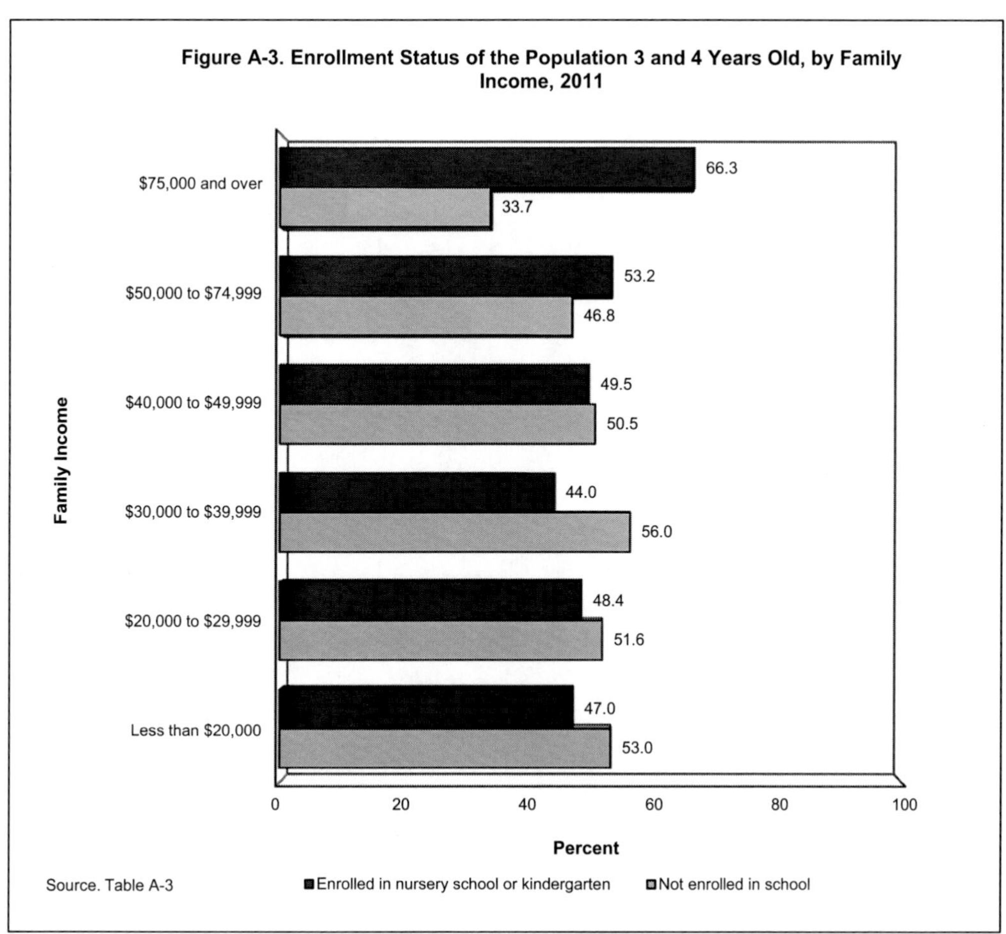

In 2011, more than 20 million students 15 years old and over were enrolled in colleges and universities. More than 16 million of them were undergraduates. Those attending four-year colleges were far more likely to be full-time students (83 percent) than those attending 2-year colleges (65 percent). Younger students continued to be more likely to attend school full-time, although the percentage of students 35 years old and over attending school full-time has increased considerably. Among students 15 to 24 years old, 85.4 percent were enrolled full-time, while 42.4 percent of students 35 years old and over were enrolled full-time. The number of students 35 and over enrolled full-time has increased almost 10 percentage points since 2008. Among graduate students, 55.5 percent were full-time students in 2010. Until 2000, part-time students outnumbered full-time students in graduate programs, but the proportion of full-time students has been increasing in the past decade. (Table A-5, A-16, and A-34)

Figure A-4. Percent Distribution of Undergraduate Students, by Type of School and Age, 2011

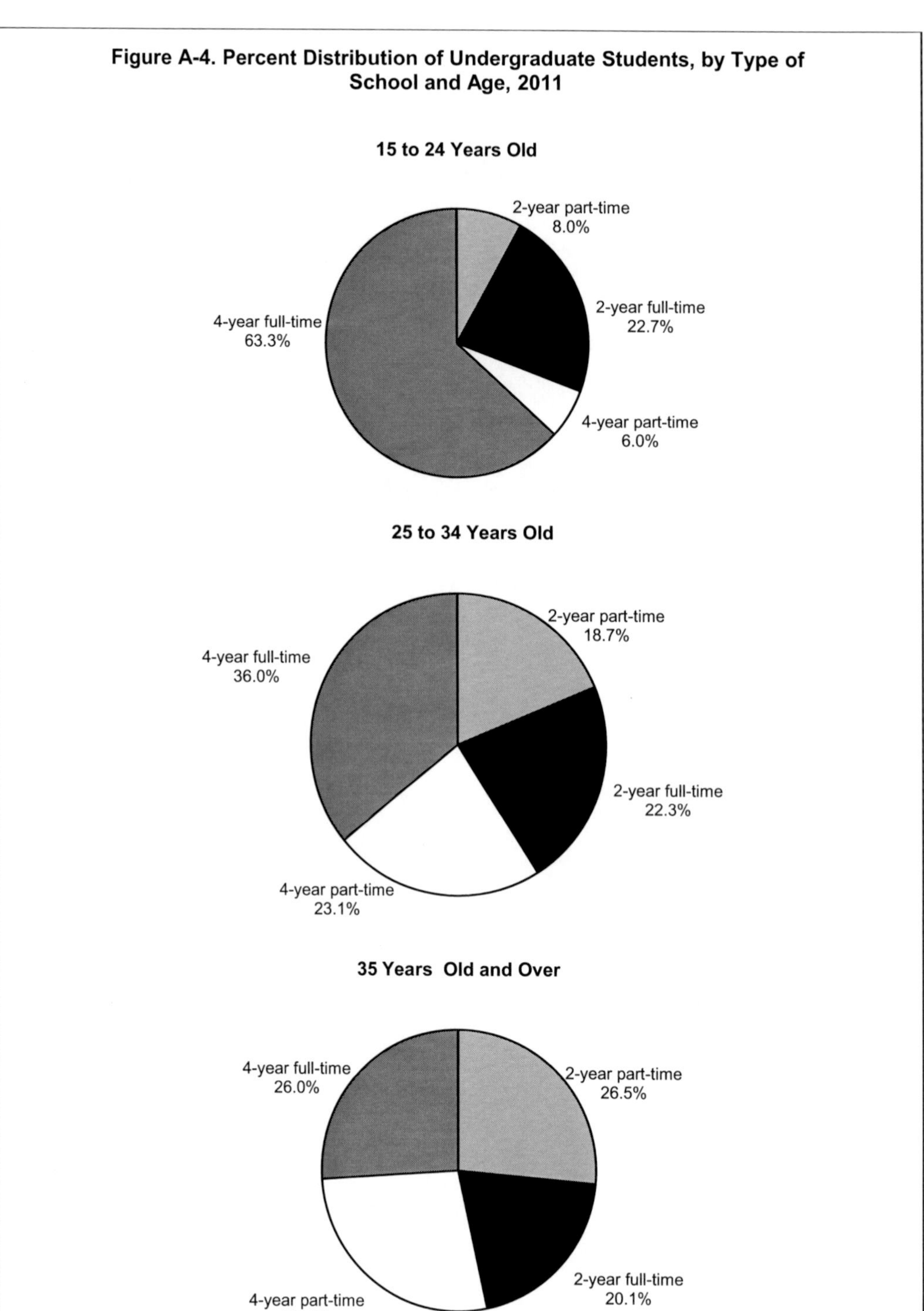

Sources. Tables A-3 and A-9

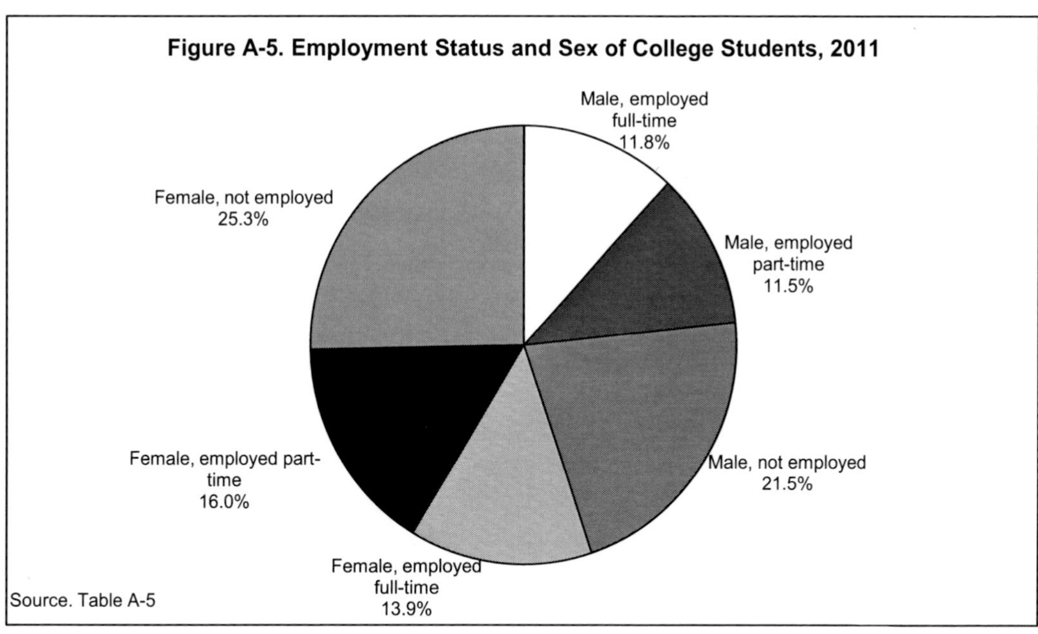

Figure A-5. Employment Status and Sex of College Students, 2011

In 2011, women made up 55.2 percent of all college students, a slight decrease in percentage from recent years. In contrast, less than 35 percent of all college students in 1960 were women. By the end of the 1970s, the proportions of men and women were equal; since then, women's share has steadily increased, staying above 55 percent in most years since the early 1990s and reaching a high of 56.9 percent in 2005. The greatest disparity between the number of male and female college students was among Black students—61.5 percent were women. Among Hispanic college students, 51.3 percent were women, making it the race or ethnic group with the most equal enrollment levels for males and females. Asian students had a slightly higher proportion of women at 52.9 percent. Among graduate students, women accounted for 57.1 percent of enrollment in 2011. (Tables A-15 and A-16)

In 2011, 52.1 percent of male college students were employed—either full- or part-time—and 54.2 percent of female college students were employed. Among college students who are also enrolled in vocational courses, 56.3 percent were employed, compared with 53.2 percent for all college students. (Table A-6)

Over the past 30 years, total college enrollment has gradually increased. For Blacks and Hispanics, this increase was substantial. In 1981, 1.1 million Black students were enrolled in college. By 2008, this number had jumped to almost 2.5 million, and by 2011, the number had jumped another half million, to 3.1 million. For Hispanics, the increase was even more dramatic, partly reflecting the growth in the Hispanic population during those years. From 1981 to 2008, enrollment for Hispanics more than quadrupled, with numbers rising from 510,000 to nearly 2.2 million, and in 2011, it had increased to almost 3 million. During this same time period, enrollment for Whites increased from 9.1 million college students to 15.4 million. (Table A-9)

Figure A-6. Percent of High School Dropouts Among the Population Age 18 to 24 Years, by Race and Hispanic Origin, 1970–2011

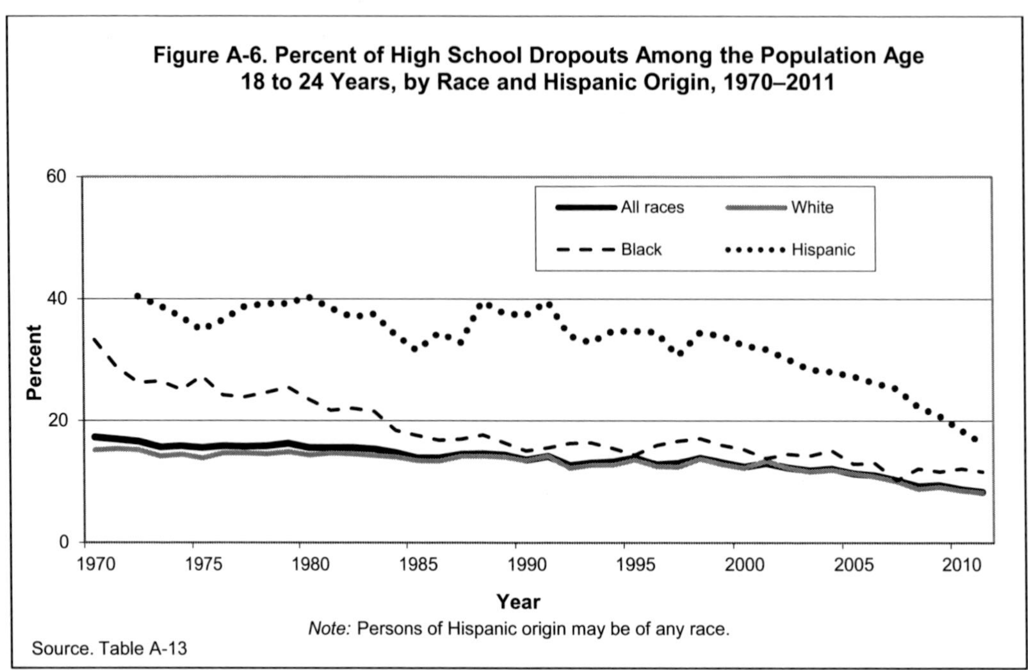

Note: Persons of Hispanic origin may be of any race.

Source. Table A-13

The high school dropout rate has continually declined between 1970 and 2011. In 1970, slightly more than 17 percent of the population between the ages of 18 and 24 years had dropped out of high school. By 2011, that rate had declined to just more than 8 percent. Although the proportion of dropouts has declined for all races, it declined most dramatically for Blacks. In 1970, 33 percent of Blacks between the ages of 18 and 24 years were high school dropouts. By 2011, that rate had dropped to 8.9 percent. During that same period, the dropout rate for Whites was 15.2 percent in 1970, and by 2011 the rate had dropped to 8.2 percent. Hispanics continue to have the highest dropout rate for the 18- to 24-year-old population, at 16.3 percent in 2011. The dropout rate is lowest among Asians, at 5.2 percent. (Table A-13)

In 2011, the high school dropout rate for grades 10 to 12 was 3.2 percent. This rate has been around 3 percent for most of the past decade after a steady decline from 5 or 6 percent throughout the 1970s and 1980s. In addition, in 2008 the dropout rate for women (3.8 percent) was higher than the rate for men (2.9 percent). By 2011 the rate had reversed back to the previous trend in which the female dropout rate (2.9 percent) was lower than the rate for males (3.4 percent). When compared by grade, the dropout rate for grade 10 was 1.2 percent, compared with 1.9 percent for grade 11 and 7.2 percent for grade 12. (Table A-12)

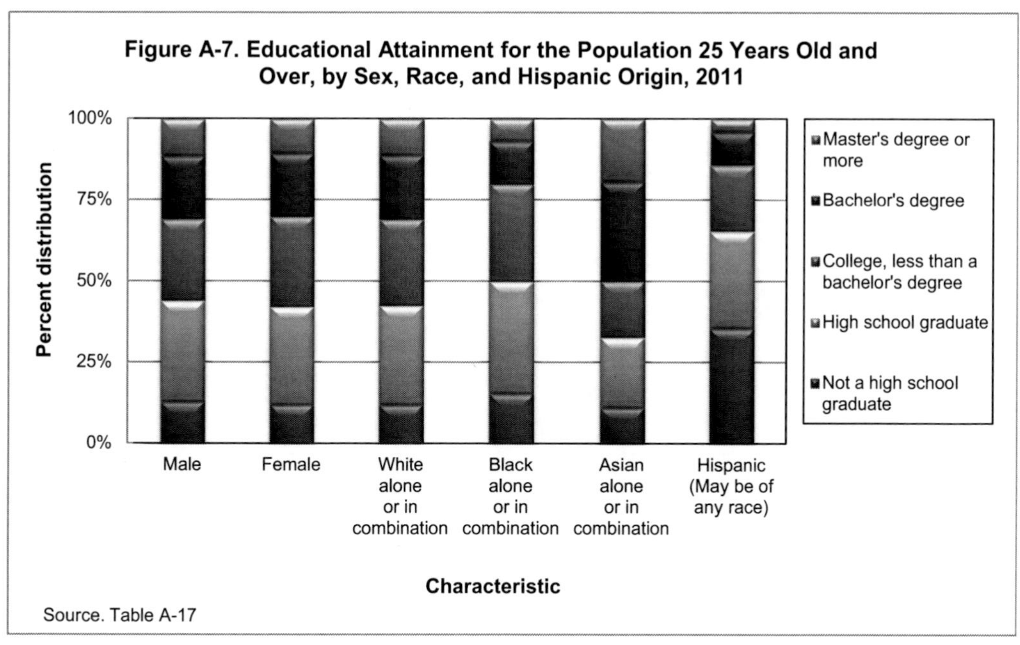

In 2011, almost 88 percent of Americans 25 years old and over were high school graduates and 30.4 percent held a bachelor's degree or higher. This proportion marked an increase of 13 percentage points from the 1980 college attainment levels, reflecting steady increases through the entire 30-year period. For people age 25 to 34 years, 89 percent had a high school diploma or higher and 33 percent held a bachelor's degree or higher. Women 25 years of age and over had slightly higher rates of high school attainment, while men had slightly higher rates of college attainment. Among race and ethnic groups in 2011, Asians had the highest high school graduation rate (88.9 percent), followed by Whites (88.0 percent), Blacks (84.6 percent), and Hispanics (64.3 percent). Nearly half (49.9 percent) of Asians had graduated from college, followed by Whites (30.9 percent), Blacks (20.1 percent), and Hispanics (14.1 percent). (Tables A-17, A-18, and A-26)

More than 35 percent of civilians over 25 years of age in the labor force held a bachelor's degree or more, a proportion higher than that of the general population in 2011. About ten percent of these civilians had not graduated from high school, compared with 13.9 percent of all people over 25 years of age. (Table A-21)

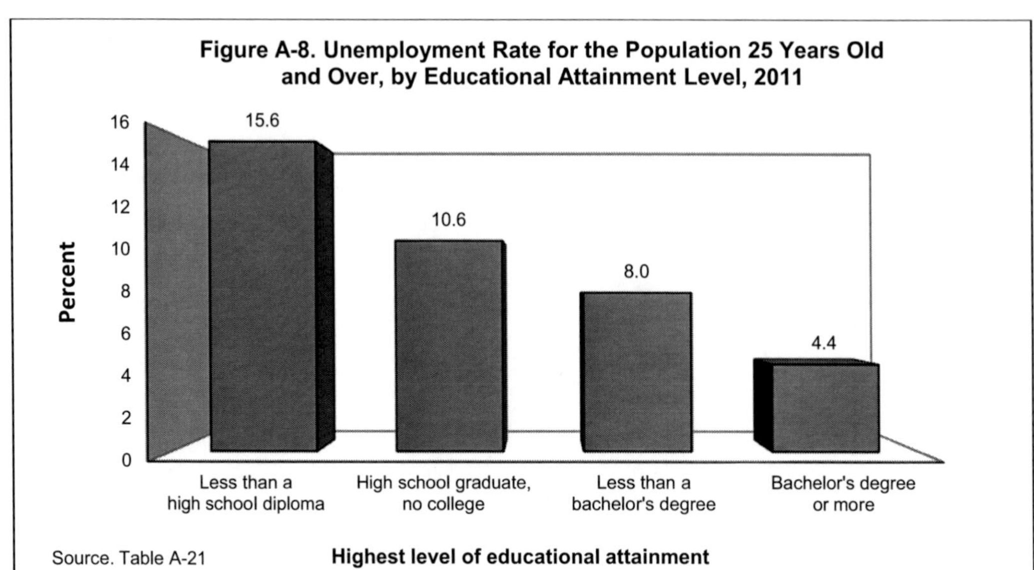

The more education a person had obtained, the less likely he or she was to be unemployed. The rate for the population age 25 and over with less than a high school diploma, was 15.7 percent in 2011. The unemployment rate for people with a bachelor's degree or more was only 4.4 percent. The overall unemployment rate in 2011 was 8.1 percent. The unemployment rate for men (9.1) was higher than that of women (7.1). In 2011, the labor force participation rate was 72.7 percent for men, but only 59.2 percent for women. (Table A-21)

For persons 25 years old and over, professional and related occupations provided the most jobs. This category includes teachers, lawyers, scientists, artists, doctors, nurses, and other healthcare professionals. More than 71 percent of those employed in professional and related occupations held a bachelor's degree or more. In contrast, less than 9 percent of those employed in farming, forestry and fishing, construction, maintenance, production, and transportation occupations had reached this level of educational attainment. Service occupations employed the highest number of people without a high school diploma (3.2 million). (Table A-22)

The educational and health services industry was the largest employer in the United States and employed more than 29.4 million people in 2011. More than half of the population in the education and health services industry held a bachelor's degree or higher (over 15 million), and more than 26 percent of workers in this field had a master's degree or higher. Mining was the smallest industry in terms of employment, with 664 thousand workers, with fewer than 150 thousand holding a bachelor's degree or higher. (Table A-23)

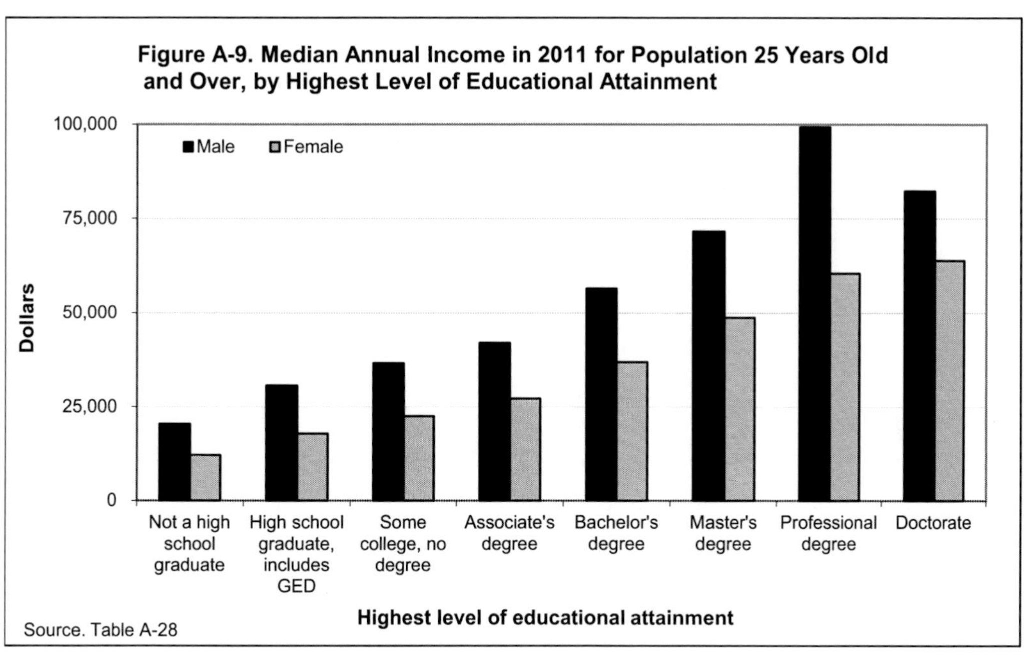

In 2011, the median income from all sources for men 25 years old and over was $37,653; for women it was $23,395, with half of the men or women earning more than this amount and half earning less. For those who attended but did not finish high school, the median income was $20,437 for men, and $12,193 for women. For high school graduates, including GED, median income was $30,616 for men and $17,887 for women. Men with bachelor's degrees had a median income of $56,404, while women with bachelor's degrees had a median income of $36,812. Workers with a professional degree had the highest median income, $98,883 for men and $61,206 for women. Men continued to earn more than women at all levels of educational attainment. (Table A-28)

Among workers 18 years old and over, the mean earnings in 2010 were $42,922. Mean earnings represents the average of income from wages, salaries, and self-employment. Non-Hispanic White males with advanced degrees had the highest mean earnings ($107,125), followed closely by Asian males with advanced degrees ($96,699) and Hispanic and Black males with advanced degrees, at $82,797 and $81,199, respectively. Asian women with advanced degrees earned an average of $67,690, more than the averages for similarly educated Black women ($64,586), White women ($63,021), and Hispanic women ($61,967). At the other end of the education spectrum, White men who were not high school graduates earned an average of $25,100, followed by Asian men ($24,355), Hispanic men ($23,384), and Black men ($19,452). Asian women who did not graduate from high school earned an average of $17,142, followed by Black women ($15,589), White women ($14,791), and Hispanic women ($14,763). (Table A-27)

Figure A-10. Percent of People Who Have Completed 4 or More Years of High School or College, by Sex and Educational Attainment Level, 1940–2011

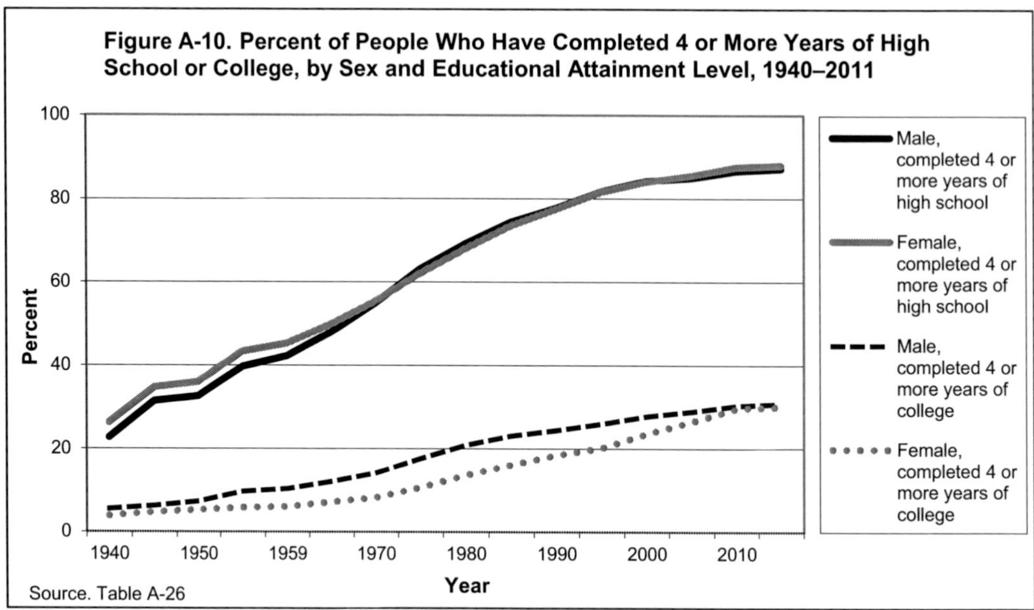

Source. Table A-26

In 1940, only one in four Americans had completed high school. By 1966, the ratio had only increased to 1 in 2—less than half of the U.S. population 25 years old and over. As of 2011, 87.6 percent of Americans in this age group were high school graduates. The high school graduation rate for women continued to exceed that of men, just as it has done each year since 2001.

The percentage of college graduates, which constituted less than 5 percent of the population in 1940, had risen to 9.8 percent by 1966. By 2011, the percentage of graduates included 30.4 percent of the population 25 years old and over. Women have continued to narrow the gap between the percentage of female and male graduates. In 1985, 23.1 percent of men and 16.0 percent of women age 25 years and over had graduated from college. By 2011, the proportions were essentially equal, at 30.8 percent for men and 30.1 percent for women. (Table A-26)

In 2011, 70.8 percent of foreign-born people 25 years old and over in the United States were high school graduates. However, this percentage was significantly different when comparing foreign-born people who were naturalized citizens and those who were not citizens. Among those who were naturalized citizens, 81.7 percent were high school graduates, whereas among non-citizens, only 61.0 percent were high school graduates. Among all foreign-born people, 10.7 percent held master's degrees or higher. Of those, 13.1 percent of foreign-born naturalized citizens held advanced degrees, while 8.5 percent of non-citizens held advanced degrees. In comparison, 11.0 percent of U.S. natives held advanced degrees. Among the native-born, 13.6 percent of those with foreign or mixed parents held advanced degrees, compared with 10.7 percent of those with native-born parents. (Table A-24)

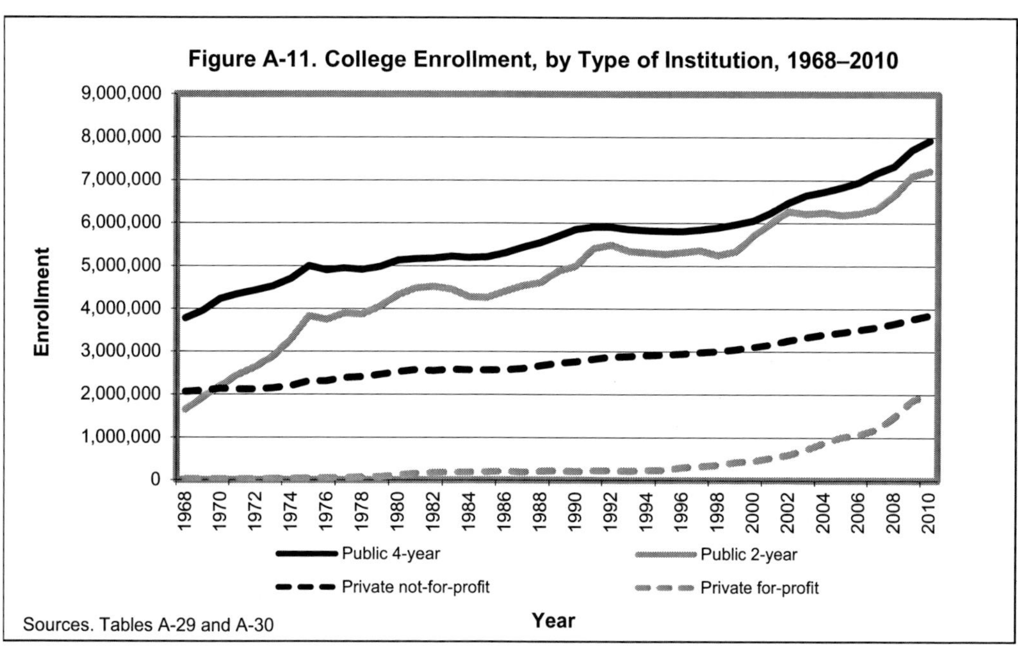

College enrollment increased 37 percent between 2000 and 2010, after only an 11 percent increase in the 1990s. In 2010, more than 21 million students were enrolled in college, with 15 million (72 percent) in public colleges and universities. Enrollment in private for-profit colleges quadrupled during the decade, enrolling about 2.0 million students in 2010. Public 4-year colleges continued to enroll the most students, increasing 31 percent since 2000 to 7.9 million students, while public 2-year colleges followed closely behind, increasing to 7.2 million students, an increase of 26.7 percent. Private not-for-profit colleges served 3.9 million students, 24.0 percent more than in 2000. (Tables A-29 and A-30)

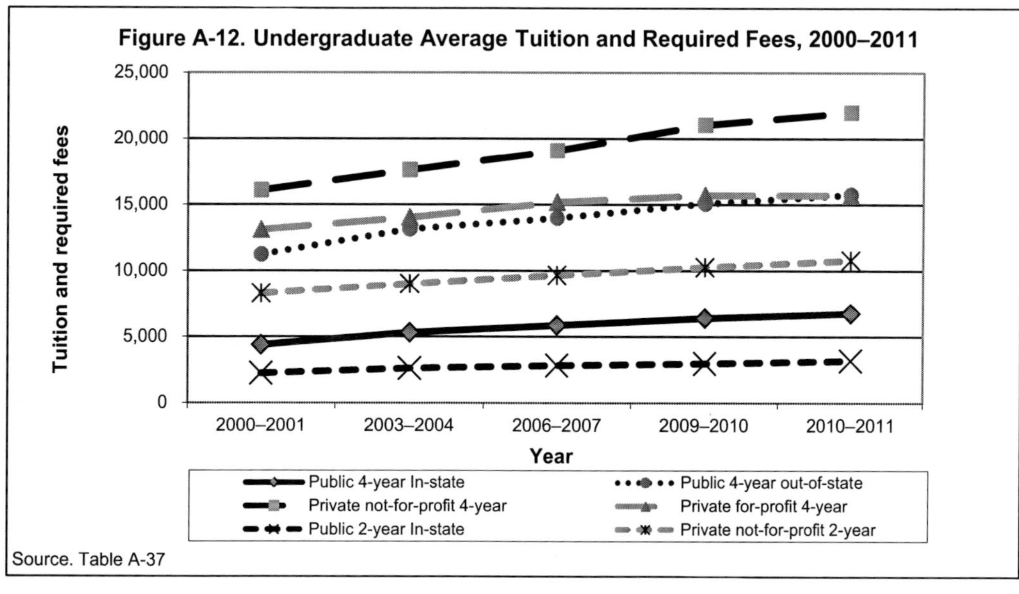

College costs have continued to increase during the decade. Most expensive are the private not-for-profit colleges—about 1,300 of them—whose average tuition and fees have increased 30.9 percent since 2000. Though much less expensive, the biggest proportional increase has been in-state tuition in the approximately 650 public 4-year colleges and universities, where tuition and fees have increased 47.3 percent. Slightly fewer than 1,000 in number, public 2-year colleges have offered the most affordable option through the decade, though even they have increased their tuition and fees 36.0 percent. The number of for-profit 4-year colleges tripled during the decade. Their tuition and fees were high, but their proportional increase was not as great as the average tuition increases for not-for-profit colleges and public 4-year out-of-state tuitions. Also of note, although the number of public 2-year colleges has declined 10 percent, the cost of tuition and fees at these colleges has increased 52.2 percent. And while the number of public less-than-2-year colleges has dropped 74 percent, the tuition costs at these colleges have increased 13.5 percent. (Table A-37)

PART A

NATIONAL EDUCATION STATISTICS

■ Enrollment Tables

Table A-1. Enrollment Status of the Population 3 Years Old and Over, by Age, Sex, Race, Hispanic Origin, Foreign Born, and Foreign-Born Parentage, October 2011

(Numbers in thousands; percent)

Age, sex, race, Hispanic origin, and nativity	Population[1]	Enrolled in school									
		Total		Nursery or kindergarten		Elementary		High school		College undergraduate or graduate	
	Number	Number	Percent	Number	Percent	Number	Percent	Number	Percent	Number	Percent
ALL RACES											
Both Sexes											
Total	294,138	79,043	26.9	9,160	3.1	32,872	11.2	16,613	5.6	20,397	6.9
3 and 4 years old	8,765	4,597	52.4	4,597	52.4	*	*	*	*	*	*
5 and 6 years old	8,419	8,009	95.1	4,534	53.9	3,475	41.3	*	*	*	*
7 to 9 years old	12,571	12,319	98.0	30	0.2	12,290	97.8	*	*	*	*
10 to 13 years old	16,180	15,941	98.5	*	*	15,731	97.2	211	1.3	*	*
14 and 15 years old	7,934	7,825	98.6	*	*	1,270	16.0	6,537	82.4	19	0.2
16 and 17 years old	8,263	7,906	95.7	*	*	66	0.8	7,655	92.7	185	2.2
18 and 19 years old	8,465	6,017	71.1	*	*	3	*	1,772	20.9	4,242	50.1
20 and 21 years old	8,760	4,618	52.7	*	*	24	0.3	135	1.5	4,459	50.9
22 to 24 years old	12,717	3,961	31.1	*	*	1	*	92	0.7	3,869	30.4
25 to 29 years old	21,139	3,139	14.8	*	*	2	*	71	0.3	3,066	14.5
30 to 34 years old	20,413	1,571	7.7	*	*	3	*	17	0.1	1,551	7.6
35 to 44 years old	39,438	1,688	4.3	*	*	3	*	52	0.1	1,632	4.1
45 to 54 years old	43,761	1,012	2.3	*	*	4	*	46	0.1	961	2.2
55 years old and over	77,312	438	0.6	*	*	*	*	25	*	413	0.5
Male											
Total	144,190	39,245	27.2	4,748	3.3	16,812	11.7	8,553	5.9	9,132	6.3
3 and 4 years old	4,468	2,358	52.8	2,358	52.8	*	*	*	*	*	*
5 and 6 years old	4,358	4,143	95.1	2,380	54.6	1,763	40.5	*	*	*	*
7 to 9 years old	6,372	6,253	98.1	10	0.2	6,243	98.0	*	*	*	*
10 to 13 years old	8,273	8,161	98.6	*	*	8,066	97.5	95	1.1	*	*
14 and 15 years old	4,054	3,990	98.4	*	*	683	16.8	3,298	81.3	9	0.2
16 and 17 years old	4,219	4,025	95.4	*	*	41	1.0	3,885	92.1	99	2.3
18 and 19 years old	4,341	2,987	68.8	*	*	*	*	1,038	23.9	1,949	44.9
20 and 21 years old	4,498	2,213	49.2	*	*	11	0.2	75	1.7	2,127	47.3
22 to 24 years old	6,372	1,931	30.3	*	*	1	*	53	0.8	1,877	29.5
25 to 29 years old	10,688	1,378	12.9	*	*	*	*	34	0.3	1,343	12.6
30 to 34 years old	10,131	653	6.4	*	*	3	*	6	0.1	643	6.3
35 to 44 years old	19,420	656	3.4	*	*	*	*	27	0.1	628	3.2
45 to 54 years old	21,417	343	1.6	*	*	1	*	32	0.2	310	1.4
55 years old and over	35,578	155	0.4	*	*	*	*	9	*	146	0.4
Female											
Total	149,948	39,798	26.5	4,412	2.9	16,060	10.7	8,060	5.4	11,266	7.5
3 and 4 years old	4,296	2,239	52.1	2,239	52.1	*	*	*	*	*	*
5 and 6 years old	4,060	3,866	95.2	2,154	53.0	1,712	42.2	*	*	*	*
7 to 9 years old	6,199	6,066	97.9	19	0.3	6,047	97.5	*	*	*	*
10 to 13 years old	7,907	7,780	98.4	*	*	7,664	96.9	116	1.5	*	*
14 and 15 years old	3,880	3,836	98.9	*	*	587	15.1	3,239	83.5	10	0.2
16 and 17 years old	4,044	3,882	96.0	*	*	26	0.6	3,770	93.2	86	2.1
18 and 19 years old	4,124	3,029	73.5	*	*	3	0.1	734	17.8	2,293	55.6
20 and 21 years old	4,262	2,406	56.4	*	*	13	0.3	60	1.4	2,333	54.7
22 to 24 years old	6,345	2,031	32.0	*	*	*	*	39	0.6	1,992	31.4
25 to 29 years old	10,451	1,761	16.8	*	*	2	*	37	0.4	1,722	16.5
30 to 34 years old	10,282	919	8.9	*	*	*	*	11	0.1	908	8.8
35 to 44 years old	20,019	1,032	5.2	*	*	3	*	25	0.1	1,004	5.0
45 to 54 years old	22,344	669	3.0	*	*	3	*	14	0.1	651	2.9
55 years old and over	41,734	283	0.7	*	*	*	*	16	-	267	0.6
WHITE ALONE OR IN COMBINATION											
Both Sexes											
Total	238,932	61,979	25.9	7,226	3.0	25,989	10.9	12,979	5.4	15,785	6.6
3 and 4 years old	6,812	3,515	51.6	3,515	51.6	*	*	*	*	*	*
5 and 6 years old	6,698	6,405	95.6	3,689	55.1	2,716	40.5	*	*	*	*
7 to 9 years old	9,925	9,747	98.2	22	0.2	9,725	98.0	*	*	*	*
10 to 13 years old	12,808	12,629	98.6	*	*	12,477	97.4	152	1.2	*	*
14 and 15 years old	6,270	6,185	98.7	*	*	989	15.8	5,184	82.7	12	0.2
16 and 17 years old	6,489	6,208	95.7	*	*	45	0.7	6,034	93.0	130	2.0
18 and 19 years old	6,686	4,691	70.2	*	*	3	*	1,307	19.5	3,381	50.6
20 and 21 years old	6,974	3,748	53.7	*	*	21	0.3	97	1.4	3,631	52.1
22 to 24 years old	10,019	3,085	30.8	*	*	1	*	54	0.5	3,031	30.3
25 to 29 years old	16,807	2,373	14.1	*	*	2	*	55	0.3	2,316	13.8
30 to 34 years old	16,180	1,138	7.0	*	*	3	*	11	0.1	1,124	6.9
35 to 44 years old	31,368	1,151	3.7	*	*	3	*	29	0.1	1,119	3.6
45 to 54 years old	35,839	789	2.2	*	*	4	*	39	0.1	745	2.1
55 years old and over	66,057	314	0.5	*	*	*	*	18	*	296	0.4

[1]Civilian noninstitutionalized population.
* = Quantity zero or rounds to zero.

Table A-1. Enrollment Status of the Population 3 Years Old and Over, by Age, Sex, Race, Hispanic Origin, Foreign Born, and Foreign-Born Parentage, October 2011—*Continued*

(Numbers in thousands; percent)

Age, sex, race, Hispanic origin, and nativity	Not enrolled in school					
	Total		High school graduate		Not high school graduate	
	Number	Percent	Number	Percent	Number	Percent
ALL RACES						
Both Sexes						
Total	215,095	73.1	182,627	62.1	32,468	11.0
3 and 4 years old	4,168	47.6	*	*	4,168	47.6
5 and 6 years old	410	4.9	*	*	410	4.9
7 to 9 years old	252	2.0	*	*	252	2.0
10 to 13 years old	239	1.5	*	*	239	1.5
14 and 15 years old	109	1.4	2	*	107	1.3
16 and 17 years old	356	4.3	124	1.5	233	2.8
18 and 19 years old	2,449	28.9	1,903	22.5	545	6.4
20 and 21 years old	4,142	47.3	3,387	38.7	755	8.6
22 to 24 years old	8,756	68.9	7,575	59.6	1,181	9.3
25 to 29 years old	18,001	85.2	15,861	75.0	2,139	10.1
30 to 34 years old	18,842	92.3	16,541	81.0	2,301	11.3
35 to 44 years old	37,750	95.7	33,540	85.0	4,210	10.7
45 to 54 years old	42,749	97.7	38,185	87.3	4,564	10.4
55 years old and over	76,874	99.4	65,508	84.7	11,366	14.7
Male						
Total	104,945	72.8	88,569	61.4	16,376	11.4
3 and 4 years old	2,110	47.2	*	*	2,110	47.2
5 and 6 years old	215	4.9	*	*	215	4.9
7 to 9 years old	119	1.9	*	*	119	1.9
10 to 13 years old	112	1.4	*	*	112	1.4
14 and 15 years old	65	1.6	*	*	65	1.6
16 and 17 years old	194	4.6	67	1.6	127	3.0
18 and 19 years old	1,354	31.2	1,060	24.4	293	6.8
20 and 21 years old	2,285	50.8	1,871	41.6	414	9.2
22 to 24 years old	4,442	69.7	3,775	59.2	667	10.5
25 to 29 years old	9,310	87.1	8,090	75.7	1,220	11.4
30 to 34 years old	9,479	93.6	8,161	80.6	1,317	13.0
35 to 44 years old	18,764	96.6	16,466	84.8	2,299	11.8
45 to 54 years old	21,074	98.4	18,653	87.1	2,421	11.3
55 years old and over	35,423	99.6	30,426	85.5	4,998	14.0
Female						
Total	110,150	73.5	94,058	62.7	16,092	10.7
3 and 4 years old	2,058	47.9	*	*	2,058	47.9
5 and 6 years old	195	4.8	*	*	195	4.8
7 to 9 years old	133	2.1	*	*	133	2.1
10 to 13 years old	127	1.6	*	*	127	1.6
14 and 15 years old	44	1.1	2	0.1	42	1.1
16 and 17 years old	162	4.0	56	1.4	106	2.6
18 and 19 years old	1,095	26.5	843	20.4	252	6.1
20 and 21 years old	1,857	43.6	1,516	35.6	341	8.0
22 to 24 years old	4,314	68.0	3,800	59.9	514	8.1
25 to 29 years old	8,690	83.2	7,771	74.4	919	8.8
30 to 34 years old	9,363	91.1	8,379	81.5	984	9.6
35 to 44 years old	18,986	94.8	17,075	85.3	1,911	9.5
45 to 54 years old	21,675	97.0	19,533	87.4	2,142	9.6
55 years old and over	41,451	99.3	35,083	84.1	6,368	15.3
WHITE ALONE OR IN COMBINATION						
Both Sexes						
Total	176,953	74.1	151,252	63.3	25,701	10.8
3 and 4 years old	3,297	48.4	*	*	3,297	48.4
5 and 6 years old	293	4.4	*	*	293	4.4
7 to 9 years old	178	1.8	*	*	178	1.8
10 to 13 years old	179	1.4	*	*	179	1.4
14 and 15 years old	85	1.3	2	*	82	1.3
16 and 17 years old	281	4.3	104	1.6	176	2.7
18 and 19 years old	1,995	29.8	1,540	23.0	455	6.8
20 and 21 years old	3,226	46.3	2,644	37.9	582	8.3
22 to 24 years old	6,933	69.2	6,029	60.2	904	9.0
25 to 29 years old	14,434	85.9	12,697	75.5	1,737	10.3
30 to 34 years old	15,042	93.0	13,086	80.9	1,956	12.1
35 to 44 years old	30,217	96.3	26,696	85.1	3,521	11.2
45 to 54 years old	35,050	97.8	31,504	87.9	3,547	9.9
55 years old and over	65,743	99.5	56,950	86.2	8,793	13.3

[1]Civilian noninstitutionalized population.
* = Quantity zero or rounds to zero.

Table A-1. Enrollment Status of the Population 3 Years Old and Over, by Age, Sex, Race, Hispanic Origin, Foreign Born, and Foreign-Born Parentage, October 2011—*Continued*

(Numbers in thousands; percent)

Age, sex, race, Hispanic origin, and nativity	Population[1]	Enrolled in school									
		Total		Nursery or kindergarten		Elementary		High school		College undergraduate or graduate	
	Number	Number	Percent	Number	Percent	Number	Percent	Number	Percent	Number	Percent
Male											
Total	118,245	31,075	26.3	3,787	3.2	13,316	11.3	6,734	5.7	7,239	6.1
3 and 4 years old	3,482	1,827	52.5	1,827	52.5	*	*	*	*	*	*
5 and 6 years old	3,451	3,298	95.6	1,949	56.5	1,348	39.1	*	*	*	*
7 to 9 years old	5,064	4,983	98.4	10	0.2	4,972	98.2	*	*	*	*
10 to 13 years old	6,576	6,490	98.7	*	*	6,420	97.6	69	1.1	*	*
14 and 15 years old	3,210	3,162	98.5	*	*	534	16.6	2,622	81.7	6	0.2
16 and 17 years old	3,340	3,195	95.6	*	*	24	0.7	3,098	92.7	72	2.2
18 and 19 years old	3,457	2,329	67.4	*	*	*	*	776	22.4	1,554	44.9
20 and 21 years old	3,556	1,787	50.3	*	*	11	0.3	57	1.6	1,719	48.3
22 to 24 years old	5,140	1,546	30.1	*	*	1	*	28	0.6	1,517	29.5
25 to 29 years old	8,609	1,073	12.5	*	*	*	*	27	0.3	1,046	12.1
30 to 34 years old	8,165	503	6.2	*	*	3	*	4	*	496	6.1
35 to 44 years old	15,704	481	3.1	*	*	-	*	16	0.1	465	3.0
45 to 54 years old	17,771	292	1.6	*	*	1	*	29	0.2	262	1.5
55 years old and over	30,718	110	0.4	*	*	*	*	7	*	103	0.3
Female											
Total	120,688	30,904	25.6	3,440	2.9	12,673	10.5	6,245	5.2	8,545	7.1
3 and 4 years old	3,330	1,688	50.7	1,688	50.7	*	*	*	*	*	*
5 and 6 years old	3,247	3,107	95.7	1,740	53.6	1,367	42.1	*	*	*	*
7 to 9 years old	4,861	4,765	98.0	12	0.2	4,753	97.8	*	*	*	*
10 to 13 years old	6,232	6,139	98.5	*	*	6,056	97.2	83	1.3	*	*
14 and 15 years old	3,060	3,023	98.8	*	*	455	14.9	2,562	83.7	6	0.2
16 and 17 years old	3,149	3,014	95.7	*	*	21	0.7	2,935	93.2	57	1.8
18 and 19 years old	3,228	2,361	73.1	*	*	2	0.1	531	16.4	1,828	56.6
20 and 21 years old	3,418	1,961	57.4	*	*	10	0.3	40	1.2	1,912	55.9
22 to 24 years old	4,879	1,540	31.6	*	*	*	*	25	0.5	1,514	31.0
25 to 29 years old	8,198	1,300	15.9	*	*	2	*	28	0.3	1,270	15.5
30 to 34 years old	8,015	635	7.9	*	*	*	*	7	0.1	627	7.8
35 to 44 years old	15,664	670	4.3	*	*	3	*	13	0.1	654	4.2
45 to 54 years old	18,068	497	2.7	*	*	3	*	10	0.1	483	2.7
55 years old and over	35,339	204	0.6	*	*	*	*	11	*	193	0.5
BLACK ALONE OR IN COMBINATION											
Both Sexes											
Total	39,559	13,288	33.6	1,600	4.0	5,524	14.0	2,847	7.2	3,317	8.4
3 and 4 years old	1,632	880	53.9	880	53.9	*	*	*	*	*	*
5 and 6 years old	1,443	1,329	92.1	712	49.3	618	42.8	*	*	*	*
7 to 9 years old	2,145	2,088	97.3	9	0.4	2,080	96.9	*	*	*	*
10 to 13 years old	2,646	2,607	98.5	*	*	2,562	96.8	46	1.7	*	*
14 and 15 years old	1,296	1,278	98.7	*	*	247	19.0	1,029	79.4	3	0.3
16 and 17 years old	1,355	1,301	96.0	*	*	18	1.3	1,248	92.0	35	2.6
18 and 19 years old	1,381	1,023	74.1	*	*	*	*	409	29.6	615	44.5
20 and 21 years old	1,354	566	41.8	*	*	*	*	26	1.9	540	39.9
22 to 24 years old	2,059	638	31.0	*	*	*	*	33	1.6	605	29.4
25 to 29 years old	3,035	549	18.1	*	*	*	*	16	0.5	533	17.6
30 to 34 years old	2,899	329	11.3	*	*	*	*	8	0.3	321	11.1
35 to 44 years old	5,144	395	7.7	*	*	*	*	23	0.4	372	7.2
45 to 54 years old	5,539	206	3.7	*	*	*	*	7	0.1	198	3.6
55 years old and over	7,631	98	1.3	*	*	*	*	4	0.1	94	1.2
Male											
Total	18,341	6,325	34.5	811	4.4	2,819	15.4	1,415	7.7	1,279	7.0
3 and 4 years old	802	423	52.8	423	52.8	*	*	*	*	*	*
5 and 6 years old	798	740	92.8	387	48.5	353	44.3	*	*	*	*
7 to 9 years old	1,039	1,012	97.5	1	0.1	1,012	97.4	*	*	*	*
10 to 13 years old	1,343	1,324	98.6	*	*	1,309	97.5	15	1.1	*	*
14 and 15 years old	643	629	97.9	*	*	130	20.3	496	77.1	3	0.5
16 and 17 years old	678	641	94.5	*	*	15	2.2	607	89.4	19	2.8
18 and 19 years old	681	488	71.6	*	*	*	*	238	35.0	250	36.6
20 and 21 years old	709	276	38.9	*	*	*	*	12	1.7	264	37.2
22 to 24 years old	899	270	30.0	*	*	*	*	21	2.3	249	27.7
25 to 29 years old	1,442	203	14.1	*	*	*	*	7	0.5	196	13.6
30 to 34 years old	1,329	102	7.7	*	*	*	*	2	0.2	100	7.5
35 to 44 years old	2,267	132	5.8	*	*	*	*	12	0.5	120	5.3
45 to 54 years old	2,520	47	1.8	*	*	*	*	3	0.1	43	1.7
55 years old and over	3,192	36	1.1	*	*	*	*	2	0.1	34	1.1

[1]Civilian noninstitutionalized population.
* = Quantity zero or rounds to zero.

Table A-1. Enrollment Status of the Population 3 Years Old and Over, by Age, Sex, Race, Hispanic Origin, Foreign Born, and Foreign-Born Parentage, October 2011—*Continued*

(Numbers in thousands; percent)

Age, sex, race, Hispanic origin, and nativity	Not enrolled in school					
	Total		High school graduate		Not high school graduate	
	Number	Percent	Number	Percent	Number	Percent
Male						
Total	87,169	73.7	73,995	62.6	13,174	11.1
3 and 4 years old	1,655	47.5	*	*	1,655	47.5
5 and 6 years old	153	4.4	*	*	153	4.4
7 to 9 years old	82	1.6	*	*	82	1.6
10 to 13 years old	86	1.3	*	*	86	1.3
14 and 15 years old	48	1.5	*	*	48	1.5
16 and 17 years old	146	4.4	55	1.6	91	2.7
18 and 19 years old	1,128	32.6	881	25.5	247	7.1
20 and 21 years old	1,769	49.7	1,445	40.6	324	9.1
22 to 24 years old	3,595	69.9	3,060	59.5	535	10.4
25 to 29 years old	7,536	87.5	6,521	75.7	1,015	11.8
30 to 34 years old	7,661	93.8	6,527	79.9	1,134	13.9
35 to 44 years old	15,223	96.9	13,276	84.5	1,946	12.4
45 to 54 years old	17,479	98.4	15,536	87.4	1,943	10.9
55 years old and over	30,608	99.6	26,693	86.9	3,915	12.7
Female						
Total	89,784	74.4	77,257	64.0	12,527	10.4
3 and 4 years old	1,642	49.3	*	*	1,642	49.3
5 and 6 years old	140	4.3	*	*	140	4.3
7 to 9 years old	97	2.0	*	*	97	2.0
10 to 13 years old	93	1.5	*	*	93	1.5
14 and 15 years old	36	1.2	2	0.1	34	1.1
16 and 17 years old	135	4.3	49	1.6	85	2.7
18 and 19 years old	867	26.9	659	20.4	209	6.5
20 and 21 years old	1,457	42.6	1,199	35.1	258	7.5
22 to 24 years old	3,339	68.4	2,969	60.9	369	7.6
25 to 29 years old	6,898	84.1	6,175	75.3	722	8.8
30 to 34 years old	7,381	92.1	6,559	81.8	822	10.3
35 to 44 years old	14,995	95.7	13,420	85.7	1,575	10.1
45 to 54 years old	17,571	97.3	15,967	88.4	1,604	8.9
55 years old and over	35,135	99.4	30,257	85.6	4,878	13.8
BLACK ALONE OR IN COMBINATION						
Both Sexes						
Total	26,271	66.4	21,309	53.9	4,962	12.5
3 and 4 years old	753	46.1	*	*	753	46.1
5 and 6 years old	114	7.9	*	*	114	7.9
7 to 9 years old	57	2.7	*	*	57	2.7
10 to 13 years old	39	1.5	*	*	39	1.5
14 and 15 years old	17	1.3	*	*	17	1.3
16 and 17 years old	54	4.0	14	1.0	40	3.0
18 and 19 years old	357	25.9	292	21.2	65	4.7
20 and 21 years old	788	58.2	637	47.1	151	11.1
22 to 24 years old	1,421	69.0	1,213	58.9	208	10.1
25 to 29 years old	2,486	81.9	2,148	70.8	337	11.1
30 to 34 years old	2,571	88.7	2,298	79.3	272	9.4
35 to 44 years old	4,749	92.3	4,263	82.9	486	9.5
45 to 54 years old	5,333	96.3	4,637	83.7	696	12.6
55 years old and over	7,532	98.7	5,806	76.1	1,727	22.6
Male						
Total	12,016	65.5	9,628	52.5	2,388	13.0
3 and 4 years old	379	47.2	*	*	379	47.2
5 and 6 years old	58	7.2	*	*	58	7.2
7 to 9 years old	26	2.5	*	*	26	2.5
10 to 13 years old	18	1.4	*	*	18	1.4
14 and 15 years old	13	2.1	*	*	13	2.1
16 and 17 years old	38	5.5	9	1.4	28	4.2
18 and 19 years old	193	28.4	149	21.9	44	6.5
20 and 21 years old	433	61.1	353	49.8	80	11.3
22 to 24 years old	629	70.0	535	59.5	94	10.5
25 to 29 years old	1,238	85.9	1,057	73.3	182	12.6
30 to 34 years old	1,226	92.3	1,102	82.9	125	9.4
35 to 44 years old	2,135	94.2	1,890	83.4	245	10.8
45 to 54 years old	2,473	98.2	2,148	85.3	325	12.9
55 years old and over	3,155	98.9	2,385	74.7	770	24.1

[1]Civilian noninstitutionalized population.
* = Quantity zero or rounds to zero.

Table A-1. Enrollment Status of the Population 3 Years Old and Over, by Age, Sex, Race, Hispanic Origin, Foreign Born, and Foreign-Born Parentage, October 2011—*Continued*

(Numbers in thousands; percent)

Age, sex, race, Hispanic origin, and nativity	Population[1]	Enrolled in school									
		Total		Nursery or kindergarten		Elementary		High school		College undergraduate or graduate	
	Number	Number	Percent	Number	Percent	Number	Percent	Number	Percent	Number	Percent
Female											
Total	21,218	6,963	32.8	789	3.7	2,704	12.7	1,432	6.8	2,037	9.6
3 and 4 years old	830	456	55.0	456	55.0	*	*	*	*	*	*
5 and 6 years old	645	589	91.3	325	50.4	264	41.0	*	*	*	*
7 to 9 years old	1,106	1,076	97.2	8	0.7	1,068	96.5	*	*	*	*
10 to 13 years old	1,303	1,283	98.4	*	*	1,252	96.1	31	2.4	*	*
14 and 15 years old	653	649	99.4	*	*	116	17.8	533	81.6	*	*
16 and 17 years old	677	660	97.5	*	*	3	0.5	641	94.7	16	2.4
18 and 19 years old	699	535	76.5	*	*	*	*	170	24.3	365	52.2
20 and 21 years old	645	290	45.0	*	*	*	*	14	2.1	276	42.9
22 to 24 years old	1,160	368	31.7	*	*	*	*	12	1.0	356	30.7
25 to 29 years old	1,593	346	21.7	*	*	*	*	9	0.6	337	21.1
30 to 34 years old	1,571	226	14.4	*	*	*	*	6	0.4	221	14.0
35 to 44 years old	2,878	263	9.1	*	*	*	*	11	0.4	252	8.8
45 to 54 years old	3,019	159	5.3	*	*	*	*	4	0.1	155	5.1
55 years old and over	4,439	62	1.4	*	*	*	*	2	-	60	1.4
ASIAN ALONE OR IN COMBINATION											
Both Sexes											
Total	15,393	4,571	29.7	531	3.4	1,860	12.1	825	5.4	1,356	8.8
3 and 4 years old	483	267	55.4	267	55.4	*	*	*	*	*	*
5 and 6 years old	493	476	96.6	263	53.4	213	43.2	*	*	*	*
7 to 9 years old	732	716	97.9	*	*	716	97.9	*	*	*	*
10 to 13 years old	909	885	97.4	*	*	877	96.5	8	0.9	*	*
14 and 15 years old	402	395	98.2	*	*	49	12.3	343	85.3	3	0.7
16 and 17 years old	430	419	97.6	*	*	1	0.3	399	93.0	19	4.3
18 and 19 years old	399	321	80.4	*	*	-	-	55	13.6	267	66.8
20 and 21 years old	438	338	77.1	*	*	3	0.7	12	2.8	323	73.6
22 to 24 years old	597	247	41.4	*	*	*	*	4	0.6	243	40.7
25 to 29 years old	1,276	220	17.2	*	*	*	*	*	*	220	17.2
30 to 34 years old	1,328	121	9.1	*	*	*	*	*	*	121	9.1
35 to 44 years old	2,603	123	4.7	*	*	*	*	1	*	122	4.7
45 to 54 years old	2,130	23	1.1	*	*	*	*	*	*	23	1.1
55 years old and over	3,173	19	0.6	*	*	*	*	3	0.1	16	0.5
Male											
Total	7,434	2,286	30.7	274	3.7	945	12.7	408	5.5	658	8.9
3 and 4 years old	250	139	55.9	139	55.9	*	*	*	*	*	*
5 and 6 years old	250	244	97.4	135	54.0	109	43.4	*	*	*	*
7 to 9 years old	360	350	97.3	*	*	350	97.3	*	*	*	*
10 to 13 years old	463	456	98.6	*	*	452	97.7	4	0.9	*	*
14 and 15 years old	203	200	98.6	*	*	34	16.6	166	82.0	*	*
16 and 17 years old	208	201	96.9	*	*	*	*	195	94.1	6	2.8
18 and 19 years old	214	178	83.3	*	*	*	*	33	15.5	145	67.9
20 and 21 years old	211	168	79.5	*	*	*	*	6	2.8	162	76.7
22 to 24 years old	323	126	39.1	*	*	*	*	4	1.2	123	37.9
25 to 29 years old	645	110	17.0	*	*	*	*	*	*	110	17.0
30 to 34 years old	635	60	9.5	*	*	*	*	*	*	60	9.5
35 to 44 years old	1,243	36	2.9	*	*	*	*	*	*	36	2.9
45 to 54 years old	1,012	9	0.9	*	*	*	*	*	*	9	0.9
55 years old and over	1,418	9	0.6	*	*	*	*	*	*	9	0.6
Female											
Total	7,959	2,285	28.7	256	3.2	915	11.5	417	5.2	697	8.8
3 and 4 years old	233	128	54.9	128	54.9	*	*	*	*	*	*
5 and 6 years old	243	232	95.7	128	52.8	104	42.9	*	*	*	*
7 to 9 years old	372	366	98.5	*	*	366	98.5	*	*	*	*
10 to 13 years old	446	429	96.2	*	*	425	95.2	4	1.0	*	*
14 and 15 years old	199	195	97.9	*	*	16	7.8	177	88.6	3	1.5
16 and 17 years old	222	218	98.3	*	*	1	0.6	204	92.0	13	5.7
18 and 19 years old	186	143	77.1	*	*	*	*	21	11.6	122	65.6
20 and 21 years old	228	170	74.8	*	*	3	1.4	6	2.7	161	70.7
22 to 24 years old	274	121	44.0	*	*	*	*	*	*	121	44.0
25 to 29 years old	631	110	17.4	*	*	*	*	*	*	110	17.4
30 to 34 years old	693	61	8.7	*	*	*	*	*	*	61	8.7
35 to 44 years old	1,360	87	6.4	*	*	*	*	1	0.1	86	6.3
45 to 54 years old	1,118	14	1.3	*	*	*	*	*	*	14	1.3
55 years old and over	1,755	10	0.6	*	*	*	*	3	0.2	7	0.4

[1]Civilian noninstitutionalized population.
* = Quantity zero or rounds to zero.

Table A-1. Enrollment Status of the Population 3 Years Old and Over, by Age, Sex, Race, Hispanic Origin, Foreign Born, and Foreign-Born Parentage, October 2011—*Continued*

(Numbers in thousands; percent)

Age, sex, race, Hispanic origin, and nativity	Not enrolled in school					
	Total		High school graduate		Not high school graduate	
	Number	Percent	Number	Percent	Number	Percent
Female						
Total	14,255	67.2	11,681	55.0	2,575	12.1
3 and 4 years old	374	45.0	*	*	374	45.0
5 and 6 years old	56	8.7	*	*	56	8.7
7 to 9 years old	31	2.8	*	*	31	2.8
10 to 13 years old	20	1.6	*	*	20	1.6
14 and 15 years old	4	0.6	*	*	4	0.6
16 and 17 years old	17	2.5	5	0.7	12	1.7
18 and 19 years old	164	23.5	143	20.5	21	3.0
20 and 21 years old	355	55.0	284	44.1	71	11.0
22 to 24 years old	792	68.3	678	58.5	114	9.8
25 to 29 years old	1,247	78.3	1,092	68.5	156	9.8
30 to 34 years old	1,344	85.6	1,196	76.2	148	9.4
35 to 44 years old	2,615	90.9	2,373	82.5	242	8.4
45 to 54 years old	2,860	94.7	2,488	82.4	371	12.3
55 years old and over	4,377	98.6	3,421	77.1	956	21.5
ASIAN ALONE OR IN COMBINATION						
Both Sexes						
Total	10,822	70.3	9,304	60.4	1,518	9.9
3 and 4 years old	215	44.6	*	*	215	44.6
5 and 6 years old	17	3.4	*	*	17	3.4
7 to 9 years old	15	2.1	*	*	15	2.1
10 to 13 years old	23	2.6	*	*	23	2.6
14 and 15 years old	7	1.8	*	*	7	1.8
16 and 17 years old	10	2.4	4	1.0	6	1.4
18 and 19 years old	78	19.6	66	16.4	13	3.1
20 and 21 years old	101	22.9	85	19.3	16	3.6
22 to 24 years old	350	58.6	312	52.2	38	6.4
25 to 29 years old	1,056	82.8	1,013	79.4	43	3.4
30 to 34 years old	1,207	90.9	1,161	87.4	46	3.5
35 to 44 years old	2,481	95.3	2,327	89.4	154	5.9
45 to 54 years old	2,107	98.9	1,896	89.0	211	9.9
55 years old and over	3,154	99.4	2,441	76.9	713	22.5
Male						
Total	5,148	69.3	4,500	60.5	648	8.7
3 and 4 years old	110	44.1	*	*	110	44.1
5 and 6 years old	6	2.6	*	*	6	2.6
7 to 9 years old	10	2.7	*	*	10	2.7
10 to 13 years old	6	1.4	*	*	6	1.4
14 and 15 years old	3	1.4	*	*	3	1.4
16 and 17 years old	6	3.1	3	1.5	3	1.6
18 and 19 years old	36	16.7	36	16.7	*	*
20 and 21 years old	43	20.5	36	17.1	7	3.5
22 to 24 years old	197	60.9	173	53.4	24	7.4
25 to 29 years old	535	83.0	513	79.4	23	3.5
30 to 34 years old	575	90.5	545	85.9	29	4.6
35 to 44 years old	1,208	97.1	1,136	91.4	71	5.7
45 to 54 years old	1,004	99.1	909	89.8	95	9.3
55 years old and over	1,410	99.4	1,150	81.1	260	18.3
Female						
Total	5,674	71.3	4,804	60.4	870	10.9
3 and 4 years old	105	45.1	*	*	105	45.1
5 and 6 years old	10	4.3	*	*	10	4.3
7 to 9 years old	6	1.5	*	*	6	1.5
10 to 13 years old	17	3.8	*	*	17	3.8
14 and 15 years old	4	2.1	*	*	4	2.1
16 and 17 years old	4	1.7	1	0.5	3	1.2
18 and 19 years old	43	22.9	30	16.1	13	6.8
20 and 21 years old	57	25.2	49	21.4	9	3.8
22 to 24 years old	154	56.0	140	50.9	14	5.2
25 to 29 years old	521	82.6	500	79.3	21	3.3
30 to 34 years old	633	91.3	616	88.8	17	2.4
35 to 44 years old	1,273	93.6	1,191	87.5	82	6.1
45 to 54 years old	1,104	98.7	987	88.3	116	10.4
55 years old and over	1,744	99.4	1,291	73.6	453	25.8

[1]Civilian noninstitutionalized population.
* = Quantity zero or rounds to zero.

Table A-1. Enrollment Status of the Population 3 Years Old and Over, by Age, Sex, Race, Hispanic Origin, Foreign Born, and Foreign-Born Parentage, October 2011—*Continued*

(Numbers in thousands; percent)

Age, sex, race, Hispanic origin, and nativity	Population[1]	Enrolled in school									
		Total		Nursery or kindergarten		Elementary		High school		College undergraduate or graduate	
	Number	Number	Percent	Number	Percent	Number	Percent	Number	Percent	Number	Percent
HISPANIC[2]											
Both Sexes											
Total	47,417	16,131	34.0	2,052	4.3	7,716	16.3	3,410	7.2	2,953	6.2
3 and 4 years old	2,295	956	41.6	956	41.6	*	*	*	*	*	*
5 and 6 years old	2,145	2,050	95.6	1,094	51.0	956	44.6	*	*	*	*
7 to 9 years old	3,059	3,005	98.2	2	0.1	3,003	98.2	*	*	*	*
10 to 13 years old	3,559	3,506	98.5	*	*	3,462	97.3	44	1.2	*	*
14 and 15 years old	1,634	1,604	98.2	*	*	264	16.2	1,335	81.7	5	0.3
16 and 17 years old	1,682	1,591	94.6	*	*	20	1.2	1,540	91.6	31	1.8
18 and 19 years old	1,743	1,136	65.2	*	*	*	0.0	370	21.3	765	43.9
20 and 21 years old	1,695	775	45.7	*	*	4	0.2	30	1.8	740	43.7
22 to 24 years old	2,536	598	23.6	*	*	*	*	25	1.0	574	22.6
25 to 29 years old	4,088	429	10.5	*	*	*	*	22	0.5	407	10.0
30 to 34 years old	4,048	183	4.5	*	*	3	0.1	5	0.1	175	4.3
35 to 44 years old	7,155	186	2.6	*	*	*	*	15	0.2	172	2.4
45 to 54 years old	5,467	73	1.3	*	*	3	0.1	14	0.3	55	1.0
55 years old and over	6,311	39	0.6	*	*	*	*	10	0.2	29	0.5
Male											
Total	24,395	8,271	33.9	1,062	4.4	3,970	16.3	1,802	7.4	1,438	5.9
3 and 4 years old	1,163	508	43.6	508	43.6	*	*	*	*	*	*
5 and 6 years old	1,114	1,068	95.9	552	49.6	516	46.3	*	*	*	*
7 to 9 years old	1,545	1,527	98.8	2	0.1	1,525	98.7	*	*	*	*
10 to 13 years old	1,827	1,805	98.8	*	*	1,788	97.9	16	0.9	*	*
14 and 15 years old	838	827	98.7	*	*	121	14.5	703	83.9	2	0.3
16 and 17 years old	873	826	94.6	*	*	11	1.3	794	90.9	21	2.4
18 and 19 years old	952	580	61.0	*	*	*	*	229	24.1	351	36.9
20 and 21 years old	923	397	43.1	*	*	4	0.5	17	1.9	376	40.7
22 to 24 years old	1,376	289	21.0	*	*	*	*	10	0.7	279	20.3
25 to 29 years old	2,221	220	9.9	*	*	*	*	9	0.4	212	9.5
30 to 34 years old	2,176	73	3.4	*	*	3	0.2	3	0.1	67	3.1
35 to 44 years old	3,731	101	2.7	*	*	*	*	9	0.2	92	2.5
45 to 54 years old	2,750	34	1.2	*	*	*	*	8	0.3	26	0.9
55 years old and over	2,907	15	0.5	*	*	*	*	3	0.1	12	0.4
Female											
Total	23,022	7,860	34.1	990	4.3	3,747	16.3	1,608	7.0	1,515	6.6
3 and 4 years old	1,132	448	39.6	448	39.6	*	*	*	*	*	*
5 and 6 years old	1,031	982	95.3	542	52.6	440	42.7	*	*	*	*
7 to 9 years old	1,515	1,478	97.6	*	*	1,478	97.6	*	*	*	*
10 to 13 years old	1,732	1,701	98.2	*	*	1,673	96.6	28	1.6	*	*
14 and 15 years old	796	777	97.6	*	*	143	17.9	631	79.3	3	0.3
16 and 17 years old	809	765	94.6	*	*	9	1.1	746	92.3	10	1.2
18 and 19 years old	791	556	70.3	*	*	*	*	142	17.9	414	52.4
20 and 21 years old	772	377	48.8	*	*	*	*	13	1.7	364	47.2
22 to 24 years old	1,160	309	26.6	*	*	*	*	15	1.3	294	25.4
25 to 29 years old	1,867	209	11.2	*	*	*	*	13	0.7	196	10.5
30 to 34 years old	1,872	109	5.8	*	*	*	*	2	0.1	108	5.8
35 to 44 years old	3,424	85	2.5	*	*	*	*	6	0.2	79	2.3
45 to 54 years old	2,717	39	1.4	*	*	3	0.1	6	0.2	30	1.1
55 years old and over	3,404	24	0.7	*	*	*	*	7	0.2	17	0.5
FOREIGN-BORN											
Both Sexes											
Total	38,826	4,729	12.2	194	0.5	1,214	3.1	1,088	2.8	2,233	5.7
3 and 4 years old	148	77	52.2	77	52.2	*	*	*	*	*	*
5 and 6 years old	212	197	92.8	117	55.1	80	37.7	*	*	*	*
7 to 9 years old	399	390	97.7	*	0.1	389	97.6	*	*	*	*
10 to 13 years old	667	645	96.8	*	*	642	96.3	3	0.5	*	*
14 and 15 years old	447	436	97.7	*	*	93	20.8	343	76.8	*	0.1
16 and 17 years old	548	514	93.8	*	*	6	1.1	495	90.3	13	2.4
18 and 19 years old	693	455	65.7	*	*	*	*	150	21.6	305	44.0
20 and 21 years old	765	363	47.4	*	*	*	*	16	2.1	347	45.4
22 to 24 years old	1,600	444	27.7	*	*	*	*	11	0.7	433	27.0
25 to 29 years old	3,578	448	12.5	*	*	*	*	21	0.6	426	11.9
30 to 34 years old	4,108	195	4.7	*	*	*	*	5	0.1	189	4.6
35 to 44 years old	8,665	351	4.0	*	*	*	*	18	0.2	333	3.8
45 to 54 years old	7,226	152	2.1	*	*	3	*	7	0.1	142	2.0
55 years old and over	9,772	62	0.6	*	*	*	*	18	0.2	44	0.5

[1]Civilian noninstitutionalized population.
[2]May be of any race.
* = Quantity zero or rounds to zero.

Table A-1. Enrollment Status of the Population 3 Years Old and Over, by Age, Sex, Race, Hispanic Origin, Foreign Born, and Foreign-Born Parentage, October 2011—*Continued*

(Numbers in thousands; percent)

Age, sex, race, Hispanic origin, and nativity	Not enrolled in school					
	Total		High school graduate		Not high school graduate	
	Number	Percent	Number	Percent	Number	Percent
HISPANIC[2]						
Both Sexes						
Total	31,286	66.0	19,111	40.3	12,175	25.7
3 and 4 years old	1,339	58.4	*	*	1,339	58.4
5 and 6 years old	94	4.4	*	*	94	4.4
7 to 9 years old	55	1.8	*	*	55	1.8
10 to 13 years old	53	1.5	*	*	53	1.5
14 and 15 years old	30	1.8	*	*	30	1.8
16 and 17 years old	91	5.4	26	1.5	65	3.9
18 and 19 years old	607	34.8	441	25.3	166	9.5
20 and 21 years old	920	54.3	670	39.5	250	14.8
22 to 24 years old	1,938	76.4	1,379	54.4	559	22.1
25 to 29 years old	3,659	89.5	2,544	62.2	1,115	27.3
30 to 34 years old	3,865	95.5	2,571	63.5	1,295	32.0
35 to 44 years old	6,969	97.4	4,550	63.6	2,419	33.8
45 to 54 years old	5,394	98.7	3,544	64.8	1,850	33.8
55 years old and over	6,272	99.4	3,387	53.7	2,885	45.7
Male						
Total	16,124	66.1	9,742	39.9	6,381	26.2
3 and 4 years old	655	56.4	*	*	655	56.4
5 and 6 years old	46	4.1	*	*	46	4.1
7 to 9 years old	18	1.2	*	*	18	1.2
10 to 13 years old	23	1.2	*	*	23	1.2
14 and 15 years old	11	1.3	*	*	11	1.3
16 and 17 years old	47	5.4	13	1.5	34	3.9
18 and 19 years old	371	39.0	269	28.3	102	10.7
20 and 21 years old	525	56.9	380	41.2	146	15.8
22 to 24 years old	1,086	79.0	766	55.7	320	23.3
25 to 29 years old	2,001	90.1	1,331	59.9	670	30.1
30 to 34 years old	2,102	96.6	1,337	61.5	765	35.2
35 to 44 years old	3,630	97.3	2,295	61.5	1,334	35.8
45 to 54 years old	2,716	98.8	1,730	62.9	986	35.9
55 years old and over	2,892	99.5	1,620	55.7	1,272	43.7
Female						
Total	15,163	65.9	9,369	40.7	5,794	25.2
3 and 4 years old	684	60.4	*	*	684	60.4
5 and 6 years old	48	4.7	*	*	48	4.7
7 to 9 years old	37	2.4	*	*	37	2.4
10 to 13 years old	31	1.8	*	*	31	1.8
14 and 15 years old	19	2.4	*	*	19	2.4
16 and 17 years old	44	5.4	13	1.5	31	3.9
18 and 19 years old	235	29.7	172	21.7	64	8.1
20 and 21 years old	395	51.2	291	37.6	104	13.5
22 to 24 years old	852	73.4	613	52.8	239	20.6
25 to 29 years old	1,658	88.8	1,212	64.9	446	23.9
30 to 34 years old	1,763	94.2	1,233	65.9	530	28.3
35 to 44 years old	3,339	97.5	2,254	65.8	1,085	31.7
45 to 54 years old	2,678	98.6	1,814	66.8	864	31.8
55 years old and over	3,380	99.3	1,767	51.9	1,613	47.4
FOREIGN-BORN						
Both Sexes						
Total	34,098	87.8	23,732	61.1	10,366	26.7
3 and 4 years old	71	47.8	*	*	71	47.8
5 and 6 years old	15	7.2	*	*	15	7.2
7 to 9 years old	9	2.3	*	*	9	2.3
10 to 13 years old	21	3.2	*	*	21	3.2
14 and 15 years old	10	2.3	*	*	10	2.3
16 and 17 years old	34	6.2	14	2.6	20	3.6
18 and 19 years old	238	34.3	164	23.7	74	10.6
20 and 21 years old	402	52.6	259	33.8	143	18.7
22 to 24 years old	1,156	72.3	748	46.7	408	25.5
25 to 29 years old	3,130	87.5	2,241	62.6	889	24.9
30 to 34 years old	3,913	95.3	2,784	67.8	1,129	27.5
35 to 44 years old	8,314	96.0	5,965	68.8	2,349	27.1
45 to 54 years old	7,073	97.9	5,158	71.4	1,915	26.5
55 years old and over	9,710	99.4	6,399	65.5	3,311	33.9

[1]Civilian noninstitutionalized population.
[2]May be of any race.
* = Quantity zero or rounds to zero.

Table A-1. Enrollment Status of the Population 3 Years Old and Over, by Age, Sex, Race, Hispanic Origin, Foreign Born, and Foreign-Born Parentage, October 2011—*Continued*

(Numbers in thousands; percent)

Age, sex, race, Hispanic origin, and nativity	Population[1]	Enrolled in school									
		Total		Nursery or kindergarten		Elementary		High school		College undergraduate or graduate	
	Number	Number	Percent	Number	Percent	Number	Percent	Number	Percent	Number	Percent
Male											
Total	19,280	2,341	12.1	79	0.4	633	3.3	593	3.1	1,036	5.4
3 and 4 years old	62	22	35.8	22	35.8	*	*	*	*	*	*
5 and 6 years old	107	99	92.3	57	53.4	42	38.9	*	*	*	*
7 to 9 years old	197	188	95.3	*	*	188	95.3	*	*	*	*
10 to 13 years old	359	356	99.3	*	*	356	99.3	*	*	*	*
14 and 15 years old	216	216	100.0	*	*	45	20.7	171	79.3	*	*
16 and 17 years old	301	280	93.1	*	*	2	0.8	269	89.3	9	3.0
18 and 19 years old	394	263	66.9	*	*	*	0.1	96	24.5	167	42.3
20 and 21 years old	406	172	42.5	*	*	*	*	12	3.0	160	39.6
22 to 24 years old	850	222	26.1	*	*	*	*	11	1.3	211	24.8
25 to 29 years old	1,919	219	11.4	*	*	*	*	8	0.4	211	11.0
30 to 34 years old	2,113	77	3.6	*	*	*	*	4	0.2	73	3.5
35 to 44 years old	4,366	131	3.0	*	*	*	*	12	0.3	119	2.7
45 to 54 years old	3,603	62	1.7	*	*	*	*	4	0.1	58	1.6
55 years old and over	4,388	33	0.8	*	*	*	*	6	0.1	27	0.6
Female											
Total	19,546	2,388	12.2	115	0.6	581	3.0	494	2.5	1,197	6.1
3 and 4 years old	86	55	64.1	55	64.1	*	*	*	*	*	*
5 and 6 years old	105	98	93.3	60	56.8	38	36.5	*	*	*	*
7 to 9 years old	202	202	100.0	*	0.2	202	99.8	*	*	*	*
10 to 13 years old	308	289	93.9	*	*	286	92.8	3	1.1	*	*
14 and 15 years old	231	220	95.5	*	*	48	21.0	172	74.4	*	0.1
16 and 17 years old	247	234	94.7	*	*	3	1.4	227	91.6	4	1.7
18 and 19 years old	299	192	64.1	*	*	*	*	53	17.9	138	46.2
20 and 21 years old	359	190	53.0	*	*	*	*	4	1.0	187	52.0
22 to 24 years old	749	222	29.6	*	*	*	*	*	*	222	29.6
25 to 29 years old	1,658	228	13.8	*	*	*	*	13	0.8	215	13.0
30 to 34 years old	1,995	118	5.9	*	*	*	*	2	0.1	116	5.8
35 to 44 years old	4,299	219	5.1	*	*	*	*	6	0.1	213	5.0
45 to 54 years old	3,622	90	2.5	*	*	3	0.1	3	0.1	84	2.3
55 years old and over	5,384	29	0.5	*	*	*	*	12	0.2	17	0.3
CHILDREN OF FOREIGN-BORN PARENTS											
Both Sexes											
Total	70,633	19,546	27.7	2,221	3.1	8,240	11.7	3,915	5.5	5,168	7.3
3 and 4 years old	2,264	1,063	47.0	1,063	47.0	*	*	*	*	*	*
5 and 6 years old	2,245	2,166	96.5	1,156	51.5	1,010	45.0	*	*	*	*
7 to 9 years old	3,299	3,230	97.9	2	0.1	3,227	97.8	*	*	*	*
10 to 13 years old	3,865	3,794	98.2	*	*	3,733	96.6	62	1.6	*	*
14 and 15 years old	1,753	1,716	97.9	*	*	240	13.7	1,470	83.9	6	0.3
16 and 17 years old	1,955	1,878	96.1	*	*	16	0.8	1,810	92.6	52	2.7
18 and 19 years old	2,062	1,501	72.8	*	*	*	*	433	21.0	1,068	51.8
20 and 21 years old	2,072	1,129	54.5	*	*	7	0.4	32	1.5	1,089	52.6
22 to 24 years old	3,277	1,058	32.3	*	*	*	*	27	0.8	1,032	31.5
25 to 29 years old	5,729	845	14.8	*	*	*	*	30	0.5	816	14.2
30 to 34 years old	5,906	372	6.3	*	*	3	0.1	6	0.1	363	6.1
35 to 44 years old	11,327	488	4.3	*	*	*	*	21	0.2	467	4.1
45 to 54 years old	9,361	206	2.2	*	*	3	*	7	0.1	196	2.1
55 years old and over	15,518	99	0.6	*	*	*	*	18	0.1	81	0.5
Male											
Total	35,395	9,979	28.2	1,179	3.3	4,258	12.0	2,077	5.9	2,464	7.0
3 and 4 years old	1,155	566	49.0	566	49.0	*	*	*	*	*	*
5 and 6 years old	1,179	1,143	96.9	613	52.0	529	44.9	*	*	*	*
7 to 9 years old	1,665	1,628	97.8	*	*	1,628	97.8	*	*	*	*
10 to 13 years old	1,997	1,975	98.9	*	*	1,955	97.9	20	1.0	*	*
14 and 15 years old	927	911	98.3	*	*	128	13.8	783	84.4	*	*
16 and 17 years old	1,023	974	95.2	*	*	10	0.9	938	91.7	26	2.6
18 and 19 years old	1,125	792	70.4	*	*	*	*	264	23.4	528	47.0
20 and 21 years old	1,114	567	50.9	*	*	4	0.4	18	1.7	545	48.9
22 to 24 years old	1,713	509	29.7	*	*	*	*	15	0.9	494	28.9
25 to 29 years old	3,052	415	13.6	*	*	*	*	13	0.4	402	13.2
30 to 34 years old	3,056	170	5.6	*	*	3	0.1	4	0.1	164	5.4
35 to 44 years old	5,720	196	3.4	*	*	*	*	12	0.2	184	3.2
45 to 54 years old	4,687	95	2.0	*	*	*	*	4	0.1	91	1.9
55 years old and over	6,983	36	0.5	*	*	*	*	6	0.1	30	0.4

[1]Civilian noninstitutionalized population.
* = Quantity zero or rounds to zero.

Table A-1. Enrollment Status of the Population 3 Years Old and Over, by Age, Sex, Race, Hispanic Origin, Foreign Born, and Foreign-Born Parentage, October 2011—*Continued*

(Numbers in thousands; percent)

Age, sex, race, Hispanic origin, and nativity	Not enrolled in school					
	Total		High school graduate		Not high school graduate	
	Number	Percent	Number	Percent	Number	Percent
Male						
Total	16,939	87.9	11,585	60.1	5,354	27.8
3 and 4 years old	40	64.2	*	*	40	64.2
5 and 6 years old	8	7.7	*	*	8	7.7
7 to 9 years old	9	4.7	*	*	9	4.7
10 to 13 years old	2	0.7	*	*	2	0.7
14 and 15 years old	*	*	*	*	*	*
16 and 17 years old	21	6.9	10	3.2	11	3.7
18 and 19 years old	130	33.1	90	22.8	41	10.3
20 and 21 years old	233	57.5	131	32.3	102	25.2
22 to 24 years old	629	73.9	390	45.9	238	28.0
25 to 29 years old	1,700	88.6	1,151	60.0	549	28.6
30 to 34 years old	2,036	96.4	1,372	65.0	664	31.4
35 to 44 years old	4,234	97.0	2,953	67.6	1,281	29.3
45 to 54 years old	3,541	98.3	2,527	70.1	1,014	28.1
55 years old and over	4,355	99.2	2,960	67.5	1,394	31.8
Female						
Total	17,159	87.8	12,147	62.1	5,011	25.6
3 and 4 years old	31	35.9	*	*	31	35.9
5 and 6 years old	7	6.7	*	*	7	6.7
7 to 9 years old	*	*	*	*	*	*
10 to 13 years old	19	6.1	*	*	19	6.1
14 and 15 years old	10	4.5	*	*	10	4.5
16 and 17 years old	13	5.3	5	1.9	8	3.4
18 and 19 years old	107	35.9	74	24.9	33	11.0
20 and 21 years old	169	47.0	128	35.6	41	11.4
22 to 24 years old	527	70.4	357	47.7	170	22.7
25 to 29 years old	1,430	86.2	1,090	65.7	340	20.5
30 to 34 years old	1,877	94.1	1,412	70.8	465	23.3
35 to 44 years old	4,080	94.9	3,012	70.1	1,068	24.8
45 to 54 years old	3,532	97.5	2,631	72.6	901	24.9
55 years old and over	5,355	99.5	3,439	63.9	1,917	35.6
CHILDREN OF FOREIGN-BORN PARENTS						
Both Sexes						
Total	51,087	72.3	37,806	53.5	13,281	18.8
3 and 4 years old	1,201	53.0	*	*	1,201	53.0
5 and 6 years old	78	3.5	*	*	78	3.5
7 to 9 years old	70	2.1	*	*	70	2.1
10 to 13 years old	71	1.8	*	*	71	1.8
14 and 15 years old	37	2.1	*	*	37	2.1
16 and 17 years old	77	3.9	30	1.5	47	2.4
18 and 19 years old	561	27.2	405	19.6	156	7.6
20 and 21 years old	943	45.5	701	33.8	242	11.7
22 to 24 years old	2,218	67.7	1,714	52.3	504	15.4
25 to 29 years old	4,884	85.2	3,823	66.7	1,061	18.5
30 to 34 years old	5,534	93.7	4,270	72.3	1,265	21.4
35 to 44 years old	10,839	95.7	8,313	73.4	2,526	22.3
45 to 54 years old	9,155	97.8	7,116	76.0	2,039	21.8
55 years old and over	15,419	99.4	11,435	73.7	3,984	25.7
Male						
Total	25,417	71.8	18,634	52.6	6,782	19.2
3 and 4 years old	589	51.0	*	*	589	51.0
5 and 6 years old	36	3.1	*	*	36	3.1
7 to 9 years old	36	2.2	*	*	36	2.2
10 to 13 years old	22	1.1	*	*	22	1.1
14 and 15 years old	16	1.7	*	*	16	1.7
16 and 17 years old	49	4.8	19	1.8	30	3.0
18 and 19 years old	333	29.6	239	21.2	94	8.4
20 and 21 years old	546	49.1	389	34.9	158	14.1
22 to 24 years old	1,203	70.3	909	53.1	295	17.2
25 to 29 years old	2,637	86.4	1,990	65.2	646	21.2
30 to 34 years old	2,886	94.4	2,143	70.1	743	24.3
35 to 44 years old	5,525	96.6	4,156	72.7	1,369	23.9
45 to 54 years old	4,592	98.0	3,517	75.0	1,074	22.9
55 years old and over	6,946	99.5	5,272	75.5	1,674	24.0

[1]Civilian noninstitutionalized population.
* = Quantity zero or rounds to zero.

Table A-1. Enrollment Status of the Population 3 Years Old and Over, by Age, Sex, Race, Hispanic Origin, Foreign Born, and Foreign-Born Parentage, October 2011—*Continued*

(Numbers in thousands; percent)

Age, sex, race, Hispanic origin, and nativity	Population[1]	Enrolled in school									
		Total		Nursery or kindergarten		Elementary		High school		College undergraduate or graduate	
	Number	Number	Percent	Number	Percent	Number	Percent	Number	Percent	Number	Percent
Female											
Total	35,238	9,567	27.1	1,042	3.0	3,982	11.3	1,838	5.2	2,704	7.7
3 and 4 years old	1,108	497	44.9	497	44.9	*	*	*	*	*	*
5 and 6 years old	1,066	1,024	96.0	543	50.9	481	45.1	*	*	*	*
7 to 9 years old	1,635	1,601	97.9	2	0.1	1,599	97.8	*	*	*	*
10 to 13 years old	1,869	1,820	97.4	*	*	1,778	95.1	42	2.2	*	*
14 and 15 years old	825	805	97.5	*	*	111	13.5	687	83.3	6	0.7
16 and 17 years old	932	904	97.1	*	*	6	0.7	872	93.6	26	2.8
18 and 19 years old	937	708	75.6	*	*	*	*	169	18.0	539	57.6
20 and 21 years old	958	561	58.6	*	*	3	0.3	14	1.4	545	56.8
22 to 24 years old	1,564	549	35.1	*	*	*	*	12	0.8	537	34.4
25 to 29 years old	2,678	430	16.1	*	*	*	*	17	0.6	414	15.4
30 to 34 years old	2,850	202	7.1	*	*	*	*	2	0.1	199	7.0
35 to 44 years old	5,607	292	5.2	*	*	*	*	9	0.2	283	5.0
45 to 54 years old	4,674	111	2.4	*	*	3	0.1	3	0.1	104	2.2
55 years old and over	8,536	63	0.7	*	*	*	*	12	0.1	51	0.6

[1]Civilian noninstitutionalized population.
* = Quantity zero or rounds to zero.

Table A-1. Enrollment Status of the Population 3 Years Old and Over, by Age, Sex, Race, Hispanic Origin, Foreign Born, and Foreign-Born Parentage, October 2011—*Continued*

(Numbers in thousands; percent)

Age, sex, race, Hispanic origin, and nativity	Not enrolled in school					
	Total		High school graduate		Not high school graduate	
	Number	Percent	Number	Percent	Number	Percent
Female						
Total	25,671	72.9	19,172	54.4	6,499	18.4
3 and 4 years old	611	55.1	*	*	611	55.1
5 and 6 years old	42	4.0	*	*	42	4.0
7 to 9 years old	34	2.1	*	*	34	2.1
10 to 13 years old	49	2.6	*	*	49	2.6
14 and 15 years old	21	2.5	*	*	21	2.5
16 and 17 years old	27	2.9	11	1.2	17	1.8
18 and 19 years old	229	24.4	167	17.8	62	6.6
20 and 21 years old	397	41.4	312	32.6	84	8.8
22 to 24 years old	1,015	64.9	805	51.5	210	13.4
25 to 29 years old	2,247	83.9	1,833	68.5	414	15.5
30 to 34 years old	2,649	92.9	2,127	74.6	522	18.3
35 to 44 years old	5,314	94.8	4,157	74.1	1,157	20.6
45 to 54 years old	4,563	97.6	3,598	77.0	965	20.6
55 years old and over	8,473	99.3	6,163	72.2	2,310	27.1

[1]Civilian noninstitutionalized population.
* = Quantity zero or rounds to zero.

Table A-2. Single Grade of Enrollment and High School Graduation Status for Population 3 Years Old and Over, by Sex, Age (Single Years for 3 to 24 Years), Race, and Hispanic Origin, October 2011

(Numbers in thousands; percent)

Age, sex, race, and Hispanic origin	Population[1]	Enrolled		Enrolled									
				Nursery	Kinder-garten	Elementary grades							
		Number	Percent			1	2	3	4	5	6	7	8
ALL RACES													
Both Sexes													
Total	294,138	79,043	26.9	4,946	4,214	4,250	4,265	4,261	4,048	4,121	4,100	3,920	3,907
3 years old	4,292	1,651	38.5	1,570	81	*	*	*	*	*	*	*	*
4 years old	4,473	2,946	65.9	2,599	346	*	*	*	*	*	*	*	*
5 years old	4,201	3,889	92.6	742	2,921	193	33	*	*	*	*	*	*
6 years old	4,218	4,120	97.7	35	836	3,084	143	22	*	*	*	*	*
7 years old	4,268	4,173	97.8	*	30	892	3,017	201	33	*	*	*	*
8 years old	4,157	4,074	98.0	*	*	69	964	2,829	177	34	*	*	*
9 years old	4,146	4,073	98.2	*	*	12	82	1,083	2,690	184	23	*	*
10 years old	4,085	4,001	97.9	*	*	*	25	111	990	2,693	159	22	*
11 years old	4,177	4,131	98.9	*	*	*	*	14	120	1,079	2,716	180	21
12 years old	3,935	3,888	98.8	*	*	*	*	*	38	119	1,051	2,516	146
13 years old	3,983	3,922	98.4	*	*	*	*	*	*	12	125	1,021	2,570
14 years old	3,915	3,855	98.5	*	*	*	*	*	*	*	14	98	1,001
15 years old	4,019	3,970	98.8	*	*	*	*	*	*	*	5	38	114
16 years old	4,163	4,035	96.9	*	*	*	*	*	*	*	8	7	32
17 years old	4,100	3,871	94.4	*	*	*	*	*	*	*	*	10	9
18 years old	4,232	3,295	77.9	*	*	*	*	*	*	*	*	3	*
19 years old	4,234	2,722	64.3	*	*	*	*	*	*	*	*	*	*
20 years old	4,281	2,433	56.8	*	*	*	*	*	*	*	*	14	3
21 years old	4,479	2,185	48.8	*	*	*	*	*	*	*	*	7	*
22 years old	4,263	1,675	39.3	*	*	*	*	*	*	*	*	*	*
23 years old	4,331	1,289	29.8	*	*	*	*	*	*	*	*	*	*
24 years old	4,123	997	24.2	*	*	*	*	*	*	*	*	*	*
25 to 29 years old	21,139	3,139	14.8	*	*	*	*	*	*	*	*	*	2
30 to 34 years old	20,413	1,571	7.7	*	*	*	*	*	*	*	*	*	3
35 to 39 years old	18,934	999	5.3	*	*	*	*	*	*	*	*	3	*
40 to 44 years old	20,505	689	3.4	*	*	*	*	*	*	*	*	*	*
45 to 49 years old	21,657	575	2.7	*	*	*	*	*	*	*	*	*	*
50 to 54 years old	22,105	438	2.0	*	*	*	*	*	*	*	*	*	4
55 to 59 years old	19,796	266	1.3	*	*	*	*	*	*	*	*	*	*
60 to 64 years old	17,479	86	0.5	*	*	*	*	*	*	*	*	*	*
65 years and over	40,037	86	0.2	*	*	*	*	*	*	*	*	*	*
Male													
Total	144,190	39,245	27.2	2,544	2,205	2,251	2,103	2,191	2,105	2,075	2,160	1,941	1,987
3 years old	2,200	894	40.7	843	51	*	*	*	*	*	*	*	*
4 years old	2,269	1,464	64.5	1,278	186	*	*	*	*	*	*	*	*
5 years old	2,150	1,991	92.6	412	1,474	95	10	*	*	*	*	*	*
6 years old	2,208	2,152	97.5	10	484	1,590	54	14	*	*	*	*	*
7 years old	2,128	2,081	97.8	*	10	518	1,441	97	14	*	*	*	*
8 years old	2,142	2,098	97.9	*	*	36	534	1,405	102	21	*	*	*
9 years old	2,103	2,075	98.7	*	*	12	47	605	1,318	78	14	*	*
10 years old	2,020	1,986	98.3	*	*	*	16	59	560	1,269	75	8	*
11 years old	2,204	2,195	99.6	*	*	*	*	10	90	615	1,394	78	8
12 years old	2,006	1,974	98.4	*	*	*	*	*	21	84	585	1,202	78
13 years old	2,044	2,005	98.1	*	*	*	*	*	*	8	75	569	1,262
14 years old	2,017	1,978	98.1	*	*	*	*	*	*	*	7	45	552
15 years old	2,037	2,011	98.7	*	*	*	*	*	*	*	5	20	54
16 years old	2,138	2,061	96.4	*	*	*	*	*	*	*	6	*	25
17 years old	2,080	1,964	94.4	*	*	*	*	*	*	*	*	7	2
18 years old	2,164	1,657	76.6	*	*	*	*	*	*	*	*	*	*
19 years old	2,177	1,331	61.1	*	*	*	*	*	*	*	*	*	*
20 years old	2,175	1,147	52.8	*	*	*	*	*	*	*	*	7	*
21 years old	2,323	1,065	45.9	*	*	*	*	*	*	*	*	4	*
22 years old	2,171	831	38.3	*	*	*	*	*	*	*	*	*	*
23 years old	2,108	596	28.2	*	*	*	*	*	*	*	*	*	*
24 years old	2,094	504	24.1	*	*	*	*	*	*	*	*	*	*
25 to 29 years old	10,688	1,378	12.9	*	*	*	*	*	*	*	*	*	*
30 to 34 years old	10,131	653	6.4	*	*	*	*	*	*	*	*	*	3
35 to 39 years old	9,330	400	4.3	*	*	*	*	*	*	*	*	*	*
40 to 44 years old	10,089	255	2.5	*	*	*	*	*	*	*	*	*	*
45 to 49 years old	10,620	225	2.1	*	*	*	*	*	*	*	*	*	*
50 to 54 years old	10,798	118	1.1	*	*	*	*	*	*	*	*	*	1
55 to 59 years old	9,541	85	0.9	*	*	*	*	*	*	*	*	*	*
60 to 64 years old	8,407	30	0.4	*	*	*	*	*	*	*	*	*	*
65 years and over	17,630	39	0.2	*	*	*	*	*	*	*	*	*	*

[1] Civilian noninstitutionalized population.
* = Quantity zero or rounds to zero.

Table A-2. Single Grade of Enrollment and High School Graduation Status for Population 3 Years Old and Over, by Sex, Age (Single Years for 3 to 24 Years), Race, and Hispanic Origin, October 2011—*Continued*

(Numbers in thousands; percent)

Age, sex, race, and Hispanic origin	Enrolled										Not enrolled		Not enrolled	
	High school				Undergraduate college				Graduate school		H.S. grad	Not grad	Number	Percent
	9	10	11	12	1	2	3	4	1	2+				
ALL RACES														
Both Sexes														
Total	3,872	4,261	4,032	4,448	4,706	5,186	4,037	2,696	1,420	2,353	182,627	32,468	215,095	73.1
3 years old	*	*	*	*	*	*	*	*	*	*	*	2,641	2,641	61.5
4 years old	*	*	*	*	*	*	*	*	*	*	*	1,527	1,527	34.1
5 years old	*	*	*	*	*	*	*	*	*	*	*	312	312	7.4
6 years old	*	*	*	*	*	*	*	*	*	*	*	98	98	2.3
7 years old	*	*	*	*	*	*	*	*	*	*	*	95	95	2.2
8 years old	*	*	*	*	*	*	*	*	*	*	*	83	83	2.0
9 years old	*	*	*	*	*	*	*	*	*	*	*	74	74	1.8
10 years old	*	*	*	*	*	*	*	*	*	*	*	84	84	2.1
11 years old	*	*	*	*	*	*	*	*	*	*	*	45	45	1.1
12 years old	17	*	*	*	*	*	*	*	*	*	*	47	47	1.2
13 years old	181	13	*	*	*	*	*	*	*	*	*	62	62	1.6
14 years old	2,464	250	29	*	*	*	*	*	*	*	*	60	60	1.5
15 years old	986	2,492	260	56	13	*	3	*	3	*	2	47	49	1.2
16 years old	169	1,171	2,330	280	37	*	*	*	*	*	37	90	127	3.1
17 years old	28	222	1,058	2,398	131	8	7	*	2	*	86	142	229	5.6
18 years old	10	41	209	1,244	1,648	104	29	*	6	*	710	227	937	22.1
19 years old	5	13	48	200	869	1,389	183	14	*	*	1,193	318	1,512	35.7
20 years old	*	18	14	63	338	994	910	72	8	*	1,492	356	1,848	43.2
21 years old	*	*	15	25	187	497	707	664	31	52	1,895	398	2,294	51.2
22 years old	*	2	13	15	159	305	403	531	149	98	2,200	388	2,588	60.7
23 years old	*	3	5	20	101	211	289	338	153	168	2,626	416	3,042	70.2
24 years old	3	5	7	19	98	172	198	195	145	156	2,749	377	3,126	75.8
25 to 29 years old	1	10	20	40	403	607	520	403	412	721	15,861	2,139	18,001	85.2
30 to 34 years old	*	*	2	15	239	356	332	160	149	315	16,541	2,301	18,842	92.3
35 to 39 years old	*	3	3	20	176	172	137	122	126	237	15,892	2,043	17,935	94.7
40 to 44 years old	*	6	*	19	103	128	102	60	88	183	17,649	2,167	19,816	96.6
45 to 49 years old	*	8	6	11	81	105	94	58	57	155	18,711	2,370	21,082	97.3
50 to 54 years old	1	4	5	12	81	66	62	38	39	125	19,474	2,193	21,667	98.0
55 to 59 years old	4	*	3	5	31	40	44	26	39	74	17,480	2,050	19,530	98.7
60 to 64 years old	3	*	1	2	6	15	10	12	5	32	15,450	1,943	17,394	99.5
65 years and over	*	*	3	4	7	19	7	2	8	36	32,578	7,373	39,951	99.8
Male														
Total	2,042	2,217	2,031	2,262	2,166	2,298	1,870	1,181	598	1,019	88,569	16,376	104,945	72.8
3 years old	*	*	*	*	*	*	*	*	*	*	*	1,305	1,305	59.3
4 years old	*	*	*	*	*	*	*	*	*	*	*	805	805	35.5
5 years old	*	*	*	*	*	*	*	*	*	*	*	159	159	7.4
6 years old	*	*	*	*	*	*	*	*	*	*	*	56	56	2.5
7 years old	*	*	*	*	*	*	*	*	*	*	*	47	47	2.2
8 years old	*	*	*	*	*	*	*	*	*	*	*	44	44	2.1
9 years old	*	*	*	*	*	*	*	*	*	*	*	28	28	1.3
10 years old	*	*	*	*	*	*	*	*	*	*	*	34	34	1.7
11 years old	*	*	*	*	*	*	*	*	*	*	*	9	9	0.4
12 years old	4	*	*	*	*	*	*	*	*	*	*	32	32	1.6
13 years old	85	6	*	*	*	*	*	*	*	*	*	38	38	1.9
14 years old	1,238	119	17	*	*	*	*	*	*	*	*	39	39	1.9
15 years old	576	1,221	105	21	9	*	*	*	*	*	*	26	26	1.3
16 years old	108	661	1,084	147	29	*	*	*	*	*	27	51	77	3.6
17 years old	15	137	620	1,113	60	4	6	*	*	*	41	76	117	5.6
18 years old	4	28	118	731	717	32	21	*	6	*	392	115	507	23.4
19 years old	3	7	30	117	474	613	78	9	*	*	669	178	847	38.9
20 years old	*	13	4	31	182	462	416	28	4	*	832	195	1,027	47.2
21 years old	*	*	7	20	111	259	367	267	9	22	1,039	219	1,258	54.1
22 years old	*	1	9	6	81	154	222	232	71	53	1,132	208	1,340	61.7
23 years old	*	*	5	3	32	114	137	169	86	49	1,268	244	1,513	71.8
24 years old	3	5	7	14	57	95	105	76	73	70	1,375	215	1,589	75.9
25 to 29 years old	1	5	11	17	178	265	233	182	153	333	8,090	1,220	9,310	87.1
30 to 34 years old	*	*	*	6	90	121	139	78	55	161	8,161	1,317	9,479	93.6
35 to 39 years old	*	*	3	13	65	68	38	58	51	105	7,819	1,111	8,930	95.7
40 to 44 years old	*	6	*	5	35	33	47	20	40	70	8,647	1,187	9,834	97.5
45 to 49 years old	*	7	3	10	24	36	30	30	20	64	9,126	1,269	10,395	97.9
50 to 54 years old	1	*	4	5	11	16	10	18	12	39	9,527	1,152	10,679	98.9
55 to 59 years old	*	*	3	2	7	14	13	7	10	28	8,446	1,010	9,456	99.1
60 to 64 years old	3	*	*	*	4	6	3	6	3	5	7,457	920	8,377	99.6
65 years and over	*	*	*	1	*	6	6	*	5	21	14,524	3,067	17,591	99.8

[1] Civilian noninstitutionalized population.
* = Quantity zero or rounds to zero.

Table A-2. Single Grade of Enrollment and High School Graduation Status for Population 3 Years Old and Over, by Sex, Age (Single Years for 3 to 24 Years), Race, and Hispanic Origin, October 2011—*Continued*

(Numbers in thousands; percent)

Age, sex, race, and Hispanic origin	Population[1]	Enrolled		Enrolled									
				Nursery	Kinder-garten	Elementary grades							
		Number	Percent			1	2	3	4	5	6	7	8
Female													
Total	149,948	39,798	26.5	2,402	2,010	1,999	2,162	2,070	1,943	2,046	1,940	1,979	1,920
3 years old	2,092	757	36.2	727	30	*	*	*	*	*	*	*	*
4 years old	2,204	1,482	67.2	1,321	161	*	*	*	*	*	*	*	*
5 years old	2,051	1,898	92.5	330	1,448	98	22	*	*	*	*	*	*
6 years old	2,010	1,968	97.9	25	352	1,494	89	8	*	*	*	*	*
7 years old	2,140	2,092	97.7	*	19	374	1,576	103	19	*	*	*	*
8 years old	2,015	1,976	98.1	*	*	33	431	1,424	75	13	*	*	*
9 years old	2,044	1,998	97.8	*	*	*	34	478	1,372	105	9	*	*
10 years old	2,065	2,015	97.6	*	*	*	9	52	430	1,425	84	15	*
11 years old	1,973	1,936	98.1	*	*	*	*	4	30	464	1,322	103	12
12 years old	1,929	1,914	99.2	*	*	*	*	*	17	35	466	1,313	69
13 years old	1,940	1,916	98.8	*	*	*	*	*	*	4	50	452	1,308
14 years old	1,898	1,877	98.9	*	*	*	*	*	*	*	7	53	449
15 years old	1,982	1,958	98.8	*	*	*	*	*	*	*	*	18	60
16 years old	2,024	1,974	97.5	*	*	*	*	*	*	*	2	7	7
17 years old	2,020	1,907	94.4	*	*	*	*	*	*	*	*	3	6
18 years old	2,068	1,638	79.2	*	*	*	*	*	*	*	*	2	*
19 years old	2,056	1,391	67.7	*	*	*	*	*	*	*	*	*	*
20 years old	2,107	1,286	61.0	*	*	*	*	*	*	*	*	7	3
21 years old	2,156	1,120	51.9	*	*	*	*	*	*	*	*	3	*
22 years old	2,092	845	40.4	*	*	*	*	*	*	*	*	*	*
23 years old	2,223	694	31.2	*	*	*	*	*	*	*	*	*	*
24 years old	2,029	492	24.3	*	*	*	*	*	*	*	*	*	*
25 to 29 years old	10,451	1,761	16.8	*	*	*	*	*	*	*	*	*	2
30 to 34 years old	10,282	919	8.9	*	*	*	*	*	*	*	*	*	*
35 to 39 years old	9,603	599	6.2	*	*	*	*	*	*	*	*	3	*
40 to 44 years old	10,415	434	4.2	*	*	*	*	*	*	*	*	*	*
45 to 49 years old	11,037	350	3.2	*	*	*	*	*	*	*	*	*	*
50 to 54 years old	11,307	319	2.8	*	*	*	*	*	*	*	*	*	3
55 to 59 years old	10,255	180	1.8	*	*	*	*	*	*	*	*	*	*
60 to 64 years old	9,073	56	0.6	*	*	*	*	*	*	*	*	*	*
65 years and over	22,407	47	0.2	*	*	*	*	*	*	*	*	*	*
WHITE ALONE NON-HISPANIC													
Both Sexes													
Total	190,428	44,951	23.6	2,743	2,238	2,156	2,286	2,237	2,221	2,294	2,272	2,222	2,143
3 years old	2,202	1,002	45.5	954	48	*	*	*	*	*	*	*	*
4 years old	2,215	1,482	66.9	1,380	103	*	*	*	*	*	*	*	*
5 years old	2,211	2,063	93.3	398	1,561	86	19	*	*	*	*	*	*
6 years old	2,194	2,156	98.2	11	508	1,555	73	9	*	*	*	*	*
7 years old	2,212	2,171	98.1	*	19	494	1,556	87	16	*	*	*	*
8 years old	2,241	2,196	98.0	*	*	19	579	1,510	63	25	*	*	*
9 years old	2,231	2,198	98.5	*	*	2	41	592	1,476	73	15	*	*
10 years old	2,303	2,250	97.7	*	*	*	19	35	574	1,527	80	16	*
11 years old	2,231	2,207	98.9	*	*	*	*	5	62	600	1,454	78	8
12 years old	2,256	2,216	98.2	*	*	*	*	*	29	60	639	1,416	71
13 years old	2,235	2,218	99.2	*	*	*	*	*	*	10	71	611	1,424
14 years old	2,260	2,218	98.2	*	*	*	*	*	*	*	8	60	580
15 years old	2,301	2,290	99.5	*	*	*	*	*	*	*	*	13	47
16 years old	2,345	2,262	96.4	*	*	*	*	*	*	*	6	4	2
17 years old	2,386	2,273	95.3	*	*	*	*	*	*	*	*	4	6
18 years old	2,430	1,897	78.1	*	*	*	*	*	*	*	*	2	*
19 years old	2,460	1,628	66.2	*	*	*	*	*	*	*	*	*	*
20 years old	2,571	1,557	60.5	*	*	*	*	*	*	*	*	14	3
21 years old	2,679	1,396	52.1	*	*	*	*	*	*	*	*	*	*
22 years old	2,504	1,063	42.4	*	*	*	*	*	*	*	*	*	*
23 years old	2,617	805	30.7	*	*	*	*	*	*	*	*	*	*
24 years old	2,366	598	25.3	*	*	*	*	*	*	*	*	*	*
25 to 29 years old	12,657	1,927	15.2	*	*	*	*	*	*	*	*	*	2
30 to 34 years old	12,103	939	7.8	*	*	*	*	*	*	*	*	*	*
35 to 39 years old	11,256	537	4.8	*	*	*	*	*	*	*	*	3	*
40 to 44 years old	13,090	426	3.3	*	*	*	*	*	*	*	*	*	*
45 to 49 years old	14,616	409	2.8	*	*	*	*	*	*	*	*	*	*
50 to 54 years old	15,712	292	1.9	*	*	*	*	*	*	*	*	*	1
55 to 59 years old	14,595	161	1.1	*	*	*	*	*	*	*	*	*	*
60 to 64 years old	13,237	46	0.3	*	*	*	*	*	*	*	*	*	*
65 years and over	31,710	68	0.2	*	*	*	*	*	*	*	*	*	*

[1] Civilian noninstitutionalized population.
* = Quantity zero or rounds to zero.

Table A-2. Single Grade of Enrollment and High School Graduation Status for Population 3 Years Old and Over, by Sex, Age (Single Years for 3 to 24 Years), Race, and Hispanic Origin, October 2011—*Continued*

(Numbers in thousands; percent)

Age, sex, race, and Hispanic origin	Enrolled										Not enrolled		Not enrolled	
	High school				Undergraduate college				Graduate school		H.S. grad	Not grad		
	9	10	11	12	1	2	3	4	1	2+			Number	Percent
Female														
Total	1,829	2,044	2,001	2,186	2,539	2,888	2,166	1,516	822	1,333	94,058	16,092	110,150	73.5
3 years old	*	*	*	*	*	*	*	*	*	*	*	1,335	1,335	63.8
4 years old	*	*	*	*	*	*	*	*	*	*	*	722	722	32.8
5 years old	*	*	*	*	*	*	*	*	*	*	*	153	153	7.5
6 years old	*	*	*	*	*	*	*	*	*	*	*	42	42	2.1
7 years old	*	*	*	*	*	*	*	*	*	*	*	48	48	2.3
8 years old	*	*	*	*	*	*	*	*	*	*	*	39	39	1.9
9 years old	*	*	*	*	*	*	*	*	*	*	*	46	46	2.2
10 years old	*	*	*	*	*	*	*	*	*	*	*	50	50	2.4
11 years old	*	*	*	*	*	*	*	*	*	*	*	37	37	1.9
12 years old	13	*	*	*	*	*	*	*	*	*	*	15	15	0.8
13 years old	96	7	*	*	*	*	*	*	*	*	*	24	24	1.2
14 years old	1,225	131	12	*	*	*	*	*	*	*	*	21	21	1.1
15 years old	410	1,271	155	34	4	*	3	*	3	*	2	21	24	1.2
16 years old	61	510	1,246	133	8	*	*	*	*	*	10	40	50	2.5
17 years old	13	84	438	1,285	72	3	1	*	2	*	46	66	112	5.6
18 years old	6	13	91	514	931	72	9	*	*	*	318	112	430	20.8
19 years old	1	7	18	84	395	776	105	5	*	*	525	140	665	32.3
20 years old	*	5	10	32	156	532	494	44	4	*	659	161	821	39.0
21 years old	*	*	8	5	76	238	340	397	22	30	857	179	1,036	48.1
22 years old	*	1	4	9	78	151	182	298	78	44	1,068	180	1,248	59.6
23 years old	*	3	*	17	70	97	152	169	66	119	1,358	172	1,530	68.8
24 years old	*	*	*	5	41	76	92	120	72	86	1,374	163	1,537	75.7
25 to 29 years old	*	5	10	23	224	342	287	222	259	388	7,771	919	8,690	83.2
30 to 34 years old	*	*	2	9	149	235	193	82	94	154	8,379	984	9,363	91.1
35 to 39 years old	*	3	*	7	111	104	100	64	75	133	8,073	932	9,004	93.8
40 to 44 years old	*	*	*	14	68	95	55	40	48	113	9,002	980	9,982	95.8
45 to 49 years old	*	*	3	1	57	68	64	27	38	91	9,586	1,101	10,687	96.8
50 to 54 years old	*	3	*	7	69	50	52	21	27	86	9,947	1,041	10,988	97.2
55 to 59 years old	4	*	*	3	23	26	31	19	29	46	9,034	1,040	10,074	98.2
60 to 64 years old	*	*	1	2	2	9	7	5	2	27	7,994	1,023	9,017	99.4
65 years and over	*	*	3	3	7	14	*	2	3	16	18,054	4,306	22,360	99.8
WHITE ALONE NON-HISPANIC														
Both Sexes														
Total	2,217	2,389	2,316	2,515	2,580	3,186	2,497	1,930	917	1,594	131,668	13,808	145,476	76.4
3 years old	*	*	*	*	*	*	*	*	*	*	*	1,200	1,200	54.5
4 years old	*	*	*	*	*	*	*	*	*	*	*	732	732	33.1
5 years old	*	*	*	*	*	*	*	*	*	*	*	148	148	6.7
6 years old	*	*	*	*	*	*	*	*	*	*	*	39	39	1.8
7 years old	*	*	*	*	*	*	*	*	*	*	*	41	41	1.9
8 years old	*	*	*	*	*	*	*	*	*	*	*	46	46	2.0
9 years old	*	*	*	*	*	*	*	*	*	*	*	33	33	1.5
10 years old	*	*	*	*	*	*	*	*	*	*	*	53	53	2.3
11 years old	*	*	*	*	*	*	*	*	*	*	*	24	24	1.1
12 years old	1	*	*	*	*	*	*	*	*	*	*	40	40	1.8
13 years old	99	4	-	*	*	*	*	*	*	*	*	17	17	0.8
14 years old	1,444	116	12	*	*	*	*	*	*	*	*	41	41	1.8
15 years old	600	1,470	128	25	7	*	*	*	*	*	2	9	11	0.5
16 years old	55	647	1,402	131	15	*	*	*	*	*	27	57	83	3.6
17 years old	9	85	622	1,464	71	6	4	*	2	*	53	60	113	4.7
18 years old	4	24	99	719	969	53	20	*	6	*	393	140	533	21.9
19 years old	1	1	17	69	453	967	109	11	*	*	681	151	832	33.8
20 years old	*	14	6	31	180	602	655	51	*	*	853	162	1,015	39.5
21 years old	*	*	8	9	93	283	433	516	17	38	1,113	170	1,283	47.9
22 years old	*	1	5	8	74	166	245	400	115	47	1,329	112	1,441	57.6
23 years old	*	3	*	*	58	121	148	247	99	127	1,647	166	1,813	69.3
24 years old	3	*	4	12	47	84	125	104	104	114	1,667	101	1,768	74.7
25 to 29 years old	1	6	6	20	207	337	269	282	269	529	10,060	670	10,730	84.8
30 to 34 years old	*	*	*	3	127	197	200	108	87	216	10,461	702	11,164	92.2
35 to 39 years old	*	*	*	*	94	88	77	85	58	131	10,204	515	10,719	95.2
40 to 44 years old	*	6	*	7	47	84	57	39	57	128	11,967	697	12,664	96.7
45 to 49 years old	*	8	3	8	54	92	63	39	43	99	13,339	867	14,207	97.2
50 to 54 years old	*	4	*	2	55	48	49	21	28	83	14,520	901	15,421	98.1
55 to 59 years old	*	*	3	3	21	32	25	18	22	37	13,624	810	14,434	98.9
60 to 64 years old	*	*	1	*	5	6	9	8	3	15	12,370	820	13,191	99.7
65 years and over	*	*	*	1	1	19	7	2	8	31	27,359	4,283	31,642	99.8

[1] Civilian noninstitutionalized population.
* = Quantity zero or rounds to zero.

Table A-2. Single Grade of Enrollment and High School Graduation Status for Population 3 Years Old and Over, by Sex, Age (Single Years for 3 to 24 Years), Race, and Hispanic Origin, October 2011—*Continued*

(Numbers in thousands; percent)

Age, sex, race, and Hispanic origin	Population[1]	Enrolled		Enrolled											
				Nursery	Kinder-garten	Elementary grades							
		Number	Percent			1	2	3	4	5	6	7	8
Male													
Total	93,323	22,336	23.9	1,397	1,197	1,110	1,146	1,137	1,158	1,169	1,203	1,113	1,089
3 years old	1,123	555	49.4	526	29	*	*	*	*	*	*	*	*
4 years old	1,126	714	63.4	649	65	*	*	*	*	*	*	*	*
5 years old	1,136	1,061	93.4	216	798	45	2	*	*	*	*	*	*
6 years old	1,115	1,087	97.5	6	297	752	23	9	*	*	*	*	*
7 years old	1,134	1,114	98.2	*	7	299	759	39	9	*	*	*	*
8 years old	1,146	1,119	97.7	*	*	12	330	733	29	15	*	*	*
9 years old	1,135	1,124	99.0	*	*	2	19	340	718	36	9	*	*
10 years old	1,165	1,140	97.9	*	*	*	12	14	347	724	38	5	*
11 years old	1,173	1,165	99.3	*	*	*	*	3	43	346	740	33	*
12 years old	1,177	1,149	97.7	*	*	*	*	*	12	39	366	685	46
13 years old	1,131	1,121	99.1	*	*	*	*	*	*	8	40	339	683
14 years old	1,164	1,134	97.4	*	*	*	*	*	*	*	3	35	328
15 years old	1,193	1,185	99.4	*	*	*	*	*	*	*	*	3	30
16 years old	1,183	1,139	96.3	*	*	*	*	*	*	*	6	*	*
17 years old	1,244	1,186	95.4	*	*	*	*	*	*	*	*	4	*
18 years old	1,224	937	76.6	*	*	*	*	*	*	*	*	*	*
19 years old	1,246	789	63.3	*	*	*	*	*	*	*	*	*	*
20 years old	1,309	725	55.4	*	*	*	*	*	*	*	*	7	*
21 years old	1,324	671	50.7	*	*	*	*	*	*	*	*	*	*
22 years old	1,323	565	42.7	*	*	*	*	*	*	*	*	*	*
23 years old	1,270	378	29.7	*	*	*	*	*	*	*	*	*	*
24 years old	1,168	303	25.9	*	*	*	*	*	*	*	*	*	*
25 to 29 years old	6,336	835	13.2	*	*	*	*	*	*	*	*	*	*
30 to 34 years old	5,993	417	7.0	*	*	*	*	*	*	*	*	*	*
35 to 39 years old	5,580	207	3.7	*	*	*	*	*	*	*	*	*	*
40 to 44 years old	6,482	172	2.7	*	*	*	*	*	*	*	*	*	*
45 to 49 years old	7,228	173	2.4	*	*	*	*	*	*	*	*	*	*
50 to 54 years old	7,750	77	1.0	*	*	*	*	*	*	*	*	*	1
55 to 59 years old	7,153	44	0.6	*	*	*	*	*	*	*	*	*	*
60 to 64 years old	6,442	15	0.2	*	*	*	*	*	*	*	*	*	*
65 years and over	14,152	34	0.2	*	*	*	*	*	*	*	*	*	*
Female													
Total	97,104	22,616	23.3	1,346	1,041	1,046	1,140	1,100	1,063	1,125	1,069	1,108	1,054
3 years old	1,080	447	41.4	429	18	*	*	*	*	*	*	*	*
4 years old	1,088	769	70.6	731	37	*	*	*	*	*	*	*	*
5 years old	1,075	1,002	93.1	182	763	40	17	*	*	*	*	*	*
6 years old	1,080	1,068	99.0	4	210	803	50	*	*	*	*	*	*
7 years old	1,079	1,058	98.1	*	12	195	796	47	7	*	*	*	*
8 years old	1,096	1,076	98.3	*	*	7	249	778	34	9	*	*	*
9 years old	1,096	1,074	98.0	*	*	*	21	252	758	36	6	*	*
10 years old	1,138	1,110	97.5	*	*	*	6	21	227	803	42	10	*
11 years old	1,058	1,041	98.4	*	*	*	*	2	19	254	714	45	7
12 years old	1,079	1,067	98.8	*	*	*	*	*	17	21	273	731	25
13 years old	1,103	1,097	99.4	*	*	*	*	*	*	1	31	272	740
14 years old	1,096	1,084	99.0	*	*	*	*	*	*	*	4	24	251
15 years old	1,109	1,105	99.7	*	*	*	*	*	*	*	*	10	17
16 years old	1,163	1,124	96.6	*	*	*	*	*	*	*	*	4	2
17 years old	1,142	1,087	95.2	*	*	*	*	*	*	*	*	*	6
18 years old	1,206	960	79.6	*	*	*	*	*	*	*	*	2	*
19 years old	1,213	839	69.1	*	*	*	*	*	*	*	*	*	*
20 years old	1,263	832	65.9	*	*	*	*	*	*	*	*	7	3
21 years old	1,356	725	53.5	*	*	*	*	*	*	*	*	*	*
22 years old	1,181	498	42.2	*	*	*	*	*	*	*	*	*	*
23 years old	1,347	427	31.7	*	*	*	*	*	*	*	*	*	*
24 years old	1,198	295	24.6	*	*	*	*	*	*	*	*	*	*
25 to 29 years old	6,321	1,091	17.3	*	*	*	*	*	*	*	*	*	2
30 to 34 years old	6,110	522	8.5	*	*	*	*	*	*	*	*	*	*
35 to 39 years old	5,676	331	5.8	*	*	*	*	*	*	*	*	3	*
40 to 44 years old	6,609	254	3.8	*	*	*	*	*	*	*	*	*	*
45 to 49 years old	7,387	236	3.2	*	*	*	*	*	*	*	*	*	*
50 to 54 years old	7,962	215	2.7	*	*	*	*	*	*	*	*	*	*
55 to 59 years old	7,442	117	1.6	*	*	*	*	*	*	*	*	*	*
60 to 64 years old	6,795	31	0.5	*	*	*	*	*	*	*	*	*	*
65 years and over	17,558	34	0.2	*	*	*	*	*	*	*	*	*	*

[1] Civilian noninstitutionalized population.
* = Quantity zero or rounds to zero.

Table A-2. Single Grade of Enrollment and High School Graduation Status for Population 3 Years Old and Over, by Sex, Age (Single Years for 3 to 24 Years), Race, and Hispanic Origin, October 2011—*Continued*

(Numbers in thousands; percent)

Age, sex, race, and Hispanic origin	Enrolled										Not enrolled		Not enrolled	
	High school				Undergraduate college				Graduate school		H.S. grad	Not grad		
	9	10	11	12	1	2	3	4	1	2+			Number	Percent
Male														
Total	1,157	1,281	1,160	1,287	1,199	1,419	1,178	872	385	679	64,037	6,951	70,988	76.1
3 years old	*	*	*	*	*	*	*	*	*	*	*	568	568	50.6
4 years old	*	*	*	*	*	*	*	*	*	*	*	413	413	36.6
5 years old	*	*	*	*	*	*	*	*	*	*	*	75	75	6.6
6 years old	*	*	*	*	*	*	*	*	*	*	*	27	27	2.5
7 years old	*	*	*	*	*	*	*	*	*	*	*	20	20	1.8
8 years old	*	*	*	*	*	*	*	*	*	*	*	27	27	2.3
9 years old	*	*	*	*	*	*	*	*	*	*	*	11	11	1.0
10 years old	*	*	*	*	*	*	*	*	*	*	*	24	24	2.1
11 years old	*	*	*	*	*	*	*	*	*	*	*	8	8	0.7
12 years old	1	*	*	*	*	*	*	*	*	*	*	27	27	2.3
13 years old	46	4	*	*	*	*	*	*	*	*	*	11	11	0.9
14 years old	700	60	6	*	*	*	*	*	*	*	*	30	30	2.6
15 years old	372	723	41	11	3	*	*	*	*	*	*	8	8	0.6
16 years old	31	387	634	71	9	*	*	*	*	*	16	28	44	3.7
17 years old	2	59	400	678	37	3	3	*	*	*	25	32	58	4.6
18 years old	*	15	50	429	408	16	14	*	6	*	217	70	287	23.4
19 years old	*	*	8	40	261	435	38	6	*	*	382	75	457	36.7
20 years old	*	13	4	18	99	274	294	17	*	*	493	91	584	44.6
21 years old	*	*	*	5	61	141	241	203	5	15	565	88	653	49.3
22 years old	*	1	5	3	46	77	151	196	58	27	697	61	758	57.3
23 years old	*	*	*	*	22	70	69	135	47	34	789	103	893	70.3
24 years old	3	*	4	7	24	46	66	43	58	51	800	66	865	74.1
25 to 29 years old	1	5	*	13	93	153	112	132	90	237	5,131	370	5,501	86.8
30 to 34 years old	*	*	*	*	45	82	95	51	35	109	5,174	402	5,576	93.0
35 to 39 years old	*	*	*	*	44	27	22	38	24	52	5,093	281	5,374	96.3
40 to 44 years old	*	6	*	1	18	28	27	16	24	53	5,907	402	6,309	97.3
45 to 49 years old	*	7	3	8	19	32	24	18	20	43	6,557	498	7,055	97.6
50 to 54 years old	*	*	*	2	5	13	8	8	7	32	7,191	483	7,674	99.0
55 to 59 years old	*	*	3	*	1	14	4	6	4	11	6,690	419	7,109	99.4
60 to 64 years old	*	*	*	*	4	3	3	3	3	*	5,996	431	6,427	99.8
65 years and over	*	*	*	1	*	6	6	*	5	15	12,314	1,805	14,118	99.8
Female														
Total	1,060	1,108	1,156	1,228	1,381	1,767	1,318	1,058	532	915	67,631	6,857	74,489	76.7
3 years old	*	*	*	*	*	*	*	*	*	*	*	632	632	58.6
4 years old	*	*	*	*	*	*	*	*	*	*	*	320	320	29.4
5 years old	*	*	*	*	*	*	*	*	*	*	*	74	74	6.9
6 years old	*	*	*	*	*	*	*	*	*	*	*	11	11	1.0
7 years old	*	*	*	*	*	*	*	*	*	*	*	21	21	1.9
8 years old	*	*	*	*	*	*	*	*	*	*	*	19	19	1.7
9 years old	*	*	*	*	*	*	*	*	*	*	*	22	22	2.0
10 years old	*	*	*	*	*	*	*	*	*	*	*	29	29	2.5
11 years old	*	*	*	*	*	*	*	*	*	*	*	17	17	1.6
12 years old	*	*	*	*	*	*	*	*	*	*	*	12	12	1.2
13 years old	53	*	*	*	*	*	*	*	*	*	*	6	6	0.6
14 years old	744	56	5	*	*	*	*	*	*	*	*	11	11	1.0
15 years old	228	747	86	14	4	*	*	*	*	*	2	1	4	0.3
16 years old	24	260	768	60	6	*	*	*	*	*	10	29	39	3.4
17 years old	7	26	222	786	35	3	1	*	2	*	27	28	55	4.8
18 years old	4	9	49	290	561	37	6	*	*	*	176	70	246	20.4
19 years old	1	*	9	29	192	532	71	5	*	*	299	75	375	30.9
20 years old	*	1	2	14	82	328	362	34	*	*	359	71	431	34.1
21 years old	*	*	8	5	32	142	192	313	12	23	548	83	630	46.5
22 years old	*	*	*	5	28	89	94	204	57	20	632	51	683	57.8
23 years old	*	3	*	*	36	52	79	112	52	93	858	62	920	68.3
24 years old	*	*	*	5	24	38	59	61	46	62	868	35	903	75.4
25 to 29 years old	*	1	6	8	114	184	157	149	179	292	4,929	301	5,230	82.7
30 to 34 years old	*	*	*	3	82	116	105	57	52	107	5,287	300	5,588	91.5
35 to 39 years old	*	*	*	*	50	60	55	48	35	79	5,111	235	5,346	94.2
40 to 44 years old	*	*	*	6	30	56	30	23	33	75	6,060	295	6,355	96.2
45 to 49 years old	*	*	*	*	35	60	40	21	24	56	6,782	369	7,152	96.8
50 to 54 years old	*	3	*	*	50	35	41	13	21	52	7,329	418	7,747	97.3
55 to 59 years old	*	*	*	3	20	17	20	12	18	26	6,933	391	7,325	98.4
60 to 64 years old	*	*	1	*	1	3	6	5	*	15	6,374	389	6,764	99.5
65 years and over	*	*	*	*	*	14	*	2	3	16	15,045	2,479	17,524	99.8

[1] Civilian noninstitutionalized population.
* = Quantity zero or rounds to zero.

Table A-2. Single Grade of Enrollment and High School Graduation Status for Population 3 Years Old and Over, by Sex, Age (Single Years for 3 to 24 Years), Race, and Hispanic Origin, October 2011—*Continued*

(Numbers in thousands; percent)

Age, sex, race, and Hispanic origin	Population[1]	Enrolled		Enrolled									
				Nursery	Kinder-garten	Elementary grades							
		Number	Percent			1	2	3	4	5	6	7	8
BLACK ALONE													
Both Sexes													
Total	37,269	12,037	32.3	794	559	658	594	645	582	536	682	585	620
3 years old	658	240	36.4	231	9	*	*	*	*	*	*	*	*
4 years old	740	533	72.0	446	86	*	*	*	*	*	*	*	*
5 years old	561	492	87.8	103	355	31	3	*	*	*	*	*	*
6 years old	645	617	95.7	14	101	478	18	6	*	*	*	*	*
7 years old	665	643	96.7	*	8	129	449	46	10	*	*	*	*
8 years old	572	565	98.7	*	*	17	111	402	29	5	*	*	*
9 years old	616	592	96.1	*	*	2	13	169	361	44	3	*	*
10 years old	509	501	98.5	*	*	*	*	20	162	293	26	*	*
11 years old	707	706	99.9	*	*	*	*	2	13	169	483	40	*
12 years old	610	607	99.5	*	*	*	*	*	6	26	141	408	19
13 years old	573	549	95.9	*	*	*	*	*	*	*	29	106	377
14 years old	590	584	98.9	*	*	*	*	*	*	*	*	14	190
15 years old	595	584	98.2	*	*	*	*	*	*	*	*	12	21
16 years old	632	621	98.3	*	*	*	*	*	*	*	*	3	10
17 years old	628	584	93.1	*	*	*	*	*	*	*	*	3	2
18 years old	673	563	83.7	*	*	*	*	*	*	*	*	*	*
19 years old	643	412	64.1	*	*	*	*	*	*	*	*	*	*
20 years old	617	303	49.1	*	*	*	*	*	*	*	*	*	*
21 years old	636	212	33.3	*	*	*	*	*	*	*	*	*	*
22 years old	633	226	35.7	*	*	*	*	*	*	*	*	*	*
23 years old	676	200	29.6	*	*	*	*	*	*	*	*	*	*
24 years old	624	177	28.4	*	*	*	*	*	*	*	*	*	*
25 to 29 years old	2,907	527	18.1	*	*	*	*	*	*	*	*	*	*
30 to 34 years old	2,736	313	11.4	*	*	*	*	*	*	*	*	*	*
35 to 39 years old	2,424	240	9.9	*	*	*	*	*	*	*	*	*	*
40 to 44 years old	2,567	151	5.9	*	*	*	*	*	*	*	*	*	*
45 to 49 years old	2,718	103	3.8	*	*	*	*	*	*	*	*	*	*
50 to 54 years old	2,652	92	3.5	*	*	*	*	*	*	*	*	*	*
55 to 59 years old	2,196	63	2.9	*	*	*	*	*	*	*	*	*	*
60 to 64 years old	1,813	30	1.6	*	*	*	*	*	*	*	*	*	*
65 years and over	3,452	6	0.2	*	*	*	*	*	*	*	*	*	*
Male													
Total	17,285	5,699	33.0	383	289	374	266	360	268	263	380	264	323
3 years old	339	107	31.6	102	5	*	*	*	*	*	*	*	*
4 years old	360	266	73.9	221	45	*	*	*	*	*	*	*	*
5 years old	289	253	87.5	60	179	11	3	*	*	*	*	*	*
6 years old	362	349	96.4	*	60	275	12	2	*	*	*	*	*
7 years old	299	288	96.2	*	*	74	183	28	2	*	*	*	*
8 years old	316	314	99.3	*	*	12	58	219	20	5	*	*	*
9 years old	286	277	96.9	*	*	2	10	100	150	12	3	*	*
10 years old	230	228	99.0	*	*	*	*	12	78	121	17	*	*
11 years old	386	386	100.0	*	*	*	*	*	11	105	259	11	*
12 years old	298	298	100.0	*	*	*	*	*	6	20	80	179	12
13 years old	302	285	94.7	*	*	*	*	*	*	*	21	59	190
14 years old	299	295	98.8	*	*	*	*	*	*	*	*	3	100
15 years old	298	288	96.7	*	*	*	*	*	*	*	*	9	9
16 years old	328	317	96.7	*	*	*	*	*	*	*	*	*	10
17 years old	301	274	91.1	*	*	*	*	*	*	*	*	3	2
18 years old	309	253	81.9	*	*	*	*	*	*	*	*	*	*
19 years old	336	215	64.0	*	*	*	*	*	*	*	*	*	*
20 years old	299	128	42.9	*	*	*	*	*	*	*	*	*	*
21 years old	372	127	34.1	*	*	*	*	*	*	*	*	*	*
22 years old	249	87	34.8	*	*	*	*	*	*	*	*	*	*
23 years old	287	79	27.5	*	*	*	*	*	*	*	*	*	*
24 years old	312	87	28.0	*	*	*	*	*	*	*	*	*	*
25 to 29 years old	1,384	196	14.2	*	*	*	*	*	*	*	*	*	*
30 to 34 years old	1,251	94	7.5	*	*	*	*	*	*	*	*	*	*
35 to 39 years old	1,073	86	8.0	*	*	*	*	*	*	*	*	*	*
40 to 44 years old	1,148	45	4.0	*	*	*	*	*	*	*	*	*	*
45 to 49 years old	1,234	22	1.8	*	*	*	*	*	*	*	*	*	*
50 to 54 years old	1,209	17	1.4	*	*	*	*	*	*	*	*	*	*
55 to 59 years old	955	25	2.6	*	*	*	*	*	*	*	*	*	*
60 to 64 years old	828	8	1.0	*	*	*	*	*	*	*	*	*	*
65 years and over	1,347	3	0.2	*	*	*	*	*	*	*	*	*	*

[1] Civilian noninstitutionalized population.
* = Quantity zero or rounds to zero.

Table A-2. Single Grade of Enrollment and High School Graduation Status for Population 3 Years Old and Over, by Sex, Age (Single Years for 3 to 24 Years), Race, and Hispanic Origin, October 2011—*Continued*

(Numbers in thousands; percent)

Age, sex, race, and Hispanic origin	Enrolled										Not enrolled		Not enrolled	
	High school				Undergraduate college				Graduate school		H.S. grad	Not grad		
	9	10	11	12	1	2	3	4	1	2+			Number	Percent
BLACK ALONE														
Both Sexes														
Total	537	673	654	772	899	801	617	281	230	319	20,510	4,722	25,232	67.7
3 years old	*	*	*	*	*	*	*	*	*	*	*	419	419	63.6
4 years old	*	*	*	*	*	*	*	*	*	*	*	207	207	28.0
5 years old	*	*	*	*	*	*	*	*	*	*	*	69	69	12.2
6 years old	*	*	*	*	*	*	*	*	*	*	*	28	28	4.3
7 years old	*	*	*	*	*	*	*	*	*	*	*	22	22	3.3
8 years old	*	*	*	*	*	*	*	*	*	*	*	7	7	1.3
9 years old	*	*	*	*	*	*	*	*	*	*	*	24	24	3.9
10 years old	*	*	*	*	*	*	*	*	*	*	*	8	8	1.5
11 years old	*	*	*	*	*	*	*	*	*	*	*	1	1	0.1
12 years old	7	*	*	*	*	*	*	*	*	*	*	3	3	0.5
13 years old	37	*	*	*	*	*	*	*	*	*	*	23	23	4.1
14 years old	336	37	7	*	*	*	*	*	*	*	*	6	6	1.1
15 years old	111	392	33	12	3	*	*	*	*	*	*	11	11	1.8
16 years old	35	167	331	60	16	*	*	*	*	*	7	4	11	1.7
17 years old	7	50	181	322	19	*	*	*	*	*	7	36	44	6.9
18 years old	*	9	58	236	239	19	3	*	*	*	91	19	110	16.3
19 years old	3	8	13	70	152	144	22	*	*	*	190	40	231	35.9
20 years old	*	4	3	15	66	135	75	2	4	*	243	70	314	50.9
21 years old	*	*	4	*	25	72	74	36	*	1	356	69	425	66.7
22 years old	*	1	4	4	37	42	60	47	9	22	321	86	407	64.3
23 years old	*	*	5	8	18	32	44	38	38	17	405	72	476	70.4
24 years old	*	3	3	7	27	22	41	40	21	13	406	42	447	71.6
25 to 29 years old	*	*	10	6	101	148	119	35	54	55	2,058	322	2,380	81.9
30 to 34 years old	*	*	*	6	62	79	70	22	35	38	2,162	261	2,423	88.6
35 to 39 years old	*	3	3	9	54	51	33	20	23	44	1,983	201	2,183	90.1
40 to 44 years old	*	*	*	7	32	32	25	9	18	27	2,155	261	2,416	94.1
45 to 49 years old	*	*	*	1	12	5	26	12	8	39	2,248	367	2,615	96.2
50 to 54 years old	*	*	*	7	20	12	11	11	7	24	2,233	327	2,560	96.5
55 to 59 years old	*	*	*	2	9	6	13	5	10	18	1,786	347	2,133	97.1
60 to 64 years old	*	*	*	2	1	3	*	4	2	17	1,471	312	1,783	98.4
65 years and over	*	*	*	*	3	*	*	*	*	3	2,388	1,058	3,446	99.8
Male														
Total	277	332	343	364	360	304	248	102	82	115	9,309	2,278	11,587	67.0
3 years old	*	*	*	*	*	*	*	*	*	*	*	232	232	68.4
4 years old	*	*	*	*	*	*	*	*	*	*	*	94	94	26.1
5 years old	*	*	*	*	*	*	*	*	*	*	*	36	36	12.5
6 years old	*	*	*	*	*	*	*	*	*	*	*	13	13	3.6
7 years old	*	*	*	*	*	*	*	*	*	*	*	11	11	3.8
8 years old	*	*	*	*	*	*	*	*	*	*	*	2	2	0.7
9 years old	*	*	*	*	*	*	*	*	*	*	*	9	9	3.1
10 years old	*	*	*	*	*	*	*	*	*	*	*	2	2	1.0
11 years old	*	*	*	*	*	*	*	*	*	*	*	*	*	*
12 years old	*	*	*	*	*	*	*	*	*	*	*	*	*	*
13 years old	15	*	*	*	*	*	*	*	*	*	*	16	16	5.3
14 years old	180	9	4	*	*	*	*	*	*	*	*	3	3	1.2
15 years old	56	195	13	3	3	*	*	*	*	*	*	10	10	3.3
16 years old	21	83	159	29	14	*	*	*	*	*	7	4	11	3.3
17 years old	1	30	94	138	5	*	*	*	*	*	2	24	27	8.9
18 years old	*	9	36	121	83	1	3	*	*	*	46	10	56	18.1
19 years old	3	4	11	42	77	73	5	*	*	*	93	28	121	36.0
20 years old	*	*	*	8	31	53	32	*	4	*	133	38	171	57.1
21 years old	*	*	4	*	10	46	51	15	*	1	207	38	245	65.9
22 years old	*	*	4	*	12	23	29	10	3	5	128	35	163	65.2
23 years old	*	*	5	*	1	8	21	8	28	8	174	33	208	72.5
24 years old	*	3	3	7	16	14	22	20	3	*	203	22	225	72.0
25 to 29 years old	*	*	7	*	45	49	48	8	15	23	1,022	166	1,188	85.8
30 to 34 years old	*	*	*	2	26	14	10	10	9	23	1,036	120	1,157	92.5
35 to 39 years old	*	*	3	4	13	21	8	8	8	21	863	124	986	92.0
40 to 44 years old	*	*	*	4	9	3	9	1	6	14	989	113	1,103	96.0
45 to 49 years old	*	*	*	*	3	*	4	8	*	7	1,047	165	1,212	98.2
50 to 54 years old	*	*	*	3	4	*	*	8	2	1	1,034	158	1,192	98.6
55 to 59 years old	*	*	*	2	6	*	6	1	3	6	746	184	930	97.4
60 to 64 years old	*	*	*	*	*	*	*	4	*	5	693	126	819	99.0
65 years and over	*	*	*	*	*	*	*	*	*	3	886	459	1,345	99.8

[1] Civilian noninstitutionalized population.
* = Quantity zero or rounds to zero.

Table A-2. Single Grade of Enrollment and High School Graduation Status for Population 3 Years Old and Over, by Sex, Age (Single Years for 3 to 24 Years), Race, and Hispanic Origin, October 2011—*Continued*

(Numbers in thousands; percent)

Age, sex, race, and Hispanic origin	Population[1]	Enrolled		Enrolled									
				Nursery	Kinder-garten	Elementary grades							
		Number	Percent			1	2	3	4	5	6	7	8
Female													
Total	19,983	6,338	31.7	411	270	284	328	285	315	273	303	321	296
3 years old	319	132	41.5	129	3	*	*	*	*	*	*	*	*
4 years old	380	267	70.2	226	41	*	*	*	*	*	*	*	*
5 years old	271	239	88.0	42	176	20	*	*	*	*	*	*	*
6 years old	283	268	94.8	14	41	204	5	4	*	*	*	*	*
7 years old	366	355	97.1	*	8	55	266	18	8	*	*	*	*
8 years old	256	251	98.0	*	*	5	53	183	10	*	*	*	*
9 years old	330	315	95.5	*	*	*	3	69	211	32	*	*	*
10 years old	279	274	98.2	*	*	*	*	9	84	172	9	*	*
11 years old	321	320	99.7	*	*	*	*	2	2	64	224	29	*
12 years old	313	310	99.1	*	*	*	*	*	*	5	62	229	7
13 years old	271	264	97.3	*	*	*	*	*	*	*	8	46	187
14 years old	292	289	99.0	*	*	*	*	*	*	*	*	11	90
15 years old	297	296	99.7	*	*	*	*	*	*	*	*	2	12
16 years old	304	304	100.0	*	*	*	*	*	*	*	*	3	*
17 years old	327	311	94.9	*	*	*	*	*	*	*	*	*	*
18 years old	364	311	85.2	*	*	*	*	*	*	*	*	*	*
19 years old	307	197	64.2	*	*	*	*	*	*	*	*	*	*
20 years old	318	175	55.0	*	*	*	*	*	*	*	*	*	*
21 years old	264	85	32.0	*	*	*	*	*	*	*	*	*	*
22 years old	384	139	36.3	*	*	*	*	*	*	*	*	*	*
23 years old	390	121	31.0	*	*	*	*	*	*	*	*	*	*
24 years old	312	90	28.7	*	*	*	*	*	*	*	*	*	*
25 to 29 years old	1,523	331	21.7	*	*	*	*	*	*	*	*	*	*
30 to 34 years old	1,485	219	14.7	*	*	*	*	*	*	*	*	*	*
35 to 39 years old	1,351	154	11.4	*	*	*	*	*	*	*	*	*	*
40 to 44 years old	1,419	105	7.4	*	*	*	*	*	*	*	*	*	*
45 to 49 years old	1,484	81	5.4	*	*	*	*	*	*	*	*	*	*
50 to 54 years old	1,443	75	5.2	*	*	*	*	*	*	*	*	*	*
55 to 59 years old	1,241	38	3.0	*	*	*	*	*	*	*	*	*	*
60 to 64 years old	985	21	2.2	*	*	*	*	*	*	*	*	*	*
65 years and over	2,105	3	0.2	*	*	*	*	*	*	*	*	*	*
ASIAN ALONE													
Both Sexes													
Total	14,050	3,779	26.9	212	209	181	219	186	184	211	188	142	158
3 years old	190	74	39.0	74	*	*	*	*	*	*	*	*	*
4 years old	203	129	63.8	104	25	*	*	*	*	*	*	*	*
5 years old	196	191	97.5	31	145	13	2	*	*	*	*	*	*
6 years old	213	204	96.0	3	39	144	18	*	*	*	*	*	*
7 years old	201	198	98.5	*	*	17	161	17	3	*	*	*	*
8 years old	188	178	94.9	*	*	3	38	125	12	*	*	*	*
9 years old	196	193	98.5	*	*	4	*	40	133	16	*	*	*
10 years old	204	202	98.9	*	*	*	*	3	36	138	22	2	*
11 years old	182	174	95.5	*	*	*	*	*	*	52	114	7	*
12 years old	172	169	98.6	*	*	*	*	*	*	5	52	99	12
13 years old	157	146	93.3	*	*	*	*	*	*	*	*	29	112
14 years old	153	153	100.0	*	*	*	*	*	*	*	*	1	30
15 years old	185	178	96.2	*	*	*	*	*	*	*	*	*	2
16 years old	198	194	98.1	*	*	*	*	*	*	*	*	*	1
17 years old	153	147	96.0	*	*	*	*	*	*	*	*	*	*
18 years old	173	140	80.8	*	*	*	*	*	*	*	*	*	*
19 years old	164	145	88.4	*	*	*	*	*	*	*	*	*	*
20 years old	189	146	77.4	*	*	*	*	*	*	*	*	*	*
21 years old	185	149	80.6	*	*	*	*	*	*	*	*	3	*
22 years old	187	95	51.1	*	*	*	*	*	*	*	*	*	*
23 years old	155	72	46.5	*	*	*	*	*	*	*	*	*	*
24 years old	198	62	31.5	*	*	*	*	*	*	*	*	*	*
25 to 29 years old	1,153	189	16.4	*	*	*	*	*	*	*	*	*	*
30 to 34 years old	1,196	99	8.3	*	*	*	*	*	*	*	*	*	*
35 to 39 years old	1,260	61	4.9	*	*	*	*	*	*	*	*	*	*
40 to 44 years old	1,245	51	4.1	*	*	*	*	*	*	*	*	*	*
45 to 49 years old	1,092	13	1.2	*	*	*	*	*	*	*	*	*	*
50 to 54 years old	951	8	0.9	*	*	*	*	*	*	*	*	*	*
55 to 59 years old	854	10	1.1	*	*	*	*	*	*	*	*	*	*
60 to 64 years old	730	*	*	*	*	*	*	*	*	*	*	*	*
65 years and over	1,529	6	0.4	*	*	*	*	*	*	*	*	*	*

[1] Civilian noninstitutionalized population.
* = Quantity zero or rounds to zero.

Table A-2. Single Grade of Enrollment and High School Graduation Status for Population 3 Years Old and Over, by Sex, Age (Single Years for 3 to 24 Years), Race, and Hispanic Origin, October 2011—*Continued*

(Numbers in thousands; percent)

Age, sex, race, and Hispanic origin	Enrolled										Not enrolled		Not enrolled	
	High school				Undergraduate college				Graduate school		H.S. grad	Not grad	Number	Percent
	9	10	11	12	1	2	3	4	1	2+				
Female														
Total	260	341	311	407	539	497	368	179	147	204	11,201	2,444	13,645	68.3
3 years old	*	*	*	*	*	*	*	*	*	*	*	187	187	58.5
4 years old	*	*	*	*	*	*	*	*	*	*	*	113	113	29.8
5 years old	*	*	*	*	*	*	*	*	*	*	*	32	32	12.0
6 years old	*	*	*	*	*	*	*	*	*	*	*	15	15	5.2
7 years old	*	*	*	*	*	*	*	*	*	*	*	11	11	2.9
8 years old	*	*	*	*	*	*	*	*	*	*	*	5	5	2.0
9 years old	*	*	*	*	*	*	*	*	*	*	*	15	15	4.5
10 years old	*	*	*	*	*	*	*	*	*	*	*	5	5	1.8
11 years old	*	*	*	*	*	*	*	*	*	*	*	1	1	0.3
12 years old	7	*	*	*	*	*	*	*	*	*	*	3	3	0.9
13 years old	22	*	*	*	*	*	*	*	*	*	*	7	7	2.7
14 years old	156	28	3	*	*	*	*	*	*	*	*	3	3	1.0
15 years old	55	198	20	9	*	*	*	*	*	*	*	1	1	0.3
16 years old	13	84	172	30	2	*	*	*	*	*	*	*	*	*
17 years old	6	20	87	184	14	*	*	*	*	*	5	12	17	5.1
18 years old	*	*	22	115	156	18	*	*	*	*	45	9	54	14.8
19 years old	*	4	1	28	75	71	17	*	*	*	98	12	110	35.8
20 years old	*	4	3	6	35	82	43	2	*	*	111	32	143	45.0
21 years old	*	*	*	*	15	26	23	21	*	1	148	31	180	68.0
22 years old	*	1	*	4	25	19	31	36	6	17	193	51	244	63.7
23 years old	*	*	*	8	17	24	23	30	10	9	230	38	269	69.0
24 years old	*	*	*	*	11	8	19	20	18	13	203	20	222	71.3
25 to 29 years old	*	*	4	5	56	99	70	27	38	32	1,036	156	1,192	78.3
30 to 34 years old	*	*	*	3	36	66	61	12	26	15	1,126	141	1,267	85.3
35 to 39 years old	*	3	*	5	41	30	25	13	15	22	1,120	77	1,197	88.6
40 to 44 years old	*	*	*	3	23	29	16	7	12	14	1,166	148	1,314	92.6
45 to 49 years old	*	*	*	1	9	5	22	4	8	32	1,201	203	1,403	94.6
50 to 54 years old	*	*	*	4	16	12	11	4	5	24	1,199	169	1,368	94.8
55 to 59 years old	*	*	*	*	3	6	7	4	6	12	1,040	163	1,203	97.0
60 to 64 years old	*	*	*	2	1	3	*	*	2	12	778	186	964	97.8
65 years and over	*	*	*	*	3	*	*	*	*	*	1,502	599	2,102	99.8
ASIAN ALONE														
Both Sexes														
Total	164	190	163	168	229	231	270	124	127	224	8,806	1,464	10,270	73.1
3 years old	*	*	*	*	*	*	*	*	*	*	*	116	116	61.0
4 years old	*	*	*	*	*	*	*	*	*	*	*	73	73	36.2
5 years old	*	*	*	*	*	*	*	*	*	*	*	5	5	2.5
6 years old	*	*	*	*	*	*	*	*	*	*	*	9	9	4.0
7 years old	*	*	*	*	*	*	*	*	*	*	*	3	3	1.5
8 years old	*	*	*	*	*	*	*	*	*	*	*	10	10	5.1
9 years old	*	*	*	*	*	*	*	*	*	*	*	3	3	1.5
10 years old	*	*	*	*	*	*	*	*	*	*	*	2	2	1.1
11 years old	*	*	*	*	*	*	*	*	*	*	*	8	8	4.5
12 years old	1	*	*	*	*	*	*	*	*	*	*	2	2	1.4
13 years old	4	1	*	*	*	*	*	*	*	*	*	10	10	6.7
14 years old	103	17	2	*	*	*	*	*	*	*	*	*	*	*
15 years old	34	116	22	*	*	*	*	*	3	*	*	7	7	3.8
16 years old	16	44	104	27	3	*	*	*	*	*	3	*	4	1.9
17 years old	3	11	27	91	15	*	*	*	*	*	*	6	6	4.0
18 years old	2	*	4	29	103	*	*	*	*	*	25	9	33	19.2
19 years old	*	2	1	5	37	85	15	*	*	*	15	4	19	11.6
20 years old	*	*	*	7	15	41	76	7	*	*	35	8	43	22.6
21 years old	*	*	3	3	6	25	67	34	3	5	28	8	36	19.4
22 years old	*	*	*	*	8	20	29	17	15	6	86	5	91	48.9
23 years old	*	*	*	3	2	2	26	19	1	20	73	10	83	53.5
24 years old	*	*	*	*	*	9	8	12	12	22	114	21	136	68.5
25 to 29 years old	*	*	*	*	4	27	18	14	42	84	924	40	964	83.6
30 to 34 years old	*	*	*	*	17	16	16	6	11	33	1,056	41	1,097	91.7
35 to 39 years old	*	*	*	*	5	1	7	3	19	26	1,137	62	1,199	95.1
40 to 44 years old	*	*	*	*	10	3	8	5	9	16	1,105	88	1,193	95.9
45 to 49 years old	*	*	*	*	2	3	*	4	4	1	966	113	1,080	98.8
50 to 54 years old	*	*	*	*	*	*	*	1	4	3	849	93	942	99.1
55 to 59 years old	*	*	*	*	*	*	*	*	4	5	709	135	844	98.9
60 to 64 years old	*	*	*	*	*	*	*	*	*	*	586	143	730	100.0
65 years and over	*	*	*	3	*	*	*	*	*	3	1,094	429	1,523	99.6

[1] Civilian noninstitutionalized population.
* = Quantity zero or rounds to zero.

Table A-2. Single Grade of Enrollment and High School Graduation Status for Population 3 Years Old and Over, by Sex, Age (Single Years for 3 to 24 Years), Race, and Hispanic Origin, October 2011—*Continued*

(Numbers in thousands; percent)

Age, sex, race, and Hispanic origin	Population[1]	Enrolled		Enrolled										
				Nursery	Kinder-garten	Elementary grades							
		Number	Percent			1	2	3	4	5	6	7	8
Male													
Total	6,759	1,894	28.0	112	105	92	117	95	94	106	87	68	95
3 years old	94	38	40.3	38	*	*	*	*	*	*	*	*	*
4 years old	112	68	61.2	56	12	*	*	*	*	*	*	*	*
5 years old	91	90	99.2	14	74	2	*	*	*	*	*	*	*
6 years old	118	112	95.1	3	19	81	8	*	*	*	*	*	*
7 years old	103	100	97.1	*	*	6	83	8	3	*	*	*	*
8 years old	104	100	96.3	*	*	*	25	68	7	*	*	*	*
9 years old	96	93	96.9	*	*	4	*	19	65	6	*	*	*
10 years old	101	99	97.7	*	*	*	*	*	19	65	12	2	*
11 years old	95	95	100.0	*	*	*	*	*	*	33	59	3	*
12 years old	66	63	96.3	*	*	*	*	*	*	1	15	41	4
13 years old	89	88	98.1	*	*	*	*	*	*	*	*	20	66
14 years old	94	94	100.0	*	*	*	*	*	*	*	*	1	24
15 years old	83	80	96.6	*	*	*	*	*	*	*	*	*	*
16 years old	107	104	96.7	*	*	*	*	*	*	*	*	*	*
17 years old	75	72	96.1	*	*	*	*	*	*	*	*	*	*
18 years old	100	86	85.8	*	*	*	*	*	*	*	*	*	*
19 years old	78	73	93.5	*	*	*	*	*	*	*	*	*	*
20 years old	85	69	81.5	*	*	*	*	*	*	*	*	*	*
21 years old	97	78	79.7	*	*	*	*	*	*	*	*	*	*
22 years old	95	49	51.3	*	*	*	*	*	*	*	*	*	*
23 years old	74	34	45.4	*	*	*	*	*	*	*	*	*	*
24 years old	109	27	25.0	*	*	*	*	*	*	*	*	*	*
25 to 29 years old	583	92	15.8	*	*	*	*	*	*	*	*	*	*
30 to 34 years old	553	45	8.1	*	*	*	*	*	*	*	*	*	*
35 to 39 years old	592	18	3.1	*	*	*	*	*	*	*	*	*	*
40 to 44 years old	606	13	2.2	*	*	*	*	*	*	*	*	*	*
45 to 49 years old	514	5	1.0	*	*	*	*	*	*	*	*	*	*
50 to 54 years old	450	3	0.7	*	*	*	*	*	*	*	*	*	*
55 to 59 years old	374	3	0.7	*	*	*	*	*	*	*	*	*	*
60 to 64 years old	346	*	*	*	*	*	*	*	*	*	*	*	*
65 years and over	675	3	0.4	*	*	*	*	*	*	*	*	*	*
Female													
Total	7,291	1,885	25.9	100	104	89	103	91	90	105	101	74	64
3 years old	96	36	37.8	36	*	*	*	*	*	*	*	*	*
4 years old	91	61	67.0	48	13	*	*	*	*	*	*	*	*
5 years old	105	101	96.1	16	71	11	2	*	*	*	*	*	*
6 years old	95	92	97.0	*	20	63	9	*	*	*	*	*	*
7 years old	99	99	100.0	*	*	12	78	9	*	*	*	*	*
8 years old	84	78	93.3	*	*	3	13	57	5	*	*	*	*
9 years old	100	100	100.0	*	*	*	0	21	68	10	*	*	*
10 years old	103	103	100.0	*	*	*	*	3	17	73	10	*	*
11 years old	87	79	90.5	*	*	*	*	*	*	19	55	5	*
12 years old	106	106	100.0	*	*	*	*	*	*	4	36	58	8
13 years old	67	59	87.0	*	*	*	*	*	*	*	*	9	46
14 years old	59	59	100.0	*	*	*	*	*	*	*	*	*	6
15 years old	102	98	95.8	*	*	*	*	*	*	*	*	*	2
16 years old	91	90	99.8	*	*	*	*	*	*	*	*	*	1
17 years old	78	75	96.0	*	*	*	*	*	*	*	*	*	*
18 years old	73	54	74.0	*	*	*	*	*	*	*	*	*	*
19 years old	86	72	83.7	*	*	*	*	*	*	*	*	*	*
20 years old	104	77	74.0	*	*	*	*	*	*	*	*	*	*
21 years old	88	72	81.6	*	*	*	*	*	*	*	*	3	*
22 years old	92	47	50.8	*	*	*	*	*	*	*	*	*	*
23 years old	81	38	47.5	*	*	*	*	*	*	*	*	*	*
24 years old	89	35	39.6	*	*	*	*	*	*	*	*	*	*
25 to 29 years old	570	97	17.0	*	*	*	*	*	*	*	*	*	*
30 to 34 years old	643	54	8.5	*	*	*	*	*	*	*	*	*	*
35 to 39 years old	668	43	6.4	*	*	*	*	*	*	*	*	*	*
40 to 44 years old	639	38	6.0	*	*	*	*	*	*	*	*	*	*
45 to 49 years old	578	8	1.4	*	*	*	*	*	*	*	*	*	*
50 to 54 years old	501	5	1.0	*	*	*	*	*	*	*	*	*	*
55 to 59 years old	480	7	1.5	*	*	*	*	*	*	*	*	*	*
60 to 64 years old	383	*	*	*	*	*	*	*	*	*	*	*	*
65 years and over	855	3	0.4	*	*	*	*	*	*	*	*	*	*

[1] Civilian noninstitutionalized population.
* = Quantity zero or rounds to zero.

Table A-2. Single Grade of Enrollment and High School Graduation Status for Population 3 Years Old and Over, by Sex, Age (Single Years for 3 to 24 Years), Race, and Hispanic Origin, October 2011—*Continued*

(Numbers in thousands; percent)

Age, sex, race, and Hispanic origin	Enrolled										Not enrolled		Not enrolled	
	High school				Undergraduate college				Graduate school		H.S. grad	Not grad		
	9	10	11	12	1	2	3	4	1	2+			Number	Percent
Male														
Total	94	90	93	81	124	104	137	55	55	93	4,236	628	4,864	72.0
3 years old	*	*	*	*	*	*	*	*	*	*	*	56	56	59.7
4 years old	*	*	*	*	*	*	*	*	*	*	*	43	43	38.8
5 years old	*	*	*	*	*	*	*	*	*	*	*	1	1	0.8
6 years old	*	*	*	*	*	*	*	*	*	*	*	6	6	4.9
7 years old	*	*	*	*	*	*	*	*	*	*	*	3	3	2.9
8 years old	*	*	*	*	*	*	*	*	*	*	*	4	4	3.7
9 years old	*	*	*	*	*	*	*	*	*	*	*	3	3	3.1
10 years old	*	*	*	*	*	*	*	*	*	*	*	2	2	2.3
11 years old	*	*	*	*	*	*	*	*	*	*	*	*	*	*
12 years old	1	*	*	*	*	*	*	*	*	*	*	2	2	3.7
13 years old	1	*	*	*	*	*	*	*	*	*	*	2	2	1.9
14 years old	64	4	2	*	*	*	*	*	*	*	*	*	*	*
15 years old	14	53	13	*	*	*	*	*	*	*	*	3	3	3.4
16 years old	11	23	55	11	3	*	*	*	*	*	3	*	4	3.3
17 years old	3	7	17	42	3	*	*	*	*	*	*	3	3	3.9
18 years old	*	*	2	20	64	*	*	*	*	*	14	*	14	14.2
19 years old	*	2	1	2	25	31	11	*	*	*	5	*	5	6.5
20 years old	*	*	*	1	5	24	34	5	*	*	9	6	16	18.5
21 years old	*	*	3	3	6	14	36	10	3	2	19	1	20	20.3
22 years old	*	*	*	*	5	9	14	11	4	6	45	1	46	48.7
23 years old	*	*	*	3	2	2	13	10	*	3	33	7	41	54.6
24 years old	*	*	*	*	*	5	3	*	7	11	68	14	82	75.0
25 to 29 years old	*	*	*	*	4	12	4	7	27	38	470	20	491	84.2
30 to 34 years old	*	*	*	*	6	6	12	4	3	14	479	29	508	91.9
35 to 39 years old	*	*	*	*	*	*	6	3	*	9	550	24	573	96.9
40 to 44 years old	*	*	*	*	*	*	3	1	6	4	549	44	592	97.8
45 to 49 years old	*	*	*	*	*	*	*	4	*	1	461	48	509	99.0
50 to 54 years old	*	*	*	*	*	*	*	*	3	*	401	46	446	99.3
55 to 59 years old	*	*	*	*	*	*	*	*	*	3	332	39	371	99.3
60 to 64 years old	*	*	*	*	*	*	*	*	*	*	284	62	346	100.0
65 years and over	*	*	*	*	*	*	*	*	*	3	514	158	672	99.6
Female														
Total	70	101	69	87	105	127	133	68	72	131	4,570	836	5,406	74.1
3 years old	*	*	*	*	*	*	*	*	*	*	*	60	60	62.2
4 years old	*	*	*	*	*	*	*	*	*	*	*	30	30	33.0
5 years old	*	*	*	*	*	*	*	*	*	*	*	4	4	3.9
6 years old	*	*	*	*	*	*	*	*	*	*	*	3	3	3.0
7 years old	*	*	*	*	*	*	*	*	*	*	*	*	*	*
8 years old	*	*	*	*	*	*	*	*	*	*	*	6	6	6.7
9 years old	*	*	*	*	*	*	*	*	*	*	*	*	*	*
10 years old	*	*	*	*	*	*	*	*	*	*	*	*	*	*
11 years old	*	*	*	*	*	*	*	*	*	*	*	8	8	9.5
12 years old	*	*	*	*	*	*	*	*	*	*	*	*	*	*
13 years old	3	1	*	*	*	*	*	*	*	*	*	9	9	13.0
14 years old	39	13	*	*	*	*	*	*	*	*	*	*	*	*
15 years old	20	63	9	*	*	*	*	*	3	*	*	4	4	4.2
16 years old	4	20	49	15	*	*	*	*	*	*	*	*	*	0.2
17 years old	*	4	9	49	13	*	*	*	*	*	*	3	3	4.0
18 years old	2	*	2	10	40	*	*	*	*	*	10	9	19	26.0
19 years old	*	*	*	3	11	54	3	*	*	*	10	4	14	16.3
20 years old	*	*	*	6	10	17	41	3	*	*	25	2	27	26.0
21 years old	*	*	*	*	1	10	31	24	*	3	10	7	16	18.4
22 years old	*	*	*	*	4	11	14	7	11	*	41	4	45	49.2
23 years old	*	*	*	*	*	*	13	8	*	16	40	3	43	52.5
24 years old	*	*	*	*	*	3	5	12	4	11	46	7	54	60.4
25 to 29 years old	*	*	*	*	*	15	15	6	14	46	454	20	473	83.0
30 to 34 years old	*	*	*	*	11	10	4	2	8	19	577	12	589	91.5
35 to 39 years old	*	*	*	*	5	1	1	*	19	17	587	38	625	93.6
40 to 44 years old	*	*	*	*	10	3	5	5	3	13	557	44	601	94.0
45 to 49 years old	*	*	*	*	1	3	*	*	4	*	505	65	570	98.6
50 to 54 years old	*	*	*	*	*	*	*	1	1	3	448	48	496	99.0
55 to 59 years old	*	*	*	*	*	*	*	*	4	3	377	95	473	98.5
60 to 64 years old	*	*	*	*	*	*	*	*	*	*	302	81	383	100.0
65 years and over	*	*	*	3	*	*	*	*	*	*	580	272	851	99.6

[1] Civilian noninstitutionalized population.
* = Quantity zero or rounds to zero.

Table A-2. Single Grade of Enrollment and High School Graduation Status for Population 3 Years Old and Over, by Sex, Age (Single Years for 3 to 24 Years), Race, and Hispanic Origin, October 2011—*Continued*

(Numbers in thousands; percent)

Age, sex, race, and Hispanic origin	Population[1]	Enrolled		Enrolled									
				Nursery	Kinder-garten	Elementary grades							
		Number	Percent			1	2	3	4	5	6	7	8
HISPANIC[2]													
Both Sexes													
Total	47,417	16,131	34.0	1,010	1,042	1,167	1,038	1,057	926	953	854	857	862
3 years old	1,091	247	22.6	225	22	*	*	*	*	*	*	*	*
4 years old	1,204	709	58.9	582	127	*	*	*	*	*	*	*	*
5 years old	1,072	999	93.1	198	724	68	8	*	*	*	*	*	*
6 years old	1,072	1,052	98.1	5	167	838	34	8	*	*	*	*	*
7 years old	1,065	1,041	97.8	*	2	229	767	40	3	*	*	*	*
8 years old	1,023	1,007	98.4	*	*	28	197	699	74	9	*	*	*
9 years old	971	957	98.6	*	*	5	26	259	620	43	4	*	*
10 years old	939	921	98.0	*	*	*	6	45	189	652	24	4	*
11 years old	937	926	98.8	*	*	*	*	7	37	223	593	57	10
12 years old	785	783	99.7	*	*	*	*	*	3	23	194	505	50
13 years old	897	875	97.6	*	*	*	*	*	*	3	26	251	559
14 years old	814	802	98.6	*	*	*	*	*	*	*	6	19	188
15 years old	820	802	97.8	*	*	*	*	*	*	*	5	14	34
16 years old	865	836	96.7	*	*	*	*	*	*	*	2	*	15
17 years old	817	755	92.4	*	*	*	*	*	*	*	*	3	*
18 years old	856	631	73.7	*	*	*	*	*	*	*	*	*	*
19 years old	887	506	57.0	*	*	*	*	*	*	*	*	*	*
20 years old	822	389	47.4	*	*	*	*	*	*	*	*	*	*
21 years old	873	385	44.1	*	*	*	*	*	*	*	*	4	*
22 years old	844	254	30.1	*	*	*	*	*	*	*	*	*	*
23 years old	820	203	24.7	*	*	*	*	*	*	*	*	*	*
24 years old	873	142	16.2	*	*	*	*	*	*	*	*	*	*
25 to 29 years old	4,088	429	10.5	*	*	*	*	*	*	*	*	*	*
30 to 34 years old	4,048	183	4.5	*	*	*	*	*	*	*	*	*	3
35 to 39 years old	3,758	138	3.7	*	*	*	*	*	*	*	*	*	*
40 to 44 years old	3,396	48	1.4	*	*	*	*	*	*	*	*	*	*
45 to 49 years old	2,994	29	1.0	*	*	*	*	*	*	*	*	*	*
50 to 54 years old	2,473	43	1.8	*	*	*	*	*	*	*	*	*	3
55 to 59 years old	1,910	30	1.6	*	*	*	*	*	*	*	*	*	*
60 to 64 years old	1,454	3	0.2	*	*	*	*	*	*	*	*	*	*
65 years and over	2,947	6	0.2	*	*	*	*	*	*	*	*	*	*
Male													
Total	24,395	8,271	33.9	536	526	638	503	541	514	475	438	435	425
3 years old	555	143	25.8	127	17	*	*	*	*	*	*	*	*
4 years old	608	364	59.9	302	62	*	*	*	*	*	*	*	*
5 years old	544	508	93.5	108	361	34	5	*	*	*	*	*	*
6 years old	570	560	98.2	*	84	463	10	4	*	*	*	*	*
7 years old	513	506	98.6	*	2	124	358	21	*	*	*	*	*
8 years old	522	516	98.9	*	*	12	109	347	42	5	*	*	*
9 years old	510	505	99.0	*	*	5	17	134	324	24	1	*	*
10 years old	477	472	99.1	*	*	*	4	29	115	318	6	*	*
11 years old	478	478	100.0	*	*	*	*	6	29	109	297	29	8
12 years old	405	403	99.5	*	*	*	*	*	3	18	111	251	17
13 years old	467	451	96.6	*	*	*	*	*	*	*	15	140	282
14 years old	417	412	98.7	*	*	*	*	*	*	*	3	3	92
15 years old	420	415	98.7	*	*	*	*	*	*	*	5	7	11
16 years old	468	450	96.0	*	*	*	*	*	*	*	*	*	11
17 years old	405	377	93.0	*	*	*	*	*	*	*	*	*	*
18 years old	475	346	72.7	*	*	*	*	*	*	*	*	*	*
19 years old	477	235	49.2	*	*	*	*	*	*	*	*	*	*
20 years old	443	221	49.9	*	*	*	*	*	*	*	*	*	*
21 years old	480	177	36.8	*	*	*	*	*	*	*	*	4	*
22 years old	448	107	23.9	*	*	*	*	*	*	*	*	*	*
23 years old	449	98	21.8	*	*	*	*	*	*	*	*	*	*
24 years old	479	84	17.6	*	*	*	*	*	*	*	*	*	*
25 to 29 years old	2,221	220	9.9	*	*	*	*	*	*	*	*	*	*
30 to 34 years old	2,176	73	3.4	*	*	*	*	*	*	*	*	*	3
35 to 39 years old	1,977	81	4.1	*	*	*	*	*	*	*	*	*	*
40 to 44 years old	1,754	20	1.1	*	*	*	*	*	*	*	*	*	*
45 to 49 years old	1,517	14	0.9	*	*	*	*	*	*	*	*	*	*
50 to 54 years old	1,233	20	1.6	*	*	*	*	*	*	*	*	*	*
55 to 59 years old	936	12	1.3	*	*	*	*	*	*	*	*	*	*
60 to 64 years old	696	3	0.5	*	*	*	*	*	*	*	*	*	*
65 years and over	1,276	*	*	*	*	*	*	*	*	*	*	*	*

[1] Civilian noninstitutionalized population.
[2] May be of any race.
* = Quantity zero or rounds to zero.

Table A-2. Single Grade of Enrollment and High School Graduation Status for Population 3 Years Old and Over, by Sex, Age (Single Years for 3 to 24 Years), Race, and Hispanic Origin, October 2011—*Continued*

(Numbers in thousands; percent)

Age, sex, race, and Hispanic origin	Enrolled										Not enrolled		Not enrolled	
	High school				Undergraduate college				Graduate school		H.S. grad	Not grad	Number	Percent
	9	10	11	12	1	2	3	4	1	2+				
HISPANIC[1]														
Both Sexes														
Total	810	903	794	902	924	868	594	276	114	178	19,111	12,175	31,286	66.0
3 years old	*	*	*	*	*	*	*	*	*	*	*	844	844	77.4
4 years old	*	*	*	*	*	*	*	*	*	*	*	495	495	41.1
5 years old	*	*	*	*	*	*	*	*	*	*	*	74	74	6.9
6 years old	*	*	*	*	*	*	*	*	*	*	*	20	20	1.9
7 years old	*	*	*	*	*	*	*	*	*	*	*	24	24	2.3
8 years old	*	*	*	*	*	*	*	*	*	*	*	17	17	1.7
9 years old	*	*	*	*	*	*	*	*	*	*	*	14	14	1.4
10 years old	*	*	*	*	*	*	*	*	*	*	*	18	18	1.9
11 years old	*	*	*	*	*	*	*	*	*	*	*	11	11	1.2
12 years old	8	*	*	*	*	*	*	*	*	*	*	2	2	0.3
13 years old	28	8	*	*	*	*	*	*	*	*	*	22	22	2.5
14 years old	499	81	9	*	*	*	*	*	*	*	*	12	12	1.5
15 years old	218	441	70	17	2	*	3	*	*	*	*	18	18	2.2
16 years old	44	286	425	62	2	*	*	*	*	*	*	28	29	3.4
17 years old	5	73	206	439	24	2	3	*	*	*	25	37	62	7.6
18 years old	*	3	45	240	310	26	6	*	*	*	170	56	225	26.3
19 years old	*	3	15	65	215	173	32	3	*	*	271	110	382	43.1
20 years old	*	*	4	13	67	199	97	6	4	*	330	103	433	52.7
21 years old	*	*	*	13	60	108	118	64	11	7	341	147	488	55.9
22 years old	*	*	4	2	28	76	72	55	3	15	397	193	590	69.9
23 years old	*	*	*	11	21	50	73	34	9	4	453	164	617	75.2
24 years old	*	5	*	3	23	54	21	27	7	2	528	203	731	83.7
25 to 29 years old	*	3	4	14	78	86	111	51	35	46	2,544	1,115	3,659	89.5
30 to 34 years old	*	*	2	3	36	52	31	11	17	27	2,571	1,295	3,865	95.5
35 to 39 years old	*	*	*	10	24	25	11	12	21	35	2,341	1,279	3,620	96.3
40 to 44 years old	*	*	*	4	14	4	7	5	3	11	2,208	1,140	3,349	98.6
45 to 49 years old	*	*	3	3	10	3	2	*	*	8	1,946	1,018	2,964	99.0
50 to 54 years old	1	*	4	3	5	8	*	5	2	12	1,598	832	2,430	98.3
55 to 59 years old	4	*	*	*	*	3	6	3	3	12	1,148	732	1,880	98.4
60 to 64 years old	3	*	*	*	*	*	*	*	*	*	827	624	1,451	99.8
65 years and over	*	*	3	*	3	*	*	*	*	*	1,412	1,528	2,941	99.8
Male														
Total	439	474	403	486	446	434	268	122	56	112	9,742	6,381	16,124	66.1
3 years old	*	*	*	*	*	*	*	*	*	*	*	412	412	74.2
4 years old	*	*	*	*	*	*	*	*	*	*	*	243	243	40.1
5 years old	*	*	*	*	*	*	*	*	*	*	*	35	35	6.5
6 years old	*	*	*	*	*	*	*	*	*	*	*	10	10	1.8
7 years old	*	*	*	*	*	*	*	*	*	*	*	7	7	1.4
8 years old	*	*	*	*	*	*	*	*	*	*	*	6	6	1.1
9 years old	*	*	*	*	*	*	*	*	*	*	*	5	5	1.0
10 years old	*	*	*	*	*	*	*	*	*	*	*	4	4	0.9
11 years old	*	*	*	*	*	*	*	*	*	*	*	*	*	*
12 years old	2	*	*	*	*	*	*	*	*	*	*	2	2	0.5
13 years old	12	2	*	*	*	*	*	*	*	*	*	16	16	3.4
14 years old	263	44	6	*	*	*	*	*	*	*	*	5	5	1.3
15 years old	128	221	35	6	2	*	*	*	*	*	*	5	5	1.3
16 years old	24	159	218	35	2	*	*	*	*	*	*	18	19	4.0
17 years old	5	43	99	212	13	2	3	*	*	*	13	16	28	7.0
18 years old	*	*	30	155	142	14	4	*	*	*	96	33	130	27.3
19 years old	*	*	7	37	103	67	18	3	*	*	173	69	242	50.8
20 years old	*	*	*	4	47	108	57	4	*	*	167	55	222	50.1
21 years old	*	*	*	13	33	58	34	32	*	4	213	91	304	63.2
22 years old	*	*	*	2	10	41	26	19	*	8	227	114	341	76.1
23 years old	*	*	*	*	6	33	34	15	6	4	252	99	351	78.2
24 years old	*	5	*	3	17	29	14	11	4	2	287	107	394	82.4
25 to 29 years old	*	*	4	4	36	47	59	22	18	30	1,331	670	2,001	90.1
30 to 34 years old	*	*	*	3	13	12	10	4	7	21	1,337	765	2,102	96.6
35 to 39 years old	*	*	*	9	12	16	*	9	14	23	1,198	698	1,896	95.9
40 to 44 years old	*	*	*	*	7	2	7	2	3	*	1,098	636	1,734	98.9
45 to 49 years old	*	*	*	3	*	3	*	*	*	8	957	546	1,503	99.1
50 to 54 years old	1	*	4	*	1	3	*	2	2	6	773	440	1,213	98.4
55 to 59 years old	*	*	*	*	*	*	3	*	3	7	565	359	924	98.7
60 to 64 years old	3	*	*	*	*	*	*	*	*	*	410	282	692	99.5
65 years and over	*	*	*	*	*	*	*	*	*	*	645	630	1,276	100.0

[1]May be of any race.
* = Quantity zero or rounds to zero.

Table A-2. Single Grade of Enrollment and High School Graduation Status for Population 3 Years Old and Over, by Sex, Age (Single Years for 3 to 24 Years), Race, and Hispanic Origin, October 2011—*Continued*

(Numbers in thousands; percent)

Age, sex, race, and Hispanic origin	Population[1]	Enrolled		Enrolled										
				Nursery	Kinder-garten	Elementary grades								
		Number	Percent			1	2	3	4	5	6	7	8
Female														
Total	23,022	7,860	34.1	474	516	529	536	516	412	478	416	422	437
3 years old	536	104	19.3	98	5	*	*	*	*	*	*	*	*
4 years old	596	345	57.8	280	65	*	*	*	*	*	*	*	*
5 years old	528	490	92.8	90	363	34	3	*	*	*	*	*	*
6 years old	502	492	98.0	5	83	376	24	4	*	*	*	*	*
7 years old	552	536	97.0	*	*	104	409	19	3	*	*	*	*
8 years old	501	490	97.8	*	*	15	88	352	32	4	*	*	*
9 years old	461	452	98.0	*	*	*	9	125	296	19	3	*	*
10 years old	462	448	97.0	*	*	*	3	16	73	334	18	4	*
11 years old	459	448	97.6	*	*	*	*	*	8	114	296	28	2
12 years old	381	381	100.0	*	*	*	*	*	*	5	83	254	33
13 years old	430	424	98.7	*	*	*	*	*	*	3	11	111	277
14 years old	396	390	98.4	*	*	*	*	*	*	*	3	16	96
15 years old	400	387	96.8	*	*	*	*	*	*	*	*	6	23
16 years old	397	387	97.5	*	*	*	*	*	*	*	2	*	4
17 years old	412	378	91.7	*	*	*	*	*	*	*	*	3	*
18 years old	381	285	74.9	*	*	*	*	*	*	*	*	*	*
19 years old	411	271	66.0	*	*	*	*	*	*	*	*	*	*
20 years old	380	169	44.4	*	*	*	*	*	*	*	*	*	*
21 years old	393	209	53.1	*	*	*	*	*	*	*	*	*	*
22 years old	395	147	37.2	*	*	*	*	*	*	*	*	*	*
23 years old	371	105	28.2	*	*	*	*	*	*	*	*	*	*
24 years old	394	57	14.5	*	*	*	*	*	*	*	*	*	*
25 to 29 years old	1,867	209	11.2	*	*	*	*	*	*	*	*	*	*
30 to 34 years old	1,872	109	5.8	*	*	*	*	*	*	*	*	*	*
35 to 39 years old	1,781	57	3.2	*	*	*	*	*	*	*	*	*	*
40 to 44 years old	1,643	28	1.7	*	*	*	*	*	*	*	*	*	*
45 to 49 years old	1,477	15	1.0	*	*	*	*	*	*	*	*	*	*
50 to 54 years old	1,240	23	1.9	*	*	*	*	*	*	*	*	*	3
55 to 59 years old	974	18	1.8	*	*	*	*	*	*	*	*	*	*
60 to 64 years old	759	*	*	*	*	*	*	*	*	*	*	*	*
65 years and over	1,672	6	0.4	*	*	*	*	*	*	*	*	*	*

[1] Civilian noninstitutionalized population.
* = Quantity zero or rounds to zero.

Table A-2. Single Grade of Enrollment and High School Graduation Status for Population 3 Years Old and Over, by Sex, Age (Single Years for 3 to 24 Years), Race, and Hispanic Origin, October 2011—*Continued*

(Numbers in thousands; percent)

Age, sex, race, and Hispanic origin	Enrolled										Not enrolled		Not enrolled	
	High school				Undergraduate college				Graduate school		H.S. grad	Not grad		
	9	10	11	12	1	2	3	4	1	2+			Number	Percent
Female														
Total	371	429	391	416	478	434	326	153	58	66	9,369	5,794	15,163	65.9
3 years old	*	*	*	*	*	*	*	*	*	*	*	432	432	80.7
4 years old	*	*	*	*	*	*	*	*	*	*	*	252	252	42.2
5 years old	*	*	*	*	*	*	*	*	*	*	*	38	38	7.2
6 years old	*	*	*	*	*	*	*	*	*	*	*	10	10	2.0
7 years old	*	*	*	*	*	*	*	*	*	*	*	17	17	3.0
8 years old	*	*	*	*	*	*	*	*	*	*	*	11	11	2.2
9 years old	*	*	*	*	*	*	*	*	*	*	*	9	9	2.0
10 years old	*	*	*	*	*	*	*	*	*	*	*	14	14	3.0
11 years old	*	*	*	*	*	*	*	*	*	*	*	11	11	2.4
12 years old	6	*	*	*	*	*	*	*	*	*	*	*	*	*
13 years old	16	6	*	*	*	*	*	*	*	*	*	6	6	1.3
14 years old	236	36	4	*	*	*	*	*	*	*	*	6	6	1.6
15 years old	90	219	35	11	*	*	3	*	*	*	*	13	13	3.2
16 years old	20	127	207	27	*	*	*	*	*	*	*	10	10	2.5
17 years old	*	31	107	227	10	*	*	*	*	*	13	22	34	8.3
18 years old	*	3	15	85	168	11	3	*	*	*	73	22	96	25.1
19 years old	*	3	8	28	113	106	14	*	*	*	98	41	140	34.0
20 years old	*	*	4	9	20	90	40	2	4	*	163	48	211	55.6
21 years old	*	*	*	*	27	50	85	33	11	4	128	56	184	46.9
22 years old	*	*	4	*	17	35	45	35	3	7	170	79	249	62.8
23 years old	*	*	*	11	15	17	39	19	4	*	201	65	266	71.8
24 years old	*	*	*	*	6	25	7	16	3	*	242	95	337	85.5
25 to 29 years old	*	3	*	10	42	39	53	29	16	16	1,212	446	1,658	88.8
30 to 34 years old	*	*	2	*	23	41	22	7	10	6	1,233	530	1,763	94.2
35 to 39 years old	*	*	*	2	13	10	11	3	7	12	1,144	581	1,724	96.8
40 to 44 years old	*	*	*	4	7	3	*	3	*	11	1,111	504	1,615	98.3
45 to 49 years old	*	*	3	*	10	*	2	*	*	*	989	472	1,461	99.0
50 to 54 years old	*	*	*	3	3	4	*	3	*	6	825	392	1,217	98.1
55 to 59 years old	4	*	*	*	*	3	3	3	*	5	582	373	956	98.2
60 to 64 years old	*	*	*	*	*	*	*	*	*	*	417	342	759	100.0
65 years and over	*	*	3	*	3	*	*	*	*	*	767	898	1,665	99.6

[1] Civilian noninstitutionalized population.
* = Quantity zero or rounds to zero.

Table A-3. Nursery and Primary School Enrollment of Population 3 to 6 Years Old, by Control of School, Attendance Status, Age, Race, Hispanic Origin, Mother's Labor Force Status and Education, and Family Income, October 2011

(Numbers in thousands)

Characteristic	Total[1]	Not enrolled	Enrolled in nursery school								
			Total			Public			Private		
			Total	Part-day	Full-day	Total	Part-day	Full-day	Total	Part-day	Full-day
3 TO 6 YEARS OLD											
Total	17,183	4,578	4,946	2,591	2,355	2,904	1,521	1,383	2,042	1,070	972
Race											
White alone	12,797	3,401	3,624	2,026	1,598	1,997	1,124	873	1,627	902	725
White alone non-Hispanic	8,823	2,120	2,743	1,542	1,200	1,332	742	590	1,411	800	610
Black alone	2,604	722	794	285	509	562	216	346	232	70	163
Asian alone	801	202	212	122	90	120	78	43	92	44	47
Hispanic[2]	4,440	1,433	1,010	555	455	766	440	326	244	115	130
Labor force status of mother											
Children not living with mother	1,409	408	364	169	195	272	136	136	92	32	59
Mother employed part-time	2,452	577	769	441	329	393	220	172	377	220	156
Mother employed full-time	6,557	1,536	2,067	831	1,236	1,158	492	665	909	338	571
Mother unemployed	1,068	351	220	116	104	176	99	78	44	17	27
Mother not in the labor force	5,697	1,706	1,526	1,035	491	905	573	331	621	462	159
Education of mother											
Children not living with mother	1,409	408	364	169	195	272	136	136	92	32	59
Elementary: 0 to 8 years	734	290	120	70	50	111	62	49	9	8	1
High School: 9 to 11 years	1,394	419	287	137	150	263	123	140	24	14	10
High school graduate	4,019	1,236	1,035	568	467	796	425	370	239	143	97
Some college or associate's degree	4,610	1,271	1,336	681	655	814	423	391	522	258	265
Bachelor's degree or more	5,018	954	1,804	967	838	648	351	297	1,156	615	541
Family income											
Less than $20,000	3,074	926	764	355	409	675	312	363	89	43	46
$20,000 to $29,999	1,979	593	534	311	223	443	263	180	91	47	44
$30,000 to $39,999	1,590	511	400	206	194	317	166	151	83	40	43
$40,000 to $49,999	989	293	280	157	123	162	75	86	119	82	37
$50,000 to $74,999	2,305	623	648	357	291	368	196	173	280	161	118
$75,000 and over	4,477	812	1,651	862	790	506	284	222	1,145	577	568
Not reported	2,770	820	668	344	325	433	224	209	236	119	116
3 AND 4 YEARS OLD											
Total	8,765	4,168	4,169	2,163	2,006	2,395	1,239	1,157	1,774	925	849
Race											
White alone	6,439	3,128	3,028	1,687	1,341	1,629	915	714	1,399	772	627
White alone non-Hispanic	4,417	1,933	2,334	1,299	1,035	1,118	610	509	1,216	690	526
Black alone	1,398	626	677	243	434	477	182	295	200	61	139
Asian alone	392	189	178	91	87	93	54	40	85	37	47
Hispanic[2]	2,295	1,339	807	445	362	596	350	245	211	95	116
Labor force status of mother											
Children not living with mother	735	370	314	142	172	231	114	117	83	28	55
Mother employed part-time	1,220	525	648	373	275	313	178	136	335	196	139
Mother employed full-time	3,390	1,425	1,770	710	1,060	981	417	564	789	292	496
Mother unemployed	528	329	186	94	92	145	76	68	41	17	24
Mother not in the labor force	2,892	1,520	1,252	844	407	725	453	272	527	391	136
Education of mother											
Children not living with mother	735	370	314	142	172	231	114	117	83	28	55
Elementary: 0 to 8 years	368	261	93	52	42	85	44	41	8	7	1
High School: 9 to 11 years	643	375	232	125	107	211	111	100	21	14	7
High school graduate	2,133	1,122	869	461	408	645	328	317	224	133	92
Some college or associate's degree	2,416	1,176	1,145	581	563	698	362	337	446	220	227
Bachelor's degree or more	2,470	864	1,516	802	714	525	279	246	991	523	468
Family income											
Less than $20,000	1,581	838	636	298	337	562	259	303	74	39	35
$20,000 to $29,999	1,036	535	443	263	179	362	220	141	81	43	38
$30,000 to $39,999	844	473	340	169	171	268	130	138	72	38	33
$40,000 to $49,999	513	259	235	129	106	137	66	71	98	63	35
$50,000 to $74,999	1,207	565	573	310	264	313	158	155	261	152	109
$75,000 and over	2,221	749	1,398	722	676	409	238	171	989	484	505
Not reported	1,363	749	545	272	273	345	167	178	200	105	95

[1]Civilian noninstitutionalized population.
[2]May be of any race.
* = Quantity zero or rounds to zero.

Table A-3. Nursery and Primary School Enrollment of Population 3 to 6 Years Old, by Control of School, Attendance Status, Age, Race, Hispanic Origin, Mother's Labor Force Status and Education, and Family Income, October 2011—*Continued*

(Numbers in thousands)

Characteristic	Enrolled in kindergarten									Enrolled in elementary school		
	Total			Public			Private					
	Total	Part-day	Full-day	Total	Part-day	Full-day	Total	Part-day	Full-day	Total	Public	Private
3 TO 6 YEARS OLD												
Total	4,185	965	3,220	3,702	840	2,862	482	125	358	3,475	3,186	289
Race												
White alone	3,177	766	2,411	2,784	656	2,129	393	110	282	2,596	2,360	236
White alone non-Hispanic	2,219	547	1,672	1,883	443	1,440	335	104	232	1,742	1,532	209
Black alone	552	62	490	496	61	435	56	*	55	536	504	31
Asian alone	209	59	151	189	49	140	21	10	11	177	158	19
Hispanic[2]	1,040	249	791	982	242	740	58	6	51	956	922	34
Labor force status of mother												
Children not living with mother	322	75	247	300	68	232	22	6	15	315	295	20
Mother employed part-time	608	152	456	526	116	410	82	36	46	498	435	63
Mother employed full-time	1,628	326	1,303	1,440	292	1,148	188	34	154	1,326	1,233	94
Mother unemployed	291	51	240	277	51	226	14	*	14	206	202	4
Mother not in the labor force	1,335	361	974	1,159	313	846	176	48	128	1,130	1,022	108
Education of mother												
Children not living with mother	322	75	247	300	68	232	22	6	15	315	295	20
Elementary: 0 to 8 years	153	42	112	147	38	109	6	4	2	170	153	17
High School: 9 to 11 years	347	56	292	337	50	287	10	6	5	342	328	14
High school graduate	978	226	752	915	206	709	64	21	43	770	724	45
Some college or associate's degree	1,151	234	916	1,044	212	832	107	23	84	852	812	41
Bachelor's degree or more	1,233	332	901	960	267	693	273	65	208	1,026	874	152
Family income												
Less than $20,000	787	134	653	747	123	624	40	11	29	597	582	15
$20,000 to $29,999	415	85	330	390	75	315	25	10	15	437	424	13
$30,000 to $39,999	392	90	302	364	84	280	28	6	22	286	270	16
$40,000 to $49,999	216	58	157	195	58	136	21	*	21	199	191	8
$50,000 to $74,999	637	173	464	549	137	412	88	36	52	397	373	25
$75,000 and over	1,052	271	781	850	225	625	202	46	156	961	801	160
Not reported	685	153	532	607	137	469	78	16	62	598	545	52
3 AND 4 YEARS OLD												
Total	428	113	314	337	93	244	91	20	70	*	*	*
Race												
White alone	283	78	205	225	62	163	58	16	42	*	*	*
White alone non-Hispanic	150	45	105	106	29	77	45	16	29	*	*	*
Black alone	95	8	87	68	8	60	27	*	27	*	*	*
Asian alone	25	14	11	20	10	10	6	4	1	*	*	*
Hispanic[2]	149	45	104	136	45	91	13	*	13	*	*	*
Labor force status of mother												
Children not living with mother	51	15	36	46	15	32	4	*	4	*	*	*
Mother employed part-time	48	17	31	27	9	19	21	8	12	*	*	*
Mother employed full-time	195	31	164	165	31	134	30	*	30	*	*	*
Mother unemployed	13	5	8	13	5	8	*	*	*	*	*	*
Mother not in the labor force	121	46	75	85	34	51	36	12	24	*	*	*
Education of mother												
Children not living with mother	51	15	36	46	15	32	4	*	4	*	*	*
Elementary: 0 to 8 years	14	6	9	14	6	9	*	*	*	*	*	*
High School: 9 to 11 years	37	5	31	37	5	31	*	*	*	*	*	*
High school graduate	142	29	113	114	24	90	27	5	22	*	*	*
Some college or associate's degree	95	15	80	74	12	62	22	3	19	*	*	*
Bachelor's degree or more	89	44	45	52	31	20	37	12	25	*	*	*
Family income												
Less than $20,000	107	25	82	94	23	71	13	2	11	*	*	*
$20,000 to $29,999	58	12	46	55	12	43	3	0	3	*	*	*
$30,000 to $39,999	31	9	22	24	9	14	7	*	7	*	*	*
$40,000 to $49,999	19	*	19	16	*	16	3	*	3	*	*	*
$50,000 to $74,999	69	20	49	46	12	34	23	8	15	*	*	*
$75,000 and over	74	32	42	45	22	23	30	10	20	*	*	*
Not reported	69	15	54	58	15	43	11	*	11	*	*	*

[1]Civilian noninstitutionalized population.
[2]May be of any race.
* = Quantity zero or rounds to zero.

Table A-3. Nursery and Primary School Enrollment of Population 3 to 6 Years Old, by Control of School, Attendance Status, Age, Race, Hispanic Origin, Mother's Labor Force Status and Education, and Family Income, October 2008—*Continued*

(Numbers in thousands)

Characteristic	Total[1]	Not enrolled	Enrolled in nursery school								
			Total			Public			Private		
			Total	Part-day	Full-day	Total	Part-day	Full-day	Total	Part-day	Full-day
5 YEARS OLD											
Total	4,201	312	742	415	326	481	270	211	261	145	116
Race											
White alone	3,197	215	580	332	248	354	202	152	226	130	96
White alone non-Hispanic	2,211	148	398	235	162	205	125	79	193	110	83
Black alone	561	69	103	42	61	76	34	43	27	8	18
Asian alone	196	5	31	27	3	24	20	3	7	7	*
Hispanic[2]	1,072	74	198	109	89	165	90	75	33	20	13
Labor force status of mother											
Children not living with mother	332	28	47	23	24	38	19	19	9	5	4
Mother employed part-time	651	33	118	64	54	76	39	37	42	25	18
Mother employed full-time	1,530	86	284	121	163	166	75	91	118	45	73
Mother unemployed	265	16	35	22	13	32	22	9	3	*	3
Mother not in the labor force	1,423	149	258	185	73	170	115	55	89	71	18
Education of mother											
Children not living with mother	332	28	47	23	24	38	19	19	9	5	4
Elementary: 0 to 8 years	194	25	27	18	8	26	17	8	1	1	*
High School: 9 to 11 years	360	33	50	12	37	47	12	35	3	*	3
High school graduate	918	79	159	107	52	146	97	49	13	10	4
Some college or associate's degree	1,106	71	175	94	81	105	56	49	70	38	32
Bachelor's degree or more	1,291	76	284	161	124	119	69	51	165	92	73
Family income											
Less than $20,000	763	64	123	56	67	108	52	56	15	4	11
$20,000 to $29,999	425	43	73	39	34	68	35	34	5	4	*
$30,000 to $39,999	405	33	58	38	21	48	36	13	10	2	8
$40,000 to $49,999	240	27	41	28	13	20	9	11	21	19	2
$50,000 to $74,999	571	48	73	47	26	54	38	16	19	9	10
$75,000 and over	1,089	46	254	140	114	97	46	51	157	93	64
Not reported	709	51	120	68	52	85	54	30	35	14	21
6 YEARS OLD											
Total	4,218	98	35	12	23	28	12	16	7	*	7
Race											
White alone	3,161	58	16	8	8	14	7	7	2	*	1
White alone non-Hispanic	2,194	39	11	8	3	9	7	2	2	*	1
Black alone	645	28	14	*	14	9	*	9	5	*	5
Asian alone	213	9	3	3	*	3	3	*	*	*	*
Hispanic[2]	1,072	20	5	*	5	5	*	5	*	*	*
Labor force status of mother											
Children not living with mother	342	10	3	3	*	3	3	*	*	*	*
Mother employed part-time	581	20	3	3	*	3	3	*	*	*	*
Mother employed full-time	1,637	25	12	*	12	11	*	11	2	*	1
Mother unemployed	275	6	*	*	*	*	*	*	*	*	*
Mother not in the labor force	1,382	37	16	5	11	10	5	5	5	*	5
Education of mother											
Children not living with mother	342	10	3	3	*	3	3	*	*	*	*
Elementary: 0 to 8 years	172	5	*	*	*	*	*	*	*	*	*
High School: 9 to 11 years	391	12	5	*	5	5	*	5	*	*	*
High school graduate	968	34	7	*	6	5	*	5	1	*	1
Some college or associate's degree	1,088	24	16	5	11	10	5	5	6	*	5
Bachelor's degree or more	1,257	14	4	3	*	4	3	0	*	*	*
Family income											
Less than $20,000	730	23	5	*	5	5	0	5	*	*	*
$20,000 to $29,999	518	14	19	8	11	13	8	5	5	*	5
$30,000 to $39,999	341	6	2	*	2	*	*	*	1	*	1
$40,000 to $49,999	236	8	4	*	4	4	*	4	*	*	*
$50,000 to $74,999	527	11	1	*	1	1	*	1	*	*	*
$75,000 and over	1,167	16	*	*	*	*	*	*	*	*	*
Not reported	699	19	4	4	*	4	3	*	*	*	*

[1]Civilian noninstitutionalized population.
[2]May be of any race.
* = Quantity zero or rounds to zero.

Table A-3. Nursery and Primary School Enrollment of Population 3 to 6 Years Old, by Control of School, Attendance Status, Age, Race, Hispanic Origin, Mother's Labor Force Status and Education, and Family Income, October 2008—*Continued*

(Numbers in thousands)

Characteristic	Enrolled in kindergarten									Enrolled in elementary school		
	Total			Public			Private			Total	Public	Private
	Total	Part-day	Full-day	Total	Part-day	Full-day	Total	Part-day	Full-day			
5 YEARS OLD												
Total	2,921	684	2,237	2,610	602	2,007	312	82	230	225	209	17
Race												
White alone	2,237	549	1,688	1,981	477	1,504	256	72	184	166	153	13
White alone non-Hispanic	1,561	391	1,170	1,340	325	1,015	221	66	155	104	92	13
Black alone	355	43	312	327	43	284	28	*	28	34	31	3
Asian alone	145	31	114	130	26	104	15	6	10	15	15	*
Hispanic[2]	724	174	551	689	167	522	35	6	28	76	76	*
Labor force status of mother												
Children not living with mother	228	51	178	217	47	169	12	3	8	29	29	*
Mother employed part-time	484	119	365	431	95	336	53	24	29	16	16	*
Mother employed full-time	1,097	232	865	959	206	753	138	27	111	62	62	*
Mother unemployed	210	32	178	196	32	164	14	*	14	5	5	*
Mother not in the labor force	902	250	652	807	222	585	95	28	67	113	97	16
Education of mother												
Children not living with mother	228	51	178	217	47	169	12	3	8	29	29	*
Elementary: 0 to 8 years	120	32	89	117	28	89	4	4	*	22	19	3
High School: 9 to 11 years	248	38	209	241	35	205	7	3	4	30	28	2
High school graduate	624	163	462	591	149	442	34	14	20	55	48	7
Some college or associate's degree	804	173	631	732	160	572	72	13	59	56	52	4
Bachelor's degree or more	896	227	669	712	183	530	184	44	140	34	34	0
Family income												
Less than $20,000	527	84	443	505	77	428	22	7	15	49	42	7
$20,000 to $29,999	277	61	216	260	55	205	17	6	11	31	31	*
$30,000 to $39,999	285	67	219	267	64	203	18	3	15	29	22	7
$40,000 to $49,999	160	54	106	145	54	90	16	*	16	12	12	*
$50,000 to $74,999	427	110	317	372	83	289	55	26	28	23	20	3
$75,000 and over	758	192	566	626	164	462	132	28	104	31	31	*
Not reported	487	115	371	434	105	329	52	10	42	51	51	*
6 YEARS OLD												
Total	836	168	668	756	145	611	80	23	57	3,250	2,977	272
Race												
White alone	657	139	518	578	117	462	79	22	57	2,430	2,207	223
White alone non-Hispanic	508	111	397	438	89	349	70	22	48	1,637	1,441	197
Black alone	101	10	91	100	10	91	1	*	*	502	474	28
Asian alone	39	14	26	39	14	26	*	*	*	162	143	19
Hispanic[2]	167	30	137	158	30	127	9	*	9	880	846	34
Labor force status of mother												
Children not living with mother	43	9	34	37	6	31	6	3	3	286	266	20
Mother employed part-time	76	16	60	67	12	55	9	4	4	482	420	63
Mother employed full-time	337	62	274	317	56	261	20	7	13	1,264	1,171	93
Mother unemployed	68	15	53	68	15	53	*	*	*	201	197	4
Mother not in the labor force	312	65	247	267	56	210	45	9	37	1,017	925	92
Education of mother												
Children not living with mother	43	9	34	37	6	31	6	3	3	286	266	20
Elementary: 0 to 8 years	18	4	15	16	4	12	2	*	2	148	135	14
High School: 9 to 11 years	63	12	51	60	10	50	3	3	1	312	300	12
High school graduate	212	35	178	209	33	177	3	2	1	715	677	38
Some college or associate's degree	251	46	205	238	40	198	14	7	7	797	760	37
Bachelor's degree or more	248	62	186	196	53	143	52	9	43	992	841	151
Family income												
Less than $20,000	153	25	128	148	23	125	5	2	3	549	540	8
$20,000 to $29,999	80	11	69	75	8	67	4	3	1	405	392	13
$30,000 to $39,999	76	14	62	73	11	62	3	3	*	257	248	9
$40,000 to $49,999	36	4	32	34	4	30	2	*	2	187	180	8
$50,000 to $74,999	141	44	97	131	42	89	10	1	9	375	353	22
$75,000 and over	220	47	173	180	39	140	40	7	33	930	770	160
Not reported	129	23	106	114	17	97	15	6	9	546	495	52

[1]Civilian noninstitutionalized population.
[2]May be of any race.
* = Quantity zero or rounds to zero.

Table A-4. Current Grade for People 15 to 24 Years Old Enrolled in School, and Highest Grade Completed for People with Selected Enrollment and Completion Status, by Sex, Age, Race, and Hispanic Origin, October 2011

(Numbers in thousands)

Age, sex, race, and Hispanic origin	Enrolled[1]							Not enrolled[1]						
	Current grade							Enrolled last year						Not enrolled last year
								Highest grade completed						
	Less than 9th grade	9th grade	10th grade	11th grade	12th grade	College, (graduated this year)	Other college	Less than 9th grade	9th grade	10th grade	11th or 12th, no diploma	New HS graduate	Other	
ALL RACES														
Both Sexes														
Total	251	1,201	3,968	3,959	4,320	2,114	10,659	17	48	84	243	978	2,324	12,057
15 years old	157	986	2,492	260	56	13	6	*	14	5	*	*	*	30
16 years old	48	169	1,171	2,330	280	24	13	6	9	30	18	14	10	40
17 years old	18	28	222	1,058	2,398	88	60	1	7	17	46	41	7	109
18 years old	3	10	41	209	1,244	1,317	470	*	8	15	67	483	85	278
19 years old	*	5	13	48	200	531	1,924	2	*	4	50	301	257	898
20 to 24 years old	25	3	28	54	142	141	8,187	8	10	12	61	140	1,964	10,702
Male														
Total	131	710	2,074	1,989	2,202	1,050	5,011	9	26	52	129	569	1,121	6,394
15 years old	79	576	1,221	105	21	9	*	*	7	5	*	*	*	14
16 years old	31	108	661	1,084	147	16	13	4	9	16	12	9	7	21
17 years old	9	15	137	620	1,113	32	38	1	3	11	24	13	7	57
18 years old	*	4	28	118	731	594	182	*	*	6	32	266	56	147
19 years old	*	3	7	30	117	326	848	*	*	3	33	185	138	488
20 to 24 years old	11	3	19	32	74	74	3,929	4	7	10	28	95	913	5,668
Female														
Total	120	491	1,894	1,970	2,118	1,064	5,649	8	22	32	114	409	1,204	5,663
15 years old	78	410	1,271	155	34	4	6	*	8	*	*	*	*	16
16 years old	17	61	510	1,246	133	8	*	2	*	14	6	4	3	19
17 years old	9	13	84	438	1,285	56	22	*	3	6	22	27	*	52
18 years old	2	6	13	91	514	724	288	*	8	9	35	217	29	131
19 years old	*	1	7	18	84	205	1,076	2	*	1	17	115	119	410
20 to 24 years old	13	*	9	21	68	67	4,257	4	3	2	33	44	1,051	5,034
WHITE ALONE														
Total	179	917	2,963	3,018	3,252	1,581	8,373	17	22	68	172	753	1,827	9,284
15 years old	112	803	1,862	197	39	9	3	*	3	5	*	*	*	21
16 years old	30	92	897	1,797	186	7	11	6	5	30	17	10	7	37
17 years old	13	14	153	820	1,872	65	46	1	3	12	30	35	7	80
18 years old	3	4	28	140	942	1,005	354	*	3	12	59	358	68	241
19 years old	*	1	3	32	121	396	1,543	2	*	*	40	236	179	731
20 to 24 years old	21	3	21	32	92	99	6,416	8	7	8	27	112	1,567	8,175
WHITE ALONE NON-HISPANIC														
Total	103	672	2,246	2,291	2,469	1,200	6,788	9	11	42	119	554	1,480	6,676
15 years old	61	600	1,470	128	25	7	*	*	*	*	*	*	*	11
16 years old	12	55	647	1,402	131	7	8	4	1	23	7	10	7	33
17 years old	11	9	85	622	1,464	58	26	1	3	5	25	23	7	49
18 years old	2	4	24	99	719	772	277	*	3	10	49	269	45	156
19 years old	*	1	1	17	69	301	1,239	*	*	*	26	169	135	502
20 to 24 years old	17	3	19	24	60	55	5,239	4	3	4	13	83	1,287	5,925
BLACK ALONE														
Total	51	157	633	634	733	333	1,344	*	11	15	51	158	294	1,946
15 years old	33	111	392	33	12	3	*	*	4	*	*	*	*	7
16 years old	13	35	167	331	60	13	3	*	4	*	*	3	4	*
17 years old	5	7	50	181	322	12	7	*	3	5	16	4	*	15
18 years old	*	*	9	58	236	186	75	*	*	3	6	77	8	17
19 years old	*	3	8	13	70	88	230	*	*	3	9	48	60	111
20 to 24 years old	*	*	7	19	33	30	1,029	*	*	4	21	26	222	1,796

[1]Civilian noninstitutionalized population.
* = Quantity zero or rounds to zero.

Table A-4. Current Grade for People 15 to 24 Years Old Enrolled in School, and Highest Grade Completed for People with Selected Enrollment and Completion Status, by Sex, Age, Race, and Hispanic Origin, October 2011—*Continued*

(Numbers in thousands)

Age, sex, race, and Hispanic origin	Enrolled[1]							Not enrolled[1]						
	Current grade							Enrolled last year						Not enrolled last year
								Highest grade completed						
	Less than 9th grade	9th grade	10th grade	11th grade	12th grade	College, (graduated this year)	Other college	Less than 9th grade	9th grade	10th grade	11th or 12th, no diploma	New HS graduate	Other	
ASIAN ALONE														
Total	7	56	173	161	165	124	645	*	12	*	5	19	104	318
15 years old	2	34	116	22	0	*	3	*	7	*	*	*	*	*
16 years old	1	16	44	104	27	3	*	*	*	*	*	*	*	4
17 years old	*	3	11	27	91	9	6	*	*	*	*	*	*	5
18 years old	*	2	*	4	29	82	22	*	5	*	3	16	4	6
19 years old	*	*	2	1	5	24	112	*	*	*	1	2	4	11
20 to 24 years old	3	*	*	3	12	6	502	*	*	*	1	1	95	291
HISPANIC[2]														
Total	76	267	811	768	865	417	1,697	8	14	26	60	208	389	2,869
15 years old	52	218	441	70	17	2	3	*	3	5	*	*	*	10
16 years old	17	44	286	425	62	*	2	2	4	7	11	*	*	4
17 years old	3	5	73	206	439	8	21	*	*	8	7	13	*	34
18 years old	*	*	3	45	240	257	85	*	*	2	10	95	31	87
19 years old	*	*	3	15	65	106	317	2	*	*	14	70	51	244
20 to 24 years old	4	*	5	8	42	44	1,269	4	7	4	18	29	307	2,490

[1]Civilian noninstitutionalized population.
[2]May be of any race.
* = Quantity zero or rounds to zero.

Table A-5. Type of College and Year Enrolled for College Students 15 Years Old and Over, by Age, Sex, Race, Attendance Status, Control of School, Disability Status, and Enrollment Status, October 2011

(Numbers in thousands)

Characteristic	Total enrolled[1]	Undergraduate college								Graduate school	
		All colleges				Two-year college		Four-year college			
		1st year	2nd year	3rd year	4th year	1st year	2nd or higher	1st year	2nd or higher	1st year	2nd or higher
BOTH SEXES											
Full-Time Students											
Total	14,903	3,683	3,896	3,003	2,157	1,590	2,127	2,093	6,929	856	1,310
Age											
15–19 years old	4,064	2,446	1,396	205	11	888	453	1,557	1,160	6	*
20–24 years old	6,850	606	1,705	2,135	1,643	298	1,042	307	4,442	377	384
25–34 years old	2,713	396	552	446	364	245	427	151	935	341	613
35 years old and over	1,276	235	242	216	138	158	205	77	392	132	312
Race											
White alone	11,205	2,642	3,000	2,249	1,740	1,111	1,612	1,531	5,376	615	960
White alone non-Hispanic	9,333	2,028	2,474	1,869	1,528	767	1,238	1,261	4,633	553	880
Black alone	2,279	716	587	462	224	343	352	373	921	132	158
Asian alone	963	197	192	235	109	60	101	137	435	81	149
Hispanic[2]	2,041	681	562	413	232	380	396	301	812	66	86
Employment Status											
Full-time	2,063	296	475	402	307	128	335	168	850	167	414
Part-time	4,434	764	1,300	1,030	836	391	761	373	2,404	217	286
Not employed	8,407	2,622	2,121	1,570	1,014	1,070	1,030	1,551	3,674	471	609
Control of School											
Public	11,768	3,063	3,345	2,437	1,663	1,450	1,979	1,612	5,465	499	762
Private	3,135	620	551	566	494	140	147	480	1,464	357	547
Disability Status											
Any disability	352	90	83	79	46	51	49	38	159	21	34
No disability	14,551	3,593	3,813	2,923	2,111	1,539	2,077	2,054	6,769	835	1,276
Part-Time Students											
Total	5,494	1,023	1,290	1,034	540	742	1,247	281	1,617	564	1,043
Age											
15–19 years old	381	252	104	17	3	182	73	71	50	5	*
20–24 years old	1,478	277	473	372	157	208	485	69	518	108	90
25–34 years old	1,905	246	411	405	200	169	396	77	620	220	423
35 years old and over	1,731	248	302	240	179	184	293	64	429	231	530
Race											
White alone	4,207	780	996	792	443	558	970	222	1,261	399	797
White alone non-Hispanic	3,370	552	711	627	402	390	667	162	1,074	364	714
Black alone	867	183	215	155	57	141	185	42	241	97	161
Asian alone	241	31	39	35	15	22	35	9	54	46	75
Hispanic[2]	912	243	306	181	43	181	310	62	220	47	92
Employment Status											
Full-time	3,182	441	630	584	291	316	608	125	897	435	801
Part-time	1,179	274	330	261	147	210	329	64	409	59	108
Not employed	1,134	309	331	189	102	216	311	93	311	70	134
Control of School											
Public	4,366	894	1,152	878	385	679	1,157	215	1,259	372	685
Private	1,128	129	138	156	155	63	90	66	358	192	358
Disability Status											
Any disability	209	37	72	37	22	22	44	15	87	12	29
No disability	5,286	986	1,218	997	518	720	1,203	266	1,530	553	1,014

[1]Civilian noninstitutionalized population.
[2]May be of any race.
* = Quantity zero or rounds to zero.

Table A-5. Type of College and Year Enrolled for College Students 15 Years Old and Over, by Age, Sex, Race, Attendance Status, Control of School, Disability Status, and Enrollment Status, October 2011—*Continued*

(Numbers in thousands)

Characteristic	Total enrolled[1]	Undergraduate college								Graduate school	
		All colleges				Two-year college		Four-year college			
		1st year	2nd year	3rd year	4th year	1st year	2nd or higher	1st year	2nd or higher	1st year	2nd or higher
MALE											
Full-Time Students											
Total	6,734	1,711	1,756	1,426	937	708	956	1,003	3,163	374	531
Age											
15–19 years old	1,872	1,165	600	99	6	437	204	729	501	1	*
20–24 years old	3,271	310	857	1,054	709	140	530	170	2,090	201	141
25–34 years old	1,172	167	225	195	174	89	168	78	427	122	289
35 years old and over	418	69	73	78	48	42	53	26	146	49	101
Race											
White alone	5,142	1,259	1,404	1,060	758	525	765	734	2,457	264	397
White alone non-Hispanic	4,253	959	1,146	880	668	351	569	608	2,124	242	358
Black alone	916	287	234	209	82	133	116	154	410	53	52
Asian alone	455	109	80	118	48	26	42	83	204	40	59
Hispanic[2]	967	331	269	195	109	182	204	149	369	23	41
Employment Status											
Full-time	898	144	221	177	131	68	144	75	384	66	160
Part-time	1,879	312	531	486	331	183	318	129	1,029	73	146
Not employed	3,957	1,254	1,005	763	475	456	493	798	1,750	234	225
Control of School											
Public	5,367	1,424	1,531	1,178	726	650	899	774	2,536	193	315
Private	1,367	286	225	248	211	58	57	229	627	180	216
Disability Status											
Any disability	182	47	51	49	17	25	28	22	88	4	15
No disability	6,552	1,664	1,705	1,377	920	683	927	981	3,075	370	516
Part-Time Students											
Total	2,398	456	542	444	244	317	472	139	757	224	488
Age											
15–19 years old	185	123	49	6	3	79	27	44	30	5	*
20–24 years old	732	153	227	194	63	118	215	35	268	42	54
25–34 years old	814	102	160	176	86	66	158	36	264	86	205
35 years old and over	666	78	107	69	92	55	72	23	195	91	230
Race											
White alone	1,912	354	424	367	217	246	386	108	623	167	382
White alone non-Hispanic	1,479	239	273	298	204	164	236	75	539	144	320
Black alone	296	74	71	39	20	54	53	20	76	30	63
Asian alone	113	15	24	19	7	10	17	5	34	14	34
Hispanic[1]	471	115	165	73	13	82	153	33	98	33	71
Employment Status											
Full-time	1,508	209	277	268	167	156	261	52	452	190	397
Part-time	470	111	148	103	51	78	124	32	177	17	41
Not employed	419	137	117	74	25	83	87	54	129	18	50
Control of School											
Public	1,889	401	479	386	171	292	443	109	594	135	316
Private	509	55	63	58	72	25	30	30	163	89	172
Disability Status											
Any disability	101	13	44	18	4	7	13	6	54	3	18
No disability	2,297	443	497	426	240	310	459	132	704	221	470

[1]Civilian noninstitutionalized population.
[2]May be of any race.
* = Quantity zero or rounds to zero.

Table A-5. Type of College and Year Enrolled for College Students 15 Years Old and Over, by Age, Sex, Race, Attendance Status, Control of School, Disability Status, and Enrollment Status, October 2011—*Continued*

(Numbers in thousands)

Characteristic	Total enrolled[1]	Undergraduate college								Graduate school	
		All colleges				Two-year college		Four-year college			
		1st year	2nd year	3rd year	4th year	1st year	2nd or higher	1st year	2nd or higher	1st year	2nd or higher
FEMALE											
Full-Time Students											
Total	8,169	1,972	2,140	1,576	1,220	882	1,171	1,090	3,765	482	779
Age											
15–19 years old	2,192	1,280	796	106	5	451	249	829	659	5	*
20–24 years old	3,579	296	848	1,082	934	158	512	138	2,352	176	243
25–34 years old	1,541	229	327	251	190	156	259	73	508	220	324
35 years old and over	857	167	169	137	91	116	151	51	246	82	211
Race											
White alone	6,063	1,383	1,596	1,189	982	587	847	797	2,920	350	563
White alone non-Hispanic	5,081	1,069	1,329	989	860	416	669	653	2,509	312	522
Black alone	1,363	429	353	252	142	210	236	219	511	80	107
Asian alone	508	88	112	117	61	34	59	54	230	40	90
Hispanic[2]	1,074	350	293	218	123	198	192	152	443	44	45
Employment Status											
Full-time	1,164	152	255	226	176	60	191	93	466	101	254
Part-time	2,555	452	769	544	505	208	443	244	1,376	144	140
Not employed	4,450	1,367	1,116	807	539	614	537	753	1,924	237	384
Control of School											
Public	6,401	1,638	1,814	1,259	937	800	1,081	838	2,929	306	448
Private	1,768	333	326	318	283	82	90	252	837	176	331
Disability Status											
Any disability	170	43	32	31	29	26	21	16	71	17	19
No disability	7,999	1,929	2,108	1,546	1,191	856	1,150	1,073	3,695	465	760
Part-Time Students											
Total	3,097	568	748	590	296	425	774	143	860	340	555
Age											
15–19 years old	196	129	55	11	*	103	47	26	20	*	*
20–24 years old	746	124	247	178	94	90	269	34	250	66	36
25–34 years old	1,090	144	251	229	114	103	237	41	356	134	218
35 years old and over	1,065	170	196	172	88	129	221	41	234	140	300
Race											
White alone	2,295	426	571	425	226	312	584	114	638	232	414
White alone non-Hispanic	1,891	312	438	329	198	225	431	87	534	221	393
Black alone	571	110	144	116	37	88	132	22	165	68	97
Asian alone	128	17	15	16	8	13	18	4	21	32	41
Hispanic[2]	441	128	140	108	30	99	157	29	121	14	21
Employment Status											
Full-time	1,673	232	352	315	124	160	346	72	445	246	403
Part-time	709	163	182	159	96	132	204	31	232	43	67
Not employed	715	172	214	116	76	133	224	39	182	52	85
Control of School											
Public	2,478	493	673	492	213	387	714	106	665	237	369
Private	619	75	75	98	82	38	60	36	195	103	186
Disability Status											
Any disability	108	24	28	19	17	15	31	9	33	8	11
No disability	2,989	543	721	571	278	410	744	134	827	332	543

[1]Civilian noninstitutionalized population.
[2]May be of any race.
* = Quantity zero or rounds to zero.

Table A-6. Employment Status and Enrollment in Vocational Courses for the Population 15 Years Old and Over, by Sex, Age, Educational Attainment, and College Enrollment, October 2011

(Numbers in thousands; percent)

Characteristic	Total[1]			Employed full-time			Employed part-time			Not employed		
	Total	Enrolled in vocational courses[2] Number	Enrolled in vocational courses[2] Percent	Total	Enrolled in vocational courses[2] Number	Enrolled in vocational courses[2] Percent	Total	Enrolled in vocational courses[2] Number	Enrolled in vocational courses[2] Percent	Total	Enrolled in vocational courses[2] Number	Enrolled in vocational courses[2] Percent
BOTH SEXES												
Total	244,289	4,143	1.7	113,734	1,995	1.8	27,942	717	2.6	102,613	1,431	1.4
Age												
15 to 19 years old	20,747	306	1.5	1,179	31	2.6	3,455	87	2.5	16,113	188	1.2
20 to 24 years old	21,477	792	3.7	8,149	219	2.7	5,164	235	4.5	8,165	339	4.1
25 to 34 years old	41,552	994	2.4	26,233	513	2.0	4,532	119	2.6	10,788	362	3.4
35 to 44 years old	39,438	741	1.9	26,432	473	1.8	3,904	76	1.9	9,103	192	2.1
45 to 64 years old	81,036	1,123	1.4	47,692	719	1.5	7,960	171	2.1	25,384	234	0.9
65 years and over	40,037	187	0.5	4,050	40	1.0	2,928	30	1.0	33,059	116	0.4
Educational attainment												
Not a high school graduate	41,139	236	0.6	9,167	80	0.9	4,071	19	0.5	27,901	137	0.5
High school graduate only	71,184	900	1.3	31,541	317	1.0	7,414	152	2.1	32,229	431	1.3
Some college or associate's degree	66,991	1,727	2.6	31,756	739	2.3	10,055	376	3.7	25,180	613	2.4
Bachelor's degree or more	64,974	1,280	2.0	41,270	859	2.1	6,402	171	2.7	17,303	250	1.4
College enrollment												
Enrolled in college	20,397	1,365	6.7	5,244	423	8.1	5,612	346	6.2	9,541	596	6.2
Not enrolled in college	223,891	2,778	1.2	108,490	1,572	1.4	22,330	372	1.7	93,071	835	0.9
MALE												
Total	118,701	1,956	1.6	64,949	1,084	1.7	10,350	278	2.7	43,401	595	1.4
Age												
15 to 19 years old	10,597	159	1.5	703	18	2.5	1,524	37	2.4	8,369	104	1.2
20 to 24 years old	10,870	447	4.1	4,551	141	3.1	2,396	141	5.9	3,924	165	4.2
25 to 34 years old	20,819	431	2.1	15,282	287	1.9	1,617	35	2.2	3,920	109	2.8
35 to 44 years old	19,420	334	1.7	15,393	255	1.7	981	9	0.9	3,046	70	2.3
45 to 64 years old	39,365	501	1.3	26,605	370	1.4	2,348	38	1.6	10,413	92	0.9
65 years and over	17,630	85	0.5	2,416	14	0.6	1,484	16	1.1	13,730	55	0.4
Educational attainment												
Not a high school graduate	20,913	115	0.5	6,363	47	0.7	1,785	13	0.7	12,765	55	0.4
High school graduate only	35,633	479	1.3	19,203	204	1.1	2,844	66	2.3	13,585	209	1.5
Some college or associate's degree	30,843	775	2.5	16,976	377	2.2	3,738	152	4.1	10,129	246	2.4
Bachelor's degree or more	31,313	588	1.9	22,407	457	2.0	1,983	46	2.3	6,923	84	1.2
College enrollment												
Enrolled in college	9,132	644	7.1	2,407	217	9.0	2,348	165	7.0	4,377	263	6.0
Not enrolled in college	109,570	1,312	1.2	62,543	867	1.4	8,002	113	1.4	39,025	332	0.9
FEMALE												
Total	125,587	2,187	1.7	48,785	911	1.9	17,591	440	2.5	59,211	836	1.4
Age												
15 to 19 years old	10,150	147	1.4	476	13	2.7	1,931	50	2.6	7,744	84	1.1
20 to 24 years old	10,607	345	3.3	3,598	78	2.2	2,768	93	3.4	4,242	173	4.1
25 to 34 years old	20,733	563	2.7	10,950	226	2.1	2,915	84	2.9	6,868	253	3.7
35 to 44 years old	20,019	408	2.0	11,039	218	2.0	2,923	67	2.3	6,057	123	2.0
45 to 64 years old	41,671	622	1.5	21,087	348	1.7	5,612	132	2.4	14,971	142	0.9
65 years and over	22,407	101	0.5	1,635	27	1.6	1,443	14	0.9	19,329	61	0.3
Educational attainment												
Not a high school graduate	20,227	121	0.6	2,804	34	1.2	2,286	6	0.3	15,136	82	0.5
High school graduate only	35,551	421	1.2	12,338	113	0.9	4,570	86	1.9	18,644	222	1.2
Some college or associate's degree	36,148	952	2.6	14,780	362	2.4	6,317	223	3.5	15,051	366	2.4
Bachelor's degree or more	33,661	692	2.1	18,863	402	2.1	4,418	125	2.8	10,380	166	1.6
College enrollment												
Enrolled in college	11,266	721	6.4	2,838	206	7.3	3,264	181	5.5	5,164	333	6.5
Not enrolled in college	114,322	1,466	1.3	45,947	704	1.5	14,327	259	1.8	54,047	503	0.9

[1]Civilian noninstitutionalized population.
[2]People enrolled in vocational courses are not considered to be enrolled in school for all tables.

Table A-7. Enrollment Status of High School Graduates 15 to 24 Years Old, by Type of School, Attendance Status, and Sex, October 2011

(Numbers in thousands)

Characteristic	Total[1]	Enrolled in college or vocational school						Not enrolled	
		2-year college		4-year college		Graduate school	Vocational school	Employed	Not employed
		Full-time	Part-time	Full-time	Part-time				
ALL RACES									
Both sexes	25,681	2,657	930	7,431	707	966	271	8,774	3,946
Graduated this year	3,092	692	115	1,245	56	7	25	441	512
Graduated earlier	22,589	1,965	815	6,187	651	959	247	8,332	3,434
Male	12,786	1,300	428	3,466	378	439	160	4,743	1,870
Graduated this year	1,620	348	59	612	29	2	17	273	279
Graduated earlier	11,166	953	369	2,854	349	437	144	4,470	1,591
Female	12,896	1,356	501	3,965	329	526	111	4,031	2,076
Graduated this year	1,472	344	56	633	26	4	8	168	233
Graduated earlier	11,423	1,012	446	3,333	302	522	103	3,862	1,843
WHITE ALONE									
Both sexes	19,953	2,015	739	5,844	581	721	207	7,077	2,769
Graduated this year	2,334	507	94	928	46	6	16	359	378
Graduated earlier	17,619	1,509	644	4,917	535	715	191	6,717	2,392
Male	10,031	1,027	334	2,731	317	323	134	3,840	1,325
Graduated this year	1,243	262	49	460	24	2	11	227	208
Graduated earlier	8,788	765	286	2,271	293	321	123	3,613	1,117
Female	9,923	988	404	3,113	264	398	73	3,237	1,445
Graduated this year	1,091	245	46	467	22	4	4	132	170
Graduated earlier	8,831	743	359	2,646	242	394	68	3,104	1,275
WHITE ALONE, NON-HISPANIC									
Both sexes	15,712	1,425	468	4,942	446	668	172	5,589	2,003
Graduated this year	1,754	345	57	765	29	4	11	296	247
Graduated earlier	13,958	1,080	411	4,176	418	664	161	5,293	1,756
Male	7,768	698	208	2,328	249	301	111	2,937	936
Graduated this year	915	170	29	380	17	*	7	180	134
Graduated earlier	6,853	527	180	1,948	232	301	105	2,758	802
Female	7,944	727	260	2,614	197	367	61	2,651	1,068
Graduated this year	838	174	28	385	12	4	4	116	113
Graduated earlier	7,106	553	231	2,228	185	362	56	2,535	955
BLACK ALONE									
Both sexes	3,684	431	125	913	68	122	36	1,128	862
Graduated this year	490	117	14	197	4	*	3	50	104
Graduated earlier	3,194	314	111	716	63	122	33	1,077	758
Male	1,723	173	63	421	25	48	13	595	384
Graduated this year	219	52	7	76	*	*	3	29	52
Graduated earlier	1,504	121	56	346	25	48	10	566	332
Female	1,962	258	62	491	43	74	23	532	477
Graduated this year	271	65	7	121	4	*	*	21	52
Graduated earlier	1,691	193	55	370	39	74	23	511	425
ASIAN ALONE									
Both sexes	1,142	115	37	500	22	87	16	235	129
Graduated this year	143	34	*	88	2	*	5	5	9
Graduated earlier	999	81	37	412	21	87	11	230	120
Male	578	57	23	245	17	38	6	117	74
Graduated this year	94	19	*	60	2	*	2	3	8
Graduated earlier	484	38	23	185	16	38	4	114	66
Female	564	58	14	256	5	49	10	118	55
Graduated this year	50	15	*	28	*	*	3	2	1
Graduated earlier	514	43	14	227	5	49	7	116	54
HISPANIC[2]									
Both sexes	4,616	634	281	963	162	62	39	1,641	836
Graduated this year	625	179	41	178	18	2	5	73	131
Graduated earlier	3,991	455	240	785	144	60	34	1,568	705
Male	2,452	341	130	443	83	27	27	989	413
Graduated this year	346	96	20	88	8	2	5	54	74
Graduated earlier	2,107	245	110	355	76	25	22	935	339
Female	2,164	293	151	520	78	34	12	652	423
Graduated this year	280	83	21	90	10	*	*	18	57
Graduated earlier	1,884	209	130	430	68	34	12	633	366

[1]Civilian noninstitutionalized population.
[2]May be of any race.
* = Quantity zero or rounds to zero.

Table A-8. Enrollment Status for Families with Children 5 to 24 Years Old, by Control of School, Race, Type of Family, and Family Income, October 2011

(Numbers in thousands)

Characteristic	Total[1]	Families with no dependents 5 to 24 years old[2]	Families with dependents 5 to 24 years old[2]: Kindergarten, elementary, and high school enrollment status				College enrollment status		
			None enrolled in elementary or high school	Public only	Public and private	Private only	None enrolled in college	One enrolled in college	Two or more enrolled in college
ALL RACES									
All families	79,647	40,721	7,790	28,199	733	2,205	32,308	5,602	1,017
Less than $20,000	9,810	4,219	873	4,509	45	165	5,059	479	53
$20,000 to $74,999	31,614	16,429	2,967	11,285	253	680	12,802	2,069	315
$75,000 and over	20,789	10,179	2,136	7,213	289	972	8,295	1,889	425
Not reported	17,434	9,894	1,813	5,191	146	389	6,151	1,165	224
Married-couple families	58,693	33,009	4,685	18,706	548	1,745	21,025	3,856	804
Less than $20,000	4,320	2,446	238	1,570	13	54	1,688	163	24
$20,000 to $74,999	22,541	13,128	1,601	7,177	168	467	7,924	1,271	218
$75,000 and over	18,822	9,447	1,750	6,447	259	919	7,362	1,618	395
Not reported	13,011	7,989	1,096	3,513	108	305	4,051	804	167
Unmarried householder[3]	20,954	7,712	3,104	9,492	185	460	11,284	1,746	213
Less than $20,000	5,491	1,773	635	2,940	32	111	3,372	316	29
$20,000 to $74,999	9,073	3,300	1,366	4,109	86	212	4,878	798	97
$75,000 and over	1,967	733	387	766	29	53	933	271	30
Not reported	4,423	1,905	717	1,679	38	84	2,100	361	57
WHITE ALONE									
All families	64,639	34,498	6,032	21,714	600	1,795	25,013	4,346	783
Less than $20,000	6,855	3,133	586	2,997	33	106	3,397	296	29
$20,000 to $74,999	25,676	13,956	2,274	8,703	200	543	9,940	1,555	225
$75,000 and over	17,901	9,029	1,761	6,030	256	826	6,951	1,575	346
Not reported	14,206	8,380	1,412	3,984	112	320	4,725	920	182
Married-couple families	50,410	29,015	3,943	15,488	478	1,486	17,556	3,184	656
Less than $20,000	3,449	1,947	199	1,249	13	41	1,369	119	13
$20,000 to $74,999	19,300	11,579	1,314	5,875	139	393	6,553	1,004	164
$75,000 and over	16,406	8,453	1,491	5,444	232	786	6,247	1,373	333
Not reported	11,256	7,035	938	2,921	95	267	3,387	688	145
Unmarried householder[3]	14,229	5,483	2,090	6,226	122	308	7,456	1,162	127
Less than $20,000	3,407	1,186	386	1,749	21	65	2,027	177	16
$20,000 to $74,999	6,376	2,377	960	2,829	60	150	3,387	551	61
$75,000 and over	1,496	575	270	586	24	40	704	202	13
Not reported	2,951	1,344	473	1,063	17	53	1,338	232	37
WHITE ALONE NON-HISPANIC									
All families	54,058	30,783	4,930	16,212	519	1,614	19,175	3,504	596
Less than $20,000	4,456	2,315	382	1,649	14	96	1,958	166	17
$20,000 to $74,999	20,754	12,310	1,775	6,043	174	452	7,181	1,147	117
$75,000 and over	16,608	8,524	1,595	5,482	235	771	6,345	1,418	321
Not reported	12,241	7,635	1,178	3,038	95	295	3,692	773	141
Married-couple families	43,425	26,469	3,325	11,839	434	1,358	13,818	2,645	494
Less than $20,000	2,212	1,467	132	571	6	36	676	62	7
$20,000 to $74,999	15,918	10,413	1,028	4,018	125	334	4,697	742	66
$75,000 and over	15,340	8,042	1,363	4,975	219	740	5,742	1,247	309
Not reported	9,956	6,547	802	2,275	84	248	2,702	594	113
Unmarried householder[3]	10,633	4,315	1,605	4,373	84	256	5,357	859	102
Less than $20,000	2,244	848	250	1,078	8	60	1,281	105	10
$20,000 to $74,999	4,836	1,897	747	2,026	49	118	2,484	405	51
$75,000 and over	1,268	483	232	507	16	31	602	170	13
Not reported	2,285	1,087	376	763	12	47	989	179	28

[1]Civilian noninstitutionalized population.
[2]Dependents may be unmarried (or married with spouse absent) child, grandchild, brother, sister, or other relative.
[3]No spouse present.
* = Quantity zero or rounds to zero.

Table A-8. Enrollment Status for Families with Children 5 to 24 Years Old, by Control of School, Race, Type of Family, and Family Income, October 2011—*Continued*

(Numbers in thousands)

Characteristic	Total[1]	Families with no dependents 5 to 24 years old[2]	Families with dependents 5 to 24 years old[2]						
			Kindergarten, elementary, and high school enrollment status				College enrollment status		
			None enrolled in elementary or high school	Public only	Public and private	Private only	None enrolled in college	One enrolled in college	Two or more enrolled in college
BLACK ALONE									
All families	9,645	3,764	1,167	4,375	99	240	5,017	740	123
Less than $20,000	2,228	718	244	1,203	12	51	1,365	130	15
$20,000 to $74,999	3,912	1,534	466	1,789	37	85	1,995	334	49
$75,000 and over	1,296	514	192	509	22	59	620	124	38
Not reported	2,209	998	265	875	28	44	1,036	153	22
Married-couple families	4,372	2,133	399	1,691	40	110	1,852	324	64
Less than $20,000	485	247	27	203	1	8	209	23	7
$20,000 to $74,999	1,862	877	168	770	15	33	810	152	24
$75,000 and over	1,004	440	119	378	16	51	455	89	21
Not reported	1,020	570	85	340	8	19	378	60	12
Unmarried householder[3]	5,272	1,631	768	2,685	59	129	3,165	417	59
Less than $20,000	1,743	471	217	1,000	11	43	1,156	107	8
$20,000 to $74,999	2,049	658	298	1,019	22	52	1,186	181	25
$75,000 and over	291	74	73	130	5	8	165	35	17
Not reported	1,189	428	180	535	20	26	658	93	10
ASIAN ALONE									
All families	3,609	1,766	399	1,310	18	117	1,356	384	103
Less than $20,000	379	218	28	129	*	4	117	36	8
$20,000 to $74,999	1,240	651	137	417	7	28	427	122	41
$75,000 and over	1,249	525	137	519	4	64	531	154	38
Not reported	742	373	97	245	6	21	282	71	16
Married-couple families	2,823	1,377	262	1,060	18	107	1,086	280	81
Less than $20,000	263	176	9	74	*	4	65	18	4
$20,000 to $74,999	889	466	82	310	7	24	304	89	30
$75,000 and over	1,122	457	114	485	4	63	501	127	38
Not reported	549	278	57	192	6	16	216	46	9
Unmarried householder[3]	786	389	137	250	*	10	270	104	22
Less than $20,000	116	41	19	55	*	*	51	18	4
$20,000 to $74,999	351	185	54	108	*	4	123	32	11
$75,000 and over	127	68	24	34	*	1	31	28	*
Not reported	192	94	40	53	*	5	65	26	7
HISPANIC[4]									
All families	11,348	3,979	1,221	5,860	86	202	6,261	917	191
Less than $20,000	2,566	872	225	1,436	19	14	1,535	147	13
$20,000 to $74,999	5,275	1,761	563	2,822	28	101	2,949	456	109
$75,000 and over	1,411	537	188	600	22	62	680	164	29
Not reported	2,096	809	245	1,002	17	25	1,097	150	41
Married-couple families	7,379	2,694	667	3,831	46	142	3,949	574	163
Less than $20,000	1,288	505	73	698	7	5	719	58	6
$20,000 to $74,999	3,570	1,237	306	1,947	15	65	1,948	287	98
$75,000 and over	1,163	441	144	512	14	52	565	131	26
Not reported	1,359	511	144	675	11	19	718	98	33
Unmarried householder[3]	3,969	1,285	554	2,029	40	60	2,312	343	28
Less than $20,000	1,279	367	153	738	12	8	817	89	6
$20,000 to $74,999	1,705	524	257	875	14	35	1,001	169	10
$75,000 and over	248	96	44	89	8	10	115	33	4
Not reported	737	298	101	327	6	6	379	52	8

[1]Civilian noninstitutionalized population.
[2]Dependents may be unmarried (or married with spouse absent) child, grandchild, brother, sister, or other relative.
[3]No spouse present.
[4]May be of any race.
* = Quantity zero or rounds to zero.

PART A

NATIONAL EDUCATION STATISTICS

■ Historical Enrollment Tables

Table A-9. School Enrollment of the Population 3 Years Old and Over, by Level and Control of School, Race, and Hispanic Origin, October 1955–2011

(Numbers in thousands)

Year, race, and Hispanic origin	Total enrolled[1]	Nursery school			Kindergarten			Elementary school		
		Total	Public	Private	Total	Public	Private	Total	Public	Private
ALL RACES										
2011	79,043	4,946	2,904	2,042	4,214	3,732	482	32,872	29,965	2,907
2010	78,519	4,835	2,776	2,059	4,172	3,764	408	32,663	29,841	2,822
2009	77,288	4,708	2,744	1,964	4,132	3,767	365	32,238	29,365	2,874
2008	76,353	4,614	2,632	1,982	4,047	3,578	469	32,344	29,162	3,182
2007	75,967	4,628	2,570	2,058	4,132	3,656	476	32,169	29,052	3,117
2006	75,197	4,688	2,519	2,169	4,039	3,552	487	32,089	28,975	3,113
2005	75,780	4,603	2,480	2,123	3,912	3,349	563	32,438	29,072	3,366
2004	75,461	4,739	2,487	2,252	3,992	3,417	575	32,556	29,166	3,389
2003[2]	74,911	4,928	2,567	2,361	3,719	3,098	622	32,565	29,204	3,361
2002	74,046	4,471	2,246	2,225	3,571	2,976	594	33,132	29,658	3,474
2001	73,124	4,289	2,161	2,128	3,737	3,145	591	33,166	29,800	3,366
2000	72,214	4,401	2,217	2,184	3,832	3,173	659	32,898	29,378	3,520
1999	72,395	4,578	2,269	2,309	3,825	3,167	658	32,873	29,264	3,609
1998	72,109	4,577	2,265	2,313	3,828	3,128	700	32,573	29,124	3,449
1997	72,031	4,500	2,254	2,246	3,933	3,271	663	32,369	29,308	3,061
1996	70,297	4,212	1,868	2,344	4,034	3,353	681	31,515	28,153	3,362
1995	69,769	4,399	2,012	2,387	3,877	3,174	704	31,815	28,384	3,431
1994[3]	69,272	4,259	1,940	2,319	3,863	3,278	585	31,512	28,131	3,381
1993[r]	64,414	3,032	1,258	1,774	4,275	3,589	686	31,219	28,278	2,941
1993	62,730	3,018	1,230	1,788	4,180	3,499	681	30,604	27,688	2,914
1992	62,082	2,899	1,098	1,801	4,130	3,507	623	30,165	27,066	3,102
1991	61,276	2,933	1,094	1,839	4,152	3,531	621	29,591	26,632	2,958
1990	60,588	3,401	1,212	2,188	3,899	3,332	567	29,265	26,591	2,674
1989	59,236	2,877	971	1,906	3,868	3,293	575	28,637	25,897	2,740
1988	58,847	2,639	838	1,770	3,958	3,420	538	28,223	25,443	2,778
1987	58,691	2,587	848	1,739	4,018	3,423	595	27,524	24,760	2,765
1986	58,153	2,554	835	1,719	3,961	3,328	633	27,121	24,163	2,958
1985	58,014	2,491	854	1,637	3,815	3,221	594	26,866	23,803	3,063
1984	57,313	2,354	761	1,593	3,484	2,953	531	26,838	24,120	2,718
1983	57,745	2,350	809	1,541	3,361	2,706	656	27,198	24,203	2,994
1982	57,905	2,153	729	1,423	3,299	2,746	553	27,412	24,381	3,031
1981	58,390	2,058	663	1,396	3,161	2,616	545	27,795	24,758	3,037
1980	57,348	1,987	633	1,354	3,176	2,690	486	27,449	24,398	3,051
1979	57,854	1,869	636	1,233	3,025	2,593	432	27,865	24,756	3,109
1978	58,616	1,824	587	1,237	2,989	2,493	496	28,490	25,252	3,238
1977	60,013	1,618	562	1,056	3,191	2,665	526	29,234	25,983	3,251
1976	60,482	1,526	476	1,050	3,490	2,962	528	29,774	26,698	3,075
1975	60,969	1,748	574	1,174	3,393	2,851	542	30,446	27,166	3,279
1974	60,259	1,607	423	1,184	3,252	2,726	526	31,126	27,956	3,169
1973	59,392	1,324	400	924	3,074	2,582	493	31,469	28,201	3,268
1972	60,142	1,283	402	881	3,135	2,636	499	32,242	28,693	3,549
1971	61,106	1,066	317	749	3,263	2,689	574	33,507	29,829	3,678
1970	60,357	1,096	333	763	3,183	2,647	536	33,950	30,001	3,949
1969	59,913	860	245	615	3,276	2,682	594	33,788	29,825	3,964
1968	58,791	816	262	554	3,268	2,709	559	33,761	29,527	4,234
1967	57,656	713	230	484	3,312	2,678	635	33,440	28,877	4,562
1966	56,167	688	215	473	3,115	2,527	588	32,916	28,208	4,706
1965	54,701	520	127	393	3,057	2,439	618	32,474	27,596	4,878
1964	52,490	471	91	380	2,830	2,349	481	31,734	26,811	4,923
1963	50,356	...	...	...	2,340	1,936	404	31,245	26,502	4,742
1962	48,704	...	...	...	2,319	1,914	405	30,661	26,148	4,513
1961	47,708	...	...	...	2,299	1,926	373	30,718	26,221	4,497
1960	46,260	...	...	...	2,092	1,691	401	30,349	25,814	4,535
1959	44,370	...	...	...	2,032	1,678	354	29,382	24,680	4,702
1958	42,900	...	...	...	1,991	1,569	422	28,184	23,800	4,385
1957	41,166	...	...	...	1,824	1,471	353	27,248	23,076	4,172
1956	39,353	...	...	...	1,758	1,566	192	26,169	22,474	3,695
1955	37,426	...	...	...	1,628	1,365	263	25,458	22,078	3,379

Note: Data shown for 1955 to 1966 for the Black population are for Black and Other races.
[1]Civilian noninstitutionalized population.
[2]Starting in 2003 respondents could identify more than one race. Except as noted, the race data in this table from 2003 onward represent those respondents who indicated only one race category.
[3]Prior to 1994, total enrolled does not include the 35 years old and over population.
r = Revised, controlled to 1990 census based population estimates; previous 1993 data controlled to 1980 census based population estimates.
... = Not available.

Table A-9. School Enrollment of the Population 3 Years Old and Over, by Level and Control of School, Race, and Hispanic Origin, October 1955–2011—*Continued*

(Numbers in thousands)

Year, race, and Hispanic origin	High school			College			
	Total	Public	Private	Total	Public	Private	Full-time
ALL RACES							
2011	16,613	15,426	1,187	20,397	16,134	4,263	14,903
2010	16,574	15,338	1,236	20,275	16,153	4,122	14,600
2009	16,445	15,269	1,177	19,764	15,722	4,042	14,364
2008	16,715	15,397	1,319	18,632	14,739	3,893	13,245
2007	17,082	15,804	1,278	17,956	14,072	3,884	12,656
2006	17,149	15,617	1,532	17,232	13,466	3,766	12,070
2005	17,354	15,934	1,420	17,472	13,435	4,037	12,237
2004	16,791	15,498	1,293	17,383	13,652	3,731	11,990
2003[2]	17,062	15,785	1,276	16,638	13,109	3,529	11,490
2002	16,374	15,064	1,310	16,497	12,834	3,664	11,141
2001	16,059	14,830	1,230	15,873	12,421	3,452	10,404
2000	15,770	14,431	1,339	15,314	12,008	3,305	10,159
1999	15,916	14,638	1,278	15,203	11,659	3,544	10,112
1998	15,584	14,299	1,285	15,547	11,984	3,563	10,184
1997	15,793	14,634	1,159	15,436	12,091	3,345	10,236
1996	15,309	14,113	1,197	15,226	12,014	3,212	9,839
1995	14,963	13,750	1,213	14,715	11,372	3,343	9,544
1994[3]	14,616	13,539	1,077	15,022	11,694	3,329	9,573
1993[r]	13,989	12,985	1,004	11,901	9,440	2,461	8,706
1993	13,522	12,542	977	11,409	9,031	2,374	8,308
1992	13,219	12,268	952	11,671	9,282	2,386	8,503
1991	13,010	12,069	945	11,589	9,078	2,511	8,461
1990	12,719	11,818	903	11,306	8,889	2,417	8,154
1989	12,786	11,980	806	11,066	8,576	2,490	7,905
1988	13,093	12,095	998	10,937	8,663	2,278	7,771
1987	13,647	12,577	1,070	10,915	8,556	2,361	7,560
1986	13,912	12,746	1,166	10,605	8,153	2,452	7,507
1985	13,979	12,764	1,215	10,863	8,379	2,483	7,720
1984	13,777	12,721	1,057	10,859	8,467	2,392	7,822
1983	14,010	12,792	1,218	10,825	8,185	2,640	7,711
1982	14,123	13,004	1,118	10,919	8,354	2,565	7,736
1981	14,642	13,523	1,119	10,734	8,159	2,576	7,569
1980	14,556	...	...	10,180	...	...	7,147
1979	15,116	13,994	1,122	9,978	7,699	2,280	7,010
1978	15,475	14,231	1,244	9,838	7,427	2,410	6,979
1977	15,753	14,505	1,248	10,217	7,925	2,292	7,196
1976	15,742	14,541	1,201	9,950	7,739	2,211	7,176
1975	15,683	14,503	1,180	9,697	7,704	1,994	7,105
1974	15,447	14,275	1,172	8,827	6,905	1,922	6,351
1973	15,347	14,162	1,184	8,179	6,224	1,955	6,089
1972	15,169	14,015	1,155	8,313	6,337	1,976	6,314
1971	15,183	14,057	1,126	8,087	6,271	1,816	6,204
1970	14,715	13,545	1,170	7,413	5,699	1,714	5,763
1969	14,553	13,400	1,153	7,435	5,439	1,995	5,810
1968	14,145	12,793	1,352	6,801	4,948	1,854	5,357
1967	13,790	12,498	1,292	6,401	4,540	1,861	4,976
1966	13,364	11,985	1,377	6,085	4,178	1,908	4,847
1965	12,975	11,517	1,457	5,675	3,840	1,835	4,414
1964	12,812	11,403	1,410	4,643	3,025	1,618	3,556
1963	12,438	11,186	1,251	4,336	2,897	1,439	3,260
1962	11,516	10,431	1,085	4,208	2,820	1,388	3,237
1961	10,959	9,817	1,141	3,731	2,376	1,354	2,902
1960	10,249	9,215	1,033	3,570	2,307	1,262	2,681
1959	9,616	8,571	1,045	3,340	2,120	1,220	2,464
1958	9,482	8,485	998	3,242	2,088	1,155	...
1957	8,956	8,059	897	3,138	2,054	1,084	...
1956	8,543	7,668	875	2,883	1,824	1,059	...
1955	7,961	7,181	780	2,379	1,515	864	...

Note: Data shown for 1955 to 1966 for the Black population are for Black and Other races.
[2]Starting in 2003 respondents could identify more than one race. Except as noted, the race data in this table from 2003 onward represent those respondents who indicated only one race category.
[3]Prior to 1994, total enrolled does not include the 35 years old and over population.
r = Revised, controlled to 1990 census based population estimates; previous 1993 data controlled to 1980 census based population estimates.
... = Not available.

Table A-9. School Enrollment of the Population 3 Years Old and Over, by Level and Control of School, Race, and Hispanic Origin, October 1955–2011—*Continued*

(Numbers in thousands)

Year, race, and Hispanic origin	Total enrolled[1]	Nursery school			Kindergarten			Elementary school		
		Total	Public	Private	Total	Public	Private	Total	Public	Private
WHITE ALONE										
2011	59,647	3,624	1,997	1,627	3,198	2,806	393	24,864	22,419	2,445
2010	59,236	3,659	1,992	1,668	3,069	2,745	324	24,680	22,395	2,284
2009	58,586	3,404	1,832	1,572	3,154	2,860	293	24,575	22,257	2,319
2008	58,244	3,479	1,830	1,649	3,121	2,748	373	24,552	21,986	2,565
2007	58,021	3,545	1,880	1,665	3,223	2,836	387	24,431	21,869	2,562
2006	57,419	3,624	1,815	1,809	3,084	2,701	382	24,472	21,923	2,549
2005	58,013	3,542	1,767	1,775	3,056	2,611	445	24,562	21,858	2,795
2004	57,585	3,566	1,703	1,863	3,043	2,571	472	24,773	21,889	2,883
2003[2]	57,391	3,909	1,918	1,990	2,866	2,367	499	24,711	21,893	2,818
2002	57,501	3,473	1,613	1,860	2,760	2,240	520	25,625	22,703	2,922
2001	56,649	3,278	1,484	1,794	2,893	2,394	499	25,729	22,848	2,881
2000	56,344	3,392	1,539	1,853	2,998	2,453	545	25,562	22,538	3,024
1999	56,713	3,590	1,571	2,019	2,956	2,422	534	25,628	22,552	3,076
1998	56,515	3,549	1,598	1,951	2,933	2,356	577	25,489	22,547	2,942
1997	56,587	3,489	1,572	1,917	3,078	2,532	546	25,289	22,679	2,610
1996	55,378	3,284	1,314	1,970	3,163	2,596	567	24,692	21,785	2,907
1995	55,186	3,553	1,435	2,118	3,032	2,440	592	24,963	22,010	2,954
1994[3]	54,823	3,376	1,330	2,046	3,010	2,505	505	24,786	21,903	2,883
1993[r]	51,034	2,434	851	1,583	3,323	2,730	593	24,637	22,078	2,559
1993	49,985	2,447	843	1,604	3,273	2,681	592	24,249	21,714	2,535
1992	49,713	2,387	785	1,602	3,256	2,727	529	23,932	21,213	2,718
1991	49,156	2,447	810	1,637	3,274	2,766	508	23,547	20,948	2,599
1990	48,897	2,830	869	1,961	3,081	2,609	472	23,343	20,984	2,359
1989	47,923	2,393	712	1,681	3,118	2,611	506	22,867	20,468	2,399
1988	47,672	2,234	651	1,583	3,192	2,722	471	22,541	20,086	2,455
1987	47,471	2,204	630	1,574	3,120	2,591	529	22,037	19,538	2,498
1986	47,267	2,144	601	1,543	3,161	2,589	572	21,761	19,090	2,671
1985	47,452	2,087	617	1,470	3,060	2,545	515	21,593	18,817	2,776
1984	46,941	1,915	543	1,372	2,788	2,319	469	21,730	19,282	2,449
1983	47,423	1,932	563	1,369	2,769	2,181	588	22,054	19,340	2,714
1982	47,662	1,783	504	1,279	2,677	2,189	489	22,297	19,583	2,713
1981	48,169	1,685	447	1,238	2,597	2,130	467	22,663	19,924	2,739
1980	47,673	1,637	432	1,205	2,595	2,172	423	22,510	19,743	2,768
1979	48,225	1,537	428	1,110	2,437	2,069	368	22,959	20,174	2,785
1978	48,843	1,456	351	1,105	2,452	2,009	444	23,524	20,551	2,973
1977	50,151	1,314	372	942	2,611	2,153	458	24,262	21,312	2,950
1976	50,761	1,246	318	929	2,881	2,423	457	24,776	21,947	2,829
1975	51,430	1,432	392	1,040	2,845	2,363	483	25,412	22,351	3,059
1974	50,992	1,340	293	1,048	2,745	2,268	477	26,051	23,063	2,990
1973	50,617	1,087	242	845	2,584	2,139	445	26,531	23,506	3,025
1972	51,314	1,079	285	794	2,633	2,185	448	27,185	23,869	3,316
1971	52,081	888	225	664	2,735	2,207	527	28,187	24,720	3,466
1970	51,719	893	198	695	2,706	2,233	473	28,638	24,923	3,715
1969	51,465	676	136	539	2,803	2,289	515	28,572	24,803	3,768
1968	50,608	664	163	501	2,775	2,272	504	28,634	24,580	4,054
1967	49,721	564	134	429	2,840	2,254	587	28,415	24,044	4,371
1966	48,620	564	127	437	2,693	2,163	530	28,012	23,469	4,542
1965	47,451	451	93	358	2,648	2,086	562	27,679	22,976	4,703
1964	44,850	...	...	...	2,157	1,795	362	27,099	22,381	4,718
1963	43,815	...	...	...	2,064	1,699	365	26,709	22,181	4,527
1962	42,501	...	...	...	2,025	1,667	358	26,272	21,922	4,350
1961	42,498	...	...	...	1,968	1,618	350	26,294	22,014	4,281
1960	40,348	...	...	...	1,849	1,485	364	26,035	21,696	4,339
1959	38,857	...	...	...	1,758	1,434	324	25,395	20,854	4,541
1958	37,662	...	...	...	1,769	1,383	386	24,380	20,178	4,203
1957	36,132	...	...	...	1,595	1,258	337	23,610	19,595	4,015
1956	34,641	...	...	...	1,544	1,364	180	22,740	19,186	3,554
1955	32,929	...	...	...	1,484	1,244	240	22,185	18,947	3,238

Note: Data shown for 1955 to 1966 for the Black population are for Black and Other races.
[1]Civilian noninstitutionalized population.
[2]Starting in 2003 respondents could identify more than one race. Except as noted, the race data in this table from 2003 onward represent those respondents who indicated only one race category.
[3]Prior to 1994, total enrolled does not include the 35 years old and over population.
r = Revised, controlled to 1990 census based population estimates; previous 1993 data controlled to 1980 census based population estimates.
... = Not available.

Table A-9. School Enrollment of the Population 3 Years Old and Over, by Level and Control of School, Race, and Hispanic Origin, October 1955–2011—*Continued*

(Numbers in thousands)

Year, race, and Hispanic origin	High school			College			
	Total	Public	Private	Total	Public	Private	Full-time
WHITE ALONE							
2011	12,548	11,542	1,007	15,412	12,161	3,251	11,205
2010	12,570	11,525	1,045	15,258	12,179	3,079	10,818
2009	12,425	11,419	1,006	15,027	11,948	3,079	10,847
2008	12,687	11,585	1,103	14,405	11,432	2,973	10,256
2007	12,986	11,886	1,100	13,835	10,855	2,979	9,696
2006	12,966	11,694	1,273	13,273	10,338	2,936	9,236
2005	13,296	12,109	1,187	13,466	10,303	3,163	9,392
2004	12,823	11,684	1,138	13,381	10,478	2,904	9,257
2003[2]	13,036	11,939	1,097	12,870	10,101	2,769	8,855
2002	12,862	11,730	1,132	12,781	9,774	3,007	8,613
2001	12,540	11,473	1,067	12,208	9,503	2,705	7,909
2000	12,392	11,259	1,133	11,999	9,364	2,636	7,945
1999	12,487	11,374	1,113	12,053	9,185	2,868	7,886
1998	12,142	11,013	1,130	12,401	9,518	2,883	8,012
1997	12,290	11,287	1,003	12,442	9,713	2,729	8,127
1996	12,052	10,999	1,053	12,188	9,567	2,622	7,849
1995	11,617	10,574	1,042	12,021	9,311	2,711	7,773
1994[3]	11,430	10,514	916	12,222	9,472	2,751	7,722
1993[r]	10,960	10,124	836	9,685	7,695	1,990	6,996
1993	10,651	9,834	819	9,366	7,428	1,940	6,739
1992	10,480	9,648	833	9,658	7,653	2,001	6,985
1991	10,309	9,467	841	9,579	7,464	2,118	6,919
1990	10,177	9,370	807	9,466	7,411	2,056	6,776
1989	10,172	9,443	730	9,374	7,219	2,158	6,658
1988	10,462	9,571	890	9,245	7,302	1,940	6,488
1987	10,967	10,019	947	9,143	7,113	2,034	6,275
1986	11,259	10,229	1,030	8,943	6,821	2,122	6,253
1985	11,378	10,258	1,120	9,334	7,131	2,203	6,597
1984	11,240	10,266	974	9,269	7,163	2,105	6,672
1983	11,425	10,339	1,086	9,242	6,949	2,293	6,532
1982	11,577	10,541	1,036	9,328	7,102	2,227	6,579
1981	12,062	11,035	1,027	9,162	6,906	2,256	6,452
1980	12,056	...	...	8,875	...	...	6,212
1979	12,583	11,549	1,033	8,709	6,672	2,037	6,058
1978	12,897	11,741	1,156	8,514	6,368	2,145	5,974
1977	13,152	11,980	1,172	8,812	6,743	2,069	6,165
1976	13,214	12,093	1,121	8,644	6,657	1,987	6,170
1975	13,224	12,112	1,112	8,516	6,724	1,792	6,183
1974	13,073	11,966	1,107	7,781	6,049	1,732	5,575
1973	13,091	11,967	1,124	7,324	5,550	1,773	5,408
1972	12,959	11,876	1,083	7,458	5,644	1,814	5,678
1971	12,998	11,937	1,061	7,273	5,624	1,650	5,560
1970	12,723	11,599	1,124	6,759	5,168	1,591	5,221
1969	12,588	11,502	1,085	6,827	4,967	1,860	5,307
1968	12,280	11,007	1,272	6,255	4,501	1,753	4,919
1967	11,997	10,769	1,228	5,905	4,155	1,750	4,604
1966	11,643	10,312	1,329	5,708	3,914	1,795	4,556
1965	11,356	9,961	1,395	5,317	3,568	1,749	4,111
1964	11,257	9,898	1,359	4,338	2,798	1,540	...
1963	10,994	9,782	1,212	4,050	2,680	1,370	...
1962	10,270	9,217	1,053	3,934	2,620	1,314	...
1961	9,737	8,635	1,102	3,498	2,205	1,293	...
1960	9,122	8,124	999	3,342	2,126	1,215	...
1959	8,586	7,572	1,014	3,118	1,960	1,158	...
1958	8,484	7,501	982	3,030	1,928	1,101	...
1957	7,995	7,121	874	2,932	1,924	1,006	...
1956	7,670	6,825	845	2,687	1,704	983	...
1955	7,036	6,303	733	2,224	1,429	795	...

Note: Data shown for 1955 to 1966 for the Black population are for Black and Other races.
[2]Starting in 2003 respondents could identify more than one race. Except as noted, the race data in this table from 2003 onward represent those respondents who indicated only one race category.
[3]Prior to 1994, total enrolled does not include the 35 years old and over population.
r = Revised, controlled to 1990 census based population estimates; previous 1993 data controlled to 1980 census based population estimates.
... = Not available.

Table A-9. School Enrollment of the Population 3 Years Old and Over, by Level and Control of School, Race, and Hispanic Origin, October 1955–2011—*Continued*

(Numbers in thousands)

Year, race, and Hispanic origin	Total enrolled[1]	Nursery school			Kindergarten			Elementary school		
		Total	Public	Private	Total	Public	Private	Total	Public	Private
WHITE ALONE NON-HISPANIC										
2011	44,951	2,743	1,332	1,411	2,238	1,903	335	17,830	15,670	2,160
2010	44,968	2,766	1,274	1,492	2,120	1,842	278	17,942	15,960	1,981
2009	45,470	2,575	1,188	1,387	2,252	1,990	262	18,244	16,198	2,046
2008	45,373	2,710	1,213	1,497	2,206	1,884	323	18,349	16,029	2,320
2007	45,334	2,711	1,225	1,486	2,279	1,929	351	18,306	15,998	2,307
2006	45,386	2,769	1,152	1,616	2,288	1,940	348	18,622	16,322	2,301
2005	46,338	2,810	1,211	1,599	2,308	1,936	372	18,858	16,335	2,523
2004	46,095	2,840	1,153	1,687	2,325	1,917	408	19,093	16,437	2,646
2003[2]	46,440	3,184	1,382	1,802	2,245	1,804	440	19,252	16,735	2,517
2002	46,725	2,881	1,172	1,709	2,065	1,585	480	20,124	17,495	2,628
2001	46,110	2,725	1,054	1,671	2,203	1,781	422	20,298	17,693	2,605
2000	46,660	2,854	1,149	1,705	2,346	1,846	500	20,574	17,747	2,827
1999	47,292	3,044	1,146	1,898	2,307	1,839	468	20,779	17,960	2,819
1998	47,386	2,964	1,136	1,828	2,336	1,790	547	20,806	18,107	2,699
1997	47,776	2,956	1,143	1,813	2,456	1,970	486	20,839	18,426	2,413
1996	46,947	2767	922	1845	2590	2081	509	20,447	17,808	2,639
1995	48,019	3,104	1,129	1,975	2,551	2,047	504	21,256	18,518	2,738
1994[3]	47,679	3,024	1,090	1,934	2,522	2,059	462	21,170	18,555	2,615
1993	43,827	2,277	720	1,557	2,779	2,239	540	20,961	18,617	2,344
BLACK ALONE										
2011	12,037	794	562	232	559	503	56	4,902	4,658	245
2010	11,969	698	522	175	736	682	54	4,795	4,498	298
2009	11,748	811	640	171	619	578	41	4,749	4,424	325
2008	11,421	706	548	158	601	545	56	4,993	4,665	329
2007	11,475	700	485	215	605	548	56	4,926	4,572	353
2006	11,400	715	513	202	608	536	71	4,952	4,608	344
2005	11,384	719	542	177	538	486	52	5,106	4,747	359
2004	11,540	825	600	224	596	535	61	5,159	4,905	254
2003[2]	11,408	697	484	212	558	495	63	5,245	4,942	302
2002	11,703	725	503	221	598	543	55	5,545	5,210	335
2001	11,630	787	537	250	605	536	69	5,478	5,160	318
2000	11,503	726	531	195	629	547	82	5,481	5,133	347
1999	11,282	729	569	160	632	558	74	5,388	5,002	386
1998	11,411	761	528	233	689	592	97	5,332	5,031	301
1997	11,270	796	582	214	632	571	61	5,332	5,049	284
1996	10,851	702	459	243	634	545	89	5,171	4,846	325
1995	10,753	663	478	185	653	564	89	5,185	4,845	340
1994[3]	10,702	721	513	208	662	603	59	5,086	4,709	378
1993[r]	9,786	433	320	113	721	649	72	5,009	4,733	276
1993	9,470	414	307	107	687	618	69	4,865	4,599	266
1992	9,150	374	250	124	688	625	63	4,730	4,494	234
1991	9,031	360	244	117	676	598	79	4,672	4,445	229
1990	8,854	431	283	148	636	574	62	4,627	4,428	199
1989	8,707	366	216	150	601	557	44	4,528	4,296	232
1988	8,609	286	168	118	591	547	44	4,538	4,289	250
1987	8,712	277	164	113	699	658	41	4,402	4,206	194
1986	8,556	315	200	115	647	600	47	4,326	4,134	193
1985	8,444	332	212	120	625	562	63	4,307	4,131	175
1984	8,226	340	179	161	563	513	51	4,123	3,947	177
1983	8,199	326	215	111	476	427	48	4,153	3,964	189
1982	8,262	305	192	113	508	463	45	4,194	3,974	220
1981	8,350	284	182	102	474	412	62	4,291	4,087	204
1980	8,251	294	180	115	490	440	50	4,259	4,058	202
1979	8,317	278	185	95	497	443	54	4,296	4,053	243
1978	8,416	312	210	102	451	414	38	4,356	4,154	202
1977	8,564	250	171	78	496	447	50	4,387	4,166	221
1976	8,518	226	146	80	542	482	60	4,430	4,256	175
1975	8,400	276	171	105	468	426	42	4,509	4,344	165
1974	8,215	227	121	106	463	416	47	4,585	4,455	131
1973	7,834	210	146	64	423	391	32	4,473	4,277	196
1972	7,959	185	113	72	448	402	46	4,573	4,382	191
1971	8,179	151	90	61	464	422	42	4,877	4,712	165
1970	7,829	178	129	49	426	374	53	4,868	4,668	200

Note: Data shown for 1955 to 1966 for the Black population are for Black and Other races.
[1]Civilian noninstitutionalized population.
[2]Starting in 2003 respondents could identify more than one race. Except as noted, the race data in this table from 2003 onward represent those respondents who indicated only one race category.
[3]Prior to 1994, total enrolled does not include the 35 years old and over population.
r = Revised, controlled to 1990 census based population estimates; previous 1993 data controlled to 1980 census based population estimates.

Table A-9. School Enrollment of the Population 3 Years Old and Over, by Level and Control of School, Race, and Hispanic Origin, October 1955–2011—*Continued*

(Numbers in thousands)

Year, race, and Hispanic origin	High school			College			
	Total	Public	Private	Total	Public	Private	Full-time
WHITE ALONE NON-HISPANIC							
2011	9,437	8,535	902	12,703	9,842	2,861	9,333
2010	9,528	8,598	930	12,613	9,900	2,713	9,122
2009	9,573	8,655	919	12,826	10,022	2,803	9,368
2008	9,783	8,798	986	12,324	9,630	2,694	8,925
2007	10,171	9,204	966	11,867	9,141	2,726	8,379
2006	10,222	9,072	1,150	11,485	8,821	2,664	8,105
2005	10,647	9,566	1,081	11,715	8,852	2,863	8,246
2004	10,266	9,144	1,029	11,571	8,928	2,643	8,082
2003[2]	10,463	9,473	990	11,295	8,742	2,553	7,810
2002	10,419	9,388	1,031	11,236	8,488	2,749	7,673
2001	10,281	9,331	950	10,602	8,133	2,469	6,980
2000	10,250	9,222	1,029	10,636	8,202	2,434	7,105
1999	10,344	9,314	1,030	10,818	8,158	2,660	7,162
1998	10,170	9,131	1,039	11,109	8,435	2,674	7,251
1997	10,280	9,358	922	11,245	8,688	2,558	7,378
1996	10,107	9,148	959	11,034	8,584	2,450	7,178
1995	10,084	9,094	991	11,024	8,439	2,585	7,194
1994[3]	9,786	8,951	835	11,178	8,568	2,610	7,152
1993	9,216	8,449	767	8,594	6,772	1,822	6,247
BLACK ALONE							
2011	2,635	2,545	91	3,146	2,541	605	2,279
2010	2,657	2,552	105	3,083	2,495	587	2,223
2009	2,680	2,592	89	2,889	2,322	567	2,061
2008	2,639	2,524	115	2,481	1,975	506	1,690
2007	2,743	2,627	116	2,501	1,968	533	1,683
2006	2,792	2,628	165	2,334	1,816	518	1,628
2005	2,723	2,592	131	2,298	1,800	498	1,526
2004	2,660	2,584	76	2,301	1,831	470	1,504
2003[2]	2,765	2,691	74	2,144	1,773	371	1,416
2002	2,558	2,451	107	2,278	1,868	410	1,468
2001	2,531	2,412	119	2,230	1,766	463	1,475
2000	2,502	2,350	152	2,164	1,721	443	1,351
1999	2,536	2,427	109	1,998	1,587	411	1,372
1998	2,614	2,515	99	2,016	1,595	421	1,284
1997	2,605	2,516	89	1,903	1,546	357	1,280
1996	2,443	2,338	105	1,901	1,519	381	1,179
1995	2,481	2,370	111	1,772	1,353	419	1,117
1994[3]	2,434	2,313	121	1,800	1,439	361	1,147
1993[r]	2,317	2,197	120	1,305	1,006	299	951
1993	2,244	2,128	115	1,261	973	288	914
1992	2,152	2,072	72	1,217	980	237	904
1991	2,100	2,044	56	1,220	1,004	217	900
1990	1,975	1,909	65	1,188	963	227	869
1989	2,069	2,027	42	1,139	932	208	833
1988	2,079	2,016	62	1,114	894	220	801
1987	2,140	2,056	84	1,193	977	218	852
1986	2,130	2,040	91	1,138	896	242	859
1985	2,131	2,068	63	1,049	860	190	767
1984	2,061	2,002	59	1,138	918	220	810
1983	2,143	2,057	86	1,102	858	245	806
1982	2,128	2,073	55	1,127	865	263	800
1981	2,168	2,102	65	1,133	898	235	815
1980	2,200	...	...	1,007	...	...	723
1979	2,245	2,171	74	1,002	814	188	748
1978	2,276	2,211	65	1,020	822	199	753
1977	2,327	2,269	59	1,103	916	187	803
1976	2,258	2,187	71	1,062	887	175	817
1975	2,199	2,140	59	948	782	166	742
1974	2,125	2,072	54	814	659	155	589
1973	2,044	1,988	56	685	537	147	536
1972	2,025	1,971	54	727	582	145	525
1971	2,006	1,951	55	680	532	148	534
1970	1,834	1,794	41	522	422	100	427

Note: Data shown for 1955 to 1966 for the Black population are for Black and Other races.
[2]Starting in 2003 respondents could identify more than one race. Except as noted, the race data in this table from 2003 onward represent those respondents who indicated only one race category.
[3]Prior to 1994, total enrolled does not include the 35 years old and over population.
r = Revised, controlled to 1990 census based population estimates; previous 1993 data controlled to 1980 census based population estimates.
... = Not available.

Table A-9. School Enrollment of the Population 3 Years Old and Over, by Level and Control of School, Race, and Hispanic Origin, October 1955–2011—*Continued*

(Numbers in thousands)

Year, race, and Hispanic origin	Total enrolled[1]	Nursery school			Kindergarten			Elementary school		
		Total	Public	Private	Total	Public	Private	Total	Public	Private
BLACK ALONE— *(Continued)*										
1969	7,680	170	102	68	425	361	64	4,785	4,633	151
1968	7,448	132	89	43	448	397	51	4,716	4,569	146
1967	7,196	140	92	47	418	375	44	4,618	4,444	173
1966	7,547	125	88	37	420	364	56	4,904	4,739	165
1965	7,252	72	37	35	407	353	54	4,796	4,620	176
1964	6,807	...	...	...	312	275	37	4,634	4,430	205
1963	6,541	...	...	...	276	237	39	4,536	4,321	215
1962	6,203	...	...	...	294	247	47	4,389	4,226	163
1961	6,210	...	...	...	331	308	23	4,424	4,207	216
1960	5,910	...	...	...	243	206	37	4,313	4,118	195
1959	5,513	...	...	...	274	244	30	3,987	3,826	161
1958	5,238	...	...	...	222	186	36	3,804	3,621	182
1957	5,034	...	...	...	229	213	16	3,638	3,483	155
1956	4,712	...	...	...	214	202	12	3,429	3,287	142
1955	4,498	...	...	...	144	121	23	3,273	3,131	142
ASIAN[4]										
2011	3,779	212	120	92	209	189	21	1,469	1,336	133
2010	3,815	223	97	127	196	181	15	1,488	1,358	130
2009	3,515	239	107	132	167	146	21	1,296	1,170	125
2008	3,545	205	110	95	144	119	24	1,356	1,168	188
2007	3,470	171	77	94	137	112	25	1,421	1,305	115
2006	3,287	143	65	78	162	149	13	1,235	1,105	130
2005	3,377	185	80	105	138	99	39	1,228	1,137	91
2004	3,409	165	72	93	164	152	12	1,239	1,153	86
2003[2]	3,312	138	56	82	122	93	29	1,258	1,122	136
2002	3,787	217	85	132	157	137	20	1,431	1,237	195
2001	3,803	161	91	70	181	161	20	1,409	1,263	146
2000	3,442	222	91	132	152	124	28	1,350	1,257	93
1999	3,621	205	96	109	195	148	47	1,461	1,343	118
1998	3,386	196	77	118	145	120	25	1,380	1,190	189
1997	3,261	168	59	108	161	110	51	1,329	1,186	144
1996	3,258	183	63	120	177	158	19	1,255	1,144	111
1995	1,863	76	28	47	75	62	13	697	622	74
1994[3]	2,057	76	27	50	74	60	14	785	707	78
1993	2,321	100	38	62	139	125	14	1,012	930	82
HISPANIC[5]										
2011	16,131	1,010	766	244	1,042	984	58	7,716	7,401	315
2010	15,670	994	794	200	1,050	1,002	49	7,403	7,052	351
2009	14,528	930	717	213	965	933	32	7,058	6,716	342
2008	13,967	844	668	177	961	910	51	6,742	6,450	292
2007	13,708	905	711	194	990	954	37	6,582	6,299	284
2006	13,111	911	707	205	846	798	48	6,394	6,109	285
2005	12,809	797	601	196	804	725	79	6,330	5,991	339
2004	12,509	787	591	196	769	699	70	6,184	5,895	290
2003[2]	11,929	768	561	206	694	633	61	5,974	5,651	322
2002	11,544	637	476	161	727	688	39	5,909	5,585	324
2001	11,163	593	452	141	728	641	87	5,779	5,478	301
2000	10,163	574	419	154	687	639	48	5,224	5,012	213
1999	9,936	585	458	127	666	594	73	5,088	4,829	259
1998	9,528	618	492	126	639	608	31	4,831	4,568	262
1997	9,220	548	436	112	648	589	59	4,644	4,427	217
1996	8,818	533	403	130	602	539	63	4,443	4,162	281
1995	8,563	510	350	160	558	465	93	4,434	4,165	269
1994[3]	8,183	400	278	122	559	516	43	4,162	3,848	314
1993[r]	7,651	231	169	62	639	576	63	4,027	3,779	248
1993	6,689	194	142	52	538	484	53	3,534	3,317	217
1992	6,598	209	139	70	554	493	60	3,525	3,271	252
1991	6,306	215	146	69	552	525	27	3,461	3,240	221
1990	6,072	242	153	88	475	446	29	3,301	3,107	197
1989	5,722	181	95	86	404	382	21	3,219	3,031	188
1988	5,588	151	111	40	461	445	16	3,160	2,954	207
1987	5,619	226	138	88	439	399	39	3,048	2,861	187
1986	5,513	179	114	65	465	421	44	2,995	2,787	208

Note: Data shown for 1955 to 1966 for the Black population are for Black and Other races.
[1]Civilian noninstitutionalized population.
[2]Starting in 2003 respondents could identify more than one race. Except as noted, the race data in this table from 2003 onward represent those respondents who indicated only one race category.
[3]Prior to 1994, total enrolled does not include the 35 years old and over population.
[4]The data shown prior to 2003 consists of those identifying themselves as "Asian or Pacific Islanders."
[5]May be of any race.
r = Revised, controlled to 1990 census based population estimates; previous 1993 data controlled to 1980 census based population estimates.
... = Not available.

Table A-9. School Enrollment of the Population 3 Years Old and Over, by Level and Control of School, Race, and Hispanic Origin, October 1955–2011—*Continued*

(Numbers in thousands)

Year, race, and Hispanic origin	High school			College			
	Total	Public	Private	Total	Public	Private	Full-time
BLACK ALONE—*(Continued)*							
1969	1,808	1,751	57	492	372	120	401
1968	1,718	1,656	62	434	359	75	338
1967	1,651	1,605	46	370	280	90	271
1966	1,721	1,673	48	282	...	...	210
1965	1,619	1,556	62	358	272	86	218
1964	1,556	1,505	51	306	227	78	...
1963	1,444	1,404	39	286	217	69	...
1962	1,246	1,214	32	274	200	74	...
1961	1,222	1,182	39	233	171	61	...
1960	1127	1092	34	227	180	46	...
1959	1,030	999	31	222	160	62	...
1958	998	981	17	212	160	53	...
1957	961	939	22	206	132	74	...
1956	873	843	30	196	120	76	...
1955	926	878	48	155	86	69	...
ASIAN[4]							
2011	685	635	50	1,204	936	268	963
2010	586	542	43	1,322	969	353	1,090
2009	582	530	53	1,231	950	282	972
2008	620	564	56	1,220	918	301	917
2007	638	616	23	1,103	841	261	896
2006	663	611	51	1,084	862	223	866
2005	642	596	46	1,184	904	279	948
2004	650	619	31	1,191	928	263	881
2003[2]	632	585	47	1,162	833	328	901
2002	723	664	59	1,258	1,040	218	951
2001	771	736	35	1,280	1,026	254	921
2000	668	622	46	1,049	831	218	792
1999	719	666	53	1,041	779	261	787
1998	650	599	51	1,016	783	233	821
1997	656	600	57	947	712	235	721
1996	644	606	38	999	816	183	710
1995	399	375	24	617	470	147	456
1994[3]	399	365	34	723	548	174	530
1993	428	390	37	641	519	122	542
HISPANIC[5]							
2011	3,410	3,294	116	2,953	2,515	438	2,041
2010	3,344	3,219	125	2,879	2,478	401	1,868
2009	3,142	3,052	90	2,434	2,122	312	1,651
2008	3,192	3,066	126	2,227	1,919	308	1,434
2007	3,058	2,902	156	2,172	1,888	284	1,459
2006	2,990	2,856	134	1,968	1,664	304	1,246
2005	2,937	2,824	113	1,942	1,625	316	1,255
2004	2,793	2,685	108	1,975	1,676	299	1,276
2003[2]	2,779	2,667	112	1,714	1,480	235	1,139
2002	2,614	2,513	101	1,656	1,374	283	1,004
2001	2,363	2,246	117	1,700	1,445	255	1,005
2000	2,253	2,144	108	1,426	1,219	207	873
1999	2,290	2,200	91	1,307	1,093	214	765
1998	2,077	1,978	98	1,363	1,137	226	801
1997	2,119	2,035	84	1,260	1,079	181	797
1996	2,018	1,922	96	1,223	1,031	192	708
1995	1,854	1,772	83	1,207	1,037	170	709
1994[3]	1,874	1,781	92	1,187	1,019	169	640
1993[r]	1,722	1,653	69	1,029	872	157	686
1993	1,556	1,496	60	867	731	134	573
1992	1,494	1,435	59	813	710	104	487
1991	1,357	1,299	61	721	607	115	481
1990	1,437	1,374	64	617	515	100	380
1989	1,278	1,231	48	642	557	82	416
1988	1,163	1,113	49	654	592	60	414
1987	1,239	1,160	80	668	551	115	414
1986	1,197	1,116	81	677	540	137	418

Note: Data shown for 1955 to 1966 for the Black population are for Black and Other races.

[2]Starting in 2003 respondents could identify more than one race. Except as noted, the race data in this table from 2003 onward represent those respondents who indicated only one race category.

[3]Prior to 1994, total enrolled does not include the 35 years old and over population.

[4]The data shown prior to 2003 consists of those identifying themselves as "Asian or Pacific Islanders."

[5]May be of any race.

r = Revised, controlled to 1990 census based population estimates; previous 1993 data controlled to 1980 census based population estimates.

... = Not available.

Table A-9. School Enrollment of the Population 3 Years Old and Over, by Level and Control of School, Race, and Hispanic Origin, October 1955–2011—*Continued*

(Numbers in thousands)

Year, race, and Hispanic origin	Total enrolled[1]	Nursery school			Kindergarten			Elementary school		
		Total	Public	Private	Total	Public	Private	Total	Public	Private
HISPANIC[5]—*(Continued)*										
1985	5,070	168	105	63	364	315	49	2,803	2,607	196
1984	4,284	117	78	39	293	267	26	2,384	2,218	166
1983	4,618	108	60	48	335	285	50	2,548	2,323	225
1982	4,478	83	46	37	329	291	37	2,501	2,276	225
1981	4,551	131	68	63	306	282	24	2,474	2,239	235
1980	4,263	146	70	75	263	234	30	2,363	2,134	228
1979	3,608	89	50	39	226	210	16	1,934	1,745	189
1978	3,455	87	47	39	231	198	33	1,893	1,704	188
1977	3,516	75	30	46	220	206	14	1,874	1,654	220
1976	3,623	68	38	30	262	242	20	1,934	1,768	165
1975	3,741	85	47	39	235	218	17	2,062	1,858	204
1974	3,620	85	37	48	225	207	18	2,040	1,780	260
1973	3,171	68	41	27	171	165	6	1,884	1,712	172
1972	3,257	61	43	18	241	227	14	1,879	1,705	173
WHITE ALONE OR IN COMBINATION										
2011	61,979	3,833	2,132	1,702	3,393	2,988	405	25,989	23,474	2,516
2010	61,498	3,880	2,130	1,749	3,188	2,848	339	25,844	23,469	2,375
2009	60,778	3,582	1,931	1,651	3,271	2,974	298	25,629	23,238	2,391
2008	60,309	3,642	1,927	1,715	3,247	2,863	385	25,498	22,849	2,649
2007	59,896	3,689	1,959	1,730	3,339	2,946	393	25,321	22,689	2,632
2006	59,391	3,765	1,895	1,871	3,213	2,820	393	25,424	22,809	2,615
2005	60,035	3,642	1,819	1,823	3,179	2,715	463	25,682	22,794	2,888
2004	59,427	3,682	1,762	1,920	3,169	2,670	498	25,691	22,682	3,009
2003[2]	59,184	4,039	1,989	2,050	3,002	2,477	525	25,581	22,686	2,895
BLACK ALONE OR IN COMBINATION										
2011	13,288	904	649	255	696	628	68	5,524	5,253	271
2010	13,105	798	589	210	809	743	66	5,402	5,069	333
2009	12,825	894	687	206	674	632	42	5,295	4,942	353
2008	12,542	776	589	187	668	609	59	5,593	5,225	368
2007	12,401	788	546	242	673	617	57	5,395	5,030	365
2006	12,261	801	568	234	678	607	71	5,365	5,002	363
2005	12,118	763	563	200	593	531	62	5,504	5,122	382
2004	12,303	864	622	242	676	606	70	5,540	5,251	289
2003[2]	12,144	787	526	262	637	559	78	5,604	5,276	327
ASIAN ALONE OR IN COMBINATION										
2011	4,571	273	139	134	257	235	22	1,860	1,686	173
2010	4,591	297	132	165	230	212	18	1,876	1,696	180
2009	4,117	316	140	175	195	170	25	1,571	1,410	160
2008	4,122	267	143	123	188	156	32	1,570	1,351	219
2007	4,025	219	94	125	179	151	28	1,664	1,513	151
2006	3,849	189	78	111	203	181	22	1,497	1,331	166
2005	3,964	220	94	126	159	118	41	1,495	1,362	133
2004	3,943	208	82	127	191	169	21	1,497	1,350	148
2003[2]	3,817	164	73	90	148	111	38	1,507	1,346	161

[1]Civilian noninstitutionalized population.
[2]Starting in 2003 respondents could identify more than one race. Except as noted, the race data in this table from 2003 onward represent those respondents who indicated only one race category.
[5]May be of any race.

Table A-9. School Enrollment of the Population 3 Years Old and Over, by Level and Control of School, Race, and Hispanic Origin, October 1955–2011—*Continued*

(Numbers in thousands)

Year, race, and Hispanic origin	High school			College			
	Total	Public	Private	Total	Public	Private	Full-time
HISPANIC[5]—*(Continued)*							
1985	1,156	1,090	167	579	464	116	381
1984	966	909	57	524	433	91	356
1983	1,104	1,027	77	523	441	82	335
1982	1,072	995	77	493	398	96	312
1981	1,130	1,056	74	510	398	112	343
1980	1,048	. . .	. . .	443	. . .	. . .	294
1979	920	875	45	440	365	75	314
1978	868	825	43	377	315	62	231
1977	928	836	92	418	357	60	287
1976	932	867	65	427	354	73	297
1975	948	886	61	411	358	53	287
1974	916	858	59	354	297	57	247
1973	758	707	51	290	247	43	201
1972	834	784	50	242	213	29	178
WHITE ALONE OR IN COMBINATION							
2011	12,979	11,952	1,027	15,785	12,449	3,336	11,476
2010	13,001	11,924	1,077	15,586	12,460	3,127	11,062
2009	12,905	11,877	1,029	15,391	12,236	3,155	11,150
2008	13,184	12,050	1,133	14,738	11,692	3,046	10,511
2007	13,433	12,302	1,131	14,114	11,058	3,056	9,912
2006	13,425	12,115	1,309	13,564	10,569	2,995	9,433
2005	13741	12516	1225	13,791	10,561	3230	9,618
2004	13,218	12,047	1,170	13,668	10,711	2,957	9,468
2003[2]	13,398	12,267	1,131	13,164	10,366	2,798	9,048
BLACK ALONE OR IN COMBINATION							
2011	2,847	2,752	95	3,317	2,676	641	2,401
2010	2,846	2,724	122	3,250	2,641	610	2,354
2009	2,932	2,836	97	3,030	2,434	596	2,178
2008	2,886	2,769	118	2,619	2,065	554	1,779
2007	2,915	2,792	122	2,630	2,059	571	1,774
2006	2,971	2,798	174	2,444	1,907	537	1,702
2005	2,870	2,729	141	2,387	1,866	521	1,585
2004	2,811	2,762	85	2,412	1,922	490	1,591
2003[2]	2,889	2,800	89	2,227	1,846	381	1,482
ASIAN ALONE OR IN COMBINATION							
2011	825	757	68	1,356	1,053	302	1,063
2010	722	668	54	1,467	1,089	378	1,205
2009	701	636	65	1,334	1,033	301	1,061
2008	758	690	68	1,340	1,009	331	1,009
2007	760	718	42	1,204	917	287	988
2006	806	743	63	1,154	918	235	900
2005	792	726	67	1,297	993	305	1,036
2004	786	743	43	1,260	980	281	936
2003[2]	736	674	62	1,262	925	337	965

[1]Civilian noninstitutionalized population.
[2]Starting in 2003 respondents could identify more than one race. Except as noted, the race data in this table from 2003 onward represent those respondents who indicated only one race category.
[5]May be of any race.

Table A-10. Percentage of the Population 3 Years Old and Over Enrolled in School, by Age, Sex, Race, and Hispanic Origin, October 1947–2011

(Percent)

Year, sex, race, and Hispanic origin	Total enrolled 3 to 34 years old	Total enrolled 3 years old and over	Years of age[1]											
			3 and 4	5 and 6	7 to 9	10 to 13	14 and 15	16 and 17	18 and 19	20 and 21	22 to 24	25 to 29	30 to 34	35 and over
ALL RACES														
Both Sexes														
2011	56.8	26.9	52.4	95.1	98.0	98.5	98.6	95.7	71.1	52.7	31.1	14.8	7.7	2.0
2010	56.5	26.9	53.2	94.5	97.7	98.2	98.1	96.1	69.2	52.4	28.9	14.6	8.3	2.1
2009	56.5	26.7	52.4	94.1	97.7	98.5	98.0	94.6	68.9	51.7	30.4	13.5	8.1	2.1
2008	56.2	26.6	52.8	93.8	98.3	98.9	98.6	95.2	66.0	50.1	28.2	13.2	7.3	2.0
2007	56.1	26.6	54.5	94.7	98.1	98.6	98.7	94.3	66.8	48.4	27.3	12.4	7.2	1.9
2006	56.2	26.7	55.7	94.6	98.2	98.3	98.3	94.5	65.5	47.5	26.7	11.7	7.2	1.9
2005	56.5	27.1	53.6	95.4	98.6	98.6	98.0	95.1	67.6	48.7	27.3	11.9	6.9	2.0
2004	56.2	27.2	54.0	95.4	98.1	98.6	98.5	94.5	64.4	48.9	26.3	13.0	6.6	2.0
2003	56.2	27.2	55.1	94.5	98.1	98.4	97.5	94.9	64.5	48.3	27.8	11.8	6.8	1.9
2002	56.1	27.3	54.5	95.2	98.0	98.5	98.4	94.3	63.3	47.8	25.6	12.1	6.6	2.1
2001	55.7	27.2	52.2	95.3	98.2	98.4	98.1	93.4	61.0	45.5	25.1	11.7	6.8	2.0
2000	55.9	27.5	52.1	95.6	98.1	98.3	98.7	92.8	61.2	44.1	24.6	11.4	6.7	1.9
1999	56.0	27.7	54.2	96.0	98.5	98.8	98.2	93.6	60.6	45.3	24.5	11.1	6.2	2.1
1998	55.8	27.9	52.1	95.6	98.8	99.0	98.4	93.9	62.2	44.8	24.9	11.9	6.6	2.1
1997	55.6	28.3	52.6	96.6	98.8	99.3	98.9	94.3	61.5	45.9	26.4	11.8	5.7	2.3
1996	54.1	27.8	48.3	94.0	97.2	98.1	98.0	92.8	61.5	44.4	24.8	11.9	6.1	2.3
1995	53.7	27.8	48.7	96.0	98.7	99.1	98.9	93.6	59.4	44.9	23.2	11.6	6.0	2.2
1994	53.3	27.9	47.3	96.7	99.3	99.4	98.8	94.4	60.2	44.9	24.1	10.8	6.7	2.3
1993r	51.9	...	40.1	95.3	99.5	99.5	98.9	93.9	61.4	42.6	23.5	10.2	5.9	...
1993	51.8	26.9	40.4	95.4	99.5	99.5	98.9	94.0	61.6	42.7	23.6	10.2	5.9	2.2
1992	51.4	26.9	39.7	95.5	99.4	99.4	99.1	94.1	61.4	44.0	23.7	9.8	6.1	2.1
1991	50.7	26.9	40.5	95.4	99.6	99.7	98.8	93.3	59.6	42.0	22.2	10.2	6.2	2.2
1990	50.2	26.8	44.4	96.5	99.7	99.6	99.0	92.5	57.3	39.7	21.0	9.7	5.8	2.1
1989	49.1	26.4	39.1	95.2	99.2	99.4	98.8	92.7	56.0	38.5	19.9	9.3	5.7	2.0
1988	48.7	26.5	38.2	96.0	99.6	99.7	98.9	91.6	55.7	39.1	18.3	8.3	5.9	2.1
1987	48.6	26.6	38.3	95.1	99.6	99.5	98.6	91.7	55.6	38.7	17.5	9.0	5.9	1.8
1986	48.2	26.6	39.0	95.3	99.3	99.1	97.6	92.3	54.6	33.0	17.9	8.8	6.0	1.8
1985	48.3	26.8	38.9	96.1	99.1	99.3	98.1	91.7	51.6	35.3	16.9	9.2	6.1	1.7
1984	47.9	26.6	36.3	94.5	99.0	99.4	97.8	91.5	50.1	33.9	17.3	9.1	6.3	1.5
1983	48.4	27.1	37.6	95.4	98.9	99.4	98.3	91.7	50.4	32.5	16.6	9.6	6.4	1.7
1982	48.6	27.4	36.4	95.0	99.2	99.1	98.5	90.6	47.8	34.0	16.8	9.6	6.3	1.6
1981	48.9	27.9	36.0	94.0	99.2	99.3	98.0	90.6	49.0	31.6	16.5	9.0	6.9	1.7
1980	49.7	28.2	36.7	95.7	99.1	99.4	98.2	89.0	46.4	31.0	16.3	9.3	6.5	1.6
1979	50.3	28.7	35.1	95.8	99.2	99.1	98.1	89.2	45.0	30.2	15.8	9.6	6.4	1.7
1978	51.2	29.3	34.2	95.3	99.3	99.0	98.4	89.1	45.4	29.5	16.3	9.4	6.4	1.6
1977	52.5	...	32.0	95.8	99.5	99.4	98.5	88.9	46.2	31.8	16.5	10.8	6.9	...
1976	53.1	31.7	31.3	95.5	99.2	99.2	98.2	89.1	46.2	32.0	17.1	10.0	6.0	3.9
1975	53.7	...	31.5	94.7	99.3	99.3	98.2	89.0	46.9	31.2	16.2	10.1	6.6	...
1974	53.6	...	28.8	94.2	99.1	99.5	97.9	87.9	43.1	30.2	15.1	9.6	5.7	...
1973	53.5	...	24.2	92.5	99.1	99.2	97.5	88.3	42.9	30.1	14.5	8.5	4.5	...
1972	54.9	...	24.4	91.9	99.0	99.3	97.6	88.9	46.3	31.4	14.8	8.6	4.6	...
1971	56.2	...	21.2	91.6	99.1	99.2	98.6	90.2	49.2	32.2	15.4	8.0	4.9	...
1970	56.4	...	20.5	89.5	99.3	99.2	98.1	90.0	47.7	31.9	14.9	7.5	4.2	...
1969	57.0	...	16.1	88.4	99.3	99.1	98.1	89.7	50.2	34.1	15.4	7.9	4.8	...
1968	56.7	...	15.7	87.6	99.1	99.1	98.0	90.2	50.4	31.2	13.8	7.0	3.9	...
1967	56.6	...	14.2	87.4	99.4	99.1	98.2	88.8	47.6	33.3	13.6	6.6	4.0	...
1966	56.1	...	12.5	85.1	99.3	99.3	98.6	88.5	47.2	29.9	13.2	6.5	2.7	...
1965	55.5	...	10.6	84.4	99.3	99.4	98.9	87.4	46.3	27.6	13.2	6.1	3.2	...
1964	54.5	...	9.5	83.3	99.0	99.0	98.6	87.7	41.6	26.3	9.9	5.2	2.6	...
1963	58.5	...	...	82.7	99.4	99.3	98.4	87.1	40.9	25.0	11.4	4.9	2.5	...
1962	57.8	...	...	82.2	99.2	99.3	98.0	84.3	41.8	23.0	10.3	5.0	2.6	...
1961	56.8	...	...	81.7	99.4	99.3	97.6	83.6	38.0	21.5	8.4	4.4	2.0	...
1960	56.4	...	...	80.7	99.6	99.5	97.8	82.6	38.4	19.4	8.7	4.9	2.4	...
1959	55.5	...	...	80.0	99.4	99.4	97.5	82.9	36.8	18.8	8.6	5.1	2.2	...
1958	54.8	...	...	80.4	99.5	99.5	96.9	80.6	37.6	----13.4----		5.7	2.2	...
1957	53.6	...	...	78.6	99.5	99.5	97.1	80.5	34.9	----14.0----		5.5	1.8	...
1956	52.3	...	...	77.6	99.4	99.2	96.9	78.4	35.4	----12.8----		5.1	1.9	...
1955	50.8	...	...	78.1	99.2	99.2	95.9	77.4	31.5	----11.1----		4.2	1.6	...
1954	50.0	...	...	77.3	99.2	99.5	95.8	78.0	32.4	----11.2----		4.1	1.5	...

Note: Data for 1947 to 1953 exclude kindergarten. Nursery school was first collected in 1964. Data shown for 1947 to 1966 for the Black population are for Black and other races.

[1]Civilian noninstitutionalized population.

r = Revised, controlled to 1990 census based population estimates; previous 1993 data controlled to 1980 census based population estimates.

… = Not available.

Table A-10. Percentage of the Population 3 Years Old and Over Enrolled in School, by Age, Sex, Race, and Hispanic Origin, October 1947–2011—*Continued*

(Percent)

Year, sex, race, and Hispanic origin	Total enrolled 3 to 34 years old	Total enrolled 3 years old and over	Years of age[1]											
			3 and 4	5 and 6	7 to 9	10 to 13	14 and 15	16 and 17	18 and 19	20 and 21	22 to 24	25 to 29	30 to 34	35 and over
Both Sexes— *(Continued)*														
1953	48.8	...	...	55.7	99.4	99.4	96.5	74.7	31.2	----11.1----		2.9	1.7	...
1952	46.8	...	...	54.7	98.7	98.9	96.2	73.4	28.7	-----9.5----		2.6	1.1	...
1951	45.4	...	...	54.5	99.0	99.2	94.8	75.1	26.3	-----8.3----		2.5	...	...
1950	44.2	...	...	58.2	98.9	98.6	94.7	71.3	29.4	-----9.0----		3.0	...	...
1949	43.9	...	...	59.3	98.5	98.7	93.5	69.5	25.3	-----9.2----		3.8	1.1	...
1948	43.1	...	...	56.0	98.3	98.0	92.7	71.2	26.9	-----9.7----		2.6	0.9	...
1947	42.3	...	...	58.0	98.4	98.6	91.6	67.6	24.3	----10.2----		3.0	1.0	...
Male														
2011	56.2	27.2	52.8	95.1	98.1	98.6	98.4	95.4	68.8	49.2	30.3	12.9	6.4	1.5
2010	55.9	27.1	53.0	93.7	97.6	97.9	98.0	94.9	66.9	49.2	27.0	13.5	6.7	1.6
2009	55.7	26.9	51.6	93.9	97.6	98.6	97.6	94.5	65.0	48.7	29.0	11.7	6.9	1.5
2008	55.6	26.9	52.3	93.8	98.0	98.7	99.0	94.9	64.0	47.4	26.3	12.1	6.3	1.4
2007	55.4	26.9	54.4	94.0	98.1	98.4	98.4	94.4	66.3	43.7	25.4	10.2	6.4	1.5
2006	55.5	27.0	56.0	94.4	98.1	98.2	98.2	94.1	63.6	44.0	25.0	10.4	5.9	1.5
2005	55.8	27.4	52.8	94.8	98.2	98.4	97.5	95.1	66.5	45.3	25.2	9.6	5.9	1.5
2004	55.0	27.6	54.7	95.5	97.8	98.5	98.7	94.9	60.3	46.6	24.1	11.5	5.6	1.6
2003	55.9	27.8	55.9	94.7	97.9	98.3	97.5	95.0	62.4	43.4	26.1	10.8	6.3	1.5
2002	55.8	27.9	54.6	95.3	98.1	98.3	98.4	94.0	61.8	44.8	23.8	10.7	5.5	1.7
2001	55.4	27.8	51.6	95.2	98.5	98.1	98.1	93.0	58.9	44.0	23.8	10.3	5.7	1.5
2000	55.8	28.0	50.8	95.1	98.0	98.3	98.7	92.7	58.3	41.0	23.9	10.0	5.6	1.5
1999	56.6	28.6	53.3	95.9	98.3	98.7	98.0	93.7	60.3	44.7	23.6	10.7	5.8	1.6
1998	55.9	28.6	53.3	95.2	98.7	99.0	98.3	93.5	60.1	42.7	24.6	10.9	5.5	1.6
1997	55.8	28.8	51.9	96.7	98.6	99.4	99.1	94.2	60.6	44.4	25.4	11.7	4.7	1.6
1996	54.4	28.5	46.9	93.8	97.2	98.0	98.5	93.2	60.8	43.9	25.2	11.4	4.9	1.8
1995	54.3	28.7	49.4	95.3	98.9	99.1	99.0	94.5	59.5	44.7	22.8	11.0	5.4	1.8
1994	53.7	28.7	47.6	97.0	99.2	99.4	98.8	94.3	60.4	42.7	24.2	10.5	5.9	1.7
1993r	52.6	...	41.1	95.5	99.5	99.6	99.0	94.9	61.1	42.3	25.3	9.6	5.2	...
1993	52.6	27.9	41.5	95.5	99.5	99.6	99.0	95.0	61.6	42.6	25.5	9.6	5.2	1.6
1992	51.9	27.7	40.3	95.7	99.5	99.5	99.2	95.4	61.6	41.7	23.8	9.1	5.2	1.5
1991	51.5	27.9	39.9	95.0	99.7	99.8	99.1	93.7	59.8	41.8	24.0	10.6	5.6	1.6
1990	50.9	27.7	43.9	96.5	99.7	99.6	99.1	92.7	58.2	40.3	22.3	9.2	4.8	1.5
1989	49.7	27.3	38.8	95.1	99.3	99.2	99.2	93.2	56.6	37.3	20.4	9.3	5.0	1.4
1988	49.6	27.6	38.3	95.9	99.6	99.7	98.9	92.1	56.2	39.0	20.5	8.1	5.5	1.5
1987	49.9	27.9	40.0	95.7	99.7	99.7	98.7	92.3	57.9	41.2	18.7	9.1	5.0	1.3
1986	49.3	27.8	38.8	96.0	99.4	98.9	97.6	92.3	57.1	33.4	19.0	9.4	5.6	1.3
1985	49.2	27.9	36.8	95.3	99.1	99.2	98.3	92.4	52.2	36.5	18.8	9.4	5.4	1.3
1984	49.1	28.0	35.9	94.0	98.8	99.3	97.5	91.8	52.4	36.2	20.1	9.6	5.8	1.1
1983	49.7	28.6	38.1	95.1	98.8	99.3	98.4	91.8	50.4	35.2	19.4	10.7	5.8	1.2
1982	49.7	28.8	36.4	94.7	99.2	99.0	98.7	91.3	48.9	35.2	18.5	10.1	5.6	1.2
1981	50.2	29.3	36.8	94.2	98.9	99.2	98.2	90.7	50.5	32.1	19.2	9.6	6.2	1.2
1980	50.9	29.6	37.8	95.0	99.0	99.4	98.7	89.1	47.0	32.6	17.8	9.8	5.9	1.2
1979	51.8	30.2	34.6	96.3	99.0	98.9	98.3	90.8	46.6	31.6	17.6	10.4	6.0	1.3
1978	52.9	31.0	34.0	95.1	99.1	98.8	98.4	89.5	47.8	31.7	19.1	10.9	6.5	1.3
1977	54.3	...	32.1	94.7	99.5	99.2	98.7	90.0	48.4	34.6	19.7	12.6	7.1	...
1976	55.1	33.6	30.9	95.6	98.9	99.1	98.6	90.5	48.2	33.6	20.7	13.0	6.8	3.6
1975	56.0	...	30.6	94.3	99.2	98.9	98.4	90.7	49.9	35.3	20.0	13.1	7.7	...
1974	56.0	...	28.1	94.4	99.1	99.3	98.0	88.6	45.8	34.8	19.4	12.7	6.7	...
1973	56.1	...	24.5	92.2	99.0	99.2	97.9	89.4	47.9	34.4	19.1	11.8	5.6	...
1972	57.8	...	24.4	91.7	98.9	99.3	97.7	90.2	51.2	37.3	21.3	12.1	5.8	...
1971	59.3	...	20.0	90.9	99.0	98.8	98.7	91.7	55.4	38.9	23.3	11.9	6.3	...
1970	59.7	...	21.2	88.9	99.3	98.8	98.2	91.3	54.4	42.7	21.2	11.0	5.3	...
1969	60.5	...	15.5	87.7	99.0	98.9	98.1	91.6	59.4	46.5	22.9	11.4	5.9	...
1968	60.4	...	15.4	87.3	98.9	98.9	98.2	91.7	60.4	45.0	20.5	10.8	5.0	...
1967	60.0	...	14.2	86.6	99.4	98.9	98.3	91.0	56.3	44.3	21.0	9.9	5.4	...
1966	59.7	...	12.3	84.5	99.2	99.1	98.7	89.9	57.8	41.4	21.3	9.6	3.8	...
1965	58.8	...	10.2	84.4	99.3	99.3	99.0	88.0	55.6	37.6	21.1	9.4	4.5	...
1964	57.5	...	8.9	83.4	98.7	98.9	99.0	89.8	50.9	34.4	16.1	8.1	3.6	...
1963	62.3	...	...	82.7	99.2	99.0	98.7	89.4	51.0	33.6	19.5	7.8	3.7	...

Note: Data for 1947 to 1953 exclude kindergarten. Nursery school was first collected in 1964. Data shown for 1947 to 1966 for the Black population are for Black and other races.

[1]Civilian noninstitutionalized population.

r = Revised, controlled to 1990 census based population estimates; previous 1993 data controlled to 1980 census based population estimates.

... = Not available.

Table A-10. Percentage of the Population 3 Years Old and Over Enrolled in School, by Age, Sex, Race, and Hispanic Origin, October 1947–2011—*Continued*

(Percent)

Year, sex, race, and Hispanic origin	Total enrolled 3 to 34 years old	Total enrolled 3 years old and over	Years of age[1]											
			3 and 4	5 and 6	7 to 9	10 to 13	14 and 15	16 and 17	18 and 19	20 and 21	22 to 24	25 to 29	30 to 34	35 and over
Male— *(Continued)*														
1962	61.7	...	...	82.6	99.1	99.2	98.7	87.1	51.2	31.3	17.7	8.5	3.9	...
1961	60.4	...	...	82.0	99.5	99.2	98.1	84.7	48.6	29.5	13.9	7.1	2.9	...
1960	60.0	...	...	80.8	99.6	99.4	97.9	84.5	47.8	27.1	15.0	8.4	3.7	...
1959	59.1	...	...	79.5	99.2	99.4	97.8	84.8	45.6	28.3	13.7	8.9	3.3	...
1958	58.7	...	...	80.6	99.6	99.4	96.9	83.8	47.5	----21.0----		9.5	2.9	...
1957	57.5	...	...	78.3	99.4	99.6	98.0	82.8	43.3	----21.3----		9.5	2.6	...
1956	56.3	...	...	77.1	99.2	99.1	97.1	79.9	45.1	----20.6----		8.9	2.7	...
1955	54.9	...	...	78.1	99.1	99.4	95.7	81.1	42.5	----18.1----		7.0	2.1	...
1954	54.0	...	...	76.3	99.0	99.4	96.1	80.9	40.6	----19.1----		6.7	1.9	...
1953	50.2	...	...	55.0	99.3	99.1	96.4	76.5	37.7	----18.5----		5.5	2.0	...
1952	49.4	...	...	54.8	98.6	98.9	96.2	73.9	37.2	----16.9----		4.7	1.7	...
1951	56.8	...	...	55.1	99.1	99.1	95.1	74.3	32.4	----14.3----		4.2	...	...
1950	54.8	...	...	56.8	98.8	98.7	95.2	72.8	35.7	----14.3----		5.9	...	...
1949	45.8	...	...	60.1	98.5	98.6	93.9	70.8	31.6	----15.4----		6.8	1.9	...
1948	44.8	...	...	55.1	99.5	98.1	92.0	72.1	34.3	----16.5----		5.1	1.5	...
1947	44.3	...	...	57.4	98.5	98.7	90.3	67.6	31.4	----17.0----		5.8	1.7	...
Female														
2011	57.4	26.5	52.1	95.2	97.9	98.4	98.9	96.0	73.5	56.4	32.0	16.8	8.9	2.4
2010	57.4	26.7	53.4	95.3	98.0	98.6	98.3	97.3	71.5	56.0	30.8	15.8	9.9	2.6
2009	57.3	26.6	53.2	94.4	97.9	98.4	98.5	94.7	72.9	54.9	31.8	15.3	9.3	2.7
2008	56.7	26.3	53.3	93.7	98.7	99.2	98.2	95.4	68.1	53.0	30.1	14.3	8.3	2.5
2007	56.8	26.3	54.7	95.3	98.1	98.7	99.0	94.1	67.2	53.3	29.2	14.7	7.9	2.4
2006	56.6	26.3	55.4	94.8	98.3	98.4	98.4	95.0	67.4	51.1	28.5	13.0	8.5	2.3
2005	57.2	26.8	54.4	96.1	99.0	98.9	98.4	95.1	68.8	52.3	29.2	14.2	7.9	2.4
2004	56.5	26.8	53.2	95.3	98.5	98.7	98.3	94.1	68.5	51.3	28.4	14.4	7.7	2.5
2003	56.4	26.6	54.1	94.4	98.3	98.6	97.5	94.8	66.6	52.9	29.5	12.8	7.3	2.2
2002	56.4	26.8	54.4	95.1	97.9	98.7	98.5	94.7	65.0	50.9	27.3	13.5	7.7	2.5
2001	55.9	26.7	52.9	95.4	97.8	98.8	98.2	93.8	63.2	46.9	26.5	13.0	7.9	2.5
2000	56.0	26.9	53.4	96.1	98.2	98.3	98.6	92.9	64.2	47.3	25.3	12.7	7.7	2.3
1999	55.5	27.0	55.2	96.1	98.7	98.9	98.3	93.5	60.9	45.8	25.4	11.4	6.6	2.4
1998	55.6	27.3	50.9	95.9	98.8	99.1	98.5	94.3	64.4	47.2	25.2	12.9	7.7	2.6
1997	55.4	27.6	53.2	96.4	99.1	99.3	98.7	94.4	62.4	47.4	27.4	11.9	6.6	2.9
1996	53.8	27.1	49.8	94.3	97.3	98.2	97.5	92.4	62.2	44.8	24.5	12.5	7.3	2.8
1995	53.2	27.0	48.1	96.8	98.5	99.1	98.8	92.6	59.2	45.1	23.6	12.2	6.5	2.7
1994	52.9	27.2	46.9	96.4	99.5	99.4	98.7	94.4	60.0	47.0	23.9	11.1	7.5	2.8
1993[r]	51.1	...	39.0	95.2	99.4	99.5	98.7	92.8	61.7	42.8	21.7	10.8	6.6	...
1993	51.0	25.9	39.3	95.2	99.4	99.5	98.7	92.9	61.7	42.9	21.8	10.8	6.6	2.6
1992	51.0	26.1	39.1	95.2	99.2	99.2	99.1	92.7	61.2	46.1	23.6	10.5	7.0	2.6
1991	49.9	26.0	41.1	95.8	99.5	99.6	98.4	92.8	59.4	42.2	20.4	9.8	6.8	2.8
1990	49.5	25.9	44.9	96.4	99.6	99.7	98.9	92.4	56.3	39.2	19.9	10.2	6.9	2.7
1989	48.4	25.5	39.5	95.2	99.2	99.6	98.4	92.2	55.5	39.7	19.5	9.3	6.4	2.5
1988	47.7	25.5	38.1	96.0	99.6	99.7	98.8	91.2	55.2	39.1	16.2	8.6	6.4	2.6
1987	47.4	25.3	36.6	94.5	99.5	99.2	98.4	91.1	53.4	36.4	16.5	9.0	6.7	2.2
1986	47.1	25.4	39.0	94.6	99.2	99.3	97.5	92.3	52.1	32.7	16.8	8.2	6.4	2.2
1985	47.4	25.7	41.2	97.0	99.2	99.4	97.9	90.9	51.0	34.1	15.1	9.1	6.8	2.1
1984	46.6	25.3	36.7	95.1	99.3	99.4	98.2	91.2	48.0	31.7	14.6	8.6	6.7	1.9
1983	47.0	25.7	36.9	95.8	99.0	99.5	98.2	91.6	50.3	29.9	13.9	8.5	7.0	2.0
1982	47.5	26.1	36.4	95.3	99.2	99.3	98.3	89.9	46.8	32.9	15.1	9.0	6.9	1.9
1981	47.7	26.6	35.2	93.8	99.5	99.4	97.7	90.5	47.5	31.2	13.9	8.4	7.5	2.0
1980	48.5	26.9	35.5	96.4	99.2	99.4	97.7	88.8	45.8	29.5	14.9	8.8	7.0	1.9
1979	49.0	27.3	35.6	95.2	99.4	99.4	97.9	87.6	43.4	28.9	14.1	8.8	6.7	2.0
1978	49.5	27.8	34.5	95.5	99.5	99.2	98.4	88.8	43.0	27.5	13.6	7.9	6.2	2.0
1977	50.7	...	32.0	96.9	99.5	99.6	98.3	87.7	44.0	29.1	13.6	9.1	6.7	...
1976	51.0	29.8	31.6	95.5	99.4	99.3	97.8	87.7	44.4	30.6	13.8	7.3	5.2	4.2
1975	51.5	...	32.4	95.2	99.5	99.6	98.0	87.2	44.2	27.4	12.6	7.2	5.6	...
1974	51.3	...	29.5	93.9	99.2	99.7	97.9	87.1	40.7	26.0	11.1	6.7	4.6	...
1973	50.9	...	23.8	92.9	99.3	99.2	97.1	87.2	38.2	26.3	10.2	5.4	3.6	...
1972	52.0	...	24.4	92.2	99.1	99.4	97.5	87.6	41.8	26.3	8.9	5.3	3.6	...

Note: Data for 1947 to 1953 exclude kindergarten. Nursery school was first collected in 1964. Data shown for 1947 to 1966 for the Black population are for Black and other races.

[1]Civilian noninstitutionalized population.

r = Revised, controlled to 1990 census based population estimates; previous 1993 data controlled to 1980 census based population estimates.

... = Not available.

Table A-10. Percentage of the Population 3 Years Old and Over Enrolled in School, by Age, Sex, Race, and Hispanic Origin, October 1947–2011—*Continued*

(Percent)

Year, sex, race, and Hispanic origin	Total enrolled 3 to 34 years old	Total enrolled 3 years old and over	Years of age[1] 3 and 4	5 and 6	7 to 9	10 to 13	14 and 15	16 and 17	18 and 19	20 and 21	22 to 24	25 to 29	30 to 34	35 and over
Female— *(Continued)*														
1971	53.2	...	22.4	92.3	99.2	99.5	98.5	88.7	43.4	26.8	8.4	4.4	3.6	...
1970	53.2	...	19.8	90.2	99.3	99.5	98.0	88.6	41.6	23.6	9.4	4.3	3.1	...
1969	53.6	...	16.8	89.1	99.6	99.4	98.2	87.7	41.8	25.3	9.1	4.6	3.8	...
1968	53.2	...	16.1	88.0	99.3	99.3	97.8	88.7	41.3	21.5	8.3	3.4	2.9	...
1967	53.3	...	14.1	88.2	99.5	99.3	98.2	86.7	40.3	24.9	7.4	3.6	2.8	...
1966	52.7	...	12.7	85.7	99.4	99.5	98.4	87.1	37.7	20.9	6.6	3.6	1.7	...
1965	52.3	...	10.9	84.4	99.3	99.5	98.7	86.9	37.7	19.5	6.5	3.1	2.1	...
1964	51.5	...	10.2	83.2	99.3	99.2	98.2	85.6	33.7	19.5	4.4	2.6	1.6	...
1963	54.9	...	...	82.6	99.6	99.6	98.0	84.8	32.3	17.8	4.4	2.4	1.5	...
1962	54.0	...	...	81.7	99.3	99.4	97.3	81.5	33.7	16.1	3.9	1.8	1.4	...
1961	53.4	...	...	81.4	99.3	99.4	97.2	82.4	28.6	14.9	3.7	1.9	1.2	...
1960	52.8	...	...	80.6	99.6	99.5	97.6	80.6	30.0	13.1	3.4	1.8	1.2	...
1959	52.0	...	...	80.5	99.6	99.5	97.1	81.0	29.2	11.1	4.4	1.7	1.3	...
1958	51.0	...	...	80.2	99.4	99.5	96.9	77.3	29.4	----7.3----		2.2	1.5	...
1957	50.0	...	...	79.0	99.6	99.5	96.2	78.1	28.1	----8.2----		1.9	1.1	...
1956	48.7	...	...	78.2	99.5	99.4	96.8	76.9	27.4	----6.8----		1.7	1.2	...
1955	47.0	...	...	78.1	99.3	99.0	96.1	73.8	22.5	----6.1----		1.8	1.1	...
1954	46.3	...	...	78.3	99.5	99.7	95.4	75.2	25.4	----6.0----		1.7	1.1	...
1953	43.0	...	...	56.6	99.5	99.7	96.6	72.9	25.9	----6.4----		0.5	1.4	...
1952	41.9	...	...	54.6	98.9	98.9	96.6	72.9	22.1	----4.9----		0.6	0.7	...
1951	49.1	...	...	54.0	98.9	99.3	94.5	75.4	21.3	----4.3----		1.0	...	...
1950	48.4	...	...	59.5	99.0	98.4	94.3	69.8	24.3	----4.6----		0.4	...	...
1949	39.2	...	...	58.4	98.5	98.8	93.1	68.2	19.9	----3.7----		1.1	0.4	...
1948	38.4	...	...	56.8	98.2	97.8	93.5	70.3	20.3	----3.4----		0.4	0.4	...
1947	38.0	...	...	58.7	98.4	98.5	92.8	67.5	18.5	----3.9----		0.4	0.3	...
WHITE ALONE														
Both Sexes														
2011	56.2	25.5	51.4	95.7	98.2	98.6	98.6	95.5	70.3	53.8	30.9	14.0	6.9	1.7
2010	55.8	25.4	52.1	94.2	97.7	98.1	98.0	96.2	70.0	51.6	28.1	13.9	7.8	1.9
2009	55.7	25.3	51.1	94.0	97.9	98.7	98.1	94.4	68.7	52.6	28.9	12.9	7.3	1.9
2008	55.5	25.3	52.0	94.0	98.2	98.9	98.7	95.4	67.1	51.2	28.1	12.3	6.2	1.8
2007	55.5	25.3	54.1	94.8	98.0	98.7	98.7	94.6	67.1	50.1	26.3	11.5	6.6	1.8
2006	55.5	25.3	55.6	95.0	98.4	98.4	98.4	95.0	64.9	48.2	25.5	11.3	6.7	1.7
2005	55.9	25.7	54.2	95.3	98.6	98.7	98.3	95.4	68.0	49.3	26.0	11.3	6.2	1.8
2004	55.5	25.7	52.8	95.5	98.1	98.3	98.5	94.2	64.9	49.3	25.3	12.2	6.4	1.8
2003	55.4	25.8	55.3	94.7	98.0	98.4	97.3	95.0	64.4	48.2	26.7	11.0	6.2	1.8
2002	55.4	26.0	53.9	95.1	98.0	98.5	98.5	94.6	63.8	47.4	24.6	11.4	5.9	2.0
2001	54.8	25.8	51.7	94.8	98.3	98.7	98.2	93.5	60.4	45.9	23.3	10.7	6.0	1.8
2000	55.1	26.1	50.2	95.3	98.2	98.3	98.4	92.8	61.3	44.9	23.7	10.4	6.0	1.8
1999	55.2	26.4	53.7	95.6	98.5	98.8	98.2	93.5	60.5	45.6	24.1	10.5	5.8	1.9
1998	55.0	26.6	50.7	95.4	98.8	99.1	98.6	94.1	61.9	44.8	24.1	11.0	6.2	2.0
1997	54.8	26.8	50.9	96.8	98.8	99.3	98.8	94.5	61.5	46.4	25.8	11.3	5.4	2.2
1996	53.4	26.4	47.9	94.8	97.1	98.2	98.0	92.8	62.5	44.9	24.6	11.3	5.7	2.2
1995	53.2	26.6	49.6	96.2	98.9	99.0	98.8	93.7	59.3	46.2	23.1	11.5	5.5	2.1
1994	52.6	26.6	47.0	96.6	99.2	99.3	98.7	94.3	60.9	46.2	23.5	10.4	6.6	2.2
1993r	51.2	...	40.4	95.4	99.5	99.5	98.9	93.9	61.4	43.7	23.1	9.7	5.9	...
1993	51.1	25.7	40.8	95.5	99.5	99.5	98.9	94.1	61.7	44.0	23.3	9.8	5.9	2.1
1992	50.7	...	40.1	95.4	99.4	99.3	99.2	94.2	61.7	45.3	23.3	9.6	6.0	...
1991	50.0	...	41.3	95.3	99.6	99.7	98.7	93.3	59.7	43.2	21.7	9.9	6.0	...
1990	49.5	...	44.9	96.5	99.7	99.6	99.1	92.5	57.1	41.0	20.2	9.9	5.9	...
1989	48.4	...	39.4	95.2	99.2	99.4	98.8	92.3	56.4	39.5	20.0	9.4	5.6	...
1988	48.0	...	38.9	96.1	99.7	99.7	98.8	91.4	55.8	40.2	18.6	8.2	5.9	...
1987	47.7	...	38.2	94.8	99.6	99.4	98.5	91.8	55.3	39.6	17.3	8.7	5.7	...
1986	47.7	...	39.1	95.3	99.3	97.8	99.0	92.2	55.3	33.9	17.7	9.1	6.2	...
1985	47.8	...	38.6	96.4	99.3	99.3	98.1	91.6	52.4	36.1	17.0	9.2	5.9	...
1984	47.3	...	36.0	94.6	99.0	99.4	97.8	91.2	51.1	34.3	17.2	9.1	6.2	...
1983	47.7	...	37.6	95.7	98.9	99.3	98.4	91.4	50.9	33.4	16.4	9.4	6.1	...

Note: Data for 1947 to 1953 exclude kindergarten. Nursery school was first collected in 1964. Data shown for 1947 to 1966 for the Black population are for Black and other races.

[1]Civilian noninstitutionalized population.

r = Revised, controlled to 1990 census based population estimates; previous 1993 data controlled to 1980 census based population estimates.

. . . = Not available.

Table A-10. Percentage of the Population 3 Years Old and Over Enrolled in School, by Age, Sex, Race, and Hispanic Origin, October 1947–2011—*Continued*

(Percent)

Year, sex, race, and Hispanic origin	Total enrolled 3 to 34 years old	Total enrolled 3 years old and over	Years of age[1] 3 and 4	5 and 6	7 to 9	10 to 13	14 and 15	16 and 17	18 and 19	20 and 21	22 to 24	25 to 29	30 to 34	35 and over
Both Sexes— *(Continued)*														
1982	47.9	...	35.9	94.9	99.2	99.2	98.6	90.3	47.9	35.1	16.2	9.6	6.2	...
1981	48.2	...	35.6	93.9	99.3	99.3	98.1	90.4	48.5	32.6	16.2	8.5	6.1	...
1980	48.9	...	36.3	95.8	99.0	99.4	98.3	88.6	46.3	31.9	16.4	9.2	6.3	...
1979	49.6	...	33.9	95.8	99.2	99.2	98.2	89.0	44.5	31.1	15.7	9.7	6.3	...
1978	50.3	...	32.7	95.4	99.3	99.0	98.4	88.7	44.9	29.6	16.1	9.4	6.2	...
1977	51.6	...	31.1	95.6	99.5	99.4	98.5	88.5	45.5	31.8	16.3	10.6	6.6	...
1976	52.3	...	30.4	95.8	99.1	99.2	98.1	89.1	45.4	32.5	17.0	10.0	5.7	...
1975	53.1	...	30.9	94.8	99.4	99.3	98.3	89.3	46.5	31.8	16.8	10.0	6.6	...
1974	53.0	...	28.6	94.4	99.2	99.4	98.1	87.9	42.6	30.7	15.2	9.6	5.5	...
1973	53.1	...	23.2	93.0	99.1	99.3	97.6	88.3	43.4	31.3	14.6	8.7	4.5	...
1972	54.4	...	23.8	92.2	99.1	99.3	97.6	88.9	46.6	32.6	15.0	8.7	4.5	...
1971	55.8	...	20.9	91.9	99.1	99.2	98.7	90.5	49.4	32.7	15.9	8.1	4.8	...
1970	56.2	...	19.9	90.3	99.3	99.1	98.2	90.6	48.7	33.1	15.7	7.7	4.2	...
1969	56.8	...	15.1	89.2	99.4	99.2	98.2	90.2	50.9	35.4	16.2	8.2	5.0	...
1968	56.6	...	15.0	88.5	99.1	99.1	98.1	90.8	50.9	32.8	14.5	7.4	3.9	...
1967	56.5	...	13.3	88.2	99.5	99.2	98.5	89.5	48.4	34.7	14.1	6.7	4.1	...
1966	56.1	...	12.3	85.7	99.3	99.3	98.8	89.0	48.2	32.2	14.0	6.9	2.7	...
1965	55.5	...	10.3	85.3	99.4	99.4	99.0	87.8	47.1	29.4	14.1	6.5	3.2	...
1964	54.4	...	9.3	84.0	99.0	99.0	98.8	88.3	42.3	27.8	10.6	5.4	2.6	...
1963	58.4	...	...	83.7	99.5	99.3	98.5	87.8	41.0	26.2	12.2	5.2	2.6	...
1962	57.9	...	...	83.2	99.3	99.4	98.2	85.9	43.0	24.1	10.9	5.2	2.7	...
1961	56.9	...	...	82.2	99.6	99.5	98.0	84.5	39.0	22.4	9.0	4.6	2.1	...
1960	56.4	...	...	82.0	99.7	99.5	98.1	83.3	38.9	20.6	9.3	5.2	2.6	...
1959	55.5	...	...	81.0	99.5	99.5	97.9	83.8	37.3	19.9	8.9	5.4	2.3	...
1958	54.9	...	...	81.4	------99.6------		-------- 90.0 --------		38.1	------14.1------		5.9	2.3	...
1957	53.7	...	...	79.3	------99.7------		--------90.1 --------		34.6	------14.7------		5.7	1.9	...
1956	52.5	...	...	78.4	------99.4------		--------89.2--------		35.9	------13.4------		5.4	2.1	...
1955	50.8	...	...	79.2	------99.3------		--------87.5--------		32.1	------11.6------		4.2	1.6	...
1954	50.2	...	...	78.6	------99.6------		--------88.3--------		33.6	------12.0------		4.0	1.5	...
1953	46.6	...	...	67.1	------99.7------		--------86.4--------		31.7	------11.9------		3.1	1.8	...
1952	45.4	...	...	54.8	------99.1------		--------86.1--------		28.9	-------9.8------		2.7	1.2	...
1951	52.8	...	...	54.5	------99.3------		--------86.3--------		26.9	-------8.8------		2.8	...	...
1950	51.6	...	...	-------- 89.0--------			--------84.4--------		30.5	-------9.5------		3.0	...	...
1949	42.6	...	...	-------- 88.8--------			--------83.0--------		25.9	-------9.6------		4.0	1.2	...
1948	41.8	...	...	--------87.8--------			--------83.9--------		27.3	------10.0------		2.8	0.9	...
1947	41.2	...	...	--------88.7--------			--------80.2--------		24.8	------10.5------		3.0	1.1	...
Male														
2011	55.5	25.8	52.0	95.5	98.4	98.6	98.5	95.5	67.6	50.3	30.1	12.3	6.0	1.4
2010	54.9	25.5	51.8	93.2	97.3	97.6	98.0	95.0	67.5	48.2	25.9	13.0	6.5	1.5
2009	54.8	25.4	50.0	93.7	97.7	98.9	97.9	94.1	64.6	48.8	28.3	11.2	6.4	1.4
2008	54.8	25.5	51.8	93.8	97.9	98.7	99.0	94.9	64.3	48.4	26.5	11.5	5.5	1.3
2007	54.4	25.4	52.9	94.1	97.9	98.6	98.3	94.5	66.4	44.6	24.2	9.6	5.7	1.4
2006	54.6	25.5	55.9	94.8	98.3	98.4	98.2	94.7	62.7	43.8	24.0	10.2	5.5	1.3
2005	54.9	25.9	53.1	94.6	98.2	98.6	98.3	95.1	66.1	45.1	24.4	8.9	5.5	1.4
2004	54.8	26.0	53.4	95.8	97.9	98.2	98.8	94.5	60.0	46.0	23.3	11.2	5.5	1.4
2003[2]	54.8	26.2	56.2	95.0	97.6	98.2	97.2	95.3	61.7	43.2	25.6	9.9	5.6	1.4
2002	54.9	26.5	54.0	95.0	98.0	98.3	98.4	94.2	62.5	44.1	23.5	10.2	5.0	1.6
2001	54.3	26.2	51.8	94.7	98.6	98.4	98.0	92.8	58.2	43.6	21.5	9.8	5.0	1.4
2000	54.8	26.5	49.1	94.8	97.8	98.3	98.4	93.1	58.5	41.8	23.2	9.5	4.9	1.4
1999	55.5	27.1	53.5	95.4	98.5	98.6	98.2	93.1	60.0	44.5	23.7	10.3	5.4	1.5
1998	54.9	27.1	52.4	94.9	98.8	99.1	98.7	93.3	59.7	42.1	24.5	10.2	5.2	1.6
1997	54.7	27.3	50.4	97.4	98.5	99.4	99.1	94.2	60.0	45.0	24.9	10.8	4.3	1.5
1996	53.3	27.0	46.5	94.6	96.9	98.0	98.6	93.0	60.9	43.6	25.4	10.6	4.3	1.7
1995	53.5	27.3	49.6	95.5	99.0	99.0	98.8	94.2	59.4	46.3	22.7	11.3	5.0	1.7
1994	52.7	27.2	46.2	97.0	99.1	99.3	98.7	94.3	61.3	43.4	23.6	9.9	5.8	1.7
1993r	51.6	...	41.2	95.1	99.5	99.5	98.9	95.0	60.1	44.4	24.5	9.1	5.2	...
1993	51.6	26.4	41.7	95.2	99.5	99.5	99.0	95.1	60.6	44.8	24.9	9.1	5.2	1.5
1992	50.8	...	39.8	95.1	99.5	99.5	99.0	99.5	60.7	44.0	23.6	8.6	5.2	...

Note: Data for 1947 to 1953 exclude kindergarten. Nursery school was first collected in 1964. Data shown for 1947 to 1966 for the Black population are for Black and other races.

[1]Civilian noninstitutionalized population.

[2]Starting in 2003 respondents could identify more than one race. Except as noted, the race data in this table from 2003 onward represent those respondents who indicated only one race category.

r = Revised, controlled to 1990 census based population estimates; previous 1993 data controlled to 1980 census based population estimates.

... = Not available.

Table A-10. Percentage of the Population 3 Years Old and Over Enrolled in School, by Age, Sex, Race, and Hispanic Origin, October 1947–2011—*Continued*

(Percent)

Year, sex, race, and Hispanic origin	Total enrolled 3 to 34 years old	Total enrolled 3 years old and over	Years of age[1]											
			3 and 4	5 and 6	7 to 9	10 to 13	14 and 15	16 and 17	18 and 19	20 and 21	22 to 24	25 to 29	30 to 34	35 and over
Male— *(Continued)*														
1991	50.4	...	40.6	94.9	99.7	99.8	98.9	94.2	58.4	42.4	23.3	10.0	5.4	...
1990	50.0	...	44.9	96.7	99.7	99.6	99.2	92.3	57.3	41.2	21.8	9.4	4.9	...
1989	48.9	...	38.7	95.4	99.3	99.2	99.3	92.6	57.3	39.3	20.4	9.3	5.0	...
1988	48.7	...	39.0	96.1	99.7	99.6	98.9	91.6	56.5	40.9	20.7	7.8	5.4	...
1987	48.8	...	39.8	95.2	99.6	99.7	98.8	92.5	57.3	42.1	18.4	8.6	5.0	...
1986	48.6	...	39.3	95.6	99.4	99.0	99.1	92.1	57.5	34.2	19.2	9.6	5.7	...
1985	48.5	...	37.3	95.7	99.3	99.2	98.2	92.5	51.9	37.2	19.0	9.5	5.4	...
1984	48.3	...	35.8	94.1	98.7	99.3	97.6	91.5	52.6	36.3	20.2	9.2	5.4	...
1983	48.9	...	38.2	95.1	98.8	99.3	98.3	91.6	50.7	36.6	19.2	10.4	5.6	...
1982	48.9	...	36.3	94.8	99.2	99.1	98.8	91.0	48.5	36.5	18.0	10.2	5.4	...
1981	49.2	...	36.8	94.3	99.1	99.2	98.3	90.5	49.2	33.3	19.1	9.1	5.5	...
1980	50.0	...	38.0	95.2	98.8	99.4	98.7	88.8	47.5	33.7	18.2	9.6	5.6	...
1979	50.7	...	33.5	96.3	99.0	99.0	98.3	90.3	46.1	32.2	17.6	10.5	5.9	...
1978	51.9	...	33.1	95.3	99.2	98.9	98.3	88.9	47.2	32.0	19.2	10.9	6.4	...
1977	53.3	...	31.7	94.3	99.6	99.3	98.7	89.5	47.7	34.7	19.4	12.6	6.8	...
1976	54.2	...	29.9	95.8	98.8	99.1	98.5	90.6	46.9	34.2	20.4	12.9	6.5	...
1975	55.4	...	30.8	94.3	99.2	99.0	98.5	91.0	49.6	36.3	20.5	13.1	7.5	...
1974	55.2	...	27.7	94.8	99.1	99.2	98.2	88.2	45.5	35.0	19.2	12.8	6.4	...
1973	55.6	...	23.5	92.7	99.0	99.3	98.0	89.4	48.4	35.7	19.6	12.1	5.4	...
1972	57.3	...	23.4	91.7	98.9	99.2	97.7	90.4	51.5	38.4	21.6	12.5	5.8	...
1971	59.0	...	20.1	91.2	99.0	98.9	98.9	92.0	55.9	39.7	24.6	12.1	6.2	...
1970	59.6	...	20.7	89.7	99.3	98.8	98.3	92.2	56.0	45.0	22.6	11.2	5.4	...
1969	60.5	...	14.5	88.5	99.1	98.9	98.2	92.2	60.9	48.9	24.2	12.2	6.2	...
1968	60.4	...	14.8	87.9	99.0	99.0	98.2	92.1	61.5	47.8	21.9	11.4	5.0	...
1967	60.0	...	13.6	87.5	99.5	99.0	98.5	91.4	57.2	46.9	22.0	10.5	5.4	...
1966	59.8	...	12.2	85.0	99.2	99.1	98.8	90.3	59.0	44.9	23.0	10.3	3.8	...
1965	59.0	...	10.4	84.8	99.3	99.3	99.1	88.6	56.6	39.9	23.3	10.0	4.5	...
1964	57.6	...	8.8	84.0	98.8	98.9	99.0	90.4	52.4	36.6	17.7	8.3	3.6	...
1963	62.3	...	...	84.1	99.4	99.0	98.8	89.8	51.6	35.2	21.1	8.2	3.8	...
1962	61.9	...	...	83.9	99.1	99.3	98.7	88.5	52.7	33.7	18.8	8.9	4.2	...
1961	60.4	...	...	82.6	99.7	99.4	98.3	85.5	49.6	31.1	15.0	7.5	3.1	...
1960	60.3	...	...	82.3	99.7	99.5	98.1	85.2	49.5	29.2	16.3	8.9	4.0	...
1959	59.2	...	...	80.1	99.3	99.4	98.1	85.9	47.1	30.8	14.1	9.5	3.4	...
1958	58.8	...	...	81.5	99.6		91.1		48.1	22.3		9.9	3.0	...
1957	57.7	...	...	79.1	99.7		91.9		44.0	22.9		9.9	2.7	...
1956	56.5	...	...	78.2	99.4		90.1		46.4	21.8		9.3	2.9	...
1955	54.9	...	...	79.0	99.4		89.1		43.9	19.3		7.1	2.2	...
1954	54.3	...	...	78.0	99.4		89.6		43.3	20.5		6.5	1.9	...
1953	50.5	...	...	56.8	99.4		87.9		38.1	20.3		5.7	2.2	...
1952	49.4	...	...	55.2	99.1		87.0		38.3	17.8		5.0	1.6	...
1951	56.8	...	...	55.4	99.3		86.6		33.8	14.9		4.2	...	...
1950	54.7	...	...	88.6			85.0		37.3	14.6		5.9	...	...
1949	45.9	...	...	89.1			84.1		32.1	15.7		7.1	2.0	...
1948	45.3	...	...	87.6			84.4		35.9	17.2		5.3	1.5	...
1947	44.4	...	...	88.6			79.6		32.6	17.4		5.9	1.8	...
Female														
2011	56.9	25.2	50.8	96.0	97.9	98.5	98.8	95.6	73.2	57.5	31.7	15.8	7.9	2.0
2010	56.8	25.3	52.5	95.1	98.0	98.5	98.1	97.4	72.5	55.5	30.2	14.9	9.0	2.2
2009	56.7	25.2	52.2	94.3	98.1	98.4	98.4	94.8	73.0	56.6	29.5	14.7	8.3	2.4
2008	56.3	25.1	52.3	94.2	98.6	99.1	98.5	95.9	69.9	54.3	29.8	13.1	6.9	2.3
2007	56.7	25.2	55.4	95.6	98.1	98.8	99.2	94.7	67.8	55.7	28.5	13.6	7.6	2.2
2006	56.3	25.1	55.3	95.2	98.5	98.5	98.7	95.3	67.2	52.6	27.1	12.4	8.0	2.1
2005	57.0	25.6	55.4	96.0	98.9	98.8	98.4	95.7	70.1	53.8	27.7	13.8	7.0	2.2
2004	56.2	25.4	52.0	95.2	98.4	98.5	98.2	93.9	69.8	52.6	27.4	13.3	7.2	2.2
2003[2]	55.9	25.4	54.3	94.4	98.4	98.6	97.4	94.8	67.3	53.1	27.8	12.1	6.8	2.1
2002	55.8	25.6	53.7	95.1	98.0	98.7	98.5	95.0	65.1	50.8	25.7	12.7	6.9	2.3
2001	55.3	25.4	51.5	94.9	97.9	98.9	98.4	94.3	62.7	48.2	25.1	11.7	7.0	2.2
2000	55.4	25.7	51.4	95.8	98.5	98.4	98.3	92.5	64.2	48.2	24.2	11.3	7.1	2.2

Note: Data for 1947 to 1953 exclude kindergarten. Nursery school was first collected in 1964. Data shown for 1947 to 1966 for the Black population are for Black and other races.

[1]Civilian noninstitutionalized population.

[2]Starting in 2003 respondents could identify more than one race. Except as noted, the race data in this table from 2003 onward represent those respondents who indicated only one race category.

... = Not available.

Table A-10. Percentage of the Population 3 Years Old and Over Enrolled in School, by Age, Sex, Race, and Hispanic Origin, October 1947–2011—*Continued*

(Percent)

Year, sex, race, and Hispanic origin	Total enrolled 3 to 34 years old	Total enrolled 3 years old and over	Years of age[1] 3 and 4	5 and 6	7 to 9	10 to 13	14 and 15	16 and 17	18 and 19	20 and 21	22 to 24	25 to 29	30 to 34	35 and over
Female— *(Continued)*														
1999	55.0	25.8	53.9	95.8	98.7	98.9	98.3	93.8	60.9	46.8	24.5	10.7	6.3	2.3
1998	55.0	26.0	49.0	96.0	98.8	99.2	98.5	94.9	64.2	47.9	23.8	11.9	7.2	2.4
1997	54.9	26.3	51.3	96.2	99.1	99.2	98.6	94.8	63.1	47.9	26.7	11.8	6.4	2.8
1996	53.5	25.9	49.3	95.0	97.4	98.3	97.3	92.7	64.1	46.1	23.6	12.0	7.1	2.6
1995	52.9	25.8	49.6	96.9	98.8	99.1	98.8	93.3	59.2	46.0	23.6	11.7	6.0	2.6
1994	52.6	26.0	47.9	96.1	99.4	99.4	98.8	94.4	60.5	49.0	23.5	11.0	7.4	2.7
1993[r]	50.7	...	39.5	95.7	99.5	99.5	98.9	92.8	62.8	43.0	21.7	10.4	6.5	...
1993	50.6	24.9	39.9	95.8	99.5	99.5	98.9	93.0	62.9	43.3	21.8	10.4	6.5	2.6
1992	50.5	...	40.4	95.7	99.2	99.1	99.4	92.8	62.7	46.6	22.9	10.6	6.7	...
1991	49.5	...	42.0	95.7	99.5	99.6	98.5	92.5	60.9	43.9	20.2	9.7	6.7	...
1990	49.0	...	44.8	96.4	99.7	99.7	98.9	92.8	57.0	40.9	18.7	10.4	6.9	...
1989	47.8	...	40.2	94.9	99.2	99.6	98.1	92.1	55.6	39.7	19.6	9.6	6.3	...
1988	47.2	...	38.8	96.1	99.6	99.8	98.8	91.1	55.1	39.6	16.5	8.6	6.3	...
1987	46.7	...	36.4	94.4	99.5	99.2	98.3	91.0	53.3	37.3	16.2	8.7	6.4	...
1986	46.8	...	39.0	94.9	99.1	99.3	98.8	92.2	53.0	33.7	16.2	8.7	6.7	...
1985	47.0	...	39.9	97.1	99.3	99.3	97.9	90.8	52.9	35.0	15.0	9.0	6.4	...
1984	46.3	...	36.1	95.2	99.3	99.4	98.0	91.0	49.6	32.3	14.2	8.9	6.9	...
1983	46.6	...	36.0	96.5	99.0	99.4	98.4	91.2	51.1	30.5	13.6	8.5	6.7	...
1982	46.9	...	35.5	95.0	99.2	99.4	98.4	89.6	47.4	33.7	14.5	9.0	6.9	...
1981	47.1	...	34.3	93.5	99.5	99.4	97.8	90.4	47.8	31.9	13.4	7.9	6.7	...
1980	47.9	...	34.6	96.4	99.2	99.4	97.8	88.4	45.1	30.2	14.8	8.9	7.0	...
1979	48.4	...	34.4	95.3	99.5	99.5	98.1	87.7	43.0	30.0	13.9	9.0	6.7	...
1978	48.7	...	32.2	95.6	99.5	99.2	98.5	88.4	42.7	27.4	13.0	7.9	6.0	...
1977	49.9	...	30.5	96.9	99.5	99.6	98.4	87.4	43.4	29.0	13.3	8.8	6.3	...
1976	50.4	...	31.0	95.8	99.5	99.3	97.6	87.7	44.0	30.9	13.7	7.1	4.8	...
1975	50.9	...	30.9	95.3	99.5	99.6	98.1	87.5	43.5	27.5	12.2	7.0	5.7	...
1974	50.9	...	29.5	94.0	99.3	99.7	97.9	87.6	39.9	26.6	11.4	6.5	4.6	...
1973	50.5	...	22.9	93.2	99.3	99.3	97.1	87.3	38.7	27.4	9.9	5.4	3.6	...
1972	51.5	...	24.4	92.7	99.2	99.4	97.5	87.3	41.9	27.5	8.9	5.1	3.2	...
1971	52.6	...	21.7	92.6	99.3	99.5	98.4	88.9	43.2	27.0	8.1	4.3	3.5	...
1970	52.9	...	19.1	90.9	99.3	99.5	98.1	89.0	41.8	24.1	9.7	4.4	3.1	...
1969	53.2	...	15.8	89.8	99.6	99.5	98.2	88.2	41.8	25.8	9.4	4.5	3.7	...
1968	52.9	...	15.2	89.0	99.3	99.3	98.0	89.4	41.3	22.3	8.2	3.7	2.8	...
1967	53.0	...	13.1	89.0	99.6	99.4	98.5	87.4	41.0	25.6	7.5	3.3	2.9	...
1966	52.5	...	12.4	86.4	99.5	99.5	98.7	87.6	38.6	22.3	6.6	3.9	1.7	...
1965	52.2	...	10.3	85.7	99.4	99.5	98.9	87.0	38.3	20.9	6.3	3.2	2.0	...
1964	51.3	...	9.9	83.9	99.2	99.1	98.6	86.1	33.7	20.3	4.5	2.6	1.6	...
1963	54.7	...	...	83.8	99.7	99.5	98.2	85.7	32.1	18.6	4.4	2.4	1.5	...
1962	54.0	...	...	82.4	99.5	99.5	97.6	83.3	34.6	16.3	4.1	1.8	1.4	...
1961	53.4	...	...	81.7	99.5	99.5	97.7	83.5	29.7	15.3	3.8	2.1	1.3	...
1960	52.7	...	...	81.6	99.7	99.6	98.1	81.4	29.7	13.5	3.5	1.8	1.2	...
1959	52.0	...	...	81.9	99.7	99.6	97.7	81.6	28.8	11.1	4.6	1.7	1.3	...
1958	51.1	...	...	81.2	99.6		88.9		29.9	7.5		2.2	1.6	...
1957	49.8	...	...	79.5	99.7		88.2		27.0	8.3		1.7	1.1	...
1956	48.6	...	...	78.6	99.5		88.2		27.3	7.0		1.8	1.3	...
1955	46.9	...	...	79.5	99.3		85.9		22.4	6.2		1.5	1.0	...
1954	46.4	...	...	79.1	99.8		87.0		25.3	6.4		1.7	1.1	...
1953	42.9	...	...	57.4	99.9		84.9		26.5	6.5		0.6	1.5	...
1952	41.7	...	...	54.3	99.1		85.3		21.1	4.3		0.6	0.7	...
1951	49.0	...	...	53.6	99.4		86.0		21.7	4.3		0.9	...	...
1950	48.6	...	...	89.4			83.7		24.2	4.8		0.4	...	...
1949	39.4	...	...	88.6			81.9		20.5	3.8		1.2	0.4	...
1948	38.4	...	...	87.9			83.4		19.7	3.5		0.4	0.4	...
1947	38.1	...	...	88.9			80.8		18.3	4.1		0.4	0.4	...

Note: Data for 1947 to 1953 exclude kindergarten. Nursery school was first collected in 1964. Data shown for 1947 to 1966 for the Black population are for Black and other races.

[1]Civilian noninstitutionalized population.

r = Revised, controlled to 1990 census based population estimates; previous 1993 data controlled to 1980 census based population estimates.

... = Not available.

Table A-10. Percentage of the Population 3 Years Old and Over Enrolled in School, by Age, Sex, Race, and Hispanic Origin, October 1947–2011—*Continued*

(Percent)

Year, sex, race, and Hispanic origin	Total enrolled 3 to 34 years old	Total enrolled 3 years old and over	Years of age[1]											
			3 and 4	5 and 6	7 to 9	10 to 13	14 and 15	16 and 17	18 and 19	20 and 21	22 to 24	25 to 29	30 to 34	35 and over
WHITE ALONE NON-HISPANIC														
Both Sexes														
2011	56.4	23.6	56.2	95.8	98.2	98.5	98.9	95.9	72.1	56.2	32.9	15.2	7.8	1.7
2010	56.1	23.6	56.1	94.2	97.4	98.3	98.0	96.2	71.0	55.5	29.1	14.6	8.5	1.8
2009	56.8	23.9	55.5	94.1	98.4	98.9	98.3	95.0	72.4	56.4	31.1	14.0	8.1	1.9
2008	56.7	23.9	56.0	94.9	98.8	98.9	98.8	95.9	70.0	55.8	30.3	13.3	6.9	1.8
2007	56.6	23.9	56.3	95.0	98.6	98.6	98.8	95.6	69.7	54.5	28.4	12.5	7.4	1.8
2006	56.8	24.0	58.2	95.6	98.5	98.6	98.4	95.9	67.9	52.9	27.4	12.5	7.4	1.7
2005	57.6	24.6	58.5	95.9	99.0	99.0	98.6	96.1	71.6	54.4	27.8	12.5	6.9	1.8
2004	56.9	24.5	56.0	96.2	98.3	98.6	98.5	95.1	68.1	54.0	27.0	13.5	6.7	1.8
2003[2]	57.0	24.7	58.8	95.8	98.2	98.5	97.5	95.6	67.9	51.8	29.4	12.5	6.8	1.8
2002	56.8	24.9	57.8	95.3	98.1	98.6	98.6	95.3	67.1	53.1	27.3	12.2	6.3	1.9
2001	56.2	24.7	55.1	95.3	98.5	98.8	98.2	94.6	64.2	50.8	25.5	11.7	6.4	1.8
2000	56.0	25.0	54.6	95.5	98.4	98.5	98.9	94.0	63.9	49.2	24.9	11.1	6.1	1.8
1999	56.2	25.4	58.6	96.0	98.5	98.9	98.4	94.5	64.1	50.0	26.3	10.9	5.9	1.9
1998	55.9	25.6	54.0	96.1	98.8	99.2	98.9	95.1	66.6	49.2	26.1	11.5	6.3	2.0
1997	55.6	25.9	54.9	96.9	98.9	99.2	98.9	95.1	64.1	49.9	27.8	12.2	5.6	2.2
1996	54.0	25.5	50.3	96.1	97.3	98.3	98.2	93.6	65.5	48.9	25.9	11.8	5.8	2.2
1995	53.8	25.9	52.3	96.6	99.0	99.0	98.8	94.4	61.8	49.7	24.4	12.3	5.7	2.1
1994	54.5	25.9	50.1	96.7	99.2	99.3	99.2	95.1	62.6	50.1	24.9	10.8	6.7	2.2
1993	51.4	25.0	43.1	95.7	99.5	99.5	99.1	95.0	63.6	46.1	24.9	10.2	6.0	2.1
Male														
2011	56.1	23.9	56.4	95.5	98.3	98.5	98.4	95.8	69.9	53.0	33.1	13.2	7.0	1.3
2010	55.5	23.9	55.9	93.3	97.1	97.7	98.0	94.7	67.8	52.1	27.8	13.8	7.2	1.4
2009	56.2	24.2	54.9	93.3	98.2	99.0	97.9	94.7	68.4	53.2	30.8	12.4	7.1	1.4
2008	56.5	24.3	57.2	94.7	98.5	98.7	99.1	95.5	66.8	52.4	29.1	12.6	6.2	1.3
2007	56.0	24.2	53.8	94.0	98.5	98.5	98.3	95.2	69.3	49.9	26.9	10.6	6.7	1.3
2006	56.4	24.4	58.3	95.9	98.5	98.6	97.9	95.5	65.4	49.2	26.2	11.9	6.3	1.3
2005	57.1	24.9	56.8	95.4	98.9	99.1	98.4	95.9	69.8	50.5	26.4	10.2	6.5	1.3
2004	56.7	25.0	57.2	96.2	98.2	98.4	98.7	95.6	63.8	50.6	25.1	12.7	6.2	1.4
2003[2]	57.1	25.4	60.6	96.2	97.7	98.2	97.4	96.1	65.4	47.9	28.9	11.7	6.3	1.4
2002	56.8	25.5	57.8	94.9	98.1	98.5	98.5	95.2	66.3	49.2	27.6	11.1	5.5	1.6
2001	56.0	25.2	54.4	94.8	98.8	98.4	97.8	94.0	62.7	49.1	23.7	10.8	5.3	1.3
2000	55.8	25.5	54.1	94.5	98.1	98.2	98.8	94.7	61.2	45.8	25.0	10.5	4.7	1.4
1999	56.7	26.2	59.2	96.1	98.4	98.7	98.2	94.3	63.7	48.9	26.8	10.7	5.8	1.5
1998	55.7	26.3	54.8	95.5	98.8	99.0	99.0	94.4	65.2	46.4	27.4	10.9	5.3	1.6
1997	55.9	26.5	54.9	97.4	98.8	99.3	99.0	94.5	63.3	48.5	27.5	12.0	4.6	1.5
1996	54.2	26.1	48.0	95.5	97.2	98.1	98.8	93.5	63.7	48.7	27.3	11.4	4.3	1.6
1995	54.2	26.6	51.1	95.9	99.0	99.0	98.9	95.0	61.9	50.0	24.1	12.2	5.0	1.6
1994	53.5	26.6	49.0	97.1	99.2	99.4	99.4	95.4	62.5	47.6	25.5	10.3	6.0	1.6
1993	52.2	25.9	44.1	95.4	99.5	99.6	99.3	96.2	62.5	47.0	26.7	9.9	5.2	1.5
Female														
2011	56.8	23.3	56.1	96.1	98.1	98.5	99.3	95.9	74.3	59.5	32.7	17.3	8.5	2.0
2010	56.7	23.4	56.3	95.2	97.7	98.9	98.1	97.8	74.3	59.2	30.4	15.4	9.8	2.2
2009	57.4	23.7	56.2	95.0	98.7	98.7	98.7	95.4	76.5	59.8	31.4	15.6	9.0	2.4
2008	57.0	23.5	54.8	95.0	99.1	99.2	98.4	96.3	73.4	59.5	31.5	14.0	7.6	2.2
2007	57.3	23.7	58.9	96.0	98.8	98.7	99.2	96.0	70.1	59.2	29.9	14.4	8.0	2.2
2006	57.1	23.7	58.1	95.3	98.6	98.5	99.0	96.2	70.5	56.5	28.7	13.2	8.5	2.1
2005	58.0	24.3	60.3	96.3	99.0	98.8	98.7	96.3	73.5	58.5	29.1	14.7	7.4	2.2
2004	57.1	24.1	54.7	96.2	98.5	98.7	98.3	94.5	72.5	57.4	28.8	14.4	7.2	2.1
2003[2]	57.0	24.1	56.9	95.3	98.6	98.8	97.6	95.1	70.3	55.6	29.9	13.2	7.3	2.1
2002	56.8	24.3	57.7	95.6	98.0	98.6	98.6	95.5	67.9	57.0	27.0	13.4	7.2	2.2
2001	56.4	24.2	55.9	95.9	98.3	99.1	98.6	95.3	65.8	52.4	27.3	12.5	7.4	2.2
2000	56.1	24.6	55.2	96.4	98.6	98.8	99.0	93.3	66.7	52.7	24.8	11.8	7.4	2.1
1999	55.7	24.7	57.9	96.0	98.5	99.1	98.6	94.8	64.6	51.1	25.7	11.0	6.1	2.3

Note: Data for 1947 to 1953 exclude kindergarten. Nursery school was first collected in 1964. Data shown for 1947 to 1966 for the Black population are for Black and other races.

[1]Civilian noninstitutionalized population.

[2]Starting in 2003 respondents could identify more than one race. Except as noted, the race data in this table from 2003 onward represent those respondents who indicated only one race category.

Table A-10. Percentage of the Population 3 Years Old and Over Enrolled in School, by Age, Sex, Race, and Hispanic Origin, October 1947–2011—*Continued*

(Percent)

Year, sex, race, and Hispanic origin	Total enrolled 3 to 34 years old	Total enrolled 3 years old and over	Years of age[1] 3 and 4	5 and 6	7 to 9	10 to 13	14 and 15	16 and 17	18 and 19	20 and 21	22 to 24	25 to 29	30 to 34	35 and over
Female— *(Continued)*														
1998	55.7	25.0	53.1	96.7	98.7	99.3	98.8	95.7	68.0	52.2	24.8	12.1	7.3	2.4
1997	55.2	25.4	55.0	96.4	99.0	99.1	98.8	95.7	64.9	51.3	28.1	12.4	6.6	2.9
1996	53.8	25.0	52.9	96.7	97.3	98.6	97.7	93.7	67.3	49.0	24.5	12.1	7.3	2.6
1995	53.4	25.1	53.5	97.4	98.9	99.0	98.7	93.8	61.8	49.3	24.8	12.3	6.3	2.5
1994	52.9	25.3	51.3	96.3	99.3	99.3	98.9	94.8	62.7	52.4	24.3	11.4	7.3	2.7
1993	50.6	24.3	42.0	96.0	99.5	99.5	98.9	93.7	64.8	45.2	23.1	10.5	6.7	2.6
BLACK ALONE														
Both Sexes														
2011	58.4	32.3	55.2	92.0	97.1	98.5	98.5	95.7	74.1	41.1	31.2	18.1	11.4	3.8
2010	58.4	32.5	56.2	94.3	97.1	98.6	98.5	95.5	62.7	50.2	29.0	16.0	10.9	4.0
2009	58.5	32.4	57.7	93.6	97.4	98.6	97.8	94.1	65.2	44.7	31.9	14.6	11.0	3.7
2008	57.8	31.7	54.6	93.1	98.9	99.0	97.9	94.2	59.2	40.3	24.9	14.7	11.5	2.8
2007	58.4	32.2	58.5	94.0	98.2	97.9	99.0	93.4	61.7	38.7	28.0	15.0	9.4	3.0
2006	58.1	32.3	59.2	92.6	97.1	97.2	97.5	93.3	64.7	39.1	27.2	11.8	8.6	3.1
2005	58.4	32.7	52.2	95.9	98.6	98.6	95.8	93.1	62.8	37.6	28.0	11.7	10.0	3.1
2004	59.0	33.4	59.6	94.1	97.5	99.4	99.0	95.7	59.2	40.0	25.1	14.3	7.2	3.3
2003[2]	59.2	33.4	55.5	94.4	98.3	98.2	97.9	94.3	61.9	41.4	27.4	12.2	8.6	2.8
2002	59.6	34.1	57.5	95.7	98.1	98.1	98.2	93.3	57.7	43.5	23.5	13.6	9.8	3.1
2001	59.5	34.3	58.8	96.0	97.8	97.0	97.6	92.1	59.6	37.2	26.0	12.2	11.5	3.2
2000	59.0	34.0	59.9	96.3	97.5	98.4	99.6	91.4	57.2	36.6	24.2	14.3	9.6	2.6
1999	58.1	33.7	56.3	97.5	98.2	98.7	98.2	93.3	57.4	39.4	21.7	10.4	7.8	2.5
1998	58.9	34.6	58.5	95.3	98.7	98.6	98.9	92.9	60.2	39.2	21.5	13.6	8.5	2.6
1997	58.4	34.6	60.0	95.8	99.2	99.4	99.2	93.4	58.2	35.9	25.4	10.7	6.5	2.8
1996	56.2	33.8	49.9	90.5	97.4	97.4	98.9	92.1	52.8	37.0	21.0	13.7	7.1	3.0
1995	56.1	33.9	47.5	95.5	97.7	99.2	99.0	92.9	57.4	37.4	19.9	10.0	7.8	2.7
1994	56.4	34.4	51.9	97.2	99.7	99.6	99.2	95.4	54.0	34.9	22.6	10.5	7.2	2.9
1993r	53.8	...	39.8	94.5	99.0	99.8	98.5	94.8	57.6	30.1	18.0	10.4	5.5	...
1993	53.6	32.4	39.8	94.6	99.0	99.8	98.5	94.7	57.7	30.0	18.1	10.4	5.5	2.6
1992	53.0	...	38.6	95.9	99.4	99.7	99.4	93.0	56.2	33.3	20.3	7.9	5.3	...
1991	52.5	...	37.2	95.8	99.6	100.0	99.1	91.7	55.6	30.0	18.2	8.7	6.5	...
1990	51.9	...	41.6	96.3	99.9	99.9	99.2	91.7	55.2	28.4	20.0	6.1	4.4	...
1989	51.3	...	38.9	94.9	99.0	99.4	99.4	93.7	50.2	30.7	17.2	6.4	4.9	...
1988	50.6	...	33.4	95.5	99.7	99.7	98.9	91.5	50.3	28.1	13.2	7.2	5.6	...
1987	51.7	...	36.8	95.8	99.7	99.8	98.3	91.5	53.2	28.7	15.0	9.3	6.0	...
1986	51.6	...	38.6	95.4	99.8	99.0	98.3	93.9	50.7	25.6	17.1	8.0	6.2	...
1985	50.9	...	42.7	95.7	98.4	99.5	97.9	91.7	44.1	27.7	13.7	7.5	5.9	...
1984	50.1	...	38.2	94.1	99.5	99.3	97.9	92.4	44.3	27.7	15.7	7.4	5.1	...
1983	50.8	...	36.2	94.7	99.1	99.7	97.8	92.6	46.1	23.4	15.6	7.4	6.5	...
1982	51.6	...	38.6	95.4	99.2	98.9	98.1	91.6	43.6	24.3	17.0	7.8	7.6	...
1981	52.5	...	36.7	94.5	98.8	99.4	97.1	91.3	48.2	23.4	14.7	8.4	7.0	...
1980	53.9	...	38.2	95.4	99.4	99.4	97.9	90.6	45.7	23.4	13.6	8.8	6.8	...
1979	55.0	...	40.8	96.0	99.4	98.7	97.4	90.8	46.6	23.7	15.0	7.9	6.8	...
1978	56.3	...	41.3	93.9	99.5	98.9	98.5	91.2	46.2	25.6	15.0	8.7	7.9	...
1977	57.7	...	35.2	96.5	99.3	99.0	98.8	90.8	48.3	29.5	15.2	11.3	9.0	...
1976	57.9	...	34.5	94.0	99.3	98.8	99.0	89.0	50.4	28.2	16.4	9.4	8.1	...
1975	57.7	...	33.5	94.3	99.3	99.2	97.4	86.9	47.1	27.1	14.2	9.4	7.1	...
1974	57.3	...	29.1	92.8	99.2	99.8	97.0	87.1	44.0	23.4	12.1	8.9	6.9	...
1973	55.8	...	28.9	89.9	99.2	99.0	96.7	87.7	37.8	20.5	12.4	6.1	5.0	...
1972	57.8	...	28.3	90.0	98.7	99.3	97.4	89.5	42.8	22.0	13.1	6.5	5.9	...
1971	58.6	...	21.5	89.8	99.0	98.8	98.4	89.2	46.6	27.3	11.4	6.2	5.2	...
1970	57.4	...	22.7	84.9	99.3	99.3	97.6	85.7	40.1	22.8	8.0	4.8	3.4	...
1969	57.8	...	21.2	84.1	98.8	99.1	97.9	85.8	44.5	23.3	8.6	4.3	3.4	...
1968	57.4	...	18.7	82.7	99.2	99.0	97.7	86.4	45.4	18.2	7.9	3.1	3.3	...
1967	56.8	...	17.7	82.2	99.1	98.7	86.1	84.1	40.7	21.2	7.2	5.0	2.4	...
1966	55.5	...	13.7	80.8	99.2	99.2	97.4	85.2	37.7	11.6	6.1	2.3	2.3	...
1965	55.6	...	11.8	79.1	98.9	99.3	98.1	83.9	39.6	12.8	6.2	2.1	2.4	...
1964	54.5	...	10.5	80.3	99.0	99.0	96.9	82.4	35.6	14.0	3.8	3.1	2.9	...

Note: Data for 1947 to 1953 exclude kindergarten. Nursery school was first collected in 1964. Data shown for 1947 to 1966 for the Black population are for Black and other races.

[1]Civilian noninstitutionalized population.

[2]Starting in 2003 respondents could identify more than one race. Except as noted, the race data in this table from 2003 onward represent those respondents who indicated only one race category.

r = Revised, controlled to 1990 census based population estimates; previous 1993 data controlled to 1980 census based population estimates.

... = Not available.

Table A-10. Percentage of the Population 3 Years Old and Over Enrolled in School, by Age, Sex, Race, and Hispanic Origin, October 1947–2011—*Continued*

(Percent)

Year, sex, race, and Hispanic origin	Total enrolled 3 to 34 years old	Total enrolled 3 years old and over	Years of age[1]										
			3 and 4	5 and 6	7 to 9	10 to 13	14 and 15	16 and 17	18 and 19	20 and 21	22 to 24	25 to 29	30 to 34	35 and over
Both Sexes— *(Continued)*														
1963	58.8	...	...	76.6	98.5	99.5	97.6	82.0	39.8	16.2	5.5	3.3	2.0	...
1962	57.1	...	...	76.0	98.6	98.8	97.1	73.2	33.4	14.9	6.1	3.8	1.5	...
1961	56.8	...	...	79.1	98.0	98.3	95.1	76.8	30.6	15.9	4.3	2.4	1.1	...
1960	55.9	...	...	73.3	99.3	99.0	95.9	76.9	34.6	11.9	4.4	2.9	1.0	...
1959	55.1	...	...	74.3	98.9	99.1	93.9	76.3	33.6	11.6	6.3	2.8	1.3	...
1958	54.0	...	...	73.9	98.8		82.8		34.3	8.7		3.9	1.3	...
1957	53.5	...	...	74.3	98.2		84.8		36.7	8.8		4.6	1.2	...
1956	51.5	...	...	72.8	98.4		81.2		31.8	8.7		3.1	0.7	...
1955	50.7	...	...	71.1	98.2		82.8		27.6	7.2		4.9	1.8	...
1954	48.6	...	...	68.8	98.0		78.8		24.0	5.8		4.8	1.4	...
1953	45.5	...	...	46.3	97.3		82.3		27.6	5.4		1.7	0.8	...
1952	46.4	...	...	54.0	96.4		77.3		6.3					...
1951	53.4	...	...	54.9	97.3		77.1		20.8	6.2		2.7	...	...
1950	51.2	...	...	86.8			75.5		23.3	6.3		3.0	...	...
1949	40.9	...	...	83.7			69.5		20.0	6.2		1.8	0.5	...
1948	39.2	...	...	80.1			66.8		24.6	6.3		1.5	0.6	...
1947	41.0	...	...	84.8			71.9		20.2	6.9		2.5	0.5	...
Male														
2011	57.9	33.0	53.4	92.4	97.5	98.5	97.8	94.0	72.6	38.0	29.8	14.2	7.5	2.7
2010	57.9	33.1	55.5	93.7	97.5	98.4	97.7	93.5	60.8	44.5	28.5	13.2	6.5	2.7
2009	58.0	32.9	56.3	93.7	96.8	98.5	96.4	95.2	60.5	42.2	26.6	11.7	7.9	2.2
2008	58.0	32.7	53.3	95.5	98.5	98.5	98.9	94.0	57.9	37.8	23.2	10.6	8.5	1.5
2007	59.5	33.9	59.6	93.9	98.3	97.2	99.2	95.2	61.9	37.8	28.0	10.4	9.4	2.0
2006	58.7	33.7	56.6	93.5	97.2	96.8	97.7	91.8	63.9	38.0	24.2	9.3	6.9	2.5
2005	58.9	34.0	54.0	94.8	97.7	97.7	93.6	93.6	67.2	35.1	23.4	9.3	6.3	2.4
2004	59.2	34.6	61.1	93.7	96.7	99.2	98.8	96.5	58.1	37.8	20.2	8.7	4.0	2.2
2003[2]	60.0	34.9	56.5	92.4	98.8	98.1	98.3	94.0	61.5	34.3	23.5	9.7	7.4	1.9
2002	60.2	35.4	57.5	96.2	99.1	97.9	97.6	92.9	54.9	39.5	16.6	10.1	7.5	2.1
2001	60.1	35.7	55.4	95.6	98.3	96.0	99.0	93.2	57.3	36.2	22.7	8.2	8.3	2.3
2000	59.5	35.3	57.6	95.8	98.3	98.7	99.6	89.1	52.4	30.5	21.8	11.3	8.3	2.2
1999	59.9	35.8	53.0	98.4	97.7	99.0	97.9	94.4	60.3	42.3	16.1	9.0	6.5	2.0
1998	60.1	36.2	57.8	95.0	98.5	98.6	97.7	93.9	58.2	40.7	15.1	12.6	5.6	1.8
1997	59.5	36.2	57.3	94.2	98.7	99.1	99.6	93.9	56.7	34.1	21.5	10.5	5.6	2.0
1996	57.8	35.7	47.0	90.1	98.1	97.2	98.1	93.7	55.2	39.0	18.6	12.8	5.4	2.4
1995	58.3	36.2	51.5	94.7	98.2	99.5	99.6	95.2	59.1	36.1	20.3	6.1	6.7	2.3
1994	58.4	36.5	56.8	97.1	99.6	99.5	99.7	95.3	53.4	33.7	21.3	10.8	5.7	2.1
1993r	56.0	...	41.6	96.8	99.3	100.0	99.0	96.1	63.4	23.7	19.6	10.4	3.1	...
1993	55.8	34.8	41.7	96.9	99.3	100.0	99.0	96.0	63.6	23.9	19.6	10.3	3.1	2.0
1992	54.8	...	41.3	97.6	99.9	99.7	99.9	94.5	60.7	27.1	18.7	7.6	3.3	...
1991	54.5	...	35.2	95.4	99.8	100.0	100.0	90.4	62.2	30.1	19.3	8.6	4.8	...
1990	53.9	...	38.3	96.1	99.9	99.9	99.7	93.2	60.7	31.1	20.0	4.6	2.3	...
1989	52.6	...	40.2	92.9	98.9	98.8	99.3	95.6	51.0	23.2	15.5	5.5	3.2	...
1988	52.4	...	34.5	96.0	99.6	100.0	99.1	93.2	49.7	20.7	14.7	6.3	4.1	...
1987	54.0	...	39.0	97.4	100.0	99.8	98.1	91.8	58.7	30.3	15.5	8.4	3.4	...
1986	53.8	...	38.7	97.1	99.6	98.8	98.4	94.7	54.1	25.4	17.3	7.1	5.9	...
1985	52.6	...	34.6	94.6	98.2	99.1	98.2	91.8	49.5	29.7	13.2	6.9	5.7	...
1984	52.6	...	37.2	92.8	99.5	99.1	96.9	93.2	48.6	29.7	17.5	5.7	3.9	...
1983	52.9	...	37.1	95.8	98.9	99.4	98.4	91.8	46.6	23.5	17.2	9.1	6.6	...
1982	53.2	...	37.4	93.9	99.3	98.4	97.8	92.2	46.5	20.9	17.4	8.5	7.1	...
1981	54.5	...	34.8	94.5	98.5	99.2	97.3	92.1	51.9	20.6	14.7	8.4	5.6	...
1980	56.1	...	36.6	94.1	99.5	99.4	98.5	90.8	42.8	23.0	13.3	10.6	7.3	...
1979	57.8	...	40.4	96.6	99.0	98.4	98.5	94.6	48.0	26.9	14.6	8.1	6.3	...
1978	58.7	...	37.9	93.2	99.4	98.8	99.0	92.8	50.5	25.2	14.7	9.5	7.8	...
1977	60.3	...	32.4	96.0	99.1	98.6	99.0	92.5	50.5	31.0	18.5	12.1	9.2	...
1976	61.1	...	36.3	94.4	99.5	98.8	99.5	90.9	54.9	28.0	18.7	11.0	8.8	...
1975	60.3	...	29.5	94.6	99.3	99.0	97.6	88.2	49.9	28.7	14.7	11.8	8.6	...
1974	60.7	...	30.3	91.8	99.5	99.6	96.1	90.1	46.1	27.7	16.0	10.4	9.7	...
1973	58.6	...	29.2	89.0	99.2	99.1	96.9	89.0	43.5	24.5	13.9	6.9	6.5	...

Note: Data for 1947 to 1953 exclude kindergarten. Nursery school was first collected in 1964. Data shown for 1947 to 1966 for the Black population are for Black and other races.

[1]Civilian noninstitutionalized population.

[2]Starting in 2003 respondents could identify more than one race. Except as noted, the race data in this table from 2003 onward represent those respondents who indicated only one race category.

r = Revised, controlled to 1990 census based population estimates; previous 1993 data controlled to 1980 census based population estimates.

... = Not available.

Table A-10. Percentage of the Population 3 Years Old and Over Enrolled in School, by Age, Sex, Race, and Hispanic Origin, October 1947–2011—*Continued*

(Percent)

Year, sex, race, and Hispanic origin	Total enrolled 3 to 34 years old	Total enrolled 3 years old and over	Years of age[1] 3 and 4	5 and 6	7 to 9	10 to 13	14 and 15	16 and 17	18 and 19	20 and 21	22 to 24	25 to 29	30 to 34	35 and over
Male— *(Continued)*														
1972	60.9	...	32.1	90.8	98.4	99.4	97.6	88.9	47.7	27.1	18.4	7.3	5.2	...
1971	60.4	...	19.0	88.7	99.1	98.1	97.7	90.0	50.7	31.3	12.9	8.5	6.4	...
1970	59.5	...	22.3	84.2	99.2	99.1	98.0	85.4	41.3	27.8	9.6	6.1	3.6	...
1969	60.0	...	21.3	83.1	98.3	98.9	98.0	87.4	49.5	28.4	10.7	2.8	2.9	...
1968	60.0	...	16.9	84.1	98.8	98.4	98.5	88.5	53.1	23.4	7.5	5.2	3.4	...
1967	59.2	...	17.0	81.0	99.0	98.3	96.5	86.7	48.6	24.5	9.0	3.5	3.5	...
1966	58.1	...	12.7	80.0	99.1	99.0	98.2	87.4	46.3	14.4	9.1	2.6	2.7	...
1965	57.7	...	9.5	81.0	99.3	99.4	98.7	82.2	47.5	18.5	4.3	2.6	2.3	...
1964	56.8	...	9.4	80.7	98.2	98.7	98.8	84.3	39.9	14.2	3.8	3.5	4.0	...
1963	61.9	...	...	74.3	97.7	99.2	98.2	85.9	46.5	21.7	7.1	4.7	2.7	...
1962	60.4	...	...	74.5	98.9	98.6	99.1	77.1	40.3	15.0	10.1	5.8	1.7	...
1961	60.0	...	...	78.7	98.4	97.6	96.6	78.6	41.7	19.9	6.1	4.0	1.9	...
1960	58.3	...	...	71.8	99.4	98.7	97.0	79.1	36.9	13.7	6.3	3.9	1.0	...
1959	58.0	...	...	76.0	98.7	99.1	95.8	76.3	35.5	12.5	10.6	4.5	1.8	...
1958	58.0	...	...	74.2	--------98.8--------		---------87.6---------		43.4	-------11.8-------		6.3	2.4	...
1957	55.9	...	...	73.1	--------98.2--------		---------84.7---------		38.5	-------10.3-------		6.0	1.2	...
1956	54.3	...	...	70.4	--------97.6--------		---------81.3---------		36.8	-------12.5-------		5.3	0.9	...
1955	54.4	...	...	72.8	--------98.2--------		---------85.2---------		32.9	--------9.8-------		6.2	1.9	...
1954	52.0	...	...	64.7	--------97.5--------		---------82.8---------		21.6	-------10.1-------		7.9	1.9	...
1953	47.8	...	...	41.6	--------97.1--------		---------79.1---------		34.6	--------5.8-------		3.3	0.9	...
1952	49.7	...	...	51.4	--------96.0--------		---------72.5---------		-------------------------6.0-------------------------					...
1951	56.9	...	...	52.8	--------98.0--------		---------74.9---------		23.6	--------9.0-------		4.3	...	...
1950	56.0	...	...	-----------87.0---------------			---------79.3---------		19.9	-------11.1-------		6.1	...	...
1949	45.0	...	...	-----------83.1---------------			---------68.8---------		26.1	-------11.8-------		3.3	1.1	...
1948	40.4	...	...	-----------78.9---------------			---------63.9---------		24.0	-------10.5-------		2.5	1.4	...
1947	45.1	...	...	-----------84.6---------------			---------72.6---------		20.7	-------12.3-------		5.1	0.8	...
Female														
2011	58.9	31.7	57.1	91.5	96.8	98.6	99.3	97.3	75.6	44.6	32.2	21.7	14.7	4.8
2010	58.8	31.9	56.8	95.0	96.8	98.8	99.3	97.5	64.5	55.4	29.6	18.5	14.6	4.9
2009	58.9	31.9	59.0	93.6	98.0	98.8	99.3	92.9	69.7	47.3	36.2	17.2	13.5	4.8
2008	57.6	30.9	55.8	90.8	99.4	99.4	96.9	94.4	60.5	42.6	26.3	18.3	13.8	3.8
2007	57.4	30.8	57.3	94.2	98.1	98.6	98.8	91.7	61.6	39.5	27.9	18.9	9.4	3.8
2006	57.6	31.1	61.5	91.7	96.9	97.6	97.2	94.7	65.4	40.2	30.0	14.0	9.9	3.6
2005	57.9	31.5	50.6	97.1	99.5	99.5	98.0	92.5	58.5	40.1	31.8	13.8	13.0	3.6
2004	58.7	32.3	57.7	94.5	98.2	99.6	99.1	94.8	60.2	41.9	29.5	19.0	9.8	4.2
2003[2]	58.4	32.1	54.5	96.4	97.7	98.3	97.5	94.6	62.2	47.4	30.8	14.2	9.6	3.5
2002	59.1	33.0	57.4	95.2	97.2	98.3	98.8	93.7	60.6	47.1	28.8	16.3	11.7	3.8
2001	58.9	33.1	62.1	96.5	97.2	98.1	96.2	91.0	62.0	37.9	29.0	15.3	14.0	3.9
2000	58.7	32.9	62.3	96.8	96.8	98.2	99.6	93.8	61.5	41.3	26.4	16.5	10.7	2.9
1999	56.5	32.0	59.1	96.5	98.7	98.6	98.5	92.1	54.7	36.9	25.9	11.5	8.9	2.9
1998	57.8	33.2	59.1	95.6	98.9	98.7	100.0	91.8	62.2	37.8	26.2	14.4	10.9	3.2
1997	57.4	33.3	62.9	97.2	99.8	99.7	98.9	92.9	59.6	37.3	28.7	10.8	7.2	3.5
1996	54.7	32.2	52.6	90.8	96.7	97.6	99.6	90.4	50.5	35.5	23.2	14.4	8.6	3.5
1995	54.1	31.9	43.6	96.3	97.2	99.0	98.3	90.4	55.9	38.5	19.5	13.0	8.7	3.0
1994	54.4	32.5	47.0	97.2	99.7	99.7	98.6	95.5	54.6	35.9	23.6	10.3	8.5	3.4
1993r	51.6	...	37.9	92.0	98.7	99.7	97.9	93.4	52.0	35.3	16.6	10.5	7.4	...
1993	51.6	30.4	37.8	92.1	98.7	99.7	97.9	93.4	51.9	35.1	16.7	10.5	7.5	3.0
1992	51.3	...	35.8	94.1	98.9	99.6	98.8	91.5	51.8	38.6	21.6	8.2	6.9	...
1991	50.6	...	39.5	96.1	99.5	100.0	98.2	93.1	49.4	29.9	17.3	8.8	7.9	...
1990	50.1	...	45.0	96.5	99.8	99.8	98.7	90.2	50.0	26.0	20.1	7.3	6.2	...
1989	50.1	...	37.6	97.1	99.2	99.9	99.5	91.7	49.4	37.3	18.6	7.1	6.3	...
1988	49.0	...	32.3	94.9	99.8	99.3	98.6	89.8	50.9	34.3	11.9	7.9	6.9	...
1987	49.6	...	34.4	94.1	99.3	99.7	98.6	91.2	48.2	27.4	14.6	10.0	8.1	...
1986	49.5	...	38.6	93.7	100.0	99.3	98.2	93.1	47.6	25.7	16.9	8.6	6.5	...
1985	49.4	...	50.2	97.1	98.7	99.9	97.6	91.6	39.0	26.0	14.1	7.9	6.1	...
1984	47.8	...	39.2	95.3	99.5	99.4	99.0	91.7	40.3	25.9	14.1	8.8	6.2	...
1983	48.8	...	35.2	93.6	99.3	100.0	97.1	93.4	45.7	23.3	14.2	6.0	6.5	...

Note: Data for 1947 to 1953 exclude kindergarten. Nursery school was first collected in 1964. Data shown for 1947 to 1966 for the Black population are for Black and other races.

[1]Civilian noninstitutionalized population.

[2]Starting in 2003 respondents could identify more than one race. Except as noted, the race data in this table from 2003 onward represent those respondents who indicated only one race category.

r = Revised, controlled to 1990 census based population estimates; previous 1993 data controlled to 1980 census based population estimates.

... = Not available.

* = Quantity zero or rounds to zero.

Table A-10. Percentage of the Population 3 Years Old and Over Enrolled in School, by Age, Sex, Race, and Hispanic Origin, October 1947–2011—*Continued*

(Percent)

Year, sex, race, and Hispanic origin	Total enrolled 3 to 34 years old	Total enrolled 3 years old and over	Years of age[1] 3 and 4	5 and 6	7 to 9	10 to 13	14 and 15	16 and 17	18 and 19	20 and 21	22 to 24	25 to 29	30 to 34	35 and over
Female— *(Continued)*														
1982	50.2	...	39.8	97.0	99.1	99.5	98.3	91.0	41.0	27.2	16.6	7.2	8.0	...
1981	50.6	...	38.7	94.4	99.1	99.6	97.0	90.5	44.9	25.7	14.7	8.4	8.1	...
1980	52.0	...	39.7	96.7	99.3	99.3	97.4	90.4	48.2	23.7	13.9	7.4	6.5	...
1979	52.5	...	41.2	95.5	99.7	99.0	96.4	87.1	45.4	21.1	15.3	7.7	7.3	...
1978	54.1	...	44.8	94.7	99.6	99.1	98.0	89.6	42.4	26.0	15.2	8.1	8.0	...
1977	55.4	...	38.1	97.0	99.4	99.4	98.5	89.1	46.3	28.2	12.6	10.7	8.9	...
1976	55.0	...	32.6	93.6	99.1	98.8	98.4	87.0	46.4	28.4	14.5	8.1	7.6	...
1975	55.3	...	37.6	93.9	99.3	99.4	97.2	85.6	44.7	25.8	13.8	7.5	5.9	...
1974	54.2	...	28.0	93.8	98.9	100.0	97.9	84.2	42.1	20.1	9.0	7.7	4.8	...
1973	53.3	...	28.5	90.9	99.2	98.9	96.5	86.4	32.8	17.3	11.1	5.5	3.8	...
1972	54.9	...	24.5	89.1	99.0	99.3	97.3	90.1	38.7	17.9	8.5	5.9	6.5	...
1971	56.9	...	24.1	90.9	98.9	99.4	99.0	88.4	43.1	24.1	10.1	4.2	4.2	...
1970	55.5	...	23.2	85.7	99.5	99.5	97.2	85.9	38.9	18.9	6.7	3.6	3.3	...
1969	55.8	...	21.1	85.0	99.4	99.2	97.7	84.3	40.1	19.6	6.9	5.5	3.7	...
1968	54.9	...	20.5	81.3	99.7	99.5	96.9	84.3	38.6	14.5	8.3	1.5	3.2	...
1967	54.6	...	18.5	83.4	99.2	99.0	95.8	81.6	34.0	18.5	5.6	6.1	1.5	...
1966	53.2	...	14.7	81.6	99.3	99.4	96.5	83.1	30.3	9.3	3.6	2.0	2.0	...
1965	53.6	...	14.1	77.3	98.6	99.2	97.6	85.6	32.5	8.0	7.8	1.7	2.4	...
1964	52.5	...	11.7	79.9	99.9	99.3	95.0	80.6	31.7	13.7	3.8	2.8	2.0	...
1963	56.0	...	...	79.0	99.2	99.8	96.9	78.2	33.9	11.5	4.3	2.2	1.5	...
1962	54.1	...	...	77.5	98.3	99.1	95.2	69.5	27.3	14.9	3.0	2.2	1.3	...
1961	53.8	...	...	79.5	97.6	99.0	93.5	75.1	20.6	12.4	2.7	1.0	0.4	...
1960	53.7	...	...	74.9	99.1	99.3	94.8	74.7	32.2	10.4	2.8	2.1	1.0	...
1959	52.4	...	...	72.5	99.2	99.1	92.0	76.4	31.9	10.8	2.7	1.4	1.0	...
1958	50.3	...	...	73.7	98.7		78.1		26.4	6.0		1.9	0.4	...
1957	51.3	...	...	75.6	98.2		85.0		35.1	7.6		3.5	1.1	...
1956	49.0	...	...	75.2	99.1		81.1		27.5	5.7		1.3	0.6	...
1955	47.4	...	...	69.4	98.1		80.5		23.1	5.5		3.8	1.7	...
1954	45.6	...	...	73.0	98.6		74.7		25.7	2.9		2.3	0.9	...
1953	43.5	...	...	51.1	97.6		85.5		21.6	5.0		0.3	0.7	...
1952	43.6	...	...	56.3	97.0		82.3		6.4					...
1951	50.3	...	...	57.1	96.5		79.2		17.9	4.3		1.5	...	...
1950	47.0	...	...	86.5			71.9		25.7	3.0		0.6	...	...
1949	37.3	...	...	84.5			70.0		14.5	1.9		0.7	*	...
1948	38.2	...	...	81.3			69.6		25.2	2.7		0.6	*	...
1947	37.3	...	...	84.9			71.3		19.9	2.5		0.3	0.3	...
ASIAN[3]														
Both Sexes														
2011	56.8	26.9	51.8	96.7	97.4	96.7	97.9	97.2	84.5	79.0	42.6	16.4	8.3	2.0
2010	58.6	27.9	61.8	96.5	98.5	98.4	97.6	95.3	82.3	80.2	46.5	20.9	10.3	1.8
2009	57.8	26.9	52.4	94.7	96.4	95.4	96.2	96.6	94.1	73.0	56.7	19.3	10.8	2.0
2008	57.3	27.4	55.8	90.8	98.0	99.5	98.7	92.4	85.4	81.1	43.1	23.4	11.5	2.4
2007	55.6	26.9	53.4	94.3	98.2	99.2	99.8	92.6	86.5	66.5	47.4	19.0	9.9	1.7
2006	54.7	26.9	48.3	96.7	99.1	99.2	99.5	92.2	83.0	74.7	44.8	17.8	8.7	2.2
2005	55.6	28.2	55.0	94.7	99.5	97.6	98.8	98.3	88.3	80.5	42.7	21.0	9.3	2.2
2004	56.8	29.3	58.3	97.2	99.9	99.1	97.5	98.6	82.6	79.7	46.8	21.5	9.5	2.6
2003[2]	56.8	29.3	54.5	89.4	99.0	99.3	99.0	97.6	87.3	79.8	48.1	22.5	9.2	2.2
2002	57.3	30.8	56.1	95.6	96.9	98.8	98.4	94.9	78.9	72.8	49.5	18.3	8.3	2.4
2001	57.7	31.7	41.9	99.4	96.3	99.6	98.4	95.7	84.0	72.6	50.8	22.6	7.8	2.2
2000	58.3	32.6	56.0	97.6	97.8	97.6	99.6	98.4	78.8	66.2	45.3	18.7	8.9	2.8
1999	60.9	34.3	55.8	98.9	99.6	100.0	95.8	97.3	78.5	61.7	45.6	20.3	7.8	3.0
1998	59.9	34.2	53.4	97.9	97.9	98.1	95.3	95.6	83.3	70.6	49.0	21.3	8.7	2.6
1997	60.6	34.6	60.2	94.0	97.7	100.0	99.4	94.7	80.2	73.2	41.8	24.2	9.6	2.7
1996	58.6	35.0	50.4	95.7	98.9	99.3	96.8	94.3	78.3	65.8	39.5	18.6	9.9	3.6
1995	57.3	32.5	42.1	95.9	99.5	99.8	100.0	95.9	83.1	63.4	46.7	21.2	11.1	3.2
1994	60.9	33.1	42.3	97.8	99.5	99.7	100.0	97.3	81.8	67.4	53.5	23.8	8.4	2.7
1993	62.2	34.7	39.6	97.1	99.7	100.0	99.9	91.1	82.5	76.1	55.3	21.0	8.6	3.4

Note: Data for 1947 to 1953 exclude kindergarten. Nursery school was first collected in 1964. Data shown for 1947 to 1966 for the Black population are for Black and other races.

[1]Civilian noninstitutionalized population.

[2]Starting in 2003 respondents could identify more than one race. Except as noted, the race data in this table from 2003 onward represent those respondents who indicated only one race category.

[3]The data shown prior to 2003 consists of those identifying themselves as "Asian or Pacific Islanders."

... = Not available.

* = Quantity zero or rounds to zero.

Table A-10. Percentage of the Population 3 Years Old and Over Enrolled in School, by Age, Sex, Race, and Hispanic Origin, October 1947–2011—*Continued*

(Percent)

Year, sex, race, and Hispanic origin	Total enrolled 3 to 34 years old	Total enrolled 3 years old and over	Years of age[1]											
			3 and 4	5 and 6	7 to 9	10 to 13	14 and 15	16 and 17	18 and 19	20 and 21	22 to 24	25 to 29	30 to 34	35 and over
Male														
2011	57.7	28.0	51.6	96.9	96.8	98.2	98.4	96.5	89.2	80.5	39.4	15.8	8.1	1.3
2010	59.8	29.4	63.2	97.5	98.8	97.8	97.1	96.0	77.6	82.9	42.7	22.8	10.8	1.8
2009	58.0	28.2	51.9	94.2	95.6	94.5	97.3	95.1	92.6	71.8	56.9	19.6	9.5	2.3
2008	57.1	27.9	54.2	91.1	96.8	99.1	100.0	96.0	89.0	74.1	38.0	25.2	10.3	1.9
2007	57.2	28.6	56.7	96.9	99.0	99.0	99.7	93.5	91.8	67.6	46.0	18.1	10.3	1.9
2006	55.5	28.3	56.7	96.8	98.3	98.8	99.4	91.0	79.7	76.1	42.2	16.3	8.5	2.4
2005	56.9	29.7	53.2	96.8	99.8	96.9	97.8	97.8	85.2	84.0	42.6	21.1	10.3	2.0
2004	59.3	31.9	58.3	96.0	99.7	99.8	96.5	99.0	85.9	84.2	49.8	24.1	11.4	2.9
2003[2]	59.6	31.8	53.3	90.8	97.9	99.9	97.8	100.0	90.4	77.0	47.8	28.9	11.9	2.3
2002	58.7	32.3	54.1	97.7	95.6	98.4	99.5	94.3	80.0	70.2	50.1	20.6	9.5	2.4
2001	59.1	33.6	35.9	99.6	96.0	100.0	97.1	94.5	83.3	74.9	58.9	22.9	10.6	1.7
2000	60.5	35.0	56.0	96.8	99.5	97.0	99.3	97.8	75.5	67.2	49.1	16.0	10.2	2.7
1999	62.0	35.8	53.5	97.9	99.2	100.0	93.7	98.7	74.4	59.6	50.5	21.4	10.6	3.1
1998	60.8	35.2	51.5	100.0	97.9	98.5	95.0	96.8	74.8	68.0	51.3	21.4	11.1	2.2
1997	63.4	36.6	61.3	89.7	99.4	100.0	98.6	95.5	88.2	71.6	46.9	31.0	10.6	2.5
1996	62.1	38.0	51.0	94.0	99.0	99.6	97.9	93.7	81.0	70.7	37.3	24.4	14.4	3.6
1995	60.0	35.6	38.0	94.5	98.9	99.6	100.0	96.9	81.9	60.3	47.8	24.8	15.7	3.5
1994	64.7	35.8	45.5	98.2	99.0	100.0	100.0	96.9	81.5	70.9	57.0	31.3	10.7	2.1
1993	65.9	37.9	43.0	95.9	99.8	99.9	100.0	93.4	79.4	78.5	65.4	21.0	11.2	3.4
Female														
2011	55.9	25.9	52.0	96.5	98.0	95.3	97.3	98.0	79.2	77.5	46.0	17.0	8.5	2.5
2010	57.3	26.5	60.5	95.6	98.2	99.0	98.1	94.3	87.2	77.8	50.3	19.1	9.9	1.8
2009	57.5	25.8	53.1	95.3	97.3	96.2	94.5	98.3	95.8	74.1	56.5	19.1	12.0	1.8
2008	57.4	26.8	57.8	90.4	99.0	100.0	97.5	88.7	81.8	89.5	47.5	21.7	12.7	2.9
2007	54.0	25.3	49.1	91.9	97.3	99.5	100.0	91.7	81.0	65.4	48.5	19.8	9.6	1.5
2006	53.8	25.6	39.1	96.5	100.0	99.5	99.0	93.3	87.3	72.9	47.0	19.1	8.9	2.0
2005	54.4	26.8	56.8	92.3	99.3	98.3	100.0	98.8	91.7	75.9	42.9	20.9	8.4	2.4
2004	54.1	26.9	58.4	99.1	100.0	98.2	98.5	98.1	79.0	74.7	43.9	19.1	7.6	2.4
2003[2]	54.0	27.1	55.8	87.4	100.0	98.4	100.0	94.9	84.6	82.5	48.3	16.6	6.7	2.1
2002	56.1	29.5	58.1	93.4	97.9	99.2	97.5	95.5	77.9	75.8	48.9	16.1	7.2	2.3
2001	56.2	29.9	47.7	99.1	96.6	99.2	100.0	97.2	84.6	70.0	42.5	22.3	5.1	2.6
2000	56.0	30.4	55.9	98.6	96.2	98.2	100.0	99.1	82.0	65.1	41.7	20.6	7.5	2.9
1999	59.8	32.9	57.8	100.0	100.0	100.0	97.6	95.8	82.0	63.7	42.2	19.4	5.2	2.9
1998	59.0	33.2	55.0	95.6	97.8	97.7	95.6	94.4	91.5	73.6	46.6	21.2	6.5	3.0
1997	57.9	32.7	59.5	98.4	95.5	100.0	100.0	93.8	71.6	74.3	36.5	17.4	8.8	2.9
1996	54.9	32.0	49.5	97.9	98.8	99.0	95.5	95.0	75.4	80.8	42.2	13.5	6.1	3.7
1995	54.5	29.6	46.0	98.1	100.0	100.0	100.0	94.8	84.4	67.0	46.2	17.8	6.8	3.1
1994	57.3	30.6	39.0	97.4	100.0	99.4	100.0	97.7	81.9	64.2	49.3	16.9	6.7	3.2
1993	58.6	31.9	36.1	98.5	99.6	100.0	99.8	88.7	87.0	74.5	43.4	20.9	6.3	3.4
HISPANIC[4]														
Both Sexes														
2011	55.6	34.0	41.6	95.6	98.2	98.5	98.2	94.6	65.2	45.7	23.6	10.5	4.5	1.6
2010	55.1	33.8	44.2	94.3	98.5	97.3	97.9	96.0	66.2	37.0	23.8	11.4	5.7	2.3
2009	52.8	32.3	41.9	93.7	96.5	98.0	97.9	92.6	57.1	37.2	20.4	9.5	5.6	2.2
2008	51.9	31.9	43.6	91.8	97.1	98.6	98.7	93.8	55.1	32.1	19.8	9.2	4.2	2.2
2007	51.7	32.1	48.2	94.3	96.3	99.0	98.4	90.6	57.2	32.3	18.8	8.3	4.5	2.1
2006	51.3	31.9	48.8	93.4	98.1	98.2	98.4	91.1	53.4	30.6	17.9	7.3	5.3	1.8
2005	50.9	32.1	43.0	93.8	97.4	97.9	97.3	92.6	54.3	30.0	19.5	7.8	4.2	2.0
2004	50.7	32.4	43.9	93.9	97.2	97.5	99.0	89.2	43.9	30.6	17.2	6.7	3.3	1.5
2003	49.6	31.6	43.7	91.6	97.5	98.3	96.7	92.1	50.5	33.7	16.1	6.2	4.6	1.8
2002	49.9	32.3	41.0	94.4	97.9	98.1	98.1	90.9	50.6	24.6	15.3	8.4	4.4	2.4
2001	49.5	32.4	39.7	93.6	97.4	98.3	97.8	88.2	45.5	27.9	15.5	7.7	4.4	2.5
2000	51.3	32.6	35.9	94.3	97.5	97.4	96.2	87.0	49.5	26.1	18.2	7.4	5.6	2.0
1999	51.1	32.9	36.9	93.9	99.0	98.3	97.6	88.1	44.5	22.6	15.0	9.1	5.6	2.3
1998	50.4	32.6	36.7	98.2	98.8	99.1	96.8	89.1	40.3	25.6	16.3	8.7	5.5	2.3
1997	50.8	32.7	36.6	96.6	98.6	99.6	98.4	91.1	49.4	28.9	16.4	7.3	3.7	1.8

Note: Data for 1947 to 1953 exclude kindergarten. Nursery school was first collected in 1964. Data shown for 1947 to 1966 for the Black population are for Black and other races.

[1]Civilian noninstitutionalized population.

[2]Starting in 2003 respondents could identify more than one race. Except as noted, the race data in this table from 2003 onward represent those respondents who indicated only one race category.

[4]May be of any race.

Table A-10. Percentage of the Population 3 Years Old and Over Enrolled in School, by Age, Sex, Race, and Hispanic Origin, October 1947–2011—*Continued*

(Percent)

Year, sex, race, and Hispanic origin	Total enrolled 3 to 34 years old	Total enrolled 3 years old and over	Years of age[1]											
			3 and 4	5 and 6	7 to 9	10 to 13	14 and 15	16 and 17	18 and 19	20 and 21	22 to 24	25 to 29	30 to 34	35 and over
Both Sexes— *(Continued)*														
1996	50.3	32.8	38.1	89.5	96.6	97.6	96.6	88.7	47.0	25.3	17.6	8.6	5.0	2.5
1995	49.7	32.9	36.9	93.9	98.5	99.2	98.9	88.2	46.1	27.1	15.6	7.1	4.7	2.7
1994	49.0	32.6	30.8	96.1	99.2	99.4	96.1	88.3	51.4	24.9	15.1	8.1	5.7	2.7
1993r	48.6	...	26.8	93.6	99.6	99.2	97.6	88.1	50.0	31.8	13.8	7.7	5.1	...
1993	48.9	31.6	26.8	93.8	99.6	99.2	97.6	88.3	50.0	31.8	13.7	7.7	5.1	1.9
1992	49.2	...	28.8	96.0	99.5	99.1	98.8	87.2	53.7	30.1	14.5	6.7	6.0	...
1991	47.9	...	30.6	92.4	99.9	99.4	97.2	82.6	47.9	26.4	11.6	6.9	5.9	...
1990	47.4	...	29.8	94.8	99.6	99.2	99.0	85.4	44.1	27.2	9.9	6.3	3.1	...
1989	45.8	...	23.8	92.8	98.0	99.3	96.5	86.4	44.6	18.8	12.0	6.6	3.5	...
1988	46.0	...	24.5	95.7	99.6	99.8	98.8	78.8	44.1	16.7	12.1	5.8	6.2	...
1987	47.2	...	30.7	93.0	99.2	99.4	97.6	87.1	39.1	26.5	12.3	7.5	4.9	...
1986	48.2	...	28.8	93.7	99.4	99.3	97.2	84.0	46.0	21.4	13.7	9.2	5.6	...
1985	47.7	...	27.0	94.5	98.4	99.4	96.1	84.5	41.8	24.0	11.6	8.6	5.6	...
1984	47.7	...	24.2	93.9	98.7	99.4	94.9	85.7	39.9	28.1	11.3	6.6	7.5	...
1983	49.3	...	23.5	95.1	98.5	99.7	96.0	88.6	44.3	24.0	12.5	7.1	5.7	...
1982	49.4	...	21.8	92.2	98.7	98.8	96.9	85.5	39.2	22.7	10.4	8.2	4.4	...
1981	49.0	...	24.5	90.4	99.2	99.1	94.0	82.8	37.8	20.6	12.3	8.0	4.7	...
1980	49.8	...	28.5	94.5	98.4	99.7	94.3	81.8	37.8	19.5	11.7	6.9	4.1	...
1979	48.6	...	22.5	92.5	98.7	99.0	96.3	82.3	39.9	22.6	10.0	7.8	7.1	...
1978	48.3	...	22.5	91.4	99.5	98.0	95.2	83.0	35.7	16.8	11.8	8.0	4.1	...
1977	50.8	...	19.5	93.7	99.0	99.3	97.6	83.6	40.6	23.1	10.8	9.3	5.6	...
1976	51.8	...	22.2	95.0	97.5	99.1	95.4	81.3	45.2	24.0	14.8	7.9	2.7	...
1975	54.8	...	27.3	92.1	99.6	99.2	95.6	86.2	44.0	27.5	14.1	8.3	4.1	...
1974	54.3	...	25.3	92.1	98.8	99.2	96.1	78.3	45.2	23.2	11.3	6.7	2.2	...
1973	52.8	...	18.8	90.7	98.7	99.1	94.4	80.2	39.2	21.5	10.0	6.8	1.3	...
1972	53.0	...	20.5	90.0	98.7	99.1	96.7	83.9	41.4	17.0	9.9	5.2	3.5	...
Male														
2011	54.1	33.9	43.6	95.9	98.8	98.8	98.7	94.6	61.0	43.1	21.0	9.9	3.4	1.6
2010	52.9	32.8	43.3	93.4	98.1	96.9	97.5	96.0	64.9	34.0	18.6	9.6	4.9	1.9
2009	50.9	31.3	39.4	94.1	96.2	98.8	98.1	92.5	51.8	32.1	18.6	7.8	5.2	1.6
2008	50.0	31.1	40.5	91.0	96.7	98.6	98.6	93.1	54.7	30.8	16.6	8.2	4.1	1.6
2007	49.4	31.1	50.7	94.1	96.4	99.0	97.8	91.1	55.2	24.6	14.4	6.7	3.1	1.8
2006	49.0	30.9	49.1	91.7	97.7	97.9	99.0	91.7	51.5	24.1	16.0	5.4	3.5	1.2
2005	48.4	31.0	43.0	92.4	96.0	97.2	97.8	92.5	51.8	25.2	17.5	5.6	2.6	1.6
2004	48.5	31.5	43.8	93.9	97.2	97.5	99.0	89.2	43.9	30.6	17.2	6.7	3.3	1.5
2003	47.3	30.8	42.9	91.3	97.5	98.4	96.7	90.4	47.0	27.2	13.3	4.9	3.8	1.3
2002	48.1	31.9	41.7	95.1	97.8	97.6	98.2	88.8	48.4	24.5	11.5	7.0	3.1	2.2
2001	48.4	32.2	42.9	94.9	97.9	98.6	98.4	87.8	40.0	24.4	14.6	6.5	3.5	2.2
2000	50.5	32.5	31.9	95.4	96.6	98.4	96.9	85.7	48.0	24.2	15.2	5.1	5.7	1.4
1999	50.3	32.9	33.5	92.8	98.8	98.5	98.1	87.9	45.3	21.5	11.2	8.6	3.9	2.0
1998	49.0	32.4	44.9	92.8	98.8	99.3	97.0	88.0	33.7	24.6	12.9	6.9	4.7	1.8
1997	49.0	32.3	35.5	97.7	97.7	99.8	99.5	92.5	45.4	27.6	14.0	5.9	2.7	1.6
1996	49.2	33.0	39.6	91.0	95.4	97.9	98.0	90.4	46.8	19.5	16.2	6.8	4.3	2.6
1995	49.1	33.1	40.8	93.6	98.8	98.8	98.4	88.4	47.4	24.8	14.8	5.6	4.5	2.1
1994	48.0	32.5	32.6	96.5	98.6	99.3	94.6	86.6	54.2	23.7	14.0	7.1	4.2	2.3
1993r	46.6	...	26.9	93.4	99.8	98.8	96.9	88.7	47.8	31.6	13.0	5.5	5.4	...
1993	47.4	31.5	27.0	93.6	99.8	98.8	96.9	89.1	47.7	31.6	12.8	5.5	5.4	1.5
1992	47.9	...	24.9	96.5	100.0	99.2	98.1	89.2	52.6	24.3	13.8	5.3	3.5	...
1991	46.4	...	30.7	92.3	99.8	99.7	97.8	83.6	42.1	20.8	9.9	6.8	3.3	...
1990	47.1	...	27.3	95.6	99.5	99.0	99.1	85.5	40.7	21.7	11.2	4.6	4.0	...
1989	45.8	...	21.3	92.5	97.7	98.6	98.0	88.7	44.2	17.1	12.2	7.3	4.1	...
1988	46.2	...	27.9	96.7	99.2	100.0	98.1	80.9	44.7	21.6	12.5	4.5	5.0	...
1987	47.8	...	30.5	92.8	99.7	100.0	98.1	90.9	42.3	30.1	11.4	7.8	5.1	...
1986	47.3	...	29.4	93.0	100.0	99.4	96.8	85.0	45.8	19.2	13.0	9.1	4.4	...
1985	47.5	...	26.4	95.3	98.9	99.1	96.2	88.9	38.6	20.3	12.6	8.7	3.8	...
1984	48.6	...	20.0	93.6	98.2	100.0	95.7	85.1	38.8	27.5	12.3	8.2	4.0	...
1983	50.7	...	25.0	91.9	98.8	99.6	97.8	88.2	40.4	26.2	15.1	6.9	4.6	...

Note: Data for 1947 to 1953 exclude kindergarten. Nursery school was first collected in 1964. Data shown for 1947 to 1966 for the Black population are for Black and other races.

[1]Civilian noninstitutionalized population.

r = Revised, controlled to 1990 census based population estimates; previous 1993 data controlled to 1980 census based population estimates.

... = Not available.

Table A-10. Percentage of the Population 3 Years Old and Over Enrolled in School, by Age, Sex, Race, and Hispanic Origin, October 1947–2011—*Continued*

(Percent)

Year, sex, race, and Hispanic origin	Total enrolled 3 to 34 years old	Total enrolled 3 years old and over	Years of age[1]											
			3 and 4	5 and 6	7 to 9	10 to 13	14 and 15	16 and 17	18 and 19	20 and 21	22 to 24	25 to 29	30 to 34	35 and over
Male— *(Continued)*														
1982	50.4	...	25.2	90.3	99.6	98.4	96.8	87.8	39.7	21.6	11.2	10.8	3.1	...
1981	49.6	...	25.5	89.6	98.8	99.0	92.3	84.5	36.0	24.4	11.4	8.3	4.3	...
1980	49.9	...	30.1	94.0	97.7	99.4	96.7	81.5	36.9	21.4	10.7	6.8	6.2	...
1979	51.0	...	22.8	93.8	98.7	99.0	96.6	85.1	42.6	24.0	12.4	8.7	6.1	...
1978	50.5	...	22.6	93.2	99.1	97.8	94.0	80.4	40.0	18.1	13.6	9.5	4.4	...
1977	54.2	...	23.2	91.4	100.0	98.7	99.1	89.4	43.1	22.8	16.0	13.1	6.4	...
1976	55.0	...	22.1	94.6	97.4	98.5	97.3	85.5	46.3	27.1	18.6	11.4	5.6	...
1975	58.1	...	26.7	89.7	99.6	98.8	97.4	88.3	51.9	31.3	15.9	11.9	7.2	...
1974	56.0	...	23.5	93.1	98.3	98.5	97.9	78.6	46.8	22.3	14.5	8.4	7.4	...
1973	55.5	...	23.1	92.4	99.1	99.1	96.5	86.6	45.8	23.8	10.8	9.9	6.7	...
1972	54.7	...	20.4	90.3	98.8	99.1	98.1	87.8	40.5	20.0	13.9	5.8	2.5	...
Female														
2011	57.2	34.1	39.6	95.3	97.6	98.2	97.6	94.6	70.3	48.8	26.6	11.2	5.8	1.6
2010	57.4	34.8	45.0	95.2	98.9	97.7	98.3	96.0	67.6	40.5	29.2	13.6	6.6	2.7
2009	55.0	33.3	44.4	93.2	96.7	97.2	97.6	92.6	62.5	43.1	22.2	11.6	6.0	2.8
2008	53.9	32.8	46.9	92.6	97.4	98.7	98.8	94.5	55.5	33.5	23.4	10.4	4.4	2.7
2007	54.3	33.1	45.6	94.5	96.2	99.0	99.1	90.0	59.2	41.0	23.7	10.3	6.1	2.3
2006	53.9	33.1	48.5	95.3	98.5	98.6	97.7	90.4	55.4	37.5	20.1	9.7	7.3	2.3
2005	58.0	33.3	43.0	95.3	98.8	98.6	96.7	92.6	57.2	35.3	21.8	10.4	6.1	2.4
2004	53.1	33.3	44.0	92.2	97.9	97.5	97.5	91.3	56.9	34.0	22.0	9.7	7.5	2.8
2003	52.2	32.5	44.7	92.0	97.5	98.2	96.8	93.8	54.4	41.1	19.4	7.9	5.6	2.2
2002	51.8	32.8	40.3	93.8	98.1	98.7	97.9	92.8	53.2	24.6	20.2	9.9	6.0	2.7
2001	50.6	32.6	36.3	92.4	96.9	98.1	97.2	88.7	51.1	31.6	16.7	9.1	5.3	2.8
2000	52.2	32.8	40.0	93.1	98.4	96.4	95.4	88.3	51.1	28.1	21.6	9.5	5.5	2.6
1999	52.1	32.8	40.5	95.0	99.3	98.0	96.9	88.3	43.6	23.6	19.2	9.5	7.3	2.7
1998	51.9	32.8	34.3	93.7	98.8	98.9	96.7	90.5	46.8	26.8	20.0	10.6	6.5	2.8
1997	52.7	33.0	37.7	95.7	99.6	99.5	97.3	89.6	53.9	30.4	19.2	8.8	4.9	2.0
1996	51.4	32.7	36.8	87.8	97.9	97.4	95.0	86.9	47.2	31.1	19.3	10.5	5.7	2.5
1995	50.3	32.7	32.7	94.3	98.2	99.6	99.4	88.0	44.8	29.2	16.6	8.7	4.9	3.2
1994	50.2	32.7	28.9	95.7	99.8	99.4	97.6	90.2	48.6	26.4	16.5	9.1	7.3	3.0
1993[r]	50.7	...	26.7	93.9	99.4	99.6	98.2	87.3	51.9	31.9	14.7	10.2	4.7	...
1993	50.6	31.6	26.7	93.9	99.4	99.6	98.2	87.4	51.9	32.0	14.5	10.2	4.8	2.2
1992	50.6	...	32.7	95.4	99.0	99.1	99.6	85.0	54.9	35.6	15.4	8.2	6.0	...
1991	49.5	...	30.5	92.6	100.0	99.2	96.6	81.5	53.7	32.0	13.6	7.0	5.9	...
1990	47.7	...	32.3	93.9	99.7	99.4	98.8	85.3	47.2	33.1	8.4	8.1	3.1	...
1989	45.9	...	26.5	93.3	98.3	100.0	95.1	83.7	45.0	20.8	11.9	5.8	3.5	...
1988	45.8	...	20.7	94.6	100.0	99.6	99.6	76.6	43.5	11.2	11.5	7.2	6.2	...
1987	46.5	...	30.8	93.2	98.7	98.9	97.1	82.6	36.2	22.0	13.2	7.3	4.9	...
1986	49.0	...	28.2	94.4	98.7	99.2	97.5	83.0	46.2	23.7	14.5	9.2	5.6	...
1985	47.9	...	27.7	93.7	98.0	99.7	96.0	80.0	44.7	27.4	10.4	8.6	5.6	...
1984	46.8	...	28.2	94.2	99.2	98.7	94.0	86.3	40.8	28.7	10.4	4.9	7.5	...
1983	48.0	...	22.0	98.3	98.1	99.8	94.1	89.1	47.6	21.7	10.1	7.4	5.7	...
1982	48.4	...	16.3	93.9	97.8	99.2	97.1	82.8	38.7	23.7	9.7	5.7	4.4	...
1981	48.4	...	23.4	91.3	99.6	99.3	95.7	80.8	39.4	16.8	13.1	7.7	4.7	...
1980	49.8	...	26.6	94.9	99.0	99.9	92.1	82.2	38.8	17.6	12.6	6.9	4.1	...
1979	46.3	...	22.3	91.1	98.7	98.9	95.9	79.5	37.1	21.5	7.8	7.0	7.1	...
1978	46.2	...	22.5	89.4	100.0	98.2	96.6	86.2	31.9	15.7	10.1	6.5	4.1	...
1977	47.6	...	15.8	96.3	97.9	99.9	95.9	77.4	38.5	23.4	6.2	5.9	5.6	...
1976	48.8	...	22.3	95.5	97.6	99.7	93.6	77.6	44.2	21.4	12.1	4.8	2.7	...
1975	51.7	...	27.9	94.4	99.5	99.7	93.8	84.0	37.1	24.3	12.5	5.3	4.1	...
1974	52.5	...	27.4	91.1	99.2	100.0	94.1	77.9	43.7	23.9	8.4	4.9	2.2	...
1973	50.1	...	14.0	88.9	98.3	99.1	92.5	74.9	32.9	19.4	9.2	3.9	1.3	...
1972	51.4	...	20.5	89.7	98.5	99.0	95.4	80.0	42.4	14.6	6.8	4.7	3.5	...

Note: Data for 1947 to 1953 exclude kindergarten. Nursery school was first collected in 1964. Data shown for 1947 to 1966 for the Black population are for Black and other races.

[1]Civilian noninstitutionalized population.

r = Revised, controlled to 1990 census based population estimates; previous 1993 data controlled to 1980 census based population estimates.

... = Not available.

Table A-10. Percentage of the Population 3 Years Old and Over Enrolled in School, by Age, Sex, Race, and Hispanic Origin, October 1947–2011—*Continued*

(Percent)

Year, sex, race, and Hispanic origin	Total enrolled 3 to 34 years old	Total enrolled 3 years old and over	Years of age[1]											
			3 and 4	5 and 6	7 to 9	10 to 13	14 and 15	16 and 17	18 and 19	20 and 21	22 to 24	25 to 29	30 to 34	35 and over
WHITE ALONE OR IN COMBINATION														
Both Sexes														
2011	56.5	25.9	51.6	95.6	98.2	98.6	98.7	95.7	70.2	53.7	30.8	14.1	7.0	1.7
2010	56.1	25.8	52.3	94.3	97.8	98.1	98.1	96.2	70.0	51.4	28.0	14.0	7.7	1.9
2009	56.0	25.7	51.3	94.2	98.0	98.7	98.1	94.6	68.4	52.5	28.8	13.0	7.4	1.9
2008	55.9	25.7	52.4	94.0	98.2	98.9	98.7	95.5	67.0	51.0	28.1	12.4	6.3	1.8
2007	55.7	25.7	54.0	94.8	98.0	98.7	98.7	94.6	67.1	49.7	26.2	16.2	9.4	1.8
2006	55.8	25.7	55.5	94.8	98.4	98.5	98.4	94.9	65.0	47.9	25.6	11.4	6.8	1.7
2005	56.2	26.1	53.9	95.3	98.6	98.7	98.3	95.3	67.7	49.3	26.2	11.3	6.2	1.8
2004	55.7	26.1	52.7	95.5	98.2	98.4	98.5	94.0	64.8	49.4	25.2	12.2	6.4	1.8
2003	55.6	26.1	55.2	94.8	98.0	98.4	97.4	95.0	64.2	48.3	26.8	11.0	6.3	1.7
Male														
2011	55.9	26.3	52.5	95.6	98.4	98.7	98.5	95.6	67.4	50.3	30.1	12.5	6.2	1.4
2010	55.2	26.0	52.2	93.4	97.4	97.7	98.1	95.0	67.5	48.2	25.9	13.1	6.4	1.5
2009	55.1	25.8	50.5	93.8	97.8	98.9	97.8	94.3	64.3	49.2	27.9	11.3	6.5	1.4
2008	55.2	25.9	52.1	93.6	97.9	98.7	99.0	95.0	64.4	48.1	26.4	11.6	5.7	1.3
2007	54.6	25.8	53.2	94.0	97.9	98.6	98.3	94.4	66.4	44.1	24.0	12.9	9.4	1.4
2006	54.9	25.9	56.0	94.5	98.3	98.4	98.2	94.7	62.7	43.5	24.1	10.3	5.6	1.3
2005	55.2	26.2	52.6	94.7	98.2	98.6	98.3	95.2	65.7	45.1	24.6	8.9	5.4	1.4
2004	55.0	26.3	53.4	95.8	98.0	98.2	98.8	94.3	59.9	46.5	23.2	11.1	5.5	1.4
2003	55.0	26.5	55.9	95.2	97.7	98.2	97.3	95.1	61.6	43.4	25.5	9.8	5.7	1.4
Female														
2011	57.2	25.6	50.7	95.7	98.0	98.5	98.8	95.7	73.1	57.4	31.6	15.9	7.9	2.0
2010	57.1	25.7	52.5	95.2	98.1	98.5	98.1	97.4	72.5	55.0	30.1	15.0	9.1	2.3
2009	57.0	25.7	52.1	94.5	98.1	98.4	98.4	94.8	72.7	56.0	29.7	14.8	8.3	2.4
2008	56.6	25.5	52.7	94.4	98.6	99.1	98.5	96.0	69.7	54.0	29.8	13.2	7.0	2.3
2007	56.9	25.6	54.9	95.6	98.1	98.7	99.2	94.9	67.9	55.5	28.4	19.2	9.4	2.2
2006	56.6	25.5	55.0	95.2	98.5	98.5	98.6	95.2	67.3	52.4	27.1	12.4	8.1	2.1
2005	57.4	26.0	55.3	96.0	98.9	98.8	98.4	95.5	70.0	53.8	27.9	13.8	7.1	2.3
2004	56.5	25.8	51.9	95.3	98.4	98.5	98.2	93.8	69.7	52.4	27.1	13.4	7.3	2.2
2003	56.3	25.7	54.4	94.5	98.3	98.7	97.5	94.9	66.8	53.1	28.1	12.2	7.0	2.1
BLACK ALONE OR IN COMBINATION														
Both Sexes														
2011	59.3	33.6	53.9	92.1	97.3	98.5	98.7	96.0	74.1	41.8	31.0	18.1	11.3	3.8
2010	59.2	33.6	55.8	94.8	97.5	98.7	98.6	95.7	63.2	49.9	28.9	16.0	10.8	3.9
2009	59.4	33.5	57.1	93.8	97.4	98.6	97.7	94.4	64.7	44.2	31.6	14.7	11.1	3.7
2008	58.8	33.0	54.5	92.9	98.8	99.1	98.1	94.5	59.7	40.4	24.8	15.1	11.4	2.8
2007	59.0	33.2	58.2	94.2	98.2	98.0	99.1	93.7	62.0	38.1	27.3	15.3	9.6	3.0
2006	58.8	33.3	59.0	92.4	96.9	97.2	97.4	93.2	64.9	38.9	27.8	11.9	8.9	3.2
2005	59.0	33.5	51.3	96.1	98.5	98.6	95.9	92.9	62.5	38.1	27.8	11.7	9.9	3.1
2004	59.6	34.3	58.6	94.5	97.4	99.4	98.6	95.3	59.7	40.8	25.3	14.8	7.0	3.3
2003	59.8	34.2	56.5	94.6	98.1	98.3	98.0	94.2	60.9	42.1	27.2	12.4	8.4	2.8
Male														
2011	59.0	34.5	52.8	92.8	97.5	98.6	97.9	94.5	71.6	38.9	30.0	14.1	7.7	2.7
2010	58.8	34.4	55.0	94.2	97.7	98.6	97.8	93.8	62.0	44.9	28.0	12.9	6.3	2.7
2009	58.9	34.0	57.4	93.8	97.2	98.3	95.9	95.6	60.4	42.3	25.7	11.5	8.1	2.2
2008	58.8	34.0	53.1	94.0	98.3	98.7	99.0	94.3	58.0	38.1	22.7	11.0	8.6	1.6
2007	60.1	35.0	60.5	93.9	98.1	97.5	99.2	95.2	61.5	37.8	27.8	10.7	9.7	2.0
2006	59.5	34.8	57.0	92.5	97.0	97.1	97.8	91.9	64.1	38.8	25.6	9.5	7.0	2.5
2005	59.2	34.6	52.5	95.1	97.5	97.9	93.8	93.8	66.2	34.9	23.9	9.3	6.1	2.3
2004	59.7	35.3	59.9	93.9	96.8	99.2	98.8	96.3	57.9	38.2	21.0	9.3	3.9	2.2
2003	60.6	35.7	57.6	93.2	98.8	98.2	98.3	93.8	61.1	35.6	23.4	9.4	7.2	1.9

Note: Data for 1947 to 1953 exclude kindergarten. Nursery school was first collected in 1964. Data shown for 1947 to 1966 for the Black population are for Black and other races.

[1]Civilian noninstitutionalized population.

Table A-10. Percentage of the Population 3 Years Old and Over Enrolled in School, by Age, Sex, Race, and Hispanic Origin, October 1947–2011—*Continued*

(Percent)

Year, sex, race, and Hispanic origin	Total enrolled 3 to 34 years old	Total enrolled 3 years old and over	Years of age[1]											
			3 and 4	5 and 6	7 to 9	10 to 13	14 and 15	16 and 17	18 and 19	20 and 21	22 to 24	25 to 29	30 to 34	35 and over
Female														
2011	59.5	32.8	55.0	91.3	97.2	98.4	99.4	97.5	76.5	45.0	31.7	21.7	14.4	4.7
2010	59.6	33.0	56.7	95.4	97.2	98.8	99.4	97.6	64.3	54.2	29.7	18.7	14.5	4.9
2009	59.8	33.0	56.9	93.9	97.6	98.9	99.4	93.1	68.9	46.1	36.5	17.5	13.5	4.8
2008	58.8	32.1	55.7	91.7	99.4	99.5	97.2	94.7	61.3	42.5	26.6	18.6	13.8	3.8
2007	57.9	31.7	55.7	94.5	98.2	98.4	98.9	92.2	62.6	38.5	26.8	19.4	9.5	3.8
2006	58.2	32.0	60.9	92.3	96.9	97.4	97.0	94.6	65.6	39.0	29.8	14.0	10.5	3.6
2005	58.8	32.4	50.0	97.1	99.4	99.3	97.8	92.0	59.1	41.3	31.1	13.8	12.8	3.7
2004	59.6	33.4	57.0	95.0	98.1	99.6	98.4	94.2	61.3	43.1	29.3	19.3	9.5	4.2
2003	59.1	32.9	55.3	95.9	97.3	98.4	97.6	94.5	60.7	47.5	30.7	14.7	9.4	3.5
ASIAN ALONE OR IN COMBINATION														
Both Sexes														
2011	58.8	29.7	55.4	96.6	97.9	97.4	98.2	97.6	80.4	77.1	41.4	17.2	9.1	2.1
2010	60.5	30.6	62.4	96.7	98.9	98.4	98.0	96.1	81.9	76.9	46.5	21.3	10.1	1.8
2009	59.3	29.0	55.3	95.6	97.2	95.8	96.8	97.0	90.1	73.6	53.5	18.7	10.8	2.1
2008	59.2	29.5	57.4	92.6	98.3	99.6	98.8	93.5	85.9	79.4	43.0	23.0	11.9	2.5
2007	57.0	28.8	54.1	93.9	98.4	99.3	99.7	93.4	86.3	64.3	45.9	19.6	9.5	1.8
2006	56.3	29.0	51.5	94.6	99.0	99.3	99.6	92.0	82.3	72.2	43.1	17.3	8.8	2.2
2005	57.6	30.5	54.4	95.5	99.6	97.5	98.7	98.2	86.2	77.1	44.4	20.9	9.4	2.3
2004	58.5	31.4	57.7	97.6	99.9	99.2	98.0	97.1	79.9	77.7	46.2	20.8	9.3	2.7
2003	58.2	31.3	51.4	89.3	99.2	99.4	99.1	95.7	87.1	77.0	48.1	21.6	9.4	2.2
Male														
2011	59.4	30.7	55.9	97.4	97.3	98.6	98.6	96.9	83.3	79.5	39.1	17.0	9.5	1.4
2010	61.5	32.2	63.1	97.9	99.0	98.0	97.6	96.5	78.1	80.7	43.1	23.5	10.3	1.7
2009	59.5	30.5	54.9	95.3	96.6	95.3	97.8	96.1	91.4	74.3	51.5	17.9	9.7	2.3
2008	59.4	30.2	56.1	92.8	97.3	99.2	100.0	96.4	89.7	74.2	39.0	24.5	11.3	2.0
2007	58.6	30.4	58.9	95.4	99.1	99.1	99.7	93.5	90.6	62.7	47.0	19.5	9.8	2.1
2006	57.0	30.2	60.4	94.7	98.2	99.0	0.0	90.1	78.1	74.6	43.0	14.9	8.5	2.4
2005	58.3	31.7	51.1	97.4	99.7	96.5	98.0	97.3	83.6	82.1	42.2	20.2	9.9	2.0
2004	60.8	33.9	57.2	96.5	99.8	99.9	97.1	96.9	83.5	83.6	49.6	23.0	10.9	2.9
2003	60.2	33.4	49.3	91.9	98.2	99.9	98.2	95.9	89.6	74.0	47.3	27.9	12.1	2.4
Female														
2011	58.3	28.7	54.9	95.7	98.5	96.2	97.9	98.3	77.1	74.8	44.0	17.4	8.7	2.6
2010	59.4	29.1	61.7	95.5	98.7	98.9	98.4	95.7	86.2	73.1	50.0	19.1	9.9	2.0
2009	59.2	27.7	55.8	95.9	97.8	96.3	95.2	98.1	88.8	73.0	55.6	19.5	11.9	1.9
2008	58.9	28.8	59.1	92.3	99.2	100.0	97.5	90.8	82.4	85.7	46.8	21.7	12.5	2.9
2007	55.5	27.4	48.3	92.5	97.6	99.5	99.7	93.2	82.2	66.1	45.0	19.7	9.2	1.5
2006	55.7	27.9	41.4	94.5	100.0	99.6	99.1	93.6	87.8	69.4	43.2	19.4	9.0	2.1
2005	57.0	29.3	57.5	93.2	99.5	98.5	99.7	99.1	89.2	71.2	46.2	21.6	8.9	2.5
2004	56.1	29.0	58.4	99.2	99.9	98.5	98.9	97.2	76.3	71.5	42.9	18.8	7.8	2.5
2003	56.2	29.3	54.2	86.0	100.0	98.7	100.0	95.4	85.1	79.7	48.8	15.8	6.9	2.1

Note: Data for 1947 to 1953 exclude kindergarten. Nursery school was first collected in 1964. Data shown for 1947 to 1966 for the Black population are for Black and other races.

[1]Civilian noninstitutionalized population.

Table A-11. Population 6 to 17 Years Old Enrolled Below Modal Grade, 1971–2011

(Numbers in thousands; percent)

Year, sex, race, and Hispanic origin	Percent below modal grade, by years of age				Dropout rate, 15 to 17	Population in age group[1]			
	6 to 8	9 to 11	12 to 14	15 to 17		6 to 8	9 to 11	12 to 14	15 to 17
ALL RACES									
Both Sexes									
2011	22.4	28.3	29.4	31.4	2.3	12,643	12,408	11,834	12,282
2010	18.2	24.6	28.6	28.9	2.2	12,618	12,190	11,963	12,273
2009	18.9	26.3	29.7	29.5	3.0	12,305	11,819	12,030	12,391
2008	19.8	27.0	31.0	30.5	2.7	12,104	11,793	12,128	12,746
2007	20.1	26.2	27.9	30.0	2.9	12,011	11,805	12,398	12,857
2006	20.1	26.1	27.9	30.5	3.0	11,776	11,902	12,473	12,926
2005	20.7	25.4	28.3	30.6	2.8	11,784	11,998	12,689	13,204
2004	21.7	25.4	28.2	32.0	3.5	11,799	12,034	12,870	12,766
2003	21.3	28.1	28.8	30.6	3.2	11,866	12,124	12,951	12,753
2002	18.0	25.5	27.1	30.1	3.3	12,029	12,421	12,592	12,187
2001	18.6	23.7	25.9	29.7	3.8	11,972	12,738	12,357	12,031
2000	19.2	24.0	27.8	30.2	4.3	12,079	12,713	12,003	11,933
1999	17.4	25.3	26.5	30.8	4.0	12,159	12,537	11,921	12,048
1998	19.0	23.8	26.7	31.9	3.8	12,165	11,960	11,600	11,314
1997	18.6	24.2	28.5	32.1	3.6	12,325	11,866	11,650	11,953
1996	17.9	23.3	28.8	31.0	4.8	12,191	11,845	11,653	11,617
1995	17.5	25.6	30.8	32.8	4.1	11,728	11,812	11,582	11,401
1994	18.9	26.2	31.3	30.9	3.8	11,601	11,528	11,462	10,560
1993[r]	18.7	28.1	31.0	32.3	3.8	11,363	11,283	10,981	10,247
1993	18.7	28.0	30.8	32.0	3.7	11,363	11,283	10,981	10,247
1992	19.4	28.4	30.9	30.5	3.6	11,260	11,183	10,723	10,114
1991	21.2	26.9	29.6	30.0	4.6	11,120	11,099	10,440	9,923
1990	21.5	27.6	31.0	30.1	4.7	11,015	10,914	10,152	9,912
1989	21.4	29.0	31.8	28.0	4.5	11,007	10,673	9,928	10,020
1988	20.4	28.4	28.7	26.2	5.1	10,906	10,350	9,869	10,379
1987	20.9	26.7	27.6	24.8	5.1	10,702	10,053	9,795	10,944
1986	19.2	26.5	27.3	25.8	4.9	10,389	9,959	9,908	11,149
1985	17.9	24.9	25.7	25.5	5.1	10,076	9,673	10,442	11,024
1984	16.6	23.9	27.0	24.6	5.3	9,707	9,594	10,858	10,711
1983	15.4	24.4	24.8	23.7	5.2	9,605	9,730	11,123	10,768
1982	16.6	22.8	23.9	23.0	5.4	9,492	10,169	10,989	11,131
1981	14.4	23.3	23.0	23.8	6.1	9,519	10,657	10,712	11,757
1980	14.3	20.3	22.6	22.5	6.6	9,350	10,681	10,537	11,835
1979	13.0	20.2	20.3	21.6	6.5	9,804	10,545	10,886	12,190
1978	12.4	19.5	19.2	21.8	6.5	10,246	10,448	11,391	12,346
1977	10.7	18.9	18.9	21.2	6.4	10,449	10,537	11,826	12,472
1976	10.6	18.1	19.8	22.2	6.3	10,334	10,872	12,137	12,550
1975	11.1	17.4	21.3	22.5	6.4	10,256	11,343	12,372	12,531
1974	10.3	17.8	21.7	21.6	7.1	10,343	11,789	12,415	12,566
1973	10.7	18.4	21.5	21.3	7.1	10,614	11,946	12,542	12,309
1972	10.7	19.6	21.9	22.3	6.6	11,119	12,152	12,451	12,283
1971	11.1	19.7	22.0	22.5	5.7	11,938	12,648	12,429	11,906
Male									
2011	24.6	31.9	32.1	35.8	2.4	6,478	6,326	6,067	6,256
2010	20.0	27.4	30.7	31.5	2.9	6,451	6,213	6,104	6,300
2009	20.0	29.7	32.4	33.2	3.2	6,260	6,058	6,144	6,334
2008	22.0	28.3	34.0	33.3	2.8	6,174	6,005	6,220	6,502
2007	23.0	28.1	29.8	33.7	2.9	6,159	6,031	6,310	6,572
2006	21.7	28.2	31.1	35.0	3.3	5,991	6,115	6,374	6,574
2005	23.2	28.6	30.7	34.3	3.0	6,014	6,126	6,523	6,645
2004	23.9	28.2	31.7	36.8	3.5	6,075	6,120	6,685	6,395
2003	23.9	32.0	31.8	35.1	3.4	6,198	6,331	6,426	6,569
2002	20.3	29.2	31.0	35.6	3.5	6,156	6,349	6,436	6,210
2001	22.1	26.1	28.7	34.0	4.3	6,147	6,540	6,311	6,182
2000	22.1	27.2	31.3	34.3	4.5	6,181	6,504	6,148	6,136
1999	18.8	28.9	30.2	36.2	3.9	6,211	6,471	6,048	6,195
1998	21.4	26.6	30.4	37.4	4.1	6,234	6,125	5,897	5,791
1997	21.9	27.7	33.4	37.8	3.7	6,295	6,112	5,932	6,126
1996	20.7	26.0	33.9	36.9	4.5	6,268	6,043	5,934	5,985
1995	20.2	28.0	35.2	38.5	3.5	5,999	6,027	5,930	5,840
1994	21.1	28.0	35.6	35.7	3.9	5,894	6,026	5,874	5,640
1993[r]	21.2	32.1	35.4	40.3	3.3	5,837	5,736	5,629	5,262
1993	21.1	32.0	35.0	38.7	3.1	5,837	5,736	5,629	5,262
1992	21.6	32.6	37.0	35.2	2.7	5,738	5,742	5,502	5,166
1991	24.0	30.7	34.7	35.5	4.3	5,674	5,704	5,343	5,085

[1]Civilian noninstitutionalized population.
r = Revised, controlled to 1990 census based population estimates; previous 1993 data controlled to 1980 census based population estimates.

Table A-11. Population 6 to 17 Years Old Enrolled Below Modal Grade, 1971–2011—*Continued*

(Numbers in thousands; percent)

Year, sex, race, and Hispanic origin	Percent below modal grade, by years of age				Dropout rate, 15 to 17	Population in age group[1]			
	6 to 8	9 to 11	12 to 14	15 to 17		6 to 8	9 to 11	12 to 14	15 to 17
Male— *(Continued)*									
1990	23.9	32.0	36.2	35.3	4.6	5,629	5,603	5,200	5,078
1989	25.1	32.9	36.7	33.4	4.3	5,632	5,472	5,088	5,151
1988	23.5	33.2	33.7	30.6	4.8	5,580	5,298	5,065	5,286
1987	23.7	31.8	31.8	29.2	4.6	5,496	5,147	5,036	5,535
1986	22.9	30.4	32.2	30.2	4.9	5,311	5,113	5,066	5,697
1985	20.6	28.3	29.0	30.2	4.9	5,159	4,946	5,340	5,623
1984	18.8	27.7	31.1	30.2	5.5	4,963	4,905	5,521	5,469
1983	17.8	28.7	30.3	28.5	5.3	4,913	4,974	5,690	5,463
1982	19.2	26.4	28.0	27.9	5.2	4,852	5,198	5,566	5,688
1981	17.2	27.9	25.6	28.1	6.2	4,866	5,447	5,510	5,914
1980	16.4	23.4	27.3	26.8	6.4	4,774	5,453	5,282	6,067
1979	15.5	23.4	24.1	27.4	5.9	5,004	5,379	5,555	6,174
1978	14.7	22.9	22.9	26.2	6.7	5,227	5,326	5,797	6,265
1977	12.5	22.4	22.6	25.3	6.1	5,327	5,371	6,044	6,297
1976	12.5	20.9	23.4	27.5	5.7	5,265	5,540	6,185	6,356
1975	12.6	21.2	25.8	26.8	5.7	5,223	5,782	6,336	6,309
1974	12.2	21.2	25.9	26.3	7.0	5,267	6,011	6,329	6,352
1973	12.8	20.8	25.2	26.4	6.8	5,403	6,082	6,397	6,215
1972	12.5	23.3	26.8	26.8	6.2	5,662	6,188	6,322	6,232
1971	13.5	22.8	26.1	27.2	5.0	6,088	6,440	6,293	6,019
Female									
2011	20.0	24.7	26.6	26.9	2.1	6,165	6,082	5,767	6,026
2010	16.4	21.7	26.4	26.1	1.5	6,166	5,977	5,860	5,973
2009	17.8	22.8	26.9	25.6	2.8	6,046	5,761	5,886	6,057
2008	17.5	25.6	27.7	27.7	2.4	5,930	5,787	5,908	6,244
2007	17.2	24.1	25.9	26.2	2.9	5,852	5,773	6,088	6,285
2006	18.4	23.9	24.6	25.9	2.6	5,785	5,787	6,099	6,352
2005	18.2	22.0	25.8	26.8	2.6	5,769	5,872	6,167	6,559
2004	19.4	22.5	24.4	27.1	3.5	5,724	5,914	6,185	6,371
2003	18.5	23.8	25.8	25.8	3.0	5,668	5,793	6,524	6,184
2002	15.6	21.7	23.0	24.4	3.1	5,872	6,072	6,156	5,977
2001	14.9	21.3	23.0	25.2	3.3	5,825	6,197	6,046	5,849
2000	16.1	20.6	24.2	25.8	4.2	5,897	6,209	5,855	5,797
1999	16.1	21.6	22.7	25.1	4.2	5,948	6,066	5,872	5,852
1998	16.5	20.9	22.8	26.2	3.5	5,931	5,835	5,703	5,523
1997	15.1	20.4	23.3	26.1	3.5	6,030	5,754	5,718	5,827
1996	14.9	20.4	23.4	24.7	5.3	5,923	5,802	5,719	5,632
1995	14.6	23.1	26.0	26.7	4.4	5,728	5,786	5,653	5,552
1994	16.5	24.2	26.7	24.8	3.6	5,705	5,644	5,666	5,384
1993[r]	16.3	24.0	26.4	26.4	4.4	5,526	5,545	5,353	4,984
1993	16.1	23.9	26.2	24.9	4.3	5,526	5,545	5,353	4,984
1992	17.1	23.5	24.6	25.6	4.5	5,523	5,441	5,220	4,947
1991	18.2	22.8	24.6	24.2	5.1	5,445	5,395	5,098	4,838
1990	19.1	23.2	25.7	24.7	4.7	5,387	5,312	4,951	4,834
1989	18.1	22.6	26.6	22.3	4.6	5,375	5,201	4,840	4,869
1988	17.3	23.6	23.4	21.7	5.4	5,327	5,052	4,803	5,093
1987	17.8	21.5	23.2	20.2	5.6	5,206	4,906	4,759	5,408
1986	15.2	22.4	22.1	21.1	4.9	5,078	4,846	4,842	5,452
1985	15.1	21.4	22.1	20.6	5.5	4,917	4,727	5,102	5,401
1984	14.2	19.8	22.9	18.7	5.1	4,744	4,689	5,337	5,242
1983	12.9	19.9	19.1	18.6	5.2	4,692	4,756	5,433	5,305
1982	13.8	19.0	19.7	17.9	5.7	4,640	4,971	5,423	5,443
1981	11.6	18.4	20.1	19.6	6.1	4,653	5,210	5,202	5,843
1980	12.1	17.0	17.8	18.0	6.7	4,576	5,228	5,255	5,768
1979	10.4	16.9	16.4	15.6	7.1	4,800	5,166	5,331	6,016
1978	10.1	16.0	15.3	17.2	6.4	5,019	5,122	5,594	6,081
1977	8.9	15.2	15.0	17.1	6.6	5,122	5,166	5,782	6,175
1976	8.6	15.1	16.0	16.8	7.0	5,069	5,332	5,952	6,194
1975	9.4	13.5	16.7	18.2	7.2	5,033	5,561	6,036	6,222
1974	8.3	14.4	17.4	16.8	7.1	5,076	5,778	6,086	6,214
1973	8.7	15.8	16.5	16.1	7.4	5,211	5,864	6,145	6,094
1972	8.9	15.7	17.0	17.7	7.1	5,457	5,964	6,129	6,051
1971	8.7	12.3	17.8	17.6	6.5	5,850	6,208	6,136	5,887

[1]Civilian noninstitutionalized population.

r = Revised, controlled to 1990 census based population estimates; previous 1993 data controlled to 1980 census based population estimates.

Table A-11. Population 6 to 17 Years Old Enrolled Below Modal Grade, 1971–2011—*Continued*

(Numbers in thousands; percent)

Year, sex, race, and Hispanic origin	Percent below modal grade, by years of age				Dropout rate, 15 to 17	Population in age group[1]			
	6 to 8	9 to 11	12 to 14	15 to 17		6 to 8	9 to 11	12 to 14	15 to 17
WHITE ALONE									
Both Sexes									
2011	23.1	28.3	30.2	31.4	2.2	9,488	9,401	9,020	9,337
2010	19.1	24.7	28.3	28.5	2.3	9,455	9,276	9,110	9,344
2009	19.1	26.2	29.0	28.6	3.3	9,377	9,006	9,167	9,495
2008	20.3	27.1	29.4	29.7	2.6	9,288	8,967	9,250	9,658
2007	21.3	26.2	27.6	28.3	2.8	9,118	9,021	9,432	9,834
2006	20.6	25.5	26.8	29.9	3.0	8,981	9,074	9,542	9,813
2005	21.4	23.8	28.0	29.5	2.6	8,929	9,194	9,680	10,131
2004	22.4	25.6	27.6	30.7	3.8	9,051	9,173	9,853	9,784
2003[2]	21.5	27.6	28.3	29.4	3.2	9,102	9,112	9,875	9,889
2002	18.1	25.7	26.2	29.6	3.1	9,230	9,682	9,832	9,520
2001	19.2	22.7	25.2	28.9	3.8	9,330	9,826	9,651	9,480
2000	19.4	23.7	26.3	29.7	4.5	9,404	9,937	9,368	9,449
1999	18.3	24.6	25.8	30.0	4.2	9,539	9,768	9,323	9,428
1998	19.5	23.5	25.8	30.5	3.8	9,481	9,413	9,130	8,926
1997	18.8	24.0	27.9	30.3	3.5	9,555	9,390	9,167	9,352
1996	18.1	22.6	27.6	30.1	4.9	9,458	9,420	9,184	9,135
1995	17.7	24.9	29.2	31.0	3.9	9,221	9,340	9,130	8,933
1994	19.4	25.8	30.1	29.6	3.7	9,087	9,261	9,121	8,668
1993[r]	18.8	27.3	29.4	31.2	3.9	9,018	8,967	8,728	8,160
1993	18.7	27.2	29.2	29.7	3.6	9,074	9,017	8,783	8,159
1992	19.5	27.5	29.6	28.1	3.5	8,956	8,996	8,520	8,031
1991	21.3	25.7	27.7	27.2	4.7	8,874	8,840	8,328	7,903
1990	21.9	26.8	28.4	27.3	4.6	8,860	8,752	8,140	7,909
1989	22.4	26.8	29.9	25.7	4.6	8,858	8,527	7,994	8,026
1988	21.0	27.6	27.2	23.9	5.4	8,758	8,323	7,929	8,353
1987	21.1	25.9	26.0	22.7	5.1	8,606	8,117	7,846	8,887
1986	19.1	25.1	25.3	23.7	5.0	8,395	8,000	8,054	9,037
1985	18.0	23.3	23.3	23.0	5.3	8,136	7,840	8,429	9,045
1984	16.3	22.1	24.7	22.7	5.6	7,915	7,781	8,827	8,853
1983	15.5	22.4	23.1	21.1	5.4	7,821	7,906	9,152	8,831
1982	16.4	21.8	22.1	21.1	5.6	7,729	8,294	9,035	9,184
1981	14.7	22.2	21.0	21.6	6.1	7,782	8,741	8,813	9,762
1980	14.1	19.0	21.1	19.3	6.7	7,635	8,823	8,739	10,132
1979	12.9	18.4	18.5	19.4	6.5	8,041	8,747	9,026	10,239
1978	12.4	18.0	17.9	19.3	6.8	8,460	8,686	9,522	10,358
1977	10.6	17.7	17.5	19.3	6.6	8,675	8,771	9,918	10,510
1976	10.5	17.2	18.7	19.7	6.3	8,612	9,066	10,187	10,622
1975	11.0	16.0	20.0	20.4	6.3	8,566	9,486	10,466	10,583
1974	10.2	16.5	19.7	19.4	6.9	8,656	9,912	10,508	10,678
1973	10.6	17.3	19.9	19.1	7.0	8,929	10,117	10,704	10,481
1972	10.3	18.2	20.1	20.0	6.6	9,359	10,313	10,606	10,506
1971	10.5	18.3	20.4	19.9	5.5	9,988	10,692	10,682	10,231
Male									
2011	25.7	31.6	32.9	36.5	2.2	4,861	4,816	4,626	4,809
2010	21.3	27.2	30.3	31.2	3.0	4,825	4,746	4,666	4,805
2009	20.4	29.5	31.7	31.9	3.5	4,816	4,611	4,697	4,866
2008	22.5	29.3	32.6	32.9	2.7	4,764	4,568	4,748	4,966
2007	24.3	28.4	29.5	31.8	2.9	4,671	4,620	4,851	5,022
2006	22.5	27.0	29.8	34.2	3.3	4,596	4,652	4,900	5,011
2005	24.3	27.4	31.0	33.2	2.7	4,576	4,715	4,995	5,116
2004	24.9	28.0	31.4	35.2	3.8	4,706	4,647	5,168	4,905
2003[2]	24.4	31.6	31.2	34.0	3.4	4,785	4,795	4,961	5,026
2002	21.7	29.5	30.4	34.7	3.2	4,737	4,965	5,044	4,875
2001	22.7	25.3	28.3	32.8	4.4	4,789	5,040	4,949	4,862
2000	22.5	27.6	29.6	34.0	4.4	4,815	5,094	4,798	4,861
1999	19.9	28.2	29.7	35.8	4.2	4,883	5,009	4,777	4,851
1998	21.9	26.4	30.2	36.2	4.4	4,851	4,823	4,686	4,571
1997	22.3	27.8	32.7	37.0	3.8	4,897	4,819	4,702	4,821
1996	20.8	25.9	32.3	36.5	4.5	4,849	4,836	4,706	4,694
1995	20.5	28.0	33.4	36.5	3.8	4,727	4,797	4,680	4,592
1994	22.0	27.9	34.4	35.2	4.0	4,659	4,758	4,679	4,457
1993[r]	21.4	31.8	33.8	37.6	3.2	4,625	4,601	4,476	4,178
1993	21.4	31.6	33.6	36.1	3.1	4,662	4,614	4,485	4,178
1992	21.5	31.8	35.8	32.4	2.8	4,602	4,607	4,359	4,115
1991	24.4	29.1	32.5	32.5	4.2	4,556	4,568	4,270	4,047

[1]Civilian noninstitutionalized population.
[2]Starting in 2003 respondents could identify more than one race. Except as noted, the race data in this table from 2003 onward represent those respondents who indicated only one race category.
r = Revised, controlled to 1990 census based population estimates; previous 1993 data controlled to 1980 census based population estimates.

Table A-11. Population 6 to 17 Years Old Enrolled Below Modal Grade, 1971–2011—*Continued*

(Numbers in thousands; percent)

Year, sex, race, and Hispanic origin	Percent below modal grade, by years of age				Dropout rate, 15 to 17	Population in age group[1]			
	6 to 8	9 to 11	12 to 14	15 to 17		6 to 8	9 to 11	12 to 14	15 to 17
Male— *(Continued)*									
1990	24.6	31.3	33.3	32.6	4.8	4,555	4,482	4,186	4,054
1989	26.0	32.1	35.0	30.8	4.6	4,544	4,378	4,112	4,107
1988	24.7	32.8	32.2	28.8	5.1	4,493	4,272	4,062	4,281
1987	24.6	30.5	30.4	26.6	4.5	4,415	4,167	4,069	4,504
1986	22.9	28.9	30.1	27.9	5.2	4,307	4,108	4,125	4,624
1985	21.1	26.5	26.7	28.0	4.9	4,175	4,024	4,307	4,634
1984	18.1	25.8	28.7	28.1	5.8	4,061	3,994	4,501	4,542
1983	18.1	26.3	28.0	26.3	5.6	4,002	4,054	4,697	4,481
1982	19.3	26.2	26.2	26.1	5.3	3,956	4,260	4,591	4,711
1981	17.3	26.9	24.2	25.4	6.3	3,990	4,480	4,556	4,937
1980	16.3	21.9	25.7	23.9	6.7	3,907	4,517	4,399	5,066
1979	15.4	20.8	22.3	24.8	6.2	4,114	4,475	4,616	5,201
1978	14.7	21.2	22.0	23.1	7.2	4,328	4,441	4,843	5,287
1977	12.5	21.1	21.2	23.5	6.3	4,436	4,484	5,079	5,325
1976	12.6	20.2	22.1	24.8	5.6	4,402	4,632	5,200	5,398
1975	12.9	19.7	24.7	24.7	5.4	4,376	4,848	5,385	5,332
1974	12.1	19.5	23.7	23.8	7.0	4,422	5,066	5,383	5,402
1973	12.5	19.6	23.1	24.0	6.6	4,559	5,165	5,469	5,319
1972	12.2	21.9	24.6	24.3	6.1	4,778	5,266	5,410	5,340
1971	12.6	21.6	23.9	24.4	4.6	5,106	5,461	5,455	5,185
Female									
2011	20.4	24.8	27.4	26.1	2.2	4,627	4,585	4,394	4,528
2010	16.9	22.1	26.1	25.7	1.4	4,630	4,530	4,444	4,539
2009	17.8	22.8	26.2	25.1	3.0	4,561	4,394	4,470	4,629
2008	18.0	24.8	26.0	26.3	2.4	4,524	4,398	4,502	4,692
2007	18.2	23.9	25.7	24.6	2.7	4,447	4,401	4,582	4,812
2006	18.6	24.0	23.8	25.5	2.6	4,385	4,422	4,643	4,801
2005	18.3	20.1	24.8	25.8	2.5	4,353	4,479	4,685	5,015
2004	19.7	23.3	23.4	26.1	3.8	4,345	4,527	4,686	4,878
2003[2]	18.3	23.1	25.3	24.7	3.0	4,317	4,317	4,914	4,863
2002	14.4	21.7	21.9	24.3	3.0	4,493	4,717	4,788	4,645
2001	15.5	20.0	21.8	24.9	3.1	4,541	4,786	4,701	4,618
2000	16.1	19.7	22.9	25.2	4.5	4,587	4,843	4,570	4,588
1999	16.7	20.7	21.8	23.9	4.1	4,655	4,579	4,546	4,578
1998	16.9	20.5	21.2	24.4	3.2	4,629	4,589	4,444	4,355
1997	15.1	20.0	22.7	23.2	3.3	4,658	4,571	4,464	4,530
1996	15.3	19.2	22.7	23.2	5.3	4,609	4,583	4,477	4,441
1995	14.7	21.6	24.8	25.0	4.1	4,494	4,543	4,449	4,342
1994	16.7	23.5	25.7	23.6	3.4	4,427	4,504	4,443	4,212
1993r	15.9	22.6	24.8	24.4	4.3	4,393	4,366	4,252	3,982
1993	15.8	22.5	24.6	23.1	4.2	4,412	4,404	4,298	3,982
1992	17.3	22.9	23.2	23.6	4.3	4,354	4,389	4,161	3,916
1991	18.1	22.1	22.6	21.5	5.2	4,318	4,272	4,058	3,856
1990	19.0	22.2	23.2	21.8	4.5	4,305	4,270	3,954	3,855
1989	18.6	21.3	24.5	20.3	4.7	4,314	4,149	3,882	3,919
1988	17.1	22.2	21.9	18.8	5.6	4,265	4,051	3,867	4,072
1987	17.3	21.0	21.3	18.7	5.8	4,191	3,950	3,777	4,383
1986	15.0	21.1	20.2	19.3	4.8	4,088	3,892	3,929	4,413
1985	14.8	19.9	19.7	17.6	5.7	3,961	3,816	4,122	4,411
1984	14.3	18.3	20.5	17.0	5.4	3,854	3,787	4,326	4,311
1983	12.7	18.3	17.9	15.8	5.2	3,819	3,852	4,455	4,350
1982	13.4	17.2	17.8	15.8	6.0	3,773	4,034	4,444	4,473
1981	11.9	17.3	17.6	17.6	5.9	3,792	4,261	4,257	4,825
1980	11.7	16.0	16.5	14.7	6.6	3,728	4,306	4,340	5,066
1979	10.3	15.8	14.5	13.8	6.9	3,927	4,272	4,410	5,038
1978	10.0	14.7	13.7	15.2	6.4	4,132	4,245	4,679	5,071
1977	8.5	14.1	13.7	14.9	6.8	4,239	4,287	4,839	5,185
1976	8.4	14.1	15.1	14.5	6.9	4,210	4,434	4,987	5,224
1975	9.1	12.2	15.1	16.0	7.1	4,190	4,638	5,081	5,251
1974	8.2	13.4	15.5	15.0	6.7	4,234	4,846	5,125	5,276
1973	8.5	14.8	16.5	14.0	7.4	4,370	4,952	5,235	5,162
1972	8.3	14.2	15.4	15.5	7.2	4,581	5,047	5,196	5,166
1971	8.4	14.9	16.6	15.2	6.3	4,882	5,231	5,227	5,046

[1]Civilian noninstitutionalized population.

[2]Starting in 2003 respondents could identify more than one race. Except as noted, the race data in this table from 2003 onward represent those respondents who indicated only one race category.

r = Revised, controlled to 1990 census based population estimates; previous 1993 data controlled to 1980 census based population estimates.

Table A-11. Population 6 to 17 Years Old Enrolled Below Modal Grade, 1971–2011—*Continued*

(Numbers in thousands; percent)

Year, sex, race, and Hispanic origin	Percent below modal grade, by years of age				Dropout rate, 15 to 17	Population in age group[1]			
	6 to 8	9 to 11	12 to 14	15 to 17		6 to 8	9 to 11	12 to 14	15 to 17
WHITE ALONE NON-HISPANIC									
Both Sexes									
2011	24.5	28.5	30.6	29.9	1.8	6,648	6,765	6,750	7,033
2010	20.3	24.7	28.0	26.8	2.2	6,707	6,836	6,821	7,243
2009	19.4	26.3	29.3	27.8	2.8	6,768	6,755	6,989	7,437
2008	21.2	27.7	29.4	28.4	2.2	6,798	6,768	7,008	7,534
2007	21.3	25.3	26.5	26.8	2.1	6,763	6,783	7,182	7,784
2006	20.5	24.5	25.1	28.6	2.3	6,748	6,887	7,368	7,827
2005	22.4	23.2	26.3	29.0	2.1	6,728	7,052	7,584	8,150
2004	22.7	25.1	27.0	29.8	3.3	6,878	7,090	7,768	7,892
2003[2]	21.8	27.1	27.3	28.7	2.8	7,006	7,102	7,889	7,980
2002	18.9	24.9	25.8	28.1	2.5	7,118	7,627	7,913	7,803
2001	19.9	23.1	25.3	28.1	3.1	7,325	7,726	7,773	7,829
2000	19.4	23.7	26.1	28.8	3.5	7,418	8,045	7,727	7,852
1999	18.9	24.2	25.3	28.9	3.6	7,717	7,938	7,669	7,879
1998	20.5	23.7	26.0	28.9	3.0	7,755	7,794	7,697	7,859
1997	19.7	24.6	27.3	28.4	3.2	7,729	7,775	7,789	7,866
1996	18.8	22.7	26.2	28.6	4.2	7,803	7,792	7,731	7,716
1995	18.2	24.5	28.0	29.2	3.4	7,853	8,000	7,872	7,795
1994	19.8	25.6	30.0	28.0	3.1	7,779	7,864	7,845	7,490
1993	18.8	27.2	28.8	29.5	3.0	7,736	7,802	7,600	7,022
Male									
2011	28.1	32.4	33.8	35.8	1.9	3,394	3,473	3,472	3,619
2010	23.3	27.7	30.6	30.5	3.1	3,414	3,498	3,487	3,728
2009	21.8	30.1	31.9	32.0	3.1	3,489	3,453	3,593	3,793
2008	24.4	29.9	33.2	31.8	2.4	3,485	3,459	3,599	3,862
2007	24.1	28.4	28.1	30.3	2.2	3,457	3,473	3,715	3,970
2006	23.1	26.0	27.6	32.4	2.9	3,449	3,537	3,775	3,984
2005	25.4	26.8	28.2	32.5	2.2	3,450	3,618	3,902	4,136
2004	25.0	27.9	30.6	35.0	3.4	3,548	3,605	4,054	3,994
2003[2]	24.6	31.7	30.7	33.4	2.9	3,668	3,725	3,960	4,101
2002	22.7	29.0	30.7	33.6	2.4	3,667	3,969	4,005	4,038
2001	23.1	26.2	28.5	31.6	3.7	3,808	3,971	3,920	4,020
2000	22.5	27.7	30.0	33.4	3.4	3,795	4,135	3,970	4,034
1999	20.3	27.7	29.7	35.1	3.5	3,955	4,076	3,913	4,058
1998	23.1	26.5	30.8	34.3	3.6	4,016	4,003	3,894	3,981
1997	24.1	29.0	32.5	35.3	3.8	3,977	3,971	3,996	4,020
1996	22.5	25.9	30.8	35.1	4.1	3,964	4,035	3,957	3,959
1995	22.1	27.3	31.9	34.9	3.1	4,038	4,094	4,017	4,010
1994	22.8	28.0	34.3	33.6	2.9	3,993	4,010	4,030	3,866
1993	22.0	31.5	33.2	35.6	2.4	3,952	4,021	3,889	3,578
Female									
2011	20.8	24.4	27.3	23.6	1.7	3,254	3,292	3,278	3,414
2010	17.2	21.5	25.3	23.0	1.3	3,294	3,338	3,334	3,515
2009	16.9	22.4	26.6	23.5	2.4	3,280	3,301	3,396	3,644
2008	18.0	25.3	25.4	24.9	2.1	3,313	3,309	3,408	3,673
2007	18.4	22.0	24.7	23.1	2.0	3,306	3,310	3,467	3,814
2006	17.6	22.8	22.6	24.6	1.8	3,299	3,350	3,593	3,843
2005	19.2	19.4	24.2	25.3	2.0	3,277	3,434	3,682	4,014
2004	20.3	22.2	23.1	24.5	3.3	3,330	3,485	3,714	3,898
2003[2]	18.6	22.2	24.0	23.7	2.6	3,337	3,377	3,929	3,878
2002	14.8	20.4	20.9	22.2	2.6	3,451	3,658	3,908	3,765
2001	16.4	19.8	22.0	24.4	2.6	3,517	3,755	3,853	3,809
2000	16.2	19.6	21.9	23.9	3.7	3,623	3,910	3,757	3,818
1999	17.4	20.5	20.8	22.3	3.6	3,761	3,864	3,757	3,840
1998	17.6	20.8	21.2	23.5	2.5	3,740	3,791	3,803	3,878
1997	15.0	19.9	21.8	21.3	2.6	3,752	3,804	3,793	3,846
1996	15.0	19.3	21.3	21.7	4.3	3,839	3,757	3,773	3,757
1995	14.1	21.5	23.8	23.1	3.8	3,815	3,906	3,854	3,784
1994	16.6	23.1	25.5	22.1	3.2	3,786	3,854	3,814	3,624
1993	15.4	22.6	24.2	23.1	3.6	3,784	3,782	3,710	3,444

[1] Civilian noninstitutionalized population.

[2] Starting in 2003 respondents could identify more than one race. Except as noted, the race data in this table from 2003 onward represent those respondents who indicated only one race category.

Table A-11. Population 6 to 17 Years Old Enrolled Below Modal Grade, 1971–2011—*Continued*

(Numbers in thousands; percent)

Year, sex, race, and Hispanic origin	Percent below modal grade, by years of age				Dropout rate, 15 to 17	Population in age group[1]			
	6 to 8	9 to 11	12 to 14	15 to 17		6 to 8	9 to 11	12 to 14	15 to 17
BLACK ALONE									
Both Sexes									
2011	20.2	30.0	28.9	32.4	2.7	1,882	1,831	1,773	1,855
2010	16.7	26.3	33.0	31.5	2.2	1,871	1,710	1,809	1,911
2009	20.1	30.7	32.7	34.8	2.7	1,692	1,814	1,801	1,943
2008	18.6	27.3	40.9	37.8	3.1	1,781	1,797	1,851	1,994
2007	17.7	28.1	33.0	39.2	3.0	1,797	1,770	1,937	2,021
2006	19.1	29.9	35.7	35.7	3.1	1,813	1,811	1,960	2,059
2005	20.8	35.6	34.1	38.8	4.2	1,806	1,826	2,011	2,085
2004	19.8	27.4	34.1	40.1	2.3	1,775	1,906	2,034	1,992
2003[2]	22.7	34.2	33.9	37.4	3.7	1,760	2,043	2,110	1,950
2002	19.6	28.6	32.8	36.2	3.9	2,017	2,048	2,036	1,943
2001	17.3	29.7	31.1	35.6	4.0	1,937	2,144	1,998	1,823
2000	19.6	26.9	37.8	34.6	4.7	1,976	2,082	1,961	1,852
1999	16.1	30.2	31.7	34.8	3.5	1,948	2,108	1,912	1,911
1998	18.3	26.6	31.4	38.4	3.6	2,019	1,934	1,840	1,801
1997	18.4	26.1	33.5	40.0	3.8	2,061	1,908	1,845	1,938
1996	18.4	29.2	36.8	36.9	4.8	2,054	1,847	1,839	1,858
1995	16.8	31.1	38.3	41.3	4.1	1,909	1,890	1,822	1,851
1994	18.4	35.1	36.1	37.7	3.3	1,912	1,795	1,835	1,809
1993[r]	20.0	33.6	34.8	45.1	3.6	1,767	1,763	1,747	1,641
1993	19.9	33.4	38.8	43.3	3.6	1,709	1,710	1,695	1,642
1992	20.6	28.7	38.0	40.6	4.2	1,761	1,635	1,686	1,621
1991	21.0	34.3	40.7	43.4	5.3	1,674	1,701	1,643	1,574
1990	21.9	33.1	46.1	42.9	5.2	1,645	1,712	1,574	1,571
1989	19.6	34.0	41.3	39.3	3.9	1,642	1,682	1,554	1,618
1988	18.6	33.1	37.6	38.4	4.7	1,680	1,629	1,545	1,637
1987	19.8	33.1	35.6	35.3	5.1	1,679	1,554	1,552	1,654
1986	12.7	34.6	38.5	38.3	4.6	1,611	1,542	1,530	1,692
1985	18.0	33.9	37.9	37.7	4.6	1,568	1,498	1,635	1,627
1984	17.9	32.3	38.1	34.6	4.1	1,445	1,442	1,652	1,536
1983	15.3	34.9	34.4	35.8	4.7	1,429	1,450	1,601	1,617
1982	17.2	27.1	32.5	32.6	4.6	1,765	1,874	1,953	1,947
1981	13.9	26.2	33.7	36.1	6.3	1,437	1,594	1,615	1,679
1980	14.9	27.8	30.5	37.6	5.1	1,460	1,606	1,568	1,728
1979	12.5	29.5	29.2	34.3	6.4	1,515	1,576	1,636	1,722
1978	12.6	27.8	26.6	35.4	5.7	1,557	1,523	1,664	1,764
1977	11.3	24.9	26.3	32.2	5.4	1,552	1,558	1,698	1,754
1976	10.5	23.2	26.1	35.6	6.7	1,493	1,633	1,724	1,726
1975	11.9	26.1	29.2	34.9	8.0	1,489	1,656	1,720	1,760
1974	11.6	26.2	33.2	34.4	8.2	1,509	1,684	1,750	1,682
1973	12.0	25.8	31.7	35.4	8.2	1,525	1,650	1,671	1,671
1972	13.2	30.5	33.1	37.3	6.6	1,585	1,638	1,691	1,636
1971	14.2	27.9	34.7	40.2	7.0	1,794	1,787	1,638	1,533
Male									
2011	20.9	35.2	32.2	34.5	4.1	977	902	898	927
2010	16.8	30.9	34.7	35.0	3.0	954	856	912	961
2009	19.2	34.6	34.4	42.3	2.6	805	954	911	980
2008	19.4	26.2	46.3	41.3	3.4	917	908	934	992
2007	22.7	31.6	35.4	43.5	2.2	946	886	964	1,027
2006	20.3	35.1	40.3	43.9	3.3	929	920	991	1,032
2005	22.6	37.9	35.8	43.0	5.2	912	913	1,011	1,041
2004	21.0	31.4	37.8	46.5	2.0	885	992	1,012	1,009
2003[2]	23.6	36.8	38.7	43.4	3.9	927	1,059	975	1,047
2002	17.5	32.5	37.0	44.7	5.0	1,044	1,036	1,012	973
2001	21.1	31.1	33.3	42.8	3.5	978	1,108	1,010	924
2000	20.8	27.5	43.3	37.0	6.4	1,003	1,057	994	941
1999	15.9	34.2	36.3	37.6	3.0	964	1,085	969	992
1998	20.9	29.3	33.3	41.9	3.0	1,027	973	926	928
1997	21.3	29.3	39.4	43.8	3.1	1,019	994	934	979
1996	21.3	30.4	45.1	43.2	4.5	1,054	925	931	943
1995	18.8	31.2	45.0	47.5	2.9	982	944	922	952
1994	19.4	30.3	39.9	39.8	3.2	951	928	928	898
1993[r]	21.8	36.5	44.3	53.0	2.5	903	884	891	832
1993	21.6	36.5	44.2	51.8	2.5	864	857	867	832
1992	24.5	28.7	44.5	47.0	2.8	864	862	860	813
1991	22.9	39.6	46.2	50.6	5.4	846	878	839	798

[1]Civilian noninstitutionalized population.

[2]Starting in 2003 respondents could identify more than one race. Except as noted, the race data in this table from 2003 onward represent those respondents who indicated only one race category.

r = Revised, controlled to 1990 census based population estimates; previous 1993 data controlled to 1980 census based population estimates.

Table A-11. Population 6 to 17 Years Old Enrolled Below Modal Grade, 1971–2011—*Continued*

(Numbers in thousands; percent)

Year, sex, race, and Hispanic origin	Percent below modal grade, by years of age				Dropout rate, 15 to 17	Population in age group[1]			
	6 to 8	9 to 11	12 to 14	15 to 17		6 to 8	9 to 11	12 to 14	15 to 17
Male— *(Continued)*									
1990	23.2	37.3	52.7	49.1	4.3	828	877	791	795
1989	21.7	38.8	44.8	46.7	2.8	831	858	785	828
1988	18.9	37.2	43.7	41.4	4.1	851	828	780	828
1987	21.6	41.1	39.7	42.3	4.9	861	779	802	818
1986	15.0	39.0	45.2	45.9	4.0	806	792	770	855
1985	19.5	38.2	41.4	40.3	5.4	778	775	830	816
1984	24.1	38.1	42.5	42.8	4.2	729	727	832	769
1983	16.8	42.0	43.1	40.6	4.4	721	723	808	799
1982	18.8	27.5	36.2	36.9	4.8	898	937	975	977
1981	17.7	34.2	33.3	42.4	5.4	723	811	814	832
1980	16.8	31.8	36.2	43.3	4.9	736	807	770	876
1979	14.7	37.3	33.8	43.6	4.0	762	796	828	853
1978	15.4	33.0	30.3	43.1	4.1	774	767	847	870
1977	12.1	29.8	31.1	35.3	4.8	776	782	858	868
1976	11.5	26.1	30.9	43.3	5.7	755	816	870	855
1975	12.8	30.7	32.5	40.2	7.6	743	849	845	879
1974	13.5	31.0	40.9	41.1	7.2	747	858	861	849
1973	14.1	29.5	38.0	42.0	8.5	752	831	837	824
1972	14.5	36.8	41.3	43.8	6.6	787	828	836	818
1971	18.1	30.9	38.5	47.6	7.4	890	900	810	757
Female									
2011	19.5	25.0	25.4	30.4	1.4	905	930	875	928
2010	16.5	21.6	31.4	28.0	1.4	917	853	897	951
2009	20.9	26.4	30.9	27.1	2.8	887	860	891	963
2008	17.7	28.4	35.5	34.2	2.9	864	889	917	1,003
2007	12.2	24.7	30.5	34.5	3.9	851	885	972	993
2006	17.7	24.7	31.0	27.5	2.8	884	891	968	1,027
2005	19.0	33.3	32.4	34.7	3.3	893	913	999	1,044
2004	18.6	23.1	30.5	33.4	2.6	890	914	1,022	983
2003[2]	21.7	31.5	39.8	30.3	3.4	833	983	1,135	903
2002	22.0	24.7	28.7	27.8	2.8	973	1,012	1,024	970
2001	13.3	28.2	29.0	27.9	4.5	959	1,036	988	900
2000	18.2	26.4	32.0	32.3	2.9	974	1,025	968	911
1999	16.3	25.8	27.0	31.6	4.0	984	1,022	944	919
1998	15.6	23.8	29.6	34.6	4.3	992	960	914	873
1997	15.9	22.8	27.4	36.0	4.5	1,041	915	911	959
1996	13.4	28.1	28.4	30.3	4.9	1,000	922	909	915
1995	14.8	23.6	30.9	34.6	5.3	928	946	901	898
1994	17.5	29.1	32.3	35.4	3.6	961	867	908	911
1993[r]	18.0	30.8	33.1	36.6	4.7	864	879	856	809
1993	18.1	30.3	33.2	34.6	4.7	844	854	828	809
1992	16.7	28.7	31.2	34.2	5.6	897	773	826	808
1991	19.0	28.6	35.0	36.0	5.2	828	823	804	776
1990	20.7	28.7	39.3	36.6	6.1	817	835	783	776
1989	17.5	29.0	37.7	31.5	5.1	811	824	769	790
1988	18.2	28.8	31.4	35.2	5.3	829	801	765	809
1987	18.0	25.2	31.3	28.5	5.3	818	775	750	836
1986	16.6	29.3	34.2	35.1	3.8	790	723	805	811
1985	11.5	26.4	33.5	26.3	4.0	716	715	820	767
1984	13.8	27.8	25.5	31.2	5.0	708	727	793	818
1983	15.5	26.7	28.7	28.1	4.3	867	937	978	970
1982	10.1	17.9	34.2	29.9	7.1	714	783	801	847
1981	12.8	23.8	25.1	31.7	5.3	724	799	798	852
1980	10.4	21.5	24.5	25.2	8.7	753	780	808	869
1979	9.8	22.6	22.6	27.9	7.2	783	756	817	894
1978	10.6	20.0	21.3	29.1	6.0	776	776	840	886
1977	9.5	20.3	21.2	28.1	7.7	738	817	854	871
1976	11.0	21.3	25.9	29.6	8.3	746	807	875	881
1975	9.7	21.3	25.8	27.5	9.2	762	826	889	833
1974	10.0	22.1	25.4	28.9	7.9	773	819	834	847
1973	11.9	24.1	25.1	30.9	6.6	798	810	855	818
1972	10.4	24.9	31.0	33.1	6.7	904	887	828	776
1971									

[1]Civilian noninstitutionalized population.
[2]Starting in 2003 respondents could identify more than one race. Except as noted, the race data in this table from 2003 onward represent those respondents who indicated only one race category.
r = Revised, controlled to 1990 census based population estimates; previous 1993 data controlled to 1980 census based population estimates.

Table A-11. Population 6 to 17 Years Old Enrolled Below Modal Grade, 1971–2011—*Continued*

(Numbers in thousands; percent)

Year, sex, race, and Hispanic origin	Percent below modal grade, by years of age				Dropout rate, 15 to 17	Population in age group[1]			
	6 to 8	9 to 11	12 to 14	15 to 17		6 to 8	9 to 11	12 to 14	15 to 17
ASIAN ALONE[3]									
Both Sexes									
2011	16.8	23.1	24.3	25.6	2.4	602	582	481	536
2010	8.9	20.3	22.3	18.9	3.1	618	575	495	424
2009	8.8	11.7	25.5	20.0	1.5	522	491	448	421
2008	17.2	22.7	26.7	18.8	4.4	491	517	482	507
2007	11.3	21.9	17.0	24.2	3.7	545	534	497	463
2006	15.2	19.7	20.9	23.0	3.2	425	472	490	476
2005	12.8	12.2	16.3	19.1	1.2	502	429	486	457
2004	12.1	11.4	20.9	23.6	1.7	417	468	490	491
2003[2]	7.5	13.6	19.7	24.5	1.6	486	453	459	458
2002	11.1	12.3	20.4	18.6	2.7	602	490	530	553
2001	11.9	17.9	20.3	21.0	2.8	503	565	523	565
2000	10.7	15.5	17.5	22.2	0.6	524	490	490	475
1999	7.5	16.5	17.9	25.5	3.2	533	496	560	555
Male									
2011	16.5	25.3	24.9	28.6	2.3	324	293	249	266
2010	8.0	20.0	24.1	20.7	2.6	327	296	247	237
2009	9.2	12.7	25.2	21.3	0.7	272	232	227	233
2008	23.8	20.4	24.3	17.4	2.4	227	257	249	253
2007	7.6	20.5	18.2	26.0	4.0	278	272	240	246
2006	14.3	18.4	23.5	21.7	3.3	206	256	264	227
2005	12.3	13.8	13.2	18.1	1.6	261	202	265	228
2004	10.9	16.0	20.9	23.5	2.4	220	216	282	231
2003[2]	7.3	15.9	20.3	19.3	*	226	223	261	231
2002	9.6	12.4	23.3	18.9	1.7	274	239	267	287
2001	15.2	16.6	19.0	22.2	4.9	265	294	256	313
2000	14.7	14.2	16.1	30.3	1.0	286	243	267	261
1999	8.4	16.4	17.6	30.3	2.2	277	269	246	276
Female									
2011	17.1	20.9	23.7	22.7	2.6	278	289	232	270
2010	10.0	20.6	20.6	16.6	3.7	290	279	248	187
2009	8.5	10.9	25.9	18.5	2.4	251	259	220	188
2008	11.5	25.0	29.3	20.3	6.5	264	260	233	254
2007	15.2	23.5	15.8	22.2	3.4	268	263	257	217
2006	16.1	21.2	17.9	24.2	3.1	218	216	226	249
2005	13.4	10.8	20.0	20.1	0.9	241	227	221	229
2004	13.5	7.3	20.8	23.7	1.1	196	253	208	260
2003[2]	7.6	11.3	18.8	29.9	3.2	259	230	198	227
2002	12.4	12.2	17.5	18.2	3.7	327	251	263	266
2001	8.3	19.3	21.4	19.6	0.2	238	270	268	252
2000	5.9	16.7	19.2	12.3	0.1	239	247	224	215
1999	6.6	16.7	18.5	20.6	4.0	256	227	314	278
HISPANIC[4]									
Both Sexes									
2011	19.8	28.0	28.6	36.1	3.3	3,161	2,847	2,496	2,502
2010	15.6	23.4	27.9	34.3	2.5	3,046	2,681	2,494	2,307
2009	18.1	26.0	28.3	32.1	4.7	2,893	2,524	2,418	2,254
2008	17.8	25.2	29.1	34.2	3.5	2,690	2,402	2,422	2,321
2007	20.9	28.9	31.1	34.0	5.7	2,541	2,414	2,418	2,211
2006	20.6	29.2	32.6	35.3	5.7	2,441	2,382	2,361	2,165
2005	18.1	26.2	33.2	32.1	4.9	2,390	2,317	2,322	2,202
2004	21.5	28.1	30.0	34.6	6.1	2,382	2,250	2,283	2,072
2003	20.2	28.7	31.3	32.7	5.2	2,280	2,221	2,167	2,063
2002	15.5	28.4	27.9	35.6	5.9	2,258	2,204	2,079	1,841
2001	16.7	22.1	25.0	34.6	6.9	2,143	2,198	2,011	1,733
2000	19.4	23.2	27.3	34.4	8.8	2,067	1,965	1,744	1,671
1999	15.7	25.9	27.9	36.5	7.3	1,902	1,922	1,734	1,653
1998	15.4	23.2	24.6	33.8	7.6	1,903	1,740	1,542	1,424
1997	15.2	21.5	31.0	41.4	5.5	1,909	1,666	1,444	1,575
1996	14.9	22.9	35.5	39.0	8.4	1,711	1,680	1,550	1,478
1995	14.4	26.1	38.5	43.6	7.4	1,597	1,628	1,496	1,373
1994	16.8	28.4	32.3	39.9	8.8	1,526	1,593	1,442	1,347

[1]Civilian noninstitutionalized population.
[2]Starting in 2003 respondents could identify more than one race. Except as noted, the race data in this table from 2003 onward represent those respondents who indicated only one race category.
[3]The data shown prior to 2003 consists of those identifying themselves as "Asian or Pacific Islanders."
[4]May be of any race.
* = Quantity zero or rounds to zero.

Table A-11. Population 6 to 17 Years Old Enrolled Below Modal Grade, 1971–2011—*Continued*

(Numbers in thousands; percent)

Year, sex, race, and Hispanic origin	Percent below modal grade, by years of age				Dropout rate, 15 to 17	Population in age group[1]			
	6 to 8	9 to 11	12 to 14	15 to 17		6 to 8	9 to 11	12 to 14	15 to 17
Both Sexes— *(Continued)*									
1993r	18.9	29.2	33.2	42.2	8.2	1,390	1,255	1,204	1,225
1993	18.9	29.2	32.7	38.3	7.9	1,455	1,295	1,243	1,226
1992	16.2	25.3	34.3	39.9	8.1	1,272	1,371	1,141	1,110
1991	21.8	30.7	35.8	38.4	11.3	1,290	1,356	1,088	1,023
1990	21.5	34.8	37.7	39.8	9.0	1,270	1,230	1,095	1,062
1989	21.9	33.8	39.9	39.5	10.6	1,257	1,154	1,079	1,001
1988	23.2	37.0	45.0	36.8	13.7	1,248	1,107	1,052	953
1987	16.9	31.2	38.9	37.3	9.1	1,181	1,054	1,063	981
1986	19.1	33.3	42.5	35.5	11.0	1,067	1,119	1,025	1,018
1985	18.7	32.4	35.8	35.7	11.3	1,035	1,047	957	946
1984	20.2	32.7	34.7	38.5	10.7	901	829	806	816
1983	20.2	32.7	39.5	38.0	8.3	903	909	949	860
1982	21.9	32.6	37.3	37.0	10.9	923	875	924	883
1981	17.9	34.7	34.9	34.9	13.3	882	939	866	963
1980	20.8	26.1	34.8	35.8	12.6	881	949	863	889
1979	18.2	33.6	33.0	30.3	10.9	729	712	697	755
1978	19.8	29.1	33.6	37.8	12.3	723	684	666	751
1977	13.0	24.1	25.1	35.2	11.0	676	693	662	773
Male									
2011	29.3	20.7	30.5	30.0	3.0	1,605	1,465	1,290	1,294
2010	16.3	24.2	28.4	33.6	3.1	1,544	1,381	1,290	1,178
2009	16.4	27.7	31.8	32.5	4.9	1,458	1,322	1,216	1,165
2008	17.8	26.6	30.9	36.3	3.7	1,377	1,218	1,233	1,198
2007	24.3	28.5	34.1	37.4	5.9	1,302	1,252	1,217	1,130
2006	20.0	31.0	37.7	40.6	4.9	1,251	1,214	1,208	1,111
2005	20.5	29.2	39.2	37.0	4.7	1,219	1,192	1,202	1,087
2004	25.2	28.8	34.3	36.6	6.4	1,247	1,142	1,202	1,001
2003	23.0	31.2	32.3	35.9	6.2	1,205	1,178	1,081	1,020
2002	17.4	31.6	28.7	38.5	7.4	1,140	1,090	1,137	911
2001	21.2	23.4	27.8	40.8	7.7	1,065	1,128	1,093	895
2000	23.1	26.7	27.7	36.9	9.0	1,048	993	875	872
1999	17.9	29.5	29.7	38.9	7.6	973	990	893	854
1998	16.8	26.6	26.9	44.9	8.1	933	887	841	792
1997	15.3	22.3	33.7	45.8	3.7	969	863	735	836
1996	13.5	25.8	40.5	45.1	6.8	914	808	798	764
1995	11.4	31.1	42.4	47.6	7.5	794	839	776	697
1994	16.4	27.5	36.3	45.1	11.4	778	845	721	676
1993r	19.1	35.1	37.2	50.4	7.6	722	612	618	658
1993	19.1	34.3	36.9	46.0	7.3	778	637	648	658
1992	15.6	27.2	42.5	46.2	6.8	636	687	602	576
1991	22.7	31.5	43.9	42.6	10.7	651	691	544	521
1990	22.2	36.4	40.2	43.8	9.0	676	616	590	564
1989	23.7	36.1	40.0	45.2	7.8	642	584	560	511
1988	26.9	42.0	53.8	40.5	12.4	676	566	470	523
1987	19.8	31.7	44.8	38.7	6.4	600	524	569	517
1986	22.2	38.0	49.3	37.8	10.8	544	555	535	471
1985	16.7	36.8	38.4	43.4	7.8	521	527	502	449
1984	18.3	35.7	33.1	42.8	10.0	443	420	423	432
1983	22.2	38.8	45.7	41.8	8.2	445	479	479	428
1982	23.1	36.4	39.1	43.4	10.1	428	426	466	477
1981	19.9	39.8	38.0	40.0	14.3	438	480	439	495
1980	22.5	29.9	40.5	40.7	13.5	418	481	415	445
1979	19.0	34.6	36.4	31.3	8.8	368	358	349	386
1978	23.5	29.9	33.9	37.3	13.6	388	335	339	413
1977	11.5	31.4	23.3	38.4	6.7	365	325	330	406
Female									
2011	19.0	25.3	27.1	34.2	3.7	1,556	1,382	1,206	1,209
2010	15.0	22.6	27.3	35.1	2.0	1,502	1,301	1,204	1,129
2009	19.9	24.0	24.8	31.6	4.6	1,435	1,202	1,202	1,089
2008	17.8	23.7	27.2	32.1	3.2	1,313	1,184	1,189	1,123
2007	17.3	29.4	28.2	30.5	5.4	1,239	1,162	1,202	1,080
2006	21.3	27.4	27.3	29.5	6.5	1,190	1,168	1,153	1,054
2005	15.6	23.0	26.7	27.3	5.1	1,171	1,126	1,119	1,115
2004	17.6	27.3	25.1	32.8	5.7	1,135	1,108	1,080	1,070
2003	17.1	25.7	30.3	29.7	4.3	1,075	1,043	1,086	1,042
2002	13.6	25.3	27.0	32.7	4.5	1,118	1,115	942	930

[1]Civilian noninstitutionalized population.
r = Revised, controlled to 1990 census based population estimates; previous 1993 data controlled to 1980 census based population estimates.

Table A-11. Population 6 to 17 Years Old Enrolled Below Modal Grade, 1971–2011—*Continued*

(Numbers in thousands; percent)

Year, sex, race, and Hispanic origin	Percent below modal grade, by years of age				Dropout rate, 15 to 17	Population in age group[1]			
	6 to 8	9 to 11	12 to 14	15 to 17		6 to 8	9 to 11	12 to 14	15 to 17
Female— *(Continued)*									
2001	12.2	20.8	21.6	28.0	6.0	1,078	1,070	918	838
2000	15.7	19.7	26.9	31.8	8.6	1,020	974	869	800
1999	13.5	22.0	26.1	33.8	6.9	930	932	841	800
1998	14.1	19.7	21.8	31.1	7.0	970	853	701	632
1997	15.0	20.4	28.8	36.1	7.4	939	803	710	739
1996	16.6	20.3	30.4	32.4	10.4	798	871	753	712
1995	17.5	20.6	34.5	39.5	7.2	802	789	721	677
1994	17.2	29.2	28.5	34.9	6.1	748	747	722	671
1993[r]	18.9	24.2	29.0	32.3	8.7	667	643	586	567
1993	18.7	24.3	28.3	29.3	8.6	678	658	597	567
1992	16.8	23.4	25.0	33.1	9.6	636	684	539	534
1991	20.8	29.8	27.6	34.1	12.0	639	665	544	502
1990	20.7	33.2	34.9	35.3	9.0	594	614	505	498
1989	20.0	31.4	39.7	33.5	13.5	615	570	519	490
1988	18.7	31.8	37.8	32.3	15.3	572	541	582	430
1987	13.8	30.8	32.2	35.8	12.1	581	530	494	464
1986	15.9	28.7	35.1	33.5	11.2	523	564	490	547
1985	20.8	27.9	33.0	28.8	14.5	514	520	455	497
1984	22.1	29.6	36.6	33.6	11.5	458	409	383	384
1983	18.1	25.8	33.2	34.3	8.3	458	430	470	432
1982	20.8	29.0	35.6	29.6	11.8	495	449	458	406
1981	16.0	29.4	31.6	29.5	12.2	444	459	427	468
1980	19.2	22.2	29.5	30.9	11.7	463	468	448	444
1979	17.5	32.5	29.6	29.3	13.0	361	354	348	369
1978	15.5	28.4	33.3	38.5	10.7	335	349	327	338
1977	14.8	17.7	26.8	31.6	15.8	311	368	332	367
WHITE ALONE OR IN COMBINATION									
Both Sexes									
2011	23.1	28.4	30.0	31.5	2.1	9,956	9,824	9,378	9,652
2010	19.0	24.7	28.1	28.5	2.2	9,935	9,712	9,435	9,699
2009	19.2	26.3	29.2	28.7	3.2	9,887	9,345	9,515	9,832
2008	20.2	27.1	29.2	29.6	2.5	9,680	9,298	9,577	10,043
2007	21.1	26.1	27.4	28.5	2.8	9,502	9,326	9,734	10,169
2006	20.6	25.6	26.7	29.9	3.0	9,346	9,444	9,850	10,175
2005	21.1	23.9	27.9	29.4	2.6	9,314	9,588	10,026	10,479
2004	22.4	25.6	27.4	30.5	3.9	9,422	9,506	10,175	10,079
2003	21.7	27.4	28.1	29.4	3.2	9,447	9,446	10,194	10,151
Male									
2011	25.8	31.6	32.6	36.4	2.1	5,089	5,042	4,820	4,956
2010	21.2	27.3	30.1	31.0	3.0	5,039	4,970	4,824	4,996
2009	20.6	29.5	32.3	31.8	3.4	5,072	4,776	4,866	5,039
2008	22.3	29.1	32.3	32.4	2.7	4,963	4,744	4,934	5,163
2007	24.0	28.2	29.1	32.0	2.9	4,857	4,770	4,997	5,203
2006	22.4	27.2	29.6	34.1	3.4	4,769	4,842	5,042	5,193
2005	23.9	27.3	30.9	33.1	2.7	4,751	4,925	5,151	5,268
2004	24.9	28.1	31.2	35.1	3.9	4,876	4,823	5,318	5,043
2003	24.5	31.6	31.0	33.8	3.4	4,965	4,946	5,108	5,172
Female									
2011	20.4	25.0	27.2	26.4	2.2	4,867	4,782	4,558	4,696
2010	16.8	21.9	26.0	25.9	1.4	4,896	4,743	4,610	4,703
2009	17.7	22.9	26.0	25.4	2.9	4,815	4,569	4,649	4,792
2008	17.9	25.0	26.0	26.6	2.4	4,717	4,554	4,643	4,880
2007	18.1	23.9	25.5	24.7	2.7	4,646	4,555	4,737	4,966
2006	18.7	23.8	23.6	25.5	2.6	4,577	4,602	4,808	4,982
2005	18.2	20.2	24.7	25.7	2.6	4,563	4,663	4,875	5,211
2004	19.6	23.0	23.2	25.9	3.9	4,545	4,683	4,857	5,037
2003	18.6	22.7	25.2	24.8	3.0	4,482	4,500	5,086	4,979

[1]Civilian noninstitutionalized population.
r = Revised, controlled to 1990 census based population estimates; previous 1993 data controlled to 1980 census based population estimates.

Table A-11. Population 6 to 17 Years Old Enrolled Below Modal Grade, 1971–2011—*Continued*

(Numbers in thousands; percent)

Year, sex, race, and Hispanic origin	Percent below modal grade, by years of age				Dropout rate, 15 to 17	Population in age group[1]			
	6 to 8	9 to 11	12 to 14	15 to 17		6 to 8	9 to 11	12 to 14	15 to 17
BLACK ALONE OR IN COMBINATION									
Both Sexes									
2011	21.0	30.1	28.1	33.1	2.5	2,186	2,061	1,945	2,003
2010	16.9	25.9	32.4	31.6	2.1	2,122	1,938	1,971	2,067
2009	20.7	30.2	32.6	34.8	2.5	1,939	2,006	2,001	2,116
2008	18.3	26.8	39.4	37.1	3.0	2,026	2,002	2,036	2,179
2007	17.6	27.3	32.1	38.8	2.8	1,998	1,950	2,071	2,146
2006	18.9	28.3	34.8	35.0	3.1	1,982	1,988	2,074	2,202
2005	20.3	34.8	33.4	37.9	4.4	1,970	1,982	2,137	2,194
2004	20.3	27.0	33.2	39.1	2.5	1,950	2,022	2,174	2,107
2003	23.2	33.5	33.4	36.8	3.8	1,921	2,183	2,220	2,034
Male									
2011	22.9	35.0	31.6	35.1	3.8	1,135	1,017	991	994
2010	16.7	30.4	34.1	34.2	3.0	1,085	961	978	1,041
2009	21.2	33.0	35.9	41.5	2.4	934	1,042	1,006	1,059
2008	19.8	25.6	44.8	39.7	3.3	1,026	1,020	1,032	1,090
2007	21.7	29.9	34.4	42.6	2.1	1,053	983	1,034	1,086
2006	20.0	33.5	39.0	42.8	3.5	1,013	1,018	1,050	1,094
2005	22.1	37.0	35.5	41.8	5.0	981	999	1,061	1,082
2004	21.1	30.6	37.3	45.3	1.9	966	1,042	1,065	1,056
2003	24.2	36.6	38.5	42.9	4.0	1,014	1,116	1,033	1,083
Female									
2011	18.8	25.4	24.4	31.2	1.3	1,051	1,044	954	1,009
2010	17.0	21.4	30.7	28.9	1.3	1,037	977	993	1,026
2009	20.3	27.1	29.3	28.1	2.5	1,004	965	995	1,058
2008	16.8	28.1	34.0	34.5	2.7	1,000	982	1,004	1,089
2007	13.2	24.6	29.9	34.8	3.6	945	967	1,037	1,061
2006	17.8	23.0	30.6	27.3	2.7	969	969	1,024	1,108
2005	18.6	32.6	31.4	34.1	3.7	990	983	1,076	1,112
2004	17.8	23.0	30.6	27.3	2.7	969	969	1,024	1,108
2003	22.0	30.4	29.0	29.8	3.4	907	1,067	1,187	951

[1]Civilian noninstitutionalized population.

Table A-11. Population 6 to 17 Years Old Enrolled Below Modal Grade, 1971–2011—*Continued*

(Numbers in thousands; percent)

Year, sex, race, and Hispanic origin	Percent below modal grade, by years of age				Dropout rate, 15 to 17	Population in age group[1]			
	6 to 8	9 to 11	12 to 14	15 to 17		6 to 8	9 to 11	12 to 14	15 to 17
ASIAN ALONE OR IN COMBINATION									
Both Sexes									
2011	16.9	22.1	25.2	27.1	2.0	744	718	614	650
2010	10.6	19.6	22.2	19.1	2.5	779	728	603	532
2009	9.2	13.2	25.7	19.3	1.2	690	563	513	508
2008	16.4	23.5	24.7	19.7	3.9	599	587	558	603
2007	11.4	20.6	15.6	25.3	3.6	650	613	600	548
2006	15.0	19.9	19.2	22.2	3.2	528	574	574	603
2005	13.0	12.3	16.5	18.4	1.2	600	531	576	581
2004	13.9	12.4	20.3	24.6	2.6	494	576	585	599
2003	8.8	14.9	18.4	23.5	2.4	579	548	552	543
Male									
2011	17.0	22.6	26.7	29.9	2.0	380	368	324	300
2010	9.5	19.3	24.9	20.9	2.1	397	385	309	291
2009	10.1	16.4	25.6	20.1	0.6	363	269	271	285
2008	21.3	22.6	20.4	15.5	2.1	285	291	299	289
2007	8.4	20.2	16.7	28.4	4.3	316	307	287	289
2006	15.4	15.4	15.4	15.4	4.1	259	311	291	285
2005	12.5	13.2	14.5	16.5	1.6	318	254	307	286
2004	12.4	16.2	19.3	22.3	3.6	254	278	324	286
2003	9.3	19.8	19.4	19.2	1.8	263	268	299	277
Female									
2011	16.9	21.5	23.6	24.7	2.0	364	35	290	350
2010	11.8	19.9	19.3	16.9	2.9	382	344	294	242
2009	8.2	10.2	25.9	18.3	2.1	326	293	242	223
2008	12.0	24.3	29.6	23.6	5.5	314	295	259	314
2007	14.3	21.1	14.6	21.8	2.9	334	306	314	259
2006	14.6	20.6	15.4	22.2	2.4	269	263	283	318
2005	13.7	11.5	18.8	20.2	0.9	282	276	269	295
2004	15.5	8.8	21.6	26.7	1.6	241	298	261	313
2003	8.4	10.3	17.2	28.0	3.1	316	280	253	266

[1]Civilian noninstitutionalized population.

Table A-12 Annual High School Dropout Rates of 15 to 24 Year Olds by Sex, Race, Grade, and Hispanic Origin, October 1967–2011

(Numbers in thousands; percent)

Year, grade, race, and Hispanic origin	Total[1]			Male			Female		
	Total students	Dropouts	Dropout rate	Total students	Dropouts	Dropout rate	Total students	Dropouts	Dropout rate
ALL RACES									
Grades 10–12									
2011	11,726	375	3.2	5,804	206	3.4	5,548	169	2.9
2010	11,647	326	2.8	6,006	172	2.9	5,641	154	2.7
2009	11,651	373	3.2	5,798	189	3.3	5,853	184	3.1
2008	11,750	390	3.3	5,999	174	2.9	5,751	216	3.8
2007	11,584	383	3.3	5,879	206	3.5	5,705	177	3.1
2006	11,604	407	3.5	5,932	227	3.8	5,672	180	3.2
2005	11,494	414	3.6	5,843	233	4.0	5,651	181	3.2
2004	11,166	486	4.4	5,624	266	4.7	5,542	220	4.0
2003	11,378	429	3.8	5,705	225	4.0	5,674	203	3.6
2002	10,989	367	3.3	5,504	193	3.5	5,484	174	3.2
2001	10,777	507	4.7	5,534	293	5.3	5,243	214	4.1
2000	10,773	488	4.5	5,417	280	5.2	5,356	208	3.9
1999	11,067	520	4.7	5,659	243	4.3	5,411	277	5.1
1998	10,791	479	4.4	5,486	237	4.3	5,305	243	4.6
1997	10,645	454	4.3	5,330	251	4.7	5,313	203	3.8
1996	10,249	485	4.7	5,175	240	4.6	5,072	244	4.8
1995	10,106	544	5.4	5,161	297	5.8	4,946	247	5.0
1994	9,922	497	5.0	5,048	249	4.9	4,873	247	5.1
1993[r]	9,430	404	4.3	4,787	211	4.4	4,640	192	4.1
1993	9,021	382	4.2	4,570	199	4.4	4,452	183	4.1
1992	8,939	384	4.3	4,580	175	3.8	4,357	207	4.8
1991	8,612	348	4.0	4,380	167	3.8	4,231	180	4.3
1990	8,679	347	4.0	4,356	177	4.1	4,323	170	3.9
1989	8,974	404	4.5	4,519	203	4.5	4,453	199	4.5
1988	9,590	461	4.8	4,960	256	5.2	4,628	206	4.5
1987	9,802	403	4.1	4,921	215	4.4	4,879	187	3.8
1986	9,829	421	4.3	4,910	213	4.3	4,917	208	4.2
1985	9,704	504	5.2	4,831	259	5.4	4,874	245	5.0
1984	10,041	507	5.0	4,986	268	5.4	5,054	238	4.7
1983	10,331	535	5.2	5,130	294	5.7	5,200	241	4.6
1982	10,611	577	5.4	5,310	305	5.7	5,301	271	5.1
1981	10,868	639	5.9	5,379	322	6.0	5,487	316	5.8
1980	10,891	658	6.0	5,445	362	6.6	5,448	296	5.4
1979	11,136	744	6.7	5,479	369	6.7	5,658	377	6.7
1978	11,116	743	6.7	5,558	415	7.5	5,558	328	5.9
1977	11,300	734	6.5	5,657	392	6.9	5,643	342	6.1
1976	10,996	644	5.9	5,534	360	6.5	5,463	285	5.2
1975	11,033	639	5.8	5,485	296	5.4	5,548	343	6.2
1974	11,026	742	6.7	5,421	402	7.4	5,605	340	6.1
1973	10,851	683	6.3	5,407	370	6.8	5,444	313	5.7
1972	10,664	659	6.2	5,305	317	6.0	5,358	341	6.4
1971	10,451	562	5.4	5,193	297	5.7	5,258	266	5.1
1970	10,281	588	5.7	5,145	288	5.6	5,138	302	5.9
1969	10,212	551	5.4	5,069	273	5.4	5,142	278	5.4
1968	9,814	506	5.2	4,831	247	5.1	4,983	259	5.2
1967	9,350	486	5.2	4,605	237	5.1	4,745	249	5.2
Grade 10									
2011	3,998	48	1.2	2,009	26	1.3	1,989	22	1.1
2010	3,983	27	0.7	2,008	17	0.8	1,976	10	0.5
2009	3,983	50	1.2	1,993	28	1.4	1,989	22	1.1
2008	4,154	56	1.4	2,104	25	1.2	2,050	31	1.5
2007	4,064	63	1.6	2,027	32	1.6	2,037	31	1.5
2006	4,179	31	0.7	2,053	19	0.9	2,126	12	0.5
2005	4,483	72	1.6	2,244	49	2.2	2,239	23	1.0
2004	4,028	99	2.5	2,096	56	2.7	1,931	42	2.2
2003	4,107	64	1.6	2,111	26	1.2	1,995	37	1.9
2002	3,896	55	1.4	1,963	36	1.8	1,934	19	1.0
2001	3,900	90	2.3	1,988	50	2.5	1,913	41	2.1
2000	3,957	77	1.9	2,036	48	2.4	1,920	28	1.5
1999	3,910	104	2.7	2,036	54	2.7	1,875	50	2.7
1998	3,883	90	2.3	1,971	36	1.8	1,911	54	2.8
1997	3,738	79	2.1	1,894	44	2.3	1,843	35	1.9
1996	3,691	94	2.5	1,906	50	2.6	1,784	43	2.4

[1]Civilian noninstitutionalized population.

r = Revised, controlled to 1990 census based population estimates; previous 1993 data controlled to 1980 census based population estimates.

Table A-12 Annual High School Dropout Rates of 15 to 24 Year Olds by Sex, Race, Grade, and Hispanic Origin, October 1967–2011—*Continued*

(Numbers in thousands; percent)

Year, grade, race, and Hispanic origin	Total[1]			Male			Female		
	Total students	Dropouts	Dropout rate	Total students	Dropouts	Dropout rate	Total students	Dropouts	Dropout rate
Grade 10— *(Continued)*									
1995	3,552	88	2.5	1,823	40	2.2	1,728	47	2.7
1994	3,474	76	2.2	1,793	45	2.5	1,681	31	1.8
1993[r]	3,265	86	2.6	1,696	52	3.1	1,567	33	2.1
1993	3,139	81	2.6	1,627	50	3.1	1,513	31	2.0
1992	3,197	81	2.5	1,657	37	2.2	1,539	43	2.8
1991	3,132	105	3.4	1,571	46	2.9	1,561	59	3.8
1990	3,215	90	2.8	1,660	43	2.6	1,555	47	3.0
1989	3,071	99	3.2	1,567	56	3.6	1,504	43	2.9
1988	3,308	112	3.4	1,716	63	3.7	1,592	49	3.1
1987	3,492	106	3.0	1,818	45	2.5	1,674	61	3.6
1986	3,555	119	3.3	1,820	56	3.1	1,734	63	3.6
1985	3,491	143	4.1	1,797	74	4.1	1,695	69	4.1
1984	3,415	135	4.0	1,735	76	4.4	1,680	59	3.5
1983	3,468	129	3.7	1,755	70	4.0	1,713	59	3.4
1982	3,540	144	4.1	1,792	69	3.9	1,747	74	4.2
1981	3,735	144	3.9	1,816	65	3.6	1,918	78	4.1
1980	3,817	166	4.3	1,957	95	4.9	1,861	71	3.8
1979	3,920	217	5.5	1,985	102	5.1	1,934	114	5.9
1978	3,878	185	4.8	1,943	96	4.9	1,935	89	4.6
1977	3,970	177	4.5	2,021	96	4.8	1,949	81	4.2
1976	3,914	145	3.7	1,960	79	4.0	1,955	67	3.4
1975	3,983	183	4.6	2,017	87	4.3	1,967	97	4.9
1974	3,901	223	5.7	1,951	122	6.3	1,949	101	5.2
1973	3,899	210	5.4	1,930	112	5.8	1,969	98	5.0
1972	3,868	203	5.2	1,940	106	5.5	1,928	97	5.0
1971	3,762	174	4.6	1,925	95	4.9	1,838	79	4.3
1970	3,686	186	5.0	1,865	90	4.8	1,822	97	5.3
1969	3,485	159	4.6	1,756	84	4.8	1,729	75	4.3
1968	3,615	151	4.2	1,849	75	4.1	1,767	76	4.3
1967	3,370	129	3.8	1,726	64	3.7	1,644	65	4.0
Grade 11									
2011	4,358	84	1.9	2,234	52	2.3	2,124	32	1.5
2010	4,247	84	2.0	2,201	50	2.3	2,046	34	1.7
2009	4,444	106	2.4	2,226	51	2.3	2,218	55	2.5
2008	4,186	96	2.3	2,113	60	2.9	2,073	36	1.7
2007	4,388	118	2.7	2,280	64	2.8	2,108	55	2.6
2006	4,324	112	2.6	2,209	62	2.7	2,053	50	2.4
2005	4,080	72	1.8	2,184	46	2.1	1,896	26	1.4
2004	4,010	141	3.5	2,012	76	3.8	1,998	65	3.3
2003	4,327	117	2.7	2,158	68	3.2	2,169	49	2.3
2002	4,137	99	2.4	2,111	54	2.6	2,026	45	2.2
2001	4,114	139	3.4	2,134	72	3.4	1,979	67	3.4
2000	3,833	170	4.4	1,933	78	4.0	1,901	93	4.9
1999	4,036	150	3.7	2,052	69	3.4	1,984	81	4.0
1998	3,735	110	2.9	1,902	55	2.9	1,833	55	3.0
1997	3,882	142	3.7	1,957	71	3.6	1,925	71	3.7
1996	3,606	138	3.8	1,828	76	4.2	1,778	62	3.5
1995	3,568	159	4.5	1,846	89	4.8	1,724	71	4.1
1994	3,587	132	3.7	1,864	61	3.3	1,722	70	4.1
1993[r]	3,375	106	3.1	1,725	43	2.5	1,650	63	3.8
1993	3,218	100	3.1	1,643	40	2.4	1,575	60	3.8
1992	3,213	120	3.7	1,642	52	3.2	1,570	67	4.3
1991	3,083	101	3.3	1,598	42	2.6	1,484	58	3.9
1990	2,976	98	3.3	1,462	57	3.9	1,514	41	2.7
1989	3,302	125	3.8	1,683	67	4.0	1,618	57	3.5
1988	3,447	161	4.7	1,819	89	4.9	1,627	72	4.4
1987	3,566	122	3.4	1,766	71	4.0	1,800	51	2.8
1986	3,433	116	3.4	1,700	51	3.0	1,733	65	3.8
1985	3,274	139	4.2	1,618	70	4.3	1,656	69	4.2
1984	3,328	163	4.9	1,682	87	5.2	1,646	76	4.6
1983	3,601	162	4.5	1,825	87	4.8	1,775	75	4.2
1982	3,694	218	5.9	1,872	122	6.5	1,822	96	5.3
1981	3,787	262	6.9	1,937	144	7.4	1,850	118	6.4

[1]Civilian noninstitutionalized population.

r = Revised, controlled to 1990 census based population estimates; previous 1993 data controlled to 1980 census based population estimates.

Table A-12 Annual High School Dropout Rates of 15 to 24 Year Olds by Sex, Race, Grade, and Hispanic Origin, October 1967–2011—*Continued*

(Numbers in thousands; percent)

Year, grade, race, and Hispanic origin	Total[1]			Male			Female		
	Total students	Dropouts	Dropout rate	Total students	Dropouts	Dropout rate	Total students	Dropouts	Dropout rate
Grade 11— *(Continued)*									
1980	3,670	225	6.1	1,832	120	6.6	1,839	105	5.7
1979	3,718	229	6.2	1,840	102	5.5	1,879	128	6.8
1978	3,708	230	6.2	1,905	113	5.9	1,803	117	6.5
1977	3,832	244	6.4	1,964	133	6.8	1,867	110	5.9
1976	3,786	227	6.0	1,955	123	6.3	1,831	104	5.7
1975	3,596	230	6.4	1,828	103	5.6	1,767	126	7.1
1974	3,721	237	6.4	1,819	123	6.8	1,902	114	6.0
1973	3,631	237	6.5	1,877	126	6.7	1,754	111	6.3
1972	3,581	241	6.7	1,825	107	5.9	1,756	134	7.6
1971	3,585	185	5.2	1,772	82	4.6	1,811	103	5.7
1970	3,456	198	5.7	1,750	96	5.5	1,706	102	6.0
1969	3,489	190	5.4	1,779	100	5.6	1,710	90	5.3
1968	3,255	179	5.5	1,640	91	5.5	1,614	88	5.5
1967	3,068	169	5.5	1,557	76	4.9	1,511	93	6.2
Grade 12									
2011	3,370	243	7.2	1,767	129	7.3	1,603	114	7.1
2010	3,417	215	6.3	1,798	106	5.9	1,620	110	6.8
2009	3,224	217	6.7	1,578	109	6.9	1,646	108	6.5
2008	3,409	237	7.0	1,781	89	5.0	1,628	149	9.1
2007	3,133	202	6.4	1,572	111	7.0	1,561	91	5.8
2006	3,101	265	8.5	1,608	146	9.1	1,492	119	8.0
2005	2,931	270	9.2	1,415	138	9.7	1,516	132	8.7
2004	3,130	247	7.9	1,516	133	8.8	1,614	114	7.1
2003	2,945	248	8.4	1,435	131	9.1	1,510	117	7.7
2002	2,956	214	7.2	1,432	104	7.3	1,524	110	7.2
2001	2,762	277	10.0	1,411	171	12.1	1,351	106	7.8
2000	2,983	241	8.1	1,447	154	10.6	1,535	87	5.7
1999	3,121	266	8.5	1,571	120	7.6	1,552	146	9.4
1998	3,173	279	8.8	1,613	146	9.0	1,560	133	8.5
1997	3,025	233	7.7	1,479	136	9.2	1,545	97	6.3
1996	2,952	253	8.6	1,441	114	7.9	1,510	139	9.2
1995	2,986	297	9.9	1,492	168	11.3	1,494	129	8.6
1994	2,861	289	10.1	1,391	143	10.3	1,470	146	9.9
1993r	2,790	212	7.6	1,366	116	8.5	1,423	96	6.7
1993	2,664	201	7.5	1,300	109	8.4	1,364	92	6.7
1992	2,529	183	7.2	1,281	86	6.7	1,248	97	7.8
1991	2,397	142	5.9	1,211	79	6.5	1,186	63	5.3
1990	2,488	159	6.4	1,234	77	6.2	1,254	82	6.5
1989	2,601	180	6.9	1,269	80	6.3	1,331	99	7.4
1988	2,835	188	6.6	1,425	104	7.3	1,409	85	6.0
1987	2,744	175	6.4	1,337	99	7.4	1,405	75	5.3
1986	2,841	186	6.5	1,390	106	7.6	1,450	80	5.5
1985	2,939	222	7.6	1,416	115	8.1	1,523	107	7.0
1984	3,298	209	6.3	1,569	105	6.7	1,728	103	6.0
1983	3,262	244	7.5	1,550	137	8.8	1,712	107	6.3
1982	3,377	215	6.4	1,646	114	6.9	1,732	101	5.8
1981	3,346	233	7.0	1,626	113	6.9	1,719	120	7.0
1980	3,404	267	7.8	1,656	147	8.9	1,748	120	6.9
1979	3,498	298	8.5	1,654	164	9.9	1,845	135	7.3
1978	3,530	328	9.3	1,710	206	12.0	1,820	122	6.7
1977	3,498	313	8.9	1,672	163	9.7	1,827	151	8.3
1976	3,296	272	8.3	1,619	158	9.8	1,677	114	6.8
1975	3,454	226	6.5	1,640	106	6.5	1,814	120	6.6
1974	3,404	282	8.3	1,651	157	9.5	1,754	125	7.1
1973	3,321	236	7.1	1,600	132	8.3	1,721	104	6.0
1972	3,215	215	6.7	1,540	104	6.8	1,674	110	6.6
1971	3,104	203	6.5	1,496	120	8.0	1,609	84	5.2
1970	3,139	204	6.5	1,530	102	6.7	1,610	103	6.4
1969	3,238	202	6.2	1,534	89	5.8	1,703	113	6.6
1968	2,944	176	6.0	1,342	81	6.0	1,602	95	5.9
1967	2,912	188	6.5	1,322	97	7.3	1,590	91	5.7

[1]Civilian noninstitutionalized population.
r = Revised, controlled to 1990 census based population estimates; previous 1993 data controlled to 1980 census based population estimates.

Table A-12 Annual High School Dropout Rates of 15 to 24 Year Olds by Sex, Race, Grade, and Hispanic Origin, October 1967–2011—*Continued*

(Numbers in thousands; percent)

Year, grade, race, and Hispanic origin	Total[1]			Male			Female		
	Total students	Dropouts	Dropout rate	Total students	Dropouts	Dropout rate	Total students	Dropouts	Dropout rate
WHITE ALONE									
Grades 10–12									
2011	8,815	261	3.0	4,414	145	3.2	4,140	116	2.7
2010	8,793	221	2.5	4,592	127	2.8	4,201	94	2.2
2009	8,886	269	3.0	4,459	146	3.3	4,427	123	2.8
2008	8,942	246	2.8	4,588	123	2.7	4,353	123	2.8
2007	8,927	246	2.8	4,518	126	2.8	4,409	120	2.7
2006	8,924	311	3.5	4,568	177	3.9	4,355	133	3.1
2005	8,855	271	3.1	4,472	151	3.4	4,382	120	2.7
2004	8,585	359	4.2	4,344	211	4.9	4,241	148	3.5
2003	8,781	321	3.7	4,434	172	3.9	4,347	148	3.4
2002	8,636	259	3.0	4,371	133	3.0	4,265	126	3.0
2001	8,490	388	4.6	4,363	230	5.3	4,126	158	3.8
2000	8,540	371	4.3	4,368	204	4.7	4,172	167	4.0
1999	8,665	380	4.4	4,426	180	4.1	4,238	198	4.7
1998	8,487	371	4.4	4,306	188	4.4	4,181	183	4.4
1997	8,402	355	4.2	4,220	208	4.9	4,180	145	3.5
1996	8,005	361	4.5	4,077	198	4.8	3,928	163	4.1
1995	7,926	402	5.1	4,079	220	5.4	3,849	183	4.8
1994	7,862	371	4.7	4,014	184	4.6	3,848	188	4.9
1993[r]	7,442	306	4.1	3,790	157	4.1	3,654	150	4.1
1993	7,152	290	4.1	3,623	147	4.1	3,530	143	4.1
1992	7,077	292	4.1	3,646	140	3.8	3,430	151	4.4
1991	6,856	254	3.7	3,514	127	3.6	3,343	128	3.8
1990	6,984	266	3.8	3,522	144	4.1	3,462	122	3.5
1989	7,243	286	3.9	3,653	149	4.1	3,589	136	3.8
1988	7,727	362	4.7	4,016	203	5.1	3,712	161	4.3
1987	7,979	299	3.7	4,023	163	4.1	3,953	135	3.4
1986	8,011	333	4.2	4,007	168	4.2	4,007	166	4.1
1985	7,967	384	4.8	3,963	195	4.9	4,003	188	4.7
1984	8,221	410	5.0	4,119	220	5.3	4,101	190	4.6
1983	8,531	410	4.8	4,264	232	5.4	4,264	177	4.2
1982	8,769	444	5.1	4,381	231	5.3	4,390	214	4.9
1981	9,067	478	5.3	4,532	254	5.6	4,536	224	4.9
1980	9,177	517	5.6	4,624	294	6.4	4,554	224	4.9
1979	9,437	588	6.2	4,694	311	6.6	4,742	277	5.8
1978	9,360	574	6.1	4,747	329	6.9	4,611	244	5.3
1977	9,536	594	6.2	4,766	327	6.9	4,770	267	5.6
1976	9,362	532	5.7	4,708	297	6.3	4,654	235	5.0
1975	9,440	507	5.4	4,709	234	5.0	4,732	274	5.8
1974	9,403	566	6.0	4,650	326	7.0	4,754	241	5.1
1973	9,359	537	5.7	4,708	288	6.1	4,649	248	5.3
1972	9,173	520	5.7	4,588	247	5.4	4,583	272	5.9
1971	9,140	470	5.1	4,577	244	5.3	4,562	226	5.0
1970	8,959	449	5.0	4,496	212	4.7	4,462	237	5.3
1969	8,878	429	4.8	4,438	208	4.7	4,439	221	5.0
1968	8,580	387	4.5	4,246	190	4.5	4,331	196	4.5
1967	8,186	379	4.6	4,060	189	4.7	4,126	190	4.6
WHITE ALONE NON-HISPANIC									
Grades 10–12									
2011	6,647	171	2.6	3,315	89	2.6	3,161	82	2.5
2010	6,851	150	2.2	3,568	97	2.7	3,284	53	1.6
2009	6,944	160	2.3	3,491	91	2.6	3,453	68	2.0
2008	7,079	156	2.2	3,638	83	2.3	3,441	73	2.1
2007	7,274	155	2.1	3,684	82	2.2	3,590	73	2.0
2006	7,171	200	2.8	3,693	120	3.2	3,478	80	2.3
2005	7,227	196	2.7	3,652	103	2.8	3,575	93	2.6
2004	7,015	245	3.5	3,582	130	3.6	3,434	115	3.4
2003[2]	7,139	214	3.0	3,665	116	3.2	3,474	98	2.8
2002	7,124	173	2.4	3,620	84	2.3	3,504	89	2.6
2001	7,070	272	3.8	3,647	173	4.7	3,423	98	2.9

[1]Civilian noninstitutionalized population.
[2]Starting in 2003 respondents could identify more than one race. Except as noted, the race data in this table from 2003 onward represent those respondents who indicated only one race category.
r = Revised, controlled to 1990 census based population estimates; previous 1993 data controlled to 1980 census based population estimates.

Table A-12 Annual High School Dropout Rates of 15 to 24 Year Olds by Sex, Race, Grade, and Hispanic Origin, October 1967–2011—*Continued*

(Numbers in thousands; percent)

Year, grade, race, and Hispanic origin	Total[1]			Male			Female		
	Total students	Dropouts	Dropout rate	Total students	Dropouts	Dropout rate	Total students	Dropouts	Dropout rate
Grades 10–12— *(Continued)*									
2000	7,159	276	3.9	3,648	150	4.1	3,511	126	3.6
1999	7,265	274	3.8	3,744	130	3.5	3,523	145	4.1
1998	7,174	266	3.7	3,605	130	3.6	3,570	137	3.8
1997	7,090	242	3.4	3,533	140	4.0	3,558	103	2.9
1996	6,850	267	3.9	3,511	145	4.1	3,337	121	3.6
1995	6,905	296	4.3	3,564	164	4.6	3,341	131	3.9
1994	6,839	274	4.0	3,496	137	3.9	3,343	137	4.1
1993	6,277	237	3.8	3,229	128	4.0	3,047	108	3.5
BLACK									
Grades 10–12									
2011	1,944	78	4.0	911	54	5.6	954	24	2.4
2010	1,898	62	3.2	946	36	3.8	952	26	2.7
2009	1,797	81	4.5	870	38	4.4	927	42	4.6
2008	1,868	114	6.1	925	42	4.6	943	72	7.6
2007	1,781	76	4.3	914	45	4.9	867	31	3.6
2006	1,767	65	3.7	902	29	3.2	864	37	4.3
2005	1,763	122	6.9	943	71	7.5	820	51	6.2
2004	1,716	90	5.2	833	40	4.8	883	50	5.7
2003[2]	1,698	76	4.5	812	33	4.1	886	43	4.9
2002	1,664	73	4.4	782	40	5.1	882	33	3.8
2001	1,655	95	5.7	828	51	6.2	827	45	5.4
2000	1,706	96	5.6	819	62	7.6	888	34	3.8
1999	1,794	107	6.0	925	48	5.2	870	59	6.8
1998	1,759	88	5.0	918	42	4.6	841	46	5.5
1997	1,678	80	4.8	813	33	4.1	866	49	5.7
1996	1,704	107	6.3	803	37	4.6	901	70	7.8
1995	1,598	97	6.1	797	63	7.9	802	35	4.4
1994	1,559	96	6.1	763	50	6.5	795	45	5.7
1993r	1,499	80	5.3	740	43	5.8	758	37	4.9
1993	1,447	78	5.4	724	41	5.7	722	36	5.0
1992	1,422	70	4.9	702	23	3.3	720	48	6.7
1991	1,366	85	6.2	685	38	5.5	683	48	7.0
1990	1,303	66	5.1	636	26	4.1	666	40	6.0
1989	1,384	106	7.7	684	47	6.9	701	60	8.6
1988	1,468	93	6.3	751	50	6.7	717	43	6.0
1987	1,463	93	6.4	730	45	6.2	732	47	6.4
1986	1,449	68	4.7	711	34	4.8	737	34	4.6
1985	1,422	110	7.7	703	58	8.3	719	52	7.2
1984	1,524	88	5.8	711	44	6.2	813	43	5.3
1983	1,498	103	6.9	687	48	7.0	810	55	6.8
1982	1,553	121	7.8	786	71	9.0	767	50	6.5
1981	1,516	146	9.6	704	66	9.4	815	83	10.2
1980	1,496	124	8.3	714	57	8.0	781	66	8.5
1979	1,479	142	9.6	679	51	7.5	802	92	11.5
1978	1,542	160	10.4	706	78	11.0	835	81	9.7
1977	1,588	133	8.4	746	62	8.3	789	71	9.0
1976	1,449	105	7.2	729	62	8.5	721	45	6.2
1975	1,416	123	8.7	673	56	8.3	743	67	9.0
1974	1,441	167	11.6	679	73	10.8	761	93	12.2
1973	1,372	138	10.1	650	78	12.0	725	61	8.4
1972	1,373	133	9.7	644	65	10.1	756	68	9.0
1971	1,195	87	7.3	552	51	9.2	643	37	5.8
1970	1,192	133	11.2	587	74	12.6	606	60	9.9
1969	1,209	113	9.3	562	58	10.3	646	55	8.5
1968	1,123	113	10.1	523	52	9.9	600	61	10.2
1967	1,066	106	9.9	485	47	9.7	578	58	10.0

[1]Civilian noninstitutionalized population.
[2]Starting in 2003 respondents could identify more than one race. Except as noted, the race data in this table from 2003 onward represent those respondents who indicated only one race category.
r = Revised, controlled to 1990 census based population estimates; previous 1993 data controlled to 1980 census based population estimates.

Table A-12 Annual High School Dropout Rates of 15 to 24 Year Olds by Sex, Race, Grade, and Hispanic Origin, October 1967–2011—*Continued*

(Numbers in thousands; percent)

Year, grade, race, and Hispanic origin	Total[1]			Male			Female		
	Total students	Dropouts	Dropout rate	Total students	Dropouts	Dropout rate	Total students	Dropouts	Dropout rate
ASIAN[3]									
Grades 10–12									
2011	495	17	3.5	268	4	1.5	209	13	6.0
2010	419	12	2.8	220	6	2.9	199	5	2.6
2009	426	7	1.7	215	2	0.8	210	5	2.6
2008	429	17	3.9	219	*	0.2	210	16	7.8
2007	404	30	7.5	202	13	6.6	202	17	8.3
2006	445	19	4.2	237	11	4.5	208	8	3.7
2005	425	6	1.5	219	5	2.4	206	1	0.5
2004	452	4	0.9	233	*	*	219	4	1.9
2003[2]	457	11	2.4	237	3	1.4	221	7	3.4
2002	515	12	2.3	266	8	3.0	249	4	1.6
2001	470	10	2.1	274	9	3.3	197	1	0.5
2000	399	13	3.3	178	12	6.7	221	1	0.5
1999	523	25	4.8	269	13	4.8	253	12	4.7
HISPANIC[4]									
Grades 10–12									
2011	2,376	100	4.2	1,204	56	4.4	1,072	44	4.0
2010	2,130	80	3.8	1,113	30	2.7	1,018	51	5.0
2009	2,129	114	5.3	1,039	55	5.3	1,090	59	5.4
2008	2,062	101	4.9	1,052	44	4.2	1,011	57	5.6
2007	1,785	99	5.5	904	49	5.5	882	49	5.6
2006	1,923	124	6.4	958	61	6.3	965	63	6.6
2005	1,814	86	4.7	910	51	5.6	904	35	3.9
2004	1,723	138	8.0	842	97	11.5	881	40	4.6
2003	1,792	116	6.5	846	65	7.7	945	51	5.4
2002	1,614	86	5.3	801	50	6.2	814	36	4.4
2001	1,487	121	8.1	755	57	7.5	732	64	8.7
2000	1,465	100	6.8	761	54	7.1	704	46	6.5
1999	1,482	105	7.1	729	50	6.9	751	55	7.3
1998	1,368	115	8.4	731	63	8.6	637	52	8.2
1997	1,377	119	8.6	710	74	10.4	668	45	6.7
1996	1,195	100	8.4	588	54	9.2	608	46	7.6
1995	1,251	145	11.6	644	70	10.9	608	76	12.5
1994	1,179	109	9.2	607	51	8.4	572	58	10.1
1993[r]	1,061	69	6.5	488	25	5.1	573	44	7.5
1993	943	60	6.4	436	21	4.8	508	39	7.7
1992	917	72	7.9	468	27	5.8	441	38	8.6
1991	809	59	7.3	396	41	10.4	417	20	4.8
1990	811	65	8.0	379	33	8.7	428	31	7.2
1989	762	59	7.7	394	30	7.6	366	28	7.7
1988	730	77	10.5	398	49	12.3	333	28	8.4
1987	769	43	5.6	380	19	5.0	389	24	6.2
1986	764	91	11.9	376	44	11.7	388	48	12.4
1985	729	71	9.7	333	31	9.3	396	39	9.8
1984	706	77	10.9	311	38	12.2	396	40	10.1
1983	691	68	9.8	351	48	13.7	340	21	6.2
1982	692	65	9.4	370	35	9.5	321	29	9.0
1981	717	77	10.7	350	37	10.6	367	40	10.9
1980	646	74	11.5	295	50	16.9	350	24	6.9
1979	593	58	9.8	295	30	10.2	298	27	9.1
1978	567	70	12.3	295	46	15.6	271	23	8.5
1977	627	50	8.0	341	35	10.3	287	15	5.2
1976	638	46	7.2	300	22	7.3	336	23	6.8
1975	614	67	10.9	317	32	10.1	294	34	11.6
1974	547	53	9.7	271	34	12.5	278	20	7.2
1973	499	50	10.0	240	19	7.9	259	31	12.0
1972	498	55	11.0	253	28	11.1	247	27	10.9

[1]Civilian noninstitutionalized population.
[2]Starting in 2003 respondents could identify more than one race. Except as noted, the race data in this table from 2003 onward represent those respondents who indicated only one race category.
[3]The data shown prior to 2003 consists of those identifying themselves as "Asian or Pacific Islanders."
[4]May be of any race.
r = Revised, controlled to 1990 census based population estimates; previous 1993 data controlled to 1980 census based population estimates.
* = Quantity zero or rounds to zero.

Table A-12 Annual High School Dropout Rates of 15 to 24 Year Olds by Sex, Race, Grade, and Hispanic Origin, October 1967–2011—*Continued*

(Numbers in thousands; percent)

Year, grade, race, and Hispanic origin	Total[1]			Male			Female		
	Total students	Dropouts	Dropout rate	Total students	Dropouts	Dropout rate	Total students	Dropouts	Dropout rate
WHITE ALONE OR IN COMBINATION									
Grades 10–12									
2011	9,087	272	3.0	4,551	145	3.1	4,264	127	2.9
2010	9,112	242	2.7	4,764	130	2.7	4,348	112	2.6
2009	9,216	280	3.0	4,610	148	3.2	4,606	132	2.9
2008	9,277	257	2.8	4,766	129	2.7	4,511	128	2.8
2007	9,199	251	2.7	4,664	131	2.8	4,535	120	2.7
2006	9,212	320	3.5	4,695	185	3.9	4,517	136	3.0
2005	9,158	281	3.1	4,610	155	3.4	4,548	126	2.8
2004	8,821	382	4.3	4,464	222	5.0	4,357	160	3.7
2003	9,045	335	3.7	4,573	183	4.0	4,471	151	3.4
BLACK ALONE OR IN COMBINATION									
Grades 10–12									
2011	2,051	82	4.0	970	54	5.3	999	28	2.8
2010	2,038	76	3.7	1,021	38	3.7	1,017	39	3.8
2009	1,985	86	4.3	958	40	4.2	1,026	46	4.5
2008	2,033	121	5.9	1,012	46	4.5	1,021	75	7.3
2007	1,900	78	4.1	977	47	4.8	923	31	3.4
2006	1,891	66	3.5	952	29	3.0	939	38	4.0
2005	1,870	129	6.9	979	71	7.3	890	58	6.5
2004	1,797	99	5.5	869	40	4.6	928	59	6.3
2003	1,808	79	4.4	853	36	4.2	955	43	4.5
ASIAN ALONE OR IN COMBINATION									
Grades 10–12									
2011	579	17	3.0	300	4	1.3	262	13	4.9
2010	520	16	3.2	270	6	2.4	250	10	4.0
2009	525	8	1.4	255	2	0.8	270	5	2.0
2008	511	17	3.3	256	*	0.2	255	16	6.4
2007	483	30	6.2	233	13	5.8	250	17	6.7
2006	542	23	4.2	279	15	5.4	263	8	3.0
2005	525	8	1.5	270	6	2.3	255	2	0.6
2004	516	8	1.6	273	3	1.2	243	5	2.1
2003	533	17	3.1	278	8	3.0	254	8	3.3

[1]Civilian noninstitutionalized population.

* = Quantity zero or rounds to zero.

Table A-13. Population 14 to 24 Years Old, by High School Graduate Status, College Enrollment, Attainment, Sex, Race, and Hispanic Origin, October 1967–2011

(Numbers in thousands; percent)

Year, race, and Hispanic origin	Population 18 to 24 years old[1]								High school graduates, 14 to 24 years old		
	Total	High school graduates		Percent			High school dropouts		All graduates	Percent	
		Total	Enrolled in college	High school graduates	Enrolled in college	High school graduate enrolled in college	Number	Percent		Enrolled in college	Enrolled or completed some college
ALL RACES											
Both Sexes											
2011	29,943	25,435	12,570	84.9	42.0	49.4	2,481	8.3	25,765	49.6	73.1
2010	29,659	25,224	12,213	85.0	41.2	48.4	2,590	8.7	25,564	48.7	72.6
2009	29,223	24,647	12,073	84.3	41.3	49.0	2,733	9.4	25,015	49.1	72.0
2008	28,950	24,568	11,466	84.9	39.6	46.7	2,702	9.3	24,922	47.0	70.6
2007	28,778	24,146	11,161	83.9	38.8	46.2	2,937	10.2	24,491	46.3	69.7
2006	28,372	23,430	10,586	82.6	37.3	45.2	3,128	11.0	23,800	45.4	69.3
2005	27,855	23,103	10,834	82.9	38.9	49.3	3,154	11.3	23,445	47.0	69.8
2004	27,948	23,086	10,611	82.6	38.0	46.0	3,836	12.1	23,379	46.2	69.0
2003	27,404	22,603	10,364	82.5	37.8	45.9	3,228	11.8	22,898	45.9	68.8
2002	27,367	22,319	10,033	81.6	36.7	45.0	3,375	12.3	22,639	45.2	67.6
2001	26,965	21,836	9,629	81.0	35.7	44.1	3,519	13.0	22,136	44.1	66.7
2000	26,658	21,822	9,452	81.9	35.5	43.3	3,315	12.4	22,080	43.5	66.7
1999	26,041	21,127	9,259	81.1	35.6	43.8	3,413	13.1	21,390	44.0	67.2
1998	25,507	20,567	9,322	80.6	36.6	45.3	3,544	13.9	20,775	45.5	68.0
1997	24,973	20,338	9,204	81.4	36.9	45.2	3,236	13.0	20,577	45.6	67.3
1996	24,671	20,131	8,767	81.6	35.5	43.5	3,147	12.8	20,465	44.0	67.2
1995	24,900	20,125	8,539	80.8	34.3	42.4	3,471	13.9	20,359	42.7	67.1
1994	25,254	20,581	8,729	81.5	34.6	42.4	3,365	13.3	20,779	42.7	66.9
1993[r]	25,522	20,844	8,630	81.7	33.8	41.4	3,349	13.1	21,060	41.6	65.3
1993	24,100	19,772	8,193	82.0	34.0	41.4	3,070	12.7	19,979	41.6	65.4
1992	24,278	19,921	8,343	82.1	34.4	41.9	3,083	12.7	20,194	42.3	65.6
1991	24,572	19,883	8,172	80.9	33.3	41.1	3,486	14.2	20,065	41.4	60.7
1990	24,852	20,311	7,964	82.3	32.0	39.1	3,379	13.6	20,571	39.6	58.9
1989	25,261	20,461	7,804	81.0	30.9	38.1	3,644	14.4	20,749	38.5	57.9
1988	25,733	20,900	7,791	81.2	30.3	37.3	3,749	14.6	21,204	37.6	57.4
1987	25,950	21,118	7,693	81.4	29.6	36.4	3,751	14.5	21,477	36.9	56.2
1986	26,512	21,768	7,477	82.1	28.2	34.3	3,687	13.9	22,086	34.8	55.0
1985	27,122	22,349	7,537	82.4	27.8	33.7	3,687	13.9	22,722	34.3	54.3
1984	28,031	22,870	7,591	81.6	27.1	33.2	4,142	14.8	23,252	33.7	53.0
1983	28,580	22,988	7,477	80.4	26.2	32.5	4,410	15.4	23,359	33.1	52.8
1982	28,846	23,291	7,678	80.7	26.6	33.0	4,500	15.6	23,708	33.5	52.7
1981	28,965	23,343	7,575	80.6	26.2	32.5	4,520	15.6	23,705	32.9	51.7
1980	28,957	23,413	7,400	80.9	25.6	31.6	4,515	15.6	23,856	32.1	51.1
1979	27,974	22,421	6,991	80.1	25.0	31.2	4,560	16.3	22,911	31.9	51.6
1978	27,647	22,309	6,995	80.7	25.3	31.4	4,388	15.9	22,759	31.9	51.4
1977	27,331	22,008	7,142	80.5	26.1	32.5	4,313	15.8	22,499	33.0	52.0
1976	26,919	21,677	7,181	80.5	26.7	33.1	4,276	15.9	22,158	33.7	53.4
1975	26,387	21,326	6,935	80.8	26.3	32.5	4,110	15.6	21,824	33.1	52.5
1974	25,670	20,725	6,316	80.7	24.6	30.5	4,070	15.9	21,267	31.2	51.3
1973	25,237	20,377	6,055	80.7	24.0	29.7	3,973	15.7	20,895	30.4	50.7
1972	24,579	19,618	6,257	79.8	25.5	31.9	4,068	16.6	20,107	32.6	52.9
1971	23,668	18,691	6,210	79.0	26.2	33.2	4,025	17.0	19,130	33.9	53.1
1970	22,552	17,768	5,805	78.8	25.7	32.7	3,908	17.3	18,218	33.5	52.3
1969	21,362	16,703	5,840	78.2	27.3	35.0	3,769	17.6	17,152	35.7	52.5
1968	20,562	15,683	5,356	76.3	26.0	34.2	3,929	19.1	16,165	35.2	51.5
1967	20,009	15,114	5,100	75.5	25.5	33.7	3,967	19.8	15,642	34.9	50.5
Male											
2011	15,211	12,659	5,953	83.2	39.1	47.0	1,374	9.0	12,834	47.2	69.0
2010	14,887	12,371	5,698	83.1	38.3	46.1	1,473	9.9	12,540	46.2	68.4
2009	14,677	12,111	5,640	82.5	38.4	46.6	1,568	10.7	12,277	46.7	68.5
2008	14,559	12,181	5,383	83.7	37.0	44.2	1,445	9.9	12,374	44.6	66.7
2007	14,515	11,825	5,156	81.5	35.5	43.6	1,680	11.6	11,972	43.7	66.0
2006	14,300	11,508	4,874	80.5	34.1	42.4	1,741	12.2	11,659	42.5	65.1
2005	14,077	11,182	4,973	79.4	35.3	43.2	1,852	13.2	11,330	44.4	65.9
2004	14,018	11,258	4,865	80.3	34.7	43.2	1,942	13.9	11,364	43.5	65.0
2003	13,681	10,919	4,697	79.8	34.3	43.0	1,875	13.7	11,040	43.1	65.0

Note: The change in the educational attainment question and the college completion categories from "4 or more years of college" to "at least some college" in 1992 caused an increase in the proportion of 14-to-24-year-old high school graduates enrolled in college or completed some college, of approximately 5 percentage points. High school graduates are people who have completed 4 years of high school or more, for 1967 to 1991. Beginning in 1992, they were people whose highest degree was a high school diploma (including equivalency) or higher.

[1]Civilian noninstitutionalized population.

r = Revised, controlled to 1990 census based population estimates; previous 1993 data controlled to 1980 census based population estimates.

Table A-13. Population 14 to 24 Years Old, by High School Graduate Status, College Enrollment, Attainment, Sex, Race, and Hispanic Origin, October 1967–2011—*Continued*

(Numbers in thousands; percent)

Year, race, and Hispanic origin	Population 18 to 24 years old[1]								High school graduates, 14 to 24 years old		
	Total	High school graduates		Percent			High school dropouts		All graduates	Percent	
		Total	Enrolled in college	High school graduates	Enrolled in college	High school graduate enrolled in college	Number	Percent		Enrolled in college	Enrolled or completed some college
Male— *(Continued)*											
2002	13,744	10,823	4,629	78.7	33.7	42.8	1,925	14.0	10,975	42.9	64.6
2001	13,434	10,461	4,437	77.9	33.0	42.4	2,028	15.1	10,587	42.4	63.9
2000	13,338	10,622	4,343	79.6	32.6	40.9	1,837	13.8	10,736	41.0	63.1
1999	12,905	10,201	4,396	79.1	34.0	43.1	1,818	14.9	10,331	43.3	64.5
1998	12,764	9,915	4,403	77.7	34.5	44.4	2,018	15.8	10,006	44.5	64.9
1997	12,513	9,933	4,374	79.4	35.0	44.0	1,765	14.1	10,025	44.2	64.9
1996	12,285	9,815	4,187	80.0	34.1	42.6	1,628	13.2	9,960	43.0	65.6
1995	12,351	9,789	4,089	79.3	33.1	41.8	1,791	14.5	9,884	42.1	64.2
1994	12,557	9,970	4,152	79.4	33.1	41.6	1,804	14.4	10,051	41.9	64.9
1993[r]	12,712	10,142	4,237	79.8	33.3	41.8	1,745	13.7	10,229	42.0	63.9
1993	11,898	9,541	3,994	80.2	33.6	41.9	1,575	13.2	9,625	42.0	64.1
1992	11,965	9,576	3,912	80.0	32.7	40.9	1,617	13.5	9,706	41.3	64.1
1991	12,036	9,493	3,954	78.9	32.9	41.7	1,810	15.0	9,564	41.9	59.2
1990	12,134	9,778	3,922	80.6	32.3	40.1	1,689	13.9	9,894	40.5	58.0
1989	12,325	9,700	3,717	78.7	30.2	38.3	1,941	15.7	9,810	38.6	57.2
1988	12,491	9,832	3,770	78.7	30.2	38.3	1,950	15.6	9,947	38.5	56.5
1987	12,626	10,030	3,867	79.4	30.6	38.6	1,948	15.4	10,207	39.0	56.0
1986	12,921	10,338	3,702	80.0	28.7	35.8	1,924	14.9	10,465	36.2	54.4
1985	13,199	10,614	3,749	80.4	28.4	35.3	2,015	15.3	10,784	36.0	54.6
1984	13,744	10,914	3,929	79.4	28.6	36.0	2,184	15.9	11,052	36.4	53.6
1983	14,003	10,906	3,820	77.9	27.3	35.0	2,379	17.0	10,959	35.5	52.7
1982	14,083	11,120	3,837	79.0	27.2	34.5	2,329	16.5	11,295	35.0	53.0
1981	14,127	11,052	3,833	78.2	27.1	34.7	2,424	17.2	11,203	35.1	52.1
1980	14,107	11,125	3,717	78.9	26.3	33.4	2,390	16.9	11,309	33.7	51.4
1979	13,571	10,657	3,508	78.5	25.8	32.9	2,320	17.1	10,838	33.6	52.4
1978	13,385	10,614	3,621	79.3	27.1	34.1	2,200	16.4	10,789	34.5	52.6
1977	13,218	10,440	3,712	79.0	28.1	35.6	2,170	16.4	10,626	36.0	54.2
1976	13,012	10,312	3,673	79.2	28.2	35.6	2,109	16.2	10,492	36.0	55.7
1975	12,724	10,214	3,693	80.3	29.0	36.2	1,928	15.2	10,415	36.7	56.1
1974	12,315	9,835	3,411	79.9	27.7	34.7	1,958	15.9	10,073	35.3	55.6
1973	12,111	9,716	3,360	80.2	27.7	34.6	1,853	15.3	9,908	35.1	55.4
1972	11,712	9,247	3,534	79.0	30.2	38.2	1,898	16.2	9,461	38.8	59.0
1971	11,092	8,669	3,599	78.2	32.4	41.5	1,865	16.8	8,855	42.1	60.1
1970	10,385	8,087	3,331	77.9	32.1	41.2	1,746	16.8	8,279	41.8	59.2
1969	9,649	7,445	3,392	77.2	35.2	45.6	1,640	17.0	7,609	46.2	61.2
1968	9,251	6,864	3,152	74.2	34.1	45.9	1,777	19.2	8,038	46.7	61.1
1967	8,999	6,678	2,982	74.2	33.1	44.7	1,804	20.0	6,829	45.1	58.8
Female											
2011	14,732	12,776	6,617	86.7	44.9	51.8	1,107	7.5	12,930	51.9	77.2
2010	14,772	12,854	6,515	87.0	44.1	50.7	1,116	7.6	13,024	51.1	76.7
2009	14,546	12,536	6,432	86.2	44.2	51.3	1,165	8.0	12,738	51.4	75.5
2008	14,391	12,387	6,083	86.1	42.3	49.1	1,257	8.7	12,548	49.3	74.5
2007	14,263	12,321	6,005	86.4	42.1	48.7	1,256	8.8	12,519	48.8	73.3
2006	14,073	11,922	5,712	84.7	40.6	47.9	1,387	9.9	12,141	48.1	73.3
2005	13,778	11,921	5,861	86.5	42.5	55.8	1,302	9.5	12,115	49.4	73.4
2004	13,930	11,828	5,746	84.9	41.2	48.6	1,444	10.4	12,015	48.8	72.8
2003	13,724	11,684	5,667	85.1	41.3	48.5	1,354	9.9	11,858	48.5	72.2
2002	13,623	11,496	5,404	84.4	39.7	47.0	1,450	10.6	11,664	47.3	70.3
2001	13,531	11,375	5,192	84.1	38.4	45.7	1,491	11.0	11,549	45.7	69.4
2000	13,319	11,200	5,109	84.1	38.4	45.6	1,478	11.1	11,344	45.8	70.1
1999	13,136	10,926	4,863	83.2	37.0	44.5	1,594	12.1	11,058	44.6	69.8
1998	12,743	10,651	4,919	83.6	38.6	46.2	1,526	12.0	10,768	46.4	70.7
1997	12,460	10,403	4,829	83.5	38.8	46.4	1,471	11.8	10,549	46.8	69.6
1996	12,386	10,317	4,582	83.3	37.0	44.4	1,519	12.3	10,507	44.9	68.6
1995	12,548	10,338	4,452	82.4	35.5	43.1	1,679	13.4	10,477	43.4	69.8
1994	12,696	10,611	4,576	83.6	36.0	43.1	1,561	12.3	10,729	43.4	68.7
1993[r]	12,810	10,702	4,393	83.5	34.3	41.0	1,604	12.5	10,831	41.3	66.6

Note: The change in the educational attainment question and the college completion categories from "4 or more years of college" to "at least some college" in 1992 caused an increase in the proportion of 14-to-24-year-old high school graduates enrolled in college or completed some college, of approximately 5 percentage points. High school graduates are people who have completed 4 years of high school or more, for 1967 to 1991. Beginning in 1992, they were people whose highest degree was a high school diploma (including equivalency) or higher.

[1]Civilian noninstitutionalized population.

r = Revised, controlled to 1990 census based population estimates; previous 1993 data controlled to 1980 census based population estimates.

Table A-13. Population 14 to 24 Years Old, by High School Graduate Status, College Enrollment, Attainment, Sex, Race, and Hispanic Origin, October 1967–2011—*Continued*

(Numbers in thousands; percent)

Year, race, and Hispanic origin	Population 18 to 24 years old[1]								High school graduates, 14 to 24 years old		
	Total	High school graduates		Percent			High school dropouts		All graduates	Percent	
		Total	Enrolled in college	High school graduates	Enrolled in college	High school graduate enrolled in college	Number	Percent		Enrolled in college	Enrolled or completed some college
Female— *(Continued)*											
1993	12,202	10,232	4,199	83.9	34.4	41.0	1,494	12.2	10,355	41.2	66.7
1992	12,313	10,344	4,429	84.0	36.0	42.8	1,466	11.9	10,486	43.3	66.9
1991	12,536	10,391	4,218	82.9	33.6	40.6	1,676	13.4	10,502	41.0	62.1
1990	12,718	10,533	4,042	82.8	31.8	38.4	1,690	13.3	10,676	38.7	59.8
1989	12,936	10,758	4,085	83.2	31.6	38.0	1,702	13.2	10,936	38.4	58.6
1988	13,242	11,068	4,021	83.6	30.4	36.3	1,799	13.5	11,257	36.8	58.2
1987	13,324	11,086	3,826	83.2	28.7	34.5	1,803	13.5	11,268	35.0	56.4
1986	13,591	11,430	3,775	84.1	27.8	33.0	1,751	12.9	11,623	33.5	55.5
1985	13,923	11,736	3,788	84.3	27.2	32.3	1,804	13.0	11,937	32.8	54.0
1984	14,287	11,956	3,662	83.7	25.6	30.6	1,958	13.7	12,199	31.3	52.4
1983	14,577	12,082	3,657	82.9	25.1	30.3	2,031	13.9	12,294	31.0	52.8
1982	14,763	12,171	3,841	82.4	26.0	31.6	2,171	14.7	12,411	32.1	52.4
1981	14,838	12,290	3,741	82.8	25.2	30.4	2,097	14.1	12,503	31.0	51.3
1980	14,851	12,287	3,682	82.7	24.8	30.0	2,124	14.3	12,547	30.6	50.8
1979	14,403	11,763	3,482	81.7	24.2	29.6	2,240	15.6	12,074	30.4	50.8
1978	14,262	11,694	3,373	82.0	23.7	28.8	2,188	15.3	11,969	29.6	50.3
1977	14,113	11,569	3,431	82.0	24.3	29.7	2,143	15.2	11,875	30.3	50.0
1976	13,907	11,365	3,508	81.7	25.2	30.9	2,168	15.6	11,666	31.6	51.4
1975	13,663	11,113	3,243	81.3	23.7	29.2	2,181	16.0	11,407	29.9	49.2
1974	13,355	10,889	2,905	81.5	21.8	26.7	2,112	15.8	11,194	27.4	47.5
1973	13,126	10,663	2,696	81.2	20.5	25.3	2,119	16.1	10,986	26.1	46.5
1972	12,867	10,371	2,724	80.6	21.2	26.3	2,170	16.9	10,644	27.0	47.4
1971	12,576	10,020	2,610	79.7	20.8	26.0	2,159	17.2	10,272	26.9	47.1
1970	12,167	9,680	2,474	79.6	20.3	25.6	2,163	17.8	9,908	26.3	46.6
1969	11,713	9,259	2,448	79.0	20.9	26.4	2,128	18.2	9,499	27.1	45.7
1968	11,311	8,820	2,205	78.0	19.5	25.0	2,150	19.0	9,072	25.9	44.4
1967	11,011	8,436	2,117	76.6	19.2	25.1	2,162	19.6	8,694	26.0	44.7
WHITE ALONE											
Both Sexes											
2011	23,089	19,760	9,813	85.6	42.5	49.7	1,885	8.2	20,007	49.8	74.0
2010	22,851	19,517	9,325	85.4	40.8	47.8	1,941	8.5	19,741	48.0	73.0
2009	22,606	19,241	9,327	85.1	41.3	48.5	2,059	9.1	19,512	48.6	72.1
2008	22,530	19,334	9,141	85.8	40.6	47.3	1,991	8.8	19,586	47.5	71.6
2007	22,392	18,913	8,780	84.5	39.2	46.4	2,248	10.0	19,170	46.5	70.3
2006	22,169	18,489	8,298	83.4	37.4	44.9	2,399	10.8	18,751	45.1	69.9
2005	21,777	18,130	8,498	83.3	39.0	50.4	2,466	11.3	18,352	46.9	70.0
2004	21,896	18,213	8,351	82.6	38.0	45.9	2,599	11.9	18,414	46.1	69.1
2003[2]	21,502	17,901	8,150	83.3	37.9	45.5	2,489	11.6	18,123	45.5	69.1
2002	21,704	17,793	7,921	82.0	36.5	44.5	2,641	12.2	17,995	44.6	67.5
2001	21,372	17,348	7,548	81.2	35.3	43.5	2,865	13.4	17,547	43.5	67.0
2000	21,257	17,512	7,566	82.4	35.6	43.2	2,598	12.2	17,714	43.4	66.9
1999	20,866	17,052	7,447	81.7	35.7	43.7	2,680	12.8	17,220	43.8	67.5
1998	20,465	16,701	7,541	81.6	36.9	45.2	2,810	13.7	16,855	45.3	68.3
1997	20,020	16,557	7,495	82.7	37.4	45.3	2,476	12.4	16,733	45.6	67.7
1996	19,676	16,199	7,123	82.3	36.2	44.0	2,458	12.5	16,436	44.3	68.4
1995	19,866	16,269	7,011	81.9	35.3	43.1	2,711	13.6	16,439	43.4	68.3
1994	20,171	16,670	7,118	82.6	35.3	42.7	2,553	12.7	16,814	42.9	67.6
1993[r]	20,493	16,989	7,074	82.9	34.5	41.6	2,595	12.7	17,161	41.8	66.5
1993	19,430	16,196	6,763	83.4	34.8	41.8	2,369	12.2	16,361	41.9	66.7
1992	19,671	16,379	6,916	83.3	35.2	42.2	2,398	12.2	16,586	42.7	67.0
1991	19,980	16,324	6,813	81.7	34.1	41.7	2,845	14.2	16,467	42.0	62.3
1990	20,393	16,823	6,635	82.5	32.5	39.4	2,751	13.5	17,022	39.8	60.1
1989	20,825	17,089	6,631	82.1	31.8	38.8	2,926	14.1	17,329	39.1	58.9
1988	21,261	17,491	6,659	82.3	31.3	38.1	3,012	14.2	17,720	38.4	58.5
1987	21,493	17,689	6,483	82.3	30.2	36.6	3,042	14.2	17,982	37.1	56.8

Note: The change in the educational attainment question and the college completion categories from "4 or more years of college" to "at least some college" in 1992 caused an increase in the proportion of 14-to-24-year-old high school graduates enrolled in college or completed some college, of approximately 5 percentage points. High school graduates are people who have completed 4 years of high school or more, for 1967 to 1991. Beginning in 1992, they were people whose highest degree was a high school diploma (including equivalency) or higher.

[1]Civilian noninstitutionalized population.

[2]Starting in 2003 respondents could identify more than one race. Except as noted, the race data in this table from 2003 onward represent those respondents who indicated only one race category.

r = Revised, controlled to 1990 census based population estimates; previous 1993 data controlled to 1980 census based population estimates.

Table A-13. Population 14 to 24 Years Old, by High School Graduate Status, College Enrollment, Attainment, Sex, Race, and Hispanic Origin, October 1967–2011—*Continued*

(Numbers in thousands; percent)

Year, race, and Hispanic origin	Population 18 to 24 years old[1]								High school graduates, 14 to 24 years old		
	Total	High school graduates		Percent			High school dropouts		All graduates	Percent	
		Total	Enrolled in college	High school graduates	Enrolled in college	High school graduate enrolled in college	Number	Percent		Enrolled in college	Enrolled or completed some college
Both Sexes— *(Continued)*											
1986	22,020	18,291	6,307	83.1	28.6	34.5	2,961	13.4	18,554	34.9	55.5
1985	22,632	18,916	6,500	83.6	28.7	34.4	3,050	13.5	19,229	35.0	55.3
1984	23,347	19,373	6,256	83.0	28.0	33.7	3,281	14.1	19,686	34.2	53.8
1983	23,899	19,643	6,463	82.2	27.0	32.9	3,428	14.3	19,948	33.5	53.4
1982	24,206	19,944	6,694	82.4	27.2	33.1	3,523	14.6	20,292	33.6	53.1
1981	24,486	20,123	6,549	82.2	26.7	32.5	3,590	14.7	20,439	33.0	52.1
1980	24,482	20,214	6,423	82.6	26.2	31.8	3,525	14.4	20,583	32.3	51.4
1979	23,895	19,616	6,120	82.1	25.6	31.2	3,571	14.9	20,033	31.8	51.7
1978	23,650	19,526	6,077	82.6	25.7	31.1	3,464	14.6	19,911	31.7	51.3
1977	23,430	19,291	6,209	82.3	26.5	32.2	3,445	14.7	19,712	32.6	52.1
1976	23,119	19,045	6,276	82.4	27.1	33.0	3,407	14.7	19,462	33.5	53.5
1975	22,703	18,883	6,116	83.2	26.9	32.4	3,149	13.9	19,298	33.0	52.7
1974	22,141	18,318	5,589	82.7	25.2	30.5	3,212	14.5	18,794	31.2	51.7
1973	21,766	18,023	5,438	82.8	25.0	30.2	3,085	14.2	18,470	30.8	51.6
1972	21,315	17,410	5,624	81.7	26.4	32.3	3,241	15.2	17,838	33.0	53.9
1971	20,533	16,593	5,594	81.3	27.2	33.5	3,156	15.4	17,087	34.2	54.1
1970	19,608	15,960	5,305	81.4	27.1	33.2	2,974	15.2	16,334	33.9	53.4
1969	18,606	15,031	5,347	80.8	28.7	35.6	2,915	15.7	15,383	36.2	53.5
1968	17,951	14,127	4,929	78.7	27.5	34.9	3,107	17.3	14,506	35.7	52.5
1967	17,500	13,657	4,708	78.0	26.9	34.5	3,141	17.9	14,022	35.2	51.4
Male											
2011	11,850	9,928	4,685	83.8	39.5	47.2	1,077	9.1	10,061	47.3	70.0
2010	11,579	9,651	4,369	83.3	37.7	45.3	1,124	9.7	9,754	45.4	68.6
2009	11,449	9,535	4,404	83.3	38.5	46.2	1,201	10.5	9,662	46.4	68.3
2008	11,432	9,646	4,340	84.4	38.0	45.0	1,122	9.8	9,784	45.2	67.8
2007	11,387	9,311	4,040	81.8	35.5	43.4	1,333	11.7	9,430	43.5	66.0
2006	11,264	9,139	3,842	81.1	34.1	42.0	1,396	12.4	9,237	42.2	66.0
2005	11,116	8,885	3,924	79.9	35.3	44.1	1,469	13.2	8,986	44.1	65.9
2004	11,107	9,001	3,855	81.0	34.7	42.8	1,524	13.7	9,067	43.1	64.4
2003[2]	10,885	8,763	3,726	80.5	34.2	42.5	1,452	13.3	8,862	42.6	65.1
2002	10,986	8,717	3,701	79.4	33.7	42.5	1,506	13.7	8,833	42.5	64.6
2001	10,817	8,490	3,521	78.5	32.6	41.5	1,659	15.3	8,582	41.5	64.0
2000	10,739	8,603	3,522	80.1	32.8	40.9	1,450	13.5	8,690	41.1	63.5
1999	10,532	8,382	3,585	79.6	34.0	42.7	1,462	13.9	8,457	42.8	64.8
1998	10,400	8,194	3,634	78.8	34.9	44.3	1,628	15.7	8,256	44.4	65.5
1997	10,173	8,204	3,633	80.6	35.7	44.3	1,406	13.8	8,274	44.5	65.3
1996	9,897	8,000	3,419	80.8	34.5	42.7	1,275	12.9	8,104	43.0	66.0
1995	9,980	8,001	3,398	80.2	34.0	42.5	1,430	14.3	8,067	42.7	65.3
1994	10,123	8,168	3,406	80.7	33.6	41.7	1,377	13.6	8,227	41.9	65.4
1993[r]	10,294	8,338	3,498	81.0	34.0	42.0	1,388	13.5	8,411	42.1	65.1
1993	9,641	7,857	3,313	81.5	34.4	42.2	1,379	12.9	7,926	42.3	65.4
1992	9,744	7,911	3,291	81.2	33.8	41.6	1,300	13.3	8,016	42.1	65.8
1991	9,896	7,843	3,270	79.3	33.0	41.7	1,520	15.4	7,899	41.9	59.9
1990	10,053	8,157	3,292	81.1	32.7	40.3	1,430	14.2	8,246	40.7	58.8
1989	10,240	8,177	3,223	79.9	31.5	39.4	1,572	15.4	8,271	39.7	58.5
1988	10,380	8,268	3,260	79.7	31.4	39.4	1,594	15.4	8,365	39.6	57.8
1987	10,549	8,498	3,289	80.6	31.2	38.7	1,593	15.1	8,647	39.2	56.4
1986	10,814	8,780	3,168	81.2	29.3	36.1	1,575	14.6	8,886	36.4	55.1
1985	11,108	9,077	3,254	81.7	29.3	35.8	1,637	14.7	9,229	36.6	55.5
1984	11,521	9,348	3,406	81.1	29.6	36.4	1,744	15.1	9,459	36.8	54.2
1983	11,787	9,411	3,335	79.8	28.3	35.4	1,865	15.8	9,534	35.9	53.5
1982	11,874	9,611	3,308	80.9	27.9	34.4	1,810	15.2	9,761	34.9	53.2
1981	12,040	9,619	3,340	79.9	27.7	34.7	1,960	16.3	9,754	35.1	52.8
1980	12,011	9,686	3,275	80.6	27.3	33.8	1,883	15.7	9,838	34.1	51.8
1979	11,721	9,457	3,104	80.7	26.5	32.8	1,830	15.6	9,615	33.4	52.7
1978	11,572	9,438	3,195	81.6	27.6	33.9	1,722	14.9	9,582	34.3	52.5
1977	11,445	9,263	3,286	80.9	28.7	35.5	1,779	15.5	9,422	35.8	54.5

Note: The change in the educational attainment question and the college completion categories from "4 or more years of college" to "at least some college" in 1992 caused an increase in the proportion of 14-to-24-year-old high school graduates enrolled in college or completed some college, of approximately 5 percentage points. High school graduates are people who have completed 4 years of high school or more, for 1967 to 1991. Beginning in 1992, they were people whose highest degree was a high school diploma (including equivalency) or higher.

[1]Civilian noninstitutionalized population.

[2]Starting in 2003 respondents could identify more than one race. Except as noted, the race data in this table from 2003 onward represent those respondents who indicated only one race category.

r = Revised, controlled to 1990 census based population estimates; previous 1993 data controlled to 1980 census based population estimates.

Table A-13. Population 14 to 24 Years Old, by High School Graduate Status, College Enrollment, Attainment, Sex, Race, and Hispanic Origin, October 1967–2011—*Continued*

(Numbers in thousands; percent)

Year, race, and Hispanic origin	Population 18 to 24 years old[1]								High school graduates, 14 to 24 years old		
	Total	High school graduates		Percent			High school dropouts		All graduates	Percent	
		Total	Enrolled in college	High school graduates	Enrolled in college	High school graduate enrolled in college	Number	Percent		Enrolled in college	Enrolled or completed some college
Male— *(Continued)*											
1976	11,279	9,186	3,250	81.4	28.8	35.4	1,691	15.0	9,340	35.7	55.9
1975	11,050	9,139	3,326	82.7	30.1	36.4	1,490	13.5	9,310	36.9	56.6
1974	10,722	8,768	3,035	81.8	28.3	34.6	1,579	14.7	8,980	35.2	55.9
1973	10,511	8,637	3,032	82.2	28.8	35.1	1,453	13.8	8,817	35.6	56.5
1972	10,212	8,278	3,195	81.1	31.3	38.6	1,506	14.7	8,462	39.2	60.1
1971	9,653	7,807	3,284	80.9	34.0	42.1	1,429	14.8	7,978	42.6	61.4
1970	9,053	7,324	3,096	80.9	34.2	42.3	1,297	14.3	7,496	42.9	60.9
1969	8,420	6,740	3,146	80.0	37.4	46.7	1,248	14.8	6,882	47.3	62.8
1968	8,084	6,221	2,949	77.0	36.5	47.4	1,401	17.3	6,372	48.1	62.7
1967	7,864	6,073	2,761	77.2	35.1	45.5	1,391	17.7	6,210	45.9	60.0
Female											
2011	11,238	9,832	5,128	87.5	45.6	51.8	808	7.2	9,946	52.2	78.0
2010	11,271	9,867	4,956	87.5	44.0	50.2	817	7.2	13,024	51.1	76.7
2009	11,157	9,706	4,923	87.0	44.1	50.7	858	7.7	9,850	50.8	75.8
2008	11,098	9,688	4,801	87.3	43.3	49.6	869	7.8	9,802	49.9	75.4
2007	11,005	9,603	4,741	87.3	43.1	49.4	915	8.3	9,741	49.5	74.4
2006	10,905	9,350	4,456	85.7	40.9	47.7	1,003	9.2	9,513	47.9	73.7
2005	10,661	9,245	4,574	86.7	42.9	57.3	997	9.4	9,366	49.7	73.9
2004	10,789	9,212	4,496	85.4	41.7	48.8	1,075	10.0	9,347	49.0	73.5
2003[2]	10,617	9,138	4,424	86.1	41.7	48.4	1,037	9.8	9,260	48.3	72.9
2002	10,718	9,075	4,220	84.7	39.4	46.5	1,135	10.6	9,162	46.6	70.4
2001	10,555	8,859	4,027	83.9	38.1	45.5	1,206	11.4	8,965	45.5	69.8
2000	10,517	8,909	4,044	84.7	38.5	45.4	1,148	10.9	9,024	45.6	70.2
1999	10,334	8,671	3,862	83.9	37.4	44.5	1,218	11.8	8,763	44.7	70.1
1998	10,065	8,507	3,907	84.5	38.8	45.9	1,181	11.7	8,599	46.2	71.0
1997	9,847	8,352	3,863	84.8	39.2	46.3	1,072	10.9	8,458	46.6	70.1
1996	9,778	8,200	3,705	83.9	37.9	45.2	1,182	12.1	8,333	45.6	70.7
1995	9,886	8,271	3,615	83.7	36.6	43.7	1,281	13.0	8,376	44.0	71.3
1994	10,048	8,503	3,714	84.6	37.0	43.7	1,175	11.7	8,588	43.9	69.7
1993r	10,199	8,651	3,576	84.8	35.1	41.3	1,207	11.8	8,750	41.5	67.9
1993	9,790	8,339	3,450	85.2	35.2	41.4	1,125	11.5	8,435	41.6	68.0
1992	9,928	8,468	3,625	85.3	36.5	42.8	1,098	11.1	8,569	43.2	68.1
1991	10,119	8,481	3,544	83.8	35.0	41.8	1,324	13.1	8,568	42.1	64.5
1990	10,340	8,666	3,344	83.8	32.3	38.6	1,322	12.8	8,775	38.9	61.4
1989	10,586	8,913	3,409	84.2	32.2	38.2	1,354	12.8	9,059	38.6	59.2
1988	10,881	9,223	3,399	84.8	31.2	36.9	1,418	13.0	9,355	37.3	59.1
1987	10,944	9,189	3,192	84.0	29.2	34.7	1,449	13.2	9,334	36.2	57.2
1986	11,205	9,509	3,139	84.9	28.0	33.0	1,388	12.4	9,667	33.6	55.8
1985	11,524	9,840	3,247	85.4	28.2	33.0	1,413	12.3	10,001	33.6	55.2
1984	11,826	10,026	3,120	84.8	26.4	31.1	1,535	13.0	10,089	31.8	53.4
1983	12,112	10,233	3,129	84.5	25.8	30.6	1,563	12.9	10,233	31.3	53.4
1982	12,332	10,333	3,285	83.8	26.6	31.8	1,713	13.0	10,530	32.3	52.9
1981	12,446	10,504	3,208	84.4	25.8	30.5	1,629	13.1	10,687	31.1	51.6
1980	12,471	10,528	3,147	84.4	25.2	29.9	1,642	13.2	10,749	30.6	50.9
1979	12,174	10,157	3,015	83.4	24.8	29.7	1,741	14.3	10,417	30.3	50.8
1978	12,078	10,088	2,882	83.5	23.9	28.6	1,742	14.4	10,327	29.3	50.3
1977	11,985	10,029	2,923	83.7	24.4	29.1	1,666	13.9	10,292	29.7	50.0
1976	11,840	9,860	3,026	83.3	25.6	30.7	1,717	14.5	10,118	31.4	51.3
1975	11,653	9,743	2,790	83.6	23.9	28.6	1,658	14.2	9,986	29.4	49.1
1974	11,419	9,551	2,555	83.6	22.4	26.8	1,633	14.3	9,811	27.5	47.8
1973	11,255	9,387	2,406	83.4	21.4	25.6	1,632	14.5	9,653	26.4	47.1
1972	11,103	9,132	2,428	82.2	21.9	26.6	1,735	15.6	9,377	27.4	48.3
1971	10,880	8,887	2,310	81.7	21.2	26.0	1,726	15.9	9,107	26.8	47.7
1970	10,555	8,634	2,209	81.8	20.9	25.6	1,675	15.9	8,837	26.3	47.2
1969	10,186	8,291	2,200	81.4	21.6	26.5	1,668	16.4	8,501	27.2	46.3
1968	9,866	7,906	1,980	80.1	20.1	25.0	1,706	17.3	8,135	26.0	45.1
1967	9,637	7,586	1,949	78.7	20.2	25.7	1,750	18.2	7,815	26.6	45.7

Note: The change in the educational attainment question and the college completion categories from "4 or more years of college" to "at least some college" in 1992 caused an increase in the proportion of 14-to-24-year-old high school graduates enrolled in college or completed some college, of approximately 5 percentage points. High school graduates are people who have completed 4 years of high school or more, for 1967 to 1991. Beginning in 1992, they were people whose highest degree was a high school diploma (including equivalency) or higher.

[1]Civilian noninstitutionalized population.

[2]Starting in 2003 respondents could identify more than one race. Except as noted, the race data in this table from 2003 onward represent those respondents who indicated only one race category.

r = Revised, controlled to 1990 census based population estimates; previous 1993 data controlled to 1980 census based population estimates.

Table A-13. Population 14 to 24 Years Old, by High School Graduate Status, College Enrollment, Attainment, Sex, Race, and Hispanic Origin, October 1967–2011—*Continued*

(Numbers in thousands; percent)

Year, race, and Hispanic origin	Population 18 to 24 years old[1]								High school graduates, 14 to 24 years old		
	Total	High school graduates		Percent			High school dropouts		All graduates	Percent	
		Total	Enrolled in college	High school graduates	Enrolled in college	High school graduate enrolled in college	Number	Percent		Enrolled in college	Enrolled or completed some college
WHITE ALONE NON-HISPANIC											
Both Sexes											
2011	17,627	15,565	7,882	88.3	44.7	50.6	1,002	5.7	15,752	50.7	76.2
2010	17,693	15,761	7,663	89.1	43.3	48.6	1,003	5.7	15,927	48.8	75.4
2009	17,750	15,839	7,983	89.2	45.0	50.4	1,029	5.8	16,051	50.5	75.2
2008	17,839	16,038	7,894	89.9	44.2	49.2	960	5.4	16,224	49.4	74.2
2007	17,669	15,727	7,533	89.0	42.6	47.9	1,064	6.0	15,921	48.0	72.9
2006	17,565	15,452	7,200	88.0	41.0	46.6	1,189	6.8	15,642	46.8	72.5
2005	17,293	15,187	7,393	87.8	42.8	54.9	1,216	7.0	15,368	48.7	72.6
2004	17,326	15,224	7,228	87.9	41.7	47.5	1,313	7.6	15,382	47.7	71.8
2003[2]	17,158	15,070	7,129	87.8	41.6	47.3	1,267	7.4	15,255	47.3	71.5
2002	17,131	14,910	7,004	87.0	40.9	47.0	1,289	7.5	15,089	47.1	70.4
2001	16,721	14,480	6,565	86.6	39.3	45.3	1,390	8.3	14,646	45.3	69.7
2000	17,327	15,187	6,709	87.7	38.7	44.2	1,316	7.6	15,344	44.3	69.0
1999	17,080	14,812	6,735	86.7	39.4	45.5	1,404	8.2	14,952	45.6	70.2
1998	16,634	14,402	6,757	86.6	40.6	46.9	1,491	9.0	14,542	47.0	70.6
1997	16,575	14,414	6,728	87.0	40.6	46.7	1,432	8.6	14,527	46.9	70.0
1996	16,339	14,288	6,447	87.5	39.5	45.1	1,303	8.0	14,501	45.5	70.7
1995	16,867	14,523	6,393	86.1	37.9	44.0	1,647	9.8	14,672	44.3	70.2
1994	17,114	14,916	6,521	87.2	38.1	43.7	1,505	8.8	15,049	44.0	69.2
1993	16,895	14,665	6,221	86.8	36.8	42.4	1,524	9.0	14,801	42.6	68.1
Male											
2011	8,864	7,697	3,754	86.8	42.4	48.8	554	6.2	7,794	48.9	72.7
2010	8,919	7,808	3,617	87.5	40.6	46.3	569	6.4	7,884	46.4	70.9
2009	8,957	7,818	3,787	87.3	42.3	48.4	632	7.1	7,915	48.5	71.9
2008	9,032	8,028	3,766	88.9	41.7	46.9	546	6.0	8,126	47.1	70.4
2007	8,940	7,786	3,541	87.1	39.6	45.5	622	7.0	7,883	45.5	68.8
2006	8,842	7,660	3,354	86.6	37.9	43.8	647	7.3	7,734	43.9	68.4
2005	8,700	7,443	3,429	85.5	39.4	48.7	685	7.9	7,526	46.0	68.6
2004	8,644	7,527	3,322	87.1	38.4	44.1	691	8.0	7,576	44.4	66.7
2003[2]	8,538	7,325	3,291	85.8	38.5	44.9	721	8.4	7,401	45.0	68.5
2002	8,453	7,244	3,287	85.7	38.9	45.4	668	7.9	7,352	45.5	67.9
2001	8,343	7,112	3,094	85.3	37.1	43.4	741	8.9	7,191	43.4	67.1
2000	8,670	7,493	3,136	86.4	36.2	41.9	677	7.8	7,556	42.0	65.4
1999	8,580	7,301	3,284	85.1	38.3	45.0	753	8.8	7,369	45.0	67.7
1998	8,380	7,094	3,300	84.7	39.4	46.5	826	9.9	7,151	46.6	68.2
1997	8,326	7,112	3,276	85.4	39.3	46.1	797	9.6	7,154	46.3	68.1
1996	8,168	7,050	3,130	86.3	38.3	44.4	651	8.0	7,143	44.7	68.6
1995	8,399	7,089	3,105	84.4	37.0	43.8	883	10.5	7,147	44.0	67.3
1994	8,457	7,261	3,126	85.9	37.0	43.1	777	9.2	7,317	43.3	67.0
1993	8,403	7,138	3,071	84.9	36.6	43.0	811	9.7	7,191	43.2	67.1
Female											
2011	8,763	7,868	4,128	89.8	47.1	52.5	448	5.1	7,958	52.5	79.6
2010	8,774	7,953	4,046	90.6	46.1	50.9	434	4.9	8,044	51.2	79.8
2009	8,793	8,021	4,195	91.2	47.7	52.3	398	4.5	8,136	52.4	78.3
2008	8,808	8,010	4,127	90.9	46.9	51.5	414	4.7	8,099	51.7	78.0
2007	8,728	7,941	3,992	91.0	45.7	50.3	442	5.1	8,039	50.4	76.9
2006	8,724	7,791	3,846	89.3	44.1	49.4	542	6.2	7,908	49.5	76.4
2005	8,593	7,744	3,964	90.1	46.1	61.4	531	6.2	7,842	51.4	76.4
2004	8,628	7,697	3,906	89.2	45.3	50.7	622	7.2	7,805	50.9	76.8
2003[2]	8,620	7,745	3,838	89.9	44.5	49.6	546	6.3	7,854	49.5	74.4
2002	8,678	7,666	3,717	88.3	42.8	48.5	621	7.2	7,736	48.6	72.8
2001	8,378	7,368	3,471	87.9	41.4	47.2	648	7.7	7,455	47.2	72.3
2000	8,657	7,693	3,573	88.9	41.3	46.4	638	7.4	7,789	46.6	72.5
1999	8,500	7,510	3,451	88.4	40.6	46.0	651	7.7	7,583	46.2	72.5

Note: The change in the educational attainment question and the college completion categories from "4 or more years of college" to "at least some college" in 1992 caused an increase in the proportion of 14-to-24-year-old high school graduates enrolled in college or completed some college, of approximately 5 percentage points. High school graduates are people who have completed 4 years of high school or more, for 1967 to 1991. Beginning in 1992, they were people whose highest degree was a high school diploma (including equivalency) or higher.

[1]Civilian noninstitutionalized population.

[2]Starting in 2003 respondents could identify more than one race. Except as noted, the race data in this table from 2003 onward represent those respondents who indicated only one race category.

Table A-13. Population 14 to 24 Years Old, by High School Graduate Status, College Enrollment, Attainment, Sex, Race, and Hispanic Origin, October 1967–2011—*Continued*

(Numbers in thousands; percent)

Year, race, and Hispanic origin	Population 18 to 24 years old[1]								High school graduates, 14 to 24 years old		
	Total	High school graduates		Percent			High school dropouts		All graduates	Percent	
		Total	Enrolled in college	High school graduates	Enrolled in college	High school graduate enrolled in college	Number	Percent		Enrolled in college	Enrolled or completed some college
Female— *(Continued)*											
1998	8,254	7,308	3,457	88.5	41.9	47.3	665	8.1	7,391	47.5	73.0
1997	8,249	7,302	3,452	88.5	41.9	47.3	636	7.7	7,373	47.5	71.9
1996	8,171	7,238	3,317	88.6	40.6	45.8	652	8.0	7,358	46.3	72.8
1995	8,467	7,433	3,288	87.8	38.8	44.2	764	9.0	7,525	44.6	73.1
1994	8,657	7,655	3,395	88.4	39.2	44.4	728	8.4	7,732	44.6	71.3
1993	8,492	7,527	3,150	88.6	37.1	41.9	714	8.4	7,610	42.0	69.1
BLACK ALONE											
Both Sexes											
2011	4,503	3,649	1,639	81.0	36.4	44.9	399	8.9	3,702	45.3	66.3
2010	4,457	3,669	1,692	82.3	38.0	46.1	258	12.1	3,731	46.2	66.2
2009	4,346	3,458	1,604	79.6	36.9	46.4	505	11.6	3,532	46.4	67.5
2008	4,265	3,387	1,349	79.4	31.6	40.0	548	12.1	3,445	40.2	60.7
2007	4,182	3,423	1,396	81.8	33.4	40.8	425	10.2	3,483	40.9	61.4
2006	4,085	3,156	1,321	77.3	32.3	41.9	532	13.0	3,224	41.9	60.8
2005	3,964	3,137	1,297	79.1	32.7	40.0	512	12.9	3,212	41.3	63.5
2004	3,940	3,050	1,238	77.4	31.4	40.6	596	15.1	3,112	41.1	63.2
2003[2]	3,837	2,948	1,225	76.8	31.9	41.6	545	14.2	2,997	41.8	62.5
2002	3,924	3,040	1,226	77.5	31.3	40.3	571	14.5	3,117	41.1	61.2
2001	3,916	3,016	1,206	77.0	30.8	40.0	540	13.8	3,095	40.0	59.0
2000	4,013	3,090	1,216	77.0	30.3	39.4	615	15.3	3,129	39.5	61.0
1999	3,827	2,911	1,145	76.1	29.9	39.4	613	16.0	2,985	39.9	60.4
1998	3,745	2,747	1,116	73.4	29.8	40.6	642	17.1	2,790	40.8	61.8
1997	3,650	2,725	1,085	74.7	29.7	39.8	611	16.7	2,762	40.2	60.0
1996	3,637	2,738	983	75.3	27.0	35.9	581	16.0	2,805	36.6	54.6
1995	3,625	2,788	988	76.9	27.3	35.4	522	14.4	2,828	35.8	58.0
1994	3,661	2,818	1,001	77.0	27.3	35.5	568	15.5	2,859	36.3	59.2
1993[r]	3,666	2,747	897	74.9	24.5	32.7	600	16.4	2,771	32.8	54.0
1993	3,516	2,629	861	74.8	24.5	32.8	578	16.4	2,653	32.9	53.9
1992	3,521	2,625	886	74.6	25.2	33.8	575	16.3	2,668	34.3	53.3
1991	3,504	2,630	828	75.1	23.6	31.5	545	15.6	2,658	31.8	46.0
1990	3,520	2,710	894	77.0	25.4	33.0	530	15.1	2,759	33.7	48.0
1989	3,559	2,708	835	76.1	23.5	30.8	583	16.4	2,750	31.5	49.2
1988	3,568	2,680	752	75.1	21.1	28.1	631	17.7	2,741	28.6	46.3
1987	3,603	2,739	823	76.0	22.8	30.0	611	17.0	2,790	30.6	48.1
1986	3,653	2,795	812	76.5	22.2	29.1	617	16.8	2,837	29.3	47.8
1985	3,716	2,810	734	75.6	19.8	26.1	655	17.6	2,848	26.5	43.8
1984	3,862	2,885	786	74.7	20.4	27.2	712	18.4	2,950	28.0	45.2
1983	3,865	2,740	741	70.9	19.2	27.0	832	21.5	2,790	27.7	45.0
1982	3,872	2,744	767	70.9	19.8	28.0	851	22.0	2,793	28.2	45.5
1981	3,778	2,678	750	70.9	19.9	28.0	821	21.7	2,718	28.7	44.8
1980	3,721	2,592	715	69.7	19.2	27.6	876	23.5	2,656	28.1	45.9
1979	3,510	2,356	696	67.1	19.8	29.5	895	25.5	2,415	30.6	48.4
1978	3,452	2,340	694	67.8	20.1	29.7	850	24.6	2,396	30.6	47.8
1977	3,387	2,286	721	67.5	21.3	31.5	808	23.9	2,342	32.4	46.9
1976	3,315	2,239	749	67.5	22.6	33.5	803	24.2	2,291	34.2	50.4
1975	3,213	2,081	665	64.8	20.7	32.0	877	27.3	2,149	32.6	48.1
1974	3,105	2,083	555	67.1	17.9	26.6	780	25.1	2,145	27.5	44.8
1973	3,114	2,079	498	66.8	16.0	24.0	826	26.5	2,139	25.0	41.6
1972	2,986	1,992	540	66.7	18.1	27.1	782	26.2	2,044	28.0	42.0
1971	2,866	1,789	522	62.4	18.2	29.2	825	28.8	1,833	30.0	42.3
1970	2,692	1,602	416	59.5	15.5	26.0	897	33.3	1,635	26.7	39.4
1969	2,542	1,497	407	58.9	16.0	27.2	828	32.6	1,547	27.5	40.1
1968	2,421	1,399	352	57.8	14.5	25.2	799	33.0	1,432	26.0	38.1
1967	2,283	1,276	297	55.9	13.0	23.3	788	34.5	1,316	23.7	35.0

Note: The change in the educational attainment question and the college completion categories from "4 or more years of college" to "at least some college" in 1992 caused an increase in the proportion of 14-to-24-year-old high school graduates enrolled in college or completed some college, of approximately 5 percentage points. High school graduates are people who have completed 4 years of high school or more, for 1967 to 1991. Beginning in 1992, they were people whose highest degree was a high school diploma (including equivalency) or higher.

[1]Civilian noninstitutionalized population.

[2]Starting in 2003 respondents could identify more than one race. Except as noted, the race data in this table from 2003 onward represent those respondents who indicated only one race category.

r = Revised, controlled to 1990 census based population estimates; previous 1993 data controlled to 1980 census based population estimates.

Table A-13. Population 14 to 24 Years Old, by High School Graduate Status, College Enrollment, Attainment, Sex, Race, and Hispanic Origin, October 1967–2011—*Continued*

(Numbers in thousands; percent)

Year, race, and Hispanic origin	Population 18 to 24 years old[1]								High school graduates, 14 to 24 years old		
	Total	High school graduates		Percent			High school dropouts		All graduates	Percent	
		Total	Enrolled in college	High school graduates	Enrolled in college	High school graduate enrolled in college	Number	Percent		Enrolled in college	Enrolled or completed some college
Male											
2011	2,165	1,701	717	78.6	33.1	42.2	205	9.5	1,732	42.7	60.9
2010	2,140	1,692	734	79.1	34.3	43.4	258	12.1	1,730	43.2	61.4
2009	2,082	1,592	673	76.5	32.3	42.3	289	13.9	1,617	42.0	63.5
2008	2,045	1,641	595	80.2	29.1	36.3	210	10.2	1,668	36.9	54.8
2007	2,011	1,622	649	80.6	32.3	40.0	202	10.0	1,642	40.1	59.3
2006	1,959	1,488	541	76.0	27.6	36.4	219	11.2	1,519	36.3	53.4
2005	1,897	1,393	530	73.4	27.9	35.0	280	14.8	1,420	37.9	58.4
2004	1,852	1,341	479	72.4	25.9	35.7	331	17.9	1,363	36.1	60.9
2003[2]	1,801	1,331	499	73.9	27.7	37.5	300	16.7	1,346	37.8	57.1
2002	1,843	1,354	475	73.5	25.8	35.1	311	16.9	1,372	35.6	56.1
2001	1,818	1,287	470	70.8	25.8	36.4	308	16.9	1,310	36.4	53.1
2000	1,885	1,389	470	73.7	24.9	33.8	329	17.4	1,409	34.1	53.5
1999	1,747	1,292	501	73.9	28.7	38.8	285	16.3	1,336	40.2	57.7
1998	1,724	1,163	445	67.5	25.8	38.2	354	20.5	1,186	38.5	57.5
1997	1,701	1,214	425	71.4	25.0	35.0	297	17.5	1,232	35.1	56.3
1996	1,682	1,199	422	71.3	25.1	35.2	292	17.4	1,225	35.8	53.7
1995	1,660	1,247	430	75.1	25.9	34.4	235	14.2	1,262	35.1	56.2
1994	1,733	1,277	440	73.7	25.4	34.5	303	17.5	1,293	35.3	57.9
1993[r]	1,703	1,240	387	72.8	22.7	31.2	266	15.6	1,247	31.4	50.1
1993	1,659	1,207	379	72.8	22.8	31.4	258	15.6	1,214	31.5	50.0
1992	1,676	1,211	356	72.3	21.2	29.4	259	15.5	1,226	29.7	49.4
1991	1,635	1,174	378	71.8	23.1	32.2	252	15.4	1,188	32.4	47.0
1990	1,634	1,240	426	75.9	26.1	34.4	223	13.6	1,260	35.1	48.8
1989	1,654	1,195	324	72.2	19.6	27.1	307	18.6	1,207	27.5	45.8
1988	1,653	1,189	297	71.9	18.0	25.0	312	18.9	1,205	25.1	42.5
1987	1,666	1,188	377	71.3	22.6	31.7	312	18.7	1,209	32.3	48.0
1986	1,687	1,220	349	72.3	20.7	28.6	300	17.8	1,239	29.1	44.4
1985	1,720	1,244	345	72.3	20.1	27.7	323	18.8	1,258	28.2	43.6
1984	1,811	1,272	367	70.2	20.3	28.9	362	20.2	1,295	29.6	45.2
1983	1,807	1,202	331	66.5	18.3	27.5	435	24.1	1,228	27.9	43.6
1982	1,786	1,171	331	65.6	18.5	28.3	458	25.6	1,188	28.6	44.5
1981	1,730	1,154	325	66.7	18.8	28.2	419	24.2	1,165	28.5	42.3
1980	1,690	1,115	293	66.0	17.3	26.3	440	26.0	1,141	26.9	44.1
1979	1,577	973	304	61.7	19.3	31.2	457	29.0	988	32.0	46.7
1978	1,554	956	305	61.5	19.6	31.9	451	29.0	981	32.4	49.3
1977	1,528	970	309	63.5	20.2	31.9	369	24.1	991	33.0	47.6
1976	1,503	936	331	62.3	22.0	35.4	393	26.1	952	35.9	50.3
1975	1,451	897	294	61.8	20.3	32.8	404	27.8	923	33.4	50.5
1974	1,396	919	280	65.8	20.1	30.5	346	24.8	941	31.1	47.3
1973	1,434	952	266	66.4	18.5	27.9	371	25.9	962	28.4	44.2
1972	1,373	870	287	63.4	20.9	33.0	373	27.2	897	34.0	47.4
1971	1,318	769	262	58.3	19.9	34.1	416	31.6	783	34.9	45.8
1970	1,220	668	192	54.8	15.7	28.7	436	35.7	684	29.5	41.4
1969	1,141	631	202	55.3	17.7	32.0	383	33.6	653	32.5	44.6
1968	1,087	582	170	53.5	15.6	29.2	370	34.0	600	30.3	43.2
1967	1,032	525	167	50.9	16.2	31.8	397	38.5	539	32.3	41.6
Female											
2011	2,339	1,949	921	83.3	39.4	47.3	194	8.3	1,970	47.6	71.0
2010	2,317	1,977	958	85.3	41.3	48.4	192	8.3	2,001	48.8	70.4
2009	2,263	1,865	931	82.4	41.1	49.9	216	9.5	1,915	50.1	70.9
2008	2,220	1,746	754	78.7	34.0	43.2	304	13.7	1,777	43.3	66.2
2007	2,171	1,801	747	82.9	34.4	41.5	223	10.3	1,841	41.5	63.3
2006	2,126	1,668	780	78.5	36.7	46.7	313	14.7	1,705	46.9	67.3
2005	2,067	1,745	767	84.4	37.1	44.9	232	11.2	1,793	44.0	67.5
2004	2,088	1,709	759	81.8	36.3	44.4	266	12.7	1,749	44.9	65.0

Note: The change in the educational attainment question and the college completion categories from "4 or more years of college" to "at least some college" in 1992 caused an increase in the proportion of 14-to-24-year-old high school graduates enrolled in college or completed some college, of approximately 5 percentage points. High school graduates are people who have completed 4 years of high school or more, for 1967 to 1991. Beginning in 1992, they were people whose highest degree was a high school diploma (including equivalency) or higher.

[1]Civilian noninstitutionalized population.

[2]Starting in 2003 respondents could identify more than one race. Except as noted, the race data in this table from 2003 onward represent those respondents who indicated only one race category.

r = Revised, controlled to 1990 census based population estimates; previous 1993 data controlled to 1980 census based population estimates.

Table A-13. Population 14 to 24 Years Old, by High School Graduate Status, College Enrollment, Attainment, Sex, Race, and Hispanic Origin, October 1967–2011—*Continued*

(Numbers in thousands; percent)

Year, race, and Hispanic origin	Population 18 to 24 years old[1]								High school graduates, 14 to 24 years old		
	Total	High school graduates		Percent			High school dropouts		All graduates	Percent	
		Total	Enrolled in college	High school graduates	Enrolled in college	High school graduate enrolled in college	Number	Percent		Enrolled in college	Enrolled or completed some college
Female— *(Continued)*											
2003[2]	2,035	1,618	726	79.5	35.7	44.9	245	12.0	1,652	45.1	66.8
2002	2,081	1,686	751	81.0	36.1	44.5	260	12.5	1,745	45.5	65.2
2001	2,098	1,729	736	82.4	35.1	42.7	232	11.0	1,785	42.7	63.3
2000	2,128	1,700	747	79.9	35.1	43.9	287	13.5	1,720	43.9	67.1
1999	2,080	1,619	644	77.9	31.0	39.8	327	15.7	1,650	39.6	62.6
1998	2,021	1,584	671	78.4	33.2	42.4	288	14.3	1,604	42.4	65.0
1997	1,949	1,511	659	77.5	33.8	43.6	314	16.1	1,529	43.1	63.0
1996	1,956	1,539	561	78.7	28.7	36.4	288	14.7	1,580	37.3	55.3
1995	1,965	1,541	558	78.4	28.4	36.2	287	14.6	1,566	36.3	59.5
1994	1,928	1,542	561	80.0	29.1	36.4	265	13.7	1,567	37.1	60.3
1993[r]	1,965	1,508	511	76.7	26.0	33.9	337	17.2	1,526	34.1	57.2
1993	1,857	1,425	484	76.7	26.1	34.0	319	17.2	1,441	34.1	57.1
1992	1,845	1,417	531	76.8	28.8	37.5	315	17.1	1,446	38.2	56.6
1991	1,869	1,455	450	77.8	24.1	30.9	296	15.8	1,468	31.4	45.2
1990	1,886	1,468	467	77.8	24.8	31.8	306	16.2	1,498	32.4	47.3
1989	1,905	1,511	511	79.3	26.8	33.8	277	14.5	1,541	34.7	51.8
1988	1,915	1,492	455	77.9	23.8	30.5	318	16.6	1,538	31.3	49.2
1987	1,937	1,550	445	80.0	23.0	28.7	298	15.4	1,579	29.4	48.9
1986	1,966	1,574	462	80.1	23.5	29.4	306	15.6	1,598	29.3	50.4
1985	1,996	1,565	389	78.4	19.5	24.9	332	16.6	1,592	25.1	44.0
1984	2,052	1,613	419	78.6	20.4	26.0	349	17.0	1,655	26.8	45.1
1983	2,058	1,539	411	74.8	20.0	26.7	398	19.3	1,561	27.5	46.3
1982	2,086	1,572	436	75.4	20.9	27.7	393	18.8	1,604	27.9	46.3
1981	2,049	1,526	424	74.5	20.7	27.8	402	19.6	1,554	28.8	46.6
1980	2,031	1,475	422	72.6	20.8	28.6	436	21.5	1,511	29.1	47.4
1979	1,934	1,383	392	71.5	20.3	28.3	439	22.7	1,426	29.7	49.8
1978	1,897	1,384	390	73.0	20.6	28.2	398	21.0	1,415	29.3	46.7
1977	1,859	1,317	413	70.8	22.2	31.4	439	23.6	1,354	31.9	46.2
1976	1,813	1,302	417	71.8	23.0	32.0	410	22.6	1,338	32.9	50.3
1975	1,761	1,182	372	67.1	21.1	31.5	473	26.9	1,224	32.0	46.4
1974	1,709	1,167	277	68.3	16.2	23.7	434	25.4	1,207	24.8	42.9
1973	1,681	1,125	231	66.9	13.7	20.5	456	27.1	1,177	22.2	39.4
1972	1,613	1,123	253	69.6	15.7	22.5	408	25.3	1,150	23.2	37.9
1971	1,547	1,019	259	65.9	16.7	25.4	409	26.4	1,049	26.4	39.8
1970	1,471	935	225	63.6	15.3	24.1	461	31.3	955	24.7	39.3
1969	1,402	867	206	61.8	14.7	23.8	444	31.7	896	24.0	38.6
1968	1,334	819	183	61.4	13.7	22.3	430	32.2	834	22.9	35.9
1967	1,249	751	130	60.1	10.4	17.3	391	31.3	778	17.9	33.2
ASIAN ALONE[3]											
Both Sexes											
2011	1,252	1,123	748	89.8	59.7	66.5	65	5.2	1,149	66.9	88.1
2010	1,303	1,193	811	91.5	62.2	68.0	64	4.9	1,232	68.4	89.8
2009	1,181	1,080	768	91.4	65.0	71.1	26	2.2	1,096	71.0	91.8
2008	1,113	1,021	655	91.8	58.9	64.1	42	3.8	1,056	64.6	90.4
2007	1,165	1,010	658	86.7	56.4	65.1	86	7.4	1,026	65.1	91.6
2006	1,148	1,046	661	91.1	57.6	63.2	46	4.0	1,064	63.0	87.0
2005	1,145	1,072	693	93.6	60.5	74.9	34	3.0	1,098	65.1	87.0
2004	1,152	1,066	695	92.5	60.3	65.2	49	4.3	1,090	65.7	89.1
2003[2]	1,144	1,030	693	90.1	60.6	67.3	56	4.9	1,046	67.7	88.2
2002	1,339	1,230	803	91.8	60.0	65.3	57	4.2	1,265	65.7	86.9
2001	1,312	1,197	794	91.2	60.5	66.5	47	3.6	1,218	66.5	87.6
2000	1,143	1,038	639	90.8	55.9	61.6	52	4.6	1,053	61.8	83.9
1999	1,130	1,019	626	90.2	55.4	61.4	58	5.1	1,035	62.0	85.5

Note: The change in the educational attainment question and the college completion categories from "4 or more years of college" to "at least some college" in 1992 caused an increase in the proportion of 14-to-24-year-old high school graduates enrolled in college or completed some college, of approximately 5 percentage points. High school graduates are people who have completed 4 years of high school or more, for 1967 to 1991. Beginning in 1992, they were people whose highest degree was a high school diploma (including equivalency) or higher.

[1]Civilian noninstitutionalized population.

[2]Starting in 2003 respondents could identify more than one race. Except as noted, the race data in this table from 2003 onward represent those respondents who indicated only one race category.

[3]The data shown prior to 2003 consists of those identifying themselves as "Asian or Pacific Islanders."

r = Revised, controlled to 1990 census based population estimates; previous 1993 data controlled to 1980 census based population estimates.

Table A-13. Population 14 to 24 Years Old, by High School Graduate Status, College Enrollment, Attainment, Sex, Race, and Hispanic Origin, October 1967–2011—*Continued*

(Numbers in thousands; percent)

Year, race, and Hispanic origin	Population 18 to 24 years old[1]								High school graduates, 14 to 24 years old		
	Total	High school graduates		Percent			High school dropouts		All graduates	Percent	
		Total	Enrolled in college	High school graduates	Enrolled in college	High school graduate enrolled in college	Number	Percent		Enrolled in college	Enrolled or completed some college
Male											
2011	639	573	379	89.6	59.3	66.2	30	4.7	582	66.1	87.6
2010	651	597	390	91.7	59.9	65.3	29	4.5	619	65.7	87.5
2009	590	546	383	92.4	64.9	70.2	7	1.2	559	69.9	90.1
2008	547	487	295	89.1	53.9	60.5	21	3.9	510	62.0	89.9
2007	560	481	318	85.8	56.9	66.3	38	6.8	483	66.4	91.8
2006	591	525	338	88.8	57.2	64.4	34	5.8	536	64.0	84.0
2005	590	552	366	93.5	62.0	68.9	17	2.9	565	66.4	88.2
2004	586	549	373	93.7	63.6	67.9	15	2.5	561	68.4	88.2
2003[2]	543	483	337	88.9	62.0	69.8	43	7.8	486	69.9	90.0
2002	707	637	417	90.0	59.0	65.5	38	5.4	652	65.3	86.7
2001	661	583	417	88.1	63.1	72.0	35	5.3	594	72.0	88.9
2000	571	521	337	91.1	58.9	64.7	34	6.0	527	64.7	85.6
1999	505	443	284	87.8	56.2	64.0	39	7.7	454	64.9	82.5
Female											
2011	612	551	369	89.9	60.2	66.9	35	5.8	567	67.8	88.7
2010	653	596	422	91.3	64.6	70.7	192	8.3	614	71.2	92.1
2009	591	534	384	90.4	65.1	72.0	19	3.3	538	72.2	93.7
2008	566	534	360	94.4	63.7	67.5	21	3.6	546	67.0	90.9
2007	605	529	339	87.4	56.0	64.1	48	7.9	543	63.9	91.5
2006	557	521	324	93.6	58.1	62.2	11	2.1	528	61.9	90.0
2005	555	521	327	93.8	58.9	81.4	17	3.0	533	63.7	85.8
2004	567	517	323	91.3	56.9	62.4	35	6.1	529	62.8	90.0
2003[2]	601	547	356	91.2	59.3	65.1	13	2.2	561	65.9	86.7
2002	632	593	386	93.8	61.0	65.1	19	2.9	613	66.1	87.2
2001	651	614	377	94.3	57.9	61.3	12	1.8	625	61.3	86.3
2000	572	517	302	90.4	52.9	58.5	18	3.1	526	58.9	82.3
1999	626	576	342	92.1	54.7	59.4	19	3.1	582	59.7	87.8
HISPANIC[4]											
Both Sexes											
2011	5,974	4,569	2,079	76.5	34.8	45.5	975	16.3	4,630	45.7	65.4
2010	5,685	4,138	1,814	72.8	31.9	43.8	1,050	18.5	4,199	44.2	63.2
2009	5,332	3,747	1,465	70.3	27.5	39.1	1,112	20.8	3,813	39.6	57.8
2008	5,176	3,618	1,338	69.9	25.8	37.0	1,155	22.3	3,691	37.7	58.7
2007	5,175	3,487	1,375	67.4	26.6	39.4	1,310	25.3	3,553	39.9	58.0
2006	5,006	3,301	1,182	65.9	23.6	35.8	1,313	26.2	3,379	36.6	57.2
2005	4,898	3,230	1,215	66.0	24.8	32.4	1,335	27.3	3,280	38.0	57.3
2004	4,941	3,244	1,221	65.6	24.7	37.7	1,386	28.0	3,287	37.9	55.9
2003	4,754	3,096	1,115	65.1	23.5	36.0	1,353	28.4	3,135	36.0	56.5
2002	4,918	3,078	979	62.6	19.9	31.8	1,479	30.1	3,109	32.0	53.1
2001	4,892	3,031	1,035	62.0	21.1	34.2	1,548	31.7	3,068	34.2	52.8
2000	4,134	2,462	899	59.6	21.7	36.5	1,335	32.3	2,509	36.8	53.1
1999	3,953	2,325	739	58.8	18.7	31.8	1,340	33.9	2,359	31.7	49.6
1998	4,014	2,403	820	59.8	20.4	34.1	1,383	34.4	2,419	34.3	53.2
1997	3,606	2,236	806	62.0	22.4	36.0	1,103	30.6	2,302	37.1	54.3
1996	3,510	2,019	706	57.5	20.1	35.0	1,210	34.5	2,046	34.5	52.5
1995	3,603	2,112	745	58.6	20.7	35.3	1,250	34.7	2,142	35.7	55.8
1994	3,523	1,995	662	56.6	18.8	33.2	1,224	34.7	2,009	33.4	54.3
1993[r]	3,363	2,049	728	60.9	21.6	35.5	1,103	32.8	2,081	35.8	55.6
1993	2,772	1,682	602	60.7	21.7	35.8	907	32.7	1,712	36.0	55.8
1992	2,754	1,579	586	57.3	21.3	37.1	936	33.9	1,603	37.6	55.0
1991	2,874	1,498	516	52.1	18.0	34.4	1,139	39.6	1,519	34.6	47.6
1990	2,749	1,498	435	54.5	15.8	29.0	1,025	37.3	1,523	29.4	44.7
1989	2,818	1,576	453	55.9	16.1	28.7	1,062	37.7	1,600	29.4	43.6
1988	2,642	1,458	450	55.2	17.0	30.9	1,046	39.6	1,481	31.3	47.0

Note: The change in the educational attainment question and the college completion categories from "4 or more years of college" to "at least some college" in 1992 caused an increase in the proportion of 14-to-24-year-old high school graduates enrolled in college or completed some college, of approximately 5 percentage points. High school graduates are people who have completed 4 years of high school or more, for 1967 to 1991. Beginning in 1992, they were people whose highest degree was a high school diploma (including equivalency) or higher.

[1]Civilian noninstitutionalized population.

[2]Starting in 2003 respondents could identify more than one race. Except as noted, the race data in this table from 2003 onward represent those respondents who indicated only one race category.

[4]May be of any race.

r = Revised, controlled to 1990 census based population estimates; previous 1993 data controlled to 1980 census based population estimates.

Table A-13. Population 14 to 24 Years Old, by High School Graduate Status, College Enrollment, Attainment, Sex, Race, and Hispanic Origin, October 1967–2011—*Continued*

(Numbers in thousands; percent)

Year, race, and Hispanic origin	Population 18 to 24 years old[1]								High school graduates, 14 to 24 years old		
	Total	High school graduates		Percent			High school dropouts		All graduates	Percent	
		Total	Enrolled in college	High school graduates	Enrolled in college	High school graduate enrolled in college	Number	Percent		Enrolled in college	Enrolled or completed some college
Both Sexes— *(Continued)*											
1987	2,592	1,597	455	61.6	17.6	28.5	849	32.8	1,612	28.7	44.0
1986	2,514	1,507	458	59.9	18.2	30.4	864	34.4	1,535	30.9	45.6
1985	2,221	1,396	375	62.9	16.9	26.9	700	31.5	1,419	27.6	46.7
1984	2,018	1,212	362	60.1	17.9	29.9	691	34.2	1,223	30.0	46.0
1983	2,025	1,110	349	54.8	17.2	31.4	759	37.5	1,134	32.3	48.4
1982	2,001	1,153	337	57.6	16.8	29.2	740	37.0	1,173	30.0	47.3
1981	2,052	1,144	342	55.8	16.7	29.9	790	38.5	1,166	30.5	45.8
1980	2,033	1,099	327	54.1	16.1	29.8	820	40.3	1,117	30.1	47.3
1979	1,754	968	292	55.2	16.6	30.2	687	39.2	1,001	31.2	45.7
1978	1,672	935	254	55.9	15.2	27.2	656	39.2	965	28.0	43.2
1977	1,609	880	277	54.7	17.2	31.5	622	38.7	900	32.4	43.8
1976	1,551	862	309	55.6	19.9	35.8	566	36.5	891	36.3	48.9
1975	1,446	832	295	57.5	20.4	35.5	505	34.9	849	36.5	50.8
1974	1,506	842	272	55.9	18.1	32.3	558	37.1	858	33.1	47.8
1973	1,285	709	206	55.2	16.0	29.1	500	38.9	732	30.3	43.0
1972	1,338	694	179	51.9	13.4	25.8	541	40.4	709	27.2	36.7
Male											
2011	3,250	2,421	1,006	74.5	31.0	41.6	568	17.5	2,458	41.9	60.2
2010	2,930	2,034	819	69.4	27.9	40.2	623	21.3	2,065	40.6	58.5
2009	2,741	1,894	663	69.1	24.2	35.0	616	22.5	1,925	35.6	51.3
2008	2,675	1,797	615	67.2	23.0	34.2	649	24.3	1,841	35.1	54.4
2007	2,706	1,689	560	62.4	20.7	33.1	790	29.2	1,711	33.6	52.2
2006	2,618	1,600	523	61.1	20.0	32.7	812	31.0	1,628	33.2	53.2
2005	2,613	1,569	540	60.1	20.7	26.2	838	32.1	1,589	34.6	52.4
2004	2,648	1,597	574	60.3	21.7	36.0	888	33.5	1,614	35.9	53.0
2003	2,541	1,548	465	60.9	18.3	30.0	805	31.7	1,571	30.0	48.7
2002	2,707	1,562	439	57.7	16.2	28.1	914	33.8	1,572	28.1	48.4
2001	2,596	1,455	449	56.1	17.3	31.0	962	37.1	1,468	31.0	48.1
2000	2,171	1,172	401	54.0	18.5	34.2	800	36.8	1,197	34.5	50.8
1999	2,045	1,122	322	54.9	15.8	28.7	746	36.4	1,131	28.7	45.7
1998	2,109	1,146	346	54.3	16.4	30.2	838	39.7	1,153	30.0	47.2
1997	1,937	1,140	371	58.9	19.2	32.5	643	33.2	1,168	33.0	49.2
1996	1,815	994	300	54.8	16.5	30.2	657	36.2	1,005	30.6	48.8
1995	1,907	1,106	356	58.0	18.7	32.2	653	34.2	1,022	36.2	52.3
1994	1,896	1,021	312	53.8	16.5	30.6	685	36.1	1,026	30.7	52.7
1993[r]	1,710	1,005	338	58.8	19.8	33.6	591	34.6	1,023	33.7	51.2
1993	1,354	786	266	58.1	19.6	33.8	470	34.7	803	33.9	51.1
1992	1,384	720	247	52.0	17.8	34.3	531	38.4	736	34.8	52.2
1991	1,503	719	211	47.8	14.0	29.3	668	44.4	728	29.7	42.2
1990	1,403	753	214	53.7	15.3	28.4	559	39.8	770	29.4	46.5
1989	1,439	756	211	52.5	14.7	27.9	580	40.3	767	28.2	42.7
1988	1,375	724	228	52.7	16.6	31.5	553	40.2	736	32.2	48.3
1987	1,337	795	247	59.5	18.5	31.1	461	34.5	803	31.1	45.1
1986	1,339	769	233	57.4	17.4	30.3	499	37.3	776	30.5	44.4
1985	1,132	659	168	58.2	14.8	25.5	405	35.8	675	26.4	44.9
1984	956	549	154	57.4	16.1	28.1	338	35.4	554	28.2	45.7
1983	968	476	152	49.2	15.7	31.9	396	40.9	489	33.1	47.4
1982	944	519	141	55.0	14.9	27.2	347	36.8	525	28.0	44.8
1981	988	498	164	50.4	16.6	32.9	428	43.3	506	33.6	48.6
1980	1,012	518	160	51.2	15.8	30.9	431	42.6	521	31.1	49.5
1979	837	454	153	54.2	18.3	33.7	328	39.2	469	34.3	49.5
1978	781	420	126	53.8	16.1	30.0	313	40.1	438	30.4	46.3

Note: The change in the educational attainment question and the college completion categories from "4 or more years of college" to "at least some college" in 1992 caused an increase in the proportion of 14-to-24-year-old high school graduates enrolled in college or completed some college, of approximately 5 percentage points. High school graduates are people who have completed 4 years of high school or more, for 1967 to 1991. Beginning in 1992, they were people whose highest degree was a high school diploma (including equivalency) or higher.

[1]Civilian noninstitutionalized population.

[4] May be of any race.

r = Revised, controlled to 1990 census based population estimates; previous 1993 data controlled to 1980 census based population estimates.

Table A-13. Population 14 to 24 Years Old, by High School Graduate Status, College Enrollment, Attainment, Sex, Race, and Hispanic Origin, October 1967–2011—*Continued*

(Numbers in thousands; percent)

Year, race, and Hispanic origin	Population 18 to 24 years old[1]								High school graduates, 14 to 24 years old		
	Total	High school graduates		Percent			High school dropouts		All graduates	Percent	
		Total	Enrolled in college	High school graduates	Enrolled in college	High school graduate enrolled in college	Number	Percent		Enrolled in college	Enrolled or completed some college
Male— *(Continued)*											
1977	754	396	139	52.5	18.4	35.1	295	39.1	404	35.9	46.5
1976	701	378	150	53.9	21.4	39.7	253	36.1	403	39.8	51.8
1975	678	383	145	56.5	21.4	37.9	221	32.6	390	37.9	55.4
1974	720	390	141	54.2	19.6	36.2	279	38.8	401	36.7	51.4
1973	625	348	105	55.7	16.8	30.2	228	36.5	361	32.1	45.4
1972	609	301	92	49.4	15.1	30.6	253	41.5	309	32.0	44.3
Female											
2011	2,724	2,147	1,073	78.8	39.4	50.0	407	15.0	2,173	50.0	71.4
2010	2,755	2,104	995	76.4	36.1	47.3	426	15.5	2,134	47.7	67.8
2009	2,591	1,853	803	71.5	31.0	43.3	496	19.1	1,888	43.6	64.5
2008	2,501	1,821	723	72.8	28.9	39.7	506	20.2	1,850	40.3	63.1
2007	2,469	1,798	816	72.8	33.0	45.4	520	21.1	1,842	45.6	63.4
2006	2,388	1,701	660	71.2	27.6	38.8	501	21.0	1,751	39.7	61.0
2005	2,285	1,661	675	72.7	29.5	39.3	498	21.8	1,691	41.2	62.0
2004	2,293	1,647	647	71.8	28.2	39.3	498	21.7	1,673	39.8	58.6
2003	2,213	1,548	651	69.9	29.4	42.1	548	24.7	1,563	41.9	64.4
2002	2,211	1,516	540	68.6	24.4	35.6	565	25.6	1,537	35.9	57.9
2001	2,296	1,576	585	68.6	25.5	37.1	586	25.5	1,600	37.1	57.0
2000	1,963	1,290	498	65.7	25.4	38.6	535	27.3	1,312	38.9	55.2
1999	1,908	1,203	417	63.0	21.8	34.7	593	31.1	1,228	34.4	53.3
1998	1,906	1,257	474	66.0	24.9	37.7	545	28.6	1,266	38.2	58.7
1997	1,669	1,097	436	65.7	26.1	39.7	460	27.6	1,135	41.4	59.6
1996	1,694	1,026	406	60.6	24.0	39.6	554	32.7	1,043	40.4	56.0
1995	1,696	1,011	389	59.6	22.9	38.4	598	35.4	1,022	38.6	59.6
1994	1,628	973	350	59.8	21.5	36.0	539	33.1	983	36.2	55.9
1993[r]	1,652	1,045	390	63.3	23.6	37.3	510	30.9	1,059	37.8	60.1
1993	1,418	895	336	63.1	23.7	37.5	439	31.0	907	38.0	60.4
1992	1,369	860	339	62.8	24.8	39.4	405	29.6	867	39.9	57.4
1991	1,372	780	305	56.9	22.2	39.1	473	34.5	791	39.2	52.5
1990	1,346	745	221	55.3	16.4	29.7	465	34.5	753	29.5	43.0
1989	1,377	823	244	59.8	17.7	29.6	482	35.0	836	30.5	44.5
1988	1,267	736	224	58.1	17.7	30.4	492	38.8	747	30.5	45.8
1987	1,256	801	208	63.8	16.6	26.0	387	30.8	808	26.4	43.2
1986	1,175	739	226	62.9	19.2	30.6	365	31.1	759	31.4	46.8
1985	1,091	734	205	67.3	18.8	27.9	295	27.0	743	28.4	48.0
1984	1,061	661	207	62.3	19.5	31.3	353	33.2	667	31.5	46.6
1983	1,057	634	198	60.0	18.7	31.2	363	34.3	644	31.8	49.7
1982	1,056	634	196	60.0	18.6	30.9	393	37.2	648	31.8	49.2
1981	1,064	646	178	60.7	16.7	27.6	362	34.0	662	28.2	43.4
1980	1,021	579	165	56.7	16.2	28.5	389	38.1	595	29.1	45.4
1979	917	516	140	56.3	15.3	27.1	358	39.0	534	28.1	42.3
1978	891	516	128	57.9	14.4	24.8	343	38.5	528	25.8	40.0
1977	855	483	139	56.5	16.3	28.8	326	38.1	495	29.7	41.6
1976	850	483	160	56.8	18.8	33.1	313	36.8	489	33.5	46.5
1975	769	449	150	58.4	19.5	33.4	283	36.8	460	34.8	46.7
1974	786	451	129	57.4	16.4	28.6	280	35.6	459	29.2	43.4
1973	658	362	102	55.0	15.5	28.2	272	41.3	372	28.8	41.1
1972	728	394	88	54.1	12.1	22.3	288	39.6	402	23.6	31.1

Note: The change in the educational attainment question and the college completion categories from "4 or more years of college" to "at least some college" in 1992 caused an increase in the proportion of 14-to-24-year-old high school graduates enrolled in college or completed some college, of approximately 5 percentage points. High school graduates are people who have completed 4 years of high school or more, for 1967 to 1991. Beginning in 1992, they were people whose highest degree was a high school diploma (including equivalency) or higher.

[1]Civilian noninstitutionalized population.

r = Revised, controlled to 1990 census based population estimates; previous 1993 data controlled to 1980 census based population estimates.

Table A-13. Population 14 to 24 Years Old, by High School Graduate Status, College Enrollment, Attainment, Sex, Race, and Hispanic Origin, October 1967–2011—*Continued*

(Numbers in thousands; percent)

Year, race, and Hispanic origin	Population 18 to 24 years old[1]								High school graduates, 14 to 24 years old		
	Total	High school graduates		Percent			High school dropouts		All graduates	Percent	
		Total	Enrolled in college	High school graduates	Enrolled in college	High school graduate enrolled in college	Number	Percent		Enrolled in college	Enrolled or completed some college
WHITE ALONE OR IN COMBINATION											
Both Sexes											
2011	23,679	20,256	10,043	85.5	42.4	49.6	1,941	8.2	20,504	49.7	73.9
2010	23,381	19,949	9,524	85.3	40.7	47.7	2,013	8.6	20,180	48.0	72.9
2009	23,256	19,784	9,562	85.1	41.1	48.3	2,127	9.1	20,060	48.5	72.0
2008	23,120	19,810	9,360	85.7	40.5	47.2	2,072	9.0	20,067	47.5	71.6
2007	22,928	19,330	8,958	84.3	39.1	46.3	2,338	10.2	19,595	46.5	70.3
2006	22,670	18,882	8,465	83.3	37.3	44.8	2,458	10.8	19,153	45.1	69.9
2005	22,345	18,583	8,721	83.2	39.0	50.1	2,539	11.4	18,818	47.0	70.0
2004	22,411	18,663	8,544	83.3	38.1	45.8	2,639	11.8	18,868	46.0	69.0
2003	22,029	18,335	8,358	83.2	37.9	45.6	2,558	11.6	18,565	45.6	69.0
Male											
2011	12,153	10,175	4,789	83.7	39.4	47.1	1,105	9.1	10,308	47.2	69.7
2010	11,832	9,869	4,472	83.4	37.8	45.3	1,152	9.7	9,976	45.4	68.5
2009	11,774	9,824	4,513	83.4	38.3	45.9	1,224	10.4	9,952	46.1	68.3
2008	11,738	9,891	4,444	84.3	37.9	44.9	1,165	9.9	10,031	45.2	67.8
2007	11,670	9,511	4,116	81.5	35.3	43.3	1,397	12.0	9,634	43.4	66.0
2006	11,502	9,331	3,923	81.1	34.1	42.0	1,427	12.4	9,435	42.2	66.1
2005	11,394	9,086	4,018	79.7	35.3	43.5	1,519	13.3	9,193	44.2	60.0
2004	11,371	9,227	3,956	81.1	34.8	42.9	1,548	13.6	9,296	43.1	64.4
2003	11,147	8,967	3,815	80.4	34.2	42.5	1,493	13.4	9,070	42.6	65.1
Female											
2011	11,525	10,081	5,254	87.5	45.6	52.1	836	7.3	10,196	52.1	78.1
2010	11,549	10,080	5,052	87.3	43.7	50.1	861	7.5	10,204	50.5	77.1
2009	11,482	9,960	5,049	86.7	44.0	50.7	903	7.9	10,108	50.8	75.6
2008	11,381	9,919	4,916	87.2	43.2	49.6	908	8.0	10,036	49.9	75.4
2007	11,258	9,820	4,842	87.2	43.0	49.3	941	8.4	9,960	49.4	74.4
2006	11,168	9,551	4,542	85.5	40.7	47.6	1,032	9.2	9,718	47.8	73.6
2005	10,952	9,497	4,702	86.7	42.9	57.1	1,020	9.3	9,625	49.7	73.9
2004	11,040	9,436	4,588	85.5	41.6	48.6	1,091	9.9	9,572	48.8	73.5
2003	10,882	9,367	4,543	86.1	41.7	48.5	1,065	9.8	9,495	48.5	72.7
BLACK ALONE OR IN COMBINATION											
Both Sexes											
2011	4,793	3,902	1,759	81.4	36.7	45.1	424	8.8	3,955	45.5	67.3
2010	4,745	3,898	1,808	82.1	38.1	46.4	493	10.4	3,965	46.6	66.7
2009	4,623	3,688	1,699	79.8	36.8	46.1	532	11.5	3,766	46.0	67.2
2008	4,531	3,588	1,435	79.2	31.7	40.0	548	12.1	3,646	40.3	60.9
2007	4,425	3,603	1,468	81.4	33.2	40.7	477	10.8	3,671	40.9	61.8
2006	4,264	3,287	1,387	77.1	32.5	42.2	560	13.1	3,359	42.2	61.1
2005	4,158	3,303	1,371	79.4	33.0	31.7	530	12.7	3,378	41.5	63.5
2004	4,115	3,190	1,318	77.5	32.0	41.3	620	15.1	3,253	41.8	63.5
2003	4,016	3,091	1,285	77.0	32.0	41.6	563	14.0	3,141	41.9	62.0
Male											
2011	2,289	1,800	762	78.6	33.3	42.4	218	9.5	1,831	42.9	61.4
2010	2,250	1,781	779	79.2	34.6	43.7	269	11.9	1,823	43.7	61.9
2009	2,211	1,702	712	76.9	32.2	41.9	301	13.6	1,726	41.6	63.7
2008	2,190	1,743	633	79.6	28.9	36.3	235	10.7	1,770	36.9	54.9
2007	2,132	1,703	686	79.9	32.2	40.3	234	11.0	1,728	40.4	59.6
2006	2,032	1,545	577	76.0	28.4	37.3	225	11.0	1,576	37.2	54.5
2005	1,988	1,466	557	73.7	28.0	42.5	290	14.6	1,492	37.9	58.2
2004	1,951	1,418	521	72.7	26.7	36.7	347	17.8	1,442	37.0	61.3
2003	1,868	1,382	525	74.0	28.1	38.0	311	16.6	1,397	38.3	57.4

Note: The change in the educational attainment question and the college completion categories from "4 or more years of college" to "at least some college" in 1992 caused an increase in the proportion of 14-to-24-year-old high school graduates enrolled in college or completed some college, of approximately 5 percentage points. High school graduates are people who have completed 4 years of high school or more, for 1967 to 1991. Beginning in 1992, they were people whose highest degree was a high school diploma (including equivalency) or higher.

[1]Civilian noninstitutionalized population.

Table A-13. Population 14 to 24 Years Old, by High School Graduate Status, College Enrollment, Attainment, Sex, Race, and Hispanic Origin, October 1967–2011—*Continued*

(Numbers in thousands; percent)

Year, race, and Hispanic origin	Population 18 to 24 years old[1]								High school graduates, 14 to 24 years old		
	Total	High school graduates		Percent			High school dropouts		All graduates	Percent	
		Total	Enrolled in college	High school graduates	Enrolled in college	High school graduate enrolled in college	Number	Percent		Enrolled in college	Enrolled or completed some college
Female											
2011	2,504	2,102	997	84.0	39.8	47.4	206	8.2	2,124	47.7	72.3
2010	2,495	2,117	1,029	84.8	41.3	48.6	224	9.0	2,142	49.0	70.7
2009	2,411	1,987	987	82.4	40.9	49.7	231	9.6	2,040	49.8	70.1
2008	2,341	1,845	802	78.8	34.2	43.5	313	13.4	1,876	43.5	66.5
2007	2,293	1,900	782	82.9	34.1	41.2	243	10.6	1,942	41.3	63.7
2006	2,232	1,742	810	78.1	36.3	46.5	335	15.0	1,783	46.5	66.8
2005	2,170	1,837	814	84.7	37.5	21.2	240	11.1	1,885	44.3	67.7
2004	2,164	1,772	797	81.9	36.8	45.0	272	12.6	1,811	45.5	65.3
2003	2,148	1,708	760	79.5	35.4	44.5	252	11.7	1,744	44.7	65.7
ASIAN ALONE OR IN COMBINATION											
Both Sexes											
2011	1,435	1,295	833	90.2	58.0	64.3	67	4.6	1,149	66.9	88.1
2010	1,465	1,338	904	91.3	61.7	67.6	80	5.5	1,382	68.0	88.9
2009	1,345	1,231	844	91.5	62.8	68.5	29	2.1	1,249	68.5	90.8
2008	1,251	1,153	738	92.1	59.0	64.0	42	3.4	1,188	64.4	89.7
2007	1,293	1,126	720	87.1	55.7	63.9	94	7.3	1,143	63.9	90.3
2006	1,270	1,158	705	91.2	55.5	60.9	49	3.9	1,180	60.6	86.1
2005	1,299	1,214	773	93.5	59.5	63.7	38	2.9	1,243	64.2	86.0
2004	1,263	1,167	750	92.5	59.4	64.3	53	4.2	1,191	64.6	87.6
2003	1,280	1,162	774	90.8	60.5	66.6	56	4.4	1,184	66.9	87.8
Male											
2011	747	673	429	90.1	57.4	63.7	31	4.2	582	66.1	87.6
2010	750	685	453	91.4	60.4	66.1	40	5.3	711	66.5	87.4
2009	673	624	418	92.8	62.2	67.0	7	1.1	637	66.8	89.8
2008	626	560	340	89.4	54.4	60.8	22	3.4	582	62.2	89.2
2007	560	481	318	85.8	56.9	66.3	38	6.8	483	66.4	91.8
2006	649	578	362	89.1	55.8	62.7	34	5.3	591	62.3	83.8
2005	653	603	392	92.4	59.9	65.0	20	3.1	621	65.1	86.3
2004	634	588	398	92.8	62.7	67.7	18	2.9	601	68.0	87.8
2003	609	545	370	89.5	60.8	67.9	43	7.1	551	67.7	88.7
Female											
2011	688	622	403	90.4	58.7	64.9	35	5.1	567	67.8	88.7
2010	715	652	451	91.2	63.1	69.1	41	5.7	671	69.7	90.4
2009	673	607	426	90.3	63.3	70.1	21	3.2	611	70.2	91.8
2008	625	593	397	94.9	63.6	67.0	21	3.3	605	66.5	90.3
2007	605	529	339	87.4	56.0	64.1	48	7.9	543	63.9	91.5
2006	621	580	343	93.4	55.3	59.2	14	2.3	589	58.8	88.5
2005	645	610	381	94.6	59.1	62.5	17	2.7	622	63.3	85.8
2004	628	579	352	92.1	56.0	60.8	35	5.5	591	61.2	87.5
2003	671	617	404	92.0	60.2	65.5	13	1.9	633	66.3	87.0

Note: The change in the educational attainment question and the college completion categories from "4 or more years of college" to "at least some college" in 1992 caused an increase in the proportion of 14-to-24-year-old high school graduates enrolled in college or completed some college, of approximately 5 percentage points. High school graduates are people who have completed 4 years of high school or more, for 1967 to 1991. Beginning in 1992, they were people whose highest degree was a high school diploma (including equivalency) or higher.

[1]Civilian noninstitutionalized population.

Table A-14. Population 18 and 19 Years Old, by School Enrollment Status, Sex, Race, and Hispanic Origin, October 1967–2011

(Numbers in thousands)

Year, race, and Hispanic origin	Total[1]	Population 18 and 19 years old							
		Still in high school	Percent	Dropped out	Percent	High school graduate only	Percent	In college	Percent
ALL RACES									
Both Sexes									
2011	8,465	1,775	21.0	545	6.4	1,903	22.5	4,242	50.1
2010	8,529	1,540	18.1	622	7.3	2,003	23.5	4,364	51.2
2009	8,615	1,645	19.1	736	8.5	1,944	22.6	4,289	49.8
2008	8,492	1,481	17.4	750	8.8	2,134	25.1	4,126	48.6
2007	8,338	1,491	17.9	675	8.1	2,097	25.2	4,075	48.9
2006	8,102	1,560	19.3	743	9.2	2,053	25.3	3,746	46.2
2005	7,559	1,372	18.1	661	8.7	1,694	22.4	3,832	50.7
2004	7,701	1,266	16.4	840	10.9	1,910	24.8	3,685	47.8
2003	7,533	1,345	17.9	817	10.8	1,859	24.7	3,512	46.6
2002	7,907	1,427	18.0	884	11.2	2,015	25.5	3,581	45.3
2001	7,985	1,394	17.5	1,034	12.9	2,079	26.0	3,478	43.6
2000	8,045	1,327	16.5	1,012	12.6	2,107	26.2	3,599	44.7
1999	7,991	1,321	16.5	1,047	13.1	2,103	26.3	3,520	44.0
1998	7,902	1,244	15.7	1,104	14.0	1,884	23.8	3,670	46.4
1997	7,510	1,256	16.7	1,038	13.8	1,854	24.7	3,362	44.8
1996	7,376	1,230	16.7	940	12.7	1,897	25.7	3,309	44.9
1995	7,198	1,173	16.3	1,051	14.6	1,873	26.0	3,101	43.1
1994	6,946	1,129	16.3	929	13.4	1,837	26.4	3,051	43.9
1993	6,594	1,137	17.2	778	11.8	1,753	26.6	2,926	44.4
1992	6,535	1,121	17.2	780	11.9	1,742	26.7	2,892	44.3
1991	6,664	1,040	15.6	889	13.3	1,806	27.1	2,929	44.0
1990	7,064	1,024	14.5	1,003	14.2	2,018	28.6	3,019	42.7
1989	7,361	1,058	14.4	1,033	14.0	2,204	29.9	3,066	41.7
1988	7,294	1,013	13.9	1,063	14.6	2,172	29.8	3,046	41.8
1987	7,160	937	13.1	954	13.3	2,224	31.1	3,045	42.5
1986	7,095	930	13.1	872	12.3	2,351	33.1	2,942	41.5
1985	7,204	809	11.2	1,031	14.3	2,457	34.1	2,907	40.4
1984	7,428	857	11.5	1,129	15.2	2,575	34.7	2,867	38.6
1983	7,819	999	12.8	1,132	14.5	2,748	35.1	2,940	37.6
1982	8,023	908	11.3	1,336	16.7	2,850	35.5	2,929	36.5
1981	8,115	932	11.5	1,299	16.0	2,840	35.0	3,044	37.5
1980	8,160	855	10.5	1,284	15.7	3,088	37.8	2,933	35.9
1979	8,214	849	10.3	1,382	16.8	3,139	38.2	2,844	34.6
1978	8,153	801	9.8	1,361	16.7	3,092	37.9	2,899	35.6
1977	8,151	849	10.4	1,355	16.6	3,034	37.2	2,913	35.7
1976	8,148	831	10.2	1,355	16.6	3,025	37.1	2,937	36.0
1975	8,024	822	10.2	1,286	16.0	2,973	37.1	2,943	36.7
1974	7,822	777	9.9	1,302	16.6	3,146	40.2	2,597	33.2
1973	7,649	766	10.0	1,228	16.1	3,138	41.0	2,517	32.9
1972	7,462	778	10.4	1,100	14.7	2,904	38.9	2,680	35.9
1971	7,231	830	11.5	1,108	15.3	2,567	35.5	2,726	37.7
1970	6,958	728	10.5	1,125	16.2	2,511	36.1	2,594	37.3
1969	6,677	749	11.2	1,007	15.1	2,320	34.7	2,601	39.0
1968	6,587	816	12.4	1,033	15.7	2,237	34.0	2,501	38.0
1967	6,358	741	11.7	1,086	17.1	2,245	35.3	2,286	36.0
Male									
2011	4,341	1,038	23.9	293	6.8	1,060	24.4	1,949	44.9
2010	4,296	867	20.2	347	8.1	1,073	25.0	2,009	46.8
2009	4,352	899	20.7	410	9.4	1,114	25.6	1,928	44.3
2008	4,289	834	19.5	376	8.8	1,169	27.3	1,909	44.5
2007	4,222	895	21.2	354	8.4	1,070	25.3	1,903	45.1
2006	4,103	907	22.1	414	10.1	1,079	26.3	1,703	41.5
2005	3,880	899	23.2	392	10.1	914	23.6	1,675	43.2
2004	3,861	714	18.5	522	13.5	1,015	26.3	1,610	41.7
2003	3,764	781	20.7	480	12.8	935	24.8	1,568	41.7
2002	4,042	862	21.3	523	12.9	1,022	25.3	1,635	40.5
2001	4,027	801	19.9	614	15.2	1,042	25.9	1,570	39.0
2000	4,037	783	19.4	571	14.1	1,113	27.6	1,570	38.9
1999	4,026	780	19.4	550	13.7	1,048	26.0	1,648	40.9
1998	3,994	732	18.3	611	15.3	984	24.6	1,667	41.7
1997	3,816	750	19.7	585	15.3	920	24.1	1,561	40.9
1996	3,711	769	20.7	488	13.2	965	26.0	1,489	40.1

Note: High school graduates are people who have completed 4 years of high school or more, for 1967 to 1991. Beginning in 1992, they were people whose highest degree was a high school diploma (including equivalency) or higher.

[1]Civilian noninstitutionalized population.

Table A-14. Population 18 and 19 Years Old, by School Enrollment Status, Sex, Race, and Hispanic Origin, October 1967–2011—*Continued*

(Numbers in thousands)

Year, race, and Hispanic origin	Total[1]	Population 18 and 19 years old							
		Still in high school	Percent	Dropped out	Percent	High school graduate only	Percent	In college	Percent
Male—*(Continued)*									
1995	3,611	719	19.9	532	14.7	929	25.7	1,431	39.6
1994	3,485	688	19.7	499	14.3	882	25.3	1,416	40.6
1993	3,329	712	21.4	403	12.1	877	26.3	1,337	40.2
1992	3,275	694	21.2	400	12.2	856	26.1	1,325	40.5
1991	3,307	650	19.7	453	13.7	878	26.5	1,326	40.1
1990	3,503	595	17.0	512	14.6	953	27.2	1,443	41.2
1989	3,640	640	17.6	531	14.6	1,047	28.8	1,422	39.1
1988	3,618	666	18.4	566	15.6	1,021	28.2	1,365	37.7
1987	3,537	564	15.9	493	13.9	997	28.2	1,483	41.9
1986	3,502	594	17.0	459	13.1	1,045	29.8	1,404	40.1
1985	3,550	503	14.2	580	16.3	1,118	31.5	1,349	38.0
1984	3,674	551	15.0	594	16.2	1,156	31.5	1,373	37.4
1983	3,877	616	15.9	630	16.2	1,291	33.3	1,340	34.6
1982	3,961	562	14.2	709	17.9	1,314	33.2	1,376	34.7
1981	3,996	567	14.2	706	17.7	1,273	31.9	1,450	36.3
1980	3,993	510	12.8	673	16.9	1,441	36.1	1,369	34.3
1979	4,023	533	13.2	739	18.4	1,410	35.0	1,341	33.3
1978	3,975	511	12.9	692	17.4	1,381	34.7	1,391	35.0
1977	3,961	522	13.2	702	17.7	1,341	33.9	1,396	35.2
1976	3,957	516	13.0	684	17.3	1,366	34.5	1,391	35.2
1975	3,891	514	13.2	603	15.5	1,348	34.6	1,426	36.6
1974	3,782	469	12.4	706	18.7	1,345	35.6	1,262	33.4
1973	3,720	490	13.2	589	15.8	1,348	36.2	1,293	34.8
1972	3,630	492	13.6	555	15.3	1,217	33.5	1,366	37.6
1971	3,503	496	14.2	551	15.7	1,012	28.9	1,444	41.2
1970	3,349	485	14.5	537	16.0	981	29.3	1,346	40.2
1969	3,173	489	15.4	473	14.9	814	25.7	1,397	44.0
1968	3,133	535	17.1	485	15.5	756	24.1	1,357	43.3
1967	2,908	438	15.1	500	17.2	772	26.5	1,198	41.2
Female									
2011	4,124	737	17.9	252	6.1	843	20.4	2,293	55.6
2010	4,233	673	15.9	275	6.5	930	22.0	2,355	55.6
2009	4,263	746	17.5	325	7.6	830	19.5	2,361	55.4
2008	4,203	647	15.4	374	8.9	965	23.0	2,217	52.7
2007	4,116	595	14.5	321	7.8	1,027	25.0	2,172	52.8
2006	3,999	654	16.3	328	8.2	974	24.4	2,043	51.1
2005	3,679	472	12.8	269	7.3	886	24.1	2,052	55.8
2004	3,840	553	14.4	318	8.3	895	23.3	2,074	54.0
2003	3,769	565	15.0	337	8.9	923	24.5	1,944	51.6
2002	3,865	565	14.6	361	9.3	993	25.7	1,946	50.3
2001	3,958	594	15.0	420	10.6	1,037	26.2	1,907	48.2
2000	4,008	544	13.6	440	11.0	995	24.8	2,029	50.6
1999	3,965	540	13.6	497	12.5	1,056	26.6	1,872	47.2
1998	3,908	513	13.1	492	12.6	900	23.0	2,003	51.3
1997	3,694	506	13.7	453	12.3	934	25.3	1,801	48.8
1996	3,665	460	12.6	452	12.3	932	25.4	1,821	49.7
1995	3,587	453	12.6	519	14.5	944	26.3	1,671	46.6
1994	3,461	440	12.7	430	12.4	956	27.6	1,635	47.2
1993	3,265	425	13.0	375	11.5	877	26.9	1,588	48.6
1992	3,260	428	13.1	380	11.7	886	27.2	1,566	48.0
1991	3,357	389	11.6	436	13.0	929	27.7	1,603	47.8
1990	3,561	429	12.0	491	13.8	1,065	29.9	1,576	44.3
1989	3,721	421	11.3	501	13.5	1,156	31.1	1,643	44.2
1988	3,676	346	9.4	497	13.5	1,151	31.3	1,682	45.8
1987	3,623	374	10.3	461	12.7	1,226	33.8	1,562	43.1
1986	3,593	337	9.4	413	11.5	1,306	36.3	1,537	42.8
1985	3,654	304	8.3	451	12.3	1,340	36.7	1,559	42.7
1984	3,754	306	8.2	535	14.3	1,419	37.8	1,494	39.8
1983	3,942	383	9.7	502	12.7	1,457	37.0	1,600	40.6
1982	4,062	346	8.5	627	15.4	1,536	37.8	1,553	38.2
1981	4,119	364	8.8	594	14.4	1,567	38.0	1,594	38.7
1980	4,167	345	8.3	611	14.7	1,646	39.5	1,565	37.6
1979	4,191	317	7.6	643	15.3	1,728	41.2	1,503	35.9

Note: High school graduates are people who have completed 4 years of high school or more, for 1967 to 1991. Beginning in 1992, they were people whose highest degree was a high school diploma (including equivalency) or higher.
[1]Civilian noninstitutionalized population.

Table A-14. Population 18 and 19 Years Old, by School Enrollment Status, Sex, Race, and Hispanic Origin, October 1967–2011—*Continued*

(Numbers in thousands)

Year, race, and Hispanic origin	Total[1]	Population 18 and 19 years old							
		Still in high school	Percent	Dropped out	Percent	High school graduate only	Percent	In college	Percent
Female—*(Continued)*									
1978	4,178	291	7.0	669	16.0	1,711	41.0	1,507	36.1
1977	4,190	326	7.8	654	15.6	1,693	40.4	1,517	36.2
1976	4,191	314	7.5	672	16.0	1,659	39.6	1,546	36.9
1975	4,133	308	7.5	683	16.5	1,625	39.3	1,517	36.7
1974	4,040	309	7.6	596	14.8	1,800	44.6	1,335	33.0
1973	3,929	276	7.0	638	16.2	1,791	45.6	1,224	31.2
1972	3,832	287	7.5	545	14.2	1,686	44.0	1,314	34.3
1971	3,728	337	9.0	556	14.9	1,554	41.7	1,281	34.4
1970	3,609	253	7.0	589	16.3	1,519	42.1	1,248	34.6
1969	3,504	260	7.4	534	15.2	1,506	43.0	1,204	34.4
1968	3,454	281	8.1	548	15.9	1,481	42.9	1,144	33.1
1967	3,450	302	8.8	586	17.0	1,474	42.7	1,088	31.5
WHITE									
Both Sexes									
2011	6,501	1,274	19.6	449	6.9	1,480	22.8	3,298	50.7
2010	6,523	1,168	17.9	435	6.7	1,522	23.3	3,398	52.1
2009	6,594	1,194	18.1	526	8.0	1,536	23.3	3,337	50.6
2008	6,589	1,067	16.2	558	8.5	1,611	24.4	3,353	50.9
2007	6,446	1,083	16.8	517	8.0	1,605	24.9	3,242	50.3
2006	6,321	1,121	17.7	600	9.5	1,619	25.6	2,982	47.2
2005	5,893	1,023	17.4	515	8.7	1,383	23.5	2,972	50.4
2004	6,043	963	15.9	634	10.5	1,500	24.8	2,946	48.8
2003[2]	5,915	979	16.6	659	11.1	1,444	24.4	2,833	47.9
2002	6,252	1,096	17.5	663	10.6	1,602	25.6	2,891	46.2
2001	6,254	1,022	16.3	843	13.5	1,634	26.1	2,755	44.1
2000	6,399	1,010	15.8	795	12.4	1,680	26.3	2,914	45.5
1999	6,383	1,009	15.8	810	12.7	1,715	26.9	2,849	44.6
1998	6,266	884	14.1	848	13.5	1,540	24.6	2,994	47.8
1997	5,995	896	14.9	816	13.6	1,491	24.9	2,792	46.6
1996	5,833	914	15.7	735	12.6	1,453	24.9	2,731	46.8
1995	5,698	803	14.1	809	14.2	1,509	26.5	2,577	45.2
1994	5,559	817	14.7	681	12.3	1,493	26.9	2,568	46.2
1993	5,252	786	15.0	628	12.0	1,382	26.3	2,456	46.8
1992	5,203	793	15.2	582	11.2	1,409	27.1	2,419	46.5
1991	5,358	709	13.2	722	13.5	1,440	26.9	2,487	46.4
1990	5,725	724	12.6	799	14.0	1,654	28.9	2,548	44.5
1989	6,013	744	12.4	819	13.6	1,802	30.0	2,648	44.0
1988	5,981	699	11.7	855	14.3	1,788	29.9	2,639	44.1
1987	5,845	667	11.4	762	13.0	1,852	31.7	2,564	43.9
1986	5,825	669	11.5	693	11.9	1,940	33.3	2,523	43.3
1985	5,922	566	9.6	815	13.8	2,002	33.8	2,539	42.9
1984	6,139	594	9.7	913	14.9	2,091	34.1	2,541	41.4
1983	6,452	688	10.7	884	13.7	2,283	35.4	2,597	40.3
1982	6,666	647	9.7	1,051	15.8	2,419	36.3	2,549	38.2
1981	6,794	656	9.7	1,054	15.5	2,445	36.0	2,639	38.8
1980	6,913	621	9.0	1,032	14.9	2,682	38.8	2,578	37.3
1979	6,980	607	8.7	1,115	16.0	2,760	39.5	2,498	35.8
1978	6,933	560	8.1	1,082	15.6	2,738	39.5	2,553	36.8
1977	6,944	581	8.4	1,103	15.9	2,681	38.6	2,579	37.1
1976	6,951	581	8.4	1,131	16.3	2,662	38.3	2,577	37.1
1975	6,855	572	8.3	1,005	14.7	2,665	38.9	2,613	38.1
1974	6,707	551	8.2	1,045	15.6	2,803	41.8	2,308	34.4
1973	6,559	568	8.7	962	14.7	2,748	41.9	2,281	34.8
1972	6,424	582	9.1	857	13.3	2,574	40.1	2,411	37.5
1971	6,243	596	9.5	875	14.0	2,287	36.6	2,485	39.8
1970	6,009	563	9.4	845	14.1	2,240	37.3	2,361	39.3
1969	5,762	557	9.7	772	13.4	2,056	35.7	2,377	41.3
1968	5,692	614	10.8	822	14.4	1,972	34.6	2,284	40.1
1967	5,506	558	10.1	875	15.9	1,968	35.7	2,105	38.2

Note: High school graduates are people who have completed 4 years of high school or more, for 1967 to 1991. Beginning in 1992, they were people whose highest degree was a high school diploma (including equivalency) or higher.

[1]Civilian noninstitutionalized population.

[2]Starting in 2003 respondents could identify more than one race. Except as noted, the race data in this table from 2003 onward represent those respondents who indicated only one race category.

Table A-14. Population 18 and 19 Years Old, by School Enrollment Status, Sex, Race, and Hispanic Origin, October 1967–2011—*Continued*

(Numbers in thousands)

Year, race, and Hispanic origin	Total[1]	Population 18 and 19 years old							
		Still in high school	Percent	Dropped out	Percent	High school graduate only	Percent	In college	Percent
Male									
2011	3,352	748	22.3	240	7.2	845	25.2	1,520	45.3
2010	3,316	667	20.1	246	7.4	830	25.0	1,573	47.4
2009	3,349	652	19.5	291	8.7	894	26.7	1,511	45.1
2008	3,350	589	17.6	299	8.9	896	26.7	1,566	46.7
2007	3,277	668	20.4	281	8.6	819	25.0	1,508	46.0
2006	3,211	645	20.1	351	10.9	848	26.4	1,367	42.6
2005	3,049	665	21.8	304	10.0	737	24.2	1,343	44.1
2004	3,062	524	17.1	406	13.3	824	26.9	1,308	42.7
2003[2]	3,003	594	19.8	381	12.7	770	25.6	1,258	41.9
2002	3,186	661	20.7	366	11.5	830	26.1	1,329	41.7
2001	3,192	585	18.3	494	15.5	840	26.3	1,273	39.9
2000	3,248	612	18.8	447	13.8	900	27.7	1,289	39.7
1999	3,242	609	18.8	423	13.0	874	27.0	1,336	41.2
1998	3,197	533	16.7	472	14.8	816	25.5	1,376	43.0
1997	3,060	523	17.1	473	15.5	750	24.5	1,314	42.9
1996	2,953	575	19.5	382	12.9	773	26.2	1,223	41.4
1995	2,886	519	18.0	408	14.1	764	26.5	1,195	41.4
1994	2,813	512	18.2	355	12.6	734	26.1	1,212	43.1
1993	2,641	497	18.8	338	12.8	703	26.6	1,103	41.8
1992	2,608	482	18.5	304	11.7	720	27.6	1,102	42.3
1991	2,677	451	16.8	381	14.2	733	27.4	1,112	41.5
1990	2,852	416	14.6	421	14.8	797	27.9	1,218	42.7
1989	2,997	463	15.4	433	14.4	848	28.3	1,253	41.8
1988	2,976	487	16.4	461	15.5	834	28.0	1,194	40.1
1987	2,906	404	13.9	400	13.8	842	29.0	1,260	43.4
1986	2,888	411	14.2	370	12.8	866	30.0	1,241	43.0
1985	2,937	349	11.9	478	16.3	934	31.8	1,176	40.0
1984	3,047	378	12.4	480	15.8	965	31.7	1,224	40.2
1983	3,216	434	13.5	500	15.5	1,085	33.7	1,197	37.2
1982	3,301	412	12.5	549	16.6	1,151	34.9	1,189	36.0
1981	3,356	394	11.7	599	17.8	1,104	32.9	1,259	37.5
1980	3,407	385	11.3	549	16.1	1,241	36.4	1,232	36.2
1979	3,445	395	11.5	610	17.7	1,248	36.2	1,192	34.6
1978	3,405	368	10.8	554	16.3	1,244	36.5	1,239	36.4
1977	3,396	348	10.2	577	17.0	1,199	35.3	1,272	37.5
1976	3,393	348	10.3	582	17.2	1,219	35.9	1,244	36.7
1975	3,343	374	11.2	458	13.7	1,228	36.7	1,283	38.4
1974	3,265	343	10.5	568	17.4	1,211	37.1	1,143	35.0
1973	3,208	375	11.7	454	14.2	1,202	37.5	1,177	36.7
1972	3,137	374	11.9	423	13.5	1,098	35.0	1,242	39.6
1971	3,035	367	12.1	432	14.2	908	29.9	1,328	43.8
1970	2,901	374	12.9	384	13.2	892	30.7	1,251	43.1
1969	2,745	374	13.6	345	12.6	728	26.5	1,298	47.3
1968	2,710	403	14.9	387	14.3	658	24.3	1,262	46.6
1967	2,511	340	13.5	386	15.4	688	27.4	1,097	43.7
Female									
2011	3,148	526	16.7	209	6.6	635	20.2	1,779	56.5
2010	3,206	501	15.6	188	5.9	692	21.6	1,825	56.9
2009	3,245	542	16.7	235	7.2	642	19.8	1,826	56.3
2008	3,239	478	14.8	259	8.0	715	22.1	1,787	55.2
2007	3,169	414	13.1	235	7.4	785	24.8	1,734	54.7
2006	3,111	476	15.3	249	8.0	771	24.8	1,615	51.9
2005	2,844	358	12.6	210	7.4	647	22.7	1,629	57.3
2004	2,980	440	14.7	227	7.6	675	22.7	1,638	55.0
2003[2]	2,913	385	13.2	279	9.6	674	23.1	1,575	54.1
2002	3,066	435	14.2	297	9.7	772	25.2	1,562	50.9
2001	3,062	438	14.3	349	11.4	794	25.9	1,481	48.4
2000	3,151	397	12.6	348	11.0	781	24.8	1,625	51.6
1999	3,141	400	12.7	387	12.3	841	26.8	1,513	48.2
1998	3,069	351	11.4	376	12.3	724	23.6	1,618	52.7
1997	2,934	371	12.6	344	11.7	740	25.2	1,479	50.4
1996	2,879	338	11.7	353	12.3	680	23.6	1,508	52.4
1995	2,812	283	10.1	401	14.3	745	26.5	1,383	49.2
1994	2,746	305	11.1	325	11.8	759	27.6	1,357	49.4

Note: High school graduates are people who have completed 4 years of high school or more, for 1967 to 1991. Beginning in 1992, they were people whose highest degree was a high school diploma (including equivalency) or higher.

[1]Civilian noninstitutionalized population.

[2]Starting in 2003 respondents could identify more than one race. Except as noted, the race data in this table from 2003 onward represent those respondents who indicated only one race category.

Table A-14. Population 18 and 19 Years Old, by School Enrollment Status, Sex, Race, and Hispanic Origin, October 1967–2011—*Continued*

(Numbers in thousands)

Year, race, and Hispanic origin	Total[1]	Population 18 and 19 years old							
		Still in high school	Percent	Dropped out	Percent	High school graduate only	Percent	In college	Percent
Female—*(Continued)*									
1993	2,611	289	11.1	290	11.1	679	26.0	1,353	51.8
1992	2,595	311	12.0	278	10.7	689	26.6	1,317	50.8
1991	2,681	259	9.7	341	12.7	706	26.3	1,375	51.3
1990	2,873	307	10.7	378	13.2	857	29.8	1,331	46.3
1989	3,016	281	9.3	386	12.8	954	31.6	1,395	46.3
1988	3,005	212	7.1	394	13.1	954	31.7	1,445	48.1
1987	2,939	263	8.9	362	12.3	1,010	34.4	1,304	44.4
1986	2,937	257	8.8	323	11.0	1,074	36.6	1,283	43.7
1985	2,985	217	7.3	337	11.3	1,068	35.8	1,363	45.7
1984	3,092	216	7.0	432	14.0	1,127	36.4	1,317	42.6
1983	3,236	255	7.9	383	11.8	1,198	37.0	1,400	43.3
1982	3,365	234	7.0	502	14.9	1,269	37.7	1,360	40.4
1981	3,438	262	7.6	454	13.2	1,342	39.0	1,380	40.1
1980	3,506	237	6.8	483	13.8	1,440	41.1	1,346	38.4
1979	3,535	213	6.0	505	14.3	1,511	42.7	1,306	36.9
1978	3,528	193	5.5	528	15.0	1,493	42.3	1,314	37.2
1977	3,548	232	6.5	526	14.8	1,483	41.8	1,307	36.8
1976	3,558	230	6.5	550	15.5	1,444	40.6	1,334	37.5
1975	3,512	199	5.7	547	15.6	1,436	40.9	1,330	37.9
1974	3,442	207	6.0	477	13.9	1,592	46.3	1,166	33.9
1973	3,351	192	5.7	508	15.2	1,547	46.2	1,104	32.9
1972	3,287	208	6.3	434	13.2	1,476	44.9	1,169	35.6
1971	3,208	229	7.1	442	13.8	1,380	43.0	1,157	36.1
1970	3,108	190	6.1	460	14.8	1,348	43.4	1,110	35.7
1969	3,017	183	6.1	427	14.2	1,328	44.0	1,079	35.8
1968	2,981	210	7.0	435	14.6	1,314	44.1	1,022	34.3
1967	2,996	218	7.3	489	16.3	1,280	42.7	1,009	33.7
WHITE NON-HISPANIC									
Both Sexes									
2011	4,889	937	19.2	291	5.9	1,074	22.0	2,588	52.9
2010	4,935	804	16.3	277	5.6	1,156	23.4	2,699	54.7
2009	5,068	826	16.3	288	5.7	1,112	21.9	2,842	56.1
2008	5,185	780	15.0	296	5.7	1,258	24.3	2,850	55.0
2007	5,067	793	15.7	283	5.6	1,252	24.7	2,739	54.1
2006	5,018	843	16.8	361	7.2	1,251	24.9	2,564	51.1
2005	4,770	790	16.6	297	6.2	1,065	22.3	2,618	54.9
2004	4,885	731	15.0	363	7.4	1,195	24.5	2,596	53.1
2003[2]	4,780	758	15.9	379	7.9	1,157	24.2	2,486	52.0
2002	5,016	817	16.3	369	7.4	1,281	25.5	2,549	50.8
2001	4,928	780	15.8	467	9.5	1,298	26.3	2,383	48.4
2000	5,221	757	14.5	500	9.6	1,384	26.5	2,580	49.4
1999	5,228	779	14.9	491	9.4	1,384	26.5	2,574	49.2
1998	5,080	691	13.6	475	9.4	1,211	23.8	2,703	53.2
Male									
2011	2,470	543	22.0	145	5.9	599	24.2	1,184	47.9
2010	2,516	470	18.7	166	6.6	645	25.6	1,236	49.1
2009	2,573	473	18.4	173	6.7	641	24.9	1,286	50.0
2008	2,649	423	16.0	170	6.4	709	26.8	1,346	50.8
2007	2,587	496	19.2	150	5.8	643	24.9	1,298	50.2
2006	2,553	501	19.6	204	8.0	679	26.6	1,168	45.7
2005	2,449	515	21.0	168	6.9	573	23.4	1,193	48.7
2004	2,443	408	16.7	204	8.4	681	27.9	1,150	47.1
2003[2]	2,407	460	19.1	230	9.6	602	25.0	1,115	46.3
2002	2,502	481	19.2	182	7.3	660	26.4	1,179	47.1
2001	2,526	453	17.9	257	10.2	685	27.1	1,131	44.8
2000	2,628	471	17.9	274	10.4	745	28.3	1,138	43.3
1999	2,648	473	17.9	255	9.6	706	26.7	1,214	45.8
1998	2,613	432	16.5	254	9.7	653	25.0	1,274	48.8

Note: High school graduates are people who have completed 4 years of high school or more, for 1967 to 1991. Beginning in 1992, they were people whose highest degree was a high school diploma (including equivalency) or higher.
[1]Civilian noninstitutionalized population.
[2]Starting in 2003 respondents could identify more than one race. Except as noted, the race data in this table from 2003 onward represent those respondents who indicated only one race category.

Table A-14. Population 18 and 19 Years Old, by School Enrollment Status, Sex, Race, and Hispanic Origin, October 1967–2011—*Continued*

(Numbers in thousands)

Year, race, and Hispanic origin	Total[1]	Population 18 and 19 years old							
		Still in high school	Percent	Dropped out	Percent	High school graduate only	Percent	In college	Percent
Female									
2011	2,470	543	22.0	145	5.9	599	24.2	1,184	47.9
2010	2,419	334	13.8	111	4.6	511	21.1	1,463	60.5
2009	2,495	353	14.1	115	4.6	471	18.9	1,556	62.4
2008	2,536	357	14.1	126	5.0	549	21.7	1,504	59.3
2007	2,480	298	12.0	132	5.3	609	24.6	1,441	58.1
2006	2,466	341	13.8	157	6.4	571	23.2	1,396	56.6
2005	2,321	275	11.9	129	5.6	491	21.2	1,425	61.4
2004	2,441	323	13.2	159	6.5	513	21.0	1,446	59.2
2003[2]	2,373	298	12.6	149	6.3	555	23.4	1,371	57.8
2002	2,514	336	13.4	187	7.4	621	24.7	1,370	54.5
2001	2,402	328	13.7	209	8.7	613	25.5	1,252	52.1
2000	2,593	286	11.0	225	8.7	639	24.6	1,443	55.6
1999	2,580	307	11.9	236	9.1	677	26.2	1,360	52.7
1998	2,467	259	10.5	221	9.0	558	22.6	1,429	57.9
BLACK									
Both Sexes									
2011	1,316	396	30.1	60	4.5	281	21.3	580	44.0
2010	1,336	271	20.3	144	10.8	355	26.5	567	42.4
2009	1,346	319	23.7	180	13.4	288	21.4	559	41.5
2008	1,335	311	23.3	145	10.8	400	30.0	479	35.9
2007	1,284	300	23.4	112	8.7	380	29.6	492	38.3
2006	1,230	332	27.0	103	8.3	332	27.0	464	37.7
2005	1,126	256	22.7	110	9.8	309	27.4	451	40.0
2004	1,112	218	19.6	162	14.5	292	26.3	440	39.6
2003[2]	1,052	277	26.3	128	12.2	273	26.0	374	35.6
2002	1,181	251	21.3	180	15.2	320	27.1	430	36.4
2001	1,246	299	24.0	152	12.2	351	28.2	444	35.6
2000	1,251	262	20.9	187	14.9	348	27.8	454	36.3
1999	1,199	259	21.6	190	15.8	320	26.7	430	35.9
1998	1,246	290	23.3	224	18.0	271	21.7	461	37.0
1997	1,133	278	24.5	172	15.2	302	26.7	381	33.6
1996	1,161	268	23.1	175	15.1	373	32.1	345	29.7
1995	1,099	287	26.1	177	16.1	291	26.5	344	31.3
1994	1,017	239	23.5	199	19.6	269	26.5	310	30.5
1993	1,040	290	27.9	133	12.8	306	29.4	311	29.9
1992	1,007	275	27.3	166	16.5	275	27.3	291	28.9
1991	1,041	276	26.5	146	14.0	316	30.4	303	29.1
1990	1,079	246	22.8	178	16.5	306	28.4	349	32.3
1989	1,078	239	22.2	194	18.0	343	31.8	302	28.0
1988	1,057	251	23.7	189	17.9	336	31.8	281	26.6
1987	1,043	213	20.4	166	15.9	323	31.0	341	32.7
1986	1,048	212	20.2	156	14.9	374	35.7	306	29.2
1985	1,072	213	19.9	186	17.4	414	38.6	259	24.2
1984	1,092	218	20.0	186	17.0	423	38.7	265	24.3
1983	1,134	265	23.4	199	17.5	412	36.3	258	22.8
1982	1,146	226	19.7	253	22.1	393	34.3	274	23.9
1981	1,128	238	21.1	218	19.3	366	32.4	306	27.1
1980	1,081	211	19.5	229	21.2	358	33.1	283	26.2
1979	1,072	221	20.6	246	22.9	326	30.4	279	26.0
1978	1,065	221	20.8	258	24.2	316	29.7	270	25.4
1977	1,072	249	23.2	235	21.9	319	29.8	269	25.1
1976	1,055	230	21.8	211	20.0	312	29.6	302	28.6
1975	1,030	225	21.8	262	25.4	283	27.5	260	25.2
1974	1,004	209	20.8	235	23.4	327	32.6	233	23.2
1973	997	182	18.3	252	25.3	369	37.0	194	19.5
1972	958	181	18.9	229	23.9	319	33.3	229	23.9
1971	908	219	24.1	219	24.1	266	29.3	204	22.5
1970	878	161	18.3	274	31.2	252	28.7	191	21.8
1969	837	179	21.4	227	27.1	238	28.4	193	23.1
1968	830	195	23.5	202	24.3	251	30.2	182	21.9
1967	780	175	22.4	203	26.0	261	33.5	141	18.1

Note: High school graduates are people who have completed 4 years of high school or more, for 1967 to 1991. Beginning in 1992, they were people whose highest degree was a high school diploma (including equivalency) or higher.
[1]Civilian noninstitutionalized population.
[2]Starting in 2003 respondents could identify more than one race. Except as noted, the race data in this table from 2003 onward represent those respondents who indicated only one race category.

Table A-14. Population 18 and 19 Years Old, by School Enrollment Status, Sex, Race, and Hispanic Origin, October 1967–2011—*Continued*

(Numbers in thousands)

Year, race, and Hispanic origin	Total[1]	Population 18 and 19 years old							
		Still in high school	Percent	Dropped out	Percent	High school graduate only	Percent	In college	Percent
Male									
2011	645	226	35.0	39	6.0	138	21.4	242	37.6
2010	654	159	24.4	83	12.6	174	26.5	238	36.4
2009	659	174	26.4	102	15.5	158	24.0	225	34.1
2008	653	173	26.5	53	8.1	222	34.0	205	31.4
2007	628	161	25.7	54	8.6	186	29.6	227	36.2
2006	600	210	35.0	42	7.0	174	29.0	174	28.9
2005	552	178	32.2	60	10.9	121	21.9	193	35.0
2004	519	137	26.4	91	17.6	126	24.3	165	31.7
2003[2]	502	143	28.5	77	15.3	116	23.1	166	33.1
2002	608	155	25.5	123	20.2	151	24.8	179	29.4
2001	624	179	28.7	97	15.5	169	27.1	179	28.7
2000	593	148	25.0	105	17.7	177	29.8	163	27.5
1999	586	144	24.6	97	16.6	136	23.2	209	35.7
1998	613	163	26.6	128	20.9	128	20.9	194	31.6
1997	554	172	31.0	90	16.2	150	27.1	142	25.6
1996	564	167	29.6	90	16.0	162	28.7	145	25.7
1995	519	162	31.2	94	18.1	118	22.7	145	27.9
1994	497	134	27.0	116	23.3	115	23.1	132	26.6
1993	517	181	35.0	53	10.3	135	26.1	148	28.6
1992	499	180	36.1	82	16.4	114	22.8	123	24.6
1991	504	176	34.9	62	12.3	129	25.6	137	27.2
1990	520	152	29.2	80	15.4	124	23.8	164	31.5
1989	516	137	26.6	90	17.4	163	31.6	126	24.4
1988	510	145	28.4	92	18.0	165	32.4	108	21.2
1987	501	140	27.9	80	16.0	127	25.3	154	30.7
1986	506	149	29.4	74	14.6	165	32.6	118	23.3
1985	518	135	26.1	92	17.8	170	32.8	121	23.4
1984	524	143	27.3	103	19.7	166	31.7	112	21.4
1983	539	158	29.3	106	19.7	182	33.8	93	17.3
1982	549	132	24.0	145	26.4	148	27.0	124	22.6
1981	538	145	27.0	102	19.0	158	29.4	133	24.7
1980	503	118	23.5	114	22.7	173	34.4	98	19.5
1979	497	128	25.8	122	24.5	137	27.6	110	22.1
1978	493	135	27.4	127	25.8	117	23.7	114	23.1
1977	496	161	32.5	118	23.8	127	25.6	90	18.1
1976	499	153	30.7	96	19.2	129	25.9	121	24.2
1975	476	127	26.7	132	27.7	106	22.3	111	23.3
1974	474	116	24.5	128	27.0	128	27.0	102	21.5
1973	467	106	22.7	130	27.8	135	28.9	96	20.6
1972	445	110	24.7	121	27.2	112	25.2	102	22.9
1971	423	120	28.4	110	26.0	99	23.4	94	22.2
1970	414	98	23.7	151	36.5	92	22.2	73	17.6
1969	394	109	27.7	124	31.5	75	19.0	86	21.8
1968	390	124	31.8	93	23.8	90	23.1	83	21.3
1967	356	95	26.7	109	30.6	74	20.8	78	21.9
Female									
2011	671	170	25.4	21	3.1	143	21.3	337	50.3
2010	682	111	16.3	61	9.0	181	26.5	329	48.2
2009	687	145	21.1	78	11.3	130	19.0	334	48.6
2008	681	138	20.3	92	13.5	178	26.1	274	40.2
2007	655	139	21.2	58	8.8	194	29.6	265	40.4
2006	631	122	19.3	60	9.6	158	25.0	291	46.1
2005	574	78	13.6	49	8.6	189	32.9	258	44.9
2004	593	81	13.7	70	11.9	167	28.2	275	46.5
2003[2]	550	133	24.2	51	9.3	157	28.5	209	38.0
2002	574	97	16.9	57	9.9	169	29.4	251	43.7
2001	623	122	19.6	54	8.7	182	29.2	265	42.5
2000	658	113	17.2	82	12.5	172	26.1	291	44.2
1999	613	114	18.6	94	15.3	184	30.0	221	36.1
1998	633	127	20.1	96	15.2	143	22.6	267	42.2
1997	579	107	18.5	82	14.2	152	26.3	238	41.1
1996	597	102	17.1	85	14.2	211	35.3	199	33.3
1995	581	126	21.7	83	14.3	173	29.8	199	34.3
1994	520	105	20.2	83	16.0	154	29.6	178	34.2

Note: High school graduates are people who have completed 4 years of high school or more, for 1967 to 1991. Beginning in 1992, they were people whose highest degree was a high school diploma (including equivalency) or higher.

[1]Civilian noninstitutionalized population.

[2]Starting in 2003 respondents could identify more than one race. Except as noted, the race data in this table from 2003 onward represent those respondents who indicated only one race category.

Table A-14. Population 18 and 19 Years Old, by School Enrollment Status, Sex, Race, and Hispanic Origin, October 1967–2011—*Continued*

(Numbers in thousands)

Year, race, and Hispanic origin	Total[1]	Population 18 and 19 years old							
		Still in high school	Percent	Dropped out	Percent	High school graduate only	Percent	In college	Percent
Female—*(Continued)*									
1993	523	108	20.7	80	15.3	172	32.9	163	31.2
1992	508	95	18.7	84	16.5	161	31.7	168	33.1
1991	537	99	18.4	85	15.8	187	34.8	166	30.9
1990	559	95	17.0	98	17.5	181	32.4	185	33.1
1989	562	102	18.1	104	18.5	180	32.0	176	31.3
1988	547	105	19.2	97	17.7	172	31.4	173	31.6
1987	542	75	13.8	85	15.7	196	36.2	186	34.3
1986	542	62	11.4	83	15.3	209	38.6	188	34.7
1985	554	78	14.1	94	17.0	244	44.0	138	24.9
1984	568	76	13.4	82	14.4	257	45.2	153	26.9
1983	595	108	18.2	93	15.6	230	38.7	164	27.6
1982	597	95	15.9	108	18.1	244	40.9	150	25.1
1981	590	93	15.8	116	19.7	209	35.4	172	29.2
1980	578	93	16.1	115	19.9	185	32.0	185	32.0
1979	576	93	16.1	125	21.7	189	32.8	169	29.3
1978	572	88	15.4	130	22.7	199	34.8	155	27.1
1977	576	88	15.3	117	20.3	192	33.3	179	31.1
1976	556	77	13.8	115	20.7	183	32.9	181	32.6
1975	553	97	17.5	130	23.5	176	31.8	150	27.1
1974	530	92	17.4	107	20.2	200	37.7	131	24.7
1973	530	77	14.5	122	23.0	234	44.2	97	18.3
1972	513	71	13.8	108	21.1	207	40.4	127	24.8
1971	485	100	20.6	109	22.5	167	34.4	109	22.5
1970	464	62	13.4	124	26.7	160	34.5	118	25.4
1969	443	70	15.8	102	23.0	163	36.8	108	24.4
1968	439	69	15.7	109	24.8	161	36.7	100	22.8
1967	424	81	19.1	93	21.9	187	44.1	63	14.9
ASIAN ALONE[3]									
Both Sexes									
2011	337	44	13.2	13	3.7	40	11.8	240	71.3
2010	331	38	11.5	12	3.7	46	14.0	234	70.8
2009	327	64	19.7	2	0.7	17	5.2	243	74.4
2008	259	49	19.0	7	2.7	31	12.0	172	66.4
2007	296	55	18.4	12	4.2	27	9.3	201	68.1
2006	297	43	14.4	9	3.0	41	14.0	204	68.6
2005	251	34	13.4	4	1.5	25	10.0	188	74.9
2004	257	31	11.9	10	3.8	34	13.2	182	70.7
2003[2]	286	41	14.3	3	1.0	33	11.5	209	73.1
2002	353	42	11.9	14	4.0	61	17.3	236	66.9
2001	353	50	14.2	18	5.1	38	10.8	247	70.0
2000	326	45	13.8	17	5.2	52	16.0	212	65.0
1999	339	43	12.7	22	6.5	51	15.0	223	65.8
Male									
2011	178	28	15.4	. . .	. . .	19	10.8	131	73.7
2010	170	16	9.6	8	5.0	30	17.4	116	68.1
2009	178	31	17.6	*	*	13	7.4	134	75.0
2008	128	39	30.2	6	5.1	8	5.9	75	58.9
2007	150	33	22.1	2	1.1	11	7.1	104	69.7
2006	167	20	12.2	8	4.7	26	15.7	113	67.5
2005	131	21	16.3	3	2.0	17	13.0	90	68.9
2004	133	22	16.7	1	0.7	18	13.5	92	69.3
2003[2]	129	14	10.9	3	2.3	9	7.0	103	79.8
2002	179	22	12.3	10	5.6	26	14.5	121	67.6
2001	168	27	16.1	14	8.3	14	8.3	113	67.3
2000	162	14	8.6	14	8.6	26	16.0	108	66.7
1999	156	23	14.7	17	10.9	23	14.7	93	59.6

Note: High school graduates are people who have completed 4 years of high school or more, for 1967 to 1991. Beginning in 1992, they were people whose highest degree was a high school diploma (including equivalency) or higher.

[1]Civilian noninstitutionalized population.

[2]Starting in 2003 respondents could identify more than one race. Except as noted, the race data in this table from 2003 onward represent those respondents who indicated only one race category.

[3]The data shown prior to 2003 consists of those identifying themselves as "Asian or Pacific Islanders."

* = Quantity zero or rounds to zero.

. . . = Not available

Table A-14. Population 18 and 19 Years Old, by School Enrollment Status, Sex, Race, and Hispanic Origin, October 1967–2011—*Continued*

(Numbers in thousands)

Year, race, and Hispanic origin	Total[1]	Population 18 and 19 years old							
		Still in high school	Percent	Dropped out	Percent	High school graduate only	Percent	In college	Percent
Female									
2011	158	17	10.7	13	7.9	20	12.8	109	68.6
2010	161	22	13.6	4	2.4	17	10.4	118	73.6
2009	149	33	22.2	2	1.6	4	2.7	109	73.6
2008	132	11	8.0	*	0.4	24	17.9	97	73.7
2007	146	21	14.6	11	7.5	17	11.5	97	66.4
2006	130	23	17.3	1	0.9	15	11.8	91	70.0
2005	120	12	10.3	1	0.9	9	7.5	98	81.4
2004	124	8	6.8	9	7.1	18	14.5	89	72.2
2003[2]	157	26	16.6	*	*	24	15.3	107	68.2
2002	173	20	11.6	3	1.7	35	20.2	115	66.5
2001	185	23	12.4	4	2.2	24	13.0	134	72.4
2000	164	30	18.3	4	2.4	26	15.9	104	63.4
1999	183	20	10.9	5	2.7	28	15.3	130	71.0
HISPANIC[4]									
Both Sexes									
2011	1,743	371	21.3	166	9.5	441	25.3	765	43.9
2010	1,768	389	22.0	179	10.1	418	23.6	783	44.3
2009	1,680	409	24.3	261	15.5	460	27.4	550	32.7
2008	1,539	320	20.8	296	19.3	395	25.7	528	34.3
2007	1,523	311	20.4	254	16.7	399	26.2	559	36.7
2006	1,406	307	21.8	253	18.0	402	28.6	444	31.6
2005	1,253	272	21.7	227	18.1	348	27.8	406	32.4
2004	1,270	244	19.2	296	23.3	346	27.2	384	30.2
2003	1,214	229	18.9	291	24.0	315	25.9	379	31.2
2002	1,309	303	23.1	310	23.7	336	25.7	360	27.5
2001	1,391	246	17.7	399	28.7	359	25.8	387	27.8
2000	1,248	268	21.5	311	24.9	320	25.6	349	28.0
1999	1,220	246	20.2	337	27.6	340	27.9	297	24.3
1998	1,209	199	16.5	402	33.3	320	26.5	288	23.8
1997	1,087	221	20.3	274	25.2	276	25.4	316	29.1
1996	1,000	229	22.9	295	29.5	236	23.6	240	24.0
1995	1,012	203	20.1	312	30.8	233	23.0	264	26.1
1994	925	250	27.0	237	25.6	213	23.0	225	24.3
1993	710	159	22.4	201	28.3	155	21.8	195	27.5
1992	778	188	24.2	197	25.3	163	21.0	230	29.6
1991	823	206	25.0	269	32.7	160	19.4	188	22.8
1990	746	181	24.3	255	34.2	162	21.7	148	19.8
1989	733	150	20.5	205	28.0	201	27.4	177	24.1
1988	734	121	16.5	229	31.2	181	24.7	203	27.7
1987	699	121	17.3	195	27.9	231	33.0	152	21.7
1986	614	114	18.6	164	26.7	171	27.9	165	26.9
1985	570	111	19.5	175	30.7	157	27.5	127	22.3
1984	561	88	15.7	146	26.0	191	34.0	136	24.2
1983	573	119	20.8	166	29.0	154	26.9	134	23.4
1982	600	92	15.3	198	33.0	167	27.8	143	23.8
1981	606	100	16.5	220	36.3	157	25.9	129	21.3
1980	597	89	14.9	233	39.0	138	23.1	137	22.9
1979	507	78	15.4	157	31.0	148	29.2	124	24.5
1978	478	61	12.8	183	38.3	125	26.2	109	22.8
1977	515	86	16.7	168	32.6	138	26.8	123	23.9
1976	534	98	18.4	164	30.7	129	24.2	143	26.8
1975	489	97	19.8	147	30.1	127	26.0	118	24.1
1974	467	99	21.2	139	29.8	117	25.1	112	24.0
1973	387	70	18.1	142	36.7	93	24.0	82	21.2
1972	381	88	23.1	117	30.7	106	27.8	70	18.4

Note: High school graduates are people who have completed 4 years of high school or more, for 1967 to 1991. Beginning in 1992, they were people whose highest degree was a high school diploma (including equivalency) or higher.
[1]Civilian noninstitutionalized population.
[2]Starting in 2003 respondents could identify more than one race. Except as noted, the race data in this table from 2003 onward represent those respondents who indicated only one race category.
[4]May be of any race.
* = Quantity zero or rounds to zero.

Table A-14. Population 18 and 19 Years Old, by School Enrollment Status, Sex, Race, and Hispanic Origin, October 1967–2011—*Continued*

(Numbers in thousands)

Year, race, and Hispanic origin	Total[1]	Population 18 and 19 years old							
		Still in high school	Percent	Dropped out	Percent	High school graduate only	Percent	In college	Percent
Male									
2011	952	229	24.1	102	10.7	269	28.3	351	36.9
2010	896	201	22.4	97	10.9	217	24.2	381	42.5
2009	853	200	23.4	129	15.2	282	33.0	242	28.4
2008	779	190	24.4	141	18.1	212	27.2	236	30.3
2007	780	185	23.7	145	18.5	205	26.3	246	31.5
2006	708	152	21.4	150	21.2	193	27.3	213	30.1
2005	663	166	25.1	144	21.7	180	27.1	173	26.2
2004	668	117	17.5	214	32.0	166	24.9	171	25.6
2003	635	142	22.4	161	25.4	179	28.2	153	24.1
2002	716	191	26.7	200	27.9	169	23.6	156	21.8
2001	701	131	18.7	254	36.2	167	23.8	149	21.3
2000	656	154	23.5	183	27.9	159	24.2	160	24.4
1999	642	148	23.1	180	28.0	171	26.6	143	22.3
1998	598	104	17.4	234	39.1	163	27.3	97	16.2
1997	579	130	22.5	162	28.0	154	26.6	133	23.0
1996	506	139	27.5	154	30.4	115	22.7	98	19.4
1995	535	132	24.7	145	27.1	137	25.6	121	22.6
1994	454	157	34.6	118	26.0	90	19.8	89	19.6
1993	325	86	26.5	105	32.3	65	20.0	69	21.2
1992	385	110	28.6	99	25.7	83	21.6	93	24.2
1991	416	107	25.7	161	38.7	80	19.2	68	16.3
1990	358	76	21.2	141	39.4	71	19.8	70	19.6
1989	371	89	24.0	96	25.9	111	29.9	75	20.2
1988	364	88	24.2	128	35.2	73	20.1	75	20.6
1987	333	66	19.8	105	31.5	86	25.8	76	22.8
1986	326	58	17.8	95	29.1	86	26.4	87	26.7
1985	275	62	22.5	116	42.2	53	19.3	44	16.0
1984	249	55	22.1	65	26.1	87	34.9	42	16.9
1983	266	66	24.8	87	32.7	72	27.1	41	15.4
1982	304	69	22.7	106	34.9	77	25.3	52	17.1
1981	288	47	16.3	127	44.1	57	19.8	57	19.8
1980	310	46	14.8	134	43.2	62	20.0	68	21.9
1979	256	42	16.4	89	34.8	58	22.7	67	26.2
1978	221	35	15.8	81	36.7	52	23.5	53	24.0
1977	238	49	20.6	80	33.6	55	23.1	54	22.7
1976	258	51	19.8	82	31.8	56	21.7	69	26.7
1975	229	66	28.8	60	26.2	50	21.8	53	23.1
1974	222	49	22.1	78	35.1	40	18.0	55	24.8
1973	190	48	25.3	62	32.6	41	21.6	39	20.5
1972	190	49	25.8	67	35.3	46	24.2	28	14.7
Female									
2011	791	142	17.9	64	8.1	172	21.7	414	52.4
2010	872	188	21.5	82	9.4	201	23.0	402	46.1
2009	827	209	25.3	132	15.9	179	21.6	308	37.2
2008	760	130	17.1	156	20.5	183	24.0	292	38.4
2007	743	126	17.0	109	14.7	193	26.1	313	42.2
2006	698	156	22.3	102	14.7	209	30.0	231	33.1
2005	591	105	17.8	83	14.0	171	28.9	232	39.3
2004	602	127	21.1	82	13.6	180	29.9	213	35.4
2003	579	87	15.0	130	22.5	136	23.5	226	39.0
2002	593	112	18.9	110	18.5	167	28.2	204	34.4
2001	691	116	16.8	145	21.0	192	27.8	238	34.4
2000	591	114	19.3	128	21.7	161	27.2	188	31.8
1999	577	99	17.2	157	27.2	168	29.1	153	26.5
1998	611	95	15.5	169	27.7	156	25.5	191	31.3
1997	508	91	17.9	112	22.0	122	24.0	183	36.0
1996	494	91	18.4	140	28.3	121	24.5	142	28.7

Note: High school graduates are people who have completed 4 years of high school or more, for 1967 to 1991. Beginning in 1992, they were people whose highest degree was a high school diploma (including equivalency) or higher.

[1]Civilian noninstitutionalized population.

Table A-14. Population 18 and 19 Years Old, by School Enrollment Status, Sex, Race, and Hispanic Origin, October 1967–2011—*Continued*

(Numbers in thousands)

Year, race, and Hispanic origin	Total[1]	Population 18 and 19 years old							
		Still in high school	Percent	Dropped out	Percent	High school graduate only	Percent	In college	Percent
Female—*(Continued)*									
1995	478	71	14.9	167	34.9	97	20.3	143	29.9
1994	471	93	19.7	119	25.3	123	26.1	136	28.9
1993	385	74	19.2	96	24.9	89	23.1	126	32.7
1992	393	78	19.8	98	24.9	80	20.4	137	34.9
1991	407	98	24.1	109	26.8	80	19.7	120	29.5
1990	388	105	27.1	114	29.4	91	23.5	78	20.1
1989	362	60	16.6	108	29.8	91	25.1	103	28.5
1988	370	32	8.6	101	27.3	108	29.2	129	34.9
1987	367	58	15.8	89	24.3	144	39.2	76	20.7
1986	288	54	18.8	69	24.0	86	29.9	79	27.4
1985	296	51	17.2	59	19.9	104	35.1	82	27.7
1984	311	33	10.6	81	26.0	103	33.1	94	30.2
1983	307	53	17.3	79	25.7	82	26.7	93	30.3
1982	296	23	7.8	92	31.1	90	30.4	91	30.7
1981	318	53	16.7	93	29.2	100	31.4	72	22.6
1980	287	44	15.3	99	34.5	76	26.5	68	23.7
1979	251	35	13.9	68	27.1	90	35.9	58	23.1
1978	257	26	10.1	102	39.7	73	28.4	56	21.8
1977	277	37	13.4	88	31.8	82	29.6	70	25.3
1976	276	49	17.8	81	29.3	72	26.1	74	26.8
1975	261	32	12.3	87	33.3	77	29.5	65	24.9
1974	245	50	20.4	62	25.3	77	31.4	56	22.9
1973	197	21	10.7	80	40.6	52	26.4	44	22.3
1972	191	37	19.4	50	26.2	61	31.9	43	22.5
WHITE ALONE OR IN COMBINATION									
Both Sexes									
2011	6,686	1,309	19.6	455	6.8	1,540	23.0	3,381	50.6
2010	6,679	1,195	17.9	450	6.7	1,556	23.3	3,478	52.1
2009	6,780	1,227	18.1	538	7.9	1,601	23.6	3,414	50.3
2008	6,762	1,093	16.2	581	8.6	1,647	24.4	3,440	50.9
2007	6,595	1,108	16.8	525	8.0	1,644	24.9	3,318	50.3
2006	6,466	1,160	17.9	615	9.5	1,648	25.5	3,043	47.1
2005	6,078	1,064	17.5	537	8.8	1,442	23.7	3,035	49.9
2004	6,191	988	16.0	643	10.4	1,548	25.0	3,012	48.7
2003	6,093	994	16.3	675	11.1	1,519	24.9	2,905	47.7
Male									
2011	3,457	776	22.4	247	7.1	881	25.5	1,554	44.9
2010	3,396	674	19.8	251	7.4	852	25.1	1,620	47.7
2009	3,422	665	19.4	297	8.7	925	27.0	1,535	44.9
2008	3,435	605	17.6	305	8.9	917	26.7	1,607	46.8
2007	3,350	684	20.4	284	8.5	842	25.1	1,540	46.0
2006	3,278	657	20.0	357	10.9	864	26.4	1,399	42.7
2005	3,149	692	22.0	321	10.2	358	11.4	1,778	56.5
2004	3,129	538	17.2	415	13.3	845	27.0	1,331	42.5
2003	3,078	604	19.6	390	12.7	801	26.0	1,283	41.7
Female									
2011	3,228	533	16.5	209	6.5	659	20.4	1,828	56.6
2010	3,282	521	15.9	200	6.1	704	21.4	1,858	56.6
2009	3,358	562	16.7	242	7.2	676	20.1	1,879	55.9
2008	3,328	488	14.7	277	8.3	730	21.9	1,833	55.1
2007	3,245	424	13.1	241	7.4	801	24.7	1,779	54.8
2006	3,188	503	15.8	258	8.1	784	24.6	1,643	51.5
2005	2,929	372	12.7	216	7.4	669	22.8	1,672	57.1
2004	3,062	450	14.7	228	7.4	702	22.9	1,682	54.9
2003	3,015	390	12.9	284	9.4	719	23.8	1,622	53.8

Note: High school graduates are people who have completed 4 years of high school or more, for 1967 to 1991. Beginning in 1992, they were people whose highest degree was a high school diploma (including equivalency) or higher.
[1]Civilian noninstitutionalized population.

Table A-14. Population 18 and 19 Years Old, by School Enrollment Status, Sex, Race, and Hispanic Origin, October 1967–2011—*Continued*

(Numbers in thousands)

Year, race, and Hispanic origin	Total[1]	Population 18 and 19 years old							
		Still in high school	Percent	Dropped out	Percent	High school graduate only	Percent	In college	Percent
BLACK ALONE OR IN COMBINATION									
Both Sexes									
2011	1,381	409	29.6	65	4.7	292	21.2	615	44.5
2010	1,439	287	20.0	158	11.0	371	25.8	622	43.2
2009	1,450	335	23.1	191	13.1	321	22.1	604	41.7
2008	1,431	339	23.7	155	10.8	422	29.5	515	36.0
2007	1,347	306	22.7	116	8.6	395	29.3	530	39.3
2006	1,287	343	26.6	111	8.6	341	26.5	492	38.2
2005	1,195	266	22.3	112	9.4	336	28.1	481	40.2
2004	1,163	229	19.7	163	14.0	305	26.2	466	40.1
2003	1,129	288	25.5	131	11.6	310	27.5	400	35.4
Male									
2011	681	238	35.0	44	6.5	149	21.9	250	36.6
2010	700	170	24.3	86	12.3	180	25.7	264	37.7
2009	708	182	25.8	110	15.5	171	24.1	245	34.6
2008	706	191	27.0	58	8.3	238	33.7	219	31.1
2007	657	164	25.0	56	8.5	197	30.0	240	36.5
2006	623	213	34.3	45	7.3	178	28.6	186	29.8
2005	586	187	31.8	62	10.7	136	23.2	201	34.3
2004	549	142	25.9	93	17.0	139	25.3	175	31.9
2003	525	146	27.8	81	15.4	123	23.4	175	33.3
Female									
2011	699	170	24.3	21	3.0	143	20.5	365	52.2
2010	739	117	15.9	72	9.8	192	25.9	358	48.4
2009	742	152	20.5	81	11.3	150	20.2	359	48.4
2008	724	148	20.5	96	13.3	184	25.4	296	40.8
2007	690	142	20.6	61	8.8	198	28.6	290	42.0
2006	665	130	19.5	66	9.9	163	24.5	307	46.1
2005	609	80	13.1	49	8.1	200	32.8	280	45.9
2004	615	86	14.0	70	11.4	169	27.5	290	47.2
2003	604	142	23.5	51	8.4	186	30.8	225	37.3
ASIAN ALONE OR IN COMBINATION									
Both Sexes									
2011	399	55	13.6	13	3.1	66	16.4	267	66.8
2010	369	39	10.5	13	3.6	53	14.4	264	71.5
2009	384	74	19.3	3	0.9	35	9.0	271	70.8
2008	309	52	16.8	7	2.3	37	11.8	214	69.1
2007	336	58	17.2	12	3.7	34	10.0	232	69.1
2006	318	47	14.8	9	2.8	47	14.9	215	67.5
2005	286	42	14.7	4	1.3	36	12.6	204	71.5
2004	299	36	12.0	14	4.5	46	15.4	203	67.9
2003	320	43	13.4	3	1.1	38	11.9	236	73.8
Male									
2011	214	33	15.5	*	*	36	16.7	145	67.9
2010	196	17	8.6	9	4.6	34	17.2	136	69.5
2009	188	34	18.3	1	0.3	16	8.3	138	73.2
2008	150	41	27.6	6	4.3	9	6.0	93	62.1
2007	161	33	20.7	2	1.0	14	8.4	113	69.9
2006	179	22	12.4	8	4.3	31	17.5	118	65.8
2005	152	30	19.5	3	1.7	22	14.5	97	64.1
2004	149	27	18.1	5	3.2	20	13.4	97	65.1
2003	144	17	11.8	3	2.3	12	8.3	112	77.8
Female									
2011	186	21	11.6	13	6.8	30	16.1	122	65.6
2010	174	22	12.6	4	2.5	20	11.3	128	73.7
2009	196	40	20.4	3	1.5	19	9.7	134	68.4
2008	159	11	6.6	*	0.3	28	17.3	121	75.8
2007	174	24	13.9	11	6.3	20	11.5	119	68.3
2006	139	25	18.0	1	0.8	16	11.4	97	69.7
2005	134	12	9.2	1	0.9	14	10.4	107	80.0
2004	150	8	5.3	9	5.9	27	18.0	106	70.7
2003	176	25	14.2	*	*	27	15.3	124	70.5

Note: High school graduates are people who have completed 4 years of high school or more, for 1967 to 1991. Beginning in 1992, they were people whose highest degree was a high school diploma (including equivalency) or higher.

[1]Civilian noninstitutionalized population.

Table A-15. Age Distribution of College Students 14 Years Old and Over, by Sex, October 1947–2011

(Numbers in thousands)

Year, sex, race, and Hispanic origin	All students[1]								Male							
	Total	14 to 17 years	18 and 19 years	20 and 21 years	22 to 24 years	25 to 29 years	30 to 34 years	35 years and over	Total	14 to 17 years	18 and 19 years	20 and 21 years	22 to 24 years	25 to 29 years	30 to 34 years	35 years and over
ALL RACES																
2011	20,397	203	4,242	4,459	3,869	3,066	1,551	3,007	9,132	108	1,949	2,127	1,877	1,343	643	1,084
2010	20,275	229	4,364	4,348	3,501	2,992	1,632	3,210	9,007	94	2,009	2,108	1,580	1,396	659	1,160
2009	19,764	206	4,289	4,034	3,749	2,769	1,524	3,193	8,642	89	1,928	1,943	1,770	1,194	649	1,069
2008	18,632	241	4,126	3,920	3,420	2,657	1,356	2,911	8,311	133	1,909	1,908	1,566	1,229	577	989
2007	17,956	186	4,075	3,794	3,292	2,496	1,342	2,772	7,826	76	1,903	1,729	1,524	1,029	596	968
2006	17,232	212	3,746	3,675	3,166	2,312	1,346	2,776	7,506	79	1,703	1,682	1,489	1,033	537	982
2005	17,472	181	3,727	3,945	3,162	2,291	1,309	2,857	7,539	62	1,675	1,878	1,420	923	562	1,019
2004	17,383	198	3,685	3,777	3,149	2,403	1,287	2,884	7,575	75	1,610	1,811	1,444	1,068	533	1,033
2003	16,638	150	3,512	3,533	3,320	2,164	1,330	2,630	7,318	61	1,568	1,551	1,578	982	607	970
2002	16,497	195	3,581	3,525	2,927	2,093	1,308	2,867	7,240	80	1,635	1,640	1,354	918	542	1,071
2001	15,873	138	3,478	3,421	2,731	2,084	1,337	2,685	6,875	54	1,570	1,579	1,287	917	559	908
2000	15,314	149	3,599	3,169	2,683	1,962	1,244	2,507	6,682	61	1,570	1,472	1,300	844	517	918
1999	15,203	151	3,520	3,120	2,620	1,940	1,155	2,697	6,956	78	1,648	1,525	1,224	911	547	1,023
1998	15,546	123	3,670	3,092	2,561	2,148	1,266	2,685	6,905	48	1,667	1,517	1,219	979	521	953
1997	15,436	171	3,362	3,143	2,699	2,154	1,116	2,791	6,843	59	1,561	1,521	1,292	1,052	457	899
1996	15,226	237	3,309	2,907	2,551	2,215	1,228	2,778	6,820	97	1,489	1,379	1,319	1,038	485	1,013
1995	14,715	158	3,101	2,940	2,498	2,143	1,206	2,669	6,703	68	1,431	1,423	1,235	1,008	553	985
1994[2]	15,022	150	3,051	3,028	2,650	2,026	1,393	2,725	6,764	65	1,416	1,414	1,322	972	617	958
1993[r]	14,394	130	3,070	2,892	2,668	1,914	1,226	2,493	6,599	55	1,407	1,405	1,425	892	534	880
1993	13,898	123	2,926	2,734	2,533	1,867	1,227	2,488	6,324	52	1,337	1,312	1,345	872	534	873
1992	14,035	205	2,892	2,938	2,512	1,829	1,296	2,364	6,192	97	1,325	1,344	1,243	845	547	789
1991	14,057	132	2,929	2,939	2,304	1,983	1,302	2,468	6,439	49	1,326	1,390	1,238	1,018	587	832
1990	13,621	178	3,019	2,767	2,178	1,927	1,235	2,319	6,192	86	1,443	1,364	1,115	910	502	772
1989	13,180	183	3,066	2,570	2,168	1,889	1,192	2,112	5,950	73	1,422	1,228	1,067	926	517	716
1988	13,116	182	3,046	2,681	2,064	1,735	1,228	2,179	5,950	58	1,365	1,295	1,110	835	560	727
1987	12,719	239	3,045	2,642	2,006	1,826	1,159	1,802	6,030	116	1,483	1,350	1,034	921	500	625
1986	12,651	201	2,967	2,374	2,136	1,860	1,245	1,867	5,957	82	1,421	1,161	1,120	968	577	628
1985	12,524	262	2,907	2,616	2,014	1,884	1,180	1,661	5,906	131	1,349	1,313	1,087	942	522	561
1984	12,304	253	2,867	2,597	2,127	1,857	1,158	1,445	5,989	91	1,373	1,337	1,219	965	527	476
1983	12,320	260	2,940	2,495	2,042	1,921	1,167	1,495	6,010	108	1,340	1,310	1,170	1,055	521	506
1982	12,308	254	2,929	2,689	2,060	1,859	1,129	1,389	5,899	112	1,376	1,346	1,115	968	492	490
1981	12,127	232	3,044	2,545	1,986	1,717	1,211	1,393	5,825	96	1,450	1,239	1,144	909	533	453
1980	11,387	249	2,933	2,423	1,870	1,641	1,062	1,207	5,430	96	1,369	1,246	989	853	472	405
1979	11,380	311	2,844	2,353	1,794	1,679	996	1,402	5,480	129	1,341	1,192	975	893	463	487
1978	11,141	274	2,899	2,298	1,798	1,619	950	1,303	5,580	106	1,391	1,202	1,028	922	474	457
1977	11,546	274	2,913	2,430	1,799	1,809	992	1,329	5,889	112	1,396	1,280	1,036	1,035	511	520
1976	11,139	281	2,937	2,398	1,846	1,686	803	1,189	5,785	105	1,391	1,209	1,073	1,067	451	489
1975	10,880	293	2,943	2,313	1,679	1,616	853	1,183	5,911	128	1,426	1,256	1,011	1,025	496	569
1974	9,852	309	2,597	2,192	1,527	1,482	720	1,025	5,402	145	1,262	1,206	943	951	420	476
1973	8,966	295	2,517	2,073	1,465	1,278	551	787	5,048	121	1,293	1,130	937	867	329	371
1972	9,096	295	2,680	2,116	1,461	1,229	531	783	5,218	141	1,366	1,170	998	848	330	365
1971	8,087	284	2,726	1,997	1,487	1,067	527	...	4,850	129	1,444	1,090	1,065	787	334	...
1970	7,413	260	2,594	1,857	1,354	939	410	...	4,401	130	1,346	1,083	902	684	256	...
1969	7,435	242	2,601	1,945	1,294	918	435	...	4,448	120	1,397	1,112	883	671	265	...
1968	6,801	281	2,501	1,826	1,029	790	373	...	4,124	134	1,357	1,093	702	603	236	...
1967	6,401	239	2,286	1,816	998	707	356	...	3,841	96	1,198	1,066	718	524	239	...
1966	6,085	254	2,440	1,472	987	679	254	...	3,749	105	1,355	899	722	494	174	...
1965	5,675	264	2,215	1,326	940	614	316	...	3,503	113	1,218	804	699	458	211	...
1964	4,643	291	1,616	1,287	670	523	256	...	2,888	165	866	769	510	396	182	...
1963	4,336	180	1,504	1,212	717	482	241	...	2,742	99	796	734	574	365	174	...
1962	4,208	233	1,612	996	630	486	251	...	2,742	125	891	617	508	406	195	...
1961	3,731	213	1,470	892	507	437	212	...	2,356	84	834	554	393	337	154	...
1960	3,570	222	1,299	790	509	491	259	...	2,339	99	734	503	411	399	193	...
1959	3,340	210	1,175	739	489	503	224	...	2,187	92	651	501	355	422	166	...
1958	3,242	167	1,114	------1,221------		534	206	...	2,129	73	621	-----850-----		439	146	...
1957	3,138	176	989	------1,236------		553	184	...	2,028	77	538	-----827-----		459	127	...
1956	2,883	167	934	------1,105------		494	183	...	1,932	77	512	-----781-----		429	133	...
1955	2,379	147	745	--------931------		406	150	...	1,579	57	432	-----647-----		337	107	...
1950	2,175	180	733	--------939------		324	...	...	1,474	74	395	-----692-----		314	...	...
1947	2,311	188	620	------1,088------		321	94	...	1,687	87	343	-----872-----		301	84	...

[1]Civilian noninstitutionalized population.
[2] Before 1994, total enrolled does not include the 35 and over population.
[6] May be of any race.
r = Revised, controlled to 1990 census based population estimates; previous 1993 data controlled to 1980 census based population estimates.
... = Not available.

Table A-15. Age Distribution of College Students 14 Years Old and Over, by Sex, October 1947–2011—*Continued*

(Numbers in thousands)

Year, sex, race, and Hispanic origin	Female							
	Total	14 to 17 years	18 and 19 years	20 and 21 years	22 to 24 years	25 to 29 years	30 to 34 years	35 years and over
ALL RACES								
2011	11,266	95	2,293	2,333	1,992	1,722	908	1,923
2010	11,268	135	2,355	2,240	1,920	1,596	973	2,049
2009	11,123	116	2,361	2,091	1,980	1,575	875	2,124
2008	10,321	108	2,217	2,013	1,854	1,428	779	1,922
2007	10,130	109	2,172	2,065	1,768	1,466	746	1,804
2006	9,726	133	2,043	1,993	1,677	1,278	809	1,793
2005	9,934	119	2,052	2,067	1,742	1,368	747	1,838
2004	9,808	123	2,074	1,966	1,705	1,335	753	1,850
2003	9,319	89	1,944	1,982	1,742	1,181	723	1,660
2002	9,258	116	1,946	1,885	1,573	1,175	766	1,797
2001	8,998	84	1,907	1,841	1,444	1,167	778	1,776
2000	8,631	88	2,029	1,697	1,383	1,118	728	1,589
1999	8,247	73	1,872	1,595	1,396	1,029	608	1,674
1998	8,641	74	2,003	1,574	1,342	1,170	745	1,732
1997	8,593	112	1,801	1,622	1,406	1,102	658	1,892
1996	8,406	140	1,821	1,528	1,233	1,177	743	1,765
1995	8,013	90	1,671	1,518	1,263	1,135	653	1,684
1994[2]	8,258	85	1,635	1,613	1,328	1,054	776	1,766
1993[r]	7,795	75	1,663	1,487	1,243	1,022	692	1,613
1993	7,574	71	1,588	1,422	1,189	995	693	1,616
1992	7,844	107	1,566	1,594	1,269	984	748	1,575
1991	7,618	83	1,603	1,549	1,066	965	715	1,636
1990	7,429	91	1,576	1,403	1,063	1,017	732	1,546
1989	7,231	110	1,643	1,342	1,100	964	675	1,396
1988	7,166	124	1,682	1,386	953	900	668	1,452
1987	6,689	123	1,562	1,292	972	905	659	1,176
1986	6,694	120	1,546	1,213	1,016	892	667	1,240
1985	6,618	129	1,559	1,303	926	941	658	1,100
1984	6,315	161	1,494	1,260	908	892	630	970
1983	6,310	153	1,600	1,185	872	865	645	989
1982	6,410	141	1,553	1,343	945	891	637	900
1981	6,303	136	1,594	1,305	842	808	677	940
1980	5,957	153	1,565	1,178	882	788	590	802
1979	5,900	183	1,503	1,161	818	786	533	914
1978	5,559	168	1,507	1,096	770	697	476	845
1977	5,657	162	1,517	1,151	763	774	481	809
1976	5,354	176	1,546	1,189	773	619	352	700
1975	4,969	164	1,517	1,058	668	590	357	614
1974	4,449	165	1,335	986	584	531	300	548
1973	3,918	174	1,224	944	528	411	222	416
1972	3,877	153	1,314	946	464	381	200	418
1971	3,236	154	1,281	906	423	280	192	...
1970	3,013	130	1,248	774	452	255	154	...
1969	2,987	122	1,204	833	411	247	171	...
1968	2,677	147	1,144	733	328	187	138	...
1967	2,560	143	1,088	749	280	183	117	...
1966	2,337	149	1,085	573	265	185	80	...
1965	2,172	151	997	522	241	156	105	...
1964	1,755	126	750	518	160	127	74	...
1963	1,594	81	708	478	143	117	67	...
1962	1,466	108	721	379	122	80	56	...
1961	1,375	129	636	338	114	100	58	...
1960	1,231	123	565	287	98	92	66	...
1959	1,153	118	524	238	134	81	58	...
1958	1,113	94	493	371		95	60	...
1957	1,110	99	451	409		94	57	...
1956	951	90	422	324		65	50	...
1955	800	90	313	285		69	43	...
1950	701	106	338	247		10	...	...
1947	624	101	277	216		20	10	...

[1]Civilian noninstitutionalized population.
[2] Before 1994, total enrolled does not include the 35 and over population.
r = Revised, controlled to 1990 census based population estimates; previous 1993 data controlled to 1980 census based population estimates.
... = Not available.

Table A-15. Age Distribution of College Students 14 Years Old and Over, by Sex, October 1947–2011—*Continued*

(Numbers in thousands)

Year, sex, race, and Hispanic origin	All students[1]								Male							
	Total	14 to 17 years	18 and 19 years	20 and 21 years	22 to 24 years	25 to 29 years	30 to 34 years	35 years and over	Total	14 to 17 years	18 and 19 years	20 and 21 years	22 to 24 years	25 to 29 years	30 to 34 years	35 years and over
WHITE ALONE																
2011	15,412	141	3,298	3,545	2,970	2,254	1,085	2,120	7,054	78	1,520	1,679	1,486	1,013	470	808
2010	15,258	154	3,398	3,297	2,629	2,217	1,197	2,366	6,883	59	1,573	1,624	1,172	1,051	511	893
2009	15,027	160	3,337	3,205	2,784	2,066	1,097	2,377	6,681	77	1,511	1,533	1,360	904	483	814
2008	14,405	171	3,353	3,119	2,669	1,952	907	2,234	6,570	85	1,566	1,524	1,250	938	413	794
2007	13,835	141	3,242	3,053	2,485	1,817	952	2,144	6,050	62	1,508	1,359	1,172	770	413	766
2006	13,273	161	2,982	2,958	2,358	1,740	985	2,090	5,829	57	1,367	1,344	1,131	799	396	734
2005	13,466	116	2,972	3,176	2,350	1,708	939	2,205	5,843	38	1,343	1,488	1,092	685	420	777
2004	13,381	134	2,946	3,016	2,389	1,776	974	2,146	5,944	49	1,308	1,437	1,110	837	421	782
2003[3]	12,870	100	2,833	2,796	2,521	1,585	960	2,075	5,714	48	1,258	1,236	1,232	723	435	783
2002	12,781	109	2,891	2,810	2,220	1,582	933	2,236	5,719	57	1,329	1,306	1,066	712	394	855
2001	12,208	88	2,755	2,774	2,019	1,514	956	2,103	5,383	36	1,273	1,305	943	693	401	731
2000	11,999	117	2,914	2,590	2,062	1,433	906	1,978	5,311	47	1,289	1,225	1,008	662	367	713
1999	12,053	87	2,849	2,519	2,074	1,474	870	2,173	5,562	32	1,335	1,226	1,026	715	414	804
1998	12,401	93	2,994	2,537	2,010	1,604	964	2,199	5,602	30	1,376	1,256	1,002	746	396	795
1997	12,442	127	2,792	2,602	2,101	1,666	856	2,289	5,552	48	1,314	1,289	1,030	802	345	725
1996	12,189	167	2,731	2,362	2,030	1,704	940	2,254	5,453	70	1,223	1,117	1,079	797	357	811
1995	12,021	116	2,577	2,437	1,997	1,745	941	2,208	5,535	44	1,195	1,201	1,002	857	432	804
1994[2]	12,222	101	2,568	2,459	2,091	1,592	1,143	2,267	5,524	44	1,212	1,140	1,054	749	512	815
1993[r]	11,735	103	2,566	2,356	2,152	1,507	1,003	2,049	5,403	44	1,157	1,196	1,145	705	451	705
1993	11,434	98	2,456	2,243	2,064	1,490	1,015	2,068	5,222	41	1,103	1,120	1,090	699	457	711
1992	11,710	158	2,419	2,466	2,031	1,512	1,070	2,053	5,210	82	1,102	1,162	1,027	689	471	678
1991	11,686	104	2,487	2,449	1,877	1,598	1,063	2,107	5,304	41	1,112	1,146	1,012	809	480	703
1990	11,488	132	2,548	2,341	1,746	1,638	1,060	2,023	5,235	63	1,218	1,151	923	782	434	665
1989	11,243	147	2,648	2,170	1,813	1,611	986	1,868	5,136	63	1,253	1,070	900	789	438	623
1988	11,140	137	2,639	2,270	1,750	1,425	1,023	1,896	5,078	50	1,194	1,114	952	685	470	613
1987	10,731	194	2,564	2,254	1,665	1,483	985	1,584	5,104	97	1,260	1,156	873	740	436	541
1986	10,707	173	2,549	2,015	1,743	1,580	1,037	1,609	5,074	69	1,254	982	932	835	475	528
1985	10,781	229	2,539	2,257	1,704	1,590	1,014	1,448	5,103	120	1,176	1,137	941	812	449	468
1984	10,520	209	2,541	2,206	1,779	1,566	967	1,252	5,111	73	1,224	1,143	1,039	796	434	402
1983	10,565	214	2,597	2,161	1,705	1,603	961	1,324	5,162	87	1,197	1,149	989	875	421	444
1982	10,551	216	2,549	2,348	1,697	1,581	938	1,222	5,077	95	1,189	1,188	931	831	415	428
1981	10,353	197	2,639	2,239	1,671	1,390	1,027	1,190	5,010	86	1,259	1,104	977	745	448	391
1980	9,925	212	2,578	2,131	1,625	1,413	915	1,051	4,804	79	1,232	1,114	878	735	400	366
1979	9,956	256	2,498	2,079	1,543	1,474	859	1,247	4,823	110	1,192	1,058	854	788	398	423
1978	9,661	229	2,553	1,993	1,531	1,399	808	1,148	4,913	90	1,239	1,056	900	810	413	405
1977	9,962	227	2,579	2,099	1,531	1,550	827	1,149	5,156	91	1,272	1,124	890	907	433	439
1976	9,679	237	2,577	2,108	1,591	1,458	673	1,035	5,084	89	1,244	1,073	933	936	382	427
1975	9,546	252	2,613	2,042	1,461	1,410	737	1,031	5,263	111	1,283	1,134	909	911	426	489
1974	8,689	271	2,308	1,940	1,341	1,308	613	908	4,782	128	1,143	1,067	825	855	350	414
1973	8,014	253	2,281	1,865	1,292	1,152	481	690	4,218	111	1,177	1,017	838	789	286	. . .
1972	7,458	259	2,411	1,917	1,296	1,119	456	. . .	4,395	120	1,242	1,062	891	784	296	. . .
1971	7,273	251	2,485	1,758	1,351	965	463	. . .	4,407	117	1,328	964	992	712	293	. . .
1970	6,759	230	2,361	1,684	1,260	853	371	. . .	4,066	117	1,251	995	850	622	231	. . .
1969	6,827	222	2,377	1,762	1,208	855	404	. . .	4,146	110	1,298	1,021	827	637	252	. . .
1968	6,255	251	2,284	1,691	954	741	333	. . .	3,843	117	1,262	1,021	666	564	213	. . .
1967	5,905	220	2,105	1,688	915	646	329	. . .	3,560	88	1,097	998	666	494	217	. . .
1966	5,708	233	2,293	----2,313----		-----869-----		. . .	3,536	93	1,281	----1,541----		------621-----		. . .
1965	5,317	233	2,074	----2,139----		-----871-----		. . .	3,326	104	1,152	----1,441----		------629-----		. . .
1964	4,337	257	1,519	----1,850----		-----711-----		. . .	2,720	147	823	----1,226----		------524-----		. . .
1963	4,050	171	1,391	----1,817----		-----671-----		. . .	2,593	94	746	----1,246----		------507-----		. . .
1962	3,934	217	1,509	----1,517----		-----691-----		. . .	2,586	120	836	----1,066----		------564-----		. . .
1961	3,498	204	1,388	----1,296----		-----610-----		. . .	2,208	79	786	------883----		------460-----		. . .
1960	3,342	214	1,211	----1,209----		-----709-----		. . .	2,214	97	691	------859----		------567-----		. . .
1959	3,118	193	1,101	----1,134----		-----690-----		. . .	2,067	88	620	------798----		------561-----		. . .
1958	3,030	155	1,044	----1,136----		-----695-----		. . .	1,999	68	577	------802----		------552-----		. . .
1957	2,932	161	921	----1,165----		-----685-----		. . .	1,938	68	510	------797----		------563-----		. . .
1956	2,687	152	869	----1,025----		-----641-----		. . .	1,808	68	474	------733----		------533-----		. . .
1955	2,224	125	715	------880----		-----504-----		. . .	1,495	47	418	------621----		-----409-----		. . .

[1]Civilian noninstitutionalized population.
[2] Before 1994, total enrolled does not include the 35 and over population.
[3]Starting in 2003 respondents could identify more than one race. Except as noted, the race data in this table from 2003 onward represent those respondents who indicated only one race category.
r = Revised, controlled to 1990 census based population estimates; previous 1993 data controlled to 1980 census based population estimates.
. . . = Not available.

Table A-15. Age Distribution of College Students 14 Years Old and Over, by Sex, October 1947–2011—*Continued*

(Numbers in thousands)

Year, sex, race, and Hispanic origin	Female							
	Total	14 to 17 years	18 and 19 years	20 and 21 years	22 to 24 years	25 to 29 years	30 to 34 years	35 years and over
WHITE ALONE								
2011	8,358	63	1,779	1,866	1,484	1,241	615	1,311
2010	8,375	95	1,825	1,673	1,458	1,166	686	1,472
2009	8,346	84	1,826	1,672	1,424	1,162	614	1,564
2008	7,835	85	1,787	1,595	1,419	1,014	493	1,440
2007	7,785	80	1,734	1,694	1,313	1,047	539	1,378
2006	7,445	104	1,615	1,613	1,227	941	588	1,355
2005	7,624	79	1,629	1,688	1,258	1,024	519	1,428
2004	7,438	86	1,638	1,579	1,279	939	553	1,364
2003[3]	7,155	53	1,575	1,560	1,289	862	525	1,291
2002	7,062	52	1,562	1,504	1,154	870	539	1,381
2001	6,826	52	1,481	1,468	1,077	820	555	1,372
2000	6,689	70	1,625	1,365	1,054	770	539	1,266
1999	6,491	55	1,513	1,296	1,053	760	455	1,358
1998	6,799	63	1,618	1,281	1,008	858	567	1,405
1997	6,890	79	1,479	1,313	1,071	864	511	1,573
1996	6,735	97	1,508	1,246	951	906	583	1,443
1995	6,486	72	1,383	1,237	995	887	508	1,404
1994[2]	6,698	57	1,357	1,320	1,037	844	631	1,453
1993[r]	6,331	59	1,409	1,160	1,007	802	552	1,344
1993	6,212	57	1,353	1,123	974	791	558	1,357
1992	6,499	76	1,317	1,303	1,005	823	599	1,376
1991	6,382	63	1,375	1,304	865	789	583	1,404
1990	6,253	69	1,331	1,190	823	856	627	1,358
1989	6,107	84	1,395	1,101	913	822	548	1,245
1988	6,063	87	1,445	1,156	798	740	554	1,283
1987	5,627	97	1,304	1,097	791	743	550	1,044
1986	5,632	105	1,295	1,033	811	745	562	1,081
1985	5,679	110	1,363	1,120	764	778	565	979
1984	5,410	136	1,317	1,063	740	770	533	851
1983	5,404	127	1,400	1,012	717	728	540	880
1982	5,472	120	1,360	1,159	766	749	523	795
1981	5,342	111	1,380	1,134	694	646	578	799
1980	5,121	133	1,346	1,017	747	678	514	686
1979	5,131	146	1,306	1,021	688	686	461	823
1978	4,748	139	1,314	937	631	590	395	742
1977	4,806	135	1,307	975	641	643	394	711
1976	4,593	147	1,334	1,034	658	521	291	608
1975	4,284	141	1,330	908	552	500	311	542
1974	3,907	143	1,166	873	516	453	263	493
1973	3,107	142	1,104	848	454	363	196	...
1972	3,061	138	1,169	855	404	334	160	...
1971	2,867	134	1,157	794	359	252	170	...
1970	2,693	113	1,110	689	410	231	140	...
1969	2,681	112	1,079	741	380	218	151	...
1968	2,412	134	1,022	670	288	177	120	...
1967	2,345	133	1,009	690	250	152	112	...
1966	2,172	140	1,012	772		248		...
1965	1,991	129	922	698		242		...
1964	1,617	110	696	624		187		...
1963	1,457	77	645	571		164		...
1962	1,348	97	673	451		127		...
1961	1,290	125	602	413		150		...
1960	1,128	117	520	350		142		...
1959	1,051	105	481	336		129		...
1958	1,031	87	467	334		143		...
1957	994	93	411	368		122		...
1956	879	84	395	292		108		...
1955	729	78	297	259		95		...

[1]Civilian noninstitutionalized population.
[2] Before 1994, total enrolled does not include the 35 and over population.
[3]Starting in 2003 respondents could identify more than one race. Except as noted, the race data in this table from 2003 onward represent those respondents who indicated only one race category.
r = Revised, controlled to 1990 census based population estimates; previous 1993 data controlled to 1980 census based population estimates.
... = Not available.

Table A-15. Age Distribution of College Students 14 Years Old and Over, by Sex, October 1947–2011—*Continued*

(Numbers in thousands)

Year, sex, race, and Hispanic origin	All students[1]								Male							
	Total	14 to 17 years	18 and 19 years	20 and 21 years	22 to 24 years	25 to 29 years	30 to 34 years	35 years and over	Total	14 to 17 years	18 and 19 years	20 and 21 years	22 to 24 years	25 to 29 years	30 to 34 years	35 years and over
WHITE ALONE NON-HISPANIC																
2011	12,703	105	2,588	2,867	2,427	1,892	936	1,888	5,731	55	1,184	1,349	1,221	817	417	689
2010	12,613	114	2,699	2,813	2,152	1,818	996	2,022	5,673	39	1,236	1,395	986	854	416	747
2009	12,826	120	2,842	2,755	2,385	1,736	913	2,074	5,709	54	1,286	1,327	1,174	765	397	706
2008	12,324	121	2,850	2,734	2,309	1,625	779	1,906	5,602	58	1,346	1,322	1,098	766	347	664
2007	11,867	104	2,739	2,677	2,117	1,509	816	1,904	5,269	45	1,298	1,223	1,021	639	370	674
2006	11,485	114	2,564	2,606	2,030	1,494	830	1,848	5,085	41	1,168	1,208	979	702	347	640
2005	11,715	93	2,618	2,769	2,006	1,445	806	1,977	5,114	30	1,193	1,308	928	590	373	692
2004	11,571	111	2,596	2,618	2,014	1,513	814	1,905	5,146	44	1,150	1,242	930	710	372	698
2003[3]	11,295	90	2,486	2,419	2,225	1,371	832	1,872	5,067	41	1,115	1,082	1,094	639	386	710
2002	11,236	97	2,549	2,525	1,931	1,317	812	2,007	5,060	57	1,179	1,162	947	596	350	770
2001	10,602	74	2,383	2,450	1,732	1,283	827	1,854	4,691	30	1,131	1,170	794	587	348	632
2000	10,636	92	2,580	2,333	1,796	1,275	770	1,790	4,716	35	1,138	1,109	890	603	296	646
1999	10,818	80	2,574	2,324	1,837	1,283	755	1,965	5,033	30	1,214	1,141	929	627	368	722
1998	11,109	84	2,715	2,281	1,760	1,408	840	2,020	5,084	30	1,280	1,123	897	668	348	738
1997	11,246	81	2,491	2,361	1,876	1,504	779	2,153	5,024	33	1,184	1,161	930	732	314	669
1996	11,034	147	2,504	2,156	1,788	1,514	834	2,091	4,961	61	1,136	1,039	955	727	303	740
1995	11,024	103	2,372	2,226	1,796	1,618	859	2,051	5,068	36	1,111	1,103	892	799	380	749
1994[2]	11,178	93	2,362	2,255	1,904	1,444	1,018	2,101	5,053	41	1,132	1,039	955	689	457	741
1993	10,554	83	2,270	2,026	1,924	1,367	923	1,960	4,838	36	1,038	1,016	1,017	663	399	670
BLACK[4]																
2011	3,146	38	580	489	570	511	307	651	1,212	23	242	243	232	189	92	191
2010	3,083	33	567	622	503	438	277	643	1,185	14	238	262	234	180	77	180
2009	2,889	34	559	495	550	410	253	587	1,058	5	225	237	212	151	81	147
2008	2,481	36	479	463	408	377	269	451	919	21	205	217	174	115	82	106
2007	2,501	27	492	436	468	400	229	449	1,016	10	227	213	209	126	102	130
2006	2,334	30	464	416	441	303	199	480	896	10	174	182	186	112	70	163
2005	2,217	28	431	393	435	282	217	430	832	6	182	178	153	99	64	150
2004	2,301	40	440	398	400	352	170	501	776	13	165	169	146	92	41	151
2003[3]	2,144	28	374	415	435	289	214	388	798	10	166	153	180	100	84	105
2002	2,278	56	430	418	379	301	241	454	802	14	179	175	121	97	83	133
2001	2,230	33	444	383	379	283	279	429	781	7	179	137	153	88	90	126
2000	2,164	19	454	375	387	325	242	361	815	10	163	137	169	110	92	133
1999	1,998	45	430	389	325	254	199	354	833	34	210	193	98	93	79	123
1998	2,016	22	461	354	300	328	211	340	770	12	194	162	88	140	67	105
1997	1,903	24	381	321	383	258	165	372	723	7	142	137	146	110	65	117
1996	1,901	45	345	346	292	337	182	354	764	17	145	155	122	142	64	120
1995	1,772	24	344	339	305	233	193	334	710	13	145	142	143	65	80	122
1994	1,800	36	310	347	344	256	184	323	745	16	132	161	147	118	72	99
1993[r]	1,599	13	322	311	264	253	143	293	652	4	151	109	127	118	36	107
1993	1,545	13	311	297	253	245	141	284	636	4	148	107	124	116	36	102
1992	1,424	28	291	316	279	170	132	208	527	8	123	114	119	73	37	54
1991	1,477	18	303	302	223	216	157	257	629	7	137	138	103	99	55	90
1990	1,393	35	349	287	258	150	108	207	587	16	164	151	111	52	26	65
1989	1,287	32	302	290	243	156	119	146	480	8	126	104	94	65	37	47
1988	1,321	33	281	273	198	188	142	206	494	6	108	90	99	75	48	68
1987	1,351	32	341	264	218	220	121	155	587	13	154	124	99	99	37	62
1986	1,359	19	308	242	262	187	143	198	580	12	120	111	118	81	64	74
1985	1,263	21	259	274	201	183	112	213	552	10	121	140	84	64	40	93
1984	1,332	40	265	274	247	182	131	193	618	16	112	129	126	99	62	74
1983	1,273	31	258	242	241	179	151	171	560	12	93	112	126	91	64	62
1982	1,294	22	274	242	251	196	142	167	544	9	124	92	115	91	51	62
1981	1,335	31	306	232	212	219	132	203	566	7	133	92	100	115	57	62
1980	1,163	30	283	225	180	176	113	156	476	14	98	101	79	92	53	39
1979	1,156	43	279	224	193	150	112	155	498	12	110	110	84	71	47	64

[1]Civilian noninstitutionalized population.
[2] Before 1994, total enrolled does not include the 35 and over population.
[3]Starting in 2003 respondents could identify more than one race. Except as noted, the race data in this table from 2003 onward represent those respondents who indicated only one race category.
[4] Data for 1955 to 1963 are for Black and other races.
r = Revised, controlled to 1990 census based population estimates; previous 1993 data controlled to 1980 census based population estimates.

Table A-15. Age Distribution of College Students 14 Years Old and Over, by Sex, October 1947–2011—*Continued*

(Numbers in thousands)

Year, sex, race, and Hispanic origin	Female							
	Total	14 to 17 years	18 and 19 years	20 and 21 years	22 to 24 years	25 to 29 years	30 to 34 years	35 years and over
WHITE ALONE NON-HISPANIC								
2011	6,972	50	1,404	1,517	1,206	1,075	519	1,199
2010	6,940	75	1,463	1,417	1,166	964	581	1,275
2009	7,116	66	1,556	1,429	1,211	971	516	1,368
2008	6,722	63	1,504	1,412	1,211	859	432	1,242
2007	6,598	59	1,441	1,455	1,096	870	447	1,230
2006	6,400	73	1,396	1,398	1,051	792	483	1,208
2005	6,601	63	1,425	1,461	1,078	855	433	1,285
2004	6,425	67	1,446	1,375	1,085	803	442	1,207
2003[3]	6,228	49	1,371	1,337	1,130	732	446	1,163
2002	6,177	40	1,370	1,364	984	721	462	1,237
2001	5,912	44	1,252	1,280	938	695	479	1,222
2000	5,921	57	1,443	1,224	906	672	474	1,145
1999	5,785	49	1,360	1,183	908	656	387	1,241
1998	6,025	54	1,435	1,158	863	740	493	1,282
1997	6,222	48	1,307	1,200	946	771	465	1,485
1996	6,073	86	1,367	1,117	833	787	531	1,352
1995	5,956	67	1,261	1,123	904	819	479	1,302
1994[2]	6,124	53	1,229	1,216	950	755	561	1,361
1993	5,715	48	1,232	1,010	907	704	524	1,290
BLACK[4]								
2011	1,934	16	337	246	338	322	215	460
2010	1,898	20	329	360	269	258	199	463
2009	1,831	29	334	258	338	259	172	441
2008	1,562	15	274	246	234	261	188	345
2007	1,485	18	265	223	259	274	127	320
2006	1,438	20	291	234	255	191	130	318
2005	1,385	22	249	215	282	183	153	281
2004	1,525	27	275	229	254	259	130	350
2003[3]	1,346	19	209	262	255	188	130	283
2002	1,476	42	251	243	257	204	158	321
2001	1,449	26	265	245	226	195	190	302
2000	1,349	9	291	238	218	215	150	228
1999	1,164	10	221	196	227	161	120	229
1998	1,247	9	267	192	212	188	144	234
1997	1,180	17	238	184	237	149	100	255
1996	1,136	28	199	192	170	195	119	234
1995	1,062	11	199	197	162	168	113	212
1994	1,054	21	178	186	197	138	112	224
1993[r]	947	9	172	202	137	135	107	186
1993	909	8	163	191	130	129	106	182
1992	897	21	168	202	161	97	95	154
1991	848	11	166	164	120	118	102	167
1990	807	19	185	136	146	98	82	141
1989	807	24	176	186	149	91	82	99
1988	827	27	173	183	99	113	94	138
1987	764	19	186	140	119	121	84	93
1986	779	7	187	131	144	106	79	124
1985	712	11	138	134	117	119	72	121
1984	714	24	153	145	121	83	69	119
1983	714	19	164	131	116	88	87	109
1982	750	12	150	150	136	105	92	105
1981	769	24	172	140	112	105	75	141
1980	686	16	185	124	101	84	60	116
1979	659	31	169	114	109	79	66	91

[1]Civilian noninstitutionalized population.
[2] Before 1994, total enrolled does not include the 35 and over population.
[3]Starting in 2003 respondents could identify more than one race. Except as noted, the race data in this table from 2003 onward represent those respondents who indicated only one race category.
[4] Data for 1955 to 1963 are for Black and other races.
r = Revised, controlled to 1990 census based population estimates; previous 1993 data controlled to 1980 census based population estimates.

Table A-15. Age Distribution of College Students 14 Years Old and Over, by Sex, October 1947–2011—*Continued*

(Numbers in thousands)

Year, sex, race, and Hispanic origin	All students[1]								Male							
	Total	14 to 17 years	18 and 19 years	20 and 21 years	22 to 24 years	25 to 29 years	30 to 34 years	35 years and over	Total	14 to 17 years	18 and 19 years	20 and 21 years	22 to 24 years	25 to 29 years	30 to 34 years	35 years and over
BLACK[4]— *(Continued)*																
1978..........	1,175	38	270	238	186	167	121	155	504	13	114	106	85	82	52	52
1977..........	1,284	37	269	262	190	210	136	180	571	18	90	115	104	101	62	81
1976..........	1,217	34	302	252	195	171	109	154	551	11	121	113	97	90	57	62
1975..........	1,099	34	260	237	168	151	97	152	523	14	111	107	76	82	53	80
1974..........	930	34	233	190	132	136	88	117	485	13	102	100	78	70	60	62
1973..........	781	37	194	164	140	89	60	97	358	7	96	93	77	49	36	...
1972..........	727	32	229	168	143	87	68	...	384	18	102	91	94	49	30	...
1971..........	680	29	204	199	119	79	50	...	363	11	94	106	62	58	31	...
1970..........	522	21	191	152	73	54	31	...	253	10	73	81	38	33	19	...
1969..........	492	19	193	149	65	39	26	...	236	10	86	75	41	15	10	...
1968..........	434	20	182	112	58	33	29	...	221	12	83	61	26	27	13	...
1967..........	370	16	141	105	51	42	15	...	199	7	78	57	32	15	11	...
1966..........	282	17	112	-----112-----		------41----		...	154	10	47	-----72-----		-----25-----		...
1965..........	274	30	111	------99-----		------34-----		...	126	8	52	-----47-----		-----19-----		...
1964..........	234	30	78	------79-----		------47-----		...	120	16	35	-----36-----		-----33-----		...
1963..........	286	9	113	-----112-----		------52-----		...	149	5	50	-----62-----		-----32-----		...
1962..........	274	16	103	-----109-----		------46-----		...	156	5	55	-----59-----		-----37-----		...
1961..........	233	9	82	-----103-----		------39-----		...	148	5	48	-----64-----		-----31-----		...
1960..........	227	8	88	------90-----		------41-----		...	125	2	43	-----55-----		-----25-----		...
1959..........	222	17	74	------94-----		------37-----		...	120	4	31	-----58-----		-----27-----		...
1958..........	212	12	70	------85-----		------45-----		...	130	5	44	-----48-----		-----33-----		...
1957..........	206	15	68	------71-----		------52-----		...	90	9	28	-----30-----		-----23-----		...
1956..........	196	15	65	------80-----		------36-----		...	124	9	38	-----48-----		-----29-----		...
1955..........	155	21	31	------51-----		------52-----		...	84	9	15	-----25-----		-----35-----		...
ASIAN[5]																
2011..........	1,204	21	240	281	227	189	99	147	567	6	131	141	107	92	45	45
2010..........	1,322	32	234	308	269	237	117	126	647	17	116	150	124	126	58	57
2009..........	1,231	11	243	216	308	197	114	141	613	8	134	97	153	96	53	73
2008..........	1,220	27	172	247	236	245	137	156	567	22	75	123	96	132	61	58
2007..........	1,103	10	201	204	252	206	123	105	533	2	104	106	108	98	60	54
2006..........	1,084	8	204	215	242	187	103	125	535	5	113	121	104	80	51	61
2005..........	1,184	22	188	272	234	226	114	129	605	10	90	163	113	110	61	58
2004..........	1,191	20	182	245	269	217	113	146	636	11	92	135	145	116	65	71
2003[2]..........	1,162	16	209	219	264	228	108	116	606	3	103	104	130	141	67	59
2002..........	1,258	28	236	269	299	182	105	140	649	8	121	137	160	101	56	67
2001..........	1,280	17	247	245	302	265	90	115	664	10	113	127	177	134	63	40
2000..........	1,049	12	212	200	227	188	81	130	517	4	108	109	120	66	51	60
1999..........	1,041	16	223	192	211	187	71	142	506	11	93	95	96	97	47	67
HISPANIC[6]																
2011..........	2,953	36	765	740	574	407	175	256	1,438	23	351	376	279	212	67	130
2010..........	2,879	41	783	517	514	424	228	373	1,302	19	381	242	196	197	108	159
2009..........	2,434	43	550	482	433	373	217	336	1,080	23	242	221	200	159	108	127
2008..........	2,227	53	528	407	402	359	141	337	1,042	31	236	210	169	186	76	135
2007..........	2,172	41	559	412	404	332	155	269	880	16	246	154	160	145	57	102
2006..........	1,968	54	444	386	353	271	190	271	808	19	213	146	164	109	64	94
2005..........	1,942	31	406	420	389	288	150	257	804	10	173	183	183	111	52	92
2004..........	1,975	23	384	431	407	280	179	271	852	5	171	212	191	131	53	89
2003..........	1,714	12	379	407	329	224	156	207	703	7	153	167	145	93	61	77
2002..........	1,656	15	360	303	316	274	140	249	705	3	156	151	132	118	49	97
2001..........	1,700	14	387	342	306	255	136	260	731	6	149	145	156	116	57	102
2000..........	1,426	24	349	268	282	167	142	194	619	12	160	118	123	61	75	70
1999..........	1,307	7	297	197	247	207	127	225	568	2	143	84	96	94	54	95
1998..........	1,363	9	288	263	269	206	130	198	550	...	97	139	110	86	54	64
1997..........	1,260	49	316	254	236	174	80	151	555	15	133	132	106	78	31	60
1996..........	1,223	22	240	213	253	198	112	184	529	8	98	78	124	79	54	90
1995..........	1,207	20	264	245	236	153	97	193	568	14	121	111	124	71	55	73
1994[2]..........	1,187	9	225	230	207	180	132	205	529	3	89	115	108	73	55	86
1993[r]..........	1,169	17	222	299	207	178	106	139	539	7	81	154	103	71	67	56
1993..........	995	15	195	241	166	149	100	129	442	6	69	118	79	57	63	51
1992..........	918	17	230	200	156	124	90	102	388	9	93	80	74	57	35	40

[1]Civilian noninstitutionalized population.
[2] Before 1994, total enrolled does not include the 35 and over population.
[4] Data for 1955 to 1963 are for Black and other races.
[5] The data shown before 2003 consists of those identifying themselves as "Asian or Pacific Islanders."
[6] May be of any race.
r = Revised, controlled to 1990 census based population estimates; previous 1993 data controlled to 1980 census based population estimates.
... = Not available.

Table A-15. Age Distribution of College Students 14 Years Old and Over, by Sex, October 1947–2011—*Continued*

(Numbers in thousands)

Year, sex, race, and Hispanic origin	Female							
	Total	14 to 17 years	18 and 19 years	20 and 21 years	22 to 24 years	25 to 29 years	30 to 34 years	35 years and over
BLACK[4]—*(Continued)*								
1978	671	25	155	133	102	85	68	103
1977	712	19	179	147	87	108	74	98
1976	665	23	181	139	97	81	52	92
1975	577	20	150	130	92	69	44	72
1974	448	22	131	91	55	66	28	55
1973	325	30	97	71	63	40	24	...
1972	343	14	127	77	49	38	38	...
1971	317	18	109	93	57	21	19	...
1970	269	11	118	71	36	22	11	...
1969	256	9	108	74	24	25	17	...
1968	213	8	100	51	32	7	15	...
1967	171	9	63	48	19	27	4	...
1966	128	7	65	40		16		...
1965	148	22	59	52		15		...
1964	114	14	43	43		14		...
1963	137	4	63	50		20		...
1962	118	11	48	50		9		...
1961	85	4	34	39		8		...
1960	102	6	45	35		16		...
1959	102	13	43	36		10		...
1958	82	7	26	37		12		...
1957	116	6	40	41		29		...
1956	72	6	27	32		7		...
1955	71	12	16	26		17		...
ASIAN[5]								
2011	637	16	109	140	120	97	54	101
2010	676	15	118	158	145	111	59	69
2009	619	4	109	120	155	101	61	68
2008	653	5	97	123	140	113	76	98
2007	569	8	97	98	144	108	63	51
2006	549	3	91	94	139	107	52	64
2005	579	12	98	109	120	116	53	71
2004	556	9	89	110	124	101	48	75
2003[2]	556	13	107	115	134	88	42	57
2002	609	19	115	132	139	82	49	73
2001	616	6	134	118	125	131	27	75
2000	532	8	104	91	107	122	30	69
1999	534	5	130	97	115	89	24	74
HISPANIC[6]								
2011	1,515	13	414	364	294	196	108	126
2010	1,576	21	402	275	319	227	119	213
2009	1,354	20	308	261	234	214	108	209
2008	1,185	23	292	197	233	173	65	202
2007	1,292	25	313	258	244	187	98	167
2006	1,161	36	231	240	189	162	126	177
2005	1,137	21	232	237	206	178	98	165
2004	1,123	19	213	219	216	150	126	182
2003	1,011	5	226	240	185	131	95	130
2002	951	12	204	152	184	156	92	152
2001	969	8	238	197	150	139	80	157
2000	807	13	188	150	160	106	67	124
1999	739	5	154	113	151	113	73	130
1998	814	9	191	124	159	120	77	134
1997	704	34	183	123	130	96	49	91
1996	693	15	142	136	128	119	59	95
1995	639	6	143	134	112	82	42	120
1994[2]	659	6	136	119	99	106	78	119
1993[r]	630	10	141	145	104	107	40	83
1993	553	9	126	123	87	93	38	78
1992	530	7	137	120	82	67	55	62

[1]Civilian noninstitutionalized population.
[2] Before 1994, total enrolled does not include the 35 and over population.
[4] Data for 1955 to 1963 are for Black and other races.
[5] The data shown before 2003 consists of those identifying themselves as "Asian or Pacific Islanders."
[6] May be of any race.
r = Revised, controlled to 1990 census based population estimates; previous 1993 data controlled to 1980 census based population estimates.
... = Not available.

Table A-15. Age Distribution of College Students 14 Years Old and Over, by Sex, October 1947–2011—*Continued*

(Numbers in thousands)

Year, sex, race, and Hispanic origin	All students[1]								Male							
	Total	14 to 17 years	18 and 19 years	20 and 21 years	22 to 24 years	25 to 29 years	30 to 34 years	35 years and over	Total	14 to 17 years	18 and 19 years	20 and 21 years	22 to 24 years	25 to 29 years	30 to 34 years	35 years and over
HISPANIC[6]— *(Continued)*																
1991	830	10	188	203	125	124	72	109	347	5	68	79	64	64	30	37
1990	748	13	148	188	99	109	59	130	364	12	70	80	64	39	30	67
1989	754	17	177	134	142	112	58	114	353	5	75	66	70	63	31	42
1988	747	13	203	110	137	118	73	93	355	9	75	76	77	48	29	43
1987	739	8	152	155	148	137	67	73	390	3	76	100	71	77	42	21
1986	794	16	171	146	141	164	67	89	377	4	92	67	74	80	26	34
1985	580	16	127	128	120	111	78	...	279	10	44	53	71	72	29	...
1984	524	5	136	133	93	100	57	...	231	2	42	63	49	49	26	...
1983	521	17	134	124	91	114	41	...	253	10	41	61	50	74	17	...
1982	494	16	143	104	90	94	47	...	216	6	52	47	42	49	20	...
1981	510	15	129	123	90	103	50	...	258	6	57	68	39	55	33	...
1980	443	10	137	94	84	69	49	...	222	2	68	52	34	36	30	...
1979	439	18	124	95	73	73	56	...	225	8	67	43	43	39	25	...
1978	377	15	109	68	77	78	30	...	196	7	53	30	43	49	14	...
1977	417	14	123	95	59	81	45	...	224	6	54	45	40	56	23	...
1976	426	13	143	83	83	73	31	...	223	3	69	39	42	50	20	...
1975	411	13	118	101	76	68	35	...	218	3	53	52	40	45	25	...
1974	354	11	112	96	64	39	32	...	195	6	55	44	42	24	24	...
1973	289	15	82	69	55	45	23	...	168	11	39	37	29	32	20	...
1972	242	14	70	60	49	34	15	...	126	7	28	35	29	20	7	...
WHITE ALONE OR IN COMBINATION																
2011	15,785	141	3,381	3,631	3,031	2,316	1,124	2,160	7,239	78	1,554	1,719	1,517	1,046	496	830
2010	15,586	157	3,478	3,359	2,687	2,287	1,220	2,399	7,030	60	1,620	1,656	1,196	1,080	516	902
2009	15,391	160	3,414	3,289	2,859	2,125	1,133	2,411	6,848	77	1,535	1,591	1,387	930	501	826
2008	14,738	175	3,440	3,181	2,738	2,003	936	2,264	6,730	87	1,607	1,550	1,286	966	426	807
2007	14,114	147	3,318	3,111	2,529	1,857	978	2,174	6,169	64	1,540	1,390	1,186	789	425	774
2006	13,564	166	3,043	3,006	2,416	1,791	1,016	2,125	5,966	61	1,399	1,363	1,161	827	411	744
2005	13,791	125	3,043	3,244	2,433	1,740	954	2,251	5,978	43	1,371	1,519	1,128	696	424	796
2004	13,688	135	3,012	3,106	2,425	1,807	989	2,192	6,068	49	1,331	1,494	1,131	847	425	792
2003	13,164	106	2,905	2,868	2,584	1,613	989	2,099	5,837	48	1,283	1,274	1,257	730	446	798
BLACK ALONE OR IN COMBINATION																
2011	3,317	39	615	540	605	533	321	665	1,279	23	250	264	249	196	100	198
2010	3,250	38	622	653	533	463	286	655	1,241	19	264	271	244	186	78	180
2009	3,030	34	604	520	574	428	268	601	1,109	5	245	250	217	155	88	149
2008	2,619	36	515	490	429	400	278	470	983	21	219	229	184	127	85	116
2007	2,630	33	530	459	479	432	243	455	1,077	12	240	229	217	139	110	130
2006	2,444	30	492	423	471	318	217	493	951	10	186	186	206	120	74	170
2005	2,387	31	481	428	462	299	229	458	895	9	201	189	167	109	66	154
2004	2,412	40	466	436	416	371	170	512	827	13	175	187	159	100	41	153
2003	2,227	30	400	440	445	303	214	395	826	10	175	165	186	100	84	107
ASIAN ALONE OR IN COMBINATION																
2011	1,356	21	267	323	243	220	121	161	658	6	145	162	123	110	60	53
2010	1,467	37	264	343	298	268	125	133	740	20	136	177	141	149	61	57
2009	1,334	11	271	242	330	207	122	150	656	8	138	115	165	98	57	76
2008	1,340	27	214	265	259	260	149	167	632	22	93	134	113	135	70	65
2007	1,204	11	232	220	268	232	126	116	592	2	113	116	123	113	61	64
2006	1,154	9	215	227	263	198	110	131	566	6	118	122	122	81	55	62
2005	1,297	25	204	292	277	240	122	137	640	13	97	170	124	113	63	60
2004	1,260	20	203	266	281	222	116	152	662	11	97	147	153	117	65	72
2003	1,262	19	236	248	290	232	117	121	649	3	112	115	143	142	72	61

[1]Civilian noninstitutionalized population.
[6]May be of any race.
... = Not available.

Table A-15. Age Distribution of College Students 14 Years Old and Over, by Sex, October 1947–2011—*Continued*

(Numbers in thousands)

Year, sex, race, and Hispanic origin	Female							
	Total	14 to 17 years	18 and 19 years	20 and 21 years	22 to 24 years	25 to 29 years	30 to 34 years	35 years and over
HISPANIC[6]—*(Continued)*								
1991	483	5	120	124	61	59	42	72
1990	384	1	78	108	35	70	29	63
1989	401	11	103	69	72	49	27	71
1988	391	4	129	35	60	70	43	51
1987	349	5	76	56	76	60	25	51
1986	417	12	79	80	67	84	41	54
1985	299	6	82	75	48	39	49	...
1984	292	3	94	70	43	51	31	...
1983	270	7	93	64	41	40	25	...
1982	278	10	91	57	48	45	27	...
1981	252	9	72	55	51	48	17	...
1980	221	8	63	42	50	33	20	...
1979	215	10	58	52	30	34	31	...
1978	181	8	56	38	34	29	16	...
1977	194	8	70	50	19	25	22	...
1976	203	9	74	45	41	23	11	...
1975	193	10	65	49	36	23	10	...
1974	157	5	56	51	22	15	8	...
1973	123	5	44	33	25	13	3	...
1972	117	7	43	25	20	14	8	...
WHITE ALONE OR IN COMBINATION								
2011	8,545	63	1,828	1,912	1,514	1,270	627	1,330
2010	8,556	97	1,858	1,702	1,491	1,207	703	1,497
2009	8,544	84	1,879	1,698	1,473	1,195	631	1,585
2008	8,008	88	1,833	1,631	1,452	1,037	510	1,457
2007	7,945	82	1,779	1,721	1,343	1,068	553	1,400
2006	7,598	105	1,643	1,643	1,255	964	605	1,382
2005	7,813	82	1,672	1,725	1,305	1,044	530	1,454
2004	7,600	86	1,682	1,612	1,295	960	564	1,401
2003	7,328	57	1,622	1,594	1,327	883	543	1,302
BLACK ALONE OR IN COMBINATION								
2011	2,037	16	365	276	356	337	221	467
2010	2,009	20	358	383	289	277	208	474
2009	1,921	29	359	270	357	274	180	451
2008	1,636	15	296	261	245	272	193	354
2007	1,553	20	290	230	263	292	133	325
2006	1,493	20	307	238	265	198	143	323
2005	1,493	22	280	239	295	190	164	303
2004	1,584	27	290	249	258	271	130	359
2003	1,401	20	225	275	260	203	130	288
ASIAN ALONE OR IN COMBINATION								
2011	697	16	122	161	121	110	61	108
2010	727	17	128	166	157	119	63	76
2009	678	4	134	127	165	109	65	74
2008	708	5	121	131	146	125	79	102
2007	612	9	119	104	145	118	65	52
2006	588	3	97	105	141	117	55	69
2005	657	12	107	122	153	128	59	77
2004	598	9	106	118	128	105	51	80
2003	613	16	124	133	147	89	44	60

[1]Civilian noninstitutionalized population.
[6]May be of any race.
... = Not available.

Table A-16. College Enrollment of Students 14 Years Old and Over, by Type of College, Attendance Status, Age, and Sex, October 1970–2011

(Numbers in thousands)

Year and type of college	All students[1]								Male			Female		
	Total	14 to 19 years	20 to 21 years	22 to 24 years	25 to 34 years	35 years and over	Public	Private	Total	Full-time	Part-time	Total	Full-time	Part-time
ALL UNDERGRADUATES														
2011	16,625	4,435	4,368	3,000	3,019	1,802	13,816	2,809	7,515	5,830	1,685	9,110	6,908	2,202
2010	16,354	4,546	4,225	2,671	2,912	2,000	13,701	2,653	7,300	5,582	1,718	9,054	6,773	2,282
2009	16,012	4,463	3,965	2,849	2,737	1,999	13,356	2,656	7,121	5,632	1,488	8,891	6,686	2,205
2008	14,955	4,347	3,862	2,600	2,430	1,716	12,340	2,616	6,737	5,220	1,517	8,218	6,158	2,060
2007	14,365	4,237	3,732	2,513	2,277	1,605	11,811	2,554	6,405	5,053	1,353	7,959	5,813	2,146
2006	13,854	3,940	3,591	2,437	2,178	1,709	11,269	2,585	6,135	4,686	1,450	7,719	5,695	2,024
2005	14,169	3,901	3,847	2,588	2,142	1,690	11,292	2,876	6,189	4,799	1,391	7,979	5,852	2,127
2004	14,004	3,863	3,700	2,431	2,257	1,753	11,384	2,620	6,156	4,714	1,442	7,848	5,704	3,102
2003	13,370	3,633	3,449	2,687	2,094	1,506	10,980	2,389	5,902	4,476	1,425	7,468	5,391	2,077
2002	13,426	3,743	3,457	2,355	2,106	1,764	10,830	2,595	5,929	4,462	1,467	7,497	5,273	2,223
2001	12,552	3,568	3,329	2,136	1,979	1,540	10,188	2,364	5,522	4,057	1,464	7,030	4,949	2,082
2000	12,401	3,710	3,093	2,113	1,988	1,498	10,044	2,357	5,520	4,059	1,461	6,881	4,832	2,049
1999	12,046	3,625	3,043	2,000	1,885	1,493	9,689	2,357	5,554	4,143	1,411	6,492	4,548	1,945
1998	12,509	3,749	3,019	2,025	2,101	1,616	10,100	2,410	5,621	4,051	1,570	6,888	4,765	2,123
1997	12,409	3,504	3,080	2,137	1,970	1,718	10,074	2,335	5,539	4,165	1,375	6,870	4,752	2,118
1996	12,305	3,526	2,856	2,017	2,226	1,680	10,121	2,183	5,533	4,032	1,502	6,772	4,502	2,269
1995	11,966	3,251	2,881	2,033	2,151	1,651	9,570	2,396	5,413	3,911	1,501	6,554	4,433	2,121
1994	12,410	3,192	3,006	2,099	2,281	1,832	9,983	2,427	5,526	3,969	1,557	6,883	4,480	2,404
1993r	11,959	3,197	2,879	2,131	2,118	1,634	9,706	2,253	5,442	4,020	1,422	6,517	4,346	2,171
1993	11,507	3,045	2,721	2,020	2,088	1,633	9,330	2,176	5,194	3,812	1,382	6,313	4,182	2,130
1992	11,643	3,097	2,902	2,004	2,090	1,550	9,519	2,124	5,091	3,724	1,365	6,553	4,338	2,214
1991	11,374	3,061	2,902	1,757	2,120	1,534	9,257	2,117	5,120	3,724	1,395	6,254	4,145	2,109
1990	11,108	3,194	2,740	1,681	2,067	1,425	9,031	2,076	5,030	3,628	1,402	6,077	3,967	2,109
1989	10,661	3,250	2,529	1,658	1,921	1,304	8,633	2,027	4,730	3,436	1,295	5,931	3,880	2,051
1988	10,605	3,229	2,645	1,600	1,865	1,266	8,617	1,988	4,763	3,441	1,322	5,842	3,816	2,026
1987	10,304	3,283	2,585	1,512	1,848	1,076	8,306	1,998	4,878	3,476	1,403	5,426	3,445	1,981
1986	10,036	3,158	2,298	1,583	1,932	1,065	7,955	2,081	4,663	3,350	1,312	5,373	3,474	1,899
1985	10,097	3,169	2,586	1,475	1,884	984	8,042	2,055	4,667	3,454	1,213	5,430	3,578	1,852
1984	9,910	3,120	2,564	1,547	1,826	852	7,944	1,966	4,725	3,573	1,152	5,185	3,419	1,766
1983	9,925	3,200	2,464	1,475	1,873	914	7,808	2,117	4,759	3,472	1,287	5,166	3,424	1,742
1982	9,952	3,183	2,657	1,526	1,745	843	7,908	2,044	4,703	3,485	1,218	5,249	3,480	1,769
1981	9,969	3,276	2,511	1,458	1,808	916	7,789	2,180	4,724	3,452	1,273	5,245	3,490	1,755
1980	9,279	3,182	2,393	1,316	1,598	791	...	...	4,353	3,247	1,105	4,927	3,210	1,717
1979	9,193	3,156	2,308	1,297	1,526	905	7,331	1,861	4,387	3,219	1,168	4,805	3,163	1,642
1978	8,947	3,173	2,246	1,233	1,505	790	7,008	1,939	4,445	3,269	1,176	4,502	3,031	1,471
1977[2]	8,408	3,184	2,376	1,206	1,640	...	6,683	1,724	4,372	3,304	1,068	4,027	3,002	1,025
1976	8,988	3,216	2,358	1,224	1,472	718	7,196	1,787	4,569	3,353	1,213	4,419	3,166	1,253
1975	8,108	3,237	2,255	1,072	1,546	...	6,598	1,510	4,393	3,394	999	3,715	2,902	813
1974	7,338	2,906	2,131	1,028	1,272	...	5,843	1,494	4,030	3,128	902	3,307	2,561	746
1973	6,794	2,812	2,031	924	1,028	...	5,279	1,516	3,791	3,035	756	3,004	2,423	581
1972	6,992	2,974	2,065	944	1,011	...	5,460	1,532	3,982	3,231	751	3,010	2,445	565
1971	6,895	3,008	1,936	1,019	931	...	5,472	1,423	4,017	3,240	777	2,878	2,348	530
1970	6,274	2,854	1,803	866	750	...	4,910	1,363	3,627	3,045	582	2,646	2,164	482
TWO-YEAR COLLEGE STUDENTS														
2011	5,705	1,596	1,187	845	1,237	840	5,265	440	2,453	1,664	790	3,252	2,053	1,199
2010	5,904	1,754	1,230	836	1,170	915	5,450	454	2,693	1,803	890	3,211	2,066	1,144
2009	5,551	1,636	960	813	1,221	920	5,095	456	2,363	1,573	790	3,188	2,060	1,128
2008	5,345	1,731	1,001	726	1,095	792	5,006	339	2,331	1,487	844	3,014	1,910	1,104
2007	4,814	1,496	856	774	963	725	4,418	396	2,061	1,322	739	2,753	1,666	1,087
2006	4,294	1,367	788	573	836	731	3,878	416	1,788	1,169	620	2,506	1,531	975
2005	4,327	1,259	833	603	882	751	3,890	437	1,866	1,197	669	2,462	1,436	1,026
2004	4,340	1,243	802	568	898	829	3,939	401	1,756	1,141	615	2,584	1,461	1,123
2003	4,384	1,178	746	843	834	784	3,999	385	1,782	1,055	726	2,603	1,507	1,095
2002	4,378	1,227	777	656	880	838	3,948	431	1,884	1,102	783	2,494	1,363	1,131
2001	4,159	1,200	776	605	832	746	3,749	410	1,802	1,057	745	2,357	1,252	1,105
2000	3,881	1,232	710	525	673	741	3,590	291	1,655	969	686	2,226	1,224	1,002
1999	3,794	1,187	715	460	683	749	3,482	312	1,637	949	688	2,157	1,157	1,000
1998	4,234	1,301	701	619	839	774	3,865	369	1,845	1,049	796	2,389	1,287	1,103
1997	4,078	1,178	760	528	806	807	3,780	298	1,663	983	680	2,415	1,307	1,108
1996	4,174	1,223	669	515	922	845	3,890	284	1,752	974	778	2,423	1,235	1,187
1995	3,882	1,028	608	593	892	761	3,553	330	1,626	898	728	2,256	1,124	1,132
1994	4,208	1,063	623	621	1,011	890	3,846	362	1,704	937	766	2,504	1,234	1,270
1993r	4,345	1,131	745	648	978	843	4,024	321	1,825	1,061	764	2,520	1,317	1,203
1993	4,196	1,077	696	614	965	844	3,884	311	1,748	1,006	742	2,448	1,268	1,179

[1]Civilian noninstitutionalized population.
[2]Data for 1970–1975 and 1977 do not include people ages 35 and over.
r = Revised, controlled to 1990 census based population estimates; previous 1993 data controlled to 1980 census based population estimates.
... = Not available.

Table A-16. College Enrollment of Students 14 Years Old and Over, by Type of College, Attendance Status, Age, and Sex, October 1970–2011—*Continued*

(Numbers in thousands)

Year and type of college	Full-time						Part-time					
	Total	14 to 19 years	20 to 21 years	22 to 24 years	25 to 34 years	35 years and over	Total	14 to 19 years	20 to 21 years	22 to 24 years	25 to 34 years	35 years and over
ALL UNDERGRADUATES												
2011	12,738	4,059	3,855	2,235	1,758	832	3,887	376	514	766	1,261	970
2010	12,354	4,032	3,653	2,071	1,674	924	4,000	514	572	599	1,237	1,077
2009	12,318	4,128	3,534	2,276	1,547	833	3,694	335	431	573	1,189	1,165
2008	11,378	3,999	3,445	2,017	1,240	676	3,577	347	417	583	1,190	1,040
2007	10,866	3,879	3,282	1,858	1,285	562	3,499	358	450	656	992	1,043
2006	10,380	3,567	3,150	1,810	1,242	612	3,474	373	441	627	936	1,097
2005	10,651	3,540	3,369	1,977	1,139	625	3,518	360	479	611	1,003	1,065
2004	10,418	3,533	3,251	1,836	1,150	648	3,586	330	449	595	1,107	1,105
2003	9,868	3,299	2,992	1,948	1,081	547	3,502	334	457	739	1,013	959
2002	9,735	3,356	3,058	1,737	1,073	511	3,690	387	399	619	1,033	1,253
2001	9,006	3,190	2,840	1,524	976	476	3,546	378	489	612	1,003	1,064
2000	8,891	3,368	2,658	1,479	930	457	3,510	342	435	633	1,058	1,041
1999	8,691	3,280	2,625	1,485	888	412	3,355	345	418	514	997	1,081
1998	8,816	3,327	2,619	1,461	956	452	3,693	421	400	563	1,145	1,164
1997	8,917	3,144	2,704	1,576	960	532	3,492	360	376	560	1,010	1,186
1996	8,534	3,131	2,460	1,516	990	437	3,771	394	396	501	1,236	1,243
1995	8,344	2,902	2,462	1,444	1,004	533	3,622	349	419	589	1,147	1,118
1994	8,449	2,843	2,585	1,455	981	586	3,961	350	421	644	1,300	1,245
1993[r]	8,366	2,866	2,513	1,513	941	533	3,593	332	366	619	1,176	1,102
1993	7,994	2,732	2,380	1,429	927	527	3,513	314	342	590	1,161	1,106
1992	8,063	2,838	2,506	1,427	834	458	3,580	259	396	578	1,255	1,092
1991	7,869	2,809	2,534	1,248	878	400	3,505	252	368	509	1,242	1,134
1990	7,597	2,912	2,333	1,165	824	363	3,511	282	408	515	1,244	1,062
1989	7,314	2,989	2,209	1,122	655	341	3,346	260	321	536	1,266	963
1988	7,257	2,925	2,275	1,079	691	285	3,348	303	371	521	1,173	981
1987	6,920	2,892	2,179	1,005	610	235	3,384	391	406	507	1,238	841
1986	6,825	2,880	1,973	1,055	680	237	3,212	278	324	528	1,254	828
1985	7,033	2,900	2,237	1,017	701	178	3,065	269	349	457	1,184	806
1984	6,992	2,846	2,221	1,067	689	170	2,918	274	344	480	1,139	683
1983	6,896	2,895	2,124	993	718	166	3,029	305	340	482	1,153	748
1982	6,965	2,880	2,286	979	662	159	2,987	302	372	547	1,083	684
1981	6,942	2,983	2,157	986	613	202	3,027	293	353	471	1,195	715
1980	6,457	2,897	2,107	810	500	142	2,822	283	287	505	1,098	649
1979	6,383	2,892	1,994	815	523	158	2,810	264	314	482	1,003	748
1978	6,300	2,872	1,918	820	559	132	2,647	302	328	412	947	658
1977[2]	6,304	2,855	2,075	775	598	...	2,104	329	301	431	1,042	...
1976	6,519	2,963	2,033	821	563	138	2,466	253	325	403	909	577
1975	6,296	2,987	1,958	696	655	...	1,812	250	297	376	891	...
1974	5,689	2,661	1,842	697	488	...	1,649	245	289	331	784	...
1973	5,460	2,629	1,801	630	398	...	1,334	183	230	294	630	...
1972	5,678	2,797	1,845	624	412	...	1,314	177	220	320	599	...
1971	5,588	2,801	1,729	700	357	...	1,307	207	207	319	574	...
1970	5,208	2,685	1,628	591	301	...	1,066	169	175	275	449	...
TWO-YEAR COLLEGE STUDENTS												
2011	3,716	1,341	882	458	672	363	1,989	255	306	387	564	477
2010	3,870	1,422	868	554	654	372	2,034	332	362	282	516	542
2009	3,633	1,409	689	540	641	354	1,918	227	271	274	580	566
2008	3,397	1,450	763	455	466	263	1,948	281	239	271	628	529
2007	2,988	1,276	627	425	443	219	1,826	221	230	349	520	506
2006	2,699	1,145	600	312	401	241	1,595	221	188	261	435	490
2005	2,632	1,031	605	373	393	231	1,695	228	228	230	489	520
2004	2,602	1,027	553	327	425	269	1,738	216	249	241	472	560
2003	2,563	973	516	386	429	258	1,822	205	230	457	404	526
2002	2,464	975	571	344	374	200	1,914	252	206	312	506	638
2001	2,310	951	529	301	307	222	1,850	250	247	304	524	525
2000	2,193	993	507	278	230	184	1,688	239	202	247	444	557
1999	2,105	955	498	261	230	161	1,688	231	217	199	453	588
1998	2,336	1,024	495	331	302	184	1,899	277	206	288	537	591
1997	2,290	947	522	283	327	212	1,788	231	238	245	479	595
1996	2,209	995	457	271	315	171	1,965	227	212	244	607	674
1995	2,022	810	397	298	321	195	1,860	218	211	295	571	565
1994	2,172	848	407	319	341	256	2,036	215	216	302	669	634
1993[r]	2,378	891	515	348	365	259	1,967	240	230	300	613	585
1993	2,274	850	483	325	360	256	1,922	227	213	288	605	588

[1]Civilian noninstitutionalized population.
[2]Data for 1970–1975 and 1977 do not include people ages 35 and over.
r = Revised, controlled to 1990 census based population estimates; previous 1993 data controlled to 1980 census based population estimates.
... = Not available.

Table A-16. College Enrollment of Students 14 Years Old and Over, by Type of College, Attendance Status, Age, and Sex, October 1970–2011—*Continued*

(Numbers in thousands)

Year and type of college	All students[1]								Male			Female		
	Total	14 to 19 years	20 to 21 years	22 to 24 years	25 to 34 years	35 years and over	Public	Private	Total	Full-time	Part-time	Total	Full-time	Part-time
TWO-YEAR COLLEGE STUDENTS— *(Continued)*														
1992	4,239	1,084	789	581	988	797	3,937	302	1,688	936	751	2,551	1,268	1,283
1991	4,277	1,120	732	560	1,084	781	4,025	252	1,798	973	825	2,479	1,239	1,239
1990	3,965	1,059	689	475	967	775	3,689	276	1,624	849	775	2,340	1,103	1,237
1989	3,627	1,048	557	467	880	676	3,382	245	1,464	777	688	2,163	949	1,214
1988	3,837	1,134	665	497	879	662	3,609	228	1,542	847	695	2,295	1,054	1,241
1987	3,648	1,111	624	457	851	605	3,405	243	1,522	780	742	2,127	937	1,190
1986	3,391	1,023	506	427	875	559	3,089	302	1,466	752	714	1,924	856	1,068
1985	3,289	959	558	403	851	518	3,009	281	1,336	702	634	1,954	914	1,040
1984	3,172	994	525	442	795	417	2,875	298	1,436	834	601	1,738	829	909
1983	3,416	1,050	595	405	882	485	3,136	280	1,498	807	691	1,919	897	1,022
1982	3,448	1,088	604	494	826	437	3,164	283	1,477	854	623	1,971	961	1,011
1981	3,347	1,144	566	414	768	455	3,091	255	1,475	837	638	1,872	909	963
1980	3,107	1,079	450	417	721	441	...	...	1,331	768	563	1,777	798	979
1979	2,897	933	403	407	664	490	2,710	187	1,251	684	567	1,646	725	921
1978	2,904	966	427	391	670	451	2,686	218	1,368	698	669	1,537	701	835
1977[2]	2,510	933	455	380	741	...	2,362	148	1,253	681	572	1,256	691	565
1976	2,854	907	444	367	718	419	2,688	165	1,400	760	640	1,454	743	711
1975	2,561	1,024	431	354	752	...	2,437	123	1,412	850	562	1,148	717	431
1974	2,072	834	369	305	565	...	1,917	154	1,172	709	463	899	528	371
1973	1,797	816	278	254	449	...	1,669	128	1,012	629	383	785	471	314
1972	1,910	883	334	267	426	...	1,816	94	1,125	770	355	785	484	301
1971	1,830	928	307	263	331	...	1,726	105	1,087	726	361	743	473	270
1970	1,692	895	281	234	283	...	1,559	133	1,001	726	275	691	452	239
GRADUATE STUDENTS														
2011	3,773	11	91	868	1,598	1,205	2,318	1,454	1,617	905	712	2,156	1,261	895
2010	3,921	47	123	830	1,712	1,209	2,453	1,468	1,708	1,050	658	2,214	1,196	1,017
2009	3,752	32	70	901	1,556	1,194	2,366	1,386	1,521	852	669	2,232	1,194	1,038
2008	3,676	20	58	819	1,583	1,195	2,399	1,277	1,574	880	694	2,103	987	1,116
2007	3,591	24	62	779	1,560	1,166	2,261	1,330	1,420	819	601	2,171	971	1,200
2006	3,378	18	84	729	1,480	1,067	2,197	1,181	1,371	692	678	2,007	998	1,009
2005	3,304	7	98	574	1,458	1,167	2,143	1,161	1,349	711	638	1,955	875	1,079
2004	3,378	20	77	718	1,433	1,131	2,267	1,111	1,419	726	693	1,959	845	1,114
2003	3,268	29	84	632	1,399	1,123	2,129	1,139	1,416	774	643	1,852	849	1,003
2002	3,072	33	68	572	1,296	1,104	2,003	1,068	1,311	632	679	1,761	774	987
2001	3,321	48	91	595	1,442	1,145	2,233	1,088	1,353	614	739	1,968	784	1,184
2000	2,913	38	77	571	1,218	1,009	1,965	948	1,162	546	616	1,750	722	1,028
1999	3,157	45	77	620	1,211	1,205	1,970	1,188	1,403	699	703	1,755	722	1,033
1998	3,037	45	73	536	1,313	1,070	1,884	1,153	1,284	614	669	1,753	758	995
1997	3,027	30	63	562	1,299	1,073	2,016	1,010	1,304	651	653	1,723	668	1,055
1996	2,922	21	52	534	1,217	1,098	1,893	1,029	1,288	650	638	1,634	655	979
1995	2,749	8	60	465	1,198	1,018	1,802	947	1,290	646	644	1,459	554	905
1994	2,613	9	21	551	1,138	893	1,710	902	1,238	619	619	1,375	505	870
1993[r]	2,435	3	14	537	1,022	859	1,611	824	1,156	601	555	1,278	458	820
1993	2,391	3	13	514	1,006	856	1,580	812	1,130	579	551	1,261	446	815
1992	2,392	*	36	508	1,035	814	1,546	846	1,102	606	496	1,291	521	770
1991	2,683	*	37	547	1,165	934	1,824	859	1,320	688	631	1,364	491	872
1990	2,514	2	27	497	1,095	893	1,722	792	1,162	569	593	1,352	531	820
1989	2,520	*	40	509	1,161	809	1,662	857	1,219	626	594	1,300	515	786
1988	2,511	*	36	464	1,098	913	1,716	795	1,187	522	666	1,324	435	889
1987	2,415	1	57	494	1,137	725	1,655	760	1,152	579	573	1,263	462	801
1986	2,365	*	44	530	1,057	732	1,624	741	1,184	596	589	1,181	479	702
1985	2,427	*	31	540	1,179	678	1,652	775	1,239	607	632	1,188	395	793
1984	2,395	*	32	580	1,190	594	1,648	747	1,263	654	610	1,132	440	692
1983	2,442	*	32	568	1,214	629	1,614	829	1,279	665	614	1,163	438	725
1982	2,393	1	31	534	1,244	584	1,587	806	1,216	626	590	1,178	421	756
1981	2,205	*	34	528	1,120	523	1,478	726	1,127	546	581	1,078	347	731
1980	2,173	2	31	554	1,104	481	...	...	1,106	526	581	1,066	372	694
1979	2,214	*	45	497	1,149	523	1,537	678	1,105	503	602	1,109	355	754
1978	2,217	*	51	565	1,064	536	1,454	762	1,149	516	633	1,068	366	702
1977[2]	1,810	2	53	593	1,161	...	1,241	568	995	548	447	813	338	475
1976	2,152	*	40	622	1,017	472	1,516	634	1,216	576	638	937	292	644
1975	1,590	*	59	607	923	...	1,105	484	949	542	407	640	267	373
1974	1,490	*	61	499	930	...	1,061	428	897	457	440	593	205	388
1973	1,385	*	42	541	801	...	945	439	887	467	420	498	163	335
1972	1,320	1	52	517	749	...	877	443	872	481	391	450	155	295
1971	1,192	1	60	468	663	...	799	393	833	480	353	359	136	223
1970	1,140	*	54	488	599	...	789	351	774	432	342	366	123	243

[1]Civilian noninstitutionalized population.
[2]Data for 1970–1975 and 1977 do not include people ages 35 and over.
r = Revised, controlled to 1990 census based population estimates; previous 1993 data controlled to 1980 census based population estimates.
* = Quantity zero or rounds to zero.
... = Not available.

Table A-16. College Enrollment of Students 14 Years Old and Over, by Type of College, Attendance Status, Age, and Sex, October 1970–2011—*Continued*

(Numbers in thousands)

Year and type of college	Full-time						Part-time					
	Total	14 to 19 years	20 to 21 years	22 to 24 years	25 to 34 years	35 years and over	Total	14 to 19 years	20 to 21 years	22 to 24 years	25 to 34 years	35 years and over
TWO-YEAR COLLEGE STUDENTS— *(Continued)*												
1992	2,205	897	528	287	304	188	2,034	187	261	294	683	609
1991	2,212	915	476	269	361	191	2,065	205	256	291	723	589
1990	1,953	847	408	227	310	160	2,012	212	281	247	657	615
1989	1,725	860	368	160	210	128	1,902	188	189	307	669	548
1988	1,901	926	410	209	227	128	1,936	207	256	288	651	534
1987	1,716	839	368	192	212	105	1,932	272	256	264	639	500
1986	1,608	814	296	170	223	105	1,783	209	210	257	652	454
1985	1,615	779	341	174	244	78	1,674	180	217	229	607	440
1984	1,663	812	330	190	247	84	1,509	182	195	252	548	333
1983	1,703	855	374	159	250	65	1,713	195	221	245	631	420
1982	1,814	883	381	214	260	77	1,634	205	223	280	566	356
1981	1,745	927	357	170	188	102	1,601	217	209	243	579	353
1980	1,566	884	287	160	167	67	1,542	195	163	256	554	374
1979	1,408	749	251	156	185	68	1,489	184	152	251	480	423
1978	1,400	776	243	157	167	57	1,505	190	184	234	503	394
1977[2]	1,372	718	283	162	208	...	1,138	216	172	218	533	...
1976	1,503	764	261	177	228	74	1,351	143	183	190	490	346
1975	1,567	865	274	155	274	...	994	159	157	199	478	...
1974	1,237	702	233	151	152	...	835	132	136	154	413	...
1973	1,100	702	164	121	111	...	697	114	113	133	338	...
1972	1,255	772	223	134	126	...	655	111	111	133	300	...
1971	1,199	797	209	124	70	...	631	131	98	139	261	...
1970	1,177	786	197	114	80	...	515	109	84	120	203	...
GRADUATE STUDENTS												
2011	2,165	6	77	684	955	444	1,607	5	14	185	643	761
2010	2,246	35	120	697	1,027	367	1,675	12	4	133	685	842
2009	2,046	26	49	704	916	351	1,707	6	20	197	641	843
2008	1,867	20	53	646	851	296	1,810	*	5	173	732	899
2007	1,790	23	59	569	815	324	1,801	1	4	210	745	842
2006	1,690	16	70	542	809	254	1,688	3	14	187	671	813
2005	1,587	4	98	423	767	294	1,717	3	*	150	691	873
2004	1,571	20	76	548	675	252	1,807	*	1	170	757	878
2003	1,622	26	76	479	738	304	1,646	3	8	153	662	820
2002	1,406	31	61	432	631	251	1,666	2	6	140	666	852
2001	1,398	38	77	455	630	197	1,923	10	14	139	812	947
2000	1,268	32	67	414	544	211	1,645	6	10	156	674	798
1999	1,421	38	71	487	539	287	1,736	8	6	133	672	918
1998	1,372	45	58	429	579	262	1,665	*	15	107	734	808
1997	1,319	26	57	401	605	229	1,708	3	6	160	694	844
1996	1,305	18	42	420	570	254	1,617	3	9	114	647	844
1995	1,199	8	43	352	571	225	1,550	*	17	112	627	793
1994	1,124	9	19	377	544	175	1,489	*	2	174	594	718
1993[r]	1,059	3	11	376	482	186	1,376	*	3	161	540	673
1993	1,025	3	10	358	469	184	1,366	*	3	156	536	672
1992	1,126	*	33	387	478	228	1,266	*	3	120	557	586
1991	1,180	*	29	423	539	188	1,504	*	8	124	626	746
1990	1,100	2	25	376	518	180	1,413	*	2	121	577	714
1989	1,140	*	33	375	525	208	1,380	*	7	135	637	601
1988	956	*	31	304	465	157	1,555	*	5	160	634	756
1987	1,041	1	52	343	477	167	1,374	*	5	151	660	558
1986	1,074	*	40	412	465	157	1,291	*	4	120	593	575
1985	1,002	*	27	385	449	141	1,424	*	4	155	728	537
1984	1,093	*	27	427	544	95	1,302	*	6	153	644	498
1983	1,103	*	32	420	530	121	1,339	*	*	148	685	507
1982	1,047	*	28	381	522	116	1,346	1	4	153	721	467
1981	893	*	28	355	447	64	1,312	*	6	173	673	459
1980	898	2	24	403	403	66	1,275	*	6	152	702	415
1979	858	*	32	358	397	72	1,356	*	14	140	752	451
1978	882	*	38	396	376	71	1,335	*	14	169	688	465
1977[2]	886	2	43	382	459	...	922	*	10	211	702	...
1976	869	*	35	405	355	73	1,282	*	5	217	662	398
1975	809	*	43	382	386	...	780	*	16	225	537	...
1974	662	*	41	289	330	...	828	*	20	210	600	...
1973	630	*	33	350	248	...	755	*	9	191	553	...
1972	636	1	44	332	262	...	686	*	8	185	487	...
1971	616	1	57	299	261	...	576	*	3	169	402	...
1970	555	*	42	304	212	...	585	*	12	184	387	...

[1]Civilian noninstitutionalized population.
[2]Data for 1970–1975 and 1977 do not include people ages 35 and over.
r = Revised, controlled to 1990 census based population estimates; previous 1993 data controlled to 1980 census based population estimates.
* = Quantity zero or rounds to zero.
... = Not available.

PART A

NATIONAL EDUCATION STATISTICS

■ Attainment Tables

Table A-17. Educational Attainment of the Population 18 Years Old and Over, by Age, Sex, Race, and Hispanic Origin, 2011

(Numbers in thousands)

Age, sex, race, and Hispanic origin	Educational attainment								
	Total[1]	None	1st to 4th grade	5th to 6th grade	7th to 8th grade	9th grade	10th grade	11th grade[2]	High school graduate
ALL RACES									
Both Sexes									
18 years old and over	231,194	914	1,793	3,587	4,554	3,852	5,026	11,126	70,316
18 to 24 years old	29,651	57	61	145	308	388	841	4,012	8,406
25 years old and over	201,543	857	1,732	3,442	4,246	3,464	4,185	7,114	61,911
25 to 29 years old	21,382	51	85	253	261	374	389	930	5,757
30 to 34 years old	20,202	43	139	344	282	340	374	691	5,493
35 to 39 years old	19,255	65	142	316	277	321	312	683	5,117
40 to 44 years old	20,587	62	147	350	268	379	385	655	5,881
45 to 49 years old	21,989	65	154	342	309	382	354	749	6,893
50 to 54 years old	21,965	99	164	326	287	297	420	744	7,148
55 to 59 years old	19,554	70	139	304	277	228	362	587	6,042
60 to 64 years old	17,430	69	151	250	338	234	319	500	5,355
65 to 69 years old	12,160	81	112	222	368	250	285	384	4,154
70 to 74 years old	9,254	61	156	194	369	202	276	370	3,495
75 years old and over	17,764	191	343	540	1,211	456	708	820	6,576
Male									
18 years old and over	112,301	425	881	1,855	2,303	1,913	2,550	5,839	35,082
18 to 24 years old	15,081	45	26	88	188	229	458	2,172	4,712
25 years old and over	97,220	380	855	1,767	2,115	1,684	2,092	3,667	30,370
25 to 29 years old	10,917	37	44	168	142	197	229	550	3,352
30 to 34 years old	10,067	21	88	184	163	188	231	396	3,092
35 to 39 years old	9,542	34	66	178	147	167	161	358	2,847
40 to 44 years old	10,172	34	75	192	151	196	192	353	3,162
45 to 49 years old	10,800	31	78	181	163	196	203	433	3,636
50 to 54 years old	10,695	48	80	148	131	136	227	406	3,605
55 to 59 years old	9,499	20	79	163	147	112	203	302	2,898
60 to 64 years old	8,447	30	69	122	151	115	165	255	2,347
65 to 69 years old	5,600	28	55	101	190	121	106	160	1,813
70 to 74 years old	4,242	28	70	92	196	85	115	158	1,387
75 years old and over	7,239	68	149	237	534	172	259	297	2,232
Female									
18 years old and over	118,893	489	912	1,732	2,251	1,939	2,476	5,287	35,234
18 to 24 years old	14,570	12	35	57	120	159	384	1,840	3,694
25 years old and over	104,323	477	877	1,675	2,130	1,780	2,093	3,447	31,541
25 to 29 years old	10,464	14	41	85	119	177	160	380	2,405
30 to 34 years old	10,135	21	52	160	119	153	142	295	2,401
35 to 39 years old	9,713	31	75	138	130	155	151	325	2,270
40 to 44 years old	10,415	29	72	158	117	184	193	303	2,720
45 to 49 years old	11,189	34	76	161	146	185	151	316	3,256
50 to 54 years old	11,270	51	83	177	156	161	194	337	3,543
55 to 59 years old	10,055	50	59	141	130	116	159	286	3,145
60 to 64 years old	8,983	40	82	129	186	119	154	245	3,008
65 to 69 years old	6,561	52	56	121	178	129	179	224	2,341
70 to 74 years old	5,012	32	86	102	172	117	161	212	2,108
75 years old and over	10,525	123	194	303	677	284	449	524	4,344

[1]Civilian noninstitutionalized population, plus armed forces living off post or with their families on post.
[2]Population who attained the 12th grade but received no diploma are included in this category.

Table A-17. Educational Attainment of the Population 18 Years Old and Over, by Age, Sex, Race, and Hispanic Origin, 2011—*Continued*

(Numbers in thousands)

Age, sex, race, and Hispanic origin	Educational attainment						
	Some college, no degree	Associate's degree, occupational	Associate's degree, academic	Bachelor's degree	Master's degree	Professional degree	Doctoral degree
ALL RACES							
Both Sexes							
18 years old and over	45,245	9,227	11,384	41,943	16,154	2,993	3,079
18 to 24 years old	11,042	677	888	2,657	139	13	17
25 years old and over	34,203	8,550	10,497	39,286	16,015	2,980	3,062
25 to 29 years old	4,277	923	1,203	5,398	1,134	213	133
30 to 34 years old	3,564	881	1198	4,549	1,715	302	287
35 to 39 years old	3,280	910	1,121	4,385	1,745	252	328
40 to 44 years old	3,423	944	1,183	4,452	1,818	316	321
45 to 49 years old	3,562	1,127	1,247	4,455	1,740	353	257
50 to 54 years old	3,685	976	1,338	4,163	1,685	302	333
55 to 59 years old	3,421	900	1033	3,811	1,790	274	315
60 to 64 years old	3,105	760	916	3,066	1,685	343	339
65 to 69 years old	1,903	401	489	1,808	1180	206	316
70 to 74 years old	1,369	280	324	1,222	610	162	165
75 years old and over	2,615	448	444	1,978	912	256	266
Male							
18 years old and over	21,393	4,169	4,736	20,137	7,231	1,870	1,916
18 to 24 years old	5,256	308	416	1,120	50	8	6
25 years old and over	16,137	3,861	4,321	19,017	7,181	1,862	1,911
25 to 29 years old	2,153	424	522	2,541	418	90	50
30 to 34 years old	1,722	415	514	2,101	652	148	151
35 to 39 years old	1,548	391	491	2,087	762	117	186
40 to 44 years old	1,636	437	488	2,084	804	168	201
45 to 49 years old	1,649	525	458	2,108	767	231	139
50 to 54 years old	1,711	488	517	2,007	792	203	196
55 to 59 years old	1,651	388	404	1,941	822	179	190
60 to 64 years old	1,534	332	423	1,632	792	250	230
65 to 69 years old	800	185	210	909	536	156	227
70 to 74 years old	644	116	130	623	352	117	130
75 years old and over	1089	160	163	984	483	202	211
Female							
18 years old and over	23,852	5,058	6,648	21,806	8,923	1,123	1163
18 to 24 years old	5,786	369	472	1,537	89	5	11
25 years old and over	18,065	4,689	6,176	20,269	8,834	1,118	1151
25 to 29 years old	2,123	499	681	2,857	717	124	83
30 to 34 years old	1,842	467	684	2,447	1062	154	135
35 to 39 years old	1,732	519	630	2,298	983	135	142
40 to 44 years old	1,787	507	695	2,368	1014	148	121
45 to 49 years old	1,913	602	789	2,347	974	122	118
50 to 54 years old	1,974	487	821	2,156	892	98	138
55 to 59 years old	1,769	512	629	1,869	968	95	126
60 to 64 years old	1,571	428	493	1,434	892	93	109
65 to 69 years old	1,103	217	279	899	644	49	88
70 to 74 years old	725	164	194	599	258	45	36
75 years old and over	1,526	287	281	994	429	54	56

[1]Civilian noninstitutionalized population, plus armed forces living off post or with their families on post.
[2]Population who attained the 12th grade but received no diploma are included in this category.

Table A-17. Educational Attainment of the Population 18 Years Old and Over, by Age, Sex, Race, and Hispanic Origin, 2011—*Continued*

(Numbers in thousands)

Age, sex, race, and Hispanic origin	Educational attainment								
	Total[1]	None	1st to 4th grade	5th to 6th grade	7th to 8th grade	9th grade	10th grade	11th grade[2]	High school graduate
WHITE ALONE OR IN COMBINATION									
Both Sexes									
18 years old and over	189,609	639	1,506	3,046	3,781	3,206	3,878	8,272	57,632
18 to 24 years old	23,428	40	53	126	246	308	607	3,066	6,704
25 years old and over	166,181	599	1,453	2,920	3,535	2,897	3,271	5,206	50,928
25 to 29 years old	16,994	40	81	237	232	335	292	669	4,501
30 to 34 years old	15,997	36	128	310	245	310	272	503	4,223
35 to 39 years old	15,258	45	120	284	247	295	244	506	3,961
40 to 44 years old	16,575	41	137	315	240	330	319	499	4,627
45 to 49 years old	17,927	37	146	297	247	302	277	506	5,608
50 to 54 years old	18,198	64	147	282	228	245	310	527	5,894
55 to 59 years old	16,384	52	114	256	228	172	268	408	5,042
60 to 64 years old	14,780	62	132	207	262	182	244	353	4,457
65 to 69 years old	10,418	53	91	165	302	213	220	271	3,617
70 to 74 years old	7,972	41	117	163	294	155	213	296	3,077
75 years old and over	15,677	127	242	403	1,011	357	611	670	5,923
Male									
18 years old and over	93,198	336	765	1,603	1,987	1,596	1,973	4,424	28,889
18 to 24 years old	12,022	34	24	81	148	178	326	1,671	3,801
25 years old and over	81,176	302	741	1,522	1,839	1,418	1,648	2,754	25,088
25 to 29 years old	8,772	30	42	160	130	175	181	414	2,646
30 to 34 years old	8,108	19	80	161	143	168	163	305	2,448
35 to 39 years old	7,705	26	62	156	141	155	135	274	2,244
40 to 44 years old	8,347	28	71	179	141	175	156	285	2,531
45 to 49 years old	8,927	18	75	157	142	157	166	288	3,026
50 to 54 years old	8,981	37	78	128	103	113	167	302	2,977
55 to 59 years old	8,024	16	64	143	126	85	155	225	2,432
60 to 64 years old	7,281	27	60	106	126	95	129	179	1,938
65 to 69 years old	4,853	22	51	76	161	100	80	113	1,595
70 to 74 years old	3,717	24	55	75	167	64	83	130	1,233
75 years old and over	6,461	56	105	182	459	132	232	239	2,018
Female									
18 years old and over	96,411	302	741	1,443	1,794	1,610	1,905	3,848	28,744
18 to 24 years old	11,407	6	29	45	98	130	282	1,395	2,903
25 years old and over	85,004	297	712	1,398	1,696	1,480	1,623	2,453	25,840
25 to 29 years old	8,222	9	38	77	101	160	111	255	1,855
30 to 34 years old	7,889	17	48	149	101	143	109	198	1,775
35 to 39 years old	7,553	20	58	128	105	140	109	232	1,716
40 to 44 years old	8,228	13	66	136	99	156	163	213	2,096
45 to 49 years old	9,000	19	71	141	105	146	111	218	2,582
50 to 54 years old	9,217	27	69	155	125	132	142	226	2,917
55 to 59 years old	8,360	37	50	112	102	87	113	183	2,610
60 to 64 years old	7,498	35	72	101	136	87	115	174	2,519
65 to 69 years old	5,565	30	40	89	140	112	140	158	2,022
70 to 74 years old	4,256	18	62	88	127	91	131	165	1,844
75 years old and over	9,216	70	138	222	553	226	379	431	3,905

[1]Civilian noninstitutionalized population, plus armed forces living off post or with their families on post.
[2]Population who attained the 12th grade but received no diploma are included in this category.

Table A-17. Educational Attainment of the Population 18 Years Old and Over, by Age, Sex, Race, and Hispanic Origin, 2011—*Continued*

(Numbers in thousands)

Age, sex, race, and Hispanic origin	Educational attainment						
	Some college, no degree	Associate's degree, occupational	Associate's degree, academic	Bachelor's degree	Master's degree	Professional degree	Doctoral degree
WHITE ALONE OR IN COMBINATION							
Both Sexes							
18 years old and over	36,801	7,700	9,386	35,167	13,526	2,544	2,524
18 to 24 years old	8,664	544	718	2,224	103	7	15
25 years old and over	28,137	7,155	8,668	32,943	13,422	2,537	2,508
25 to 29 years old	3,282	749	976	4,441	897	154	109
30 to 34 years old	2,796	721	968	3,695	1,324	252	214
35 to 39 years old	2,588	737	892	3,543	1,361	198	237
40 to 44 years old	2,724	759	979	3,646	1,451	259	248
45 to 49 years old	2,887	946	1,007	3,761	1,425	287	195
50 to 54 years old	3,079	835	1,116	3,481	1,464	260	267
55 to 59 years old	2,875	742	837	3,263	1,602	252	275
60 to 64 years old	2,662	667	787	2,680	1,486	312	287
65 to 69 years old	1,659	354	426	1,540	1044	181	283
70 to 74 years old	1,201	234	270	1,082	542	140	147
75 years old and over	2,382	413	410	1,812	826	242	246
Male							
18 years old and over	17,607	3,552	3,972	17,164	6,087	1,645	1,596
18 to 24 years old	4,163	254	357	934	40	5	6
25 years old and over	13,444	3,298	3,615	16,229	6,048	1,640	1,590
25 to 29 years old	1,672	343	431	2,125	316	66	41
30 to 34 years old	1,404	354	415	1,727	494	121	108
35 to 39 years old	1,239	326	409	1,711	589	97	141
40 to 44 years old	1,319	368	397	1,774	627	145	152
45 to 49 years old	1,352	460	376	1,790	633	184	105
50 to 54 years old	1,465	426	438	1,699	701	185	162
55 to 59 years old	1,384	320	332	1,688	724	169	164
60 to 64 years old	1,351	294	366	1,459	711	239	201
65 to 69 years old	679	169	189	783	486	142	206
70 to 74 years old	571	97	118	560	323	103	114
75 years old and over	1,009	141	145	914	444	190	195
Female							
18 years old and over	19,193	4,148	5,414	18,004	7,438	899	928
18 to 24 years old	4,501	290	361	1,290	63	2	10
25 years old and over	14,692	3,858	5,053	16,714	7,375	896	918
25 to 29 years old	1,610	406	545	2,317	581	88	68
30 to 34 years old	1,393	367	554	1,968	831	131	106
35 to 39 years old	1,349	411	483	1,831	771	101	96
40 to 44 years old	1,405	391	582	1,873	824	114	96
45 to 49 years old	1,535	485	630	1,970	792	103	91
50 to 54 years old	1,614	409	678	1,781	763	74	104
55 to 59 years old	1,491	423	505	1,575	878	83	111
60 to 64 years old	1,311	373	422	1,221	775	73	86
65 to 69 years old	980	185	237	757	558	40	77
70 to 74 years old	630	137	152	523	219	37	33
75 years old and over	1,373	271	265	898	382	52	51

[1]Civilian noninstitutionalized population, plus armed forces living off post or with their families on post.
[2]Population who attained the 12th grade but received no diploma are included in this category.

Table A-17. Educational Attainment of the Population 18 Years Old and Over, by Age, Sex, Race, and Hispanic Origin, 2011—*Continued*

(Numbers in thousands)

Age, sex, race, and Hispanic origin	Educational attainment								
	Total[1]	None	1st to 4th grade	5th to 6th grade	7th to 8th grade	9th grade	10th grade	11th grade[2]	High school graduate
BLACK ALONE OR IN COMBINATION									
Both Sexes									
18 years old and over	28,870	98	151	286	529	460	923	2,411	9,782
18 to 24 years old	4,743	9	2	11	57	62	199	794	1,435
25 years old and over	24,127	90	149	275	473	398	724	1,616	8,348
25 to 29 years old	3,096	7	1	14	26	21	75	230	1,033
30 to 34 years old	2,817	4	4	18	12	21	83	165	986
35 to 39 years old	2,561	13	4	16	21	14	52	152	876
40 to 44 years old	2,659	6	6	9	9	23	41	124	964
45 to 49 years old	2,796	14	4	21	33	59	57	192	983
50 to 54 years old	2,666	8	9	18	38	30	87	190	921
55 to 59 years old	2,174	1	15	21	32	44	75	147	739
60 to 64 years old	1,858	3	9	27	48	42	56	126	691
65 to 69 years old	1,198	10	7	34	45	27	56	95	401
70 to 74 years old	860	6	17	14	52	39	58	62	303
75 years old and over	1,442	18	72	82	157	78	86	134	453
Male									
18 years old and over	13,054	36	74	147	221	229	460	1,179	4,867
18 to 24 years old	2,294	7	*	5	30	41	111	418	780
25 years old and over	10,759	29	74	142	191	188	350	761	4,087
25 to 29 years old	1,486	4	1	9	9	10	34	119	567
30 to 34 years old	1,293	1	3	15	4	11	60	79	513
35 to 39 years old	1,141	2	1	12	6	7	19	69	452
40 to 44 years old	1,195	*	2	4	3	14	24	51	504
45 to 49 years old	1,269	5	3	9	15	30	29	112	481
50 to 54 years old	1,192	4	2	10	15	12	48	89	472
55 to 59 years old	1014	*	11	12	18	24	34	67	363
60 to 64 years old	799	3	6	10	18	16	24	61	318
65 to 69 years old	513	3	3	15	23	14	25	44	164
70 to 74 years old	344	3	10	10	23	19	29	24	109
75 years old and over	512	5	35	38	56	29	25	47	143
Female									
18 years old and over	15,816	62	77	139	309	231	463	1,232	4,915
18 to 24 years old	2,448	2	2	7	27	21	89	376	655
25 years old and over	13,368	60	75	133	282	211	374	856	4,261
25 to 29 years old	1,610	3	1	6	16	11	41	111	465
30 to 34 years old	1,524	3	2	3	7	10	23	87	474
35 to 39 years old	1,419	11	4	5	15	8	32	83	424
40 to 44 years old	1,464	6	4	5	7	9	16	73	460
45 to 49 years old	1,527	9	1	12	18	29	28	80	502
50 to 54 years old	1,474	4	7	8	23	18	39	101	449
55 to 59 years old	1,160	1	4	10	13	20	42	80	375
60 to 64 years old	1059	*	3	17	30	25	32	65	373
65 to 69 years old	686	6	5	20	22	13	31	51	236
70 to 74 years old	515	4	7	4	29	20	29	38	193
75 years old and over	930	13	37	43	101	49	60	87	309

[1]Civilian noninstitutionalized population, plus armed forces living off post or with their families on post.
[2]Population who attained the 12th grade but received no diploma are included in this category.
* = Quantity zero or rounds to zero.

Table A-17. Educational Attainment of the Population 18 Years Old and Over, by Age, Sex, Race, and Hispanic Origin, 2011—*Continued*

(Numbers in thousands)

Age, sex, race, and Hispanic origin	Educational attainment						
	Some college, no degree	Associate's degree, occupational	Associate's degree, academic	Bachelor's degree	Master's degree	Professional degree	Doctoral degree
BLACK ALONE OR IN COMBINATION							
Both Sexes							
18 years old and over	6,504	1155	1,487	3,437	1,275	189	181
18 to 24 years old	1,710	97	128	223	14	1	*
25 years old and over	4,794	1058	1,358	3,214	1,262	188	181
25 to 29 years old	780	130	168	492	82	31	8
30 to 34 years old	620	117	179	443	137	13	13
35 to 39 years old	539	127	166	393	140	17	30
40 to 44 years old	556	130	146	421	182	23	19
45 to 49 years old	546	130	187	377	150	27	17
50 to 54 years old	500	113	165	392	139	28	28
55 to 59 years old	437	127	141	270	106	8	11
60 to 64 years old	339	78	97	172	135	21	17
65 to 69 years old	191	43	51	126	82	9	20
70 to 74 years old	124	32	41	51	50	3	9
75 years old and over	161	30	17	78	59	8	9
Male							
18 years old and over	2,797	443	552	1,409	467	70	102
18 to 24 years old	737	38	34	92	2	*	*
25 years old and over	2,060	405	518	1,317	465	70	102
25 to 29 years old	364	59	68	217	23	2	*
30 to 34 years old	252	36	74	189	46	4	7
35 to 39 years old	230	45	64	167	50	2	16
40 to 44 years old	243	49	64	145	71	7	14
45 to 49 years old	239	42	60	156	63	17	9
50 to 54 years old	198	53	53	164	49	11	13
55 to 59 years old	215	53	53	107	45	5	6
60 to 64 years old	129	28	46	76	47	10	8
65 to 69 years old	91	13	20	51	27	4	16
70 to 74 years old	47	10	11	21	20	2	8
75 years old and over	51	17	6	23	23	7	6
Female							
18 years old and over	3,707	712	935	2,028	808	119	79
18 to 24 years old	974	59	95	131	11	1	*
25 years old and over	2,734	653	840	1,897	797	118	79
25 to 29 years old	415	72	100	275	59	28	8
30 to 34 years old	367	81	105	254	91	10	7
35 to 39 years old	309	82	103	226	90	15	13
40 to 44 years old	313	82	82	276	111	16	5
45 to 49 years old	307	88	126	221	87	10	8
50 to 54 years old	302	60	112	228	90	17	15
55 to 59 years old	222	74	88	162	61	3	5
60 to 64 years old	210	50	51	95	88	11	9
65 to 69 years old	101	30	32	75	55	5	4
70 to 74 years old	77	21	30	30	30	1	1
75 years old and over	110	13	11	55	36	2	3

[1]Civilian noninstitutionalized population, plus armed forces living off post or with their families on post.
[2]Population who attained the 12th grade but received no diploma are included in this category.
* = Quantity zero or rounds to zero.

Table A-17. Educational Attainment of the Population 18 Years Old and Over, by Age, Sex, Race, and Hispanic Origin, 2011—*Continued*

(Numbers in thousands)

Age, sex, race, and Hispanic origin	Educational attainment								
	Total[1]	None	1st to 4th grade	5th to 6th grade	7th to 8th grade	9th grade	10th grade	11th grade[2]	High school graduate
ASIAN ALONE OR IN COMBINATION									
Both Sexes									
18 years old and over	11,673	156	118	213	204	126	158	378	2,449
18 to 24 years old	1,496	6	5	8	15	12	28	145	249
25 years old and over	10,177	150	113	205	189	114	129	233	2,200
25 to 29 years old	1,236	5	3	2	2	8	16	29	180
30 to 34 years old	1,274	2	4	7	11	8	7	22	227
35 to 39 years old	1,319	6	17	3	10	8	9	19	228
40 to 44 years old	1,209	16	3	26	17	17	17	23	237
45 to 49 years old	1,116	14	4	17	26	10	13	37	250
50 to 54 years old	971	23	6	17	13	19	18	19	270
55 to 59 years old	868	15	9	24	15	10	9	27	224
60 to 64 years old	702	5	6	15	21	6	18	16	172
65 to 69 years old	506	15	13	22	17	6	7	17	125
70 to 74 years old	392	13	21	17	21	6	5	14	102
75 years old and over	585	36	26	56	37	16	11	10	184
Male									
18 years old and over	5,511	45	35	74	72	59	77	202	1,087
18 to 24 years old	782	2	2	2	13	6	13	78	132
25 years old and over	4,729	43	33	71	59	53	64	123	955
25 to 29 years old	601	3	2	*	2	6	11	20	107
30 to 34 years old	608	2	4	4	6	8	3	14	98
35 to 39 years old	618	6	5	1	*	3	4	11	117
40 to 44 years old	573	6	2	8	7	4	8	11	104
45 to 49 years old	530	9	*	10	7	5	6	23	95
50 to 54 years old	458	7	*	5	5	12	9	9	124
55 to 59 years old	389	3	5	7	*	2	7	9	79
60 to 64 years old	319	*	1	3	5	2	11	12	76
65 to 69 years old	220	3	2	10	4	2	*	3	49
70 to 74 years old	171	2	3	7	5	2	3	6	39
75 years old and over	242	4	10	16	17	7	2	6	66
Female									
18 years old and over	6,163	111	83	139	132	67	81	176	1,362
18 to 24 years old	714	4	3	5	2	6	15	66	117
25 years old and over	5,449	107	80	134	130	62	66	110	1,245
25 to 29 years old	635	2	2	2	*	2	5	10	73
30 to 34 years old	665	1	*	3	5	*	4	9	130
35 to 39 years old	701	*	13	2	10	5	5	8	112
40 to 44 years old	635	10	1	18	9	13	9	12	133
45 to 49 years old	586	5	4	7	19	4	7	13	155
50 to 54 years old	513	16	6	12	8	7	9	10	146
55 to 59 years old	479	12	4	17	15	9	3	18	145
60 to 64 years old	383	5	5	12	15	5	7	4	96
65 to 69 years old	286	13	11	12	13	4	7	13	76
70 to 74 years old	221	11	18	10	16	4	1	8	63
75 years old and over	343	33	17	39	20	9	9	4	118

[1]Civilian noninstitutionalized population, plus armed forces living off post or with their families on post.
[2]Population who attained the 12th grade but received no diploma are included in this category.
* = Quantity zero or rounds to zero.

Table A-17. Educational Attainment of the Population 18 Years Old and Over, by Age, Sex, Race, and Hispanic Origin, 2011—*Continued*

(Numbers in thousands)

Age, sex, race, and Hispanic origin	Educational attainment						
	Some college, no degree	Associate's degree, occupational	Associate's degree, academic	Bachelor's degree	Master's degree	Professional degree	Doctoral degree
ASIAN ALONE OR IN COMBINATION							
Both Sexes							
18 years old and over	1,806	296	451	3,332	1,344	268	375
18 to 24 years old	707	32	44	217	24	3	2
25 years old and over	1,099	263	407	3,116	1,320	265	374
25 to 29 years old	210	39	54	485	155	32	16
30 to 34 years old	126	34	51	419	257	40	59
35 to 39 years old	122	37	59	453	245	39	64
40 to 44 years old	105	41	51	373	197	36	51
45 to 49 years old	123	35	44	306	154	38	46
50 to 54 years old	88	19	50	293	81	15	41
55 to 59 years old	89	26	32	263	80	16	30
60 to 64 years old	89	9	25	214	63	10	34
65 to 69 years old	54	2	13	144	47	13	12
70 to 74 years old	31	16	16	86	17	19	9
75 years old and over	64	6	13	82	25	7	11
Male							
18 years old and over	917	141	193	1,556	674	160	221
18 to 24 years old	376	17	25	102	10	3	*
25 years old and over	541	125	168	1,454	664	157	221
25 to 29 years old	101	16	20	209	74	21	9
30 to 34 years old	55	23	27	193	112	24	37
35 to 39 years old	57	14	19	209	121	20	32
40 to 44 years old	56	14	27	165	115	16	32
45 to 49 years old	65	16	16	150	70	31	26
50 to 54 years old	46	6	22	141	43	7	21
55 to 59 years old	38	16	10	133	54	6	21
60 to 64 years old	44	7	9	93	32	3	21
65 to 69 years old	31	1	6	75	21	9	5
70 to 74 years old	22	8	4	41	8	13	8
75 years old and over	27	2	8	44	16	7	10
Female							
18 years old and over	889	154	258	1,777	671	108	155
18 to 24 years old	331	15	19	115	14	*	2
25 years old and over	558	139	239	1,662	656	108	153
25 to 29 years old	109	22	33	276	81	11	8
30 to 34 years old	71	11	24	226	145	16	23
35 to 39 years old	66	22	40	244	124	19	32
40 to 44 years old	49	27	24	208	82	19	19
45 to 49 years old	58	18	28	156	84	7	20
50 to 54 years old	41	13	28	151	38	7	20
55 to 59 years old	52	11	22	130	26	9	9
60 to 64 years old	44	2	17	120	30	8	13
65 to 69 years old	23	1	7	69	26	5	7
70 to 74 years old	8	8	12	45	9	7	1
75 years old and over	37	3	4	38	10	*	2

[1]Civilian noninstitutionalized population, plus armed forces living off post or with their families on post.
[2]Population who attained the 12th grade but received no diploma are included in this category.
* = Quantity zero or rounds to zero.

Table A-17. Educational Attainment of the Population 18 Years Old and Over, by Age, Sex, Race, and Hispanic Origin, 2011—*Continued*

(Numbers in thousands)

Age, sex, race, and Hispanic origin	Educational attainment								
	Total[1]	None	1st to 4th grade	5th to 6th grade	7th to 8th grade	9th grade	10th grade	11th grade[2]	High school graduate
HISPANIC[3]									
Both Sexes									
18 years old and over	32,434	456	1,231	2,604	1,524	1,641	1,072	2,647	9,825
18 to 24 years old	5,762	26	30	122	126	183	235	940	1,867
25 years old and over	26,672	429	1,201	2,482	1,398	1,458	838	1,707	7,957
25 to 29 years old	4,182	22	75	236	148	241	118	353	1,366
30 to 34 years old	3,948	22	115	319	176	229	139	275	1,236
35 to 39 years old	3,715	39	108	282	173	222	117	256	1,172
40 to 44 years old	3,354	24	129	302	173	235	100	211	1,020
45 to 49 years old	2,962	31	129	294	151	162	90	152	943
50 to 54 years old	2,399	44	130	271	109	89	57	145	721
55 to 59 years old	1,801	43	104	210	92	85	65	95	454
60 to 64 years old	1,453	48	115	167	110	55	52	73	385
65 to 69 years old	977	41	68	125	87	51	28	49	237
70 to 74 years old	733	25	83	82	57	39	22	49	176
75 years old and over	1,148	91	145	192	121	50	50	50	246
Male									
18 years old and over	16,720	234	618	1,362	800	857	572	1,485	5,361
18 to 24 years old	3,120	23	16	78	84	102	122	548	1,085
25 years old and over	13,599	210	601	1,284	716	755	450	937	4,276
25 to 29 years old	2,321	20	39	157	86	130	77	205	805
30 to 34 years old	2,093	11	80	173	103	122	77	171	699
35 to 39 years old	1,950	23	53	153	98	122	66	142	674
40 to 44 years old	1,737	16	69	167	94	124	37	118	541
45 to 49 years old	1,507	15	69	155	74	86	56	75	523
50 to 54 years old	1,186	23	63	127	56	37	27	85	383
55 to 59 years old	889	11	56	113	50	47	43	48	213
60 to 64 years old	684	21	52	82	41	32	26	34	175
65 to 69 years old	419	17	36	53	27	19	10	16	102
70 to 74 years old	319	14	28	28	31	13	5	20	72
75 years old and over	493	39	56	77	55	24	28	23	89
Female									
18 years old and over	15,714	222	613	1,241	724	785	500	1,162	4,464
18 to 24 years old	2,642	3	14	43	42	81	112	392	783
25 years old and over	13,072	219	599	1,198	683	703	388	770	3,681
25 to 29 years old	1,862	2	36	79	61	111	41	148	561
30 to 34 years old	1,854	11	35	147	73	106	62	104	537
35 to 39 years old	1,765	16	55	130	76	100	52	114	498
40 to 44 years old	1,617	8	60	136	79	112	63	92	479
45 to 49 years old	1,455	16	60	139	78	77	34	78	420
50 to 54 years old	1,213	22	66	144	53	53	31	60	339
55 to 59 years old	912	32	48	97	42	38	22	47	241
60 to 64 years old	769	27	63	85	69	23	27	39	210
65 to 69 years old	558	24	32	72	59	32	19	33	135
70 to 74 years old	413	11	55	54	26	26	17	29	104
75 years old and over	655	52	89	115	67	26	22	27	157

[1]Civilian noninstitutionalized population, plus armed forces living off post or with their families on post.
[2]Population who attained the 12th grade but received no diploma are included in this category.
[3]May be of any race.

Table A-17. Educational Attainment of the Population 18 Years Old and Over, by Age, Sex, Race, and Hispanic Origin, 2011—*Continued*

(Numbers in thousands)

Age, sex, race, and Hispanic origin	Educational attainment						
	Some college, no degree	Associate's degree, occupational	Associate's degree, academic	Bachelor's degree	Master's degree	Professional degree	Doctoral degree
HISPANIC[3]							
Both Sexes							
18 years old and over	5,388	875	1,174	2,895	780	147	174
18 to 24 years old	1,745	102	149	225	8	4	*
25 years old and over	3,642	774	1,025	2,669	772	144	174
25 to 29 years old	761	131	196	424	76	21	14
30 to 34 years old	584	115	165	432	105	21	14
35 to 39 years old	504	105	131	464	96	19	24
40 to 44 years old	467	118	109	318	111	13	24
45 to 49 years old	359	95	111	315	93	19	17
50 to 54 years old	308	81	112	232	70	11	19
55 to 59 years old	250	37	57	208	69	13	17
60 to 64 years old	175	37	57	102	51	10	15
65 to 69 years old	88	28	45	83	29	4	14
70 to 74 years old	63	13	22	45	44	6	7
75 years old and over	84	12	20	45	27	6	10
Male							
18 years old and over	2,663	363	527	1,358	346	80	94
18 to 24 years old	846	36	77	97	3	1	*
25 years old and over	1,817	328	450	1,261	343	79	94
25 to 29 years old	426	51	101	182	19	14	8
30 to 34 years old	299	44	71	182	45	11	6
35 to 39 years old	233	46	63	213	45	4	15
40 to 44 years old	241	57	51	160	51	3	9
45 to 49 years old	169	44	46	144	31	11	10
50 to 54 years old	140	34	47	119	32	6	9
55 to 59 years old	121	15	20	97	37	8	10
60 to 64 years old	87	16	18	65	21	7	8
65 to 69 years old	39	9	13	51	18	4	6
70 to 74 years old	23	8	13	24	28	6	5
75 years old and over	40	4	6	24	17	4	8
Female							
18 years old and over	2,724	512	647	1,537	434	67	80
18 to 24 years old	899	66	71	128	5	2	*
25 years old and over	1,825	446	576	1,409	429	65	80
25 to 29 years old	335	81	94	242	57	7	7
30 to 34 years old	285	72	94	251	60	10	8
35 to 39 years old	271	59	68	252	52	15	9
40 to 44 years old	226	60	58	158	60	11	15
45 to 49 years old	190	51	65	171	63	8	7
50 to 54 years old	168	48	65	113	38	4	10
55 to 59 years old	129	22	37	111	32	5	8
60 to 64 years old	88	21	39	37	30	3	6
65 to 69 years old	49	19	32	33	11	*	7
70 to 74 years old	40	5	9	21	16	*	2
75 years old and over	44	9	14	20	10	2	2

[1]Civilian noninstitutionalized population, plus armed forces living off post or with their families on post.
[2]Population who attained the 12th grade but received no diploma are included in this category.
[3]May be of any race.
* = Quantity zero or rounds to zero.

Table A-18. Percent of High School and College Graduates of the Population 15 Years Old and Over, by Age, Sex, Race, and Hispanic Origin, 2011

(Percent, except where noted)

Age, sex, race, and Hispanic origin	Total population (thousands)[1]	High school graduate status			Bachelor's degree status		
		Total	Not high school graduate	High school graduate or more[2]	Total	Less than Bachelor's degree	Bachelor's degree or more
ALL RACES							
Both Sexes							
18 years old and over	231,194	100.0	13.3	86.7	100.0	72.2	27.8
18 to 24 years old	29,651	100.0	19.6	80.4	100.0	90.5	9.5
25 years old and over	201,543	100.0	12.4	87.6	100.0	69.6	30.4
25 to 29 years old	21,382	100.0	11.0	89.0	100.0	67.8	32.2
30 to 34 years old	20,202	100.0	11.0	89.0	100.0	66.1	33.9
35 to 39 years old	19,255	100.0	11.0	89.0	100.0	65.2	34.8
40 to 44 years old	20,587	100.0	10.9	89.1	100.0	66.4	33.6
45 to 49 years old	21,989	100.0	10.7	89.3	100.0	69.1	30.9
50 to 54 years old	21,965	100.0	10.6	89.4	100.0	70.5	29.5
55 to 59 years old	19,554	100.0	10.1	89.9	100.0	68.3	31.7
60 to 64 years old	17,430	100.0	10.7	89.3	100.0	68.8	31.2
65 to 69 years old	12,160	100.0	14.0	86.0	100.0	71.1	28.9
70 to 74 years old	9,254	100.0	17.6	82.4	100.0	76.7	23.3
75 years old and over	17,764	100.0	24.0	76.0	100.0	80.8	19.2
Male							
18 years old and over	112,301	100.0	14.0	86.0	100.0	72.3	27.7
18 to 24 years old	15,081	100.0	21.3	78.7	100.0	92.1	7.9
25 years old and over	97,220	100.0	12.9	87.1	100.0	69.2	30.8
25 to 29 years old	10,917	100.0	12.5	87.5	100.0	71.6	28.4
30 to 34 years old	10,067	100.0	12.6	87.4	100.0	69.7	30.3
35 to 39 years old	9,542	100.0	11.7	88.3	100.0	67.0	33.0
40 to 44 years old	10,172	100.0	11.7	88.3	100.0	68.0	32.0
45 to 49 years old	10,800	100.0	11.9	88.1	100.0	70.0	30.0
50 to 54 years old	10,695	100.0	11.0	89.0	100.0	70.1	29.9
55 to 59 years old	9,499	100.0	10.8	89.2	100.0	67.0	33.0
60 to 64 years old	8,447	100.0	10.7	89.3	100.0	65.6	34.4
65 to 69 years old	5,600	100.0	13.6	86.4	100.0	67.4	32.6
70 to 74 years old	4,242	100.0	17.5	82.5	100.0	71.2	28.8
75 years old and over	7,239	100.0	23.7	76.3	100.0	74.0	26.0
Female							
18 years old and over	118,893	100.0	12.7	87.3	100.0	72.2	27.8
18 to 24 years old	14,570	100.0	17.9	82.1	100.0	88.7	11.3
25 years old and over	104,323	100.0	12.0	88.0	100.0	69.9	30.1
25 to 29 years old	10,464	100.0	9.3	90.7	100.0	63.9	36.1
30 to 34 years old	10,135	100.0	9.3	90.7	100.0	62.5	37.5
35 to 39 years old	9,713	100.0	10.3	89.7	100.0	63.4	36.6
40 to 44 years old	10,415	100.0	10.1	89.9	100.0	64.9	35.1
45 to 49 years old	11,189	100.0	9.5	90.5	100.0	68.2	31.8
50 to 54 years old	11,270	100.0	10.3	89.7	100.0	70.9	29.1
55 to 59 years old	10,055	100.0	9.4	90.6	100.0	69.6	30.4
60 to 64 years old	8,983	100.0	10.6	89.4	100.0	71.9	28.1
65 to 69 years old	6,561	100.0	14.3	85.7	100.0	74.4	25.6
70 to 74 years old	5,012	100.0	17.6	82.4	100.0	81.3	18.7
75 years old and over	10,525	100.0	24.3	75.7	100.0	85.4	14.6
WHITE ALONE OR IN COMBINATION							
Both Sexes							
18 years old and over	189,609	100.0	12.8	87.2	100.0	71.6	28.4
18 to 24 years old	23,428	100.0	19.0	81.0	100.0	90.0	10.0
25 years old and over	166,181	100.0	12.0	88.0	100.0	69.1	30.9
25 to 29 years old	16,994	100.0	11.1	88.9	100.0	67.0	33.0
30 to 34 years old	15,997	100.0	11.3	88.7	100.0	65.7	34.3
35 to 39 years old	15,258	100.0	11.4	88.6	100.0	65.0	35.0
40 to 44 years old	16,575	100.0	11.4	88.6	100.0	66.2	33.8
45 to 49 years old	17,927	100.0	10.1	89.9	100.0	68.4	31.6
50 to 54 years old	18,198	100.0	9.9	90.1	100.0	69.9	30.1
55 to 59 years old	16,384	100.0	9.1	90.9	100.0	67.1	32.9
60 to 64 years old	14,780	100.0	9.8	90.2	100.0	67.8	32.2
65 to 69 years old	10,418	100.0	12.6	87.4	100.0	70.7	29.3
70 to 74 years old	7,972	100.0	16.0	84.0	100.0	76.0	24.0
75 years old and over	15,677	100.0	21.8	78.2	100.0	80.1	19.9

[1]Civilian noninstitutionalized population, plus armed forces living off post or with their families on post.
[2]Population in the 12th grade with no diploma are included in this category.

Table A-18. Percent of High School and College Graduates of the Population 15 Years Old and Over, by Age, Sex, Race, and Hispanic Origin, 2011—*Continued*

(Percent, except where noted)

Age, sex, race, and Hispanic origin	Total population (thousands)[1]	High school graduate status			Bachelor's degree status		
		Total	Not high school graduate	High school graduate or more[2]	Total	Less than Bachelor's degree	Bachelor's degree or more
Male							
18 years old and over	93,198	100.0	13.6	86.4	100.0	71.6	28.4
18 to 24 years old	12,022	100.0	20.5	79.5	100.0	91.8	8.2
25 years old and over	81,176	100.0	12.6	87.4	100.0	68.6	31.4
25 to 29 years old	8,772	100.0	12.9	87.1	100.0	71.0	29.0
30 to 34 years old	8,108	100.0	12.8	87.2	100.0	69.8	30.2
35 to 39 years old	7,705	100.0	12.3	87.7	100.0	67.1	32.9
40 to 44 years old	8,347	100.0	12.4	87.6	100.0	67.7	32.3
45 to 49 years old	8,927	100.0	11.2	88.8	100.0	69.6	30.4
50 to 54 years old	8,981	100.0	10.3	89.7	100.0	69.4	30.6
55 to 59 years old	8,024	100.0	10.1	89.9	100.0	65.8	34.2
60 to 64 years old	7,281	100.0	9.9	90.1	100.0	64.2	35.8
65 to 69 years old	4,853	100.0	12.4	87.6	100.0	66.7	33.3
70 to 74 years old	3,717	100.0	16.1	83.9	100.0	70.4	29.6
75 years old and over	6,461	100.0	21.7	78.3	100.0	73.0	27.0
Female							
18 years old and over	96,411	100.0	12.1	87.9	100.0	71.7	28.3
18 to 24 years old	11,407	100.0	17.4	82.6	100.0	88.0	12.0
25 years old and over	85,004	100.0	11.4	88.6	100.0	69.5	30.5
25 to 29 years old	8,222	100.0	9.1	90.9	100.0	62.9	37.1
30 to 34 years old	7,889	100.0	9.7	90.3	100.0	61.5	38.5
35 to 39 years old	7,553	100.0	10.5	89.5	100.0	62.9	37.1
40 to 44 years old	8,228	100.0	10.3	89.7	100.0	64.7	35.3
45 to 49 years old	9,000	100.0	9.0	91.0	100.0	67.2	32.8
50 to 54 years old	9,217	100.0	9.5	90.5	100.0	70.5	29.5
55 to 59 years old	8,360	100.0	8.2	91.8	100.0	68.3	31.7
60 to 64 years old	7,498	100.0	9.6	90.4	100.0	71.3	28.7
65 to 69 years old	5,565	100.0	12.7	87.3	100.0	74.3	25.7
70 to 74 years old	4,256	100.0	16.0	84.0	100.0	80.9	19.1
75 years old and over	9,216	100.0	21.9	78.1	100.0	85.0	15.0
BLACK ALONE OR IN COMBINATION							
Both Sexes							
18 years old and over	28,870	100.0	16.8	83.2	100.0	82.4	17.6
18 to 24 years old	4,743	100.0	23.9	76.1	100.0	95.0	5.0
25 years old and over	24,127	100.0	15.4	84.6	100.0	79.9	20.1
25 to 29 years old	3,096	100.0	12.0	88.0	100.0	80.2	19.8
30 to 34 years old	2,817	100.0	11.0	89.0	100.0	78.5	21.5
35 to 39 years old	2,561	100.0	10.7	89.3	100.0	77.4	22.6
40 to 44 years old	2,659	100.0	8.2	91.8	100.0	75.7	24.3
45 to 49 years old	2,796	100.0	13.6	86.4	100.0	79.6	20.4
50 to 54 years old	2,666	100.0	14.3	85.7	100.0	78.0	22.0
55 to 59 years old	2,174	100.0	15.4	84.6	100.0	81.8	18.2
60 to 64 years old	1,858	100.0	16.6	83.4	100.0	81.4	18.6
65 to 69 years old	1,198	100.0	23.0	77.0	100.0	80.2	19.8
70 to 74 years old	860	100.0	28.7	71.3	100.0	86.9	13.1
75 years old and over	1,442	100.0	43.5	56.5	100.0	89.3	10.7
Male							
18 years old and over	13,054	100.0	18.0	82.0	100.0	84.3	15.7
18 to 24 years old	2,294	100.0	26.6	73.4	100.0	95.9	4.1
25 years old and over	10,759	100.0	16.1	83.9	100.0	81.8	18.2
25 to 29 years old	1,486	100.0	12.5	87.5	100.0	83.7	16.3
30 to 34 years old	1,293	100.0	13.3	86.7	100.0	81.0	19.0
35 to 39 years old	1,141	100.0	10.1	89.9	100.0	79.4	20.6
40 to 44 years old	1,195	100.0	8.2	91.8	100.0	80.2	19.8
45 to 49 years old	1,269	100.0	15.9	84.1	100.0	80.7	19.3
50 to 54 years old	1,192	100.0	15.0	85.0	100.0	80.1	19.9
55 to 59 years old	1,014	100.0	16.5	83.5	100.0	83.9	16.1
60 to 64 years old	799	100.0	17.1	82.9	100.0	82.4	17.6
65 to 69 years old	513	100.0	24.8	75.2	100.0	80.9	19.1
70 to 74 years old	344	100.0	33.7	66.3	100.0	85.2	14.8
75 years old and over	512	100.0	46.1	53.9	100.0	88.5	11.5

[1]Civilian noninstitutionalized population, plus armed forces living off post or with their families on post.
[2]Population in the 12th grade with no diploma are included in this category.

Table A-18. Percent of High School and College Graduates of the Population 15 Years Old and Over, by Age, Sex, Race, and Hispanic Origin, 2011—*Continued*

(Percent, except where noted)

Age, sex, race, and Hispanic origin	Total population (thousands)[1]	High school graduate status			Bachelor's degree status		
		Total	Not high school graduate	High school graduate or more[2]	Total	Less than Bachelor's degree	Bachelor's degree or more
Female							
18 years old and over	15,816	100.0	15.9	84.1	100.0	80.8	19.2
18 to 24 years old	2,448	100.0	21.3	78.7	100.0	94.2	5.8
25 years old and over	13,368	100.0	14.9	85.1	100.0	78.4	21.6
25 to 29 years old	1,610	100.0	11.7	88.3	100.0	77.0	23.0
30 to 34 years old	1,524	100.0	8.9	91.1	100.0	76.2	23.8
35 to 39 years old	1,419	100.0	11.1	88.9	100.0	75.8	24.2
40 to 44 years old	1,464	100.0	8.1	91.9	100.0	72.1	27.9
45 to 49 years old	1,527	100.0	11.7	88.3	100.0	78.7	21.3
50 to 54 years old	1,474	100.0	13.6	86.4	100.0	76.3	23.7
55 to 59 years old	1,160	100.0	14.7	85.3	100.0	80.1	19.9
60 to 64 years old	1,059	100.0	16.2	83.8	100.0	80.8	19.2
65 to 69 years old	686	100.0	21.6	78.4	100.0	79.7	20.3
70 to 74 years old	515	100.0	25.6	74.4	100.0	88.0	12.0
75 years old and over	930	100.0	42.0	58.0	100.0	89.7	10.3
ASIAN ALONE OR IN COMBINATION							
Both Sexes							
18 years old and over	11,673	100.0	11.6	88.4	100.0	54.4	45.6
18 to 24 years old	1,496	100.0	14.6	85.4	100.0	83.6	16.4
25 years old and over	10,177	100.0	11.1	88.9	100.0	50.1	49.9
25 to 29 years old	1,236	100.0	5.3	94.7	100.0	44.3	55.7
30 to 34 years old	1,274	100.0	4.8	95.2	100.0	39.2	60.8
35 to 39 years old	1,319	100.0	5.5	94.5	100.0	39.3	60.7
40 to 44 years old	1,209	100.0	9.8	90.2	100.0	45.7	54.3
45 to 49 years old	1,116	100.0	10.8	89.2	100.0	51.3	48.7
50 to 54 years old	971	100.0	11.7	88.3	100.0	55.7	44.3
55 to 59 years old	868	100.0	12.4	87.6	100.0	55.2	44.8
60 to 64 years old	702	100.0	12.3	87.7	100.0	54.3	45.7
65 to 69 years old	506	100.0	19.0	81.0	100.0	57.3	42.7
70 to 74 years old	392	100.0	24.5	75.5	100.0	66.6	33.4
75 years old and over	585	100.0	33.0	67.0	100.0	78.6	21.4
Male							
18 years old and over	5,511	100.0	10.2	89.8	100.0	52.6	47.4
18 to 24 years old	782	100.0	15.0	85.0	100.0	85.3	14.7
25 years old and over	4,729	100.0	9.4	90.6	100.0	47.2	52.8
25 to 29 years old	601	100.0	7.3	92.7	100.0	47.9	52.1
30 to 34 years old	608	100.0	6.4	93.6	100.0	39.8	60.2
35 to 39 years old	618	100.0	4.7	95.3	100.0	38.2	61.8
40 to 44 years old	573	100.0	7.7	92.3	100.0	42.8	57.2
45 to 49 years old	530	100.0	11.5	88.5	100.0	47.7	52.3
50 to 54 years old	458	100.0	10.5	89.5	100.0	53.7	46.3
55 to 59 years old	389	100.0	8.2	91.8	100.0	45.0	55.0
60 to 64 years old	319	100.0	10.7	89.3	100.0	53.3	46.7
65 to 69 years old	220	100.0	10.5	89.5	100.0	50.0	50.0
70 to 74 years old	171	100.0	16.4	83.6	100.0	59.1	40.9
75 years old and over	242	100.0	25.6	74.4	100.0	68.2	31.8
Female							
18 years old and over	6,163	100.0	12.8	87.2	100.0	56.0	44.0
18 to 24 years old	714	100.0	14.1	85.9	100.0	81.7	18.3
25 years old and over	5,449	100.0	12.6	87.4	100.0	52.7	47.3
25 to 29 years old	635	100.0	3.5	96.5	100.0	40.8	59.2
30 to 34 years old	665	100.0	2.9	97.1	100.0	38.3	61.7
35 to 39 years old	701	100.0	6.0	94.0	100.0	40.2	59.8
40 to 44 years old	635	100.0	11.7	88.3	100.0	48.3	51.7
45 to 49 years old	586	100.0	10.2	89.8	100.0	54.4	45.6
50 to 54 years old	513	100.0	13.5	86.5	100.0	57.9	42.1
55 to 59 years old	479	100.0	15.7	84.3	100.0	63.7	36.3
60 to 64 years old	383	100.0	13.8	86.2	100.0	55.4	44.6
65 to 69 years old	286	100.0	25.2	74.8	100.0	62.6	37.4
70 to 74 years old	221	100.0	30.8	69.2	100.0	71.9	28.1
75 years old and over	343	100.0	38.2	61.8	100.0	85.4	14.6

[1]Civilian noninstitutionalized population, plus armed forces living off post or with their families on post.
[2]Population in the 12th grade with no diploma are included in this category.

Table A-18. Percent of High School and College Graduates of the Population 15 Years Old and Over, by Age, Sex, Race, and Hispanic Origin, 2011—*Continued*

(Percent, except where noted)

Age, sex, race, and Hispanic origin	Total population (thousands)[1]	High school graduate status			Bachelor's degree status		
		Total	Not high school graduate	High school graduate or more[2]	Total	Less than Bachelor's degree	Bachelor's degree or more
HISPANIC[3]							
Both Sexes							
18 years old and over	32,434	100.0	34.5	65.5	100.0	87.7	12.3
18 to 24 years old	5,762	100.0	28.8	71.2	100.0	95.9	4.1
25 years old and over	26,672	100.0	35.7	64.3	100.0	85.9	14.1
25 to 29 years old	4,182	100.0	28.5	71.5	100.0	87.2	12.8
30 to 34 years old	3,948	100.0	32.3	67.7	100.0	85.5	14.5
35 to 39 years old	3,715	100.0	32.3	67.7	100.0	83.8	16.2
40 to 44 years old	3,354	100.0	35.0	65.0	100.0	86.1	13.9
45 to 49 years old	2,962	100.0	34.1	65.9	100.0	85.0	15.0
50 to 54 years old	2,399	100.0	35.2	64.8	100.0	86.2	13.8
55 to 59 years old	1,801	100.0	38.6	61.4	100.0	83.0	17.0
60 to 64 years old	1,453	100.0	42.7	57.3	100.0	87.7	12.3
65 to 69 years old	977	100.0	46.0	54.0	100.0	86.7	13.3
70 to 74 years old	733	100.0	48.7	51.3	100.0	86.1	13.9
75 years old and over	1,148	100.0	60.8	39.2	100.0	92.3	7.7
Male							
18 years old and over	16,720	100.0	35.5	64.5	100.0	88.8	11.2
18 to 24 years old	3,120	100.0	31.3	68.8	100.0	96.8	3.2
25 years old and over	13,599	100.0	36.4	63.6	100.0	86.9	13.1
25 to 29 years old	2,321	100.0	30.8	69.2	100.0	90.4	9.6
30 to 34 years old	2,093	100.0	35.2	64.8	100.0	88.3	11.7
35 to 39 years old	1,950	100.0	33.7	66.3	100.0	85.8	14.2
40 to 44 years old	1,737	100.0	35.9	64.1	100.0	87.2	12.8
45 to 49 years old	1,507	100.0	35.1	64.9	100.0	87.0	13.0
50 to 54 years old	1,186	100.0	35.1	64.9	100.0	86.0	14.0
55 to 59 years old	889	100.0	41.4	58.6	100.0	82.9	17.1
60 to 64 years old	684	100.0	42.0	58.0	100.0	85.2	14.8
65 to 69 years old	419	100.0	42.2	57.8	100.0	81.1	18.9
70 to 74 years old	319	100.0	43.9	56.1	100.0	80.3	19.7
75 years old and over	493	100.0	61.1	38.9	100.0	89.2	10.8
Female							
18 years old and over	15,714	100.0	33.4	66.6	100.0	86.5	13.5
18 to 24 years old	2,642	100.0	26.0	74.0	100.0	94.9	5.1
25 years old and over	13,072	100.0	34.9	65.1	100.0	84.8	15.2
25 to 29 years old	1,862	100.0	25.7	74.3	100.0	83.2	16.8
30 to 34 years old	1,854	100.0	29.0	71.0	100.0	82.3	17.7
35 to 39 years old	1,765	100.0	30.7	69.3	100.0	81.4	18.6
40 to 44 years old	1,617	100.0	34.0	66.0	100.0	84.9	15.1
45 to 49 years old	1,455	100.0	33.0	67.0	100.0	82.9	17.1
50 to 54 years old	1,213	100.0	35.3	64.7	100.0	86.4	13.6
55 to 59 years old	912	100.0	35.9	64.1	100.0	82.9	17.1
60 to 64 years old	769	100.0	43.6	56.4	100.0	90.1	9.9
65 to 69 years old	558	100.0	48.7	51.3	100.0	90.9	9.1
70 to 74 years old	413	100.0	52.3	47.7	100.0	90.6	9.4
75 years old and over	655	100.0	60.6	39.4	100.0	94.8	5.2

[1]Civilian noninstitutionalized population, plus armed forces living off post or with their families on post.
[2]Population in the 12th grade with no diploma are included in this category.
[3]May be of any race.

Table A-19. Educational Attainment of the Population 25 Years Old and Over, by Marital Status and Sex, 2011

(Numbers in thousands)

Sex and marital status	Educational attainment									
	Total[1]		None to 8th grade		9th to 11th grade[2]		High school graduate		Some college, no degree	
	Number	Percent	Number	Percent	Number	Percent	Number	Percent	Number	Percent
Both Sexes										
Total	201,543	100.0	10,277	100.0	14,763	100.0	61,911	100.0	34,203	100.0
Married spouse present	117,727	58.4	5,274	51.3	6,786	46.0	34,651	56.0	18,862	55.1
Married spouse absent, not separated	3,265	1.6	391	3.8	403	2.7	981	1.6	505	1.5
Separated	4,996	2.5	444	4.3	663	4.5	1,706	2.8	916	2.7
Widowed	14,215	7.1	1,722	16.8	1,805	12.2	5,455	8.8	2,133	6.2
Divorced	24,134	12.0	747	7.3	1,858	12.6	7,893	12.7	5,193	15.2
Never married	37,205	18.5	1,699	16.5	3,247	22.0	11,224	18.1	6,595	19.3
Male										
Total	97,220	100.0	5,117	100.0	7,443	100.0	30,370	100.0	16,137	100.0
Married spouse present	59,242	60.9	2,871	56.1	3,669	49.3	17,480	57.6	9,368	58.1
Married spouse absent, not separated	1,679	1.7	253	4.9	227	3.0	531	1.7	216	1.3
Separated	2,182	2.2	194	3.8	318	4.3	752	2.5	381	2.4
Widowed	2,928	3.0	448	8.8	382	5.1	990	3.3	437	2.7
Divorced	10,556	10.9	341	6.7	900	12.1	3,796	12.5	2,161	13.4
Never married	20,633	21.2	1,011	19.8	1,947	26.2	6,821	22.5	3,573	22.1
Female										
Total	104,323	100.0	5,160	100.0	7,320	100.0	31,541	100.0	18,065	100.0
Married spouse present	58,486	56.1	2,403	46.6	3,117	42.6	17,171	54.4	9,494	52.6
Married spouse absent, not separated	1,585	1.5	138	2.7	176	2.4	450	1.4	289	1.6
Separated	2,814	2.7	250	4.8	346	4.7	954	3.0	534	3.0
Widowed	11,287	10.8	1,275	24.7	1,424	19.5	4,465	14.2	1,695	9.4
Divorced	13,578	13.0	406	7.9	958	13.1	4,098	13.0	3,031	16.8
Never married	16,572	15.9	688	13.3	1,299	17.7	4,404	14.0	3,022	16.7

Note. Percentages may not sum to total because of rounding.
[1]Civilian noninstitutionalized population, plus armed forces living off post or with their families on post.
[2]Population who attained the 12th grade but received no diploma are included in this category.

Table A-19. Educational Attainment of the Population 25 Years Old and Over, by Marital Status and Sex, 2011—*Continued*

(Numbers in thousands)

Sex and marital status	Educational attainment									
	Associate degree		Bachelor's degree		Master's degree		Professional degree		Doctoral degree	
	Number	Percent	Number	Percent	Number	Percent	Number	Percent	Number	Percent
Both Sexes										
Total	19,047	100.0	39,286	100.0	16,015	100.0	2,980	100.0	3,062	100.0
Married spouse present	11,589	60.8	25,176	64.1	10,975	68.5	2,150	72.1	2,265	74.0
Married spouse absent, not separated	201	1.1	501	1.3	216	1.3	30	1.0	36	1.2
Separated	452	2.4	552	1.4	200	1.2	36	1.2	28	0.9
Widowed	871	4.6	1,422	3.6	605	3.8	105	3.5	96	3.1
Divorced	2,662	14.0	3,801	9.7	1,484	9.3	244	8.2	253	8.3
Never married	3,271	17.2	7,834	19.9	2,536	15.8	415	13.9	385	12.6
Male										
Total	8,182	100.0	19,017	100.0	7,181	100.0	1,862	100.0	1,911	100.0
Married spouse present	5,234	64.0	12,359	65.0	5,288	73.6	1,461	78.5	1,511	79.1
Married spouse absent, not separated	87	1.1	239	1.3	80	1.1	23	1.2	23	1.2
Separated	152	1.9	255	1.3	85	1.2	27	1.5	18	0.9
Widowed	127	1.6	313	1.6	141	2.0	42	2.3	48	2.5
Divorced	949	11.6	1,641	8.6	511	7.1	124	6.7	133	7.0
Never married	1,633	20.0	4,210	22.1	1,076	15.0	185	9.9	177	9.3
Female										
Total	10,865	100.0	20,269	100.0	8,834	100.0	1,118	100.0	1,151	100.0
Married spouse present	6,355	58.5	12,817	63.2	5,686	64.4	689	61.6	754	65.5
Married spouse absent, not separated	114	1.0	262	1.3	136	1.5	7	0.6	13	1.1
Separated	300	2.8	297	1.5	115	1.3	9	0.8	10	0.9
Widowed	744	6.8	1,109	5.5	464	5.3	63	5.6	47	4.1
Divorced	1,712	15.8	2,160	10.7	973	11.0	120	10.7	119	10.3
Never married	1,639	15.1	3,623	17.9	1,460	16.5	230	20.6	208	18.1

Note. Percentages may not sum to total because of rounding.
[1]Civilian noninstitutionalized population, plus armed forces living off post or with their families on post.
[2]Population who attained the 12th grade but received no diploma are included in this category.

Table A-20. Educational Attainment of the Population 25 Years Old and Over, by Household Relationship and Sex, 2011

(Numbers in thousands)

Sex and Household Relationship	Educational attainment											
	Total[1]		None to 8th grade		9th to 11th grade[2]		High school graduate		Some college, no degree		Associate degree	
	Number	Percent	Number	Percent	Number	Percent	Number	Percent	Number	Percent	Number	Percent
BOTH SEXES												
Total	201,543	100.0	10,277	100.0	14,763	100.0	61,911	100.0	34,203	100.0	19,047	100.0
Family householder												
Married spouse present	56,969	28.3	2,315	22.5	3,131	21.2	15,812	25.5	9,610	28.1	5,648	29.7
Other family householder	18,348	9.1	1,043	10.1	2,063	14.0	5,996	9.7	3,759	11.0	1,931	10.1
Nonfamily householder												
Living alone	31,316	15.5	1,575	15.3	2,503	17.0	9,354	15.1	5,680	16.6	2,813	14.8
Living with nonrelatives	5,972	3.0	166	1.6	368	2.5	1,578	2.5	1,184	3.5	565	3.0
Relative of householder												
Spouse	56,882	28.2	2,374	23.1	3,308	22.4	17,450	28.2	8,702	25.4	5,676	29.8
Other	21,094	10.5	2,122	20.6	2,375	16.1	8,069	13.0	3,298	9.6	1,605	8.4
Nonrelative	10,962	5.4	683	6.6	1,016	6.9	3,651	5.9	1,970	5.8	807	4.2
MALE												
Total	97,220	100.0	5,117	100.0	7,443	100.0	30,370	100.0	16,137	100.0	8,182	100.0
Family householder												
Married spouse present	35,033	36.0	1,574	30.8	1,906	25.6	9,828	32.4	5,696	35.3	3,178	38.8
Other family householder	4,736	4.9	259	5.1	511	6.9	1,744	5.7	864	5.4	413	5.0
Nonfamily householder												
Living alone	13,821	14.2	683	13.3	1,079	14.5	4,092	13.5	2,515	15.6	1,147	14.0
Living with nonrelatives	3,561	3.7	111	2.2	221	3.0	1,018	3.4	719	4.5	328	4.0
Relative of householder												
Spouse	22,229	22.9	1,001	19.6	1,585	21.3	6,905	22.7	3,401	21.1	1,950	23.8
Other	11,568	11.9	987	19.3	1,451	19.5	4,577	15.1	1,879	11.6	790	9.7
Nonrelative	6,272	6.5	502	9.8	690	9.3	2,206	7.3	1,064	6.6	376	4.6
FEMALE												
Total	104,323	100.0	5,160	100.0	7,320	100.0	31,541	100.0	18,065	100.0	10,865	100.0
Family householder												
Married spouse present	21,937	21.0	741	14.4	1,225	16.7	5,983	19.0	3,914	21.7	2,470	22.7
Other family householder	13,612	13.0	784	15.2	1,552	21.2	4,252	13.5	2,896	16.0	1,518	14.0
Nonfamily householder												
Living alone	17,495	16.8	893	17.3	1,423	19.4	5,263	16.7	3,165	17.5	1,666	15.3
Living with nonrelatives	2,411	2.3	56	1.1	147	2.0	560	1.8	465	2.6	238	2.2
Relative of householder												
Spouse	34,652	33.2	1,372	26.6	1,722	23.5	10,546	33.4	5,301	29.3	3,726	34.3
Other	9,525	9.1	1,135	22.0	924	12.6	3,492	11.1	1,419	7.9	815	7.5
Nonrelative	4,691	4.5	180	3.5	326	4.5	1,445	4.6	905	5.0	432	4.0

Note. Percentages may not sum to total because of rounding.
[1]Civilian noninstitutionalized population, plus armed forces living off post or with their families on post.
[2]Population who attained the 12th grade but received no diploma are included in this category.

Table A-20. Educational Attainment of the Population 25 Years Old and Over, by Household Relationship and Sex, 2011—*Continued*

(Numbers in thousands)

Sex and Household Relationship	Educational attainment							
	Bachelor's degree		Master's degree		Professional degree		Doctoral degree	
	Number	Percent	Number	Percent	Number	Percent	Number	Percent
BOTH SEXES								
Total	39,286	100.0	16,015	100.0	2,980	100.0	3,062	100.0
Family householder								
Married spouse present	12,595	32.1	5,527	34.5	1,117	37.5	1,215	39.7
Other family householder	2,463	6.3	891	5.6	106	3.6	96	3.1
Nonfamily householder								
Living alone	5,948	15.1	2,549	15.9	470	15.8	424	13.8
Living with nonrelatives	1,456	3.7	475	3.0	72	2.4	106	3.5
Relative of householder								
Spouse	12,032	30.6	5,312	33.2	1,008	33.8	1,022	33.4
Other	2,774	7.1	654	4.1	101	3.4	96	3.1
Nonrelative	2,018	5.1	607	3.8	107	3.6	103	3.4
MALE								
Total	19,017	100.0	7,181	100.0	1,862	100.0	1,911	100.0
Family householder								
Married spouse present	7,656	40.3	3,407	47.4	886	47.6	902	47.2
Other family householder	683	3.6	202	2.8	37	2.0	23	1.2
Nonfamily householder								
Living alone	2,850	15.0	1,006	14.0	234	12.6	214	11.2
Living with nonrelatives	863	4.5	206	2.9	30	1.6	67	3.5
Relative of householder								
Spouse	4,425	23.3	1,820	25.3	555	29.8	588	30.8
Other	1,493	7.9	277	3.9	58	3.1	55	2.9
Nonrelative	1,047	5.5	262	3.6	61	3.3	62	3.2
FEMALE								
Total	20,269	100.0	8,834	100.0	1,118	100.0	1,151	100.0
Family householder								
Married spouse present	4,939	24.4	2,121	24.0	230	20.6	313	27.2
Other family householder	1,779	8.8	688	7.8	69	6.2	72	6.3
Nonfamily householder								
Living alone	3,098	15.3	1,543	17.5	235	21.0	209	18.2
Living with nonrelatives	593	2.9	270	3.1	42	3.8	40	3.5
Relative of householder								
Spouse	7,607	37.5	3,491	39.5	453	40.5	434	37.7
Other	1,281	6.3	377	4.3	42	3.8	40	3.5
Nonrelative	971	4.8	345	3.9	45	4.0	42	3.6

Note. Percentages may not sum to total because of rounding.

Table A-21. Educational Attainment of the Population 25 Years Old and Over, by Labor Force Status and Sex, 2011

(Numbers in thousands)

Sex and labor force status	Total[1]	Educational attainment								
		None to 8th grade	9th to 11th grade[2]	High school graduate	Some college, no degree	Associate's degree	Bachelor's degree	Master's degree	Professional degree	Doctoral degree
BOTH SEXES										
Total	201,543	10,277	14,763	61,911	34,203	19,047	39,286	16,015	2,980	3,062
Employed	121,646	3,658	5,904	33,444	20,573	13,145	28,448	11,817	2,281	2,376
Unemployed	10,789	543	1,234	3,980	2,035	912	1,525	457	42	59
Unemployment Rate	8.1	12.9	17.3	10.6	9.0	6.5	5.1	3.7	1.8	2.4
Not in Labor Force	69,108	6,077	7,624	24,486	11,594	4,989	9,313	3,740	657	627
Percent	34.3	59.1	51.6	39.6	33.9	26.2	23.7	23.4	22.0	20.5
MALE										
Total	97,220	5,117	7,443	30,370	16,137	8,182	19,017	7,181	1,862	1,911
Employed	64,306	2,431	3,655	18,820	10,364	5,925	14,712	5,476	1,470	1,452
Unemployed	6,400	346	842	2,550	1,108	443	843	221	14	34
Unemployment Rate	9.1	12.5	18.7	11.9	9.7	7.0	5.4	3.9	0.9	2.3
Not in Labor Force	26,514	2,340	2,946	9,000	4,666	1,813	3,463	1,484	378	425
Percent	27.3	45.7	39.6	29.6	28.9	22.2	18.2	20.7	20.3	22.2
FEMALE										
Total	104,323	5,160	7,320	31,541	18,065	10,865	20,269	8,834	1,118	1,151
Employed	57,340	1,227	2,249	14,624	10,209	7,220	13,736	6,341	811	924
Unemployed	4,389	197	393	1,430	928	469	683	237	28	26
Unemployment Rate	7.1	13.8	14.9	8.9	8.3	6.1	4.7	3.6	3.3	2.7
Not in Labor Force	42,594	3,737	4,678	15,486	6,929	3,176	5,850	2,256	279	202
Percent	40.8	72.4	63.9	49.1	38.4	29.2	28.9	25.5	25.0	17.5

[1]Civilian noninstitutionalized population, plus armed forces living off post or with their families on post. May be of any race.
[2]Population who attained the 12th grade but received no diploma are included in this category.

Table A-22. Educational Attainment of Employed Civilians 25 Years Old and Over, by Occupation and Sex, 2011

(Numbers in thousands)

Occupation and sex	Total[1]	Educational attainment								
		Percent	None to 8th grade	Percent	9th to 11th grade[2]	Percent	High school graduate	Percent	Some college, no degree	Percent
BOTH SEXES										
Total Employed Civilians	121,646	100.0	3,658	100.0	5,904	100.0	33,444	100.0	20,573	100.0
Occupation										
Management, business, and financial occupations	20,604	16.9	107	2.9	335	5.7	3,412	10.2	3,086	15.0
Professional and related occupations	29,285	24.1	49	1.3	137	2.3	2,031	6.1	2,694	13.1
Service occupations	18,921	15.6	1,336	36.5	1,843	31.2	7,067	21.1	3,903	19.0
Sales and related occupations	12,054	9.9	179	4.9	469	7.9	3,628	10.8	2,603	12.7
Office and administrative occupations	15,488	12.7	121	3.3	438	7.4	5,319	15.9	4,072	19.8
Farming, fishing, and forestry occupations	665	0.5	193	5.3	112	1.9	239	0.7	57	0.3
Construction and extraction occupations	6,262	5.1	612	16.7	845	14.3	2,852	8.5	986	4.8
Installation, maintenance, and repair occupations	4,250	3.5	133	3.6	253	4.3	1,900	5.7	842	4.1
Production occupations	7,213	5.9	536	14.7	768	13.0	3,473	10.4	1,166	5.7
Transportation and material moving occupations	6,902	5.7	391	10.7	702	11.9	3,522	10.5	1,163	5.7
MALE										
Total Employed Civilians	64,306	100.0	2,431	100.0	3,655	100.0	18,820	100.0	10,364	100.0
Occupation										
Management, business, and financial occupations	11,771	18.3	83	3.4	217	5.9	1,979	10.5	1,659	16.0
Professional and related occupations	12,489	19.4	21	0.9	79	2.2	741	3.9	1,136	11.0
Service occupations	8,176	12.7	656	27.0	717	19.6	2,909	15.5	1,675	16.2
Sales and related occupations	6,386	9.9	83	3.4	195	5.3	1,760	9.4	1,254	12.1
Office and administrative occupations	3,836	6.0	54	2.2	161	4.4	1,225	6.5	971	9.4
Farming, fishing, and forestry occupations	524	0.8	142	5.8	94	2.6	193	1.0	51	0.5
Construction and extraction occupations	6,105	9.5	606	24.9	833	22.8	2,778	14.8	964	9.3
Installation, maintenance, and repair occupations	4,083	6.3	123	5.1	246	6.7	1,842	9.8	802	7.7
Production occupations	5,112	7.9	328	13.5	516	14.1	2,432	12.9	878	8.5
Transportation and material moving occupations	5,824	9.1	335	13.8	597	16.3	2,961	15.7	974	9.4
FEMALE										
Total Employed Civilians	57,340	100.0	1,227	100.0	2,249	99.9	14,624	100.0	10,209	100.0
Occupation										
Management, business, and financial occupations	8,833	15.4	24	2.0	118	5.2	1,432	9.8	1,428	14.0
Professional and related occupations	16,796	29.3	28	2.3	58	2.6	1,290	8.8	1,558	15.3
Service occupations	10,745	18.7	681	55.5	1,126	50.1	4,159	28.4	2,228	21.8
Sales and related occupations	5,668	9.9	97	7.9	274	12.2	1,868	12.8	1,350	13.2
Office and administrative occupations	11,652	20.3	67	5.5	277	12.3	4,094	28.0	3,100	30.4
Farming, fishing, and forestry occupations	142	0.2	51	4.2	18	0.8	47	0.3	6	0.1
Construction and extraction occupations	158	0.3	6	0.5	12	0.5	74	0.5	22	0.2
Installation, maintenance, and repair occupations	167	0.3	9	0.7	7	0.3	59	0.4	40	0.4
Production occupations	2,102	3.7	208	17.0	252	11.2	1,041	7.1	288	2.8
Transportation and material moving occupations	1,078	1.9	56	4.6	105	4.7	561	3.8	189	1.9

[1]Civilian noninstitutionalized population plus armed forces living off post or with their families on post.
[2]Population who attained 12th grade but received no diploma are included in this category.

Table A-22. Educational Attainment of Employed Civilians 25 Years Old and Over, by Occupation and Sex, 2011—*Continued*

(Numbers in thousands)

Occupation and sex	Educational attainment									
	Associate's degree	Percent	Bachelor's degree	Percent	Master's degree	Percent	Professional degree	Percent	Doctoral degree	Percent
BOTH SEXES										
Total Employed Civilians	13,145	100.0	28,448	100.0	11,817	100.0	2,281	100.0	2,376	100.0
Occupation										
Management, business, and financial occupations	1,876	14.3	7,878	27.7	3,373	28.5	221	9.7	315	13.3
Professional and related occupations	3,468	26.4	10,334	36.3	6,749	57.1	1,879	82.4	1,945	81.9
Service occupations	2,144	16.3	2,196	7.7	360	3.0	37	1.6	34	1.4
Sales and related occupations	1,139	8.7	3,366	11.8	595	5.0	43	1.9	31	1.3
Office and administrative occupations	2,138	16.3	2,848	10.0	467	4.0	51	2.2	34	1.4
Farming, fishing, and forestry occupations	22	0.2	33	0.1	6	0.1	1	0.0	2	0.1
Construction and extraction occupations	486	3.7	409	1.4	55	0.5	17	0.7	*	*
Installation, maintenance, and repair occupations	728	5.5	346	1.2	42	0.4	5	0.2	*	*
Production occupations	643	4.9	493	1.7	104	0.9	17	0.7	14	0.6
Transportation and material moving occupations	500	3.8	547	1.9	66	0.6	10	0.4	1	0.0
MALE										
Total Employed Civilians	5,925	100.0	14,712	100.0	5,476	100.0	1,470	100.0	1,452	100.0
Occupation										
Management, business, and financial occupations	917	15.5	4,556	31.0	1,982	36.2	160	10.9	218	15.0
Professional and related occupations	1,090	18.4	4,466	30.4	2,587	47.2	1,199	81.6	1,170	80.6
Service occupations	892	15.1	1,092	7.4	192	3.5	21	1.4	23	1.6
Sales and related occupations	589	9.9	2,102	14.3	363	6.6	24	1.6	16	1.1
Office and administrative occupations	355	6.0	896	6.1	139	2.5	22	1.5	12	0.8
Farming, fishing, and forestry occupations	15	0.3	23	0.2	4	0.1	*	*	1	0.1
Construction and extraction occupations	471	7.9	388	2.6	50	0.9	14	1.0	*	*
Installation, maintenance, and repair occupations	693	11.7	332	2.3	41	0.7	5	0.3	*	*
Production occupations	490	8.3	380	2.6	60	1.1	17	1.2	11	0.8
Transportation and material moving occupations	414	7.0	475	3.2	58	1.1	8	0.5	1	0.1
FEMALE										
Total Employed Civilians	7,220	100.0	13,736	100.0	6,341	100.0	811	100.0	924	100.1
Occupation										
Management, business, and financial occupations	960	13.3	3,322	24.2	1,390	21.9	61	7.5	97	10.5
Professional and related occupations	2,378	32.9	5,867	42.7	4,162	65.6	680	83.8	775	83.9
Service occupations	1,253	17.4	1,104	8.0	168	2.6	16	2.0	11	1.2
Sales and related occupations	550	7.6	1,263	9.2	233	3.7	19	2.3	15	1.6
Office and administrative occupations	1,782	24.7	1,951	14.2	329	5.2	29	3.6	23	2.5
Farming, fishing, and forestry occupations	7	0.1	9	0.1	2	0.0	1	0.1	1	0.1
Construction and extraction occupations	15	0.2	21	0.2	5	0.1	3	0.4	*	*
Installation, maintenance, and repair occupations	36	0.5	14	0.1	2	0.0	*	*	*	*
Production occupations	153	2.1	112	0.8	44	0.7	*	*	3	0.3
Transportation and material moving occupations	85	1.2	72	0.5	8	0.1	2	0.2	*	*

* = Quantity zero or rounds to zero.

Table A-23. Educational Attainment of the Population 25 Years Old and Older, by Industry and Sex, 2011

(Numbers in thousands)

Occupation and sex	Total[1]	Educational attainment								
		Percent	None to 8th grade	Percent	9th to 11th grade[2]	Percent	High school graduate	Percent	Some college, no degree	Percent
BOTH SEXES										
Total Employed Civilians	121,646	100.0	3,658	100.0	5,904	100.0	33,444	100.0	20,573	100.0
Industry										
Agriculture, forestry, fishing, and hunting	1,866	1.5	244	6.7	178	3.0	717	2.1	254	1.2
Mining	664	0.5	27	0.7	53	0.9	293	0.9	95	0.5
Construction	7,964	6.5	620	16.9	906	15.3	3,254	9.7	1,288	6.3
Manufacturing	13,073	10.7	541	14.8	841	14.2	4,722	14.1	2,125	10.3
Wholesale and retail trade	15,711	12.9	416	11.4	862	14.6	5,697	17.0	3,224	15.7
Transportation and utilities	6,436	5.3	119	3.3	366	6.2	2,466	7.4	1,432	7.0
Information	2,785	2.3	13	0.4	24	0.4	554	1.7	545	2.6
Financial activities	8,612	7.1	48	1.3	158	2.7	1,808	5.4	1,638	8.0
Professional and business services	14,413	11.8	509	13.9	535	9.1	2,681	8.0	2,093	10.2
Educational and health services	29,393	24.2	291	8.0	769	13.0	5,142	15.4	3,897	18.9
Leisure and hospitality	8,321	6.8	528	14.4	763	12.9	2,804	8.4	1,669	8.1
Other services	5,750	4.7	275	7.5	371	6.3	1,991	6.0	916	4.5
Public administration	6,658	5.5	27	0.7	77	1.3	1,317	3.9	1,397	6.8
MALE										
Total Employed Civilians	64,306	100.0	2,431	100.0	3,655	100.0	18,820	100.0	10,364	100.0
Industry										
Agriculture, forestry, fishing, and hunting	1,423	2.2	192	7.9	155	4.2	576	3.1	167	1.6
Mining	588	0.9	27	1.1	51	1.4	282	1.5	76	0.7
Construction	7,191	11.2	608	25.0	878	24.0	2,968	15.8	1,147	11.1
Manufacturing	9,167	14.3	352	14.5	592	16.2	3,247	17.3	1,509	14.6
Wholesale and retail trade	8,838	13.7	271	11.1	478	13.1	3,179	16.9	1,671	16.1
Transportation and utilities	4,942	7.7	101	4.2	300	8.2	1,983	10.5	1,041	10.0
Information	1,731	2.7	13	0.5	17	0.5	358	1.9	339	3.3
Financial activities	3,883	6.0	27	1.1	87	2.4	536	2.8	532	5.1
Professional and business services	8,456	13.1	342	14.1	346	9.5	1,524	8.1	1,038	10.0
Educational and health services	7,377	11.5	62	2.6	180	4.9	1,054	5.6	763	7.4
Leisure and hospitality	4,205	6.5	273	11.2	353	9.7	1,392	7.4	868	8.4
Other services	2,828	4.4	149	6.1	190	5.2	1,025	5.4	408	3.9
Public administration	3,676	5.7	13	0.5	29	0.8	694	3.7	804	7.8
FEMALE										
Total Employed Civilians	57,340	100.0	1,227	100.0	2,249	100.0	14,624	100.0	10,209	100.0
Industry										
Agriculture, forestry, fishing, and hunting	443	0.8	52	4.2	23	1.0	141	1.0	87	0.9
Mining	76	0.1	*	*	2	0.1	11	0.1	19	0.2
Construction	773	1.3	11	0.9	28	1.2	286	2.0	141	1.4
Manufacturing	3,906	6.8	189	15.4	249	11.1	1,475	10.1	616	6.0
Wholesale and retail trade	6,874	12.0	145	11.8	385	17.1	2,518	17.2	1,553	15.2
Transportation and utilities	1,493	2.6	18	1.5	66	2.9	482	3.3	391	3.8
Information	1,053	1.8	*	*	7	0.3	196	1.3	206	2.0
Financial activities	4,730	8.2	21	1.7	72	3.2	1,272	8.7	1,105	10.8
Professional and business services	5,957	10.4	167	13.6	189	8.4	1,156	7.9	1,055	10.3
Educational and health services	22,016	38.4	229	18.7	589	26.2	4,087	27.9	3,134	30.7
Leisure and hospitality	4,116	7.2	254	20.7	410	18.2	1,411	9.6	801	7.8
Other services	2,922	5.1	126	10.3	181	8.0	966	6.6	508	5.0
Public administration	2,982	5.2	14	1.1	48	2.1	623	4.3	592	5.8

[1]Civilian noninstitutionalized population plus armed forces living off post or with their families on post.
[2]Population who attained 12th grade but received no diploma are included in this category.
* = Quantity zero or rounds to zero.

Table A-23. Educational Attainment of the Population 25 Years Old and Older, by Industry and Sex, 2011

(Numbers in thousands)

Occupation and sex	Educational attainment									
	Associate's degree	Percent	Bachelor's degree	Percent	Master's degree	Percent	Professional degree	Percent	Doctoral degree	Percent
BOTH SEXES										
Total Employed Civilians	13,145	100.0	28,448	100.0	11,817	100.0	2,281	100.0	2,376	100.0
Industry										
Agriculture, forestry, fishing, and hunting	139	1.1	269	0.9	52	0.4	5	0.2	8	0.3
Mining	54	0.4	108	0.4	22	0.2	*	*	11	0.5
Construction	702	5.3	968	3.4	195	1.7	21	0.9	10	0.4
Manufacturing	1,265	9.6	2,474	8.7	916	7.8	57	2.5	132	5.6
Wholesale and retail trade	1,502	11.4	3,248	11.4	601	5.1	66	2.9	96	4.0
Transportation and utilities	737	5.6	1026	3.6	257	2.2	21	0.9	11	0.5
Information	297	2.3	1007	3.5	315	2.7	13	0.6	16	0.7
Financial activities	880	6.7	3,118	11.0	795	6.7	118	5.2	49	2.1
Professional and business services	1,289	9.8	4,434	15.6	1,708	14.5	750	32.9	413	17.4
Educational and health services	3,896	29.6	7,520	26.4	5,471	46.3	1,018	44.6	1,389	58.5
Leisure and hospitality	762	5.8	1,466	5.2	289	2.4	17	0.7	24	1.0
Other services	726	5.5	953	3.3	421	3.6	43	1.9	55	2.3
Public administration	896	6.8	1,856	6.5	775	6.6	153	6.7	161	6.8
MALE										
Total Employed Civilians	5,925	100.0	14,712	100.0	5,476	100.0	1,470	100.0	1,452	100.0
Industry										
Agriculture, forestry, fishing, and hunting	98	1.7	186	1.3	38	0.7	2	0.1	8	0.6
Mining	50	0.8	81	0.6	13	0.2	*	*	8	0.6
Construction	615	10.4	796	5.4	154	2.8	16	1.1	8	0.6
Manufacturing	931	15.7	1,751	11.9	648	11.8	46	3.1	90	6.2
Wholesale and retail trade	831	14.0	1,976	13.4	350	6.4	38	2.6	44	3.0
Transportation and utilities	551	9.3	756	5.1	183	3.3	17	1.2	8	0.6
Information	177	3.0	645	4.4	170	3.1	3	0.2	9	0.6
Financial activities	266	4.5	1,788	12.2	539	9.8	73	5.0	34	2.3
Professional and business services	612	10.3	2,668	18.1	1,110	20.3	530	36.1	286	19.7
Educational and health services	654	11.0	1,786	12.1	1,476	27.0	604	41.1	799	55.0
Leisure and hospitality	348	5.9	805	5.5	140	2.6	11	0.7	14	1.0
Other services	301	5.1	440	3.0	233	4.3	35	2.4	47	3.2
Public administration	491	8.3	1035	7.0	420	7.7	95	6.5	95	6.5
FEMALE										
Total Employed Civilians	7,220	100.0	13,736	100.0	6,341	100.0	811	100.0	924	100.0
Industry										
Agriculture, forestry, fishing, and hunting	41	0.6	83	0.6	14	0.2	3	0.4	*	*
Mining	4	0.1	27	0.2	9	0.1	*	*	4	0.4
Construction	87	1.2	172	1.3	41	0.6	5	0.6	2	0.2
Manufacturing	334	4.6	723	5.3	268	4.2	11	1.4	41	4.4
Wholesale and retail trade	670	9.3	1,272	9.3	252	4.0	27	3.3	52	5.6
Transportation and utilities	187	2.6	270	2.0	73	1.2	3	0.4	2	0.2
Information	119	1.6	362	2.6	145	2.3	10	1.2	8	0.9
Financial activities	614	8.5	1,330	9.7	256	4.0	46	5.7	15	1.6
Professional and business services	677	9.4	1,766	12.9	598	9.4	221	27.3	127	13.7
Educational and health services	3,242	44.9	5,735	41.8	3,996	63.0	414	51.0	590	63.9
Leisure and hospitality	413	5.7	661	4.8	149	2.3	6	0.7	10	1.1
Other services	425	5.9	513	3.7	188	3.0	8	1.0	7	0.8
Public administration	405	5.6	821	6.0	355	5.6	58	7.2	66	7.1

* = Quantity zero or rounds to zero.

Table A–24. Educational Attainment of the Population 25 Years Old and Over, by Citizenship, Nativity, Period of Entry, and Sex, 2011

(Numbers in thousands)

Citizenship, Nativity, Period of Entry, and Sex	Educational attainment									
	Total[1]		None to 8th grade		9th to 11th grade[2]		High school graduate		Some college, no degree	
	Number	Percent	Number	Percent	Number	Percent	Number	Percent	Number	Percent
BOTH SEXES										
Total	201,543	100.0	10,277	100.0	14,763	100.0	61,911	100.0	34,203	100.0
Native	168,998	83.9	4,261	41.5	11,264	76.3	53,355	86.2	30,834	90.1
Foreign-Born	32,545	16.1	6,016	58.5	3,499	23.7	8,556	13.8	3,368	9.8
Native										
Native Parentage[3]	154,106	76.5	3,770	36.7	10,211	69.2	49,211	79.5	28,195	82.4
Foreign or Mixed Parentage[4]	14,892	7.4	491	4.8	1,053	7.1	4,144	6.7	2,639	7.7
Foreign Born										
Naturalized Citizen	15,448	7.7	1,747	17.0	1,096	7.4	4,048	6.5	1,989	5.8
Not a Citizen	17,096	8.5	4,269	41.5	2,403	16.3	4,507	7.3	1,379	4.0
Year of Entry										
2000 or later	9,817	4.9	1,746	17.0	1,116	7.6	2,526	4.1	889	2.6
1990-1999	8,827	4.4	1,620	15.8	1,085	7.3	2,363	3.8	833	2.4
1980-1989	6,817	3.4	1,325	12.9	729	4.9	1,729	2.8	767	2.2
1970-1979	3,893	1.9	756	7.4	347	2.4	1,000	1.6	424	1.2
Before 1970	3,190	1.6	569	5.5	221	1.5	938	1.5	455	1.3
MALE										
Total	97,220	100.0	5,117	100.0	7,443	100.0	30,370	100.0	16,137	100.0
Native	81,177	83.5	2,214	43.3	5,561	74.7	26,169	86.2	14,441	89.5
Foreign-Born	16,043	16.5	2,903	56.7	1,882	25.3	4,201	13.8	1,696	10.5
Native										
Native Parentage[3]	73,920	76.0	1,967	38.4	5,032	67.6	24,253	79.9	13,137	81.4
Foreign or Mixed Parentage[4]	7,258	7.5	248	4.8	529	7.1	1,916	6.3	1,304	8.1
Foreign Born										
Naturalized Citizen	7,207	7.4	757	14.8	539	7.2	1,837	6.0	952	5.9
Not a Citizen	8,836	9.1	2,146	41.9	1,344	18.1	2,364	7.8	744	4.6
Year of Entry										
2000 or later	5,010	5.2	869	17.0	613	8.2	1,353	4.5	474	2.9
1990-1999	4,361	4.5	752	14.7	592	8.0	1,211	4.0	409	2.5
1980-1989	3,419	3.5	675	13.2	391	5.3	831	2.7	418	2.6
1970-1979	1,890	1.9	351	6.9	186	2.5	462	1.5	212	1.3
Before 1970	1,363	1.4	255	5.0	101	1.4	343	1.1	184	1.1
FEMALE										
Total	104,323	100.0	5,160	100.0	7,320	100.0	31,541	100.0	18,065	100.0
Native	87,821	84.2	2,047	39.7	5,703	77.9	27,186	86.2	16,393	90.7
Foreign-Born	16,502	15.8	3,113	60.3	1,616	22.1	4,355	13.8	1,672	9.3
Native										
Native Parentage[3]	80,187	76.9	1,804	35.0	5,180	70.8	24,958	79.1	15,058	83.4
Foreign or Mixed Parentage[4]	7,635	7.3	243	4.7	524	7.2	2,227	7.1	1,335	7.4
Foreign Born										
Naturalized Citizen	8,241	7.9	990	19.2	557	7.6	2,211	7.0	1,037	5.7
Not a Citizen	8,261	7.9	2,123	41.1	1,059	14.5	2,144	6.8	635	3.5
Year of Entry										
2000 or later	4,808	4.6	877	17.0	503	6.9	1,172	3.7	415	2.3
1990-1999	4,466	4.3	867	16.8	493	6.7	1,152	3.7	424	2.3
1980-1989	3,398	3.3	650	12.6	337	4.6	898	2.8	349	1.9
1970-1979	2,004	1.9	405	7.8	162	2.2	538	1.7	213	1.2
Before 1970	1,827	1.8	314	6.1	121	1.7	595	1.9	271	1.5

[1]Civilian noninstitutionalized population plus armed forces living off post or with their families on post.
[2]Population who attained 12th grade but received no diploma are included in this category.
[3]Native parentage: Both parents born in the United States.
[4]Foreign or mixed parentage: One or both parents born outside of the United States.

Table A–24. Educational Attainment of the Population 25 Years Old and Over, by Citizenship, Nativity, Period of Entry, and Sex, 2011—*Continued*

(Numbers in thousands)

Citizenship, Nativity, Period of Entry, and Sex	Educational attainment									
	Associate's degree		Bachelor's degree		Master's degree		Professional degree		Doctoral degree	
	Number	Percent	Number	Percent	Number	Percent	Number	Percent	Number	Percent
BOTH SEXES										
Total	19,047	100.0	39,286	100.0	16,015	100.0	2,980	100.0	3,062	100.0
Native	17,031	89.4	33,664	85.7	13,638	85.2	2,515	84.4	2,437	79.6
Foreign-Born	2,016	10.6	5,623	14.3	2,377	14.8	465	15.6	625	20.4
Native										
Native Parentage[3]	15,626	82.0	30,527	77.7	12,276	76.7	2,191	73.5	2,098	68.5
Foreign or Mixed Parentage[4]	1,405	7.4	3,136	8.0	1,362	8.5	324	10.9	338	11.0
Foreign Born										
Naturalized Citizen	1,249	6.6	3,300	8.4	1,366	8.5	295	9.9	358	11.7
Not a Citizen	767	4.0	2,323	5.9	1,011	6.3	170	5.7	267	8.7
Year of Entry										
2000 or later	492	2.6	1,895	4.8	819	5.1	148	5.0	187	6.1
1990-1999	524	2.8	1,499	3.8	625	3.9	114	3.8	164	5.4
1980-1989	473	2.5	1,157	2.9	444	2.8	74	2.5	119	3.9
1970-1979	280	1.5	672	1.7	258	1.6	69	2.3	86	2.8
Before 1970	247	1.3	400	1.0	230	1.4	60	2.0	69	2.3
MALE										
Total	8,182	100.0	19,017	100.0	7,181	100.0	1,862	100.0	1,911	100.0
Native	7,356	89.9	16,350	86.0	5,949	82.8	1,606	86.3	1,532	80.2
Foreign-Born	826	10.1	2,667	14.0	1,232	17.2	256	13.7	379	19.8
Native										
Native Parentage[3]	6,716	82.1	14,775	77.7	5,330	74.2	1,390	74.7	1,321	69.1
Foreign or Mixed Parentage[4]	640	7.8	1,575	8.3	619	8.6	216	11.6	210	11.0
Foreign Born										
Naturalized Citizen	515	6.3	1,542	8.1	692	9.6	174	9.3	199	10.4
Not a Citizen	311	3.8	1,125	5.9	540	7.5	82	4.4	180	9.4
Year of Entry										
2000 or later	202	2.5	890	4.7	417	5.8	68	3.7	123	6.4
1990-1999	220	2.7	673	3.5	329	4.6	65	3.5	109	5.7
1980-1989	197	2.4	585	3.1	221	3.1	42	2.3	59	3.1
1970-1979	106	1.3	339	1.8	154	2.1	37	2.0	43	2.3
Before 1970	100	1.2	181	1.0	111	1.5	43	2.3	46	2.4
FEMALE										
Total	10,865	100.0	20,269	100.0	8,834	100.0	1,118	100.0	1,151	100.0
Native	9,675	89.0	17,313	85.4	7,690	87.1	909	81.3	905	78.6
Foreign-Born	1,190	11.0	2,956	14.6	1,145	13.0	209	18.7	246	21.4
Native										
Native Parentage[3]	8,910	82.0	15,752	77.7	6,946	78.6	801	71.6	777	67.5
Foreign or Mixed Parentage[4]	765	7.0	1,562	7.7	744	8.4	107	9.6	128	11.1
Foreign Born										
Naturalized Citizen	734	6.8	1,758	8.7	674	7.6	122	10.9	159	13.8
Not a Citizen	456	4.2	1,198	5.9	471	5.3	87	7.8	87	7.6
Year of Entry										
2000 or later	289	2.7	1,005	5.0	402	4.6	80	7.2	64	5.6
1990-1999	304	2.8	826	4.1	295	3.3	49	4.4	55	4.8
1980-1989	275	2.5	573	2.8	223	2.5	32	2.9	60	5.2
1970-1979	175	1.6	332	1.6	104	1.2	31	2.8	44	3.8
Before 1970	147	1.4	219	1.1	120	1.4	17	1.5	23	2.0

[3]Native parentage: Both parents born in the United States.

[4]Foreign or mixed parentage: One or both parents born outside of the United States.

Table A-25. Years of School Completed by People 25 Years Old and Over, by Age and Sex, Selected Years, 1940–2011

(Numbers in thousands)

Year, sex, and age	Total[1]	Years of school completed						
		Elementary		High school[2]		College[3]		Median years[3,4]
		0 to 4 years	5 to 8 years	1 to 3 years	4 years	1 to 3 years	4 years or more	
25 YEARS OLD AND OVER								
Both Sexes								
2011	201,543	2,589	7,688	14,763	61,911	53,249	61,343	...
2010	199,928	2,615	7,836	15,260	62,456	51,920	59,840	...
2009	198,285	2,785	8,043	15,587	61,626	51,670	58,574	...
2008	196,305	2,599	8,226	15,516	61,183	50,994	57,787	...
2007	194,318	2,830	8,462	16,451	61,490	49,243	55,842	...
2006	191,884	2,951	8,791	16,154	60,898	49,371	53,720	...
2005	189,367	2,983	8,935	16,099	60,893	48,076	52,381	...
2004	186,876	2,858	8,888	15,999	59,811	47,571	51,749	...
2003	185,183	2,915	9,361	16,323	59,292	46,910	50,383	...
2002	182,142	2,902	9,668	16,378	58,456	46,042	48,696	...
2001[5]	180,389	2,810	9,518	16,279	58,272	46,281	47,228	...
2000	175,230	2,742	9,438	15,674	58,086	44,445	44,845	...
1999	173,754	2,742	9,655	15,674	57,935	43,176	43,803	...
1998	172,211	2,834	9,948	16,776	58,174	42,506	41,973	...
1997	170,581	2,840	10,472	17,211	57,586	41,774	40,697	...
1996	168,323	3,027	10,595	17,102	56,559	41,372	39,668	...
1995	166,438	3,074	10,873	16,566	56,450	41,249	38,226	...
1994	164,512	3,156	11,359	16,925	56,515	40,014	36,544	...
1993	162,826	3,380	11,747	17,067	57,589	37,451	35,590	...
1992[3,4]	160,827	3,449	11,989	17,672	57,860	35,520	34,337	...
1991	158,694	3,803	13,046	17,379	61,272	29,170	34,026	12.7
1990	156,538	3,833	13,758	17,461	60,119	28,075	33,291	12.7
1989	154,155	3,861	14,061	17,719	59,336	26,614	32,565	12.7
1988	151,635	3,714	14,550	17,847	58,940	25,799	30,787	12.7
1987	149,144	3,640	15,301	17,417	57,669	25,479	29,637	12.7
1986	146,606	3,894	15,672	17,484	56,338	24,729	28,489	12.6
1985	143,524	3,873	16,020	17,553	54,866	23,405	27,808	12.6
1984	140,794	3,884	16,258	17,433	54,073	22,281	26,862	12.6
1983	138,020	4,119	16,714	17,681	52,060	21,531	25,915	12.6
1982	135,526	4,119	17,232	18,006	51,426	20,692	24,050	12.6
1981	132,899	4,358	17,868	18,041	49,915	20,042	22,674	12.5
1980	130,409	4,390	18,426	18,086	47,934	19,379	22,193	12.5
1979	125,295	4,324	18,504	17,579	45,915	18,393	20,579	12.5
1978	123,019	4,445	19,309	18,175	44,381	17,379	19,332	12.4
1977	120,870	4,509	19,567	18,318	43,602	16,247	18,627	12.4
1976	118,848	4,601	19,912	18,204	43,157	15,477	17,496	12.4
1975	116,897	4,912	20,633	18,237	42,353	14,518	16,244	12.3
1974	115,005	5,106	21,200	18,274	41,460	13,665	15,300	12.3
1973	112,866	5,100	21,838	18,420	40,448	12,831	14,228	12.3
1972	111,133	5,124	22,503	18,855	39,171	12,117	13,364	12.2
1971	110,627	5,574	24,029	18,601	38,029	11,782	12,612	12.2
1970	109,310	5,747	24,519	18,682	37,134	11,164	12,062	12.2
1969	107,750	6,014	24,976	18,527	36,133	10,564	11,535	12.1
1968	106,469	6,248	25,467	18,724	34,603	10,254	11,171	12.1
1967	104,864	6,400	26,178	18,647	33,173	9,914	10,550	12.0
1966	103,876	6,705	26,478	18,859	32,391	9,235	10,212	12.0
1965	103,245	6,982	27,063	18,617	31,703	9,139	9,742	11.8
1964	102,421	7,295	27,551	18,419	30,728	9,085	9,345	11.7
1962	100,664	7,826	28,438	17,751	28,477	9,170	9,002	11.4
1960	99,465	8,303	31,218	19,140	24,440	8,747	7,617	10.6
1959	97,478	7,816	28,490	17,520	26,219	7,888	7,734	11.0
1957	95,630	8,561	29,316	16,951	24,832	6,985	7,172	10.6
1952	88,358	8,004	30,274	15,228	21,074	6,714	6,118	10.1
1950	87,484	9,491	31,617	14,817	17,625	6,246	5,272	9.3
1947	82,578	8,611	32,308	13,487	16,926	5,533	4,424	9.0
1940	74,776	10,105	34,413	11,182	10,552	4,075	3,407	8.6

[1]Civilian noninstitutionalized population, except where noted.
Total includes persons who did not report "Years of school completed."
[2]Data shown as "High school, 4 years" is now collected by the category "High School Graduate."
[3]Data shown as "College 1 to 3 years" is now collected by "Some College" and "Associate degree" categories. Data shown as "College 4 years or more" is now collected by the categories "Bachelor's degree," "Master's degree," "Doctorate degree," and "Professional degree." Due to the change in question format, median years of schooling cannot be derived after 1992.
[4]Beginning with data for 1992, a new question results in different categories than for earlier years.
[5]Starting in 2001, data are from the expanded Current Population Survey (CPS) sample and were created using population controls based on data from the 2000 Census.
... = Not available.

Table A-25. Years of School Completed by People 25 Years Old and Over, by Age and Sex, Selected Years, 1940–2011—*Continued*

(Numbers in thousands)

Year, sex, and age	Total[1]	Years of school completed						
		Elementary		High school[2]		College[3]		Median years[3,4]
		0 to 4 years	5 to 8 years	1 to 3 years	4 years	1 to 3 years	4 years or more	
Male								
2011	97,220	1,234	3,883	7,443	30,370	24,319	29,971	...
2010	96,325	1,279	3,931	7,705	30,682	23,570	29,158	...
2009	95,518	1,372	4,027	7,754	30,025	23,634	28,706	...
2008	94,470	1,310	4,136	7,853	29,491	23,247	28,433	...
2007	93,421	1,458	4,249	8,294	29,604	22,219	27,596	...
2006	92,233	1,472	4,395	7,940	29,380	22,136	26,910	...
2005	90,899	1,505	4,402	7,787	29,151	21,794	26,259	...
2004	89,558	1,496	4,308	7,766	27,889	21,763	26,336	...
2003	88,597	1,482	4,566	8,026	27,356	21,568	25,598	...
2002	86,996	1,457	4,743	7,894	26,947	21,127	24,828	...
2001[5]	86,096	1,419	4,673	7,615	26,956	21,120	24,313	...
2000	83,611	1,341	4,577	7,298	26,651	20,493	23,252	...
1999	82,917	1,339	4,651	7,736	26,368	20,043	22,782	...
1998	82,376	1,431	4,727	8,017	26,575	19,792	21,832	...
1997	81,620	1,454	5,023	8,212	26,226	19,332	21,374	...
1996	80,339	1,537	5,067	7,930	25,649	19,301	20,854	...
1995	79,463	1,598	5,231	7,691	25,378	18,933	20,631	...
1994	78,539	1,669	5,427	7,789	25,404	18,544	19,705	...
1993	77,644	1,709	5,594	7,821	25,766	17,521	19,234	...
1992[3,4]	76,579	1,737	5,726	8,085	25,774	16,631	18,627	...
1991	75,487	2,018	6,299	7,887	27,189	13,720	18,373	12.8
1990	74,421	2,004	6,557	8,000	26,426	13,271	18,164	12.8
1989	73,225	1,956	6,659	8,076	25,897	12,725	17,913	12.8
1988	71,911	1,852	6,849	8,247	25,638	12,057	17,268	12.7
1987	70,677	1,794	7,259	7,909	24,998	12,062	16,654	12.7
1986	69,503	1,978	7,446	7,872	24,260	11,856	16,091	12.7
1985	67,756	1,947	7,629	7,783	23,552	11,164	15,682	12.7
1984	66,350	1,945	7,688	7,837	22,990	10,678	15,211	12.7
1983	65,004	2,103	7,750	7,867	22,048	10,310	14,926	12.7
1982	63,764	2,074	7,987	7,960	21,749	10,020	13,974	12.6
1981	62,509	2,141	8,322	8,084	21,019	9,734	13,208	12.6
1980	61,389	2,212	8,627	8,046	20,080	9,593	12,832	12.6
1979	58,986	2,190	8,785	7,636	19,250	9,100	12,025	12.6
1978	57,922	2,230	9,195	7,821	18,620	8,657	11,398	12.5
1977	56,917	2,296	9,330	7,969	18,290	8,104	10,926	12.5
1976	55,902	2,371	9,463	7,923	18,048	7,699	10,397	12.5
1975	55,036	2,568	9,760	7,985	17,769	7,274	9,679	12.4
1974	54,167	2,637	10,186	7,966	17,488	6,756	9,135	12.4
1973	53,067	2,598	10,488	8,120	17,011	6,376	8,473	12.3
1972	52,351	2,634	10,854	8,413	16,424	5,972	8,055	12.3
1971	52,357	2,933	11,703	8,264	16,008	5,798	7,653	12.2
1970	51,784	3,031	11,925	8,355	15,571	5,580	7,321	12.2
1969	51,031	3,095	12,182	8,398	15,177	5,263	6,917	12.1
1968	50,510	3,261	12,407	8,564	14,613	4,945	6,721	12.1
1967	49,756	3,417	12,736	8,463	14,015	4,755	6,372	12.0
1966	49,410	3,614	12,992	8,611	13,672	4,342	6,180	11.8
1965	49,242	3,774	13,308	8,529	13,334	4,370	5,923	11.7
1964	48,975	3,959	13,467	8,537	12,902	4,394	5,714	11.5
1962	48,283	4,213	13,927	8,399	11,932	4,315	5,497	11.1
1960	47,997	4,522	15,562	8,988	10,175	4,127	4,626	10.3
1959	47,041	4,257	14,039	8,326	10,870	3,801	4,765	10.7
1957	46,208	4,610	14,634	8,003	10,230	3,347	4,359	10.3
1952	42,368	4,396	14,876	7,048	8,760	3,164	3,480	9.7
1950	42,627	5,074	15,852	6,974	7,511	2,888	3,008	9.0
1947	40,483	4,615	16,086	6,535	7,353	2,625	2,478	8.9
1940	37,463	5,550	17,639	5,333	4,507	1,824	2,021	8.6
Female								
2011	104,323	1,355	3,806	7,320	31,541	28,930	31,372	...
2010	103,603	1,336	3,904	7,555	31,774	28,350	30,683	...
2009	102,767	1,413	4,016	7,833	31,601	28,036	29,868	...
2008	101,835	1,289	4,090	7,663	31,692	27,747	29,354	...
2007	100,897	1,371	4,213	8,157	31,887	27,024	28,245	...
2006	99,651	1,479	4,395	8,215	31,518	27,234	26,810	...

[1]Civilian noninstitutionalized population, except where noted.
Total includes persons who did not report "Years of school completed."
[2]Data shown as "High school, 4 years" is now collected by the category "High School Graduate."
[3]Data shown as "College 1 to 3 years" is now collected by "Some College" and "Associate degree" categories. Data shown as "College 4 years or more" is now collected by the categories "Bachelor's degree," "Master's degree," "Doctorate degree," and "Professional degree." Due to the change in question format, median years of schooling cannot be derived after 1992.
[4]Beginning with data for 1992, a new question results in different categories than for earlier years.
[5]Starting in 2001, data are from the expanded Current Population Survey (CPS) sample and were created using population controls based on data from the 2000 Census.
... = Not available.

Table A-25. Years of School Completed by People 25 Years Old and Over, by Age and Sex, Selected Years, 1940–2011—*Continued*

(Numbers in thousands)

Year, sex, and age	Total[1]	Years of school completed						
		Elementary		High school[2]		College[3]		Median years[3,4]
		0 to 4 years	5 to 8 years	1 to 3 years	4 years	1 to 3 years	4 years or more	
Female—*(Continued)*								
2005	98,467	1,477	4,532	8,311	31,742	26,283	26,122	...
2004	97,319	1,363	4,580	8,233	31,921	25,808	25,413	...
2003	96,586	1,433	4,795	8,297	31,936	25,342	24,784	...
2002	95,146	1,445	4,926	8,484	31,509	24,915	23,868	...
2001[5]	94,293	1,392	4,845	8,664	31,316	25,161	22,915	...
2000	91,620	1,400	4,861	8,378	31,435	23,953	21,594	...
1999	90,837	1,404	5,004	8,707	31,566	23,133	21,021	...
1998	89,835	1,403	5,220	8,758	31,599	22,714	20,142	...
1997	88,961	1,387	5,450	8,999	31,360	22,442	19,323	...
1996	87,984	1,491	5,528	9,171	30,911	22,071	18,813	...
1995	86,975	1,476	5,642	8,874	31,072	22,317	17,594	...
1994	85,973	1,487	5,932	9,135	31,111	21,470	16,838	...
1993	85,181	1,672	6,154	9,246	31,823	19,930	16,357	...
1992[3,4]	84,248	1,712	6,263	9,587	32,086	18,889	15,709	...
1991	83,207	1,784	6,747	9,491	34,083	15,449	15,652	12.7
1990	82,116	1,829	7,200	9,462	33,693	14,806	15,126	12.7
1989	80,930	1,904	7,402	9,643	33,440	13,888	14,652	12.6
1988	79,724	1,862	7,700	9,599	33,303	13,741	13,519	12.6
1987	78,467	1,846	8,042	9,508	32,671	13,417	12,983	12.6
1986	77,102	1,916	8,226	9,612	32,078	12,874	12,399	12.6
1985	75,768	1,926	8,390	9,770	31,314	12,242	12,126	12.6
1984	74,444	1,939	8,571	9,596	31,083	11,603	11,651	12.6
1983	73,016	2,015	8,964	9,814	30,012	11,220	10,990	12.5
1982	71,762	2,045	9,245	10,046	29,677	10,673	10,076	12.5
1981	70,390	2,217	9,545	9,957	28,896	10,309	9,466	12.5
1980	69,020	2,178	9,800	10,040	27,854	9,786	9,362	12.4
1979	66,309	2,133	9,720	9,945	26,665	9,293	8,554	12.4
1978	65,097	2,214	10,114	10,353	25,761	8,721	7,934	12.4
1977	63,953	2,213	10,236	10,349	25,312	8,142	7,701	12.4
1976	62,946	2,230	10,449	10,281	25,109	7,779	7,098	12.3
1975	61,861	2,344	10,871	10,252	24,584	7,243	6,565	12.3
1974	60,838	2,469	11,015	10,308	23,972	6,910	6,165	12.3
1973	59,799	2,502	11,350	10,300	23,437	6,454	5,755	12.2
1972	58,782	2,490	11,649	10,442	22,746	6,145	5,309	12.2
1971	58,270	2,641	12,327	10,339	22,021	5,984	4,959	12.2
1970	57,527	2,716	12,595	10,327	21,563	5,584	4,743	12.1
1969	56,719	2,919	12,796	10,131	20,955	5,301	4,619	12.1
1968	55,959	2,987	13,060	10,160	19,991	5,309	4,450	12.1
1967	55,107	2,985	13,439	10,185	19,157	5,162	4,178	12.0
1966	54,467	3,090	13,488	10,246	18,719	4,892	4,032	12.0
1965	54,004	3,207	13,753	10,085	18,369	4,767	3,820	12.0
1964	53,447	3,333	14,086	9,881	17,825	4,686	3,629	11.8
1962	52,381	3,613	14,511	9,352	16,545	4,855	3,505	11.6
1960	51,468	3,781	15,656	10,151	14,267	4,620	2,991	10.9
1959	50,437	3,559	14,451	9,194	15,349	4,087	2,969	11.2
1957	49,422	3,951	14,682	8,948	14,602	3,638	2,813	10.9
1952	45,990	3,608	15,398	8,180	12,314	3,550	2,638	10.4
1950	44,857	4,417	15,824	7,843	10,114	3,358	2,264	9.6
1947	42,095	3,996	16,222	6,952	9,573	2,908	1,946	8.9
1940	37,313	4,554	16,773	5,849	6,044	2,251	1,386	8.7
25 to 34 YEARS OLD								
Both Sexes								
2011	41,584	318	1,140	3,098	11,250	12,046	13,731	...
2010	41,085	323	1,169	3,271	11,186	11,655	13,480	...
2009	40,520	321	1,226	3,202	11,351	11,409	13,010	...
2008	40,146	282	1,189	3,296	11,297	11,113	12,969	...
2007	39,868	380	1,283	3,462	11,408	10,961	12,375	...
2006	39,481	359	1,410	3,375	11,302	11,229	11,806	...
2005	39,310	414	1,375	3,422	11,269	10,865	11,965	...
2004	39,201	430	1,399	3,239	11,244	11,044	11,844	...
2003	39,242	370	1,370	3,336	11,392	10,986	11,791	...

[1]Civilian noninstitutionalized population, except where noted.
Total includes persons who did not report "Years of school completed."
[2]Data shown as "High school, 4 years" is now collected by the category "High School Graduate."
[3]Data shown as "College 1 to 3 years" is now collected by "Some College" and "Associate degree" categories. Data shown as "College 4 years or more" is now collected by the categories "Bachelor's degree," "Master's degree," "Doctorate degree," and "Professional degree." Due to the change in question format, median years of schooling cannot be derived after 1992.
[4]Beginning with data for 1992, a new question results in different categories than for earlier years.
[5]Starting in 2001, data are from the expanded Current Population Survey (CPS) sample and were created using population controls based on data from the 2000 Census.
... = Not available.

Table A-25. Years of School Completed by People 25 Years Old and Over, by Age and Sex, Selected Years, 1940–2011—*Continued*

(Numbers in thousands)

Year, sex, and age	Total[1]	Years of school completed						
		Elementary		High school[2]		College[3]		Median years[3,4]
		0 to 4 years	5 to 8 years	1 to 3 years	4 years	1 to 3 years	4 years or more	
Both Sexes—*(Continued)*								
2002	38,670	433	1,393	3,245	10,988	10,776	11,834	...
2001[5]	38,865	380	1,317	3,202	11,294	11,146	11,526	...
2000	37,786	287	1,135	3,052	11,546	10,700	11,066	...
1999	38,474	280	1,142	3,296	11,826	10,893	11,040	...
1998	39,354	319	1,207	3,228	12,569	11,220	10,811	...
1997	40,256	334	1,163	3,624	12,710	11,524	10,892	...
1996	40,919	418	1,169	3,780	13,087	11,624	10,841	...
1995	41,388	394	1,264	3,667	14,061	11,659	10,342	...
1994	41,946	367	1,297	4,057	14,483	11,913	9,829	...
1993	41,864	382	1,223	3,894	15,036	11,361	9,968	...
1992[3,4]	42,493	433	1,250	4,071	16,021	10,860	9,861	...
1991	42,905	465	1,322	4,178	17,503	9,283	10,153	12.9
1990	43,240	505	1,413	4,041	17,635	9,320	10,326	12.9
1989	43,240	446	1,352	4,013	17,901	9,072	10,454	12.9
1988	42,953	430	1,308	4,095	17,887	9,076	10,155	12.9
1987	42,635	390	1,360	3,995	17,539	9,157	10,196	12.9
1986	42,053	387	1,359	3,797	17,311	9,104	10,094	12.9
1985	40,858	362	1,328	3,703	16,748	8,980	9,737	12.9
1984	40,173	404	1,371	3,638	16,431	8,555	9,771	12.9
1983	39,342	376	1,324	3,664	15,804	8,567	9,605	12.9
1982	38,703	337	1,371	3,598	15,893	8,304	9,200	12.9
1981	37,828	337	1,428	3,665	15,419	8,198	8,782	12.9
1980	36,615	362	1,424	3,571	14,481	7,942	8,836	12.9
1979	34,053	370	1,381	3,452	13,338	7,415	8,096	12.9
1978	33,120	325	1,459	3,515	12,993	7,008	7,821	12.9
1977	32,284	269	1,383	3,715	12,845	6,398	7,676	12.8
1976	31,148	247	1,508	3,619	12,920	5,813	7,041	12.8
1975	30,092	313	1,644	3,743	12,544	5,403	6,443	12.7
1974	28,972	352	1,654	3,763	12,362	5,056	5,785	12.7
1973	27,793	333	1,850	3,915	12,194	4,454	5,047	12.6
1972	26,517	285	1,791	3,981	11,635	4,090	4,734	12.6
1971	25,545	327	2,011	3,986	11,232	3,822	4,169	12.6
1970	24,865	329	1,937	4,251	10,929	3,491	3,926	12.5
1969	24,072	359	2,086	4,140	10,592	3,202	3,693	12.5
1968	23,285	350	2,246	4,129	10,157	2,989	3,413	12.5
1967	22,388	319	2,293	4,017	9,645	2,946	3,169	12.5
1966	22,023	430	2,208	4,158	9,546	2,647	3,037	12.4
1965	21,980	543	2,437	4,058	9,500	2,561	2,880	12.4
1964	21,997	502	2,591	4,176	9,370	2,529	2,830	12.4
1962	22,130	597	2,936	4,371	8,815	2,552	2,859	12.4
1960	22,821	709	3,738	5,135	8,166	2,572	2,499	12.4
1959	22,922	761	3,348	4,741	8,979	2,398	2,480	12.3
1957	23,437	750	3,971	4,965	8,927	2,275	2,351	12.2
1952	23,138	844	4,362	4,898	8,620	2,220	2,052	12.2
1950	23,626	1,147	5,308	5,050	7,660	2,198	1,252	11.9
1947	22,627	1,015	5,523	4,997	7,630	1,908	1,378	11.9
1940	21,339	1,377	7,676	4,553	4,702	1,554	1,288	10.0
Male								
2011	20,985	190	657	1,791	6,444	5,750	6,151	...
2010	20,689	186	641	1,866	6,458	5,587	5,951	...
2009	20,440	184	695	1,806	6,495	5,508	5,752	...
2008	20,210	172	714	1,874	6,356	5,277	5,816	...
2007	20,024	246	757	1,930	6,361	5,137	5,593	...
2006	19,827	218	834	1,835	6,233	5,336	5,371	...
2005	19,677	241	769	1,827	6,216	5,198	5,426	...
2004	19,598	280	793	1,723	6,020	5,286	5,495	...
2003	19,564	216	771	1,831	6,028	5,252	5,466	...
2002	19,234	280	809	1,782	5,751	5,131	5,480	...
2001[5]	19,330	233	748	1,677	6,099	5,161	5,411	...
2000	18,563	155	593	1,637	5,989	4,870	5,318	...
1999	18,294	157	616	1,724	6,114	5,052	5,260	...

[1]Civilian noninstitutionalized population, except where noted.
Total includes persons who did not report "Years of school completed."
[2]Data shown as "High school, 4 years" is now collected by the category "High School Graduate."
[3]Data shown as "College 1 to 3 years" is now collected by "Some College" and "Associate degree" categories. Data shown as "College 4 years or more" is now collected by the categories "Bachelor's degree," "Master's degree," "Doctorate degree," and "Professional degree." Due to the change in question format, median years of schooling cannot be derived after 1992.
[4]Beginning with data for 1992, a new question results in different categories than for earlier years.
[5]Starting in 2001, data are from the expanded Current Population Survey (CPS) sample and were created using population controls based on data from the 2000 Census.
... = Not available.

Table A-25. Years of School Completed by People 25 Years Old and Over, by Age and Sex, Selected Years, 1940–2011—*Continued*

(Numbers in thousands)

Year, sex, and age	Total[1]	Years of school completed						
		Elementary		High school[2]		College[3]		Median years[3,4]
		0 to 4 years	5 to 8 years	1 to 3 years	4 years	1 to 3 years	4 years or more	
Male—*(Continued)*								
1998	19,526	190	654	1,735	6,592	5,233	5,125	...
1997	20,039	193	629	2,007	6,482	5,477	5,249	...
1996	20,390	225	601	2,055	6,701	5,536	5,274	...
1995	20,589	229	708	1,930	7,176	5,373	5,174	...
1994	20,873	230	716	2,134	7,408	5,510	4,873	...
1993	20,856	237	679	1,986	7,604	5,308	5,041	...
1992[3,4]	21,125	231	682	2,057	8,113	5,116	4,927	...
1991	21,319	270	694	2,095	8,810	4,441	5,009	12.9
1990	21,462	295	759	2,153	8,649	4,392	5,215	12.9
1989	21,461	251	698	2,129	8,659	4,391	5,335	12.9
1988	21,277	237	651	2,227	8,569	4,273	5,319	12.9
1987	21,142	223	698	2,030	8,544	4,384	5,263	12.9
1986	20,956	227	715	1,887	8,359	4,488	5,279	12.9
1985	20,184	194	700	1,823	7,955	4,433	5,080	12.9
1984	19,876	231	721	1,739	7,798	4,238	5,150	12.9
1983	19,438	213	659	1,724	7,351	4,284	5,207	13.0
1982	19,090	182	659	1,654	7,380	4,162	5,053	13.0
1981	18,625	176	733	1,679	6,991	4,185	4,863	13.0
1980	18,051	198	699	1,639	6,393	4,166	4,957	13.0
1979	16,719	197	695	1,476	5,852	3,862	4,637	13.0
1978	16,263	154	717	1,526	5,701	3,698	4,471	13.1
1977	15,863	134	672	1,625	5,634	3,403	4,396	13.0
1976	15,266	134	724	1,566	5,672	3,085	4,087	12.9
1975	14,776	177	815	1,605	5,508	2,915	3,757	12.9
1974	14,222	211	859	1,617	5,491	2,672	3,372	12.8
1973	13,638	204	966	1,760	5,363	2,416	2,927	12.7
1972	13,030	157	927	1,796	5,150	2,191	2,809	12.7
1971	12,596	170	1,092	1,771	5,049	2,005	2,506	12.6
1970	12,236	189	1,063	1,896	4,833	1,842	2,412	12.6
1969	11,788	204	1,121	1,849	4,652	1,719	2,241	12.6
1968	11,381	193	1,192	1,880	4,473	1,505	2,136	12.5
1967	10,876	170	1,209	1,814	4,187	1,522	1,973	12.5
1966	10,701	241	1,162	1,839	4,191	1,374	1,894	12.5
1965	10,693	325	1,240	1,802	4,188	1,316	1,822	12.5
1964	10,729	297	1,344	1,962	4,008	1,306	1,812	12.4
1962	10,762	334	1,569	2,008	3,700	1,309	1,842	12.4
1960	11,184	420	2,026	2,441	3,356	1,316	1,624	12.2
1959	11,226	416	1,822	2,238	3,682	1,256	1,658	12.3
1957	11,368	423	2,097	2,446	3,542	1,181	1,556	12.2
1952	10,936	502	2,202	2,268	3,458	1,118	1,268	12.1
1950	11,454	631	2,705	2,426	3,250	1,117	1,037	11.5
1947	10,894	544	2,665	2,494	3,337	993	738	11.7
1940	10,521	779	3,932	2,220	2,049	692	744	9.7
Female								
2011	20,599	128	483	1,307	4,806	6,296	7,580	...
2010	20,396	137	527	1,405	4,728	6,068	7,530	...
2009	20,079	137	531	1,395	4,856	5,901	7,258	...
2008	19,937	111	475	1,421	4,941	5,836	7,153	...
2007	19,843	134	527	1,532	5,047	5,824	6,781	...
2006	19,654	140	577	1,538	5,069	5,894	6,435	...
2005	19,633	173	607	1,594	5,053	5,667	6,539	...
2004	19,603	150	606	1,516	5,224	5,758	6,349	...
2003	19,679	153	598	1,503	5,364	5,734	6,325	...
2002	19,436	153	584	1,463	5,237	5,645	6,353	...
2001[5]	19,536	147	569	1,525	5,195	5,985	6,115	...
2000	19,222	130	542	1,415	5,557	5,831	5,750	...
1999	19,551	122	525	1,572	5,712	5,842	5,779	...
1998	19,828	130	553	1,493	5,977	5,986	5,688	...
1997	20,217	149	533	1,615	6,227	6,047	5,643	...
1996	20,528	195	569	1,734	6,386	6,090	5,568	...

[1]Civilian noninstitutionalized population, except where noted.
Total includes persons who did not report "Years of school completed."
[2]Data shown as "High school, 4 years" is now collected by the category "High School Graduate."
[3]Data shown as "College 1 to 3 years" is now collected by "Some College" and "Associate degree" categories. Data shown as "College 4 years or more" is now collected by the categories "Bachelor's degree," "Master's degree," "Doctorate degree," and "Professional degree." Due to the change in question format, median years of schooling cannot be derived after 1992.
[4]Beginning with data for 1992, a new question results in different categories than for earlier years.
[5]Starting in 2001, data are from the expanded Current Population Survey (CPS) sample and were created using population controls based on data from the 2000 Census.
... = Not available.

Table A-25. Years of School Completed by People 25 Years Old and Over, by Age and Sex, Selected Years, 1940–2011—*Continued*

(Numbers in thousands)

Year, sex, and age	Total[1]	Years of school completed						
		Elementary		High school[2]		College[3]		Median years[3,4]
		0 to 4 years	5 to 8 years	1 to 3 years	4 years	1 to 3 years	4 years or more	
Female—*(Continued)*								
1995	20,800	165	556	1,738	6,885	6,286	5,170	...
1994	21,073	138	581	1,923	7,075	6,404	4,953	...
1993	21,007	143	543	1,907	7,432	6,054	4,928	...
1992[3,4]	21,368	203	567	2,014	7,908	5,744	4,933	...
1991	21,586	195	629	2,085	8,693	4,841	5,143	12.9
1990	21,779	209	653	1,889	8,986	4,927	5,112	12.9
1989	21,777	195	654	1,885	9,242	4,681	5,119	12.9
1988	21,675	193	657	1,869	9,319	4,801	4,836	12.9
1987	21,494	168	662	1,965	8,995	4,772	4,932	12.9
1986	21,097	160	644	1,910	8,952	4,616	4,813	12.9
1985	20,673	168	627	1,880	8,794	4,547	4,657	12.9
1984	20,297	173	649	1,904	8,634	4,319	4,621	12.9
1983	19,903	161	665	1,941	8,452	4,285	4,398	12.9
1982	19,614	155	713	1,942	8,512	4,140	4,148	12.8
1981	19,203	161	698	1,986	8,427	4,013	3,918	12.8
1980	18,565	164	725	1,932	8,087	3,777	3,879	12.8
1979	17,334	173	685	1,977	7,486	3,553	3,460	12.8
1978	16,857	172	742	1,989	7,292	3,311	3,351	12.6
1977	16,421	136	710	2,088	7,212	2,995	3,280	12.7
1976	15,882	112	784	2,054	7,248	2,731	2,954	12.7
1975	15,316	135	833	2,139	7,037	2,489	2,686	12.6
1974	14,750	142	796	2,145	6,871	2,383	2,413	12.6
1973	14,155	129	884	2,154	6,830	2,037	2,121	12.6
1972	13,487	128	862	2,184	6,485	1,899	1,926	12.5
1971	12,950	156	919	2,212	6,183	1,816	1,663	12.5
1970	12,629	140	876	2,355	6,096	1,648	1,512	12.5
1969	12,285	155	965	2,291	5,941	1,481	1,451	12.4
1968	11,904	157	1,053	2,246	5,684	1,484	1,278	12.4
1967	11,512	149	1,084	2,200	5,458	1,426	1,195	12.4
1966	11,322	186	1,047	2,319	5,355	1,273	1,134	12.4
1965	11,284	218	1,197	2,256	5,310	1,244	1,060	12.4
1964	11,269	202	1,248	2,216	5,362	1,221	1,018	12.4
1962	11,368	263	1,367	2,363	5,115	1,243	1,017	12.3
1960	11,637	289	1,712	2,694	4,810	1,256	875	12.2
1959	11,696	345	1,526	2,503	5,297	1,142	822	12.3
1957	12,069	327	1,874	2,519	5,385	1,094	795	12.2
1952	12,202	342	2,160	2,630	5,162	1,102	784	12.2
1950	12,172	516	2,603	2,624	4,410	1,081	714	12.1
1947	11,733	471	2,858	2,503	4,293	915	640	12.0
1940	10,818	598	3,744	2,333	2,653	862	544	10.3
35 to 54 YEARS OLD								
Both Sexes								
2011	83,796	899	2,474	5,682	25,039	22,796	26,907	...
2010	84,834	852	2,549	5,937	26,145	22,911	26,440	...
2009	85,688	909	2,716	6,046	26,121	23,384	26,513	...
2008	86,067	905	2,742	5,882	26,108	23,504	26,926	...
2007	86,224	874	2,720	6,310	26,675	22,777	26,869	...
2006	85,918	965	2,769	6,274	26,636	23,317	25,958	...
2005	85,311	954	2,757	5,892	27,232	23,129	25,347	...
2004	84,642	963	2,582	5,938	26,649	23,093	25,417	...
2003	84,308	957	2,620	6,112	26,346	23,039	25,234	...
2002	83,829	941	2,636	5,874	26,740	23,148	24,489	...
2001[5]	83,286	886	2,612	5,899	26,356	23,271	24,262	...
2000	81,435	932	2,521	5,702	26,481	22,618	23,183	...
1999	79,976	872	2,535	6,052	26,367	21,561	22,589	...
1998	78,520	890	2,613	6,164	26,079	21,267	21,506	...
1997	76,973	867	2,686	6,045	26,054	20,684	20,635	...
1996	74,661	968	2,710	5,803	24,924	20,105	20,152	...
1995	73,028	927	2,561	5,664	24,070	19,926	19,878	...
1994	71,049	987	2,680	5,415	23,804	19,210	18,956	...

[1]Civilian noninstitutionalized population, except where noted.
Total includes persons who did not report "Years of school completed."
[2]Data shown as "High school, 4 years" is now collected by the category "High School Graduate."
[3]Data shown as "College 1 to 3 years" is now collected by "Some College" and "Associate degree" categories. Data shown as "College 4 years or more" is now collected by the categories "Bachelor's degree," "Master's degree," "Doctorate degree," and "Professional degree." Due to the change in question format, median years of schooling cannot be derived after 1992.
[4]Beginning with data for 1992, a new question results in different categories than for earlier years.
[5]Starting in 2001, data are from the expanded Current Population Survey (CPS) sample and were created using population controls based on data from the 2000 Census.
... = Not available.

Table A-25. Years of School Completed by People 25 Years Old and Over, by Age and Sex, Selected Years, 1940–2011—*Continued*

(Numbers in thousands)

Year, sex, and age	Total[1]	Years of school completed						
		Elementary		High school[2]		College[3]		Median years[3,4]
		0 to 4 years	5 to 8 years	1 to 3 years	4 years	1 to 3 years	4 years or more	
Both Sexes—*(Continued)*								
1993	68,845	942	2,486	5,538	23,927	17,984	17,970	...
1992[3,4]	66,594	899	2,608	5,845	23,442	16,658	17,144	...
1991	64,351	995	3,057	5,522	24,815	13,348	16,614	12.9
1990	62,499	980	3,104	5,529	24,434	12,553	15,899	12.9
1989	60,494	999	3,315	5,800	23,334	11,627	15,417	12.9
1988	58,555	958	3,272	5,889	23,049	11,017	14,369	12.8
1987	56,650	842	3,398	5,656	22,820	10,523	13,409	12.8
1986	55,170	896	3,614	5,769	22,151	10,110	12,629	12.8
1985	53,697	899	3,639	5,978	21,600	9,217	12,363	12.8
1984	52,297	893	3,754	6,158	21,290	8,702	11,500	12.7
1983	50,956	973	4,044	6,313	20,788	8,045	10,795	12.7
1982	49,722	963	4,320	6,657	20,445	7,580	9,756	12.6
1981	48,680	1,038	4,531	6,773	20,032	7,115	9,181	12.6
1980	48,124	1,034	4,676	7,063	19,584	6,943	8,822	12.6
1979	47,437	1,030	4,895	7,132	19,488	6,655	8,237	12.5
1978	46,921	1,107	5,262	7,590	19,012	6,286	7,667	12.5
1977	46,409	1,192	5,445	7,781	18,781	6,013	7,196	12.5
1976	46,271	1,245	5,729	7,671	18,893	5,957	6,776	12.5
1975	46,193	1,296	5,942	7,765	19,010	5,673	6,506	12.4
1974	46,217	1,293	6,244	7,896	19,038	5,375	6,372	12.4
1973	45,910	1,344	6,519	8,001	18,651	5,318	6,076	12.4
1972	45,956	1,367	7,004	8,521	18,400	5,074	5,589	12.3
1971	46,294	1,439	7,588	8,393	18,334	5,082	5,460	12.3
1970	46,319	1,461	7,935	8,555	18,200	4,875	5,294	12.3
1969	46,255	1,644	8,313	8,586	17,773	4,749	5,190	12.3
1968	46,396	1,654	8,698	8,838	17,362	4,642	5,200	12.2
1967	46,321	1,771	9,036	9,138	16,906	4,525	4,947	12.2
1966	46,313	1,837	9,528	9,309	16,605	4,230	4,805	12.1
1965	46,296	1,827	9,812	9,266	16,359	4,384	4,647	12.1
1964	46,089	1,905	10,259	9,289	15,760	4,397	4,482	12.1
1962	45,287	2,181	10,795	8,938	14,668	4,452	4,253	12.0
1960	44,742	2,424	12,536	9,502	12,517	4,123	3,639	11.3
1959	43,989	2,303	11,657	8,719	13,244	3,715	3,709	11.8
1957	42,645	2,658	12,349	8,384	12,041	3,248	3,360	11.3
1952	39,014	2,606	13,274	7,348	9,374	3,148	2,802	10.5
1950	38,432	3,404	14,420	6,976	7,262	2,878	2,516	9.7
1947	36,717	3,203	15,184	6,311	6,715	2,622	2,221	9.0
1940	33,845	4,549	16,270	4,972	4,217	1,836	1,540	8.6
Male								
2011	41,209	447	1,292	3,027	13,250	10,339	12,854	...
2010	41,858	446	1,367	3,227	13,824	10,311	12,682	...
2009	42,263	500	1,458	3,278	13,644	10,670	12,713	...
2008	42,419	507	1,490	3,228	13,625	10,711	12,858	...
2007	42,476	491	1,433	3,480	13,737	10,359	12,976	...
2006	42,344	549	1,472	3,356	13,660	10,608	12,701	...
2005	42,024	547	1,476	3,063	14,017	10,429	12,491	...
2004	41,612	577	1,323	3,157	13,238	10,636	12,682	...
2003	41,340	538	1,372	3,282	12,903	10,622	12,622	...
2002	41,154	513	1,333	3,063	13,133	10,739	12,373	...
2001[5]	40,858	488	1,368	2,974	12,784	10,827	12,417	...
2000	40,024	479	1,288	2,845	12,845	10,716	11,854	...
1999	39,300	470	1,290	3,101	12,544	10,233	11,664	...
1998	38,654	486	1,333	3,284	12,239	10,098	11,214	...
1997	37,912	486	1,370	3,143	12,326	9,713	10,870	...
1996	36,596	520	1,319	2,877	11,749	9,514	10,526	...
1995	35,994	529	1,368	2,781	11,223	9,305	10,784	...
1994	34,998	545	1,383	2,621	11,009	9,073	10,369	...
1993	33,751	478	1,316	2,660	10,983	8,624	9,687	...
1992[3,4]	32,619	472	1,368	2,750	10,670	7,968	9,389	...
1991	31,460	530	1,624	2,612	11,092	6,430	9,169	13.0
1990	30,623	527	1,658	2,573	10,790	6,169	8,905	13.0
1989	29,597	504	1,762	2,628	10,235	5,719	8,749	13.0

[1]Civilian noninstitutionalized population, except where noted.
Total includes persons who did not report "Years of school completed."
[2]Data shown as "High school, 4 years" is now collected by the category "High School Graduate."
[3]Data shown as "College 1 to 3 years" is now collected by "Some College" and "Associate degree" categories. Data shown as "College 4 years or more" is now collected by the categories "Bachelor's degree," "Master's degree," "Doctorate degree," and "Professional degree." Due to the change in question format, median years of schooling cannot be derived after 1992.
[4]Beginning with data for 1992, a new question results in different categories than for earlier years.
[5]Starting in 2001, data are from the expanded Current Population Survey (CPS) sample and were created using population controls based on data from the 2000 Census.
... = Not available.

Table A-25. Years of School Completed by People 25 Years Old and Over, by Age and Sex, Selected Years, 1940–2011—*Continued*

(Numbers in thousands)

Year, sex, and age	Total[1]	Years of school completed						
		Elementary		High school[2]		College[3]		Median years[3,4]
		0 to 4 years	5 to 8 years	1 to 3 years	4 years	1 to 3 years	4 years or more	
Male—*(Continued)*								
1988	28,645	498	1,725	2,654	10,100	5,327	8,340	12.9
1987	27,680	412	1,801	2,617	9,781	5,173	7,895	12.9
1986	26,925	475	1,919	2,699	9,393	5,013	7,426	12.9
1985	26,181	501	1,928	2,726	9,210	4,502	7,314	12.9
1984	25,460	506	2,014	2,831	8,926	4,257	6,929	12.8
1983	24,796	548	2,108	2,862	8,795	3,884	6,601	12.8
1982	24,164	530	2,302	2,989	8,609	3,757	5,977	12.7
1981	23,646	572	2,425	3,112	8,431	3,519	5,588	12.7
1980	23,373	590	2,492	3,202	8,278	3,442	5,370	12.7
1979	22,976	545	2,612	3,194	8,232	3,306	5,090	12.6
1978	22,719	609	2,779	3,377	8,001	3,136	4,817	12.6
1977	22,445	661	2,889	3,554	7,822	3,000	4,520	12.5
1976	22,403	730	3,004	3,473	7,904	2,969	4,323	12.5
1975	22,358	763	3,100	3,510	7,952	2,879	4,153	12.5
1974	22,367	733	3,286	3,532	8,004	2,730	4,081	12.6
1973	22,166	716	3,413	3,586	7,836	2,714	3,901	12.4
1972	22,200	749	3,674	3,917	7,663	2,564	3,631	12.4
1971	22,474	849	3,985	3,823	7,674	2,578	3,567	12.3
1970	22,475	834	4,208	3,876	7,612	2,555	3,390	12.3
1969	22,420	889	4,359	4,012	7,427	2,456	3,277	12.3
1968	22,521	931	4,487	4,160	7,324	2,364	3,257	12.2
1967	22,482	1,000	4,700	4,270	7,143	2,244	3,128	12.2
1966	22,508	1,085	4,886	4,455	6,990	2,029	3,063	12.1
1965	22,534	1,081	5,076	4,462	6,815	2,161	2,937	12.1
1964	22,457	1,158	5,226	4,416	6,657	2,212	2,789	12.2
1962	22,081	1,235	5,545	4,359	6,202	2,142	2,598	11.9
1960	21,919	1,397	6,415	4,579	5,364	1,957	2,206	11.1
1959	21,511	1,350	5,781	4,329	5,604	1,827	2,250	11.5
1957	20,873	1,491	6,293	3,987	5,195	1,558	1,972	11.0
1952	18,888	1,466	6,512	3,462	4,040	1,518	1,576	10.3
1950	18,896	1,834	7,338	3,339	3,151	1,271	1,403	9.6
1947	18,165	1,678	7,765	3,102	2,907	1,168	1,258	8.6
1940	17,127	2,480	8,458	2,388	1,798	819	917	8.5
Female								
2011	42,587	452	1,183	2,654	11,789	12,457	14,053	...
2010	42,976	406	1,181	2,710	12,321	12,600	13,758	...
2009	43,424	409	1,258	2,768	12,476	12,713	13,800	...
2008	43,648	398	1,253	2,654	12,483	12,792	14,067	...
2007	43,748	382	1,288	2,830	12,938	12,419	13,892	...
2006	43,573	417	1,298	2,915	12,976	12,710	13,255	...
2005	43,287	407	1,280	2,829	13,215	12,700	12,856	...
2004	43,030	386	1,259	2,781	13,411	12,458	12,736	...
2003	42,968	419	1,248	2,830	13,443	12,417	12,611	...
2002	42,675	428	1,303	2,811	13,607	12,410	12,116	...
2001[5]	42,428	398	1,244	2,926	13,572	12,444	11,844	...
2000	41,411	452	1,235	2,858	13,635	11,905	11,330	...
1999	40,676	402	1,248	2,950	13,825	11,326	10,925	...
1998	39,866	403	1,279	2,879	13,841	11,168	10,293	...
1997	39,061	381	1,319	2,902	13,726	10,969	9,766	...
1996	38,065	449	1,301	2,924	13,174	10,592	9,623	...
1995	37,034	396	1,192	2,881	12,846	10,623	9,096	...
1994	36,051	443	1,298	2,792	12,795	10,140	8,587	...
1993	35,093	462	1,169	2,877	12,944	9,358	8,283	...
1992[3,4]	33,975	427	1,240	3,096	12,770	8,687	7,756	...
1991	32,891	464	1,431	2,910	13,723	6,919	7,443	12.8
1990	31,876	454	1,448	2,955	13,643	6,383	6,997	12.8
1989	30,898	498	1,552	3,171	13,099	5,908	6,669	12.8
1988	29,908	462	1,547	3,234	12,949	5,689	6,029	12.7
1987	28,969	430	1,598	3,039	13,038	5,349	5,513	12.7
1986	28,244	420	1,694	3,071	12,759	5,098	5,202	12.7
1985	27,516	398	1,710	3,252	12,391	4,715	5,049	12.7

[1]Civilian noninstitutionalized population, except where noted.
Total includes persons who did not report "Years of school completed."
[2]Data shown as "High school, 4 years" is now collected by the category "High School Graduate."
[3]Data shown as "College 1 to 3 years" is now collected by "Some College" and "Associate degree" categories. Data shown as "College 4 years or more" is now collected by the categories "Bachelor's degree," "Master's degree," "Doctorate degree," and "Professional degree." Due to the change in question format, median years of schooling cannot be derived after 1992.
[4]Beginning with data for 1992, a new question results in different categories than for earlier years.
[5]Starting in 2001, data are from the expanded Current Population Survey (CPS) sample and were created using population controls based on data from the 2000 Census.
... = Not available.

Table A-25. Years of School Completed by People 25 Years Old and Over, by Age and Sex, Selected Years, 1940–2011—*Continued*

(Numbers in thousands)

Year, sex, and age	Total[1]	Years of school completed						
		Elementary		High school[2]		College[3]		Median years[3,4]
		0 to 4 years	5 to 8 years	1 to 3 years	4 years	1 to 3 years	4 years or more	
Female—*(Continued)*								
1984	26,838	389	1,740	3,331	12,364	4,444	4,570	12.6
1983	26,161	427	1,935	3,450	11,993	4,161	4,193	12.6
1982	25,555	433	2,017	3,666	11,833	3,827	3,778	12.6
1981	25,034	467	2,105	3,661	11,599	3,605	3,595	12.5
1980	24,751	444	2,186	3,862	11,307	3,501	3,452	12.5
1979	24,461	486	2,282	3,935	11,258	3,353	3,147	12.5
1978	24,202	497	2,483	4,212	11,012	3,149	2,849	12.5
1977	23,964	534	2,557	4,227	10,959	3,014	2,678	12.4
1976	23,868	517	2,721	4,198	10,989	2,988	2,455	12.4
1975	23,835	533	2,842	4,256	11,058	2,793	2,352	12.4
1974	23,850	559	2,956	4,364	11,033	2,647	2,290	12.4
1973	23,744	628	3,106	4,415	10,815	2,603	2,174	12.3
1972	23,756	618	3,330	4,604	10,736	2,509	1,958	12.3
1971	23,821	590	3,604	4,570	10,660	2,505	1,894	12.3
1970	23,845	629	3,728	4,679	10,588	2,318	1,903	12.3
1969	23,834	755	3,953	4,575	10,349	2,293	1,913	12.3
1968	23,874	725	4,212	4,676	10,038	2,281	1,943	12.2
1967	23,839	773	4,334	4,868	9,762	2,282	1,819	12.2
1966	23,806	752	4,644	4,853	9,615	2,200	1,741	12.2
1965	23,765	746	4,735	4,803	9,545	2,223	1,712	12.2
1964	23,632	748	5,033	4,871	9,103	2,183	1,691	12.1
1962	23,206	946	5,250	4,579	8,466	2,310	1,655	12.1
1960	22,823	1,027	6,121	4,923	7,153	2,166	1,433	11.6
1959	22,478	953	5,876	4,390	7,640	1,888	1,459	12.0
1957	21,772	1,167	6,056	4,397	6,846	1,690	1,388	11.5
1952	20,126	1,140	6,762	3,886	5,334	1,630	1,226	10.7
1950	19,536	1,570	7,082	3,637	4,111	1,607	1,113	9.7
1947	18,552	1,525	7,419	3,209	3,808	1,454	963	9.3
1940	16,718	2,070	7,812	2,584	2,419	1,017	623	8.7
55 YEARS OLD AND OVER								
Both Sexes								
2011	76,163	1,372	4,073	5,983	25,622	18,408	20,705	...
2010	74,008	1,440	4,118	6,051	25,125	17,354	19,920	...
2009	72,077	1,555	4,101	6,338	24,154	16,877	19,051	...
2008	70,092	1,411	4,294	6,338	23,779	16,378	17,892	...
2007	68,226	1,576	4,458	6,680	23,408	15,505	16,599	...
2006	66,485	1,628	4,610	6,508	22,961	14,824	15,956	...
2005	64,745	1,614	4,803	6,784	22,392	14,083	15,069	...
2004	63,034	1,465	4,907	6,821	21,918	13,434	14,488	...
2003	61,633	1,589	5,372	6,876	21,554	12,884	13,358	...
2002	59,644	1,528	5,639	7,258	20,728	12,117	12,374	...
2001[5]	58,238	1,544	5,589	7,178	20,622	11,864	11,440	...
2000	56,008	1,524	5,780	6,921	20,059	11,126	10,598	...
1999	55,303	1,589	5,978	7,096	19,742	10,722	10,174	...
1998	54,337	1,624	6,126	7,385	19,526	10,022	9,654	...
1997	53,352	1,628	6,622	7,543	18,823	9,565	9,169	...
1996	52,742	1,642	6,716	7,520	18,549	9,642	8,677	...
1995	52,022	1,755	7,048	7,232	18,320	9,662	8,005	...
1994	51,516	1,802	7,382	7,454	18,228	8,890	7,761	...
1993	52,117	2,058	8,038	7,637	18,626	8,106	7,652	...
1992[3,4]	51,740	2,118	8,133	7,756	18,397	8,005	7,332	...
1991	51,439	2,341	8,668	7,675	18,954	6,540	7,258	12.6
1990	50,798	2,349	9,239	7,893	18,050	6,202	7,064	12.3
1989	50,421	2,412	9,395	7,907	18,102	5,914	6,693	12.3
1988	50,128	2,325	9,969	7,860	18,004	5,705	6,263	12.3
1987	49,858	2,408	10,544	7,766	17,310	5,799	6,033	12.2
1986	49,383	2,611	10,699	7,917	16,876	5,515	5,767	12.2
1985	48,969	2,612	11,052	7,872	16,516	5,208	5,708	12.2
1984	48,324	2,584	11,131	7,636	16,353	5,026	5,593	12.2
1983	47,723	2,769	11,348	7,703	15,470	4,915	5,514	12.1

[1]Civilian noninstitutionalized population, except where noted.
Total includes persons who did not report "Years of school completed."
[2]Data shown as "High school, 4 years" is now collected by the category "High School Graduate."
[3]Data shown as "College 1 to 3 years" is now collected by "Some College" and "Associate degree" categories. Data shown as "College 4 years or more" is now collected by the categories "Bachelor's degree," "Master's degree," "Doctorate degree," and "Professional degree." Due to the change in question format, median years of schooling cannot be derived after 1992.
[4]Beginning with data for 1992, a new question results in different categories than for earlier years.
[5]Starting in 2001, data are from the expanded Current Population Survey (CPS) sample and were created using population controls based on data from the 2000 Census.
... = Not available.

Table A-25. Years of School Completed by People 25 Years Old and Over, by Age and Sex, Selected Years, 1940–2011—*Continued*

(Numbers in thousands)

Year, sex, and age	Total[1]	Years of school completed						
		Elementary		High school[2]		College[3]		Median years[3,4]
		0 to 4 years	5 to 8 years	1 to 3 years	4 years	1 to 3 years	4 years or more	
Both Sexes—*(Continued)*								
1982	47,102	2,818	11,541	7,751	15,091	4,807	5,095	12.1
1981	46,391	2,983	11,909	7,600	14,464	4,721	4,711	12.0
1980	45,670	2,994	12,326	7,451	13,869	4,494	4,535	12.0
1979	43,806	2,924	12,230	6,999	13,088	4,321	4,245	12.0
1978	42,977	3,013	12,593	7,069	12,376	4,086	3,843	11.6
1977	42,176	3,047	12,740	6,823	11,977	3,835	3,754	11.3
1976	41,429	3,107	12,674	6,915	11,346	3,709	3,677	11.1
1975	40,613	3,303	13,045	6,730	10,798	3,442	3,295	10.8
1974	39,817	3,461	13,302	6,615	10,060	3,233	3,145	10.4
1973	39,163	3,424	13,467	6,504	9,604	3,060	3,105	10.2
1972	38,659	3,471	13,706	6,351	9,136	2,952	3,042	10.0
1971	38,787	3,808	14,430	6,225	8,463	2,878	2,982	9.6
1970	38,126	3,957	14,647	5,877	8,005	2,797	2,843	9.2
1969	37,424	4,012	14,576	5,801	7,768	2,615	2,653	9.1
1968	36,789	4,244	14,522	5,760	7,085	2,624	2,558	8.9
1967	36,155	4,310	14,849	5,495	6,622	2,443	2,434	8.7
1966	35,540	4,438	14,742	5,392	6,240	2,358	2,370	8.6
1965	34,969	4,612	14,814	5,293	5,844	2,194	2,215	8.5
1964	34,335	4,888	14,701	4,954	5,598	2,159	2,033	8.3
1962	33,247	5,048	14,707	4,442	4,994	2,166	1,890	8.1
1960	31,902	5,169	14,944	4,503	3,757	2,051	1,479	8.5
1959	30,567	4,752	13,485	4,060	3,996	1,775	1,545	8.1
1957	29,548	5,153	12,996	3,602	3,864	1,462	1,461	8.0
1952	26,206	4,554	12,638	2,982	3,080	1,346	1,264	7.7
1950	25,427	4,940	11,947	2,791	2,704	1,170	1,005	8.3
1947	23,234	4,393	11,601	2,179	2,581	1,003	825	7.5
1940	19,592	4,178	10,467	1,656	1,633	685	579	8.2
Male								
2011	35,027	597	1,934	2,625	10,676	8,230	10,966	...
2010	33,778	647	1,923	2,611	10,399	7,672	10,525	...
2009	32,814	689	1,874	2,669	9,886	7,456	10,241	...
2008	31,841	631	1,932	2,751	9,510	7,259	9,759	...
2007	30,920	721	2,060	2,884	9,505	6,723	9,026	...
2006	30,060	705	2,090	2,784	9,488	6,193	8,837	...
2005	29,198	717	2,157	2,896	8,918	6,167	8,341	...
2004	28,347	639	2,192	2,885	8,631	5,841	8,159	...
2003	27,694	729	2,423	2,912	8,425	5,694	7,510	...
2002	26,608	664	2,601	3,048	8,063	5,257	6,975	...
2001[5]	25,908	697	2,558	2,964	8,073	5,131	6,485	...
2000	25,023	706	2,696	2,817	7,816	4,906	6,079	...
1999	24,694	712	2,746	2,911	7,712	4,756	5,856	...
1998	24,197	755	2,740	3,000	7,745	4,461	5,496	...
1997	23,668	773	3,026	3,060	7,417	4,139	5,255	...
1996	23,352	795	3,058	2,998	7,198	4,254	5,055	...
1995	22,881	839	3,153	2,980	6,980	4,254	4,675	...
1994	22,669	894	3,327	3,037	6,987	3,962	4,462	...
1993	23,038	992	3,595	3,174	7,178	3,587	4,508	...
1992[3,4]	22,836	1,033	3,676	3,277	6,991	3,549	4,312	...
1991	22,708	1,217	3,980	3,183	7,287	2,850	4,193	12.4
1990	22,337	1,182	4,141	3,274	6,986	2,707	4,046	12.4
1989	22,167	1,202	4,198	3,317	7,003	2,616	3,829	12.3
1988	21,989	1,117	4,471	3,366	6,968	2,455	3,609	12.3
1987	21,855	1,160	4,762	3,261	6,673	2,504	3,496	12.3
1986	21,622	1,275	4,813	3,286	6,509	2,355	3,385	12.2
1985	21,391	1,252	5,001	3,234	6,387	2,229	3,289	12.2
1984	21,014	1,209	4,951	3,270	6,265	2,185	3,132	12.2
1983	20,769	1,343	4,986	3,282	5,906	2,141	3,117	12.1
1982	20,508	1,362	5,026	3,313	5,759	2,102	2,946	12.1

[1]Civilian noninstitutionalized population, except where noted.
Total includes persons who did not report "Years of school completed."
[2]Data shown as "High school, 4 years" is now collected by the category "High School Graduate."
[3]Data shown as "College 1 to 3 years" is now collected by "Some College" and "Associate degree" categories. Data shown as "College 4 years or more" is now collected by the categories "Bachelor's degree," "Master's degree," "Doctorate degree," and "Professional degree." Due to the change in question format, median years of schooling cannot be derived after 1992.
[4]Beginning with data for 1992, a new question results in different categories than for earlier years.
[5]Starting in 2001, data are from the expanded Current Population Survey (CPS) sample and were created using population controls based on data from the 2000 Census.
... = Not available.

Table A-25. Years of School Completed by People 25 Years Old and Over, by Age and Sex, Selected Years, 1940–2011—*Continued*

(Numbers in thousands)

Year, sex, and age	Total[1]	Years of school completed						
		Elementary		High school[2]		College[3]		Median years[3,4]
		0 to 4 years	5 to 8 years	1 to 3 years	4 years	1 to 3 years	4 years or more	
Male—*(Continued)*								
1981	20,237	1,394	5,165	3,292	5,597	2,032	2,758	12.0
1980	19,967	1,424	5,436	3,206	5,409	1,986	2,506	11.9
1979	19,292	1,446	5,479	2,964	5,167	1,935	2,301	11.8
1978	18,939	1,467	5,701	2,919	4,919	1,824	2,110	11.4
1977	18,608	1,502	5,770	2,787	4,835	1,700	2,011	11.2
1976	18,233	1,507	5,733	2,884	4,473	1,646	1,989	11.0
1975	17,903	1,628	5,845	2,871	4,308	1,480	1,768	10.5
1974	17,579	1,693	6,042	2,817	3,993	1,356	1,682	10.1
1973	17,263	1,678	6,111	2,774	3,811	1,245	1,645	9.9
1972	17,120	1,728	6,252	2,698	3,612	1,215	1,614	9.6
1971	17,288	1,913	6,629	2,668	3,285	1,214	1,579	9.1
1970	17,074	2,011	6,655	2,583	3,127	1,182	1,516	9.0
1969	16,822	2,003	6,701	2,536	3,099	1,086	1,397	8.8
1968	16,609	2,137	6,728	2,523	2,816	1,078	1,328	8.7
1967	16,398	2,247	6,827	2,379	2,685	989	1,271	8.5
1966	16,201	2,288	6,944	2,317	2,491	939	1,223	8.3
1965	16,015	2,368	6,992	2,265	2,331	893	1,164	8.2
1964	15,789	2,504	6,897	2,159	2,237	876	1,113	8.1
1962	15,440	2,644	6,813	2,032	2,030	864	1,057	8.0
1960	14,895	2,704	7,121	1,969	1,453	853	796	8.4
1959	14,304	2,491	6,436	1,759	1,584	718	857	7.9
1957	13,967	2,696	6,244	1,570	1,493	608	831	7.7
1952	12,544	2,428	6,162	1,318	1,262	528	636	7.5
1950	12,277	2,609	5,808	1,209	1,111	500	569	8.2
1947	11,424	2,393	5,656	939	1,109	464	482	7.3
1940	9,815	2,293	5,249	724	660	313	361	8.1
Female								
2011	41,136	775	2,140	3,358	14,946	10,178	9,739	...
2010	40,230	793	2,195	3,440	14,725	9,682	9,395	...
2009	39,263	867	2,228	3,669	14,268	9,421	8,810	...
2008	38,251	780	2,362	3,588	14,269	9,119	8,133	...
2007	37,306	855	2,398	3,796	13,902	8,781	7,573	...
2006	36,425	922	2,521	3,761	13,472	8,630	7,119	...
2005	35,547	897	2,645	3,887	13,474	7,916	6,728	...
2004	34,687	826	2,715	3,936	13,287	7,593	6,329	...
2003	33,939	860	2,949	3,964	13,129	7,190	5,848	...
2002	33,035	864	3,038	4,210	12,664	6,860	5,399	...
2001[5]	32,329	847	3,032	4,213	12,549	6,733	4,956	...
2000	30,985	817	3,085	4,105	12,243	6,218	4,517	...
1999	30,609	879	3,232	4,186	12,031	5,965	4,319	...
1998	30,140	868	3,386	4,386	11,780	5,560	4,160	...
1997	29,684	855	3,596	4,483	11,407	5,427	3,916	...
1996	29,390	848	3,659	4,523	11,350	5,387	3,623	...
1995	29,142	915	3,894	4,255	11,340	5,410	3,330	...
1994	28,848	909	4,054	4,419	11,242	4,926	3,298	...
1993	29,080	1,066	4,442	4,462	11,447	4,519	3,149	...
1992[3,4]	28,904	1,084	4,456	4,478	11,409	4,455	3,021	...
1991	28,729	1,125	4,687	4,495	11,667	3,690	3,066	12.3
1990	28,461	1,167	5,098	4,619	11,063	3,495	3,019	12.3
1989	28,255	1,211	5,195	4,587	11,099	3,300	2,863	12.3
1988	28,139	1,208	5,498	4,495	11,034	3,250	2,655	12.3
1987	28,004	1,248	5,782	4,504	10,637	3,294	2,539	12.2
1986	27,762	1,336	5,886	4,630	10,367	3,160	2,382	12.2
1985	27,578	1,360	6,052	4,638	10,129	2,979	2,420	12.2
1984	27,309	1,377	6,183	4,363	10,086	2,843	2,459	12.2
1983	26,954	1,428	6,364	4,423	9,567	2,774	2,398	12.1
1982	26,593	1,458	6,511	4,435	9,330	2,705	2,150	12.1
1981	26,152	1,589	6,742	4,308	8,868	2,690	1,954	12.0

[1]Civilian noninstitutionalized population, except where noted.
Total includes persons who did not report "Years of school completed."
[2]Data shown as "High school, 4 years" is now collected by the category "High School Graduate."
[3]Data shown as "College 1 to 3 years" is now collected by "Some College" and "Associate degree" categories. Data shown as "College 4 years or more" is now collected by the categories "Bachelor's degree," "Master's degree," "Doctorate degree," and "Professional degree." Due to the change in question format, median years of schooling cannot be derived after 1992.
[4]Beginning with data for 1992, a new question results in different categories than for earlier years.
[5]Starting in 2001, data are from the expanded Current Population Survey (CPS) sample and were created using population controls based on data from the 2000 Census.
... = Not available.

Table A-25. Years of School Completed by People 25 Years Old and Over, by Age and Sex, Selected Years, 1940–2011—*Continued*

(Numbers in thousands)

Year, sex, and age	Total[1]	Years of school completed						
		Elementary		High school[2]		College[3]		Median years[3,4]
		0 to 4 years	5 to 8 years	1 to 3 years	4 years	1 to 3 years	4 years or more	
Female—*(Continued)*								
1980	25,703	1,571	6,889	4,245	8,460	2,509	2,030	12.0
1979	24,514	1,474	6,750	4,034	7,920	2,389	1,944	12.0
1978	24,038	1,545	6,889	4,149	7,457	2,263	1,733	11.6
1977	23,568	1,546	6,972	4,034	7,141	2,135	1,742	11.0
1976	23,196	1,602	6,942	4,029	6,871	2,063	1,690	11.0
1975	22,710	1,675	7,198	3,858	6,490	1,962	1,527	10.9
1974	22,238	1,762	7,261	3,799	6,068	1,880	1,463	10.7
1973	21,900	1,746	7,359	3,729	5,790	1,814	1,461	10.5
1972	21,539	1,743	7,455	3,654	5,526	1,737	1,425	10.3
1971	21,500	1,896	7,805	3,556	5,179	1,665	1,402	9.9
1970	21,052	1,946	7,993	3,292	4,879	1,615	1,327	9.5
1969	20,601	2,009	7,878	3,264	4,669	1,526	1,255	9.4
1968	20,180	2,106	7,795	3,237	4,269	1,544	1,229	9.2
1967	19,756	2,063	8,021	3,117	3,937	1,454	1,164	8.9
1966	19,339	2,152	7,797	3,074	3,749	1,419	1,147	8.9
1965	18,955	2,243	7,821	3,026	3,514	1,300	1,048	8.7
1964	18,546	2,383	7,805	2,794	3,360	1,282	920	8.5
1962	17,807	2,404	7,894	2,410	2,964	1,302	833	8.3
1960	17,007	2,465	7,823	2,534	2,304	1,198	683	8.6
1959	16,263	2,261	7,049	2,301	2,412	1,057	688	8.3
1957	15,581	2,457	6,752	2,032	2,371	854	630	8.2
1952	13,662	2,126	6,476	1,664	1,818	818	628	7.9
1950	13,150	2,331	6,139	1,582	1,593	670	436	8.4
1947	11,810	2,000	5,945	1,240	1,472	539	343	7.6
1940	9,777	1,886	5,217	932	973	372	219	8.3

[1]Civilian noninstitutionalized population, except where noted.
Total includes persons who did not report "Years of school completed."
[2]Data shown as "High school, 4 years" is now collected by the category "High School Graduate."
[3]Data shown as "College 1 to 3 years" is now collected by "Some College" and "Associate degree" categories. Data shown as "College 4 years or more" is now collected by the categories "Bachelor's degree," "Master's degree," "Doctorate degree," and "Professional degree." Due to the change in question format, median years of schooling cannot be derived after 1992.
[4]Beginning with data for 1992, a new question results in different categories than for earlier years.

Table A-26. Percent of People 25 Years Old and Over Who Have Completed High School or College, by Race, Hispanic Origin, and Sex, Selected Years, 1940–2011

(Noninstitutionalized population)

Age, educational attainment level, and year	All races			White			Non-Hispanic White			Black[1]			Asian		
	Both sexes	Male	Female	Both sexes	Male	Female	Both sexes	Male	Female	Both sexes	Male	Female	Both sexes	Male	Female
25 YEARS OLD AND OVER															
Completed 4 Years of High School or More															
2011	87.6	87.1	88.0	88.1	87.4	88.6	92.4	92.0	92.8	84.5	83.8	85.0	88.6	90.4	87.1
2010	87.1	86.6	87.6	87.6	86.9	88.2	92.1	91.8	92.3	84.2	83.6	84.6	88.9	91.2	87.0
2009	86.7	86.2	87.1	87.1	86.5	87.7	91.6	91.4	91.9	84.1	84.0	84.1	88.2	90.4	86.2
2008	86.6	85.9	87.2	87.1	86.3	87.8	91.5	91.1	91.8	83.0	81.8	84.0	88.7	90.8	86.9
2007	85.7	85.0	86.4	86.2	85.3	87.1	90.6	90.2	91.0	82.3	81.9	82.6	87.8	89.8	85.9
2006	85.5	85.0	85.9	86.1	85.5	86.7	90.5	90.2	90.8	80.7	80.1	81.2	87.4	89.6	85.5
2005	85.2	84.9	85.5	85.8	85.2	86.2	90.1	89.9	90.3	81.1	81.0	81.2	87.6	90.4	85.2
2004	85.2	84.8	85.4	85.8	85.3	86.3	90.0	89.9	90.1	80.6	80.4	80.8	86.8	88.7	85.0
2003[3]	84.6	84.1	85.0	85.1	84.5	85.7	89.4	89.0	89.7	80.0	79.6	80.3	87.6	89.5	86.0
2002	84.1	83.8	84.4	84.8	84.3	85.2	88.7	88.5	88.9	78.7	78.5	78.9	...	...	...
2001[4]	84.1	84.1	84.2	84.8	84.4	85.1	88.6	88.6	88.6	78.8	79.2	78.5	...	...	...
2000	84.1	84.2	84.0	84.9	84.8	85.0	88.4	88.5	88.4	78.5	78.7	78.3	...	...	...
1999	83.4	83.4	83.4	84.3	84.2	84.3	87.7	87.7	87.7	77.0	76.7	77.2	...	...	...
1998	82.8	82.8	82.9	83.7	83.6	83.8	87.1	87.1	87.1	76.0	75.2	76.7	...	...	...
1997	82.1	82.0	82.2	83.0	82.9	83.2	86.3	86.3	86.3	74.9	73.5	76.0	...	...	...
1996	81.7	81.9	81.6	82.8	82.7	82.8	86.0	86.1	85.9	74.3	74.3	74.2	...	...	...
1995	81.7	81.7	81.6	83.0	83.0	83.0	85.9	86.0	85.8	73.8	73.4	74.1	...	...	...
1994	80.9	81.0	80.7	82.0	82.1	81.9	84.9	85.1	84.7	72.9	71.7	73.8	...	...	...
1993	80.2	80.5	80.0	81.5	81.8	81.3	84.1	84.5	83.8	70.4	69.6	71.1	...	...	...
1992[5]	79.4	79.7	79.2	80.9	81.1	80.7	...	...	...	67.7	67.0	68.2	...	...	...
1991	78.4	78.5	78.3	79.9	79.8	79.9	...	...	...	66.7	66.7	66.7	...	...	...
1990	77.6	77.7	77.5	79.1	79.1	79.0	...	...	...	66.2	65.8	66.5	...	...	...
1989	76.9	77.2	76.6	78.4	78.6	78.2	...	...	...	64.6	64.2	65.0	...	...	...
1988	76.2	76.4	76.0	77.7	77.7	77.6	...	...	...	63.5	63.7	63.4	...	...	...
1987	75.6	76.0	75.3	77.0	77.3	76.7	...	...	...	63.4	63.0	63.7	...	...	...
1986	74.7	75.1	74.4	76.2	76.5	75.9	...	...	...	62.3	61.5	63.0	...	...	...
1985	73.9	74.4	73.5	75.5	76.0	75.1	...	...	...	59.8	58.4	60.8	...	...	...
1984	73.3	73.7	73.0	75.0	75.4	74.6	...	...	...	58.5	57.1	59.7	...	...	...
1983	72.1	72.7	71.5	73.8	74.4	73.3	...	...	...	56.8	56.5	57.1	...	...	...
1982	71.0	71.7	70.3	72.8	73.4	72.3	...	...	...	54.9	55.7	54.3	...	...	...
1981	69.7	70.3	69.1	71.6	72.1	71.2	...	...	...	52.9	53.2	52.6	...	...	...
1980	68.6	69.2	68.1	70.5	71.0	70.1	...	...	...	51.2	51.1	51.3	...	...	...
1979	67.7	68.4	67.1	69.7	70.3	69.2	...	...	...	49.4	49.2	49.5	...	...	...
1978	65.9	66.8	65.2	67.9	68.6	67.2	...	...	...	47.6	47.9	47.3	...	...	...
1977	64.9	65.6	64.4	67.0	67.5	66.5	...	...	...	45.5	45.6	45.4	...	...	...
1976	64.1	64.7	63.5	66.1	66.7	65.5	...	...	...	43.8	42.3	45.0	...	...	...
1975	62.5	63.1	62.1	64.5	65.0	64.1	...	...	...	42.5	41.6	43.3	...	...	...
1974	61.2	61.6	60.9	63.3	63.6	63.0	...	...	...	40.8	39.9	41.5	...	...	...
1973	59.8	60.0	59.6	61.9	62.1	61.7	...	...	...	39.2	38.2	40.1	...	...	...
1972	58.2	58.2	58.2	60.4	60.3	60.5	...	...	...	36.6	35.7	37.2	...	...	...
1971	56.4	56.3	56.6	58.6	58.4	58.8	...	...	...	34.7	33.8	35.4	...	...	...
1970	55.2	55.0	55.4	57.4	57.2	57.6	...	...	...	33.7	32.4	34.8	...	...	...
1969	54.0	53.6	54.4	56.3	55.7	56.7	...	...	...	32.3	31.9	32.6	...	...	...
1968	52.6	52.0	53.2	54.9	54.3	55.5	...	...	...	30.1	28.9	31.0	...	...	...
1967	51.1	50.5	51.7	53.4	52.8	53.8	...	...	...	29.5	27.1	31.5	...	...	...
1966	49.9	49.0	50.8	52.2	51.3	53.0	...	...	...	27.8	25.8	29.5	...	...	...
1965	49.0	48.0	49.9	51.3	50.2	52.2	...	...	...	27.2	25.8	28.4	...	...	...
1964	48.0	47.0	48.9	50.3	49.3	51.2	...	...	...	25.7	23.7	27.4	...	...	...
1962	46.3	45.0	47.5	48.7	47.4	49.9	...	...	...	24.8	23.2	26.2	...	...	...
1959	43.7	42.2	45.2	46.1	44.5	47.7	...	...	...	20.7	19.6	21.6	...	...	...
1957	41.6	39.7	43.3	43.2	41.1	45.1	...	...	...	18.4	16.9	19.7	...	...	...
1952	38.8	36.9	40.5	...	...	...	...	...	...	15.0	14.0	15.7	...	...	...
1950	34.3	32.6	36.0	...	...	...	...	...	...	13.7	12.5	14.7	...	...	...
1947	33.1	31.4	34.7	35.0	33.2	36.7	...	...	...	13.6	12.7	14.5	...	...	...
1940	24.5	22.7	26.3	26.1	24.2	28.1	...	...	...	7.7	6.9	8.4	...	...	...

[1]Data include Black and other races from 1940 to 1962; from 1963 to 2003, data are for the Black population only.
[3]Starting in 2003, respondents could choose more than one race. The race data in this table from 2003 onward represent respondents who indicated only one race. Prior to 2003, Asians were grouped with Pacific Islanders.
[4]Starting in 2001, data are from the expanded Current Population Survey (CPS) sample and were calculated using population controls based on data from the 2000 Census.
[5]Beginning with data for 1992, a new question results in different categories than for earlier years. Data shown as "Completed 4 Years of High School or More" are now collected by the category "High School Graduate." Data shown as "Completed 4 Years of College or more" are now collected by the categories, Bachelor's degree; Master's degree; Doctorate degree; and Professional degree. Due to the change in question format, median years of schooling cannot be derived.
... = Not available.

Table A-26. Percent of People 25 Years Old and Over Who Have Completed High School or College, by Race, Hispanic Origin, and Sex, Selected Years, 1940–2011—*Continued*

(Noninstitutionalized population)

Age, educational attainment level, and year	Hispanic[2]			White alone or in combination			Non-Hispanic White alone or in combination			Black alone or in combination			Asian alone or in combination		
	Both sexes	Male	Female	Both sexes	Male	Female	Both sexes	Male	Female	Both sexes	Male	Female	Both sexes	Male	Female
25 YEARS OLD AND OVER															
Completed 4 Years of High School or More															
2011	64.3	63.6	65.1	88.0	87.4	88.6	92.4	92.0	92.7	84.6	83.9	85.1	88.9	90.6	87.4
2010	62.9	61.4	64.4	87.6	86.8	88.2	92.0	91.7	92.3	84.2	83.5	84.8	89.1	91.2	87.3
2009	61.9	60.6	63.3	87.1	86.4	87.7	91.6	91.4	91.8	84.1	83.9	84.2	88.3	90.6	86.4
2008	62.3	60.9	63.7	87.1	86.3	87.8	91.4	91.1	91.8	83.2	81.9	84.1	89.0	90.9	87.2
2007	60.3	58.2	62.5	86.2	85.3	87.0	90.6	90.2	91.0	82.4	82.0	82.6	87.8	89.2	86.5
2006	59.3	58.5	60.1	86.1	85.5	86.7	90.5	90.2	90.8	80.8	80.3	81.2	87.6	89.6	85.8
2005	58.5	57.9	59.1	85.7	85.2	86.2	90.1	89.9	90.3	81.3	81.2	81.3	87.9	90.5	85.6
2004	58.4	57.3	59.5	85.8	85.3	86.2	90.0	89.9	90.1	80.6	80.3	80.9	86.9	88.8	85.2
2003[3]	57.0	56.3	57.8	85.1	84.5	85.7	89.4	89.0	89.6	80.0	79.5	80.3	87.8	89.7	86.1
2002	57.0	56.1	57.9	...	...	...	...	...	...	...	...	...	...	...	...
2001[4]	56.8	55.5	58.0	...	...	...	...	...	...	...	...	...	...	...	...
2000	57.0	56.6	57.5	...	...	...	...	...	...	...	...	...	...	...	...
1999	56.1	56.0	56.3	...	...	...	...	...	...	...	...	...	...	...	...
1998	55.5	55.7	55.3	...	...	...	...	...	...	...	...	...	...	...	...
1997	54.7	54.9	54.6	...	...	...	...	...	...	...	...	...	...	...	...
1996	53.1	53.0	53.3	...	...	...	...	...	...	...	...	...	...	...	...
1995	53.4	52.9	53.8	...	...	...	...	...	...	...	...	...	...	...	...
1994	53.3	53.4	53.2	...	...	...	...	...	...	...	...	...	...	...	...
1993	53.1	52.9	53.2	...	...	...	...	...	...	...	...	...	...	...	...
1992[5]	52.6	53.7	51.5	...	...	...	...	...	...	...	...	...	...	...	...
1991	51.3	51.4	51.2	...	...	...	...	...	...	...	...	...	...	...	...
1990	50.8	50.3	51.3	...	...	...	...	...	...	...	...	...	...	...	...
1989	50.9	51.0	50.7	...	...	...	...	...	...	...	...	...	...	...	...
1988	51.0	52.0	50.0	...	...	...	...	...	...	...	...	...	...	...	...
1987	50.9	51.8	50.0	...	...	...	...	...	...	...	...	...	...	...	...
1986	48.5	49.2	47.8	...	...	...	...	...	...	...	...	...	...	...	...
1985	47.9	48.5	47.4	...	...	...	...	...	...	...	...	...	...	...	...
1984	47.1	48.6	45.7	...	...	...	...	...	...	...	...	...	...	...	...
1983	46.2	48.6	44.2	...	...	...	...	...	...	...	...	...	...	...	...
1982	45.9	48.1	44.1	...	...	...	...	...	...	...	...	...	...	...	...
1981	44.5	45.5	43.6	...	...	...	...	...	...	...	...	...	...	...	...
1980	45.3	46.4	44.1	...	...	...	...	...	...	...	...	...	...	...	...
1979	42.0	42.3	41.7	...	...	...	...	...	...	...	...	...	...	...	...
1978	40.8	42.2	39.6	...	...	...	...	...	...	...	...	...	...	...	...
1977	39.6	42.3	37.2	...	...	...	...	...	...	...	...	...	...	...	...
1976	39.3	41.4	37.3	...	...	...	...	...	...	...	...	...	...	...	...
1975	37.9	39.5	36.7	...	...	...	...	...	...	...	...	...	...	...	...
1974	36.5	38.3	34.9	...	...	...	...	...	...	...	...	...	...	...	...
1973	...	...	...	...	...	...	...	...	...	...	...	...	...	...	...
1972	...	...	...	...	...	...	...	...	...	...	...	...	...	...	...
1971	...	...	...	...	...	...	...	...	...	...	...	...	...	...	...
1970	...	...	...	...	...	...	...	...	...	...	...	...	...	...	...
1969	...	...	...	...	...	...	...	...	...	...	...	...	...	...	...
1968	...	...	...	...	...	...	...	...	...	...	...	...	...	...	...
1967	...	...	...	...	...	...	...	...	...	...	...	...	...	...	...
1966	...	...	...	...	...	...	...	...	...	...	...	...	...	...	...
1965	...	...	...	...	...	...	...	...	...	...	...	...	...	...	...
1964	...	...	...	...	...	...	...	...	...	...	...	...	...	...	...
1962	...	...	...	...	...	...	...	...	...	...	...	...	...	...	...
1959	...	...	...	...	...	...	...	...	...	...	...	...	...	...	...
1957	...	...	...	...	...	...	...	...	...	...	...	...	...	...	...
1952	...	...	...	...	...	...	...	...	...	...	...	...	...	...	...
1950	...	...	...	...	...	...	...	...	...	...	...	...	...	...	...
1947	...	...	...	...	...	...	...	...	...	...	...	...	...	...	...
1940	...	...	...	...	...	...	...	...	...	...	...	...	...	...	...

[2]May be of any race.

[3]Starting in 2003, respondents could choose more than one race. The race data in this table from 2003 onward represent respondents who indicated only one race. Prior to 2003, Asians were grouped with Pacific Islanders.

[4]Starting in 2001, data are from the expanded Current Population Survey (CPS) sample and were calculated using population controls based on data from the 2000 Census.

[5]Beginning with data for 1992, a new question results in different categories than for earlier years. Data shown as "Completed 4 Years of High School or More" are now collected by the category "High School Graduate." Data shown as "Completed 4 Years of College or more" are now collected by the categories, Bachelor's degree; Master's degree; Doctorate degree; and Professional degree. Due to the change in question format, median years of schooling cannot be derived.

... = Not available.

Table A-26. Percent of People 25 Years Old and Over Who Have Completed High School or College, by Race, Hispanic Origin, and Sex, Selected Years, 1940–2011—*Continued*

(Noninstitutionalized population)

Age, educational attainment level, and year	All races			White			Non-Hispanic White			Black[1]			Asian		
	Both sexes	Male	Female	Both sexes	Male	Female	Both sexes	Male	Female	Both sexes	Male	Female	Both sexes	Male	Female
25 YEARS OLD AND OVER— *(Continued)* **Completed 4 Years of College or More**															
2011	30.4	30.8	30.1	31.0	31.5	30.5	34.0	35.0	33.1	19.9	18.0	21.4	50.3	53.4	47.7
2010	29.9	30.3	29.6	30.3	30.8	29.9	33.2	34.2	32.4	19.8	17.7	21.4	52.4	55.6	49.5
2009	29.5	30.1	29.1	29.9	30.6	29.3	32.9	33.9	31.9	19.3	17.8	20.6	52.3	55.7	49.3
2008	29.4	30.1	28.8	29.8	30.5	29.1	32.6	33.8	31.5	19.6	18.7	20.4	52.6	55.8	49.8
2007	28.7	29.5	28.0	29.1	29.9	28.3	31.8	33.2	30.6	18.5	18.0	19.0	52.1	55.2	49.3
2006	28.0	29.2	26.9	28.4	29.7	27.1	31.0	32.8	29.3	18.5	17.2	19.4	49.7	52.5	47.1
2005	27.7	28.9	26.5	28.1	29.4	26.8	30.6	32.4	28.9	17.6	16.0	18.8	50.2	54.0	46.8
2004	27.7	29.4	26.1	28.2	30.0	26.4	30.6	32.9	28.4	17.6	16.6	18.5	49.4	53.7	45.6
2003[3]	27.2	28.9	25.7	27.6	29.4	25.9	30.0	32.3	27.9	17.3	16.7	17.8	49.8	53.9	46.1
2002	26.7	28.5	25.1	27.2	29.1	25.4	29.4	31.7	27.3	17.0	16.4	17.5	...	...	...
2001[4]	26.2	28.2	24.3	26.6	28.7	24.6	28.7	31.3	26.3	15.7	15.3	16.1	...	...	...
2000	25.6	27.8	23.6	26.1	28.5	23.9	28.1	30.8	25.5	16.5	16.3	16.7	...	...	...
1999	25.2	27.5	23.1	25.9	28.5	23.5	27.7	30.6	25.0	15.4	14.2	16.4	...	...	...
1998	24.4	26.5	22.4	25.0	27.3	22.8	26.6	29.3	24.1	14.7	13.9	15.4	...	...	...
1997	23.9	26.2	21.7	24.6	27.0	22.3	26.2	29.0	23.7	13.3	12.5	13.9	...	...	...
1996	23.6	26.0	21.4	24.3	26.9	21.8	25.9	28.8	23.2	13.6	12.4	14.6	...	...	...
1995	23.0	26.0	20.2	24.0	27.2	21.0	25.4	28.9	22.1	13.2	13.6	12.9	...	...	...
1994	22.2	25.1	19.6	22.9	26.1	20.0	24.3	27.8	21.1	12.9	12.8	13.0	...	...	...
1993	21.9	24.8	19.2	22.6	25.7	19.7	23.8	27.2	20.7	12.2	11.9	12.4	...	...	...
1992[5]	21.4	24.3	18.6	22.1	25.2	19.1	...	...	...	11.9	11.9	12.0	...	...	...
1991	21.4	24.3	18.8	22.2	25.4	19.3	...	...	...	11.5	11.4	11.6	...	...	...
1990	21.3	24.4	18.4	22.0	25.3	19.0	...	...	...	11.3	11.9	10.8	...	...	...
1989	21.1	24.5	18.1	21.8	25.4	18.5	...	...	...	11.8	11.7	11.9	...	...	...
1988	20.3	24.0	17.0	20.9	25.0	17.3	...	...	...	11.2	11.1	11.4	...	...	...
1987	19.9	23.6	16.5	20.5	24.5	16.9	...	...	...	10.7	11.0	10.4	...	...	...
1986	19.4	23.2	16.1	20.1	24.1	16.4	...	...	...	10.9	11.2	10.7	...	...	...
1985	19.4	23.1	16.0	20.0	24.0	16.3	...	...	...	11.1	11.2	11.0	...	...	...
1984	19.1	22.9	15.7	19.8	23.9	16.0	...	...	...	10.4	10.4	10.4	...	...	...
1983	18.8	23.0	15.1	19.5	24.0	15.4	...	...	...	9.5	10.0	9.2	...	...	...
1982	17.7	21.9	14.0	18.5	23.0	14.4	...	...	...	8.8	9.1	8.5	...	...	...
1981	17.1	21.1	13.4	17.8	22.2	13.8	...	...	...	8.2	8.2	8.2	...	...	...
1980	17.0	20.9	13.6	17.8	22.1	14.0	...	...	...	7.9	7.7	8.1	...	...	...
1979	16.4	20.4	12.9	17.2	21.4	13.3	...	...	...	7.9	8.3	7.5	...	...	...
1978	15.7	19.7	12.2	16.4	20.7	12.6	...	...	...	7.2	7.3	7.1	...	...	...
1977	15.4	19.2	12.0	16.1	20.2	12.4	...	...	...	7.2	7.0	7.4	...	...	...
1976	14.7	18.6	11.3	15.4	19.6	11.6	...	...	...	6.6	6.3	6.8	...	...	...
1975	13.9	17.6	10.6	14.5	18.4	11.0	...	...	...	6.4	6.7	6.2	...	...	...
1974	13.3	16.9	10.1	14.0	17.7	10.6	...	...	...	5.5	5.7	5.3	...	...	...
1973	12.6	16.0	9.6	13.1	16.8	9.9	...	...	...	6.0	5.9	6.0	...	...	...
1972	12.0	15.4	9.0	12.6	16.2	9.4	...	...	...	5.1	5.5	4.8	...	...	...
1971	11.4	14.6	8.5	12.0	15.5	8.9	...	...	...	4.5	4.7	4.3	...	...	...
1970	11.0	14.1	8.2	11.6	15.0	8.6	...	...	...	4.5	4.6	4.4	...	...	...
1969	10.7	13.6	8.1	11.2	14.3	8.5	...	...	...	4.6	4.8	4.5	...	...	...
1968	10.5	13.3	8.0	11.0	14.1	8.3	...	...	...	4.3	3.7	4.8	...	...	...
1967	10.1	12.8	7.6	10.6	13.6	7.9	...	...	...	4.0	3.4	4.4	...	...	...
1966	9.8	12.5	7.4	10.4	13.3	7.7	...	...	...	3.8	3.9	3.7	...	...	...
1965	9.4	12.0	7.1	9.9	12.7	7.3	...	...	...	4.7	4.9	4.5	...	...	...
1964	9.1	11.7	6.8	9.6	12.3	7.1	...	...	...	3.9	4.5	3.4	...	...	...
1962	8.9	11.4	6.7	9.5	12.2	7.0	...	...	...	4.0	3.9	4.0	...	...	...
1959	8.1	10.3	6.0	8.6	11.0	6.2	...	...	...	3.3	3.8	2.9	...	...	...
1957	7.6	9.6	5.8	8.0	10.1	6.0	...	...	...	2.9	2.7	3.0	...	...	...
1952	7.0	8.3	5.8	...	...	...	...	...	...	2.4	2.0	2.7	...	...	...
1950	6.2	7.3	5.2	...	...	...	...	...	...	2.3	2.1	2.4	...	...	...
1947	5.4	6.2	4.7	5.7	6.6	4.9	...	...	...	2.5	2.4	2.6	...	...	...
1940	4.6	5.5	3.8	4.9	5.9	4.0	...	...	...	1.3	1.4	1.2	...	...	...

[1]Data include Black and other races from 1940 to 1962; from 1963 to 2003, data are for the Black population only.
[3]Starting in 2003, respondents could choose more than one race. The race data in this table from 2003 onward represent respondents who indicated only one race. Prior to 2003, Asians were grouped with Pacific Islanders.
[4]Starting in 2001, data are from the expanded Current Population Survey (CPS) sample and were calculated using population controls based on data from the 2000 Census.
[5]Beginning with data for 1992, a new question results in different categories than for earlier years. Data shown as "Completed 4 Years of High School or More" are now collected by the category "High School Graduate." Data shown as "Completed 4 Years of College or more" are now collected by the categories, Bachelor's degree; Master's degree; Doctorate degree; and Professional degree. Due to the change in question format, median years of schooling cannot be derived.
... = Not available.

Table A-26. Percent of People 25 Years Old and Over Who Have Completed High School or College, by Race, Hispanic Origin, and Sex, Selected Years, 1940–2011—*Continued*

(Noninstitutionalized population)

Age, educational attainment level, and year	Hispanic[2]			White alone or in combination			Non-Hispanic White alone or in combination			Black alone or in combination			Asian alone or in combination		
	Both sexes	Male	Female	Both sexes	Male	Female	Both sexes	Male	Female	Both sexes	Male	Female	Both sexes	Male	Female
25 YEARS OLD AND OVER— *(Continued)*															
Completed 4 Years of College or More															
2011	14.1	13.1	15.2	30.9	31.4	30.5	33.9	34.9	33.1	20.1	18.2	21.6	49.9	52.8	47.3
2010	13.9	12.9	14.9	30.2	30.7	29.8	33.2	34.1	32.3	19.9	17.7	21.6	51.8	54.7	49.3
2009	13.2	12.5	14.0	29.8	30.4	29.3	32.8	33.8	31.8	19.4	17.8	20.7	51.8	54.8	49.2
2008	13.3	12.6	14.1	29.7	30.3	29.0	32.5	33.6	31.4	19.8	18.8	20.5	52.0	54.6	49.8
2007	12.7	11.8	13.7	29.0	29.8	28.3	31.7	33.0	30.5	18.7	18.2	19.1	47.1	49.1	45.4
2006	12.4	11.9	12.9	28.3	29.6	27.0	30.9	32.7	29.2	18.7	17.4	19.7	49.0	51.4	46.8
2005	12.0	11.8	12.1	28.0	29.3	26.7	30.5	32.3	28.9	17.6	16.0	18.9	49.8	53.3	46.6
2004	12.1	11.8	12.3	28.0	29.9	26.3	30.5	32.8	28.3	17.7	16.5	18.6	48.9	52.8	45.4
2003[3]	11.4	11.2	11.6	27.5	29.3	25.8	29.9	32.2	27.9	17.5	16.8	18.0	49.2	52.7	46.0
2002	11.1	11.0	11.2	...	...	...	...	...	...	...	...	...	...	...	...
2001[4]	11.1	10.8	11.4	...	...	...	...	...	...	...	...	...	...	...	...
2000	10.6	10.7	10.6	...	...	...	...	...	...	...	...	...	...	...	...
1999	10.9	10.7	11.0	...	...	...	...	...	...	...	...	...	...	...	...
1998	11.0	11.1	10.9	...	...	...	...	...	...	...	...	...	...	...	...
1997	10.3	10.6	10.1	...	...	...	...	...	...	...	...	...	...	...	...
1996	9.3	10.3	8.3	...	...	...	...	...	...	...	...	...	...	...	...
1995	9.3	10.1	8.4	...	...	...	...	...	...	...	...	...	...	...	...
1994	9.1	9.6	8.6	...	...	...	...	...	...	...	...	...	...	...	...
1993	9.0	9.5	8.5	...	...	...	...	...	...	...	...	...	...	...	...
1992[5]	9.3	10.2	8.5	...	...	...	...	...	...	...	...	...	...	...	...
1991	9.7	10.0	9.4	...	...	...	...	...	...	...	...	...	...	...	...
1990	9.2	9.8	8.7	...	...	...	...	...	...	...	...	...	...	...	...
1989	9.9	11.0	8.8	...	...	...	...	...	...	...	...	...	...	...	...
1988	10.1	12.3	8.1	...	...	...	...	...	...	...	...	...	...	...	...
1987	8.6	9.7	7.5	...	...	...	...	...	...	...	...	...	...	...	...
1986	8.4	9.5	7.4	...	...	...	...	...	...	...	...	...	...	...	...
1985	8.5	9.7	7.3	...	...	...	...	...	...	...	...	...	...	...	...
1984	8.2	9.5	7.0	...	...	...	...	...	...	...	...	...	...	...	...
1983	7.9	9.2	6.8	...	...	...	...	...	...	...	...	...	...	...	...
1982	7.8	9.6	6.2	...	...	...	...	...	...	...	...	...	...	...	...
1981	7.7	9.7	5.9	...	...	...	...	...	...	...	...	...	...	...	...
1980	7.9	9.7	6.2	...	...	...	...	...	...	...	...	...	...	...	...
1979	6.7	8.2	5.3	...	...	...	...	...	...	...	...	...	...	...	...
1978	7.0	8.6	5.7	...	...	...	...	...	...	...	...	...	...	...	...
1977	6.2	8.1	4.4	...	...	...	...	...	...	...	...	...	...	...	...
1976	6.1	8.6	4.0	...	...	...	...	...	...	...	...	...	...	...	...
1975	6.3	8.3	4.6	...	...	...	...	...	...	...	...	...	...	...	...
1974	5.5	7.1	4.0	...	...	...	...	...	...	...	...	...	...	...	...
1973	...	...	...	...	...	...	...	...	...	...	...	...	...	...	...
1972	...	...	...	...	...	...	...	...	...	...	...	...	...	...	...
1971	...	...	...	...	...	...	...	...	...	...	...	...	...	...	...
1970	...	...	...	...	...	...	...	...	...	...	...	...	...	...	...
1969	...	...	...	...	...	...	...	...	...	...	...	...	...	...	...
1968	...	...	...	...	...	...	...	...	...	...	...	...	...	...	...
1967	...	...	...	...	...	...	...	...	...	...	...	...	...	...	...
1966	...	...	...	...	...	...	...	...	...	...	...	...	...	...	...
1965	...	...	...	...	...	...	...	...	...	...	...	...	...	...	...
1964	...	...	...	...	...	...	...	...	...	...	...	...	...	...	...
1962	...	...	...	...	...	...	...	...	...	...	...	...	...	...	...
1959	...	...	...	...	...	...	...	...	...	...	...	...	...	...	...
1957	...	...	...	...	...	...	...	...	...	...	...	...	...	...	...
1952	...	...	...	...	...	...	...	...	...	...	...	...	...	...	...
1950	...	...	...	...	...	...	...	...	...	...	...	...	...	...	...
1947	...	...	...	...	...	...	...	...	...	...	...	...	...	...	...
1940	...	...	...	...	...	...	...	...	...	...	...	...	...	...	...

[2]May be of any race.

[3]Starting in 2003, respondents could choose more than one race. The race data in this table from 2003 onward represent respondents who indicated only one race. Prior to 2003, Asians were grouped with Pacific Islanders.

[4]Starting in 2001, data are from the expanded Current Population Survey (CPS) sample and were calculated using population controls based on data from the 2000 Census.

[5]Beginning with data for 1992, a new question results in different categories than for earlier years. Data shown as "Completed 4 Years of High School or More" are now collected by the category "High School Graduate." Data shown as "Completed 4 Years of College or more" are now collected by the categories, Bachelor's degree; Master's degree; Doctorate degree; and Professional degree. Due to the change in question format, median years of schooling cannot be derived.

... = Not available.

Table A-26. Percent of People 25 Years Old and Over Who Have Completed High School or College, by Race, Hispanic Origin, and Sex, Selected Years, 1940–2011—*Continued*

(Noninstitutionalized population)

Age, educational attainment level, and year	All races			White			Non-Hispanic White			Black[1]			Asian		
	Both sexes	Male	Female	Both sexes	Male	Female	Both sexes	Male	Female	Both sexes	Male	Female	Both sexes	Male	Female
25 TO 29 YEARS OLD															
Completed 4 Years of High School or More															
2011	89.0	87.5	90.7	88.9	87.1	90.8	94.4	93.4	95.5	87.7	87.6	87.8	95.2	93.6	96.7
2010	88.8	87.4	90.2	88.5	87.3	89.9	94.5	94.6	94.4	89.0	86.7	91.0	93.2	92.3	94.1
2009	88.6	87.5	89.8	88.4	87.0	89.9	94.6	94.4	94.8	88.9	88.6	89.1	95.2	95.6	94.9
2008	87.8	85.8	89.9	87.6	85.5	89.8	93.7	92.6	94.7	87.4	85.4	89.2	95.6	95.4	95.7
2007	87.0	84.9	89.1	86.5	84.2	89.0	93.5	92.7	94.2	87.4	87.0	87.8	97.2	95.8	98.5
2006	86.4	84.4	88.5	86.1	84.1	88.3	93.4	92.3	94.6	85.6	83.1	87.8	96.6	97.2	96.0
2005	86.2	85.0	87.4	85.7	84.3	87.1	92.8	91.8	93.8	86.5	86.4	86.6	95.5	96.7	94.5
2004	86.6	85.2	88.0	85.9	83.7	88.1	93.3	92.1	94.5	87.9	90.1	86.1	96.2	96.9	95.4
2003[3]	86.5	84.9	88.2	85.7	83.8	87.6	93.7	92.8	94.5	87.6	86.4	88.5	97.1	97.4	96.8
2002	86.4	84.7	88.1	85.9	84.1	87.7	93.0	92.1	93.8	86.6	85.0	88.0	...	...	...
2001[4]	86.8	85.3	88.3	86.4	84.6	88.3	93.4	93.1	93.7	86.3	85.4	87.0	...	...	...
2000	88.1	86.7	89.4	88.3	86.6	90.0	94.0	92.9	95.2	85.9	86.6	85.3	...	...	...
1999	87.8	86.1	89.5	87.6	85.8	89.3	93.0	91.9	94.1	88.2	87.7	88.6	...	...	...
1998	88.1	86.6	89.6	88.1	86.3	90.0	93.6	92.5	94.6	87.6	87.6	87.6	...	...	...
1997	87.4	85.8	88.9	87.6	85.8	89.4	92.9	91.7	94.0	86.2	85.2	87.1	...	...	...
1996	87.3	86.5	88.1	87.5	86.3	88.8	92.6	92.0	93.1	85.6	87.2	84.2	...	...	...
1995	86.8	86.3	87.4	87.4	86.6	88.2	92.5	92.0	93.0	86.5	88.1	85.1	...	...	...
1994	86.1	84.5	87.6	86.5	84.7	88.3	91.1	90.0	92.3	84.1	82.9	85.0	...	...	...
1993	86.7	86.0	87.4	87.3	86.1	88.5	91.2	90.6	91.8	82.8	85.0	80.9	...	...	...
1992[5]	86.3	86.1	86.5	87.0	86.5	87.6	...	...	...	80.9	82.5	79.5	...	...	...
1991	85.4	84.9	85.8	85.8	85.1	86.6	...	...	...	81.7	83.5	80.1	...	...	...
1990	85.7	84.4	87.0	86.3	84.6	88.1	...	...	...	81.7	81.5	81.8	...	...	...
1989	85.5	84.4	86.5	86.0	84.8	87.1	...	...	...	82.2	80.6	83.6	...	...	...
1988	85.7	84.4	87.0	86.5	84.8	88.2	...	...	...	80.7	80.6	80.7	...	...	...
1987	86.0	85.5	86.4	86.3	85.6	87.0	...	...	...	83.3	84.8	82.1	...	...	...
1986	86.1	85.9	86.4	86.5	85.6	87.4	...	...	...	83.4	86.5	80.6	...	...	...
1985	86.1	85.9	86.4	86.8	86.4	87.3	...	...	...	80.6	80.8	80.4	...	...	...
1984	85.9	85.6	86.3	86.9	86.8	87.0	...	...	...	78.9	75.9	81.5	...	...	...
1983	86.0	86.0	86.0	86.9	86.9	86.9	...	...	...	79.4	78.9	79.8	...	...	...
1982	86.2	86.3	86.1	86.9	87.0	86.8	...	...	...	80.9	80.5	81.3	...	...	...
1981	86.3	86.5	86.1	87.6	87.6	87.6	...	...	...	77.3	78.4	76.4	...	...	...
1980	85.4	85.4	85.5	86.9	86.8	87.0	...	...	...	76.6	74.8	78.1	...	...	...
1979	85.6	86.3	84.9	87.0	87.7	86.4	...	...	...	74.8	73.9	75.4	...	...	...
1978	85.3	86.0	84.6	86.3	86.8	85.8	...	...	...	77.3	78.5	76.3	...	...	...
1977	85.4	86.6	84.2	86.8	87.6	86.0	...	...	...	74.4	77.5	72.0	...	...	...
1976	84.7	86.0	83.5	85.9	87.3	84.6	...	...	...	73.8	72.5	74.9	...	...	...
1975	83.1	84.5	81.8	84.4	85.7	83.2	...	...	...	71.0	72.2	70.1	...	...	...
1974	81.9	83.1	80.8	83.4	84.1	82.7	...	...	...	68.2	71.1	66.0	...	...	...
1973	80.2	80.6	79.8	82.0	82.4	81.6	...	...	...	64.2	63.1	64.9	...	...	...
1972	79.8	80.5	79.2	81.5	82.3	80.8	...	...	...	64.1	61.8	66.2	...	...	...
1971	77.2	78.1	76.4	79.5	80.8	78.3	...	...	...	57.5	54.1	60.7	...	...	...
1970	75.4	76.6	74.2	77.8	79.2	76.4	...	...	...	56.2	54.5	57.9	...	...	...
1969	74.7	75.6	73.8	77.0	77.5	76.6	...	...	...	55.8	59.8	52.3	...	...	...
1968	73.2	73.7	72.7	75.3	75.5	75.0	...	...	...	55.8	58.1	53.6	...	...	...
1967	72.5	72.1	72.9	74.8	74.3	75.3	...	...	...	53.4	51.7	55.0	...	...	...
1966	71.0	70.9	71.2	73.8	73.2	74.4	...	...	...	47.9	48.9	47.0	...	...	...
1965	70.3	70.5	70.1	72.8	72.7	72.8	...	...	...	50.3	50.3	50.4	...	...	...
1964	69.2	68.8	69.5	72.1	71.8	72.4	...	...	...	45.0	41.6	47.9	...	...	...
1962	65.9	65.8	66.1	69.2	69.2	69.3	...	...	...	41.6	38.9	43.8	...	...	...
1959	63.9	63.9	64.0	67.2	66.9	67.4	...	...	...	39.5	40.6	38.6	...	...	...
1957	60.2	57.9	62.4	63.3	60.7	65.7	...	...	...	31.6	27.4	35.2	...	...	...
1952	57.1	55.3	58.7	...	...	...	...	...	...	28.1	27.9	28.3	...	...	...
1950	52.8	50.6	55.0	...	...	...	...	...	...	23.6	21.3	25.5	...	...	...
1947	51.4	49.4	53.3	54.9	52.9	56.8	...	...	...	22.3	19.6	24.7	...	...	...
1940	38.1	36.0	40.1	41.2	38.9	43.4	...	...	...	12.3	10.6	13.6	...	...	...

[1]Data include Black and other races from 1940 to 1962; from 1963 to 2003, data are for the Black population only.
[3]Starting in 2003, respondents could choose more than one race. The race data in this table from 2003 onward represent respondents who indicated only one race. Prior to 2003, Asians were grouped with Pacific Islanders.
[4]Starting in 2001, data are from the expanded Current Population Survey (CPS) sample and were calculated using population controls based on data from the 2000 Census.
[5]Beginning with data for 1992, a new question results in different categories than for earlier years. Data shown as "Completed 4 Years of High School or More" are now collected by the category "High School Graduate." Data shown as "Completed 4 Years of College or more" are now collected by the categories, Bachelor's degree; Master's degree; Doctorate degree; and Professional degree. Due to the change in question format, median years of schooling cannot be derived.
... = Not available.

Table A-26. Percent of People 25 Years Old and Over Who Have Completed High School or College, by Race, Hispanic Origin, and Sex, Selected Years, 1940–2011—*Continued*

(Noninstitutionalized population)

Age, educational attainment level, and year	Hispanic[2]			White alone or in combination			Non-Hispanic White alone or in combination			Black alone or in combination			Asian alone or in combination		
	Both sexes	Male	Female	Both sexes	Male	Female	Both sexes	Male	Female	Both sexes	Male	Female	Both sexes	Male	Female
25 TO 29 YEARS OLD															
Completed 4 Years of High School or More															
2011	71.5	69.2	74.3	88.9	87.1	90.8	94.4	93.3	95.5	87.9	87.6	88.3	94.7	92.8	96.5
2010	69.4	65.7	74.1	88.5	87.3	89.8	94.4	94.5	94.3	89.9	86.5	91.0	93.1	92.3	93.9
2009	68.9	66.2	72.5	88.4	87.0	89.9	94.5	94.4	94.6	88.8	88.5	89.1	95.1	95.7	94.6
2008	68.3	65.6	71.9	87.6	85.5	89.8	93.7	92.6	94.8	87.7	85.6	89.4	95.7	95.5	95.9
2007	65.0	60.5	70.7	86.5	84.2	88.8	93.4	92.7	94.1	87.4	87.0	87.8	96.3	95.8	96.8
2006	63.3	60.6	66.7	86.0	83.9	88.2	93.3	92.2	94.5	85.6	83.2	87.7	96.0	96.4	95.7
2005	63.3	63.2	63.4	85.6	84.2	87.0	92.8	91.7	93.8	86.6	86.4	86.7	95.5	96.7	94.4
2004	62.4	60.1	65.2	85.9	83.9	87.9	93.2	92.1	94.4	87.8	89.9	86.2	95.7	97.0	94.5
2003[3]	61.7	59.6	64.2	85.7	83.9	87.6	93.6	92.8	94.4	87.4	86.4	88.5	97.2	97.5	97.0
2002	62.4	60.2	65.0	...	...	...	...	...	...	...	...	...	...	...	...
2001[4]	62.4	58.3	67.3	...	...	...	...	...	...	...	...	...	...	...	...
2000	62.8	59.2	66.4	...	...	...	...	...	...	...	...	...	...	...	...
1999	61.6	57.4	66.0	...	...	...	...	...	...	...	...	...	...	...	...
1998	62.8	59.9	66.3	...	...	...	...	...	...	...	...	...	...	...	...
1997	61.8	59.2	64.9	...	...	...	...	...	...	...	...	...	...	...	...
1996	61.1	59.7	62.9	...	...	...	...	...	...	...	...	...	...	...	...
1995	57.1	55.7	58.7	...	...	...	...	...	...	...	...	...	...	...	...
1994	60.3	58.0	63.0	...	...	...	...	...	...	...	...	...	...	...	...
1993	60.9	58.3	64.0	...	...	...	...	...	...	...	...	...	...	...	...
1992[5]	60.9	61.1	60.6	...	...	...	...	...	...	...	...	...	...	...	...
1991	56.7	56.4	57.1	...	...	...	...	...	...	...	...	...	...	...	...
1990	58.2	56.6	59.9	...	...	...	...	...	...	...	...	...	...	...	...
1989	61.0	61.0	61.0	...	...	...	...	...	...	...	...	...	...	...	...
1988	62.0	59.4	65.0	...	...	...	...	...	...	...	...	...	...	...	...
1987	59.8	58.6	61.0	...	...	...	...	...	...	...	...	...	...	...	...
1986	59.1	58.2	60.0	...	...	...	...	...	...	...	...	...	...	...	...
1985	60.9	58.6	63.1	...	...	...	...	...	...	...	...	...	...	...	...
1984	58.6	56.8	60.2	...	...	...	...	...	...	...	...	...	...	...	...
1983	58.3	57.8	58.9	...	...	...	...	...	...	...	...	...	...	...	...
1982	60.9	60.7	61.2	...	...	...	...	...	...	...	...	...	...	...	...
1981	59.8	59.1	60.4	...	...	...	...	...	...	...	...	...	...	...	...
1980	58.6	58.3	58.8	...	...	...	...	...	...	...	...	...	...	...	...
1979	57.0	55.5	58.5	...	...	...	...	...	...	...	...	...	...	...	...
1978	56.6	58.5	54.7	...	...	...	...	...	...	...	...	...	...	...	...
1977	58.1	62.1	54.8	...	...	...	...	...	...	...	...	...	...	...	...
1976	58.1	57.6	58.4	...	...	...	...	...	...	...	...	...	...	...	...
1975	51.7	51.1	52.1	...	...	...	...	...	...	...	...	...	...	...	...
1974	52.5	55.1	49.9	...	...	...	...	...	...	...	...	...	...	...	...
1973	...	...	...	...	...	...	...	...	...	...	...	...	...	...	...
1972	...	...	...	...	...	...	...	...	...	...	...	...	...	...	...
1971	...	...	...	...	...	...	...	...	...	...	...	...	...	...	...
1970	...	...	...	...	...	...	...	...	...	...	...	...	...	...	...
1969	...	...	...	...	...	...	...	...	...	...	...	...	...	...	...
1968	...	...	...	...	...	...	...	...	...	...	...	...	...	...	...
1967	...	...	...	...	...	...	...	...	...	...	...	...	...	...	...
1966	...	...	...	...	...	...	...	...	...	...	...	...	...	...	...
1965	...	...	...	...	...	...	...	...	...	...	...	...	...	...	...
1964	...	...	...	...	...	...	...	...	...	...	...	...	...	...	...
1962	...	...	...	...	...	...	...	...	...	...	...	...	...	...	...
1959	...	...	...	...	...	...	...	...	...	...	...	...	...	...	...
1957	...	...	...	...	...	...	...	...	...	...	...	...	...	...	...
1952	...	...	...	...	...	...	...	...	...	...	...	...	...	...	...
1950	...	...	...	...	...	...	...	...	...	...	...	...	...	...	...
1947	...	...	...	...	...	...	...	...	...	...	...	...	...	...	...
1940	...	...	...	...	...	...	...	...	...	...	...	...	...	...	...

[2]May be of any race.
[3]Starting in 2003, respondents could choose more than one race. The race data in this table from 2003 onward represent respondents who indicated only one race. Prior to 2003, Asians were grouped with Pacific Islanders.
[4]Starting in 2001, data are from the expanded Current Population Survey (CPS) sample and were calculated using population controls based on data from the 2000 Census.
[5]Beginning with data for 1992, a new question results in different categories than for earlier years. Data shown as "Completed 4 Years of High School or More" are now collected by the category "High School Graduate." Data shown as "Completed 4 Years of College or more" are now collected by the categories, Bachelor's degree; Master's degree; Doctorate degree; and Professional degree. Due to the change in question format, median years of schooling cannot be derived.
... = Not available.

Table A-26. Percent of People 25 Years Old and Over Who Have Completed High School or College, by Race, Hispanic Origin, and Sex, Selected Years, 1940–2011—*Continued*

(Noninstitutionalized population)

Age, educational attainment level, and year	All races			White			Non-Hispanic White			Black[1]			Asian		
	Both sexes	Male	Female	Both sexes	Male	Female	Both sexes	Male	Female	Both sexes	Male	Female	Both sexes	Male	Female
25 TO 29 YEARS OLD — *(Continued)*															
Completed 4 Years of College or More															
2011	32.2	28.4	36.1	33.1	29.2	37.4	39.2	35.5	43.0	19.6	16.1	22.8	56.2	51.5	60.6
2010	31.7	27.8	35.7	32.7	28.8	37.0	38.6	34.8	42.4	19.0	14.8	22.9	55.4	52.0	58.6
2009	30.6	26.6	34.8	31.3	27.0	36.0	37.2	32.6	42.0	19.0	15.2	22.4	59.3	58.0	60.6
2008	30.8	26.8	34.9	31.1	26.7	35.9	37.1	32.6	41.7	20.6	18.7	22.3	59.4	55.1	63.5
2007	29.6	26.3	33.0	29.8	25.8	34.0	35.5	31.9	39.2	18.9	17.9	19.9	60.9	59.8	62.0
2006	28.4	25.3	31.6	28.3	25.0	31.7	34.3	31.4	37.2	18.6	14.9	21.6	60.9	59.8	61.9
2005	28.8	25.5	32.2	28.9	25.3	32.7	34.5	30.7	38.2	17.4	14.1	20.1	61.6	60.5	62.5
2004	28.7	26.1	31.4	28.9	25.8	32.1	34.5	31.4	37.5	16.9	13.4	19.7	61.4	62.0	60.9
2003[3]	28.4	26.0	30.9	28.3	25.3	31.5	34.2	31.4	37.1	17.2	17.5	17.0	61.6	60.9	62.3
2002	29.3	26.9	31.8	29.7	26.5	33.1	35.9	32.6	39.2	17.5	17.4	17.7	...	...	...
2001[4]	28.4	25.5	31.3	28.5	25.1	32.1	33.7	30.4	36.9	16.8	15.6	17.9	...	...	...
2000	29.1	27.9	30.1	29.6	27.8	31.3	34.0	32.3	35.8	17.5	18.1	17.0	...	...	...
1999	28.2	26.8	29.5	29.3	27.6	30.9	33.6	32.0	35.1	15.0	13.1	16.5	...	...	...
1998	27.3	25.6	29.0	28.4	26.5	30.4	32.3	30.5	34.2	15.8	14.2	17.0	...	...	...
1997	27.8	26.3	29.3	28.9	27.2	30.7	32.6	31.2	34.1	14.4	12.1	16.4	...	...	...
1996	27.1	26.1	28.2	28.1	27.2	29.1	31.6	30.9	32.3	14.6	12.4	16.4	...	...	...
1995	24.7	24.5	24.9	26.0	25.4	26.6	28.8	28.4	29.2	15.3	17.2	13.6	...	...	...
1994	23.3	22.5	24.0	24.2	23.6	24.8	27.1	26.8	27.4	13.7	11.7	15.4	...	...	...
1993	23.7	23.4	23.9	24.7	24.4	25.1	27.2	27.2	27.1	13.2	12.6	13.8	...	...	...
1992[5]	23.6	23.2	24.0	25.0	24.2	25.7	...	...	...	11.3	12.0	10.6	...	...	...
1991	23.2	23.0	23.4	24.6	24.1	25.0	...	...	...	11.0	11.5	10.6	...	...	...
1990	23.2	23.7	22.8	24.2	24.2	24.3	...	...	...	13.4	15.1	11.9	...	...	...
1989	23.4	23.9	22.9	24.4	24.8	24.0	...	...	...	12.7	12.0	13.3	...	...	...
1988	22.5	23.2	21.9	23.5	24.0	22.9	...	...	...	12.2	12.6	11.9	...	...	...
1987	22.0	22.3	21.7	23.0	23.3	22.8	...	...	...	11.4	11.6	11.1	...	...	...
1986	22.4	22.9	21.9	23.5	24.1	22.9	...	...	...	11.8	10.1	13.3	...	...	...
1985	22.2	23.1	21.3	23.2	24.2	22.2	...	...	...	11.5	10.3	12.6	...	...	...
1984	21.9	23.2	20.7	23.1	24.3	21.9	...	...	...	11.6	12.9	10.5	...	...	...
1983	22.5	23.9	21.1	23.4	25.0	21.8	...	...	...	12.9	13.1	12.8	...	...	...
1982	21.7	23.3	20.2	22.7	24.5	20.9	...	...	...	12.6	11.8	13.2	...	...	...
1981	21.3	23.1	19.6	22.4	24.3	20.5	...	...	...	11.6	12.1	11.1	...	...	...
1980	22.5	24.0	21.0	23.7	25.5	22.0	...	...	...	11.6	10.5	12.5	...	...	...
1979	23.1	25.6	20.5	24.3	27.1	21.5	...	...	...	12.4	13.3	11.7	...	...	...
1978	23.3	26.0	20.6	24.5	27.6	21.4	...	...	...	11.8	10.7	12.6	...	...	...
1977	24.0	27.0	21.1	25.3	28.5	22.1	...	...	...	12.6	12.8	12.4	...	...	...
1976	23.7	27.5	20.1	24.6	28.7	20.6	...	...	...	13.0	12.0	13.6	...	...	...
1975	21.9	25.1	18.7	22.8	26.3	19.4	...	...	...	10.7	11.4	10.1	...	...	...
1974	20.7	23.9	17.6	22.0	25.3	18.8	...	...	...	7.9	8.8	7.2	...	...	...
1973	19.0	21.6	16.4	19.9	22.8	17.0	...	...	...	8.1	7.1	8.8	...	...	...
1972	19.0	22.0	16.0	19.9	23.1	16.7	...	...	...	8.3	7.1	9.4	...	...	...
1971	16.9	20.1	13.8	17.9	21.3	14.6	...	...	...	6.4	6.4	6.5	...	...	...
1970	16.4	20.0	12.9	17.3	21.3	13.3	...	...	...	7.3	6.7	8.0	...	...	...
1969	16.0	19.4	12.8	17.0	20.6	13.4	...	...	...	6.7	8.1	5.5	...	...	...
1968	14.7	18.0	11.6	15.6	19.1	12.3	...	...	...	5.3	5.3	5.3	...	...	...
1967	14.6	17.2	12.1	15.5	18.3	12.7	...	...	...	5.4	4.2	6.3	...	...	...
1966	14.0	16.8	11.3	14.7	17.9	11.8	...	...	...	5.9	5.4	6.4	...	...	...
1965	12.4	15.6	9.5	13.0	16.4	9.8	...	...	...	6.8	7.3	6.8	...	...	...
1964	12.8	16.6	9.2	13.6	17.5	9.9	...	...	...	5.5	7.5	3.9	...	...	...
1962	13.1	17.2	9.2	14.3	18.7	10.0	...	...	...	4.2	5.7	3.0	...	...	...
1959	11.1	14.8	7.6	11.9	15.9	8.1	...	...	...	4.6	5.6	3.7	...	...	...
1957	10.4	13.5	7.5	11.1	14.5	7.8	...	...	...	4.1	3.3	5.0	...	...	...
1952	10.1	13.8	6.7	...	...	...	...	...	...	4.6	3.2	5.8	...	...	...
1950	7.7	9.6	5.9	...	...	...	...	...	...	2.9	2.4	3.2	...	...	...
1947	5.6	5.8	5.4	5.9	6.2	5.7	...	...	...	2.8	2.6	2.9	...	...	...
1940	5.9	6.9	4.9	6.4	7.5	5.3	...	...	...	1.6	1.5	1.7	...	...	...

[1]Data include Black and other races from 1940 to 1962; from 1963 to 2003, data are for the Black population only.
[3]Starting in 2003, respondents could choose more than one race. The race data in this table from 2003 onward represent respondents who indicated only one race. Prior to 2003, Asians were grouped with Pacific Islanders.
[4]Starting in 2001, data are from the expanded Current Population Survey (CPS) sample and were calculated using population controls based on data from the 2000 Census.
[5]Beginning with data for 1992, a new question results in different categories than for earlier years. Data shown as "Completed 4 Years of High School or More" are now collected by the category "High School Graduate." Data shown as "Completed 4 Years of College or more" are now collected by the categories, Bachelor's degree; Master's degree; Doctorate degree; and Professional degree. Due to the change in question format, median years of schooling cannot be derived.
... = Not available.

Table A-26. Percent of People 25 Years Old and Over Who Have Completed High School or College, by Race, Hispanic Origin, and Sex, Selected Years, 1940–2011—*Continued*

(Noninstitutionalized population)

Age, educational attainment level, and year	Hispanic[2]			White alone or in combination			Non-Hispanic White alone or in combination			Black alone or in combination			Asian alone or in combination		
	Both sexes	Male	Female	Both sexes	Male	Female	Both sexes	Male	Female	Both sexes	Male	Female	Both sexes	Male	Female
25 TO 29 YEARS OLD — *(Continued)*															
Completed 4 Years of College or More															
2011	12.8	9.6	16.8	33.0	29.0	37.1	39.0	35.4	42.7	19.8	16.3	22.9	55.7	52.0	59.1
2010	13.5	10.8	16.8	32.6	28.6	36.8	38.4	34.6	42.3	19.3	14.8	23.5	53.7	49.6	57.6
2009	12.2	11.0	13.8	31.1	26.8	35.9	37.1	32.4	41.9	19.0	15.0	22.6	58.0	56.7	59.3
2008	12.4	10.0	15.5	31.0	26.6	35.8	36.9	32.4	41.5	20.9	19.3	22.3	57.4	52.9	61.8
2007	11.6	8.6	15.4	29.7	25.7	33.8	35.3	31.7	39.0	19.1	18.1	19.9	59.0	57.8	60.1
2006	9.5	6.9	12.8	28.1	24.8	31.6	34.1	31.2	37.0	18.9	15.0	22.3	59.4	58.4	60.5
2005	11.2	10.2	12.4	28.8	25.3	32.5	34.3	30.6	38.1	17.6	14.6	20.3	60.3	59.0	61.5
2004	10.9	9.6	12.4	28.7	25.7	31.8	34.2	31.2	37.2	16.8	13.4	19.5	59.9	61.1	58.9
2003[3]	10.0	8.4	12.0	28.2	25.2	31.4	34.0	31.2	36.9	17.3	17.4	17.3	60.3	58.8	61.7
2002	8.9	8.3	9.7	...	...	...	...	...	...	...	...	...	...	...	...
2001[4]	10.5	8.2	13.3	...	...	...	...	...	...	...	...	...	...	...	...
2000	9.7	8.3	11.0	...	...	...	...	...	...	...	...	...	...	...	...
1999	8.9	7.5	10.4	...	...	...	...	...	...	...	...	...	...	...	...
1998	10.4	9.5	11.3	...	...	...	...	...	...	...	...	...	...	...	...
1997	11.0	9.6	10.1	...	...	...	...	...	...	...	...	...	...	...	...
1996	10.0	10.2	9.8	...	...	...	...	...	...	...	...	...	...	...	...
1995	8.9	7.8	10.1	...	...	...	...	...	...	...	...	...	...	...	...
1994	8.0	6.6	9.8	...	...	...	...	...	...	...	...	...	...	...	...
1993	8.3	7.1	9.8	...	...	...	...	...	...	...	...	...	...	...	...
1992[5]	9.5	8.8	10.3	...	...	...	...	...	...	...	...	...	...	...	...
1991	9.2	8.1	10.4	...	...	...	...	...	...	...	...	...	...	...	...
1990	8.1	7.3	9.1	...	...	...	...	...	...	...	...	...	...	...	...
1989	10.1	9.6	10.6	...	...	...	...	...	...	...	...	...	...	...	...
1988	11.4	12.1	10.6	...	...	...	...	...	...	...	...	...	...	...	...
1987	8.7	9.2	8.2	...	...	...	...	...	...	...	...	...	...	...	...
1986	9.0	8.9	9.1	...	...	...	...	...	...	...	...	...	...	...	...
1985	11.1	10.9	11.2	...	...	...	...	...	...	...	...	...	...	...	...
1984	10.6	9.6	11.6	...	...	...	...	...	...	...	...	...	...	...	...
1983	10.4	9.6	11.1	...	...	...	...	...	...	...	...	...	...	...	...
1982	9.7	10.7	8.7	...	...	...	...	...	...	...	...	...	...	...	...
1981	7.5	8.6	6.5	...	...	...	...	...	...	...	...	...	...	...	...
1980	7.7	8.4	6.9	...	...	...	...	...	...	...	...	...	...	...	...
1979	7.3	7.9	6.8	...	...	...	...	...	...	...	...	...	...	...	...
1978	9.6	9.6	9.7	...	...	...	...	...	...	...	...	...	...	...	...
1977	6.7	7.2	6.4	...	...	...	...	...	...	...	...	...	...	...	...
1976	7.4	10.3	4.8	...	...	...	...	...	...	...	...	...	...	...	...
1975	8.8	10.0	7.3	...	...	...	...	...	...	...	...	...	...	...	...
1974	5.7	7.2	4.6	...	...	...	...	...	...	...	...	...	...	...	...
1973	...	...	...	...	...	...	...	...	...	...	...	...	...	...	...
1972	...	...	...	...	...	...	...	...	...	...	...	...	...	...	...
1971	...	...	...	...	...	...	...	...	...	...	...	...	...	...	...
1970	...	...	...	...	...	...	...	...	...	...	...	...	...	...	...
1969	...	...	...	...	...	...	...	...	...	...	...	...	...	...	...
1968	...	...	...	...	...	...	...	...	...	...	...	...	...	...	...
1967	...	...	...	...	...	...	...	...	...	...	...	...	...	...	...
1966	...	...	...	...	...	...	...	...	...	...	...	...	...	...	...
1965	...	...	...	...	...	...	...	...	...	...	...	...	...	...	...
1964	...	...	...	...	...	...	...	...	...	...	...	...	...	...	...
1962	...	...	...	...	...	...	...	...	...	...	...	...	...	...	...
1959	...	...	...	...	...	...	...	...	...	...	...	...	...	...	...
1957	...	...	...	...	...	...	...	...	...	...	...	...	...	...	...
1952	...	...	...	...	...	...	...	...	...	...	...	...	...	...	...
1950	...	...	...	...	...	...	...	...	...	...	...	...	...	...	...
1947	...	...	...	...	...	...	...	...	...	...	...	...	...	...	...
1940	...	...	...	...	...	...	...	...	...	...	...	...	...	...	...

[2]May be of any race.

[3]Starting in 2003, respondents could choose more than one race. The race data in this table from 2003 onward represent respondents who indicated only one race. Prior to 2003, Asians were grouped with Pacific Islanders.

[4]Starting in 2001, data are from the expanded Current Population Survey (CPS) sample and were calculated using population controls based on data from the 2000 Census.

[5]Beginning with data for 1992, a new question results in different categories than for earlier years. Data shown as "Completed 4 Years of High School or More" are now collected by the category "High School Graduate." Data shown as "Completed 4 Years of College or more" are now collected by the categories, Bachelor's degree; Master's degree; Doctorate degree; and Professional degree. Due to the change in question format, median years of schooling cannot be derived.

... = Not available.

PART A

NATIONAL EDUCATION STATISTICS

■ Historical Attainment Tables

Table A-27. Mean Earnings of Workers 18 Years Old and Over, by Educational Attainment, Race, Hispanic Origin, and Sex, 1975–2010

(Dollars except as noted)

Race, sex, year, and Hispanic origin	Total		Not a high school graduate		High school graduate		Some college/ associate's degree[1]		Bachelor's degree[1]		Advanced degree[1]	
	Mean earnings	Number of workers (thousands)	Mean earnings	Number of workers (thousands)	Mean earnings	Number of workers (thousands)	Mean earnings	Number of workers (thousands)	Mean earnings	Number of workers (thousands)	Mean earnings	Number of workers (thousands)
ALL RACES												
Both Sexes												
2010	42,922	151,498	20,911	13,345	31,003	42,599	34,366	45,643	57,621	32,429	83,841	17,481
2009	42,469	152,707	20,241	14,083	30,627	44,396	34,773	45,239	56,665	32,127	85,818	16,860
2008	42,588	155,989	21,023	15,217	31,283	45,182	34,808	46,663	58,613	31,890	83,144	17,035
2007	42,064	155,738	21,484	15,330	31,286	45,393	35,138	46,577	57,181	31,832	80,977	16,604
2006	41,412	154,438	20,873	16,652	31,071	45,936	34,650	45,073	56,788	31,006	82,320	15,769
2005	39,579	152,215	19,915	16,317	29,448	45,652	33,496	45,434	54,689	29,658	79,946	15,152
2004	37,899	150,095	19,182	16,372	28,631	45,571	32,010	44,387	51,568	29,004	78,224	14,713
2003[2]	37,046	148,660	18,734	16,282	27,915	45,064	31,498	44,048	51,206	28,672	74,602	14,592
2002	36,308	148,492	18,826	16,931	27,280	45,407	31,046	43,776	51,194	28,257	72,824	14,119
2001	35,805	147,829	18,793	17,293	26,795	45,641	30,782	43,214	50,623	27,980	72,869	13,700
2000[3]	34,514	147,966	17,738	17,425	25,692	45,977	29,939	43,874	49,595	27,488	71,194	13,200
1999	32,356	144,640	16,121	16,737	24,572	46,082	28,403	42,860	45,678	26,215	67,697	12,749
1998	30,928	142,053	16,053	16,742	23,594	45,987	27,566	41,412	43,782	25,818	63,473	12,095
1997	29,514	140,367	16,124	16,962	22,895	45,976	26,235	40,802	40,478	25,035	63,229	11,591
1996	28,106	138,703	15,011	17,075	22,154	45,908	25,181	40,410	38,112	24,028	61,317	11,281
1995	26,792	136,221	14,013	16,990	21,431	44,546	23,862	40,142	36,980	23,285	56,667	11,258
1994	25,852	135,096	13,697	16,479	20,248	44,614	22,226	40,135	37,224	22,712	56,105	11,155
1993	24,674	133,119	12,820	16,575	19,422	44,779	21,539	39,429	35,121	21,815	55,789	10,521
1992	23,227	130,860	12,809	16,612	18,737	45,340	20,867	37,339	32,629	21,091	48,652	10,479
1991	22,332	130,371	12,613	17,553	18,261	46,508	20,551	35,732	31,323	20,475	46,039	10,103
1990	21,793	130,080	12,582	18,698	17,820	51,977	20,694	28,993	31,112	18,128	41,458	12,285
1989	21,414	129,094	12,242	19,137	17,594	51,846	20,255	28,078	30,736	17,767	41,019	12,265
1988	20,060	127,564	11,889	19,635	16,750	51,297	19,066	27,217	28,344	17,308	37,724	12,109
1987	19,016	124,874	11,824	19,748	15,939	50,815	18,054	26,404	26,919	16,497	35,968	11,411
1986	18,149	122,757	11,203	19,665	15,120	50,104	17,073	26,113	26,511	15,788	34,787	11,087
1985	17,181	120,651	10,726	19,692	14,457	49,674	16,349	25,402	24,877	15,373	32,909	10,510
1984	16,083	118,183	10,384	20,206	13,893	48,452	14,936	24,463	23,072	14,653	30,192	10,410
1983	15,137	115,095	9,853	20,020	13,044	47,560	14,245	23,208	21,532	13,929	28,333	10,377
1982	14,351	113,451	9,387	20,789	12,560	46,584	13,503	22,602	20,272	13,425	26,915	10,051
1981	13,624	113,301	9,357	22,296	12,109	47,332	13,176	21,759	19,006	12,579	25,281	9,336
1980	12,665	111,919	8,845	23,028	11,314	46,795	12,409	21,384	18,075	12,175	23,308	8,535
1979	11,795	110,826	8,420	23,783	10,624	45,497	11,377	21,174	16,514	11,751	21,874	8,621
1978	10,812	106,436	7,759	23,787	9,834	43,510	10,357	20,121	15,291	11,001	20,173	8,017
1977	9,887	103,119	7,066	24,854	9,013	41,696	9,607	18,905	14,207	10,357	19,077	7,309
1976	9,180	100,510	6,720	25,035	8,393	40,570	8,813	17,786	13,033	10,132	17,911	6,985
1975	8,552	97,881	6,198	24,916	7,843	39,827	8,388	16,917	12,332	9,764	16,725	6,457
Male												
2010	50,645	80,284	24,413	8,382	36,181	24,230	40,935	22,150	69,623	16,595	103,359	8,925
2009	50,186	80,799	23,036	8,851	35,468	25,143	41,773	21,895	69,479	16,226	105,636	8,683
2008	51,148	82,727	24,831	9,596	36,753	25,290	42,221	22,830	72,868	16,100	103,980	8,909
2007	50,110	82,932	24,985	9,780	36,839	25,396	41,709	22,916	70,898	16,109	100,550	8,730
2006	49,647	82,310	24,072	10,541	37,356	25,489	41,521	21,952	69,818	15,769	101,441	8,556
2005	48,034	81,258	23,222	10,273	35,248	25,348	40,995	22,173	67,980	15,217	100,379	8,245
2004	46,008	79,765	22,537	10,188	34,050	25,209	39,509	21,473	63,753	14,860	97,855	8,032
2003[2]	44,726	78,869	21,447	10,173	33,266	24,292	38,451	21,534	63,084	14,849	91,831	8,019
2002	44,310	78,757	22,091	10,526	32,673	24,174	38,377	21,599	63,503	14,667	90,761	7,788
2001	43,648	78,342	21,508	10,572	32,363	24,239	37,429	21,390	63,354	14,507	90,130	7,631
2000[3]	42,772	78,319	21,007	10,535	31,446	24,439	37,372	21,526	62,609	14,375	88,077	7,442
1999	40,257	76,233	18,855	9,917	30,414	24,235	35,326	21,173	57,706	13,683	84,051	7,225
1998	38,134	75,213	19,155	10,085	28,742	24,155	34,179	20,545	55,057	13,486	77,217	6,942
1997	36,556	74,596	19,575	10,348	28,307	24,152	32,641	20,359	50,056	13,008	78,032	6,728
1996	34,705	73,955	17,826	10,583	27,642	23,966	31,426	20,208	46,702	12,562	74,406	6,636
1995	33,251	72,634	16,748	10,312	26,333	23,473	29,851	19,918	46,111	12,251	69,588	6,679
1994	32,087	72,246	16,633	9,981	25,038	23,418	27,636	19,859	46,278	12,324	67,032	6,663
1993	30,568	71,183	14,946	10,151	23,973	23,388	26,614	19,532	43,499	11,810	68,221	6,302
1992	28,448	70,409	14,934	10,335	22,978	23,610	25,660	18,768	40,039	11,353	58,324	6,344
1991	27,494	70,145	15,056	10,679	22,663	24,110	25,345	18,076	38,484	11,126	54,449	6,154
1990	27,164	70,218	14,991	11,412	22,378	26,753	26,120	14,844	38,901	9,807	49,768	7,402
1989	27,025	69,798	14,727	11,774	22,508	26,469	25,555	14,384	38,692	9,737	50,144	7,434
1988	25,344	69,006	14,551	11,993	21,481	26,080	23,827	14,019	35,906	9,466	45,677	7,449
1987	24,015	67,951	14,544	12,117	20,364	25,981	22,781	13,433	33,677	9,286	43,140	7,134
1986	23,057	67,189	13,703	12,208	19,453	25,562	21,784	13,502	33,376	8,908	41,836	7,009

[1]For data prior to 1991, "Some college/Associate degree" equals 1 to 3 years of college completed; "Bachelor's degree" equals 4 years of college; "Advanced degree" equals 5 or more years of college completed.
[2]Starting in 2003, respondents could choose more than one race. The race data in this table from 2003 onward represent respondents who indicated only one race.
[3]Beginning in 2000, earnings data are from the expanded Current Population Survey (CPS) sample and were calculated using population controls based on Census 2000.

Table A-27. Mean Earnings of Workers 18 Years Old and Over, by Educational Attainment, Race, Hispanic Origin, and Sex, 1975–2010—*Continued*

(Dollars except as noted)

Race, sex, year, and Hispanic origin	Total		Not a high school graduate		High school graduate		Some college/ associate's degree[1]		Bachelor's degree[1]		Advanced degree[1]	
	Mean earnings	Number of workers (thousands)	Mean earnings	Number of workers (thousands)	Mean earnings	Number of workers (thousands)	Mean earnings	Number of workers (thousands)	Mean earnings	Number of workers (thousands)	Mean earnings	Number of workers (thousands)
Male— *(Continued)*												
1985	21,823	66,439	13,124	12,137	18,575	25,496	20,698	13,385	31,433	8,794	39,768	6,627
1984	20,452	65,005	12,775	12,325	18,016	24,827	18,863	12,818	29,203	8,387	35,804	6,648
1983	19,175	63,816	12,052	12,376	16,728	24,449	18,052	12,261	27,239	8,010	33,635	6,719
1982	18,244	63,489	11,513	12,868	16,160	24,059	17,108	12,103	25,758	7,865	32,109	6,594
1981	17,542	63,547	11,668	13,701	15,900	24,435	16,870	11,784	24,353	7,393	30,072	6,235
1980	16,382	62,825	11,042	14,273	15,002	24,023	15,871	11,663	23,340	7,132	27,846	5,733
1979	15,430	62,464	10,628	14,711	14,317	23,318	14,716	11,781	21,482	6,889	26,411	5,765
1978	14,154	60,586	9,894	14,550	13,188	22,650	13,382	11,352	19,861	6,611	24,274	5,422
1977	12,888	59,441	8,939	15,369	12,092	21,846	12,393	10,848	18,187	6,341	22,786	5,038
1976	11,923	58,419	8,522	15,634	11,189	21,499	11,376	10,282	16,714	6,135	21,202	4,868
1975	11,091	57,297	7,843	15,613	10,475	21,347	10,805	9,851	15,758	5,960	19,672	4,526
Female												
2010	34,216	71,214	14,995	4,962	24,172	18,368	28,173	23,492	45,044	15,834	63,482	8,556
2009	33,797	71,907	15,514	5,232	24,304	19,253	28,207	23,344	43,589	15,900	64,771	8,176
2008	32,922	73,262	14,521	5,621	24,329	19,892	27,708	23,833	44,078	15,789	60,301	8,126
2007	32,899	72,805	15,315	5,550	24,234	19,997	28,773	23,660	43,127	15,722	59,273	7,873
2006	32,015	72,128	15,352	6,110	23,236	20,447	28,126	23,121	43,302	15,237	59,636	7,213
2005	29,897	70,956	14,294	6,044	22,208	20,304	26,348	23,260	40,684	14,440	55,553	6,906
2004	28,691	70,285	13,655	6,183	21,923	20,361	24,983	22,914	38,776	14,143	54,623	6,680
2003[2]	28,367	69,790	14,214	6,108	21,659	20,772	24,848	22,514	38,447	13,823	53,579	6,572
2002	27,271	69,735	13,459	6,404	21,141	21,233	23,905	22,176	37,909	13,589	50,756	6,330
2001	26,962	69,487	14,524	6,720	20,489	21,402	24,268	21,824	36,913	13,472	51,160	6,068
2000[3]	25,228	69,647	12,739	6,890	19,162	21,538	22,779	22,348	35,328	13,113	49,368	5,757
1999	23,551	68,409	12,145	6,819	18,092	21,847	21,644	22,687	32,546	12,533	46,307	5,523
1998	22,818	66,840	11,353	6,657	17,898	21,832	21,056	20,867	31,452	12,332	44,954	5,153
1997	21,528	65,771	10,725	6,614	16,906	21,824	19,856	20,442	30,119	12,027	42,744	4,863
1996	20,570	64,748	10,421	6,492	16,161	21,942	18,933	20,202	28,701	11,466	42,625	4,646
1995	19,414	63,587	9,790	6,678	15,970	21,073	17,962	20,224	26,841	11,034	37,813	4,578
1994	18,684	62,850	9,189	6,498	14,955	21,195	16,928	20,276	26,483	10,388	39,905	4,493
1993	17,900	61,937	9,462	6,425	14,446	21,391	16,555	19,897	25,232	10,005	37,212	4,218
1992	17,145	60,451	9,311	6,277	14,128	21,730	16,023	18,571	23,991	9,738	33,814	4,135
1991	16,320	60,226	8,818	6,875	13,523	22,398	15,643	17,657	22,802	9,348	32,929	3,948
1990	15,493	59,862	8,808	7,286	12,986	25,224	15,002	14,149	21,933	8,321	28,862	4,883
1989	14,809	59,296	8,268	7,363	12,468	25,377	14,688	13,694	21,089	8,030	26,977	4,831
1988	13,833	58,558	7,711	7,642	11,857	25,217	14,009	13,198	19,216	7,842	25,010	4,660
1987	13,049	56,923	7,504	7,631	11,309	24,834	13,158	12,971	18,217	7,211	24,004	4,277
1986	12,214	55,568	7,109	7,457	10,606	24,542	12,029	12,611	17,623	6,880	22,672	4,078
1985	11,493	54,212	6,874	7,555	10,115	24,178	11,504	12,017	16,114	6,579	21,202	3,883
1984	10,742	53,178	6,644	7,881	9,561	23,625	10,614	11,645	14,865	6,266	20,275	3,762
1983	10,111	51,279	6,292	7,644	9,147	23,111	9,981	10,947	13,808	5,919	18,593	3,658
1982	9,403	49,962	5,932	7,921	8,715	22,525	9,348	10,499	12,511	5,560	17,009	3,457
1981	8,619	49,754	5,673	8,595	8,063	22,897	8,811	9,975	11,384	5,186	15,647	3,101
1980	7,909	49,094	5,263	8,755	7,423	22,772	8,256	9,721	10,628	5,043	14,022	2,802
1979	7,099	48,362	4,840	9,072	6,741	22,179	7,190	9,393	9,474	4,862	12,717	2,856
1978	6,396	45,850	4,397	9,237	6,192	20,860	6,441	8,769	8,408	4,390	11,603	2,595
1977	5,804	43,678	4,032	9,485	5,624	19,850	5,856	8,057	7,923	4,016	10,848	2,271
1976	5,373	42,091	3,723	9,401	5,240	19,071	5,301	7,504	7,383	3,997	10,345	2,117
1975	4,968	40,584	3,438	9,303	4,802	18,480	5,019	7,066	6,963	3,804	9,818	1,931
WHITE												
Both Sexes												
2010	44,142	123,870	21,471	10,820	32,067	34,611	35,180	37,071	59,188	26,950	85,070	14,415
2009	43,337	125,151	20,457	11,507	31,429	36,125	35,634	37,035	57,762	26,595	86,188	13,887
2008	43,666	127,552	21,590	12,379	32,126	36,819	35,622	37,891	59,866	26,487	84,739	13,973
2007	43,139	127,413	22,289	12,363	32,223	37,058	35,685	37,988	58,652	26,310	82,384	13,692
2006	42,395	126,570	21,464	13,582	32,083	37,362	35,338	36,878	57,932	25,763	83,185	12,983
2005	40,717	124,870	20,264	13,157	30,569	37,122	34,326	37,409	55,785	24,652	81,697	12,527
2004	38,946	123,452	19,367	13,289	29,605	37,114	32,751	36,547	52,877	24,061	79,071	12,397
2003[2]	38,053	122,599	19,110	13,094	28,708	36,951	32,346	36,318	52,259	24,010	75,638	12,226
2002	37,376	122,699	19,264	13,740	28,145	37,380	31,878	36,023	52,479	23,638	73,870	11,916
2001	36,844	122,930	19,120	14,012	27,700	37,969	31,482	35,722	51,631	23,531	74,398	11,694
2000[3]	35,527	123,039	18,285	14,172	26,444	38,133	30,638	36,334	50,969	23,110	71,983	11,288

[1]For data prior to 1991, "Some college/Associate degree" equals 1 to 3 years of college completed; "Bachelor's degree" equals 4 years of college; "Advanced degree" equals 5 or more years of college completed.
[2]Starting in 2003, respondents could choose more than one race. The race data in this table from 2003 onward represent respondents who indicated only one race.
[3]Beginning in 2000, earnings data are from the expanded Current Population Survey (CPS) sample and were calculated using population controls based on Census 2000.

Table A-27. Mean Earnings of Workers 18 Years Old and Over, by Educational Attainment, Race, Hispanic Origin, and Sex, 1975–2010—*Continued*

(Dollars except as noted)

Race, sex, year, and Hispanic origin	Total		Not a high school graduate		High school graduate		Some college/ associate's degree[1]		Bachelor's degree[1]		Advanced degree[1]	
	Mean earnings	Number of workers (thousands)	Mean earnings	Number of workers (thousands)	Mean earnings	Number of workers (thousands)	Mean earnings	Number of workers (thousands)	Mean earnings	Number of workers (thousands)	Mean earnings	Number of workers (thousands)
Both Sexes— *(Continued)*												
1999	33,326	120,916	16,623	13,585	25,270	38,428	29,105	35,634	46,894	22,322	68,910	10,949
1998	32,057	119,201	16,474	13,531	24,409	38,397	28,318	34,540	44,852	22,266	65,379	10,467
1997	30,515	117,985	16,596	13,780	23,618	38,409	26,906	34,274	41,439	21,528	65,058	9,994
1996	28,844	117,230	15,358	13,972	22,782	38,463	25,511	34,087	38,936	20,846	61,779	9,861
1995	27,556	115,636	14,234	13,869	22,154	37,802	24,349	33,850	37,711	20,203	57,054	9,914
1994	26,696	114,586	13,941	13,119	20,911	37,562	22,648	34,006	37,996	19,917	56,475	9,981
1993	25,440	113,342	13,171	13,480	19,918	37,826	21,924	33,728	35,846	18,922	56,964	9,386
1992	23,932	112,120	13,193	13,494	19,265	38,692	21,357	32,014	33,092	18,555	49,347	9,363
1991	22,998	111,830	12,914	14,041	18,766	39,764	21,013	30,973	31,837	18,033	46,498	9,019
1990	22,401	111,972	12,773	15,191	18,257	44,635	21,095	25,105	31,626	15,993	41,908	11,049
1989	22,035	111,243	12,654	15,628	18,011	44,726	20,678	24,212	31,266	15,723	41,610	10,952
1988	20,616	110,159	12,236	16,042	17,183	44,399	19,384	23,643	28,886	15,221	38,129	10,854
1987	19,599	108,407	12,502	16,165	16,339	44,235	18,265	23,083	27,741	14,624	36,175	10,300
1986	18,698	106,384	11,605	16,094	15,514	43,593	17,371	22,653	27,061	14,055	35,265	9,987
1985	17,709	104,818	11,115	16,149	14,815	43,347	16,701	22,131	25,376	13,670	33,401	9,522
1984	16,546	103,022	10,732	16,559	14,274	42,547	15,197	21,451	23,472	13,056	30,515	9,409
1983	15,556	101,035	10,239	16,568	13,357	42,007	14,486	20,452	21,914	12,577	28,532	9,430
1982	14,767	99,488	9,719	17,132	12,854	41,157	13,799	19,967	20,760	12,103	27,040	9,127
1981	14,027	99,510	9,737	18,298	12,355	42,080	13,424	19,102	19,389	11,450	25,564	8,582
1980	13,040	98,358	9,743	18,925	11,524	41,600	12,677	18,888	18,434	11,067	23,466	7,876
1979	12,155	97,544	8,827	19,504	10,431	40,458	11,574	18,835	16,758	10,807	22,085	7,940
1978	11,135	94,002	8,135	19,516	10,020	38,915	10,504	18,022	15,463	10,171	20,531	7,376
1977	10,191	91,254	7,415	20,492	9,173	37,521	9,771	16,968	14,462	9,534	19,337	6,739
1976	9,469	89,099	7,018	20,625	8,559	36,523	8,958	16,127	13,279	9,325	18,153	6,498
1975	8,815	86,894	6,438	20,696	8,005	35,799	8,525	15,423	12,597	8,955	16,920	6,021
Male												
2010	52,304	66,887	25,100	7,011	37,477	20,018	42,151	18,362	71,958	14,077	105,869	7,417
2009	51,287	67,464	23,353	7,426	36,418	20,855	42,884	18,273	71,286	13,740	106,571	7,168
2008	52,672	68,816	25,386	8,113	37,852	20,899	43,463	18,849	75,053	13,596	107,099	7,356
2007	51,781	69,099	25,886	8,170	38,214	21,129	42,903	18,995	73,477	13,577	103,293	7,227
2006	51,013	68,752	24,579	8,932	38,833	21,090	42,684	18,340	71,735	13,326	103,340	7,063
2005	49,611	67,874	23,556	8,582	36,753	20,914	42,206	18,583	69,852	12,900	103,144	6,893
2004	47,404	66,677	22,598	8,591	35,360	20,781	40,639	17,990	65,652	12,555	100,084	6,758
2003[2]	46,114	66,199	21,791	8,500	34,224	20,238	39,594	18,060	65,264	12,665	94,017	6,734
2002	45,793	66,202	22,539	8,841	33,920	20,156	39,605	18,068	65,439	12,512	92,733	6,623
2001	45,071	66,216	22,006	8,833	33,545	20,465	38,501	17,957	65,046	12,396	92,304	6,562
2000[3]	44,181	66,222	21,561	8,859	32,528	20,553	38,476	18,179	64,831	12,271	89,812	6,359
1999	41,598	64,856	19,320	8,286	31,279	20,526	36,518	17,928	59,606	11,851	85,345	6,265
1998	39,638	64,181	19,632	8,430	29,782	20,388	35,277	17,407	56,620	11,874	79,734	6,083
1997	37,933	63,738	20,071	8,670	29,298	20,426	33,691	17,423	51,678	11,340	80,322	5,879
1996	35,821	63,532	18,246	8,899	28,591	20,329	32,238	17,418	48,014	11,065	75,481	5,821
1995	34,276	62,520	17,032	8,660	27,467	19,982	30,529	17,136	47,016	10,851	70,155	5,891
1994	33,292	62,029	16,835	8,133	26,125	19,833	28,240	17,091	47,575	10,992	67,629	5,979
1993	31,719	61,356	15,295	8,430	24,781	19,835	27,297	16,959	44,505	10,452	70,000	5,680
1992	29,515	60,919	15,414	8,487	23,844	20,259	26,387	16,335	40,893	10,118	59,329	5,720
1991	28,516	60,770	15,499	8,720	23,475	20,765	26,090	15,873	39,547	9,893	55,257	5,519
1990	28,105	60,676	15,319	9,476	23,135	23,088	26,841	13,003	39,780	8,770	50,385	6,731
1989	28,013	60,877	15,217	9,805	23,291	23,029	26,260	12,582	39,654	8,750	51,031	6,710
1988	26,184	60,221	14,943	10,008	22,216	22,707	24,462	12,277	36,637	8,467	46,181	6,762
1987	24,898	59,468	15,303	10,132	21,012	22,682	23,310	11,771	34,865	8,384	43,440	6,499
1986	23,892	58,932	14,168	10,239	20,128	22,392	22,303	11,846	34,273	8,041	42,480	6,413
1985	22,604	58,385	13,579	10,163	19,203	22,357	21,240	11,831	32,165	7,970	40,358	6,064
1984	21,174	57,362	13,248	10,280	18,681	21,989	19,344	11,387	29,781	7,624	36,219	6,081
1983	19,812	56,641	12,573	10,387	17,281	21,733	18,388	10,974	27,726	7,379	33,981	6,168
1982	18,859	56,364	11,952	10,816	16,662	21,436	17,571	10,822	26,404	7,242	32,266	6,047
1981	18,141	56,397	12,094	11,523	16,352	21,809	17,303	10,448	24,943	6,824	30,396	5,794
1980	16,945	55,772	11,539	11,937	15,382	21,453	16,313	10,400	23,803	6,618	27,991	5,363
1979	15,971	55,556	11,127	12,291	13,916	20,834	15,043	10,572	21,785	6,464	26,645	5,395
1978	14,627	54,113	10,358	12,141	13,534	20,328	13,589	10,350	20,085	6,205	24,635	5,088
1977	13,329	53,174	9,366	12,903	12,377	19,773	12,657	9,853	18,521	5,941	23,093	4,704
1976	12,342	52,312	8,867	13,117	11,497	19,446	11,616	9,394	16,995	5,765	21,490	4,589
1975	11,448	51,510	8,110	13,191	10,726	19,361	11,028	9,096	16,079	5,587	19,858	4,275

[1]For data prior to 1991, "Some college/Associate degree" equals 1 to 3 years of college completed; "Bachelor's degree" equals 4 years of college; "Advanced degree" equals 5 or more years of college completed.
[2]Starting in 2003, respondents could choose more than one race. The race data in this table from 2003 onward represent respondents who indicated only one race.
[3]Beginning in 2000, earnings data are from the expanded Current Population Survey (CPS) sample and were calculated using population controls based on Census 2000.

Table A-27. Mean Earnings of Workers 18 Years Old and Over, by Educational Attainment, Race, Hispanic Origin, and Sex, 1975–2010—*Continued*

(Dollars except as noted)

Race, sex, year, and Hispanic origin	Total		Not a high school graduate		High school graduate		Some college/ associate's degree[1]		Bachelor's degree[1]		Advanced degree[1]	
	Mean earnings	Number of workers (thousands)	Mean earnings	Number of workers (thousands)	Mean earnings	Number of workers (thousands)	Mean earnings	Number of workers (thousands)	Mean earnings	Number of workers (thousands)	Mean earnings	Number of workers (thousands)
Female												
2010............	34,561	56,982	14,791	3,808	24,645	14,593	28,339	18,709	45,223	12,873	63,021	6,997
2009............	34,040	57,687	15,187	4,080	24,615	15,270	28,573	16,762	43,309	12,855	64,441	6,718
2008............	33,115	58,735	14,370	4,265	24,610	15,919	27,859	19,041	43,848	12,891	59,877	6,616
2007............	32,899	58,313	15,278	4,192	24,276	15,929	28,466	18,993	42,846	12,733	59,006	6,464
2006............	32,148	57,818	15,483	4,650	23,334	16,272	28,069	18,537	43,142	12,437	59,141	5,920
2005............	30,125	56,995	14,086	4,575	22,590	16,208	26,547	18,825	40,344	11,751	55,461	5,634
2004............	28,966	56,705	13,459	4,703	22,260	16,358	25,104	18,556	38,898	11,445	53,895	5,641
2003[2]...........	28,591	56,400	14,149	4,593	22,028	16,712	25,177	18,258	37,739	11,344	53,102	5,492
2002............	27,512	56,496	13,354	4,898	21,388	17,224	24,101	17,954	37,903	11,126	50,270	5,293
2001............	27,240	56,714	14,197	5,178	20,866	17,503	24,387	17,764	36,698	11,135	51,499	5,131
2000[3]...........	25,441	56,816	12,823	5,313	19,330	17,579	22,790	18,155	35,273	10,838	48,982	4,929
1999............	23,756	56,061	12,405	5,299	18,381	17,902	21,598	17,705	32,507	10,471	45,741	4,684
1998............	23,213	55,020	11,255	5,102	18,327	18,009	21,246	17,132	31,406	10,393	45,462	4,384
1997............	21,779	54,247	10,700	5,111	17,166	17,983	19,892	16,852	30,041	10,188	43,236	4,114
1996............	20,590	53,697	10,290	5,073	16,270	18,134	18,482	16,669	28,667	9,781	42,049	4,041
1995............	19,647	53,117	9,582	5,208	16,196	17,820	18,011	16,714	26,916	9,352	37,864	4,022
1994............	18,912	52,557	9,220	4,987	15,078	17,729	16,998	16,915	26,198	8,925	39,816	4,002
1993............	18,028	51,986	9,624	5,050	14,557	17,991	16,490	16,769	25,161	8,470	36,988	3,705
1992............	17,289	51,200	9,428	5,007	14,233	18,434	16,116	15,679	23,738	8,437	33,675	3,643
1991............	16,431	51,060	8,677	5,321	13,621	18,999	15,677	15,100	22,471	8,140	32,687	3,500
1990............	15,559	50,905	8,725	5,715	13,031	21,547	14,922	12,102	21,725	7,223	28,694	4,318
1989............	14,810	50,366	8,338	5,823	12,406	21,697	14,640	11,630	20,741	6,973	26,709	4,242
1988............	13,902	49,938	7,747	6,034	11,915	21,692	13,898	11,366	19,169	6,754	24,824	4,092
1987............	13,161	48,939	7,798	6,033	11,421	21,553	13,015	11,312	18,170	6,240	23,753	3,801
1986............	12,247	47,452	7,123	5,855	10,641	21,201	11,964	10,807	17,418	6,014	22,320	3,574
1985............	11,555	46,433	6,931	5,986	10,142	20,990	11,488	10,300	15,883	5,700	21,202	3,458
1984............	10,732	45,660	6,614	6,279	9,561	20,558	10,504	10,064	14,617	5,432	20,092	3,328
1983............	10,126	44,394	6,317	6,181	9,150	20,274	9,969	9,478	13,664	5,198	18,230	3,262
1982............	9,419	43,124	5,896	6,316	8,714	19,721	9,336	9,145	12,352	4,861	16,779	3,080
1981............	8,646	43,113	5,727	6,775	8,054	20,271	8,740	8,654	11,196	4,626	15,523	2,788
1980............	7,926	42,586	6,675	6,988	7,415	20,147	8,221	8,488	10,447	4,449	13,809	2,513
1979............	7,105	41,988	4,909	7,213	6,731	19,624	7,135	8,263	9,275	4,343	12,420	2,545
1978............	6,398	39,889	4,476	7,375	6,176	18,587	6,342	7,672	8,231	3,966	11,404	2,288
1977............	5,808	38,080	4,097	7,589	5,604	17,748	5,774	7,115	7,750	3,593	10,655	2,035
1976............	5,383	36,787	3,788	7,508	5,214	17,077	5,250	6,733	7,262	3,560	10,131	1,909
1975............	4,982	35,384	3,500	7,505	4,800	16,438	4,926	6,327	6,822	3,368	9,728	1,746
NON-HISPANIC WHITE												
Both Sexes												
2010............	46,878	103,829	22,557	4,877	33,279	28,369	35,903	32,184	60,119	24,823	85,840	13,574
2009............	45,939	105,137	21,229	5,216	32,562	29,860	36,249	32,430	58,487	24,533	86,770	13,095
2008............	46,179	107,294	21,765	5,798	33,159	30,598	36,158	33,221	60,866	24,445	85,017	13,230
2007............	45,542	107,434	23,015	5,908	33,094	30,855	36,290	33,431	59,727	24,366	82,900	12,871
2006............	44,813	106,828	22,206	6,876	32,931	31,345	35,872	32,403	58,917	23,855	83,785	12,347
2005............	42,963	106,337	21,134	6,603	31,445	31,484	34,866	33,355	56,462	23,013	82,205	11,879
2004............	40,943	105,505	19,742	6,754	30,197	31,793	33,192	33,200	53,411	22,544	79,166	11,961
2003[2]...........	40,094	105,214	19,769	6,768	29,571	31,831	32,825	32,460	52,856	22,474	76,200	11,680
2002............	39,220	105,706	19,423	7,380	28,756	32,365	32,318	32,344	53,185	22,221	74,122	11,395
2001............	38,711	106,384	19,659	7,812	28,426	33,050	31,905	32,118	52,300	22,204	74,932	11,198
2000[3]...........	37,346	106,709	19,147	7,957	27,122	33,231	31,217	32,836	51,351	21,824	72,356	10,859
1999............	34,838	106,573	16,957	8,219	25,847	34,121	29,557	32,454	47,401	21,272	68,910	10,507
1998............	33,336	105,523	16,837	8,488	24,801	34,344	23,897	31,459	45,342	21,175	65,461	10,059

[1]For data prior to 1991, "Some college/Associate degree" equals 1 to 3 years of college completed; "Bachelor's degree" equals 4 years of college; "Advanced degree" equals 5 or more years of college completed.
[2]Starting in 2003, respondents could choose more than one race. The race data in this table from 2003 onward represent respondents who indicated only one race.
[3]Beginning in 2000, earnings data are from the expanded Current Population Survey (CPS) sample and were calculated using population controls based on Census 2000.

Table A-27. Mean Earnings of Workers 18 Years Old and Over, by Educational Attainment, Race, Hispanic Origin, and Sex, 1975–2010—*Continued*

(Dollars except as noted)

Race, sex, year, and Hispanic origin	Total		Not a high school graduate		High school graduate		Some college/ associate's degree[1]		Bachelor's degree[1]		Advanced degree[1]	
	Mean earnings	Number of workers (thousands)	Mean earnings	Number of workers (thousands)	Mean earnings	Number of workers (thousands)	Mean earnings	Number of workers (thousands)	Mean earnings	Number of workers (thousands)	Mean earnings	Number of workers (thousands)
Male												
2010............	56,417	55,094	27,375	3,030	39,284	16,186	43,272	15,846	73,149	13,010	107,125	7,019
2009............	55,318	55,638	25,695	3,187	38,160	17,015	43,802	15,981	72,305	12,708	107,872	6,746
2008............	56,538	56,822	26,479	3,654	39,405	17,206	44,237	16,439	76,613	12,562	107,498	6,960
2007............	55,662	57,080	27,874	3,716	39,764	17,309	43,835	16,684	75,214	12,597	104,317	6,772
2006............	54,843	56,843	26,100	4,289	40,180	17,470	43,589	16,024	73,376	12,321	104,031	6,738
2005............	53,263	56,675	25,511	4,127	38,134	17,507	43,137	16,456	70,932	12,048	104,107	6,535
2004............	50,597	55,930	23,590	4,203	36,324	17,568	41,490	16,259	66,527	11,739	100,220	6,527
2003[2]............	49,386	55,774	22,957	4,224	35,589	17,225	40,316	16,048	66,390	11,849	95,029	6,427
2002............	48,817	55,994	23,250	4,580	34,909	17,218	40,368	16,121	66,638	11,764	93,686	6,309
2001............	47,973	56,528	23,096	4,749	34,627	17,672	39,133	16,114	66,196	11,692	92,954	6,299
2000[3]............	47,084	56,675	23,296	4,763	33,669	17,733	39,379	16,435	65,459	11,594	90,150	6,149
1999............	44,032	56,575	20,256	4,842	32,321	18,047	37,224	16,343	60,384	11,307	85,918	6,036
1998............	41,612	56,246	20,781	5,152	30,429	18,048	29,555	15,849	57,346	11,335	79,524	5,862
Female												
2010............	36,093	48,735	14,649	1,846	25,300	12,183	28,755	16,337	45,767	11,812	63,047	6,555
2009............	35,396	49,498	14,216	2,029	25,147	12,845	28,911	16,448	43,636	11,825	64,351	6,349
2008............	34,517	50,471	13,730	2,144	25,133	13,391	28,244	16,781	44,220	11,883	60,063	6,270
2007............	34,069	50,353	14,779	2,192	24,570	13,546	28,772	16,746	43,150	11,769	59,121	6,099
2006............	33,407	49,984	15,751	2,857	23,805	13,875	28,322	16,379	43,473	11,534	59,458	5,608
2005............	31,208	49,661	13,837	2,476	23,004	13,977	26,812	16,899	40,562	10,964	55,422	5,344
2004............	30,051	49,575	13,401	2,550	22,631	14,224	25,228	16,940	39,161	10,805	53,875	5,433
2003[2]............	29,613	49,439	14,475	2,543	22,473	14,605	25,499	16,411	37,761	10,624	53,164	5,253
2002............	28,410	49,712	13,163	2,800	21,762	15,146	24,318	16,222	38,049	10,457	49,845	5,085
2001............	28,210	49,856	14,328	3,062	21,301	15,378	24,628	16,004	36,844	10,512	51,756	4,898
2000[3]............	26,315	50,034	12,962	3,194	19,631	15,498	23,038	16,401	35,362	10,230	49,126	4,710
1999............	24,436	49,998	12,227	3,378	18,579	16,074	21,779	16,112	32,667	9,964	45,943	4,470
1998............	23,891	49,277	10,746	3,336	18,568	16,295	18,198	15,610	31,516	9,840	45,805	4,196
BLACK												
Both Sexes												
2010............	32,808	16,840	17,644	1,559	25,757	5,518	30,351	5,927	44,311	2,596	71,000	1,237
2009............	33,362	16,744	18,936	1,618	26,970	5,803	30,520	5,577	47,799	2,583	66,923	1,162
2008............	32,874	17,509	18,123	1,748	27,265	6,060	30,248	5,933	46,527	2,550	66,198	1,216
2007............	33,333	17,453	17,439	1,854	27,179	5,996	32,787	5,813	46,502	2,682	64,247	1,107
2006............	32,443	17,234	17,823	1,943	26,368	6,159	31,234	5,581	47,903	2,503	64,834	1,045
2005............	30,472	17,000	17,216	2,025	23,904	6,101	28,848	5,390	47,101	2,412	63,664	1,071
2004............	29,096	16,631	17,827	2,044	23,498	6,138	27,779	5,191	42,342	2,348	65,538	909
2003[2]............	28,838	16,389	16,201	2,095	23,777	5,941	27,187	5,119	42,968	2,321	64,164	911
2002............	28,179	16,352	16,516	2,148	22,823	5,822	27,626	5,255	42,285	2,275	59,944	851
2001............	27,031	16,683	17,248	2,382	21,743	5,729	26,907	5,481	40,165	2,212	55,771	877
2000[2]............	26,204	16,756	15,201	2,434	21,789	6,020	26,324	5,431	41,513	2,060	52,373	809
1999............	24,979	16,936	13,569	2,393	20,991	6,112	25,176	5,417	37,422	2,140	52,437	873
1998............	22,829	16,201	13,672	2,402	19,236	6,053	23,927	4,559	36,373	1,897	44,760	764
1997............	21,909	15,873	13,185	2,437	18,980	5,964	22,899	4,902	32,062	1,846	42,791	724
1996............	21,978	15,255	13,110	2,383	18,722	5,844	23,628	4,783	31,955	1,655	48,731	590
1995............	20,537	14,847	12,956	2,389	17,072	5,453	21,824	4,727	29,666	1,684	46,654	595
1994............	19,772	14,754	12,705	2,290	16,446	5,596	19,631	4,610	30,938	1,679	48,653	579
1993............	18,614	14,315	11,065	2,352	16,122	5,521	18,867	4,279	29,953	1,638	41,221	525
1992............	17,416	13,836	11,077	2,451	15,260	5,379	18,719	4,054	27,457	1,429	41,439	523
1991............	16,809	13,865	11,248	2,860	15,060	5,512	17,850	3,581	25,630	1,383	38,002	528
1990............	16,627	13,731	11,184	2,853	14,794	6,049	18,209	3,004	26,448	1,217	32,962	607
1989............	16,072	13,600	10,066	2,883	14,613	5,894	17,385	3,008	25,357	1,121	32,740	694
1988............	15,318	13,356	10,202	2,970	13,835	5,760	16,760	2,802	23,689	1,204	30,802	621
1987............	14,136	13,023	9,976	3,015	12,862	5,699	15,491	2,617	20,805	1,097	29,163	596
1986............	13,494	12,729	9,365	3,028	12,276	5,470	14,743	2,662	21,403	1,004	27,503	564
1985............	12,926	12,427	9,116	3,009	11,791	5,223	13,805	2,615	20,533	1,046	26,246	535
1984............	12,002	11,948	8,725	3,127	10,882	4,927	12,890	2,396	19,330	937	24,072	561
1983............	11,299	11,296	7,867	3,035	10,557	4,692	12,426	2,206	17,207	828	23,506	535
1982............	10,612	11,081	7,799	3,188	10,287	4,591	11,119	2,067	15,152	747	22,959	488
1981............	10,117	11,088	7,520	3,514	9,994	4,388	11,456	2,078	14,587	708	19,463	398

[1]For data prior to 1991, "Some college/Associate degree" equals 1 to 3 years of college completed; "Bachelor's degree" equals 4 years of college; "Advanced degree" equals 5 or more years of college completed.
[2]Starting in 2003, respondents could choose more than one race. The race data in this table from 2003 onward represent respondents who indicated only one race.
[3]Beginning in 2000, earnings data are from the expanded Current Population Survey (CPS) sample and were calculated using population controls based on Census 2000.

Table A-27. Mean Earnings of Workers 18 Years Old and Over, by Educational Attainment, Race, Hispanic Origin, and Sex, 1975–2010—*Continued*

(Dollars except as noted)

Race, sex, year, and Hispanic origin	Total		Not a high school graduate		High school graduate		Some college/ associate's degree[1]		Bachelor's degree[1]		Advanced degree[1]	
	Mean earnings	Number of workers (thousands)	Mean earnings	Number of workers (thousands)	Mean earnings	Number of workers (thousands)	Mean earnings	Number of workers (thousands)	Mean earnings	Number of workers (thousands)	Mean earnings	Number of workers (thousands)
Both Sexes— *(Continued)*												
1980	11,085	5,576	8,421	2,054	11,563	2,119	12,393	964	15,616	283	19,960	353
1979	8,720	10,856	6,424	3,776	8,723	4,267	9,895	1,826	13,473	622	18,182	366
1978	7,981	10,420	5,918	3,841	8,152	3,944	9,026	1,689	12,870	557	15,076	389
1977	7,271	10,014	5,406	3,946	7,553	3,604	8,321	1,578	11,088	532	14,749	354
1976	6,716	9,744	5,304	4,008	6,805	3,515	7,331	1,370	10,331	547	15,013	305
1975	6,190	9,368	4,989	3,922	6,281	3,495	7,212	1,193	9,473	517	12,333	241
Male												
2010	35,598	7,735	19,452	829	29,478	2,878	33,905	2,473	48,068	1,075	81,199	477
2009	37,553	7,657	21,828	861	30,723	2,996	35,889	2,301	55,655	1,030	78,574	467
2008	36,057	8,116	22,344	866	30,985	3,166	34,209	2,505	51,691	1,059	73,948	518
2007	35,668	8,088	19,705	985	29,640	2,994	34,035	2,492	53,029	1,155	74,351	459
2006	36,045	7,932	21,294	982	30,122	3,067	34,750	2,334	52,569	1,086	74,507	460
2005	34,165	7,836	19,890	1,056	27,360	3,050	33,544	2,273	52,070	1,011	77,210	444
2004	33,020	7,668	22,796	1,029	26,608	3,119	32,367	2,176	47,746	956	79,168	386
2003[2]	32,545	7,469	17,915	1,039	28,102	2,910	31,556	2,156	45,635	966	76,871	397
2002	31,790	7,483	19,294	1,072	25,582	2,832	32,764	2,283	47,018	974	75,050	321
2001	30,502	7,727	18,543	1,210	25,037	2,759	31,084	2,457	46,511	943	67,007	356
2000[3]	30,109	7,700	17,992	1,235	25,219	2,942	30,966	2,291	49,270	880	60,207	349
1999	28,821	7,806	16,391	1,199	25,849	2,934	28,442	2,338	42,530	971	59,587	365
1998	26,090	7,488	16,013	1,190	22,698	2,974	26,586	2,215	42,539	792	51,198	318
1997	25,080	7,370	15,423	1,304	22,440	2,862	27,215	2,108	35,792	818	49,940	278
1996	25,067	7,125	15,461	1,290	22,267	2,836	26,365	2,047	35,558	700	65,981	253
1995	23,876	7,090	14,877	1,280	19,514	2,812	26,846	2,047	36,026	659	57,186	293
1994	22,614	7,009	15,984	1,191	18,527	2,818	23,748	1,959	34,073	758	52,829	281
1993	21,108	6,833	13,074	1,305	18,668	2,775	21,734	1,804	35,147	721	47,372	228
1992	19,278	6,822	12,661	1,457	16,978	2,683	22,697	1,796	30,989	643	48,968	244
1991	18,607	6,830	15,714	1,624	17,352	2,731	20,548	1,570	26,075	650	43,927	255
1990	18,859	6,781	13,031	1,563	17,046	3,013	21,152	1,372	29,471	564	39,104	269
1989	18,108	6,654	11,827	1,614	16,658	2,848	20,253	1,352	27,493	515	38,166	326
1988	17,782	6,593	12,439	1,671	16,345	2,795	19,265	1,311	28,506	533	36,452	283
1987	16,171	6,505	11,899	1,711	14,800	2,769	18,081	1,250	23,345	482	34,073	294
1986	15,441	6,326	11,248	1,691	14,214	2,666	17,419	1,226	23,412	480	31,054	263
1985	14,932	6,237	10,802	1,716	13,721	2,572	16,415	1,230	23,818	477	31,947	243
1984	13,560	5,899	10,216	1,780	12,382	2,339	14,960	1,106	21,986	424	27,893	250
1983	12,789	5,707	9,094	1,768	11,956	2,312	15,113	996	20,370	363	25,466	268
1982	12,203	5,535	9,153	1,798	11,952	2,213	12,926	953	17,658	319	26,452	253
1981	11,937	5,651	9,266	1,925	11,905	2,191	13,740	1,002	16,624	327	21,082	205
1980	11,085	5,576	8,421	2,054	11,563	2,119	12,393	964	15,616	283	23,346	156
1979	10,403	5,581	7,938	2,138	10,662	2,087	11,971	931	16,161	259	21,092	166
1978	9,651	5,350	7,423	2,156	9,869	1,982	11,197	770	16,009	260	18,083	181
1977	8,710	5,220	6,648	2,230	9,332	1,770	10,023	799	12,978	234	16,385	188
1976	7,991	5,156	6,670	2,289	8,056	1,766	8,688	726	12,246	233	17,859	143
1975	7,541	4,864	6,364	2,247	7,847	1,684	8,505	599	11,318	213	13,720	121
Female												
2010	30,438	9,104	15,589	730	21,700	2,640	27,805	3,453	41,653	1,520	64,586	759
2009	29,831	9,087	15,644	756	22,964	2,806	26,748	3,276	42,587	1,552	59,073	694
2008	29,734	9,392	13,976	881	23,195	2,893	27,354	3,428	42,858	1,491	60,430	697
2007	31,317	9,365	14,869	868	24,724	3,001	31,850	3,320	41,560	1,526	57,076	647
2006	29,371	9,302	14,277	961	22,643	3,092	28,706	3,246	44,326	1,417	57,206	584
2005	27,314	9,163	14,300	968	20,449	3,051	25,422	3,116	43,516	1,401	54,044	626
2004	25,738	8,962	12,785	1,014	20,284	3,019	24,468	3,015	38,626	1,391	55,436	522
2003[2]	25,735	8,919	14,513	1,056	19,623	3,030	24,007	2,963	41,066	1,355	54,346	514
2002	25,131	8,868	13,748	1,075	20,209	2,989	23,679	2,972	38,741	1,301	50,766	529
2001	24,036	8,956	15,912	1,172	18,683	2,970	23,511	3,023	35,448	1,269	48,080	521
2000[3]	22,884	9,056	12,321	1,198	18,510	3,078	22,937	3,140	35,719	1,179	46,416	459
1999	21,694	9,130	10,734	1,194	16,506	3,178	22,699	3,080	33,184	1,170	47,358	509
1998	20,026	8,713	11,372	1,212	15,892	3,078	20,371	2,870	31,952	1,105	40,214	448
1997	19,161	8,503	10,607	1,132	15,789	3,102	19,643	2,794	29,091	1,027	38,392	448
1996	19,271	8,129	10,337	1,094	15,379	3,008	21,581	2,736	29,311	954	35,785	337
1995	17,485	7,757	10,739	1,108	14,473	2,641	17,985	2,679	25,577	1,025	36,585	304
1994	17,200	7,745	9,150	1,099	14,333	2,777	16,589	2,651	28,356	921	44,618	297
1993	16,336	7,481	8,562	1,048	13,550	2,746	16,778	2,475	25,865	917	36,485	296
1992	15,605	7,014	8,756	995	13,550	2,696	15,553	2,256	24,572	786	34,902	281

[1]For data prior to 1991, "Some college/Associate degree" equals 1 to 3 years of college completed; "Bachelor's degree" equals 4 years of college; "Advanced degree" equals 5 or more years of college completed.
[2]Starting in 2003, respondents could choose more than one race. The race data in this table from 2003 onward represent respondents who indicated only one race.
[3]Beginning in 2000, earnings data are from the expanded Current Population Survey (CPS) sample and were calculated using population controls based on Census 2000.

Table A-27. Mean Earnings of Workers 18 Years Old and Over, by Educational Attainment, Race, Hispanic Origin, and Sex, 1975–2010—*Continued*

(Dollars except as noted)

Race, sex, year, and Hispanic origin	Total		Not a high school graduate		High school graduate		Some college/ associate's degree[1]		Bachelor's degree[1]		Advanced degree[1]	
	Mean earnings	Number of workers (thousands)	Mean earnings	Number of workers (thousands)	Mean earnings	Number of workers (thousands)	Mean earnings	Number of workers (thousands)	Mean earnings	Number of workers (thousands)	Mean earnings	Number of workers (thousands)
Female— *(Continued)*												
1991	15,065	7,034	9,151	1,237	12,810	2,781	15,743	2,010	25,235	733	32,467	273
1990	14,449	6,950	8,946	1,290	12,560	3,036	15,734	1,632	23,837	653	28,074	338
1989	14,122	6,946	7,827	1,269	12,701	3,046	15,044	1,656	23,541	606	27,933	368
1988	12,916	6,763	7,325	1,299	11,469	2,965	14,557	1,491	19,862	671	26,072	338
1987	12,106	6,518	7,452	1,304	11,030	2,930	13,123	1,367	18,815	615	24,383	302
1986	11,571	6,403	6,984	1,337	10,434	2,804	12,459	1,436	19,562	524	24,400	301
1985	10,904	6,190	6,879	1,293	9,918	2,651	11,488	1,385	17,779	569	21,502	292
1984	10,482	6,049	6,754	1,347	9,527	2,588	11,115	1,290	17,134	513	21,000	311
1983	9,778	5,589	6,154	1,267	9,197	2,380	10,215	1,210	14,738	465	21,539	267
1982	9,024	5,546	6,047	1,390	8,737	2,378	9,574	1,114	13,284	428	19,198	235
1981	8,225	5,437	5,404	1,589	8,088	2,197	9,329	1,076	12,839	381	17,743	193
1980	7,684	...	4,685	...	7,508	...	8,544	...	12,389	...	17,278	(NA)
1979	6,940	5,275	4,448	1,638	6,866	2,180	7,735	895	11,555	363	15,766	200
ASIAN												
Both Sexes												
2010	49,894	7,244	20,922	534	28,579	1,374	31,273	1,432	57,183	2,338	84,657	1,565
2009	53,419	7,158	20,461	487	29,312	1,367	32,958	1,356	55,730	2,376	98,871	1,569
2008	51,063	7,118	21,200	540	29,390	1,213	32,671	1,466	58,524	2,298	83,721	1,600
2007	49,571	7,137	21,305	512	28,773	1,241	34,423	1,456	54,451	2,354	81,943	1,572
2006	50,940	7,073	20,573	599	29,426	1,301	33,238	1,350	56,197	2,268	88,408	1,553
2005	45,751	6,684	22,909	598	27,082	1,304	31,460	1,337	51,064	2,108	80,145	1,335
2004	44,361	6,369	19,684	497	28,289	1,192	29,524	1,364	47,912	2,118	81,259	1,196
2003[2]	42,163	6,190	19,558	539	25,704	1,162	27,209	1,355	48,333	1,878	74,046	1,254
2002	40,793	6,086	16,746	536	24,900	1,138	27,340	1,325	46,628	1,911	72,852	1,174
Male												
2010	57,937	3,814	24,355	280	31,783	695	35,347	741	65,448	1,181	96,699	915
2009	62,328	3,811	21,167	255	33,080	695	37,691	722	62,561	1,198	113,711	940
2008	60,007	3,776	23,814	279	34,904	606	37,283	773	67,088	1,186	97,068	931
2007	57,890	3,731	24,213	244	33,607	630	41,876	773	60,356	1,156	93,604	926
2006	60,516	3,757	23,311	298	32,528	710	37,263	658	67,144	1,150	101,676	939
2005	54,257	3,564	28,150	307	30,547	721	35,401	675	60,739	1,048	92,552	811
2004	52,544	3,440	20,691	235	31,710	676	33,798	679	56,998	1,078	90,870	770
2003[2]	48,890	3,333	23,745	291	28,522	582	31,775	673	52,508	992	83,098	793
2002	48,934	3,272	17,659	298	29,547	578	32,750	664	55,198	971	82,170	758
Female												
2010	40,952	3,430	17,142	254	25,295	678	26,899	690	48,745	1,157	67,690	649
2009	43,270	3,346	19,684	232	25,420	672	27,574	634	48,783	1,178	76,637	628
2008	40,954	3,341	18,395	260	23,886	607	27,528	693	49,380	1,111	65,148	669
2007	40,455	3,405	18,643	267	23,785	611	25,992	683	48,748	1,197	65,206	645
2006	40,089	3,315	17,855	300	25,696	590	29,415	692	44,932	1,118	68,084	613
2005	36,033	3,119	17,383	291	22,789	582	27,439	662	41,494	1,059	60,934	524
2004	34,748	2,928	18,780	262	23,802	515	25,280	684	38,488	1,040	63,894	426
2003[2]	34,315	2,857	14,614	247	22,876	580	22,703	682	43,655	885	58,489	461
2002	31,328	2,814	15,595	237	20,094	559	21,912	661	37,766	939	55,851	415
HISPANIC[4]												
Both Sexes												
2010	29,917	21,566	20,534	6,301	26,381	6,750	30,708	5,327	47,980	2,290	71,647	896
2009	29,565	21,551	19,816	6,667	25,998	6,753	31,004	5,036	49,017	2,256	74,675	837
2008	30,291	21,853	21,310	6,972	27,020	6,702	31,644	5,149	48,081	2,225	77,630	802
2007	29,910	21,561	21,303	6,888	27,604	6,682	31,040	5,000	44,696	2,114	73,111	874
2006	29,155	21,209	20,581	7,134	27,508	6,495	31,380	4,863	45,371	2,038	70,432	678
2005	27,760	20,025	19,294	6,995	25,659	6,080	29,836	4,467	45,933	1,775	70,916	705
2004	27,263	19,343	19,025	6,935	25,823	5,740	29,260	4,369	45,166	1,669	69,839	629
2003[2]	25,810	18,786	18,349	6,767	23,472	5,517	28,494	4,235	43,676	1,663	62,794	603
2002	25,824	18,409	18,981	6,748	24,163	5,499	27,757	4,024	40,949	1,568	67,679	569
2001	24,786	17,575	18,334	6,533	22,866	5,265	27,523	3,842	40,586	1,416	62,194	517
2000[3]	23,855	17,161	17,156	6,428	22,009	5,145	25,276	3,737	44,661	1,395	63,908	455
1999	22,096	15,122	16,106	5,601	20,704	4,539	24,577	3,392	36,212	1,117	55,352	472

[1]For data prior to 1991, "Some college/Associate degree" equals 1 to 3 years of college completed; "Bachelor's degree" equals 4 years of college; "Advanced degree" equals 5 or more years of college completed.
[2]Starting in 2003, respondents could choose more than one race. The race data in this table from 2003 onward represent respondents who indicated only one race.
[3]Beginning in 2000, earnings data are from the expanded Current Population Survey (CPS) sample and were calculated using population controls based on Census 2000.
[4]May be of any race.
... = Not available.

Table A-27. Mean Earnings of Workers 18 Years Old and Over, by Educational Attainment, Race, Hispanic Origin, and Sex, 1975–2010—*Continued*

(Dollars except as noted)

Race, sex, year, and Hispanic origin	Total		Not a high school graduate		High school graduate		Some college/ associate's degree[1]		Bachelor's degree[1]		Advanced degree[1]	
	Mean earnings	Number of workers (thousands)	Mean earnings	Number of workers (thousands)	Mean earnings	Number of workers (thousands)	Mean earnings	Number of workers (thousands)	Mean earnings	Number of workers (thousands)	Mean earnings	Number of workers (thousands)
Both Sexes— *(Continued)*												
1998	22,117	14,372	15,832	5,281	20,978	4,219	23,091	3,289	35,014	1,156	62,583	425
1997	20,766	13,972	15,069	5,238	19,558	4,082	22,001	3,075	33,465	1,140	58,571	437
1996	19,439	13,365	13,287	5,062	18,528	3,783	22,209	3,096	32,955	1,027	49,873	398
1995	18,262	12,434	13,068	4,784	18,333	3,594	19,923	2,856	30,602	866	45,612	334
1994	18,568	12,035	13,733	4,686	17,323	3,444	21,041	2,723	29,165	844	51,898	337
1993	17,102	11,644	11,852	4,425	16,591	3,367	19,043	2,728	30,359	799	45,034	325
1992	16,824	10,171	11,836	3,962	16,714	2,991	19,778	2,242	28,260	702	46,736	274
1991	16,300	10,006	11,335	3,906	16,142	3,045	19,123	2,080	26,623	665	40,154	311
1990	15,943	9,729	10,368	3,929	15,417	3,282	19,206	1,534	25,703	601	38,075	382
1989	15,714	9,570	11,500	3,985	14,901	3,188	18,707	1,513	28,157	535	39,273	349
1988	15,007	9,226	11,045	3,824	14,667	2,953	18,101	1,511	23,745	596	33,843	340
1987	14,695	8,817	10,961	3,457	13,958	2,982	16,899	1,400	23,105	644	34,413	335
1986	13,558	8,393	9,896	3,379	13,389	2,835	16,523	1,411	22,707	471	28,316	295
1985	13,120	7,840	9,956	3,223	13,044	2,661	15,318	1,226	20,878	458	28,357	273
1984	12,583	7,349	9,671	3,129	12,858	2,457	14,359	1,116	19,924	381	26,327	265
1983	11,901	6,222	9,473	2,674	12,077	2,030	13,371	976	17,972	320	24,352	222
1982	11,307	5,914	8,498	2,583	11,539	1,967	13,108	873	18,186	303	28,167	186
1981	10,872	5,930	8,645	2,648	11,046	1,966	12,971	834	16,114	320	24,082	161
1980	10,062	5,723	8,119	2,649	10,182	1,824	11,891	808	15,676	283	21,910	157
1979	9,248	5,545	7,683	2,533	9,338	1,812	10,181	768	14,940	240	18,273	190
1978	8,460	4,898	7,138	2,345	8,512	1,554	9,575	661	13,985	213	17,333	125
1977	7,761	4,752	6,547	2,306	8,079	1,461	8,172	656	12,572	210	16,660	118
1976	7,081	4,303	5,984	2,107	7,580	1,309	7,252	592	11,242	177	14,000	118
1975	6,567	4,078	5,462	2,028	6,759	1,293	7,154	474	10,573	173	15,756	111
Male												
2010	32,981	12,644	23,384	4,218	29,620	4,143	35,406	2,729	56,774	1,136	82,797	416
2009	32,279	12,643	21,588	4,486	28,908	4,109	36,071	2,485	58,570	1,122	84,368	439
2008	34,240	12,857	24,340	4,720	30,618	3,990	37,864	2,615	56,980	1,109	96,976	422
2007	33,040	12,885	23,923	4,726	30,932	4,111	35,861	2,510	50,805	1,057	87,195	478
2006	32,532	12,711	23,060	4,920	32,148	3,884	36,217	2,500	51,336	1,066	87,835	340
2005	31,008	12,015	21,623	4,744	29,471	3,667	34,754	2,326	54,700	896	84,033	380
2004	30,828	11,562	21,606	4,633	29,694	3,439	34,447	2,241	53,567	915	84,152	331
2003[2]	28,806	11,195	20,637	4,556	26,652	3,234	34,157	2,193	49,298	867	71,446	344
2002	29,084	10,979	21,611	4,506	27,992	3,205	32,935	2,112	46,115	815	73,836	338
2001	27,964	10,258	20,614	4,289	26,745	2,985	32,595	1,962	45,445	748	75,746	272
2000[3]	27,253	9,996	19,501	4,236	25,629	2,940	30,155	1,873	55,050	722	81,447	223
1999	24,970	8,713	18,020	3,592	23,736	2,597	29,387	1,698	42,733	577	66,745	250
1998	25,534	8,288	17,756	3,428	24,739	2,413	26,483	1,652	40,889	569	83,754	226
1997	23,520	8,261	17,447	3,444	22,253	2,391	25,923	1,598	37,963	557	68,097	272
1996	21,870	7,975	14,986	3,382	21,593	2,116	26,682	1,687	38,130	531	49,307	259
1995	20,312	7,337	14,774	3,140	20,882	2,039	22,171	1,475	35,109	466	50,802	215
1994	21,288	7,117	16,355	3,111	19,667	1,937	24,517	1,410	33,797	450	60,858	210
1993	19,460	6,957	13,572	2,928	18,765	1,954	22,417	1,444	37,554	438	52,441	194
1992	18,842	6,034	13,313	2,633	19,357	1,665	23,033	1,193	33,430	380	53,645	164
1991	18,516	5,932	13,133	2,548	18,582	1,705	21,974	1,131	31,699	356	45,873	193
1990	18,320	5,745	13,182	2,562	18,100	1,812	22,376	852	31,485	314	47,479	205
1989	18,087	5,641	13,167	2,632	17,579	1,711	22,374	810	32,767	292	49,088	196
1988	17,357	5,477	12,836	2,517	17,446	1,621	21,631	811	26,935	333	40,916	194
1987	17,048	5,248	12,823	2,281	16,774	1,616	19,414	758	26,581	383	39,014	211
1986	15,624	5,037	11,262	2,262	15,948	1,546	19,675	778	27,427	274	32,538	176
1985	15,293	4,702	11,671	2,111	15,602	1,491	18,168	678	24,723	267	32,831	155
1984	14,957	4,344	11,441	2,022	15,763	1,319	17,261	611	23,835	223	30,727	168
1983	14,265	3,577	11,353	1,678	14,584	1,074	16,626	514	21,911	170	28,680	141
1982	13,484	3,480	10,108	1,622	13,883	1,083	15,560	495	22,565	153	34,474	125
1981	13,052	3,504	10,447	1,686	13,513	1,037	15,432	489	19,201	177	27,619	114
1980	12,310	3,401	9,825	1,707	13,108	961	14,331	451	19,224	167	24,642	114
1979	11,332	3,269	9,393	1,615	11,714	952	12,489	441	18,923	142	21,299	118
1978	10,473	2,915	8,836	1,498	10,940	815	11,545	393	16,898	127	20,702	82
1977	9,655	2,833	8,192	1,460	10,386	776	9,924	391	15,189	120	19,025	85
1976	8,787	2,571	7,440	1,321	9,640	712	8,843	342	13,650	114	16,184	81
1975	8,162	2,456	6,745	1,287	8,546	691	8,807	279	12,881	113	17,991	86

[1]For data prior to 1991, "Some college/Associate degree" equals 1 to 3 years of college completed; "Bachelor's degree" equals 4 years of college; "Advanced degree" equals 5 or more years of college completed.
[2]Starting in 2003, respondents could choose more than one race. The race data in this table from 2003 onward represent respondents who indicated only one race.
[3]Beginning in 2000, earnings data are from the expanded Current Population Survey (CPS) sample and were calculated using population controls based on Census 2000.
[4]May be of any race.

Table A-27. Mean Earnings of Workers 18 Years Old and Over, by Educational Attainment, Race, Hispanic Origin, and Sex, 1975–2010—*Continued*

(Dollars except as noted)

Race, sex, year, and Hispanic origin	Total		Not a high school graduate		High school graduate		Some college/ associate's degree[1]		Bachelor's degree[1]		Advanced degree[1]	
	Mean earnings	Number of workers (thousands)	Mean earnings	Number of workers (thousands)	Mean earnings	Number of workers (thousands)	Mean earnings	Number of workers (thousands)	Mean earnings	Number of workers (thousands)	Mean earnings	Number of workers (thousands)
Female												
2010	25,574	8,921	14,763	2,083	21,234	2,607	25,771	2,597	39,321	1,153	61,967	479
2009	25,713	8,907	16,170	2,180	21,473	2,644	26,065	2,550	39,566	1,134	64,405	398
2008	24,646	8,995	14,960	2,552	21,725	2,712	25,226	2,534	39,231	1,115	56,175	380
2007	25,262	8,676	15,574	2,162	22,283	2,570	26,179	2,489	38,584	1,057	56,129	396
2006	24,104	8,497	15,072	2,214	20,608	2,611	26,260	2,362	38,825	971	52,896	337
2005	22,887	8,009	14,365	2,250	19,864	2,413	24,493	2,141	37,003	879	55,554	324
2004	21,967	7,781	13,830	2,302	20,037	2,300	23,796	2,127	34,949	753	53,887	297
2003[2]	21,391	7,591	13,632	2,210	18,967	2,283	22,411	2,042	37,550	795	51,294	258
2002	21,008	7,430	13,694	2,241	18,810	2,293	22,035	1,911	35,357	753	58,623	230
2001	20,330	7,316	13,976	2,243	17,786	2,279	22,229	1,879	35,142	668	47,176	245
2000[3]	19,115	7,164	12,622	2,191	17,180	2,204	20,372	1,864	33,489	672	47,057	232
1999	18,187	6,409	12,684	2,010	16,653	1,943	19,754	1,694	29,249	540	42,503	222
1998	17,461	6,804	12,273	1,854	15,952	1,806	20,460	1,639	29,317	587	38,422	200
1997	16,781	5,711	10,503	1,794	15,747	1,691	17,759	1,477	29,173	584	43,051	165
1996	15,841	5,390	9,867	1,680	14,635	1,667	16,856	1,409	27,407	495	50,960	139
1995	15,310	5,096	9,809	1,644	14,989	1,555	17,521	1,380	25,338	399	36,255	118
1994	14,631	4,918	8,559	1,576	14,313	1,508	17,309	1,313	23,867	393	37,269	127
1993	13,602	4,687	8,489	1,498	13,584	1,413	15,250	1,284	21,627	361	34,001	131
1992	13,880	4,137	8,913	1,330	13,396	1,326	16,076	1,049	22,160	322	34,551	110
1991	13,069	4,072	4,809	1,358	13,043	1,339	15,721	948	20,791	309	30,721	117
1990	12,516	3,984	5,093	1,367	12,109	1,470	15,245	682	19,378	287	27,184	177
1989	12,307	3,929	8,256	1,353	11,799	1,477	14,482	703	22,617	243	26,700	153
1988	11,573	3,749	7,597	1,307	11,284	1,332	14,012	700	19,707	263	24,444	146
1987	11,234	3,569	7,350	1,176	10,627	1,366	13,929	642	18,003	261	26,584	124
1986	10,457	3,356	7,130	1,117	10,319	1,289	12,648	633	16,142	197	22,071	119
1985	9,865	3,138	6,699	1,112	9,784	1,170	11,791	548	15,503	191	22,480	118
1984	9,150	3,005	6,438	1,107	9,492	1,138	10,848	505	14,404	158	18,706	97
1983	8,704	2,645	6,305	996	9,261	956	9,750	462	13,507	150	16,817	81
1982	8,195	2,434	5,781	961	8,668	884	9,896	378	13,719	150	15,244	61
1981	7,723	2,426	5,486	962	8,292	929	9,483	345	12,292	143	15,503	47
1980	6,770	2,322	5,028	942	6,923	863	8,808	357	10,568	116	14,668	43
1979	6,255	2,276	4,675	918	6,708	860	7,069	327	9,168	98	13,313	72
1978	5,501	1,983	4,135	847	5,834	739	6,686	268	9,684	86	10,908	43
1977	4,964	1,919	3,707	846	5,466	685	5,588	265	9,082	90	10,569	33
1976	4,548	1,732	3,537	786	5,124	597	5,075	250	6,884	63	9,218	37
1975	4,152	1,622	3,233	741	4,708	602	4,790	195	6,226	60	8,067	25
WHITE ALONE OR IN COMBINATION												
Both Sexes												
2010	44,023	125,712	21,388	11,004	31,990	35,140	35,139	37,717	59,055	27,266	84,972	14,582
2009	43,213	127,001	20,468	11,708	31,351	36,656	35,540	37,684	57,662	26,920	86,067	14,031
2008	43,550	129,419	21,483	12,630	32,072	37,299	35,528	38,593	59,824	26,784	84,687	14,111
2007	43,000	129,203	22,245	12,568	32,126	37,570	35,565	38,664	58,565	26,583	82,309	13,816
2006	42,249	128,366	21,389	13,800	31,998	37,915	35,276	37,530	57,807	26,035	83,002	13,084
2005	40,592	126,882	20,225	13,424	30,494	37,723	34,279	38,149	55,758	24,919	81,437	12,665
2004	38,855	125,387	19,365	13,539	29,595	37,639	32,736	37,287	52,790	24,361	78,747	12,560
2003[2]	37,958	124,456	18,734	16,282	27,915	45,064	31,498	44,048	51,206	28,672	74,601	14,592
2002	37,290	124,337	19,278	13,957	28,107	37,863	31,767	36,639	52,509	23,865	73,773	12,011
Male												
2010	52,152	67,831	25,023	7,117	37,378	20,333	42,130	18,666	71,793	14,222	105,700	7,492
2009	51,133	68,426	23,327	7,561	36,321	21,162	42,760	18,567	71,166	13,886	106,451	7,248
2008	52,502	69,829	25,254	8,263	37,740	21,192	43,307	19,210	75,024	13,734	107,065	7,428
2007	51,599	70,073	25,848	8,305	38,072	21,436	42,760	19,343	73,390	13,697	103,214	7,291
2006	50,826	69,702	24,524	9,055	38,699	21,401	42,605	18,686	71,602	13,443	103,097	7,116
2005	49,437	68,987	23,526	8,740	36,608	21,289	42,139	18,954	69,821	13,045	102,904	6,957
2004	47,275	67,758	22,576	8,751	35,348	21,073	40,627	18,361	65,498	12,728	99,534	6,842
2003[2]	45,989	67,198	21,787	8,682	34,225	20,534	39,555	18,421	65,237	12,774	93,792	6,785
2002	45,682	67,082	22,601	8,977	33,846	20,430	39,439	18,377	65,548	12,621	92,575	6,675

[1]For data prior to 1991, "Some college/Associate degree" equals 1 to 3 years of college completed; "Bachelor's degree" equals 4 years of college; "Advanced degree" equals 5 or more years of college completed.
[2]Starting in 2003, respondents could choose more than one race. The race data in this table from 2003 onward represent respondents who indicated only one race.
[3]Beginning in 2000, earnings data are from the expanded Current Population Survey (CPS) sample and were calculated using population controls based on Census 2000.
[4]May be of any race.

Table A-27. Mean Earnings of Workers 18 Years Old and Over, by Educational Attainment, Race, Hispanic Origin, and Sex, 1975–2010—*Continued*

(Dollars except as noted)

Race, sex, year, and Hispanic origin	Total		Not a high school graduate		High school graduate		Some college/ associate's degree[1]		Bachelor's degree[1]		Advanced degree[1]	
	Mean earnings	Number of workers (thousands)	Mean earnings	Number of workers (thousands)	Mean earnings	Number of workers (thousands)	Mean earnings	Number of workers (thousands)	Mean earnings	Number of workers (thousands)	Mean earnings	Number of workers (thousands)
Female												
2010............	34,497	57,881	14,733	3,887	24,593	14,807	28,290	19,051	45,165	13,044	63,069	7,090
2009............	33,961	58,574	15,254	4,146	24,561	15,494	28,528	19,116	43,275	13,034	64,283	6,782
2008............	33,060	59,590	14,345	4,366	24,615	16,107	27,819	19,383	43,826	13,050	59,814	6,683
2007............	32,810	59,130	15,226	4,263	24,226	16,134	28,362	19,321	42,807	12,886	58,951	6,525
2006............	32,059	58,663	15,408	4,745	23,313	16,514	28,008	18,844	43,078	12,591	59,042	5,968
2005............	30,053	57,895	14,066	4,684	22,574	16,434	25,518	19,194	40,306	11,873	55,273	5,707
2004............	28,954	57,629	13,498	4,788	22,277	16,565	25,079	18,925	38,886	11,632	53,859	5,717
2003[2]...........	28,532	57,257	14,086	4,684	22,029	16,926	25,093	18,616	37,750	11,476	53,021	5,552
2002............	27,457	57,254	13,286	4,979	21,381	17,433	24,046	18,261	37,872	11,243	50,255	5,336
NON-HISPANIC WHITE ALONE OR IN COMBINATION												
Both Sexes												
2010............	46,754	105,350	22,413	4,982	33,207	28,787	35,855	32,746	59,993	25,101	85,771	13,732
2009............	45,813	106,618	21,241	5,331	32,478	30,276	36,163	32,964	58,398	24,814	86,674	13,231
2008............	46,050	108,823	21,579	5,959	33,105	30,982	36,042	33,806	60,818	24,717	84,996	13,358
2007............	45,393	108,929	22,945	6,040	32,992	31,288	36,176	33,994	59,637	24,622	82,840	12,983
2006............	44,652	108,297	22,094	6,995	32,844	31,802	35,795	32,962	58,785	24,103	83,629	12,433
2005............	42,839	107,945	21,088	6,744	31,367	31,951	34,824	33,991	56,441	23,253	81,944	12,003
2004............	40,847	107,086	19,667	6,892	30,195	32,216	33,192	33,200	53,335	22,814	79,166	11,961
2003[2]...........	39,989	106,658	19,764	6,906	29,561	32,225	32,732	33,062	52,823	22,686	76,029	11,777
2002............	39,135	107,050	19,491	7,516	28,714	32,758	32,210	32,876	53,244	22,415	74,011	11,482
Male												
2010............	56,252	55,855	27,218	3,086	39,192	16,430	43,238	16,108	72,990	13,140	106,988	7,088
2009............	55,161	56,390	25,612	3,262	38,049	17,253	43,680	16,218	72,222	12,834	107,782	6,821
2008............	56,357	57,636	26,226	3,743	39,288	17,435	44,075	16,739	76,560	12,692	107,540	7,025
2007............	55,457	57,886	27,810	3,800	39,602	17,567	43,707	16,973	75,109	12,715	104,236	6,830
2006............	54,624	57,615	25,996	4,358	40,034	17,723	43,491	16,320	73,244	12,424	103,794	6,787
2005............	53,084	57,553	25,469	4,213	38,034	17,787	43,083	16,769	70,891	12,187	103,850	6,593
2004............	50,488	56,761	23,520	4,287	36,323	17,817	41,490	16,259	66,467	11,869	100,220	6,527
2003[2]...........	49,227	56,549	22,947	4,313	35,550	17,549	40,196	16,358	66,368	11,946	94,830	6,471
2002............	48,700	56,714	23,426	4,663	34,830	17,446	40,195	16,390	66,776	11,859	100,412	6,510
Female												
2010............	36,034	49,495	14,590	1,895	25,249	12,356	28,707	16,637	45,715	11,960	63,134	6,644
2009............	35,318	50,227	14,347	2,068	25,096	13,022	28,882	16,745	43,589	11,980	64,211	6,409
2008............	34,445	51,187	13,726	2,215	25,148	13,547	28,163	17,067	44,203	12,025	59,983	6,332
2007............	33,979	51,043	14,690	2,239	24,530	13,721	28,665	17,020	43,115	11,907	59,092	6,153
2006............	33,316	50,682	15,642	2,636	23,794	14,079	28,248	16,641	43,402	11,678	59,389	5,646
2005............	31,139	50,391	13,793	2,530	22,994	14,163	26,782	17,222	40,527	11,065	55,242	5,409
2004............	29,972	50,324	13,325	2,605	22,613	14,399	25,228	16,940	39,092	10,945	53,875	5,433
2003[2]...........	29,564	50,108	14,469	2,592	22,479	14,765	25,422	16,704	37,757	10,739	53,102	5,306
2002............	28,359	50,335	13,060	2,853	21,745	15,312	24,271	16,485	38,042	10,556	49,827	5,127
BLACK ALONE OR IN COMBINATION												
Both Sexes												
2010............	32,934	17,524	17,406	1,641	25,842	5,709	30,521	6,172	44,519	2,712	71,305	1,288
2009............	33,294	17,389	18,841	1,691	26,805	5,972	30,451	5,823	47,773	2,696	67,075	1,205
2008............	32,878	18,157	18,049	1,826	27,123	6,220	30,266	6,207	46,983	2,654	66,247	1,248
2007............	33,318	18,023	17,555	1,903	27,096	6,149	32,580	6,056	46,555	2,761	64,714	1,152
2006............	32,384	17,721	17,842	1,995	26,290	6,305	31,175	5,759	47,740	2,580	64,563	1,080
2005............	30,521	17,540	17,264	2,097	23,810	6,246	28,817	5,576	47,641	2,501	63,065	1,118
2004............	29,031	17,109	17,821	2,085	23,458	6,298	27,801	5,369	42,131	2,414	64,545	941
2003[2]...........	28,854	16,871	16,238	2,177	23,956	6,082	27,095	5,296	42,991	2,374	63,966	940
2002............	28,255	16,833	17,114	2,217	22,762	5,940	27,582	5,441	42,099	2,348	60,458	884

[1]For data prior to 1991, "Some college/Associate degree" equals 1 to 3 years of college completed; "Bachelor's degree" equals 4 years of college; "Advanced degree" equals 5 or more years of college completed.
[2]Starting in 2003, respondents could choose more than one race. The race data in this table from 2003 onward represent respondents who indicated only one race.

Table A-27. Mean Earnings of Workers 18 Years Old and Over, by Educational Attainment, Race, Hispanic Origin, and Sex, 1975–2010—*Continued*

(Dollars except as noted)

Race, sex, year, and Hispanic origin	Total		Not a high school graduate		High school graduate		Some college/ associate's degree[1]		Bachelor's degree[1]		Advanced degree[1]	
	Mean earnings	Number of workers (thousands)	Mean earnings	Number of workers (thousands)	Mean earnings	Number of workers (thousands)	Mean earnings	Number of workers (thousands)	Mean earnings	Number of workers (thousands)	Mean earnings	Number of workers (thousands)
Male												
2010	35,899	8,067	19,116	875	29,746	2,974	34,307	2,592	48,406	1,117	81,533	507
2009	37,500	7,963	21,585	912	30,541	3,087	35,842	2,409	55,824	1,068	79,551	485
2008	36,386	8,442	21,894	913	30,690	3,263	34,159	2,631	52,773	1,103	73,362	530
2007	35,669	8,405	19,932	1,019	29,508	3,083	33,845	2,621	52,951	1,200	75,355	480
2006	36,026	8,170	21,361	1,006	29,973	3,146	34,784	2,417	52,382	1,124	74,769	475
2005	34,258	8,127	19,996	1,093	27,189	3,142	33,449	2,380	53,556	1,049	76,407	462
2004	32,919	7,884	22,755	1,049	26,575	3,202	32,466	2,258	47,448	976	77,648	398
2003[2]	32,574	7,689	17,982	1,088	28,323	2,981	31,591	2,233	45,705	982	76,954	402
2002	31,967	7,734	20,537	1,114	25,510	2,902	32,696	2,375	46,942	1,009	76,003	332
Female												
2010	30,405	9,456	15,449	765	21,597	2,735	27,779	3,579	41,796	1,595	64,662	781
2009	29,740	9,426	15,631	779	22,805	2,884	26,646	3,414	42,487	1,627	58,664	719
2008	29,829	9,715	14,204	913	23,187	2,957	27,399	3,575	42,861	1,550	60,996	718
2007	31,263	9,618	14,816	884	24,669	3,065	31,614	3,435	41,636	1,561	57,105	672
2006	29,268	9,551	14,257	988	22,622	3,159	28,565	3,342	44,157	1,456	56,541	605
2005	27,295	9,413	14,289	1,003	20,389	3,104	25,366	3,195	43,369	1,452	53,669	656
2004	25,707	9,224	12,818	1,035	20,236	3,096	24,415	3,111	38,522	1,438	54,931	543
2003[2]	25,739	9,182	14,495	1,089	19,765	3,100	23,816	3,063	41,073	1,391	54,265	538
2002	25,099	9,098	13,656	1,103	20,137	3,038	23,621	3,066	38,447	1,339	51,101	552
ASIAN ALONE OR IN COMBINATION												
Both Sexes												
2010	49,145	7,711	20,791	555	28,544	1,468	30,951	1,608	56,521	2,459	84,367	1,621
2009	61,575	4,022	20,995	267	32,985	747	37,106	793	62,504	1,237	113,267	976
2008	50,622	7,553	21,195	569	29,163	1,300	32,577	1,630	58,179	2,403	84,523	1,649
2007	48,865	7,563	21,399	530	28,524	1,331	33,846	1,630	54,204	2,454	81,694	1,615
2006	50,094	7,501	20,142	631	29,502	1,413	33,050	1,495	55,827	2,375	87,887	1,585
2005	45,269	7,131	22,330	629	27,059	1,413	31,332	1,504	51,750	2,204	79,229	1,379
2004	43,856	6,771	19,536	524	27,946	1,292	29,377	1,490	47,711	2,226	81,310	1,237
2003[2]	41,563	6,560	19,548	564	25,554	1,256	27,083	1,495	47,945	1,948	73,812	1,295
2002	40,323	6,424	16,969	559	25,038	1,221	27,146	1,456	46,218	1,984	72,943	1,202
Male												
2010	56,907	4,048	24,137	292	31,788	741	34,995	827	64,573	1,253	96,286	933
2009	61,575	4,022	20,995	267	32,985	747	37,106	793	62,504	1,237	113,267	976
2008	59,565	4,007	23,204	297	34,568	655	37,228	865	66,880	1,228	98,718	959
2007	56,990	3,945	24,261	254	33,105	685	40,965	875	60,606	1,187	93,566	942
2006	59,328	3,980	22,631	318	32,716	783	37,104	736	66,740	1,191	101,474	950
2005	53,761	3,797	27,107	328	30,490	790	35,583	758	62,247	1,097	92,170	823
2004	52,032	3,633	20,799	251	31,194	730	34,237	736	56,581	1,126	91,406	788
2003[2]	48,062	3,522	23,122	308	28,514	635	31,430	746	52,179	1,024	83,131	807
2002	48,128	3,469	18,101	312	29,493	633	32,427	744	54,683	1,006	82,134	772
Female												
2010	40,566	3,663	17,055	262	25,230	726	26,667	780	48,151	1,205	68,200	687
2009	42,848	3,561	20,121	239	25,448	713	27,565	717	48,655	1,241	76,052	650
2008	40,518	3,546	18,999	272	23,665	644	27,315	764	49,076	1,174	64,802	690
2007	40,002	3,617	18,753	275	23,660	645	25,597	755	48,200	1,266	65,098	673
2006	39,652	3,520	17,610	313	25,508	630	29,116	759	44,846	1,183	67,514	634
2005	35,593	3,333	17,122	301	22,703	622	27,007	745	41,350	1,107	60,077	556
2004	34,387	3,137	18,375	273	23,721	561	24,634	754	38,618	1,099	63,553	448
2003[2]	34,031	3,038	15,233	255	22,530	621	22,750	748	43,252	924	58,391	487
2002	31,157	2,954	15,536	247	20,242	588	21,615	711	37,507	978	56,417	429

[1]For data prior to 1991, "Some college/Associate degree" equals 1 to 3 years of college completed; "Bachelor's degree" equals 4 years of college; "Advanced degree" equals 5 or more years of college completed.
[2]Starting in 2003, respondents could choose more than one race. The race data in this table from 2003 onward represent respondents who indicated only one race.

Table A-28. Educational Attainment of Persons 25 Years Old and Over, by Median Income and Sex, 1991–2011

(Dollars except as noted)

Educational attainment and year	Male			Female		
	Number with income (thousands)	Median income[1]		Number with income (thousands)	Median income[1]	
		Current dollars	2011 dollars		Current dollars	2011 dollars
2011	93,141	37,653	37,653	95,404	23,395	23,395
2010[2]	92,242	36,852	38,014	94,679	22,934	23,657
2009[3]	91,745	36,801	38,588	93,426	23,159	24,284
2008	91,653	37,463	39,134	93,143	22,944	23,967
2007	90,647	37,828	41,033	92,075	23,052	25,005
2006	89,816	36,847	41,103	91,315	21,900	24,429
2005	88,804	35,758	41,196	90,762	20,806	23,970
2004[4]	87,570	34,823	41,464	89,794	20,147	23,989
2003	86,532	33,517	40,987	89,118	19,679	24,065
2002	85,668	32,471	40,595	88,903	18,965	23,710
2001	84,389	32,494	41,280	88,075	18,549	23,564
2000[5]	83,860	32,155	41,996	87,619	18,032	23,551
1999[6]	82,795	31,545	42,580	87,229	17,022	22,977
1998	80,869	30,654	42,240	84,819	16,258	22,403
1997	80,263	28,919	40,406	83,821	15,573	21,759
1996	79,423	27,248	38,894	83,056	14,682	20,957
1995[7]	78,264	26,346	38,607	82,457	13,821	20,253
1994[8]	77,546	25,465	38,215	81,829	12,766	19,158
1993[9]	76,419	24,605	37,712	80,898	12,234	18,751
1992[10]	75,872	23,894	37,528	79,854	11,922	18,725
1991	75,137	23,686	38,145	79,383	11,580	18,649
Less than 9th grade						
2011	4,633	17,505	17,505	3,839	11,113	11,113
2010[2]	4,757	16,384	16,901	3,897	10,680	11,017
2009[3]	4,736	16,473	17,273	4,036	10,516	11,027
2008	4,973	17,043	17,803	4,201	10,625	11,099
2007	5,036	16,625	18,034	4,070	10,539	11,432
2006	5,283	17,169	19,152	4,257	10,451	11,658
2005	5,475	16,321	18,803	4,579	9,496	10,940
2004[4]	5,520	16,171	19,255	4,742	9,576	11,402
2003	5,405	15,461	18,907	4,734	9,296	11,368
2002	5,705	15,130	18,915	5,015	8,965	11,208
2001	5,809	14,594	18,540	5,196	8,846	11,238
2000[5]	5,724	14,131	18,456	5,195	8,546	11,162
1999[6]	5,728	13,529	18,262	5,397	8,261	11,151
1998	5,641	12,571	17,322	5,419	7,914	10,905
1997	5,839	12,157	16,986	5,647	7,505	10,486
1996	6,139	12,174	17,377	5,775	7,276	10,386
1995[7]	6,277	11,723	17,179	6,020	7,096	10,398
1994[8]	6,507	11,324	16,994	6,183	6,865	10,302
1993[9]	6,734	10,895	16,699	6,423	6,480	9,932
1992[10]	7,000	10,374	16,294	6,921	6,337	9,953
1991	7,143	10,319	16,618	7,065	6,268	10,094

Note. People 25 years old and over as of March of the following year.

[1] Income in current and 2011 CPI-U-RS adjusted dollars.

[2] Data reflect implementation of Census 2010-based population controls.

[3] Beginning with 2009 income data, the Census Bureau expanded the upper income interval used to calculate medians and Gini indexes to $250,000 or more. Medians falling in the upper open-ended interval are plugged with "$250,000." Before 2009, the upper open-ended interval was $100,000 and a plug of "$100,000" was used.

[4] Data reflect a correction to the weights in the 2005 Annual Social and Economic Supplement (ASEC).

[5] Data reflect implementation of a 28,000 household sample expansion.

[6] Data reflect implementation of Census 2000-based population controls.

[7] Data reflect full implementation of the 1990 census-based sample design and metropolitan definitions, 7,000 household sample reduction, and revised race edits.

[8] Data reflect introduction of 1990 census-based sample design.

[9] Data collection method changed from paper and pencil to computer-assisted interviewing. In addition, the March 1994 income supplement was revised to allow for the coding of different income amounts on selected questionnaire items. Child support and alimony limits decreased to $49,999. Limits increased in the following categories: earnings to $999,999; social security to $49,999; supplemental security income and public assistance income to $24,999; and veterans' benefits to $99,999.

[10] Data reflect implementation of 1990 census population controls.

Table A-28. Educational Attainment of Persons 25 Years Old and Over, by Median Income and Sex, 1991–2011—*Continued*

(Dollars except as noted)

Educational attainment and year	Male			Female		
	Number with income (thousands)	Median income[1]		Number with income (thousands)	Median income[1]	
		Current dollars	2011 dollars		Current dollars	2011 dollars
9th to 12th grade (no diploma)						
2011	6,650	20,437	20,437	6,235	12,193	12,193
2010[2]	6,625	19,356	19,967	6,003	12,075	12,456
2009[3]	6,948	19,720	20,678	6,175	12,278	12,874
2008	7,158	20,845	21,775	6,413	11,904	12,435
2007	7,200	20,643	22,392	6,286	11,982	12,997
2006	7,684	21,184	23,631	6,750	11,914	13,290
2005	7,276	20,934	24,118	6,812	11,136	12,830
2004[4]	7,254	19,593	23,329	6,982	10,751	12,801
2003	7,245	18,990	23,222	6,965	10,786	13,190
2002	7,488	19,802	24,756	7,103	10,613	13,268
2001	7,421	19,434	24,689	7,376	10,330	13,123
2000[5]	7,226	18,915	24,704	7,565	10,063	13,143
1999[6]	7,085	17,653	23,828	7,525	9,632	13,001
1998	7,366	17,462	24,062	7,559	9,582	13,204
1997	7,601	16,818	23,498	7,661	8,861	12,381
1996	7,671	16,058	22,921	7,929	8,544	12,196
1995[7]	7,490	15,791	23,140	8,122	8,057	11,807
1994[8]	7,286	14,584	21,886	7,943	7,618	11,432
1993[9]	7,377	14,550	22,301	8,152	7,187	11,016
1992[10]	7,524	14,218	22,331	8,248	7,293	11,454
1991	7,759	14,736	23,731	8,561	7,055	11,362
High School Graduate (includes equivalency)						
2011	28,295	30,616	30,616	28,051	17,887	17,887
2010[2]	28,307	30,250	31,204	28,314	17,826	18,388
2009[3]	28,946	30,303	31,775	28,154	18,340	19,231
2008	28,450	30,879	32,256	28,217	18,293	19,109
2007	27,988	31,337	33,992	28,134	18,162	19,701
2006	28,253	31,009	34,591	28,538	17,546	19,573
2005	28,077	30,134	34,717	28,409	16,695	19,234
2004[4]	27,799	29,332	34,926	28,561	16,165	19,248
2003	26,800	28,763	35,174	28,976	15,962	19,520
2002	26,298	27,526	34,413	29,161	15,972	19,968
2001	25,954	28,343	36,007	28,945	15,665	19,901
2000[5]	26,175	27,480	35,890	28,968	15,153	19,791
1999[6]	26,278	27,188	36,699	29,798	14,652	19,778
1998	25,636	26,542	36,574	29,330	13,786	18,997
1997	25,777	25,453	35,563	29,332	13,407	18,732
1996	25,510	24,814	35,419	29,212	12,702	18,131
1995[7]	24,909	23,365	34,239	28,785	12,046	17,652
1994[8]	24,704	22,387	33,596	29,110	11,390	17,093
1993[9]	24,682	21,782	33,386	29,171	11,089	16,996
1992[10]	25,143	21,645	33,996	29,596	10,901	17,121
1991	25,297	21,546	34,698	30,149	10,818	17,422

Note. People 25 years old and over as of March of the following year.
[1] Income in current and 2011 CPI-U-RS adjusted dollars.
[2]Data reflect implementation of Census 2010-based population controls.
[3]Beginning with 2009 income data, the Census Bureau expanded the upper income interval used to calculate medians and Gini indexes to $250,000 or more. Medians falling in the upper open-ended interval are plugged with "$250,000." Before 2009, the upper open-ended interval was $100,000 and a plug of "$100,000" was used.
[4]Data reflect a correction to the weights in the 2005 Annual Social and Economic Supplement (ASEC).
[5]Data reflect implementation of a 28,000 household sample expansion.
[6]Data reflect implementation of Census 2000-based population controls.
[7]Data reflect full implementation of the 1990 census-based sample design and metropolitan definitions, 7,000 household sample reduction, and revised race edits.
[8]Data reflect introduction of 1990 census-based sample design.
[9]Data collection method changed from paper and pencil to computer-assisted interviewing. In addition, the March 1994 income supplement was revised to allow for the coding of different income amounts on selected questionnaire items. Child support and alimony limits decreased to $49,999. Limits increased in the following categories: earnings to $999,999; social security to $49,999; supplemental security income and public assistance income to $24,999; and veterans' benefits to $99,999.
[10]Data reflect implementation of 1990 census population controls.

Table A-28. Educational Attainment of Persons 25 Years Old and Over, by Median Income and Sex, 1991–2011—*Continued*

(Dollars except as noted)

Educational attainment and year	Male			Female		
	Number with income (thousands)	Median income[1]		Number with income (thousands)	Median income[1]	
		Current dollars	2011 dollars		Current dollars	2011 dollars
Some College, No Degree[11]						
2011	15,301	36,552	36,552	16,427	22,499	22,499
2010[2]	15,395	36,226	37,369	16,661	22,808	23,527
2009[3]	15,184	36,693	38,475	16,208	23,107	24,229
2008	15,523	37,297	38,960	16,329	23,252	24,289
2007	15,321	37,447	40,620	16,600	23,532	25,526
2006	14,526	37,271	41,576	16,099	22,709	25,332
2005	14,505	36,930	42,546	16,402	21,545	24,821
2004[4]	14,405	36,162	43,058	15,791	21,159	25,194
2003	14,586	35,073	42,890	15,691	21,007	25,689
2002	14,747	35,023	43,785	15,616	20,602	25,756
2001	14,340	33,777	42,910	15,420	20,101	25,536
2000[5]	14,433	33,319	43,516	15,825	20,166	26,338
1999[6]	14,440	32,575	43,970	15,693	19,599	26,455
1998	13,935	31,627	43,581	15,173	18,445	25,417
1997	13,892	30,536	42,665	14,677	17,153	23,966
1996	13,756	29,160	41,623	14,528	16,255	23,202
1995[7]	13,715	28,004	41,037	14,619	15,552	22,790
1994[8]	13,573	26,768	40,170	14,911	14,585	21,887
1993[9]	13,247	26,323	40,346	14,390	14,489	22,208
1992[10]	12,728	26,318	41,335	13,615	14,401	22,618
1991	12,366	26,591	42,823	13,013	13,963	22,486
Associate's Degree						
2011	8,286	41,916	41,916	10,353	27,180	27,180
2010[2]	7,924	40,974	42,266	10,197	28,147	29,035
2009[3]	7,399	42,163	44,211	9,936	27,027	28,340
2008	7,375	42,608	44,508	9,662	27,715	28,951
2007	7,244	43,006	46,650	9,166	27,668	30,012
2006	6,973	41,807	46,636	9,043	26,295	29,332
2005	7,000	41,903	48,275	9,070	26,074	30,039
2004[4]	6,782	39,765	47,348	8,861	25,199	30,004
2003	6,618	39,015	47,711	8,523	24,808	30,337
2002	6,274	37,970	47,470	8,323	23,766	29,712
2001	6,352	38,870	49,380	8,177	22,638	28,759
2000[5]	6,272	38,026	49,664	8,108	23,124	30,201
1999[6]	5,939	36,558	49,347	7,482	21,916	29,583
1998	5,766	35,962	49,555	6,931	21,290	29,337
1997	5,591	32,930	46,010	6,914	21,073	29,443
1996	5,210	33,065	47,197	6,839	20,460	29,205
1995[7]	5,230	31,027	45,467	6,642	19,450	28,502
1994[8]	5,046	30,643	45,985	6,573	17,954	26,943
1993[9]	4,901	29,736	45,577	6,282	18,346	28,119
1992[10]	4,540	28,791	45,220	5,539	17,331	27,220
1991	4,083	29,358	47,279	5,236	17,364	27,964

Note. People 25 years old and over as of March of the following year.

[1] Income in current and 2011 CPI-U-RS adjusted dollars.

[2]Data reflect implementation of Census 2010-based population controls.

[3]Beginning with 2009 income data, the Census Bureau expanded the upper income interval used to calculate medians and Gini indexes to $250,000 or more. Medians falling in the upper open-ended interval are plugged with "$250,000." Before 2009, the upper open-ended interval was $100,000 and a plug of "$100,000" was used.

[4]Data reflect a correction to the weights in the 2005 Annual Social and Economic Supplement (ASEC).

[5]Data reflect implementation of a 28,000 household sample expansion.

[6]Data reflect implementation of Census 2000-based population controls.

[7]Data reflect full implementation of the 1990 census-based sample design and metropolitan definitions, 7,000 household sample reduction, and revised race edits.

[8]Data reflect introduction of 1990 census-based sample design.

[9]Data collection method changed from paper and pencil to computer-assisted interviewing. In addition, the March 1994 income supplement was revised to allow for the coding of different income amounts on selected questionnaire items. Child support and alimony limits decreased to $49,999. Limits increased in the following categories: earnings to $999,999; social security to $49,999; supplemental security income and public assistance income to $24,999; and veterans' benefits to $99,999.

[10]Data reflect implementation of 1990 census population controls.

[11]Beginning in 1991, includes people with less than one year of college. Before 1991, the category "High school, four years" included those with less than one year of college.

Table A-28. Educational Attainment of Persons 25 Years Old and Over, by Median Income and Sex, 1991–2011—*Continued*

(Dollars except as noted)

Educational attainment and year	Male			Female		
	Number with income (thousands)	Median income[1]		Number with income (thousands)	Median income[1]	
		Current dollars	2011 dollars		Current dollars	2011 dollars
Bachelor's Degree or More						
2011	29,976	62,282	62,282	30,498	41,338	41,338
2010[2]	29,234	61,522	63,463	29,606	41,112	42,409
2009[3]	28,532	61,280	64,256	28,917	40,766	42,746
2008	28,174	63,277	66,099	28,321	40,801	42,620
2007	27,857	62,421	67,710	27,820	40,712	44,161
2006	27,097	61,168	68,233	26,626	39,450	44,007
2005	26,470	58,114	66,952	25,490	37,055	42,690
2004[4]	25,810	56,434	67,196	24,857	35,726	42,539
2003	25,879	55,751	68,177	24,229	35,125	42,954
2002	25,155	55,188	68,995	23,686	34,292	42,871
2001	24,512	54,069	68,688	22,961	33,842	42,992
2000[5]	24,028	53,488	69,858	21,958	33,148	43,293
1999[6]	23,325	52,246	70,522	21,334	31,604	42,660
1998	22,525	50,272	69,273	20,409	30,692	42,293
1997	21,563	47,126	65,845	19,590	29,781	41,610
1996	21,136	44,161	63,035	18,775	27,556	39,333
1995[7]	20,644	43,322	63,484	18,269	26,843	39,336
1994[8]	20,429	42,027	63,069	17,109	26,237	39,373
1993[9]	19,479	41,649	63,836	16,480	25,246	38,695
1992[10]	18,937	40,557	63,699	15,933	25,093	39,411
1991	18,490	39,803	64,100	15,359	23,627	38,050
Bachelor's Degree						
2011	18,859	56,404	56,404	19,629	36,812	36,812
2010[2]	18,378	55,225	56,967	18,909	36,359	37,506
2009[3]	18,205	54,091	56,718	18,844	35,972	37,719
2008	17,726	57,278	59,832	18,381	36,294	37,912
2007	17,654	56,826	61,641	18,347	36,167	39,231
2006	17,129	54,403	60,687	17,931	35,094	39,147
2005	16,764	51,700	59,562	17,090	32,668	37,636
2004[4]	16,302	51,081	60,822	16,668	31,585	37,608
2003	16,295	50,916	62,264	16,198	31,309	38,287
2002	16,057	50,600	63,260	16,003	30,788	38,491
2001	15,723	49,985	63,500	15,660	30,973	39,348
2000[5]	15,452	49,080	64,101	15,102	30,418	39,727
1999[6]	14,922	47,289	63,831	14,690	28,520	38,497
1998	14,614	45,749	63,041	14,218	27,415	37,777
1997	13,900	41,949	58,611	13,787	26,401	36,888
1996	13,510	39,624	56,559	13,247	25,192	35,959
1995[7]	13,065	39,040	57,209	12,875	24,065	35,265
1994[8]	12,997	38,701	58,078	11,773	23,405	35,123
1993[9]	12,360	37,474	57,437	11,447	22,452	34,413
1992[10]	11,938	36,745	57,712	11,133	22,383	35,155
1991	11,657	36,067	58,084	10,721	20,967	33,766

Note. People 25 years old and over as of March of the following year.
[1] Income in current and 2011 CPI-U-RS adjusted dollars.
[2]Data reflect implementation of Census 2010-based population controls.
[3]Beginning with 2009 income data, the Census Bureau expanded the upper income interval used to calculate medians and Gini indexes to $250,000 or more. Medians falling in the upper open-ended interval are plugged with "$250,000." Before 2009, the upper open-ended interval was $100,000 and a plug of "$100,000" was used.
[4]Data reflect a correction to the weights in the 2005 Annual Social and Economic Supplement (ASEC).
[5]Data reflect implementation of a 28,000 household sample expansion.
[6]Data reflect implementation of Census 2000-based population controls.
[7]Data reflect full implementation of the 1990 census-based sample design and metropolitan definitions, 7,000 household sample reduction, and revised race edits.
[8]Data reflect introduction of 1990 census-based sample design.
[9]Data collection method changed from paper and pencil to computer-assisted interviewing. In addition, the March 1994 income supplement was revised to allow for the coding of different income amounts on selected questionnaire items. Child support and alimony limits decreased to $49,999. Limits increased in the following categories: earnings to $999,999; social security to $49,999; supplemental security income and public assistance income to $24,999; and veterans' benefits to $99,999.
[10]Data reflect implementation of 1990 census population controls.

Table A-28. Educational Attainment of Persons 25 Years Old and Over, by Median Income and Sex, 1991–2011—*Continued*

(Dollars except as noted)

Educational attainment and year	Male			Female		
	Number with income (thousands)	Median income[1]		Number with income (thousands)	Median income[1]	
		Current dollars	2011 dollars		Current dollars	2011 dollars
Master's Degree						
2011	7,238	71,537	71,537	8,650	48,738	48,738
2010[2]	7,100	69,576	71,771	8,507	48,488	50,017
2009[3]	6,728	69,825	73,217	7,945	50,576	73,217
2008	6,896	70,973	74,138	7,801	48,000	74,138
2007	6,759	71,097	77,121	7,590	48,077	77,121
2006	6,350	67,425	75,213	6,876	46,250	75,213
2005	6,137	64,468	74,272	6,560	44,385	74,272
2004[4]	6,059	63,260	75,324	6,464	42,243	75,324
2003	6,076	61,698	75,449	6,268	41,334	75,449
2002	5,768	60,830	76,049	6,073	40,939	76,049
2001	5,522	61,960	78,713	5,749	40,744	78,713
2000[5]	5,346	59,732	78,013	5,421	40,619	78,013
1999[6]	5,178	59,189	79,894	5,220	39,712	79,894
1998	4,772	55,784	76,869	4,837	36,888	76,869
1997	4,583	52,530	73,395	4,488	35,882	73,395
1996	4,709	50,003	71,374	4,285	33,302	71,374
1995[7]	4,774	49,076	71,916	4,205	33,509	71,916
1994[8]	4,558	46,635	69,984	4,166	32,069	69,984
1993[9]	4,320	45,597	69,887	4,003	31,389	69,887
1992[10]	4,308	44,293	69,567	3,873	30,169	69,567
1991	4,356	43,125	69,450	3,745	29,747	69,450
Professional Degree						
2011	1,903	98,883	98,883	1,098	61,206	61,206
2010[2]	1,856	96,212	99,247	1,053	60,477	62,385
2009[3]	1,844	102,398	107,372	1,142	60,259	63,186
2008	1,930	100,000[12]	n.a.	1,197	58,364	60,967
2007	1,843	100,000[12]	n.a.	1,060	61,875	67,118
2006	1,969	96,926	108,121	1,037	60,463	67,447
2005	1,912	90,878	104,698	1,090	59,934	69,048
2004[4]	1,876	90,210	107,413	991	50,311	59,905
2003	1,901	88,530	108,262	990	48,536	59,354
2002	1,816	88,216	110,287	946	44,748	55,943
2001	1,779	81,602	103,666	899	46,635	59,244
2000[5]	1,711	83,701	109,318	852	46,084	60,188
1999[6]	1,774	81,545	110,071	824	45,432	61,325
1998	1,695	76,362	105,225	788	43,490	59,928
1997	1,741	72,274	100,982	807	45,199	63,152
1996	1,702	71,869	102,586	715	42,059	60,035
1995[7]	1,657	66,257	97,093	732	38,588	56,547
1994[8]	1,691	61,739	92,651	709	35,806	53,733
1993[9]	1,650	69,678	106,796	583	32,742	50,184
1992[10]	1,639	68,429	107,476	569	36,640	57,547
1991	1,547	63,741	102,651	556	34,064	54,858

Note. People 25 years old and over as of March of the following year.
[1] Income in current and 2011 CPI-U-RS adjusted dollars.
[2]Data reflect implementation of Census 2010-based population controls.
[3]Beginning with 2009 income data, the Census Bureau expanded the upper income interval used to calculate medians and Gini indexes to $250,000 or more. Medians falling in the upper open-ended interval are plugged with "$250,000." Before 2009, the upper open-ended interval was $100,000 and a plug of "$100,000" was used.
[4]Data reflect a correction to the weights in the 2005 Annual Social and Economic Supplement (ASEC).
[5]Data reflect implementation of a 28,000 household sample expansion.
[6]Data reflect implementation of Census 2000-based population controls.
[7]Data reflect full implementation of the 1990 census-based sample design and metropolitan definitions, 7,000 household sample reduction, and revised race edits.
[8]Data reflect introduction of 1990 census-based sample design.
[9]Data collection method changed from paper and pencil to computer-assisted interviewing. In addition, the March 1994 income supplement was revised to allow for the coding of different income amounts on selected questionnaire items. Child support and alimony limits decreased to $49,999. Limits increased in the following categories: earnings to $999,999; social security to $49,999; supplemental security income and public assistance income to $24,999; and veterans' benefits to $99,999.
[10]Data reflect implementation of 1990 census population controls.
[12]Indicates that the medians were topcoded.
n.a. = Not applicable

Table A-28. Educational Attainment of Persons 25 Years Old and Over, by Median Income and Sex, 1991–2011—*Continued*

(Dollars except as noted)

Educational attainment and year	Male			Female		
	Number with income (thousands)	Median income[1]		Number with income (thousands)	Median income[1]	
		Current dollars	2011 dollars		Current dollars	2011 dollars
Doctorate Degree						
2011	1,976	82,376	82,376	1,121	63,913	63,913
2010[2]	1,900	86,200	88,919	1,136	70,417	72,638
2009[3]	1,755	89,845	94,209	987	65,587	68,773
2008	1,622	90,575	94,614	942	60,619	63,322
2007	1,601	86,171	93,472	823	61,554	66,769
2006	1,649	90,511	100,965	782	61,091	68,147
2005	1,656	76,937	88,637	749	56,820	65,461
2004[4]	1,573	80,033	95,295	734	55,996	66,674
2003	1,606	73,853	90,313	773	53,003	64,816
2002	1,514	76,147	95,198	663	52,336	65,430
2001	1,488	72,642	92,283	653	52,181	66,290
2000[5]	1,520	71,271	93,083	584	51,460	67,209
1999[6]	1,451	70,461	95,109	600	46,511	62,781
1998	1,443	65,319	90,008	567	46,275	63,766
1997	1,338	68,643	95,909	508	46,545	65,033
1996	1,215	62,255	88,863	527	42,431	60,566
1995[7]	1,149	57,356	84,049	457	39,821	58,353
1994[8]	1,183	57,478	86,256	462	40,793	61,217
1993[9]	1,149	55,751	85,450	447	42,737	65,504
1992[10]	1,053	51,681	81,171	358	39,322	61,760
1991	929	51,845	83,493	337	37,242	59,976

Note. People 25 years old and over as of March of the following year.
[1] Income in current and 2011 CPI-U-RS adjusted dollars.
[2] Data reflect implementation of Census 2010-based population controls.
[3] Beginning with 2009 income data, the Census Bureau expanded the upper income interval used to calculate medians and Gini indexes to $250,000 or more. Medians falling in the upper open-ended interval are plugged with "$250,000." Before 2009, the upper open-ended interval was $100,000 and a plug of "$100,000" was used.
[4] Data reflect a correction to the weights in the 2005 Annual Social and Economic Supplement (ASEC).
[5] Data reflect implementation of a 28,000 household sample expansion.
[6] Data reflect implementation of Census 2000-based population controls.
[7] Data reflect full implementation of the 1990 census-based sample design and metropolitan definitions, 7,000 household sample reduction, and revised race edits.
[8] Data reflect introduction of 1990 census-based sample design.
[9] Data collection method changed from paper and pencil to computer-assisted interviewing. In addition, the March 1994 income supplement was revised to allow for the coding of different income amounts on selected questionnaire items. Child support and alimony limits decreased to $49,999. Limits increased in the following categories: earnings to $999,999; social security to $49,999; supplemental security income and public assistance income to $24,999; and veterans' benefits to $99,999.
[10] Data reflect implementation of 1990 census population controls.

PART A

NATIONAL EDUCATION STATISTICS

■ Postsecondary Education Tables

Table A-29. Total Fall Enrollment in Degree-Granting Institutions, by Attendance Status, Sex of Student, and Control of Institution: Selected Years, 1947–2010

(Numbers in thousands)

Year	Total enrolled	Attendance status			Sex of student			Control of institution			
									Private		
		Full-time	Part-time	Percent part-time	Male	Female	Percent Female	Public	Total	Not-for-profit	For-profit
2010	21,016	13,082	7,934	37.8	9,045	11,971	57.0	15,143	5,873	3,855	2,018
2009	20,428	12,723	7,705	37.7	8,770	11,658	57.1	14,811	5,617	3,765	1,852
2008	19,103	11,748	7,355	38.5	8,189	10,914	57.1	13,972	5,131	3,662	1,469
2007	18,248	11,270	6,978	38.2	7,816	10,432	57.2	13,491	4,757	3,571	1,186
2006	17,759	10,957	6,802	38.3	7,575	10,184	57.3	13,180	4,579	3,513	1,066
2005	17,487	10,797	6,690	38.3	7,456	10,032	57.4	13,022	4,466	3,455	1,011
2004	17,272	10,610	6,662	38.6	7,387	9,885	57.2	12,980	4,292	3,412	880
2003	16,911	10,326	6,585	38.9	7,260	9,651	57.1	12,859	4,053	3,341	712
2002	16,612	9,946	6,665	40.1	7,202	9,410	56.6	12,752	3,860	3,265	594
2001	15,928	9,448	6,480	40.7	6,961	8,967	56.3	12,233	3,695	3,167	528
2000	15,312	9,010	6,303	41.2	6,722	8,591	56.1	11,753	3,560	3,109	450
1999	14,850	8,803	6,047	40.7	6,515	8,335	56.1	11,376	3,474	3,055	419
1998	14,507	8,563	5,944	41.0	6,369	8,138	56.1	11,138	3,369	3,005	364
1997	14,502	8,438	6,064	41.8	6,396	8,106	55.9	11,196	3,306	2,978	329
1996	14,368	8,303	6,065	42.2	6,353	8,015	55.8	11,120	3,247	2,943	304
1995	14,262	8,129	6,133	43.0	6,343	7,919	55.5	11,092	3,169	2,929	240
1994	14,279	8,138	6,141	43.0	6,372	7,907	55.4	11,134	3,145	2,910	235
1993	14,305	8,128	6,177	43.2	6,427	7,877	55.1	11,189	3,116	2,889	227
1992	14,487	8,162	6,325	43.7	6,524	7,963	55.0	11,385	3,103	2,873	230
1991	14,359	8,115	6,244	43.5	6,502	7,857	54.7	11,310	3,049	2,819	230
1990	13,819	7,821	5,998	43.4	6,284	7,535	54.5	10,845	2,974	2,760	214
1989	13,539	7,661	5,878	43.4	6,190	7,349	54.3	10,578	2,961	2,731	229
1988	13,055	7,437	5,619	43.0	6,002	7,053	54.0	10,161	2,894	2,674	220
1987	12,767	7,231	5,536	43.4	5,932	6,835	53.5	9,973	2,793	2,602	191[1]
1986	12,504	7,120	5,384	43.1	5,885	6,619	52.9	9,714	2,790	2,572	217[1]
1985	12,247	7,075	5,172	42.2	5,818	6,429	52.5	9,479	2,768	2,572	196
1984	12,242	7,098	5,144	42.0	5,864	6,378	52.1	9,477	2,765	2,574	190
1983	12,465	7,261	5,204	41.7	6,024	6,441	51.7	9,683	2,782	2,589	193
1982	12,426	7,221	5,205	41.9	6,031	6,394	51.5	9,696	2,730	2,553	177[2]
1981	12,372	7,181	5,190	42.0	5,975	6,397	51.7	9,647	2,725	2,572	152[2]
1980	12,097	7,098	4,999	41.3	5,874	6,223	51.4	9,457	2,640	2,528	112[2]
1979	11,570	6,794	4,776	41.3	5,683	5,887	50.9	9,037	2,533	2,462	71
1978	11,260	6,668	4,592	40.8	5,641	5,619	49.9	8,786	2,474	2,408	66
1977	11,286	6,793	4,493	39.8	5,789	5,497	48.7	8,847	2,439	2,387	52
1976	11,012	6,717	4,295	39.0	5,811	5,201	47.2	8,653	2,359	2,314	44
1975	11,185	6,841	4,344	38.8	6,149	5,036	45.0	8,835	2,350	2,311	39
1974	10,224	6,370	3,853	37.7	5,622	4,601	45.0	7,989	2,235	2,201	34
1973	9,602	6,189	3,413	35.5	5,371	4,231	44.1	7,420	2,183	2,149	34
1972	9,215	6,072	3,142	34.1	5,239	3,976	43.1	7,071	2,144	2,123	21
1971	8,949	6,077	2,871	32.1	5,207	3,742	41.8	6,804	2,144	2,122	22
1970	8,581	5,816	2,765	32.2	5,044	3,537	41.2	6,428	2,153	2,134	18
1969	8,005	5,499	2,506	31.3	4,746	3,258	40.7	5,897	2,108	2,088	20
1968	7,513	5,210	2,303	30.7	4,478	3,035	40.4	5,431	2,082	2,061	21
1967	6,912	4,793	2,119[3]	30.7	4,133	2,779	40.2	4,816	2,096	2,074	22
1966	6,390	4,439	1,951[3]	30.5	3,856	2,534	39.7	4,349	2,041	...	...
1965	5,921	4,096	1,825[3]	30.8	3,630	2,291	38.7	3,970	1,951	...	...
1964	5,280	3,573	1,707[3]	32.3	3,249	2,031	38.5	3,468	1,812	...	...
1963	4,780	3,184	1,596[3]	33.4	2,962	1,818	38.0	3,081	1,698	...	...
1961	4,145	2,785	1,360[3]	32.8	2,586	1,559	37.6	2,561	1,584	...	...
1959	3,640	2,421	1,219[3]	33.5	2,333	1,307	35.9	2,181	1,459	...	...
1957	3,324	...	...	...	2,171	1,153	34.7	1,973	1,351	...	...
1956[4]	2,918	...	...	...	1,911	1,007	34.5	1,656	1,262	...	...
1955[4]	2,653	...	...	...	1,733	920	34.7	1,476	1,177	...	...
1954[4]	2,447	...	...	...	1,563	883	36.1	1,354	1,093	...	...
1953[4]	2,231	...	...	...	1,423	808	36.2	1,186	1,045	...	...
1952[4]	2,134	...	...	...	1,380	754	35.3	1,101	1,033	...	...
1951[4]	2,102	...	...	...	1,391	711	33.8	1,038	1,064	...	...
1950[4]	2,281	...	...	...	1,560	721	31.6	1,140	1,142	...	...
1949[4]	2,445	...	...	...	1,722	723	29.6	1,207	1,238	...	...
1948[4]	2,403	...	...	...	1,709	694	28.9	1,186	1,218	...	...
1947[4]	2,338	...	...	...	1,659	679	29.0	1,152	1,186	...	...

Note: Data through 1995 are for institutions of higher education, while later data are for degree-granting institutions. Degree-granting institutions grant associate's or higher degrees and participate in Title IV federal financial aid programs. The degree-granting classification is very similar to the earlier higher education classification, but it includes more 2-year colleges and excludes a few higher education institutions that did not grant degrees. Some data have been revised from previously published figures.

[1]Because of imputation techniques, data are not consistent with figures for other years.

[2]Large increases are due to the addition of schools accredited by the Accrediting Commission of Career Schools and Colleges of Technology.

[3]Includes part-time resident students and all extension students (students attending courses at sites separate from the primary reporting campus).

[4]Degree-credit enrollment only.

... = Not available.

Table A-30. Total Fall Enrollment in Degree-Granting Institutions, by Control and Type of Institution: 1963–2010

(Numbers in thousands)

Year	All institutions					Public institutions					Private institutions				
	Total	4-year			2-year	Total	4-year			2-year	Total	4-year			2-year
		Total	University	Other 4-year			Total	University	Other 4-year			Total	University	Other 4-year	
2010......	21,016	13,335	3,558	9,777	7,681	15,143	7,925	2,649	5,275	7,218	5,873	5,410	909	4,502	463
2009......	20,428	12,906	3,493	9,413	7,521	14,811	7,709	2,603	5,106	7,101	5,617	5,197	890	4,307	420
2008......	19,103	12,131	3,412	8,719	6,971	13,972	7,332	2,545	4,787	6,640	5,131	4,800	868	3,932	331
2007......	18,248	11,630	3,349	8,281	6,618	13,491	7,167	2,491	4,676	6,324	4,757	4,464	859	3,605	294
2006......	17,759	11,240	3,307	7,933	6,519	13,180	6,955	2,460	4,495	6,225	4,579	4,285	847	3,438	293
2005......	17,487	10,999	3,272	7,728	6,488	13,022	6,838	2,444	4,394	6,184	4,466	4,162	828	3,334	304
2004......	17,272	10,726	3,259	7,467	6,546	12,980	6,737	2,426	4,310	6,244	4,292	3,990	832	3,157	302
2003......	16,911	10,417	3,243	7,175	6,494	12,859	6,649	2,420	4,230	6,209	4,053	3,768	823	2,945	285
2002......	16,612	10,082	3,210	6,872	6,529	12,752	6,482	2,403	4,078	6,270	3,860	3,601	807	2,794	259
2001......	15,928	9,677	3,127	6,551	6,251	12,233	6,236	2,337	3,900	5,997	3,695	3,441	790	2,651	254
2000......	15,312	9,364	3,062	6,302	5,948	11,753	6,055	2,280	3,775	5,697	3,560	3,308	782	2,527	251
1999........	14,850	9,196	3,044	6,152	5,654	11,376	5,978	2,266	3,711	5,398	3,474	3,218	778	2,441	255
1998........	14,507	9,018	3,021	5,997	5,489	11,138	5,892	2,250	3,642	5,246	3,369	3,126	771	2,355	243
1997........	14,502	8,897	2,996	5,901	5,606	11,196	5,835	2,231	3,604	5,361	3,306	3,061	765	2,297	245
1996........	14,368	8,804	2,985	5,819	5,563	11,120	5,806	2,227	3,580	5,314	3,247	2,998	758	2,240	249
1995........	14,262	8,769	3,000	5,770	5,493	11,092	5,815	2,236	3,579	5,278	3,169	2,955	764	2,191	215
1994........	14,279	8,749	3,009	5,740	5,530	11,134	5,825	2,245	3,581	5,308	3,145	2,924	764	2,159	221
1993........	14,305	8,739	3,023	5,716	5,566	11,189	5,852	2,260	3,592	5,337	3,116	2,887	763	2,124	229
1992........	14,487	8,765	3,050	5,715	5,722	11,385	5,900	2,284	3,616	5,485	3,103	2,865	767	2,098	238
1991........	14,359	8,707	3,065	5,642	5,652	11,310	5,905	2,301	3,604	5,405	3,049	2,802	764	2,038	247
1990........	13,819	8,579	3,045	5,534	5,240	10,845	5,848	2,290	3,558	4,996	2,974	2,730	754	1,976	244
1989........	13,539	8,388	3,019	5,369	5,151	10,578	5,694	2,266	3,428	4,884	2,961	2,693	753	1,940	267
1988........	13,055	8,180	2,979	5,202	4,875	10,161	5,546	2,230	3,316	4,615	2,894	2,634	749	1,886	260
1987........	12,767	7,990	2,929	5,061	4,776	9,973	5,432	2,188	3,244	4,541	2,793	2,558	741	1,817	235
1986........	12,504	7,824	2,897	4,927	4,680	9,714	5,300	2,161	3,140	4,414	2,790	2,524	737	1,787	266 [1]
1985........	12,247	7,716	2,871	4,845	4,531	9,479	5,210	2,141	3,068	4,270	2,768	2,506	730	1,777	261 [1]
1984........	12,242	7,711	2,870	4,841	4,531	9,477	5,198	2,139	3,060	4,279	2,765	2,513	732	1,781	252
1983........	12,465	7,741	2,889	4,852	4,723	9,683	5,223	2,155	3,069	4,459	2,782	2,518	734	1,784	264
1982........	12,426	7,654	2,884	4,770	4,772	9,696	5,176	2,153	3,024	4,520	2,730	2,478	731	1,746	252 [2]
1981........	12,372	7,655	2,901	4,754	4,716	9,647	5,166	2,152	3,014	4,481	2,725	2,489	749	1,740	236 [2]
1980........	12,097	7,571	2,902	4,669	4,526	9,457	5,129	2,154	2,974	4,329	2,640	2,442	748	1,694	198 [2]
1979........	11,570	7,353	2,840	4,514	4,217	9,037	4,980	2,100	2,880	4,057	2,533	2,373	740	1,633	160
1978........	11,260	7,232	2,781	4,451	4,028	8,786	4,912	2,062	2,850	3,874	2,474	2,319	718	1,601	155
1977........	11,286	7,243	2,793	4,449	4,043	8,847	4,945	2,070	2,875	3,902	2,439	2,298	723	1,574	141
1976........	11,012	7,129	2,780	4,349	3,883	8,653	4,902	2,080	2,822	3,752	2,359	2,227	700	1,527	132
1975........	11,185	7,215	2,838	4,376	3,970	8,835	4,998	2,124	2,874	3,836	2,350	2,217	714	1,503	134
1974........	10,224	6,820	2,702	4,117	3,404	7,989	4,703	2,007	2,696	3,285	2,235	2,117	696	1,421	119
1973........	9,602	6,590	2,630	3,960	3,012	7,420	4,530	1,951	2,579	2,890	2,183	2,060	679	1,381	122
1972........	9,215	6,459	2,621	3,838	2,756	7,071	4,430	1,941	2,489	2,641	2,144	2,029	680	1,349	115
1971........	8,949	6,369	2,594	3,775	2,579	6,804	4,347	1,914	2,433	2,457	2,144	2,022	681	1,342	122
1970........	8,581	6,262	2,534	3,727	2,319	6,428	4,233	1,833	2,400	2,195	2,153	2,029	702	1,327	124
1969........	8,005	5,937	2,420	3,517	2,068	5,897	3,963	1,738	2,224	1,934	2,108	1,975	682	1,293	133
1968........	7,513	5,720	2,266	3,454	1,793	5,431	3,784	1,593	2,191	1,647	2,082	1,937	673	1,263	146
1967........	6,912	5,399	2,186	3,213	1,513	4,816	3,444	1,510	1,934	1,372	2,096	1,955	676	1,279	141
1966[3].....	6,390	5,064	...	...	1,326	4,349	3,160	...	...	1,189	2,041	1,904	...	...	137
1965[3].....	5,921	4,748	...	...	1,173	3,970	2,928	...	...	1,041	1,951	1,820	...	...	132
1964[3].....	5,280	4,291	...	...	989	3,468	2,593	...	...	875	1,812	1,698	...	...	114
1963[3]........	4,780	3,929	...	...	850	3,081	2,341	...	...	740	1,698	1,588	...	...	111

Note: Data through 1995 are for institutions of higher education, while later data are for degree-granting institutions. Degree-granting institutions grant associate's or higher degrees and participate in Title IV federal financial aid programs. The degree-granting classification is very similar to the earlier higher education classification, but it includes more 2-year colleges and excludes a few higher education institutions that did not grant degrees. A university is an institution of higher education consisting of a liberal arts college, a diverse graduate program, and usually two or more professional schools or faculties. It is empowered to confer degrees in various fields of study; for purposes of maintaining trend data in this publication, the selection of university institutions has not been revised since 1982. Some data have been revised from previously published figures.

[1]Large increases are due to the addition of schools accredited by the Accrediting Commission of Career Schools and Colleges of Technology.

[2]Because of imputation techniques, data are not consistent with figures for other years.

[3]Data for 2-year branch campuses of 4-year institutions are included with the 4-year institutions.

... = Not available

Table A-31. Total Fall Enrollment in Degree-Granting Institutions, by Level of Enrollment, Sex, Age, and Attendance Status of Student, 2009

Age of student and attendance status	All levels						Undergraduate					
	Total		Males		Females		Total		Males		Females	
	Number	Percent	Number	Percent	Number	Percent	Number	Percent	Number	Percent	Number	Percent
All students	20,427,711	100.0	8,769,504	100.0	11,658,207	100.0	17,565,320	100.0	7,595,481	100.0	9,969,839	100.0
Under 18	757,239	3.7	314,150	3.6	443,089	3.8	756,952	4.3	314,045	4.1	442,907	4.4
18 and 19	4,300,248	21.1	1,946,838	22.2	2,353,410	20.2	4,298,311	24.5	1,946,160	25.6	2,352,151	23.6
20 and 21	4,003,222	19.6	1,814,622	20.7	2,188,600	18.8	3,971,829	22.6	1,802,523	23.7	2,169,306	21.8
22 to 24	3,315,227	16.2	1,520,388	17.3	1,794,839	15.4	2,725,760	15.5	1,282,572	16.9	1,443,188	14.5
25 to 29	2,961,851	14.5	1,277,580	14.6	1,684,271	14.4	2,044,157	11.6	881,057	11.6	1,163,100	11.7
30 to 34	1,635,355	8.0	663,459	7.6	971,896	8.3	1,177,534	6.7	457,992	6.0	719,542	7.2
35 to 39	1,128,666	5.5	426,387	4.9	702,279	6.0	841,719	4.8	305,628	4.0	536,091	5.4
40 to 49	1,449,671	7.1	498,553	5.7	951,118	8.2	1,097,374	6.2	371,599	4.9	725,775	7.3
50 to 64	734,572	3.6	247,034	2.8	487,538	4.2	536,289	3.1	184,110	2.4	352,179	3.5
65 and over	69,844	0.3	29,251	0.3	40,593	0.3	61,650	0.4	25,505	0.3	36,145	0.4
Age unknown	71,816	0.4	31,242	0.4	40,574	0.3	53,745	0.3	24,290	0.3	29,455	0.3
Full-time	12,722,782	100.0	5,670,644	100.0	7,052,138	100.0	11,143,499	100.0	4,976,727	100.0	6,166,772	100.0
Under 18	177,445	1.4	71,603	1.3	105,842	1.5	177,332	1.6	71,566	1.4	105,766	1.7
18 and 19	3,640,621	28.6	1,636,522	28.9	2,004,099	28.4	3,638,867	32.7	1,635,905	32.9	2,002,962	32.5
20 and 21	3,249,604	25.5	1,477,485	26.1	1,772,119	25.1	3,221,556	28.9	1,466,453	29.5	1,755,103	28.5
22 to 24	2,198,573	17.3	1,047,143	18.5	1,151,430	16.3	1,737,688	15.6	855,243	17.2	882,445	14.3
25 to 29	1,540,444	12.1	705,203	12.4	835,241	11.8	980,396	8.8	444,069	8.9	536,327	8.7
30 to 34	725,901	5.7	304,439	5.4	421,462	6.0	505,141	4.5	197,344	4.0	307,797	5.0
35 to 39	447,946	3.5	169,775	3.0	278,171	3.9	332,217	3.0	118,170	2.4	214,047	3.5
40 to 49	501,869	3.9	173,301	3.1	328,568	4.7	379,205	3.4	126,766	2.5	252,439	4.1
50 to 64	207,365	1.6	70,665	1.2	136,700	1.9	145,838	1.3	50,045	1.0	95,793	1.6
65 and over	6,642	0.1	2,871	0.1	3,771	0.1	4,378	*	1,853	*	2,525	*
Age unknown	26,372	0.2	11,637	0.2	14,735	0.2	20,881	0.2	9,313	0.2	11,568	0.2
Part-time	7,704,929	100.0	3,098,860	100.0	4,606,069	100.0	6,421,821	100.0	2,618,754	100.0	3,803,067	100.0
Under 18	579,794	7.5	242,547	7.8	337,247	7.3	579,620	9.0	242,479	9.3	337,141	8.9
18 and 19	659,627	8.6	310,316	10.0	349,311	7.6	659,444	10.3	310,255	11.8	349,189	9.2
20 and 21	753,618	9.8	337,137	10.9	416,481	9.0	750,273	11.7	336,070	12.8	414,203	10.9
22 to 24	1,116,654	14.5	473,245	15.3	643,409	14.0	988,072	15.4	427,329	16.3	560,743	14.7
25 to 29	1,421,407	18.4	572,377	18.5	849,030	18.4	1,063,761	16.6	436,988	16.7	626,773	16.5
30 to 34	909,454	11.8	359,020	11.6	550,434	12.0	672,393	10.5	260,648	10.0	411,745	10.8
35 to 39	680,720	8.8	256,612	8.3	424,108	9.2	509,502	7.9	187,458	7.2	322,044	8.5
40 to 49	947,802	12.3	325,252	10.5	622,550	13.5	718,169	11.2	244,833	9.3	473,336	12.4
50 to 64	527,207	6.8	176,369	5.7	350,838	7.6	390,451	6.1	134,065	5.1	256,386	6.7
65 and over	63,202	0.8	26,380	0.9	36,822	0.8	57,272	0.9	23,652	0.9	33,620	0.9
Age unknown	45,444	0.6	19,605	0.6	25,839	0.6	32,864	0.5	14,977	0.6	17,887	0.5

Note: Degree-granting institutions grant associate's or higher degrees and participate in Title IV federal financial aid programs. Details may not sum to totals because of rounding.

* = Quantity zero or equals zero

Table A-31. Total Fall Enrollment in Degree-Granting Institutions, by Level of Enrollment, Sex, Age, and Attendance Status of Student, 2009—*Continued*

Age of student and attendance status	Postbaccalaureate					
	Total		Males		Females	
	Number	Percent	Number	Percent	Number	Percent
All students	2,862,391	100.0	1,174,023	100.0	1,688,368	100.0
Under 18	287	*	105	*	182	*
18 and 19	1,937	0.1	678	0.1	1,259	0.1
20 and 21	31,393	1.1	12,099	1.0	19,294	1.1
22 to 24	589,467	20.6	237,816	20.3	351,651	20.8
25 to 29	917,694	32.1	396,523	33.8	521,171	30.9
30 to 34	457,821	16.0	205,467	17.5	252,354	14.9
35 to 39	286,947	10.0	120,759	10.3	166,188	9.8
40 to 49	352,297	12.3	126,954	10.8	225,343	13.3
50 to 64	198,283	6.9	62,924	5.4	135,359	8.0
65 and over	8,194	0.3	3,746	0.3	4,448	0.3
Age unknown	18,071	0.6	6,952	0.6	11,119	0.7
Full-time	1,579,283	100.0	693,917	100.0	885,366	100.0
Under 18	113	*	37	*	76	*
18 and 19	1,754	0.1	617	0.1	1,137	0.1
20 and 21	28,048	1.8	11,032	1.6	17,016	1.9
22 to 24	460,885	29.2	191,900	27.7	268,985	30.4
25 to 29	560,048	35.5	261,134	37.6	298,914	33.8
30 to 34	220,760	14.0	107,095	15.4	113,665	12.8
35 to 39	115,729	7.3	51,605	7.4	64,124	7.2
40 to 49	122,664	7.8	46,535	6.7	76,129	8.6
50 to 64	61,527	3.9	20,620	3.0	40,907	4.6
65 and over	2,264	0.1	1,018	0.1	1,246	0.1
Age unknown	5,491	0.3	2,324	0.3	3,167	0.4
Part-time	1,283,108	100.0	480,106	100.0	803,002	100.0
Under 18	174	*	68	*	106	*
18 and 19	183	*	61	*	122	*
20 and 21	3,345	0.3	1,067	0.2	2,278	0.3
22 to 24	128,582	10.0	45,916	9.6	82,666	10.3
25 to 29	357,646	27.9	135,389	28.2	222,257	27.7
30 to 34	237,061	18.5	98,372	20.5	138,689	17.3
35 to 39	171,218	13.3	69,154	14.4	102,064	12.7
40 to 49	229,633	17.9	80,419	16.8	149,214	18.6
50 to 64	136,756	10.7	42,304	8.8	94,452	11.8
65 and over	5,930	0.5	2,728	0.6	3,202	0.4
Age unknown	12,580	1.0	4,628	1.0	7,952	1.0

Note: Degree-granting institutions grant associate's or higher degrees and participate in Title IV federal financial aid programs. Details may not sum to totals because of rounding.

* = Quantity zero or equals zero

Table A-32. Total Fall Enrollment in Degree-Granting Institutions, by Control and Type of Institution, Age, and Attendance Status of Student, 2009

Age of student and attendance status	All institutions						Public institutions					
	Total		4-year		2-year		Total		4-year		2-year	
	Number	Percent	Number	Percent	Number	Percent	Number	Percent	Number	Percent	Number	Percent
All students	20,427,711	100.0	12,906,305	100.0	7,521,406	100.0	14,810,642	100.0	7,709,197	100.0	7,101,445	100.0
Under 18	757,239	3.7	252,415	2.0	504,824	6.7	685,380	4.6	183,963	2.4	501,417	7.1
18 and 19	4,300,248	21.1	2,645,704	20.5	1,654,544	22.0	3,373,060	22.8	1,776,382	23.0	1,596,678	22.5
20 and 21	4,003,222	19.6	2,759,078	21.4	1,244,144	16.5	3,025,002	20.4	1,848,966	24.0	1,176,036	16.6
22 to 24	3,315,227	16.2	2,286,382	17.7	1,028,845	13.7	2,480,545	16.7	1,523,533	19.8	957,012	13.5
25 to 29	2,961,851	14.5	1,943,572	15.1	1,018,279	13.5	1,989,236	13.4	1,051,400	13.6	937,836	13.2
30 to 34	1,635,355	8.0	1,021,005	7.9	614,350	8.2	1,050,454	7.1	484,567	6.3	565,887	8.0
35 to 39	1,128,666	5.5	683,089	5.3	445,577	5.9	708,505	4.8	295,880	3.8	412,625	5.8
40 to 49	1,449,671	7.1	841,913	6.5	607,758	8.1	920,345	6.2	349,801	4.5	570,544	8.0
50 to 64	734,572	3.6	402,822	3.1	331,750	4.4	490,101	3.3	173,439	2.2	316,662	4.5
65 and over	69,844	0.3	21,108	0.2	48,736	0.6	60,362	0.4	12,200	0.2	48,162	0.7
Age unknown	71,816	0.4	49,217	0.4	22,599	0.3	27,652	0.2	9,066	0.1	18,586	0.3
Full-time	12,722,782	100.0	9,474,059	100.0	3,248,723	100.0	8,530,344	100.0	5,649,713	100.0	2,880,631	100.0
Under 18	177,445	1.4	102,344	1.1	75,101	2.3	141,497	1.7	68,954	1.2	72,543	2.5
18 and 19	3,640,621	28.6	2,511,562	26.5	1,129,059	34.8	2,745,734	32.2	1,670,996	29.6	1,074,738	37.3
20 and 21	3,249,604	25.5	2,553,166	26.9	696,438	21.4	2,326,319	27.3	1,691,938	29.9	634,381	22.0
22 to 24	2,198,573	17.3	1,780,300	18.8	418,273	12.9	1,526,568	17.9	1,171,760	20.7	354,808	12.3
25 to 29	1,540,444	12.1	1,177,157	12.4	363,287	11.2	885,635	10.4	592,049	10.5	293,586	10.2
30 to 34	725,901	5.7	524,974	5.5	200,927	6.2	370,602	4.3	211,183	3.7	159,419	5.5
35 to 39	447,946	3.5	314,580	3.3	133,366	4.1	208,973	2.4	103,389	1.8	105,584	3.7
40 to 49	501,869	3.9	345,535	3.6	156,334	4.8	223,623	2.6	97,945	1.7	125,678	4.4
50 to 64	207,365	1.6	141,374	1.5	65,991	2.0	90,567	1.1	36,710	0.6	53,857	1.9
65 and over	6,642	0.1	4,290	*	2,352	0.1	3,010	*	1,067	*	1,943	0.1
Age unknown	26,372	0.2	18,777	0.2	7,595	0.2	7,816	0.1	3,722	0.1	4,094	0.1
Part-time	7,704,929	100.0	3,432,246	100.0	4,272,683	100.0	6,280,298	100.0	2,059,484	100.0	4,220,814	100.0
Under 18	579,794	7.5	150,071	4.4	429,723	10.1	543,883	8.7	115,009	5.6	428,874	10.2
18 and 19	659,627	8.6	134,142	3.9	525,485	12.3	627,326	10.0	105,386	5.1	521,940	12.4
20 and 21	753,618	9.8	205,912	6.0	547,706	12.8	698,683	11.1	157,028	7.6	541,655	12.8
22 to 24	1,116,654	14.5	506,082	14.7	610,572	14.3	953,977	15.2	351,773	17.1	602,204	14.3
25 to 29	1,421,407	18.4	766,415	22.3	654,992	15.3	1,103,601	17.6	459,351	22.3	644,250	15.3
30 to 34	909,454	11.8	496,031	14.5	413,423	9.7	679,852	10.8	273,384	13.3	406,468	9.6
35 to 39	680,720	8.8	368,509	10.7	312,211	7.3	499,532	8.0	192,491	9.3	307,041	7.3
40 to 49	947,802	12.3	496,378	14.5	451,424	10.6	696,722	11.1	251,856	12.2	444,866	10.5
50 to 64	527,207	6.8	261,448	7.6	265,759	6.2	399,534	6.4	136,729	6.6	262,805	6.2
65 and over	63,202	0.8	16,818	0.5	46,384	1.1	57,352	0.9	11,133	0.5	46,219	1.1
Age unknown	45,444	0.6	30,440	0.9	15,004	0.4	19,836	0.3	5,344	0.3	14,492	0.3

Note: Degree-granting institutions grant associate's or higher degrees and participate in Title IV federal financial aid programs.
Details may not sum to totals because of rounding.
* = Quantity zero or equals zero

Table A-32. Total Fall Enrollment in Degree-Granting Institutions, by Control and Type of Institution, Age, and Attendance Status of Student, 2009—*Continued*

Age of student and attendance status	Private not-for-profit institutions						Private for-profit institutions					
	Total		4-year		2-year		Total		4-year		2-year	
	Number	Percent	Number	Percent	Number	Percent	Number	Percent	Number	Percent	Number	Percent
All students	3,765,083	100.0	3,730,316	100.0	34,767	100.0	1,851,986	100.0	1,466,792	100.0	385,194	100.0
Under 18	66,151	1.8	65,185	1.7	966	2.8	5,708	0.3	3,267	0.2	2,441	0.6
18 and 19	805,278	21.4	797,161	21.4	8,117	23.3	121,910	6.6	72,161	4.9	49,749	12.9
20 and 21	802,555	21.3	797,197	21.4	5,358	15.4	175,665	9.5	112,915	7.7	62,750	16.3
22 to 24	584,991	15.5	580,104	15.6	4,887	14.1	249,691	13.5	182,745	12.5	66,946	17.4
25 to 29	571,923	15.2	566,735	15.2	5,188	14.9	400,692	21.6	325,437	22.2	75,255	19.5
30 to 34	294,681	7.8	291,397	7.8	3,284	9.4	290,220	15.7	245,041	16.7	45,179	11.7
35 to 39	201,567	5.4	199,136	5.3	2,431	7.0	218,594	11.8	188,073	12.8	30,521	7.9
40 to 49	265,064	7.0	262,089	7.0	2,975	8.6	264,262	14.3	230,023	15.7	34,239	8.9
50 to 64	132,392	3.5	131,049	3.5	1,343	3.9	112,079	6.1	98,334	6.7	13,745	3.6
65 and over	6,475	0.2	6,381	0.2	94	0.3	3,007	0.2	2,527	0.2	480	0.1
Age unknown	34,006	0.9	33,882	0.9	124	0.4	10,158	0.5	6,269	0.4	3,889	1.0
Full-time	2,806,645	100.0	2,783,162	100.0	23,483	100.0	1,385,793	100.0	1,041,184	100.0	344,609	100.0
Under 18	31,430	1.1	31,142	1.1	288	1.2	4,518	0.3	2,248	0.2	2,270	0.7
18 and 19	787,103	28.0	779,858	28.0	7,245	30.9	107,784	7.8	60,708	5.8	47,076	13.7
20 and 21	776,054	27.7	771,655	27.7	4,399	18.7	147,231	10.6	89,573	8.6	57,658	16.7
22 to 24	476,179	17.0	472,910	17.0	3,269	13.9	195,826	14.1	135,630	13.0	60,196	17.5
25 to 29	356,612	12.7	353,624	12.7	2,988	12.7	298,197	21.5	231,484	22.2	66,713	19.4
30 to 34	145,411	5.2	143,620	5.2	1,791	7.6	209,888	15.1	170,171	16.3	39,717	11.5
35 to 39	84,126	3.0	82,846	3.0	1,280	5.5	154,847	11.2	128,345	12.3	26,502	7.7
40 to 49	95,665	3.4	94,198	3.4	1,467	6.2	182,581	13.2	153,392	14.7	29,189	8.5
50 to 64	41,109	1.5	40,459	1.5	650	2.8	75,689	5.5	64,205	6.2	11,484	3.3
65 and over	1,690	0.1	1,648	0.1	42	0.2	1,942	0.1	1,575	0.2	367	0.2
Age unknown	11,266	0.4	11,202	0.4	64	0.3	7,290	0.5	3,853	0.4	3,437	1.0
Part-time	958,438	100.0	947,154	100.0	11,284	100.0	466,193	100.0	425,608	100.0	40,585	100.0
Under 18	34,721	3.6	34,043	3.6	678	6.0	1,190	0.3	1,019	0.2	171	0.4
18 and 19	18,175	1.9	17,303	1.8	872	7.7	14,126	3.0	11,453	2.7	2,673	6.6
20 and 21	26,501	2.8	25,542	2.7	959	8.5	28,434	6.1	23,342	5.5	5,092	12.5
22 to 24	108,812	11.4	107,194	11.3	1,618	14.3	53,865	11.6	47,115	11.1	6,750	16.6
25 to 29	215,311	22.5	213,111	22.5	2,200	19.5	102,495	22.0	93,953	22.1	8,542	21.0
30 to 34	149,270	15.6	147,777	15.6	1,493	13.2	80,332	17.2	74,870	17.6	5,462	13.5
35 to 39	117,441	12.3	116,290	12.3	1,151	10.2	63,747	13.7	59,728	14.0	4,019	9.9
40 to 49	169,399	17.7	167,891	17.7	1,508	13.4	81,681	17.5	76,631	18.0	5,050	12.4
50 to 64	91,283	9.5	90,590	9.6	693	6.1	36,390	7.8	34,129	8.0	2,261	5.6
65 and over	4,785	0.5	4,733	0.5	52	0.5	1,065	0.2	952	0.2	113	0.3
Age unknown	22,740	2.4	22,680	2.4	60	0.5	2,868	0.6	2,416	0.6	452	1.1

Note: Degree-granting institutions grant associate's or higher degrees and participate in Title IV federal financial aid programs.
Details may not sum to totals because of rounding.
* = Quantity zero or equals zero

Table A-33. Total Undergraduate Fall Enrollment in Degree-Granting Institutions, by Attendance Status, Sex of Student, and Control of Institution, 1967–2010

(Numbers in thousands)

Year	Total	Full-time	Part-time	Males	Females	Males		Females		Males		Females	
						Full-time	Part-time	Full-time	Part-time	Public	Private	Public	Private
2010	18,079	11,452	6,627	7,835	10,244	5,117	2,718	6,334	3,909	6,076	1,759	7,628	2,615
2009	17,565	11,143	6,422	7,595	9,970	4,977	2,619	6,167	3,803	5,917	1,678	7,469	2,501
2008	16,366	10,255	6,111	7,067	9,299	4,577	2,489	5,677	3,622	5,532	1,535	7,059	2,240
2007	15,604	9,841	5,763	6,728	8,876	4,397	2,331	5,444	3,432	5,301	1,427	6,837	2,039
2006	15,184	9,571	5,613	6,514	8,671	4,265	2,249	5,306	3,364	5,134	1,380	6,714	1,957
2005	14,964	9,446	5,518	6,409	8,555	4,201	2,208	5,246	3,310	5,046	1,363	6,652	1,903
2004	14,781	9,284	5,496	6,340	8,441	4,141	2,199	5,144	3,297	5,009	1,331	6,641	1,799
2003	14,480	9,045	5,435	6,227	8,253	4,049	2,179	4,997	3,256	4,956	1,271	6,567	1,686
2002	14,257	8,734	5,523	6,192	8,065	3,934	2,258	4,800	3,265	4,960	1,232	6,473	1,592
2001	13,716	8,328	5,388	6,004	7,711	3,769	2,236	4,559	3,152	4,804	1,200	6,182	1,529
2000	13,155	7,923	5,232	5,778	7,377	3,588	2,190	4,335	3,042	4,622	1,156	5,917	1,460
1999	12,681	7,735	4,946	5,559	7,122	3,516	2,044	4,219	2,903	4,431	1,128	5,679	1,443
1998	12,437	7,539	4,898	5,446	6,991	3,428	2,018	4,111	2,880	4,361	1,085	5,589	1,402
1997	12,451	7,419	5,032	5,469	6,982	3,380	2,089	4,039	2,943	4,408	1,060	5,599	1,383
1996	12,327	7,299	5,028	5,421	6,906	3,339	2,082	3,960	2,947	4,383	1,038	5,553	1,354
1995	12,232	7,145	5,086	5,401	6,831	3,297	2,105	3,849	2,982	4,380	1,021	5,524	1,307
1994	12,263	7,169	5,094	5,422	6,840	3,342	2,081	3,827	3,013	4,394	1,028	5,551	1,290
1993	12,324	7,179	5,144	5,484	6,840	3,382	2,102	3,797	3,043	4,447	1,036	5,565	1,276
1992	12,538	7,244	5,293	5,583	6,955	3,425	2,158	3,820	3,135	4,537	1,046	5,679	1,275
1991	12,439	7,221	5,218	5,571	6,868	3,436	2,135	3,786	3,082	4,531	1,040	5,617	1,251
1990	11,959	6,976	4,983	5,380	6,579	3,337	2,043	3,639	2,940	4,353	1,027	5,357	1,223
1989	11,743	6,841	4,902	5,311	6,432	3,279	2,032	3,562	2,869	4,272	1,039	5,216	1,216
1988	11,317	6,642	4,674	5,138	6,179	3,206	1,931	3,436	2,743	4,113	1,024	4,990	1,189
1987	11,046	6,463	4,584	5,068	5,978	3,164	1,905	3,299	2,679	4,076	992	4,842	1,136
1986	10,798	6,352	4,446	5,018	5,780	3,146	1,871	3,206	2,575	4,002	1,015	4,658	1,122
1985	10,597	6,320	4,277	4,962	5,635	3,156	1,806	3,163	2,471	3,953	1,010	4,525	1,110
1984	10,618	6,348	4,270	5,007	5,611	3,195	1,812	3,153	2,459	3,990	1,017	4,504	1,107
1983	10,846	6,514	4,332	5,158	5,688	3,304	1,854	3,210	2,478	4,117	1,042	4,580	1,107
1982	10,825	6,484	4,341	5,170	5,655	3,299	1,871	3,184	2,470	4,140	1,031	4,573	1,081
1981	10,755	6,449	4,305	5,108	5,646	3,260	1,848	3,189	2,458	4,090	1,018	4,558	1,088
1980	10,475	6,362	4,113	5,000	5,475	3,227	1,773	3,135	2,340	4,015	985	4,427	1,048
1979	9,998	6,079	3,919	4,820	5,178	3,087	1,733	2,993	2,185	3,865	955	4,182	996
1978	9,684	5,963	3,722	4,761	4,923	3,069	1,692	2,894	2,029	3,812	949	3,975	948
1977	9,717	6,094	3,623	4,897	4,820	3,188	1,709	2,906	1,914	3,937	960	3,906	914
1976	9,435	6,033	3,401	4,906	4,528	3,244	1,662	2,789	1,739	3,951	955	3,669	859
1975	9,679	6,168	3,511	5,257	4,422	3,459	1,798	2,709	1,713	4,245	1,012	3,581	841
1974	8,799	5,726	3,072	4,766	4,033	3,192	1,574	2,535	1,499	3,800	966	3,232	801
1973	8,260	5,579	2,681	4,538	3,722	3,134	1,403	2,444	1,278	3,580	958	2,943	779
1972	7,942	5,489	2,453	4,429	3,514	3,121	1,308	2,368	1,146	3,466	963	2,757	757
1971	7,744	5,513	2,231	4,418	3,326	3,201	1,217	2,312	1,015	3,427	991	2,581	746
1970	7,369	5,280	2,089	4,250	3,119	3,096	1,153	2,184	935	3,236	1,014	2,384	735
1969	6,884	4,992	1,892	4,008	2,877	2,952	1,055	2,040	837	2,996	1,012	2,162	715
1968	6,476	4,740	1,735	3,781	2,695	2,810	971	1,930	764	2,787	994	1,995	700
1967[1]	6,016	4,345	1,671	3,502	2,514	2,569	933	1,775	738	2,492	1,010	1,802	712

Note: Data include unclassified undergraduate students. Data through 1995 are for institutions of higher education, while later data are for degree-granting institutions. Degree-granting institutions grant associate's or higher degrees and participate in Title IV federal financial aid programs. The degree-granting classification is very similar to the earlier higher education classification, but it includes more 2-year colleges and excludes a few higher education institutions that did not grant degrees. Some data have been revised from previously published figures. Details may not sum to totals because of rounding.

[1]Data for part-time students are for part-time resident students and all extension students (students attending courses at sites separate from the primary reporting campus). In later years, part-time student enrollment was collected as a distinct category.

Table A-34. Total Postbaccalaureate Fall Enrollment in Degree-Granting Institutions, by Attendance Status, Sex of Student, and Control of Institution, 1967–2010

Year	Total	Full-time	Part-time	Males	Females	Males		Females		Males		Females	
						Full-time	Part-time	Full-time	Part-time	Public	Private	Public	Private
2010	2,937	1,631	1,307	1,210	1,728	720	490	911	817	603	606	835	893
2009	2,862	1,579	1,283	1,174	1,688	694	480	885	803	592	582	832	857
2008	2,737	1,493	1,244	1,122	1,615	657	465	836	779	569	554	812	802
2007	2,644	1,429	1,215	1,088	1,556	633	456	796	760	557	532	796	760
2006	2,575	1,386	1,188	1,061	1,514	615	446	772	742	546	516	787	726
2005	2,524	1,351	1,173	1,047	1,476	603	445	748	728	543	504	781	696
2004	2,491	1,326	1,166	1,047	1,444	599	448	727	717	550	497	779	665
2003	2,431	1,281	1,150	1,033	1,398	589	444	692	707	556	477	780	619
2002	2,355	1,212	1,143	1,010	1,345	567	443	645	700	552	458	767	577
2001	2,212	1,120	1,093	956	1,256	531	425	589	667	524	433	724	532
2000	2,157	1,087	1,070	944	1,213	523	421	564	650	510	433	703	510
1999	2,110	1,051	1,059	931	1,179	510	421	542	637	510	421	689	490
1998	2,070	1,025	1,045	923	1,147	505	418	519	628	508	415	680	467
1997	2,052	1,019	1,032	927	1,124	511	417	509	616	516	412	673	451
1996	2,041	1,004	1,036	932	1,108	512	420	492	616	520	412	666	443
1995	2,030	984	1,047	941	1,089	511	431	473	616	528	414	661	428
1994	2,016	969	1,047	950	1,066	514	436	455	611	536	414	653	414
1993	1,981	948	1,033	944	1,037	509	435	440	598	537	407	640	397
1992	1,950	918	1,032	941	1,009	502	439	416	593	537	404	631	378
1991	1,920	894	1,026	931	989	494	437	400	589	535	395	626	363
1990	1,860	845	1,015	904	955	471	433	374	582	522	382	613	342
1989	1,796	820	976	879	917	462	417	359	558	505	374	586	331
1988	1,739	794	944	864	875	455	409	339	536	495	369	563	312
1987	1,720	769	952	864	857	447	416	321	535	497	366	558	299
1986	1,706	767	938	867	839	453	414	315	524	503	364	550	288
1985	1,650	756	895	856	794	451	405	304	490	485	371	517	277
1984	1,624	751	873	857	767	453	404	298	469	485	372	499	268
1983	1,619	747	872	865	753	456	410	291	462	493	372	492	261
1982	1,601	737	864	861	740	454	407	283	457	493	368	490	250
1981	1,617	732	885	867	750	452	414	280	471	497	370	502	249
1980	1,622	736	886	874	748	462	412	274	474	508	367	508	240
1979	1,572	715	857	863	709	456	407	258	451	504	359	486	223
1978	1,576	705	871	880	696	459	421	246	450	519	361	479	216
1977	1,569	699	870	892	677	462	430	237	440	536	356	468	209
1976	1,578	684	894	905	673	459	445	225	448	556	349	477	196
1975	1,505	673	832	892	613	467	425	206	408	560	332	448	165
1974	1,425	644	781	857	568	455	402	189	379	539	318	418	150
1973	1,342	611	732	833	509	444	389	167	342	523	310	374	135
1972	1,272	583	689	810	462	437	374	147	315	507	303	341	121
1971	1,204	564	640	789	415	428	361	136	279	514	276	306	110
1970	1,212	536	676	794	418	408	386	129	290	497	297	311	107
1969	1,120	507	613	739	382	384	355	123	258	457	282	281	100
1968	1,037	470	568	697	341	359	338	111	230	411	286	238	103
1967	896	448	448	631	265	355	276	94	172	352	279	171	95

Note: Data include unclassified graduate students. Data through 1995 are for institutions of higher education, while later data are for degree-granting institutions. Degree-granting institutions grant associate's or higher degrees and participate in Title IV federal financial aid programs. The degree-granting classification is very similar to the earlier higher education classification, but it includes more 2-year colleges and excludes a few higher education institutions that did not grant degrees. Some data have been revised from previously published figures.

Table A-35. Total Fall Enrollment in Degree-Granting Institutions, by Race/Ethnicity, Sex, Attendance Status, and Level of Student: Selected Years, 1990–2010

(Numbers in thousands)

Race/ethnicity, sex, attendance status, and level of student	Fall enrollment							
	1990		2000		2008		2010	
	Number	Percent	Number	Percent	Number	Percent	Number	Percent
All students, total	13,819	100.00	15,312	100.00	19,103	100.00	21,016	100.00
White	10,722	77.59	10,462	68.32	12,089	63.28	12,723	60.54
Total, selected races/ethnicities	2,705	19.57	4,321	28.22	6,353	33.26	7,584	36.09
Black	1,247	9.02	1,730	11.30	2,584	13.53	3,039	14.46
Hispanic	782	5.66	1,462	9.55	2,273	11.90	2,741	13.04
Asian/Pacific Islander	572	4.14	978	6.39	1,303	6.82	1,282	6.10
American Indian/Alaska Native	103	0.74	151	0.99	193	1.01	196	0.93
Nonresident alien	391	2.83	529	3.45	661	3.46	710	3.38
Male	6,284	100.00	6,722	100.00	8,189	100.00	9,045	100.00
White	4,861	77.36	4,635	68.95	5,303	64.76	5,607	61.99
Total, selected races/ethnicities	1,177	18.72	1,790	26.63	2,533	30.93	3,058	33.81
Black	485	7.71	635	9.45	912	11.13	1,089	12.04
Hispanic	354	5.63	627	9.33	947	11.56	1,155	12.77
Asian/Pacific Islander	295	4.69	466	6.93	597	7.29	601	6.64
American Indian/Alaska Native	43	0.69	61	0.91	77	0.94	79	0.87
Nonresident alien	246	3.92	297	4.42	353	4.31	380	4.21
Female	7,535	100.00	8,591	100.00	10,914	100.00	11,971	100.00
White	5,861	77.79	5,827	67.84	6,786	62.18	7,116	59.44
Total, selected races/ethnicities	1,528	20.28	2,532	29.47	3,821	35.01	4,526	37.81
Black	762	10.12	1,095	12.75	1,673	15.33	1,950	16.29
Hispanic	429	5.69	835	9.72	1,326	12.15	1,587	13.26
Asian/Pacific Islander	278	3.68	512	5.96	705	6.46	681	5.69
American Indian/Alaska Native	60	0.79	90	1.04	116	1.07	118	0.98
Nonresident alien	145	1.93	231	2.69	307	2.82	329	2.75
Full-time	7,821	100.00	9,010	100.00	11,748	100.00	13,082	100.00
White	6,016	76.93	6,231	69.16	7,594	64.64	8,051	61.54
Total, selected races/ethnicities	1,515	19.37	2,368	26.29	3,632	30.92	4,465	34.13
Black	718	9.18	983	10.91	1,531	13.03	1,809	13.83
Hispanic	395	5.05	710	7.88	1,177	10.02	1,500	11.46
Asian/Pacific Islander	347	4.44	591	6.56	809	6.89	821	6.28
American Indian/Alaska Native	54	0.70	84	0.94	115	0.98	118	0.90
Nonresident alien	290	3.70	410	4.55	522	4.45	566	4.33
Part-time	5,998	100.00	6,303	100.00	7,355	100.00	7,934	100.00
White	4,706	78.46	4,231	67.13	4,495	61.12	4,671	58.88
Total, selected races/ethnicities	1,190	19.84	1,953	30.99	2,722	37.00	3,119	39.31
Black	529	8.81	748	11.86	1,054	14.33	1,230	15.50
Hispanic	388	6.46	751	11.92	1,096	14.90	1,242	15.65
Asian/Pacific Islander	225	3.75	387	6.14	494	6.71	461	5.81
American Indian/Alaska Native	48	0.81	67	1.06	78	1.06	78	0.99
Nonresident alien	102	1.70	119	1.88	138	1.88	143	1.81
Undergraduate, total	11,959	100.00	13,155	100.00	16,366	100.00	18,079	100.00
White	9,273	77.54	8,983	68.29	10,339	63.18	10,898	60.28
Total, selected races/ethnicities	2,468	20.63	3,884	29.52	5,666	34.62	6,781	37.51
Black	1,147	9.59	1,549	11.77	2,269	13.87	2,677	14.80
Hispanic	725	6.06	1,351	10.27	2,104	12.85	2,544	14.07
Asian/Pacific Islander	500	4.18	846	6.43	1,118	6.83	1,088	6.02
American Indian/Alaska Native	95	0.80	139	1.05	176	1.07	179	0.99
Nonresident alien	219	1.83	288	2.19	360	2.20	400	2.21

Note: Race categories exclude persons of Hispanic ethnicity. Because of underreporting and nonreporting of racial/ethnic data, some figures are slightly lower than corresponding data in other tables. Data through 1990 are for institutions of higher education, while later data are for degree-granting institutions. Degree-granting institutions grant associate's or higher degrees and participate in Title IV federal financial aid programs. The degree-granting classification is very similar to the earlier higher education classification, but it includes more 2-year colleges and excludes a few higher education institutions that did not grant degrees. Details may not sum to totals because of rounding.

Table A-35. Total Fall Enrollment in Degree-Granting Institutions, by Race/Ethnicity, Sex, Attendance Status, and Level of Student: Selected Years, 1990–2010—*Continued*

(Numbers in thousands)

Race/ethnicity, sex, attendance status, and level of student	Fall enrollment							
	1990		2000		2008		2010	
	Number	Percent	Number	Percent	Number	Percent	Number	Percent
Male	5,380	100.00	5,778	100.00	7,067	100.00	7,835	100.00
White	4,184	77.78	4,010	69.40	4,599	65.07	4,862	62.05
Total, selected races/ethnicities	1,069	19.88	1,618	28.00	2,290	32.41	2,771	35.37
Black	448	8.33	577	9.99	821	11.62	983	12.54
Hispanic	327	6.08	583	10.08	884	12.51	1,080	13.78
Asian/Pacific Islander	254	4.73	402	6.96	515	7.28	514	6.55
American Indian/Alaska Native	40	0.74	56	0.98	70	1.00	72	0.92
Nonresident alien	126	2.34	150	2.60	178	2.52	202	2.58
Female	6,579	100.00	7,377	100.00	9,299	100.00	10,244	100.00
White	5,088	77.34	4,973	67.42	5,741	61.73	6,036	58.92
Total, selected races/ethnicities	1,398	21.26	2,266	30.72	3,376	36.30	4,010	39.14
Black	699	10.63	972	13.17	1,448	15.57	1,694	16.53
Hispanic	398	6.04	768	10.42	1,219	13.11	1,464	14.29
Asian/Pacific Islander	246	3.74	444	6.01	603	6.49	574	5.61
American Indian/Alaska Native	56	0.84	82	1.11	105	1.13	107	1.04
Nonresident alien	93	1.41	138	1.87	183	1.96	198	1.93
Postbaccalaureate, total	1,860	100.00	2,157	100.00	100	100.00	2,937	100.00
White	1,450	77.97	1,479	68.55	1,750	63.92	1,825	62.13
Total, selected races/ethnicities	237	12.74	438	20.29	687	25.11	803	27.35
Black	100	5.37	181	8.41	315	11.52	362	12.33
Hispanic	58	3.11	111	5.14	169	6.19	198	6.74
Asian/Pacific Islander	72	3.87	133	6.15	185	6.76	194	6.61
American Indian/Alaska Native	7	0.39	13	0.59	18	0.65	17	0.58
Nonresident alien	173	9.29	241	11.16	300	10.97	309	10.53
Male	904	100.00	944	100.00	1,122	100.00	1,210	100.00
White	677	74.83	625	66.19	704	62.75	745	61.58
Total, selected races/ethnicities	107	11.88	172	18.21	242	21.60	287	23.69
Black	37	4.06	58	6.18	90	8.06	106	8.78
Hispanic	27	2.99	45	4.72	63	5.59	75	6.18
Asian/Pacific Islander	40	4.47	64	6.78	83	7.37	87	7.21
American Indian/Alaska Native	3	0.35	5	0.53	7	0.58	6	0.53
Nonresident alien	120	13.29	147	15.59	176	15.64	178	14.73
Female	955	100.00	1,213	100.00	1,615	100.00	1,728	100.00
White	773	80.94	854	70.39	1,045	64.73	1,080	62.51
Total, selected races/ethnicities	130	13.57	266	21.90	445	27.54	517	29.90
Black	63	6.60	123	10.14	225	13.92	256	14.82
Hispanic	31	3.23	66	5.46	107	6.61	123	7.13
Asian/Pacific Islander	32	3.30	69	5.66	102	6.33	107	6.20
American Indian/Alaska Native	4	0.43	8	0.63	11	0.69	11	0.62

Note: Race categories exclude persons of Hispanic ethnicity. Because of underreporting and nonreporting of racial/ethnic data, some figures are slightly lower than corresponding data in other tables. Data through 1990 are for institutions of higher education, while later data are for degree-granting institutions. Degree-granting institutions grant associate's or higher degrees and participate in Title IV federal financial aid programs. The degree-granting classification is very similar to the earlier higher education classification, but it includes more 2-year colleges and excludes a few higher education institutions that did not grant degrees. Details may not sum to totals because of rounding.

Table A-36. Total Fall Enrollment in Degree-Granting Institutions, by Race/Ethnicity of Student and Type and Control of Institution: Selected Years, 1990–2010

(Numbers in thousands)

Race/ethnicity of student and type and control of institution	Fall enrollment							
	1990		2000		2008		2010	
	Number	Percent	Number	Percent	Number	Percent	Number	Percent
All students, total	13,819	100.00	15,312	100.00	19,103	100.00	21,016	100.00
White	10,722	77.59	10,462	68.32	12,089	63.28	12,723	60.54
Total, selected races/ethnicities	2,705	19.57	4,321	28.22	6,353	33.26	7,584	36.09
Black	1,247	9.02	1,730	11.30	2,584	13.53	3,039	14.46
Hispanic	782	5.66	1,462	9.55	2,273	11.90	2,741	13.04
Asian/Pacific Islander	572	4.14	978	6.39	1,303	6.82	1,282	6.10
American Indian/Alaska Native	103	0.74	151	0.99	193	1.01	196	0.93
Nonresident alien	391	2.83	529	3.45	661	3.46	710	3.38
Public	10,845	100.00	11,753	100.00	13,972	100.00	15,143	100.00
White	8,385	77.32	7,963	67.76	8,818	63.11	9,187	60.67
Total, selected races/ethnicities	2,199	20.28	3,446	29.32	4,728	33.84	5,501	36.33
Black	976	9.00	1,319	11.22	1,759	12.59	1,989	13.13
Hispanic	671	6.19	1,229	10.46	1,832	13.11	2,157	14.25
Asian/Pacific Islander	461	4.25	771	6.56	983	7.03	970	6.40
American Indian/Alaska Native	90	0.83	127	1.08	153	1.10	151	1.00
Nonresident alien	260	2.40	343	2.92	427	3.06	454	3.00
Private	2,974	100.00	3,560	100.00	5,131	100.00	5,873	100.00
White	2,337	78.58	2,499	70.20	3,271	63.76	3,535	60.19
Total, selected races/ethnicities	505	17.00	875	24.59	1,626	31.69	2,083	35.46
Black	271	9.10	411	11.55	825	16.09	1,050	17.88
Hispanic	111	3.73	233	6.53	440	8.59	584	9.94
Asian/Pacific Islander	111	3.75	208	5.83	320	6.24	313	5.32
American Indian/Alaska Native	12	0.42	24	0.67	40	0.78	45	0.77
Nonresident alien	131	4.42	186	5.22	234	4.55	255	4.35
4-year, total	8,579	100.00	9,364	100.00	12,131	100.00	13,335	100.00
White	6,768	78.90	6,658	71.10	7,987	65.84	8,398	62.98
Total, selected races/ethnicities	1,486	17.32	2,266	24.20	3,588	29.58	4,328	32.46
Black	723	8.43	995	10.63	1,565	12.90	1,841	13.81
Hispanic	358	4.18	618	6.60	1,092	9.00	1,355	10.16
Asian/Pacific Islander	357	4.16	576	6.15	823	6.79	818	6.14
American Indian/Alaska Native	48	0.56	76	0.82	108	0.89	109	0.82
Nonresident alien	324	3.78	440	4.70	556	4.58	609	4.57
Public	5,848	100.00	6,055	100.00	7,332	100.00	7,925	100.00
White	4,606	78.75	4,311	71.20	4,879	66.55	5,070	63.98
Total, selected races/ethnicities	1,046	17.89	1,486	24.55	2,128	29.03	2,497	31.50
Black	495	8.47	628	10.37	827	11.28	913	11.52
Hispanic	263	4.49	420	6.94	710	9.68	869	10.97
Asian/Pacific Islander	251	4.29	381	6.30	518	7.07	523	6.60
American Indian/Alaska Native	38	0.65	57	0.94	73	0.99	70	0.88
Nonresident alien	196	3.36	258	4.26	324	4.42	358	4.51
Private	2,730	100.00	3,308	100.00	4,800	100.00	5,410	100.00
White	2,163	79.20	2,347	70.94	3,108	64.75	3,328	61.51
Total, selected races/ethnicities	440	16.11	780	23.57	1,460	30.42	1,832	33.85
Black	228	8.34	368	11.11	738	15.37	928	17.16
Hispanic	96	3.51	198	5.98	382	7.96	486	8.98
Asian/Pacific Islander	107	3.90	195	5.89	305	6.36	296	5.46
American Indian/Alaska Native	10	0.36	19	0.58	35	0.73	39	0.73
Nonresident alien	128	4.69	182	5.50	231	4.82	251	4.64

Note: Race categories exclude persons of Hispanic ethnicity. Because of underreporting and nonreporting of racial/ethnic data, some figures are slightly lower than corresponding data in other tables. Data through 1990 are for institutions of higher education, while later data are for degree-granting institutions. Degree-granting institutions grant associate's or higher degrees and participate in Title IV federal financial aid programs. The degree-granting classification is very similar to the earlier higher education classification, but it includes more 2-year colleges and excludes a few higher education institutions that did not grant degrees. Details may not sum to totals because of rounding.

Table A-36. Total Fall Enrollment in Degree-Granting Institutions, by Race/Ethnicity of Student and Type and Control of Institution: Selected Years, 1990–2010—*Continued*

(Numbers in thousands)

Race/ethnicity of student and type and control of institution	Fall enrollment							
	1990		2000		2008		2010	
	Number	Percent	Number	Percent	Number	Percent	Number	Percent
2-year, total	5,240	100.00	5,948	100.00	6,971	100.00	7,681	100.00
White	3,954	75.46	3,804	63.95	4,102	58.84	4,324	56.30
Total, selected races/ethnicities	1,219	23.26	2,055	34.55	2,765	39.66	3,256	42.39
Black	524	10.01	735	12.35	1,020	14.62	1,198	15.59
Hispanic	424	8.10	844	14.19	1,181	16.94	1,386	18.05
Asian/Pacific Islander	215	4.11	402	6.76	479	6.88	464	6.04
American Indian/Alaska Native	55	1.05	75	1.26	85	1.23	87	1.14
Nonresident alien	67	1.28	89	1.50	105	1.50	101	1.31
Public	4,996	100.00	5,697	100.00	6,640	100.00	7,218	100.00
White	3,780	75.65	3,652	64.10	3,938	59.31	4,117	57.03
Total, selected races/ethnicities	1,153	23.08	1,960	34.40	2,599	39.14	3,005	41.63
Black	481	9.63	691	12.13	932	14.03	1,076	14.91
Hispanic	409	8.18	809	14.20	1,122	16.90	1,288	17.85
Asian/Pacific Islander	210	4.21	389	6.83	465	7.00	447	6.19
American Indian/Alaska Native	52	1.05	70	1.23	80	1.21	82	1.13
Nonresident alien	64	1.27	85	1.50	103	1.54	97	1.34
Private	244	100.00	251	100.00	331	100.00	463	100.00
White	174	71.63	152	60.48	163	49.30	208	44.87
Total, selected races/ethnicities	66	26.94	95	38.02	166	50.07	251	54.24
Black	43	17.62	44	17.33	88	26.48	122	26.31
Hispanic	15	6.28	35	13.82	58	17.58	98	21.22
Asian/Pacific Islander	5	2.00	13	5.07	15	4.48	17	3.70
American Indian/Alaska Native	3	1.04	5	1.81	5	1.52	6	1.27
Nonresident alien	3	1.43	4	1.50	2	0.64	4	0.89

Note: Race categories exclude persons of Hispanic ethnicity. Because of underreporting and nonreporting of racial/ethnic data, some figures are slightly lower than corresponding data in other tables. Data through 1990 are for institutions of higher education, while later data are for degree-granting institutions. Degree-granting institutions grant associate's or higher degrees and participate in Title IV federal financial aid programs. The degree-granting classification is very similar to the earlier higher education classification, but it includes more 2-year colleges and excludes a few higher education institutions that did not grant degrees. Details may not sum to totals because of rounding.

Table A-37. Tuition and Required Fees for Full-Time Students, by Student Level, Sector, and Residency, 2001–2011

(Dollars except as noted)

Student level, sector, and residency	Academic year[1]				Percent change 2001–2002 to 2010–2011
	2001–2002	2004–2005	2007–2008	2010–2011	
AVERAGE TUITION AND REQUIRED FEES[2]					
Undergraduate					
Public 4-year					
In-district[3]	$4,584	$5,720	$6,050	$6,749	47.2
In-state	4,585	5,717	6,054	6,752	47.3
Out-of-state	11,701	14,002	14,363	15,742	34.5
Public 2-year					
In-district[3]	1,914	2,340	2,427	2,716	41.9
In-state	2,330	2,797	2,904	3,169	36.0
Out-of-state	5,528	6,176	6,248	6,516	17.9
Public less-than-2-year					
In-district[3]	5,191	5,951	5,515	6,281	21.0
In-state	5,327	6,074	5,583	6,309	18.4
Out-of-state	5,720	6,556	6,002	6,479	13.3
Private not-for-profit 4-year	16,805	18,587	20,125	21,996	30.9
Private not-for-profit 2-year	8,523	9,545	10,037	10,784	26.5
Private not-for-profit less-than-2-year	9,272	9,528	10,226	9,005	-2.9
Private for-profit 4-year	13,319	15,131	15,751	15,700	17.9
Private for-profit 2-year	11,989	13,029	13,055	14,566	21.5
Private for-profit less-than-2-year	10,860	11,381	13,001	13,451	23.9
Graduate[4]					
Public 4-year					
In-district[3]	5,239	6,707	7,329	8,363	59.6
In-state	5,240	6,707	7,330	8,366	59.7
Out-of-state	11,825	14,432	14,937	16,265	37.5
Private not-for-profit 4-year	12,942	13,867	14,604	15,564	20.3
Private for-profit 4-year	14,907	14,636	15,492	14,907	0.0
MEDIAN TUITION AND REQUIRED FEES[2]					
Undergraduate					
Public 4-year					
In-district[3]	$4,203	$5,284	$5,685	$6,224	48.1
In-state	4,203	5,280	5,695	6,231	48.3
Out-of-state	11,295	13,624	14,193	15,353	35.9
Public 2-year					
In-district[3]	1,885	2,247	2,423	2,744	45.6
In-state	2,039	2,554	2,767	3,103	52.2
Out-of-state	5,190	5,982	5,901	6,037	16.3
Public less-than-2-year					
In-district[3]	4,621	5,560	4,986	5,350	15.8
In-state	4,713	5,560	4,986	5,350	13.5
Out-of-state	5,095	5,676	4,986	5,350	5.0
Private not-for-profit 4-year	16,697	18,545	20,075	22,204	33.0
Private not-for-profit 2-year	8,500	9,268	9,298	10,252	20.6
Private not-for-profit less-than-2-year	9,116	7,705	9,203	9,325	2.3
Private for-profit 4-year	12,403	14,097	14,688	15,285	23.2
Private for-profit 2-year	10,943	11,551	11,966	13,545	23.8
Private for-profit less-than-2-year	10,311	11,569	12,388	14,679	42.4

Note: Tuition and required fees are average institutional charges for all full-time students at the institution as reported by the institution, not average amounts paid by students (i.e., charges are not weighted by enrollment). The time points displayed in this table were chosen to demonstrate the range of data available from the Integrated Postsecondary Education Data System (IPEDS) for trend analysis, not to emphasize any particular period of change. Data for years included in the range of this table, but not specifically displayed in the table, are available via the IPEDS Data Center. Institutions with academic calendars that differ by program or allow continuous enrollment (2,515 in fall 2010, 2,181 in fall 2007, 1,981 in fall 2004, and 1,980 in fall 2001) are not included. U.S. service academies are not included. All amounts from prior years were converted to 2010–2011 dollars using the average Consumer Price Index values for the 12-month period ending in October of the academic year the data represent (e.g., October 2001) and the CPI value for the 12-month period ending in October 2010. Medians were calculated using SAS, Version 9, Proc Univariate.

[1]Before the 2010–2011 survey, Title IV not primarily postsecondary institutions were not required to respond to the IPEDS survey. In addition, no such institutions in the 2001–2002 survey met the criteria to be included in this table. However, in the 2004–2005 survey, 12 out of 13 such institutions meeting the criteria to be included in this table responded voluntarily to the fall 2004 Institutional Characteristics component. In the 2007–2008 survey, 6 out of 7 such institutions responded voluntarily to the fall 2007 Institutional Characteristics component. Data for the nonresponding institutions represent 0.02 percent of the total institutions included in this table.

[2]Out-of-state average and median tuition and required fees were used for private institutions that reported varying tuitions by residency.

[3]For public institutions, *in district* refers to the charges paid by a student who lives in the locality surrounding the institution, such as a county.

Table A-37. Tuition and Required Fees for Full-Time Students, by Student Level, Sector, and Residency, 2001–2011—*Continued*

(Dollars except as noted)

Student level, sector, and residency	Academic year[1]				Percent change 2001–2002 to 2010–2011
	2001–2002	2004–2005	2007–2008	2010–2011	
Graduate[4]					
Public 4-year					
In-district[3]	4,773	5,987	6,733	7,674	60.8
In-state	4,773	6,035	6,733	7,682	60.9
Out-of-state	11,003	13,599	14,627	15,298	39
Private not-for-profit 4-year	11,054	11,769	12,391	13,100	18.5
Private for-profit 4-year	14,603	13,031	13,963	14,380	-1.5
INSTITUTIONS REPORTING TUITION AND REQUIRED FEES (Number)					
Undergraduate					
Public 4-year					
In-district[3]	600	611	631	658	9.7
In-state	600	613	631	658	9.7
Out-of-state	600	613	631	658	9.7
Public 2-year					
In-district[3]	1,094	1,087	1,050	985	-10.0
In-state	1,097	1,087	1,050	985	-10.2
Out-of-state	1,097	1,087	1,050	985	-10.2
Public less-than-2-year					
In-district[3]	90	65	53	23	-74.4
In-state	90	65	53	23	-74.4
Out-of-state	90	65	53	23	-74.4
Private not-for-profit 4-year	1,271	1,284	1,295	1,297	2.0
Private not-for-profit 2-year	212	195	153	141	-33.5
Private not-for-profit less-than-2-year	24	26	17	11	-54.2
Private for-profit 4-year	193	321	441	595	208.3
Private for-profit 2-year	379	392	387	438	15.6
Private for-profit less-than-2-year	100	152	79	48	-52.0
Graduate[4]					
Public 4-year					
In-district[3]	527	545	557	568	7.8
In-state	527	546	557	568	7.8
Out-of-state	527	547	557	568	7.8
Private not-for-profit 4-year	951	1,005	1,076	1,138	19.7
Private for-profit 4-year	120	151	203	266	121.7

Note: Tuition and required fees are average institutional charges for all full-time students at the institution as reported by the institution, not average amounts paid by students (i.e., charges are not weighted by enrollment). The time points displayed in this table were chosen to demonstrate the range of data available from the Integrated Postsecondary Education Data System (IPEDS) for trend analysis, not to emphasize any particular period of change. Data for years included in the range of this table, but not specifically displayed in the table, are available via the IPEDS Data Center. Institutions with academic calendars that differ by program or allow continuous enrollment (2,515 in fall 2010, 2,181 in fall 2007, 1,981 in fall 2004, and 1,980 in fall 2001) are not included. U.S. service academies are not included. All amounts from prior years were converted to 2010–2011 dollars using the average Consumer Price Index values for the 12-month period ending in October of the academic year the data represent (e.g., October 2001) and the CPI value for the 12-month period ending in October 2010. Medians were calculated using SAS, Version 9, Proc Univariate.

[1]Before the 2010–2011 survey, Title IV not primarily postsecondary institutions were not required to respond to the IPEDS survey. In addition, no such institutions in the 2001–2002 survey met the criteria to be included in this table. However, in the 2004–2005 survey, 12 out of 13 such institutions meeting the criteria to be included in this table responded voluntarily to the fall 2004 Institutional Characteristics component. In the 2007–2008 survey, 6 out of 7 such institutions responded voluntarily to the fall 2007 Institutional Characteristics component. Data for the nonresponding institutions represent 0.02 percent of the total institutions included in this table.

[3]For public institutions, *in district* refers to the charges paid by a student who lives in the locality surrounding the institution, such as a county.

[4]Tuition and fee charges for graduate students do not include charges for programs designated as doctor's degrees—professional practice.

Table A-38. Price of Undergraduate College Attendance, by Level and Control of Institution, Student Housing, and Residency, 2008–2009 and 2010–2011

(Dollars except as noted)

Control of institution, student housing, and residency	4-year			2-year			Less-than-2-year		
	2008–2009	2010–2011	Percent change	2008–2009	2010–2011	Percent change	2008–2009	2010–2011	Percent change
PUBLIC									
On campus[1]									
In-district[2]	17,725	19,476	9.9	11,310	12,423	9.8	...	...	...
In-state	17,726	19,478	9.9	11,536	12,664	9.8	...	...	...
Out-of-state	26,404	28,924	9.5	13,881	15,072	8.6	...	...	...
Off campus (not with family)[3]									
In-district[2]	18,987	20,454	7.7	14,171	15,130	6.8	14,556	16,264	11.7
In-state	18,990	20,457	7.7	14,620	15,588	6.6	14,557	16,265	11.7
Out-of-state	27,218	29,386	8.0	17,912	18,949	5.8	14,732	16,442	11.6
Off campus (with family)[3]									
In-district[2]	10,805	11,780	9.0	7,205	7,812	8.4	9,488	10,721	13.0
In-state	10,809	11,784	9.0	7,654	8,270	8.0	9,489	10,723	13.0
Out-of-state	19,037	20,712	8.8	10,946	11,631	6.3	9,664	10,900	12.8
PRIVATE NOT-FOR-PROFIT									
On campus[1]	33,139	35,675	7.7	22,999	25,125	9.2	21,283	22,870	7.5
Off campus (not with family)[3]	31,204	33,366	6.9	23,898	25,729	7.7	22,684	23,462	3.4
Off campus (with family)[3]	23,298	24,991	7.3	15,561	16,983	9.1	15,761	15,776	0.1
PRIVATE FOR PROFIT									
On campus[1]	33,719	34,922	3.6	26,163	28,842	10.2	...	...	...
Off campus (not with family)[3]	29,392	31,002	5.5	26,506	27,988	5.6	23,690	26,097	10.2
Off campus (with family)[3]	20,822	22,211	6.7	18,733	19,970	6.6	15,808	17,490	10.6

Note: Price of attendance includes tuition and required fees, books and supplies, room and board charges, and other expenses. Amounts are institutional averages as reported by the institution, not average amounts paid by students (i.e., charges are not weighted by enrollment). The time points displayed in this table were chosen to demonstrate the range of data available from the Integrated Postsecondary Education Data System (IPEDS) for trend analysis, not to emphasize any particular period of change. Out-of-state average tuition and required fees were used for private institutions that reported varying tuitions by residency. The 2,467 institutions with academic calendars that differ by program or allow continuous enrollment are not included. U.S. service academies are not included. All amounts from 2008–2009 were converted to 2010–2011 dollars using the average Consumer Price Index values for the 12-month periods ending in October 2008 and October 2010.

[1]On-campus average price is based on those institutions that offer on-campus housing and/or meal service.

[2]For public institutions, *in district* refers to the charges paid by a student who lives in the locality surrounding the institution, such as a county.

[3]Off-campus average price is based on those institutions that do not require full-time, first-time students to live on campus.

... = Not available

NOTES AND DEFINITIONS: NATIONAL SCHOOL ENROLLMENT, EDUCATIONAL ATTAINMENT, AND POSTSECONDARY EDUCATION

ENROLLMENT TABLES A-1 THROUGH A-16

Source: U.S. Census Bureau. School Enrollment in the United States. *Current Population Survey (CPS) Report*. www.census.gov/hhes/school/data/cps/2011/tables.html and www.census.gov/hhes/school/data/cps/historical/index.html .

ATTAINMENT TABLES A-17 THROUGH A-28

Source: U.S. Census Bureau. Educational Attainment in the United States: 2011. *Annual Social and Economic Supplement to the Current Population Survey*. www.census.gov/hhes/socdemo/education/data/cps/2011/tables.html, www.census.gov/hhes/socdemo/education/data/cps/historical/index.html and Historical Income Tables (Table P-16). www.census.gov/hhes/www/income/data/historical/people/index.html .

POSTSECONDARY EDUCATION TABLES A-29 THROUGH A-38

U.S. Department of Education, National Center for Education Statistics, Institute of Education Sciences, *Digest of Education Statistics 2011* (NCES 2011-001), www.nces.ed.gov/pubsearch/pubsinfo.asp?pubid=2012001, and *Postsecondary Institutions and Price of Attendance in the United States: 2010–11, Degrees and Other Awards Conferred: 2009–10, and 12-Month Enrollment: 2009–10* (NCES 2011-250),www.nces.ed.gov/pubsearch/pubsinfo.asp?pubid=2011250 .

SCHOOL ENROLLMENT AND EDUCATIONAL ATTAINMENT TABLES

The School Enrollment and Educational Attainment tables in Part A are derived from the Current Population Survey (CPS). The Census Bureau disseminated comparable tables in the P-20 series of *Current Population Reports* (CPR) for most years between 1947 and 1994. Since then, these tables have not been available in printed form. However, they can be found on the Census Bureau website at www.census.gov. In the historical series, data before 1992 are not strictly comparable to data after 1992. Before 1992, the CPS did not ask questions about degrees received; educational attainment was gauged only by years of school completed. For information about the availability of earlier reports, or for answers to data questions not addressed in this section, contact the Education and Social Stratification Branch, Population Division, Census Bureau at (301) 763-2464.

Age. Age classification is based on the age of the person at his or her last birthday.

Citizenship status. There are five categories of citizenship status: (1) born in the United States; (2) born in Puerto Rico or another outlying area of the United States; (3) born abroad to U.S. citizen parents; (4) naturalized citizens; and (5) non-citizens. Place of birth was asked for every household member and for the parents of every household member in the CPS sample. People born in the United States or its outlying areas, or whose parents were born in the United States or its outlying areas, were not asked citizenship questions. Citizenship statuses (1), (2), and (3) were assigned during the editing phase of data preparation, based on the place of birth of the household member or the place of birth of his or her parents. People born outside the United States and its outlying areas, whose parents were born outside the United States and its outlying areas, were asked, "Are you a citizen of the United States?" 'Yes' answers were assigned to the "naturalized citizen" category (4), and 'No' answers were assigned to the "not a citizen" category (5) during the editing process. People for whom no birthplace was provided were also assigned a citizenship status during the editing process; for example, the citizenship status of a child might have been assigned based on the citizenship status of his or her mother.

Dropouts. See School, Dropout rate, annual high school.

Earnings. See Income.

Educational attainment. Data on educational attainment are derived from a single question that asks, "What is the highest grade of school . . . completed, or the highest degree . . . received?"

The single educational attainment question now in use was introduced into the CPS in January 1992. It is similar to the question used in the 1990 Decennial Census of Population and Housing. Consequently, data on educational attainment from the 1992 CPS are not directly comparable to CPS data from earlier years. The new question replaces the previous two-part question used in the CPS, which asked respondents to report the highest grade they attended and whether or not they completed that grade.

The question concerning educational attainment applies only to progress in "regular" schools. Such schools include graded public, private, and parochial elementary and high schools (both junior and senior high schools), colleges, universities, and professional schools, and both day schools and night schools. Thus, regular schooling is that which may advance a person toward an elementary school certificate, a high school diploma, or a college, university, or professional school degree. Non-regular schooling was counted only if the credits obtained were regarded as transferable to a school within the regular school system.

Family. A family is a group of two people or more residing together (including the householder) related by birth, marriage, or adoption; all such people (including related subfamily members) are considered members of one family. Beginning with the 1980 Current Population Survey, unrelated subfamilies (formerly referred to as secondary families) are no longer included in the count of families, nor are members of unrelated subfamilies included in the count of family members. The number of families is equal to the number of family households; however, the count of family members differs from the count of family household members, as family household members include any nonrelatives living in the household.

Family household. A family household is a household maintained by a householder within a family (as defined above). It includes any unrelated people (unrelated subfamily members and/or secondary individuals) residing in the household. The number of family households is equal to the number of families; however, the count of family household members differs from the count of family members. Family household members include all people living in the household, whereas family members include only the householder and his or her relatives. (See Family for more information.)

Hispanic origin. People of Hispanic origin were identified by a question that asked respondents to self-identify their origin or descent. Respondents were asked to select their origin (and the origin of other household members) from a "flash card" listing different ethnicities. People of Hispanic origin were those who indicated that their descent was of Mexican, Puerto Rican, Cuban, Central or South American, or some other Hispanic origin. It should be noted that people of Hispanic origin may be of any race.

People who were of non-Hispanic White origin were identified by crossing the responses to two self-identification questions: (1) origin or descent; and (2) race. Respondents were asked to select their race (and the race of other household members) from a "flash card" listing racial groups. Since March 1989, the population has been divided into five groups on the basis of race: White; Black; American Indian, Eskimo, or Aleut; Asian or Pacific Islander; and Other races. The last category includes any race other than the four indicated races. Respondents who identified their race as White and did not select one of the Hispanic origin subgroups (Mexican, Puerto Rican, Cuban, Central or South American) were classified as non-Hispanic White.

Household. A household consists of all the people who occupy a housing unit. A house, apartment, group of rooms, or single room is regarded as a housing unit when it is occupied or intended for occupancy as separate living quarters (meaning that occupants do not live and eat with any other persons in the structure and have direct access to their dwelling from outside or through a common hall). A household includes related family members and all unrelated people—such as lodgers, foster children, wards, or employees—who share the housing unit. A person living alone in a housing unit, or a group of unrelated people sharing a dwelling (such as partners or roomers), are also counted as a household. The count of households excludes group quarters. There are two major categories of households: "family" and "nonfamily." (See Family household and Nonfamily household for more information.)

Householder. The householder is the person (or one of the people) in whose name the housing unit is owned or rented (maintained). If there is no such person, any adult member of the household—excluding roomers, boarders, and paid employees—can be counted as the householder. If a married couple jointly owns or rents the housing unit, the householder may be either the husband or the wife. The person designated as the householder is the "reference person" to whom the relationship of all other household members, if any, is recorded.

The number of householders is equal to the number of households. The number of family householders is also equal to the number of families.

Head versus householder. The Census Bureau discontinued the use of the terms "head of household" and "head of family" beginning with the 1980 CPS. Instead, the terms "householder" and "family householder" are used. Recent social changes have resulted in a greater sharing of household responsibilities among the adult members. This has made the term "head" increasingly inappropriate in the analysis of household and family data. Specifically, beginning in 1980, the Census Bureau discontinued its longtime practice of always classifying the husband as the reference person (head of household) when he was living with his wife.

INCOME. Definitions of income and the types of income are found below.

Income, Official definition of. For each person age 15 years and over in the sample, the CPS asks questions about the amount of money income received during the preceding calendar year from each of the following sources: earnings; unemployment compensation; workers' compensation; Social Security; Supplemental Security Income; public assistance or welfare payments; veterans' payments; survivor benefits; disability benefits; pension or retirement income; interest, dividends, rents, royalties, and estates and trusts; educational assistance; child support; alimony; financial assistance from outside the household; and other income.

Although the income statistics refer to receipts during the preceding calendar year, demographic characteristics such as age, labor force status, and family or household composition are as of the survey date. The income of the family/household does not include amounts received by members who were members of the family/household during all or part of the income year if these people no longer resided in the family/household at the time of interview. However, the CPS collects income data for people who are current residents, but who did not reside in the household during the income year.

Data on consumer income collected in the CPS by the Census Bureau cover money income (exclusive of certain money receipts, such as capital gains) received before payments for personal income taxes, Social Security, union dues, Medicare deductions, and so on. Therefore, money income does not reflect the fact that some families receive part of their income in the form of noncash benefits, such as food stamps, health benefits, rent-free housing, and goods produced and consumed on the farm. Money income also does not reflect the fact that noncash benefits are also received by some nonfarm residents. These benefits often take the form of the use of business transportation and facilities, full or partial payments by business for retirement programs, medical and educational expenses, and so on. Data users should consider these elements when comparing income levels. Moreover, readers should be aware that respondents in household surveys tend to underreport their income for many different reasons. Based on an analysis of independently derived income estimates, the Census Bureau determined that respondents report income earned from wages or salaries much more accurately than income earned from other sources of income, and that the reported wage and salary income is nearly equal to independent estimates of aggregate income.

The Census Bureau collects data for the following income sources:

Alimony. Alimony includes all periodic payments received from ex-spouses. It excludes one-time property settlements.

Child support. Child support includes all periodic payments received from an absent parent for the support of his or her children, even if these payments are made through a state or local government office.

Disability benefits. Disability benefits include payments people received due to a health problem or disability (other than those received from Social Security). Respondents can report payments from 10 sources, including workers' compensation, companies or unions, federal government (civil service), military, state or local governments, railroad retirement, accident or disability insurance, Black Lung payments, state temporary sickness, or other disability payments.

Dividends. Dividends include income received from stock holdings and mutual fund shares. The CPS does not include capital gains from the sale of stock holdings as income.

Earnings. The Census Bureau classifies earnings from respondents' longest job (or self-employment) and other employment earnings into three types:

- Money wage or salary income, is the total income people receive for work performed as an employee during the income year. This category includes wages, salary, armed forces pay, commissions, tips, piece-rate payments, and cash bonuses earned, before deductions are made for items such as taxes, bonds, pensions, and union dues.
- Net income from nonfarm self-employment is the net money income (gross receipts minus expenses) from a respondent's own business, professional enterprise, or partnership. Gross receipts include the value of all goods sold and all services rendered. Expenses include items

such as the costs of goods purchased; rent, heat, power, and depreciation charges; wages and salaries paid; and business taxes (but not personal income taxes). In general, the Census Bureau considers inventory changes in determining net income from nonfarm self-employment; replies based on income tax returns or other official records reflect inventory changes. However, when respondents do not report values of inventory changes, interviewers will accept net income figures exclusive of inventory changes. The Census Bureau does not include the value of saleable merchandise consumed by the proprietors of retail stores as part of net income.

- Net income from farm self-employment is the net money income (gross receipts minus operating expenses) from the operation of a farm by a person acting on their own account as owner, renter, or sharecropper. Gross receipts include the value of all products sold, payments from government farm programs, money received from renting farm equipment to others, rent received from farm property if payment is based on the percentage of crops produced, and incidental receipts from the sale of items such as wood, sand, and gravel.

- Operating expenses include items such as the cost of feed, fertilizer, seed, and other farming supplies; cash wages paid to farmhands; depreciation charges; cash rent; interest on farm mortgages; farm building repairs; and farm taxes (not state and federal personal income taxes). The Census Bureau does not include the value of fuel, food, or other farm products used for family living as part of net income, and only considers inventory changes in determining net income when they are accounted for in income tax returns or other official records. Otherwise, the Census Bureau does not take inventory changes into account.

Educational assistance. Educational assistance includes Pell Grants, other government educational assistance, scholarships or grants, and any financial assistance received from employers, friends, or relatives not residing in the student's household.

Financial assistance from outside the household. Financial assistance from outside the household includes periodic payments received from nonhousehold members. This type of assistance excludes gifts and sporadic assistance.

Government transfers. Government transfers include payments received from the following sources: unemployment compensation, state workers' compensation, Social Security, Supplemental Security Income (SSI), public assistance, veterans' payments, government survivor benefits, government disability benefits, government pensions, and government educational assistance.

Interest income. Interest income includes payments received or credited to accounts from bonds, treasury notes, individual retirement accounts (IRAs), certificates of deposit, interest-bearing savings and checking accounts, and all other interest-paying investments.

Other income. Other income includes any other unclassified payments received regularly. Some examples are state programs such as foster child payments, military family allotments, and income received from foreign government pensions.

Pension or retirement income. Pension or retirement income includes payments received from eight sources, including companies or unions; federal government (civil service); military; state or local governments; railroad retirement; annuities or paid-up insurance policies; IRAs, Keogh, or 401(k) payments; or other retirement income.

Public assistance or welfare payments. Public assistance or welfare payments include cash payments to low-income persons, including payments given under programs such as Aid to Families with Dependent Children (AFDC, ADC) and Temporary Assistance to Needy Families (TANF), emergency assistance, and other general assistance.

Rents, royalties, and estates and trusts. Rents, royalties, and estates and trusts include net income received from the rental of a house, a store, or other property; receipts from boarders or lodgers; net royalty income; and periodic payments from estate or trust funds.

Social Security. Social Security includes pensions, survivors' benefits, and permanent disability insurance payments made by the Social Security Administration prior to medical insurance deductions. The Census Bureau does not include Medicare reimbursements for health services as Social Security benefits.

Supplemental Security Income. Supplemental Security Income includes federal, state, and local welfare agency payments to low-income people age 65 years and over and to blind or disabled people of any age.

Survivor benefits. Survivor benefits include payments received from survivors' or widows' pensions, estates, trusts, annuities, or any other types of survivors' benefits. Respondents can report payments from 10 different sources, including private companies or unions, federal government (civil service), military, state or local governments, railroad retirement, workers' compensation, Black Lung payments, estates and trusts, annuities or paid-up insurance policies, and other survivor payments.

Unemployment compensation. Unemployment compensation includes payments made to the respondent from government unemployment agencies or private companies during periods of unemployment. It also accounts for any strike benefits the respondent received from union funds.

Veterans' payments. Veterans' payments include periodic payments from the Department of Veterans Affairs to disabled members of the armed forces or survivors of deceased veterans for education and on-the-job training. These payments also include means-tested assistance to veterans.

Workers' compensation. Workers' compensation includes periodic payments from public or private insurance companies for work-related injuries.

The Census Bureau does not count the following receipts as income: (1) capital gains (or losses) from the sale of property, including stocks, bonds, houses, or cars (unless the person was engaged in the business of selling such property, in which case the CPS counts the net proceeds as income from self-employment); (2) withdrawals of bank deposits; (3) money borrowed; (4) tax refunds; (5) gifts; and (6) lump-sum inheritances or insurance payments.

The Census Bureau combines all sources of income into two major types:

Total money earnings. Total money earnings is the algebraic sum of money wages, salary, and net income from farm and nonfarm self-employment.

Income other than earnings. Income other than earnings is the algebraic sum of all sources of money income, except wages and salaries and income from self-employment.

Mean (average) income. Mean (average) income is the amount obtained by dividing the total aggregate income of a group by the number of units in that group. The means for households, families, and unrelated individuals are based respectively on all households, all families, and all unrelated individuals. The means (averages) for people are based on people age 15 years and over with income.

Median income. Median income is the amount that divides the income distribution into two equal groups. Half of all people have incomes above the median, and half of all people have incomes below the median. The medians for households, families, and unrelated individuals are respectively based on all households, all families, and all unrelated individuals. The medians for people are based on people age 15 years and over with income.

LABOR FORCE STATUS. Definitions of labor force characteristics are found below:

Civilian labor force. Consists of people classified as employed or unemployed. Excluded are institutionalized people and people on active duty in the United States Armed Forces. The entire labor force consists of people classified as employed or unemployed and people in the armed forces.

Current job (basic data). A worker's current job is the job held during the reference week (the week before the survey). A person holding two or more jobs is classified as being in the job at which he or she spent the most hours during the reference week. The unemployed are classified according to their most recent full-time job of two weeks or more, or by the job (either the full-time or part-time job) from which they were laid off. The occupation/industry classification system for the 1990 Decennial Census of Population was first used to code CPS data for the January 1992 file. The occupation/industry classification system for the 2000 Decennial Census of Population was first used to code CPS data for the January 2003 file.

Employed. Employed persons include all civilians who, during the survey week, did any work at all (for at least one hour) as paid employees or in their own business or profession, or on their own farm, or who worked 15 hours or more as unpaid workers on a farm or a business operated by a member of the family; and all people who had jobs but were not working due to illness, bad weather, vacation, labor-management dispute, or personal reasons, whether or not they were seeking other jobs. Each employed person is counted only once. People who held two or more jobs are counted as working in the job at which they worked the greatest number of hours during the survey week. If a person worked an equal number of hours at two or more jobs, he or she is counted as working at the job that they have held the longest.

Labor force. Workers are classified as being in the labor force if they are employed, unemployed, or in the armed forces during the survey week. The "civilian labor force" includes all civilians classified as employed or unemployed. The file includes labor force data for civilians age 15 years and over. However, the official definition of the civilian labor force consists of workers age 16 years and over.

Not in labor force. All civilians age 15 years and over who are not classified as employed or unemployed are considered not to be in the labor force. These people are further classified as being engaged in a major activity such as keeping house, going to school, unable to work because of long-term physical or mental illness, and "other," which is mostly composed of retired persons. Those who report doing unpaid work on a family-owned farm or in a family-owned business for less than 15 hours are also classified as not in the labor force.

For persons not in the labor force, questions about previous work experience, intentions to seek work again, current desire for a job, and reasons for not seeking work are only asked of households in the fourth and eighth months of the sample. These are the "outgoing" groups—those that were in the sample for three previous months and would not be in it for the subsequent month.

Finally, it should be noted that the unemployment rate represents the number of unemployed persons as a percentage of the civilian labor force age 16 years and over. This measure can be computed for groups within the labor force by sex, age, marital status, race, and so on. The job loser, job leaver, reentrant, and new entrant rates are each calculated as a percentage of the civilian labor force age 16 years and over; the sum of the rates for the four groups thus equals the total unemployment rate.

Unemployed. Unemployed persons are civilians who, during the survey week, had no employment but were available for work and had engaged in any specific job-seeking activity within the past four previous weeks, such as registering at a public or private employment office, meeting with prospective employers, checking with friends or relatives, placing and answering advertisements, writing letters of application, or being on a union or professional register. Others in this category were waiting to be called back to a job from which they had been laid off or were within 30 days of starting a new wage or salary job. This category consists of job leavers, job losers, new job entrants, and job reentrants.

Work experience. A person with work experience is one who did any work for pay or profit or worked without pay on a family-operated farm or business at any time during the preceding calendar year, on a part-time or full-time basis. A full-time worker is a worker who worked 35 hours or more per week during a majority of the weeks in the preceding calendar year. A year-round worker is a worker who worked for 50 weeks or more during the preceding calendar year. A full-time, year-round worker is a person who worked full-time (35 or more hours per week) for 50 or more weeks during the previous calendar year.

Level of school completed. The statistics on level of school completed indicate the number of persons enrolled at each of five levels: nursery school, kindergarten, elementary school (first to eighth grades), high school (ninth to twelfth grades), and college or professional school. The last group includes graduate students at colleges and universities. Those enrolled in elementary school, middle school, intermediate school, or junior high through eighth grade are classified as being in elementary school. All persons enrolled in ninth through twelfth grade are classified as being in high school.

Modal grade. See School, Modal grade.

Nativity. There are two major categories of nativity, native born and foreign born. A person who is native is a citizen at birth. All people with the following citizenship status are native born: (1) born in the United States; (2) born in Puerto Rico or an outlying area of the United States; and (3) born abroad of American parents. (See Citizenship status for more information.) All other people are classified as foreign born.

Nonfamily household. A nonfamily household consists of a householder living alone (a one-person household) or a household shared exclusively by unrelated people.

Population coverage. The sample for the CPS includes the civilian noninstitutional population of the United States, along with members of the armed forces in the United States living off post or with their families on post. It excludes all other members of the armed forces. The information on the Hispanic population from the CPS was collected in the 50 states and the District of Columbia and does not include residents of outlying areas or of U.S. territories such as Guam, Puerto Rico, and the U.S. Virgin Islands.

Race. The race of individuals was identified through a question requiring self-identification of the person's race. Respondents were asked to select their race from a "flash card" listing racial groups. Since March 1989, the population has been divided into five groups on the basis of race: White; Black; American Indian, Eskimo or Aleut; Asian or Pacific Islander; and Other races. The last category includes any other race except the five mentioned. In most of the published tables, "Other races" are included in the total population data line but are not shown individually.

Reference person. The reference person serves as the central point for determining relationships within the household. The household reference person is the person listed as the householder. (See Householder for more information.) The subfamily reference person is either the single parent or the husband or wife in a married-couple situation.

Rounding. Percentages are rounded to the nearest 10th of a percent; therefore, the percentages in a distribution do not always sum to exactly 100 percent.

School, Dropout rate, annual high school. The annual high school dropout rate is an estimate of the proportion of students who drop out of school in a single year. This section briefly explains how the annual dropout rate is calculated; for further explanation and details of its derivation, see *Current Population Report (Series P-20, No. 413): "School Enrollment—Social and Economic Characteristics of Students: October 1983."*

Annual dropout rates for a single grade (X) are estimated as the ratio between the number of people enrolled in grade (X) in the year preceding the survey who did not complete grade (X) and are not currently enrolled in grade (X) at the start of the year preceding this survey. People reported as enrolled last year but not currently enrolled are presented by the highest grade completed. They are presumed to have dropped out of the succeeding grade (except for those who graduated this year). Thus, individuals counted as 10th grade dropouts are those whose highest grade completed is the 9th grade, but who are not currently enrolled in school. (The dropout classification also includes those people who finished the 9th grade in the spring preceding the survey and were not enrolled on the survey date.) These estimates form the numerator of the annual grade-specific dropout rate.

People currently enrolled in high school are presumed to have been enrolled in and have successfully completed the preceding grade during the preceding year. For example, those who have successfully completed the 10th grade would be enrolled in the 11th grade. Along with the people who dropped out of that grade, they comprise the denominator of the estimate of the annual grade-specific dropout rate:

$$\text{Dropout from Grade n} = \frac{\text{Not enrolled and highest grade completed} = \text{n-1}}{(\text{Enrolled in n+1} + \text{Not enrolled and highest grade completed} = \text{n-1})}$$

It cannot be presumed that all 12th grade graduates will enroll in college. The estimate of the number of people enrolled in the 12th grade one year before the survey is constructed as the sum of the number of people reported to have graduated from high school "this year" (whether or not they are currently enrolled in college) and those not currently enrolled who were enrolled last year and whose highest grade completed is the 11th grade (dropouts). The annual dropout rate for all grades during one year can be obtained by summing the components of the rates for the individual grades—the sum of all people previously enrolled in the 10th, 11th, or 12th grade last year, but who are not currently enrolled and do not have a high school diploma.

In addition to the annual rate, two other estimates of dropouts are frequently used. The annual dropout rate is different from a "pool" (or status) measure, such as the proportion of high school dropouts within an age group. A third measure of dropouts is the "cohort measure," most commonly from a longitudinal study, in which the proportion of a specific group of people enrolled in a specific year is calculated. These people did not receive diplomas (and are no longer in school) some years later. For example, the proportion of a cohort enrolled in 9th grade in year X, who were not enrolled and had not received a diploma by year X equals 4.

School enrollment. The school enrollment statistics from the CPS are based on replies to inquiries concerning current regular school enrollment. Those counted as enrolled had attended a public, parochial, or other private school in the regular school system at any time during the current or previous school year. Such schools include nursery schools, kindergartens, elementary schools, high schools, colleges, universities, and professional schools. Attendance could have been on either a full-time or part-time basis during the day or night. Regular schooling is that which advances a person toward an elementary or high school diploma or toward a college, university, or professional school degree. Children enrolled in nursery schools and kindergarten are included in the enrollment figures for regular schools and are shown separately.

Enrollment in schools not in the regular school system, such as trade schools, business colleges, and schools for the mentally handicapped is not included, as these schools do not advance students toward regular school degrees.

People enrolled in classes not requiring their physical presence in school, such as correspondence courses or other courses of independent study, and those enrolled in training courses given directly on the job, are also excluded from the count of those enrolled in school, unless such courses are being counted for credit at a regular school.

School enrollment in the year preceding current survey. All respondents were asked to state their school enrollment status as of October of the preceding year. Before 1988, this question was only asked of people not currently attending regular school and people who were enrolled in college. In the tabulations of previous year's secondary school enrollment, those currently enrolled in high school were assumed to have been enrolled the previous year.

Comparability of enrollment data in previous years. Changes in the edit and tabulation packages used to process the October CPS school enrollment supplement caused some minor revisions to the estimates. The current edit and tabulation package began with 1987 data. The 1986 data published in the *Current Population Report (Series P-20 No. 429)* were reprocessed with the rewritten programs in order to clarify comparability. Time series tables usually show only the revised estimates for 1986. The previous edit and tabulation package was used from 1967 to 1986.

Major changes in the data caused by the 1987 edit revisions were: (1) Among 14- and 15-year-olds, an edit improvement allowed people with unreported enrollment data, who were previously imputed as "not enrolled," to be enrolled; (2) Revisions in the tabulation of enrollment in the previous year simplified the calculation of an annual high school dropout rate; (3) Edit improvements caused increases in college enrollment estimates, most notably above the age of 24. This age group was largely ignored in earlier edits; (4) Type of college is fully allocated (discussed later in the section); (5) Tabulations of type of college (2-year and 4-year colleges) were made available by race; (6) Dependent family members became consistently defined; (7) New tabulations of employment status, vocational course enrollment, college retention and re-entry, and families with children enrolled in public and private school became available beginning in 1987.

In the series of reports on school enrollment for 1987 to 1992, race and Hispanic origin were erroneously tabulated for a small percentage of children age 3 to 14 years. Race and Hispanic origin of an adult in the household were attributed to the child, rather than using the child's reported characteristics. In the vast majority of cases, these characteristics were the same for family members, but for a small percentage of children, they were different. The correction made the following proportional changes in the numbers of children in each group: White (-0.5 percent), Black (+3.1 percent), and Hispanic (-4.6 percent).

Published data on enrollment from the October CPS for 1981 to 1993 used population controls based on the 1980 census. Beginning in 1994, estimates used 1990 census–based population controls, including adjustment for undercount. Time series tables show two sets of data for 1993; the data labeled "1993r" were processed using population controls based on the 1990 census with adjustments for undercount. The change in 1994 from a paper-and-pencil survey to a computer-assisted survey had some affect on the data. Most notably, the enrollment question for children age 3 to 5 years was different from the question for older children—it included a reference to nursery school. In 1994, reported nursery school enrollment was significantly higher than in earlier years.

Attendance, full-time and part-time. College students are classified according to their attendance status. A student is categorized as attending college full-time if he or she was taking 12 or more hours of classes during the average school week, and part-time if he or she was taking less than 12 hours of classes per average school week.

College enrollment. The college enrollment statistics are based on reports of school enrollment, including the grade in which the respondent was enrolled. Students enrolled in college at any time during the current term or school year were counted as enrolled, except those who had left for the remainder of the term. Thus, regular college enrollment includes those attending two-year or four-year colleges, universities, or professional schools (such as medical or law schools) in courses that advance students toward a recognized college or university degree (such as a B.A. or an M.A.). Attendance may be full-time or part-time during the day or night. The college student need not be working toward a degree, but he or she must be enrolled in a class for which credit would be applied toward a degree. (See school enrollment for more information.) Students are classified by year of college, based on the academic year (not calendar year). The undergraduate years are the first through fourth year, or freshman through senior years. Graduate or professional school years include the fifth year and higher.

Two-year and four-year colleges. College students were asked if their school was a two-year college (junior or community college) or a four-year college or university. Students enrolled in the first four years of college (undergraduates) were classified by the type of school that they attended. Graduate students are shown as a separate group.

Vocational school enrollment. Vocational school enrollment includes enrollment in business, vocational, technical, secretarial, trade, or correspondence courses that are not counted as regular school enrollment. This category excludes recreation or adult education classes. Courses that counted as college enrollment are also excluded.

School, Modal grade. Enrolled people are classified according to their relative progress in school and whether the grade or year in which they were enrolled was below, at, or above the modal (or typical) grade for students of their age at the time of the survey. The modal grade is the year of school in which the largest proportion of students of a given age were enrolled.

School, Nursery. A nursery school is defined as a group or class that has been organized to provide educational experiences for children during the year or years preceding kindergarten. It includes instruction as an important and integral phase of its childcare program. Private homes, in which essentially custodial care is provided, are not considered nursery schools. Children attending nursery school are classified as attending for part of the day or for the full day. Part-day attendance refers to those who attend either in the morning or in the afternoon. Full-day attendance refers to those who attend in the morning and in the afternoon. Children enrolled in Head Start programs or similar local agency-sponsored programs that provide preschool education to young children are counted as being enrolled in nursery school.

School, Public or private. A public school is defined as any educational institution operated by publicly elected or appointed school officials and supported by public funds. Private schools include educational institutions established and operated by religious bodies, as well as those that are under other private controls. In cases in which a school or college was both publicly and privately controlled or supported, enrollment was counted according to whether the school was primarily public or private.

Undocumented immigrants or illegal aliens. Since all residents of the United States living in households are represented in the sample of households interviewed by the CPS, undocumented immigrants or illegal aliens are probably included in CPS data. Because the CPS makes no attempt to ascertain the legal status of any person interviewed, these individuals cannot be identified from CPS data.

POSTSECONDARY EDUCATION TABLES

Tables A-29 through A-38 were adapted from published tables in two publications from the National Center for Education Statistics, Institute of Education Sciences: *Digest of Education Statistics: 2011* (NCES 2011-001). (www.nces.ed.gov/pubsearch/pubsinfo.asp?pubid=2012001) and *Postsecondary Institutions and Price of Attendance in the United States: 2010–11, Degrees and Other Awards Conferred: 2009–10, and 12-Month Enrollment: 2009–10* (NCES 2011-250). (www.nces.ed.gov/pubsearch/pubsinfo.asp?pubid=2011250). The data in these tables come primarily from the Integrated Postsecondary Education Data System (IPEDS) fall 2010 data collection, which included three survey components: Institutional Characteristics for the 2010–2011 academic year, Completions covering the period July 1, 2009, through June 30, 2010, and 12-Month Enrollment covering academic year 2009–2010. Enrollment data for 1967 through 1985 are from Higher Education General Information Survey (HEGIS), "Fall Enrollment in Colleges and Universities" surveys.

Control of institution describes whether an institution is operated by publicly elected or appointed officials (public control) or by privately elected or appointed officials and derives its major source of funds from private sources (private not-for-profit or private for-profit control). There are nine institutional categories resulting from dividing the universe according to control and level. Control categories are public, private not-for-profit, and private for-profit. Level categories are 4-year and higher (4 year), 2-but-less-than 4-year (2 year), and less than 2-year. For example: Public, 4-year is one of the institution sectors.

Fall enrollment. IPEDS collects data on the number of students enrolled in the fall at postsecondary institutions. Students reported are those enrolled in courses creditable toward a degree or other formal award; students enrolled in courses that are part of a vocational or occupational program, including those enrolled in off-campus or extension centers; and high school students taking regular college courses for credit. Institutions report annually the number of full- and part-time students, by gender, race/ethnicity, and level (undergraduate, graduate, first-professional); the total number of undergraduate entering students (first-time, full- and part-time students, transfer-ins, and nondegree students); and retention rates. In even-numbered years, data are collected for state of residence of first-time students and for the number of those students who graduated from high school or received high school equivalent certificates in the past 12 months. Also in even-numbered years, 4-year institutions are required to provide enrollment data by gender, race/ethnicity, and level for selected fields of study. In odd-numbered years, data are collected for enrollment by age category by student level and gender.

Data through 1995 are for institutions of higher education, while later data are for degree-granting institutions. Degree-granting institutions grant associate's or higher degrees and participate in Title IV federal financial aid programs. The degree-granting classification is very similar to the earlier higher education classification, but it includes more 2-year colleges and excludes a few higher education institutions that did not grant degrees.

Nonresident alien is a person who is not a citizen or national of the United States and who is in this country on a visa or temporary basis and does not have the right to remain indefinitely.

A **Postbaccalaureate student** is a student with a bachelor's degree who is enrolled in graduate-level or first-professional courses.

Price of attendance includes tuition and required fees, books and supplies, room and board charges, and other expenses. Amounts are institutional averages as reported by the institution, not average amounts paid by students (i.e., charges are not weighted by enrollment). Out-of-state average tuition and required fees were used for private institutions that reported varying tuitions by residency. The 2,467 institutions with academic calendars that differ by program or allow continuous enrollment are not included. U.S. service academies are not included. All amounts from 2008–2009 were converted to 2010–2011 dollars using the average Consumer Price Index values for the 12-month periods ending in October 2008 and October 2010. On-campus average price is based on those institutions that offer on-campus housing and/or meal service. Off-campus average price is based on those institutions that do not require full-time, first-time students to live on campus. For public institutions, "in district" refers to the charges paid by a student who lives in the locality surrounding the institution, such as a county.

Race/ethnicity categories were developed in 1997 by the Office of Management and Budget (OMB) and are used to describe groups to which individuals belong, identify with, or belong in the eyes of the community. The categories do not denote scientific definitions of anthropological origins. The designations are used to categorize U.S. citizens, resident aliens, and other eligible non-citizens. Individuals are asked to first designate ethnicity as Hispanic/Latino or not Hispanic/Latino. Hispanic/Latino refers to a person of Cuban, Mexican, Puerto Rican, South or Central American, or other Spanish culture or origin, regardless of race. Second, individuals are asked to indicate all races that apply among the following:

American Indian or Alaska Native (A person having origins in any of the original peoples of North and South America (including Central America) who maintains cultural identification through tribal affiliation or community attachment.)

Asian (A person having origins in any of the original peoples of the Far East, Southeast Asia, or the Indian Subcontinent, including, for example, Cambodia, China, India, Japan, Korea, Malaysia, Pakistan, the Philippine Islands, Thailand, and Vietnam.)

Black or African American (A person having origins in any of the black racial groups of Africa.)

Native Hawaiian or Other Pacific Islander (A person having origins in any of the original peoples of Hawaii, Guam, Samoa, or other Pacific Islands.)

White (A person having origins in any of the original peoples of Europe, the Middle East, or North Africa.)

Before 1997, slightly different race/ethnicity categories were used and persons could identify with only one racial category.

Tuition and required fees is the amount of tuition and required fees covering a full academic year most frequently charged to students. These values represent what a typical student would be charged and may not be the same for all students at an institution. If tuition is charged on a per-credit-hour basis, the average full-time credit hour load for an entire academic year is used to estimate average tuition. Required fees include all fixed sum charges that are required of such a large proportion of all students that the student who does not pay the charges is an exception.

PART B

REGION AND STATE EDUCATION STATISTICS

PART B—REGION AND STATE EDUCATION STATISTICS

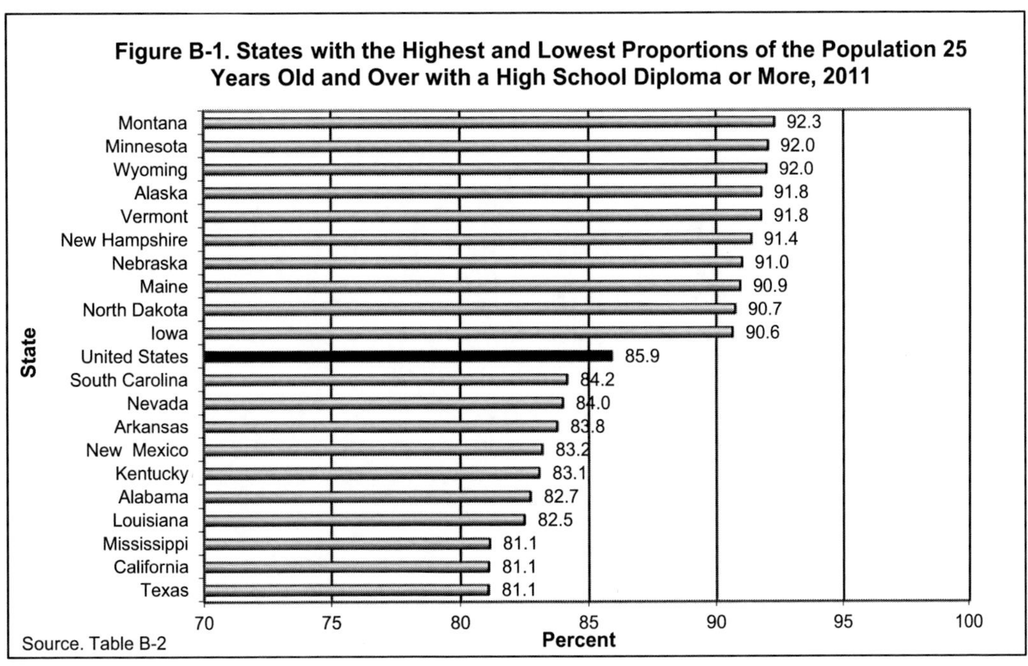

In 2011, 85.9 percent of the U.S. population 25 years old and over had graduated from high school. Seventeen states had high school attainment levels of 90 percent or higher, and all states had high school attainment levels of 80 percent or higher. In 1975, less than two-thirds of people over 25 years of age had graduated from high school. The high school graduation rate for women 25 years old and over (86.5 percent) continued to exceed that of men (85.2 percent).

Among the four regions of the United States, the Midwest had the highest proportion of high school graduates (88.8 percent), followed by the Northeast (87.5 percent), the West (84.7 percent), and the South (84.2 percent). (Source. Table B-2)

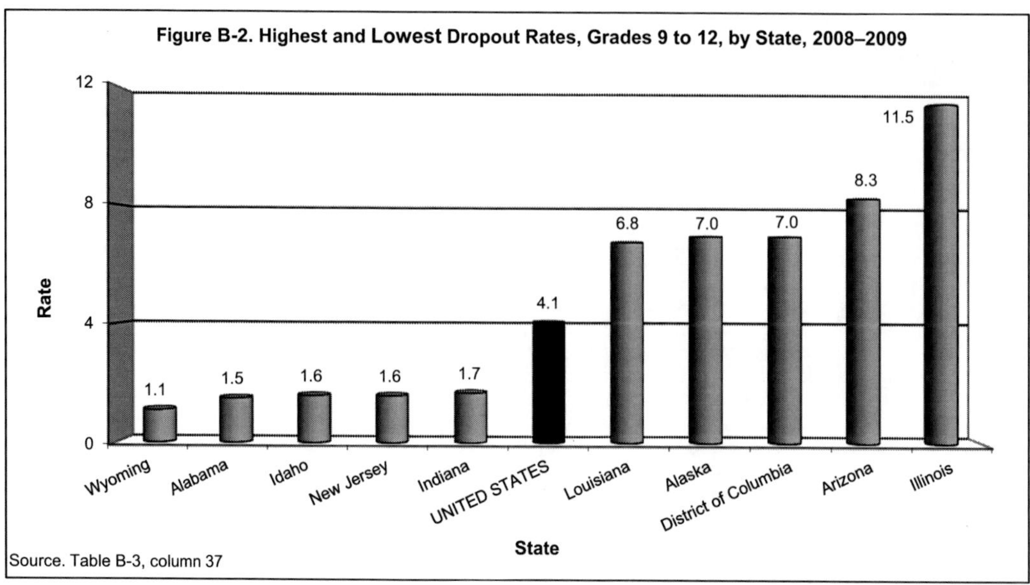

In 2011, 4.9 percent of the population 16 to 19 years old were no longer enrolled in school and not high school graduates; therefore it was estimated that this segment of the population had dropped out of school before graduation. Of the states, Wyoming had the lowest percentage of these dropouts (2.2 percent) and New Mexico had the highest percentage (8.5 percent). Among the regions, five of the six New England states ranked among the ten lowest percentages of dropout students, at 3.6 percent or below. The South Atlantic and Mountain regions each had four states in the top ten percentages of students not finishing high school, all 6.5 percent or higher. (Source. Table B-3, Column 149)

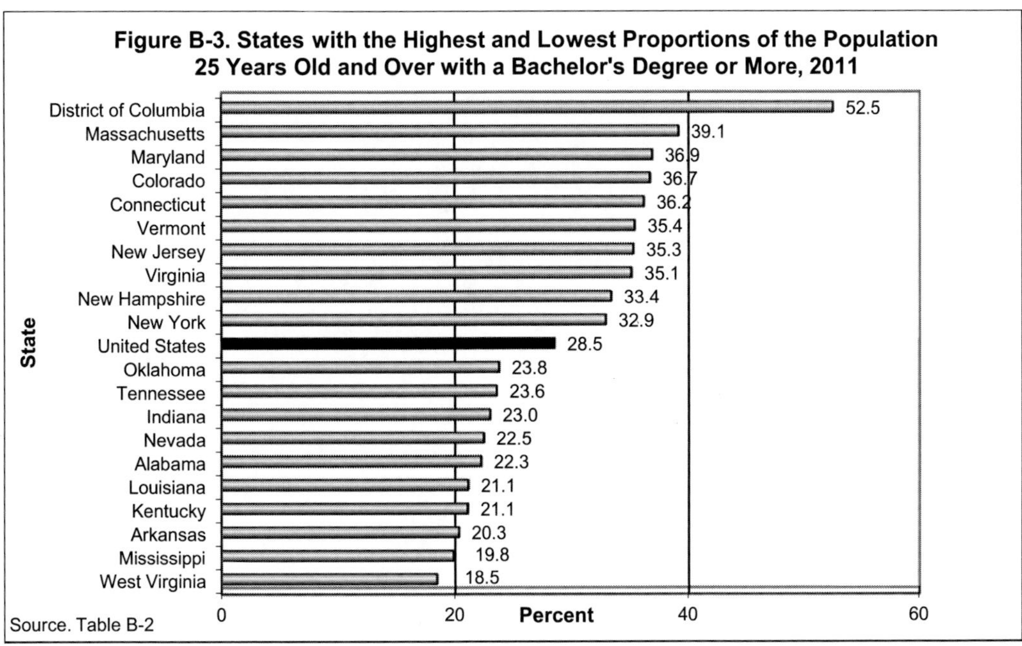

The proportion of the U.S. population with a bachelor's degree has increased slightly since 2009, from 27.9 percent to 28.5 percent in 2011. In the District of Columbia, 52.5 percent of residents held a bachelor's degree or more, the highest rate in the nation. Among the states, seven had proportions of college graduates exceeding 35 percent. Only two states had college attainment levels of less than 20 percent, with West Virginia at 18.5 percent and Mississippi at 19.8 percent. In 2011, slightly more men than women age 25 years old and over held a bachelor's degree or more (28.7 percent for men and 28.3 percent for women), but the proportion of women holding degrees is higher than men in the age groups under 45 in all four regions of the country. Nationally, 28.6 percent of men age 25 to 44 held bachelor's degrees, while 34.8 percent of women in this age group had graduated from college.

The Northeast region had the highest college attainment rate, with 32.8 percent, followed by the West region, with 29.8 percent, and the Midwest region, with 27.2 percent. The South region had the lowest proportion of its residents holding a bachelor's degree (26.4 percent).

Among the races, for the population 25 years old and older, the Asian population had the highest college attainment (50.0 percent), followed by the White (31.9 percent), Black (18.4 percent), and Hispanic (13.2 percent) populations. (Source. Table B-2)

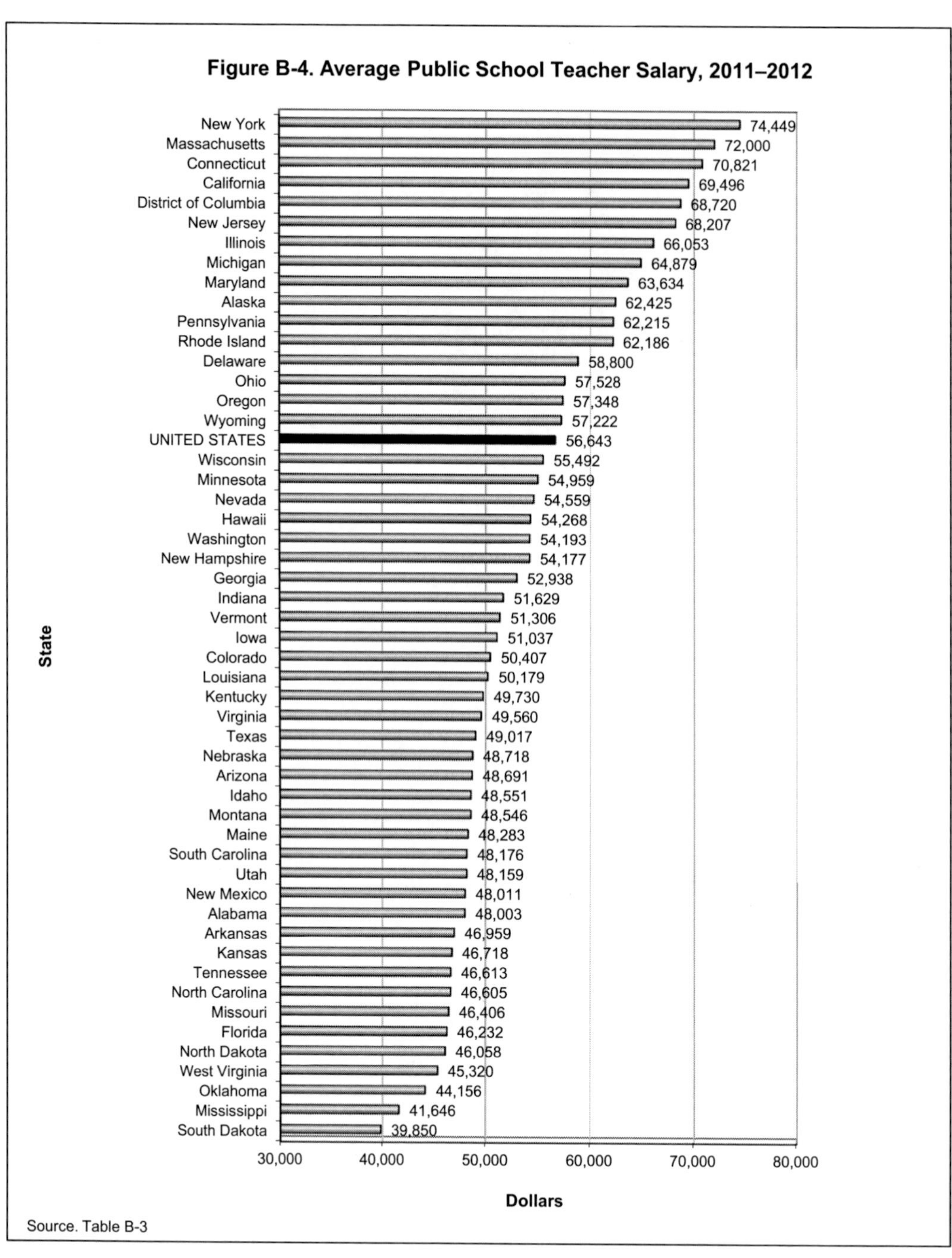

For the 2011–2012 school year, the average public school teacher's salary was $56,643, an increase of 2.3 percent from the 2009–2010 school year. Salaries ranged from $39,850 in South Dakota to $74,449 in New York. Five of the nine U.S. geographic divisions are represented in the top ten states with the highest salaries. These states were evenly divided with two states representing each division, and all four regions represented. Six of the ten states with the lowest teacher salaries were in the South region, while the other four were in the Midwest. (Source. Table B-3)

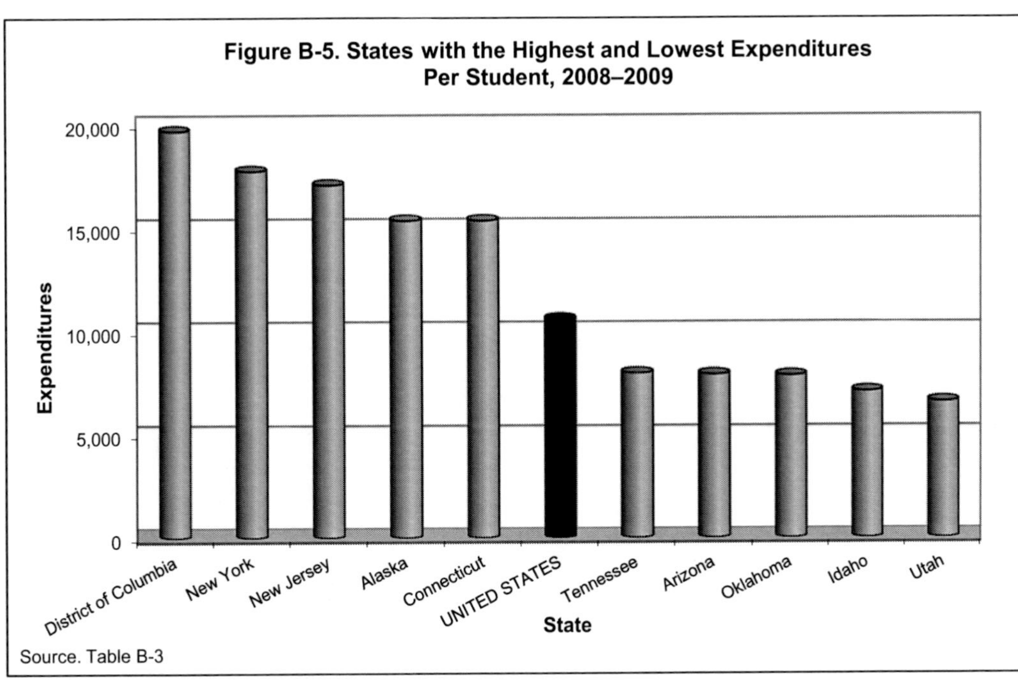

Nationally, the average expenditure per student was $10,591 for the 2008–2009 school year. The District of Columbia, with a completely urban school district, had higher expenditures per student, at $19,698, than any of the states. Among the states, New York and New Jersey had the highest expenditures, both above $17,000. Utah had the lowest expenditure per student at $6,612 and was the only state with a per student expenditure of less than $7,000. Utah also had the highest proportion of population age 5 to 17 years old, at 21.9 percent, and a very high student/teacher ratio (22.8 students per teacher). The District of Columbia had the lowest proportion of school-age population, with just 11.2 percent. Nationally, 17.3 percent of the population was 5 to 17 years old. Four of the eight Mountain states (Arizona, Idaho, Utah, and Nevada) ranked among the 10 lowest per student expenditures.

Ten states had per student expenditures of more than $13,000, and five states spent less than $8,000 per student. All six states in the New England division and all three states in the Middle Atlantic division ranked among the highest 15 per student expenditures in the nation. Three New England states (Connecticut, Massachusetts, and New Hampshire) had among the ten highest median household incomes for a family of four in 2011. Arizona, Mississippi, and Arkansas had the lowest median household incomes.

Nationally, instruction accounted for 61.0 percent of all expenses, with support services at 35.0 percent and non-instructional expenses at 4.1 percent. New York had the highest proportion of instruction and instruction-related expenditures, at 69.2 percent. The District of Columbia had the lowest at 46.1 percent. (Source. Table B-3)

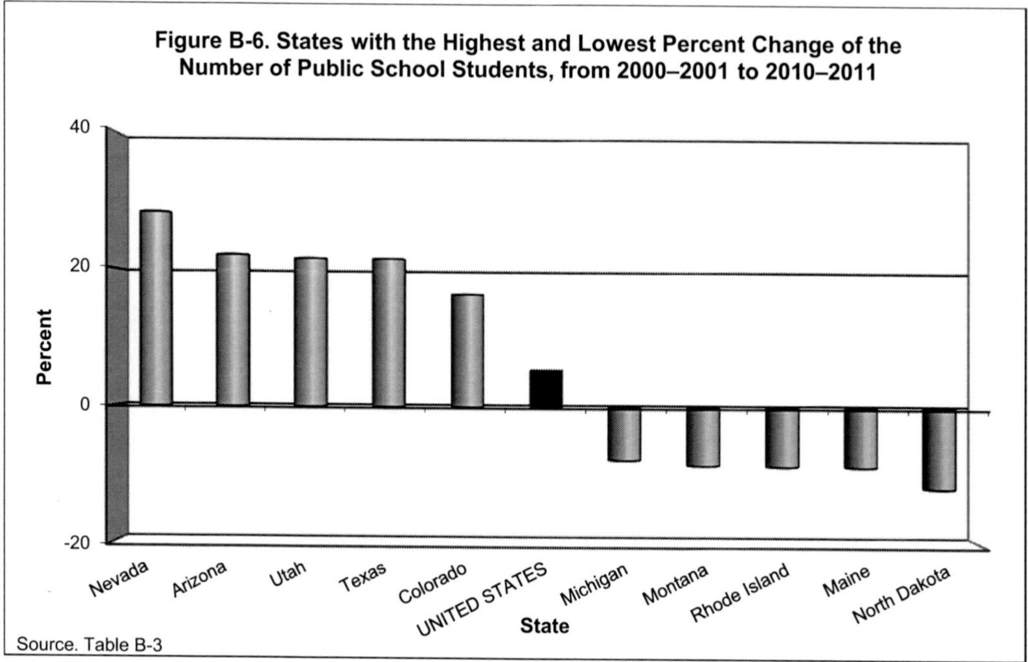

There was a huge variation by state in the percent change in the number of students from the 2000–2001 school year to the 2010–2011 school year. In the past 10 years, the number of students in the United States increased 4.8 percent. However, in Nevada, the number of students increased substantially, rising 28.3 percent. Arizona had the next-highest increase at 22.1 percent, closely followed by Texas and Utah, both at 21.6 percent. North Dakota saw the biggest decrease, at 11.8 percent. During the same ten-year period, the number of teachers also changed, often in proportions similar to the number of students. In Virginia, the number of teachers dropped 18.4 percent, while the number of students grew by 9.3 percent. Similarly, California counted 12.4 percent fewer teachers despite a 2.4 percent increase in the number of students.

Nationally, the student–teacher ratio was 16.0 during the 2010–2011 school year. California, Utah, Arizona, and Oregon exceeded 20 students per teacher. North Dakota, Vermont, the District of Columbia, Maine, and Wyoming had the five lowest student–teacher ratios in the nation. North Dakota, Vermont, Maine, and the District of Columbia also ranked among the ten states with the lowest proportion of population age 5 to 17 years old. The District of Columbia ranked lowest, at 11.2 percent. (Source. Table B-3)

During the 2009–2010 school year, 8.7 percent of students attended private elementary and secondary schools. The District of Columbia, Louisiana, Hawaii, and Delaware had the highest proportion of students attending private schools, all 15 percent or higher. Wyoming, Utah, and Alaska had the lowest proportion of students enrolled in private schools, 3.2 percent or lower. (Source. Table B-3)

Table B-1. Educational Attainment of the Population 18 Years Old and Over, by Region, Age, and Sex, 2011

Region, age, sex	Total		High school				College			
			Less than high school		High school graduate, GED or alternative		Some college or associate's degree		Bachelor's degree or higher	
	Number	Percent	Number	Percent	Number	Percent	Number	Percent	Number	Percent
ALL RACES										
Northeast										
Both sexes										
18 years and over	43,334,924	100.0	5,476,971	12.6	12,935,346	29.8	11,808,453	27.2	13,114,154	30.3
18 to 24 years	5,468,259	100.0	737,122	13.5	1,518,671	27.8	2,507,690	45.9	704,776	12.9
25 to 34 years	7,149,362	100.0	695,143	9.7	1,666,203	23.3	1,917,566	26.8	2,870,450	40.1
35 to 44 years	7,252,643	100.0	730,069	10.1	1,916,792	26.4	1,901,963	26.2	2,703,819	37.3
45 to 64 years	15,524,105	100.0	1,616,062	10.4	4,809,511	31.0	4,054,061	26.1	5,044,471	32.5
65 years and over	7,940,555	100.0	1,698,575	21.4	3,024,169	38.1	1,427,173	18.0	1,790,638	22.6
Male										
18 years and over	20,762,036	100.0	2,749,228	13.2	6,337,269	30.5	5,443,865	26.2	6,231,674	30.0
18 to 24 years	2,782,379	100.0	437,730	15.7	846,542	30.4	1,196,031	43.0	302,076	10.9
25 to 34 years	3,554,286	100.0	392,595	11.0	965,377	27.2	928,835	26.1	1,267,479	35.7
35 to 44 years	3,567,822	100.0	406,579	11.4	1,054,925	29.6	870,648	24.4	1,235,670	34.6
45 to 64 years	7,520,565	100.0	823,423	10.9	2,385,049	31.7	1,844,734	24.5	2,467,359	32.8
65 years and over	3,336,984	100.0	688,901	20.6	1,085,376	32.5	603,617	18.1	959,090	28.7
Female										
18 years and over	22,572,888	100.0	2,727,743	12.1	6,598,077	29.2	6,364,588	28.2	6,882,480	30.5
18 to 24 years	2,685,880	100.0	299,392	11.1	672,129	25.0	1,311,659	48.8	402,700	15.0
25 to 34 years	3,595,076	100.0	302,548	8.4	700,826	19.5	988,731	27.5	1,602,971	44.6
35 to 44 years	3,684,821	100.0	323,490	8.8	861,867	23.4	1,031,315	28.0	1,468,149	39.8
45 to 64 years	8,003,540	100.0	792,639	9.9	2,424,462	30.3	2,209,327	27.6	2,577,112	32.2
65 years and over	4,603,571	100.0	1,009,674	21.9	1,938,793	42.1	823,556	17.9	831,548	18.1
Midwest										
Both sexes										
18 years and over	51,203,805	100.0	5,989,459	11.7	15,796,749	30.9	16,675,452	32.6	12,742,145	24.9
18 to 24 years	6,627,224	100.0	985,090	14.9	1,902,551	28.7	3,106,545	46.9	633,038	9.6
25 to 34 years	8,649,710	100.0	826,285	9.6	2,066,975	23.9	2,963,766	34.3	2,792,684	32.3
35 to 44 years	8,463,456	100.0	782,180	9.2	2,219,177	26.2	2,777,962	32.8	2,684,137	31.7
45 to 64 years	18,272,296	100.0	1,661,487	9.1	5,909,754	32.3	5,799,091	31.7	4,901,964	26.8
65 years and over	9,191,119	100.0	1,734,417	18.9	3,698,292	40.2	2,028,088	22.1	1,730,322	18.8
Male										
18 years and over	24,890,332	100.0	3,121,347	12.5	7,910,254	31.8	7,751,029	31.1	6,107,702	24.5
18 to 24 years	3,379,774	100.0	576,693	17.1	1,066,924	31.6	1,477,171	43.7	258,986	7.7
25 to 34 years	4,355,232	100.0	469,379	10.8	1,223,914	28.1	1,427,024	32.8	1,234,915	28.4
35 to 44 years	4,227,494	100.0	441,024	10.4	1,240,063	29.3	1,307,847	30.9	1,238,560	29.3
45 to 64 years	8,978,521	100.0	888,906	9.9	2,979,478	33.2	2,681,956	29.9	2,428,181	27.0
65 years and over	3,949,311	100.0	745,345	18.9	1,399,875	35.4	857,031	21.7	947,060	24.0
Female										
18 years and over	26,313,473	100.0	2,868,112	10.9	7,886,495	30.0	8,924,423	33.9	6,634,443	25.2
18 to 24 years	3,247,450	100.0	408,397	12.6	835,627	25.7	1,629,374	50.2	374,052	11.5
25 to 34 years	4,294,478	100.0	356,906	8.3	843,061	19.6	1,536,742	35.8	1,557,769	36.3
35 to 44 years	4,235,962	100.0	341,156	8.1	979,114	23.1	1,470,115	34.7	1,445,577	34.1
45 to 64 years	9,293,775	100.0	772,581	8.3	2,930,276	31.5	3,117,135	33.5	2,473,783	26.6
65 years and over	5,241,808	100.0	989,072	18.9	2,298,417	43.8	1,171,057	22.3	783,262	14.9
South										
Both sexes										
18 years and over	88,180,370	100.0	14,091,856	16.0	25,939,480	29.4	27,020,458	30.6	21,128,576	24.0
18 to 24 years	11,643,580	100.0	2,030,937	17.4	3,560,140	30.6	5,129,788	44.1	922,715	7.9
25 to 34 years	15,422,356	100.0	2,106,543	13.7	4,012,134	26.0	4,929,325	32.0	4,374,354	28.4
35 to 44 years	15,375,254	100.0	2,058,260	13.4	4,132,273	26.9	4,645,655	30.2	4,539,066	29.5
45 to 64 years	30,367,043	100.0	4,206,128	13.9	9,203,116	30.3	8,895,789	29.3	8,062,010	26.5
65 years and over	15,372,137	100.0	3,689,988	24.0	5,031,817	32.7	3,419,901	22.2	3,230,431	21.0

Table B-1. Educational Attainment of the Population 18 Years Old and Over, by Region, Age, and Sex, 2011—*Continued*

Region, age, sex	Total		High school				College			
			Less than high school		High school graduate, GED or alternative		Some college or associate's degree		Bachelor's degree or higher	
	Number	Percent	Number	Percent	Number	Percent	Number	Percent	Number	Percent
Male										
18 years and over	42,626,030	100.0	7,376,872	17.3	12,851,345	30.1	12,275,719	28.8	10,122,094	23.7
18 to 24 years	5,957,939	100.0	1,208,137	20.3	1,982,960	33.3	2,386,805	40.1	380,037	6.4
25 to 34 years	7,692,870	100.0	1,221,508	15.9	2,293,220	29.8	2,298,915	29.9	1,879,227	24.4
35 to 44 years	7,596,342	100.0	1,172,065	15.4	2,234,637	29.4	2,121,958	27.9	2,067,682	27.2
45 to 64 years	14,705,871	100.0	2,240,795	15.2	4,486,134	30.5	4,000,868	27.2	3,978,074	27.1
65 years and over	6,673,008	100.0	1,534,367	23.0	1,854,394	27.8	1,467,173	22.0	1,817,074	27.2
Female										
18 years and over	45,554,340	100.0	6,714,984	14.7	13,088,135	28.7	14,744,739	32.4	11,006,482	24.2
18 to 24 years	5,685,641	100.0	822,800	14.5	1,577,180	27.7	2,742,983	48.2	542,678	9.5
25 to 34 years	7,729,486	100.0	885,035	11.5	1,718,914	22.2	2,630,410	34.0	2,495,127	32.3
35 to 44 years	7,778,912	100.0	886,195	11.4	1,897,636	24.4	2,523,697	32.4	2,471,384	31.8
45 to 64 years	15,661,172	100.0	1,965,333	12.5	4,716,982	30.1	4,894,921	31.3	4,083,936	26.1
65 years and over	8,699,129	100.0	2,155,621	24.8	3,177,423	36.5	1,952,728	22.4	1,413,357	16.2
West										
Both sexes										
18 years and over	54,962,119	100.0	8,488,574	15.4	13,170,074	24.0	18,550,968	33.8	14,752,503	26.8
18 to 24 years	7,470,485	100.0	1,204,406	16.1	2,207,076	29.5	3,472,967	46.5	586,036	7.8
25 to 34 years	10,318,918	100.0	1,415,239	13.7	2,361,698	22.9	3,474,054	33.7	3,067,927	29.7
35 to 44 years	9,736,357	100.0	1,585,766	16.3	2,091,002	21.5	2,965,406	30.5	3,094,183	31.8
45 to 64 years	18,555,144	100.0	2,592,500	14.0	4,156,213	22.4	6,179,940	33.3	5,626,491	30.3
65 years and over	8,881,215	100.0	1,690,663	19.0	2,354,085	26.5	2,458,601	27.7	2,377,866	26.8
Male										
18 years and over	27,169,780	100.0	4,386,810	16.1	6,687,755	24.6	8,802,158	32.4	7,293,057	26.8
18 to 24 years	3,874,898	100.0	720,810	18.6	1,240,783	32.0	1,677,684	43.3	235,621	6.1
25 to 34 years	5,289,954	100.0	810,256	15.3	1,351,655	25.6	1,737,186	32.8	1,390,857	26.3
35 to 44 years	4,916,577	100.0	854,919	17.4	1,140,941	23.2	1,441,055	29.3	1,479,662	30.1
45 to 64 years	9,131,408	100.0	1,314,265	14.4	2,078,429	22.8	2,885,776	31.6	2,852,938	31.2
65 years and over	3,956,943	100.0	686,560	17.4	875,947	22.1	1,060,457	26.8	1,333,979	33.7
Female										
18 years and over	27,792,339	100.0	4,101,764	14.8	6,482,319	23.3	9,748,810	35.1	7,459,446	26.8
18 to 24 years	3,595,587	100.0	483,596	13.4	966,293	26.9	1,795,283	49.9	350,415	9.7
25 to 34 years	5,028,964	100.0	604,983	12.0	1,010,043	20.1	1,736,868	34.5	1,677,070	33.3
35 to 44 years	4,819,780	100.0	730,847	15.2	950,061	19.7	1,524,351	31.6	1,614,521	33.5
45 to 64 years	9,423,736	100.0	1,278,235	13.6	2,077,784	22.0	3,294,164	35.0	2,773,553	29.4
65 years and over	4,924,272	100.0	1,004,103	20.4	1,478,138	30.0	1,398,144	28.4	1,043,887	21.2

Table B-2. Educational Attainment of the Population 25 Years Old and Over, by Sex, Race, Hispanic Origin, and Region or State, 2011

Region/State	Total, age 25 years and over			Male, age 25 years and over			Female, age 25 years and over		
	Population	High school graduate or higher (percent)	Bachelor's degree or higher (percent)	Population	High school graduate or higher (percent)	Bachelor's degree or higher (percent)	Population	High school graduate or higher (percent)	Bachelor's degree or higher (percent)
UNITED STATES	206,471,670	85.9	28.5	99,453,188	85.2	28.7	107,018,482	86.5	28.3
Northeast Region	37,866,665	87.5	32.8	17,979,657	87.1	33.0	19,887,008	87.8	32.6
Midwest Region	44,576,581	88.8	27.2	21,510,558	88.2	27.2	23,066,023	89.3	27.1
South Region	76,536,790	84.2	26.4	36,668,091	83.2	26.6	39,868,699	85.2	26.2
West Region	47,491,634	84.7	29.8	23,294,882	84.3	30.3	24,196,752	85.0	29.4
Alabama	3,193,078	82.7	22.3	1,508,892	81.2	22.2	1,684,186	84.1	22.3
Alaska	456,862	91.8	26.4	234,211	91.6	23.9	222,651	91.9	28.9
Arizona	4,211,223	85.7	26.6	2,059,722	85.0	27.7	2,151,501	86.4	25.5
Arkansas	1,943,427	83.8	20.3	935,804	82.9	20.4	1,007,623	84.6	20.2
California	24,443,872	81.1	30.3	11,937,927	80.8	30.6	12,505,945	81.3	30.0
Colorado	3,387,310	90.2	36.7	1,675,846	89.5	37.2	1,711,464	90.9	36.2
Connecticut	2,444,403	89.1	36.2	1,161,569	88.6	36.6	1,282,834	89.5	35.8
Delaware	611,120	87.0	28.8	289,532	85.7	29.4	321,588	88.1	28.4
District of Columbia	428,261	87.2	52.5	200,665	86.4	53.2	227,596	88.0	51.9
Florida	13,267,581	85.9	25.8	6,351,556	84.9	26.7	6,916,025	86.9	25.1
Georgia	6,308,961	84.3	27.6	3,004,726	83.3	27.6	3,304,235	85.2	27.6
Hawaii	939,512	90.6	29.1	462,509	91.1	28.1	477,003	90.1	30.1
Idaho	998,460	88.6	25.2	494,011	88.0	26.7	504,449	89.2	23.8
Illinois	8,521,694	87.2	31.0	4,090,567	86.6	31.0	4,431,127	87.8	31.0
Indiana	4,255,459	87.3	23.0	2,052,213	86.6	23.3	2,203,246	87.9	22.8
Iowa	2,027,201	90.6	25.8	985,672	89.9	25.3	1,041,529	91.3	26.3
Kansas	1,852,094	90.0	30.1	899,868	89.4	29.9	952,226	90.6	30.4
Kentucky	2,922,350	83.1	21.1	1,404,490	82.0	20.7	1,517,860	84.1	21.4
Louisiana	2,972,737	82.5	21.1	1,421,896	80.7	20.3	1,550,841	84.1	21.9
Maine	942,537	90.9	28.4	451,592	89.5	27.4	490,945	92.3	29.3
Maryland	3,915,657	88.9	36.9	1,843,965	88.1	36.8	2,071,692	89.6	36.9
Massachusetts	4,502,048	89.2	39.1	2,130,741	88.9	39.8	2,371,307	89.5	38.6
Michigan	6,588,324	88.8	25.6	3,165,493	88.0	25.8	3,422,831	89.5	25.4
Minnesota	3,560,801	92.0	32.4	1,743,571	91.6	32.0	1,817,230	92.5	32.7
Mississippi	1,912,708	81.1	19.8	903,797	78.9	18.8	1,008,911	83.2	20.8
Missouri	4,008,554	87.6	26.1	1,925,630	87.1	26.4	2,082,924	88.0	25.8
Montana	676,793	92.3	28.2	335,111	91.8	28.2	341,682	92.7	28.2
Nebraska	1,196,112	91.0	27.9	582,471	90.3	27.6	613,641	91.7	28.2
Nevada	1,810,960	84.0	22.5	907,541	83.7	22.1	903,419	84.3	22.8
New Hampshire	914,207	91.4	33.4	444,745	90.3	32.9	469,462	92.3	33.9
New Jersey	6,004,613	88.1	35.3	2,852,446	87.9	36.5	3,152,167	88.3	34.2
New Mexico	1,354,186	83.2	25.6	658,821	82.1	25.6	695,365	84.2	25.5
New York	13,197,704	85.0	32.9	6,234,632	84.8	32.6	6,963,072	85.3	33.2
North Carolina	6,399,357	84.7	26.9	3,034,749	83.0	26.5	3,364,608	86.3	27.3
North Dakota	448,145	90.7	26.3	223,043	90.3	24.5	225,102	91.2	28.1
Ohio	7,749,236	88.3	24.7	3,704,377	87.9	25.3	4,044,859	88.7	24.1
Oklahoma	2,469,196	86.3	23.8	1,198,119	85.2	23.7	1,271,077	87.4	23.9
Oregon	2,644,754	89.4	29.3	1,286,421	88.5	29.7	1,358,333	90.1	29.0
Pennsylvania	8,714,235	88.6	27.0	4,157,544	88.3	27.3	4,556,691	88.9	26.7
Rhode Island	712,266	84.8	31.1	336,083	84.1	32.4	376,183	85.4	30.0
South Carolina	3,110,532	84.2	24.1	1,474,305	82.9	24.1	1,636,227	85.3	24.0
South Dakota	537,588	90.6	26.3	264,798	89.6	25.1	272,790	91.5	27.6
Tennessee	4,294,392	84.2	23.6	2,046,502	83.1	23.4	2,247,890	85.3	23.8
Texas	16,074,391	81.1	26.4	7,818,598	80.6	26.9	8,255,793	81.6	26.0
Utah	1,608,668	90.3	29.7	798,958	89.5	32.5	809,710	91.2	27.0
Vermont	434,652	91.8	35.4	210,305	89.9	32.3	224,347	93.5	38.3
Virginia	5,418,844	87.8	35.1	2,605,062	87.0	35.8	2,813,782	88.6	34.5
Washington	4,583,426	90.1	31.9	2,254,973	89.8	33.0	2,328,453	90.5	30.8
West Virginia	1,294,198	84.2	18.5	625,433	82.9	18.4	668,765	85.4	18.6
Wisconsin	3,831,373	90.4	26.5	1,872,855	89.5	25.8	1,958,518	91.2	27.1
Wyoming	375,608	92.0	24.7	188,831	91.3	23.8	186,777	92.6	25.7

[1]Race categories do not include persons of Hispanic origin

Table B-2. Educational Attainment of the Population 25 Years Old and Over, by Sex, Race, Hispanic Origin, and Region or State, 2011—*Continued*

Region/State	White alone, not Hispanic or Latino, age 25 years and over			Black or African American alone, age 25 years and over[1]		
	Population	High school graduate or higher (percent)	Bachelor's degree or higher (percent)	Population	High school graduate or higher (percent)	Bachelor's degree or higher (percent)
UNITED STATES	140,303,930	91.1	31.9	23,898,097	82.5	18.4
Northeast Region	27,202,780	91.7	35.7	4,054,376	82.2	19.6
Midwest Region	36,276,134	91.3	28.5	4,130,052	82.7	16.5
South Region	49,218,569	89.0	30.0	13,584,375	81.6	18.1
West Region	27,606,447	93.8	35.8	2,129,294	88.0	21.8
Alabama	2,244,173	85.1	25.1	775,682	78.6	14.3
Alaska	318,668	95.4	31.3	14,143	88.4	19.8
Arizona	2,743,025	93.5	32.7	152,992	89.1	21.5
Arkansas	1,524,464	86.4	21.7	271,892	80.0	15.2
California	11,151,511	93.9	39.4	1,439,189	88.1	22.2
Colorado	2,536,575	95.4	42.4	129,110	87.8	24.4
Connecticut	1,839,505	92.9	40.2	220,634	82.2	18.3
Delaware	427,326	89.8	31.6	118,294	84.8	17.6
District of Columbia	162,595	99.8	90.5	206,037	81.2	22.8
Florida	8,269,724	91.0	29.0	1,822,207	79.0	16.0
Georgia	3,783,800	88.0	31.1	1,814,424	83.3	20.8
Hawaii	242,709	96.4	39.1	15,765	96.4	25.5
Idaho	872,822	92.0	26.8	4,100	85.3	35.8
Illinois	5,793,573	92.6	34.9	1,135,459	83.3	18.8
Indiana	3,608,453	89.0	23.8	345,403	83.5	15.0
Iowa	1,859,074	92.3	26.2	45,845	82.4	16.5
Kansas	1,527,375	93.1	32.2	97,209	87.8	19.5
Kentucky	2,591,207	83.4	21.2	213,929	82.9	15.8
Louisiana	1,903,090	86.9	24.9	863,194	74.8	12.7
Maine	904,964	91.4	28.6	6,066	74.3	10.9
Maryland	2,266,724	92.5	41.2	1,100,533	87.9	26.7
Massachusetts	3,589,266	92.5	41.5	269,257	82.5	23.2
Michigan	5,264,527	90.7	26.6	841,688	82.6	16.2
Minnesota	3,102,215	94.4	33.6	148,520	79.1	17.5
Mississippi	1,189,140	85.9	23.1	647,174	74.8	14.2
Missouri	3,356,945	88.8	27.0	418,675	82.6	16.5
Montana	614,682	92.8	29.4	...	...	...
Nebraska	1,032,339	94.7	29.7	45,717	84.9	19.9
Nevada	1,088,730	92.3	26.7	138,013	86.3	16.6
New Hampshire	857,046	91.9	33.0	8,936	82.6	38.0
New Jersey	3,739,920	92.4	38.7	749,100	85.2	21.2
New Mexico	636,971	94.2	38.8	26,378	88.3	22.8
New York	8,076,808	91.8	38.5	1,930,941	80.9	20.5
North Carolina	4,451,196	88.8	30.7	1,292,433	81.3	17.0
North Dakota	412,482	91.6	27.0	2,739	86.3	33.6
Ohio	6,501,405	89.6	25.4	850,445	82.4	14.6
Oklahoma	1,827,005	89.1	25.9	162,449	86.3	18.3
Oregon	2,194,015	92.7	30.9	40,027	86.3	20.5
Pennsylvania	7,204,475	90.6	28.3	831,734	82.7	14.8
Rhode Island	575,747	88.4	34.0	35,048	77.6	17.5
South Carolina	2,116,225	87.9	28.5	799,213	77.9	13.2
South Dakota	476,892	92.7	27.7	4,757	75.0	14.5
Tennessee	3,391,408	85.6	24.8	644,891	81.8	17.6
Texas	8,166,413	92.5	34.8	1,824,697	86.2	20.3
Utah	1,339,574	94.3	32.1	14,445	84.4	15.9
Vermont	415,049	92.1	35.4	2,660	92.6	37.7
Virginia	3,680,813	90.6	38.3	990,339	82.5	20.2
Washington	3,533,559	93.9	33.7	149,213	87.1	20.7
West Virginia	1,223,266	84.3	18.4	36,987	84.3	15.7
Wisconsin	3,340,854	92.5	27.7	193,595	79.1	11.9
Wyoming	333,606	93.4	25.8	3,609	79.6	11.5

[1]Race categories do not include persons of Hispanic origin
... = Not available.

Table B-2. Educational Attainment of the Population 25 Years Old and Over, by Sex, Race, Hispanic Origin, and Region or State, 2011—*Continued*

Region/State	Asian alone, age 25 years and over[1]			Hispanic or Latino, age 25 years and over[2]		
	Population	High school graduate or higher (percent)	Bachelor's degree or higher (percent)	Population	High school graduate or higher (percent)	Bachelor's degree or higher (percent)
UNITED STATES	10,241,927	85.1	50.0	28,157,700	63.2	13.2
Northeast Region	2,125,614	82.2	53.3	4,127,611	67.5	15.5
Midwest Region	1,104,708	86.2	56.8	2,389,912	63.1	12.9
South Region	2,205,621	85.8	52.1	10,399,760	64.3	15.0
West Region	4,805,984	85.9	46.1	11,240,417	60.6	10.8
Alabama	35,803	83.3	49.3	97,062	58.8	11.6
Alaska	25,736	77.4	21.5	19,906	86.6	21.3
Arizona	123,310	83.5	47.9	997,289	65.0	10.1
Arkansas	21,558	82.6	41.6	90,058	51.9	9.1
California	3,493,200	85.8	48.7	7,755,013	58.6	10.5
Colorado	93,835	86.8	44.1	562,149	68.0	13.0
Connecticut	90,763	87.7	61.2	269,781	68.6	14.5
Delaware	20,187	85.8	64.9	38,262	61.6	14.3
District of Columbia	16,440	84.8	74.2	37,487	64.2	36.6
Florida	322,108	84.7	45.3	2,753,603	75.0	20.4
Georgia	212,914	85.6	49.6	444,963	55.1	13.3
Hawaii	409,738	87.4	30.8	64,315	87.6	18.2
Idaho	14,209	82.9	47.9	83,199	55.3	8.3
Illinois	408,636	88.9	60.6	1,099,018	61.6	12.0
Indiana	61,147	85.8	57.8	190,872	61.2	11.5
Iowa	33,014	83.3	48.9	68,047	54.9	11.0
Kansas	41,475	82.8	46.6	143,351	61.1	12.1
Kentucky	29,388	84.6	57.4	62,497	65.8	13.7
Louisiana	47,610	72.2	33.7	120,103	73.2	17.0
Maine	8,492	78.3	37.6	9,074	81.5	25.9
Maryland	225,890	89.7	60.9	273,880	61.5	20.7
Massachusetts	236,601	82.5	55.2	344,449	65.6	17.0
Michigan	150,940	87.2	61.5	219,456	68.7	15.3
Minnesota	119,248	78.5	43.2	121,419	63.8	13.8
Mississippi	16,660	71.4	31.1	45,010	51.7	11.1
Missouri	62,800	87.6	57.4	104,549	66.4	18.1
Montana	3,287	94.9	48.8	12,876	83.7	16.8
Nebraska	20,983	72.1	39.2	80,203	53.8	9.1
Nevada	140,789	87.4	34.4	385,743	57.4	8.5
New Hampshire	18,298	85.7	58.0	19,281	78.4	24.4
New Jersey	510,945	91.3	67.2	945,616	71.4	15.3
New Mexico	16,948	89.3	48.3	557,351	71.1	12.9
New York	1,003,271	77.5	45.9	2,082,942	65.8	15.9
North Carolina	135,688	82.5	51.3	401,821	53.1	11.1
North Dakota	4,550	91.6	52.0	6,466	69.6	7.9
Ohio	127,785	89.0	65.1	180,866	72.5	17.0
Oklahoma	43,920	83.2	42.3	164,773	57.8	11.0
Oregon	100,212	86.7	45.6	224,090	59.2	11.1
Pennsylvania	232,117	81.1	51.4	382,138	67.6	13.1
Rhode Island	20,319	73.4	42.4	69,426	60.8	12.6
South Carolina	42,455	81.2	42.0	122,450	62.5	13.1
South Dakota	4,262	86.0	57.0	10,310	60.0	12.7
Tennessee	60,807	84.4	48.8	148,396	63.2	12.1
Texas	659,432	85.7	52.5	5,231,791	60.4	12.0
Utah	36,227	85.5	44.1	176,906	62.9	12.4
Vermont	4,808	75.6	39.8	4,904	92.6	45.6
Virginia	307,816	90.9	59.3	357,349	71.1	23.5
Washington	345,182	84.7	43.5	376,040	60.9	12.6
West Virginia	6,945	84.0	62.7	10,255	79.2	25.9
Wisconsin	69,868	82.0	46.5	165,355	64.4	12.4
Wyoming	3,311	98.5	57.8	25,540	77.1	13.5

[1]Race categories do not include persons of Hispanic origin
[2]May be of any race

Table B-3. Population, School, and Student Characteristics, by State, Selected Years

FIPS code	State	Population, 2011		Median income for a family of four, 2011 (dollars)	Children under 18 years old in poverty, 2011 (percent)	Poverty and health insurance, 2011		
		Total	5 to 17 years old (percent)			Total children under 19 years old (thousands)	Low-income children under 19 years old (percent)	Low-income children with no health insurance (percent)
		1	2	3	4	5	6	7
00	**UNITED STATES**	311,591,917	17.3	74,563	21.9	78,013	44.0	6.4
01	Alabama	4,802,740	17.1	63,388	22.6	1,218	41.7	4.9
02	Alaska	722,718	18.5	86,581	16.7	200	36.6	5.3
04	Arizona	6,482,505	18.1	59,786	25.2	1,698	50.9	9.5
05	Arkansas	2,937,979	17.5	55,444	25.9	718	52.4	5.4
06	California	37,691,912	17.9	74,122	24.3	9,869	48.1	7.8
08	Colorado	5,116,796	17.4	85,027	16.1	1,312	33.1	7.7
09	Connecticut	3,580,709	16.9	100,451	14.5	868	30.3	2.3
10	Delaware	907,135	16.4	83,424	22.6	220	43.0	4.4
11	District of Columbia	617,996	11.2	76,230	34.9	114	50.1	2.9
12	Florida	19,057,542	15.3	63,937	22.3	4,171	45.5	8.6
13	Georgia	9,815,210	18.4	65,851	24.8	2,651	47.6	6.8
15	Hawaii	1,374,810	15.7	82,973	16.3	330	41.8	2.6
16	Idaho	1,584,985	19.5	61,058	23.0	453	53.5	9.4
17	Illinois	12,869,257	17.6	79,138	20.1	3,281	43.8	3.9
18	Indiana	6,516,922	17.9	69,328	24.0	1,687	44.4	3.5
19	Iowa	3,062,309	17.1	76,777	14.0	763	35.4	3.3
20	Kansas	2,871,238	18.1	74,853	22.1	746	44.6	5.9
21	Kentucky	4,369,356	16.9	66,409	24.0	1,072	51.8	3.9
22	Louisiana	4,574,836	17.5	68,921	31.0	1,171	48.9	7.7
23	Maine	1,328,188	15.2	78,310	18.2	286	40.7	3.4
24	Maryland	5,828,289	16.8	106,707	11.5	1,441	28.7	5.5
25	Massachusetts	6,587,536	15.8	101,523	13.6	1,521	33.1	1.7
26	Michigan	9,876,187	17.3	72,366	23.2	2,414	40.8	3.4
27	Minnesota	5,344,861	17.3	87,319	13.8	1,338	32.2	5.2
28	Mississippi	2,978,512	18.2	58,047	24.6	813	49.3	7.0
29	Missouri	6,010,688	17.1	70,687	23.9	1,477	44.8	8.6
30	Montana	998,199	16.1	65,695	25.7	227	52.0	8.1
31	Nebraska	1,842,641	17.8	75,495	15.0	481	32.5	3.4
32	Nevada	2,723,322	17.5	65,212	20.6	687	48.1	15.0
33	New Hampshire	1,318,194	16.1	97,441	9.4	297	22.1	2.8
34	New Jersey	8,821,155	17.1	101,682	17.9	2,147	33.1	6.1
35	New Mexico	2,082,224	17.9	60,368	31.8	533	53.0	7.9
36	New York	19,465,197	16.0	81,522	23.2	4,494	42.9	4.1
37	North Carolina	9,656,401	17.2	63,665	24.1	2,454	47.2	6.1
38	North Dakota	683,932	15.5	84,896	12.2	162	25.9	3.2
39	Ohio	11,544,951	17.2	72,764	21.7	2,795	45.5	5.3
40	Oklahoma	3,791,508	17.7	63,069	21.4	985	46.4	4.2
41	Oregon	3,871,859	16.2	65,950	21.7	908	43.8	3.6
42	Pennsylvania	12,742,886	16.0	80,414	17.5	2,857	38.1	5.4
44	Rhode Island	1,051,302	15.6	82,086	18.2	239	39.6	4.4
45	South Carolina	4,679,230	16.6	60,143	27.3	1,115	52.4	9.4
46	South Dakota	824,082	17.4	72,460	22.8	209	43.0	4.5
47	Tennessee	6,403,353	17.0	63,719	24.0	1,559	45.9	4.7
48	Texas	25,674,681	19.5	65,932	25.8	7,317	51.6	10.9
49	Utah	2,817,222	21.9	65,240	14.5	934	40.9	6.8
50	Vermont	626,431	15.1	84,011	18.0	131	35.2	1.3
51	Virginia	8,096,604	16.6	89,803	14.6	1,978	30.7	3.9
53	Washington	6,830,038	16.7	81,582	19.2	1,725	45.7	6.4
54	West Virginia	1,855,364	15.2	65,403	25.2	399	50.9	5.8
55	Wisconsin	5,711,767	17.0	79,648	21.4	1,400	39.9	3.4
56	Wyoming	568,158	16.8	77,137	12.7	144	36.4	4.6

Table B-3. Population, School, and Student Characteristics, by State, Selected Years—*Continued*

FIPS code	State	Educational attainment, 2011			Public schools and school districts, 2010–2011					
							Type of school			
		Population 25 years old and over	High school graduate or more (percent)	Bachelor's degree or more (percent)	Number of school districts	Total schools	Regular schools	Special education schools	Vocational schools	Alternative schools
		8	9	10	11	12	13	14	15	16
00	**UNITED STATES**	206,471,670	85.9	28.5	17,911	98,817	88,929	2,206	1,485	6,197
01	Alabama	3,193,078	82.7	22.3	171	1,600	1,372	41	72	115
02	Alaska	456,862	91.8	26.4	54	509	441	3	3	62
04	Arizona	4,211,223	85.7	26.6	649	2,265	1,950	21	217	77
05	Arkansas	1,943,427	83.8	20.3	289	1,110	1,069	4	26	11
06	California	24,443,872	81.1	30.3	1,189	10,124	8,526	147	86	1,365
08	Colorado	3,387,310	90.2	36.7	259	1,796	1,694	8	6	88
09	Connecticut	2,444,403	89.1	36.2	200	1,157	1,046	54	16	41
10	Delaware	611,120	87.0	28.8	41	214	183	19	6	6
11	District of Columbia	428,261	87.2	52.5	54	228	204	10	4	10
12	Florida	13,267,581	85.9	25.8	75	4,131	3,468	182	53	428
13	Georgia	6,308,961	84.3	27.6	212	2,449	2,265	66	1	117
15	Hawaii	939,512	90.6	29.1	1	289	285	3	0	1
16	Idaho	998,460	88.6	25.2	146	748	637	15	11	85
17	Illinois	8,521,694	87.2	31.0	1,078	4,361	4,012	146	53	150
18	Indiana	4,255,459	87.3	23.0	391	1,936	1,862	34	28	12
19	Iowa	2,027,201	90.6	25.8	368	1,436	1,390	6	0	40
20	Kansas	1,852,094	90.0	30.1	324	1,378	1,365	10	1	2
21	Kentucky	2,922,350	83.1	21.1	194	1,554	1,249	10	126	169
22	Louisiana	2,972,737	82.5	21.1	126	1,471	1,265	34	6	166
23	Maine	942,537	90.9	28.4	252	631	601	3	27	0
24	Maryland	3,915,657	88.9	36.9	25	1,449	1,322	40	24	63
25	Massachusetts	4,502,048	89.2	39.1	394	1,829	1,748	23	39	19
26	Michigan	6,588,324	88.8	25.6	864	3,877	3,257	279	62	279
27	Minnesota	3,560,801	92.0	32.4	555	2,392	1,641	277	11	463
28	Mississippi	1,912,708	81.1	19.8	164	1,083	925	3	90	65
29	Missouri	4,008,554	87.6	26.1	567	2,410	2,172	65	66	107
30	Montana	676,793	92.3	28.2	503	827	821	2	0	4
31	Nebraska	1,196,112	91.0	27.9	290	1,096	1,067	24	0	5
32	Nevada	1,810,960	84.0	22.5	18	645	598	12	1	34
33	New Hampshire	914,207	91.4	33.4	277	480	480	0	0	0
34	New Jersey	6,004,613	88.1	35.3	690	2,607	2,355	71	56	125
35	New Mexico	1,354,186	83.2	25.6	128	862	815	7	1	39
36	New York	13,197,704	85.0	32.9	919	4,757	4,576	124	29	28
37	North Carolina	6,399,357	84.7	26.9	235	2,567	2,449	30	1	87
38	North Dakota	448,145	90.7	26.3	227	516	468	33	10	5
39	Ohio	7,749,236	88.3	24.7	1,063	3,758	3,621	59	72	6
40	Oklahoma	2,469,196	86.3	23.8	578	1,785	1,775	4	0	6
41	Oregon	2,644,754	89.4	29.3	221	1,296	1,252	2	0	42
42	Pennsylvania	8,714,235	88.6	27.0	773	3,233	3,125	9	86	13
44	Rhode Island	712,266	84.8	31.1	54	317	297	3	11	6
45	South Carolina	3,110,532	84.2	24.1	104	1,214	1,144	10	39	21
46	South Dakota	537,588	90.6	26.3	172	710	658	11	4	37
47	Tennessee	4,294,392	84.2	23.6	140	1,784	1,730	15	17	22
48	Texas	16,074,391	81.1	26.4	1,275	8,732	7,635	26	0	1,071
49	Utah	1,608,668	90.3	29.7	124	1,016	875	87	6	48
50	Vermont	434,652	91.8	35.4	360	320	304	0	15	1
51	Virginia	5,418,844	87.8	35.1	225	2,175	1,882	55	49	189
53	Washington	4,583,426	90.1	31.9	314	2,338	1,898	104	16	320
54	West Virginia	1,294,198	84.2	18.5	57	757	691	3	31	32
55	Wisconsin	3,831,373	90.4	26.5	461	2,238	2,131	9	7	91
56	Wyoming	375,608	92.0	24.7	61	360	333	3	0	24

Table B-3. Population, School, and Student Characteristics, by State, Selected Years—*Continued*

FIPS code	State	Public schools and students, 2010–2011									
		Total schools	Charter schools	Magnet schools	Title I status			Number of students	Primary schools (percent)	Middle schools (percent)	High schools (percent)
					Title I eligible schools	Title I schoolwide schools	Students in Title I schoolwide schools (percent)				
		17	18	19	20	21	22	23	24	25	26
00	**UNITED STATES**	98,817	5,274	2,722	66,646	48,990	50.5	49,484,181	40.0	29.8	29.9
01	Alabama	1,600	...	30	924	897	58.6	755,552	39.4	31.3	29.4
02	Alaska	509	27	19	366	335	50.7	132,104	40.0	29.7	30.4
04	Arizona	2,265	519	...	1,764	1,224	60.9	1,071,751	39.6	30.5	29.8
05	Arkansas	1,110	40	38	810	710	57.1	482,114	41.4	30.2	28.2
06	California	10,124	908	282	6,028	4,878	50.2	6,289,578	38.4	29.8	31.7
08	Colorado	1,796	168	24	658	447	21.8	843,316	42.1	29.1	28.7
09	Connecticut	1,157	18	54	532	186	15.7	560,546	39.1	30.0	30.9
10	Delaware	214	19	3	171	155	70.9	129,403	39.7	30.1	30.2
11	District of Columbia	228	97	7	184	177	83.1	71,284	49.7	25.2	24.7
12	Florida	4,131	458	414	2,935	2,649	71.6	2,643,347	39.9	30.4	29.7
13	Georgia	2,449	67	78	1,566	1,399	54.3	1,677,067	41.4	30.3	28.3
15	Hawaii	289	31	...	205	183	57.9	179,601	41.4	29.5	28.9
16	Idaho	748	40	2	547	519	69.3	275,859	39.7	30.7	29.6
17	Illinois	4,361	50	104	3,272	1,575	39.1	2,091,654	40.1	29.5	30.4
18	Indiana	1,936	60	26	1,460	1,095	55.8	1,047,232	39.2	30.5	30.3
19	Iowa	1,436	7	...	978	519	35.9	495,775	41.8	28.5	29.8
20	Kansas	1,378	25	36	1,148	804	55.9	483,701	41.1	29.1	28.8
21	Kentucky	1,554	...	41	1,090	1,040	78.7	673,128	41.7	29.6	28.6
22	Louisiana	1,471	78	72	1,245	1,207	81.5	696,558	44.0	29.6	26.5
23	Maine	631	...	1	526	400	57.9	189,077	38.2	30.0	31.8
24	Maryland	1,449	44	90	412	312	16.4	852,211	40.2	28.9	31.0
25	Massachusetts	1,829	63	...	1,017	521	26.8	955,563	39.6	30.0	30.3
26	Michigan	3,877	300	464	2,836	1,672	45.2	1,587,067	37.7	29.7	32.1
27	Minnesota	2,392	176	73	854	284	11.6	838,037	38.8	29.2	32.0
28	Mississippi	1,083	0	20	877	837	90.5	490,526	40.0	30.6	27.8
29	Missouri	2,410	53	30	1,165	622	24.2	918,710	40.3	29.7	30.0
30	Montana	827	...	...	692	430	48.7	141,693	39.4	30.1	30.5
31	Nebraska	1,096	...	...	524	298	24.8	298,500	42.1	28.4	29.6
32	Nevada	645	34	24	374	328	51.4	437,149	39.3	30.8	29.7
33	New Hampshire	480	14	...	415	119	18.4	194,711	36.8	30.8	32.4
34	New Jersey	2,607	76	...	1,488	416	18.3	1,402,548	38.6	28.5	28.9
35	New Mexico	862	81	...	750	728	84.0	338,122	41.2	29.6	29.2
36	New York	4,757	170	...	4,418	2,535	53.2	2,734,955	38.3	29.5	31.1
37	North Carolina	2,567	99	106	2,044	1,909	67.8	1,490,605	40.3	30.6	29.0
38	North Dakota	516	...	...	303	93	16.8	96,323	39.0	29.6	31.4
39	Ohio	3,758	339	...	2,913	2,116	51.9	1,754,191	39.2	30.6	30.3
40	Oklahoma	1,785	18	...	1,191	1,049	56.0	659,911	44.4	28.7	26.7
41	Oregon	1,296	108	...	600	446	30.9	570,720	38.5	30.3	31.2
42	Pennsylvania	3,233	145	52	2,373	1,491	42.1	1,793,284	37.2	30.2	32.5
44	Rhode Island	317	16	...	232	129	41.7	143,793	38.6	29.3	32.0
45	South Carolina	1,214	44	104	1,000	942	75.1	725,838	41.0	30.0	29.0
46	South Dakota	710	...	...	601	350	36.3	126,128	40.3	29.4	30.3
47	Tennessee	1,784	29	32	1,480	1,398	74.6	987,422	41.2	29.8	28.9
48	Texas	8,732	561	219	6,802	6,508	74.8	4,935,715	43.4	29.3	27.3
49	Utah	1,016	78	24	288	224	18.0	585,552	42.4	30.2	27.4
50	Vermont	320	...	...	243	183	52.5	96,858	43.2	27.0	29.8
51	Virginia	2,175	4	131	741	442	15.9	1,251,440	40.0	29.7	30.4
53	Washington	2,338	...	...	1,518	1,205	50.4	1,043,788	38.3	30.1	31.6
54	West Virginia	757	...	...	366	366	37.9	282,879	41.9	29.3	28.8
55	Wisconsin	2,238	207	4	1,535	547	22.6	872,286	40.5	28.1	31.4
56	Wyoming	360	3	...	185	91	23.3	89,009	40.3	30.2	29.5

... = Not available.

Table B-3. Population, School, and Student Characteristics, by State, Selected Years—*Continued*

FIPS code	State	Characteristics of public school students, 2010–2011 (percent)								
		Students in charter schools (percent)	Students eligible for free or reduced-price lunch	Students with IEP[1]	English language learners	Race and hispanic origin of students: Non-Hispanic White	Non-Hispanic Black	Hispanic or Latino[2]	Asian and Pacific Islander	American Indian, Alaska Native
		27	28	29	30	31	32	33	34	35
00	**UNITED STATES**	3.6	47.9	13.0	6.0	52.4	16.0	23.1	5.0	1.1
01	Alabama	0.0	54.9	11.0	2.4	58.3	34.6	4.7	1.3	0.8
02	Alaska	4.4	38.4	13.7	11.3	52.2	3.6	5.9	8.0	23.0
04	Arizona	11.6	45.1	11.7	7.1	42.9	5.6	42.2	3.0	5.2
05	Arkansas	2.1	60.5	13.5	6.5	64.8	21.5	9.8	1.9	0.7
06	California	5.9	53.7	10.7	...	26.6	6.7	51.4	11.7	0.7
08	Colorado	8.9	39.9	10.0	11.8	56.8	4.8	31.6	3.1	0.9
09	Connecticut	0.9	34.0	12.2	5.4	62.0	13.2	18.6	4.3	0.4
10	Delaware	7.4	47.7	14.4	5.3	50.1	32.3	12.4	3.4	0.5
11	District of Columbia	37.8	73.0	16.8	7.4	7.1	77.8	12.6	1.4	0.1
12	Florida	5.9	56.0	13.9	8.7	43.0	23.0	28.0	2.6	0.4
13	Georgia	2.5	57.4	10.6	4.9	44.4	37.0	11.9	3.4	0.2
15	Hawaii	4.6	46.8	11.0	10.6	14.5	2.5	4.5	69.6	0.6
16	Idaho	5.6	45.0	9.9	5.6	78.5	1.0	15.9	1.7	1.4
17	Illinois	2.1	44.3	14.5	8.3	51.3	18.4	22.9	4.2	0.3
18	Indiana	2.1	46.6	15.8	4.7	73.1	12.1	8.4	1.7	0.3
19	Iowa	0.1	38.9	13.8	4.4	81.5	5.1	8.5	2.1	0.5
20	Kansas	1.0	47.7	13.8	8.1	68.0	7.4	16.4	2.6	1.3
21	Kentucky	0.0	56.6	15.2	2.4	81.9	10.8	3.9	1.4	0.1
22	Louisiana	4.2	66.2	11.9	1.7	48.5	45.4	2.6	1.5	0.9
23	Maine	0.0	43.0	15.6	2.5	92.5	1.8	1.5	1.1	0.7
24	Maryland	1.7	40.1	12.1	5.3	42.9	35.8	11.5	5.9	0.4
25	Massachusetts	3.0	34.2	17.5	5.8	68.0	8.2	15.4	5.6	0.2
26	Michigan	7.2	46.3	13.7	3.6	69.8	19.0	5.8	2.7	0.8
27	Minnesota	4.4	36.5	14.7	5.8	73.8	9.2	7.2	6.1	1.9
28	Mississippi	0.0	70.6	13.0	1.1	46.0	49.9	2.5	0.9	0.2
29	Missouri	2.2	44.3	13.8	2.4	74.7	17.1	4.5	2.0	0.5
30	Montana	0.0	40.8	11.8	2.3	81.7	1.0	3.5	1.1	11.1
31	Nebraska	0.0	42.6	14.8	6.7	70.8	6.7	16.0	2.1	1.5
32	Nevada	3.2	50.3	11.0	19.1	38.7	9.9	38.7	7.1	1.3
33	New Hampshire	0.5	25.2	15.3	2.0	89.8	2.0	3.7	2.8	0.3
34	New Jersey	1.8	32.8	16.1	3.8	51.5	16.7	22.1	8.9	0.1
35	New Mexico	4.6	67.6	13.8	15.5	26.0	2.1	59.4	1.3	10.2
36	New York	2.0	48.1	16.5	7.6	49.2	19.0	22.4	8.3	0.5
37	North Carolina	2.8	50.3	12.4	6.9	53.2	26.5	12.6	2.5	1.5
38	North Dakota	0.0	31.7	13.9	3.0	83.7	2.4	0.1	1.3	9.1
39	Ohio	5.6	42.6	14.8	2.1	74.2	16.3	3.4	1.7	0.1
40	Oklahoma	1.0	60.5	14.7	6.3	54.6	10.2	12.3	2.1	17.7
41	Oregon	3.7	50.6	14.3	10.5	66.3	2.6	20.5	4.5	1.9
42	Pennsylvania	5.1	38.9	16.5	2.6	71.2	15.7	8.3	3.2	0.2
44	Rhode Island	2.8	42.9	17.6	5.3	65.2	8.0	20.8	3.0	0.7
45	South Carolina	2.3	54.5	13.8	5.0	53.4	36.2	6.4	1.4	0.3
46	South Dakota	0.0	37.1	14.3	3.5	79.8	2.5	3.5	1.5	11.6
47	Tennessee	0.7	55.0	12.1	3.0	67.3	23.9	6.1	1.7	0.2
48	Texas	3.3	50.1	9.0	15.0	31.2	12.9	50.3	3.6	0.5
49	Utah	6.8	38.2	12.0	7.3	78.0	1.4	15.1	3.4	1.3
50	Vermont	0.0	36.8	14.8	1.6	92.8	1.8	1.3	1.6	0.3
51	Virginia	0.0	36.7	13.0	7.0	54.1	24.1	11.4	6.0	0.3
53	Washington	0.0	40.1	12.3	8.7	62.8	4.8	18.0	8.1	1.7
54	West Virginia	0.0	51.5	15.9	0.6	92.0	5.2	1.1	0.7	0.1
55	Wisconsin	4.2	39.3	14.3	5.0	74.4	9.9	9.3	3.6	1.3
56	Wyoming	0.3	37.1	17.1	2.9	81.0	1.1	12.3	0.9	3.3

[1]IEP = Individual Education Program. See notes and definitions for more information.
[2]May be of any race.
... = Not available.
0.0 = Rounds to zero.

Table B-3. Population, School, and Student Characteristics, by State, Selected Years—*Continued*

FIPS code	State	Public school outcomes: Event dropout rates: Enrollment grades 9–12, 2008–2009	Event Dropouts, grades 9–12 2008-2009 (percent)	Number of graduates and averaged freshman graduation rates: Estimated first-time 9th graders, 2005–2006	High school graduates (regular diplomas), 2008–2009	Averaged freshman graduation rates, 2008–2009	Private schools: Number of schools, 2009–2010	Enrollment, 2009–2010	High school graduates, 2008–2009
		36	37	38	39	40	41	42	43
00	**UNITED STATES**	14,954,795	4.1	4,024,345	3,039,015	75.5	33,366	4,700,119	308,813
01	Alabama	217,590	1.5	60,169	42,082	69.9	578	78,351	5,277
02	Alaska	41,399	7.0	11,034	8,008	72.6	123	4,426	189
04	Arizona	316,122	8.3	85,984	62,374	72.5	360	44,559	2,755
05	Arkansas	137,358	4.1	37,912	28,057	74.0	224	23,889	1,330
06	California	2,013,687	5.0	524,273	372,310	71.0	3,644	539,726	35,256
08	Colorado	238,139	6.1	61,162	47,459	77.6	488	48,545	2,838
09	Connecticut	174,980	3.1	46,374	34,968	75.4	405	64,384	6,233
10	Delaware	38,619	5.1	10,634	7,839	73.7	135	22,758	1,847
11	District of Columbia	17,898	7.0	5,635	3,517	62.4	86	15,667	1,339
12	Florida	781,725	2.6	222,578	153,461	68.9	1,962	287,689	18,255
13	Georgia	470,108	4.2	129,797	88,003	67.8	823	130,263	8,322
15	Hawaii	53,535	4.9	15,292	11,508	75.3	135	33,536	2,659
16	Idaho	81,497	1.6	20,850	16,807	80.6	197	14,507	543
17	Illinois	640,512	11.5	169,361	131,670	77.7	1,733	243,405	15,107
18	Indiana	316,126	1.7	84,649	63,663	75.2	910	104,169	5,232
19	Iowa	151,993	3.1	39,571	33,926	85.7	230	39,694	2,249
20	Kansas	140,032	2.1	37,847	30,368	80.2	263	40,252	2,166
21	Kentucky	197,825	2.9	53,909	41,851	77.6	358	61,384	3,937
22	Louisiana	180,660	6.8	52,954	35,622	67.3	458	131,866	8,136
23	Maine	63,611	3.6	16,166	14,093	79.9	163	16,933	2,362
24	Maryland	267,388	3.0	72,759	58,304	80.1	795	126,415	9,228
25	Massachusetts	292,593	2.9	78,386	65,258	83.3	830	119,112	10,630
26	Michigan	541,231	3.8	149,640	112,742	75.3	1,069	134,125	8,519
27	Minnesota	275,864	1.9	68,329	59,729	87.4	524	78,389	4,241
28	Mississippi	139,135	4.2	39,536	24,505	62.0	316	47,361	3,358
29	Missouri	282,460	4.3	75,801	62,969	83.1	693	105,548	7,043
30	Montana	45,030	5.0	12,291	10,077	82.0	153	7,987	372
31	Nebraska	89,678	2.4	23,522	19,501	82.9	221	34,819	2,004
32	Nevada	125,117	5.1	35,336	19,904	56.3	157	20,108	824
33	New Hampshire	64,939	1.7	17,510	14,757	84.3	285	20,807	2,463
34	New Jersey	425,555	1.6	111,411	95,085	85.3	1,385	188,307	14,348
35	New Mexico	98,830	4.9	27,675	17,931	64.8	187	20,548	1,387
36	New York	875,179	4.2	245,982	180,917	73.5	2,016	430,605	31,245
37	North Carolina	429,719	5.3	115,487	86,712	75.1	667	98,582	5,727
38	North Dakota	30,773	2.5	8,270	7,232	87.4	47	6,732	**
39	Ohio	577,669	4.2	153,528	122,203	79.6	1,759	222,218	13,303
40	Oklahoma	177,132	2.5	48,143	37,219	77.3	252	28,159	1,531
41	Oregon	179,972	3.4	45,944	35,138	76.5	497	47,123	3,139
42	Pennsylvania	580,304	2.3	162,243	130,658	80.5	2,276	265,399	18,663
44	Rhode Island	47,359	4.4	13,313	10,028	75.3	163	21,871	1,818
45	South Carolina	210,511	3.4	59,274	39,114	66.0	398	49,203	3,073
46	South Dakota	38,952	1.8	9,943	8,123	81.7	75	9,394	518
47	Tennessee	287,401	3.2	77,980	60,368	77.4	525	87,754	6,219
48	Texas	1,305,637	3.2	350,368	264,275	75.4	1,852	245,568	12,903
49	Utah	155,309	3.3	38,366	30,463	79.4	184	18,038	1,270
50	Vermont	30,631	2.6	8,048	7,209	89.6	119	9,542	1,167
51	Virginia	380,787	2.5	101,607	79,651	78.4	915	103,076	6,511
53	Washington	332,224	4.7	85,123	62,764	73.7	656	77,024	4,448
54	West Virginia	83,252	4.1	22,983	17,690	77.0	137	12,321	739
55	Wisconsin	284,222	2.3	72,089	65,410	90.7	894	115,985	5,607
56	Wyoming	26,526	1.1	7,307	5,493	75.2	39	1,998	**

** = Reporting standards not met.

Table B-3. Population, School, and Student Characteristics, by State, Selected Years—*Continued*

FIPS code	State	Public and private school characteristics							
		Public schools					Private schools, 2009–2010		
		Student enrollment		Teachers					
		Total students, 2010–2011	Percent change from 2000–2001 to 2010–2011	Total teachers, 2010–2011	Percent change from 2000–2001 to 2010–2011	Student-teacher ratio, 2010–2011	Total enrollment	Total teachers	Student-teacher ratio
		44	45	46	47	48	49	50	51
00	**UNITED STATES**	49,484,181	4.8	3,099,095	5.4	16.0	4,700,119	437,414	10.7
01	Alabama	755,552	2.1	49,363	2.4	15.3	78,351	8,775	8.9
02	Alaska	132,104	-0.9	8,171	3.7	16.2	4,426	529	8.4
04	Arizona	1,071,751	22.1	50,031	12.6	21.4	44,559	3,896	11.4
05	Arkansas	482,114	7.1	34,273	7.3	14.1	23,889	2,392	10.0
06	California	6,289,578	2.4	260,806	-12.5	24.1	539,726	45,741	11.8
08	Colorado	843,316	16.4	48,543	15.6	17.4	48,545	4,793	10.1
09	Connecticut	560,546	-0.3	42,951	4.6	13.1	64,384	7,431	8.7
10	Delaware	129,403	12.8	8,933	19.6	14.5	22,758	2,064	11.0
11	District of Columbia	71,284	3.4	5,925	19.7	12.0	15,667	1,873	8.4
12	Florida	2,643,347	8.6	175,609	33.0	15.1	287,689	26,591	10.8
13	Georgia	1,677,067	16.1	112,460	23.5	14.9	130,263	13,246	9.8
15	Hawaii	179,601	-2.6	11,396	4.3	15.8	33,536	3,044	11.0
16	Idaho	275,859	12.5	15,673	14.3	17.6	14,507	1,364	10.6
17	Illinois	2,091,654	2.1	132,983	4.2	15.7	243,405	20,289	12.0
18	Indiana	1,047,232	5.9	58,121	-1.9	18.0	104,169	8,420	12.4
19	Iowa	495,775	0.1	34,642	0.0	14.3	39,694	3,218	12.3
20	Kansas	483,701	2.8	34,644	5.8	14.0	40,252	3,367	12.0
21	Kentucky	673,128	1.1	42,042	6.2	16.0	61,384	5,282	11.6
22	Louisiana	696,558	-6.3	48,655	-2.5	14.3	131,866	10,061	13.1
23	Maine	189,077	-8.7	15,384	-7.1	12.3	16,933	1,885	9.0
24	Maryland	852,211	-0.1	58,428	11.4	14.6	126,415	13,230	9.6
25	Massachusetts	955,563	-2.0	68,754	2.0	13.9	119,112	14,917	8.0
26	Michigan	1,587,067	-7.8	88,615	-8.7	17.9	134,125	10,888	12.3
27	Minnesota	838,037	-1.9	52,672	-1.5	15.9	78,389	6,424	12.2
28	Mississippi	490,526	-1.5	32,255	4.0	15.2	47,361	4,507	10.5
29	Missouri	918,710	0.7	66,735	3.1	13.8	105,548	9,028	11.7
30	Montana	141,693	-8.5	10,361	-0.5	13.7	7,987	880	9.1
31	Nebraska	298,500	4.3	22,345	6.5	13.4	34,819	2,658	13.1
32	Nevada	437,149	28.3	21,839	19.4	20.0	20,108	1,601	12.6
33	New Hampshire	194,711	-6.6	15,365	7.1	12.7	20,807	2,611	8.0
34	New Jersey	1,402,548	6.8	110,202	11.2	12.7	188,307	19,018	9.9
35	New Mexico	338,122	5.6	22,437	6.6	15.1	20,548	2,041	10.1
36	New York	2,734,955	-5.1	211,606	2.2	12.9	430,605	41,959	10.3
37	North Carolina	1,490,605	15.2	98,357	17.5	15.2	98,582	9,962	9.9
38	North Dakota	96,323	-11.8	8,417	3.4	11.4	6,732	585	11.5
39	Ohio	1,754,191	-4.4	109,282	-7.7	16.1	222,218	16,787	13.2
40	Oklahoma	659,911	5.9	41,278	-0.1	16.0	28,159	2,936	9.6
41	Oregon	570,720	4.5	28,109	0.1	20.3	47,123	4,372	10.8
42	Pennsylvania	1,793,284	-1.2	129,911	11.1	13.8	265,399	23,699	11.2
44	Rhode Island	143,793	-8.6	11,212	5.3	12.8	21,871	2,296	9.5
45	South Carolina	725,838	7.1	45,210	-0.4	16.1	49,203	5,058	9.7
46	South Dakota	126,128	-1.9	9,512	1.2	13.3	9,394	849	11.1
47	Tennessee	987,422	8.6	66,558	16.4	14.8	87,754	8,579	10.2
48	Texas	4,935,715	21.6	334,997	21.9	14.7	245,568	25,659	9.6
49	Utah	585,552	21.6	25,677	16.7	22.8	18,038	1,849	9.8
50	Vermont	96,858	-5.1	8,382	-0.4	11.6	9,542	1,317	7.2
51	Virginia	1,251,440	9.3	70,947	-18.4	17.6	103,076	11,357	9.1
53	Washington	1,043,788	3.9	53,934	5.6	19.4	77,024	6,957	11.1
54	West Virginia	282,879	-1.2	20,338	-2.8	13.9	12,321	1,279	9.6
55	Wisconsin	872,286	-0.8	57,625	-4.2	15.1	115,985	9,580	12.1
56	Wyoming	89,009	-1.0	7,127	5.1	12.5	1,998	270	7.4

Table B-3. Population, School, and Student Characteristics, by State, Selected Years—*Continued*

FIPS code	State	Average public school teacher salary, 2011–2012[3] (dollars)	Staff employed by public elementary and secondary school systems and percent of total staff, 2010–2011								
			Total staff	Teachers		Instructional aides		Instructional coordinators and supervisors		Guidance counselors/ directors	
				Number	Percent	Number	Percent	Number	Percent	Number	Percent
		52	53	54	55	56	57	58	59	60	61
00	**UNITED STATES**	56,643	6,195,207	3,099,095	50.0	731,705	11.8	69,236	1.1	105,079	1.7
01	Alabama	48,003	95,144	49,363	51.9	6,550	6.9	1,013	1.1	1,802	1.9
02	Alaska	62,425	18,102	8,171	45.1	2,537	14.0	192	1.1	327	1.8
04	Arizona	48,691	96,622	50,031	51.8	14,386	14.9	98	0.1	1,245	1.3
05	Arkansas	46,959	72,185	34,273	47.5	8,065	11.2	847	1.2	1,527	2.1
06	California	69,496	530,337	260,806	49.2	63,972	12.1	3,391	0.6	6,191	1.2
08	Colorado	50,407	101,426	48,543	47.9	14,680	14.5	2,434	2.4	2,100	2.1
09	Connecticut	70,821	93,088	42,951	46.1	15,637	16.8	3,496	3.8	1,081	1.2
10	Delaware	58,800	16,478	8,933	54.2	1,577	9.6	226	1.4	281	1.7
11	District of Columbia	68,720	11,381	5,925	52.1	1,635	14.4	377	3.3	260	2.3
12	Florida	46,232	333,183	175,609	52.7	30,031	9.0	696	0.2	5,859	1.8
13	Georgia	52,938	227,188	112,460	49.5	25,773	11.3	2,353	1.0	3,557	1.6
15	Hawaii	54,268	21,704	11,396	52.5	2,407	11.1	573	2.6	632	2.9
16	Idaho	48,551	27,783	15,673	56.4	2,991	10.8	229	0.8	564	2.0
17	Illinois	66,053	215,764	132,983	61.6	30,219	14.0	491	0.2	3,193	1.5
18	Indiana	51,629	138,802	58,121	41.9	23,589	17.0	2,219	1.6	1,688	1.2
19	Iowa	51,037	69,615	34,642	49.8	10,531	15.1	305	0.4	1,157	1.7
20	Kansas	46,718	67,751	34,644	51.1	9,163	13.5	970	1.4	1,061	1.6
21	Kentucky	49,730	99,225	42,042	42.4	14,325	14.4	1,000	1.0	1,515	1.5
22	Louisiana	50,179	100,881	48,655	48.2	11,448	11.3	2,079	2.1	1,919	1.9
23	Maine	48,283	32,549	15,384	47.3	5,744	17.6	250	0.8	575	1.8
24	Maryland	63,634	115,367	58,428	50.6	11,360	9.8	1,792	1.6	2,389	2.1
25	Massachusetts	72,000	122,057	68,754	56.3	23,484	19.2	408	0.3	2,168	1.8
26	Michigan	64,879	193,487	88,615	45.8	21,379	11.0	3,347	1.7	2,249	1.2
27	Minnesota	54,959	108,993	52,672	48.3	16,759	15.4	2,035	1.9	1,072	1.0
28	Mississippi	41,646	67,866	32,255	47.5	8,195	12.1	649	1.0	1,096	1.6
29	Missouri	46,406	128,289	66,735	52.0	13,314	10.4	1,081	0.8	2,613	2.0
30	Montana	48,546	19,249	10,361	53.8	2,397	12.5	165	0.9	457	2.4
31	Nebraska	48,718	45,509	22,345	49.1	6,506	14.3	999	2.2	811	1.8
32	Nevada	54,559	33,400	21,839	65.4	4,152	12.4	1,380	4.1	880	2.6
33	New Hampshire	54,177	32,955	15,365	46.6	7,356	22.3	264	0.8	824	2.5
34	New Jersey	68,207	202,634	110,202	54.4	26,227	12.9	3,138	1.5	3,904	1.9
35	New Mexico	48,011	46,519	22,437	48.2	6,009	12.9	659	1.4	815	1.8
36	New York	74,449	413,971	211,606	51.1	37,849	9.1	1,979	0.5	6,979	1.7
37	North Carolina	46,605	193,039	98,357	51.0	26,173	13.6	1,043	0.5	3,976	2.1
38	North Dakota	46,058	16,239	8,417	51.8	2,071	12.8	179	1.1	309	1.9
39	Ohio	57,528	241,212	109,282	45.3	19,333	8.0	1,676	0.7	3,655	1.5
40	Oklahoma	44,156	82,262	41,278	50.2	8,362	10.2	329	0.4	1,610	2.0
41	Oregon	57,348	63,603	28,109	44.2	9,837	15.5	409	0.6	1,032	1.6
42	Pennsylvania	62,215	266,796	129,911	48.7	34,314	12.9	1,671	0.6	4,763	1.8
44	Rhode Island	62,186	18,632	11,212	60.2	2,224	11.9	84	0.5	384	2.1
45	South Carolina	48,176	65,508	45,210	69.0	8,475	12.9	453	0.7	1,816	2.8
46	South Dakota	39,850	19,545	9,512	48.7	2,454	12.6	132	0.7	345	1.8
47	Tennessee	46,613	128,197	66,558	51.9	16,243	12.7	836	0.7	2,889	2.3
48	Texas	49,017	665,419	334,997	50.3	63,338	9.5	3,456	0.5	11,212	1.7
49	Utah	48,159	52,341	25,677	49.1	8,214	15.7	1,699	3.2	807	1.5
50	Vermont	51,306	18,485	8,382	45.3	4,284	23.2	235	1.3	413	2.2
51	Virginia	49,560	201,047	70,947	35.3	19,388	9.6	13,419	6.7	3,977	2.0
53	Washington	54,193	103,783	53,934	52.0	10,422	10.0	358	0.3	2,045	2.0
54	West Virginia	45,320	39,270	20,338	51.8	3,632	9.2	370	0.9	738	1.9
55	Wisconsin	55,492	103,901	57,625	55.5	10,292	9.9	1,326	1.3	1,874	1.8
56	Wyoming	57,222	16,424	7,127	43.4	2,402	14.6	424	2.6	444	2.7

[3]National Education Association. Highlights Table 2: Summary of Selected Estimates Data for 2011–2012. *Rankings & Estimates: Rankings of the States 2011 and Estimates of School Statistics, 2012*, page 67. Reprinted with permission of the National Education Association © 2012. All rights reserved. http://www.nea.org .

Table B-3. Population, School, and Student Characteristics, by State, Selected Years—*Continued*

FIPS code	State	Staff employed by public elementary and secondary school systems and percent of total staff, 2010–2011									
		Librarians		Student/other support staff		School administrators		School district administrators		School and school district administrative support staff	
		Number	Percent	Number	Percent	Number	Percent	Number	Percent	Number	Percent
		62	63	64	65	66	67	68	69	70	71
00	**UNITED STATES**	50,300	0.8	1,482,224	23.9	165,047	2.7	64,597	1.0	427,926	6.9
01	Alabama	1,413	1.5	26,655	28.0	2,606	2.7	803	0.8	4,939	5.2
02	Alaska	163	0.9	3,334	18.4	683	3.8	709	3.9	1,987	11.0
04	Arizona	529	0.5	22,006	22.8	2,471	2.6	425	0.4	5,431	5.6
05	Arkansas	1,088	1.5	18,269	25.3	1,767	2.4	668	0.9	5,681	7.9
06	California	757	0.1	123,619	23.3	15,267	2.9	3,579	0.7	52,755	9.9
08	Colorado	773	0.8	19,805	19.5	2,777	2.7	1,174	1.2	9,140	9.0
09	Connecticut	781	0.8	20,154	21.7	2,127	2.3	1,800	1.9	5,060	5.4
10	Delaware	134	0.8	3,734	22.7	413	2.5	366	2.2	813	4.9
11	District of Columbia	111	1.0	1,501	13.2	491	4.3	246	2.2	836	7.3
12	Florida	2,589	0.8	77,207	23.2	7,957	2.4	1,920	0.6	31,315	9.4
13	Georgia	2,247	1.0	60,792	26.8	6,157	2.7	2,300	1.0	11,549	5.1
15	Hawaii	208	1.0	3,952	18.2	571	2.6	218	1.0	1,747	8.0
16	Idaho	98	0.4	5,916	21.3	701	2.5	133	0.5	1,478	5.3
17	Illinois	1,960	0.9	32,539	15.1	7,362	3.4	2,828	1.3	4,190	1.9
18	Indiana	646	0.5	40,615	29.3	2,903	2.1	1,096	0.8	7,925	5.7
19	Iowa	513	0.7	15,276	21.9	1,740	2.5	1,237	1.8	4,211	6.0
20	Kansas	797	1.2	15,373	22.7	1,807	2.7	477	0.7	3,459	5.1
21	Kentucky	1,122	1.1	27,154	27.4	3,147	3.2	922	0.9	7,999	8.1
22	Louisiana	1,157	1.1	26,030	25.8	2,880	2.9	380	0.4	6,332	6.3
23	Maine	222	0.7	7,066	21.7	876	2.7	418	1.3	2,015	6.2
24	Maryland	1,245	1.1	25,095	21.8	3,635	3.2	3,328	2.9	8,095	7.0
25	Massachusetts	727	0.6	11,306	9.3	4,382	3.6	2,496	2.0	8,332	6.8
26	Michigan	746	0.4	56,584	29.2	4,751	2.5	3,132	1.6	12,683	6.6
27	Minnesota	709	0.7	25,339	23.2	2,103	1.9	2,072	1.9	6,232	5.7
28	Mississippi	872	1.3	17,546	25.9	1,912	2.8	989	1.5	4,353	6.4
29	Missouri	1,477	1.2	30,099	23.5	3,136	2.4	1,395	1.1	8,439	6.6
30	Montana	369	1.9	4,266	22.2	534	2.8	175	0.9	525	2.7
31	Nebraska	556	1.2	10,030	22.0	1,029	2.3	614	1.3	2,619	5.8
32	Nevada	376	1.1	1,455	4.4	993	3.0	30	0.1	2,295	6.9
33	New Hampshire	330	1.0	6,281	19.1	506	1.5	742	2.3	1,287	3.9
34	New Jersey	1,585	0.8	38,195	18.8	4,651	2.3	1,394	0.7	13,339	6.6
35	New Mexico	272	0.6	10,359	22.3	1,309	2.8	897	1.9	3,761	8.1
36	New York	2,775	0.7	111,280	26.9	9,282	2.2	2,921	0.7	29,300	7.1
37	North Carolina	2,290	1.2	42,034	21.8	5,101	2.6	1,565	0.8	12,500	6.5
38	North Dakota	193	1.2	3,389	20.9	447	2.8	474	2.9	760	4.7
39	Ohio	1,217	0.5	73,111	30.3	5,053	2.1	2,110	0.9	25,775	10.7
40	Oklahoma	1,072	1.3	20,318	24.7	2,147	2.6	593	0.7	6,555	8.0
41	Oregon	306	0.5	14,900	23.4	1,584	2.5	446	0.7	6,980	11.0
42	Pennsylvania	2,136	0.8	67,768	25.4	5,531	2.1	2,708	1.0	17,993	6.7
44	Rhode Island	298	1.6	2,720	14.6	452	2.4	85	0.5	1,173	6.3
45	South Carolina	1,085	1.7	3,636	5.6	2,554	3.9	704	1.1	1,574	2.4
46	South Dakota	137	0.7	4,862	24.9	430	2.2	764	3.9	909	4.7
47	Tennessee	1,933	1.5	30,648	23.9	3,360	2.6	174	0.1	5,556	4.3
48	Texas	5,097	0.8	171,399	25.8	22,360	3.4	6,563	1.0	46,997	7.1
49	Utah	279	0.5	11,007	21.0	1,300	2.5	367	0.7	2,991	5.7
50	Vermont	212	1.1	3,219	17.4	488	2.6	135	0.7	1,117	6.0
51	Virginia	1,978	1.0	73,489	36.6	4,606	2.3	1,537	0.8	11,705	5.8
53	Washington	1,134	1.1	24,409	23.5	2,800	2.7	2,416	2.3	6,266	6.0
54	West Virginia	352	0.9	10,375	26.4	1,105	2.8	771	2.0	1,589	4.0
55	Wisconsin	1,074	1.0	21,983	21.2	2,447	2.4	973	0.9	6,306	6.1
56	Wyoming	161	1.0	4,126	25.1	354	2.2	330	2.0	1,056	6.4

Table B-3. Population, School, and Student Characteristics, by State, Selected Years—*Continued*

FIPS code	State	Highest degree earned and years of experience for teachers in public elementary and secondary schools, 2007–2008								
		Number of teachers (thousands)	Highest degree earned (percent)				Years of experience (percent distribution)			
			Bachelor's degree	Master's degree or higher	Education specialist	Doctorate	Under 3 years	3–9 years	10–20 years	More than 20 years
		72	73	74	75	76	77	78	79	80
00	**UNITED STATES**	3,404,519	47.4	44.5	6.4	0.9	13.4	33.6	29.3	23.7
01	Alabama	53,241	44.3	46.9	6.9	0.6	14.4	31.3	36.1	18.2
02	Alaska	8,117	56.3	36.3	5.4	0.7	12.0	27.5	39.7	20.7
04	Arizona	66,517	49.1	41.6	7.1	0.7	21.0	34.6	26.1	18.4
05	Arkansas	35,807	58.6	34.1	5.3	0.2	10.7	25.7	32.1	31.6
06	California	310,004	52.7	34.3	10.2	1.9	13.5	35.9	30.3	20.3
08	Colorado	50,091	42.9	48.4	6.9	1.4	17.2	37.9	28.1	16.8
09	Connecticut	50,128	19.2	64.3	15.0	0.9	12.2	29.7	31.1	27.1
10	Delaware	8,283	38.2	53.0	6.2	1.2	10.6	43.3	27.9	18.2
11	District of Columbia	4,394	41.3	45.3	7.1	5.9	20.0	29.9	24.6	25.5
12	Florida	177,203	60.9	34.1	3.1	1.1	14.8	35.0	27.4	22.8
13	Georgia	121,896	38.8	43.4	15.0	2.3	10.3	32.4	35.9	21.4
15	Hawaii	12,775	46.9	32.6	17.7	1.4	18.6	34.3	28.6	18.6
16	Idaho	16,214	66.1	29.7	2.7	0.8	12.5	31.0	33.6	22.8
17	Illinois	145,010	45.5	49.8	4.0	0.3	13.4	35.6	29.3	21.6
18	Indiana	68,446	37.4	57.0	4.9	0.4	9.2	32.3	29.1	29.4
19	Iowa	39,635	59.8	37.9	1.4	...	11.4	30.5	29.9	28.2
20	Kansas	37,671	53.0	41.8	4.7	0.2	13.0	30.2	27.2	29.6
21	Kentucky	44,438	20.9	57.5	18.9	0.7	10.2	35.5	30.1	24.2
22	Louisiana	48,117	71.9	23.5	3.7	0.4	12.7	33.3	27.6	26.3
23	Maine	17,802	54.4	37.9	5.1	0.6	12.3	27.0	31.5	29.1
24	Maryland	59,878	42.6	47.0	8.2	1.5	12.0	37.1	26.2	24.8
25	Massachusetts	80,402	30.6	62.0	5.6	0.7	11.1	39.9	27.2	21.8
26	Michigan	98,299	37.2	57.6	4.4	0.3	9.4	32.5	36.3	21.8
27	Minnesota	63,984	41.6	51.4	6.1	0.8	12.7	28.5	35.3	23.6
28	Mississippi	35,470	56.6	37.2	4.2	0.7	17.1	31.8	26.1	25.1
29	Missouri	73,254	47.2	47.5	3.9	0.6	13.3	34.2	31.6	20.8
30	Montana	12,701	62.8	33.4	3.5	...	11.0	26.9	28.8	33.3
31	Nebraska	23,176	53.1	44.2	2.0	...	11.4	24.2	30.2	34.2
32	Nevada	23,653	41.5	49.5	7.5	1.0	15.6	37.3	27.8	19.4
33	New Hampshire	17,437	49.4	45.4	4.5	...	13.3	31.7	29.1	26.0
34	New Jersey	124,538	55.8	36.5	6.3	1.4	12.3	40.8	22.8	24.1
35	New Mexico	22,691	53.0	39.5	5.4	1.5	13.3	35.6	29.6	21.5
36	New York	228,142	11.8	77.6	8.9	1.1	12.8	38.0	28.5	20.6
37	North Carolina	96,047	64.6	28.0	5.4	0.4	15.6	37.3	25.0	22.0
38	North Dakota	8,921	68.2	28.1	2.8	...	12.0	23.3	30.0	34.7
39	Ohio	134,252	31.9	62.3	3.7	0.7	12.1	29.9	31.6	26.3
40	Oklahoma	46,464	66.5	28.9	2.9	0.7	10.9	31.4	30.7	27.0
41	Oregon	31,699	37.0	52.3	9.0	1.2	18.0	31.5	29.5	21.0
42	Pennsylvania	136,852	45.3	45.2	8.0	...	12.5	33.6	26.7	27.2
44	Rhode Island	13,234	44.7	48.7	5.7	...	7.7	37.0	32.2	23.1
45	South Carolina	49,009	40.9	52.1	5.1	0.5	12.8	31.5	27.3	28.5
46	South Dakota	10,591	66.8	30.9	1.1	0.8	11.4	23.7	32.5	32.4
47	Tennessee	67,104	44.9	43.0	9.3	0.9	13.6	28.8	30.8	26.8
48	Texas	340,429	70.1	26.3	2.5	0.6	17.1	31.2	27.7	24.0
49	Utah	27,220	61.1	30.3	6.1	0.5	19.9	32.9	26.0	21.2
50	Vermont	10,237	42.6	50.0	5.9	0.5	11.7	30.5	30.5	27.3
51	Virginia	94,044	57.4	36.1	4.5	1.0	14.1	32.8	26.6	26.5
53	Washington	58,108	31.4	60.7	6.4	0.6	14.1	27.8	32.6	25.5
54	West Virginia	22,894	39.5	51.6	6.7	0.5	13.1	26.4	23.1	37.4
55	Wisconsin	70,060	44.8	49.3	5.5	0.3	9.8	32.4	31.4	26.4
56	Wyoming	7,939	56.0	37.6	5.3	0.6	10.3	27.3	32.5	29.9

... = Not available.

Table B-3. Population, School, and Student Characteristics, by State, Selected Years—*Continued*

FIPS code	State	National Assessment of Educational Progress: percent of public school students at or above the proficient level					ACT, 2012[4]		Preliminary SAT (PSAT) National Merit Scholarship Qualifying Test (NMSQT) scores, 2011–2012[5]			
		Math, 2011		Reading, 2011		Science, 2011	Average score	Percent of graduates taking ACT	Number of high school juniors taking the PSAT/ NMSQT	Percent of test takers achieving scores of 65 or above		
		Grade 4	Grade 8	Grade 4	Grade 8	Grade 8				Critical reading	Math	Writing skills
		81	82	83	84	85	86	87	88	89	90	91
00	**UNITED STATES**	39	34	32	32	31	21.1	52	1,557,056	6.4	9.9	4.7
01	Alabama	28	20	32	26	20	20.3	86	11,992	7.6	8.3	5.9
02	Alaska	37	35	25	31	33	21.2	35	2,285	8.7	8.3	3.9
04	Arizona	33	31	26	28	23	19.7	35	20,386	7.0	10.1	4.6
05	Arkansas	37	29	30	28	27	20.3	88	6,231	7.3	8.4	5.1
06	California	34	25	25	24	22	22.1	25	181,557	7.1	11.5	5.9
08	Colorado	47	43	38	40	42	20.6	100	20,044	8.5	11.2	4.5
09	Connecticut	45	38	42	44	35	23.8	27	34,605	6.7	9.9	4.9
10	Delaware	39	32	36	32	27	22.6	14	7,123	4.7	6.1	3.1
11	District of Columbia	21	17	19	16	7	19.7	32	4,197	10.2	10.8	8.7
12	Florida	37	28	35	29	28	19.8	70	66,958	6.5	8.9	4.8
13	Georgia	37	28	32	28	30	20.7	52	33,280	7.9	11.4	6.7
15	Hawaii	39	30	27	26	22	21.3	27	7,530	4.2	8.9	3.3
16	Idaho	39	37	32	34	38	21.6	67	6,553	7.2	7.3	4.0
17	Illinois	38	33	34	34	26	20.9	100	39,473	9.6	17.4	6.5
18	Indiana	44	34	32	32	33	22.3	32	35,058	5.5	8.5	3.9
19	Iowa	43	34	33	33	35	22.1	63	8,145	8.8	14.1	4.5
20	Kansas	48	40	36	36	35	21.9	81	10,081	9.3	12.4	5.8
21	Kentucky	39	30	36	36	33	19.8	100	11,001	7.7	10.4	5.8
22	Louisiana	26	22	23	22	23	20.3	100	12,453	5.8	7.7	5.7
23	Maine	45	39	32	38	37	23.4	9	10,661	4.9	6.7	2.8
24	Maryland	48	41	43	40	32	22.1	21	46,081	6.6	9.8	5.3
25	Massachusetts	58	51	51	46	44	24.1	23	52,603	8.3	12.4	5.7
26	Michigan	35	31	31	32	38	20.1	100	29,675	7.3	10.9	4.5
27	Minnesota	53	47	35	39	42	22.8	74	21,190	9.9	14.7	5.2
28	Mississippi	25	19	22	21	18	18.7	100	6,376	5.4	5.3	6.7
29	Missouri	42	32	34	36	36	21.6	75	13,953	9.9	13.2	7.2
30	Montana	45	46	35	41	42	22.0	61	4,235	6.0	8.0	2.8
31	Nebraska	39	33	36	34	37	22.0	78	6,370	6.5	9.8	4.2
32	Nevada	36	29	26	26	24	21.3	34	7,871	4.9	7.3	3.5
33	New Hampshire	58	44	43	40	42	23.8	19	8,910	8.4	11.7	5.1
34	New Jersey	51	47	43	45	34	23.4	20	70,180	6.5	11.7	5.6
35	New Mexico	30	24	20	22	23	19.9	75	9,228	4.4	4.6	2.4
36	New York	35	30	35	35	29	23.3	29	153,459	4.5	8.0	3.3
37	North Carolina	45	37	34	31	26	21.9	20	46,201	5.3	9.0	3.6
38	North Dakota	46	42	36	34	44	20.7	100	1,860	5.1	8.8	2.5
39	Ohio	45	39	34	37	38	21.8	71	49,231	7.1	10.6	4.9
40	Oklahoma	34	27	26	27	27	20.7	80	8,163	9.0	10.1	6.2
41	Oregon	36	42	30	33	36	21.4	38	15,602	8.8	9.5	4.4
42	Pennsylvania	48	38	41	38	33	22.4	18	74,749	5.8	8.7	4.4
44	Rhode Island	43	34	36	34	30	22.9	13	5,938	5.9	7.5	4.1
45	South Carolina	36	32	28	27	28	20.2	57	16,557	5.8	7.8	4.0
46	South Dakota	40	41	31	35	42	21.8	81	2,516	6.4	10.7	3.8
47	Tennessee	30	24	26	27	30	19.7	100	15,841	9.0	11.5	7.8
48	Texas	39	40	29	27	32	20.8	39	207,096	4.0	6.5	3.3
49	Utah	43	35	33	36	43	20.7	97	6,104	10.7	11.1	4.7
50	Vermont	49	46	41	45	43	23.0	28	4,321	8.3	10.0	4.6
51	Virginia	46	40	39	36	40	22.4	25	51,326	7.5	9.3	5.0
53	Washington	45	40	34	37	36	22.9	21	35,692	8.3	10.1	4.7
54	West Virginia	31	21	27	24	25	20.6	68	3,641	4.9	6.4	4.3
55	Wisconsin	47	41	33	35	40	22.1	71	18,606	7.3	12.3	4.3
56	Wyoming	43	37	35	38	38	20.3	100	1,284	6.6	9.5	2.3

[4]2012 *ACT Composite Averages by State.* © 2012 by ACT, Inc. All rights reserved. Reprinted with permission. http://www.act.org . This material may not be posted, published, or distributed without permission from ACT, Inc.
[5]"PSAT/NMSQT 2010–2011 College-Bound High School Juniors Summary Reports" Copyright © 2010–2011. The College Board, www.collegeboard.org . Reproduced with permission.

Table B-3. Population, School, and Student Characteristics, by State, Selected Years—*Continued*

FIPS code	State	SAT Reasoning Test average scores, 2012[6]				Revenues for public elementary and secondary schools by source, 2008–2009 school year			
		Critical reading	Math	Writing	Percent of graduates taking SAT	Total revenue (thousands of dollars)	Percent from: Federal government	Percent from: State government	Percent from: Local government
		92	93	94	95	96	97	98	99
00	**UNITED STATES**	496	514	488	...	593,061,181	9.6	46.7	43.7
01	Alabama	538	531	527	8	7,239,083	10.7	57.5	31.7
02	Alaska	512	507	485	54	2,262,964	13.9	64.5	21.6
04	Arizona	517	525	499	27	9,771,972	11.6	47.0	41.3
05	Arkansas	565	566	549	4	4,823,956	11.5	55.6	32.8
06	California	495	512	496	55	70,687,012	13.0	57.4	29.6
08	Colorado	575	581	562	17	8,353,849	6.9	43.9	49.1
09	Connecticut	506	512	510	88	9,871,755	4.5	38.9	56.6
10	Delaware	456	462	444	100	1,755,133	8.1	62.4	29.5
11	District of Columbia	466	460	456	83	1,651,014	10.6	0.0	89.4
12	Florida	492	492	476	66	26,322,090	10.2	34.4	55.4
13	Georgia	488	489	475	81	18,017,477	9.4	43.2	47.4
15	Hawaii	478	500	467	66	2,689,757	14.6	82.0	3.4
16	Idaho	547	541	525	20	2,243,784	10.2	67.3	22.5
17	Illinois	596	615	587	5	26,512,711	11.9	27.6	60.5
18	Indiana	493	501	476	69	12,569,782	11.4	39.5	49.1
19	Iowa	603	606	580	3	5,519,854	8.0	46.1	45.8
20	Kansas	584	594	561	6	5,757,927	7.9	57.7	34.4
21	Kentucky	579	575	566	6	6,641,128	11.0	57.3	31.7
22	Louisiana	542	536	529	9	8,099,981	15.6	46.2	38.2
23	Maine	470	472	452	93	2,575,516	9.5	43.8	46.7
24	Maryland	497	502	488	74	13,097,508	5.3	43.5	51.2
25	Massachusetts	513	530	508	89	15,102,480	8.5	40.0	51.6
26	Michigan	586	603	574	4	19,585,635	11.5	55.7	32.8
27	Minnesota	592	606	573	7	10,542,303	6.0	65.6	28.4
28	Mississippi	561	544	551	4	4,360,702	15.5	53.5	31.0
29	Missouri	589	592	575	5	10,042,753	8.3	34.1	57.6
30	Montana	536	536	511	28	1,595,197	12.5	48.5	39.0
31	Nebraska	576	585	562	5	3,455,794	8.1	35.1	56.8
32	Nevada	491	493	466	49	4,450,741	9.8	30.6	59.6
33	New Hampshire	521	525	510	75	2,717,115	5.4	36.9	57.7
34	New Jersey	495	517	499	78	25,283,290	4.1	41.6	54.3
35	New Mexico	550	546	529	13	3,820,116	14.9	70.0	15.1
36	New York	483	500	475	90	55,558,190	5.8	45.6	48.6
37	North Carolina	491	506	472	68	13,322,946	10.6	63.1	26.4
38	North Dakota	588	610	568	3	1,102,479	14.6	37.0	48.3
39	Ohio	543	552	525	19	22,956,215	7.3	47.6	45.1
40	Oklahoma	568	566	546	5	5,729,610	13.5	53.1	33.4
41	Oregon	521	523	498	57	6,145,206	10.9	50.7	38.4
42	Pennsylvania	491	501	480	74	25,632,072	7.3	38.7	54.0
44	Rhode Island	490	491	485	69	2,232,149	9.7	36.6	53.7
45	South Carolina	481	488	462	73	7,702,962	9.9	47.8	42.3
46	South Dakota	589	610	570	3	1,241,892	16.4	33.0	50.6
47	Tennessee	576	570	566	10	8,283,928	11.3	46.0	42.7
48	Texas	474	499	461	62	46,962,119	10.7	42.5	46.8
49	Utah	568	566	548	6	4,542,690	12.4	52.6	35.0
50	Vermont	519	523	505	69	1,571,006	6.5	85.7	7.8
51	Virginia	510	512	495	72	14,964,444	6.1	42.1	51.8
53	Washington	519	530	503	58	11,903,510	11.6	60.0	28.3
54	West Virginia	516	502	497	17	3,281,385	11.2	59.1	29.8
55	Wisconsin	594	605	577	4	10,832,105	12.0	44.4	43.6
56	Wyoming	567	579	549	5	1,675,896	6.6	56.4	37.0

[6]2011 College Bound Seniors: Total Group Profile Report. Copyright © 2011. The College Board, www.collegeboard.org . Reproduced with permission. All rights reserved.

... = Not available.

Table B-3. Population, School, and Student Characteristics, by State, Selected Years—*Continued*

FIPS code	State	Current expenditures for public elementary and secondary schools, by function, 2008–2009				
		Total current expenditures (thousands of dollars)	Percent for:			Per student expenditures (dollars)
			Instruction and instruction-related	Support services	Non-instruction	
		100	101	102	103	104
00	**UNITED STATES**	518,997,430	61.0	35.0	4.1	10,591
01	Alabama	6,683,843	58.3	35.0	6.7	9,042
02	Alaska	2,006,114	56.0	40.9	3.1	15,353
04	Arizona	8,625,276	60.4	34.5	5.1	7,929
05	Arkansas	4,240,839	58.1	36.2	5.7	8,854
06	California	60,080,929	59.8	36.2	4.0	9,503
08	Colorado	7,187,267	57.6	38.4	3.9	8,782
09	Connecticut	8,708,294	62.5	34.2	3.3	15,353
10	Delaware	1,518,786	60.9	35.1	4.0	12,109
11	District of Columbia	1,352,905	46.1	50.7	3.2	19,698
12	Florida	23,328,028	60.5	35.1	4.4	8,867
13	Georgia	15,976,945	62.7	32.1	5.3	9,649
15	Hawaii	2,225,437	62.2	33.1	4.7	12,399
16	Idaho	1,957,740	60.9	34.1	5.0	7,118
17	Illinois	23,495,271	58.8	38.1	3.1	11,592
18	Indiana	9,680,895	58.4	37.4	4.2	9,254
19	Iowa	4,731,463	61.2	34.2	4.6	10,055
20	Kansas	4,805,310	60.4	35.0	4.6	10,201
21	Kentucky	5,886,890	59.2	34.7	6.1	9,038
22	Louisiana	7,276,651	58.0	36.6	5.4	10,625
23	Maine	2,350,447	60.2	36.2	3.6	12,183
24	Maryland	11,591,965	61.7	34.3	4.0	13,737
25	Massachusetts	13,942,586	65.1	32.3	2.6	14,540
26	Michigan	17,217,584	57.2	39.6	3.3	10,373
27	Minnesota	9,270,281	65.2	30.5	4.3	11,088
28	Mississippi	3,967,232	58.7	35.3	6.1	8,064
29	Missouri	8,827,224	60.1	35.4	4.5	9,891
30	Montana	1,436,062	60.1	35.6	4.3	10,189
31	Nebraska	3,053,575	64.9	28.3	6.8	10,846
32	Nevada	3,606,035	59.4	37.3	3.3	8,321
33	New Hampshire	2,490,623	64.2	33.0	2.7	12,583
34	New Jersey	23,589,224	59.1	37.8	3.2	17,076
35	New Mexico	3,186,252	57.7	38.1	4.2	9,648
36	New York	48,635,363	69.2	28.7	2.1	17,746
37	North Carolina	12,470,470	63.4	31.2	5.4	8,518
38	North Dakota	928,528	58.4	33.3	8.4	9,802
39	Ohio	19,397,511	57.0	39.7	3.3	10,902
40	Oklahoma	5,082,062	57.2	36.0	6.8	7,878
41	Oregon	5,529,831	58.2	38.3	3.5	9,611
42	Pennsylvania	21,831,816	60.5	35.6	3.9	12,299
44	Rhode Island	2,139,317	59.9	37.7	2.4	14,719
45	South Carolina	6,626,763	57.7	36.8	5.4	9,228
46	South Dakota	1,080,054	58.0	36.3	5.7	8,543
47	Tennessee	7,768,052	62.8	32.3	5.0	7,992
48	Texas	40,688,181	60.0	34.8	5.2	8,562
49	Utah	3,638,775	64.6	29.6	5.7	6,612
50	Vermont	1,413,329	62.4	34.8	2.8	15,096
51	Virginia	13,505,290	60.7	35.6	3.7	10,928
53	Washington	9,940,056	60.2	35.3	4.5	9,688
54	West Virginia	3,059,420	59.7	34.8	5.5	10,821
55	Wisconsin	9,696,228	61.2	35.3	3.5	11,183
56	Wyoming	1,268,407	58.8	38.1	3.1	14,628

Table B-3. Population, School, and Student Characteristics, by State, Selected Years—*Continued*

FIPS code	State	Enrollment in degree-granting institutions of higher education, fall 2010								
		Total	Attendance status		Level of enrollment			Control of institution		
			Full-time	Part-time	Undergraduate		Post-baccalaureate	Public	Private, not-for-profit	Private, for-profit
					Four-year	Two-year				
		105	106	107	108	109	110	111	112	113
00	**UNITED STATES**	21,016,126	13,082,267	7,933,859	10,397,797	7,680,875	2,937,454	15,142,809	3,854,920	2,018,397
01	Alabama	327,327	218,196	109,131	180,746	101,103	45,478	267,083	25,136	35,108
02	Alaska	33,653	14,527	19,126	29,943	836	2,874	32,303	732	618
04	Arizona	795,388	549,397	245,991	427,248	246,352	121,788	366,976	8,817	419,595
05	Arkansas	175,895	113,875	62,020	94,694	62,468	18,733	155,780	16,701	3,414
06	California	2,714,172	1,423,974	1,290,198	778,185	1,665,800	270,187	2,223,648	285,839	204,685
08	Colorado	372,025	229,656	142,369	196,002	117,432	58,591	269,407	32,938	69,680
09	Connecticut	199,384	128,028	71,356	104,166	59,125	36,093	127,194	66,750	5,440
10	Delaware	55,731	37,588	18,143	30,624	15,697	9,410	40,408	14,833	490
11	District of Columbia	91,992	61,827	30,165	50,330	0	41,662	5,840	78,215	7,937
12	Florida	1,125,469	651,966	473,503	826,192	168,044	131,233	790,027	162,285	173,157
13	Georgia	568,723	386,381	182,342	314,716	184,450	69,557	436,109	71,144	61,470
15	Hawaii	78,073	43,973	34,100	36,423	31,821	9,829	60,090	14,273	3,710
16	Idaho	85,201	60,964	24,237	61,397	15,601	8,203	64,204	18,185	2,812
17	Illinois	906,889	532,457	374,432	356,725	392,240	157,924	585,515	227,482	93,892
18	Indiana	459,423	315,300	144,123	287,660	116,303	55,460	337,705	88,928	32,790
19	Iowa	381,842	242,021	139,821	231,876	107,135	42,831	177,781	57,373	146,688
20	Kansas	214,859	130,224	84,635	99,290	89,046	26,523	185,623	25,212	4,024
21	Kentucky	291,102	182,748	108,354	144,358	112,554	34,190	229,725	37,608	23,769
22	Louisiana	263,638	180,516	83,122	143,713	86,619	33,306	224,811	27,667	11,160
23	Maine	72,985	46,068	26,917	44,105	20,073	8,807	51,482	19,578	1,925
24	Maryland	377,967	199,831	178,136	153,770	151,588	72,609	309,779	54,894	13,294
25	Massachusetts	508,302	351,451	156,851	269,337	108,453	130,512	224,493	276,163	7,646
26	Michigan	698,125	411,932	286,193	344,176	262,191	91,758	562,444	124,298	11,383
27	Minnesota	465,336	268,864	196,472	206,149	140,602	118,585	276,176	73,508	115,652
28	Mississippi	178,197	139,317	38,880	71,990	85,474	20,733	159,695	15,398	3,104
29	Missouri	444,695	274,654	170,041	242,972	123,962	77,761	256,119	153,824	34,752
30	Montana	53,312	39,550	13,762	37,242	11,234	4,836	48,261	5,051	0
31	Nebraska	144,682	93,757	50,925	70,527	50,893	23,262	107,980	32,940	3,762
32	Nevada	129,360	64,116	65,244	98,858	17,885	12,617	113,103	3,370	12,887
33	New Hampshire	75,594	54,119	21,475	47,161	15,286	13,147	44,072	26,626	4,896
34	New Jersey	444,091	282,639	161,452	197,377	182,682	64,032	358,256	75,979	9,856
35	New Mexico	162,652	85,887	76,765	57,802	90,274	14,576	150,856	1,120	10,676
36	New York	1,305,595	921,924	383,671	702,405	357,371	245,819	723,500	526,292	55,803
37	North Carolina	586,042	377,649	208,393	259,135	257,369	69,538	475,598	92,027	18,417
38	North Dakota	56,903	40,244	16,659	42,392	7,611	6,900	48,904	6,234	1,765
39	Ohio	744,947	504,119	240,828	409,442	240,936	94,569	547,551	146,386	51,010
40	Oklahoma	230,573	147,195	83,378	127,329	76,901	26,343	197,642	22,657	10,274
41	Oregon	250,331	155,396	94,935	107,258	113,190	29,883	208,002	32,811	9,518
42	Pennsylvania	803,593	577,562	226,031	463,754	199,583	140,256	432,889	299,011	71,693
44	Rhode Island	85,110	62,921	22,189	56,199	17,775	11,136	43,224	41,886	0
45	South Carolina	257,293	178,734	78,559	125,859	105,745	25,689	205,080	35,089	17,124
46	South Dakota	58,370	36,737	21,633	43,860	6,829	7,681	44,569	9,044	4,757
47	Tennessee	351,988	250,216	101,772	190,938	111,536	49,514	242,486	77,764	31,738
48	Texas	1,536,858	840,954	695,904	608,386	753,136	175,336	1,334,885	131,481	70,492
49	Utah	252,107	160,092	92,015	178,728	49,447	23,932	178,599	61,310	12,198
50	Vermont	45,572	34,285	11,287	31,383	7,225	6,964	27,524	17,433	615
51	Virginia	576,010	351,174	224,836	278,221	206,687	91,102	409,004	110,720	56,286
53	Washington	388,110	253,619	134,491	185,319	166,537	36,254	330,874	43,675	13,561
54	West Virginia	152,431	89,463	62,968	102,655	25,680	24,096	96,104	12,952	43,375
55	Wisconsin	383,986	246,051	137,935	222,669	118,834	42,483	301,212	65,281	17,493
56	Wyoming	38,298	22,224	16,074	10,206	25,260	2,832	36,292	0	2,006

Table B-3. Population, School, and Student Characteristics, by State, Selected Years—*Continued*

FIPS code	State	Race and ethnicity of students enrolled in institutions of higher education, fall 2010							Migration patterns of college freshmen, fall 2010	
		Total	Non-Hispanic White (percent)	Non-Hispanic Black (percent)	Hispanic or Latino[2] (percent)	Asian and Pacific Islander (percent)	American Indian, Alaska Native (percent)	Nonresident alien (percent)	Percent of enrolled freshmen who are from another state	Percent of state's freshmen enrolled in another state
		114	115	116	117	118	119	120	121	122
00	**UNITED STATES**	21,016,126	60.5	14.5	13.0	**6.1**	0.9	3.4	19.5	18.2
01	Alabama	327,327	61.6	31.1	2.3	1.6	0.8	1.9	24.9	9.6
02	Alaska	33,653	66.2	3.1	6.0	4.9	11.8	2.3	9.5	39.0
04	Arizona	795,388	58.2	15.6	16.5	3.3	2.7	2.3	22.3	10.6
05	Arkansas	175,895	70.7	19.2	3.5	1.6	1.0	2.5	20.5	8.9
06	California	2,714,172	37.6	7.8	31.2	16.9	0.7	3.4	7.2	10.4
08	Colorado	372,025	69.3	8.3	13.5	3.8	1.2	2.0	21.3	24.2
09	Connecticut	199,384	66.3	11.7	11.2	4.7	0.3	3.9	33.8	44.7
10	Delaware	55,731	64.2	21.8	5.1	3.7	0.3	3.7	28.7	41.8
11	District of Columbia	91,992	49.5	28.6	6.2	6.9	0.4	7.3	94.1	79.3
12	Florida	1,125,469	50.7	20.1	21.6	3.4	0.4	2.7	12.3	11.0
13	Georgia	568,723	52.1	35.4	4.0	4.0	0.3	2.5	14.3	15.4
15	Hawaii	78,073	21.6	2.5	7.8	41.4	0.4	6.3	20.5	32.5
16	Idaho	85,201	85.3	1.3	6.7	2.4	1.3	2.1	37.2	32.4
17	Illinois	906,889	60.6	15.7	13.1	5.7	0.3	3.3	15.4	28.9
18	Indiana	459,423	77.3	10.8	4.1	2.2	0.4	4.0	24.2	12.1
19	Iowa	381,842	73.7	12.2	6.1	2.8	0.7	3.1	31.5	13.2
20	Kansas	214,859	75.1	7.4	6.3	2.5	1.5	5.7	21.5	14.9
21	Kentucky	291,102	83.4	10.4	1.9	1.3	0.3	1.5	19.5	10.7
22	Louisiana	263,638	59.0	31.4	3.2	2.3	0.6	2.6	16.7	9.7
23	Maine	72,985	89.0	2.7	2.1	2.0	1.3	1.8	29.6	34.2
24	Maryland	377,967	52.0	29.8	5.7	6.6	0.4	4.0	21.0	35.4
25	Massachusetts	508,302	67.0	8.6	8.3	7.3	0.4	7.0	40.9	32.8
26	Michigan	698,125	73.0	14.8	3.2	3.3	0.7	3.6	10.7	10.7
27	Minnesota	465,336	72.9	13.0	3.6	4.2	0.9	3.0	20.5	27.8
28	Mississippi	178,197	54.9	40.3	1.4	1.1	0.4	1.4	18.3	7.2
29	Missouri	444,695	74.6	14.2	3.5	2.7	0.6	3.1	20.4	15.7
30	Montana	53,312	82.7	0.8	2.8	1.2	8.7	2.2	31.4	20.6
31	Nebraska	144,682	81.9	5.9	5.1	2.5	0.9	2.9	19.3	16.3
32	Nevada	129,360	54.6	8.5	19.6	11.1	1.1	2.0	11.4	24.5
33	New Hampshire	75,594	85.7	2.9	4.0	2.9	0.6	3.0	46.7	43.2
34	New Jersey	444,091	54.9	14.7	16.8	8.3	0.4	4.1	8.6	41.1
35	New Mexico	162,652	38.8	3.2	43.8	1.9	8.7	2.3	15.4	13.3
36	New York	1,305,595	56.5	14.0	13.4	8.5	0.4	6.3	21.2	19.3
37	North Carolina	586,042	62.8	25.9	4.2	2.5	1.2	2.5	19.7	10.6
38	North Dakota	56,903	82.8	2.3	1.5	1.2	5.9	5.6	47.4	25.1
39	Ohio	744,947	76.6	14.2	2.6	2.1	0.4	3.0	17.3	14.9
40	Oklahoma	230,573	65.9	10.2	4.6	2.8	9.8	3.8	22.1	9.8
41	Oregon	250,331	75.6	2.9	8.4	6.1	1.6	3.2	33.0	22.8
42	Pennsylvania	803,593	74.2	11.7	4.8	4.3	0.3	3.7	29.8	17.1
44	Rhode Island	85,110	73.5	6.7	8.9	4.8	0.5	4.8	62.3	36.0
45	South Carolina	257,293	63.8	29.0	2.6	1.6	0.4	1.5	24.8	10.1
46	South Dakota	58,370	82.8	2.1	1.9	1.0	8.7	2.1	32.4	23.4
47	Tennessee	351,988	70.5	21.2	2.7	2.0	0.4	1.8	17.7	15.2
48	Texas	1,536,858	45.1	13.6	30.7	5.3	0.5	3.6	6.2	11.6
49	Utah	252,107	82.9	2.3	6.8	3.2	1.1	2.7	29.0	8.4
50	Vermont	45,572	87.7	2.3	3.1	2.4	0.6	2.2	68.8	50.2
51	Virginia	576,010	61.5	22.5	5.6	5.8	0.4	2.6	22.5	18.9
53	Washington	388,110	69.3	4.7	7.9	9.4	1.6	3.6	18.2	23.9
54	West Virginia	152,431	81.4	9.1	4.0	1.6	0.5	1.9	35.6	10.9
55	Wisconsin	383,986	81.6	6.5	4.2	3.2	1.0	2.3	22.2	19.0
56	Wyoming	38,298	85.9	1.4	6.0	1.0	1.8	2.8	37.0	22.0

[2]May be of any race.

Table B-3. Population, School, and Student Characteristics, by State, Selected Years—*Continued*

FIPS code	State	Degrees conferred by institutions of higher education, 2009–2010								
		Total degrees	Associate's degrees				Bachelor's degrees			
			Total	Public	Private not-for-profit	Private for-profit	Total	Public	Private not-for-profit	Private for-profit
		123	124	125	126	127	128	129	130	131
00	**UNITED STATES**	3,351,049	849,452	640,113	46,673	162,666	1,650,014	1,049,057	503,164	97,793
01	Alabama	49,254	10,198	8,624	60	1,514	25,686	20,633	3,488	1,565
02	Alaska	3,527	1,182	994	9	179	1,619	1,498	91	30
04	Arizona	132,135	50,252	13,374	13	36,865	44,339	21,037	953	22,349
05	Arkansas	24,625	7,172	6,945	61	166	12,523	10,032	2,381	110
06	California	347,684	102,018	84,374	991	16,653	164,234	120,274	31,556	12,404
08	Colorado	58,357	14,552	6,268	342	7,942	28,546	20,826	3,883	3,837
09	Connecticut	35,479	5,523	4,346	837	340	19,483	10,135	9,197	151
10	Delaware	10,197	1,712	1,482	214	16	5,505	3,797	1,695	13
11	District of Columbia	22,053	447	109	143	195	8,927	431	8,025	471
12	Florida	201,948	79,644	63,305	2,795	13,544	83,471	54,979	21,528	6,964
13	Georgia	78,297	15,583	12,632	889	2,062	42,452	30,421	9,547	2,484
15	Hawaii	11,048	3,238	2,606	272	360	5,401	3,593	1,670	138
16	Idaho	14,942	3,490	1,943	1,252	295	9,466	5,263	4,070	133
17	Illinois	158,283	38,263	27,910	1,733	8,620	70,847	33,935	28,986	7,926
18	Indiana	75,337	16,727	10,288	1,898	4,541	41,687	26,858	14,026	803
19	Iowa	56,353	15,834	10,932	608	4,294	30,323	11,263	9,760	9,300
20	Kansas	34,369	8,424	7,617	491	316	17,835	14,005	3,796	34
21	Kentucky	41,663	11,707	8,059	553	3,095	20,389	15,535	4,241	613
22	Louisiana	35,764	5,849	4,429	394	1,026	20,893	17,939	2,592	362
23	Maine	11,983	2,718	2,085	204	429	7,088	4,280	2,808	0
24	Maryland	59,142	12,446	11,455	112	879	28,012	21,163	6,165	684
25	Massachusetts	104,240	12,396	9,831	1,590	975	52,223	16,251	35,593	379
26	Michigan	112,144	29,318	23,961	4,320	1,037	56,061	42,037	13,313	711
27	Minnesota	75,593	18,453	14,160	704	3,589	31,952	19,215	10,614	2,123
28	Mississippi	28,134	9,824	9,403	41	380	12,953	10,764	2,189	0
29	Missouri	79,526	15,802	9,953	2,380	3,469	39,670	19,683	17,596	2,391
30	Montana	8,426	1,745	1,618	127	0	5,232	4,670	562	0
31	Nebraska	23,212	4,860	4,071	244	545	12,596	7,483	5,027	86
32	Nevada	14,895	4,068	3,155	0	913	7,345	6,262	186	897
33	New Hampshire	16,246	2,933	1,869	378	686	9,396	5,116	3,856	424
34	New Jersey	72,450	19,268	18,562	186	520	36,025	25,869	9,520	636
35	New Mexico	16,609	5,234	4,805	0	429	7,774	6,639	167	968
36	New York	267,734	61,618	43,875	9,478	8,265	123,703	53,684	66,802	3,217
37	North Carolina	89,055	22,879	20,520	1,286	1,073	46,826	32,706	13,393	727
38	North Dakota	9,977	2,411	1,972	183	256	5,727	4,860	786	81
39	Ohio	118,432	29,332	19,843	2,571	6,918	61,085	39,196	20,927	962
40	Oklahoma	36,791	9,723	8,412	164	1,147	19,535	15,736	3,460	339
41	Oregon	36,630	9,129	8,156	41	932	18,873	13,614	4,686	573
42	Pennsylvania	157,716	27,517	15,365	3,172	8,980	87,162	43,911	41,347	1,904
44	Rhode Island	17,379	3,590	1,229	2,361	0	10,647	3,782	6,865	0
45	South Carolina	37,804	8,727	7,528	419	780	21,905	15,880	5,050	975
46	South Dakota	8,544	1,952	1,590	150	212	4,976	3,690	966	320
47	Tennessee	53,784	10,645	7,723	506	2,416	29,857	18,249	10,674	934
48	Texas	208,762	55,048	49,598	682	4,768	104,657	82,789	19,845	2,023
49	Utah	39,725	11,054	9,607	326	1,121	21,931	12,571	8,429	931
50	Vermont	9,779	1,266	939	211	116	5,888	3,251	2,588	49
51	Virginia	89,856	21,010	14,229	563	6,218	45,324	31,927	10,997	2,400
53	Washington	65,751	23,068	22,195	128	745	30,551	22,851	6,823	877
54	West Virginia	22,028	3,989	2,713	299	977	12,032	8,444	1,692	1,896
55	Wisconsin	58,685	12,752	11,064	292	1,396	34,110	24,766	8,753	591
56	Wyoming	5,220	2,862	2,390	0	472	1,791	1,783	0	8

... = Not available.

Table B-3. Population, School, and Student Characteristics, by State, Selected Years—*Continued*

FIPS code	State	Degrees conferred by institutions of higher education, 2009–2010					Average undergraduate tuition and fees, 2010–2011		
		Master's degrees				Doctor's degrees	Public 4-year institutions		Private 4-year institutions
		Total	Public	Private not-for-profit	Private for-profit		In-state tuition	Out-of-state tuition	
		132	133	134	135	136	137	138	139
00	**UNITED STATES**	693,025	322,243	299,911	70,871	158,558	7,136	19,622	22,771
01	Alabama	11,291	9,375	666	1,250	2,079	6,808	17,427	16,649
02	Alaska	681	620	61	0	45	5,578	16,179	21,070
04	Arizona	34,860	6,940	1,154	26,766	2,684	7,685	20,210	12,261
05	Arkansas	4,126	3,535	511	80	804	6,117	13,582	16,103
06	California	65,050	28,943	30,855	5,252	16,382	7,357	26,509	26,519
08	Colorado	13,054	5,981	4,153	2,920	2,205	6,670	24,255	19,116
09	Connecticut	8,639	3,027	5,534	78	1,834	8,854	24,981	32,581
10	Delaware	2,452	768	1,656	28	528	9,646	23,047	12,989
11	District of Columbia	9,285	62	8,818	405	3,394	7,000	14,000	32,191
12	Florida	29,726	15,689	11,141	2,896	9,107	3,720	16,327	19,242
13	Georgia	16,304	10,153	4,229	1,922	3,958	5,435	18,883	20,783
15	Hawaii	2,028	1,216	655	157	381	6,635	19,368	12,807
16	Idaho	1,680	1,455	191	34	306	5,325	15,653	6,866
17	Illinois	41,548	12,629	25,021	3,898	7,625	10,562	25,148	24,070
18	Indiana	13,673	8,321	5,203	149	3,250	7,614	23,365	24,032
19	Iowa	7,452	2,824	1,893	2,735	2,744	7,157	21,265	16,041
20	Kansas	6,722	4,713	2,008	1	1,388	6,471	16,334	19,128
21	Kentucky	7,976	5,527	2,249	200	1,591	7,561	16,853	17,867
22	Louisiana	6,641	4,526	1,934	181	2,381	4,702	14,047	25,531
23	Maine	1,829	931	898	0	348	8,876	22,058	26,092
24	Maryland	16,019	8,882	6,752	385	2,665	7,579	19,591	29,516
25	Massachusetts	32,136	5,539	26,512	85	7,485	9,444	21,778	34,315
26	Michigan	21,176	15,668	5,223	285	5,589	9,839	28,558	16,184
27	Minnesota	21,015	5,220	5,049	10,746	4,173	9,285	13,945	23,838
28	Mississippi	4,203	3,077	1,126	0	1,154	5,301	13,500	14,098
29	Missouri	19,403	5,899	13,255	249	4,651	7,120	16,103	18,286
30	Montana	1,140	1,070	70	0	309	5,753	18,458	17,356
31	Nebraska	4,364	2,443	1,918	3	1,392	6,602	15,525	17,633
32	Nevada	2,652	1,904	242	506	830	4,005	16,767	15,217
33	New Hampshire	3,458	1,120	2,295	43	459	11,807	23,113	27,958
34	New Jersey	14,146	7,525	6,619	2	3,011	11,197	22,304	28,226
35	New Mexico	3,057	2,469	156	432	544	5,021	14,996	14,996
36	New York	68,258	18,450	49,143	665	14,155	5,764	13,772	29,742
37	North Carolina	15,395	10,379	4,286	730	3,955	5,270	17,950	24,313
38	North Dakota	1,392	997	395	0	447	6,162	15,202	11,869
39	Ohio	22,187	13,716	8,121	350	5,828	8,501	20,139	24,558
40	Oklahoma	5,947	4,551	1,329	67	1,586	5,244	14,816	18,921
41	Oregon	6,779	4,068	2,586	125	1,849	7,413	22,729	27,350
42	Pennsylvania	33,902	11,607	21,903	392	9,135	11,085	21,298	29,929
44	Rhode Island	2,396	776	1,620	0	746	9,250	25,594	31,400
45	South Carolina	5,676	4,002	1,254	420	1,496	10,147	23,774	19,560
46	South Dakota	1,309	953	250	106	307	6,414	8,464	15,129
47	Tennessee	10,627	5,506	4,658	463	2,655	6,407	19,694	20,461
48	Texas	39,739	30,505	8,194	1,040	9,318	6,742	18,280	22,832
49	Utah	5,804	2,991	2,175	638	936	4,793	14,587	7,313
50	Vermont	2,244	480	1,764	0	381	12,459	29,932	29,265
51	Virginia	18,889	11,526	5,484	1,879	4,633	8,658	24,254	20,178
53	Washington	9,766	5,138	4,357	271	2,366	6,678	21,636	27,030
54	West Virginia	5,064	2,559	583	1,922	943	4,944	15,113	10,609
55	Wisconsin	9,476	5,599	3,762	115	2,347	7,391	18,610	23,287
56	Wyoming	388	388	0	0	179	3,333	9,981	...

... = Not available.

Table B-3. Population, School, and Student Characteristics, by State, Selected Years—*Continued*

FIPS code	State	School enrollment of resident population, 2011								Dropouts, 2011	
		Total enrollment		K–12 enrollment		College and graduate school enrollment				Total population 16–19 years old	Not a high school graduate, not enrolled in school (percent)
		Number	Percent public	Number	Percent public	Number	Percent public	Percent female	Percent 25 years old and over		
		140	141	142	143	144	145	146	147	148	149
00	**UNITED STATES**	83,131,910	83.6	54,248,150	90.1	23,864,830	74.7	56.3	42.8	17,623,804	4.9
01	Alabama	1,241,786	85.3	839,657	88.7	336,601	83.6	58.2	40.1	272,487	6.3
02	Alaska	196,240	88.2	136,031	92.8	51,069	80.5	57.5	57.5	39,062	6.5
04	Arizona	1,751,916	89.4	1,175,493	93.8	494,785	83.0	54.8	50.1	370,492	6.5
05	Arkansas	752,121	88.9	507,883	92.7	192,506	83.3	56.4	43.6	155,124	4.5
06	California	10,584,220	86.1	6,835,261	91.6	3,160,867	79.4	54.4	42.1	2,219,870	4.0
08	Colorado	1,377,803	86.8	885,284	92.7	402,669	80.0	54.5	49.5	272,261	5.9
09	Connecticut	943,212	80.3	622,309	90.2	260,920	63.1	56.9	38.8	203,780	3.6
10	Delaware	237,520	79.3	151,646	83.8	71,209	75.2	59.5	40.7	50,755	6.5
11	District of Columbia	160,469	56.6	73,606	83.6	75,893	28.1	58.1	41.7	34,703	6.5
12	Florida	4,682,575	82.4	2,965,169	88.9	1,418,849	74.8	56.0	44.9	994,565	5.6
13	Georgia	2,782,980	85.3	1,838,363	91.4	767,036	75.8	60.7	47.1	587,795	6.8
15	Hawaii	336,724	76.7	216,640	82.3	100,731	70.9	54.8	52.9	64,083	4.1
16	Idaho	452,340	87.4	307,782	94.1	120,734	77.3	54.1	44.6	91,421	4.4
17	Illinois	3,516,919	81.2	2,290,874	89.3	985,999	67.2	55.8	43.4	738,248	4.9
18	Indiana	1,761,848	83.8	1,167,457	89.1	487,337	77.9	56.5	41.2	381,863	6.0
19	Iowa	809,863	84.3	521,603	91.0	232,783	72.7	54.9	36.2	176,920	4.5
20	Kansas	801,598	86.2	519,181	89.2	231,001	83.7	55.9	41.8	164,758	4.1
21	Kentucky	1,127,708	86.0	755,335	89.2	309,379	82.8	58.8	44.2	237,159	4.3
22	Louisiana	1,213,228	81.2	817,972	83.0	310,887	81.4	57.7	39.5	264,377	6.9
23	Maine	304,531	82.8	205,683	90.0	83,483	70.1	57.3	42.9	68,565	3.6
24	Maryland	1,577,839	80.0	974,356	85.9	506,267	75.3	57.1	47.9	328,017	4.5
25	Massachusetts	1,764,471	72.8	1,056,556	89.2	592,754	48.8	55.9	37.8	381,941	3.1
26	Michigan	2,695,641	86.7	1,725,887	90.1	824,464	83.0	56.4	43.0	580,614	5.2
27	Minnesota	1,423,499	83.2	930,361	90.2	399,353	72.3	55.2	43.0	296,038	3.4
28	Mississippi	830,815	87.0	557,274	89.7	218,241	84.7	62.3	38.1	187,436	6.0
29	Missouri	1,569,557	79.8	1,019,482	86.5	444,836	69.7	57.3	44.1	336,492	5.4
30	Montana	242,981	85.4	158,372	90.7	67,088	84.0	54.5	41.4	52,462	6.8
31	Nebraska	515,647	83.1	331,609	87.6	150,546	78.2	56.3	40.8	105,902	3.1
32	Nevada	684,009	88.4	479,216	93.9	172,667	80.0	57.7	48.7	140,884	7.0
33	New Hampshire	324,586	79.1	212,936	90.7	93,643	61.1	58.1	38.4	74,354	2.6
34	New Jersey	2,289,399	80.7	1,510,127	89.0	605,154	68.6	55.6	38.6	471,162	3.2
35	New Mexico	571,157	90.3	374,840	93.2	166,556	87.4	55.5	49.5	116,758	8.5
36	New York	5,020,940	76.1	3,178,961	86.6	1,550,865	59.1	56.2	37.1	1,083,744	4.7
37	North Carolina	2,557,304	85.9	1,672,379	91.4	740,399	80.1	59.4	45.3	540,206	5.4
38	North Dakota	172,936	89.1	102,785	92.3	60,886	86.6	54.8	34.4	39,772	5.2
39	Ohio	3,077,214	82.0	1,988,670	87.1	896,290	75.7	57.4	45.4	642,437	4.4
40	Oklahoma	994,523	89.0	675,000	92.5	255,255	82.0	55.9	45.3	214,070	6.1
41	Oregon	973,213	85.5	623,178	91.0	299,673	80.8	55.2	49.4	201,199	4.7
42	Pennsylvania	3,177,813	75.8	2,040,128	86.4	941,435	59.0	56.8	36.9	730,158	4.0
44	Rhode Island	277,923	74.3	161,285	88.1	99,750	55.9	54.9	32.3	64,101	4.5
45	South Carolina	1,199,462	85.8	805,235	91.8	329,454	76.7	59.3	42.8	265,706	6.7
46	South Dakota	219,022	88.7	143,735	93.0	60,828	83.6	54.4	36.2	48,081	5.1
47	Tennessee	1,594,654	83.2	1,088,443	88.8	416,138	74.3	57.8	41.9	345,915	3.6
48	Texas	7,320,055	89.1	5,039,309	93.7	1,828,650	82.8	56.1	43.8	1,507,388	5.9
49	Utah	926,365	85.9	608,154	94.3	259,033	74.1	48.8	44.5	177,098	3.5
50	Vermont	155,911	80.4	94,304	90.8	53,349	64.6	58.5	34.0	36,557	2.8
51	Virginia	2,156,250	82.8	1,354,589	90.3	673,479	74.8	55.5	45.6	447,064	3.6
53	Washington	1,710,462	85.7	1,134,202	91.4	473,560	80.9	55.2	47.0	367,781	4.7
54	West Virginia	420,204	88.6	281,331	92.8	115,768	81.7	54.5	40.0	96,986	6.3
55	Wisconsin	1,506,580	83.3	994,360	87.0	434,902	78.3	57.2	42.5	324,962	4.1
56	Wyoming	145,877	90.1	97,857	94.1	38,809	87.0	58.1	44.3	30,231	2.2

NOTES AND DEFINITIONS: REGION AND STATE EDUCATION STATISTICS

This section provides details about each item's source and provides relevant definitions. Internet references are provided when available. In some cases, the Internet reference will lead to a general website instead of to the precise data included in this volume. Additional data sources, such as the U.S. Census Bureau's online FERRET (Federal Electronic Research and Review Extraction Tool) and online databases from the National Center for Education Statistics (NCES), were often used.

TABLE B-1

Source: U.S. Census Bureau. *American Community Survey, 2011*. Table B15001. Educational attainment of the population 18 years and over by region, sex, and age, 2011. http://factfinder2.census.gov .

TABLE B-2

Source: U.S. Census Bureau. *American Community Survey, 2011*. Tables C15002, C15002B, C15002D, C15002H, and C15002I. Educational attainment of the population 25 years and over by region, state, sex, race, and Hispanic origin, 2011. http://factfinder2.census.gov/faces/nav/jsf/pages/index.xhtml .

Tables B-1 and B-2 are from the American Community Survey (ACS), the sample survey that has replaced the long form of the decennial census. The sample data are estimates of the actual figures that would have been obtained from a complete count. Estimates derived from a sample are expected to be different from the 100-percent figures because they are subject to sampling and nonsampling errors. Sampling error in data arises from the selection of people and housing units included in the sample. Nonsampling error affects both sample and 100-percent data. It is introduced as a result of errors that may occur during the data collection and processing phases of the census. Conclusions should not be based on small numbers or small differences and users should consult the ACS website to determine the appropriate margins of error. The ACS is ongoing and data are released on an annual basis for all regions and states.

For additional information about the American Community Survey, see www.census.gov/acs/www/ .

Educational Attainment. In the ACS, respondents are classified according to the highest degree or the highest level of school completed. The question includes instructions for people currently enrolled in school to report the level of the previous grade attended or the highest degree received.

High school graduate or higher. This category includes persons who have received a high school diploma or its equivalent (for example, GED), and those who reported any level higher than a high school diploma.

Bachelor's degree or higher. This category includes persons who have received bachelor's degrees, master's degrees, professional school degrees (such as law school or medical school degrees), and doctoral degrees.

Graduate or professional degree. This category includes persons who have received master's degrees, professional school degrees (such as law school or medical school degrees), and doctoral degrees.

Geographic Definitions
Data are presented for the four major regions and nine divisions of the United States. These groups of states are as follows:

Northeast: Connecticut, Maine, Massachusetts, New Hampshire, New Jersey, New York, Pennsylvania, Rhode Island, and Vermont

New England—Connecticut, Maine, Massachusetts, New Hampshire, Rhode Island, and Vermont
Middle Atlantic—New Jersey, New York, and Pennsylvania

Midwest: Illinois, Indiana, Iowa, Kansas, Michigan, Minnesota, Missouri, Nebraska, North Dakota, Ohio, South Dakota, and Wisconsin

East North Central—Illinois, Indiana, Michigan, Ohio, and Wisconsin
West North Central—Iowa, Kansas, Minnesota, Missouri, Nebraska, North Dakota, and South Dakota

South: Alabama, Arkansas, Delaware, District of Columbia, Florida, Georgia, Kentucky, Louisiana, Maryland, Mississippi, North Carolina, Oklahoma, South Carolina, Tennessee, Texas, Virginia, and West Virginia

East South Central—Alabama, Kentucky, Mississippi, and Tennessee
South Atlantic—Delaware, District of Columbia, Florida, Georgia, Maryland, North Carolina, South Carolina, Virginia, and West Virginia
West South Central—Arkansas, Louisiana, Oklahoma, and Texas

West: Alaska, Arizona, California, Colorado, Hawaii, Idaho, Montana, Nevada, New Mexico, Oregon, Utah, Washington, and Wyoming

Mountain—Arizona, Colorado, Idaho, Montana, Nevada, New Mexico, Utah, and Wyoming
Pacific—Alaska, California, Hawaii, Oregon, and Washington

TABLE B-3

POPULATION, ITEMS 1–2

Source: U.S. Census Bureau. *Population Estimates Program.*
www.census.gov/popest/states/ .

The population data for 2011 are U.S. Census Bureau estimates of the resident population as of July 1, 2011.

INCOME, POVERTY, AND HEALTH INSURANCE, Items 3–7

Source: U.S. Census Bureau, September 2012. *Income, Poverty, and Health Insurance Coverage in the United States: 2011* (Current Population Reports, P60-243). www.census.gov/prod/2012pubs/p60-243.pdf .

Additional Internet sources:

- www.census.gov/acs/www/
- www.census.gov/hhes/www/cpstables/032011/pov/new46_000.htm
- www.census.gov/hhes/www/hlthins/data/revhlth/index.html

The Census Bureau reports income from several major household surveys and programs. Each of these surveys differs from the others in some way, such as the length and detail of its questionnaire, the number of households included (sample size), and the methodology used to collect and process the data. The Current Population Survey Annual Social and Economic Supplement (CPS ASEC) is the preferred source for national analysis. It provides the most timely and most accurate cross-section of data for the nation on income and poverty and is the official source of national poverty estimates. The American Community Survey (ACS) is preferred for subnational data on income and poverty by detailed demographic characteristics, because of its large sample size. The Census Bureau recommends using the ACS for single-year estimates of income and poverty at the state level, but still produces some state-level estimates from the CPS ASEC.

The median income for a family of four is from ACS table B19119 on American FactFinder. "Total income" is the sum of the amounts reported separately for wages, salary, commissions, bonuses, or tips; self-employment income from own nonfarm or farm businesses, including proprietorships and partnerships; interest, dividends, net rental income, royalty income, or income from estates and trusts; Social Security or Railroad Retirement income; Supplemental Security Income (SSI); any public assistance or welfare payments from the state or local welfare office; retirement, survivor, or disability pensions; and any other sources of income received regularly such as Veterans' (VA) payments, unemployment compensation, child support, or alimony. Receipts not counted as income include various "lump sum" payments, such as capital gains or inheritances. The total represents the amount of income received before deductions for personal income taxes, Social Security, bond purchases, union dues, Medicare deductions, and the like.

Family income includes the income of all family members 15 years old and over. Median family income is usually higher than median household income because many households consist of only one person. The median divides the income distribution into two equal parts—one part consisting of families with incomes above the median and the other part consisting of families with incomes below the median.

The poverty and health insurance estimates are from the CPS ASEC. Poverty status is based on the definition prescribed by the U.S. Office of Management and Budget as the standard to be used by federal agencies for statistical purposes. A family is classified as below the poverty level (or "in poverty") if its total family income was less than the poverty threshold specified for the applicable family size, age of householder, and number of related children under 18 years old present in the family. The poverty threshold for a four-person family with two children under 18 years old was $22,811in 2011. A child is defined as low income if his or her family's income was less than 200 percent of the poverty threshold. Persons lacking health insurance coverage include those not covered by a private health plan or by Medicaid, Medicare, or a military health plan.

EDUCATIONAL ATTAINMENT, Items 8–10

Source: U.S. Census Bureau, September 2012, American Community Survey. www.census.gov/acs/www/ , Table C15002 on American FactFinder.

Statistics for educational attainment only include persons 25 years old and over. Respondents are classified according to the highest degree or the highest level of school completed. The question includes instructions for people currently enrolled in school to report the level of the previous grade attended or the highest degree received.

High school graduate or more. This category includes persons who have received a high school diploma or its equivalent, and those who reported any level higher than a high school diploma.

Bachelor's degree or more. This category includes persons who have received bachelor's degrees, master's degrees, professional school degrees (such as law school or medical school degrees), and doctoral degrees.

SCHOOL DISTRICTS, Item 11

Source: U.S. Department of Education. National Center for Education Statistics. *Common Core of Data, 2010–2011* (Local Education Agency Universe, 2010–2011, version 1a). http://nces.ed.gov/ccd/ , as published in *Numbers and Types of Public Elementary and Secondary Education Agencies from the Common Core of Data: School Year 2008–09* (NCES 2012-326).

A school district or Local Education Agency (LEA) is a local-level education agency that exists primarily to operate public schools or to contract for public school services. A public school is controlled and operated by publicly elected or appointed officials, and it derives its primary support from public funds.

The state numbers are aggregated from the Common Core of Data (CCD) Local Education Agency universe, which includes nearly 18,000 school districts. These school districts include regular local school districts, local school district components of supervisory unions, supervisory union administrative centers, regional education service agencies, state-operated institutions, federally operated institutions, and other agencies. The CCD data now include charter schools. Since charter schools are typically managed independently from the local school district, each one is considered a single district.

NUMBER AND TYPE OF SCHOOLS, Items 12–22

Sources: U.S. Department of Education. National Center for Education Statistics. *Common Core of Data, 2010-2011.* http://nces.ed.gov/ccd ; as published in *Numbers and Types of Public Elementary and Secondary Schools from the Common Core of Data: School Year 2010–2011: First Look* (NCES 2012-325)

The state data are from the CCD school universe. There are almost 99,000 schools represented, including all those that were operating in 2010–2011.

Regular schools do not focus primarily on special, vocational, or alternative education, though they may offer these programs in addition to the regular curriculum. Special education schools focus primarily on special education, with materials and instructional approaches adapted to meet students' needs. Vocational education schools focus on vocational, technical, or career education. They provide education or training in at least one semi-skilled or technical occupation. Alternative education schools address students' needs that typically cannot be met in a regular school setting. These schools provide nontraditional educational experiences.

A charter school is a school that provides free public elementary and/or secondary education to eligible students under a specific charter granted by the state legislature or other appropriate authority; the school must have also been designated as a charter school by these authorities. Charter schools can be administered by regular school districts, State Education Agencies (SEAs), or chartering organizations.

A magnet school or program is a special school or program designed to attract students of different racial and ethnic backgrounds for the purpose of reducing, preventing, or eliminating racial isolation and/or to provide an academic or social focus on a particular theme.

A Title I eligible school is a school designated under appropriate state and federal regulations as being high poverty and eligible for participation in programs authorized by Title I of P.L. 107–110. A Title I school is one in which the percentage of children from low-income families is at least as high as the percentage of children from low-income families served by the LEA as a whole, or a school designated by the LEA as Title I eligible because 35 percent or more of the children are from low-income families. A Title I schoolwide school is a school in which all the students are designated under appropriate state and federal regulations as eligible for participation in Title I programs authorized by Title I of P.L. 107–110.

NUMBER AND GRADE LEVEL OF STUDENTS, Items 23–26

Sources: U.S. Department of Education. National Center for Education Statistics. *Common Core of Data State Nonfiscal Survey of Public Elementary/Secondary Education:*

School Year 2010–2011 v.1a. http://nces.ed.gov/ccd/stnfis.asp , as published in *Public Elementary and Secondary School Student Enrollment and Staff Counts from the Common Core of Data: School Year 2010–2011*. http://nces.ed.gov/pubsearch/pubsinfo.asp?pubid=2012327 .

The primary grades include pre-kindergarten through grade 4. Middle school grades include grades 5–8. High school grades include grades 9–12. Ungraded students are included in the total but are not separately listed. Some states have no ungraded students.

STUDENTS IN CHARTER SCHOOLS, Item 27
Source: U.S. Department of Education, National Center for Education Statistics, *Common Core of Data (CCD), Local Education Agency Universe Survey, 2010–11, v.1a.* as published in *Numbers and Types of Public Elementary and Secondary Schools from the Common Core of Data: School Year 2010–2011: First Look* (NCES 2012-325).

A charter school is a school providing free public elementary and/or secondary education to eligible students under a specific charter granted by the state legislature or other appropriate authority, and designated by such authority to be a charter school.

STUDENTS WHO ARE ELIGIBLE FOR FREE OR REDUCED-PRICE LUNCH, Item 28
Source: U.S. Department of Education. National Center for Education Statistics. *Common Core of Data, Public Elementary/Secondary School Universe Survey, 2010–2011 v.2a.* http://nces.ed.gov/ccd/pubschuniv.asp . Accessed through the Build-a-Table data tool.

The Free and Reduced-Price Lunch Program is a program under the National School Lunch Act that provides cash subsidies for free or reduced-price meals to students based on family size and income criteria. Participation in the Free and Reduced-Price Lunch Program depends on income, and eligibility is often used to estimate student needs.

STUDENTS WITH INDIVIDUAL EDUCATION PROGRAMS, Item 29
Source: U.S. Department of Education. National Center for Education Statistics. *Common Core of Data, Local Education Agency Universe Survey, 2010–2011 v.2a.* http://nces.ed.gov/ccd/pubagency.asp . Accessed through the Build-a-Table data tool.

An Individualized Education Program (IEP) is a written instructional plan for students with disabilities who are designated as special education students under IDEA (Individuals with Disabilities Education Act). An IEP includes a statement of present levels of educational performance of a child; a statement of annual goals, including short-term instructional objectives; a statement of specific educational services to be provided and the extent to which the child will be able to participate in regular educational programs; a projected date for initiation and the anticipated duration of services; appropriate objectives, criteria, and evaluation procedures; and schedules for determining, on at least an annual basis, whether instructional objectives are being achieved.

STUDENTS WHO ARE ENGLISH-LANGUAGE LEARNERS, Item 30
Source: U.S. Department of Education. National Center for Education Statistics. *Local Education Agency Universe Survey, 2010–2011 v.2a.* http://nces.ed.gov/ccd/pubagency.asp. Accessed through the Build-a-Table data tool.

This category includes the number of students who are served in appropriate programs of language assistance (e.g., English as a Second Language, High Intensity Language Training, and bilingual education). This designation changed from Limited-English Proficient

(LEP) to English-Language Learners (ELL) in the 2001–2002 school year.

RACE AND HISPANIC ORIGIN, Items 31–35
Sources: U.S. Department of Education. National Center for Education Statistics. *Common Core of Data State Nonfiscal Survey of Public Elementary/Secondary Education: School Year 2010–2011 v.1a.* http://nces.ed.gov/ccd/stnfis.asp , as published in *Public Elementary and Secondary School Student Enrollment and Staff from the Common Core of Data: School Year 2010–2011.* http://nces.ed.gov/pubsearch/pubsinfo.asp?pubid=2012327 .

The racial and ethnic categories used in the CCD are those approved by the U.S. Office of Management and Budget at the time these data were collected. These categories are mutually exclusive. Because some students do not report their race or ethnicity, the percentages do not always add to 100 percent.

EVENT DROPOUT RATES, Items 36–37
Source: U.S. Department of Education. National Center for Education Statistics. *Common Core of Data, 2008–2009, Public School Graduates and Dropouts from the Common Core of Data: School Year 2008–09: First Look* (NCES Report 2011-312). http://nces.ed.gov/pubsearch/pubsinfo.asp?pubid=2011312 .

A dropout is a student who was enrolled in school at some time during the previous school year who was not enrolled at the beginning of the current school year and who had not graduated from high school or completed a state or district-approved educational program and who did not meet any of the following exclusionary conditions: transferral to another public school district, private school, or state- or district-approved educational program; temporary absence due to suspension or school-approved illness; or death. The school year is the 12-month period of time from the first day of school (operationally set as October 1), with dropouts from the previous summer reported for the year and grade in which they fail to enroll. Individuals who are not accounted for on October 1 are considered dropouts.

Most of the states that reported on dropouts used an October through September cycle; however, some states used a different cycle, and there is variation among the states in definitions and record-keeping methods concerning graduates and dropouts.

NUMBER OF GRADUATES AND AVERAGED FRESHMAN GRADUATION RATE, Items 38–40
Source: U.S. Department of Education. National Center for Education Statistics. *Common Core of Data, Public School Graduates and Dropouts from the Common Core of Data: School Year 2008–2009: First Look* (NCES Report 2011-312). http://nces.ed.gov/pubsearch/pubsinfo.asp?pubid=2011312 .

The number of graduates includes individuals who received a regular diploma, but does not include individuals who received a diploma from a program different than the regular school program, and individuals who received a certificate of attendance or other certificate of completion in lieu of a diploma during the previous school year and subsequent summer school session. Recipients of high school equivalency certificates are also not included.

The averaged freshman graduation rate provides an estimate of the percentage of high school students who graduate on time. The rate uses aggregate student enrollment data (to estimate the size of an incoming freshman class) and aggregate counts of the number of diplomas awarded four years later. The incoming freshman class size is estimated by summing the enrollment in 8th grade in one year, 9th grade in the next year, and

10th grade in the year after that, and then dividing by three. The averaging is intended to account for prior-year retentions in the 9th grade.

PRIVATE SCHOOLS, Items 41–43

Source: U.S. Department of Education. National Center for Education Statistics. *Characteristics of Private Schools in the United States: Results from the 2009–2010 Private School Universe Survey* (NCES Report 2011-339). http://nces.ed.gov/pubsearch/pubsinfo.asp?pubid=2011339 .

Since 1989, the Census Bureau has conducted the biennial Private School Universe Survey (PSS) for NCES. The PSS is designed to generate biennial data on the total number of private schools, students, and teachers and to build a universe of private schools in all of the states and the District of Columbia to serve as a sampling frame of private schools for NCES sample surveys. The target population for the PSS is every school in all of the states and the District of Columbia that is not primarily supported by public funds, provides instruction for one or more grades between kindergarten and grade 12 (or comparable ungraded levels), and has one or more teachers. Organizations or institutions that provide support for home schooling, but do not provide classroom instruction, are not included. Although the PSS has begun to collect limited data on the many private schools for which kindergarten is the highest grade, the data in this volume are for (traditional) schools that include at least one grade between grades 1 and 12.

A private school is controlled by an individual or agency other than a state, a subdivision of a state, or the federal government; is usually supported primarily by nonpublic funds; and the operation of its program does not rest with publicly elected or appointed officials. Private schools include both nonprofit and proprietary institutions.

Data for private schools in Alaska, Idaho, Montana, and Ohio, and for students in Idaho should be interpreted with caution. The coefficient of variation for these estimates is larger than 25 percent. Reporting standards were not met for private high school graduates in North Dakota and Wyoming.

PUBLIC AND PRIVATE SCHOOL CHARACTERISTICS, Items 44–51

Sources: U.S. Department of Education. National Center for Education Statistics. *Common Core of Data, 2000–2001* and *2010–2011.* http://nces.ed.gov/ccd/ ; *State Nonfiscal Survey of Public Elementary/Secondary Education*; *Private School Universe Survey, 2009–2010.* http://nces.ed.gov/surveys/pss/ ; *Characteristics of Private Schools in the United States: Results from the 2009–2010 Private School Universe Survey: First Look* (NCES Report 2011-339).

The public school numbers are from the CCD state universe. Teacher counts measure the number of full-time equivalent teachers, including teachers who are employed by agencies and not assigned to specific schools. The student-teacher ratio is calculated by dividing the number of students in all schools by the number of full-time equivalent teachers employed by all schools and agencies.

The private school numbers are derived from the Private School Survey Universe (PSS). These estimates measured full-time equivalent teachers. The student-teacher ratio is calculated by dividing the number of students enrolled in all schools by the number of full-time equivalent teachers employed by all schools.

TEACHER SALARIES, Item 52

Source: National Education Association. Rankings & Estimates Database. *Rankings & Estimates: Rankings of the States 2011 and Estimates of School Statistics, 2012.* (Washington, DC: NEA, 2012). www.nea.org/assets/docs/NEA_Rankings_And_Estimates

_FINAL_20120209.pdf . Reprinted with permission of the National Education Association © 2012. All rights reserved.

The National Education Association (NEA) publishes average teacher salaries by state in its annual *Estimates of School Statistics*. The information is compiled from surveys conducted by the state departments of education. If a state does not provide a salary amount, the NEA develops an estimate. The states then have the option of replacing this estimate with one of their own. At the time of this publication, about half of the states used NEA estimates.

The average salary for public school teachers is defined as the arithmetic mean of the salaries of the group described. This figure is the average gross salary before deductions for Social Security, retirement, health insurance, and the like.

PUBLIC SCHOOL STAFF, Items 53–71

Sources: U.S. Department of Education. National Center for Education Statistics. *Common Core of Data, 2010–2011.* http://nces.ed.gov/ccd/ . *State Nonfiscal Survey of Public Elementary/Secondary Education, 2010–2011*, as published in *Public Elementary and Secondary School Student Enrollment and Staff Counts from the Common Core of Data: School Year 2010–2011: First Look* (NCES Report 2012-327). http://nces.ed.gov/pubsearch/pubsinfo.asp?pubid=2012327 .

The number of teachers represents full-time equivalent teachers employed within the state. Instructional aides directly assist teachers in providing instruction. Instructional coordinators help teachers through curriculum development and in-service training. Support staff includes those involved with food, health, library, maintenance, transportation, security, and other services in public schools. School administrators are principals and assistant principals. School district administrators include the Local Education Agency (LEA) superintendents, deputies, assistant superintendents, and other persons with district-wide responsibilities.

CHARACTERISTICS OF TEACHERS, Items 72–80

Source: U.S. Department of Education. National Center for Education Statistics. Schools and Staffing Survey, Public Teacher Questionnaire, 2007–2008. Table 72, *Digest of Education Statistics, 2011*. http://nces.ed.gov/programs/digest/d11/tables/dt11_072.asp .

The highest degree earned and years of experience are from the Schools and Staffing Survey (SASS), "Public Teacher Questionnaire," 2007–2008, as published in the *Digest of Education Statistics, 2011*. Data are based on a head count of all teachers and exclude prekindergarten teachers. Detail may not sum to totals because of rounding, cell suppression, and omitted categories (less than bachelor's). Elementary teachers are those who taught self-contained classes at the elementary level, and secondary teachers are those who taught departmentalized classes (e.g., science, art, social science, or other course subjects) at the secondary level. Teachers were classified as elementary or secondary on the basis of the grades they taught, rather than on the level of the school in which they taught. Education specialist includes certificate of advanced graduate studies.

NATIONAL ASSESSMENT OF EDUCATIONAL PROGRESS, Items 81–85

Source: U.S. Department of Education. Institute of Education Sciences, National Center for Education Statistics. *National Assessment of Educational Progress, 2011*. http://nces.ed.gov/nationsreportcard/ .

The National Assessment of Educational Progress (NAEP) is a congressionally mandated project of the National Center for

Education Statistics (NCES) that has, for more than a quarter of a century, continually collected and reported information on what American students know and what they can do. It is the nation's only ongoing, comparable, and representative assessment of student achievement. Its assessments are based on a national probability sample of public and nonpublic school students enrolled in grades 4, 8, or 12. Results are only provided for group performance, as NAEP is forbidden by law to report results at an individual or school level. The assessment questions are written around a framework prepared for each content area—reading, writing, mathematics, science, and other; this framework represents the consensus of groups of curriculum experts, educators, and members of the general public on what such a test should cover.

In response to legislation passed by the Congress in 1988, the NAEP program includes voluntary state-by-state assessments. To help ensure valid state-by-state results, NCES applies minimum school and student participation rate standards for its reporting activities. Results are not reported for jurisdictions that failed to meet these standards.

This volume includes the proportion of students in specific grades whose NAEP mathematics, reading, and science assessment results were designated as "proficient" or better for their grades. The achievement level results describe what students participating in the NAEP assessment should know and what they should be able to do. The National Assessment Governing Board (NAGB) adopted three achievement levels: basic, proficient, and advanced. The basic level denotes partial mastery of fundamental knowledge and skills, the proficient level shows solid academic performance and competency in challenging subject matter, and the advanced level signifies superior performance. Achievement levels are based on collective judgments gathered from a broadly representative panel of teachers, education specialists, and members of the general public about what students should know and be able to do relative to the body of content reflected in the NAEP assessment framework.

ACT ASSESSMENT COMPOSITE SCORES, Items 86–87

Source: ACT, Inc. *2012 ACT Composite Averages by State*. www.act.org/newsroom/data/2012/states.html . © 2012 by ACT, Inc. All rights reserved. Reprinted with permission. This material may not be posted, published, or distributed without permission from ACT, Inc.

Totals for graduating seniors were obtained from: ACT, Inc. *Knocking at the College Door—March 2009, Projections of High School Graduates by State and Race/Ethnicity, 1992–2022*. (Boulder, CO: Western Interstate Commission for Higher Education, 2008).

Founded in 1959 as the American College Testing Program, ACT, Inc., is an independent, not-for-profit organization that provides more than 100 assessment, research, information, and program management services in the broad areas of educational planning, career planning, and workforce development. The ACT Assessment is designed to assess high school students' general educational development and their ability to complete college-level work. The test covers four skill areas: English, mathematics, reading, and science reasoning. Data in this volume are based on all high school graduates in the class of 2010 who took the ACT Assessment during their sophomore, junior, or senior year. For students who took the test more than once, only their most recent scores are used. Students who tested on campus, used extended time testing, or failed to list a valid high school code are not included.

College-bound students who take the ACT Assessment are not representative of college-bound students nationally. Students residing in the Midwest, the Mountain West, the Plains, and the South are overrepresented among ACT-tested students, compared with college-bound students nationally. ACT-tested students also tend to enroll in public colleges and universities more frequently than college-bound students nationally.

In Spring 2011, all public high school eleventh graders in the states of Colorado, Illinois, Kentucky, Michigan, North Dakota, Tennessee, and Wyoming were tested with the ACT as required by each state. Colorado, Illinois, Kentucky, Michigan, North Dakota, Tennessee, and Wyoming students who met ACT's 2012 graduating class criteria are included in the 2012 graduating class average score results. Consistent with ACT's reporting policies, graduating class test results are reported only for students tested under standard time conditions.

Caution should be used in comparing state and national norms. State norms may differ from national norms for non-educational reasons, such as the representativeness of the ACT-tested population and the demographic makeup of a state.

PSAT/NMSQT® (PRELIMINARY SAT/ NATIONAL MERIT SCHOLARSHIP QUALIFYING TEST), Items 88–91

Source: The College Entrance Examination Board. *PSAT/NMSQT® 2011–2012 College-Bound High School Juniors State Summary Reports.* http://research.collegeboard.org/programs/psat/data/cb-jr . Reproduced with permission. All rights reserved.

The PSAT/NMSQT (Preliminary SAT/National Merit Scholarship Qualifying Test) is a program co-sponsored by the College Board and the National Merit Scholarship Corporation. The test serves several functions: it helps assess skills necessary for college-level work, prepares students for the SAT, enters students in competitions for national scholarships (including the National Merit Scholarship Corporation scholarship programs), and helps students receive access to information and applications for educational and financial aid information from colleges, universities, and scholarship programs.

Verbal, math, and writing skills scores are each reported on a 20 to 80 scale. The average scores of juniors in each section are between 47 and 49. Unless students earn scores that are much lower than average, the PSAT/NMSQT shows that they are likely developing the kinds of critical reading, math problem-solving, and writing skills needed for academic success in college.

The sum of the verbal, math, and writing skills scores makes up the Selection Index, which is used by National Merit Scholarship Corporation to designate those who will be honored in its scholarship programs. The qualifying score varies from state to state, depending on the scores and the proportion of test takers in each state. Scores between 65 and 80 on each skill mark the approximate level of the achievement needed to qualify. In states with higher percentages of scores in this range, a student must achieve a higher Selection Index to be designated a National Merit semifinalist.

SAT REASONING TEST SCORES, Items 92–95

Source: The College Board. *The SAT Report on College and Career Readiness, 2012.* (New York: The College Board, 2012). http://media.collegeboard.com/homeOrg/content/pdf/sat-report-college-career-readiness-2012.pdf . Reprinted with permission. All rights reserved.

The percentage of high school graduates is based on the projection of high school graduates in 2012 by the Western Interstate Commission for Higher Education (*Knocking at the College Door: Projections of High School Graduates by State and Race/Ethnicity, 1992–2022*, Western Interstate Commission for Higher Education, March 2008), and the number of students in the class of 2012 who took the SAT in each state through March 2012. Senior test-takers in May and June are not included in the analysis.

The SAT is an examination administered by the Educational Testing Service that is used to predict the facility with which an individual will progress in college-level academic classes.

The *SAT Report on College and Career Readiness, 2012* presents data for high school graduates who participated in the SAT program during their high school years. Students are counted once no matter how often they tested, and only their most recent scores are included in the data. The class of 2006 was the first to take the new SAT, which includes writing as well as critical reading and math. Each test is scored on a scale of 200 to 800.

The College Board cautions that relationships between test scores and other factors, such as educational background, gender, race/ethnic background, parental education, and household income, are complex and interdependent. These factors do not directly affect test performance; rather, they are associated with educational experiences both on tests such as the SAT and in school work. Moreover, not all students in a high school, school district, or state take the SAT. Since the population of test takers is self-selected, using aggregate SAT scores to compare or evaluate teachers, schools, districts, states, or other educational units is not valid, and the College Board strongly discourages such uses.

Interpreting SAT scores for states requires unique considerations. The most significant factor to consider in interpreting SAT scores for any group or subgroup of test takers is the proportion of students taking the test. For example, it is important to recognize that some states have lower participation rates. Typically, test takers in these low-participation states have strong academic backgrounds and apply to the nation's most selective colleges and scholarship programs. For these states, it is expected that the SAT mean scores reported for students will be higher than the national average.

REVENUES, Items 96–99

Source: U.S. Department of Education. National Center for Education Statistics. *Common Core of Data,* "National Public Education Financial Survey (State Fiscal)" 2008–2009 (FY 2009) v.1a. http://nces.ed.gov/ccd/ . *Revenues and Expenditures for Public Elementary and Secondary Education: School Year 2008–2009 (Fiscal Year 2009)* (NCES 2011-329)

The state data include adjustments made by NCES. Values that were missing and not reported elsewhere in the survey were imputed based on corresponding proportions in reporting states. Other adjustments were made when a single value was reported that included two or more categories. NCES distributed portions of the single reported value to the missing items. In addition to these adjustments, the NPEFS may also include state-run education programs. Consequently, these numbers may differ from the state totals in Table C-1, which are derived from a different survey.

Charter school systems' reporting requirements vary from state to state and data are not currently reported uniformly to the State Education Agencies (SEAs). Note that some charter school data may be missing from this volume, since some charter schools were not required to submit finance data to their SEAs. Only those charter schools that submit data to the SEAs, and whose SEAs maintain the data, are included in the CCD fiscal files.

Revenues from federal sources include direct grants-in-aid from the federal government, federal grants-in-aid through the state or an intermediate agency, and other revenue in lieu of taxes to compensate a school district for nontaxable federal institutions within a district's boundaries.

State revenues include revenues that can be used without restriction, revenues for categorical purposes, and revenues in lieu of taxation. Also included are revenues from payments made by a state for the benefit of the Local Education Agency (LEA) or contributions of equipment or supplies. Such revenues include the payment of a pension fund by the state on behalf of an LEA employee for services rendered and contributions of fixed assets (property, plant, or equipment), such as school buses and textbooks.

Revenues from local sources include local property and non-property tax revenues, taxes levied or assessed by an LEA, revenues from a local government to the LEA, tuition received, transportation fees, earnings on investments from LEA holdings, net revenues from food services (gross receipts less gross expenditures), net revenues from student activities (gross receipts less gross expenditures), and other revenues (textbook sales, donations, and property rentals). Intermediate revenues were included in local revenue totals. Intermediate revenues are derived from sources other than Local or State Education Agencies; these sources operate at an intermediate level between Local and State Education Agencies and possess independent fundraising capabilities (such as county or municipal agencies).

EXPENDITURES, Items 100–104

Sources: U.S. Department of Education. National Center for Education Statistics. "National Public Education Financial Survey (State Fiscal)" 2008–2009 (FY 2009) v.1a. http://nces.ed.gov/ccd/ . *Revenues and Expenditures for Public Elementary and Secondary Education: School Year 2008–2009 (Fiscal Year 2009)* (NCES 2011-329).

The state data include adjustments made by NCES. Values that were missing and not reported elsewhere in the survey were imputed based on proportions in reporting states. Other adjustments were made when a single value was reported that included two or more categories. NCES distributed portions of the single reported value to the missing items. In addition to these adjustments, the NPEFS may include state-run education programs. Consequently, these numbers may differ from the state totals in Table C-1, which come from a different survey.

Current expenditures consist of expenditures for the categories of instruction, support services, and non-instructional services for salaries; employee benefits; purchased services and supplies; and payments by the state made for or on behalf of school systems. These expenditures do not include expenditures for debt service, capital outlay, and property (e.g., equipment), or direct costs (e.g., Head Start, adult education, community colleges, etc.) and community services expenditures.

Instructional and instruction-related expenses comprise current expenditures for activities that deal directly with the interaction between students and teachers. These expenditures include teacher salaries and benefits, supplies (such as textbooks), instructional staff support (i.e., salaries for librarians and instructional specialists), and purchased instructional services.

Support services expenditures consist of current expenditures for activities supporting instruction. These services include operation and maintenance of buildings, school administration, student support services (e.g., nurses, therapists, and guidance counselors), student transportation, school district administration, business services, research, and data processing.

Noninstructional expenditures are mostly for food service, but also consist of expenditures for enterprise operations, such as bookstores and interscholastic athletics.

Current expenditures per student are derived by dividing total current expenditures by the fall student membership count from the CCD. Student membership consists of the count of students enrolled on or about October 1 and is comparable across all states.

HIGHER EDUCATION, Items 105–139

Sources: U.S. Department of Education. National Center for Education Statistics. Integrated Postsecondary Education Data System (IPEDS). *Digest of Education Statistics, 2011*. http://nces.ed.gov/programs/digest/d11/tables_3.asp .

The Integrated Postsecondary Education Data System (IPEDS) surveys approximately 10,000 postsecondary institutions, including universities, colleges, and institutions offering technical and vocational education beyond the high school level. This survey, which began in 1986, replaced the Higher Education General Information Survey (HEGIS). IPEDS is made up of eight integrated components that obtain information on who provides postsecondary education (institutions), who participates in it and completes it (students), what programs are offered and which ones are completed, and the specific human and financial resources involved in the provision of institutionally based postsecondary education. These components are organized into the following categories: Institutional Characteristics, including instructional activity; Fall Enrollment, including age and residence; Enrollment in Occupationally Specific Programs; Completions; Finance; Staff; Salaries of Full-Time Instructional Faculty; and Academic Libraries.

Institutions of higher education include those with courses leading to an associate's degree or higher, or those with courses accepted for credit toward such degrees. A public institution is controlled and operated by publicly elected or appointed officials and derives its primary support from public funds. A private institution is controlled by an individual or agency other than a state, a subdivision of a state, or the federal government; it is usually primarily supported by nonpublic funds, and the operation of its program does not rest with publicly elected or appointed officials. Private institutions comprise both not-for-profit and proprietary institutions.

Full-time students include undergraduate students enrolled for 12 or more semester credits, 12 or more quarter credits, or 24 or more contact hours a week each term; graduate students enrolled for 9 or more semester credits or 9 or more quarter credits, or students involved in thesis or dissertation preparation who are considered full-time students by the institution; and first-professional students (as defined by the institution).

Types of institutions include the following:

- Degree-granting institutions, which offer associate's, bachelor's, master's, doctoral and/or first-professional degrees.

- Level categories include four-year and higher (four-year) institutions, at least two but less than four-year (two-year) institutions, and less than two-year institutions.

  A four-year institution is a postsecondary institution that offers programs of at least four years' duration or programs at or above the baccalaureate level. This category includes schools that only offer postbaccalaureate certificates and those that only offer graduate programs. Also included are freestanding medical, law, and other first-professional schools.

A two-year institution is a postsecondary institution that offers programs of at least two years' duration but less than four years' duration. This category includes occupational and vocational schools with programs of at least 1,800 hours and academic institutions with programs of less than four years' duration. It does not include bachelor's degree–granting institutions where the baccalaureate program can be completed in three years.

Control categories are public, private not-for-profit, and private for-profit.

Undergraduate students are registered at an institution of higher education and are working in a program leading to a baccalaureate degree or other formal award below the baccalaureate, such as an associate degree.

Postbaccalaureate students are working toward a master's or doctor's degree or are enrolled in graduate-level classes, but not enrolled in degree programs.

Race/ethnicity categories are categories used to describe groups to which individuals belong, identify with, or belong to in the eyes of the community. A person may be counted in only one group. Classification is based on self-identification. Race categories exclude persons of Hispanic ethnicity.

A nonresident alien is a person who is not a citizen or national of the United States, and who is in this country on a visa or temporary basis; a nonresident alien does not have the right to remain in the United States indefinitely.

Migration refers to the movement of students from their home state of residence to another state to attend a postsecondary institution. The percentages in columns 121 and 122 refer to freshmen who had graduated from high school within the previous 12 months and who were enrolled in 4-year degree granting institutions in Fall 2010.

An associate's degree is a degree granted for the successful completion of a sub-baccalaureate program of studies, and usually requires at least two years (or the equivalent) of full-time college-level study. This category also includes degrees granted in a cooperative or work-study program.

A bachelor's degree is a degree granted for the successful completion of a baccalaureate program of studies, and usually requires at least four years (or the equivalent) of full-time college-level study. This category includes degrees granted in a cooperative or work-study program.

A master's degree is awarded for successful completion of a program generally requiring 1 or 2 years of full-time, college-level study beyond the bachelor's degree. One type of master's degree, including the master of arts degree (M.A.), and the master of science degree (M.S.), is awarded in the liberal arts and sciences for advanced scholarship in a subject field or discipline and demonstrated ability to perform scholarly research. A second type of master's degree is awarded for the completion of a professionally oriented program. These include master's degrees in education (M.Ed.), business administration (M.B.A.), fine arts (M.F.A.), music (M.M.), social work (M.S.W.), and public administration (M.P.A.) A third type of master's degree is awarded in professional fields for study beyond the first-professional degree, such as the master of laws (LL.M.) and the masters of science in various medical specializations. Some master's degrees—such as divinity degrees (M.Div. or M.H.L./Rav), which were formerly classified as "first-professional"—may require more than 2 years of full-time study beyond the bachelor's degree.

A doctor's degree is an earned degree that generally carries the title of Doctor. The Doctor of Philosophy degree (Ph.D.) is the highest academic degree and requires mastery within a field of knowledge and demonstrated ability to perform scholarly research. Other doctor's degrees are awarded for fulfilling specialized requirements in professional fields, such as education (Ed.D.), musical arts (D.M.A.), business administration (D.B.A.), and engineering (D.Eng. or D.E.S.). Many doctor's degrees in academic and professional fields require an earned master's degree as a prerequisite. The doctor's degree classification includes most degrees that NCES formerly classified as first-professional degrees. Such degrees are awarded in the fields of dentistry (D.D.S. or D.M.D.), medicine (M.D.), optometry (O.D.), osteopathic medicine (D.O.), pharmacy (Pharm.D.), podiatry (D.P.M., Pod.D., or D.P.), veterinary medicine (D.V.M.), chiropractic (D.C. or D.C.M.), and law (L.L.B. or J.D.).

Tuition and required fees are payments or charges for instruction or compensation for services, privileges, or the use of equipment, books, or other goods. Data are for the entire academic year and are average charges. In-state tuition and fees were weighted by the number of full-time-equivalent undergraduates, but were not adjusted to reflect student residency. Out-of-state tuition and fees were weighted by the number of first-time freshmen attending the institution in fall 2010 from out of state.

SCHOOL ENROLLMENT OF RESIDENT POPULATION, Items 140–147

Source: U.S. Census Bureau. *2011 American Community Survey.* http://www.census.gov/acs/www/ ; Tables C14002 and B14004 from American FactFinder.

School enrollment is enrollment in a regular school, either public or private, including nursery schools, kindergarten, and elementary schools, as well as schooling that leads to a high school diploma or college degree. Schools supported and controlled primarily by the federal, state, or local government are defined as public schools (including tribal schools). Schools primarily supported and controlled by religious organizations or other private groups are considered private schools.

DROPOUTS, Items 148–149

Source: U.S. Census Bureau. 2011 *American Community Survey.* http://www.census.gov/acs/www/ ; Table B14005 from American FactFinder.

The "high school dropout" category includes people of compulsory school attendance age or older who were not enrolled in school and were not high school graduates. However, there is no criterion regarding when they dropped out of school, thus, some may have never attended high school. This column includes only persons 16 to 19 years old.

PART C
COUNTY EDUCATION STATISTICS

PART C—COUNTY EDUCATION STATISTICS

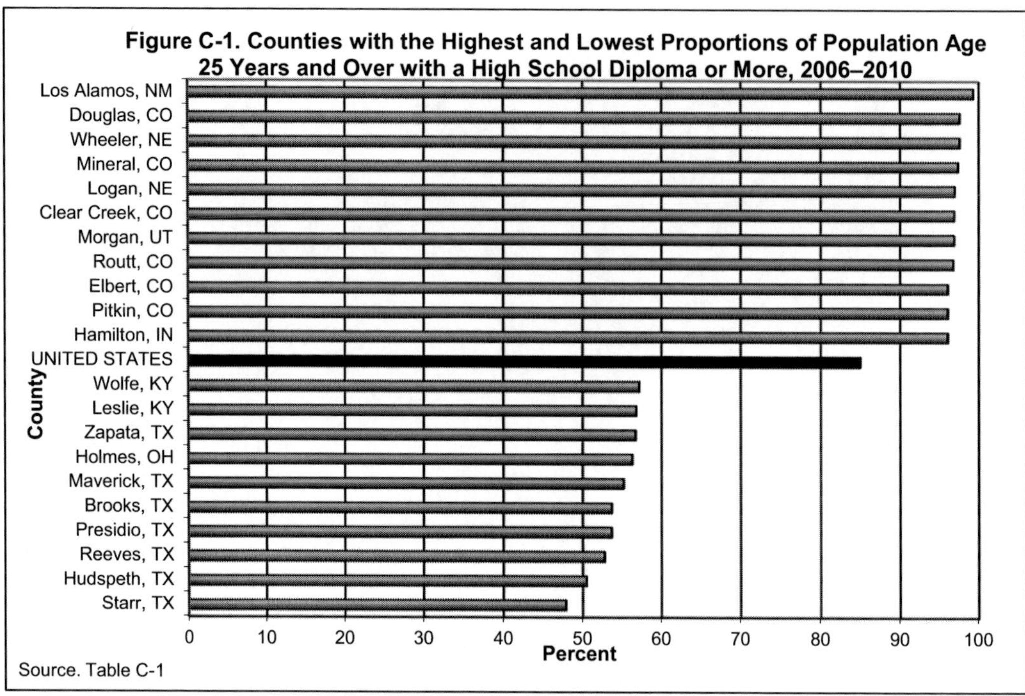

There were 35 counties in which more than 95 percent of the population age 25 years old and over had graduated from high school. The highest proportion was 99.3 percent in Los Alamos County, NM, home of the Los Alamos National Laboratory. Twenty-three counties had high school attainment levels of less than 60 percent, including five counties in Texas, where less than 55 percent of the population had graduated from high school. In the 2006–2010 time period, 23 counties had college attainment levels that exceeded 50 percent, with Los Alamos, NM, and 3 Virginia counties in the Washington, DC area exceeding 60 percent. Twenty-three counties had college attainment levels below 7 percent, four of them below 5 percent, in Georgia, Mississippi, and Kentucky.

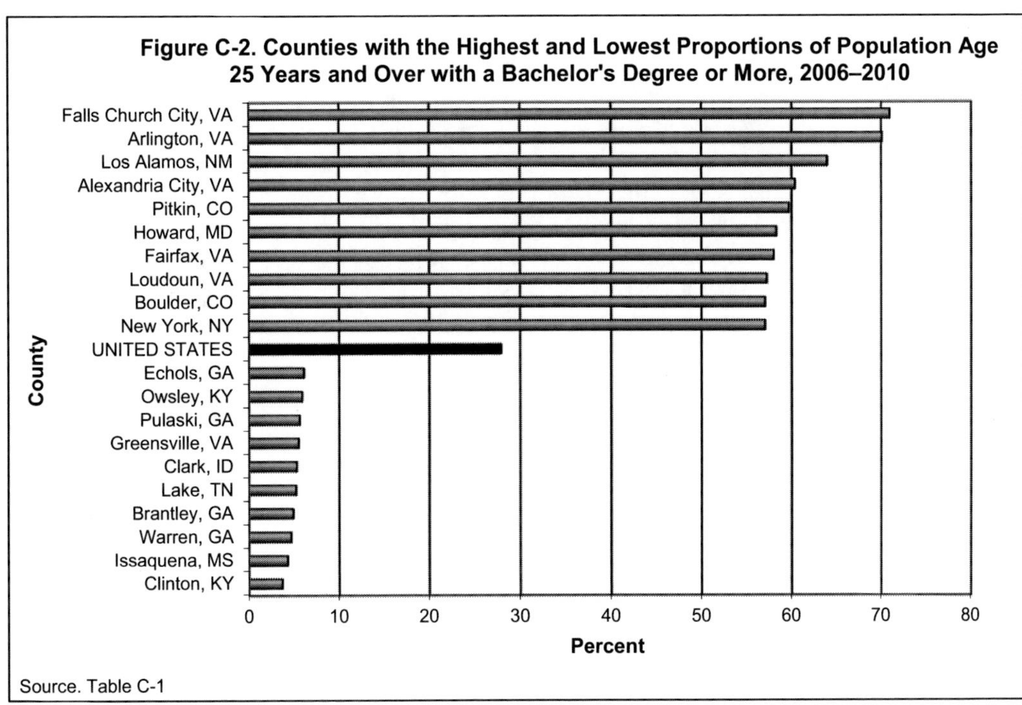
Figure C-2. Counties with the Highest and Lowest Proportions of Population Age 25 Years and Over with a Bachelor's Degree or More, 2006–2010
Falls Church City, VA
Arlington, VA
Los Alamos, NM
Alexandria City, VA
Pitkin, CO
Howard, MD
Fairfax, VA
Loudoun, VA
Boulder, CO
New York, NY
UNITED STATES
Echols, GA
Owsley, KY
Pulaski, GA
Greensville, VA
Clark, ID
Lake, TN
Brantley, GA
Warren, GA
Issaquena, MS
Clinton, KY
County
0
10
20
30
40
50
60
70
80
Percent
Source. Table C-1

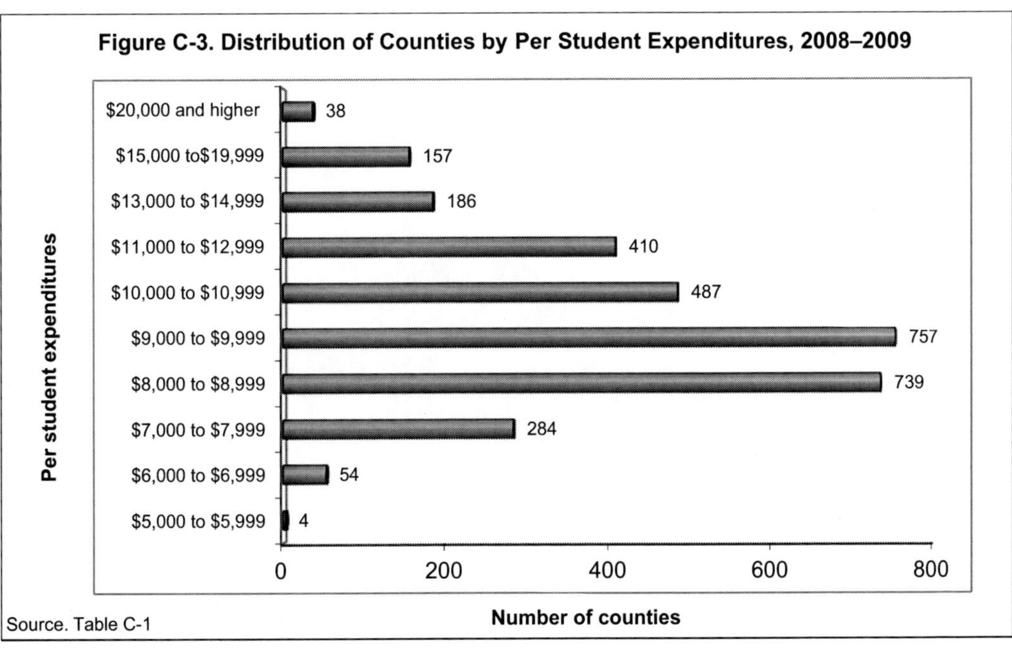
Figure C-3. Distribution of Counties by Per Student Expenditures, 2008–2009
$20,000 and higher
38
$15,000 to$19,999
157
$13,000 to $14,999
186
$11,000 to $12,999
410
$10,000 to $10,999
487
$9,000 to $9,999
757
$8,000 to $8,999
739
$7,000 to $7,999
284
$6,000 to $6,999
54
$5,000 to $5,999
4
Per student expenditures
0
200
400
600
800
Number of counties
Source. Table C-1

Expenditures per student range from almost $40,810 in Billings County, North Dakota, to less than $5,500 in Utah, Morgan, and Tooele Counties in Utah, and Franklin County, in Idaho, counties with high proportions of children age 5 to 17 years old. With the highest proportion of student-age population of all the states, Utah has many counties with low expenditures per student. At the other extreme, the 13 counties with expenditures above $30,000 per student have small student populations. The median per student expenditure was $9,541 (with half of the counties spending more and half spending less). Los Angeles County had the largest enrollment (1,589,543 students), but New York City had the highest educational expenditures with $18.8 billion spent in fiscal year 2008–2009, followed closely by Los Angeles with $16.5 billion. Slope County, North Dakota, and Keweenaw County, Michigan, each spent less than $1 million.

In the United States, there were 3,143 counties (including county equivalents), about 18,000 Local Education Agencies (school districts), nearly 100,000 public schools, and 49.4 million public school students. Some counties—even large counties, such as Miami–Dade County in Florida—had only one school district, while others had many. For example, Arizona's Maricopa County had 310 school districts and Cook County in Illinois had 171 school districts.

Student–teacher ratios varied greatly from county to county, ranging from 15 counties that exceeded 25 students per teacher to a low of 3.3 students per teacher in Billings, North Dakota. Some counties have small populations and very high student–teacher ratios, possibly because some of their teachers are not counted in the NCES data. Many of California's counties have student–teacher ratios of 24 or higher because of recent reductions in the number of teachers. The median student–teacher ratio was 14.3.

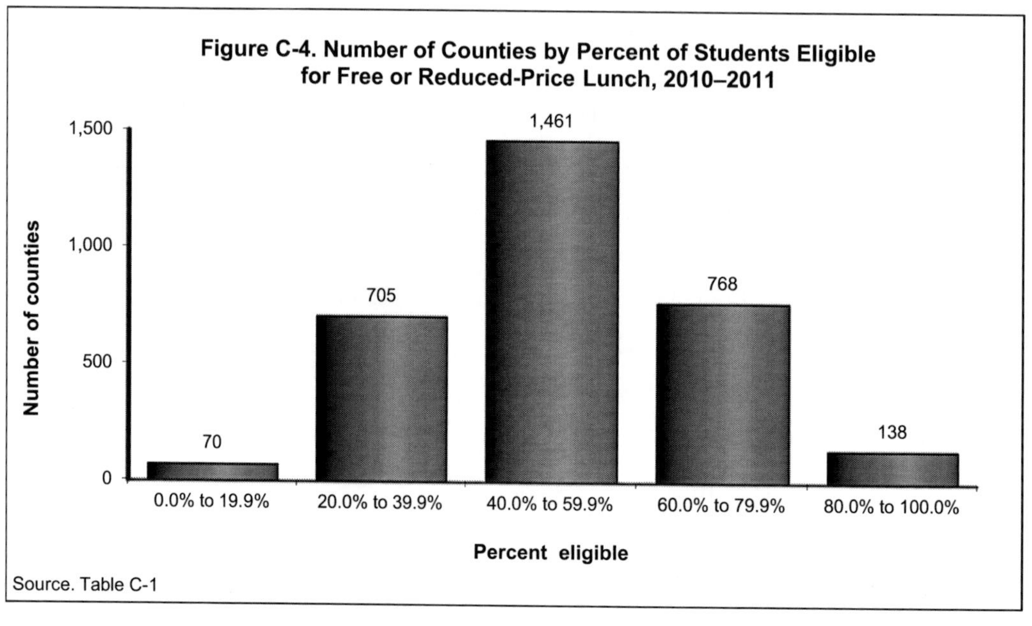

Based on family size and income, nearly half of all public school students qualify for free or reduced price school lunches. Fifty-three counties (most located in the South), had 90 percent or more students who were eligible for free or reduced-price lunches in the 2010–2011 school year. Among the six counties with proportions exceeding 99 percent, four were in Mississippi. Only a few counties had less than 10 percent of students whose income was low enough to qualify for these federal programs.

Fifteen counties had 35 percent or higher proportions of English-language learners. Six were in Kansas, four in Texas, and two in Alaska. Most of these counties had populations of less than 10,000, but two Texas counties on the Mexican border had large populations, including Webb County (the city of Laredo) with 250,000 residents. In many of these counties, the students' native language was Spanish. In many others, the students spoke Native American languages at home.

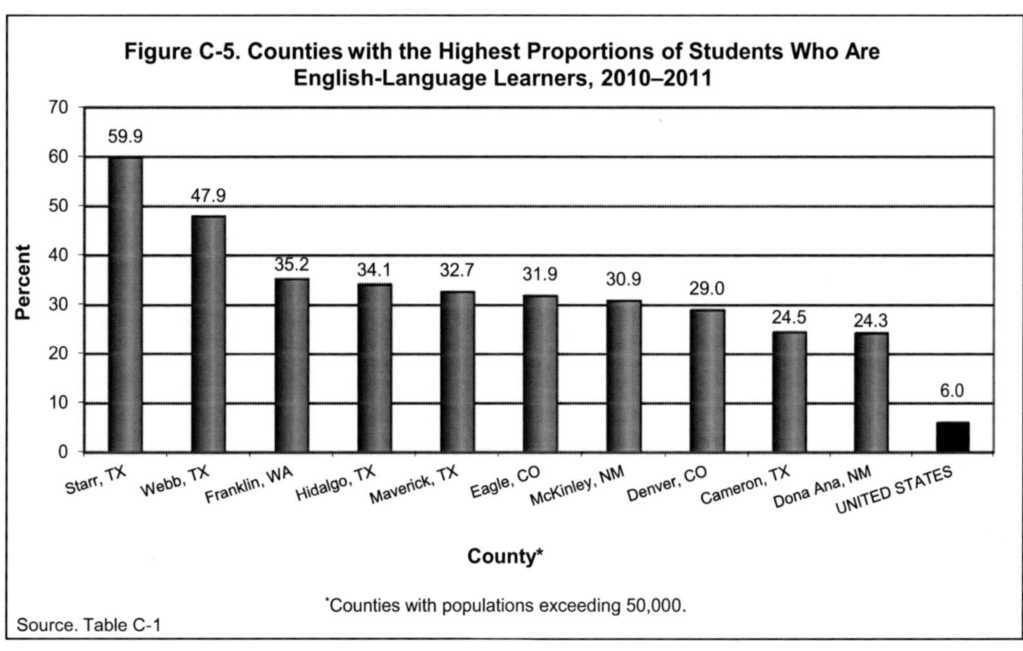

Table C-1. Population, School, and Student Characteristics by County, Selected Years

County	State/ County Code	County Type[1]	Population, 2010		Percent of related children 5–17 years in poverty, 2010	Percent of children under 19 years with no health insurance, 2010	Number of schools and students, 2010–2011			Resident enrollment, 2006–2010 K–12 enrollment	
			Total	Percent 5–17 years			School districts	Schools	Students	Number	Percent public
			1	2	3	4	5	6	7	8	9
UNITED STATES	00000	X	308,745,538	17.5	19.8	8.5	18,045	98,817	49,367,108	54,224,838	89.5
ALABAMA	01000	X	4,779,736	17.3	25.6	6.3	171	1,600	738,322	832,101	89.1
Autauga, AL	01001	2	54,571	20.2	16.4	5.3	1	15	9,904	11,384	89.0
Baldwin, AL	01003	4	182,265	16.9	18.9	9.1	1	46	28,199	29,759	88.1
Barbour, AL	01005	6	27,457	15.7	34.3	6.4	2	10	3,841	4,698	88.1
Bibb, AL	01007	1	22,915	16.7	25.3	6.1	2	11	3,512	3,870	92.5
Blount, AL	01009	1	57,322	18.3	21.3	8.1	2	19	9,946	10,433	92.0
Bullock, AL	01011	6	10,914	15.5	39.5	5.2	1	5	1,579	1,833	91.3
Butler, AL	01013	6	20,947	17.6	38.9	5.5	1	7	3,368	4,009	88.4
Calhoun, AL	01015	3	118,572	16.8	30.8	5.4	5	40	18,636	19,501	90.0
Chambers, AL	01017	6	34,215	16.8	38.2	5.9	2	14	4,881	6,184	90.3
Cherokee, AL	01019	8	25,989	16.1	30.2	7.0	1	8	4,081	3,836	92.1
Chilton, AL	01021	1	43,643	18.2	30.8	7.0	1	12	7,859	7,657	93.8
Choctaw, AL	01023	9	13,859	17.3	26.2	7.3	1	5	1,769	2,538	76.4
Clarke, AL	01025	7	25,833	19.0	29.8	6.7	2	11	4,928	5,647	92.0
Clay, AL	01027	9	13,932	16.8	28.1	7.7	1	4	2,066	2,463	90.4
Cleburne, AL	01029	8	14,972	17.5	25.5	6.8	1	8	2,669	2,577	97.2
Coffee, AL	01031	6	49,948	17.6	30.5	7.4	4	19	9,283	8,377	96.9
Colbert, AL	01033	3	54,428	16.4	30.0	5.6	4	27	8,430	9,200	95.4
Conecuh, AL	01035	9	13,228	17.1	38.6	6.5	2	7	1,709	2,503	89.8
Coosa, AL	01037	8	11,539	15.7	26.9	6.3	1	4	1,277	1,918	95.4
Covington, AL	01039	7	37,765	16.6	28.5	6.4	3	15	6,194	6,092	94.0
Crenshaw, AL	01041	8	13,906	17.8	27.7	8.5	1	4	2,299	2,569	90.8
Cullman, AL	01043	6	80,406	17.1	24.7	6.9	2	36	12,793	13,478	91.6
Dale, AL	01045	4	50,251	17.5	24.4	5.1	3	16	6,521	8,674	89.0
Dallas, AL	01047	4	43,820	19.2	53.8	4.8	2	28	8,033	9,126	90.9
De Kalb, AL	01049	6	71,109	18.7	30.8	7.6	2	19	11,955	12,705	96.2
Elmore, AL	01051	2	79,303	17.5	17.2	5.8	2	18	12,956	14,427	83.4
Escambia, AL	01053	6	38,319	16.4	32.5	6.8	3	18	5,850	6,770	91.2
Etowah, AL	01055	3	104,430	17.1	26.3	6.6	7	45	16,489	17,616	90.1
Fayette, AL	01057	6	17,241	16.5	34.3	6.0	1	6	2,415	3,052	93.7
Franklin, AL	01059	6	31,704	17.7	33.0	8.5	2	13	5,768	5,506	98.8
Geneva, AL	01061	3	26,790	16.5	31.3	7.3	2	12	3,979	4,438	96.9
Greene, AL	01063	3	9,045	18.1	38.3	7.4	1	5	1,348	1,893	89.5
Hale, AL	01065	3	15,760	18.8	31.4	5.9	1	7	2,895	3,346	91.6
Henry, AL	01067	3	17,302	17.2	26.0	7.0	1	8	2,860	2,955	82.4
Houston, AL	01069	3	101,547	17.9	26.8	5.7	3	31	15,677	17,832	85.8
Jackson, AL	01071	6	53,227	16.9	28.0	6.2	3	25	8,500	9,110	92.9
Jefferson, AL	01073	1	658,466	16.8	26.7	6.2	20	220	104,319	113,783	89.5
Lamar, AL	01075	9	14,564	16.2	30.2	6.8	1	5	2,365	2,491	99.2
Lauderdale, AL	01077	3	92,709	16.0	23.8	6.2	2	22	13,141	14,860	89.6
Lawrence, AL	01079	3	34,339	16.9	23.3	7.3	2	15	5,207	6,081	91.7
Lee, AL	01081	3	140,247	16.3	18.9	6.2	4	32	20,710	22,087	91.5
Limestone, AL	01083	2	82,782	17.5	17.8	7.1	2	20	11,954	13,632	89.5
Lowndes, AL	01085	2	11,299	17.6	44.1	6.6	1	9	1,853	2,274	79.5
Macon, AL	01087	6	21,452	15.2	42.4	4.9	3	7	2,629	3,622	90.5
Madison, AL	01089	2	334,811	17.5	16.5	5.4	6	88	51,740	57,300	86.5
Marengo, AL	01091	7	21,027	18.5	30.9	6.5	3	13	4,351	4,342	92.8
Marion, AL	01093	8	30,776	16.1	29.9	5.8	2	15	4,943	4,824	96.6
Marshall, AL	01095	4	93,019	18.0	28.1	7.9	5	34	16,869	15,805	94.4
Mobile, AL	01097	2	412,992	18.3	26.7	6.2	6	115	63,988	77,360	82.9
Monroe, AL	01099	7	23,068	19.3	41.3	6.9	1	11	3,963	4,769	84.7
Montgomery, AL	01101	2	229,363	17.6	29.3	5.8	6	75	31,464	40,501	82.0
Morgan, AL	01103	3	119,490	17.7	20.0	7.9	3	45	11,063	20,957	92.5
Perry, AL	01105	8	10,591	17.7	52.5	6.0	1	5	1,833	1,853	91.5
Pickens, AL	01107	8	19,746	17.3	33.0	7.1	1	10	2,905	3,669	88.3
Pike, AL	01109	6	32,899	14.7	35.1	6.2	2	11	4,369	5,082	90.0
Randolph, AL	01111	6	22,913	17.8	33.1	6.2	2	11	3,908	3,921	92.6
Russell, AL	01113	2	52,947	17.9	34.1	5.3	2	19	9,808	9,545	90.8
St. Clair, AL	01115	1	83,593	17.1	19.5	6.4	2	27	12,753	14,115	90.2
Shelby, AL	01117	1	195,085	18.9	11.7	5.2	3	40	28,063	35,310	82.8
Sumter, AL	01119	8	13,763	16.8	38.6	6.9	1	7	2,053	2,904	93.8

[1]County type codes are from the Economic Research Service of the United States Department of Agriculture. See notes and definitions for more information.
. . . = Not available.

Table C-1. Population, School, and Student Characteristics by County, Selected Years—*Continued*

County	State/ County Code	Characteristics of students, 2010–2011				Number of graduates, 2008–2009	Staff and students, 2010–2011			
		Percent with IEP[2]	Percent eligible for free or reduced lunch	Percent minority	Percent English-language learners		Total staff	Number of teachers	Student/ teacher ratio	Central admin. staff
		10	11	12	13	14	15	16	17	18
UNITED STATES	00000	13.0	47.9	47.5	6.0	2,637,749	6,068,314	3,086,404	16.0	245,266
ALABAMA	01000	11.0	54.9	41.5	2.4	42,082	94,312	49,327	15.0	2,418
Autauga, AL	01001	8.8	43.0	27.7	0.7	593	1,095	551	18.0	17
Baldwin, AL	01003	13.6	42.3	21.3	2.4	1,549	3,404	1,793	15.7	72
Barbour, AL	01005	11.7	71.0	69.0	2.4	220	508	261	14.7	17
Bibb, AL	01007	13.7	62.8	25.1	0.1	194	456	229	15.3	7
Blount, AL	01009	10.4	52.0	14.3	4.7	553	1,177	655	15.2	18
Bullock, AL	01011	12.2	90.2	99.7	5.0	69	220	101	15.6	7
Butler, AL	01013	11.8	75.1	61.8	0.2	223	419	220	15.3	18
Calhoun, AL	01015	9.7	58.1	32.1	1.7	1,063	2,326	1,193	15.6	55
Chambers, AL	01017	12.8	70.9	56.3	0.2	258	637	340	14.4	15
Cherokee, AL	01019	8.6	60.5	9.7	0.4	215	539	294	13.9	13
Chilton, AL	01021	10.4	59.1	22.8	4.8	395	975	549	14.3	17
Choctaw, AL	01023	11.3	76.4	67.0	0.5	109	229	105	16.8	12
Clarke, AL	01025	9.4	67.4	59.5	0.1	307	670	345	14.3	19
Clay, AL	01027	12.1	64.3	25.4	0.8	115	247	109	19.0	8
Cleburne, AL	01029	12.2	58.8	7.7	0.8	195	350	172	15.6	8
Coffee, AL	01031	8.6	44.3	31.4	2.5	569	1,075	547	17.0	34
Colbert, AL	01033	10.4	51.8	24.4	1.1	461	1,072	586	14.4	35
Conecuh, AL	01035	12.5	84.6	83.7	0.1	115	261	112	15.3	8
Coosa, AL	01037	10.2	72.9	47.1	0.9	74	185	91	14.1	4
Covington, AL	01039	12.3	53.0	20.3	0.3	368	783	428	14.5	24
Crenshaw, AL	01041	11.4	59.7	36.7	1.0	144	289	156	14.7	11
Cullman, AL	01043	11.5	53.7	7.6	2.8	700	1,695	938	13.6	28
Dale, AL	01045	10.0	58.4	37.4	1.1	405	850	442	14.8	32
Dallas, AL	01047	11.8	81.6	88.1	0.2	450	501	262	30.7	15
De Kalb, AL	01049	10.1	65.9	35.3	16.3	624	339	195	61.5	10
Elmore, AL	01051	12.0	47.7	30.0	1.5	763	1,530	780	16.6	30
Escambia, AL	01053	10.0	68.9	46.4	0.2	360	797	396	14.8	19
Etowah, AL	01055	12.2	56.7	27.2	2.9	927	2,024	1,113	14.8	42
Fayette, AL	01057	10.8	57.6	16.0	0.2	142	320	166	14.5	13
Franklin, AL	01059	10.9	65.8	24.1	10.3	345	801	458	12.6	23
Geneva, AL	01061	13.4	60.2	19.6	1.5	216	504	269	14.8	12
Greene, AL	01063	9.3	92.9	99.9	0.1	76	213	109	12.4	11
Hale, AL	01065	10.8	74.9	73.2	0.2	192	404	203	14.3	13
Henry, AL	01067	11.2	60.6	40.4	0.7	125	305	142	20.1	8
Houston, AL	01069	11.3	59.8	43.6	1.0	867	1,810	916	17.1	33
Jackson, AL	01071	8.8	59.8	12.8	1.9	533	1,247	626	13.6	30
Jefferson, AL	01073	11.2	47.4	59.6	2.0	5,945	13,535	7,264	14.4	416
Lamar, AL	01075	11.0	57.9	18.9	0.7	114	308	166	14.2	7
Lauderdale, AL	01077	9.6	48.9	17.7	1.3	872	1,696	891	14.8	31
Lawrence, AL	01079	10.3	58.4	31.5	0.9	367	727	353	14.7	15
Lee, AL	01081	9.0	46.5	38.5	1.4	1,174	2,665	1,401	14.8	65
Limestone, AL	01083	9.2	45.0	23.4	4.9	713	1,537	800	14.9	40
Lowndes, AL	01085	12.4	92.7	98.5	...	112	287	131	14.2	11
Macon, AL	01087	10.7	98.1	98.9	...	167	357	162	16.2	15
Madison, AL	01089	10.3	36.8	40.0	2.5	3,156	6,480	3,487	14.8	168
Marengo, AL	01091	9.4	68.2	64.2	0.6	314	596	341	12.8	18
Marion, AL	01093	9.4	56.1	7.3	0.9	252	607	337	14.7	19
Marshall, AL	01095	9.5	55.0	20.6	7.2	894	2,185	1,192	14.2	57
Mobile, AL	01097	12.6	68.1	55.1	1.6	3,369	8,354	4,169	15.3	159
Monroe, AL	01099	8.2	68.0	55.4	...	223	525	262	15.1	12
Montgomery, AL	01101	11.0	69.9	84.7	3.7	1,279	3,910	1,916	16.4	161
Morgan, AL	01103	11.3	44.1	16.4	2.8	1,163	2,967	1,622	6.8	56
Perry, AL	01105	9.7	96.9	99.2	0.2	120	254	128	14.3	14
Pickens, AL	01107	10.7	73.9	61.1	0.5	182	389	190	15.3	9
Pike, AL	01109	12.3	69.4	59.1	1.5	231	577	305	14.3	24
Randolph, AL	01111	10.9	63.9	29.0	1.8	239	491	269	14.5	16
Russell, AL	01113	9.2	69.0	57.8	0.2	468	1,234	588	16.7	31
St. Clair, AL	01115	11.2	48.8	14.5	1.3	739	1,518	836	15.3	34
Shelby, AL	01117	6.7	28.0	26.2	5.3	1,597	3,724	1,926	14.6	59
Sumter, AL	01119	13.2	90.9	99.6	...	159	160	0	...	18

[2]IEP= Individual Education Program. See notes and definitions for more information

... Not available

Table C-1. Population, School, and Student Characteristics by County, Selected Years—*Continued*

County	State/ County Code	Revenues, 2008–2009				Current expenditures, 2008–2009			Resident population 16 to 19 years, 2006–2010			
			Percentage of revenue from									
		Total revenue ($1,000's)	Federal government	State government	Local government	Amount ($1,000's)	Amount per student	Percent for instruction	Total population 16 to 19 years	Percent enrolled in school	Percent high school graduates, not enrolled in school	Percent not enrolled, not grads, not employed, or not in labor force
		19	20	21	22	23	24	25	26	27	28	29
UNITED STATES	00000	608,170,448	9.3	45.6	45.1	512,981,346	10,473	60.6	17,793,067	84.0	9.8	4.1
ALABAMA	01000	7,186,390	10.1	57.9	32.0	6,614,077	8,870	58.0	276,194	81.7	9.8	5.9
Autauga, AL	01001	82,536	7.1	71.3	21.7	73,631	7,420	61.5	3,528	84.9	8.3	4.9
Baldwin, AL	01003	260,391	7.3	46.7	46.0	254,904	9,399	58.3	9,139	81.0	11.9	5.5
Barbour, AL	01005	35,604	15.7	59.5	24.9	35,263	8,896	58.4	1,507	82.0	7.3	8.4
Bibb, AL	01007	33,403	11.5	65.7	22.8	30,933	8,677	55.5	1,240	72.5	15.1	7.5
Blount, AL	01009	78,443	8.3	71.2	20.4	75,165	7,665	61.3	3,183	76.8	12.4	4.4
Bullock, AL	01011	15,409	19.7	64.3	16.0	15,390	9,524	50.5	753	55.6	12.2	32.1
Butler, AL	01013	30,996	15.8	63.8	20.5	30,615	9,147	57.0	1,008	84.5	13.0	1.9
Calhoun, AL	01015	166,941	10.4	60.4	29.3	155,162	8,370	57.7	6,962	83.1	8.8	6.2
Chambers, AL	01017	44,378	12.0	67.2	20.8	40,803	8,112	56.6	1,865	74.7	16.7	3.8
Cherokee, AL	01019	41,043	9.0	67.1	23.9	37,217	9,113	57.3	1,173	62.2	7.7	16.9
Chilton, AL	01021	64,826	10.6	71.5	17.9	58,992	7,745	60.6	2,286	67.9	21.4	7.7
Choctaw, AL	01023	20,412	13.5	54.3	32.3	17,094	9,064	52.4	798	84.2	8.0	6.8
Clarke, AL	01025	47,048	12.9	66.0	21.1	43,252	8,628	57.0	2,121	82.6	12.5	5.0
Clay, AL	01027	19,928	9.0	71.9	19.1	17,789	8,352	60.9	586	84.3	11.6	2.7
Cleburne, AL	01029	28,507	8.1	74.9	17.0	22,354	8,413	57.0	793	74.4	11.4	12.2
Coffee, AL	01031	82,454	11.0	63.1	25.9	76,950	8,431	60.2	2,459	82.7	9.9	3.2
Colbert, AL	01033	84,679	9.0	57.4	33.6	80,184	9,469	55.7	2,987	82.4	12.3	3.4
Conecuh, AL	01035	19,409	14.4	61.0	24.6	19,533	11,753	50.1	668	64.5	20.2	15.3
Coosa, AL	01037	12,386	17.4	61.7	20.9	12,333	9,142	53.3	571	76.7	20.7	2.3
Covington, AL	01039	57,974	11.7	62.9	25.3	52,839	8,571	58.9	2,200	82.3	6.5	8.4
Crenshaw, AL	01041	21,974	12.5	68.0	19.6	20,129	8,094	59.1	666	79.7	12.9	5.1
Cullman, AL	01043	120,816	9.0	61.9	29.1	110,462	8,627	60.4	4,109	81.0	11.8	4.6
Dale, AL	01045	62,267	12.1	62.3	25.5	58,828	8,934	57.0	2,794	72.6	22.2	2.7
Dallas, AL	01047	76,537	16.9	65.5	17.6	72,898	8,892	55.3	2,663	85.4	9.4	4.5
De Kalb, AL	01049	102,017	12.1	65.4	22.5	101,846	8,538	62.0	3,736	79.8	6.5	10.2
Elmore, AL	01051	110,321	10.3	64.8	24.9	103,152	8,037	61.9	4,535	78.9	12.5	7.2
Escambia, AL	01053	57,691	12.3	60.5	27.2	52,474	8,933	57.4	2,165	83.8	7.9	5.1
Etowah, AL	01055	150,970	11.9	64.2	23.9	135,154	8,299	58.9	5,916	78.7	10.4	7.4
Fayette, AL	01057	23,364	12.0	63.8	24.2	22,564	8,983	56.2	1,042	87.3	9.8	2.8
Franklin, AL	01059	52,115	11.7	63.6	24.7	49,329	8,586	58.9	1,620	77.4	11.4	4.9
Geneva, AL	01061	33,338	12.0	68.6	19.4	31,429	7,933	58.5	1,490	76.5	14.3	6.2
Greene, AL	01063	15,944	18.6	57.2	24.3	14,309	10,027	50.1	735	83.0	13.3	3.7
Hale, AL	01065	30,905	14.2	67.5	18.4	26,840	8,914	59.2	1,008	77.6	8.9	8.3
Henry, AL	01067	26,697	11.1	71.6	17.3	22,404	8,103	56.9	1,100	88.5	6.7	4.8
Houston, AL	01069	131,035	12.6	60.1	27.3	131,573	8,519	60.4	5,400	78.4	11.5	7.4
Jackson, AL	01071	86,128	10.1	63.0	27.0	81,163	9,382	54.6	2,965	84.0	6.9	5.3
Jefferson, AL	01073	1,103,012	8.9	49.9	41.1	1,001,298	9,540	56.4	36,783	81.3	9.8	6.3
Lamar, AL	01075	22,628	9.6	70.0	20.4	19,491	8,308	57.1	677	72.7	7.1	13.3
Lauderdale, AL	01077	125,895	9.4	57.5	33.1	118,781	9,012	61.7	5,155	87.5	8.1	3.3
Lawrence, AL	01079	54,927	10.4	65.8	23.8	48,497	8,949	58.1	1,802	82.5	12.8	3.8
Lee, AL	01081	198,049	6.9	52.3	40.9	176,115	8,847	60.4	11,074	90.6	4.8	3.1
Limestone, AL	01083	113,698	6.6	60.1	33.3	104,431	8,870	63.1	3,856	80.8	6.1	10.1
Lowndes, AL	01085	22,673	26.2	55.7	18.1	22,454	11,497	53.4	885	74.7	17.0	8.0
Macon, AL	01087	29,038	18.3	61.2	20.4	26,925	9,205	50.3	2,383	93.2	3.3	3.1
Madison, AL	01089	481,422	7.1	54.5	38.4	469,325	9,121	59.0	19,272	84.8	8.4	4.2
Marengo, AL	01091	44,490	11.8	62.6	25.7	38,875	8,582	59.0	1,164	83.3	15.9	0.2
Marion, AL	01093	46,140	8.8	69.9	21.2	41,050	8,097	61.6	1,446	86.7	7.5	5.7
Marshall, AL	01095	147,597	11.2	62.7	26.2	140,563	8,653	58.5	4,845	74.7	13.6	8.7
Mobile, AL	01097	609,389	12.8	57.8	29.4	565,199	8,822	55.6	24,444	81.2	9.9	7.9
Monroe, AL	01099	37,903	13.0	69.6	17.5	36,346	8,625	60.0	1,474	86.8	7.6	1.1
Montgomery, AL	01101	331,136	11.9	54.6	33.5	276,562	8,834	56.5	13,105	82.2	6.8	6.8
Morgan, AL	01103	194,238	8.0	53.1	39.0	185,855	9,396	60.5	5,965	79.4	10.9	5.5
Perry, AL	01105	18,010	20.3	66.0	13.7	18,261	9,336	56.4	1,012	83.4	6.7	8.4
Pickens, AL	01107	27,411	13.6	69.3	17.1	27,074	8,929	59.0	1,226	85.1	4.9	8.6
Pike, AL	01109	42,594	13.9	58.9	27.3	41,432	9,357	57.8	2,998	93.0	2.1	2.2
Randolph, AL	01111	33,700	11.4	65.3	23.4	31,371	8,136	59.8	1,381	82.7	11.4	5.4
Russell, AL	01113	84,909	13.1	62.1	24.8	82,675	8,733	57.3	2,921	68.9	12.5	13.1
St. Clair, AL	01115	108,953	8.8	66.6	24.5	98,951	7,910	62.2	4,210	77.8	12.7	3.9
Shelby, AL	01117	269,297	5.3	51.9	42.7	233,333	8,580	58.7	9,645	88.4	8.8	1.4
Sumter, AL	01119	21,610	20.0	61.3	18.7	21,889	9,386	53.1	1,217	82.9	12.8	4.3

Note. Data in columns 26 through 41 from the American Community Survey are subject to sampling error, which can be especially large in small counties and small population groups. See notes and definitions for more information.

Table C-1. Population, School, and Student Characteristics by County, Selected Years—*Continued*

County	State/ County Code	High school graduates, 2006–2010			College enrollment, 2006–2010		College graduates, 2006–2010 (percent)						
		Population 25 years and over	High school diploma or less (percent)	High school diploma or more (percent)	Number	Percent public	Bachelor's degree or more	+/- U.S. percent with Bachelor's degree or more	Non-Hispanic White	Black or African American	American Indian and Alaska Native	Asian, Hawaiian, and Pacific Islander	Hispanic or Latino[3]
		30	31	32	33	34	35	36	37	38	39	40	41
UNITED STATES	00000	199,726,659	44.0	85.0	21,790,019	73.9	27.9	0.0	30.9	17.7	13.0	49.2	13.0
ALABAMA	01000	3,108,132	50.4	81.4	305,547	83.8	21.7	-6.2	24.1	14.4	13.4	50.2	12.3
Autauga, AL	01001	33,884	49.9	85.3	3,076	72.3	21.8	-6.1	23.0	14.2	22.2	46.9	28.6
Baldwin, AL	01003	121,560	42.3	87.6	7,056	82.2	26.8	-1.1	29.1	8.6	10.6	51.1	10.3
Barbour, AL	01005	18,879	63.5	71.9	1,046	91.9	13.5	-14.4	20.2	5.1	0.0	0.0	20.3
Bibb, AL	01007	15,082	67.8	74.6	730	100.0	10.0	-17.9	10.7	6.6	0.0	33.3	0.0
Blount, AL	01009	38,085	61.8	74.7	2,265	84.1	12.5	-15.4	12.8	23.2	8.7	94.4	1.1
Bullock, AL	01011	7,301	61.9	74.7	484	96.1	12.0	-15.9	21.8	6.0	70.8	42.3	0.0
Butler, AL	01013	14,039	63.9	74.8	969	94.1	11.0	-16.9	13.7	6.1	0.0	60.0	0.0
Calhoun, AL	01015	77,722	56.0	78.5	8,357	91.9	16.1	-11.8	16.6	12.3	21.5	53.9	16.1
Chambers, AL	01017	23,737	62.5	71.9	1,353	91.3	10.8	-17.1	14.4	4.4	0.0	21.3	17.7
Cherokee, AL	01019	18,554	61.9	73.4	877	92.6	10.5	-17.4	10.8	2.2	2.0	0.0	29.0
Chilton, AL	01021	28,554	64.6	75.9	1,149	82.4	12.2	-15.7	13.2	7.7	3.6	64.6	1.8
Choctaw, AL	01023	9,793	68.2	71.1	546	84.1	10.9	-17.0	13.0	7.1	0.0	66.7	0.0
Clarke, AL	01025	16,839	65.9	76.1	1,106	87.1	13.5	-14.4	17.7	7.4	0.0	68.6	0.0
Clay, AL	01027	9,828	67.4	71.4	402	89.3	9.5	-18.4	10.5	6.6	0.0	0.0	0.0
Cleburne, AL	01029	10,130	69.2	70.3	395	90.4	8.4	-19.5	8.6	7.9	0.0	0.0	0.0
Coffee, AL	01031	32,426	49.0	79.3	2,341	86.8	22.1	-5.8	24.4	10.8	15.8	27.0	17.0
Colbert, AL	01033	37,986	54.2	80.1	2,209	94.2	16.4	-11.5	16.6	16.1	1.9	45.7	8.6
Conecuh, AL	01035	8,917	65.7	71.3	430	88.8	9.7	-18.2	13.0	5.5	0.0	0.0	0.0
Coosa, AL	01037	8,169	69.4	73.1	349	100.0	10.6	-17.3	13.2	5.0	0.0	0.0	0.0
Covington, AL	01039	26,024	60.9	76.5	1,428	90.3	13.1	-14.8	14.5	4.4	0.0	0.0	2.1
Crenshaw, AL	01041	9,548	64.5	73.7	611	94.4	10.1	-17.8	11.5	3.3	0.0	31.3	3.6
Cullman, AL	01043	54,240	56.7	76.9	4,375	91.3	13.8	-14.1	14.1	10.7	4.9	20.7	5.7
Dale, AL	01045	32,541	47.4	82.2	2,747	88.6	17.5	-10.4	18.9	11.0	14.6	27.9	17.6
Dallas, AL	01047	28,045	59.8	76.8	2,454	79.2	14.3	-13.6	18.7	11.7	0.0	39.4	0.0
De Kalb, AL	01049	46,314	65.7	68.1	2,579	93.8	10.9	-17.0	11.5	4.5	5.6	45.2	3.4
Elmore, AL	01051	51,758	51.4	83.8	3,422	80.1	20.2	-7.7	23.4	8.1	22.9	12.8	13.7
Escambia, AL	01053	25,907	62.3	73.0	1,391	89.1	10.9	-17.0	13.1	6.3	2.8	65.5	17.7
Etowah, AL	01055	71,016	52.0	81.2	4,502	90.0	15.8	-12.1	16.6	12.1	6.0	29.3	7.2
Fayette, AL	01057	12,082	62.9	74.7	526	91.3	9.5	-18.4	9.6	8.2	0.0	0.0	21.4
Franklin, AL	01059	20,876	62.6	69.6	1,020	92.5	11.8	-16.1	12.7	4.1	0.0	39.0	6.1
Geneva, AL	01061	18,274	65.1	72.3	865	90.4	8.0	-19.9	9.0	0.3	0.0	0.0	5.9
Greene, AL	01063	6,088	64.3	72.6	345	91.3	9.9	-18.0	12.9	9.3	0.0	0.0	0.0
Hale, AL	01065	10,552	64.2	69.9	739	79.7	10.0	-17.9	16.6	4.7	0.0	0.0	19.2
Henry, AL	01067	11,969	61.8	76.1	710	88.3	15.0	-12.9	18.5	6.6	0.0	16.2	0.0
Houston, AL	01069	66,161	51.3	82.0	4,007	84.6	19.0	-8.9	22.0	9.4	13.6	21.2	12.0
Jackson, AL	01071	36,997	62.4	74.0	2,143	94.4	12.0	-15.9	12.4	3.0	14.8	46.2	4.9
Jefferson, AL	01073	436,589	41.5	86.6	44,402	72.1	28.8	0.9	36.5	16.7	14.7	73.4	19.7
Lamar, AL	01075	10,283	66.3	75.3	433	91.2	9.3	-18.6	9.6	5.4	33.3	0.0	0.0
Lauderdale, AL	01077	61,976	51.1	82.9	6,785	89.0	21.5	-6.4	22.6	10.3	33.5	49.6	7.0
Lawrence, AL	01079	23,169	64.0	75.2	1,416	86.7	10.7	-17.2	9.8	9.9	27.1	69.2	22.3
Lee, AL	01081	75,568	41.5	85.2	26,670	94.8	30.9	3.0	34.9	15.4	20.8	69.3	19.0
Limestone, AL	01083	53,419	52.2	80.5	3,925	90.8	20.8	-7.1	21.8	15.3	6.3	46.4	13.2
Lowndes, AL	01085	7,626	65.8	73.4	309	82.5	12.8	-15.1	24.0	7.8	100.0	0.0	0.0
Macon, AL	01087	13,185	50.4	78.8	3,897	32.1	20.9	-7.0	18.5	21.3	0.0	0.0	0.0
Madison, AL	01089	212,171	34.4	87.8	28,730	82.5	37.4	9.5	40.5	27.7	27.1	59.0	17.9
Marengo, AL	01091	13,985	58.0	79.7	622	93.1	17.9	-10.0	25.8	9.5	21.1	0.0	6.5
Marion, AL	01093	21,843	64.2	71.0	1,332	87.4	8.8	-19.1	9.1	2.8	57.1	0.0	2.7
Marshall, AL	01095	60,272	58.5	73.7	3,443	90.8	14.5	-13.4	15.4	19.9	2.6	29.6	2.8
Mobile, AL	01097	263,796	52.0	82.3	25,298	78.2	19.8	-8.1	22.9	13.6	13.0	25.2	14.9
Monroe, AL	01099	15,390	64.5	75.4	799	82.2	11.2	-16.7	16.8	2.7	0.0	41.9	0.0
Montgomery, AL	01101	145,359	42.8	84.7	19,537	78.9	30.5	2.6	41.7	19.9	20.0	50.9	15.9
Morgan, AL	01103	79,297	50.8	80.8	5,458	85.6	19.1	-8.8	21.1	9.0	18.8	31.1	4.0
Perry, AL	01105	6,633	66.4	71.5	748	43.9	13.3	-14.6	28.0	6.0	0.0	0.0	0.0
Pickens, AL	01107	13,351	63.2	78.7	852	96.6	11.5	-16.4	14.0	7.5	21.4	0.0	20.8
Pike, AL	01109	18,646	56.1	79.4	6,011	96.1	23.7	-4.2	31.7	9.3	0.0	69.9	9.7
Randolph, AL	01111	15,319	64.7	71.6	995	93.9	12.2	-15.7	13.4	7.5	38.0	0.0	0.0
Russell, AL	01113	33,442	58.4	76.9	2,875	88.0	11.9	-16.0	11.7	11.5	51.6	20.9	16.7
St. Clair, AL	01115	54,763	57.2	79.3	2,924	82.3	14.5	-13.4	14.9	9.9	6.3	46.5	7.2
Shelby, AL	01117	124,951	30.8	91.5	11,021	85.7	39.6	11.7	41.0	36.7	21.3	50.4	14.0
Sumter, AL	01119	8,634	64.8	75.4	1,092	87.7	12.8	-15.1	28.4	7.4	0.0	0.0	0.0

Note. Data in columns 26 through 41 from the American Community Survey are subject to sampling error, which can be especially large in small counties and small population groups. See notes and definitions for more information.
. . . = Not available.
[3]May be of any race.

Table C-1. Population, School, and Student Characteristics by County, Selected Years—*Continued*

County	State/ County Code	County Type[1]	Population, 2010		Percent of related children 5–17 years in poverty, 2010	Percent of children under 19 years with no health insurance, 2010	Number of schools and students, 2010–2011			Resident enrollment, 2006–2010 K–12 enrollment	
			Total	Percent 5–17 years			School districts	Schools	Students	Number	Percent public
			1	2	3	4	5	6	7	8	9
ALABAMA—*(Continued)*											
Talladega, AL	01121	4	82,291	17.4	30.7	5.0	4	35	12,499	14,270	94.6
Tallapoosa, AL	01123	6	41,616	16.4	27.6	6.8	2	12	6,181	7,264	94.3
Tuscaloosa, AL	01125	3	194,656	15.5	21.7	6.5	4	61	28,133	29,782	91.1
Walker, AL	01127	1	67,023	16.8	34.2	5.5	2	29	10,985	11,255	94.7
Washington, AL	01129	8	17,581	19.5	26.0	7.5	1	8	3,418	3,675	96.0
Wilcox, AL	01131	8	11,670	20.9	47.5	7.3	1	7	1,991	2,584	88.0
Winston, AL	01133	6	24,484	16.2	29.8	6.1	2	14	4,395	4,208	99.1
ALASKA	02000	X	710,231	18.8	12.1	13.1	54	509	132,104	134,806	92.3
Aleutians East Borough, AK	02013	9	3,141	7.9	14.1	27.4	1	6	275	258	95.4
Aleutians West Census Area, AK	02016	7	5,561	11.0	8.6	20.5	2	4	497	404	100.0
Anchorage, AK	02020	2	291,826	18.4	9.5	11.2	3	103	49,522	53,301	93.6
Bethel, AK	02050	7	17,013	26.0	25.9	13.9	3	40	4,989	4,747	99.2
Bristol Bay, AK	02060	9	997	17.8	7.6	15.1	2	17	556	287	93.7
Denali Borough	02068	8	1,826	16.3	5.4	14.1	1	4	768	205	84.9
Dillingham, AK	02070	9	4,847	23.6	25.6	16.1	2	11	1,124	1,368	98.8
Fairbanks North Star, AK	02090	3	97,581	17.5	11.1	13.1	2	45	15,672	16,749	88.2
Haines, AK	02100	9	2,508	14.8	16.8	20.1	1	4	310	329	96.4
Hoonah-Angoon, AK	02105		2,150	13.9	23.4	23.2	3	8	294	258	100.0
Juneau, AK	02110	5	31,275	17.1	7.7	11.4	1	14	5,094	5,533	93.2
Kenai Peninsula, AK	02122	7	55,400	17.4	12.0	15.7	1	44	9,327	10,249	91.2
Ketchikan Gateway, AK	02130	7	13,477	17.2	12.2	14.2	1	10	2,247	2,425	86.9
Kodiak Island, AK	02150	7	13,592	20.2	8.3	18.7	1	15	2,565	2,608	87.2
Lake and Peninsula Borough, AK	02164	9	1,631	21.7	21.8	19.2	...	...	...	543	94.8
Matanuska-Susitna, AK	02170	2	88,995	21.1	11.4	13.0	1	44	17,079	18,305	86.8
Nome, AK	02180	7	9,492	23.6	25.8	15.2	2	20	2,556	2,356	99.7
North Slope, AK	02185	7	9,430	15.9	11.0	13.1	1	11	1,879	2,002	99.9
Northwest Arctic Borough, AK	02188	7	7,523	23.6	18.7	15.4	1	12	1,930	2,013	98.4
Petersburg, AK	02195		3,815	17.4	12.3	17.2	2	4	576	687	98.5
Prince of Wales-Hyder, AK	02198		5,559	18.1	20.1	22.9	5	19	1,280	987	95.0
Sitka, AK	02220	7	8,881	16.5	9.7	16.0	2	7	1,788	1,609	100.0
Skagway Municipality, AK	02230		968	10.6	6.1	18.4	1	1	96	156	71.8
Southeast Fairbanks, AK	02240	8	7,029	19.4	17.4	16.5	2	14	1,386	1,436	87.7
Valdez-Cordova, AK	02261	9	9,636	17.9	9.3	16.3	3	12	1,513	1,788	95.5
Wade Hampton, AK	02270	9	7,459	29.5	39.5	11.4	3	13	2,471	2,349	99.6
Wrangell City and Borough, AK	02275		2,369	16.5	15.9	18.0	1	4	346	520	97.1
Yakutat Borough	02282	9	662	18.4	20.3	21.2	1	1	119	170	100.0
Yukon-Koyukuk, AK	02290	8	5,588	19.8	29.1	17.4	5	22	5,845	1,164	93.2
ARIZONA	04000	X	6,392,017	18.4	23.0	13.1	673	2,265	1,071,690	1,145,594	93.2
Apache, AZ	04001	6	71,518	23.4	36.4	14.1	14	40	12,857	17,555	95.4
Cochise, AZ	04003	4	131,346	16.6	24.7	11.8	30	72	20,044	21,909	92.2
Coconino, AZ	04005	3	134,421	17.0	26.2	12.9	21	62	19,524	22,684	96.3
Gila, AZ	04007	4	53,597	15.7	30.3	14.6	14	33	8,128	8,263	90.6
Graham, AZ	04009	6	37,220	19.8	26.0	12.3	15	34	6,434	7,112	94.0
Greenlee, AZ	04011	7	8,437	21.4	15.0	10.6	8	8	1,562	1,736	93.4
La Paz, AZ	04012	6	20,489	12.9	35.8	18.1	7	13	2,540	2,568	98.2
Maricopa, AZ	04013	1	3,817,117	19.0	21.5	12.8	310	1,171	685,440	706,838	93.2
Mohave, AZ	04015	4	200,186	15.1	30.7	14.5	24	64	25,653	30,612	91.4
Navajo, AZ	04017	4	107,449	21.6	33.3	11.0	22	82	19,105	24,830	95.3
Pima, AZ	04019	2	980,263	16.6	22.8	12.3	90	378	145,499	161,582	91.8
Pinal, AZ	04021	1	375,770	18.5	17.9	15.9	33	116	51,277	58,677	93.4
Santa Cruz, AZ	04023	4	47,420	23.0	38.8	16.0	13	27	10,328	12,058	98.2
Yavapai, AZ	04025	3	211,033	14.1	24.7	15.6	50	96	24,946	29,861	92.6
Yuma, AZ	04027	3	195,751	20.5	31.6	14.4	17	63	37,626	39,309	95.0

[1]County type codes are from the Economic Research Service of the United States Department of Agriculture. See notes and definitions for more information.
. . . = Not available.

Table C-1. Population, School, and Student Characteristics by County, Selected Years—*Continued*

County	State/ County Code	Characteristics of students, 2010–2011				Number of graduates, 2008–2009	Staff and students, 2010–2011			
		Percent with IEP[2]	Percent eligible for free or reduced lunch	Percent minority	Percent English-language learners		Total staff	Number of teachers	Student/ teacher ratio	Central admin. staff
		10	11	12	13	14	15	16	17	18
ALABAMA—*(Continued)*										
Talladega, AL	01121	12.9	69.6	42.6	0.6	735	1,728	904	13.8	37
Tallapoosa, AL	01123	13.3	60.0	38.0	1.5	365	744	417	14.8	27
Tuscaloosa, AL	01125	13.8	55.3	48.7	1.7	1,430	3,612	1,912	14.7	77
Walker, AL	01127	12.9	55.6	11.5	0.8	533	1,509	784	14.0	50
Washington, AL	01129	10.3	60.0	39.8	0.4	238	488	285	12.0	8
Wilcox, AL	01131	9.3	96.4	99.5	...	132	284	129	15.4	11
Winston, AL	01133	12.9	57.5	4.7	1.5	286	611	314	14.0	22
ALASKA	02000	13.7	38.4	47.8	11.3	8,006	17,741	8,110	16.3	1,445
Aleutians East Borough, AK	02013	14.9	42.9	86.9	...	16	59	32	8.7	4
Aleutians West Census Area, AK	02016	8.9	20.7	75.5	13.9	19	88	41	12.2	5
Anchorage, AK	02020	14.1	39.2	52.6	10.8	2,981	6,291	2,989	16.6	530
Bethel, AK	02050	12.1	72.8	96.3	62.4	180	862	360	13.9	105
Bristol Bay, AK	02060	12.6	38.9	65.0	...	27	152	58	9.6	18
Denali Borough	02068	5.3	...	24.1	...	21	52	23	32.8	5
Dillingham, AK	02070	15.4	75.9	94.6	13.3	60	251	91	12.3	29
Fairbanks North Star, AK	02090	15.0	21.4	31.4	2.8	938	2,083	891	17.6	160
Haines, AK	02100	16.1	58.7	21.6	0.3	20	60	25	12.7	4
Hoonah-Angoon, AK	02105	19.0	43.9	75.5	...	14	79	29	10.0	3
Juneau, AK	02110	16.0	26.7	46.2	7.4	348	740	336	15.2	51
Kenai Peninsula, AK	02122	14.2	34.6	21.6	2.2	680	1,182	594	15.7	68
Ketchikan Gateway, AK	02130	8.9	38.2	47.4	3.6	155	325	151	14.9	12
Kodiak Island, AK	02150	12.5	43.6	58.0	11.4	197	400	182	14.1	41
Lake and Peninsula Borough, AK	02164	...	68.4	85.1	...	...	...	...	...	...
Matanuska-Susitna, AK	02170	15.0	32.5	20.0	2.5	1,012	1,956	993	17.2	143
Nome, AK	02180	10.2	77.3	94.7	33.1	129	597	231	11.1	38
North Slope, AK	02185	10.2	42.6	96.1	28.4	122	426	163	11.5	45
Northwest Arctic Borough, AK	02188	10.5	74.5	97.1	29.9	97	358	141	13.6	37
Petersburg, AK	02195	17.2	52.0	41.4	2.8	51	100	46	12.4	10
Prince of Wales-Hyder, AK	02198	16.6	58.1	55.6	...	70	224	96	13.3	17
Sitka, AK	02220	10.6	37.6	57.0	6.4	180	239	122	14.7	18
Skagway Municipality, AK	02230	8.3	7.3	14.6	...	5	17	9	10.7	1
Southeast Fairbanks, AK	02240	13.7	41.9	29.5	17.9	71	204	93	14.9	15
Valdez-Cordova, AK	02261	13.9	30.2	39.0	1.4	123	266	109	13.8	22
Wade Hampton, AK	02270	12.7	73.0	99.8	79.2	111	449	194	12.7	36
Wrangell City and Borough, AK	02275	14.5	54.6	40.5	...	31	60	24	14.3	7
Yakutat Borough	02282	16.8	80.7	82.4	...	8	25	12	9.7	3
Yukon-Koyukuk, AK	02290	7.6	29.8	65.2	2.7	340	194	75	78.0	19
ARIZONA	04000	11.7	45.1	57.1	7.1	62,287	96,567	50,022	21.4	1,275
Apache, AZ	04001	13.3	71.0	84.3	3.3	781	1,854	773	16.6	30
Cochise, AZ	04003	11.2	49.8	59.8	8.6	1,331	2,126	998	20.1	56
Coconino, AZ	04005	14.3	36.3	57.3	4.5	1,298	2,235	1,069	18.3	45
Gila, AZ	04007	14.3	60.3	52.2	2.4	486	992	460	17.7	27
Graham, AZ	04009	12.0	46.8	43.4	0.2	419	680	365	17.6	21
Greenlee, AZ	04011	12.7	31.7	60.6	0.1	111	210	96	16.3	12
La Paz, AZ	04012	16.7	75.9	75.6	5.9	178	357	138	18.5	13
Maricopa, AZ	04013	11.0	41.4	55.3	7.5	39,493	58,008	31,303	21.9	620
Mohave, AZ	04015	12.0	56.0	30.9	2.3	1,522	2,157	1,109	23.1	31
Navajo, AZ	04017	13.0	58.2	59.8	4.2	1,440	2,222	1,073	17.8	52
Pima, AZ	04019	14.3	44.6	63.4	6.0	8,991	13,983	6,978	20.9	167
Pinal, AZ	04021	13.6	51.4	55.6	3.5	1,658	4,952	2,400	21.4	80
Santa Cruz, AZ	04023	7.6	75.5	95.7	18.9	677	1,025	529	19.5	13
Yavapai, AZ	04025	12.4	42.4	30.0	3.0	1,533	2,241	1,129	22.1	55
Yuma, AZ	04027	10.0	71.9	83.6	17.8	2,288	3,527	1,603	23.5	55

[2]IEP= Individual Education Program. See notes and definitions for more information

... Not available

Table C-1. Population, School, and Student Characteristics by County, Selected Years—*Continued*

County	State/ County Code	Revenues, 2008–2009				Current expenditures, 2008–2009			Resident population 16 to 19 years, 2006–2010			
			Percentage of revenue from									
		Total revenue ($1,000's)	Federal government	State government	Local government	Amount ($1,000's)	Amount per student	Percent for instruction	Total population 16 to 19 years	Percent enrolled in school	Percent high school graduates, not enrolled in school	Percent not enrolled, not grads, not employed, or not in labor force
		19	20	21	22	23	24	25	26	27	28	29
ALABAMA— *(Continued)*												
Talladega, AL	01121	118,355	11.3	59.7	29.0	114,375	8,952	54.8	4,844	81.5	6.9	9.5
Tallapoosa, AL	01123	59,616	10.8	58.9	30.3	58,248	8,988	61.6	2,270	82.3	5.3	8.3
Tuscaloosa, AL	01125	292,044	8.9	53.6	37.6	234,682	8,439	56.8	15,638	80.1	11.9	4.2
Walker, AL	01127	120,338	9.7	62.1	28.2	103,928	9,387	57.0	3,446	82.9	10.2	6.4
Washington, AL	01129	32,449	12.0	62.9	25.1	30,737	8,815	61.1	978	87.7	8.3	2.5
Wilcox, AL	01131	21,801	18.6	64.3	17.1	20,181	9,330	52.5	906	71.9	20.5	1.7
Winston, AL	01133	44,182	10.1	64.1	25.8	40,216	9,148	56.4	1,401	76.4	10.1	9.1
ALASKA	02000	2,158,970	14.5	62.9	22.6	2,025,407	15,552	55.8	43,185	77.8	15.0	4.8
Aleutians East Borough, AK	02013	9,201	19.5	63.1	17.4	9,012	32,771	53.0	70	71.4	28.6	0.0
Aleutians West Census Area, AK	02016	12,294	10.2	51.2	38.5	10,908	21,017	56.1	95	72.6	26.3	1.1
Anchorage, AK	02020	658,906	10.6	59.1	30.2	647,979	13,191	56.7	16,949	78.2	14.0	4.4
Bethel, AK	02050	167,783	30.8	64.8	4.4	126,738	26,453	52.7	1,445	74.2	10.5	13.4
Bristol Bay, AK	02060	19,864	21.0	64.3	14.7	20,325	35,910	45.4	61	88.5	3.3	8.2
Denali Borough	02068	6,650	3.6	69.7	26.8	7,315	17,212	52.8	51	68.6	7.8	23.5
Dillingham, AK	02070	38,525	23.9	69.8	6.3	29,843	26,224	46.2	397	78.8	15.6	5.5
Fairbanks North Star, AK	02090	227,474	14.3	63.7	22.0	227,301	14,440	57.8	5,612	78.3	16.8	3.6
Haines, AK	02100	5,960	8.7	58.8	32.5	6,106	19,571	63.6	19	79.0	15.8	5.3
Hoonah-Angoon, AK	02105	8,915	28.2	62.8	9.0	7,671	25,742	49.4	63	76.2	17.5	6.4
Juneau, AK	02110	79,124	6.3	56.3	37.4	74,846	14,862	59.5	2,056	82.7	11.9	2.9
Kenai Peninsula, AK	02122	136,831	6.0	61.7	32.3	130,297	13,734	59.1	3,149	84.2	11.2	3.3
Ketchikan Gateway, AK	02130	34,851	10.2	61.5	28.2	33,895	15,663	61.7	702	67.5	21.4	1.3
Kodiak Island, AK	02150	45,317	11.8	64.8	23.4	44,080	16,837	54.7	708	75.3	16.0	8.3
Lake and Peninsula Borough, AK	02164	...	...	...	...	...	...	...	151	85.4	8.6	6.0
Matanuska-Susitna, AK	02170	213,660	7.0	70.7	22.3	215,481	13,085	57.9	5,622	80.7	14.3	3.4
Nome, AK	02180	88,834	25.6	68.4	6.0	64,256	27,297	55.8	747	66.3	21.8	10.7
North Slope, AK	02185	61,744	18.0	32.7	49.3	69,004	37,914	50.3	1,084	59.4	24.9	12.6
Northwest Arctic Borough, AK	02188	59,895	23.0	64.5	12.5	52,720	26,216	48.0	677	68.5	18.3	10.3
Petersburg, AK	02195	12,080	13.9	65.7	20.4	12,147	19,529	54.4	199	96.0	4.0	0.0
Prince of Wales-Hyder, AK	02198	31,483	32.3	60.8	6.9	28,059	20,392	52.5	271	62.4	23.3	8.9
Sitka, AK	02220	23,038	11.9	57.8	30.3	20,973	15,710	66.2	684	91.2	7.5	1.3
Skagway Municipality, AK	02230	3,059	13.8	36.8	49.4	3,167	31,670	65.0	42	40.5	57.1	0.0
Southeast Fairbanks, AK	02240	26,004	14.4	83.8	1.9	23,875	14,629	51.8	464	73.5	23.5	3.0
Valdez-Cordova, AK	02261	32,740	10.0	60.8	29.2	30,034	18,997	54.7	548	76.6	17.9	5.5
Wade Hampton, AK	02270	85,345	26.4	70.9	2.7	64,503	25,089	50.3	747	69.9	20.9	6.3
Wrangell City and Borough, AK	02275	5,936	17.3	69.0	13.7	5,879	18,089	62.7	115	68.7	31.3	0.0
Yakutat Borough	02282	3,035	16.7	58.3	25.0	3,439	27,734	52.7	30	96.7	0.0	0.0
Yukon-Koyukuk, AK	02290	60,422	13.1	81.2	5.7	55,554	10,240	49.3	427	66.3	28.1	4.9
ARIZONA	04000	9,640,930	11.6	46.9	41.5	8,357,376	7,700	55.8	362,973	79.2	12.1	5.6
Apache, AZ	04001	176,843	47.1	36.6	16.3	148,837	11,182	47.9	5,909	76.5	16.5	6.6
Cochise, AZ	04003	180,447	16.4	54.1	29.5	166,924	8,086	55.8	7,473	72.1	17.5	8.6
Coconino, AZ	04005	223,801	21.8	35.1	43.1	191,584	9,298	54.2	11,433	85.2	8.3	5.0
Gila, AZ	04007	84,090	25.4	41.5	33.1	70,464	8,486	53.8	3,152	71.4	12.1	14.0
Graham, AZ	04009	54,445	18.9	58.0	23.1	50,344	7,825	59.5	2,278	79.7	7.4	8.8
Greenlee, AZ	04011	18,133	8.9	19.9	71.2	14,101	7,391	56.7	443	65.2	25.1	9.7
La Paz, AZ	04012	27,798	32.3	39.7	28.0	26,159	9,928	50.7	571	81.1	15.9	2.1
Maricopa, AZ	04013	5,981,411	9.0	45.5	45.5	5,206,314	7,558	56.8	214,479	79.3	12.3	5.1
Mohave, AZ	04015	216,226	12.7	45.0	42.4	187,909	7,027	55.2	9,701	67.3	16.1	9.2
Navajo, AZ	04017	230,141	33.1	43.6	23.2	197,874	9,774	52.1	7,495	76.3	13.0	6.7
Pima, AZ	04019	1,317,737	11.0	49.0	40.1	1,162,777	7,777	54.8	58,572	83.6	9.5	4.6
Pinal, AZ	04021	533,497	8.5	59.6	31.9	391,644	7,708	53.0	15,950	74.3	14.2	9.0
Santa Cruz, AZ	04023	94,784	13.9	53.5	32.6	80,164	7,541	53.7	3,270	89.1	7.5	3.3
Yavapai, AZ	04025	203,463	9.9	47.2	42.9	188,669	7,191	58.1	9,860	74.5	13.0	6.4
Yuma, AZ	04027	293,297	16.2	56.1	27.7	268,978	7,115	51.7	12,387	77.3	12.8	7.3

Note. Data in columns 26 through 41 from the American Community Survey are subject to sampling error, which can be especially large in small counties and small population groups. See notes and definitions for more information.
. . . = Not available.

Table C-1. Population, School, and Student Characteristics by County, Selected Years—*Continued*

County	State/ County Code	High school graduates, 2006–2010			College enrollment, 2006–2010		College graduates, 2006–2010 (percent)						
		Population 25 years and over	High school diploma or less (percent)	High school diploma or more (percent)	Number	Percent public	Bachelor's degree or more	+/- U.S. percent with Bachelor's degree or more	Non-Hispanic White	Black or African American	American Indian and Alaska Native	Asian, Hawaiian, and Pacific Islander	Hispanic or Latino[3]
		30	31	32	33	34	35	36	37	38	39	40	41
ALABAMA— *(Continued)*													
Talladega, AL	01121	55,620	61.4	75.7	4,528	68.0	11.9	-16.0	14.2	6.1	25.3	39.7	11.0
Tallapoosa, AL	01123	28,734	58.0	76.1	1,530	85.5	15.7	-12.2	18.9	6.7	0.0	0.0	7.9
Tuscaloosa, AL	01125	110,719	46.6	84.7	27,004	94.5	26.2	-1.7	29.5	17.7	9.4	61.4	16.2
Walker, AL	01127	46,946	60.2	75.5	2,328	90.5	9.7	-18.2	9.8	9.0	6.7	24.1	13.6
Washington, AL	01129	11,540	67.4	78.0	561	73.3	9.3	-18.6	9.9	8.8	3.3	32.4	0.0
Wilcox, AL	01131	7,676	67.2	68.5	172	80.8	13.2	-14.7	24.6	8.0	0.0	0.0	0.0
Winston, AL	01133	17,353	64.2	69.3	846	96.3	11.1	-16.8	11.4	0.0	16.2	92.3	0.0
ALASKA	02000	429,979	36.7	90.7	46,420	82.0	27.0	-0.9	32.3	19.0	6.4	22.9	18.2
Aleutians East Borough, AK	02013	3,017	63.0	64.1	43	67.4	9.7	-18.2	23.6	0.6	2.6	13.3	0.0
Aleutians West Census Area, AK	02016	5,058	64.0	70.4	162	45.1	9.0	-18.9	19.3	2.7	3.2	8.0	2.5
Anchorage, AK	02020	177,161	31.0	91.9	22,673	79.1	33.0	5.1	38.3	21.5	11.9	23.8	19.8
Bethel, AK	02050	8,617	61.2	78.4	469	93.2	13.9	-14.0	53.0	16.7	4.0	45.1	35.6
Bristol Bay, AK	02060	636	37.0	90.6	52	94.2	15.9	-12.0	19.6	0.0	8.5	100.0	0.0
Denali Borough	02068	843	33.9	95.7	53	67.9	27.5	-0.4	27.4	6.3	27.6	22.2	50.0
Dillingham, AK	02070	2,648	49.2	82.6	181	81.8	20.2	-7.7	53.9	0.0	4.4	46.7	27.8
Fairbanks North Star, AK	02090	56,644	33.6	92.9	9,313	91.2	27.1	-0.8	29.4	21.4	10.0	32.0	16.1
Haines, AK	02100	1,198	40.4	94.0	22	95.5	33.1	5.2	39.1	0.0	3.1	44.4	15.8
Hoonah-Angoon, AK	02105	1,603	42.4	87.6	72	93.1	27.9	0.0	42.6	0.0	10.4	45.5	29.3
Juneau, AK	02110	20,611	28.5	95.3	2,078	86.1	34.7	6.8	40.7	11.5	10.5	25.7	18.8
Kenai Peninsula, AK	02122	36,285	40.4	92.1	2,526	83.5	22.4	-5.5	24.0	2.1	4.8	31.2	22.8
Ketchikan Gateway, AK	02130	8,902	37.7	92.5	440	81.8	24.2	-3.7	27.6	56.9	6.6	32.0	13.9
Kodiak Island, AK	02150	8,006	39.5	87.7	798	62.5	21.8	-6.1	26.4	0.0	3.2	20.7	27.4
Lake and Peninsula Borough, AK	02164	746	53.1	78.0	34	91.2	13.5	-14.4	38.5	0.0	5.0	0.0	0.0
Matanuska-Susitna, AK	02170	52,158	39.3	91.8	4,408	75.6	20.8	-7.1	21.9	7.8	6.9	26.5	17.6
Nome, AK	02180	5,015	58.6	83.8	339	87.3	14.9	-13.0	54.3	12.0	2.8	0.0	0.0
North Slope, AK	02185	4,626	65.4	73.8	223	91.9	13.5	-14.4	64.8	72.7	1.6	23.7	80.3
Northwest Arctic Borough, AK	02188	3,827	62.7	79.6	252	93.7	12.5	-15.4	48.8	50.0	3.0	25.5	0.0
Petersburg, AK	02195	2,707	40.5	95.5	202	92.1	27.4	-0.5	32.9	0.0	7.0	10.7	39.3
Prince of Wales-Hyder, AK	02198	3,681	51.1	88.4	126	90.5	17.8	-10.1	24.8	0.0	5.3	61.5	15.6
Sitka, AK	02220	5,931	33.9	92.3	526	80.8	29.2	1.3	35.7	0.0	7.8	27.0	40.0
Skagway Municipality, AK	02230	722	23.3	95.3	92	100.0	32.3	4.4	37.3	0.0	0.0	0.0	0.0
Southeast Fairbanks, AK	02240	4,309	41.1	91.1	437	94.1	20.0	-7.9	23.0	16.7	2.1	0.0	18.0
Valdez-Cordova, AK	02261	6,359	30.2	92.6	383	76.2	23.8	-4.1	28.3	0.0	3.3	16.3	0.0
Wade Hampton, AK	02270	3,256	69.8	73.7	185	92.4	7.7	-20.2	79.4	0.0	2.9	43.8	0.0
Wrangell City and Borough, AK	02275	1,533	47.6	89.6	92	21.7	16.2	-11.7	20.0	0.0	0.0	40.0	16.0
Yakutat Borough	02282	390	40.8	90.5	12	100.0	18.0	-9.9	24.4	0.0	10.0	40.0	0.0
Yukon-Koyukuk, AK	02290	3,490	57.0	79.5	227	88.1	11.5	-16.4	28.6	0.0	3.8	33.3	21.8
ARIZONA	04000	4,017,638	40.1	85.0	427,449	83.3	26.3	-1.6	31.7	22.8	8.9	49.9	10.3
Apache, AZ	04001	40,189	59.5	72.1	3,182	87.5	10.3	-17.6	21.9	0.0	6.0	31.3	9.8
Cochise, AZ	04003	87,126	40.2	84.8	7,797	86.7	21.4	-6.5	25.4	19.8	21.0	32.9	9.9
Coconino, AZ	04005	76,643	36.5	87.0	19,546	94.9	31.1	3.2	41.3	26.6	10.2	54.7	16.6
Gila, AZ	04007	37,756	49.6	83.4	2,075	77.8	15.0	-12.9	18.1	14.0	2.2	12.5	7.6
Graham, AZ	04009	21,508	51.8	81.8	2,868	94.5	13.4	-14.5	18.8	10.6	5.1	22.2	5.6
Greenlee, AZ	04011	5,235	44.8	89.8	341	82.7	13.4	-14.5	17.0	0.0	0.0	45.8	8.3
La Paz, AZ	04012	15,848	57.2	76.9	219	84.0	9.0	-18.9	10.3	9.9	1.3	63.5	3.3
Maricopa, AZ	04013	2,376,039	38.2	85.6	256,827	81.2	29.0	1.1	34.4	23.8	12.3	53.0	10.4
Mohave, AZ	04015	143,120	51.6	83.0	7,381	87.2	12.0	-15.9	12.6	14.7	9.1	29.3	6.0
Navajo, AZ	04017	63,894	49.5	80.5	5,015	89.3	14.4	-13.5	21.7	14.1	5.7	39.5	7.6
Pima, AZ	04019	635,425	36.8	86.8	85,287	87.6	29.7	1.8	36.8	22.1	11.5	46.4	12.9
Pinal, AZ	04021	217,683	45.3	83.7	14,708	77.0	17.9	-10.0	21.8	18.1	5.6	33.0	7.4
Santa Cruz, AZ	04023	27,905	60.2	70.9	1,744	71.8	17.4	-10.5	42.1	60.6	38.4	15.4	9.0
Yavapai, AZ	04025	153,129	37.6	89.4	11,350	74.9	23.7	-4.2	25.1	31.0	15.8	39.8	9.9
Yuma, AZ	04027	116,138	55.4	71.6	9,109	87.5	13.3	-14.6	19.6	15.3	15.1	30.9	6.4

Note. Data in columns 26 through 41 from the American Community Survey are subject to sampling error, which can be especially large in small counties and small population groups. See notes and definitions for more information.

[3]May be of any race.

Table C-1. Population, School, and Student Characteristics by County, Selected Years—*Continued*

County	State/ County Code	County Type[1]	Population, 2010		Percent of related children 5–17 years in poverty, 2010	Percent of children under 19 years with no health insurance, 2010	Number of schools and students, 2010–2011			Resident enrollment, 2006–2010 K–12 enrollment	
			Total	Percent 5–17 years			School districts	Schools	Students	Number	Percent public
			1	2	3	4	5	6	7	8	9
ARKANSAS	05000	X	2,915,918	17.6	24.9	7.6	289	1,110	482,114	505,436	92.7
Arkansas, AR	05001	6	19,019	17.2	24.8	6.4	3	9	3,197	3,410	94.8
Ashley, AR	05003	7	21,853	17.9	29.9	7.5	2	9	4,043	4,206	97.8
Baxter, AR	05005	7	41,513	13.2	26.0	8.5	3	10	5,175	5,680	96.4
Benton, AR	05007	2	221,339	19.9	13.3	8.3	8	56	38,070	40,055	92.9
Boone, AR	05009	7	36,903	17.2	23.7	6.9	8	20	6,367	6,503	94.7
Bradley, AR	05011	6	11,508	16.6	38.6	8.9	2	7	2,036	2,028	98.0
Calhoun, AR	05013	9	5,368	15.6	20.3	9.3	1	2	577	824	99.0
Carroll, AR	05015	6	27,446	16.7	25.4	11.8	3	10	3,822	4,279	92.1
Chicot, AR	05017	7	11,800	16.2	41.0	7.5	2	7	1,679	2,139	94.3
Clark, AR	05019	7	22,995	14.1	26.3	6.5	4	11	3,872	3,192	98.5
Clay, AR	05021	7	16,083	16.7	24.9	8.3	3	7	2,713	2,711	97.1
Cleburne, AR	05023	6	25,970	14.6	28.1	8.7	4	9	3,383	3,711	89.3
Cleveland, AR	05025	3	8,689	18.0	20.6	8.9	2	5	1,393	1,674	100.0
Columbia, AR	05027	7	24,552	16.7	31.9	6.4	2	9	3,541	4,154	90.3
Conway, AR	05029	6	21,273	17.6	24.0	6.9	4	11	3,281	3,727	94.0
Craighead, AR	05031	3	96,443	17.7	24.6	6.8	8	36	16,942	16,171	92.9
Crawford, AR	05033	2	61,948	19.5	22.3	8.5	5	25	11,471	12,190	93.6
Crittenden, AR	05035	1	50,902	21.1	41.6	5.3	4	21	10,842	11,012	96.0
Cross, AR	05037	6	17,870	18.9	26.5	6.5	2	6	3,649	3,494	98.9
Dallas, AR	05039	6	8,116	17.8	31.0	6.5	1	3	968	1,559	85.1
Desha, AR	05041	6	13,008	18.4	40.3	6.9	2	6	2,706	2,587	95.5
Drew, AR	05043	7	18,509	17.3	28.3	6.7	3	8	3,169	3,152	97.8
Faulkner, AR	05045	2	113,237	17.5	15.5	7.4	6	38	17,837	18,290	89.5
Franklin, AR	05047	2	18,125	17.9	23.9	7.6	4	9	3,242	3,216	97.3
Fulton, AR	05049	9	12,245	15.6	29.5	10.0	3	6	1,655	1,855	99.3
Garland, AR	05051	3	96,024	15.3	33.4	8.3	8	29	14,387	14,650	93.8
Grant, AR	05053	2	17,853	18.0	16.9	6.7	2	8	4,804	3,157	96.8
Greene, AR	05055	6	42,090	18.4	23.3	6.4	3	13	7,360	7,433	95.6
Hempstead, AR	05057	6	22,609	18.2	31.9	8.9	4	9	3,714	4,272	94.5
Hot Spring, AR	05059	6	32,923	17.1	25.3	6.9	6	15	5,339	5,947	95.6
Howard, AR	05061	7	13,789	18.8	28.1	10.5	3	10	3,207	2,495	99.5
Independence, AR	05063	7	36,647	17.3	24.3	8.0	4	14	6,243	5,619	97.3
Izard, AR	05065	9	13,696	14.5	29.2	9.5	4	8	1,877	2,024	93.8
Jackson, AR	05067	6	17,997	15.1	33.3	6.6	2	6	2,450	2,710	95.9
Jefferson, AR	05069	3	77,435	17.4	30.6	5.5	6	30	12,752	13,682	94.2
Johnson, AR	05071	6	25,540	17.7	26.8	9.4	3	10	4,210	4,221	93.0
Lafayette, AR	05073	8	7,645	17.3	32.8	9.3	2	4	1,177	1,333	94.5
Lawrence, AR	05075	6	17,415	17.1	32.5	6.7	6	13	3,411	2,953	93.8
Lee, AR	05077	6	10,424	15.0	43.2	6.3	1	3	1,103	1,688	85.0
Lincoln, AR	05079	3	14,134	14.5	30.0	7.5	1	3	1,708	2,474	98.3
Little River, AR	05081	6	13,171	17.8	23.0	7.5	2	7	2,057	2,393	94.6
Logan, AR	05083	6	22,353	18.6	25.9	7.3	4	10	3,547	4,286	94.2
Lonoke, AR	05085	2	68,356	20.5	15.6	6.7	4	24	13,752	12,808	94.0
Madison, AR	05087	2	15,717	18.0	26.9	10.6	1	6	2,362	2,843	95.4
Marion, AR	05089	9	16,653	13.3	33.6	9.7	2	5	1,732	2,540	94.6
Miller, AR	05091	3	43,462	17.1	28.8	5.8	3	15	6,541	7,656	94.3
Mississippi, AR	05093	4	46,480	20.6	33.9	4.9	8	25	8,844	9,672	98.9
Monroe, AR	05095	7	8,149	16.6	34.1	6.8	2	4	1,239	1,673	92.0
Montgomery, AR	05097	8	9,487	15.7	32.1	9.9	2	4	1,144	1,613	99.4
Nevada, AR	05099	7	8,997	17.0	35.6	6.7	2	5	1,453	1,606	97.6
Newton, AR	05101	9	8,330	15.7	34.2	10.7	2	10	1,332	1,293	86.8
Ouachita, AR	05103	7	26,120	16.6	29.7	6.3	6	14	4,541	4,548	94.6
Perry, AR	05105	2	10,445	17.2	24.5	8.3	2	4	1,685	1,913	97.0
Phillips, AR	05107	7	21,757	20.5	50.0	5.1	5	14	4,328	4,933	88.9
Pike, AR	05109	9	11,291	18.2	29.1	10.1	2	6	1,209	2,132	95.2
Poinsett, AR	05111	3	24,583	17.7	35.7	6.2	5	15	4,432	4,466	97.4
Polk, AR	05113	7	20,662	17.7	32.8	9.1	3	15	3,861	3,662	93.6
Pope, AR	05115	5	61,754	16.4	21.9	7.0	5	23	10,030	10,374	94.6
Prairie, AR	05117	8	8,715	16.3	26.5	8.9	2	4	1,285	1,444	97.1

[1]County type codes are from the Economic Research Service of the United States Department of Agriculture. See notes and definitions for more information.

Table C-1. Population, School, and Student Characteristics by County, Selected Years—*Continued*

County	State/ County Code	Characteristics of students, 2010–2011				Number of graduates, 2008–2009	Staff and students, 2010–2011			
		Percent with IEP[2]	Percent eligible for free or reduced lunch	Percent minority	Percent English-language learners		Total staff	Number of teachers	Student/ teacher ratio	Central admin. staff
		10	11	12	13	14	15	16	17	18
ARKANSAS	05000	13.5	60.5	35.2	6.5	28,054	72,185	34,273	14.1	3,095
Arkansas, AR	05001	10.0	61.5	37.0	1.4	210	504	262	12.2	19
Ashley, AR	05003	7.9	79.2	39.2	4.7	243	601	294	13.7	23
Baxter, AR	05005	9.7	58.5	7.2	0.5	306	754	391	13.2	32
Benton, AR	05007	10.2	46.2	32.7	17.1	2,004	5,014	2,416	15.8	179
Boone, AR	05009	16.9	54.2	4.8	0.3	387	998	467	13.6	38
Bradley, AR	05011	8.8	73.6	51.7	7.9	126	387	170	12.0	16
Calhoun, AR	05013	10.7	63.8	32.1	2.1	53	106	45	13.0	8
Carroll, AR	05015	10.6	65.5	26.5	17.7	206	712	293	13.0	32
Chicot, AR	05017	9.2	98.2	88.7	5.7	113	349	150	11.2	21
Clark, AR	05019	26.8	60.2	40.1	5.4	258	608	286	13.5	24
Clay, AR	05021	14.4	61.7	2.6	...	196	428	214	12.7	14
Cleburne, AR	05023	10.8	54.7	4.3	0.8	236	570	267	12.7	31
Cleveland, AR	05025	9.9	49.1	19.5	1.1	81	225	106	13.1	7
Columbia, AR	05027	8.5	64.3	51.1	1.0	250	587	275	12.9	30
Conway, AR	05029	39.9	61.4	23.7	2.0	213	532	255	12.9	22
Craighead, AR	05031	11.1	55.3	29.3	2.8	953	2,307	1,177	14.4	92
Crawford, AR	05033	11.2	59.8	18.0	4.1	694	1,596	751	15.3	70
Crittenden, AR	05035	11.3	82.9	69.6	0.4	630	1,446	720	15.1	59
Cross, AR	05037	11.1	66.7	30.2	0.2	246	535	260	14.0	22
Dallas, AR	05039	19.5	65.4	53.3	0.7	55	158	74	13.1	6
Desha, AR	05041	11.4	78.1	63.3	2.9	201	485	227	11.9	24
Drew, AR	05043	31.5	61.6	35.6	1.8	229	522	238	13.3	21
Faulkner, AR	05045	11.5	44.3	21.7	2.2	1,116	2,320	1,177	15.2	84
Franklin, AR	05047	20.2	52.6	7.0	0.5	206	468	239	13.6	21
Fulton, AR	05049	15.3	62.4	5.3	0.2	111	279	135	12.2	13
Garland, AR	05051	11.9	58.8	26.1	4.0	771	1,947	1,002	14.4	82
Grant, AR	05053	8.6	47.0	6.2	2.3	282	643	311	15.5	32
Greene, AR	05055	14.7	58.0	6.3	1.3	414	1,097	508	14.5	47
Hempstead, AR	05057	20.7	77.4	61.0	12.4	237	596	276	13.5	20
Hot Spring, AR	05059	11.1	60.9	19.6	1.6	346	869	394	13.5	35
Howard, AR	05061	10.5	68.2	40.5	7.6	203	495	254	12.6	21
Independence, AR	05063	18.5	59.5	14.1	5.2	360	1,011	452	13.8	41
Izard, AR	05065	33.4	60.7	4.1	...	110	373	153	12.3	14
Jackson, AR	05067	14.3	70.2	30.2	1.3	175	416	187	13.1	15
Jefferson, AR	05069	13.2	68.9	72.3	0.3	753	2,101	903	14.1	91
Johnson, AR	05071	10.7	70.7	22.9	11.6	268	635	314	13.4	21
Lafayette, AR	05073	9.3	82.4	56.5	...	72	215	98	12.0	13
Lawrence, AR	05075	21.1	67.8	3.0	...	223	566	283	12.1	30
Lee, AR	05077	11.1	91.6	95.3	0.1	74	224	94	11.8	12
Lincoln, AR	05079	8.7	60.6	31.0	1.4	110	264	115	14.9	14
Little River, AR	05081	9.9	61.2	33.8	...	132	364	168	12.2	17
Logan, AR	05083	11.4	63.4	9.3	1.8	272	595	274	12.9	27
Lonoke, AR	05085	11.0	40.8	13.6	1.5	744	1,864	885	15.5	76
Madison, AR	05087	9.1	60.7	9.4	5.8	176	372	169	14.0	10
Marion, AR	05089	14.1	67.8	4.4	0.1	128	290	143	12.1	16
Miller, AR	05091	9.3	63.6	38.9	0.6	354	1,060	481	13.6	47
Mississippi, AR	05093	11.0	80.5	52.1	1.4	485	1,497	675	13.1	69
Monroe, AR	05095	13.5	94.3	62.5	1.7	108	240	116	10.7	17
Montgomery, AR	05097	12.1	71.8	10.6	0.2	81	195	96	11.9	7
Nevada, AR	05099	11.6	75.3	44.0	1.4	117	260	113	12.8	13
Newton, AR	05101	13.6	73.0	4.5	...	106	328	138	9.7	13
Ouachita, AR	05103	16.9	70.6	57.3	0.1	358	792	353	12.8	40
Perry, AR	05105	14.6	52.2	6.5	...	130	252	131	12.9	7
Phillips, AR	05107	23.8	91.7	83.7	...	226	760	350	12.4	45
Pike, AR	05109	11.7	66.7	13.1	1.1	76	244	122	9.9	11
Poinsett, AR	05111	24.8	78.5	15.6	1.4	294	830	367	12.1	30
Polk, AR	05113	10.0	76.4	13.3	5.4	241	615	294	13.2	31
Pope, AR	05115	10.3	56.4	17.9	5.7	633	1,538	745	13.5	63
Prairie, AR	05117	11.8	68.9	21.7	...	95	235	108	11.9	11

[2]IEP= Individual Education Program. See notes and definitions for more information
... Not available

Table C-1. Population, School, and Student Characteristics by County, Selected Years—*Continued*

County	State/ County Code	Revenues, 2008–2009				Current expenditures, 2008–2009			Resident population 16 to 19 years, 2006–2010			
		Total revenue ($1,000's)	Percentage of revenue from: Federal government	State government	Local government	Amount ($1,000's)	Amount per student	Percent for instruction	Total population 16 to 19 years	Percent enrolled in school	Percent high school graduates, not enrolled in school	Percent not enrolled, not grads, not employed, or not in labor force
		19	20	21	22	23	24	25	26	27	28	29
ARKANSAS	05000	4,787,521	11.3	55.2	33.5	4,162,868	8,695	58.4	165,933	80.4	12.5	5.0
Arkansas, AR	05001	31,360	12.8	54.3	33.0	29,236	8,696	58.6	1,240	78.4	17.1	3.3
Ashley, AR	05003	39,902	13.3	53.9	32.8	35,192	8,579	58.5	1,273	81.3	15.4	3.3
Baxter, AR	05005	44,259	11.3	44.8	43.9	41,288	8,074	60.6	1,674	81.3	12.7	3.4
Benton, AR	05007	347,777	6.6	45.4	48.0	293,668	8,066	61.2	10,940	77.3	17.8	3.8
Boone, AR	05009	64,631	9.9	57.8	32.3	57,384	9,003	59.9	1,947	79.3	12.8	4.5
Bradley, AR	05011	21,506	13.7	64.9	21.4	19,283	9,425	57.0	531	71.0	23.5	5.5
Calhoun, AR	05013	5,999	10.9	51.4	37.7	5,611	8,619	55.0	383	64.5	8.4	27.2
Carroll, AR	05015	37,291	10.2	51.8	38.0	30,846	8,073	58.7	1,289	73.7	13.7	11.4
Chicot, AR	05017	22,089	19.3	54.2	26.6	18,830	10,262	53.2	612	75.0	8.7	5.6
Clark, AR	05019	53,667	15.2	56.6	28.2	46,017	11,496	46.8	2,277	88.8	6.9	2.6
Clay, AR	05021	24,883	10.9	60.1	29.0	23,569	8,352	60.5	872	74.5	14.2	5.6
Cleburne, AR	05023	31,836	11.1	43.2	45.6	27,863	8,263	59.9	1,264	88.5	9.2	1.2
Cleveland, AR	05025	15,258	14.4	61.9	23.8	12,195	8,498	56.9	477	88.9	1.9	3.1
Columbia, AR	05027	34,828	12.3	55.4	32.3	30,353	8,228	59.2	1,952	91.6	6.1	1.9
Conway, AR	05029	44,211	9.0	55.2	35.7	36,890	10,996	47.3	1,208	83.5	11.8	3.3
Craighead, AR	05031	143,922	12.3	54.7	33.0	125,936	7,707	60.2	6,377	84.7	10.4	3.5
Crawford, AR	05033	106,011	9.9	59.2	30.9	90,463	7,940	58.7	3,310	80.9	14.8	4.2
Crittenden, AR	05035	114,729	13.1	63.3	23.6	95,341	8,565	59.4	3,016	81.4	10.5	5.3
Cross, AR	05037	36,726	11.7	65.3	23.0	29,325	7,949	61.0	1,184	72.6	19.8	7.1
Dallas, AR	05039	10,961	11.0	70.8	18.2	8,461	8,104	60.7	433	74.8	12.9	12.2
Desha, AR	05041	29,199	15.1	57.8	27.0	26,297	9,221	57.7	793	82.2	5.9	11.9
Drew, AR	05043	45,199	18.8	56.4	24.8	37,214	11,651	50.4	1,273	88.9	8.8	2.3
Faulkner, AR	05045	155,709	8.2	58.5	33.3	136,820	7,852	59.5	7,958	88.9	7.1	1.5
Franklin, AR	05047	29,846	19.8	52.4	27.8	27,101	9,682	52.6	1,122	87.4	3.8	8.1
Fulton, AR	05049	14,319	12.3	63.1	24.6	13,246	8,389	62.2	551	91.5	6.2	1.6
Garland, AR	05051	138,456	10.9	43.4	45.7	118,879	8,375	57.9	4,528	81.4	10.7	6.2
Grant, AR	05053	41,223	7.8	69.0	23.1	33,703	6,984	59.9	994	74.9	17.9	4.9
Greene, AR	05055	66,025	11.8	59.9	28.3	56,331	7,853	60.0	2,063	69.4	21.9	5.5
Hempstead, AR	05057	40,757	14.3	63.4	22.2	37,484	9,790	58.3	1,436	75.8	15.8	8.4
Hot Spring, AR	05059	50,848	10.9	58.7	30.4	44,056	8,119	58.0	1,852	79.1	15.9	5.1
Howard, AR	05061	27,812	12.6	59.2	28.1	24,908	7,930	63.4	999	76.0	5.5	6.0
Independence, AR	05063	63,286	10.7	56.7	32.7	53,225	8,830	57.6	2,056	78.5	10.6	5.3
Izard, AR	05065	22,564	11.3	56.1	32.6	19,393	10,477	51.0	642	73.5	18.7	4.7
Jackson, AR	05067	30,477	13.4	57.5	29.1	26,891	8,675	60.1	767	84.2	11.6	4.2
Jefferson, AR	05069	132,714	12.8	61.7	25.5	120,370	9,110	58.1	5,200	75.8	13.8	9.9
Johnson, AR	05071	38,415	12.2	63.0	24.8	34,756	8,081	61.3	1,418	68.0	16.8	5.2
Lafayette, AR	05073	13,568	13.8	58.2	28.0	11,022	9,485	58.2	635	91.3	7.2	1.4
Lawrence, AR	05075	35,567	13.1	63.9	23.0	31,353	9,510	57.4	1,153	85.3	8.4	3.7
Lee, AR	05077	14,888	22.9	61.7	15.4	14,525	11,491	56.4	668	69.3	22.2	8.5
Lincoln, AR	05079	15,957	12.2	64.4	23.5	13,733	7,843	57.0	1,096	80.3	10.0	6.6
Little River, AR	05081	20,761	11.3	40.6	48.1	18,544	8,941	54.7	805	77.3	22.1	0.6
Logan, AR	05083	40,889	13.3	55.9	30.8	34,923	8,327	58.2	1,297	91.0	7.7	1.3
Lonoke, AR	05085	115,648	8.0	64.8	27.2	98,545	7,438	61.1	3,383	79.7	9.0	6.0
Madison, AR	05087	21,701	11.5	64.1	24.4	19,524	8,055	58.3	818	77.6	10.5	7.3
Marion, AR	05089	18,051	13.0	56.8	30.2	16,127	8,798	60.2	789	82.4	8.2	2.5
Miller, AR	05091	69,659	16.1	55.2	28.7	60,030	9,113	54.7	2,379	72.1	22.1	4.8
Mississippi, AR	05093	89,237	14.8	60.1	25.1	79,719	8,746	57.5	2,704	74.9	15.4	5.7
Monroe, AR	05095	16,090	15.2	54.3	30.5	14,062	10,073	56.2	703	90.6	4.8	1.1
Montgomery, AR	05097	10,843	21.9	49.6	28.5	9,813	8,489	58.5	481	79.0	9.8	11.2
Nevada, AR	05099	13,872	11.9	62.1	26.0	12,683	8,681	54.1	525	83.2	4.6	12.2
Newton, AR	05101	15,333	17.7	62.5	19.8	13,399	10,014	56.4	402	51.5	10.0	18.9
Ouachita, AR	05103	51,587	14.4	63.3	22.4	47,195	10,126	53.4	1,437	84.2	10.8	4.0
Perry, AR	05105	14,750	11.1	66.1	22.9	13,621	7,901	59.5	668	94.6	5.4	0.0
Phillips, AR	05107	56,936	18.6	62.5	19.0	53,160	11,827	52.1	1,536	80.3	11.9	5.1
Pike, AR	05109	11,764	11.2	57.6	31.2	10,910	8,185	62.0	676	82.4	9.2	5.3
Poinsett, AR	05111	54,056	16.2	63.2	20.7	44,193	9,566	56.2	1,365	76.9	13.6	9.2
Polk, AR	05113	42,207	12.6	54.2	33.2	33,453	8,698	60.0	1,074	79.4	11.6	6.6
Pope, AR	05115	104,934	9.9	50.1	40.0	83,251	8,364	59.5	4,602	77.8	15.5	4.1
Prairie, AR	05117	12,273	11.0	54.1	34.8	10,689	8,172	56.1	391	73.9	11.0	4.4

Note. Data in columns 26 through 41 from the American Community Survey are subject to sampling error, which can be especially large in small counties and small population groups. See notes and definitions for more information.

Table C-1. Population, School, and Student Characteristics by County, Selected Years—*Continued*

County	State/ County Code	High school graduates, 2006–2010			College enrollment, 2006–2010		College graduates, 2006–2010 (percent)						
		Population 25 years and over	High school diploma or less (percent)	High school diploma or more (percent)	Number	Percent public	Bachelor's degree or more	+/- U.S. percent with Bachelor's degree or more	Non-Hispanic White	Black or African American	American Indian and Alaska Native	Asian, Hawaiian, and Pacific Islander	Hispanic or Latino[3]
		30	31	32	33	34	35	36	37	38	39	40	41
ARKANSAS	05000	1,885,607	53.4	81.9	173,914	83.7	19.1	-8.8	20.6	12.3	16.4	38.7	8.9
Arkansas, AR	05001	13,202	58.4	79.4	633	96.2	14.3	-13.6	17.2	4.9	0.0	43.1	0.0
Ashley, AR	05003	14,869	64.0	81.1	642	94.1	13.7	-14.2	16.6	7.0	0.0	0.0	1.6
Baxter, AR	05005	31,371	53.9	83.7	1,467	90.4	14.5	-13.4	14.7	0.0	3.5	17.5	0.0
Benton, AR	05007	133,625	46.9	84.2	9,461	74.2	25.9	-2.0	27.3	40.4	16.8	44.8	10.7
Boone, AR	05009	25,086	57.1	83.8	1,315	82.7	14.5	-13.4	14.2	1.7	32.3	72.4	15.9
Bradley, AR	05011	8,213	70.3	69.4	298	70.5	12.7	-15.2	17.6	4.9	13.2	0.0	1.3
Calhoun, AR	05013	3,805	67.7	77.8	213	100.0	6.6	-21.3	7.3	5.3	0.0	0.0	0.0
Carroll, AR	05015	18,970	57.6	79.0	541	89.6	17.4	-10.5	18.1	26.9	28.1	32.7	6.4
Chicot, AR	05017	8,167	71.4	69.3	296	84.5	12.6	-15.3	15.5	10.1	0.0	34.4	0.0
Clark, AR	05019	13,428	53.7	83.1	4,214	57.8	21.7	-6.2	26.2	8.3	0.0	20.0	11.0
Clay, AR	05021	11,410	68.7	73.2	649	70.0	8.8	-19.1	8.7	0.0	5.5	0.0	21.2
Cleburne, AR	05023	18,769	56.4	79.1	838	88.9	13.8	-14.1	14.0	0.0	0.0	0.0	1.6
Cleveland, AR	05025	5,866	60.0	85.9	269	88.5	14.0	-13.9	15.3	4.7	0.0	0.0	0.0
Columbia, AR	05027	15,618	53.8	83.7	2,952	98.2	20.8	-7.1	26.6	8.7	51.9	0.0	15.0
Conway, AR	05029	14,106	61.3	82.7	1,020	90.6	13.9	-14.0	13.9	14.5	11.1	0.0	12.6
Craighead, AR	05031	58,490	51.7	83.3	8,171	92.1	23.1	-4.8	24.0	15.7	16.0	44.5	9.8
Crawford, AR	05033	39,393	57.5	77.4	2,125	91.2	13.0	-14.9	13.1	24.9	24.3	23.8	6.4
Crittenden, AR	05035	30,785	57.5	76.3	3,389	91.1	14.2	-13.7	18.3	9.2	0.0	30.9	18.5
Cross, AR	05037	11,916	66.6	76.1	778	86.8	12.6	-15.3	14.9	3.9	23.9	0.0	9.7
Dallas, AR	05039	5,561	65.7	80.3	300	100.0	12.4	-15.5	16.2	7.0	0.0	0.0	0.0
Desha, AR	05041	8,650	65.7	72.5	591	82.9	13.6	-14.3	19.0	7.6	19.4	0.0	5.7
Drew, AR	05043	11,877	56.5	80.6	1,625	86.2	19.4	-8.5	23.5	5.9	0.0	98.1	5.6
Faulkner, AR	05045	64,243	44.6	87.4	13,407	81.9	26.4	-1.5	27.4	18.2	20.3	47.6	13.2
Franklin, AR	05047	12,239	59.9	82.6	745	96.8	11.6	-16.3	11.9	0.0	0.0	35.6	10.0
Fulton, AR	05049	8,812	63.1	79.4	449	70.4	9.7	-18.2	9.7	0.0	25.6	0.0	10.0
Garland, AR	05051	68,033	47.1	85.0	3,701	83.6	20.2	-7.7	21.4	10.0	8.9	38.0	9.5
Grant, AR	05053	11,852	61.0	84.8	560	85.7	14.7	-13.2	14.7	24.8	0.0	100.0	5.8
Greene, AR	05055	27,307	63.0	80.9	2,229	82.2	12.0	-15.9	11.7	8.8	12.3	91.1	37.3
Hempstead, AR	05057	14,683	57.1	80.7	1,160	85.3	14.7	-13.2	18.3	9.5	0.0	0.0	6.2
Hot Spring, AR	05059	22,343	57.5	81.3	1,573	89.8	12.5	-15.4	13.3	7.6	16.2	7.7	1.1
Howard, AR	05061	8,959	65.1	78.1	545	93.0	12.4	-15.5	15.8	3.9	0.0	0.0	0.0
Independence, AR	05063	24,176	56.3	82.4	1,938	65.2	14.7	-13.2	14.7	2.7	35.6	57.2	8.9
Izard, AR	05065	10,115	58.2	81.6	336	87.5	12.3	-15.6	12.2	0.0	0.0	47.3	11.1
Jackson, AR	05067	12,709	71.8	72.3	910	91.1	7.0	-20.9	7.7	4.2	0.0	0.0	6.1
Jefferson, AR	05069	50,689	56.2	81.6	6,776	93.4	16.5	-11.4	15.7	17.7	9.1	27.9	0.0
Johnson, AR	05071	16,267	64.1	76.4	1,004	50.1	14.8	-13.1	16.0	0.0	12.9	34.3	4.3
Lafayette, AR	05073	5,233	65.3	77.9	505	92.9	13.3	-14.6	18.0	5.2	0.0	0.0	0.0
Lawrence, AR	05075	11,673	67.5	74.8	1,281	35.8	9.2	-18.7	9.3	0.0	9.2	0.0	0.0
Lee, AR	05077	7,288	70.3	69.3	376	73.4	8.5	-19.4	8.1	9.4	0.0	0.0	0.0
Lincoln, AR	05079	9,437	71.4	73.2	601	84.0	8.6	-19.3	10.4	4.7	0.0	0.0	0.0
Little River, AR	05081	8,937	58.5	81.3	478	96.9	11.9	-16.0	13.3	5.5	0.0	0.0	24.1
Logan, AR	05083	15,184	65.3	76.8	820	75.1	11.7	-16.2	11.5	0.0	41.1	21.7	8.2
Lonoke, AR	05085	42,243	50.2	85.8	3,559	86.8	16.6	-11.3	17.4	10.5	10.5	19.6	9.4
Madison, AR	05087	10,431	64.9	75.8	626	90.4	13.4	-14.5	14.2	0.0	0.0	0.0	0.0
Marion, AR	05089	12,577	53.1	85.1	539	70.1	14.8	-13.1	15.2	0.0	4.0	0.0	12.1
Miller, AR	05091	28,325	58.4	83.0	1,660	90.4	12.7	-15.2	14.7	6.8	0.0	6.9	7.0
Mississippi, AR	05093	29,233	62.1	75.6	1,658	93.5	11.0	-16.9	12.6	7.3	0.0	44.2	8.8
Monroe, AR	05095	5,798	65.4	68.6	287	94.1	12.4	-15.5	13.9	8.6	37.5	40.4	0.0
Montgomery, AR	05097	6,758	58.7	82.2	285	91.6	10.1	-17.8	9.7	0.0	12.8	0.0	40.6
Nevada, AR	05099	6,223	59.6	78.3	528	92.4	10.7	-17.2	12.9	6.2	0.0	0.0	29.6
Newton, AR	05101	5,968	62.4	78.0	216	98.1	12.2	-15.7	12.0	100.0	6.7	0.0	36.4
Ouachita, AR	05103	17,914	59.0	81.8	1,221	88.6	13.2	-14.7	17.7	6.2	12.4	0.0	9.5
Perry, AR	05105	7,272	65.1	81.6	280	88.2	10.5	-17.4	10.2	30.5	0.0	0.0	0.0
Phillips, AR	05107	13,887	57.8	70.9	965	92.5	12.1	-15.8	15.4	9.8	0.0	48.0	0.0
Pike, AR	05109	7,364	61.8	77.2	366	81.1	12.4	-15.5	13.0	0.0	2.0	0.0	5.9
Poinsett, AR	05111	16,611	71.0	72.8	670	83.3	8.8	-19.1	9.2	5.7	0.0	4.1	0.0
Polk, AR	05113	14,153	57.4	80.4	790	85.7	10.0	-17.9	10.2	0.0	27.9	0.0	0.0
Pope, AR	05115	37,708	53.3	81.9	5,473	95.1	20.1	-7.8	20.6	7.7	4.1	37.0	13.0
Prairie, AR	05117	6,234	71.6	78.0	197	97.0	11.5	-16.4	12.4	3.8	0.0	0.0	100.0

Note. Data in columns 26 through 41 from the American Community Survey are subject to sampling error, which can be especially large in small counties and small population groups. See notes and definitions for more information.

[3]May be of any race.

Table C-1. Population, School, and Student Characteristics by County, Selected Years—*Continued*

County	State/ County Code	County Type[1]	Population, 2010		Percent of related children 5–17 years in poverty, 2010	Percent of children under 19 years with no health insurance, 2010	Number of schools and students, 2010–2011			Resident enrollment, 2006–2010 K–12 enrollment	
			Total	Percent 5–17 years			School districts	Schools	Students	Number	Percent public
			1	2	3	4	5	6	7	8	9
ARKANSAS—*(Continued)*											
Pulaski, AR	05119	2	382,748	17.1	23.0	6.6	19	129	57,336	65,421	84.0
Randolph, AR	05121	7	17,969	17.2	29.5	8.1	2	6	2,410	3,123	93.3
St. Francis, AR	05123	6	28,258	16.9	43.6	5.6	4	11	4,556	4,757	92.8
Saline, AR	05125	2	107,118	17.8	12.5	6.6	5	23	15,418	18,297	92.7
Scott, AR	05127	6	11,233	19.1	31.7	9.7	2	6	2,688	2,099	98.7
Searcy, AR	05129	9	8,195	15.4	39.4	10.4	2	10	1,615	1,221	81.2
Sebastian, AR	05131	2	125,744	18.1	27.4	8.4	6	39	19,642	22,243	93.2
Sevier, AR	05133	7	17,058	20.7	28.6	12.1	3	9	3,289	3,023	97.1
Sharp, AR	05135	7	17,264	16.2	35.3	8.2	2	8	3,042	2,791	95.4
Stone, AR	05137	9	12,394	15.0	35.1	10.7	1	7	1,766	1,897	87.1
Union, AR	05139	5	41,639	17.5	29.7	6.4	7	19	7,740	7,399	96.7
Van Buren, AR	05141	8	17,295	15.4	29.4	8.9	3	8	2,385	2,469	91.2
Washington, AR	05143	2	203,065	17.9	22.3	9.9	11	64	37,031	34,065	93.1
White, AR	05145	4	77,076	17.3	20.9	7.4	10	29	12,826	12,851	92.1
Woodruff, AR	05147	9	7,260	17.1	38.3	7.9	2	5	1,244	1,278	99.7
Yell, AR	05149	6	22,185	19.1	28.1	11.4	4	12	4,380	4,170	98.3
CALIFORNIA	06000	X	37,253,956	18.2	20.8	9.5	1,193	10,124	6,216,977	6,918,447	91.1
Alameda, CA	06001	1	1,510,271	16.1	17.0	7.1	35	398	218,151	244,741	89.0
Alpine, CA	06003	8	1,175	15.7	26.7	8.7	2	5	88	202	86.6
Amador, CA	06005	6	38,091	13.0	14.9	8.6	4	17	4,308	5,872	92.2
Butte, CA	06007	3	220,000	15.3	22.9	8.1	17	95	31,225	35,297	93.0
Calaveras, CA	06009	6	45,578	15.3	16.3	8.7	5	26	6,122	7,150	93.5
Colusa, CA	06011	6	21,419	21.3	21.2	11.4	6	26	4,710	4,801	98.7
Contra Costa, CA	06013	1	1,049,025	18.4	11.2	7.2	21	264	168,094	193,427	89.5
Del Norte, CA	06015	7	28,610	15.5	27.8	7.8	3	22	4,276	4,914	87.9
El Dorado, CA	06017	1	181,058	17.5	10.3	6.7	18	70	28,027	32,875	91.2
Fresno, CA	06019	2	930,450	21.3	36.2	8.4	43	335	193,737	200,698	96.2
Glenn, CA	06021	6	28,122	20.2	24.0	10.2	9	29	5,440	5,835	90.7
Humboldt, CA	06023	5	134,623	14.4	21.0	7.8	34	90	18,090	19,767	93.1
Imperial, CA	06025	3	174,528	21.5	30.4	9.7	19	69	36,435	37,904	97.6
Inyo, CA	06027	7	18,546	15.3	18.3	10.4	8	33	3,880	2,934	96.9
Kern, CA	06029	2	839,631	21.6	28.6	11.1	55	268	173,604	181,884	94.6
Kings, CA	06031	3	152,982	19.4	28.0	9.7	16	68	28,942	29,339	93.8
Lake, CA	06033	4	64,665	15.5	27.2	10.2	9	47	8,734	11,057	96.7
Lassen, CA	06035	6	34,895	13.4	17.0	6.8	13	38	4,888	5,513	86.0
Los Angeles, CA	06037	1	9,818,605	17.9	23.7	11.1	115	2,136	1,589,543	1,852,302	90.5
Madera, CA	06039	3	150,865	20.5	28.1	10.9	10	81	29,993	30,947	96.9
Marin, CA	06041	1	252,409	15.2	9.9	5.8	22	79	30,574	37,293	79.4
Mariposa, CA	06043	8	18,251	13.5	20.3	9.1	2	17	2,118	2,747	88.4
Mendocino, CA	06045	4	87,841	16.1	26.2	9.7	15	76	12,993	14,684	89.8
Merced, CA	06047	3	255,793	22.9	29.2	8.7	23	106	55,489	59,731	97.4
Modoc, CA	06049	6	9,686	16.3	29.1	12.5	4	17	1,029	1,572	93.4
Mono, CA	06051	7	14,202	14.7	14.6	11.4	4	18	1,688	2,091	90.5
Monterey, CA	06053	2	415,057	18.9	25.0	10.7	28	133	71,260	78,442	92.8
Napa, CA	06055	3	136,484	17.1	13.3	10.7	7	47	20,584	22,747	88.9
Nevada, CA	06057	4	98,764	14.9	15.4	9.1	14	62	17,076	15,518	91.8
Orange, CA	06059	1	3,010,232	18.1	15.7	10.1	36	604	503,152	552,483	89.8
Placer, CA	06061	1	348,432	18.4	10.1	6.3	20	114	64,369	62,861	89.8
Plumas, CA	06063	7	20,007	13.6	20.2	10.1	3	16	2,314	3,093	93.5
Riverside, CA	06065	1	2,189,641	20.9	22.0	11.7	26	478	425,334	459,684	93.1
Sacramento, CA	06067	1	1,418,788	18.5	22.4	6.7	14	367	235,343	268,843	90.7
San Benito, CA	06069	1	55,269	21.7	16.4	10.3	11	24	11,174	11,952	90.3
San Bernardino, CA	06071	1	2,035,210	21.4	22.9	10.8	38	547	417,214	450,530	94.2
San Diego, CA	06073	1	3,095,313	16.8	18.4	9.6	45	743	498,243	526,273	92.0
San Francisco, CA	06075	1	805,235	9.0	14.9	6.3	6	123	56,758	73,158	76.5
San Joaquin, CA	06077	2	685,306	21.4	24.5	8.2	19	227	136,304	148,359	93.2
San Luis Obispo, CA	06079	3	269,637	13.9	14.3	9.5	14	85	34,299	37,961	90.9

[1]County type codes are from the Economic Research Service of the United States Department of Agriculture. See notes and definitions for more information.

Table C-1. Population, School, and Student Characteristics by County, Selected Years—*Continued*

County	State/ County Code	Characteristics of students, 2010–2011				Number of graduates, 2008–2009	Staff and students, 2010–2011			
		Percent with IEP[2]	Percent eligible for free or reduced lunch	Percent minority	Percent English-language learners		Total staff	Number of teachers	Student/ teacher ratio	Central admin. staff
		10	11	12	13	14	15	16	17	18
ARKANSAS—*(Continued)*										
Pulaski, AR	05119	18.4	63.5	66.7	4.6	2,766	8,940	4,041	14.2	404
Randolph, AR	05121	16.3	70.5	5.7	0.2	203	368	174	13.9	15
St. Francis, AR	05123	11.5	99.3	74.6	0.4	280	738	335	13.6	40
Saline, AR	05125	10.3	38.3	14.8	2.9	824	1,709	936	16.5	78
Scott, AR	05127	10.6	66.4	17.1	5.1	168	401	191	14.1	13
Searcy, AR	05129	13.6	73.8	4.9	0.4	124	429	155	10.5	14
Sebastian, AR	05131	13.3	61.3	41.3	17.0	1,133	2,721	1,276	15.4	140
Sevier, AR	05133	17.5	72.7	55.1	30.6	176	499	244	13.5	20
Sharp, AR	05135	9.9	66.0	3.6	0.1	208	476	221	13.8	12
Stone, AR	05137	11.7	61.3	3.9	0.2	101	281	141	12.6	12
Union, AR	05139	7.8	57.8	46.7	2.0	496	1,132	615	12.6	65
Van Buren, AR	05141	14.9	68.5	6.1	0.8	151	423	205	11.7	22
Washington, AR	05143	11.6	55.4	40.2	24.3	1,932	4,946	2,404	15.4	193
White, AR	05145	15.0	53.9	13.9	1.7	739	1,878	920	13.9	77
Woodruff, AR	05147	14.3	80.1	38.8	0.4	31	232	112	11.1	11
Yell, AR	05149	14.1	72.5	33.5	20.7	245	742	346	12.7	33
CALIFORNIA	06000	10.7	53.7	73.4	...	...	523,577	258,142	24.1	24,810
Alameda, CA	06001	9.9	40.9	77.3	...	...	17,648	9,395	23.2	1,003
Alpine, CA	06003	30.7	48.9	45.5	...	...	29	11	8.0	3
Amador, CA	06005	12.4	41.0	27.1	...	...	414	200	21.5	19
Butte, CA	06007	12.5	55.3	38.2	...	...	3,403	1,346	23.2	190
Calaveras, CA	06009	11.8	45.4	21.3	...	...	601	271	22.6	34
Colusa, CA	06011	3.2	69.8	75.2	...	...	448	222	21.2	31
Contra Costa, CA	06013	11.5	36.6	62.3	...	...	13,201	7,045	23.9	536
Del Norte, CA	06015	13.7	62.4	41.5	...	...	444	201	21.3	15
El Dorado, CA	06017	11.7	28.5	28.4	...	...	2,447	1,215	23.1	157
Fresno, CA	06019	9.1	68.0	79.5	...	...	17,262	8,158	23.7	786
Glenn, CA	06021	9.5	65.5	59.2	...	...	548	241	22.6	28
Humboldt, CA	06023	15.2	53.1	38.1	...	...	1,942	868	20.8	89
Imperial, CA	06025	8.6	72.2	92.9	...	...	3,537	1,570	23.2	181
Inyo, CA	06027	4.4	48.5	55.1	...	...	417	200	19.4	42
Kern, CA	06029	9.2	66.3	73.7	...	...	15,956	7,392	23.5	909
Kings, CA	06031	8.0	65.3	74.3	...	...	2,631	1,272	22.8	168
Lake, CA	06033	11.7	66.9	41.2	...	...	787	346	25.3	55
Lassen, CA	06035	4.1	35.4	24.0	...	...	466	219	22.3	36
Los Angeles, CA	06037	11.3	58.5	85.2	...	...	140,121	68,041	23.4	5,849
Madera, CA	06039	9.2	73.3	75.1	...	...	2,749	1,260	23.8	219
Marin, CA	06041	12.0	24.1	39.3	...	...	2,984	1,552	19.7	159
Mariposa, CA	06043	19.2	49.5	27.1	...	...	243	107	19.8	13
Mendocino, CA	06045	11.2	66.1	49.9	...	...	1,569	692	18.8	92
Merced, CA	06047	9.9	74.9	79.9	...	...	5,369	2,374	23.4	257
Modoc, CA	06049	3.5	60.2	35.5	...	...	178	73	14.0	8
Mono, CA	06051	12.4	56.1	83.3	...	...	254	103	16.4	7
Monterey, CA	06053	9.3	67.0	84.3	...	...	6,294	3,016	23.6	273
Napa, CA	06055	11.5	41.7	66.5	...	...	1,769	903	22.8	77
Nevada, CA	06057	9.7	32.1	18.4	...	...	1,561	796	21.5	74
Orange, CA	06059	10.1	45.2	68.9	...	...	36,188	18,460	27.3	1,427
Placer, CA	06061	9.5	24.9	31.7	...	...	5,109	2,737	23.5	258
Plumas, CA	06063	11.6	35.1	21.8	...	...	214	101	22.9	21
Riverside, CA	06065	10.6	55.6	74.4	...	...	31,763	16,564	25.7	1,298
Sacramento, CA	06067	10.8	51.7	64.0	...	...	18,287	8,651	27.2	990
San Benito, CA	06069	10.4	51.5	75.0	...	...	838	414	27.0	52
San Bernardino, CA	06071	10.7	64.3	78.3	...	...	33,287	16,405	25.4	1,768
San Diego, CA	06073	11.2	48.7	67.1	...	...	42,606	20,346	24.5	2,189
San Francisco, CA	06075	11.2	59.4	88.8	...	...	5,641	2,720	20.9	346
San Joaquin, CA	06077	10.1	60.3	76.2	...	...	11,238	5,558	24.5	606
San Luis Obispo, CA	06079	11.5	42.9	42.5	...	...	3,231	1,448	23.7	162

[2]IEP= Individual Education Program. See notes and definitions for more information
[4]Broomfield county is included with Boulder county
... Not available

Table C-1. Population, School, and Student Characteristics by County, Selected Years—*Continued*

County	State/ County Code	Revenues, 2008–2009				Current expenditures, 2008–2009			Resident population 16 to 19 years, 2006–2010			
			Percentage of revenue from									
		Total revenue ($1,000's)	Federal government	State government	Local government	Amount ($1,000's)	Amount per student	Percent for instruction	Total population 16 to 19 years	Percent enrolled in school	Percent high school graduates, not enrolled in school	Percent not enrolled, not grads, not employed, or not in labor force
		19	20	21	22	23	24	25	26	27	28	29
ARKANSAS— *(Continued)*												
Pulaski, AR	05119	648,346	9.7	49.2	41.0	572,082	10,097	57.0	18,524	78.7	13.0	6.4
Randolph, AR	05121	25,509	11.6	66.1	22.2	23,033	8,264	61.1	1,032	83.1	11.2	5.6
St. Francis, AR	05123	48,786	17.8	63.7	18.5	47,412	9,861	56.4	1,623	69.5	11.5	13.1
Saline, AR	05125	121,372	6.7	62.2	31.1	104,225	7,198	62.7	5,181	76.7	18.1	3.6
Scott, AR	05127	26,335	16.9	62.7	20.4	22,926	8,316	59.8	566	77.0	15.7	4.2
Searcy, AR	05129	18,311	13.6	63.1	23.3	17,480	10,530	57.6	459	71.5	17.2	3.5
Sebastian, AR	05131	189,357	12.6	50.6	36.8	163,895	8,400	57.8	7,179	77.9	15.8	4.6
Sevier, AR	05133	37,577	14.0	68.1	17.8	35,133	10,237	57.8	860	69.3	11.1	17.9
Sharp, AR	05135	25,838	12.9	59.0	28.1	22,838	7,669	59.7	807	81.3	9.9	8.4
Stone, AR	05137	15,233	13.4	62.0	24.6	13,672	7,981	63.9	496	76.6	15.7	4.8
Union, AR	05139	74,403	10.4	54.2	35.4	66,031	8,312	60.0	2,309	84.4	9.3	5.3
Van Buren, AR	05141	23,438	13.9	48.0	38.2	19,394	8,105	59.1	789	79.3	7.5	12.3
Washington, AR	05143	328,829	8.7	50.0	41.3	294,237	8,442	60.7	13,900	85.1	9.3	2.4
White, AR	05145	129,765	10.5	61.2	28.3	103,404	8,200	58.3	5,048	86.4	9.5	2.6
Woodruff, AR	05147	7,177	26.6	50.0	23.4	6,567	11,603	56.8	419	82.8	15.8	1.4
Yell, AR	05149	47,979	13.8	68.1	18.1	37,640	8,487	59.4	1,243	74.7	14.4	7.7
CALIFORNIA	06000	73,868,198	13.2	54.3	32.6	59,466,302	9,538	59.9	2,249,151	84.6	9.5	3.7
Alameda, CA	06001	2,472,488	11.5	52.0	36.5	1,990,330	9,333	61.0	80,484	87.9	7.1	3.2
Alpine, CA	06003	5,831	25.0	28.7	46.3	4,374	33,907	45.5	96	90.6	0.0	0.0
Amador, CA	06005	47,908	9.6	26.2	64.2	38,787	8,434	59.7	1,996	79.7	13.0	5.5
Butte, CA	06007	396,668	19.6	50.9	29.5	319,497	9,963	58.0	15,652	88.5	8.9	1.8
Calaveras, CA	06009	85,289	7.6	33.0	59.4	66,905	10,293	57.7	2,372	71.8	23.3	4.0
Colusa, CA	06011	61,142	15.0	59.4	25.6	51,453	10,848	59.1	1,313	83.0	14.7	0.6
Contra Costa, CA	06013	1,903,425	9.1	47.5	43.4	1,488,582	8,916	62.7	58,065	87.4	8.1	3.1
Del Norte, CA	06015	48,841	20.1	58.0	21.9	46,425	10,148	63.7	1,569	82.1	15.1	2.1
El Dorado, CA	06017	326,500	11.0	45.6	43.3	264,757	9,161	59.5	10,134	91.8	6.4	1.3
Fresno, CA	06019	2,181,512	15.0	65.3	19.7	1,821,628	9,398	58.1	64,294	82.6	10.0	5.0
Glenn, CA	06021	75,741	19.2	55.8	25.0	63,881	11,502	57.9	1,787	81.3	12.1	3.8
Humboldt, CA	06023	220,860	14.2	56.4	29.4	176,221	10,084	59.3	8,274	82.8	12.8	2.2
Imperial, CA	06025	454,116	18.0	61.9	20.1	370,778	10,223	55.4	11,924	87.0	8.3	3.7
Inyo, CA	06027	51,434	13.1	32.3	54.6	38,776	12,676	54.7	877	78.2	14.8	7.0
Kern, CA	06029	2,115,422	15.3	59.7	25.0	1,663,856	9,565	56.9	55,843	78.0	13.4	6.1
Kings, CA	06031	360,824	15.9	65.9	18.1	259,059	9,137	56.7	9,090	76.6	13.8	7.0
Lake, CA	06033	116,668	15.0	52.0	33.0	96,692	10,091	55.0	3,137	79.3	4.1	15.4
Lassen, CA	06035	58,719	14.8	60.1	25.1	50,010	10,924	55.0	1,636	73.5	13.0	13.6
Los Angeles, CA	06037	20,425,074	14.8	64.0	21.2	16,525,535	10,139	59.0	602,657	85.0	8.6	4.1
Madera, CA	06039	414,428	12.1	66.0	21.9	270,515	9,198	55.9	9,514	72.9	13.6	7.4
Marin, CA	06041	503,294	5.9	24.8	69.3	345,808	11,677	59.6	9,949	89.7	6.3	2.1
Mariposa, CA	06043	26,186	12.6	31.9	55.5	24,099	10,687	58.4	773	79.8	14.6	5.6
Mendocino, CA	06045	200,640	13.6	50.2	36.2	152,934	11,689	57.2	4,700	80.8	14.2	2.4
Merced, CA	06047	651,425	16.1	66.6	17.3	547,175	9,744	58.2	18,896	81.9	12.7	3.3
Modoc, CA	06049	24,419	26.3	50.9	22.8	19,313	15,935	54.3	362	89.8	4.4	0.0
Mono, CA	06051	36,837	6.4	25.4	68.3	26,922	16,140	52.0	786	74.9	14.0	2.3
Monterey, CA	06053	905,959	13.2	46.7	40.1	726,326	10,295	58.5	26,317	78.1	12.6	4.6
Napa, CA	06055	263,612	13.8	24.9	61.2	213,635	10,595	57.8	7,523	82.4	10.1	1.7
Nevada, CA	06057	208,033	7.9	35.4	56.7	167,030	9,511	60.5	5,086	79.8	15.5	2.9
Orange, CA	06059	5,401,035	11.3	46.0	42.7	4,485,095	8,897	63.0	177,481	88.0	7.3	2.5
Placer, CA	06061	704,016	8.9	37.8	53.3	511,426	8,009	60.3	18,493	86.0	11.5	1.2
Plumas, CA	06063	41,154	16.6	27.4	56.0	27,910	11,173	53.7	1,112	85.0	6.9	6.0
Riverside, CA	06065	4,541,992	12.8	55.1	32.1	3,627,924	8,643	61.2	142,136	81.6	12.0	4.1
Sacramento, CA	06067	2,525,416	13.3	59.6	27.1	2,183,061	9,270	60.0	83,458	84.0	10.9	3.8
San Benito, CA	06069	119,846	11.4	48.3	40.4	104,354	9,191	62.7	3,585	76.0	9.3	4.0
San Bernardino, CA	06071	4,640,378	13.4	66.7	19.9	3,661,415	8,750	59.9	142,720	80.9	12.6	4.6
San Diego, CA	06073	5,768,345	11.8	43.1	45.0	4,696,545	9,538	59.1	181,315	84.3	11.2	3.1
San Francisco, CA	06075	840,855	13.6	30.7	55.7	677,038	12,269	54.1	28,357	88.7	7.2	2.0
San Joaquin, CA	06077	1,471,001	12.8	63.6	23.6	1,213,619	9,005	60.3	46,423	83.2	9.8	4.2
San Luis Obispo, CA	06079	400,086	12.5	26.1	61.4	325,927	9,391	59.9	19,316	91.3	5.8	1.1

Note. Data in columns 26 through 41 from the American Community Survey are subject to sampling error, which can be especially large in small counties and small population groups. See notes and definitions for more information.

Table C-1. Population, School, and Student Characteristics by County, Selected Years—*Continued*

County	State/ County Code	High school graduates, 2006–2010			College enrollment, 2006–2010		College graduates, 2006–2010 (percent)						
		Population 25 years and over	High school diploma or less (percent)	High school diploma or more (percent)	Number	Percent public	Bachelor's degree or more	+/- U.S. percent with Bachelor's degree or more	Non-Hispanic White	Black or African American	American Indian and Alaska Native	Asian, Hawaiian, and Pacific Islander	Hispanic or Latino[3]
		30	31	32	33	34	35	36	37	38	39	40	41
ARKANSAS— *(Continued)*													
Pulaski, AR	05119	250,377	39.6	88.2	26,331	83.9	30.7	2.8	37.6	16.6	36.2	57.3	14.1
Randolph, AR	05121	12,400	61.8	77.8	1,052	76.5	11.1	-16.8	11.3	0.0	0.0	0.0	0.0
St. Francis, AR	05123	18,911	63.9	73.3	1,131	77.3	10.5	-17.4	11.7	9.8	0.0	63.6	2.9
Saline, AR	05125	69,853	48.1	87.6	4,770	85.5	22.6	-5.3	22.7	18.1	0.0	41.3	23.5
Scott, AR	05127	7,314	69.6	73.7	454	94.5	9.0	-18.9	8.5	0.0	0.0	24.6	15.9
Searcy, AR	05129	5,982	66.8	72.7	332	100.0	9.2	-18.7	9.2	0.0	17.3	0.0	0.0
Sebastian, AR	05131	80,535	51.1	81.0	5,928	87.0	17.9	-10.0	19.8	8.7	20.5	18.1	5.2
Sevier, AR	05133	10,392	65.3	68.8	547	98.9	9.3	-18.6	12.5	0.0	0.0	1.5	2.0
Sharp, AR	05135	12,655	61.6	80.4	633	88.9	12.5	-15.4	12.4	0.0	40.9	0.0	19.0
Stone, AR	05137	8,964	63.6	75.8	374	100.0	10.4	-17.5	10.3	0.0	0.0	0.0	35.7
Union, AR	05139	28,511	55.3	81.3	1,622	84.5	16.1	-11.8	19.6	8.7	3.7	39.9	10.0
Van Buren, AR	05141	12,399	55.9	81.0	438	100.0	13.2	-14.7	13.4	0.0	8.3	100.0	1.2
Washington, AR	05143	118,442	47.0	81.7	21,690	91.5	27.4	-0.5	30.2	25.8	23.8	32.6	6.5
White, AR	05145	47,435	56.4	81.8	7,185	42.7	17.3	-10.6	17.4	16.1	5.6	67.0	10.9
Woodruff, AR	05147	5,162	71.8	73.1	223	94.6	9.0	-18.9	10.5	4.8	0.0	0.0	0.0
Yell, AR	05149	14,220	71.0	70.2	703	88.8	10.3	-17.6	10.8	0.0	0.0	8.9	8.8
CALIFORNIA	06000	23,497,945	40.8	80.7	2,960,189	79.6	30.1	2.2	38.6	21.5	13.4	47.4	10.3
Alameda, CA	06001	994,960	34.4	85.9	136,509	84.0	40.3	12.4	50.0	22.6	16.7	51.1	15.0
Alpine, CA	06003	750	34.3	92.1	127	82.7	29.7	1.8	37.3	0.0	1.8	82.4	0.0
Amador, CA	06005	29,197	43.1	87.4	1,135	67.8	19.0	-8.9	21.1	7.2	23.2	28.5	5.2
Butte, CA	06007	138,733	38.0	85.7	30,051	94.6	24.1	-3.8	26.1	14.5	9.8	28.9	10.2
Calaveras, CA	06009	33,871	39.4	90.7	1,877	79.3	19.6	-8.3	20.4	6.6	25.9	41.3	7.1
Colusa, CA	06011	12,974	56.9	70.5	619	79.6	11.8	-16.1	18.2	3.7	0.0	14.9	3.7
Contra Costa, CA	06013	681,162	31.3	88.4	67,667	77.9	38.2	10.3	44.7	22.3	18.5	54.1	13.7
Del Norte, CA	06015	19,376	50.5	81.3	1,625	86.0	14.3	-13.6	16.0	11.3	9.0	20.1	7.8
El Dorado, CA	06017	123,862	30.6	92.7	11,642	86.8	31.1	3.2	31.7	28.4	13.5	50.6	17.5
Fresno, CA	06019	529,358	50.2	73.1	68,900	85.9	19.7	-8.2	29.4	14.6	10.1	32.2	7.8
Glenn, CA	06021	17,372	50.3	73.9	1,386	91.6	16.2	-11.7	20.2	11.0	13.4	37.0	4.8
Humboldt, CA	06023	88,677	35.6	90.4	14,345	93.7	26.3	-1.6	28.0	8.6	16.4	33.4	14.9
Imperial, CA	06025	99,424	60.7	62.3	11,769	93.4	12.2	-15.7	22.9	8.0	8.6	27.5	9.3
Inyo, CA	06027	13,181	41.9	88.6	755	76.6	20.9	-7.0	24.0	0.0	7.4	62.3	6.4
Kern, CA	06029	476,168	55.7	71.1	48,276	83.3	14.7	-13.2	21.1	10.2	8.4	33.7	5.2
Kings, CA	06031	91,224	58.2	69.9	8,633	81.0	11.8	-16.1	19.1	6.9	7.0	28.7	4.1
Lake, CA	06033	45,478	46.6	86.3	2,659	92.6	16.5	-11.4	17.8	14.2	12.3	30.2	7.2
Lassen, CA	06035	24,828	46.9	79.8	1,867	78.1	12.4	-15.5	15.6	2.0	3.7	20.6	4.9
Los Angeles, CA	06037	6,268,121	45.4	75.9	806,410	75.6	29.0	1.1	44.4	22.6	15.3	48.4	9.7
Madera, CA	06039	90,204	57.6	67.9	6,658	82.5	13.5	-14.4	19.9	10.9	11.3	34.3	5.3
Marin, CA	06041	182,677	21.0	91.8	14,017	72.4	54.1	26.2	60.6	19.0	22.1	57.7	18.8
Mariposa, CA	06043	13,675	42.7	90.0	810	87.7	20.4	-7.5	21.0	16.2	25.6	36.7	19.2
Mendocino, CA	06045	60,381	42.0	83.2	4,218	88.8	22.7	-5.2	26.5	14.1	8.2	36.3	4.8
Merced, CA	06047	140,880	58.7	67.0	17,507	84.7	12.5	-15.4	18.5	6.3	13.4	27.3	5.3
Modoc, CA	06049	6,854	44.7	84.3	476	93.3	15.6	-12.3	16.5	0.0	15.8	73.2	0.9
Mono, CA	06051	9,297	37.0	87.4	689	98.1	29.9	2.0	36.3	0.0	0.0	6.1	6.0
Monterey, CA	06053	252,221	49.9	70.7	29,132	83.0	23.4	-4.5	39.8	13.2	13.0	37.1	6.1
Napa, CA	06055	90,794	38.3	82.2	8,401	68.0	30.0	2.1	36.8	28.4	10.2	42.6	7.7
Nevada, CA	06057	71,984	28.7	94.1	4,890	86.6	31.9	4.0	32.9	22.7	1.8	32.7	19.8
Orange, CA	06059	1,929,994	35.2	83.3	257,769	81.4	36.0	8.1	43.4	34.3	14.7	49.8	11.9
Placer, CA	06061	226,859	27.9	93.0	21,399	82.9	34.1	6.2	35.0	35.1	20.7	50.8	16.4
Plumas, CA	06063	15,280	37.9	92.2	934	72.9	19.8	-8.1	20.8	48.7	0.0	10.5	10.7
Riverside, CA	06065	1,284,414	47.0	79.2	133,527	78.0	20.5	-7.4	26.5	22.3	12.1	42.5	8.2
Sacramento, CA	06067	893,042	37.4	85.1	114,962	84.7	27.8	-0.1	32.0	18.6	16.7	34.5	13.5
San Benito, CA	06069	33,308	49.8	73.8	3,206	88.3	18.3	-9.6	27.6	16.8	13.5	21.7	7.9
San Bernardino, CA	06071	1,181,413	49.3	77.5	145,717	76.8	18.4	-9.5	23.3	18.3	8.9	47.5	8.1
San Diego, CA	06073	1,946,525	34.5	85.3	280,184	79.8	34.1	6.2	41.8	21.7	14.9	44.6	14.4
San Francisco, CA	06075	608,563	28.7	85.7	84,004	71.8	51.2	23.3	70.0	24.4	22.0	39.1	27.7
San Joaquin, CA	06077	403,342	50.5	76.7	42,100	73.4	17.5	-10.4	21.8	16.7	8.8	28.6	6.2
San Luis Obispo, CA	06079	174,072	33.9	88.2	33,959	94.1	30.6	2.7	34.8	12.3	13.9	44.2	11.3

Note. Data in columns 26 through 41 from the American Community Survey are subject to sampling error, which can be especially large in small counties and small population groups. See notes and definitions for more information.
[3]May be of any race.

Table C-1. Population, School, and Student Characteristics by County, Selected Years—*Continued*

County	State/ County Code	County Type[1]	Population, 2010		Percent of related children 5–17 years in poverty, 2010	Percent of children under 19 years with no health insurance, 2010	Number of schools and students, 2010–2011			Resident enrollment, 2006–2010 K–12 enrollment	
			Total	Percent 5–17 years			School districts	Schools	Students	Number	Percent public
			1	2	3	4	5	6	7	8	9
CALIFORNIA—*(Continued)*											
San Mateo, CA	06081	1	718,451	15.8	7.7	6.5	26	177	92,124	112,663	80.3
Santa Barbara, CA	06083	2	423,895	16.7	19.5	10.4	26	124	66,053	71,628	90.3
Santa Clara, CA	06085	1	1,781,642	17.1	12.6	5.6	39	394	265,851	300,415	87.4
Santa Cruz, CA	06087	2	262,382	15.4	18.1	7.9	17	79	39,387	41,097	89.5
Shasta, CA	06089	3	177,223	16.6	23.1	8.6	28	109	27,396	30,615	89.0
Sierra, CA	06091	8	3,240	12.5	18.0	12.4	3	10	427	413	90.3
Siskiyou, CA	06093	7	44,900	15.3	27.8	9.7	29	68	6,535	6,941	93.5
Solano, CA	06095	2	413,344	18.1	14.7	6.6	10	117	66,088	77,833	92.1
Sonoma, CA	06097	2	483,878	16.2	13.1	8.6	46	180	70,869	79,494	90.3
Stanislaus, CA	06099	2	514,453	20.9	26.8	7.9	31	187	104,543	109,661	95.0
Sutter, CA	06101	3	94,737	20.0	21.8	9.8	14	45	20,652	18,769	96.0
Tehama, CA	06103	4	63,463	18.5	29.7	9.7	20	51	10,786	12,150	91.3
Trinity, CA	06105	8	13,786	13.8	29.2	9.3	11	25	1,729	1,890	98.6
Tulare, CA	06107	2	442,179	23.3	32.2	10.3	49	192	97,894	102,210	95.7
Tuolumne, CA	06109	4	55,365	13.3	18.8	8.4	12	42	6,142	8,345	88.7
Ventura, CA	06111	2	823,318	19.0	14.2	8.7	25	219	141,610	159,438	90.4
Yolo, CA	06113	1	200,849	16.5	17.4	7.6	8	63	29,366	32,536	93.1
Yuba, CA	06115	3	72,155	20.5	26.4	8.1	6	42	13,923	14,868	93.8
COLORADO	08000	X	5,029,196	17.5	15.1	10.6	259	1,796	843,316	854,965	91.6
Adams, CO											
	08001	1	441,603	20.0	16.0	13.1	13	135	84,454	82,177	92.9
Alamosa, CO	08003	7	15,445	17.0	29.1	11.1	4	8	2,393	2,626	92.8
Arapahoe, CO	08005	1	572,003	18.6	13.5	10.5	12	156	111,855	102,615	91.7
Archuleta, CO	08007	7	12,084	15.0	21.8	14.3	1	4	1,492	2,776	91.7
Baca, CO	08009	9	3,788	15.9	23.8	20.8	5	13	948	659	95.3
Bent, CO	08011	7	6,499	12.4	30.0	10.9	2	6	852	843	99.1
Boulder, CO	08013	2	294,567	15.7	12.2	9.0	5[4]	104[4]	56,905[4]	44,992	91.1
Broomfield, CO	08014	1	55,889	19.2	6.3	7.0	(4)	(4)	(4)	10,049	88.4
Chaffee, CO	08015	7	17,809	12.5	17.7	12.7	2	9	2,056	2,575	93.9
Cheyenne, CO	08017	9	1,836	17.4	19.9	24.4	2	5	315	379	88.4
Clear Creek, CO	08019	1	9,088	12.4	11.6	9.2	3	5	989	1,180	95.0
Conejos, CO	08021	9	8,256	20.4	25.8	15.4	3	10	1,613	1,783	94.7
Costilla, CO	08023	9	3,524	15.9	34.4	19.4	2	6	508	709	100.0
Crowley, CO	08025	8	5,823	10.4	32.0	12.0	1	4	493	827	79.9
Custer, CO	08027	8	4,255	14.0	24.5	19.1	1	3	454	508	99.0
Delta, CO	08029	6	30,952	16.5	21.7	14.6	2	19	5,301	5,194	95.7
Denver, CO	08031	1	600,158	14.2	27.3	11.4	8	176	86,681	81,183	89.0
Dolores, CO	08033	9	2,064	15.8	14.4	20.8	1	3	309	354	98.0
Douglas, CO	08035	1	285,465	22.8	3.3	4.5	2	79	61,465	60,848	90.0
Eagle, CO	08037	5	52,197	17.0	11.3	16.3	1	20	6,181	8,060	89.0
Elbert, CO	08039	1	23,086	20.3	8.0	10.4	5	18	3,601	4,697	95.4
El Paso, CO	08041	2	622,263	18.9	15.9	9.0	27	207	110,001	113,734	91.7
Fremont, CO	08043	4	46,824	13.0	20.4	10.4	4	17	5,524	5,634	88.5
Garfield, CO	08045	5	56,389	19.0	12.7	16.9	4	28	11,325	10,463	91.4
Gilpin, CO	08047	1	5,441	12.5	7.8	9.2	1	2	386	691	96.4
Grand, CO	08049	8	14,843	14.7	12.3	15.2	2	9	1,754	2,083	90.5
Gunnison, CO	08051	7	15,324	13.1	13.7	15.6	2	7	1,864	1,601	91.8
Hinsdale, CO	08053	9	843	12.8	17.2	16.4	1	1	96	11	100.0
Huerfano, CO	08055	6	6,711	13.6	31.3	12.1	2	6	798	1,112	93.4
Jackson, CO	08057	9	1,394	14.2	24.6	19.0	1	2	211	260	99.2
Jefferson, CO	08059	1	534,543	16.6	10.4	10.0	2	164	85,979	89,949	90.8
Kiowa, CO	08061	9	1,398	17.5	15.8	16.0	2	5	272	302	100.0
Kit Carson, CO	08063	7	8,270	15.6	19.3	20.6	5	13	1,452	1,467	95.6
Lake, CO	08065	7	7,310	17.2	20.8	15.6	2	7	1,330	1,305	100.0
La Plata, CO	08067	6	51,334	14.8	13.0	11.8	5	19	6,844	7,539	91.2
Larimer, CO	08069	2	299,630	15.5	11.2	8.9	6	88	43,392	46,352	93.1
Las Animas, CO	08071	7	15,507	15.3	23.7	12.1	6	17	2,547	2,460	95.9
Lincoln, CO	08073	8	5,467	14.9	22.2	15.7	5	8	848	825	95.8
Logan, CO	08075	7	22,709	14.8	18.2	12.4	5	14	3,123	3,485	90.0
Mesa, CO	08077	3	146,723	16.7	16.4	12.7	5	51	22,716	24,030	91.4

[1]County type codes are from the Economic Research Service of the United States Department of Agriculture. See notes and definitions for more information.
[4]Broomfield county is included with Boulder county

Table C-1. Population, School, and Student Characteristics by County, Selected Years—*Continued*

County	State/ County Code	Characteristics of students, 2010–2011				Number of graduates, 2008–2009	Staff and students, 2010–2011			
		Percent with IEP[2]	Percent eligible for free or reduced lunch	Percent minority	Percent English-language learners		Total staff	Number of teachers	Student/ teacher ratio	Central admin. staff
		10	11	12	13	14	15	16	17	18
CALIFORNIA—*(Continued)*										
San Mateo, CA	06081	11.0	36.0	71.4	...	...	7,548	4,112	22.4	389
Santa Barbara, CA	06083	10.1	55.4	73.0	...	...	5,674	2,812	23.5	334
Santa Clara, CA	06085	10.1	37.4	77.0	...	...	21,044	11,524	23.1	1,082
Santa Cruz, CA	06087	12.5	49.8	59.6	...	...	3,449	1,624	24.2	180
Shasta, CA	06089	10.2	51.7	26.8	...	...	2,711	1,228	22.3	145
Sierra, CA	06091	11.5	49.2	17.6	...	...	62	30	14.4	5
Siskiyou, CA	06093	10.7	63.4	34.0	...	...	889	355	18.4	55
Solano, CA	06095	11.3	44.5	70.5	...	...	5,465	2,807	23.5	185
Sonoma, CA	06097	13.0	42.8	51.1	...	...	6,229	3,165	22.4	341
Stanislaus, CA	06099	11.7	63.0	66.6	...	...	9,202	4,349	24.0	439
Sutter, CA	06101	10.1	54.6	57.6	...	...	1,837	935	22.1	68
Tehama, CA	06103	8.4	69.8	40.6	...	...	1,207	500	21.6	96
Trinity, CA	06105	11.5	59.1	27.2	...	...	304	98	17.6	14
Tulare, CA	06107	6.8	72.1	79.5	...	...	8,432	4,051	24.2	382
Tuolumne, CA	06109	11.5	47.8	34.9	...	...	694	322	19.1	38
Ventura, CA	06111	10.5	46.1	61.6	...	...	11,264	5,795	24.4	465
Yolo, CA	06113	10.2	50.3	60.9	...	...	2,631	1,286	22.8	112
Yuba, CA	06115	13.1	67.4	52.4	...	...	1,265	655	21.3	59
COLORADO	08000	10.0	39.9	43.2	11.8	47,457	101,420	48,543	17.4	5,660
Adams, CO	08001	9.9	49.1	55.7	18.3	3,621	8,556	4,186	20.2	444
Alamosa, CO	08003	25.7	69.2	61.6	10.0	176	415	168	14.2	31
Arapahoe, CO	08005	10.6	38.4	51.5	16.9	6,262	13,001	6,062	18.5	739
Archuleta, CO	08007	...	51.2	28.4	6.0	111	173	87	17.1	11
Baca, CO	08009	...	53.0	22.7	1.5	115	170	76	12.6	16
Bent, CO	08011	...	70.3	45.0	1.8	42	127	59	14.5	9
Boulder, CO	08013	9.2[4]	25.6	33.4	10.8[4]	3,528[4]	6,830[4]	3,268[4]	17.4[4]	386[4]
Broomfield, CO	08014	(4)	19.4	24.8	(4)	(4)	(4)	(4)	(4)	(4)
Chaffee, CO	08015	...	39.8	16.9	1.1	156	313	154	13.3	19
Cheyenne, CO	08017	...	34.9	18.7	4.8	23	73	35	9.0	3
Clear Creek, CO	08019	30.9	25.2	16.0	0.4	62	158	62	15.9	8
Conejos, CO	08021	...	70.6	60.2	1.4	136	219	120	13.4	14
Costilla, CO	08023	...	80.1	86.4	9.8	28	85	41	12.5	10
Crowley, CO	08025	...	70.2	31.6	0.6	32	68	30	16.7	3
Custer, CO	08027	...	38.8	6.8	...	41	68	37	12.2	4
Delta, CO	08029	11.3	48.7	25.4	4.7	374	649	281	18.9	23
Denver, CO	08031	10.9	71.4	79.7	29.0	3,067	10,786	5,133	16.9	703
Dolores, CO	08033	...	47.9	14.9	...	24	49	22	14.0	4
Douglas, CO	08035	8.9	10.6	22.7	3.3	3,347	6,321	2,949	20.8	262
Eagle, CO	08037	...	39.7	53.0	31.9	341	839	435	14.2	48
Elbert, CO	08039	...	22.2	12.4	1.0	273	485	245	14.7	24
El Paso, CO	08041	10.0	34.7	38.9	5.4	6,556	13,896	6,737	16.3	739
Fremont, CO	08043	11.0	52.1	17.1	0.6	393	706	329	16.8	43
Garfield, CO	08045	21.0	42.5	47.8	18.1	583	1,384	717	15.8	57
Gilpin, CO	08047	...	29.5	15.5	0.5	17	67	30	12.9	6
Grand, CO	08049	...	26.0	15.8	8.0	145	250	135	13.0	16
Gunnison, CO	08051	7.2	21.3	15.6	7.0	106	254	140	13.3	13
Hinsdale, CO	08053	...	19.8	5.2	2.1	0	3	1	96.0	0
Huerfano, CO	08055	...	68.3	61.2	...	47	135	65	12.3	8
Jackson, CO	08057	...	53.6	25.1	9.0	9	26	20	10.4	2
Jefferson, CO	08059	9.2	30.1	31.6	6.1	5,767	10,520	4,869	17.7	488
Kiowa, CO	08061	...	47.1	10.7	1.1	26	54	31	8.8	4
Kit Carson, CO	08063	...	51.9	32.9	13.2	107	225	113	12.8	16
Lake, CO	08065	...	63.8	71.4	30.0	99	310	94	14.2	32
La Plata, CO	08067	17.9	31.0	27.5	2.4	463	922	448	15.3	74
Larimer, CO	08069	9.9	29.7	24.6	5.0	3,008	5,250	2,463	17.6	324
Las Animas, CO	08071	...	49.9	54.8	2.3	183	350	186	13.7	34
Lincoln, CO	08073	...	38.8	14.3	1.2	75	195	73	11.7	24
Logan, CO	08075	11.8	47.3	25.0	3.3	201	485	212	14.7	35
Mesa, CO	08077	10.8	44.0	26.4	4.6	1,416	2,865	1,360	16.7	179

[2]IEP= Individual Education Program. See notes and definitions for more information
[4]Broomfield county is included with Boulder county
... Not available

Table C-1. Population, School, and Student Characteristics by County, Selected Years—*Continued*

County	State/ County Code	Revenues, 2008–2009				Current expenditures, 2008–2009			Resident population 16 to 19 years, 2006–2010			
		Total revenue ($1,000's)	Percentage of revenue from: Federal government	State government	Local government	Amount ($1,000's)	Amount per student	Percent for instruction	Total population 16 to 19 years	Percent enrolled in school	Percent high school graduates, not enrolled in school	Percent not enrolled, not grads, not employed, or not in labor force
		19	20	21	22	23	24	25	26	27	28	29
CALIFORNIA— *(Continued)*												
San Mateo, CA	06081	1,270,673	8.0	23.6	68.4	934,143	10,449	60.8	32,188	88.4	7.2	2.3
Santa Barbara, CA	06083	718,075	12.6	42.2	45.2	626,567	9,505	60.0	31,988	88.1	5.9	2.7
Santa Clara, CA	06085	3,275,757	10.5	29.3	60.2	2,560,950	9,792	62.2	89,237	88.5	6.9	3.0
Santa Cruz, CA	06087	456,037	15.1	44.3	40.6	386,575	9,993	57.0	18,596	88.9	7.1	1.7
Shasta, CA	06089	369,607	15.9	51.2	32.9	286,515	10,107	59.5	10,416	84.1	11.3	3.3
Sierra, CA	06091	9,330	24.7	40.0	35.3	7,319	15,572	48.3	162	63.0	32.1	4.9
Siskiyou, CA	06093	108,412	18.3	51.0	30.7	85,209	12,684	54.4	2,420	87.9	8.6	3.2
Solano, CA	06095	727,387	11.9	60.1	28.1	607,626	8,818	60.2	25,115	83.7	9.7	4.7
Sonoma, CA	06097	839,372	10.2	38.8	50.9	687,272	9,781	63.4	27,276	85.4	9.6	2.6
Stanislaus, CA	06099	1,249,166	13.9	56.3	29.8	994,940	9,415	61.7	33,796	82.4	11.9	4.3
Sutter, CA	06101	206,715	14.5	56.6	28.9	168,957	8,631	57.7	6,038	78.9	11.9	5.8
Tehama, CA	06103	138,530	16.5	54.0	29.5	115,216	10,617	56.5	3,854	79.0	15.1	5.6
Trinity, CA	06105	36,088	27.1	48.5	24.4	27,427	15,836	52.1	646	82.7	16.6	0.0
Tulare, CA	06107	1,216,857	16.6	65.6	17.8	905,477	9,395	60.9	30,394	78.9	12.1	5.5
Tuolumne, CA	06109	81,597	12.0	42.8	45.2	70,632	10,250	58.5	2,499	85.8	10.5	2.4
Ventura, CA	06111	1,525,605	12.0	52.2	35.8	1,244,098	8,794	62.1	51,750	86.6	8.1	2.6
Yolo, CA	06113	370,985	11.7	57.0	31.3	271,727	9,183	57.2	18,720	91.3	6.1	1.5
Yuba, CA	06115	173,873	15.8	59.9	24.2	142,928	9,966	55.6	4,554	78.6	15.2	5.1
COLORADO	08000	8,446,178	7.1	43.7	49.2	7,186,252	8,784	57.6	274,206	82.4	10.4	4.2
Adams, CO	08001	774,825	6.3	53.5	40.2	666,046	8,401	58.5	23,033	74.1	14.4	6.6
Alamosa, CO	08003	37,875	31.7	45.8	22.5	31,722	13,022	50.2	1,491	97.0	3.0	0.0
Arapahoe, CO	08005	1,090,574	6.1	47.0	46.9	955,424	8,828	62.4	30,205	82.1	11.0	4.3
Archuleta, CO	08007	15,235	6.7	22.9	70.3	12,658	8,300	61.7	1,242	84.6	15.4	0.0
Baca, CO	08009	11,432	5.6	64.7	29.7	10,846	10,118	57.6	280	87.1	8.2	2.1
Bent, CO	08011	9,977	10.1	62.9	26.9	7,895	9,033	60.8	203	69.5	7.9	15.8
Boulder, CO	08013	574,112[4]	5.7[4]	31.5[4]	62.8[4]	480,985[4]	8,783[4]	58.5[4]	20,666	93.2	5.0	0.8
Broomfield, CO	08014	(4)	(4)	(4)	(4)	(4)	(4)	(4)	2,786	83.8	10.8	5.1
Chaffee, CO	08015	22,701	6.6	36.6	56.8	19,288	9,539	56.8	822	88.0	8.5	3.5
Cheyenne, CO	08017	6,015	1.4	43.3	55.3	4,689	15,424	53.6	141	76.6	22.0	1.4
Clear Creek, CO	08019	14,489	8.5	10.5	80.9	10,087	10,148	51.8	510	82.8	10.2	6.1
Conejos, CO	08021	17,433	8.0	74.4	17.6	15,255	9,032	59.2	504	87.5	8.7	3.2
Costilla, CO	08023	7,723	11.9	35.6	52.5	6,063	13,267	47.7	297	61.6	25.3	11.8
Crowley, CO	08025	4,970	8.8	68.9	22.2	4,396	9,045	52.2	406	82.8	9.6	5.7
Custer, CO	08027	5,232	5.5	27.7	66.8	4,608	8,965	60.1	136	94.1	5.9	0.0
Delta, CO	08029	48,725	8.8	55.4	35.8	42,331	7,683	61.9	1,593	77.1	14.1	5.3
Denver, CO	08031	931,089	10.1	32.2	57.7	756,261	9,463	51.9	25,826	75.5	10.7	8.6
Dolores, CO	08033	3,623	3.7	46.0	50.3	3,072	10,485	54.1	97	69.1	4.1	0.0
Douglas, CO	08035	568,232	2.6	43.5	53.9	487,809	8,307	58.1	12,996	89.2	7.3	1.9
Eagle, CO	08037	77,862	5.2	7.3	87.5	59,291	9,870	58.9	2,352	69.9	12.2	8.6
Elbert, CO	08039	36,577	1.7	58.2	40.0	32,066	8,377	55.5	1,441	85.8	9.9	1.9
El Paso, CO	08041	1,041,499	7.5	51.8	40.7	903,670	8,534	57.3	35,534	83.0	11.2	3.4
Fremont, CO	08043	53,721	9.1	56.1	34.8	45,548	8,025	56.6	1,917	36.9	55.1	5.8
Garfield, CO	08045	139,300	6.0	35.0	59.0	105,000	9,069	55.5	2,879	81.7	8.8	4.9
Gilpin, CO	08047	6,390	1.8	28.1	70.1	4,151	11,628	53.1	171	96.5	0.0	0.0
Grand, CO	08049	25,798	0.9	8.3	90.8	18,576	9,670	57.1	629	72.5	26.2	1.3
Gunnison, CO	08051	20,897	4.1	4.4	91.5	15,482	8,419	61.5	1,314	89.4	0.0	5.1
Hinsdale, CO	08053	1,499	3.3	26.9	69.8	1,332	12,932	54.9	0	0.0	0.0	0.0
Huerfano, CO	08055	10,686	10.2	47.8	42.0	8,611	9,083	55.5	275	91.3	2.9	0.0
Jackson, CO	08057	2,957	1.3	48.1	50.6	2,552	11,000	57.5	58	87.9	12.1	0.0
Jefferson, CO	08059	853,041	4.8	42.3	52.9	738,732	8,595	58.5	29,610	83.5	10.1	4.0
Kiowa, CO	08061	3,763	3.6	61.9	34.5	3,374	12,007	59.8	134	82.8	10.5	0.0
Kit Carson, CO	08063	16,272	3.4	56.8	39.9	13,944	9,683	59.1	548	95.8	4.0	0.0
Lake, CO	08065	26,000	24.1	43.2	32.7	19,626	13,919	48.2	359	63.2	28.4	8.4
La Plata, CO	08067	87,177	8.7	35.1	56.2	69,329	9,882	55.2	3,351	86.9	9.5	1.9
Larimer, CO	08069	407,746	5.9	41.1	53.0	362,564	8,535	56.0	19,385	89.0	6.6	2.6
Las Animas, CO	08071	29,775	6.5	58.0	35.5	24,070	8,600	53.5	988	84.0	11.6	3.0
Lincoln, CO	08073	26,010	27.9	39.5	32.7	18,556	19,889	41.2	210	79.5	20.5	0.0
Logan, CO	08075	34,751	6.2	58.1	35.7	28,098	8,960	59.9	1,741	80.5	11.4	4.3
Mesa, CO	08077	204,454	7.6	49.0	43.4	182,479	7,988	60.8	8,058	77.5	15.7	4.0

Note. Data in columns 26 through 41 from the American Community Survey are subject to sampling error, which can be especially large in small counties and small population groups. See notes and definitions for more information.
[4]Broomfield county is included with Boulder county

Table C-1. Population, School, and Student Characteristics by County, Selected Years—*Continued*

County	State/ County Code	High school graduates, 2006–2010			College enrollment, 2006–2010		College graduates, 2006–2010 (percent)						
		Population 25 years and over	High school diploma or less (percent)	High school diploma or more (percent)	Number	Percent public	Bachelor's degree or more	+/- U.S. percent with Bachelor's degree or more	Non-Hispanic White	Black or African American	American Indian and Alaska Native	Asian, Hawaiian, and Pacific Islander	Hispanic or Latino[3]
		30	31	32	33	34	35	36	37	38	39	40	41
CALIFORNIA— *(Continued)*													
San Mateo, CA	06081	492,374	29.3	88.6	53,653	76.5	44.0	16.1	52.4	25.6	27.5	52.6	15.7
Santa Barbara, CA	06083	255,722	38.3	80.1	50,771	89.5	31.0	3.1	43.2	21.5	13.4	46.6	8.6
Santa Clara, CA	06085	1,161,850	30.2	86.3	151,440	73.1	45.3	17.4	52.0	29.5	16.2	58.5	13.9
Santa Cruz, CA	06087	165,318	32.7	84.2	32,589	92.4	37.3	9.4	46.1	29.5	8.5	49.8	11.1
Shasta, CA	06089	120,092	38.7	88.1	12,497	77.6	20.0	-7.9	20.5	21.2	10.1	33.9	13.4
Sierra, CA	06091	2,602	42.9	88.3	74	86.5	23.0	-4.9	23.9	56.8	0.0	0.0	0.0
Siskiyou, CA	06093	32,115	38.8	88.4	2,884	83.6	22.6	-5.3	23.5	11.2	6.9	35.9	14.8
Solano, CA	06095	266,344	38.8	85.8	31,248	81.1	24.0	-3.9	27.4	19.1	16.5	35.8	10.5
Sonoma, CA	06097	322,558	34.8	86.2	36,585	89.5	31.5	3.6	36.5	23.4	13.9	40.5	9.9
Stanislaus, CA	06099	308,072	52.4	75.3	32,814	83.8	16.3	-11.6	20.8	16.7	7.6	27.1	6.7
Sutter, CA	06101	58,400	46.4	78.4	6,213	85.0	18.7	-9.2	21.6	36.5	11.6	23.3	6.3
Tehama, CA	06103	41,177	50.2	80.3	2,864	82.2	12.6	-15.3	14.4	10.0	5.8	30.8	2.7
Trinity, CA	06105	10,228	37.8	90.1	652	77.9	19.5	-8.4	20.4	0.0	8.7	43.8	11.3
Tulare, CA	06107	242,813	57.3	67.3	23,379	86.0	13.0	-14.9	20.6	13.3	15.2	28.1	5.1
Tuolumne, CA	06109	41,624	41.9	87.3	2,711	88.7	17.3	-10.6	18.8	2.4	13.1	25.2	8.1
Ventura, CA	06111	516,739	37.5	82.3	57,800	79.2	30.8	2.9	39.1	27.7	13.0	55.2	10.5
Yolo, CA	06113	112,707	35.8	84.3	36,752	94.1	37.8	9.9	46.3	30.1	6.7	54.6	12.5
Yuba, CA	06115	42,715	50.1	76.9	4,452	87.9	12.5	-15.4	13.0	15.1	11.9	24.9	7.6
COLORADO	08000	3,201,139	34.0	89.3	353,699	79.6	35.9	8.0	41.4	21.4	15.5	46.3	12.1
Adams, CO	08001	263,420	49.5	81.0	19,894	75.0	20.3	-7.6	25.8	19.4	11.6	27.4	7.9
Alamosa, CO	08003	9,074	41.3	86.4	2,416	95.9	26.6	-1.3	35.3	0.0	18.6	45.5	14.8
Arapahoe, CO	08005	361,581	31.3	90.4	35,543	73.6	37.9	10.0	44.3	21.2	12.5	43.8	14.2
Archuleta, CO	08007	7,061	29.2	93.2	735	64.2	39.0	11.1	41.0	0.0	68.2	25.4	17.6
Baca, CO	08009	2,753	46.9	85.0	67	91.0	19.0	-8.9	19.1	0.0	17.4	92.3	6.3
Bent, CO	08011	4,421	54.7	80.4	153	92.2	13.2	-14.7	14.4	1.7	37.6	72.1	7.5
Boulder, CO	08013	184,965	19.9	93.7	40,541	89.6	57.0	29.1	61.2	39.7	25.2	70.6	19.3
Broomfield, CO	08014	34,606	25.1	95.3	3,568	72.3	44.4	16.5	45.4	51.9	54.3	50.7	29.1
Chaffee, CO	08015	13,274	38.5	90.8	512	70.5	33.3	5.4	36.7	7.3	0.0	48.7	4.5
Cheyenne, CO	08017	1,501	46.2	87.9	77	92.2	18.5	-9.4	18.4	0.0	0.0	100.0	10.7
Clear Creek, CO	08019	6,911	28.1	96.9	382	64.1	41.6	13.7	42.1	0.0	38.1	44.4	37.8
Conejos, CO	08021	5,216	53.7	81.4	306	93.5	18.7	-9.2	22.5	100.0	0.0	0.0	14.8
Costilla, CO	08023	2,498	59.5	73.9	115	100.0	14.3	-13.6	24.5	0.0	0.0	17.1	7.4
Crowley, CO	08025	4,225	62.9	72.4	283	98.9	12.2	-15.7	16.7	0.0	0.0	18.5	7.3
Custer, CO	08027	2,976	39.1	93.7	105	81.0	29.2	1.3	30.1	100.0	0.0	24.0	0.0
Delta, CO	08029	21,710	49.9	86.0	699	77.0	18.3	-9.6	20.4	0.0	3.8	12.8	2.6
Denver, CO	08031	393,317	36.6	84.0	46,743	61.9	40.1	12.2	55.4	20.9	14.9	52.3	10.3
Dolores, CO	08033	1,452	54.7	86.0	35	54.3	14.9	-13.0	14.8	0.0	0.0	0.0	8.5
Douglas, CO	08035	174,704	16.4	97.6	12,974	73.2	54.4	26.5	55.0	51.9	45.2	68.3	38.2
Eagle, CO	08037	33,987	32.9	87.2	1,543	77.8	45.9	18.0	56.3	0.0	53.7	60.1	11.9
Elbert, CO	08039	15,564	35.1	96.1	846	73.0	29.2	1.3	29.5	0.0	40.3	26.2	35.1
El Paso, CO	08041	376,883	30.2	92.5	47,942	77.2	34.9	7.0	39.1	21.3	21.3	33.7	15.0
Fremont, CO	08043	35,288	56.1	79.2	1,240	76.7	16.2	-11.7	19.5	4.6	6.7	7.4	7.0
Garfield, CO	08045	35,345	43.1	85.6	2,326	85.5	24.4	-3.5	30.1	0.0	16.9	12.9	4.4
Gilpin, CO	08047	4,034	27.6	94.8	288	80.9	33.7	5.8	32.4	97.2	63.4	100.0	20.6
Grand, CO	08049	9,915	36.9	94.9	460	75.9	28.8	0.9	29.3	22.2	0.0	74.0	16.5
Gunnison, CO	08051	9,447	25.7	93.1	2,562	92.8	45.8	17.9	47.3	0.0	18.6	100.0	16.9
Hinsdale, CO	08053	433	22.4	90.8	0	0.0	42.0	14.1	46.0	0.0	0.0	0.0	0.0
Huerfano, CO	08055	5,358	44.2	85.1	166	59.0	27.2	-0.7	38.4	0.0	0.0	71.8	7.6
Jackson, CO	08057	1,064	42.2	91.5	61	77.0	21.7	-6.2	22.8	0.0	0.0	0.0	8.7
Jefferson, CO	08059	362,571	29.4	92.9	33,775	76.0	39.3	11.4	42.3	22.6	13.4	42.5	17.3
Kiowa, CO	08061	1,157	43.0	91.0	65	89.2	20.1	-7.8	20.3	0.0	0.0	54.6	0.0
Kit Carson, CO	08063	5,666	52.6	84.5	340	72.1	14.9	-13.0	16.6	9.9	63.2	8.6	4.9
Lake, CO	08065	4,741	43.2	79.4	374	95.5	20.7	-7.2	28.4	100.0	0.0	31.0	2.7
La Plata, CO	08067	33,377	27.5	93.6	4,901	94.3	40.6	12.7	44.3	53.3	18.8	4.8	19.2
Larimer, CO	08069	185,448	26.6	93.7	37,572	92.2	42.5	14.6	44.4	32.9	20.6	66.0	17.4
Las Animas, CO	08071	10,974	44.6	83.8	1,048	94.8	19.3	-8.6	28.0	0.0	10.1	13.8	5.7
Lincoln, CO	08073	3,881	55.6	84.5	122	85.2	15.3	-12.6	17.1	6.0	0.0	27.3	7.2
Logan, CO	08075	14,982	45.0	86.7	1,817	88.6	18.0	-9.9	19.9	6.6	0.0	59.2	5.4
Mesa, CO	08077	94,568	41.8	89.2	8,697	86.9	25.4	-2.5	27.1	14.6	7.2	36.0	11.2

Note. Data in columns 26 through 41 from the American Community Survey are subject to sampling error, which can be especially large in small counties and small population groups. See notes and definitions for more information.

[3]May be of any race.

Table C-1. Population, School, and Student Characteristics by County, Selected Years—*Continued*

County	State/ County Code	County Type[1]	Population, 2010		Percent of related children 5–17 years in poverty, 2010	Percent of children under 19 years with no health insurance, 2010	Number of schools and students, 2010–2011			Resident enrollment, 2006–2010 K–12 enrollment	
			Total	Percent 5–17 years			School districts	Schools	Students	Number	Percent public
			1	2	3	4	5	6	7	8	9
COLORADO—*(Continued)*											
Mineral, CO	08079	9	712	11.4	20.7	19.8	1	2	92	57	79.0
Moffat, CO	08081	7	13,795	19.2	13.0	12.6	2	8	2,402	2,647	96.8
Montezuma, CO	08083	6	25,535	17.2	24.0	13.8	3	17	3,987	4,220	94.2
Montrose, CO	08085	7	41,276	18.3	20.3	15.6	3	17	6,762	7,360	87.5
Morgan, CO	08087	6	28,159	20.3	18.5	14.6	5	18	5,483	5,615	96.5
Otero, CO	08089	6	18,831	18.5	27.9	11.9	8	16	3,358	3,442	96.6
Ouray, CO	08091	9	4,436	13.9	14.1	18.2	4	6	566	727	94.1
Park, CO	08093	1	16,206	14.3	12.7	14.9	2	8	1,810	2,234	90.0
Phillips, CO	08095	9	4,442	19.0	14.3	18.8	4	5	937	802	99.8
Pitkin, CO	08097	7	17,148	13.1	7.2	15.7	1	5	1,727	2,205	79.5
Prowers, CO	08099	7	12,551	19.4	29.1	15.2	6	14	2,439	2,576	99.7
Pueblo, CO	08101	3	159,063	17.8	24.1	9.9	7	63	27,279	28,209	93.4
Rio Blanco, CO	08103	9	6,666	17.0	10.3	13.5	4	5	1,147	1,132	93.8
Rio Grande, CO	08105	7	11,982	18.6	27.5	12.2	3	13	2,217	2,711	94.8
Routt, CO	08107	7	23,509	15.3	9.3	11.1	5	13	3,062	3,389	88.1
Saguache, CO	08109	9	6,108	16.3	35.9	23.7	3	11	906	1,103	98.1
San Juan, CO	08111	9	699	13.2	23.6	17.6	1	3	65	43	100.0
San Miguel, CO	08113	9	7,359	13.5	14.1	20.7	2	5	954	1,004	92.0
Sedgwick, CO	08115	9	2,379	14.2	20.5	18.7	2	5	1,907	394	98.0
Summit, CO	08117	7	27,994	11.9	11.9	13.8	1	9	3,124	3,217	88.7
Teller, CO	08119	2	23,350	15.8	12.5	10.2	4	7	3,193	4,081	89.1
Washington, CO	08121	9	4,814	17.7	17.7	21.0	5	11	918	824	91.9
Weld, CO	08123	3	252,825	19.9	15.9	11.4	17	76	37,848	46,804	93.6
Yuma, CO	08125	7	10,043	18.7	16.5	17.7	4	11	1,806	1,832	96.2
CONNECTICUT	09000	X	3,574,097	17.2	11.3	3.2	200	1,157	559,964	628,958	89.5
Fairfield, CT	09001	2	916,829	18.6	9.9	3.8	33	245	146,990	169,745	86.1
Hartford, CT	09003	1	894,014	17.2	12.9	3.0	39	321	143,894	158,797	91.4
Litchfield, CT	09005	4	189,927	16.8	7.1	3.1	24	74	26,088	33,086	88.1
Middlesex, CT	09007	1	165,676	16.2	5.6	2.8	15	70	33,832	27,310	91.6
New Haven, CT	09009	2	862,477	16.7	14.7	3.2	31	257	128,265	148,955	89.5
New London, CT	09011	2	274,055	16.3	9.9	2.9	24	98	41,005	46,359	91.7
Tolland, CT	09013	1	152,691	15.6	5.1	2.3	16	47	22,476	23,958	93.6
Windham, CT	09015	4	118,428	16.8	12.9	3.3	18	45	17,414	20,748	92.7
DELAWARE	10000	X	897,934	16.7	15.9	5.6	42	214	129,403	148,337	83.1
Kent, DE	10001	3	162,310	18.0	17.4	5.0	10	47	25,704	28,279	88.7
New Castle, DE	10003	1	538,479	17.1	13.6	5.3	23	118	75,287	92,201	79.3
Sussex, DE	10005	4	197,145	14.6	21.5	7.1	9	49	28,412	27,857	90.2
DISTRICT OF COLUMBIA	11000	X	601,723	11.3	30.9	2.6	61	228	71,277	73,999	81.6
District of Columbia	11001	1	601,723	11.3	30.9	2.6	54	228	71,277	73,999	81.6
FLORIDA	12000	X	18,801,310	15.6	21.9	13.4	75	4,131	2,643,347	2,952,360	88.3
Alachua, FL	12001	3	247,336	12.6	25.3	10.4	2	65	28,659	30,181	88.3
Baker, FL	12003	1	27,115	18.9	22.2	9.2	1	9	5,004	4,937	92.2
Oay, FL	12005	3	168,852	15.7	21.6	11.7	1	48	25,935	26,804	93.1
Bradford, FL	12007	6	28,520	13.9	25.5	10.4	1	11	3,278	3,956	86.2
Brevard, FL	12009	2	543,376	14.9	17.7	11.5	1	123	71,866	83,135	86.5
Broward, FL	12011	1	1,748,066	16.5	18.7	14.6	1	320	256,472	296,620	87.0
Calhoun, FL	12013	6	14,625	15.2	28.6	12.0	1	7	2,249	2,242	96.9
Charlotte, FL	12015	3	159,978	10.8	23.3	15.4	1	26	16,640	18,505	91.9
Citrus, FL	12017	4	141,236	11.9	28.5	13.2	1	25	15,675	17,476	90.8
Clay, FL	12019	1	190,865	20.1	13.7	9.3	1	45	35,812	38,653	91.9

[1]County type codes are from the Economic Research Service of the United States Department of Agriculture. See notes and definitions for more information.

Table C-1. Population, School, and Student Characteristics by County, Selected Years—*Continued*

County	State/ County Code	Characteristics of students, 2010–2011				Number of graduates, 2008–2009	Staff and students, 2010–2011			
		Percent with IEP[2]	Percent eligible for free or reduced lunch	Percent minority	Percent English-language learners		Total staff	Number of teachers	Student/ teacher ratio	Central admin. staff
		10	11	12	13	14	15	16	17	18
COLORADO—*(Continued)*										
Mineral, CO	08079	. . .	48.9	6.5	. . .	10	28	17	5.3	4
Moffat, CO	08081	10.4	40.5	23.9	6.7	150	339	146	16.5	15
Montezuma, CO	08083	. . .	56.9	38.7	5.7	227	570	267	14.9	36
Montrose, CO	08085	9.0	55.3	39.7	13.7	401	771	401	16.9	40
Morgan, CO	08087	5.5	60.8	55.3	18.9	281	780	357	15.4	45
Otero, CO	08089	12.2	68.0	56.0	3.8	214	509	255	13.2	31
Ouray, CO	08091	32.5	33.2	18.2	4.8	40	123	60	9.5	14
Park, CO	08093	. . .	32.4	14.2	0.3	145	281	122	14.9	19
Phillips, CO	08095	66.7	45.9	29.5	13.2	56	181	78	12.1	18
Pitkin, CO	08097	. . .	18.4	29.5	7.5	125	232	138	12.5	14
Prowers, CO	08099	14.4	63.1	54.4	6.6	145	388	188	12.9	30
Pueblo, CO	08101	13.4	56.5	58.7	4.1	1,526	2,924	1,520	17.9	142
Rio Blanco, CO	08103	11.6	26.3	15.7	4.9	74	188	81	14.2	17
Rio Grande, CO	08105	0.0	59.3	59.6	7.1	134	303	159	13.9	17
Routt, CO	08107	18.0	19.1	12.8	5.6	182	424	224	13.7	28
Saguache, CO	08109	. . .	76.2	66.9	14.9	47	183	80	11.3	20
San Juan, CO	08111	. . .	69.2	32.3	18.5	. . .	17	7	9.8	4
San Miguel, CO	08113	. . .	27.5	16.5	9.1	84	150	85	11.3	9
Sedgwick, CO	08115	. . .	18.0	34.4	. . .	39	99	61	31.4	5
Summit, CO	08117	. . .	32.1	33.1	20.4	202	428	201	15.6	22
Teller, CO	08119	12.6	30.8	13.8	0.7	258	423	201	15.9	22
Washington, CO	08121	. . .	46.1	13.4	0.5	67	177	91	10.1	8
Weld, CO	08123	10.4	45.7	45.5	15.6	1,962	4,343	2,194	17.3	222
Yuma, CO	08125	. . .	53.3	36.2	19.5	128	281	141	12.8	20
CONNECTICUT	09000	12.2	34.0	37.9	5.4	34,956	93,087	42,951	13.0	5,135
Fairfield, CT	09001	10.8	31.8	40.2	6.6	9,622	23,035	10,998	13.4	1,139
Hartford, CT	09003	12.8	37.2	45.0	6.0	8,997	23,396	10,916	13.2	1,335
Litchfield, CT	09005	14.3	19.7	12.6	2.4	1,736	4,485	2,044	12.8	248
Middlesex, CT	09007	10.2	18.4	17.9	1.9	1,785	5,557	2,861	11.8	320
New Haven, CT	09009	12.7	42.8	45.3	6.1	7,491	22,351	9,758	13.1	1,313
New London, CT	09011	13.1	29.8	30.3	4.2	2,841	7,100	3,221	12.7	390
Tolland, CT	09013	11.7	15.3	13.6	1.0	1,494	3,696	1,755	12.8	200
Windham, CT	09015	13.5	38.4	21.6	5.7	990	3,469	1,398	12.5	189
DELAWARE	10000	14.4	47.7	49.9	5.3	7,839	16,304	8,774	14.7	830
Kent, DE	10001	16.4	43.5	44.0	2.0	1,512	3,306	1,734	14.8	164
New Castle, DE	10003	13.5	46.6	55.2	5.9	4,623	9,290	5,124	14.7	471
Sussex, DE	10005	15.0	55.6	41.1	6.8	1,704	3,708	1,916	14.8	194
DISTRICT OF COLUMBIA	11000	16.8	73.0	92.9	7.4	3,517	11,339	5,925	12.0	453
District of Columbia	11001	16.8	73.0	92.9	7.4	3,517	11,339	5,925	12.0	453
FLORIDA	12000	13.9	56.0	56.9	8.7	153,461	333,183	175,609	15.1	17,368
Alachua, FL	12001	15.7	47.5	52.1	1.5	1,976	4,247	1,958	14.6	380
Baker, FL	12003	11.8	47.5	17.5	0.2	293	602	323	15.5	48
Oay, FL	12005	16.0	53.1	26.2	1.5	1,532	3,397	1,745	14.9	173
Bradford, FL	12007	21.0	63.8	30.5	0.2	214	491	235	13.9	21
Brevard, FL	12009	17.5	41.6	35.5	2.6	4,931	9,038	4,960	14.5	293
Broward, FL	12011	12.2	54.4	73.4	9.5	15,663	28,836	15,573	16.5	1,148
Calhoun, FL	12013	21.8	61.7	23.9	0.3	128	330	161	14.0	16
Charlotte, FL	12015	17.8	59.5	25.4	1.3	1,402	2,969	1,506	11.1	147
Citrus, FL	12017	14.7	54.3	18.2	1.0	1,056	2,387	1,135	13.8	126
Clay, FL	12019	18.7	35.5	29.1	1.4	2,469	4,494	2,457	14.6	276

[2]IEP=Individual Education Program. See notes and definitions for more information.
. . . = Not available.

Table C-1. Population, School, and Student Characteristics by County, Selected Years—*Continued*

County	State/ County Code	Revenues, 2008–2009				Current expenditures, 2008–2009			Resident population 16 to 19 years, 2006–2010			
			Percentage of revenue from									
		Total revenue ($1,000's)	Federal government	State government	Local government	Amount ($1,000's)	Amount per student	Percent for instruction	Total population 16 to 19 years	Percent enrolled in school	Percent high school graduates, not enrolled in school	Percent not enrolled, not grads, not employed, or not in labor force
		19	20	21	22	23	24	25	26	27	28	29
COLORADO— *(Continued)*												
Mineral, CO	08079	1,972	2.1	48.7	49.2	1,814	15,774	63.6	27	63.0	37.0	0.0
Moffat, CO	08081	24,808	5.0	21.7	73.4	20,622	8,643	61.7	730	73.3	8.6	2.3
Montezuma, CO	08083	45,169	13.0	49.2	37.8	37,863	9,041	54.5	1,393	67.1	28.5	3.1
Montrose, CO	08085	58,010	10.2	56.1	33.7	52,805	7,701	59.2	2,127	79.5	15.6	2.4
Morgan, CO	08087	52,964	9.0	51.0	40.0	45,000	8,127	57.1	1,679	81.6	15.6	2.8
Otero, CO	08089	42,388	14.1	60.3	25.5	35,036	10,390	57.1	1,165	88.2	2.8	7.8
Ouray, CO	08091	10,565	9.8	36.1	54.2	9,382	14,845	54.7	163	90.2	0.0	0.0
Park, CO	08093	20,445	4.0	35.7	60.4	17,212	9,064	56.4	714	81.4	18.6	0.0
Phillips, CO	08095	19,058	19.6	37.8	42.6	14,468	16,093	44.3	200	80.5	10.5	3.0
Pitkin, CO	08097	30,331	0.2	5.1	94.6	20,954	12,653	65.1	660	99.7	0.0	0.3
Prowers, CO	08099	32,470	19.1	54.9	26.0	26,917	10,806	56.0	824	81.2	6.1	4.1
Pueblo, CO	08101	247,849	14.1	59.1	26.8	225,832	8,235	53.9	8,979	82.9	7.6	5.3
Rio Blanco, CO	08103	20,293	6.2	21.5	72.3	15,809	12,729	59.9	291	94.2	5.8	0.0
Rio Grande, CO	08105	23,362	8.4	61.5	30.2	18,038	8,210	56.6	1,108	83.0	8.2	2.5
Routt, CO	08107	54,610	8.4	12.5	79.1	44,755	14,626	60.2	1,288	80.4	9.6	3.1
Saguache, CO	08109	12,504	12.2	61.0	26.8	10,417	11,410	55.0	314	82.5	12.7	0.3
San Juan, CO	08111	1,370	3.5	25.8	70.7	1,262	19,719	50.4	32	50.0	50.0	0.0
San Miguel, CO	08113	15,960	1.7	24.4	73.9	12,186	12,065	61.0	218	85.8	10.6	0.0
Sedgwick, CO	08115	7,950	2.2	65.9	31.9	6,896	7,504	70.2	99	90.9	2.0	2.0
Summit, CO	08117	45,892	1.9	7.3	90.9	31,459	10,257	55.6	881	76.1	13.9	0.9
Teller, CO	08119	36,243	8.0	44.3	47.7	29,208	8,740	62.7	999	87.8	9.8	1.8
Washington, CO	08121	13,172	2.3	56.9	40.8	10,916	12,062	57.2	236	90.7	0.0	2.1
Weld, CO	08123	355,922	8.6	50.0	41.4	303,922	8,353	57.2	15,452	82.1	8.3	5.8
Yuma, CO	08125	22,434	5.5	39.6	54.9	16,993	9,541	57.4	439	89.8	0.9	0.0
CONNECTICUT	09000	9,756,387	4.2	37.4	58.4	8,017,058	14,629	61.1	201,273	88.1	7.6	2.9
Fairfield, CT	09001	2,700,872	3.4	25.2	71.4	2,256,377	15,467	61.7	47,729	89.7	6.3	2.4
Hartford, CT	09003	2,469,999	4.6	42.7	52.7	2,049,279	14,557	60.9	48,928	87.2	7.3	3.6
Litchfield, CT	09005	457,215	2.4	33.3	64.3	383,153	14,098	60.5	9,963	89.0	7.5	2.5
Middlesex, CT	09007	418,061	2.5	29.7	67.8	338,968	14,350	61.2	8,222	89.9	7.8	1.7
New Haven, CT	09009	2,292,110	5.4	44.3	50.3	1,867,101	14,464	60.1	51,014	87.9	7.9	3.4
New London, CT	09011	722,033	3.5	41.5	55.0	569,684	13,896	61.4	15,108	82.6	13.0	2.8
Tolland, CT	09013	358,516	2.2	40.2	57.5	310,045	13,648	62.3	12,435	94.5	3.3	1.3
Windham, CT	09015	337,581	6.7	53.0	40.2	242,451	13,650	62.7	7,874	83.7	10.9	4.2
DELAWARE	10000	1,808,005	6.4	61.2	32.4	1,515,083	12,079	60.6	51,436	85.2	8.1	4.8
Kent, DE	10001	365,238	6.6	72.5	21.0	280,889	11,343	60.8	9,726	82.6	12.2	3.6
New Castle, DE	10003	1,029,966	6.2	55.6	38.2	900,691	12,287	60.4	33,237	87.7	6.3	4.5
Sussex, DE	10005	412,801	6.9	65.0	28.1	333,503	12,189	61.2	8,473	78.0	10.2	7.3
DISTRICT OF COLUMBIA	11000	1,255,586	9.7	0.0	90.3	1,079,789	15,826	46.2	37,888	86.6	7.0	5.1
District of Columbia	11001	1,255,586	9.7	0.0	90.3	1,079,789	15,826	46.2	37,888	86.6	7.0	5.1
FLORIDA	12000	26,494,500	10.2	34.1	55.7	22,979,072	8,760	60.4	991,504	81.7	11.2	4.9
Alachua, FL	12001	268,085	11.9	41.5	46.6	235,757	8,559	54.9	21,470	91.0	5.1	3.4
Baker, FL	12003	47,416	8.9	72.0	19.2	39,014	7,703	55.6	1,811	74.5	17.8	5.3
Oay, FL	12005	230,121	10.9	30.2	58.9	211,282	8,139	62.2	9,123	74.8	17.2	4.3
Bradford, FL	12007	32,979	12.6	57.4	30.0	31,154	9,155	58.5	1,275	79.0	9.8	7.1
Brevard, FL	12009	675,705	7.9	40.0	52.1	602,371	8,241	63.0	28,515	84.5	10.3	3.9
Broward, FL	12011	2,513,314	10.1	33.4	56.6	2,365,072	9,226	61.1	90,998	84.3	9.8	4.0
Calhoun, FL	12013	22,713	10.7	72.7	16.6	19,850	8,838	58.1	734	71.9	18.8	6.8
Charlotte, FL	12015	181,061	9.7	18.5	71.9	157,348	9,059	56.5	6,191	81.6	14.3	2.9
Citrus, FL	12017	154,171	9.9	30.1	60.0	138,243	8,624	56.5	5,624	82.3	14.3	3.0
Clay, FL	12019	313,943	6.7	59.9	33.3	299,031	8,318	64.4	11,195	84.3	10.2	3.6

Note. Data in columns 26 through 41 from the American Community Survey are subject to sampling error, which can be especially large in small counties and small population groups. See notes and definitions for more information.

Table C-1. Population, School, and Student Characteristics by County, Selected Years—*Continued*

County	State/ County Code	High school graduates, 2006–2010: Population 25 years and over	High school graduates, 2006–2010: High school diploma or less (percent)	High school graduates, 2006–2010: High school diploma or more (percent)	College enrollment, 2006–2010: Number	College enrollment, 2006–2010: Percent public	College graduates, 2006–2010 (percent): Bachelor's degree or more	College graduates, 2006–2010 (percent): +/- U.S. percent with Bachelor's degree or more	College graduates, 2006–2010 (percent): Non-Hispanic White	College graduates, 2006–2010 (percent): Black or African American	College graduates, 2006–2010 (percent): American Indian and Alaska Native	College graduates, 2006–2010 (percent): Asian, Hawaiian, and Pacific Islander	College graduates, 2006–2010 (percent): Hispanic or Latino[3]
		30	31	32	33	34	35	36	37	38	39	40	41
COLORADO— *(Continued)*													
Mineral, CO	08079	888	33.0	97.4	51	31.4	39.1	11.2	39.4	0.0	0.0	100.0	0.0
Moffat, CO	08081	8,762	49.4	88.4	911	94.4	14.9	-13.0	15.9	0.0	14.0	0.0	11.0
Montezuma, CO	08083	17,374	41.3	88.4	598	83.3	26.5	-1.4	29.4	0.0	5.8	74.0	12.4
Montrose, CO	08085	27,540	48.5	85.4	1,050	77.2	22.3	-5.6	25.1	0.0	0.0	38.9	4.6
Morgan, CO	08087	17,828	56.1	77.7	969	88.8	14.6	-13.3	19.2	0.0	0.0	9.9	4.1
Otero, CO	08089	12,482	51.5	79.8	1,164	93.8	15.4	-12.5	19.3	20.0	3.4	31.9	8.3
Ouray, CO	08091	3,206	28.2	95.2	107	64.5	41.3	13.4	42.6	0.0	0.0	48.2	4.8
Park, CO	08093	12,447	35.0	93.5	495	86.9	32.6	4.7	32.6	0.0	35.7	100.0	7.8
Phillips, CO	08095	2,922	48.2	85.3	140	74.3	16.0	-11.9	17.1	0.0	34.3	76.2	2.6
Pitkin, CO	08097	12,521	15.0	96.1	720	79.4	59.7	31.8	63.0	0.0	72.4	70.6	20.6
Prowers, CO	08099	7,969	48.6	80.5	728	92.9	18.3	-9.6	22.5	0.0	0.0	100.0	5.8
Pueblo, CO	08101	102,736	44.0	85.7	11,008	86.3	20.9	-7.0	26.9	23.5	13.7	39.9	10.1
Rio Blanco, CO	08103	4,285	41.6	91.8	313	90.1	22.7	-5.2	23.6	0.0	13.8	100.0	11.2
Rio Grande, CO	08105	7,579	47.6	83.9	561	88.9	19.2	-8.7	26.1	0.0	7.1	0.0	5.6
Routt, CO	08107	16,063	23.3	96.8	1,026	91.3	45.6	17.7	47.6	0.0	0.0	21.7	17.1
Saguache, CO	08109	4,220	53.3	76.1	124	92.7	19.4	-8.5	26.4	0.0	5.4	37.3	5.8
San Juan, CO	08111	617	26.6	93.4	45	35.6	30.8	2.9	38.8	0.0	0.0	0.0	0.0
San Miguel, CO	08113	5,380	19.7	94.7	127	64.6	48.8	20.9	53.1	0.0	0.0	0.0	6.0
Sedgwick, CO	08115	1,806	52.4	82.6	60	71.7	12.7	-15.2	12.9	0.0	0.0	25.0	8.6
Summit, CO	08117	19,584	24.7	94.6	1,134	89.4	49.9	22.0	53.8	28.1	0.0	57.5	16.7
Teller, CO	08119	16,666	32.6	94.1	834	87.2	31.0	3.1	31.4	79.3	25.6	37.7	8.8
Washington, CO	08121	3,351	47.8	85.4	196	83.2	18.3	-9.6	19.3	0.0	0.0	34.4	1.4
Weld, CO	08123	148,025	42.8	84.7	19,827	89.4	25.4	-2.5	30.1	34.0	20.2	41.3	8.3
Yuma, CO	08125	6,540	52.1	83.6	218	93.6	17.8	-10.1	20.1	0.0	7.6	0.0	5.0
CONNECTICUT	09000	2,398,283	40.2	88.4	255,861	59.3	35.2	7.3	38.7	17.4	16.0	61.5	14.2
Fairfield, CT	09001	607,347	35.5	88.3	56,618	52.6	43.6	15.7	50.9	18.0	26.2	65.8	16.0
Hartford, CT	09003	603,576	41.6	87.1	63,094	62.4	33.3	5.4	37.8	16.1	17.9	61.0	11.1
Litchfield, CT	09005	134,797	39.9	91.2	9,976	66.8	32.3	4.4	32.6	33.4	8.4	42.0	19.3
Middlesex, CT	09007	116,245	36.5	92.0	11,653	46.2	37.0	9.1	37.4	19.9	10.7	63.0	30.0
New Haven, CT	09009	577,711	43.3	87.8	67,018	50.1	31.7	3.8	34.8	18.2	16.5	64.8	13.8
New London, CT	09011	185,164	41.6	89.8	16,629	58.3	30.6	2.7	32.2	13.0	8.3	43.7	16.8
Tolland, CT	09013	95,185	34.8	92.2	22,254	89.3	36.8	8.9	37.0	18.6	16.3	68.5	18.8
Windham, CT	09015	78,258	52.6	84.5	8,619	85.1	21.3	-6.6	22.1	18.3	7.4	43.6	8.4
DELAWARE	10000	587,903	45.1	87.1	66,448	76.5	27.7	-0.2	29.6	18.4	13.8	65.7	12.5
Kent, DE	10001	100,182	49.8	84.9	12,373	78.8	20.0	-7.9	20.7	17.8	4.9	33.1	8.8
New Castle, DE	10003	350,538	41.0	88.4	46,194	76.1	32.4	4.5	35.3	20.3	19.1	73.3	14.3
Sussex, DE	10005	137,183	52.2	85.2	7,881	75.4	21.2	-6.7	23.3	9.2	12.0	43.0	9.4
DISTRICT OF COLUMBIA	11000	399,457	33.5	86.5	69,924	30.0	49.2	21.3	87.1	22.0	54.2	77.6	35.9
District of Columbia	11001	399,457	33.5	86.5	69,924	30.0	49.2	21.3	87.1	22.0	54.2	77.6	35.9
FLORIDA	12000	12,788,471	45.0	85.3	1,220,131	74.7	25.9	-2.0	28.6	16.2	16.1	45.4	21.2
Alachua, FL	12001	141,279	31.2	89.7	59,101	96.4	40.9	13.0	45.9	13.4	18.6	72.4	43.0
Baker, FL	12003	16,937	71.0	78.4	921	90.0	6.2	-21.7	6.8	0.8	100.0	19.4	9.7
Oay, FL	12005	113,422	45.2	86.3	9,349	86.3	20.4	-7.5	21.5	10.8	2.6	30.3	17.6
Bradford, FL	12007	20,068	63.3	76.4	1,283	82.7	8.6	-19.3	9.7	4.5	0.0	11.2	7.3
Brevard, FL	12009	388,573	40.1	90.6	34,423	69.5	26.2	-1.7	27.2	15.1	13.6	43.8	22.6
Broward, FL	12011	1,194,763	41.6	87.1	119,124	66.1	29.6	1.7	33.6	20.1	21.0	47.6	27.5
Calhoun, FL	12013	10,019	67.0	74.1	427	85.9	11.6	-16.3	11.7	5.0	67.7	0.0	3.7
Charlotte, FL	12015	126,849	47.0	88.3	5,360	75.7	21.3	-6.6	21.5	13.4	43.7	41.1	18.6
Citrus, FL	12017	110,041	53.8	85.0	4,200	74.4	16.5	-11.4	16.1	11.5	6.6	67.0	13.4
Clay, FL	12019	120,491	40.3	90.3	11,303	78.2	23.8	-4.1	23.5	24.5	26.4	34.9	22.3

Note. Data in columns 26 through 41 from the American Community Survey are subject to sampling error, which can be especially large in small counties and small population groups. See notes and definitions for more information.

[3]May be of any race.

Table C-1. Population, School, and Student Characteristics by County, Selected Years—*Continued*

County	State/ County Code	County Type[1]	Population, 2010		Percent of related children 5–17 years in poverty, 2010	Percent of children under 19 years with no health insurance, 2010	Number of schools and students, 2010–2011			Resident enrollment, 2006–2010 K–12 enrollment	
			Total	Percent 5–17 years			School districts	Schools	Students	Number	Percent public
			1	2	3	4	5	6	7	8	9
FLORIDA—*(Continued)*											
Collier, FL	12021	2	321,520	14.2	24.7	18.7	1	67	42,919	45,786	90.2
Columbia, FL	12023	6	67,531	16.2	27.9	11.2	1	19	9,810	11,201	90.5
De Soto, FL	12027	6	34,862	15.9	37.8	17.1	1	14	4,938	5,906	93.7
Dixie, FL	12029	6	16,422	13.9	36.4	11.4	1	7	2,022	2,203	91.3
Duval, FL	12031	1	864,263	16.7	22.7	9.9	1	187	123,997	146,805	83.6
Escambia, FL	12033	2	297,619	15.2	27.0	9.8	1	72	40,227	46,207	87.8
Flagler, FL	12035	4	95,696	14.9	20.4	14.1	1	16	12,931	13,639	89.3
Franklin, FL	12037	6	11,549	11.9	32.9	14.8	1	5	1,350	1,243	90.2
Gadsden, FL	12039	2	46,389	17.2	32.4	11.5	1	24	6,299	8,138	86.9
Gilchrist, FL	12041	3	16,939	16.1	24.7	12.9	1	6	2,636	2,999	87.6
Glades, FL	12043	6	12,884	13.2	27.8	22.6	1	10	1,441	2,104	94.8
Gulf, FL	12045	6	15,863	12.1	24.9	12.9	1	7	2,014	2,362	98.5
Hamilton, FL	12047	6	14,799	14.4	36.8	11.7	1	10	1,799	2,121	90.5
Hardee, FL	12049	6	27,731	19.6	39.8	15.7	1	11	5,036	5,225	97.0
Hendry, FL	12051	4	39,140	19.8	41.7	16.6	1	16	6,821	8,045	97.2
Hernando, FL	12053	1	172,778	14.8	22.5	14.1	1	31	22,684	25,796	90.7
Highlands, FL	12055	4	98,786	13.1	31.9	14.4	1	24	12,128	13,202	92.8
Hillsborough, FL	12057	1	1,229,226	17.4	20.7	10.6	1	298	194,525	212,349	89.6
Holmes, FL	12059	6	19,927	15.8	30.8	11.0	1	10	3,374	3,200	97.6
Indian River, FL	12061	3	138,028	14.1	23.9	16.0	1	30	17,740	19,245	88.8
Jackson, FL	12063	6	49,746	14.7	25.0	10.3	1	21	7,161	8,060	86.6
Jefferson, FL	12065	2	14,761	13.4	28.2	13.7	1	9	1,104	2,020	64.8
Lafayette, FL	12067	8	8,870	14.6	26.0	16.6	1	5	1,157	1,763	93.5
Lake, FL	12069	1	297,052	15.3	20.1	11.4	1	58	41,110	44,611	88.2
Lee, FL	12071	2	618,754	14.2	25.9	15.7	1	120	81,967	88,002	90.5
Leon, FL	12073	2	275,487	14.0	21.7	8.8	4	63	36,198	38,794	83.5
Levy, FL	12075	8	40,801	15.5	37.3	12.4	1	17	5,732	6,772	87.5
Liberty, FL	12077	8	8,365	15.7	25.9	12.1	1	10	1,462	1,146	97.6
Madison, FL	12079	6	19,224	15.5	34.6	11.8	1	11	2,720	2,776	96.8
Manatee, FL	12081	2	322,833	14.9	22.5	13.0	1	81	44,249	47,998	88.5
Marion, FL	12083	2	331,298	14.2	28.5	13.9	1	63	41,955	47,042	88.0
Martin, FL	12085	2	146,318	13.4	15.3	15.2	1	38	18,170	20,060	85.8
Miami-Dade, FL	12086	1	2,496,435	15.9	24.5	17.2	1	515	347,366	400,792	86.8
Monroe, FL	12087	4	73,090	10.7	19.1	18.2	1	22	8,356	8,376	90.4
Nassau, FL	12089	1	73,314	16.3	16.2	11.3	1	21	11,100	11,782	88.6
Okaloosa, FL	12091	3	180,822	15.9	18.3	10.5	1	54	28,695	29,172	93.1
Okeechobee, FL	12093	4	39,996	17.3	32.2	14.1	1	15	6,789	6,838	96.6
Orange, FL	12095	1	1,145,956	17.1	21.4	12.7	2	244	176,008	194,193	86.8
Osceola, FL	12097	1	268,685	19.6	21.6	13.8	1	66	53,357	51,406	92.3
Palm Beach, FL	12099	1	1,320,134	15.0	21.0	15.8	2	249	176,808	199,345	86.3
Pasco, FL	12101	1	464,697	15.7	19.0	12.0	1	108	66,994	70,929	90.9
Pinellas, FL	12103	1	916,542	13.2	18.2	11.0	1	163	104,001	125,022	87.2
Polk, FL	12105	2	602,095	17.1	25.7	13.2	1	159	95,178	100,363	91.9
Putnam, FL	12107	4	74,364	16.3	37.9	12.3	1	23	11,244	12,174	92.3
St. Johns, FL	12109	1	190,039	17.8	12.4	10.4	2	53	31,270	31,708	88.1
St. Lucie, FL	12111	2	277,789	16.4	26.4	15.0	1	51	39,259	45,134	91.8
Santa Rosa, FL	12113	2	151,372	17.8	15.1	10.9	1	38	25,533	27,182	91.3
Sarasota, FL	12115	2	379,448	11.9	18.9	15.2	1	58	40,899	45,930	88.6
Seminole, FL	12117	1	422,718	17.5	12.9	11.4	1	73	64,229	75,929	87.9
Sumter, FL	12119	4	93,420	6.7	32.2	12.6	1	12	7,626	6,599	92.0
Suwannee, FL	12121	6	41,551	16.5	27.7	13.4	1	12	6,172	7,020	91.6
Taylor, FL	12123	6	22,570	14.0	30.3	9.4	1	9	3,153	3,532	84.7
Union, FL	12125	6	15,535	14.1	23.3	11.6	1	8	2,281	2,658	95.0
Volusia, FL	12127	2	494,593	13.9	24.0	12.5	1	92	61,559	69,907	91.1
Wakulla, FL	12129	2	30,776	16.8	18.1	10.2	1	14	5,151	5,126	91.8
Walton, FL	12131	6	55,043	14.5	26.2	14.7	1	22	7,343	8,040	94.3
Washington, FL	12133	6	24,896	15.4	29.6	10.8	2	11	3,710	3,874	91.5

[1]County type codes are from the Economic Research Service of the United States Department of Agriculture. See notes and definitions for more information.

Table C-1. Population, School, and Student Characteristics by County, Selected Years—*Continued*

County	State/ County Code	Characteristics of students, 2010–2011				Number of graduates, 2008–2009	Staff and students, 2010–2011			
		Percent with IEP[2]	Percent eligible for free or reduced lunch	Percent minority	Percent English-language learners		Total staff	Number of teachers	Student/ teacher ratio	Central admin. staff
		10	11	12	13	14	15	16	17	18
FLORIDA—*(Continued)*										
Collier, FL	12021	13.8	58.6	60.0	12.6	2,477	5,336	2,777	15.5	334
Columbia, FL	12023	16.7	62.4	31.5	0.8	575	1,468	707	13.9	83
De Soto, FL	12027	16.4	73.7	55.3	11.2	241	888	456	10.8	64
Dixie, FL	12029	23.6	72.7	14.9	. . .	123	336	131	15.4	49
Duval, FL	12031	13.8	53.2	60.3	3.1	5,958	12,724	7,993	15.5	1,167
Escambia, FL	12033	16.7	59.0	50.0	1.0	2,116	6,434	3,502	11.5	318
Flagler, FL	12035	11.8	58.0	35.5	2.1	754	1,693	820	15.8	121
Franklin, FL	12037	16.9	74.9	17.5	1.3	70	186	91	14.9	16
Gadsden, FL	12039	12.1	81.7	96.4	7.7	270	986	453	13.9	49
Gilchrist, FL	12041	23.7	57.7	10.5	1.9	169	351	163	16.2	37
Glades, FL	12043	15.8	55.5	58.2	5.1	67	266	126	11.4	15
Gulf, FL	12045	17.2	51.2	20.0	. . .	149	308	147	13.7	26
Hamilton, FL	12047	14.5	76.6	56.5	5.9	92	281	114	15.8	31
Hardee, FL	12049	14.3	76.6	65.7	6.9	229	684	342	14.7	73
Hendry, FL	12051	15.7	77.7	74.8	9.6	410	908	469	14.5	57
Hernando, FL	12053	14.1	55.0	27.5	2.8	1,338	2,881	1,556	14.6	90
Highlands, FL	12055	13.2	68.2	51.6	4.5	676	1,553	727	16.7	130
Hillsborough, FL	12057	15.1	55.9	61.0	12.0	10,415	24,717	13,470	14.4	1,213
Holmes, FL	12059	14.6	63.1	9.0	0.3	207	438	221	15.3	20
Indian River, FL	12061	13.3	53.7	40.2	6.4	1,108	2,003	1,068	16.6	66
Jackson, FL	12063	15.1	57.7	38.9	0.9	402	1,099	537	13.3	56
Jefferson, FL	12065	18.7	75.5	75.2	1.6	46	160	78	14.2	14
Lafayette, FL	12067	12.8	59.0	28.0	6.7	52	180	92	12.5	15
Lake, FL	12069	12.5	54.4	41.3	3.9	2,354	5,501	2,656	15.5	382
Lee, FL	12071	14.2	62.3	51.2	6.6	4,258	9,969	4,968	16.5	417
Leon, FL	12073	15.8	42.7	53.1	1.5	2,019	4,755	2,300	15.7	199
Levy, FL	12075	22.6	69.2	27.5	2.9	292	838	371	15.5	65
Liberty, FL	12077	19.4	55.3	24.8	2.1	75	199	109	13.4	7
Madison, FL	12079	22.2	77.7	61.6	0.2	169	416	181	15.0	38
Manatee, FL	12081	17.7	53.7	47.2	8.9	2,438	6,271	3,072	14.4	362
Marion, FL	12083	16.3	62.3	43.8	4.8	2,421	6,216	2,876	14.6	313
Martin, FL	12085	15.8	39.2	35.6	11.9	1,242	2,385	1,210	15.0	144
Miami-Dade, FL	12086	10.9	70.2	91.4	17.8	19,207	38,477	21,195	16.4	1,352
Monroe, FL	12087	16.0	44.0	45.5	6.7	513	1,256	610	13.7	76
Nassau, FL	12089	14.1	44.1	16.7	0.7	736	1,418	693	16.0	65
Okaloosa, FL	12091	14.1	39.3	28.9	2.0	2,089	3,069	1,914	15.0	98
Okeechobee, FL	12093	20.1	68.5	45.6	10.2	320	951	432	15.7	41
Orange, FL	12095	12.7	57.0	68.0	16.1	9,946	23,087	12,221	14.4	1,823
Osceola, FL	12097	12.2	63.4	71.6	17.3	3,202	6,561	3,196	16.7	330
Palm Beach, FL	12099	14.9	50.9	63.5	10.5	10,672	20,841	11,424	15.5	1,224
Pasco, FL	12101	16.1	51.5	31.7	3.7	3,611	10,357	5,016	13.4	468
Pinellas, FL	12103	13.4	49.6	40.1	4.1	6,711	14,657	7,251	14.3	781
Polk, FL	12105	11.4	65.5	53.0	9.5	4,884	13,649	6,778	14.0	646
Putnam, FL	12107	17.6	77.2	43.6	5.4	607	1,612	721	15.6	106
St. Johns, FL	12109	15.0	23.1	19.5	0.9	1,923	4,510	2,235	14.0	243
St. Lucie, FL	12111	12.3	60.0	59.2	7.2	2,052	5,042	2,588	15.2	237
Santa Rosa, FL	12113	13.4	41.3	19.7	0.6	1,664	2,438	1,570	16.3	41
Sarasota, FL	12115	14.7	49.2	32.5	5.6	2,607	5,368	2,786	14.7	157
Seminole, FL	12117	13.2	41.0	43.5	3.6	4,373	8,011	4,751	13.5	336
Sumter, FL	12119	13.7	59.2	30.6	4.1	429	1,018	501	15.2	54
Suwannee, FL	12121	11.5	66.7	31.7	3.3	275	772	364	17.0	52
Taylor, FL	12123	14.5	67.6	30.6	0.1	164	458	197	16.0	32
Union, FL	12125	16.5	58.9	22.5	0.2	110	329	167	13.6	33
Volusia, FL	12127	16.1	56.4	38.4	4.8	3,633	7,640	4,044	15.2	404
Wakulla, FL	12129	19.5	47.6	17.4	0.2	243	702	324	15.9	42
Walton, FL	12131	10.2	51.4	20.1	2.9	369	1,080	518	14.2	55
Washington, FL	12133	17.8	63.9	23.7	1.1	245	664	283	13.1	75

[2]IEP=Individual Education Program. See notes and definitions for more information.
. . . = Not available.

Table C-1. Population, School, and Student Characteristics by County, Selected Years—*Continued*

County	State/ County Code	Revenues, 2008–2009				Current expenditures, 2008–2009			Resident population 16 to 19 years, 2006–2010			
		Total revenue ($1,000's)	Percentage of revenue from			Amount ($1,000's)	Amount per student	Percent for instruction	Total population 16 to 19 years	Percent enrolled in school	Percent high school graduates, not enrolled in school	Percent not enrolled, not grads, not employed, or not in labor force
			Federal government	State government	Local government							
		19	20	21	22	23	24	25	26	27	28	29
FLORIDA—*(Continued)*												
Collier, FL	12021	548,305	8.7	15.9	75.4	426,164	10,019	59.8	13,277	79.9	10.3	4.1
Columbia, FL	12023	94,089	14.2	59.4	26.4	85,652	8,575	59.0	3,949	73.3	13.1	9.3
De Soto, FL	12027	47,798	14.6	54.1	31.3	44,697	9,026	58.3	2,042	75.5	6.6	14.4
Dixie, FL	12029	19,949	15.4	57.2	27.3	18,415	8,690	53.1	884	78.9	14.1	7.0
Duval, FL	12031	1,148,276	10.0	43.9	46.1	1,053,519	8,593	59.9	47,999	78.5	13.9	5.6
Escambia, FL	12033	388,194	12.8	46.1	41.1	345,023	8,431	58.4	21,031	68.2	24.7	5.2
Flagler, FL	12035	137,781	6.5	22.0	71.5	101,394	7,866	60.5	4,053	81.2	15.6	1.6
Franklin, FL	12037	19,610	11.1	20.1	68.8	14,156	11,051	61.4	433	68.6	3.9	25.6
Gadsden, FL	12039	62,852	18.6	60.7	20.7	56,054	8,735	50.4	2,595	70.2	18.5	7.0
Gilchrist, FL	12041	26,299	10.3	62.6	27.1	24,725	8,991	55.5	1,011	64.2	19.9	9.8
Glades, FL	12043	14,246	11.6	46.0	42.4	13,213	9,520	57.1	757	71.3	11.1	12.8
Gulf, FL	12045	22,979	11.9	25.4	62.7	18,908	9,228	54.3	749	70.5	16.3	11.4
Hamilton, FL	12047	19,698	19.8	48.3	32.0	18,643	9,570	53.9	803	62.4	15.6	19.1
Hardee, FL	12049	49,855	14.8	55.8	29.5	44,153	8,644	55.5	1,802	67.9	9.0	9.9
Hendry, FL	12051	68,181	14.9	53.3	31.7	63,519	9,025	58.5	2,675	68.5	11.2	8.0
Hernando, FL	12053	214,656	8.5	43.1	48.4	179,194	7,884	58.6	7,339	79.6	13.5	4.0
Highlands, FL	12055	125,754	13.6	41.4	45.0	111,822	9,129	55.4	4,275	76.3	10.6	8.9
Hillsborough, FL	12057	1,905,911	14.1	44.8	41.1	1,645,308	8,569	61.7	68,934	80.1	11.9	5.4
Holmes, FL	12059	29,257	14.8	70.5	14.7	28,983	8,598	56.9	1,065	76.6	4.4	12.8
Indian River, FL	12061	183,855	7.3	22.0	70.8	150,622	8,555	59.4	6,281	82.2	10.5	4.4
Jackson, FL	12063	68,728	14.4	63.8	21.9	65,720	8,979	55.9	3,000	90.9	6.3	2.7
Jefferson, FL	12065	12,477	17.6	44.5	37.9	12,326	11,145	51.4	1,101	72.1	25.4	0.0
Lafayette, FL	12067	11,183	22.3	59.1	18.6	10,677	9,542	51.3	616	86.4	13.6	0.0
Lake, FL	12069	385,578	8.6	39.4	52.0	326,104	7,962	60.1	13,274	79.9	11.8	5.5
Lee, FL	12071	858,184	8.3	18.7	73.0	717,883	9,038	59.9	28,033	79.8	12.2	3.9
Leon, FL	12073	329,367	10.0	40.4	49.6	280,435	8,623	56.7	23,925	92.3	5.5	2.0
Levy, FL	12075	62,597	12.9	53.1	34.0	53,152	8,823	56.5	2,046	83.5	8.8	6.4
Liberty, FL	12077	29,203	9.7	80.6	9.7	14,254	9,605	58.1	411	65.9	30.7	3.4
Madison, FL	12079	25,765	17.3	57.5	25.2	25,365	9,370	50.4	1,185	59.9	15.0	8.3
Manatee, FL	12081	447,127	9.7	27.0	63.4	378,224	8,883	58.6	14,172	78.7	13.3	5.0
Marion, FL	12083	414,723	10.9	39.5	49.6	350,168	8,215	56.4	15,538	77.3	15.0	5.9
Martin, FL	12085	193,805	7.3	19.6	73.1	158,278	8,761	59.1	6,552	84.4	7.3	4.1
Miami-Dade, FL	12086	3,531,152	12.9	27.8	59.3	3,144,292	9,100	61.9	135,729	84.1	9.3	5.1
Monroe, FL	12087	121,505	8.3	14.1	77.5	98,703	11,924	59.3	2,302	79.7	11.0	5.6
Nassau, FL	12089	105,719	6.7	28.6	64.6	87,152	7,936	57.7	3,606	77.4	16.6	5.4
Okaloosa, FL	12091	266,215	9.7	35.7	54.6	236,577	8,123	63.4	9,824	77.1	19.0	2.4
Okeechobee, FL	12093	66,514	14.0	55.6	30.3	58,213	8,311	58.4	2,510	65.0	19.2	10.1
Orange, FL	12095	1,810,528	9.0	32.3	58.8	1,412,137	8,198	58.2	70,827	81.8	10.7	5.5
Osceola, FL	12097	500,150	9.7	41.9	48.5	429,657	8,272	57.6	16,537	79.9	13.2	4.6
Palm Beach, FL	12099	1,944,936	8.2	17.0	74.8	1,587,281	9,296	63.0	63,732	82.3	9.0	5.2
Pasco, FL	12101	647,083	8.8	49.0	42.2	566,068	8,476	59.2	21,395	80.6	10.9	6.5
Pinellas, FL	12103	1,068,296	9.5	29.2	61.4	944,508	8,905	60.7	41,014	82.7	11.1	3.8
Polk, FL	12105	915,097	10.7	48.4	40.9	815,185	8,612	64.1	32,427	75.7	13.2	7.3
Putnam, FL	12107	105,676	15.5	50.5	34.1	102,210	8,893	56.5	4,250	70.5	18.9	7.7
St. Johns, FL	12109	295,060	4.4	24.0	71.6	237,306	8,178	58.5	9,622	84.1	10.3	2.8
St. Lucie, FL	12111	394,904	9.4	38.2	52.4	337,376	8,687	55.3	13,881	82.1	10.1	4.7
Santa Rosa, FL	12113	219,995	8.7	51.1	40.2	203,127	7,998	60.6	8,629	86.3	7.7	4.6
Sarasota, FL	12115	530,237	6.0	14.8	79.3	439,503	10,701	61.2	14,448	81.6	12.7	3.3
Seminole, FL	12117	580,536	7.1	42.7	50.2	510,274	7,859	62.5	23,791	87.1	7.8	3.2
Sumter, FL	12119	74,456	10.9	25.5	63.6	67,679	8,847	64.6	1,998	58.5	29.6	5.5
Suwannee, FL	12121	55,299	14.1	55.7	30.3	46,576	7,802	57.2	1,910	72.1	16.3	9.1
Taylor, FL	12123	31,896	19.0	43.8	37.2	27,344	8,291	54.5	1,352	68.6	19.6	10.8
Union, FL	12125	21,414	12.6	71.4	16.1	20,358	8,794	58.0	1,191	68.5	17.0	11.9
Volusia, FL	12127	627,597	8.5	33.9	57.7	518,461	8,227	59.7	26,437	87.8	7.1	3.5
Wakulla, FL	12129	46,183	8.8	60.4	30.8	41,531	7,890	56.2	1,560	79.7	15.0	5.3
Walton, FL	12131	89,558	7.3	16.1	76.5	73,604	10,528	57.9	2,384	76.7	15.3	3.1
Washington, FL	12133	38,704	15.9	57.3	26.8	38,078	10,790	57.6	1,405	64.7	11.7	15.7

Note. Data in columns 26 through 41 from the American Community Survey are subject to sampling error, which can be especially large in small counties and small population groups. See notes and definitions for more information.

Table C-1. Population, School, and Student Characteristics by County, Selected Years—*Continued*

County	State/ County Code	High school graduates, 2006–2010			College enrollment, 2006–2010		College graduates, 2006–2010 (percent)						
		Population 25 years and over	High school diploma or less (percent)	High school diploma or more (percent)	Number	Percent public	Bachelor's degree or more	+/- U.S. percent with Bachelor's degree or more	Non-Hispanic White	Black or African American	American Indian and Alaska Native	Asian, Hawaiian, and Pacific Islander	Hispanic or Latino[3]
		30	31	32	33	34	35	36	37	38	39	40	41
FLORIDA— *(Continued)*													
Collier, FL	12021	232,040	43.1	84.8	12,505	71.9	30.8	2.9	37.2	13.2	17.4	41.1	10.4
Columbia, FL	12023	44,750	54.7	82.0	3,431	84.9	14.9	-13.0	15.5	10.4	11.8	62.4	14.6
De Soto, FL	12027	22,888	67.4	67.5	821	81.6	11.6	-16.3	15.0	8.9	0.0	22.8	1.2
Dixie, FL	12029	11,350	69.6	72.6	589	60.1	6.2	-21.7	6.0	7.5	0.0	100.0	4.4
Duval, FL	12031	558,743	43.1	87.2	64,283	74.9	24.9	-3.0	28.0	15.6	14.7	43.0	20.2
Escambia, FL	12033	194,162	42.9	86.7	22,997	66.5	23.4	-4.5	26.4	12.6	14.1	26.5	23.2
Flagler, FL	12035	67,418	42.9	90.2	3,990	84.0	22.0	-5.9	22.0	21.7	5.2	37.9	17.3
Franklin, FL	12037	8,692	56.4	78.3	211	94.3	18.8	-9.1	21.5	4.6	0.0	60.2	0.0
Gadsden, FL	12039	30,786	62.7	75.7	1,826	80.8	12.3	-15.6	19.7	6.7	7.5	67.1	6.9
Gilchrist, FL	12041	10,956	63.3	81.1	453	83.2	8.6	-19.3	9.0	5.0	0.0	44.8	0.0
Glades, FL	12043	9,108	61.4	71.3	220	81.4	11.3	-16.6	12.0	13.9	12.0	6.6	6.4
Gulf, FL	12045	11,785	61.7	77.7	424	91.5	13.6	-14.3	15.4	8.2	0.0	100.0	7.8
Hamilton, FL	12047	9,849	69.8	74.0	363	86.5	7.8	-20.1	10.0	3.3	0.0	51.7	9.3
Hardee, FL	12049	17,141	72.4	59.9	703	74.8	7.5	-20.4	10.4	3.3	0.0	4.1	3.6
Hendry, FL	12051	23,408	74.3	62.0	1,106	79.5	8.2	-19.7	13.3	4.7	12.4	22.8	3.9
Hernando, FL	12053	125,261	52.2	85.6	7,458	79.6	16.2	-11.7	16.1	21.8	24.6	34.3	13.8
Highlands, FL	12055	73,708	57.8	78.8	2,972	79.2	14.6	-13.3	15.1	4.8	16.5	51.9	11.7
Hillsborough, FL	12057	784,080	42.3	85.8	89,946	78.0	28.8	0.9	33.2	19.2	11.3	54.4	18.2
Holmes, FL	12059	13,897	68.1	74.1	551	84.2	11.1	-16.8	11.8	5.1	9.1	5.2	5.0
Indian River, FL	12061	100,521	42.1	86.3	5,307	80.3	26.7	-1.2	29.2	11.9	16.3	31.6	11.4
Jackson, FL	12063	34,735	57.2	77.4	2,457	67.2	12.8	-15.1	15.1	6.3	6.2	37.3	11.1
Jefferson, FL	12065	10,233	58.3	79.9	471	42.9	14.7	-13.2	18.8	5.7	0.0	0.0	40.8
Lafayette, FL	12067	5,224	63.4	81.3	343	73.2	9.0	-18.9	10.2	0.0	0.0	31.6	0.7
Lake, FL	12069	211,684	47.5	86.9	10,842	72.0	20.3	-7.6	20.8	14.2	15.0	38.0	18.0
Lee, FL	12071	439,458	45.5	86.7	27,668	78.4	24.6	-3.3	27.3	12.3	14.6	40.6	13.3
Leon, FL	12073	154,149	30.7	90.6	59,792	94.2	41.3	13.4	46.2	26.6	24.4	64.2	38.6
Levy, FL	12075	28,598	58.5	80.3	1,727	82.6	12.2	-15.7	12.6	5.2	24.6	35.4	14.0
Liberty, FL	12077	5,336	70.0	74.9	389	93.1	15.1	-12.8	17.7	4.5	0.0	0.0	0.0
Madison, FL	12079	13,265	66.5	74.8	612	86.1	10.6	-17.3	12.7	6.3	0.0	52.9	9.0
Manatee, FL	12081	229,953	45.3	86.9	12,173	76.0	25.6	-2.3	28.2	11.7	23.3	32.3	12.9
Marion, FL	12083	238,962	53.2	84.5	12,467	75.7	17.1	-10.8	17.4	12.7	19.4	45.2	13.5
Martin, FL	12085	108,901	39.7	88.6	6,482	85.4	29.4	1.5	31.7	10.4	1.6	36.9	12.3
Miami-Dade, FL	12086	1,655,557	50.4	77.0	188,242	68.8	26.3	-1.6	45.2	14.7	14.0	48.0	23.6
Monroe, FL	12087	56,634	38.9	89.8	2,894	75.5	28.7	0.8	32.6	7.4	13.1	32.0	17.4
Nassau, FL	12089	49,814	48.7	86.5	3,262	79.3	21.9	-6.0	22.2	14.8	41.6	60.4	16.2
Okaloosa, FL	12091	121,598	37.3	90.7	11,737	88.6	26.8	-1.1	28.4	14.3	17.8	28.1	20.2
Okeechobee, FL	12093	26,426	63.8	71.6	1,458	86.3	11.4	-16.5	12.5	2.5	9.7	59.1	7.8
Orange, FL	12095	707,984	40.5	86.9	100,238	74.4	30.3	2.4	37.4	19.1	19.6	44.1	20.7
Osceola, FL	12097	164,646	50.8	84.4	12,991	68.1	18.3	-9.6	21.8	15.9	16.4	30.8	13.7
Palm Beach, FL	12099	929,594	39.9	86.8	70,795	72.0	31.8	3.9	36.8	16.6	15.4	49.2	19.9
Pasco, FL	12101	327,686	49.0	86.1	20,558	71.8	20.0	-7.9	19.4	27.0	19.8	41.4	17.0
Pinellas, FL	12103	684,879	42.5	88.1	50,373	77.3	27.1	-0.8	28.6	14.4	18.4	34.1	20.2
Polk, FL	12105	397,514	54.8	81.9	27,175	64.0	18.0	-9.9	19.5	12.4	13.5	42.6	11.5
Putnam, FL	12107	51,125	63.3	78.0	1,961	88.8	12.2	-15.7	13.5	7.7	4.1	37.7	3.7
St. Johns, FL	12109	124,601	30.3	92.8	10,724	64.7	38.7	10.8	39.7	16.6	38.7	64.0	31.3
St. Lucie, FL	12111	188,029	51.6	83.4	13,045	80.6	17.8	-10.1	18.9	14.6	1.5	43.9	12.9
Santa Rosa, FL	12113	99,450	40.4	88.4	9,062	81.0	24.8	-3.1	25.1	15.5	13.9	33.8	26.8
Sarasota, FL	12115	293,562	40.6	90.6	14,736	73.6	29.1	1.2	30.1	13.7	29.8	46.8	17.9
Seminole, FL	12117	277,479	34.3	90.7	34,608	80.2	33.6	5.7	35.3	22.5	26.6	55.5	26.1
Sumter, FL	12119	73,840	53.0	84.5	1,345	71.3	19.0	-8.9	21.0	5.4	0.0	39.1	11.0
Suwannee, FL	12121	27,747	62.5	79.9	1,182	83.8	10.2	-17.7	10.3	8.1	0.0	64.6	8.5
Taylor, FL	12123	15,242	60.2	78.7	980	78.8	12.0	-15.9	13.2	5.5	17.7	61.2	17.0
Union, FL	12125	10,100	66.7	77.1	533	84.6	9.3	-18.6	11.6	1.9	15.5	11.3	4.0
Volusia, FL	12127	355,769	46.1	87.3	36,734	54.9	21.0	-6.9	21.8	15.1	20.8	44.4	15.0
Wakulla, FL	12129	20,366	52.7	84.5	1,386	72.0	17.3	-10.6	17.2	15.8	0.0	43.2	16.8
Walton, FL	12131	38,412	44.9	84.3	1,906	76.7	25.0	-2.9	26.9	7.8	18.7	40.9	5.5
Washington, FL	12133	16,934	60.6	78.7	1,136	90.0	12.8	-15.1	13.8	3.1	29.4	49.2	11.2

Note. Data in columns 26 through 41 from the American Community Survey are subject to sampling error, which can be especially large in small counties and small population groups. See notes and definitions for more information.

[3]May be of any race.

Table C-1. Population, School, and Student Characteristics by County, Selected Years—*Continued*

County	State/ County Code	County Type[1]	Population, 2010		Percent of related children 5–17 years in poverty, 2010	Percent of children under 19 years with no health insurance, 2010	Number of schools and students, 2010–2011			Resident enrollment, 2006–2010 K–12 enrollment	
			Total	Percent 5–17 years			School districts	Schools	Students	Number	Percent public
			1	2	3	4	5	6	7	8	9
GEORGIA	13000	X	9,687,653	18.6	23.0	10.3	212	2,449	1,677,067	1,780,538	90.3
Appling, GA	13001	7	18,236	18.6	33.3	12.3	1	7	3,580	3,502	96.1
Atkinson, GA	13003	9	8,375	20.6	47.9	14.9	1	4	1,734	1,838	100.0
Bacon, GA	13005	7	11,096	18.0	32.8	11.5	1	4	1,978	2,085	89.0
Baker, GA	13007	3	3,451	16.8	38.0	10.6	1	1	352	730	100.0
Baldwin, GA	13009	4	45,720	14.4	31.9	8.5	1	7	5,484	6,706	81.1
Banks, GA	13011	8	18,395	19.1	22.7	12.3	1	4	2,910	3,353	89.7
Barrow, GA	13013	1	69,367	19.8	17.6	10.4	1	15	12,703	12,983	93.7
Bartow, GA	13015	1	100,157	19.8	20.9	9.6	2	24	18,489	19,334	92.5
Ben Hill, GA	13017	7	17,634	18.5	39.8	9.8	1	5	3,330	3,369	95.6
Berrien, GA	13019	6	19,286	18.7	33.0	9.8	1	5	3,231	3,540	95.0
Bibb, GA	13021	3	155,547	18.4	36.7	8.2	1	43	24,961	29,850	83.4
Bleckley, GA	13023	6	13,063	16.8	25.0	8.2	1	5	2,486	2,603	94.9
Brantley, GA	13025	3	18,411	19.4	28.9	10.8	1	7	3,560	3,649	97.4
Brooks, GA	13027	3	16,243	17.0	37.4	11.2	1	4	2,312	2,712	96.0
Bryan, GA	13029	2	30,233	22.0	15.2	9.9	1	12	7,564	6,400	94.7
Bulloch, GA	13031	4	70,217	14.5	29.0	10.3	3	19	9,655	9,694	92.8
Burke, GA	13033	2	23,316	20.6	47.7	8.3	1	6	4,672	5,198	85.7
Butts, GA	13035	1	23,655	16.5	22.2	9.4	1	5	3,607	3,989	87.0
Calhoun, GA	13037	8	6,694	14.2	39.1	11.3	2	3	875	1,001	83.9
Camden, GA	13039	4	50,513	19.1	21.4	7.4	1	12	9,437	9,820	95.8
Candler, GA	13043	7	10,998	18.5	37.2	12.1	1	4	2,058	1,954	90.4
Carroll, GA	13045	1	110,527	18.4	22.8	9.5	2	30	19,206	20,494	92.5
Catoosa, GA	13047	2	63,942	18.5	18.5	7.6	1	17	10,959	11,834	88.5
Charlton, GA	13049	6	12,171	15.7	30.2	8.6	1	5	1,723	2,243	94.4
Chatham, GA	13051	2	265,128	15.6	24.6	9.4	1	58	35,246	41,628	82.4
Chattahoochee, GA	13053	2	11,267	17.6	20.9	5.8	1	3	945	2,239	89.8
Chattooga, GA	13055	6	26,015	16.5	26.7	9.0	2	11	4,158	4,339	97.8
Cherokee, GA	13057	1	214,346	20.1	11.0	8.1	1	40	38,760	40,740	88.7
Clarke, GA	13059	3	116,714	11.5	34.3	9.7	2	22	12,371	13,408	89.6
Clay, GA	13061	9	3,183	16.1	56.0	9.9	1	2	318	533	97.0
Clayton, GA	13063	1	259,424	20.4	31.3	11.5	2	67	50,543	54,638	94.1
Clinch, GA	13065	6	6,798	19.4	32.7	8.9	1	5	1,386	1,239	98.5
Cobb, GA	13067	1	688,078	18.6	18.0	10.3	3	132	115,371	125,072	88.8
Coffee, GA	13069	7	42,356	18.9	35.4	10.7	1	12	7,808	7,843	96.5
Colquitt, GA	13071	6	45,498	19.3	33.7	11.6	1	13	9,259	8,429	95.8
Columbia, GA	13073	2	124,053	20.6	9.3	8.9	1	31	23,722	24,315	91.0
Cook, GA	13075	6	17,212	19.6	34.7	11.2	2	4	3,376	3,292	99.7
Coweta, GA	13077	1	127,317	20.1	15.2	8.6	4	32	29,219	24,610	89.3
Crawford, GA	13079	3	12,630	16.9	26.3	12.5	1	4	1,878	2,080	90.2
Crisp, GA	13081	6	23,439	18.9	46.0	7.8	1	7	4,325	4,480	94.4
Dade, GA	13083	2	16,633	16.1	20.6	9.8	1	4	2,486	2,720	85.6
Dawson, GA	13085	1	22,330	17.1	20.2	10.7	1	8	3,486	3,652	92.1
Decatur, GA	13087	6	27,842	18.7	35.1	9.2	1	9	5,604	5,562	94.4
De Kalb, GA	13089	1	691,893	16.6	24.0	12.3	5	178	102,211	117,731	88.6
Dodge, GA	13091	7	21,796	17.1	31.5	9.4	2	6	3,401	3,406	96.5
Dooly, GA	13093	6	14,918	15.4	32.4	10.3	1	3	1,441	2,311	87.8
Dougherty, GA	13095	3	94,565	18.2	43.8	7.3	1	29	15,906	17,478	91.6
Douglas, GA	13097	1	132,403	21.0	16.9	10.2	1	35	24,601	27,099	91.5
Early, GA	13099	6	11,008	19.8	36.6	7.7	1	4	2,328	2,289	96.7
Echols, GA	13101	3	4,034	20.5	40.9	20.5	1	2	790	983	95.3
Effingham, GA	13103	2	52,250	21.5	13.7	7.7	1	14	11,553	11,106	91.5
Elbert, GA	13105	6	20,166	16.8	34.6	10.2	1	8	3,397	3,800	89.5
Emanuel, GA	13107	7	22,598	18.1	40.9	10.3	1	8	4,490	3,911	91.8
Evans, GA	13109	6	11,000	18.1	37.3	11.1	1	4	1,821	2,162	84.6
Fannin, GA	13111	8	23,682	14.4	27.3	13.7	1	5	3,049	3,189	93.5
Fayette, GA	13113	1	106,567	21.8	8.6	7.4	1	29	21,274	23,630	88.7
Floyd, GA	13115	3	96,317	17.6	25.3	9.9	3	32	16,143	16,982	91.0
Forsyth, GA	13117	1	175,511	22.7	7.7	7.9	1	35	35,920	34,704	90.3
Franklin, GA	13119	8	22,084	16.6	25.0	9.9	1	6	3,679	3,553	95.6
Fulton, GA	13121	1	920,581	17.1	22.2	11.4	8	224	142,702	150,231	85.1

[1]County type codes are from the Economic Research Service of the United States Department of Agriculture. See notes and definitions for more information.

Table C-1. Population, School, and Student Characteristics by County, Selected Years—*Continued*

County	State/ County Code	Characteristics of students, 2010–2011				Number of graduates, 2008–2009	Staff and students, 2010–2011			
		Percent with IEP[2]	Percent eligible for free or reduced lunch	Percent minority	Percent English-language learners		Total staff	Number of teachers	Student/ teacher ratio	Central admin. staff
		10	11	12	13	14	15	16	17	18
GEORGIA	13000	10.6	57.4	55.6	4.9	88,003	227,188	112,460	14.9	4,853
Appling, GA	13001	13.5	66.9	37.9	3.0	204	492	237	15.1	10
Atkinson, GA	13003	11.1	75.4	53.6	7.3	58	227	111	15.7	6
Bacon, GA	13005	13.4	60.3	31.2	3.3	72	263	122	16.2	10
Baker, GA	13007	15.3	83.2	86.4	3.7	19	55	26	13.8	2
Baldwin, GA	13009	11.3	73.0	70.1	0.9	274	768	415	13.2	15
Banks, GA	13011	16.2	66.8	19.9	2.7	161	402	190	15.3	12
Barrow, GA	13013	11.4	60.7	36.1	6.2	570	1,611	870	14.6	22
Bartow, GA	13015	10.8	58.0	26.0	4.9	991	2,408	1,231	15.0	37
Ben Hill, GA	13017	11.4	78.7	54.5	4.1	171	451	220	15.1	12
Berrien, GA	13019	10.9	69.7	22.4	2.0	159	436	209	15.5	16
Bibb, GA	13021	10.4	77.1	79.0	1.4	979	3,657	1,666	15.0	96
Bleckley, GA	13023	14.0	58.3	31.6	0.7	163	380	170	14.6	12
Brantley, GA	13025	9.7	62.5	5.3	0.4	171	505	240	14.9	10
Brooks, GA	13027	8.9	81.2	63.1	1.9	115	331	155	14.9	9
Bryan, GA	13029	7.5	38.6	27.7	1.9	372	861	446	17.0	16
Bulloch, GA	13031	11.8	59.9	43.9	2.1	581	1,538	663	14.6	54
Burke, GA	13033	10.5	83.6	69.0	0.3	244	853	329	14.2	18
Butts, GA	13035	12.9	62.7	37.2	0.3	183	506	227	15.9	14
Calhoun, GA	13037	9.3	81.7	77.9	1.5	25	158	60	14.5	7
Camden, GA	13039	10.5	46.2	35.8	0.5	595	1,276	623	15.2	21
Candler, GA	13043	11.1	72.0	49.5	3.5	105	305	136	15.2	10
Carroll, GA	13045	11.5	63.3	36.6	2.2	1,110	2,540	1,177	16.3	38
Catoosa, GA	13047	14.1	48.9	9.8	0.7	587	1,626	733	14.9	30
Charlton, GA	13049	7.3	71.6	35.6	0.2	104	235	110	15.7	8
Chatham, GA	13051	10.5	61.0	72.6	1.8	1,528	4,829	2,700	13.1	100
Chattahoochee, GA	13053	12.6	67.8	48.1	1.8	85	196	70	13.5	7
Chattooga, GA	13055	12.6	63.7	17.9	1.9	208	574	270	15.4	21
Cherokee, GA	13057	10.7	30.0	25.0	3.5	1,880	4,515	2,461	15.8	83
Clarke, GA	13059	11.9	79.0	80.9	9.2	524	2,411	1,066	11.6	75
Clay, GA	13061	9.1	92.5	98.7	...	...	72	25	12.7	5
Clayton, GA	13063	9.5	82.1	96.3	6.9	1,944	6,971	3,342	15.1	143
Clinch, GA	13065	12.0	72.2	41.9	0.8	78	196	94	14.7	6
Cobb, GA	13067	11.3	44.6	57.3	7.4	7,205	14,756	8,012	14.4	268
Coffee, GA	13069	7.9	75.0	48.9	4.3	348	1,078	515	15.2	20
Colquitt, GA	13071	11.7	72.7	52.6	10.1	447	1,322	618	15.0	22
Columbia, GA	13073	7.4	32.1	32.9	1.2	1,380	3,046	1,449	16.4	47
Cook, GA	13075	11.7	68.9	46.8	3.2	161	519	213	15.9	20
Coweta, GA	13077	9.6	44.5	34.4	1.5	1,217	3,443	1,652	17.7	69
Crawford, GA	13079	16.0	78.6	28.2	...	84	262	126	14.9	8
Crisp, GA	13081	10.7	76.1	63.9	1.2	211	672	304	14.2	17
Dade, GA	13083	14.7	54.1	4.5	0.3	154	340	154	16.2	9
Dawson, GA	13085	12.0	45.1	7.1	1.7	188	532	256	13.6	17
Decatur, GA	13087	10.7	72.5	60.8	2.7	313	843	364	15.4	21
De Kalb, GA	13089	8.8	68.3	87.5	8.8	5,307	13,790	6,856	14.9	233
Dodge, GA	13091	13.7	67.6	42.0	1.5	190	576	235	14.5	26
Dooly, GA	13093	11.9	85.5	89.9	3.0	57	239	92	15.6	7
Dougherty, GA	13095	9.3	81.2	91.0	1.2	752	2,390	1,039	15.3	51
Douglas, GA	13097	10.3	58.4	64.6	3.9	1,459	3,377	1,689	14.6	51
Early, GA	13099	12.9	75.8	68.0	1.2	143	372	190	12.3	9
Echols, GA	13101	6.7	70.5	39.7	5.9	42	123	53	15.0	6
Effingham, GA	13103	13.6	41.1	23.9	0.6	644	1,651	759	15.2	25
Elbert, GA	13105	9.1	69.4	45.8	2.9	180	570	254	13.4	13
Emanuel, GA	13107	13.3	76.4	49.3	1.7	233	619	286	15.7	18
Evans, GA	13109	12.2	80.6	58.6	10.3	100	274	128	14.2	9
Fannin, GA	13111	12.4	60.0	6.4	0.6	185	477	211	14.4	9
Fayette, GA	13113	8.2	22.4	42.9	2.3	1,829	2,914	1,456	14.6	33
Floyd, GA	13115	13.6	63.2	36.4	5.0	880	2,360	1,180	13.7	57
Forsyth, GA	13117	11.3	18.9	24.4	4.5	1,555	4,097	2,163	16.6	61
Franklin, GA	13119	11.1	58.1	19.0	1.8	448	542	238	15.5	13
Fulton, GA	13121	10.0	55.0	73.9	4.6	7,123	18,569	9,831	14.5	684

[2]IEP=Individual Education Program. See notes and definitions for more information.
. . . = Not available.

Table C-1. Population, School, and Student Characteristics by County, Selected Years—*Continued*

County	State/ County Code	Revenues, 2008–2009				Current expenditures, 2008–2009			Resident population 16 to 19 years, 2006–2010			
		Total revenue ($1,000's)	Percentage of revenue from			Amount ($1,000's)	Amount per student	Percent for instruction	Total population 16 to 19 years	Percent enrolled in school	Percent high school graduates, not enrolled in school	Percent not enrolled, not grads, not employed, or not in labor force
			Federal government	State government	Local government							
		19	20	21	22	23	24	25	26	27	28	29
GEORGIA	13000	17,979,225	9.1	43.1	47.8	15,924,560	9,649	62.7	574,283	81.2	10.4	6.0
Appling, GA	13001	36,323	9.6	49.8	40.6	34,558	9,762	63.1	725	75.0	9.8	2.2
Atkinson, GA	13003	17,146	14.4	67.5	18.1	15,474	8,929	62.6	516	62.2	16.7	9.7
Bacon, GA	13005	18,217	11.4	62.9	25.7	17,179	9,281	62.9	527	75.3	14.8	4.4
Baker, GA	13007	7,270	18.0	52.9	29.1	6,364	14,698	58.1	178	82.0	18.0	0.0
Baldwin, GA	13009	59,776	14.2	54.5	31.3	53,521	9,218	63.9	3,535	78.7	7.4	11.7
Banks, GA	13011	27,698	10.1	48.8	41.1	25,725	8,825	64.2	1,041	72.5	12.2	10.1
Barrow, GA	13013	117,907	7.9	50.7	41.4	107,943	8,690	65.6	3,813	79.4	12.0	7.8
Bartow, GA	13015	201,897	7.8	48.4	43.8	170,578	9,128	64.7	5,076	78.0	13.1	6.3
Ben Hill, GA	13017	31,696	13.7	58.7	27.6	30,722	9,130	65.4	961	79.1	11.8	4.4
Berrien, GA	13019	32,682	11.8	66.1	22.0	26,155	8,402	65.7	1,140	74.8	20.4	2.6
Bibb, GA	13021	261,862	12.8	43.4	43.8	225,299	9,024	59.3	10,903	79.6	7.3	9.8
Bleckley, GA	13023	24,625	16.2	62.2	21.6	24,035	9,684	62.1	1,225	87.3	10.8	2.0
Brantley, GA	13025	32,451	10.5	68.6	21.0	29,706	8,204	65.3	1,025	79.9	11.0	6.7
Brooks, GA	13027	23,908	17.1	49.3	33.5	23,297	9,797	59.1	1,263	74.7	12.3	6.3
Bryan, GA	13029	60,559	7.4	51.3	41.3	54,964	7,792	66.9	1,801	79.8	14.1	0.7
Bulloch, GA	13031	109,045	9.6	48.6	41.8	95,744	10,207	60.4	8,636	93.3	2.9	2.4
Burke, GA	13033	46,632	15.5	37.9	46.6	49,725	10,517	57.9	1,447	75.7	14.9	8.5
Butts, GA	13035	34,773	10.7	44.7	44.6	32,500	9,168	59.0	1,308	76.2	12.5	8.9
Calhoun, GA	13037	8,223	19.2	49.7	31.1	7,930	12,070	52.6	189	72.0	23.8	4.2
Camden, GA	13039	89,860	15.3	54.4	30.4	90,536	9,333	63.6	3,171	72.3	20.4	5.8
Candler, GA	13043	19,365	15.1	59.7	25.1	18,567	9,321	62.9	615	49.1	39.2	11.7
Carroll, GA	13045	196,398	8.6	53.5	38.0	172,643	8,923	62.5	7,688	79.3	11.7	4.9
Catoosa, GA	13047	110,252	7.6	54.1	38.3	97,916	9,187	64.3	3,672	83.0	8.4	5.8
Charlton, GA	13049	18,461	11.6	57.4	31.0	17,097	9,493	61.4	744	77.4	20.0	1.1
Chatham, GA	13051	394,106	10.3	31.6	58.2	342,523	10,076	63.6	15,726	79.6	10.1	7.7
Chattahoochee, GA	13053	10,894	16.6	61.4	22.0	9,066	9,865	54.4	826	65.1	29.1	1.6
Chattooga, GA	13055	41,530	11.3	61.0	27.7	42,118	9,834	60.9	1,363	75.4	15.9	7.0
Cherokee, GA	13057	391,795	5.1	43.8	51.1	343,215	9,208	68.9	10,432	82.3	9.2	4.8
Clarke, GA	13059	174,747	11.3	31.5	57.2	156,300	12,747	60.4	14,002	92.7	5.4	1.3
Clay, GA	13061	4,529	23.7	44.4	31.9	4,341	13,155	51.2	71	90.1	9.9	0.0
Clayton, GA	13063	543,400	10.9	45.6	43.5	506,238	10,225	60.0	16,634	76.1	14.8	6.3
Clinch, GA	13065	15,104	12.0	54.5	33.5	13,722	9,503	62.3	482	67.0	14.1	3.5
Cobb, GA	13067	1,221,077	7.1	35.8	57.1	1,109,251	9,678	67.3	37,181	85.5	8.4	3.7
Coffee, GA	13069	76,329	12.2	61.8	26.0	72,442	9,037	64.0	2,450	75.6	10.2	9.5
Colquitt, GA	13071	88,225	12.2	64.3	23.5	82,143	9,196	63.8	2,959	65.5	16.8	10.9
Columbia, GA	13073	212,886	5.4	48.9	45.6	191,568	8,414	66.1	7,133	85.8	8.5	5.3
Cook, GA	13075	36,641	14.1	59.4	26.6	31,571	9,664	55.7	754	90.7	0.9	2.3
Coweta, GA	13077	214,696	7.2	44.8	48.0	193,753	8,747	64.0	6,539	80.4	12.6	4.8
Crawford, GA	13079	16,675	17.1	57.1	25.8	18,461	9,825	63.4	584	63.9	18.5	17.6
Crisp, GA	13081	46,149	14.8	55.7	29.5	42,793	9,784	63.5	1,387	70.4	20.0	9.2
Dade, GA	13083	23,589	8.9	54.2	36.9	22,125	8,694	64.9	1,344	84.3	11.8	1.6
Dawson, GA	13085	43,180	5.1	30.6	64.3	36,386	10,486	63.7	992	75.3	15.2	6.4
Decatur, GA	13087	55,508	15.4	53.0	31.6	50,952	8,996	64.5	1,754	82.5	5.9	9.5
De Kalb, GA	13089	1,210,403	9.5	31.7	58.8	1,061,692	10,348	61.0	37,276	81.5	11.5	4.5
Dodge, GA	13091	37,274	19.1	56.9	24.0	36,894	10,896	57.0	2,051	41.7	23.4	34.7
Dooly, GA	13093	16,877	19.4	46.5	34.1	15,206	10,394	60.4	837	62.5	28.4	5.6
Dougherty, GA	13095	172,259	14.9	48.8	36.2	156,580	9,652	60.5	6,604	79.7	8.2	7.0
Douglas, GA	13097	265,011	8.1	47.0	44.9	215,186	8,677	63.9	7,841	83.4	10.0	4.5
Early, GA	13099	27,252	18.7	49.8	31.5	25,234	10,283	64.1	723	70.1	11.2	10.0
Echols, GA	13101	8,793	13.6	58.3	28.0	6,992	9,436	61.9	234	73.5	9.0	6.8
Effingham, GA	13103	117,228	6.3	58.4	35.3	97,788	8,609	65.9	3,307	81.9	12.7	3.1
Elbert, GA	13105	37,213	8.3	54.6	37.1	35,581	10,340	64.8	1,284	72.0	17.1	8.1
Emanuel, GA	13107	41,397	16.5	62.6	20.9	40,291	9,107	64.6	1,286	79.7	13.7	5.7
Evans, GA	13109	17,916	15.4	57.3	27.4	16,565	8,906	61.7	661	74.1	16.6	6.2
Fannin, GA	13111	36,312	8.0	37.9	54.1	31,313	9,912	62.2	814	84.2	13.6	0.0
Fayette, GA	13113	233,599	3.9	39.0	57.0	199,672	9,028	67.3	6,760	92.2	4.6	2.4
Floyd, GA	13115	184,711	10.6	49.7	39.7	173,045	10,682	62.7	6,195	83.7	8.9	5.8
Forsyth, GA	13117	343,827	3.7	37.2	59.2	284,126	8,776	68.0	7,628	84.9	8.7	4.3
Franklin, GA	13119	81,590	9.8	50.0	40.2	76,969	9,702	65.0	1,346	76.5	14.9	6.9
Fulton, GA	13121	1,900,523	7.9	22.3	69.8	1,563,725	11,387	55.8	49,788	86.4	6.7	5.2

Table C-1. Population, School, and Student Characteristics by County, Selected Years—*Continued*

County	State/ County Code	High school graduates, 2006–2010			College enrollment, 2006–2010		College graduates, 2006–2010 (percent)						
		Population 25 years and over	High school diploma or less (percent)	High school diploma or more (percent)	Number	Percent public	Bachelor's degree or more	+/- U.S. percent with Bachelor's degree or more	Non-Hispanic White	Black or African American	American Indian and Alaska Native	Asian, Hawaiian, and Pacific Islander	Hispanic or Latino[3]
		30	31	32	33	34	35	36	37	38	39	40	41
GEORGIA	13000	6,052,410	46.1	83.5	655,050	75.4	27.2	-0.7	30.9	19.4	19.6	50.8	13.7
Appling, GA	13001	12,192	68.6	75.1	641	94.7	8.3	-19.6	8.5	6.5	100.0	52.3	0.0
Atkinson, GA	13003	4,997	73.4	66.7	115	96.5	8.0	-19.9	10.4	3.8	0.0	0.0	3.8
Bacon, GA	13005	7,299	72.5	72.6	233	75.1	7.4	-20.5	7.3	9.5	0.0	0.0	0.0
Baker, GA	13007	2,206	63.0	75.1	155	78.1	12.2	-15.7	19.7	6.9	0.0	0.0	0.0
Baldwin, GA	13009	28,748	58.2	78.0	6,433	93.9	18.4	-9.5	24.3	9.5	0.0	50.8	18.3
Banks, GA	13011	11,769	69.4	73.0	632	79.4	10.5	-17.4	10.7	0.0	0.0	58.4	2.4
Barrow, GA	13013	41,744	54.9	78.9	2,508	85.8	14.9	-13.0	15.4	12.0	0.0	23.1	11.4
Bartow, GA	13015	62,842	61.3	78.4	3,387	74.8	16.5	-11.4	17.4	14.6	19.3	20.2	7.1
Ben Hill, GA	13017	11,363	66.7	69.9	874	76.4	12.3	-15.6	14.5	9.6	0.0	38.3	0.0
Berrien, GA	13019	12,218	63.4	68.9	1,013	94.5	10.8	-17.1	11.5	6.9	0.0	0.0	6.8
Bibb, GA	13021	98,704	50.3	81.2	12,263	65.1	23.1	-4.8	33.0	12.1	13.9	55.1	12.9
Bleckley, GA	13023	8,080	70.3	73.2	1,118	75.0	10.1	-17.8	13.9	0.0	0.0	0.0	0.0
Brantley, GA	13025	11,342	71.7	75.7	675	91.6	4.9	-23.0	4.7	0.0	0.0	0.0	34.3
Brooks, GA	13027	10,590	58.3	78.2	766	98.4	15.8	-12.1	20.3	8.1	0.0	0.0	9.1
Bryan, GA	13029	18,232	40.3	88.4	1,635	76.9	27.6	-0.3	26.4	30.7	53.6	39.6	38.9
Bulloch, GA	13031	34,486	46.7	85.2	17,157	97.7	25.3	-2.6	31.2	9.5	46.3	39.3	5.2
Burke, GA	13033	14,227	66.7	75.1	1,163	98.2	9.1	-18.8	13.3	3.7	0.0	100.0	33.6
Butts, GA	13035	15,820	68.7	76.5	712	60.7	9.1	-18.8	10.2	5.6	0.0	60.4	4.2
Calhoun, GA	13037	4,522	68.6	68.3	232	88.8	8.7	-19.2	15.0	4.8	0.0	0.0	5.3
Camden, GA	13039	29,212	44.3	89.1	3,445	78.8	20.4	-7.5	21.9	14.1	22.7	25.2	24.9
Candler, GA	13043	6,751	68.2	77.5	435	100.0	13.2	-14.7	17.5	5.2	0.0	0.0	0.0
Carroll, GA	13045	67,183	56.3	78.8	9,033	88.4	18.3	-9.6	20.0	13.0	24.5	16.1	6.9
Catoosa, GA	13047	41,944	49.5	82.1	3,045	83.5	17.3	-10.6	16.8	18.4	20.2	53.7	31.2
Charlton, GA	13049	8,363	70.0	72.6	398	74.6	7.2	-20.7	7.9	6.0	0.0	0.0	0.0
Chatham, GA	13051	164,703	42.4	87.4	23,713	65.1	29.0	1.1	39.1	12.8	28.0	43.7	18.6
Chattahoochee, GA	13053	5,946	27.8	93.2	1,453	82.9	31.5	3.6	39.1	18.3	83.3	33.7	11.0
Chattooga, GA	13055	17,736	68.7	68.4	1,305	87.2	8.0	-19.9	8.7	0.5	0.0	71.4	14.2
Cherokee, GA	13057	133,624	35.6	88.9	10,642	71.2	33.6	5.7	34.8	32.0	40.0	39.6	17.7
Clarke, GA	13059	59,171	37.6	84.3	34,130	95.8	41.2	13.3	56.8	12.4	26.6	78.5	15.5
Clay, GA	13061	2,010	68.0	78.1	57	100.0	8.5	-19.4	20.9	2.9	0.0	0.0	0.0
Clayton, GA	13063	156,190	50.5	82.6	16,649	70.1	17.9	-10.0	14.8	20.7	2.2	16.9	8.1
Clinch, GA	13065	4,485	66.8	72.9	148	100.0	17.1	-10.8	20.9	7.7	0.0	0.0	0.0
Cobb, GA	13067	440,089	30.2	90.2	50,227	73.7	43.9	16.0	49.3	36.3	28.8	58.4	18.2
Coffee, GA	13069	26,161	63.8	73.9	2,333	93.8	11.0	-16.9	13.6	4.3	14.7	0.0	4.7
Colquitt, GA	13071	27,911	66.5	71.8	1,993	97.1	11.2	-16.7	14.6	1.8	0.0	15.8	8.1
Columbia, GA	13073	75,738	36.8	89.9	7,291	81.1	33.8	5.9	33.8	27.4	28.9	56.6	31.3
Cook, GA	13075	10,813	65.6	72.2	1,058	97.0	10.4	-17.5	13.1	2.7	0.0	0.0	15.7
Coweta, GA	13077	78,826	45.5	87.2	5,384	74.2	25.7	-2.2	28.5	15.7	0.0	34.7	14.9
Crawford, GA	13079	8,653	61.3	78.8	638	91.5	13.6	-14.3	14.3	13.4	0.0	0.0	4.9
Crisp, GA	13081	14,828	65.3	73.4	983	92.0	11.8	-16.1	17.8	2.8	0.0	0.0	4.3
Dade, GA	13083	10,745	55.0	79.1	1,499	36.0	16.8	-11.1	16.6	41.3	41.3	18.6	7.1
Dawson, GA	13085	14,880	54.5	84.6	909	78.8	18.8	-9.1	19.0	0.0	45.1	0.0	12.7
Decatur, GA	13087	18,012	60.6	75.6	1,704	89.3	12.5	-15.4	18.1	3.8	17.5	100.0	4.5
De Kalb, GA	13089	449,183	34.9	87.9	56,593	56.8	38.7	10.8	63.0	23.8	12.3	57.1	15.3
Dodge, GA	13091	13,901	65.1	76.9	1,014	81.4	13.8	-14.1	17.4	4.4	0.0	100.0	4.8
Dooly, GA	13093	9,724	70.9	69.7	361	76.5	9.6	-18.3	13.3	6.3	0.0	0.0	1.7
Dougherty, GA	13095	57,684	48.6	80.7	10,048	93.7	19.6	-8.3	27.2	14.6	16.5	37.2	17.2
Douglas, GA	13097	80,733	46.4	86.4	7,564	71.4	23.7	-4.2	21.3	28.3	7.5	47.1	13.4
Early, GA	13099	7,219	64.8	77.1	610	84.8	13.5	-14.4	19.8	5.2	0.0	0.0	0.0
Echols, GA	13101	2,372	75.8	67.8	158	100.0	6.1	-21.8	7.5	0.0	0.0	50.0	0.0
Effingham, GA	13103	31,627	57.3	84.3	2,364	85.7	15.5	-12.4	16.2	9.6	68.2	13.2	10.3
Elbert, GA	13105	13,607	70.0	73.0	760	85.9	9.6	-18.3	11.3	4.1	100.0	71.1	5.1
Emanuel, GA	13107	14,409	66.8	72.4	824	90.2	9.7	-18.2	11.7	5.9	0.0	82.9	0.0
Evans, GA	13109	6,941	63.2	73.3	459	98.7	13.4	-14.5	16.1	10.9	0.0	23.5	0.0
Fannin, GA	13111	17,288	61.8	77.9	795	61.8	16.2	-11.7	16.5	0.0	13.5	13.8	0.0
Fayette, GA	13113	69,560	27.8	93.6	6,232	71.7	41.5	13.6	41.4	43.9	52.6	48.7	23.9
Floyd, GA	13115	62,548	56.8	75.9	7,153	45.0	17.9	-10.0	20.1	9.2	0.0	34.8	4.7
Forsyth, GA	13117	105,100	29.9	90.6	6,797	71.9	43.6	15.7	43.8	49.1	34.2	65.5	22.0
Franklin, GA	13119	14,829	65.4	74.3	1,250	59.0	13.6	-14.3	14.7	1.1	0.0	6.0	12.3
Fulton, GA	13121	579,297	30.2	89.7	76,104	67.3	47.6	19.7	66.9	26.6	24.8	73.6	20.9

Note. Data in columns 26 through 41 from the American Community Survey are subject to sampling error, which can be especially large in small counties and small population groups. See notes and definitions for more information.

[3]May be of any race.

Table C-1. Population, School, and Student Characteristics by County, Selected Years—*Continued*

County	State/ County Code	County Type[1]	Population, 2010		Percent of related children 5–17 years in poverty, 2010	Percent of children under 19 years with no health insurance, 2010	Number of schools and students, 2010–2011			Resident enrollment, 2006–2010 K–12 enrollment	
			Total	Percent 5–17 years			School districts	Schools	Students	Number	Percent public
			1	2	3	4	5	6	7	8	9
GEORGIA—*(Continued)*											
Gilmer, GA	13123	6	28,292	16.1	26.5	14.4	2	8	4,262	4,772	96.1
Glascock, GA	13125	9	3,082	19.9	21.1	10.1	1	1	658	582	91.6
Glynn, GA	13127	3	79,626	17.4	27.3	10.5	1	19	12,868	13,840	93.7
Gordon, GA	13129	6	55,186	19.5	23.7	10.9	2	14	10,423	10,619	94.1
Grady, GA	13131	6	25,011	18.1	36.7	11.7	1	8	4,498	4,619	96.9
Greene, GA	13133	6	15,994	15.0	38.9	10.6	1	5	2,145	2,558	83.0
Gwinnett, GA	13135	1	805,321	21.4	18.0	12.8	3	136	164,412	164,461	91.5
Habersham, GA	13137	6	43,041	17.2	23.4	14.5	1	13	6,883	7,411	93.3
Hall, GA	13139	3	179,684	20.1	24.5	13.9	2	42	32,916	33,295	93.5
Hancock, GA	13141	7	9,429	13.6	37.5	8.1	1	4	1,212	1,516	98.0
Haralson, GA	13143	1	28,780	18.7	26.2	8.8	2	10	5,775	5,500	96.2
Harris, GA	13145	2	32,024	18.3	11.9	9.9	1	8	5,011	6,012	92.0
Hart, GA	13147	6	25,213	16.1	28.4	11.8	1	6	3,447	4,014	91.1
Heard, GA	13149	1	11,834	19.5	27.8	10.0	1	5	2,119	2,467	94.4
Henry, GA	13151	1	203,922	22.5	12.9	10.0	1	50	40,909	44,064	87.7
Houston, GA	13153	3	139,900	19.5	18.7	8.2	1	39	27,061	26,978	93.9
Irwin, GA	13155	7	9,538	18.0	32.1	11.6	1	4	1,698	1,589	99.2
Jackson, GA	13157	6	60,485	19.4	20.0	10.9	3	22	11,623	11,342	92.8
Jasper, GA	13159	1	13,900	18.2	28.2	11.2	1	4	2,199	2,471	79.4
Jeff Davis, GA	13161	7	15,068	19.8	32.1	11.6	1	4	3,006	2,557	94.3
Jefferson, GA	13163	6	16,930	18.3	38.2	8.9	1	6	2,982	3,187	86.0
Jenkins, GA	13165	6	8,340	19.5	42.1	10.7	1	4	1,502	1,554	96.1
Johnson, GA	13167	9	9,980	15.4	32.8	9.7	1	3	1,198	1,709	93.1
Jones, GA	13169	3	28,669	19.5	16.5	9.3	1	10	5,606	5,555	83.6
Lamar, GA	13171	1	18,317	15.2	25.7	9.5	1	4	2,554	2,827	89.3
Lanier, GA	13173	3	10,078	18.6	32.9	10.1	1	4	1,744	1,575	97.5
Laurens, GA	13175	6	48,434	18.6	28.1	7.9	2	17	9,406	9,115	94.3
Lee, GA	13177	3	28,298	21.5	12.9	7.9	1	8	6,352	6,250	91.6
Liberty, GA	13179	3	63,453	19.9	30.0	7.4	1	14	10,525	13,186	94.8
Lincoln, GA	13181	8	7,996	15.4	29.8	12.1	1	3	1,240	1,307	93.9
Long, GA	13183	3	14,464	21.2	28.9	12.3	1	3	2,632	2,803	96.5
Lowndes, GA	13185	3	109,233	17.1	29.5	8.5	2	21	17,869	17,525	91.8
Lumpkin, GA	13187	6	29,966	14.9	23.6	11.0	1	5	3,866	4,639	94.3
McDuffie, GA	13189	2	21,875	18.9	30.1	8.4	2	7	4,201	4,415	94.3
McIntosh, GA	13191	3	14,333	16.0	30.2	10.9	1	4	1,767	2,426	87.5
Macon, GA	13193	6	14,740	16.3	36.6	10.7	1	4	1,803	2,871	88.5
Madison, GA	13195	3	28,120	18.3	23.3	11.2	1	8	4,819	5,370	89.7
Marion, GA	13197	2	8,742	17.5	34.5	14.5	1	2	1,353	1,758	95.7
Meriwether, GA	13199	1	21,992	17.2	30.7	9.7	1	8	3,276	4,107	84.4
Miller, GA	13201	8	6,125	16.5	34.8	10.3	1	4	1,093	1,020	84.4
Mitchell, GA	13205	6	23,498	17.5	38.5	8.3	3	8	4,031	4,625	90.0
Monroe, GA	13207	3	26,424	17.0	19.6	9.2	1	7	3,950	4,827	82.6
Montgomery, GA	13209	9	9,123	16.8	30.5	13.7	1	3	1,093	1,641	92.3
Morgan, GA	13211	6	17,868	19.1	21.2	11.4	1	5	3,356	3,254	88.5
Murray, GA	13213	3	39,628	19.7	24.9	12.4	1	11	7,737	7,842	96.4
Muscogee, GA	13215	2	189,885	18.1	27.3	6.4	1	61	32,288	35,016	92.2
Newton, GA	13217	1	99,958	21.3	19.3	11.4	1	24	19,478	20,239	90.3
Oconee, GA	13219	3	32,808	22.5	9.0	8.8	1	10	6,489	7,135	85.5
Oglethorpe, GA	13221	3	14,899	18.0	22.1	12.1	1	5	2,392	2,857	95.3
Paulding, GA	13223	1	142,324	22.4	10.8	8.6	1	33	28,407	29,910	93.2
Peach, GA	13225	6	27,695	16.2	31.7	10.1	2	6	3,988	4,626	91.1
Pickens, GA	13227	1	29,431	16.6	20.9	9.7	1	7	4,479	4,784	93.6
Pierce, GA	13229	6	18,758	19.1	26.7	11.5	1	5	3,615	3,583	97.9
Pike, GA	13231	1	17,869	21.4	15.5	11.5	1	4	3,556	3,798	91.8
Polk, GA	13233	6	41,475	18.7	29.3	11.1	1	11	7,598	7,414	96.2
Pulaski, GA	13235	6	12,010	15.6	26.7	9.9	1	5	1,427	1,794	97.5
Putnam, GA	13237	6	21,218	15.3	32.1	12.5	1	4	2,801	3,425	83.0
Quitman, GA	13239	9	2,513	15.2	40.5	9.4	1	2	378	461	98.9
Rabun, GA	13241	9	16,276	16.0	27.5	14.5	1	5	2,329	2,508	91.5
Randolph, GA	13243	6	7,719	15.9	37.8	8.7	1	3	1,251	1,395	85.0

[1]County type codes are from the Economic Research Service of the United States Department of Agriculture. See notes and definitions for more information.

Table C-1. Population, School, and Student Characteristics by County, Selected Years—*Continued*

County	State/ County Code	Characteristics of students, 2010–2011				Number of graduates, 2008–2009	Staff and students, 2010–2011			
		Percent with IEP[2]	Percent eligible for free or reduced lunch	Percent minority	Percent English-language learners		Total staff	Number of teachers	Student/ teacher ratio	Central admin. staff
		10	11	12	13	14	15	16	17	18
GEORGIA—*(Continued)*										
Gilmer, GA	13123	9.7	66.9	20.7	8.9	216	722	317	13.4	24
Glascock, GA	13125	10.6	53.6	9.3	...	34	96	40	16.3	5
Glynn, GA	13127	10.2	57.8	49.9	4.1	654	1,849	851	15.1	35
Gordon, GA	13129	9.4	61.0	27.1	5.6	593	1,370	670	15.6	37
Grady, GA	13131	7.7	71.6	56.3	5.0	242	619	299	15.1	13
Greene, GA	13133	11.0	76.4	75.9	3.2	113	337	162	13.3	12
Gwinnett, GA	13135	10.9	52.3	67.9	11.7	8,484	20,655	10,892	15.1	271
Habersham, GA	13137	13.8	55.4	28.6	8.9	340	1,040	508	13.6	15
Hall, GA	13139	9.8	63.0	52.7	17.7	1,479	3,972	2,131	15.4	44
Hancock, GA	13141	12.5	81.4	99.3	...	84	234	108	11.3	10
Haralson, GA	13143	14.2	49.1	9.4	0.4	322	806	401	14.4	17
Harris, GA	13145	7.0	34.7	25.6	0.1	375	716	320	15.7	12
Hart, GA	13147	10.3	60.5	34.2	2.0	187	482	232	14.9	8
Heard, GA	13149	10.8	63.5	14.8	...	124	290	138	15.4	9
Henry, GA	13151	12.9	47.6	59.9	1.8	2,395	4,998	2,631	15.5	25
Houston, GA	13153	10.8	50.4	48.9	2.9	1,523	3,685	1,773	15.3	82
Irwin, GA	13155	15.3	69.7	38.0	0.6	74	260	121	14.0	11
Jackson, GA	13157	12.5	47.8	21.9	3.3	547	1,625	792	14.7	31
Jasper, GA	13159	8.7	70.2	34.6	1.3	97	355	146	15.0	10
Jeff Davis, GA	13161	13.4	67.0	33.8	8.0	140	397	175	17.1	14
Jefferson, GA	13163	11.3	84.2	73.7	1.3	193	436	204	14.6	9
Jenkins, GA	13165	13.4	77.2	62.8	2.3	83	225	99	15.2	7
Johnson, GA	13167	11.7	72.0	49.2	0.3	54	199	82	14.7	8
Jones, GA	13169	11.0	44.4	30.4	0.3	304	747	354	15.9	12
Lamar, GA	13171	11.1	70.8	39.8	0.5	129	362	156	16.4	12
Lanier, GA	13173	8.9	73.5	35.3	1.7	71	218	102	17.1	8
Laurens, GA	13175	8.9	64.3	50.2	0.5	532	1,211	611	15.4	27
Lee, GA	13177	8.3	41.7	25.8	1.1	352	794	390	16.3	13
Liberty, GA	13179	8.8	63.1	70.4	0.8	600	1,483	652	16.2	29
Lincoln, GA	13181	13.1	64.6	44.5	...	102	206	88	14.1	7
Long, GA	13183	8.5	67.7	47.1	4.9	105	340	162	16.3	10
Lowndes, GA	13185	11.5	58.4	53.8	1.8	905	2,477	1,225	14.6	51
Lumpkin, GA	13187	13.0	53.5	10.7	2.0	224	543	253	15.3	12
McDuffie, GA	13189	13.1	71.6	55.2	1.2	242	686	295	14.3	26
McIntosh, GA	13191	11.1	79.1	47.3	0.8	127	267	119	14.9	7
Macon, GA	13193	12.3	82.3	90.2	1.9	94	305	117	15.4	9
Madison, GA	13195	15.9	58.5	19.3	1.8	265	750	325	14.9	17
Marion, GA	13197	9.5	74.0	50.0	2.7	100	208	83	16.3	7
Meriwether, GA	13199	16.5	61.3	61.2	0.6	193	564	232	14.1	11
Miller, GA	13201	7.0	70.7	38.8	0.6	89	154	68	16.1	4
Mitchell, GA	13205	10.7	74.5	59.7	2.4	208	660	300	13.4	24
Monroe, GA	13207	10.6	56.3	32.9	1.0	215	625	271	14.6	14
Montgomery, GA	13209	8.8	79.0	46.6	2.5	54	187	83	13.2	8
Morgan, GA	13211	9.1	47.6	35.6	1.9	207	480	241	13.9	11
Murray, GA	13213	9.0	72.7	23.3	5.5	389	983	479	16.1	12
Muscogee, GA	13215	11.3	62.4	70.2	1.5	1,791	5,100	2,317	13.9	142
Newton, GA	13217	12.4	62.4	59.4	2.4	858	2,602	1,275	15.3	30
Oconee, GA	13219	9.8	22.0	16.3	1.7	461	881	422	15.4	21
Oglethorpe, GA	13221	13.3	56.5	28.6	2.7	148	370	176	13.6	10
Paulding, GA	13223	9.3	39.1	32.8	1.2	1,349	3,331	1,743	16.3	45
Peach, GA	13225	9.8	72.0	65.5	4.6	202	569	268	14.9	31
Pickens, GA	13227	11.8	50.4	7.5	1.0	223	670	311	14.4	17
Pierce, GA	13229	10.3	56.2	17.0	2.8	222	476	239	15.1	16
Pike, GA	13231	6.9	46.5	17.4	...	200	442	216	16.4	13
Polk, GA	13233	13.4	64.5	35.0	5.8	352	984	505	15.0	16
Pulaski, GA	13235	12.3	68.3	50.0	2.0	94	244	111	12.9	16
Putnam, GA	13237	16.3	77.4	53.7	2.3	147	506	225	12.4	15
Quitman, GA	13239	12.2	98.4	75.4	...	...	69	31	12.2	4
Rabun, GA	13241	11.3	65.1	16.8	4.5	129	393	166	14.0	12
Randolph, GA	13243	12.0	90.2	94.2	...	63	248	101	12.4	8

[2]IEP=Individual Education Program. See notes and definitions for more information.
. . . = Not available.

Table C-1. Population, School, and Student Characteristics by County, Selected Years—*Continued*

County	State/ County Code	Revenues, 2008–2009				Current expenditures, 2008–2009			Resident population 16 to 19 years, 2006–2010			
			Percentage of revenue from									
		Total revenue ($1,000's)	Federal government	State government	Local government	Amount ($1,000's)	Amount per student	Percent for instruction	Total population 16 to 19 years	Percent enrolled in school	Percent high school graduates, not enrolled in school	Percent not enrolled, not grads, not employed, or not in labor force
		19	20	21	22	23	24	25	26	27	28	29
GEORGIA—*(Continued)*												
Gilmer, GA	13123	53,459	11.3	39.2	49.5	51,413	12,166	63.3	1,425	71.4	13.3	7.5
Glascock, GA	13125	5,709	13.9	58.3	27.8	6,123	9,377	53.7	134	92.5	1.5	6.0
Glynn, GA	13127	164,756	7.9	31.7	60.4	133,289	10,447	63.9	4,157	80.8	11.0	4.4
Gordon, GA	13129	105,331	9.2	52.7	38.2	94,468	9,143	63.0	3,129	81.8	11.1	3.5
Grady, GA	13131	40,241	14.2	57.5	28.3	37,678	8,475	64.7	1,482	71.0	14.9	8.4
Greene, GA	13133	30,435	10.3	16.0	73.6	26,084	13,411	59.6	877	72.5	15.6	2.1
Gwinnett, GA	13135	1,704,753	6.6	41.5	51.8	1,527,109	9,532	63.2	44,208	85.9	7.4	4.3
Habersham, GA	13137	70,671	8.7	49.1	42.1	66,025	9,474	64.9	3,839	93.2	4.9	1.2
Hall, GA	13139	341,241	8.9	48.8	42.4	295,454	9,238	65.5	10,027	72.4	13.6	11.0
Hancock, GA	13141	16,758	21.0	37.6	41.4	15,329	11,819	50.3	523	85.7	14.3	0.0
Haralson, GA	13143	58,802	9.3	55.2	35.5	52,907	9,038	64.7	1,630	69.4	11.7	14.6
Harris, GA	13145	50,781	5.9	42.0	52.1	46,243	9,428	62.8	1,649	89.1	9.1	1.5
Hart, GA	13147	36,117	9.8	40.6	49.5	33,209	9,394	67.3	1,295	82.2	6.1	8.7
Heard, GA	13149	30,287	6.5	47.9	45.6	19,877	9,198	65.1	732	82.1	10.7	5.7
Henry, GA	13151	424,382	5.4	46.1	48.5	339,389	8,494	66.4	11,579	83.6	12.3	3.5
Houston, GA	13153	272,381	9.0	54.2	36.8	246,120	9,364	64.6	8,592	86.7	7.9	4.2
Irwin, GA	13155	18,005	11.7	61.8	26.5	16,667	9,535	62.7	645	65.7	0.0	33.2
Jackson, GA	13157	123,491	7.1	41.5	51.4	110,928	9,794	62.0	3,421	79.5	8.6	10.5
Jasper, GA	13159	21,013	14.4	42.9	42.7	19,280	8,808	59.9	785	74.5	15.7	8.3
Jeff Davis, GA	13161	27,196	12.4	64.2	23.4	24,807	8,545	63.6	764	76.1	18.1	2.9
Jefferson, GA	13163	29,910	14.7	56.3	29.0	27,403	8,783	63.2	1,110	73.2	16.9	8.0
Jenkins, GA	13165	15,890	14.6	61.2	24.2	14,221	9,289	60.9	521	76.2	20.7	3.1
Johnson, GA	13167	12,645	20.9	56.6	22.6	12,619	10,128	60.0	467	73.2	22.5	2.4
Jones, GA	13169	49,585	9.2	57.7	33.1	47,670	8,409	64.4	1,600	85.3	11.5	3.3
Lamar, GA	13171	24,637	12.4	44.5	43.2	22,970	9,195	58.8	1,505	84.6	10.8	0.8
Lanier, GA	13173	19,093	10.2	69.3	20.4	15,243	8,765	62.2	459	70.4	13.1	16.6
Laurens, GA	13175	94,358	11.4	58.0	30.7	83,598	8,831	65.6	2,631	77.4	8.4	10.4
Lee, GA	13177	53,205	7.4	56.5	36.1	47,660	7,705	64.8	1,672	85.6	3.7	8.0
Liberty, GA	13179	113,242	18.7	55.8	25.5	100,852	9,193	62.7	4,221	75.7	16.5	6.4
Lincoln, GA	13181	22,777	7.8	65.5	26.7	14,458	10,928	62.6	528	79.6	5.9	6.4
Long, GA	13183	20,695	15.1	64.6	20.3	19,423	7,708	61.3	1,141	61.1	19.4	12.4
Lowndes, GA	13185	177,036	10.3	50.5	39.2	160,632	9,300	64.5	8,164	82.9	10.6	4.1
Lumpkin, GA	13187	37,636	9.1	40.4	50.6	35,911	9,362	61.1	2,539	90.6	7.1	2.3
McDuffie, GA	13189	47,773	11.3	55.7	33.0	43,903	10,433	60.9	1,301	80.4	7.2	10.2
McIntosh, GA	13191	17,152	12.5	42.9	44.5	17,933	9,554	57.1	938	60.9	28.4	2.6
Macon, GA	13193	20,755	17.9	47.8	34.2	19,118	10,115	59.2	892	79.9	0.5	14.4
Madison, GA	13195	48,738	8.8	57.4	33.8	46,361	9,715	64.1	1,540	86.8	5.7	5.7
Marion, GA	13197	15,001	12.2	54.9	32.9	14,126	9,899	55.9	426	77.0	0.0	18.5
Meriwether, GA	13199	37,995	15.0	54.8	30.2	35,623	10,329	60.1	1,452	71.9	19.6	8.0
Miller, GA	13201	13,104	13.0	59.1	27.9	11,322	9,984	59.8	317	78.2	4.1	2.2
Mitchell, GA	13205	49,599	15.0	58.5	26.5	42,937	10,576	61.7	1,333	88.6	3.7	4.1
Monroe, GA	13207	42,813	6.8	36.1	57.1	37,362	9,366	60.4	1,288	87.7	3.8	7.6
Montgomery, GA	13209	12,478	13.1	58.2	28.7	12,417	11,309	63.9	764	82.9	12.4	4.1
Morgan, GA	13211	34,279	8.8	39.9	51.3	31,879	9,640	70.4	681	87.7	10.3	0.6
Murray, GA	13213	71,449	11.1	59.7	29.2	66,170	8,453	64.5	2,178	76.0	15.0	8.3
Muscogee, GA	13215	356,342	11.1	50.5	38.4	312,503	9,590	61.7	13,369	71.4	21.7	5.9
Newton, GA	13217	195,317	8.2	55.3	36.6	174,843	9,052	64.4	6,438	84.0	10.1	4.9
Oconee, GA	13219	69,066	4.4	41.2	54.4	60,328	9,336	65.6	2,165	86.2	5.9	6.8
Oglethorpe, GA	13221	24,677	8.0	50.7	41.3	21,555	8,730	62.1	926	84.0	1.8	8.3
Paulding, GA	13223	279,339	5.4	53.9	40.7	234,460	8,401	66.7	7,542	78.0	12.3	8.1
Peach, GA	13225	50,623	11.5	56.6	31.9	40,732	9,991	56.4	3,065	91.4	4.6	2.6
Pickens, GA	13227	51,231	8.4	37.2	54.4	45,466	10,043	63.7	1,444	86.9	7.5	5.6
Pierce, GA	13229	32,945	10.7	62.9	26.4	32,029	8,989	64.7	1,049	74.8	19.5	5.7
Pike, GA	13231	25,910	8.0	58.9	33.0	26,795	7,715	63.3	1,013	83.1	12.7	3.4
Polk, GA	13233	75,818	9.6	59.6	30.8	65,405	8,775	66.0	2,225	72.5	15.3	11.4
Pulaski, GA	13235	15,571	13.0	56.0	31.0	15,173	9,525	63.7	689	81.0	15.2	3.8
Putnam, GA	13237	42,784	10.3	41.4	48.3	32,000	11,573	62.6	956	72.0	19.0	9.0
Quitman, GA	13239	5,725	18.0	58.9	23.1	3,845	13,587	51.3	179	69.3	22.9	2.2
Rabun, GA	13241	32,506	6.5	21.0	72.5	25,143	11,205	62.4	792	79.2	5.7	10.5
Randolph, GA	13243	15,880	24.6	48.0	27.4	15,527	11,075	54.6	742	78.7	2.8	14.6

Note. Data in columns 26 through 41 from the American Community Survey are subject to sampling error, which can be especially large in small counties and small population groups. See notes and definitions for more information.

Table C-1. Population, School, and Student Characteristics by County, Selected Years—*Continued*

County	State/ County Code	High school graduates, 2006–2010			College enrollment, 2006–2010		College graduates, 2006–2010 (percent)						
		Population 25 years and over	High school diploma or less (percent)	High school diploma or more (percent)	Number	Percent public	Bachelor's degree or more	+/- U.S. percent with Bachelor's degree or more	Non-Hispanic White	Black or African American	American Indian and Alaska Native	Asian, Hawaiian, and Pacific Islander	Hispanic or Latino[3]
		30	31	32	33	34	35	36	37	38	39	40	41
GEORGIA— *(Continued)*													
Gilmer, GA	13123	19,688	60.8	75.4	851	82.7	13.4	-14.5	13.7	0.0	0.0	0.0	10.5
Glascock, GA	13125	2,033	70.8	72.5	72	91.7	10.5	-17.4	10.5	9.9	0.0	0.0	0.0
Glynn, GA	13127	52,227	44.6	86.1	3,928	83.1	26.4	-1.5	31.5	11.5	0.0	45.2	14.1
Gordon, GA	13129	34,571	64.6	73.3	2,079	75.2	12.7	-15.2	13.8	15.7	5.2	19.6	2.4
Grady, GA	13131	16,000	67.3	74.1	1,190	86.2	10.1	-17.8	13.0	3.3	5.9	69.2	6.8
Greene, GA	13133	11,329	63.0	75.3	585	72.6	18.9	-9.0	27.4	4.4	72.2	45.5	5.1
Gwinnett, GA	13135	484,996	36.1	87.3	46,037	72.2	34.9	7.0	39.6	32.5	24.9	46.1	14.7
Habersham, GA	13137	27,267	57.7	75.0	3,770	36.3	18.7	-9.2	20.3	5.6	0.0	28.9	5.3
Hall, GA	13139	109,764	54.1	76.5	7,754	76.3	21.0	-6.9	26.0	10.1	15.7	32.4	4.6
Hancock, GA	13141	6,702	75.0	66.1	352	89.2	10.3	-17.6	17.6	8.8	0.0	0.0	0.0
Haralson, GA	13143	18,789	67.7	69.6	923	85.2	11.0	-16.9	11.2	3.1	0.0	35.5	21.9
Harris, GA	13145	21,052	42.1	88.5	1,587	77.6	27.4	-0.5	30.1	17.4	25.6	6.0	21.0
Hart, GA	13147	17,414	61.7	75.3	966	83.0	15.2	-12.7	17.5	6.7	0.0	0.0	0.0
Heard, GA	13149	7,727	68.2	71.8	424	94.3	7.3	-20.6	7.7	3.4	0.0	0.0	31.6
Henry, GA	13151	121,223	43.3	89.2	11,579	66.4	24.4	-3.5	20.9	30.5	15.0	36.4	19.4
Houston, GA	13153	85,196	41.4	87.3	10,808	87.4	24.4	-3.5	26.2	20.9	8.5	33.8	13.3
Irwin, GA	13155	6,381	66.9	70.3	366	87.2	9.3	-18.6	9.9	8.3	0.0	0.0	0.0
Jackson, GA	13157	38,166	57.7	78.9	2,635	78.4	17.7	-10.2	18.8	7.4	37.3	8.4	11.9
Jasper, GA	13159	8,994	62.6	78.3	375	92.3	13.3	-14.6	15.7	3.8	41.8	0.0	0.0
Jeff Davis, GA	13161	9,131	68.9	75.2	442	97.7	11.5	-16.4	14.2	1.1	0.0	53.6	0.0
Jefferson, GA	13163	10,928	71.4	72.6	841	75.1	8.7	-19.2	14.7	2.8	0.0	100.0	16.2
Jenkins, GA	13165	5,557	68.2	70.6	313	80.8	12.8	-15.1	12.4	11.7	0.0	0.0	11.6
Johnson, GA	13167	6,832	70.8	65.5	398	90.7	8.9	-19.0	10.4	6.1	0.0	0.0	0.0
Jones, GA	13169	18,845	53.0	85.4	1,311	87.0	17.2	-10.7	18.2	12.3	0.0	89.3	0.0
Lamar, GA	13171	11,524	65.8	76.2	1,400	86.0	9.7	-18.2	10.3	9.2	0.0	0.0	0.0
Lanier, GA	13173	5,830	61.0	76.8	418	66.3	9.4	-18.5	10.8	5.8	0.0	0.0	0.0
Laurens, GA	13175	31,374	62.4	79.6	2,058	93.1	15.9	-12.0	19.4	8.2	0.0	54.7	6.9
Lee, GA	13177	17,707	48.2	83.4	1,813	86.7	19.2	-8.7	20.2	15.3	87.0	9.0	10.5
Liberty, GA	13179	34,823	45.9	88.7	5,580	78.7	16.3	-11.6	20.8	11.7	18.5	22.3	11.1
Lincoln, GA	13181	5,582	64.9	77.4	341	97.1	9.7	-18.2	11.5	4.6	0.0	20.0	36.4
Long, GA	13183	7,311	61.3	78.7	639	80.3	9.1	-18.8	10.8	4.4	0.0	0.0	13.6
Lowndes, GA	13185	60,458	48.7	82.9	14,155	95.4	22.3	-5.6	27.9	11.7	13.6	21.4	18.7
Lumpkin, GA	13187	18,121	54.1	80.9	3,980	89.1	19.5	-8.4	20.3	5.6	19.2	45.8	1.1
McDuffie, GA	13189	14,110	65.6	70.1	863	81.0	11.5	-16.4	15.5	4.8	41.7	29.7	8.1
McIntosh, GA	13191	9,251	62.6	75.1	605	89.8	15.0	-12.9	20.4	2.5	0.0	100.0	47.9
Macon, GA	13193	9,624	69.1	67.5	675	87.4	10.7	-17.2	16.8	5.9	0.0	73.6	0.0
Madison, GA	13195	18,669	66.9	72.9	1,094	64.4	12.9	-15.0	13.5	8.6	0.0	0.0	7.6
Marion, GA	13197	5,508	70.3	80.2	207	75.4	6.8	-21.1	7.7	4.3	0.0	19.6	8.2
Meriwether, GA	13199	14,942	70.7	72.8	803	76.1	9.7	-18.2	12.2	5.8	0.0	50.0	14.2
Miller, GA	13201	4,224	65.6	73.4	378	94.2	9.5	-18.4	11.8	3.4	0.0	0.0	0.0
Mitchell, GA	13205	15,428	69.8	66.0	1,049	95.3	9.6	-18.3	15.2	3.9	20.6	0.0	0.0
Monroe, GA	13207	17,422	56.5	80.7	1,279	63.5	19.0	-8.9	21.6	10.5	0.0	78.0	6.9
Montgomery, GA	13209	5,694	60.5	81.3	884	27.8	15.5	-12.4	20.6	3.1	0.0	22.7	0.0
Morgan, GA	13211	12,267	54.9	78.9	802	80.3	23.8	-4.1	28.6	8.8	0.0	27.0	19.9
Murray, GA	13213	25,452	73.4	66.2	1,289	89.8	6.7	-21.2	7.3	0.0	5.1	22.7	0.6
Muscogee, GA	13215	116,071	45.6	83.8	15,378	88.8	21.6	-6.3	28.2	13.8	15.0	40.4	16.4
Newton, GA	13217	60,054	50.2	83.4	5,823	66.0	19.4	-8.5	19.1	19.8	17.7	31.6	15.2
Oconee, GA	13219	20,160	30.0	88.7	1,830	77.2	45.0	17.1	46.9	9.6	0.0	79.8	18.4
Oglethorpe, GA	13221	9,630	58.9	75.7	710	69.9	11.7	-16.2	13.2	4.8	100.0	54.8	1.2
Paulding, GA	13223	83,208	50.6	85.9	6,768	77.5	20.9	-7.0	20.1	24.8	0.0	42.2	19.3
Peach, GA	13225	16,134	55.7	80.1	4,131	92.1	18.0	-9.9	19.7	16.9	0.0	23.2	4.5
Pickens, GA	13227	20,387	53.3	79.3	1,061	78.5	22.0	-5.9	22.1	3.9	0.0	36.8	21.6
Pierce, GA	13229	11,968	63.1	77.4	654	92.2	8.8	-19.1	9.5	4.2	0.0	16.7	0.0
Pike, GA	13231	11,276	56.5	83.0	876	88.8	15.7	-12.2	17.0	5.5	0.0	0.0	43.6
Polk, GA	13233	26,341	66.7	71.6	1,659	78.1	11.4	-16.5	12.5	7.3	62.3	8.0	4.3
Pulaski, GA	13235	8,272	69.0	77.2	602	97.3	5.6	-22.3	7.7	1.0	0.0	0.0	0.0
Putnam, GA	13237	14,743	55.2	80.4	1,025	78.2	18.8	-9.1	23.5	6.4	0.0	81.0	0.0
Quitman, GA	13239	1,592	71.4	66.5	0	0.0	7.4	-20.5	13.7	1.5	0.0	0.0	0.0
Rabun, GA	13241	11,794	50.0	80.5	573	72.6	24.7	-3.2	26.4	0.0	0.0	52.6	1.4
Randolph, GA	13243	4,998	63.7	70.5	577	28.4	13.1	-14.8	19.6	8.8	0.0	0.0	0.0

Note. Data in columns 26 through 41 from the American Community Survey are subject to sampling error, which can be especially large in small counties and small population groups. See notes and definitions for more information.

[3]May be of any race.

Table C-1. Population, School, and Student Characteristics by County, Selected Years—*Continued*

County	State/ County Code	County Type[1]	Population, 2010		Percent of related children 5–17 years in poverty, 2010	Percent of children under 19 years with no health insurance, 2010	Number of schools and students, 2010–2011			Resident enrollment, 2006–2010 K–12 enrollment	
			Total	Percent 5–17 years			School districts	Schools	Students	Number	Percent public
			1	2	3	4	5	6	7	8	9
GEORGIA—*(Continued)*											
Richmond, GA	13245	2	200,549	17.2	36.0	6.7	1	59	32,322	34,857	90.8
Rockdale, GA	13247	1	85,215	20.1	22.0	10.7	1	19	15,864	16,719	88.9
Schley, GA	13249	8	5,010	23.7	21.4	11.5	2	2	1,426	1,120	97.1
Screven, GA	13251	6	14,593	18.5	32.9	9.6	1	4	2,473	2,993	94.3
Seminole, GA	13253	6	8,729	17.2	36.7	9.9	1	2	1,611	1,447	90.7
Spalding, GA	13255	1	64,073	18.1	32.4	9.3	2	20	10,685	11,776	91.1
Stephens, GA	13257	7	26,175	16.6	31.2	11.0	1	7	4,075	4,403	93.1
Stewart, GA	13259	8	6,058	11.2	43.4	9.5	1	3	548	1,086	89.7
Sumter, GA	13261	6	32,819	18.1	42.3	8.6	1	10	5,044	6,524	86.3
Talbot, GA	13263	8	6,865	16.1	32.6	10.1	1	1	599	1,233	74.0
Taliaferro, GA	13265	8	1,717	13.2	48.0	11.1	1	1	218	364	95.3
Tattnall, GA	13267	6	25,520	15.3	32.9	14.5	1	7	3,634	4,036	90.6
Taylor, GA	13269	8	8,906	18.4	30.6	9.4	1	5	1,543	1,864	98.8
Telfair, GA	13271	7	16,500	14.4	37.2	10.3	1	3	1,758	2,492	98.2
Terrell, GA	13273	3	9,315	17.6	40.4	7.7	1	4	1,517	1,854	82.3
Thomas, GA	13275	4	44,720	18.1	30.9	9.4	2	13	8,355	8,384	91.6
Tift, GA	13277	4	40,118	18.4	31.3	10.6	1	13	7,755	7,875	93.7
Toombs, GA	13279	7	27,223	19.8	37.7	10.6	2	10	5,608	5,321	93.2
Towns, GA	13281	9	10,471	12.0	25.7	13.5	1	3	1,150	1,151	89.8
Treutlen, GA	13283	7	6,885	17.7	39.9	9.2	1	2	1,198	1,231	91.2
Troup, GA	13285	4	67,044	19.5	28.5	8.9	1	23	12,648	12,740	93.9
Turner, GA	13287	6	8,930	18.0	38.1	9.8	1	4	1,616	1,736	92.5
Twiggs, GA	13289	3	9,023	14.8	29.7	11.3	1	3	988	1,655	81.5
Union, GA	13291	9	21,356	13.4	28.7	14.9	2	6	3,610	2,923	74.9
Upson, GA	13293	6	27,153	17.4	30.5	8.9	1	6	4,629	5,065	93.5
Walker, GA	13295	2	68,756	17.5	24.3	9.2	2	17	10,616	12,228	89.4
Walton, GA	13297	1	83,768	20.0	18.5	11.2	2	19	14,966	15,804	86.1
Ware, GA	13299	4	36,312	16.7	32.5	9.6	2	10	5,951	6,698	96.7
Warren, GA	13301	8	5,834	16.6	38.0	9.1	1	3	770	1,096	91.8
Washington, GA	13303	7	21,187	17.2	33.8	9.4	2	6	3,190	3,621	92.4
Wayne, GA	13305	6	30,099	17.5	34.8	11.5	1	8	5,446	5,615	95.4
Webster, GA	13307	8	2,799	19.5	27.2	15.2	1	2	468	578	87.7
Wheeler, GA	13309	9	7,421	13.3	35.7	11.2	1	3	1,001	943	100.0
White, GA	13311	8	27,144	17.0	22.6	11.6	2	8	3,842	4,242	91.3
Whitfield, GA	13313	3	102,599	20.6	23.9	13.0	2	33	20,440	20,472	94.8
Wilcox, GA	13315	9	9,255	14.1	35.1	10.4	1	3	1,332	1,495	97.5
Wilkes, GA	13317	6	10,593	16.3	35.3	9.7	1	5	1,662	1,727	98.8
Wilkinson, GA	13319	8	9,563	17.4	30.5	10.1	1	4	1,588	1,808	93.9
Worth, GA	13321	3	21,679	18.0	28.7	9.3	1	4	3,532	4,097	86.6
HAWAII	15000	X	1,360,301	15.9	13.0	4.1	1	289	179,601	217,247	81.0
Hawaii, HI	15001	5	185,079	16.4	22.1	5.6	(5)	(5)	(5)	30,813	82.6
Honolulu, HI	15003	2	953,207	15.7	10.8	3.6	1[5]	289[5]	179601[5]	149,965	79.3
Kalawao, HI	15005	9	90	0.0	0.0	0.0	(5)	(5)	(5)	0	0.0
Kauai, HI	15007	5	67,091	16.3	14.7	5.3	(5)	(5)	(5)	11,036	87.7
Maui, HI	15009	5	154,834	16.7	14.4	4.8	(5)	(5)	(5)	25,433	85.8
IDAHO	16000	X	1,567,582	19.6	17.2	11.1	151	748	276,081	295,085	92.0
Ada, ID	16001	2	392,365	19.2	12.9	9.6	13	126	71,330	72,495	91.8
Adams, ID	16003	8	3,976	14.4	22.5	18.4	2	3	414	756	86.4
Bannock, ID	16005	3	82,839	19.0	17.9	8.8	4	37	14,084	15,128	94.0
Bear Lake, ID	16007	7	5,986	20.5	17.6	12.7	1	6	1,102	1,150	96.5
Benewah, ID	16009	6	9,285	17.2	22.4	11.0	2	8	1,427	1,752	96.4
Bingham, ID	16011	6	45,607	23.3	17.8	12.7	7	33	9,837	10,122	96.2
Blaine, ID	16013	7	21,376	17.7	12.7	15.3	1	9	3,197	3,694	86.0
Boise, ID	16015	2	7,028	17.1	17.4	14.1	3	7	889	1,280	78.6
Bonner, ID	16017	6	40,877	16.4	21.3	11.4	2	19	5,204	6,594	83.8
Bonneville, ID	16019	3	104,234	21.9	15.2	9.0	6	47	21,040	21,154	92.1

[1]County type codes are from the Economic Research Service of the United States Department of Agriculture. See notes and definitions for more information.
[5]Hawaii, Kalawao, Kauai, and Maui counties are included with Honolulu county.

Table C-1. Population, School, and Student Characteristics by County, Selected Years—*Continued*

County	State/ County Code	Characteristics of students, 2010–2011				Number of graduates, 2008–2009	Staff and students, 2010–2011			
		Percent with IEP[2]	Percent eligible for free or reduced lunch	Percent minority	Percent English-language learners		Total staff	Number of teachers	Student/ teacher ratio	Central admin. staff
		10	11	12	13	14	15	16	17	18
GEORGIA—*(Continued)*										
Richmond, GA	13245	8.7	73.8	79.8	0.4	1,529	4,456	2,176	14.9	66
Rockdale, GA	13247	8.3	61.7	76.6	3.7	1,033	2,276	1,088	14.6	32
Schley, GA	13249	8.5	52.9	22.5	0.4	63	206	84	17.0	13
Screven, GA	13251	17.1	78.1	54.6	. . .	209	351	165	15.0	9
Seminole, GA	13253	7.7	72.8	50.0	0.7	76	236	115	14.0	4
Spalding, GA	13255	9.8	70.4	53.1	1.2	496	1,612	732	14.6	50
Stephens, GA	13257	13.1	57.1	22.6	1.7	. . .	684	314	13.0	12
Stewart, GA	13259	12.0	90.5	94.3	. . .	41	113	43	12.9	5
Sumter, GA	13261	11.5	84.6	83.5	3.2	251	785	340	14.9	18
Talbot, GA	13263	12.4	90.0	95.8	. . .	36	116	53	11.3	5
Taliaferro, GA	13265	13.3	93.6	88.1	. . .	20	48	23	9.5	3
Tattnall, GA	13267	10.7	74.7	46.0	5.5	144	532	224	16.2	13
Taylor, GA	13269	10.2	78.5	45.2	. . .	73	262	116	13.3	6
Telfair, GA	13271	9.5	74.9	45.2	1.4	84	269	121	14.5	8
Terrell, GA	13273	12.2	83.4	95.4	0.2	80	241	90	16.9	5
Thomas, GA	13275	12.0	64.8	50.3	0.8	465	1,167	559	15.0	29
Tift, GA	13277	11.1	65.3	54.5	7.0	398	1,095	519	14.9	23
Toombs, GA	13279	10.4	69.4	48.7	3.2	268	748	377	14.9	16
Towns, GA	13281	8.5	58.0	3.0	1.2	70	206	90	12.7	11
Treutlen, GA	13283	12.0	71.7	42.7	. . .	57	151	71	16.9	6
Troup, GA	13285	8.0	62.1	48.2	1.2	683	1,862	896	14.1	27
Turner, GA	13287	13.0	77.5	62.4	0.7	94	275	119	13.6	8
Twiggs, GA	13289	12.3	87.1	66.5	. . .	64	176	76	13.1	7
Union, GA	13291	12.2	42.2	5.7	1.7	370	519	256	14.1	16
Upson, GA	13293	10.1	66.0	40.9	0.6	263	665	293	15.8	11
Walker, GA	13295	12.9	64.3	10.2	0.3	544	1,617	763	13.9	33
Walton, GA	13297	9.8	49.2	31.0	0.9	690	1,818	978	15.3	46
Ware, GA	13299	12.4	66.5	44.8	1.3	346	930	424	14.0	28
Warren, GA	13301	13.0	89.1	93.0	. . .	34	137	51	15.1	7
Washington, GA	13303	8.9	67.5	70.1	0.5	218	473	215	14.8	15
Wayne, GA	13305	12.1	63.5	30.9	1.9	314	766	343	15.9	13
Webster, GA	13307	7.5	73.5	55.1	2.1	1	71	33	14.1	4
Wheeler, GA	13309	13.3	78.5	42.2	2.5	55	154	72	13.9	4
White, GA	13311	12.2	54.7	9.2	1.1	227	690	300	12.8	37
Whitfield, GA	13313	8.4	70.4	55.8	14.8	1,029	2,420	1,295	15.8	50
Wilcox, GA	13315	10.4	73.7	46.6	. . .	75	173	79	16.8	10
Wilkes, GA	13317	11.0	75.6	61.0	1.6	94	259	113	14.7	9
Wilkinson, GA	13319	10.5	83.4	61.7	1.9	81	275	120	13.3	5
Worth, GA	13321	5.8	68.9	41.1	0.2	234	460	221	16.0	14
HAWAII	15000	11.0	46.8	85.5	10.6	11,508	21,704	11,396	15.8	795
Hawaii, HI	15001	(5)	61.5	82.1	(5)	(5)	(5)	(5)	(5)	(5)
Honolulu, HI	15003	11[5]	43.7	87.0	10.6[5]	11,508[5]	21,704[5]	11,396[5]	15.8[5]	795[5]
Kalawao, HI	15005	. . .	. . .	. . .	. . .	0	0	0	0.0	0
Kauai, HI	15007	(5)	45.0	82.6	(5)	(5)	(5)	(5)	(5)	(5)
Maui, HI	15009	(5)	47.4	82.7	(5)	(5)	(5)	(5)	(5)	(5)
IDAHO	16000	9.9	45.0	21.5	5.6	16,807	27,919	15,803	17.5	716
Ada, ID	16001	10.0	30.7	16.7	4.6	4,025	6,904	3,863	18.5	155
Adams, ID	16003	13.5	58.2	5.1	1.0	25	62	40	10.4	4
Bannock, ID	16005	9.7	44.3	16.0	0.6	935	1,319	751	18.8	34
Bear Lake, ID	16007	10.4	43.6	5.9	0.1	93	140	67	16.4	4
Benewah, ID	16009	15.0	57.7	16.3	0.1	113	200	106	13.4	8
Bingham, ID	16011	9.7	49.5	29.0	13.2	625	1,029	573	17.2	28
Blaine, ID	16013	9.9	37.9	36.8	19.3	187	484	268	11.9	18
Boise, ID	16015	13.2	49.0	7.3	. . .	70	137	76	11.7	7
Bonner, ID	16017	11.1	48.4	9.6	0.2	411	636	356	14.6	16
Bonneville, ID	16019	9.5	41.9	20.3	3.9	1,310	1,977	1,107	19.0	47

[2]IEP=Individual Education Program. See notes and definitions for more information.
[5]Hawaii, Kalawao, Kauai, and Maui counties are included with Honolulu county.
. . . = Not available.

Table C-1. Population, School, and Student Characteristics by County, Selected Years—*Continued*

County	State/ County Code	Revenues, 2008–2009				Current expenditures, 2008–2009			Resident population 16 to 19 years, 2006–2010			
		Total revenue ($1,000's)	Percentage of revenue from			Amount ($1,000's)	Amount per student	Percent for instruction	Total population 16 to 19 years	Percent enrolled in school	Percent high school graduates, not enrolled in school	Percent not enrolled, not grads, not employed, or not in labor force
			Federal government	State government	Local government							
		19	20	21	22	23	24	25	26	27	28	29
GEORGIA—*(Continued)*												
Richmond, GA	13245	347,097	14.1	48.9	37.0	308,765	9,438	62.9	12,909	71.7	17.6	8.1
Rockdale, GA	13247	155,905	8.2	40.9	50.9	155,889	9,926	62.3	5,584	80.0	8.9	6.1
Schley, GA	13249	15,404	12.5	59.4	28.1	14,269	10,280	55.3	307	88.3	4.9	6.8
Screven, GA	13251	25,669	14.1	57.5	28.4	25,297	9,355	60.2	1,223	79.2	12.5	7.4
Seminole, GA	13253	16,111	14.6	57.1	28.3	16,040	9,634	63.2	574	68.8	14.1	17.1
Spalding, GA	13255	111,287	11.5	50.9	37.6	104,700	9,674	60.2	3,744	80.5	6.4	9.1
Stephens, GA	13257	...	...	...	...	...	...	...	1,613	86.4	10.7	2.9
Stewart, GA	13259	7,765	21.1	46.6	32.3	7,467	12,261	54.2	292	80.8	9.3	9.9
Sumter, GA	13261	55,335	16.6	53.4	30.1	50,155	9,625	61.7	2,395	73.8	9.0	16.2
Talbot, GA	13263	9,912	29.5	32.1	38.4	9,399	14,328	54.7	421	74.8	16.6	1.9
Taliaferro, GA	13265	3,306	16.5	48.5	35.1	3,162	13,688	59.3	84	85.7	14.3	0.0
Tattnall, GA	13267	31,901	15.2	60.1	24.6	31,128	8,940	62.6	1,614	62.5	9.2	20.0
Taylor, GA	13269	17,040	17.9	57.5	24.6	16,802	10,567	60.0	505	85.9	12.7	1.4
Telfair, GA	13271	17,810	15.4	52.4	32.3	16,535	9,443	63.5	1,057	72.4	10.0	10.4
Terrell, GA	13273	16,822	19.2	51.5	29.4	16,416	10,836	57.7	585	75.2	13.7	11.1
Thomas, GA	13275	88,650	10.6	52.2	37.2	79,579	9,323	61.3	2,677	75.6	9.5	13.0
Tift, GA	13277	72,350	12.2	52.9	34.9	66,467	8,802	68.5	2,975	85.8	4.7	2.9
Toombs, GA	13279	54,718	12.8	60.1	27.1	49,493	8,919	64.8	1,505	62.8	24.8	9.2
Towns, GA	13281	13,449	10.5	27.6	61.9	13,537	11,600	60.8	945	96.7	2.1	0.3
Treutlen, GA	13283	11,190	16.6	63.3	20.1	11,177	9,102	65.3	284	91.6	2.8	5.6
Troup, GA	13285	128,365	9.7	49.7	40.7	117,709	9,384	59.5	4,022	82.9	8.5	7.1
Turner, GA	13287	18,669	22.8	53.3	24.0	18,389	10,722	57.3	646	63.2	20.7	12.9
Twiggs, GA	13289	12,244	25.2	43.4	31.4	11,908	11,472	54.8	698	55.4	29.1	3.7
Union, GA	13291	36,916	9.0	46.1	44.9	34,147	10,211	63.0	788	77.9	12.6	3.8
Upson, GA	13293	45,160	12.7	57.6	29.7	43,364	9,047	63.2	1,647	76.3	9.0	10.0
Walker, GA	13295	105,957	9.7	57.2	33.2	96,459	8,995	64.7	3,359	69.3	12.7	14.3
Walton, GA	13297	147,445	7.9	43.6	48.4	127,595	8,714	64.8	4,282	73.5	14.1	10.5
Ware, GA	13299	68,179	12.6	58.7	28.7	66,024	10,989	62.0	2,070	82.6	7.0	9.3
Warren, GA	13301	9,187	16.0	43.0	40.9	8,269	10,601	49.0	418	88.8	1.9	9.3
Washington, GA	13303	43,638	11.4	46.4	42.2	34,509	10,366	55.9	1,201	75.1	15.7	8.0
Wayne, GA	13305	47,456	11.6	61.8	26.6	48,376	8,919	62.7	1,655	71.4	10.1	14.7
Webster, GA	13307	5,773	15.6	52.8	31.6	5,109	10,448	62.6	56	91.1	8.9	0.0
Wheeler, GA	13309	10,560	15.6	58.4	26.0	9,837	9,560	54.8	307	73.9	7.5	18.6
White, GA	13311	52,160	11.0	43.7	45.3	51,038	13,250	54.0	1,434	82.7	5.1	2.4
Whitfield, GA	13313	207,294	9.8	50.5	39.7	190,845	9,473	63.8	5,748	77.0	10.0	10.2
Wilcox, GA	13315	12,257	13.6	67.0	19.5	11,964	9,091	63.3	567	69.8	6.2	24.0
Wilkes, GA	13317	17,349	13.3	47.8	38.8	16,287	9,339	60.0	688	79.7	5.2	7.4
Wilkinson, GA	13319	21,299	20.8	35.1	44.1	20,103	12,016	56.5	575	74.6	19.0	6.4
Worth, GA	13321	35,937	13.4	61.5	25.1	32,332	8,677	61.6	1,227	69.6	15.2	11.9
HAWAII	15000	2,689,758	14.6	82.0	3.4	2,225,437	12,400	63.0	69,042	79.0	15.8	3.6
Hawaii, HI	15001	([5])	([5])	([5])	([5])	([5])	([5])	([5])	9,683	84.6	10.6	2.8
Honolulu, HI	15003	2,689,758[5]	14.6[5]	82.0[5]	3.4[5]	2,225,437[5]	12,400[5]	63.0[5]	48,744	78.8	16.3	3.6
Kalawao, HI	15005	0	0.0	0.0	0.0	0	0	0.0	0	0.0	0.0	0.0
Kauai, HI	15007	([5])	([5])	([5])	([5])	([5])	([5])	([5])	3,486	76.1	15.7	6.0
Maui, HI	15009	([5])	([5])	([5])	([5])	([5])	([5])	([5])	7,129	74.2	19.2	3.8
IDAHO	16000	2,226,585	10.0	67.3	22.7	1,941,099	7,057	61.1	92,068	79.7	13.2	4.0
Ada, ID	16001	554,301	6.5	63.3	30.2	483,335	7,001	62.2	20,520	84.6	10.1	2.7
Adams, ID	16003	4,918	12.6	75.8	11.6	4,400	9,110	60.0	234	77.8	15.8	6.4
Bannock, ID	16005	101,594	12.7	71.0	16.3	92,113	6,627	61.9	5,016	75.0	18.0	4.2
Bear Lake, ID	16007	8,558	10.8	81.3	7.9	8,105	7,185	58.5	286	74.1	16.8	4.2
Benewah, ID	16009	14,587	21.9	68.4	9.7	14,504	9,321	53.8	468	77.4	17.5	2.6
Bingham, ID	16011	73,502	12.3	76.1	11.6	66,680	6,700	60.9	2,935	78.5	16.8	3.3
Blaine, ID	16013	58,519	2.4	29.2	68.4	46,762	14,213	64.6	799	92.0	5.6	2.0
Boise, ID	16015	11,655	11.9	59.9	28.2	9,199	9,255	51.6	246	86.2	10.6	3.3
Bonner, ID	16017	49,399	9.1	62.3	28.6	40,896	7,616	58.0	2,032	73.5	15.6	4.5
Bonneville, ID	16019	147,171	8.1	71.9	20.0	127,992	6,174	61.7	5,985	76.7	14.1	4.2

Note. Data in columns 26 through 41 from the American Community Survey are subject to sampling error, which can be especially large in small counties and small population groups. See notes and definitions for more information.

[5]Hawaii, Kalawao, Kauai, and Maui counties are included with Honolulu county.

. . . = Not available.

Table C-1. Population, School, and Student Characteristics by County, Selected Years—*Continued*

County	State/ County Code	High school graduates, 2006–2010			College enrollment, 2006–2010		College graduates, 2006–2010 (percent)						
		Population 25 years and over	High school diploma or less (percent)	High school diploma or more (percent)	Number	Percent public	Bachelor's degree or more	+/- U.S. percent with Bachelor's degree or more	Non-Hispanic White	Black or African American	American Indian and Alaska Native	Asian, Hawaiian, and Pacific Islander	Hispanic or Latino[3]
		30	31	32	33	34	35	36	37	38	39	40	41
GEORGIA— *(Continued)*													
Richmond, GA	13245	123,819	48.9	82.3	16,566	78.6	20.3	-7.6	27.7	13.4	9.3	34.5	18.0
Rockdale, GA	13247	53,162	45.0	84.8	5,532	67.9	23.6	-4.3	22.1	25.7	42.2	56.7	11.8
Schley, GA	13249	2,983	64.7	71.4	195	93.8	8.7	-19.2	12.1	1.0	0.0	0.0	0.0
Screven, GA	13251	9,543	68.3	74.7	681	89.4	11.4	-16.5	15.3	5.4	0.0	37.5	53.7
Seminole, GA	13253	5,935	60.7	77.0	511	100.0	10.3	-17.6	12.6	4.5	0.0	73.3	0.0
Spalding, GA	13255	41,324	62.0	74.8	3,049	84.1	13.6	-14.3	15.4	9.1	22.5	58.8	3.5
Stephens, GA	13257	17,538	63.7	74.8	1,876	41.3	13.3	-14.6	14.9	2.3	0.0	24.8	0.0
Stewart, GA	13259	4,021	67.7	70.4	175	92.0	11.0	-16.9	17.6	6.0	0.0	100.0	0.0
Sumter, GA	13261	19,989	58.1	75.4	2,398	88.4	18.9	-9.0	27.7	8.8	24.3	78.3	7.0
Talbot, GA	13263	4,907	68.5	78.7	272	66.2	10.9	-17.0	20.6	3.6	0.0	0.0	0.0
Taliaferro, GA	13265	1,433	79.1	58.4	59	67.8	6.8	-21.1	11.9	0.6	100.0	100.0	0.0
Tattnall, GA	13267	16,179	71.3	74.0	965	73.6	11.9	-16.0	14.6	4.8	28.6	10.6	11.9
Taylor, GA	13269	5,934	72.1	63.5	230	84.3	7.4	-20.5	8.9	3.8	0.0	100.0	0.0
Telfair, GA	13271	11,249	76.1	68.9	431	84.9	8.1	-19.8	12.1	3.9	0.0	15.8	3.8
Terrell, GA	13273	6,224	66.9	65.8	435	97.5	9.9	-18.0	18.9	2.7	0.0	70.6	0.0
Thomas, GA	13275	29,518	56.2	81.4	1,687	78.9	19.6	-8.3	23.9	12.2	41.2	22.6	10.1
Tift, GA	13277	24,801	55.0	75.9	2,491	92.7	16.3	-11.6	21.1	5.4	0.0	58.3	3.8
Toombs, GA	13279	16,991	60.2	80.1	904	85.2	14.3	-13.6	17.9	6.5	0.0	21.4	4.5
Towns, GA	13281	7,691	50.9	86.5	1,170	15.2	20.8	-7.1	21.1	0.0	13.2	0.0	0.0
Treutlen, GA	13283	4,552	70.1	73.0	127	100.0	9.9	-18.0	11.0	6.1	0.0	31.4	0.0
Troup, GA	13285	41,567	55.5	79.3	3,784	63.3	19.4	-8.5	24.4	8.1	34.2	54.6	11.6
Turner, GA	13287	5,732	65.7	68.5	404	68.3	13.2	-14.7	16.2	9.0	0.0	0.0	0.0
Twiggs, GA	13289	6,352	78.1	61.4	417	87.5	6.7	-21.2	8.5	4.3	0.0	0.0	0.0
Union, GA	13291	16,053	46.0	82.9	688	68.0	21.6	-6.3	21.1	39.6	0.0	36.2	0.0
Upson, GA	13293	18,314	63.9	76.1	1,300	91.8	11.3	-16.6	13.5	5.3	0.0	61.8	0.0
Walker, GA	13295	46,088	59.2	76.3	2,385	79.2	12.9	-15.0	12.9	4.2	25.7	68.1	11.9
Walton, GA	13297	53,054	55.5	80.4	2,971	77.8	17.3	-10.6	18.1	12.1	28.8	34.0	7.7
Ware, GA	13299	23,880	61.3	79.6	1,529	94.2	12.2	-15.7	13.8	8.2	0.0	65.9	2.4
Warren, GA	13301	4,029	77.3	69.7	138	78.3	4.7	-23.2	9.2	1.4	0.0	0.0	0.0
Washington, GA	13303	14,046	67.7	74.8	694	94.5	10.7	-17.2	18.4	2.9	0.0	0.0	6.4
Wayne, GA	13305	19,710	62.3	77.9	1,387	87.2	10.9	-17.0	12.8	3.2	0.0	25.9	8.2
Webster, GA	13307	1,871	69.0	78.1	64	100.0	7.9	-20.0	12.2	0.0	0.0	60.9	0.0
Wheeler, GA	13309	5,145	76.4	69.7	264	75.0	8.6	-19.3	10.3	4.7	0.0	100.0	0.0
White, GA	13311	18,526	53.1	83.3	1,136	58.5	19.6	-8.3	19.5	12.2	30.1	0.0	27.1
Whitfield, GA	13313	61,689	62.1	67.4	5,034	85.9	15.1	-12.8	18.2	9.1	4.6	49.5	4.5
Wilcox, GA	13315	6,386	68.7	73.0	317	78.5	8.8	-19.1	12.3	3.0	0.0	7.7	0.0
Wilkes, GA	13317	7,435	66.5	71.8	537	86.0	15.5	-12.4	22.5	6.6	10.0	0.0	0.0
Wilkinson, GA	13319	6,432	68.6	79.2	337	78.9	12.1	-15.8	16.6	5.3	0.0	0.0	0.0
Worth, GA	13321	14,170	65.4	73.6	1,075	92.3	9.4	-18.5	12.1	2.0	0.0	22.9	0.0
HAWAII	15000	903,810	39.2	89.8	92,102	73.2	29.4	1.5	42.0	26.0	21.3	27.2	17.5
Hawaii, HI	15001	123,533	40.9	90.5	10,406	81.9	26.6	-1.3	37.5	32.0	27.4	22.7	10.2
Honolulu, HI	15003	631,112	38.1	89.9	72,894	70.9	31.1	3.2	45.7	25.9	18.9	29.1	20.4
Kalawao, HI	15005	74	41.9	79.7	4	100.0	24.3	-3.6	57.7	0.0	0.0	0.0	0.0
Kauai, HI	15007	45,286	42.0	88.3	2,671	87.1	22.7	-5.2	33.3	15.7	36.2	17.6	15.1
Maui, HI	15009	103,805	42.6	88.7	6,127	80.9	25.7	-2.2	38.4	25.5	14.8	19.4	14.3
IDAHO	16000	952,630	40.7	88.2	100,476	75.6	24.3	-3.6	25.7	23.6	9.8	39.4	7.8
Ada, ID	16001	244,071	30.1	92.9	28,464	84.5	35.0	7.1	35.8	21.5	10.4	46.1	20.5
Adams, ID	16003	2,852	50.8	88.4	116	75.9	21.3	-6.6	21.3	0.0	52.4	40.5	13.0
Bannock, ID	16005	47,842	35.5	90.5	7,698	93.5	27.3	-0.6	27.9	33.0	11.0	50.4	13.3
Bear Lake, ID	16007	3,954	47.7	90.4	172	84.3	16.7	-11.2	16.8	100.0	0.0	0.0	0.0
Benewah, ID	16009	6,397	56.4	87.2	228	84.2	12.1	-15.8	12.3	0.0	11.2	0.0	4.7
Bingham, ID	16011	25,743	48.7	84.6	2,145	84.8	15.9	-12.0	18.7	13.0	3.2	39.2	2.4
Blaine, ID	16013	14,768	27.0	92.0	705	70.6	43.2	15.3	48.9	100.0	5.9	30.3	9.3
Boise, ID	16015	5,123	42.3	87.2	247	96.8	23.9	-4.0	24.8	0.0	0.0	0.0	3.4
Bonner, ID	16017	29,200	42.0	91.0	1,085	74.3	22.5	-5.4	22.7	50.0	6.3	37.2	6.6
Bonneville, ID	16019	59,824	37.3	90.6	4,518	81.2	26.2	-1.7	27.8	13.8	9.5	38.6	7.0

Note. Data in columns 26 through 41 from the American Community Survey are subject to sampling error, which can be especially large in small counties and small population groups. See notes and definitions for more information.

[3]May be of any race.

Table C-1. Population, School, and Student Characteristics by County, Selected Years—*Continued*

County	State/ County Code	County Type[1]	Population, 2010		Percent of related children 5–17 years in poverty, 2010	Percent of children under 19 years with no health insurance, 2010	Number of schools and students, 2010–2011			Resident enrollment, 2006–2010 K–12 enrollment	
			Total	Percent 5–17 years			School districts	Schools	Students	Number	Percent public
			1	2	3	4	5	6	7	8	9
IDAHO—*(Continued)*											
Boundary, ID	16021	7	10,972	19.4	21.7	13.8	1	6	1,514	1,955	89.3
Butte, ID	16023	8	2,891	20.8	18.7	15.0	1	4	460	533	97.4
Camas, ID	16025	9	1,117	15.8	13.7	19.7	1	2	149	319	93.7
Canyon, ID	16027	2	188,923	22.4	22.7	11.0	15	79	35,450	39,607	91.2
Caribou, ID	16029	6	6,963	21.1	14.0	12.1	3	9	1,455	1,386	96.0
Cassia, ID	16031	7	22,952	23.7	19.0	13.6	1	17	5,071	5,287	93.8
Clark, ID	16033	8	982	23.0	23.4	19.8	1	2	195	112	100.0
Clearwater, ID	16035	6	8,761	13.5	22.6	11.4	1	6	1,089	1,276	93.7
Custer, ID	16037	9	4,368	14.6	16.4	14.9	2	6	618	609	98.2
Elmore, ID	16039	4	27,038	19.1	19.5	10.2	4	13	4,640	5,087	95.5
Franklin, ID	16041	3	12,786	25.6	13.2	14.0	2	8	3,108	3,190	96.5
Fremont, ID	16043	6	13,242	22.6	21.4	17.2	1	10	2,293	2,673	96.4
Gem, ID	16045	2	16,719	17.9	21.7	12.7	1	11	2,548	3,210	94.9
Gooding, ID	16047	7	15,464	21.2	21.4	15.1	6	12	3,172	3,011	94.9
Idaho, ID	16049	6	16,267	15.6	23.2	13.9	3	11	1,737	2,551	91.9
Jefferson, ID	16051	3	26,140	24.7	14.4	12.9	3	15	5,676	5,888	96.5
Jerome, ID	16053	7	22,374	21.5	22.2	15.6	2	8	4,188	4,602	94.8
Kootenai, ID	16055	3	138,494	18.3	15.0	10.7	5	45	21,204	24,728	87.4
Latah, ID	16057	4	37,244	13.0	13.0	8.5	7	19	4,978	4,861	88.0
Lemhi, ID	16059	7	7,936	14.5	28.6	12.5	2	8	1,008	1,120	97.2
Lewis, ID	16061	8	3,821	16.0	24.5	14.1	3	5	878	650	91.1
Lincoln, ID	16063	9	5,208	24.0	16.6	18.2	3	5	918	1,060	96.6
Madison, ID	16065	6	37,536	16.4	19.5	9.3	2	16	6,489	5,924	97.5
Minidoka, ID	16067	7	20,069	21.0	19.9	12.3	1	10	4,144	4,172	95.5
Nez Perce, ID	16069	3	39,265	16.0	15.2	8.4	3	18	5,515	6,228	91.9
Oneida, ID	16071	8	4,286	22.3	14.5	14.9	1	5	873	1,001	99.5
Owyhee, ID	16073	2	11,526	21.5	28.5	19.6	4	13	2,385	2,464	89.0
Payette, ID	16075	6	22,623	21.0	20.1	13.0	3	13	4,283	4,761	93.0
Power, ID	16077	3	7,817	21.7	22.9	15.1	3	7	1,514	1,675	99.6
Shoshone, ID	16079	6	12,765	16.0	22.6	8.7	4	11	1,932	1,997	97.5
Teton, ID	16081	9	10,170	20.1	16.7	19.7	1	7	1,576	1,787	96.3
Twin Falls, ID	16083	5	77,230	19.1	17.1	13.4	10	35	13,451	13,810	90.7
Valley, ID	16085	8	9,862	14.6	19.3	17.9	2	8	1,190	1,472	84.9
Washington, ID	16087	6	10,198	19.1	21.3	14.8	3	9	1,856	1,954	93.7
ILLINOIS	17000	X	12,830,632	17.9	18.1	4.9	1,078	4,361	2,090,403	2,317,936	88.5
Adams, IL	17001	5	67,103	16.7	16.9	3.6	9	27	9,616	11,502	84.0
Alexander, IL	17003	7	8,238	15.8	47.4	3.7	5	15	1,005	1,600	93.9
Bond, IL	17005	1	17,768	15.2	16.2	4.1	2	8	2,417	2,670	94.5
Boone, IL	17007	2	54,165	22.1	14.2	5.8	3	18	10,468	11,758	87.9
Brown, IL	17009	7	6,937	11.8	12.9	4.4	1	3	766	1,023	94.0
Bureau, IL	17011	6	34,978	17.5	15.2	4.6	15	26	5,602	6,002	90.9
Calhoun, IL	17013	1	5,089	16.5	13.4	5.6	2	4	647	876	81.7
Carroll, IL	17015	7	15,387	15.8	18.2	4.9	3	11	2,564	2,459	96.9
Cass, IL	17017	6	13,642	18.1	18.4	5.3	4	11	2,498	2,620	93.7
Champaign, IL	17019	3	201,081	13.6	20.0	5.5	19	63	24,047	26,958	90.2
Christian, IL	17021	6	34,800	16.3	17.4	4.1	7	24	6,098	5,980	92.1
Clark, IL	17023	6	16,335	17.1	17.2	4.3	3	9	2,775	2,978	97.5
Clay, IL	17025	7	13,815	16.7	19.7	4.6	4	11	2,400	2,269	100.0
Clinton, IL	17027	1	37,762	16.9	10.5	4.1	13	24	5,470	6,515	86.9
Coles, IL	17029	5	53,873	13.2	20.5	3.5	6	26	6,601	7,087	90.6
Cook, IL	17031	1	5,194,675	17.1	23.9	6.0	171	1,314	787,234	912,465	86.8
Crawford, IL	17033	6	19,817	15.4	17.6	4.2	5	12	3,010	3,388	88.1
Cumberland, IL	17035	9	11,048	16.9	16.2	4.9	2	7	1,770	1,849	94.4
De Kalb, IL	17037	1	105,160	16.0	12.9	4.4	13	46	17,252	16,823	92.0
De Witt, IL	17039	6	16,561	17.3	14.7	3.9	2	10	2,820	2,830	98.0

[1]County type codes are from the Economic Research Service of the United States Department of Agriculture. See notes and definitions for more information.

Table C-1. Population, School, and Student Characteristics by County, Selected Years—*Continued*

County	State/ County Code	Characteristics of students, 2010–2011				Number of graduates, 2008–2009	Staff and students, 2010–2011			
		Percent with IEP[2]	Percent eligible for free or reduced lunch	Percent minority	Percent English-language learners		Total staff	Number of teachers	Student/ teacher ratio	Central admin. staff
		10	11	12	13	14	15	16	17	18
IDAHO—*(Continued)*										
Boundary, ID	16021	11.1	52.8	10.3	0.1	101	180	101	15.0	6
Butte, ID	16023	13.7	42.0	6.3	1.3	24	71	44	10.5	3
Camas, ID	16025	7.4	52.3	7.4	. . .	14	35	22	6.9	2
Canyon, ID	16027	9.8	61.9	36.9	9.6	1,749	3,060	1,823	19.4	73
Caribou, ID	16029	10.2	38.8	8.6	1.0	111	182	104	14.0	7
Cassia, ID	16031	8.0	53.7	34.0	12.9	345	551	301	16.8	8
Clark, ID	16033	7.2	65.6	51.3	16.4	10	31	20	10.0	2
Clearwater, ID	16035	12.6	52.5	14.5	0.1	128	135	67	16.3	5
Custer, ID	16037	13.9	36.1	8.6	1.1	51	88	48	12.8	5
Elmore, ID	16039	13.2	42.8	30.7	6.9	282	420	236	19.7	14
Franklin, ID	16041	8.0	49.8	10.0	2.0	226	286	167	18.6	6
Fremont, ID	16043	10.1	49.1	20.1	8.5	127	216	139	16.6	4
Gem, ID	16045	11.1	54.8	16.1	2.7	186	310	151	16.8	6
Gooding, ID	16047	13.1	56.1	37.1	12.5	195	378	228	13.9	14
Idaho, ID	16049	11.3	49.6	8.2	. . .	126	239	143	12.2	7
Jefferson, ID	16051	8.1	47.4	15.9	5.3	357	531	308	18.5	12
Jerome, ID	16053	8.4	60.6	44.7	16.4	244	444	244	17.1	9
Kootenai, ID	16055	8.3	44.5	9.7	0.1	1,249	1,946	1,121	18.9	31
Latah, ID	16057	10.7	27.0	10.6	0.6	339	613	313	15.9	31
Lemhi, ID	16059	10.5	44.2	2.3	. . .	93	141	74	13.6	6
Lewis, ID	16061	14.1	52.6	18.0	. . .	72	127	79	11.2	5
Lincoln, ID	16063	9.5	70.0	36.2	20.5	55	112	65	14.1	5
Madison, ID	16065	9.8	41.8	8.9	3.8	424	601	336	19.3	10
Minidoka, ID	16067	10.6	59.0	44.1	10.4	270	418	234	17.7	9
Nez Perce, ID	16069	12.2	41.1	20.0	0.3	418	675	363	15.2	21
Oneida, ID	16071	9.2	41.1	7.7	2.1	59	90	54	16.1	3
Owyhee, ID	16073	8.6	65.7	38.4	13.3	159	270	151	15.8	9
Payette, ID	16075	10.5	54.1	27.0	8.0	271	434	255	16.8	10
Power, ID	16077	8.3	66.6	48.0	19.6	126	209	116	13.1	7
Shoshone, ID	16079	13.3	46.7	7.8	. . .	149	265	135	14.3	11
Teton, ID	16081	10.0	48.6	25.4	10.0	78	175	95	16.6	3
Twin Falls, ID	16083	9.5	54.8	23.4	5.8	722	1,391	831	16.2	41
Valley, ID	16085	9.6	38.8	7.8	1.7	98	178	103	11.6	7
Washington, ID	16087	9.6	57.1	26.7	11.9	155	232	128	14.5	6
ILLINOIS	17000	14.5	44.3	48.7	8.3	131,670	158,452	132,983	15.7	2,828
Adams, IL	17001	18.2	49.9	11.4	0.2	736	741	634	15.2	12
Alexander, IL	17003	20.2	75.8	52.9	0.1	84	128	105	9.6	10
Bond, IL	17005	16.7	44.3	9.0	0.2	152	171	152	15.9	3
Boone, IL	17007	14.5	44.7	37.6	9.7	545	735	630	16.6	10
Brown, IL	17009	16.7	35.3	2.8	0.3	. . .	64	57	13.5	1
Bureau, IL	17011	18.5	38.8	18.4	4.5	423	480	424	13.2	13
Calhoun, IL	17013	23.6	44.5	2.8	. . .	57	61	53	12.2	1
Carroll, IL	17015	16.1	43.6	9.1	. . .	236	217	191	13.4	4
Cass, IL	17017	17.4	59.8	34.3	16.3	156	202	179	13.9	3
Champaign, IL	17019	15.9	45.2	40.8	4.6	1,439	2,137	1,768	13.6	37
Christian, IL	17021	17.2	46.6	4.8	. . .	554	427	379	16.1	10
Clark, IL	17023	18.2	40.4	2.9	0.8	212	229	195	14.3	3
Clay, IL	17025	17.1	47.5	3.5	. . .	187	198	170	14.1	4
Clinton, IL	17027	18.8	29.7	8.6	1.1	307	412	366	15.0	17
Coles, IL	17029	18.8	46.1	9.2	0.5	456	593	487	13.6	11
Cook, IL	17031	13.2	57.1	74.2	12.8	46,925	58,770	48,909	16.1	946
Crawford, IL	17033	17.8	43.5	4.5	. . .	216	254	221	13.6	4
Cumberland, IL	17035	20.1	37.0	2.3	. . .	139	148	128	13.8	2
De Kalb, IL	17037	12.9	32.4	23.7	4.4	1,230	1,353	1,131	15.3	29
De Witt, IL	17039	17.9	38.4	6.0	0.2	61	222	195	14.5	2

[2]IEP=Individual Education Program. See notes and definitions for more information.
. . . = Not available.

Table C-1. Population, School, and Student Characteristics by County, Selected Years—*Continued*

County	State/ County Code	Revenues, 2008–2009				Current expenditures, 2008–2009			Resident population 16 to 19 years, 2006–2010			
			Percentage of revenue from									
		Total revenue ($1,000's)	Federal government	State government	Local government	Amount ($1,000's)	Amount per student	Percent for instruction	Total population 16 to 19 years	Percent enrolled in school	Percent high school graduates, not enrolled in school	Percent not enrolled, not grads, not employed, or not in labor force
		19	20	21	22	23	24	25	26	27	28	29
IDAHO—*(Continued)*												
Boundary, ID	16021	13,773	14.5	67.7	17.7	12,346	7,760	60.9	698	75.2	9.2	12.6
Butte, ID	16023	4,663	13.6	71.2	15.3	4,079	8,772	51.9	187	72.7	21.9	0.0
Camas, ID	16025	2,389	9.7	63.5	26.7	1,828	11,284	57.2	106	85.9	10.4	3.8
Canyon, ID	16027	277,865	10.6	69.3	20.1	231,108	6,524	60.4	11,273	68.9	18.1	9.1
Caribou, ID	16029	14,005	10.3	74.6	15.1	12,788	8,486	62.6	316	64.6	32.6	2.9
Cassia, ID	16031	40,139	12.6	72.1	15.4	33,847	6,558	60.3	1,610	77.2	16.2	2.4
Clark, ID	16033	2,996	21.5	65.6	12.9	2,454	11,686	53.0	38	42.1	0.0	10.5
Clearwater, ID	16035	11,619	15.9	67.4	16.7	11,226	9,194	57.8	342	83.3	9.4	5.0
Custer, ID	16037	7,252	19.6	70.7	9.7	6,215	9,591	57.3	158	78.5	9.5	12.0
Elmore, ID	16039	37,144	20.1	71.5	8.3	35,053	7,116	60.9	1,736	78.8	16.8	1.6
Franklin, ID	16041	20,207	11.2	80.2	8.6	17,663	5,722	62.4	810	79.0	19.4	1.0
Fremont, ID	16043	19,266	14.6	70.7	14.6	16,985	6,885	64.6	766	72.9	20.8	3.0
Gem, ID	16045	19,807	10.9	79.0	10.0	17,787	6,735	61.2	1,046	84.3	9.3	6.4
Gooding, ID	16047	24,586	13.2	75.4	11.4	22,218	7,416	61.7	871	81.9	14.8	2.3
Idaho, ID	16049	20,956	25.3	57.3	17.4	18,036	10,462	57.8	741	80.4	19.0	0.0
Jefferson, ID	16051	45,120	8.8	70.5	20.8	37,214	6,248	60.0	1,388	84.2	13.6	1.4
Jerome, ID	16053	31,651	11.8	73.9	14.3	27,036	6,357	60.4	1,383	62.7	17.3	9.3
Kootenai, ID	16055	152,155	9.2	71.3	19.6	136,063	6,463	64.0	7,647	83.1	13.8	1.8
Latah, ID	16057	46,615	6.3	63.9	29.8	43,207	8,559	58.2	4,037	94.5	3.9	0.1
Lemhi, ID	16059	9,834	17.4	76.1	6.6	8,522	7,965	62.4	562	60.3	18.9	2.1
Lewis, ID	16061	10,379	19.3	68.1	12.6	9,488	10,519	58.1	229	78.6	8.7	12.2
Lincoln, ID	16063	9,539	11.0	75.1	13.9	8,531	8,307	61.3	291	74.6	17.9	0.7
Madison, ID	16065	45,897	10.9	70.7	18.4	37,725	6,190	59.8	4,738	90.7	7.4	1.0
Minidoka, ID	16067	32,626	13.5	76.6	9.9	29,077	7,097	61.8	1,081	85.6	4.2	4.5
Nez Perce, ID	16069	52,561	13.5	59.1	27.4	50,741	8,989	61.2	2,280	74.8	19.3	3.5
Oneida, ID	16071	6,915	12.5	78.9	8.6	6,276	7,044	63.1	287	85.0	15.0	0.0
Owyhee, ID	16073	21,516	15.4	74.1	10.4	19,745	7,457	60.1	531	87.6	1.1	0.0
Payette, ID	16075	32,128	12.1	75.7	12.1	28,417	6,441	63.1	1,298	87.1	6.1	4.9
Power, ID	16077	16,607	12.3	66.5	21.2	14,842	8,909	57.2	648	61.7	36.1	2.2
Shoshone, ID	16079	22,844	12.8	58.3	29.0	19,999	9,775	57.5	673	67.3	12.6	15.9
Teton, ID	16081	13,585	9.2	60.5	30.2	11,117	6,996	59.5	364	91.2	8.2	0.6
Twin Falls, ID	16083	101,118	11.6	70.9	17.6	86,375	6,754	58.3	4,398	76.9	11.6	6.2
Valley, ID	16085	18,879	7.2	44.1	48.6	14,309	10,865	57.4	406	77.3	8.1	5.9
Washington, ID	16087	15,505	13.0	78.7	8.3	14,563	7,718	63.2	608	75.7	14.6	8.7
ILLINOIS	17000	26,988,141	12.4	26.6	61.0	22,936,395	10,833	58.4	746,998	85.5	8.9	3.9
Adams, IL	17001	98,894	16.5	37.3	46.3	89,471	9,835	56.3	3,848	84.9	12.7	0.9
Alexander, IL	17003	20,760	28.6	48.4	22.9	17,231	14,159	53.0	442	89.1	3.6	6.6
Bond, IL	17005	23,522	16.2	47.5	36.3	18,456	7,506	60.7	1,040	86.2	12.1	1.7
Boone, IL	17007	129,223	9.4	27.8	62.8	99,392	9,280	60.5	3,374	85.3	5.3	7.7
Brown, IL	17009	8,010	12.7	43.1	44.2	6,802	8,408	52.4	189	78.3	11.6	10.1
Bureau, IL	17011	66,102	13.5	37.2	49.3	54,258	9,373	55.9	1,980	80.1	8.6	6.4
Calhoun, IL	17013	7,793	16.8	42.8	40.4	7,019	9,803	56.3	223	90.1	7.6	2.2
Carroll, IL	17015	31,175	9.7	35.2	55.1	25,751	9,499	59.6	783	82.1	11.0	1.4
Cass, IL	17017	24,591	19.7	50.5	29.8	19,693	8,094	57.7	701	71.6	20.7	3.0
Champaign, IL	17019	274,407	12.5	29.5	58.1	238,136	10,143	59.0	20,109	94.6	3.3	1.3
Christian, IL	17021	77,701	16.6	40.5	42.9	63,200	9,716	61.9	1,881	78.3	15.0	6.1
Clark, IL	17023	27,897	19.5	48.4	32.1	23,865	8,090	54.0	904	90.5	9.2	0.3
Clay, IL	17025	27,976	20.6	51.8	27.7	23,996	8,292	59.3	713	83.6	16.1	0.3
Clinton, IL	17027	50,690	12.7	40.6	46.7	42,903	7,768	62.9	2,055	88.3	6.9	4.0
Coles, IL	17029	90,255	19.2	37.6	43.2	76,411	11,637	57.3	6,602	92.8	4.8	2.2
Cook, IL	17031	11,021,657	15.1	24.7	60.2	9,535,767	11,815	58.6	289,147	84.8	8.5	4.8
Crawford, IL	17033	36,361	12.0	37.3	50.7	28,504	9,060	54.1	1,283	83.9	11.4	4.8
Cumberland, IL	17035	16,429	17.3	53.8	28.9	14,446	7,920	57.3	612	72.9	14.7	6.9
De Kalb, IL	17037	218,564	8.8	26.3	64.9	190,361	10,832	55.5	9,289	92.8	5.9	0.5
De Witt, IL	17039	30,886	8.8	22.7	68.5	24,961	8,197	62.2	803	81.1	15.7	3.1

Note. Data in columns 26 through 41 from the American Community Survey are subject to sampling error, which can be especially large in small counties and small population groups. See notes and definitions for more information.

Table C-1. Population, School, and Student Characteristics by County, Selected Years—*Continued*

County	State/ County Code	High school graduates, 2006–2010			College enrollment, 2006–2010		College graduates, 2006–2010 (percent)						
		Population 25 years and over	High school diploma or less (percent)	High school diploma or more (percent)	Number	Percent public	Bachelor's degree or more	+/- U.S. percent with Bachelor's degree or more	Non-Hispanic White	Black or African American	American Indian and Alaska Native	Asian, Hawaiian, and Pacific Islander	Hispanic or Latino[3]
		30	31	32	33	34	35	36	37	38	39	40	41
IDAHO—*(Continued)*													
Boundary, ID	16021	7,329	58.4	82.9	138	59.4	12.9	-15.0	12.5	0.0	34.0	17.9	6.3
Butte, ID	16023	2,026	42.8	88.7	34	47.1	17.5	-10.4	16.5	0.0	0.0	77.8	55.8
Camas, ID	16025	774	48.3	81.9	29	79.3	22.6	-5.3	24.7	0.0	0.0	0.0	0.0
Canyon, ID	16027	107,501	50.2	82.0	8,631	64.0	16.7	-11.2	19.5	13.0	4.8	33.0	4.5
Caribou, ID	16029	4,509	48.4	88.0	130	79.2	16.2	-11.7	16.9	0.0	0.0	0.0	9.4
Cassia, ID	16031	12,907	47.9	78.8	930	91.0	15.7	-12.2	18.1	0.0	0.0	35.5	3.2
Clark, ID	16033	569	67.5	68.9	10	100.0	5.3	-22.6	8.0	0.0	0.0	0.0	0.0
Clearwater, ID	16035	6,691	57.3	84.7	217	94.5	14.4	-13.5	15.1	0.0	0.0	27.3	3.6
Custer, ID	16037	3,039	46.8	92.9	155	95.5	24.5	-3.4	25.7	0.0	0.0	0.0	0.0
Elmore, ID	16039	15,586	42.9	84.5	1,890	78.1	14.6	-13.3	17.0	14.6	4.2	8.2	2.4
Franklin, ID	16041	7,141	49.5	91.7	300	77.3	18.5	-9.4	19.4	0.0	35.4	0.0	3.0
Fremont, ID	16043	8,012	42.8	85.1	383	64.0	19.8	-8.1	22.1	0.0	9.9	34.5	0.7
Gem, ID	16045	11,388	49.6	83.5	741	82.3	12.6	-15.3	13.4	0.0	0.0	0.0	4.6
Gooding, ID	16047	9,422	59.0	76.2	371	89.2	11.5	-16.4	13.9	100.0	0.0	0.0	0.2
Idaho, ID	16049	11,562	58.2	85.7	197	75.6	12.3	-15.6	12.7	0.0	2.7	18.2	15.4
Jefferson, ID	16051	13,935	43.5	85.8	1,066	55.8	17.9	-10.0	18.9	54.6	22.5	26.8	2.2
Jerome, ID	16053	12,426	58.5	71.7	678	88.1	12.1	-15.8	14.6	0.0	10.1	0.0	2.3
Kootenai, ID	16055	89,440	38.1	91.4	6,521	89.4	23.2	-4.7	23.3	19.0	25.0	33.4	16.6
Latah, ID	16057	20,074	29.3	93.5	9,920	97.7	41.8	13.9	41.3	100.0	25.4	77.1	39.6
Lemhi, ID	16059	5,551	37.5	91.9	162	54.9	22.3	-5.6	22.2	0.0	0.0	0.0	52.0
Lewis, ID	16061	2,670	46.2	90.2	99	84.8	15.5	-12.4	16.6	0.0	0.0	18.8	0.0
Lincoln, ID	16063	3,057	56.6	76.6	116	89.7	11.5	-16.4	13.2	0.0	0.0	0.0	3.3
Madison, ID	16065	13,355	24.7	95.2	12,667	14.4	30.0	2.1	31.2	100.0	7.9	11.3	12.9
Minidoka, ID	16067	12,182	59.1	74.9	837	93.8	9.4	-18.5	11.2	0.0	0.0	0.0	3.7
Nez Perce, ID	16069	26,476	45.7	89.7	2,418	90.0	18.2	-9.7	18.4	94.0	12.5	24.9	6.2
Oneida, ID	16071	2,657	45.1	92.3	139	87.8	15.6	-12.3	15.7	0.0	27.1	0.0	0.0
Owyhee, ID	16073	7,076	61.7	75.1	278	86.0	10.3	-17.6	12.7	100.0	3.2	0.0	1.3
Payette, ID	16075	14,104	53.7	83.7	959	83.4	13.8	-14.1	14.7	0.0	0.0	37.9	3.1
Power, ID	16077	4,533	49.0	82.1	174	84.5	18.9	-9.0	22.8	0.0	26.2	0.0	0.0
Shoshone, ID	16079	9,382	55.2	82.1	307	74.9	11.9	-16.0	12.2	0.0	2.6	0.0	4.9
Teton, ID	16081	6,099	34.8	89.0	173	57.8	31.6	3.7	35.4	0.0	0.0	56.3	8.8
Twin Falls, ID	16083	47,071	46.7	83.3	3,815	89.4	16.8	-11.1	18.1	36.9	5.3	19.5	2.9
Valley, ID	16085	7,215	36.4	93.3	356	62.6	36.1	8.2	37.2	0.0	0.0	0.0	3.4
Washington, ID	16087	7,097	50.4	80.0	257	80.5	17.4	-10.5	20.0	100.0	0.0	4.7	0.0
ILLINOIS	17000	8,345,982	41.6	86.2	945,601	67.1	30.3	2.4	33.6	18.5	17.4	62.5	11.8
Adams, IL	17001	45,323	50.2	89.2	4,226	60.5	21.1	-6.8	20.9	14.3	0.0	84.8	18.9
Alexander, IL	17003	5,735	60.7	76.0	453	89.2	9.5	-18.4	9.2	7.9	0.0	88.5	0.0
Bond, IL	17005	12,050	47.0	88.0	1,679	42.5	24.7	-3.2	24.3	35.7	0.0	28.6	28.6
Boone, IL	17007	33,448	52.2	85.4	2,358	71.0	20.8	-7.1	22.5	21.8	0.0	60.1	8.3
Brown, IL	17009	5,063	59.4	75.6	282	95.7	10.9	-17.0	14.4	1.8	100.0	100.0	0.0
Bureau, IL	17011	24,313	52.8	89.2	1,385	88.0	16.1	-11.8	16.5	15.9	47.8	36.7	3.2
Calhoun, IL	17013	3,618	58.7	84.3	159	94.3	12.6	-15.3	12.3	100.0	0.0	10.0	12.5
Carroll, IL	17015	11,340	54.4	86.9	637	75.0	15.9	-12.0	15.9	0.0	100.0	56.9	5.6
Cass, IL	17017	9,069	62.5	80.6	452	82.7	12.3	-15.6	14.0	5.5	0.0	0.0	0.0
Champaign, IL	17019	110,894	31.1	92.3	49,888	97.0	41.2	13.3	41.0	18.8	12.4	79.5	36.3
Christian, IL	17021	24,168	56.8	85.8	1,529	80.4	12.1	-15.8	12.1	2.7	0.0	36.0	28.2
Clark, IL	17023	11,404	51.2	88.0	812	86.3	16.4	-11.5	16.2	0.0	0.0	60.0	43.6
Clay, IL	17025	9,626	56.2	86.2	499	88.4	13.8	-14.1	13.6	0.0	0.0	74.7	0.0
Clinton, IL	17027	25,642	44.8	85.8	2,003	77.9	18.9	-9.0	19.4	4.3	31.6	43.8	15.7
Coles, IL	17029	30,576	45.6	89.3	12,063	99.1	23.3	-4.6	23.0	20.9	47.4	64.6	18.9
Cook, IL	17031	3,413,901	41.7	83.2	391,513	55.3	33.2	5.3	44.4	18.8	19.4	59.6	11.6
Crawford, IL	17033	13,593	49.6	86.5	936	91.6	13.5	-14.4	13.9	7.4	7.4	34.2	0.0
Cumberland, IL	17035	7,485	55.0	88.1	565	96.8	13.0	-14.9	12.2	100.0	42.9	57.1	0.0
De Kalb, IL	17037	58,234	39.0	90.7	21,417	95.5	28.0	0.1	28.9	33.2	44.7	55.2	10.7
De Witt, IL	17039	11,540	56.2	90.3	751	92.0	15.7	-12.2	15.6	75.0	0.0	21.4	0.0

Note. Data in columns 26 through 41 from the American Community Survey are subject to sampling error, which can be especially large in small counties and small population groups. See notes and definitions for more information.
[3]May be of any race.

Table C-1. Population, School, and Student Characteristics by County, Selected Years—*Continued*

County	State/ County Code	County Type[1]	Population, 2010		Percent of related children 5–17 years in poverty, 2010	Percent of children under 19 years with no health insurance, 2010	Number of schools and students, 2010–2011			Resident enrollment, 2006–2010 K-12 enrollment	
			Total	Percent 5–17 years			School districts	Schools	Students	Number	Percent public
			1	2	3	4	5	6	7	8	9
ILLINOIS—*(Continued)*											
Douglas, IL	17041	6	19,980	18.9	14.5	5.4	4	11	2,918	3,610	93.4
Du Page, IL	17043	1	916,924	18.6	7.9	3.5	49	254	159,711	171,244	87.1
Edgar, IL	17045	6	18,576	16.4	19.0	4.1	6	17	3,187	3,083	95.3
Edwards, IL	17047	9	6,721	17.4	15.8	4.6	1	3	985	1,129	85.7
Effingham, IL	17049	7	34,242	18.1	13.4	4.0	5	16	5,532	6,329	86.9
Fayette, IL	17051	6	22,140	16.6	21.0	4.6	7	17	2,894	3,819	92.6
Ford, IL	17053	3	14,081	18.0	14.8	4.1	4	11	3,065	2,619	94.0
Franklin, IL	17055	5	39,561	16.7	26.7	3.9	12	23	6,673	6,656	96.4
Fulton, IL	17057	6	37,069	15.7	17.0	4.0	9	27	6,867	5,974	96.0
Gallatin, IL	17059	8	5,589	15.2	25.9	5.4	1	3	794	868	96.0
Greene, IL	17061	6	13,886	17.2	20.5	4.6	3	8	2,071	2,514	91.4
Grundy, IL	17063	1	50,063	20.0	8.5	3.6	15	32	12,713	9,772	94.1
Hamilton, IL	17065	7	8,457	16.9	20.7	4.8	1	4	1,280	1,369	92.1
Hancock, IL	17067	7	19,104	16.1	18.2	4.7	8	14	3,296	3,208	95.4
Hardin, IL	17069	9	4,320	14.7	28.0	4.9	1	3	637	682	97.1
Henderson, IL	17071	9	7,331	15.7	18.6	5.9	1	4	995	1,224	93.0
Henry, IL	17073	2	50,486	18.0	13.9	3.8	10	28	8,639	9,199	95.5
Iroquois, IL	17075	6	29,718	18.1	16.3	5.0	10	26	4,839	5,402	92.3
Jackson, IL	17077	5	60,218	12.6	31.7	4.6	10	24	7,390	7,523	83.6
Jasper, IL	17079	7	9,698	17.0	14.6	4.8	2	6	1,425	1,621	88.8
Jefferson, IL	17081	7	38,827	15.9	23.4	4.5	20	25	6,146	6,388	89.9
Jersey, IL	17083	1	22,985	17.2	12.6	4.3	2	8	2,794	3,907	86.8
Jo Daviess, IL	17085	6	22,678	15.5	13.9	5.7	9	21	3,342	3,364	92.5
Johnson, IL	17087	7	12,582	14.9	17.8	4.8	7	8	1,994	1,911	95.8
Kane, IL	17089	1	515,269	21.2	15.4	5.2	15	170	122,246	105,784	89.7
Kankakee, IL	17091	3	113,449	18.6	18.8	4.5	16	46	19,529	21,340	86.9
Kendall, IL	17093	1	114,736	22.6	5.7	4.2	7	40	25,084	22,835	91.0
Knox, IL	17095	4	52,919	15.3	22.6	3.6	8	26	7,692	8,338	95.4
Lake, IL	17097	1	703,462	20.7	10.6	5.1	51	216	139,168	146,022	90.1
La Salle, IL	17099	4	113,924	17.2	15.9	4.6	30	51	17,290	19,814	89.0
Lawrence, IL	17101	7	16,833	13.9	21.9	4.1	2	6	2,321	2,385	94.8
Lee, IL	17103	4	36,031	15.8	13.8	4.3	7	15	4,666	5,989	86.3
Livingston, IL	17105	4	38,950	16.8	13.3	4.2	14	25	6,456	6,822	94.6
Logan, IL	17107	6	30,305	14.7	16.4	3.9	10	16	3,422	4,922	91.0
McDonough, IL	17109	5	32,612	11.5	22.5	4.5	6	20	3,450	3,572	92.4
McHenry, IL	17111	1	308,760	20.8	8.5	4.2	21	80	53,095	64,788	90.6
McLean, IL	17113	3	169,572	16.4	9.8	3.4	15	56	25,605	27,178	87.1
Macon, IL	17115	3	110,768	16.6	22.8	3.4	11	50	16,864	18,688	88.7
Macoupin, IL	17117	1	47,765	16.7	16.6	3.8	9	33	8,988	8,326	95.7
Madison, IL	17119	1	269,282	16.7	18.5	3.7	19	85	41,810	45,479	88.0
Marion, IL	17121	4	39,437	16.9	24.8	3.8	16	32	6,879	6,976	93.1
Marshall, IL	17123	2	12,640	16.3	15.2	4.7	2	5	1,460	2,133	93.2
Mason, IL	17125	6	14,666	16.8	19.2	4.2	3	10	3,143	2,602	95.0
Massac, IL	17127	7	15,429	16.6	24.8	3.9	2	9	2,615	2,666	95.0
Menard, IL	17129	3	12,705	17.8	12.6	4.0	3	11	2,624	2,184	94.4
Mercer, IL	17131	2	16,434	16.8	12.5	4.3	2	11	2,892	2,886	91.2
Monroe, IL	17133	1	32,957	18.6	4.8	3.1	6	15	5,393	6,131	80.0
Montgomery, IL	17135	6	30,104	15.6	18.5	4.3	6	17	4,661	4,822	91.0
Morgan, IL	17137	4	35,547	15.9	18.7	3.7	7	24	5,075	6,000	89.6
Moultrie, IL	17139	6	14,846	18.3	15.3	4.4	3	9	2,091	2,516	89.1
Ogle, IL	17141	4	53,497	18.8	13.4	4.7	12	29	9,802	10,541	94.2
Peoria, IL	17143	2	186,494	17.3	19.3	3.5	20	80	27,906	31,960	86.5
Perry, IL	17145	7	22,350	15.4	21.1	3.9	6	8	2,848	3,883	94.4
Piatt, IL	17147	3	16,729	18.3	8.1	3.7	5	16	3,329	3,056	95.4
Pike, IL	17149	7	16,430	16.4	23.7	4.9	4	13	2,740	2,837	97.6
Pope, IL	17151	9	4,470	13.6	25.6	5.8	1	2	572	933	92.3
Pulaski, IL	17153	9	6,161	17.0	33.6	5.4	3	6	1,050	1,175	93.6
Putnam, IL	17155	8	6,006	16.1	12.3	5.4	1	4	909	981	93.7
Randolph, IL	17157	6	33,476	14.7	17.5	3.7	8	16	4,298	5,105	84.0

[1]County type codes are from the Economic Research Service of the United States Department of Agriculture. See notes and definitions for more information.

Table C-1. Population, School, and Student Characteristics by County, Selected Years—*Continued*

County	State/ County Code	Characteristics of students, 2010–2011				Number of graduates, 2008–2009	Staff and students, 2010–2011			
		Percent with IEP[2]	Percent eligible for free or reduced lunch	Percent minority	Percent English-language learners		Total staff	Number of teachers	Student/ teacher ratio	Central admin. staff
		10	11	12	13	14	15	16	17	18
ILLINOIS—*(Continued)*										
Douglas, IL	17041	21.3	32.0	14.3	2.5	190	264	230	12.7	3
Du Page, IL	17043	13.1	21.7	40.6	8.8	10,262	12,280	10,102	15.8	212
Edgar, IL	17045	20.1	43.8	3.4	0.1	198	284	248	12.8	5
Edwards, IL	17047	22.0	34.6	3.9	0.2	86	76	68	14.5	1
Effingham, IL	17049	16.7	31.5	4.5	0.7	452	429	367	15.1	10
Fayette, IL	17051	17.8	49.9	3.5	. . .	258	263	229	12.6	7
Ford, IL	17053	14.8	35.4	4.8	1.5	198	281	243	12.6	4
Franklin, IL	17055	18.1	55.1	3.0	. . .	401	501	450	14.8	14
Fulton, IL	17057	17.4	43.1	4.3	0.2	438	550	486	14.1	17
Gallatin, IL	17059	25.9	48.7	3.0	0.9	61	62	54	14.6	1
Greene, IL	17061	19.3	48.1	2.4	. . .	142	190	166	12.5	3
Grundy, IL	17063	13.6	19.5	17.6	1.6	952	867	744	17.1	21
Hamilton, IL	17065	21.6	48.3	4.0	0.2	126	94	82	15.7	2
Hancock, IL	17067	19.1	45.9	3.1	0.3	244	282	251	13.1	7
Hardin, IL	17069	19.2	58.5	5.7	. . .	46	51	45	14.0	1
Henderson, IL	17071	13.2	49.1	4.5	. . .	51	90	80	12.5	1
Henry, IL	17073	14.0	36.5	13.1	1.3	581	638	563	15.4	14
Iroquois, IL	17075	16.2	43.4	14.7	1.2	401	381	325	14.9	9
Jackson, IL	17077	17.7	55.2	32.4	3.4	475	656	532	13.9	15
Jasper, IL	17079	13.9	43.7	2.5	0.1	120	132	113	12.6	2
Jefferson, IL	17081	20.4	53.3	18.9	0.1	402	501	439	14.0	22
Jersey, IL	17083	17.1	41.8	1.5	. . .	339	194	163	17.1	4
Jo Daviess, IL	17085	15.7	33.3	7.6	0.8	236	327	281	11.9	10
Johnson, IL	17087	15.9	43.9	4.2	0.4	125	155	136	14.7	6
Kane, IL	17089	13.6	39.7	51.9	15.2	7,373	8,029	6,780	18.0	101
Kankakee, IL	17091	15.2	50.3	40.7	3.1	1,209	1,514	1,276	15.3	33
Kendall, IL	17093	13.9	20.7	35.8	4.8	1,282	1,789	1,491	16.8	17
Knox, IL	17095	13.9	51.7	21.6	1.1	481	533	472	16.3	12
Lake, IL	17097	14.5	27.0	45.3	10.6	9,460	11,238	9,330	14.9	244
La Salle, IL	17099	16.5	39.5	19.1	3.0	1,212	1,425	1,225	14.1	35
Lawrence, IL	17101	13.9	46.3	4.4	0.2	181	198	169	13.8	3
Lee, IL	17103	15.7	40.5	13.0	0.5	354	356	311	15.0	8
Livingston, IL	17105	19.0	37.1	9.1	. . .	511	545	484	13.4	10
Logan, IL	17107	16.3	40.1	6.7	0.2	222	314	275	12.4	11
McDonough, IL	17109	19.6	47.6	12.9	0.9	238	316	272	12.7	6
McHenry, IL	17111	14.4	21.0	23.5	6.0	3,671	3,997	3,260	16.3	82
McLean, IL	17113	14.8	25.5	27.6	2.5	1,513	2,017	1,709	15.0	29
Macon, IL	17115	15.2	47.7	36.1	0.5	1,015	1,111	943	17.9	23
Macoupin, IL	17117	17.7	43.4	3.6	0.1	541	623	535	16.8	12
Madison, IL	17119	17.3	43.4	22.1	1.5	2,932	3,135	2,611	16.0	57
Marion, IL	17121	23.2	58.3	12.1	0.1	512	627	528	13.0	16
Marshall, IL	17123	16.5	39.7	6.2	. . .	106	132	116	12.6	2
Mason, IL	17125	19.3	49.1	2.9	. . .	221	263	229	13.7	3
Massac, IL	17127	13.5	55.5	14.2	. . .	169	192	166	15.7	4
Menard, IL	17129	17.4	27.6	4.1	0.1	193	188	169	15.6	3
Mercer, IL	17131	15.6	28.5	6.7	. . .	209	248	214	13.5	2
Monroe, IL	17133	12.6	14.4	3.8	0.1	405	370	317	17.0	10
Montgomery, IL	17135	16.1	43.8	5.0	. . .	298	305	268	17.4	6
Morgan, IL	17137	19.3	45.5	15.2	0.6	397	460	396	12.8	9
Moultrie, IL	17139	16.2	42.1	3.9	. . .	148	173	147	14.2	3
Ogle, IL	17141	14.1	28.5	18.8	4.9	831	830	691	14.2	19
Peoria, IL	17143	16.8	51.3	45.6	2.7	1,706	2,160	1,884	14.8	37
Perry, IL	17145	17.8	43.5	10.2	. . .	203	217	193	14.8	6
Piatt, IL	17147	14.0	25.4	4.1	0.2	233	263	232	14.3	6
Pike, IL	17149	19.3	46.2	2.7	0.1	197	243	216	12.7	5
Pope, IL	17151	19.4	52.8	5.5	. . .	39	48	42	13.5	1
Pulaski, IL	17153	18.0	78.2	51.7	. . .	119	104	85	12.3	4
Putnam, IL	17155	14.9	29.0	10.6	1.3	64	80	70	13.1	1
Randolph, IL	17157	17.2	44.3	10.3	0.1	299	359	319	13.5	6

[2]IEP=Individual Education Program. See notes and definitions for more information.
. . . = Not available.

Table C-1. Population, School, and Student Characteristics by County, Selected Years—*Continued*

County	State/ County Code	Revenues, 2008–2009				Current expenditures, 2008–2009			Resident population 16 to 19 years, 2006–2010			
		Total revenue ($1,000's)	Percentage of revenue from			Amount ($1,000's)	Amount per student	Percent for instruction	Total population 16 to 19 years	Percent enrolled in school	Percent high school graduates, not enrolled in school	Percent not enrolled, not grads, not employed, or not in labor force
			Federal government	State government	Local government							
		19	20	21	22	23	24	25	26	27	28	29
ILLINOIS—*(Continued)*												
Douglas, IL	17041	27,765	10.6	33.6	55.9	25,872	8,987	61.3	1,110	73.9	9.6	10.7
Du Page, IL	17043	2,253,215	4.4	15.6	80.0	1,914,629	11,898	61.5	51,164	90.1	6.9	1.6
Edgar, IL	17045	33,262	15.6	40.2	44.2	28,402	8,772	62.4	977	77.4	7.2	12.1
Edwards, IL	17047	8,922	16.5	52.9	30.5	8,392	8,494	63.0	373	85.5	7.8	0.0
Effingham, IL	17049	51,454	14.3	42.5	43.2	45,672	8,452	57.3	1,997	84.3	10.9	2.5
Fayette, IL	17051	36,976	17.0	48.6	34.5	28,735	7,912	57.5	1,142	77.9	15.1	3.5
Ford, IL	17053	32,127	13.1	35.9	51.1	29,506	9,132	59.3	820	87.7	7.4	3.9
Franklin, IL	17055	66,209	25.6	50.4	24.0	60,611	9,139	60.9	2,191	75.2	13.4	10.2
Fulton, IL	17057	69,260	13.3	39.4	47.3	59,347	8,560	55.1	1,766	85.7	9.1	4.2
Gallatin, IL	17059	8,479	22.5	48.5	29.0	7,615	9,495	58.8	254	88.2	3.9	7.9
Greene, IL	17061	21,199	18.1	51.4	30.5	18,191	8,261	60.1	750	82.1	10.1	5.7
Grundy, IL	17063	161,088	4.5	16.1	79.4	128,737	10,313	53.6	2,791	86.6	7.5	2.8
Hamilton, IL	17065	20,484	18.9	56.7	24.5	17,702	8,746	57.5	410	92.7	6.6	0.7
Hancock, IL	17067	37,929	12.7	46.7	40.5	32,259	10,320	54.0	984	89.9	6.8	3.0
Hardin, IL	17069	5,545	20.9	58.8	20.3	5,463	8,496	58.6	95	76.8	17.9	5.3
Henderson, IL	17071	11,579	13.8	44.2	42.0	8,904	8,586	58.8	347	94.5	4.3	1.2
Henry, IL	17073	83,644	13.6	41.0	45.4	71,345	8,052	59.1	2,825	84.2	10.9	4.4
Iroquois, IL	17075	59,087	14.8	39.5	45.6	50,021	10,028	58.1	1,566	82.6	11.1	2.1
Jackson, IL	17077	97,086	18.3	39.2	42.5	80,679	11,099	58.5	5,804	92.8	4.9	2.1
Jasper, IL	17079	22,117	24.8	26.0	49.1	20,718	14,549	50.2	553	88.3	7.1	4.7
Jefferson, IL	17081	59,753	19.5	46.7	33.8	54,412	9,255	58.6	2,266	78.2	10.1	6.9
Jersey, IL	17083	43,842	15.4	46.2	38.3	39,732	8,535	59.2	1,428	93.4	2.3	2.7
Jo Daviess, IL	17085	42,219	7.7	23.9	68.4	34,842	10,432	61.2	1,096	80.8	16.5	0.6
Johnson, IL	17087	19,398	17.1	48.7	34.2	16,373	7,937	57.8	613	49.6	11.8	38.2
Kane, IL	17089	1,403,925	8.8	25.3	65.9	1,197,533	9,916	57.7	29,138	84.8	10.2	2.9
Kankakee, IL	17091	218,651	16.4	37.7	45.9	185,246	9,401	57.4	7,199	84.1	9.7	5.5
Kendall, IL	17093	283,142	5.6	25.0	69.4	214,310	9,132	56.8	5,181	86.3	6.4	2.7
Knox, IL	17095	87,069	15.6	38.5	46.0	71,513	9,219	64.7	3,075	85.1	10.6	3.5
Lake, IL	17097	2,084,268	7.4	19.2	73.4	1,694,334	12,031	57.5	44,176	80.6	15.3	2.6
La Salle, IL	17099	210,384	10.9	27.3	61.7	179,449	10,298	58.5	6,075	80.4	15.4	3.6
Lawrence, IL	17101	21,451	19.2	55.4	25.4	19,617	8,017	58.1	941	75.9	12.2	11.6
Lee, IL	17103	56,715	9.8	30.0	60.2	46,445	9,494	59.4	2,015	82.1	12.1	3.6
Livingston, IL	17105	79,805	12.2	33.3	54.4	69,636	10,406	60.1	2,105	81.8	11.9	6.3
Logan, IL	17107	39,113	14.0	32.4	53.6	35,093	10,001	61.1	2,224	91.3	3.3	4.2
McDonough, IL	17109	48,287	19.0	33.2	47.8	41,123	11,934	55.8	4,407	94.4	2.7	1.9
McHenry, IL	17111	638,980	6.7	21.6	71.7	536,249	9,898	59.7	18,527	91.1	6.7	1.7
McLean, IL	17113	297,141	7.6	22.0	70.5	232,540	9,534	57.8	12,744	91.7	5.6	1.9
Macon, IL	17115	201,239	15.7	35.7	48.6	168,631	9,936	55.3	6,501	79.1	12.5	7.1
Macoupin, IL	17117	69,807	17.1	47.8	35.1	54,870	7,393	59.7	2,798	85.5	12.0	1.6
Madison, IL	17119	459,154	14.2	34.5	51.3	398,047	9,246	56.5	15,414	87.6	7.5	4.4
Marion, IL	17121	81,912	20.8	45.6	33.6	72,126	9,924	57.9	2,459	82.3	9.5	6.0
Marshall, IL	17123	19,217	8.7	33.3	58.0	16,026	9,269	58.5	757	84.7	9.1	4.8
Mason, IL	17125	31,221	13.4	43.0	43.6	27,584	8,793	60.6	717	77.7	12.4	6.7
Massac, IL	17127	24,235	19.1	43.2	37.7	20,755	7,868	56.6	705	89.7	4.5	5.8
Menard, IL	17129	26,017	12.1	36.5	51.4	20,653	7,727	54.6	675	84.4	9.2	1.8
Mercer, IL	17131	29,666	13.6	44.4	42.0	27,664	8,855	60.6	832	85.1	10.7	1.1
Monroe, IL	17133	54,826	10.0	25.5	64.6	42,932	8,059	60.0	1,639	91.8	2.3	3.3
Montgomery, IL	17135	49,847	14.7	43.3	42.1	39,700	8,278	57.7	1,580	82.7	12.9	3.3
Morgan, IL	17137	59,950	17.4	34.9	47.7	54,024	10,346	55.4	2,183	86.4	6.0	5.1
Moultrie, IL	17139	18,943	13.2	40.0	46.8	16,162	8,101	56.3	784	80.2	7.0	3.7
Ogle, IL	17141	124,891	8.8	27.3	63.8	100,898	9,836	59.7	3,406	88.3	8.7	0.6
Peoria, IL	17143	338,944	15.5	31.0	53.4	287,145	10,321	56.3	10,762	83.8	7.5	6.3
Perry, IL	17145	27,276	17.3	46.6	36.1	23,591	7,901	62.6	1,170	79.7	9.6	6.8
Piatt, IL	17147	33,768	8.2	23.2	68.5	28,445	8,411	53.7	811	85.5	9.9	1.7
Pike, IL	17149	28,767	16.8	48.5	34.7	24,676	8,870	57.1	800	79.3	13.3	3.5
Pope, IL	17151	5,172	21.0	51.1	27.9	4,484	8,319	56.7	383	94.5	4.2	0.0
Pulaski, IL	17153	13,296	26.9	60.8	12.3	12,019	10,406	57.6	295	81.4	10.9	7.8
Putnam, IL	17155	11,662	5.0	28.2	66.9	8,716	9,433	60.4	280	73.6	18.9	0.0
Randolph, IL	17157	48,947	19.2	37.1	43.6	42,629	9,877	53.2	1,678	81.5	11.6	6.6

Note. Data in columns 26 through 41 from the American Community Survey are subject to sampling error, which can be especially large in small counties and small population groups. See notes and definitions for more information.

Table C-1. Population, School, and Student Characteristics by County, Selected Years—*Continued*

County	State/ County Code	High school graduates, 2006–2010			College enrollment, 2006–2010		College graduates, 2006–2010 (percent)						
		Population 25 years and over	High school diploma or less (percent)	High school diploma or more (percent)	Number	Percent public	Bachelor's degree or more	+/- U.S. percent with Bachelor's degree or more	Non-Hispanic White	Black or African American	American Indian and Alaska Native	Asian, Hawaiian, and Pacific Islander	Hispanic or Latino[3]
		30	31	32	33	34	35	36	37	38	39	40	41
ILLINOIS— *(Continued)*													
Douglas, IL	17041	13,031	57.4	81.7	764	88.7	14.9	-13.0	14.9	100.0	0.0	80.8	5.7
Du Page, IL	17043	602,799	28.2	92.0	69,247	58.3	45.3	17.4	46.3	34.2	13.2	70.0	17.8
Edgar, IL	17045	13,194	53.6	88.4	571	83.4	16.8	-11.1	17.0	0.0	0.0	13.0	47.5
Edwards, IL	17047	4,645	45.4	89.0	265	97.4	13.1	-14.8	13.1	0.0	0.0	0.0	0.0
Effingham, IL	17049	22,473	47.4	89.4	1,481	94.5	20.0	-7.9	20.1	0.0	0.0	37.7	4.5
Fayette, IL	17051	15,015	59.5	82.9	1,229	87.4	14.3	-13.6	14.2	0.0	0.0	6.6	22.7
Ford, IL	17053	9,688	53.8	87.3	606	87.8	17.8	-10.1	17.8	12.5	0.0	67.5	6.8
Franklin, IL	17055	27,381	49.7	83.8	1,700	94.1	12.4	-15.5	12.2	40.0	29.3	66.2	6.3
Fulton, IL	17057	26,452	54.5	83.6	1,799	88.2	13.4	-14.5	14.0	4.1	4.5	29.7	0.2
Gallatin, IL	17059	4,103	58.8	77.8	149	95.3	10.1	-17.8	9.9	37.1	0.0	11.1	22.2
Greene, IL	17061	9,606	58.5	85.2	624	74.7	13.5	-14.4	13.4	12.5	0.0	68.2	0.0
Grundy, IL	17063	31,660	44.4	90.7	2,427	80.6	18.3	-9.6	18.1	43.4	0.0	55.7	12.5
Hamilton, IL	17065	5,885	55.7	80.9	270	100.0	12.7	-15.2	12.5	0.0	57.1	0.0	16.3
Hancock, IL	17067	13,640	50.2	90.2	868	88.2	19.1	-8.8	19.0	0.0	43.3	50.0	0.0
Hardin, IL	17069	3,208	56.8	77.0	63	95.2	11.0	-16.9	10.6	12.0	0.0	100.0	0.0
Henderson, IL	17071	5,451	54.9	87.2	342	80.4	14.9	-13.0	14.9	50.0	0.0	20.0	0.0
Henry, IL	17073	34,588	47.5	87.9	2,198	79.1	20.6	-7.3	21.0	14.9	0.0	46.4	13.3
Iroquois, IL	17075	20,791	54.5	87.2	1,144	79.2	13.7	-14.2	13.7	12.4	62.1	55.8	5.3
Jackson, IL	17077	33,734	36.0	89.5	16,159	95.2	35.4	7.5	34.7	26.8	54.1	79.0	36.5
Jasper, IL	17079	6,770	51.3	88.2	513	92.6	13.0	-14.9	13.2	0.0	18.8	14.8	0.0
Jefferson, IL	17081	26,975	51.9	83.7	1,780	90.8	14.1	-13.8	14.7	4.2	9.2	47.6	2.8
Jersey, IL	17083	15,252	49.6	87.1	1,458	55.6	16.0	-11.9	15.9	16.8	0.0	59.4	28.0
Jo Daviess, IL	17085	16,575	50.2	89.1	774	64.7	23.0	-4.9	23.2	16.7	9.8	57.5	10.3
Johnson, IL	17087	8,982	54.3	78.0	429	94.9	12.9	-15.0	14.9	0.8	0.0	34.3	1.2
Kane, IL	17089	313,028	41.6	83.2	26,708	67.4	31.8	3.9	39.7	18.0	13.6	58.3	8.0
Kankakee, IL	17091	71,890	49.8	85.3	7,390	64.2	17.4	-10.5	18.7	10.5	21.4	57.5	7.9
Kendall, IL	17093	65,160	34.5	92.0	5,579	71.6	32.3	4.4	33.6	39.3	0.0	62.3	12.6
Knox, IL	17095	36,542	53.0	85.2	3,692	50.9	15.2	-12.7	16.0	3.2	0.0	55.2	15.4
Lake, IL	17097	440,297	32.8	88.5	42,268	64.7	41.3	13.4	47.6	21.6	17.7	63.9	10.2
La Salle, IL	17099	77,228	50.8	87.8	5,125	86.1	15.8	-12.1	16.1	12.2	12.5	55.3	9.9
Lawrence, IL	17101	11,830	56.5	81.1	876	95.8	11.2	-16.7	12.0	0.8	0.0	56.1	0.0
Lee, IL	17103	24,808	50.6	85.8	2,178	82.8	15.0	-12.9	15.7	9.4	0.0	36.7	3.5
Livingston, IL	17105	26,987	58.2	84.1	1,669	87.1	13.5	-14.4	14.3	1.9	0.0	51.2	6.0
Logan, IL	17107	20,925	54.6	85.4	3,004	35.1	17.1	-10.8	18.9	3.1	4.2	28.2	1.9
McDonough, IL	17109	17,975	39.7	91.2	9,715	96.3	32.6	4.7	31.1	48.0	37.8	62.5	40.5
McHenry, IL	17111	197,494	36.0	91.7	16,986	72.7	32.1	4.2	33.2	44.0	8.3	60.2	12.1
McLean, IL	17113	99,291	33.5	93.4	26,402	83.4	40.4	12.5	39.7	28.1	16.7	84.1	25.7
Macon, IL	17115	74,973	49.1	86.9	6,675	57.9	20.5	-7.4	21.5	7.8	33.1	79.6	39.8
Macoupin, IL	17117	32,900	52.3	86.8	2,565	57.7	15.1	-12.8	15.1	18.7	18.3	32.1	5.5
Madison, IL	17119	178,583	44.5	89.4	22,326	87.2	23.0	-4.9	23.4	15.3	18.4	53.5	15.6
Marion, IL	17121	26,967	52.2	84.1	2,044	88.2	13.6	-14.3	13.4	21.1	35.3	43.1	4.5
Marshall, IL	17123	9,039	52.1	90.2	553	78.7	17.1	-10.8	16.9	0.0	0.0	0.0	34.8
Mason, IL	17125	10,468	55.1	83.3	567	78.3	16.5	-11.4	16.3	0.0	0.0	75.7	3.5
Massac, IL	17127	10,816	50.4	85.0	535	90.1	14.2	-13.7	14.2	9.5	0.0	53.1	37.8
Menard, IL	17129	8,794	47.8	90.3	605	70.1	24.2	-3.7	24.3	0.0	100.0	0.0	8.1
Mercer, IL	17131	11,582	52.1	88.7	662	75.4	14.5	-13.4	14.6	0.0	28.1	0.0	6.8
Monroe, IL	17133	22,066	41.2	91.0	1,791	74.1	24.7	-3.2	24.5	100.0	63.2	68.6	23.7
Montgomery, IL	17135	21,330	58.7	83.5	1,542	85.0	13.3	-14.6	13.8	2.9	25.4	7.6	9.3
Morgan, IL	17137	24,264	52.3	86.5	2,753	49.5	20.2	-7.7	20.8	11.6	0.0	35.8	8.2
Moultrie, IL	17139	9,953	57.8	83.8	588	96.8	13.8	-14.1	14.0	0.0	0.0	5.7	0.0
Ogle, IL	17141	35,808	49.9	87.4	2,755	82.9	17.8	-10.1	18.5	16.7	0.0	32.7	7.0
Peoria, IL	17143	121,123	40.8	88.7	14,234	49.0	28.1	0.2	29.4	12.0	32.8	75.5	20.3
Perry, IL	17145	15,484	54.8	81.6	1,227	96.3	13.5	-14.4	14.6	1.7	0.0	29.6	3.1
Piatt, IL	17147	11,600	46.3	89.8	757	86.9	23.0	-4.9	23.1	0.0	0.0	0.0	27.2
Pike, IL	17149	11,495	59.5	86.0	621	73.8	12.7	-15.2	12.9	0.0	0.0	18.2	3.5
Pope, IL	17151	3,092	50.4	85.1	154	87.7	8.3	-19.6	8.1	0.0	100.0	0.0	0.0
Pulaski, IL	17153	4,176	56.7	78.9	294	92.2	11.9	-16.0	9.1	17.6	0.0	67.5	6.7
Putnam, IL	17155	4,243	48.1	88.7	194	87.1	15.0	-12.9	15.0	0.0	0.0	0.0	6.5
Randolph, IL	17157	23,942	60.5	78.5	1,197	88.2	12.0	-15.9	13.4	1.7	0.0	8.3	4.7

Note. Data in columns 26 through 41 from the American Community Survey are subject to sampling error, which can be especially large in small counties and small population groups. See notes and definitions for more information.

[3]May be of any race.

Table C-1. Population, School, and Student Characteristics by County, Selected Years—*Continued*

County	State/ County Code	County Type[1]	Population, 2010		Percent of related children 5–17 years in poverty, 2010	Percent of children under 19 years with no health insurance, 2010	Number of schools and students, 2010–2011			Resident enrollment, 2006–2010 K–12 enrollment	
			Total	Percent 5–17 years			School districts	Schools	Students	Number	Percent public
			1	2	3	4	5	6	7	8	9
ILLINOIS—*(Continued)*											
Richland, IL	17159	7	16,233	16.2	19.1	4.2	3	13	2,574	2,586	92.0
Rock Island, IL	17161	2	147,546	16.1	18.7	4.3	13	55	21,744	24,495	88.3
St. Clair, IL	17163	1	270,056	18.6	21.3	3.6	35	103	43,737	50,754	90.0
Saline, IL	17165	7	24,913	17.1	25.9	3.7	5	16	4,373	4,519	96.0
Sangamon, IL	17167	3	197,465	17.4	17.4	3.4	16	83	30,486	34,586	84.5
Schuyler, IL	17169	7	7,544	15.3	16.5	5.2	1	5	1,210	1,415	97.9
Scott, IL	17171	9	5,355	17.7	11.7	5.1	2	5	969	937	94.7
Shelby, IL	17173	6	22,363	16.9	15.4	4.6	4	11	2,424	3,843	97.2
Stark, IL	17175	2	5,994	18.2	14.5	4.4	4	7	1,184	1,137	92.8
Stephenson, IL	17177	4	47,711	16.7	18.7	4.0	7	24	6,925	8,398	91.3
Tazewell, IL	17179	2	135,394	17.1	12.3	3.3	22	55	20,064	23,816	91.1
Union, IL	17181	7	17,808	15.7	24.0	4.3	6	15	2,895	2,893	96.4
Vermilion, IL	17183	3	81,625	17.7	28.1	3.7	15	42	13,576	14,336	93.1
Wabash, IL	17185	6	11,947	16.1	18.6	4.4	2	5	1,853	2,110	91.2
Warren, IL	17187	7	17,707	16.3	17.7	4.6	4	12	2,686	3,077	88.8
Washington, IL	17189	6	14,716	16.5	11.1	3.8	7	8	1,949	2,454	89.9
Wayne, IL	17191	7	16,760	16.3	20.1	4.7	7	13	2,585	2,763	96.1
White, IL	17193	6	14,665	14.9	24.1	4.3	5	14	2,373	2,228	95.2
Whiteside, IL	17195	4	58,498	17.5	15.9	3.9	14	32	9,776	10,386	88.4
Will, IL	17197	1	677,560	21.8	10.7	4.3	36	181	118,370	143,761	90.8
Williamson, IL	17199	5	66,357	16.0	21.4	3.5	7	22	10,002	10,631	92.8
Winnebago, IL	17201	2	295,266	18.3	23.8	4.4	14	100	47,302	54,473	84.2
Woodford, IL	17203	2	38,664	19.3	8.5	3.5	12	26	8,126	7,602	91.1
INDIANA	18000	X	6,483,802	18.1	19.6	9.1	394	1,936	1,047,232	1,171,743	88.7
Adams, IN	18001	6	34,387	21.9	29.7	15.2	3	10	4,536	6,929	74.5
Allen, IN	18003	2	355,329	19.5	19.8	9.6	8	93	56,422	69,462	82.6
Bartholomew, IN	18005	3	76,794	18.4	19.4	9.4	3	19	12,394	14,333	86.5
Benton, IN	18007	3	8,854	18.8	16.0	11.7	1	4	1,860	1,724	88.7
Blackford, IN	18009	6	12,766	16.9	21.9	8.3	1	5	1,943	2,218	98.2
Boone, IN	18011	1	56,640	21.2	8.0	7.1	3	17	10,985	11,572	89.5
Brown, IN	18013	1	15,242	15.7	19.3	11.2	1	6	2,099	2,659	94.8
Carroll, IN	18015	3	20,155	18.5	14.8	9.7	2	5	2,763	3,771	91.4
Cass, IN	18017	4	38,966	19.1	20.9	10.0	3	14	6,774	7,491	91.0
Clark, IN	18019	1	110,232	17.1	17.3	8.3	5	32	16,798	18,232	89.1
Clay, IN	18021	3	26,890	18.1	18.8	9.2	1	10	4,458	4,991	93.0
Clinton, IN	18023	6	33,224	19.1	20.0	11.8	4	12	6,313	6,101	95.3
Crawford, IN	18025	8	10,713	17.2	26.2	11.1	1	6	1,632	1,776	93.4
Daviess, IN	18027	7	31,648	20.4	23.0	13.7	4	11	4,404	5,731	82.8
Dearborn, IN	18029	1	50,047	18.8	12.5	8.7	3	17	9,008	9,495	86.4
Decatur, IN	18031	6	25,740	19.0	19.4	9.4	2	7	4,478	4,933	92.0
De Kalb, IN	18033	4	42,223	19.7	14.2	8.7	4	16	7,663	8,471	87.8
Delaware, IN	18035	3	117,671	14.6	24.0	7.9	11	36	16,467	17,288	94.9
Dubois, IN	18037	7	41,889	18.9	8.7	9.1	5	18	7,300	7,835	90.3
Elkhart, IN	18039	3	197,559	20.3	24.7	14.6	7	57	35,885	40,472	89.2
Fayette, IN	18041	7	24,277	17.8	22.8	8.1	2	12	4,122	4,343	93.7
Floyd, IN	18043	1	74,578	17.9	17.9	6.9	2	17	12,156	13,517	86.9
Fountain, IN	18045	6	17,240	18.3	17.1	9.3	3	7	3,232	3,317	93.5
Franklin, IN	18047	1	23,087	19.9	15.8	10.1	2	9	5,031	4,778	84.9
Fulton, IN	18049	7	20,836	18.2	20.8	9.7	2	6	2,662	3,812	95.2
Gibson, IN	18051	2	33,503	17.8	14.4	7.5	4	14	5,148	5,734	93.3
Grant, IN	18053	4	70,061	15.9	26.9	8.3	6	30	11,523	11,872	95.0
Greene, IN	18055	3	33,165	17.8	18.7	10.2	6	14	5,484	6,044	94.0
Hamilton, IN	18057	1	274,569	22.3	5.8	6.1	10	67	53,877	57,660	87.0
Hancock, IN	18059	1	70,002	19.9	8.0	8.5	4	23	12,854	13,361	92.6
Harrison, IN	18061	1	39,364	17.6	14.4	8.7	3	15	6,115	6,881	91.8
Hendricks, IN	18063	1	145,448	20.4	7.0	6.7	6	40	26,971	29,104	89.8
Henry, IN	18065	4	49,462	16.9	21.1	8.8	5	21	8,053	8,715	97.3
Howard, IN	18067	3	82,752	17.4	21.7	7.6	5	26	13,430	15,135	94.4
Huntington, IN	18069	6	37,124	17.7	14.8	8.4	1	11	6,014	6,778	90.8
Jackson, IN	18071	4	42,376	18.1	17.6	9.7	4	15	6,848	7,577	81.6

[1]County type codes are from the Economic Research Service of the United States Department of Agriculture. See notes and definitions for more information.

Table C-1. Population, School, and Student Characteristics by County, Selected Years—*Continued*

County	State/ County Code	Characteristics of students, 2010–2011				Number of graduates, 2008–2009	Staff and students, 2010–2011			
		Percent with IEP[2]	Percent eligible for free or reduced lunch	Percent minority	Percent English-language learners		Total staff	Number of teachers	Student/ teacher ratio	Central admin. staff
		10	11	12	13	14	15	16	17	18
ILLINOIS—*(Continued)*										
Richland, IL	17159	14.7	46.7	4.1	. . .	143	215	181	14.2	5
Rock Island, IL	17161	14.9	50.6	38.7	6.4	1,333	1,630	1,361	16.0	26
St. Clair, IL	17163	17.5	48.1	50.2	0.2	3,026	3,238	2,778	15.7	61
Saline, IL	17165	18.1	51.7	13.6	. . .	264	329	289	15.1	8
Sangamon, IL	17167	19.4	39.3	28.7	0.4	1,700	2,634	2,209	13.8	44
Schuyler, IL	17169	22.1	45.2	3.2	1.3	96	96	81	15.0	2
Scott, IL	17171	16.0	33.5	1.9	. . .	63	88	78	12.4	2
Shelby, IL	17173	16.9	37.7	2.3	. . .	224	221	188	12.9	5
Stark, IL	17175	18.6	36.0	6.4	0.8	67	125	102	11.7	2
Stephenson, IL	17177	12.5	50.1	28.3	1.3	499	607	529	13.1	11
Tazewell, IL	17179	17.1	33.9	7.0	0.2	1,346	1,535	1,308	15.3	31
Union, IL	17181	19.3	53.5	11.5	2.2	222	228	202	14.3	5
Vermilion, IL	17183	15.6	58.8	28.9	0.8	788	1,055	900	15.1	20
Wabash, IL	17185	18.9	40.8	3.8	0.1	144	141	119	15.6	1
Warren, IL	17187	14.0	44.3	19.6	4.2	192	208	178	15.1	6
Washington, IL	17189	20.7	31.5	5.0	0.1	195	162	141	13.8	8
Wayne, IL	17191	17.8	44.5	3.5	. . .	187	206	180	14.4	8
White, IL	17193	21.4	44.7	3.6	0.2	124	274	215	11.1	2
Whiteside, IL	17195	17.4	44.7	22.5	2.2	723	794	676	14.5	16
Will, IL	17197	14.1	29.3	43.9	6.3	7,032	8,318	6,927	17.1	149
Williamson, IL	17199	17.1	48.4	15.3	0.4	609	627	543	18.4	9
Winnebago, IL	17201	14.9	59.2	45.7	8.0	2,678	3,616	3,052	15.5	51
Woodford, IL	17203	14.0	22.8	6.3	0.2	572	624	557	14.6	17
INDIANA	18000	15.8	46.6	26.8	4.7	63,662	109,766	56,608	18.5	1,772
Adams, IN	18001	13.7	40.9	11.5	3.5	401	532	273	16.6	13
Allen, IN	18003	13.8	51.7	38.2	6.2	3,472	5,436	3,054	18.5	88
Bartholomew, IN	18005	13.3	39.8	19.0	6.6	754	1,225	606	20.5	16
Benton, IN	18007	26.5	45.9	8.8	2.7	139	259	122	15.2	5
Blackford, IN	18009	19.5	51.8	3.8	0.5	162	256	110	17.7	5
Boone, IN	18011	15.3	22.0	8.6	0.7	728	1,237	583	18.8	17
Brown, IN	18013	21.5	51.9	4.5	. . .	164	211	138	15.2	8
Carroll, IN	18015	11.7	43.5	8.8	3.5	208	299	151	18.3	5
Cass, IN	18017	12.6	49.2	25.9	14.3	441	835	436	15.5	12
Clark, IN	18019	16.8	49.4	20.7	3.8	931	1,456	871	19.3	22
Clay, IN	18021	20.8	50.0	4.7	0.4	269	534	238	18.7	6
Clinton, IN	18023	15.3	50.5	22.4	13.8	382	700	386	16.4	14
Crawford, IN	18025	16.1	61.0	4.3	0.1	140	270	88	18.5	5
Daviess, IN	18027	18.1	45.5	11.2	6.2	273	483	268	16.4	10
Dearborn, IN	18029	16.7	30.1	3.6	0.5	650	804	457	19.7	17
Decatur, IN	18031	16.5	45.5	3.9	0.8	292	485	263	17.0	8
De Kalb, IN	18033	15.0	42.7	6.2	1.1	537	965	468	16.4	15
Delaware, IN	18035	18.8	49.6	17.7	0.6	1,162	1,920	997	16.5	48
Dubois, IN	18037	12.5	29.9	10.9	5.5	529	683	367	19.9	22
Elkhart, IN	18039	15.3	55.4	36.3	15.8	2,028	3,716	2,067	17.4	44
Fayette, IN	18041	15.4	60.7	4.9	0.1	225	452	250	16.5	8
Floyd, IN	18043	18.3	42.0	17.3	1.9	797	1,215	637	19.1	9
Fountain, IN	18045	14.7	44.1	6.6	1.4	183	430	206	15.7	12
Franklin, IN	18047	14.4	37.3	3.3	1.0	321	527	266	18.9	11
Fulton, IN	18049	14.5	47.9	10.6	0.5	180	312	145	18.4	9
Gibson, IN	18051	21.4	34.4	6.4	0.3	343	642	360	14.3	14
Grant, IN	18053	15.2	54.7	21.0	1.6	813	1,293	637	18.1	22
Greene, IN	18055	16.0	44.2	3.8	0.1	354	596	338	16.2	14
Hamilton, IN	18057	13.1	16.1	18.0	2.7	2,908	4,337	2,230	24.2	55
Hancock, IN	18059	16.2	23.7	7.3	0.5	775	765	377	34.1	16
Harrison, IN	18061	17.4	41.2	5.3	0.8	411	672	333	18.4	12
Hendricks, IN	18063	13.2	23.4	16.1	2.5	1,647	2,782	1,346	20.0	35
Henry, IN	18065	21.1	48.8	6.2	0.2	544	1,028	501	16.1	18
Howard, IN	18067	19.3	47.8	20.2	1.0	878	1,651	844	15.9	31
Huntington, IN	18069	14.5	43.2	6.0	0.4	399	618	358	16.8	9
Jackson, IN	18071	16.5	46.5	11.6	5.1	447	739	375	18.3	18

Note. Data in columns 26 through 41 from the American Community Survey are subject to sampling error, which can be especially large in small counties and small population groups. See notes and definitions for more information.
[2]IEP=Individual Education Program. See notes and definitions for more information.

Table C-1. Population, School, and Student Characteristics by County, Selected Years—*Continued*

County	State/ County Code	Revenues, 2008–2009				Current expenditures, 2008–2009			Resident population 16 to 19 years, 2006–2010			
		Total revenue ($1,000's)	Percentage of revenue from: Federal government	State government	Local government	Amount ($1,000's)	Amount per student	Percent for instruction	Total population 16 to 19 years	Percent enrolled in school	Percent high school graduates, not enrolled in school	Percent not enrolled, not grads, not employed, or not in labor force
		19	20	21	22	23	24	25	26	27	28	29
ILLINOIS—*(Continued)*												
Richland, IL	17159	20,437	17.0	45.2	37.9	18,023	8,438	55.4	869	81.8	14.4	1.0
Rock Island, IL	17161	246,814	14.7	31.1	54.2	213,957	9,958	62.2	7,829	83.9	7.7	5.1
St. Clair, IL	17163	543,106	19.1	40.6	40.3	467,386	10,525	55.5	15,885	86.2	8.6	4.2
Saline, IL	17165	40,522	21.6	53.0	25.5	35,351	8,168	61.3	1,569	85.0	12.2	2.4
Sangamon, IL	17167	366,371	14.0	31.4	54.7	302,296	10,300	55.5	10,124	84.8	9.5	3.9
Schuyler, IL	17169	13,928	13.0	53.9	33.1	12,121	9,477	54.2	348	81.0	17.2	1.7
Scott, IL	17171	8,992	16.4	50.0	33.7	8,305	8,687	59.0	270	98.5	0.0	1.5
Shelby, IL	17173	22,947	15.6	47.9	36.5	21,085	8,259	57.6	1,203	86.9	6.2	6.2
Stark, IL	17175	16,734	18.4	27.4	54.1	14,106	14,755	56.9	310	85.2	13.2	1.6
Stephenson, IL	17177	81,831	14.3	37.4	48.4	71,687	9,995	57.0	2,440	91.4	4.2	4.4
Tazewell, IL	17179	218,162	12.4	28.5	59.2	180,364	9,021	58.9	6,656	85.9	9.3	3.5
Union, IL	17181	32,913	19.4	49.9	30.8	27,660	8,753	60.4	1,006	86.3	8.9	3.4
Vermilion, IL	17183	153,609	18.4	45.1	36.5	134,465	9,713	60.9	4,855	77.7	11.8	7.5
Wabash, IL	17185	17,714	14.8	49.9	35.3	14,983	7,775	62.4	733	89.5	5.5	4.0
Warren, IL	17187	26,674	15.3	47.0	37.7	22,646	8,123	58.6	1,280	90.2	8.0	1.0
Washington, IL	17189	19,588	12.4	38.9	48.6	17,301	8,608	61.5	849	90.5	4.5	4.2
Wayne, IL	17191	25,633	19.1	53.5	27.3	22,540	8,480	61.4	941	81.1	11.6	3.8
White, IL	17193	27,674	25.5	40.0	34.5	24,588	14,481	56.9	650	77.9	16.8	2.0
Whiteside, IL	17195	110,642	14.1	34.6	51.3	93,517	9,445	61.6	3,258	81.7	13.1	1.7
Will, IL	17197	1,423,407	8.0	25.4	66.6	1,193,984	10,075	57.0	40,271	85.7	10.1	2.3
Williamson, IL	17199	116,624	15.7	42.2	42.1	89,674	8,798	57.3	3,152	82.4	11.0	5.7
Winnebago, IL	17201	572,273	14.0	32.9	53.2	473,862	9,984	59.2	16,448	79.4	10.2	7.5
Woodford, IL	17203	98,326	9.5	29.6	60.9	72,847	8,799	59.6	2,316	91.5	5.7	1.8
INDIANA	18000	13,056,485	10.8	44.7	44.5	9,681,726	9,366	57.5	382,116	84.8	7.8	4.7
Adams, IN	18001	66,847	10.0	39.5	50.6	39,238	8,306	57.2	2,019	70.7	8.6	10.3
Allen, IN	18003	635,191	12.5	47.6	39.9	515,393	9,379	60.4	20,902	85.7	8.0	4.1
Bartholomew, IN	18005	150,975	11.0	42.1	46.9	125,313	10,294	51.9	4,027	88.9	5.0	5.0
Benton, IN	18007	27,571	5.0	39.8	55.2	18,571	10,115	56.6	432	85.9	11.6	2.6
Blackford, IN	18009	24,461	11.5	53.3	35.2	19,342	9,068	58.2	692	80.2	7.5	10.8
Boone, IN	18011	140,789	6.0	37.7	56.3	95,346	8,832	57.8	2,815	86.9	7.6	4.3
Brown, IN	18013	25,054	9.8	47.6	42.6	21,531	9,800	55.5	699	88.6	7.2	1.1
Carroll, IN	18015	31,116	8.3	48.8	42.9	22,715	8,162	49.4	1,107	76.3	16.6	6.2
Cass, IN	18017	87,840	13.3	47.7	39.0	68,056	9,889	61.5	2,212	75.4	10.8	11.0
Clark, IN	18019	204,644	11.1	44.9	44.0	148,739	9,088	61.6	5,542	73.3	16.0	5.9
Clay, IN	18021	55,349	10.5	48.5	41.0	39,063	8,542	62.2	1,460	84.5	9.9	5.0
Clinton, IN	18023	73,725	13.8	48.1	38.1	57,230	9,151	58.6	1,975	78.8	13.0	6.8
Crawford, IN	18025	21,399	12.8	48.8	38.5	16,406	9,754	60.1	679	83.1	3.4	13.6
Daviess, IN	18027	53,932	12.6	45.7	41.7	41,719	9,716	61.6	1,814	69.9	8.7	6.1
Dearborn, IN	18029	123,894	8.7	37.3	54.0	80,276	8,867	60.4	2,656	87.0	9.0	2.1
Decatur, IN	18031	48,640	8.5	46.4	45.1	35,836	7,960	60.5	1,493	86.1	11.1	1.9
De Kalb, IN	18033	108,193	13.8	40.1	46.1	86,005	10,925	59.9	2,377	84.4	7.2	3.0
Delaware, IN	18035	201,891	14.0	47.7	38.3	147,597	9,481	62.1	9,746	92.5	4.2	2.4
Dubois, IN	18037	103,614	9.3	36.9	53.8	70,956	9,533	53.8	2,244	76.3	9.4	11.0
Elkhart, IN	18039	467,681	11.4	43.9	44.7	340,518	9,490	57.3	11,476	78.8	7.0	6.2
Fayette, IN	18041	48,888	17.2	50.4	32.4	40,287	9,504	58.6	1,313	85.8	4.8	4.7
Floyd, IN	18043	158,880	10.1	42.2	47.7	113,019	9,212	58.9	4,213	85.1	7.7	4.9
Fountain, IN	18045	36,137	9.9	48.3	41.8	26,779	8,353	58.4	898	91.7	5.0	1.5
Franklin, IN	18047	54,586	7.2	47.2	45.6	39,705	7,872	60.4	1,369	85.2	6.9	3.4
Fulton, IN	18049	29,204	9.2	47.5	43.2	21,338	7,903	55.4	1,182	77.2	16.2	4.9
Gibson, IN	18051	60,894	6.9	44.0	49.0	42,375	8,285	60.8	1,697	88.0	8.0	3.2
Grant, IN	18053	139,335	15.6	51.7	32.7	105,959	8,918	44.7	5,073	88.4	4.5	6.3
Greene, IN	18055	67,057	12.9	50.7	36.4	52,794	9,566	60.8	1,614	87.0	8.6	3.3
Hamilton, IN	18057	614,095	6.6	35.3	58.1	419,439	8,282	58.8	13,119	92.6	5.1	1.8
Hancock, IN	18059	160,961	7.3	39.1	53.7	106,819	8,372	57.2	3,766	78.4	12.1	7.2
Harrison, IN	18061	72,001	9.3	45.4	45.3	53,493	8,724	56.5	2,033	79.4	9.9	5.2
Hendricks, IN	18063	291,224	7.3	43.9	48.8	218,113	8,307	54.7	7,309	89.0	6.8	2.6
Henry, IN	18065	101,082	11.0	48.3	40.7	77,457	9,413	58.8	2,437	87.2	8.2	4.3
Howard, IN	18067	174,782	12.3	44.7	43.0	132,825	9,669	56.8	4,362	83.8	7.4	6.2
Huntington, IN	18069	65,504	10.4	49.0	40.6	52,074	8,609	58.1	2,238	88.2	8.8	2.7
Jackson, IN	18071	74,558	9.9	47.2	42.9	56,114	8,324	62.5	2,102	78.2	14.7	5.0

Note. Data in columns 26 through 41 from the American Community Survey are subject to sampling error, which can be especially large in small counties and small population groups. See notes and definitions for more information.

Table C-1. Population, School, and Student Characteristics by County, Selected Years—*Continued*

County	State/ County Code	High school graduates, 2006–2010			College enrollment, 2006–2010		College graduates, 2006–2010 (percent)						
		Population 25 years and over	High school diploma or less (percent)	High school diploma or more (percent)	Number	Percent public	Bachelor's degree or more	+/- U.S. percent with Bachelor's degree or more	Non-Hispanic White	Black or African American	American Indian and Alaska Native	Asian, Hawaiian, and Pacific Islander	Hispanic or Latino[3]
		30	31	32	33	34	35	36	37	38	39	40	41
ILLINOIS— *(Continued)*													
Richland, IL	17159	11,231	47.8	89.1	743	94.3	18.1	-9.8	17.8	14.0	0.0	73.0	0.0
Rock Island, IL	17161	100,302	46.5	86.8	9,701	63.8	21.1	-6.8	22.4	11.7	14.4	56.8	9.3
St. Clair, IL	17163	173,279	41.6	87.4	19,884	78.7	23.9	-4.0	27.0	15.6	21.5	43.5	17.0
Saline, IL	17165	17,270	47.9	82.1	1,342	90.5	14.3	-13.6	14.6	4.9	58.2	41.5	15.1
Sangamon, IL	17167	132,183	38.4	91.0	12,519	79.8	31.0	3.1	32.0	16.8	24.8	65.5	21.5
Schuyler, IL	17169	5,263	52.9	89.2	349	84.2	17.7	-10.2	18.0	0.0	0.0	0.0	2.6
Scott, IL	17171	3,704	55.7	88.3	208	71.6	18.0	-9.9	18.0	0.0	0.0	0.0	0.0
Shelby, IL	17173	15,567	53.7	87.7	865	91.0	14.8	-13.1	14.8	21.7	0.0	19.1	24.1
Stark, IL	17175	4,167	51.3	88.0	222	82.0	15.2	-12.7	15.3	0.0	0.0	30.8	0.0
Stephenson, IL	17177	33,339	47.8	88.5	2,284	78.7	17.2	-10.7	17.8	8.7	0.0	47.3	7.0
Tazewell, IL	17179	91,972	42.7	90.2	6,900	76.2	23.1	-4.8	23.5	3.9	8.6	28.0	14.8
Union, IL	17181	12,604	52.1	79.1	946	92.7	17.8	-10.1	18.2	0.0	0.0	0.0	20.2
Vermilion, IL	17183	54,287	55.4	84.9	3,052	90.0	13.7	-14.2	13.8	7.9	0.0	83.8	11.9
Wabash, IL	17185	8,346	47.4	86.4	720	84.3	15.3	-12.6	15.5	0.0	0.0	0.0	14.6
Warren, IL	17187	11,670	48.6	85.5	1,792	32.5	19.9	-8.0	20.8	1.6	0.0	58.6	2.4
Washington, IL	17189	10,344	48.6	86.2	751	84.8	17.1	-10.8	17.5	0.0	0.0	0.0	2.3
Wayne, IL	17191	11,713	51.4	84.3	877	86.3	12.1	-15.8	12.2	0.0	0.0	29.2	0.0
White, IL	17193	10,643	50.3	84.5	555	89.5	12.2	-15.7	11.9	42.9	0.0	28.6	4.5
Whiteside, IL	17195	40,176	53.6	85.5	2,539	72.6	16.1	-11.8	16.6	7.2	0.0	34.2	10.7
Will, IL	17197	417,951	38.2	90.0	39,650	65.8	30.7	2.8	32.1	24.2	16.1	70.8	11.9
Williamson, IL	17199	45,292	43.9	88.2	4,268	91.2	21.7	-6.2	22.0	8.1	0.0	50.5	29.2
Winnebago, IL	17201	194,604	49.3	84.4	16,395	68.7	21.1	-6.8	22.9	9.0	18.4	47.8	9.8
Woodford, IL	17203	25,002	40.3	92.4	2,341	58.7	26.0	-1.9	26.0	47.8	0.0	38.1	28.1
INDIANA	18000	4,165,617	50.0	86.2	450,727	76.8	22.4	-5.5	23.1	14.6	15.1	58.6	11.5
Adams, IN	18001	20,661	59.7	82.8	1,497	72.5	12.2	-15.7	12.5	76.0	0.0	15.6	0.0
Allen, IN	18003	223,089	43.1	88.5	23,071	78.8	26.1	-1.8	28.0	12.6	8.2	46.1	11.4
Bartholomew, IN	18005	50,606	47.0	89.2	3,333	86.7	26.7	-1.2	25.3	44.4	29.0	77.9	10.9
Benton, IN	18007	5,864	60.6	89.7	393	88.0	13.7	-14.2	13.9	0.0	0.0	0.0	8.9
Blackford, IN	18009	8,912	64.4	84.7	503	84.3	12.2	-15.7	12.4	0.0	100.0	100.0	0.0
Boone, IN	18011	35,523	36.4	92.9	2,301	79.5	38.0	10.1	38.1	46.5	0.0	64.0	18.5
Brown, IN	18013	11,028	52.6	87.5	415	82.2	21.2	-6.7	21.1	0.0	33.3	52.4	45.3
Carroll, IN	18015	13,683	59.8	88.6	670	82.7	14.9	-13.0	15.1	0.0	100.0	100.0	0.0
Cass, IN	18017	25,870	61.7	82.0	1,510	84.8	14.1	-13.8	14.6	8.7	8.9	33.5	7.3
Clark, IN	18019	72,970	51.2	85.4	5,245	82.2	17.8	-10.1	17.9	15.8	8.1	62.0	9.0
Clay, IN	18021	18,143	56.0	87.9	1,471	80.9	13.9	-14.0	14.0	0.0	0.0	0.0	0.0
Clinton, IN	18023	21,516	62.2	81.4	1,137	85.0	13.1	-14.8	14.1	12.5	0.0	0.0	2.5
Crawford, IN	18025	7,339	68.0	82.3	324	76.2	11.5	-16.4	11.7	0.0	0.0	0.0	0.0
Daviess, IN	18027	19,405	62.9	74.5	1,004	73.0	12.2	-15.7	12.0	49.2	14.3	27.2	0.7
Dearborn, IN	18029	33,210	55.4	88.5	2,349	81.3	16.9	-11.0	16.9	9.3	0.0	37.6	17.5
Decatur, IN	18031	16,966	61.0	84.6	1,165	83.4	14.8	-13.1	14.0	0.0	0.0	78.0	10.8
De Kalb, IN	18033	27,392	55.6	88.2	1,937	78.7	15.7	-12.2	15.7	12.0	15.9	100.0	13.2
Delaware, IN	18035	70,845	51.9	84.5	19,438	96.5	22.4	-5.5	22.8	8.7	4.2	73.5	16.2
Dubois, IN	18037	28,078	56.2	84.6	1,240	79.0	20.2	-7.7	20.6	25.0	0.0	19.7	10.1
Elkhart, IN	18039	122,660	56.5	80.0	8,285	71.6	18.1	-9.8	19.9	8.8	4.4	29.8	7.6
Fayette, IN	18041	16,728	66.2	76.9	1,316	90.4	8.8	-19.1	8.7	0.0	100.0	100.0	0.0
Floyd, IN	18043	49,203	48.4	87.3	4,145	78.8	22.1	-5.8	22.5	10.7	29.4	46.6	11.0
Fountain, IN	18045	11,791	62.5	83.2	488	74.0	10.8	-17.1	10.9	0.0	0.0	27.6	4.1
Franklin, IN	18047	15,433	59.5	85.4	785	65.5	16.5	-11.4	16.6	0.0	0.0	0.0	28.4
Fulton, IN	18049	14,064	60.2	85.7	642	63.7	14.0	-13.9	13.6	0.0	0.0	56.9	25.6
Gibson, IN	18051	22,541	55.2	88.6	1,698	61.2	14.3	-13.6	14.5	6.2	0.0	60.0	0.0
Grant, IN	18053	45,577	59.5	83.3	6,408	32.5	15.4	-12.5	16.2	5.5	21.4	25.5	7.4
Greene, IN	18055	22,589	60.5	83.2	1,416	89.5	11.2	-16.7	11.1	100.0	0.0	0.0	6.2
Hamilton, IN	18057	166,658	21.2	96.1	13,181	76.5	53.8	25.9	53.8	43.7	20.6	74.1	29.6
Hancock, IN	18059	45,189	46.1	90.7	2,912	77.6	24.2	-3.7	24.3	17.2	0.0	23.8	21.1
Harrison, IN	18061	26,209	56.0	88.4	2,009	80.4	14.4	-13.5	14.4	21.5	41.5	27.1	0.0
Hendricks, IN	18063	91,341	38.9	93.4	6,493	71.6	31.2	3.3	30.8	27.4	13.9	53.4	28.5
Henry, IN	18065	34,189	60.9	83.5	2,491	81.7	13.8	-14.1	14.2	3.3	0.0	20.4	6.2
Howard, IN	18067	56,747	50.9	86.3	4,249	91.0	19.7	-8.2	20.3	8.6	45.7	37.9	9.9
Huntington, IN	18069	24,531	56.5	87.8	2,534	50.5	14.8	-13.1	14.9	0.0	0.0	44.2	1.1
Jackson, IN	18071	28,195	58.6	84.2	1,298	76.3	13.8	-14.1	13.8	0.0	8.8	59.1	7.4

Note. Data in columns 26 through 41 from the American Community Survey are subject to sampling error, which can be especially large in small counties and small population groups. See notes and definitions for more information.

[3]May be of any race.

Table C-1. Population, School, and Student Characteristics by County, Selected Years—*Continued*

County	State/ County Code	County Type[1]	Population, 2010		Percent of related children 5–17 years in poverty, 2010	Percent of children under 19 years with no health insurance, 2010	Number of schools and students, 2010–2011			Resident enrollment, 2006–2010 K-12 enrollment	
			Total	Percent 5–17 years			School districts	Schools	Students	Number	Percent public
			1	2	3	4	5	6	7	8	9
INDIANA—*(Continued)*											
Jasper, IN	18073	1	33,478	19.2	12.9	9.2	2	9	5,338	6,401	90.3
Jay, IN	18075	6	21,253	19.6	23.8	9.0	1	10	3,613	4,255	97.6
Jefferson, IN	18077	6	32,428	16.9	21.0	8.6	3	10	4,630	5,652	84.3
Jennings, IN	18079	6	28,525	19.8	20.0	8.9	1	10	5,005	5,715	94.2
Johnson, IN	18081	1	139,654	19.5	13.3	7.5	8	38	25,207	26,313	89.6
Knox, IN	18083	4	38,440	15.4	21.4	8.2	4	13	5,237	5,819	91.6
Kosciusko, IN	18085	4	77,358	18.7	17.9	13.5	4	24	14,115	14,442	89.4
Lagrange, IN	18087	6	37,128	24.4	26.5	30.7	3	14	5,976	7,693	69.0
Lake, IN	18089	1	496,005	19.0	24.7	7.5	28	137	87,520	96,779	89.0
La Porte, IN	18091	3	111,467	16.8	23.5	7.8	9	37	18,211	19,949	89.7
Lawrence, IN	18093	4	46,134	17.7	20.0	9.1	2	20	7,355	8,186	91.8
Madison, IN	18095	3	131,636	16.9	25.1	8.3	6	30	19,338	21,793	92.0
Marion, IN	18097	1	903,393	17.5	28.2	9.5	45	228	143,816	157,364	86.0
Marshall, IN	18099	6	47,051	20.0	17.2	12.9	6	17	7,782	9,210	86.2
Martin, IN	18101	6	10,334	17.5	17.3	8.9	2	5	1,644	1,712	95.8
Miami, IN	18103	6	36,903	17.0	21.5	8.7	3	11	5,687	6,970	93.8
Monroe, IN	18105	3	137,974	11.6	16.7	8.5	3	29	13,743	14,991	89.9
Montgomery, IN	18107	6	38,124	17.5	20.8	9.9	3	16	6,240	6,877	98.2
Morgan, IN	18109	1	68,894	18.9	15.3	9.8	4	23	11,993	13,246	92.9
Newton, IN	18111	1	14,244	17.3	15.1	10.4	2	7	2,365	2,637	92.0
Noble, IN	18113	6	47,536	19.8	17.6	12.5	3	15	7,753	9,415	89.1
Ohio, IN	18115	1	6,128	16.3	12.4	10.1	1	2	878	1,060	97.4
Orange, IN	18117	6	19,840	18.5	22.9	8.7	5	8	3,402	3,570	88.1
Owen, IN	18119	3	21,575	17.6	21.1	10.1	1	6	2,848	3,807	94.9
Parke, IN	18121	6	17,339	15.7	26.3	13.5	3	7	2,313	2,607	90.3
Perry, IN	18123	6	19,338	15.5	15.7	8.5	3	5	2,951	2,891	94.8
Pike, IN	18125	6	12,845	16.4	17.0	8.7	1	5	1,991	2,266	94.0
Porter, IN	18127	1	164,343	18.3	12.0	7.4	9	51	27,636	30,332	91.3
Posey, IN	18129	2	25,910	18.0	11.6	7.2	3	10	3,817	4,858	87.7
Pulaski, IN	18131	6	13,402	18.0	19.6	10.8	2	6	2,132	2,722	97.7
Putnam, IN	18133	1	37,963	15.9	15.8	9.3	7	17	6,338	6,232	91.6
Randolph, IN	18135	6	26,171	18.5	24.3	9.8	6	14	4,590	5,073	95.0
Ripley, IN	18137	6	28,818	19.7	13.6	9.4	4	9	3,365	5,679	91.0
Rush, IN	18139	6	17,392	18.8	18.4	9.9	1	7	2,593	3,538	94.5
St. Joseph, IN	18141	2	266,931	18.0	20.9	8.0	8	72	39,090	48,615	81.9
Scott, IN	18143	6	24,181	17.9	26.9	8.2	2	9	4,142	4,301	97.9
Shelby, IN	18145	1	44,436	18.3	16.8	9.8	5	16	7,552	8,083	94.0
Spencer, IN	18147	8	20,952	18.3	13.0	9.6	2	10	3,524	3,826	84.0
Starke, IN	18149	6	23,363	18.0	27.5	9.6	3	8	3,991	4,338	95.7
Steuben, IN	18151	7	34,185	17.4	17.3	10.6	2	9	4,177	5,948	89.8
Sullivan, IN	18153	3	21,475	16.0	18.8	8.9	3	11	3,303	3,589	90.8
Switzerland, IN	18155	8	10,613	18.2	26.4	12.3	1	4	1,437	1,886	91.1
Tippecanoe, IN	18157	3	172,780	14.3	17.3	9.2	6	34	21,232	23,599	90.1
Tipton, IN	18159	3	15,936	18.1	12.1	8.6	2	5	2,706	3,005	92.5
Union, IN	18161	8	7,516	19.2	18.5	10.1	1	4	1,588	1,468	92.1
Vanderburgh, IN	18163	2	179,703	15.7	22.0	6.7	3	42	23,998	28,114	83.2
Vermillion, IN	18165	3	16,212	17.6	16.8	7.9	3	7	2,737	2,956	97.8
Vigo, IN	18167	3	107,848	15.5	25.4	8.6	2	30	15,891	16,816	94.1
Wabash, IN	18169	6	32,888	16.8	16.7	8.3	4	16	5,349	5,394	97.1
Warren, IN	18171	8	8,508	17.7	13.8	9.9	1	4	1,239	1,466	96.9
Warrick, IN	18173	2	59,689	19.5	9.2	7.5	1	16	9,905	11,347	83.9
Washington, IN	18175	1	28,262	19.2	22.8	9.9	3	9	4,591	5,513	90.6
Wayne, IN	18177	5	68,917	16.7	24.6	10.3	6	26	10,944	11,614	93.1
Wells, IN	18179	2	27,636	18.4	12.8	9.2	4	9	4,885	5,183	90.0
White, IN	18181	6	24,643	18.2	16.6	12.1	4	15	4,978	4,549	96.9
Whitley, IN	18183	2	33,292	18.3	11.6	8.7	3	8	4,849	5,967	91.2

[1]County type codes are from the Economic Research Service of the United States Department of Agriculture. See notes and definitions for more information.

Table C-1. Population, School, and Student Characteristics by County, Selected Years—*Continued*

County	State/ County Code	Characteristics of students, 2010–2011				Number of graduates, 2008–2009	Staff and students, 2010–2011			
		Percent with IEP[2]	Percent eligible for free or reduced lunch	Percent minority	Percent English-language learners		Total staff	Number of teachers	Student/ teacher ratio	Central admin. staff
		10	11	12	13	14	15	16	17	18
INDIANA—*(Continued)*										
Jasper, IN	18073	16.0	37.9	10.4	3.8	320	602	263	20.3	7
Jay, IN	18075	26.6	51.6	6.0	2.9	261	387	220	16.4	3
Jefferson, IN	18077	16.7	49.9	6.8	0.7	281	577	259	17.9	10
Jennings, IN	18079	22.4	56.8	5.5	0.9	312	497	307	16.3	5
Johnson, IN	18081	14.2	34.0	10.2	2.7	1,580	2,597	1,298	19.4	43
Knox, IN	18083	15.9	47.5	6.3	0.3	320	627	327	16.0	12
Kosciusko, IN	18085	15.6	47.8	17.5	7.2	914	1,579	786	18.0	26
Lagrange, IN	18087	14.2	50.4	10.1	14.7	337	685	347	17.2	10
Lake, IN	18089	13.0	54.1	58.9	5.7	5,054	9,041	4,653	18.8	118
La Porte, IN	18091	15.6	51.1	26.2	2.5	1,081	2,229	990	18.4	34
Lawrence, IN	18093	18.1	45.3	4.8	0.2	426	902	398	18.5	10
Madison, IN	18095	18.6	48.4	18.7	2.8	1,130	2,010	988	19.6	43
Marion, IN	18097	15.1	63.7	58.6	9.9	6,962	13,939	7,321	19.6	240
Marshall, IN	18099	11.6	49.1	18.6	7.8	480	914	435	17.9	18
Martin, IN	18101	20.1	43.4	3.5	0.1	126	159	95	17.3	8
Miami, IN	18103	14.1	47.7	8.6	0.8	346	586	309	18.4	12
Monroe, IN	18105	17.2	35.9	19.0	2.3	905	1,772	778	17.7	35
Montgomery, IN	18107	17.6	42.9	9.3	3.3	467	753	374	16.7	6
Morgan, IN	18109	14.8	39.1	5.0	0.4	789	1,234	631	19.0	18
Newton, IN	18111	19.0	47.8	9.7	2.9	181	328	151	15.7	5
Noble, IN	18113	14.9	53.1	21.1	11.0	514	878	426	18.2	11
Ohio, IN	18115	16.6	36.8	2.8	0.5	76	92	51	17.2	4
Orange, IN	18117	18.4	51.2	5.5	0.4	209	456	202	16.8	10
Owen, IN	18119	20.6	44.3	2.9	0.3	180	302	146	19.5	5
Parke, IN	18121	20.6	54.3	4.5	. . .	194	290	159	14.5	9
Perry, IN	18123	12.7	45.0	3.8	0.1	206	282	165	17.9	4
Pike, IN	18125	23.7	40.4	3.0	0.4	143	351	131	15.2	4
Porter, IN	18127	14.3	32.6	19.6	1.4	1,869	2,844	1,446	19.1	40
Posey, IN	18129	23.7	28.4	7.9	0.4	329	490	246	15.5	13
Pulaski, IN	18131	17.8	45.9	7.2	1.2	156	271	141	15.1	5
Putnam, IN	18133	20.4	44.8	6.2	0.3	409	765	394	16.1	20
Randolph, IN	18135	20.6	51.4	6.9	1.4	294	655	311	14.8	17
Ripley, IN	18137	16.4	43.3	2.1	0.1	210	404	226	14.9	7
Rush, IN	18139	12.1	46.3	6.5	0.4	147	302	154	16.8	3
St. Joseph, IN	18141	18.1	53.3	39.2	7.6	2,387	4,565	2,195	17.8	50
Scott, IN	18143	18.4	50.0	4.7	0.4	227	422	223	18.6	8
Shelby, IN	18145	16.1	41.5	9.6	3.3	475	722	423	17.9	13
Spencer, IN	18147	14.5	34.2	7.0	2.0	247	370	201	17.5	8
Starke, IN	18149	13.3	56.9	6.1	1.2	281	458	226	17.7	12
Steuben, IN	18151	14.4	45.7	9.9	2.8	295	499	244	17.1	12
Sullivan, IN	18153	15.5	48.3	4.4	. . .	232	227	103	32.1	3
Switzerland, IN	18155	18.0	47.0	3.8	0.4	101	154	82	17.5	3
Tippecanoe, IN	18157	16.5	42.8	28.4	8.7	1,342	2,222	1,156	18.4	13
Tipton, IN	18159	18.8	34.1	7.1	1.6	179	345	162	16.7	11
Union, IN	18161	16.6	45.2	3.3	0.2	103	185	111	14.3	1
Vanderburgh, IN	18163	18.9	56.2	28.9	1.4	1,469	2,479	1,426	16.8	42
Vermillion, IN	18165	18.2	48.9	4.4	0.1	192	281	169	16.2	6
Vigo, IN	18167	23.8	51.6	17.3	1.1	952	1,464	893	17.8	5
Wabash, IN	18169	13.0	46.3	6.6	0.7	335	785	345	15.5	11
Warren, IN	18171	20.0	35.5	2.3	. . .	90	147	74	16.7	4
Warrick, IN	18173	21.9	29.0	9.0	1.0	670	834	493	20.1	17
Washington, IN	18175	18.1	52.0	3.3	0.2	306	529	253	18.1	8
Wayne, IN	18177	17.9	56.6	16.2	1.8	646	1,183	657	16.7	30
Wells, IN	18179	15.1	34.7	5.5	1.0	364	532	305	16.0	10
White, IN	18181	17.0	48.6	13.7	6.1	313	620	312	16.0	10
Whitley, IN	18183	13.2	32.8	6.6	0.2	361	578	281	17.3	7

[2]IEP=Individual Education Program. See notes and definitions for more information.
. . . = Not available.

Table C-1. Population, School, and Student Characteristics by County, Selected Years—*Continued*

County	State/ County Code	Revenues, 2008–2009				Current expenditures, 2008–2009			Resident population 16 to 19 years, 2006–2010			
		Total revenue ($1,000's)	Percentage of revenue from: Federal government	State government	Local government	Amount ($1,000's)	Amount per student	Percent for instruction	Total population 16 to 19 years	Percent enrolled in school	Percent high school graduates, not enrolled in school	Percent not enrolled, not grads, not employed, or not in labor force
		19	20	21	22	23	24	25	26	27	28	29
INDIANA—*(Continued)*												
Jasper, IN	18073	58,694	7.4	44.1	48.5	42,649	7,867	61.1	2,000	87.0	7.5	4.8
Jay, IN	18075	45,971	10.5	51.7	37.8	34,455	9,386	58.7	1,270	83.9	8.3	6.1
Jefferson, IN	18077	71,619	14.1	40.4	45.5	54,535	11,383	57.5	2,113	89.6	7.6	1.3
Jennings, IN	18079	56,018	11.1	56.9	31.9	46,575	8,965	60.2	1,626	77.1	10.5	6.8
Johnson, IN	18081	297,921	8.4	42.3	49.3	212,556	8,580	54.9	8,252	81.2	9.6	4.6
Knox, IN	18083	67,701	12.9	45.9	41.2	52,233	10,024	60.3	2,958	90.5	5.9	2.2
Kosciusko, IN	18085	194,359	9.4	38.6	51.9	124,728	8,686	58.7	4,500	76.3	14.5	4.8
Lagrange, IN	18087	71,376	8.5	46.0	45.4	54,910	8,990	58.4	2,383	47.8	6.5	11.0
Lake, IN	18089	1,163,422	10.8	45.2	44.0	831,652	9,731	55.9	28,631	84.5	9.0	4.7
La Porte, IN	18091	207,100	12.5	46.9	40.6	166,537	9,111	57.4	5,820	81.8	6.8	9.2
Lawrence, IN	18093	84,919	11.7	49.3	39.0	65,879	8,949	60.4	2,330	74.2	16.1	7.0
Madison, IN	18095	249,167	10.9	47.1	42.0	182,477	9,370	56.0	7,121	78.0	9.7	8.3
Marion, IN	18097	1,842,794	13.1	47.9	39.0	1,449,923	10,802	55.2	50,197	81.2	8.8	7.5
Marshall, IN	18099	104,024	11.5	40.3	48.2	76,681	9,860	59.9	2,688	81.2	9.9	3.8
Martin, IN	18101	19,131	9.8	55.2	35.0	15,978	9,273	60.2	510	99.4	0.0	0.6
Miami, IN	18103	66,572	9.3	52.7	37.9	52,056	9,120	55.3	2,189	90.5	5.9	3.6
Monroe, IN	18105	181,543	9.6	36.2	54.2	126,027	9,084	56.3	13,839	96.1	2.4	1.3
Montgomery, IN	18107	87,528	11.9	39.7	48.4	59,826	9,280	53.3	2,455	83.1	8.4	5.5
Morgan, IN	18109	143,270	8.8	44.3	46.9	99,736	8,322	58.4	3,774	83.7	7.1	6.7
Newton, IN	18111	36,046	6.5	38.8	54.7	22,933	9,376	57.4	784	83.7	8.6	6.9
Noble, IN	18113	95,488	9.0	46.0	45.0	68,588	8,766	59.6	2,772	76.8	11.4	8.2
Ohio, IN	18115	10,735	6.8	48.4	44.8	8,070	8,706	64.5	296	72.3	14.9	8.1
Orange, IN	18117	45,780	14.6	45.9	39.5	36,957	10,867	64.4	1,223	70.2	13.5	14.1
Owen, IN	18119	39,181	8.2	47.5	44.3	28,891	9,708	59.6	1,257	75.0	8.8	8.0
Parke, IN	18121	32,226	10.2	48.0	41.8	23,372	9,567	60.3	956	61.9	13.3	7.6
Perry, IN	18123	34,175	8.2	51.5	40.3	26,933	8,904	62.3	996	83.0	7.8	5.0
Pike, IN	18125	37,278	15.0	30.0	55.0	32,040	15,668	44.4	653	75.0	18.4	3.4
Porter, IN	18127	354,520	7.5	35.8	56.7	229,469	8,329	57.2	9,531	90.3	6.8	1.6
Posey, IN	18129	68,577	7.7	32.4	59.8	41,993	10,575	55.6	1,515	92.1	4.0	0.6
Pulaski, IN	18131	30,825	16.8	41.8	41.4	23,260	10,714	57.1	718	93.3	5.0	1.3
Putnam, IN	18133	82,022	8.0	46.5	45.5	59,635	9,018	55.3	2,865	87.6	7.0	2.9
Randolph, IN	18135	56,077	12.8	51.8	35.4	43,336	9,004	59.4	1,344	87.2	7.3	4.7
Ripley, IN	18137	42,381	8.6	50.8	40.5	34,082	9,716	58.6	1,535	93.6	4.2	1.6
Rush, IN	18139	29,439	9.2	47.6	43.2	22,731	8,431	57.8	1,057	75.2	9.6	12.2
St. Joseph, IN	18141	536,331	12.2	46.3	41.6	401,905	9,887	58.8	17,339	90.8	4.5	3.6
Scott, IN	18143	50,794	10.1	51.6	38.3	36,859	8,636	59.1	1,233	79.1	9.7	6.2
Shelby, IN	18145	103,892	8.6	39.1	52.3	66,247	8,524	59.4	2,390	84.1	6.7	4.0
Spencer, IN	18147	42,409	8.2	42.4	49.4	29,815	8,410	60.6	1,165	85.8	10.3	3.0
Starke, IN	18149	47,389	10.3	51.9	37.8	33,276	8,130	59.2	1,379	77.8	11.0	7.0
Steuben, IN	18151	55,376	8.2	37.0	54.9	38,400	8,907	60.6	2,251	80.7	13.7	0.9
Sullivan, IN	18153	39,878	8.3	49.5	42.1	31,129	9,640	59.7	1,108	81.3	11.6	7.0
Switzerland, IN	18155	17,595	10.1	50.4	39.5	13,297	8,871	55.2	567	77.8	5.6	13.4
Tippecanoe, IN	18157	281,343	9.2	38.9	51.8	186,213	8,780	58.7	15,267	96.1	2.4	0.4
Tipton, IN	18159	29,573	7.4	49.6	43.0	22,867	8,032	58.8	808	83.9	7.9	4.1
Union, IN	18161	20,972	14.0	44.2	41.8	15,782	9,760	59.8	385	92.5	6.5	1.0
Vanderburgh, IN	18163	243,613	17.1	51.2	31.7	224,800	9,958	57.7	10,331	88.0	8.1	2.5
Vermillion, IN	18165	34,362	10.6	45.6	43.8	24,401	8,681	56.5	758	73.4	12.4	8.3
Vigo, IN	18167	188,944	13.4	50.8	35.9	149,348	9,351	61.8	7,623	86.6	7.8	4.1
Wabash, IN	18169	69,686	10.9	46.2	42.8	54,690	10,053	58.4	2,282	82.5	9.6	5.6
Warren, IN	18171	16,086	11.1	44.6	44.3	11,495	9,009	58.0	482	79.3	5.8	14.9
Warrick, IN	18173	103,302	6.7	44.3	48.9	72,266	7,491	61.1	3,216	87.8	7.0	3.4
Washington, IN	18175	53,055	9.3	55.1	35.6	38,923	8,217	60.2	1,415	79.1	13.6	6.0
Wayne, IN	18177	122,439	12.0	52.7	35.3	97,402	9,149	61.4	4,114	84.3	8.3	3.0
Wells, IN	18179	60,998	9.6	42.5	47.9	46,074	9,718	60.8	1,531	83.7	8.4	2.9
White, IN	18181	69,198	8.1	38.2	53.7	45,158	8,731	57.9	1,458	82.5	10.6	2.7
Whitley, IN	18183	59,377	7.0	43.4	49.6	41,236	8,478	56.8	1,764	83.6	11.9	3.7

Note. Data in columns 26 through 41 from the American Community Survey are subject to sampling error, which can be especially large in small counties and small population groups. See notes and definitions for more information.

Table C-1. Population, School, and Student Characteristics by County, Selected Years—*Continued*

County	State/ County Code	High school graduates, 2006–2010			College enrollment, 2006–2010		College graduates, 2006–2010 (percent)						
		Population 25 years and over	High school diploma or less (percent)	High school diploma or more (percent)	Number	Percent public	Bachelor's degree or more	+/- U.S. percent with Bachelor's degree or more	Non-Hispanic White	Black or African American	American Indian and Alaska Native	Asian, Hawaiian, and Pacific Islander	Hispanic or Latino[3]
		30	31	32	33	34	35	36	37	38	39	40	41
INDIANA— *(Continued)*													
Jasper, IN	18073	21,313	57.6	87.6	1,764	52.6	14.2	-13.7	14.6	3.2	0.0	20.5	6.0
Jay, IN	18075	13,962	64.1	84.3	895	75.5	10.7	-17.2	11.0	0.0	0.0	0.0	0.0
Jefferson, IN	18077	21,489	55.2	83.8	2,346	36.4	18.2	-9.7	18.1	25.6	0.0	39.8	10.4
Jennings, IN	18079	18,507	65.6	81.3	1,043	82.9	7.5	-20.4	7.6	0.0	0.0	46.0	0.0
Johnson, IN	18081	88,091	44.8	90.3	7,086	68.1	26.2	-1.7	25.9	22.5	34.9	42.6	21.7
Knox, IN	18083	24,865	51.9	85.3	3,767	93.8	14.9	-13.0	14.9	0.0	0.0	90.5	20.1
Kosciusko, IN	18085	49,948	53.0	84.7	3,226	72.7	20.2	-7.7	20.5	18.5	0.0	59.3	9.7
Lagrange, IN	18087	20,895	70.2	59.7	520	82.5	10.4	-17.5	10.1	0.0	0.0	49.0	14.7
Lake, IN	18089	322,775	51.2	86.1	28,284	75.4	18.9	-9.0	21.8	13.4	21.4	55.0	11.3
La Porte, IN	18091	75,996	54.1	85.4	5,175	83.2	16.7	-11.2	17.8	8.2	8.6	41.9	12.3
Lawrence, IN	18093	31,810	63.3	81.0	1,656	85.4	12.5	-15.4	12.5	0.0	16.0	51.8	8.1
Madison, IN	18095	89,020	55.7	86.4	6,968	62.6	16.6	-11.3	17.2	12.5	14.2	19.3	9.6
Marion, IN	18097	574,762	46.1	84.0	61,403	68.4	27.3	-0.6	32.4	15.4	21.6	54.6	9.6
Marshall, IN	18099	30,563	57.4	83.3	1,832	75.7	17.1	-10.8	17.7	33.7	0.0	29.5	5.8
Martin, IN	18101	7,035	61.9	81.2	419	73.0	8.5	-19.4	8.4	0.0	0.0	10.0	85.7
Miami, IN	18103	25,485	60.7	81.9	2,177	89.3	10.2	-17.7	10.9	0.0	0.0	27.0	4.7
Monroe, IN	18105	73,100	33.1	91.1	42,232	96.6	42.7	14.8	40.8	36.7	17.8	83.7	39.1
Montgomery, IN	18107	25,138	58.0	86.8	2,131	53.6	17.5	-10.4	17.7	19.8	0.0	50.0	4.1
Morgan, IN	18109	45,766	55.9	85.0	3,029	77.2	13.9	-14.0	14.1	0.0	0.0	12.1	3.2
Newton, IN	18111	9,889	61.1	85.8	615	77.4	9.5	-18.4	9.5	0.0	0.0	0.0	10.7
Noble, IN	18113	30,503	60.7	81.2	1,933	79.0	13.0	-14.9	13.8	39.2	12.5	36.0	1.6
Ohio, IN	18115	4,297	64.0	81.2	142	61.3	12.1	-15.8	10.8	0.0	0.0	0.0	84.9
Orange, IN	18117	13,397	66.2	78.7	470	89.6	12.5	-15.4	12.6	15.9	0.0	0.0	6.5
Owen, IN	18119	14,823	68.0	81.9	855	83.4	8.3	-19.6	8.4	0.0	0.0	0.0	4.6
Parke, IN	18121	12,196	58.5	80.9	579	74.3	12.7	-15.2	13.2	7.1	6.5	0.0	0.0
Perry, IN	18123	13,596	65.7	82.5	525	74.9	8.3	-19.6	8.4	0.5	0.0	0.0	15.7
Pike, IN	18125	9,073	63.1	83.9	326	84.4	8.3	-19.6	8.4	0.0	0.0	29.4	0.0
Porter, IN	18127	107,034	44.4	91.3	11,439	60.1	25.2	-2.7	25.9	25.9	15.0	47.8	10.2
Posey, IN	18129	17,601	51.7	89.0	1,293	80.7	18.5	-9.4	18.5	30.3	0.0	0.0	7.3
Pulaski, IN	18131	9,194	60.7	85.9	599	60.3	13.6	-14.3	13.6	0.0	0.0	47.5	13.9
Putnam, IN	18133	24,634	54.9	85.1	3,389	50.5	17.6	-10.3	17.7	6.2	5.8	44.3	26.5
Randolph, IN	18135	17,900	62.0	84.7	1,037	82.8	10.4	-17.5	10.7	0.0	0.0	100.0	0.0
Ripley, IN	18137	18,889	61.4	84.8	1,286	77.2	14.8	-13.1	15.0	36.8	0.0	26.7	3.1
Rush, IN	18139	11,740	64.5	84.8	600	81.0	13.3	-14.6	13.2	11.7	60.0	100.0	0.0
St. Joseph, IN	18141	169,943	47.1	86.4	27,052	45.4	25.6	-2.3	27.3	13.1	17.9	51.2	16.4
Scott, IN	18143	16,264	69.0	74.3	862	88.9	9.9	-18.0	9.8	20.4	0.0	100.0	12.2
Shelby, IN	18145	29,791	58.3	85.9	2,003	75.7	15.2	-12.7	14.7	29.5	19.1	47.2	17.9
Spencer, IN	18147	14,488	58.7	85.7	863	83.7	15.9	-12.0	16.1	6.7	0.0	42.3	1.8
Starke, IN	18149	15,680	65.7	79.1	633	80.1	11.2	-16.7	11.2	0.0	30.0	100.0	4.0
Steuben, IN	18151	22,562	53.3	89.4	2,158	52.9	18.9	-9.0	19.5	13.6	0.0	51.8	8.6
Sullivan, IN	18153	14,941	58.4	86.1	915	89.5	14.1	-13.8	14.7	5.8	6.8	58.3	0.0
Switzerland, IN	18155	6,945	69.1	78.1	285	79.3	11.4	-16.5	11.5	0.0	0.0	0.0	0.0
Tippecanoe, IN	18157	91,096	38.8	90.5	42,218	95.8	35.7	7.8	34.1	30.1	23.4	81.8	19.8
Tipton, IN	18159	11,176	57.4	87.5	590	83.2	13.5	-14.4	13.6	0.0	0.0	0.0	3.7
Union, IN	18161	5,014	59.1	84.8	464	94.8	15.2	-12.7	15.2	0.0	100.0	63.2	0.0
Vanderburgh, IN	18163	117,558	47.6	87.1	15,473	84.3	21.8	-6.1	22.6	10.2	35.5	55.6	11.9
Vermillion, IN	18165	11,435	61.3	85.4	465	86.5	12.3	-15.6	12.1	55.6	65.0	0.0	14.9
Vigo, IN	18167	68,357	49.6	84.8	12,933	77.3	21.3	-6.6	21.4	8.5	26.0	64.2	14.1
Wabash, IN	18169	22,172	59.4	85.4	2,212	40.4	16.3	-11.6	16.4	7.7	21.9	14.3	6.1
Warren, IN	18171	5,886	60.9	83.2	320	79.1	13.1	-14.8	12.5	0.0	0.0	82.6	29.4
Warrick, IN	18173	39,240	42.5	91.3	2,323	83.9	25.6	-2.3	25.3	38.1	8.7	46.5	23.2
Washington, IN	18175	18,705	66.7	79.6	910	79.5	10.5	-17.4	10.5	0.0	0.0	42.2	1.7
Wayne, IN	18177	46,676	56.7	82.7	4,113	77.9	15.8	-12.1	15.9	10.5	7.2	64.3	8.7
Wells, IN	18179	18,521	53.6	89.4	1,174	77.4	14.0	-13.9	14.3	5.7	3.7	0.0	3.0
White, IN	18181	16,957	57.2	86.8	896	78.0	14.5	-13.4	15.1	0.0	0.0	47.7	3.1
Whitley, IN	18183	22,179	50.3	90.2	1,471	68.3	16.6	-11.3	16.5	23.9	0.0	44.1	8.4

Note. Data in columns 26 through 41 from the American Community Survey are subject to sampling error, which can be especially large in small counties and small population groups. See notes and definitions for more information.
[3]May be of any race.

Table C-1. Population, School, and Student Characteristics by County, Selected Years—*Continued*

County	State/ County Code	County Type[1]	Population, 2010		Percent of related children 5–17 years in poverty, 2010	Percent of children under 19 years with no health insurance, 2010	Number of schools and students, 2010–2011			Resident enrollment, 2006–2010	
										K–12 enrollment	
			Total	Percent 5–17 years			School districts	Schools	Students	Number	Percent public
			1	2	3	4	5	6	7	8	9
IOWA	19000	X	3,046,355	17.3	14.2	4.1	368	1,436	495,775	524,375	90.6
Adair, IA	19001	8	7,682	16.6	12.7	4.6	2	5	951	1,327	100.0
Adams, IA	19003	9	4,029	15.3	19.0	6.3	2	4	580	660	94.2
Allamakee, IA	19005	6	14,330	16.5	20.9	7.6	3	10	2,303	2,565	91.1
Appanoose, IA	19007	7	12,887	16.2	21.7	4.9	3	15	2,077	2,058	97.6
Audubon, IA	19009	8	6,119	16.4	13.0	7.0	2	4	868	1,081	98.8
Benton, IA	19011	3	26,076	19.2	9.9	3.7	3	12	4,059	5,008	93.0
Black Hawk, IA	19013	3	131,090	15.3	21.3	3.4	6	39	18,027	19,827	88.6
Boone, IA	19015	6	26,306	17.9	10.2	3.2	4	14	3,994	4,756	94.4
Bremer, IA	19017	3	24,276	16.9	7.2	3.2	6	25	5,019	4,049	92.0
Buchanan, IA	19019	6	20,958	19.6	15.8	4.5	3	15	2,910	4,076	89.3
Buena Vista, IA	19021	7	20,260	17.8	16.8	5.9	5	16	3,974	3,756	94.0
Butler, IA	19023	8	14,867	17.0	11.6	4.9	4	10	1,891	2,470	99.2
Calhoun, IA	19025	9	9,670	15.5	15.9	5.3	4	7	1,961	1,484	98.3
Carroll, IA	19027	7	20,816	17.8	10.5	4.0	4	10	3,124	3,797	72.4
Cass, IA	19029	6	13,956	16.2	19.0	4.8	4	11	2,653	2,308	98.7
Cedar, IA	19031	6	18,499	18.3	8.5	3.5	5	14	3,449	3,332	98.5
Cerro Gordo, IA	19033	5	44,151	15.7	14.7	3.4	4	15	6,078	7,056	94.4
Cherokee, IA	19035	6	12,072	15.5	12.8	4.1	3	11	1,745	2,051	96.2
Chickasaw, IA	19037	6	12,439	17.8	13.8	4.9	3	9	2,141	2,168	94.3
Clarke, IA	19039	6	9,286	17.8	17.8	5.6	2	6	1,823	1,783	98.1
Clay, IA	19041	7	16,667	16.5	13.4	3.8	2	8	2,477	2,867	92.9
Clayton, IA	19043	8	18,129	17.0	17.1	7.4	4	9	2,011	3,161	93.2
Clinton, IA	19045	4	49,116	17.3	16.8	3.7	6	20	8,350	9,019	94.7
Crawford, IA	19047	6	17,096	19.0	16.2	6.9	5	15	3,409	3,345	92.8
Dallas, IA	19049	2	66,135	20.3	6.8	3.7	6	29	13,643	11,940	92.0
Davis, IA	19051	9	8,753	20.6	26.4	10.3	1	4	1,237	1,639	79.7
Decatur, IA	19053	9	8,457	16.4	24.9	6.1	2	6	1,128	1,452	93.7
Delaware, IA	19055	6	17,764	18.8	12.5	5.0	3	10	2,888	3,448	87.3
Des Moines, IA	19057	5	40,325	16.6	21.9	3.3	4	17	6,497	6,898	93.1
Dickinson, IA	19059	7	16,667	14.5	10.3	4.0	3	8	2,470	2,254	99.3
Dubuque, IA	19061	3	93,653	17.4	12.0	3.1	2	28	14,358	15,944	78.9
Emmet, IA	19063	7	10,302	16.6	17.8	4.7	2	6	1,797	1,757	94.4
Fayette, IA	19065	6	20,880	16.4	17.5	4.8	5	17	3,804	3,513	95.5
Floyd, IA	19067	7	16,303	17.5	18.7	4.9	3	9	2,509	2,808	93.8
Franklin, IA	19069	7	10,680	17.6	17.5	6.4	3	8	2,007	1,785	98.4
Fremont, IA	19071	8	7,441	16.5	15.6	4.3	3	6	914	1,345	98.9
Greene, IA	19073	6	9,336	17.5	15.9	4.6	3	7	1,637	1,645	100.0
Grundy, IA	19075	3	12,453	17.5	6.7	3.8	4	14	2,766	2,229	97.0
Guthrie, IA	19077	2	10,954	18.3	12.6	5.2	4	13	2,701	1,990	94.1
Hamilton, IA	19079	6	15,673	17.8	13.7	4.1	4	11	2,855	2,770	91.2
Hancock, IA	19081	7	11,341	17.4	11.7	4.5	4	9	1,799	1,987	91.3
Hardin, IA	19083	6	17,534	17.1	15.2	4.3	5	13	3,120	3,082	92.7
Harrison, IA	19085	2	14,928	17.9	13.2	4.1	5	11	2,987	2,722	96.4
Henry, IA	19087	7	20,145	17.4	16.6	4.3	4	13	3,549	3,597	94.6
Howard, IA	19089	7	9,566	18.0	17.9	5.2	2	9	1,739	1,773	90.3
Humboldt, IA	19091	7	9,815	16.6	13.6	4.4	3	8	1,542	1,762	88.0
Ida, IA	19093	8	7,089	17.1	14.1	4.9	2	6	1,175	1,276	99.1
Iowa, IA	19095	8	16,355	18.4	9.0	3.5	4	9	2,812	3,102	87.9
Jackson, IA	19097	6	19,848	17.5	16.9	4.4	5	15	3,177	3,714	89.0
Jasper, IA	19099	6	36,842	17.0	13.2	3.7	5	20	6,050	6,389	95.8
Jefferson, IA	19101	7	16,843	13.7	19.2	6.2	2	8	2,401	2,524	89.6
Johnson, IA	19103	3	130,882	13.6	11.8	3.3	4	35	15,510	16,837	90.6
Jones, IA	19105	3	20,638	16.6	12.3	3.9	4	12	3,309	3,600	91.8

[1]County type codes are from the Economic Research Service of the United States Department of Agriculture. See notes and definitions for more information.

Table C-1. Population, School, and Student Characteristics by County, Selected Years—*Continued*

County	State/ County Code	Characteristics of students, 2010–2011				Number of graduates, 2008–2009	Staff and students, 2010–2011			
		Percent with IEP[2]	Percent eligible for free or reduced lunch	Percent minority	Percent English-language learners		Total staff	Number of teachers	Student/ teacher ratio	Central admin. staff
		10	11	12	13	14	15	16	17	18
IOWA	19000	13.8	38.9	18.5	4.4	33,926	69,615	34,642	14.3	3,158
Adair, IA	19001	14.3	41.8	3.5	0.4	98	144	76	12.6	7
Adams, IA	19003	13.3	47.8	4.0	0.5	59	105	51	11.4	4
Allamakee, IA	19005	13.7	50.6	13.8	6.2	200	306	158	14.6	16
Appanoose, IA	19007	15.5	45.3	5.3	0.3	175	324	171	12.2	17
Audubon, IA	19009	9.3	32.8	3.9	...	76	127	67	13.0	5
Benton, IA	19011	15.6	27.7	4.9	0.1	285	535	286	14.2	18
Black Hawk, IA	19013	17.8	49.4	30.7	5.4	1,235	3,288	1,475	12.2	205
Boone, IA	19015	15.0	38.9	9.1	1.1	296	506	272	14.7	17
Bremer, IA	19017	14.2	21.2	4.1	1.3	380	547	296	16.9	21
Buchanan, IA	19019	17.3	29.6	3.5	2.4	203	400	204	14.3	15
Buena Vista, IA	19021	10.8	57.0	48.2	28.2	284	564	290	13.7	26
Butler, IA	19023	15.0	29.8	3.9	0.3	135	231	123	15.4	9
Calhoun, IA	19025	11.2	38.0	6.0	0.1	172	298	157	12.5	16
Carroll, IA	19027	12.8	35.3	6.7	0.9	260	434	223	14.0	17
Cass, IA	19029	16.3	42.5	5.1	1.1	202	358	194	13.6	12
Cedar, IA	19031	13.6	26.1	6.0	0.2	257	502	258	13.4	25
Cerro Gordo, IA	19033	16.8	40.9	13.1	0.5	389	751	418	14.5	26
Cherokee, IA	19035	16.3	36.1	8.6	1.0	141	247	130	13.5	10
Chickasaw, IA	19037	13.9	31.1	4.4	1.0	163	287	154	13.9	9
Clarke, IA	19039	14.4	44.3	19.5	8.7	101	240	125	14.6	10
Clay, IA	19041	14.4	39.4	9.6	0.5	189	346	169	14.7	12
Clayton, IA	19043	15.3	39.8	3.1	0.4	194	525	168	11.9	63
Clinton, IA	19045	16.2	42.9	13.0	0.4	560	1,140	597	14.0	40
Crawford, IA	19047	12.4	55.0	42.8	32.1	262	472	232	14.7	18
Dallas, IA	19049	9.8	21.7	15.2	3.9	787	1,673	916	14.9	76
Davis, IA	19051	12.7	42.8	4.9	...	102	145	90	13.7	7
Decatur, IA	19053	17.6	59.0	7.7	0.9	84	175	89	12.7	9
Delaware, IA	19055	11.6	33.9	2.5	0.3	267	397	207	13.9	13
Des Moines, IA	19057	17.0	49.1	20.4	0.5	431	930	465	14.0	37
Dickinson, IA	19059	12.9	28.6	5.9	0.5	214	365	184	13.5	17
Dubuque, IA	19061	16.2	35.4	12.2	1.4	990	1,918	965	14.9	60
Emmet, IA	19063	14.8	41.1	18.6	5.7	114	282	132	13.7	10
Fayette, IA	19065	16.5	43.2	6.6	0.5	322	519	265	14.4	19
Floyd, IA	19067	16.2	40.0	9.8	1.2	194	351	180	13.9	16
Franklin, IA	19069	17.2	46.0	24.1	7.6	186	289	153	13.1	12
Fremont, IA	19071	14.3	45.1	7.5	1.3	67	158	79	11.6	7
Greene, IA	19073	12.8	48.9	8.3	0.5	127	230	120	13.6	9
Grundy, IA	19075	13.6	25.7	5.3	0.3	262	331	188	14.7	13
Guthrie, IA	19077	13.2	36.1	5.0	0.5	199	403	204	13.2	18
Hamilton, IA	19079	11.8	38.3	13.0	3.4	198	409	201	14.2	15
Hancock, IA	19081	11.5	34.8	11.1	2.8	161	242	132	13.7	8
Hardin, IA	19083	16.6	39.4	8.9	1.1	209	457	223	14.0	19
Harrison, IA	19085	14.6	34.1	5.5	0.4	243	431	218	13.7	16
Henry, IA	19087	15.5	44.1	14.8	3.1	339	557	284	12.5	16
Howard, IA	19089	16.4	42.2	5.9	0.3	116	239	127	13.7	4
Humboldt, IA	19091	9.0	39.6	10.9	3.0	97	223	113	13.6	11
Ida, IA	19093	14.3	31.9	7.2	0.3	106	177	86	13.7	8
Iowa, IA	19095	12.0	27.9	6.4	2.9	209	364	199	14.2	13
Jackson, IA	19097	16.5	39.5	6.1	0.3	244	445	237	13.4	24
Jasper, IA	19099	13.1	37.8	6.6	0.3	448	799	423	14.3	25
Jefferson, IA	19101	13.5	41.2	7.9	1.7	186	369	171	14.0	13
Johnson, IA	19103	12.3	27.8	27.4	2.9	904	1,865	1,014	15.3	68
Jones, IA	19105	13.8	32.9	5.4	0.4	252	480	236	14.0	14

[2]IEP=Individual Education Program. See notes and definitions for more information.
. . . = Not available.

Table C-1. Population, School, and Student Characteristics by County, Selected Years—*Continued*

County	State/ County Code	Revenues, 2008–2009				Current expenditures, 2008–2009			Resident population 16 to 19 years, 2006–2010			
		Total revenue ($1,000's)	Percentage of revenue from			Amount ($1,000's)	Amount per student	Percent for instruction	Total population 16 to 19 years	Percent enrolled in school	Percent high school graduates, not enrolled in school	Percent not enrolled, not grads, not employed, or not in labor force
			Federal government	State government	Local government							
		19	20	21	22	23	24	25	26	27	28	29
IOWA	19000	5,732,319	7.5	44.4	48.1	4,732,655	9,707	61.6	177,476	87.5	8.3	2.4
Adair, IA	19001	11,223	5.3	44.3	50.4	9,445	9,953	63.2	361	79.2	17.2	1.7
Adams, IA	19003	7,495	7.6	43.9	48.5	5,834	10,804	65.0	216	83.3	8.8	4.6
Allamakee, IA	19005	26,591	10.1	44.7	45.2	20,940	9,172	60.4	775	91.4	7.7	0.4
Appanoose, IA	19007	23,511	7.5	53.5	39.1	19,461	8,886	65.9	661	78.4	15.1	4.1
Audubon, IA	19009	9,916	4.5	47.7	47.7	8,165	9,185	62.7	366	79.8	13.4	4.4
Benton, IA	19011	41,856	4.1	51.0	44.9	34,146	8,590	65.5	1,458	87.7	9.1	1.2
Black Hawk, IA	19013	221,772	12.5	44.7	42.8	195,501	11,077	53.0	8,583	90.3	5.6	2.1
Boone, IA	19015	45,352	4.5	43.7	51.8	34,852	9,136	65.9	1,611	87.9	8.7	2.2
Bremer, IA	19017	52,219	3.7	45.8	50.5	40,347	8,466	61.4	1,760	95.5	3.5	0.0
Buchanan, IA	19019	31,127	4.8	49.4	45.8	25,271	8,858	67.3	1,193	83.6	12.8	0.2
Buena Vista, IA	19021	45,158	9.9	43.3	46.8	36,557	9,350	66.2	1,409	91.2	7.3	1.0
Butler, IA	19023	35,496	4.0	26.3	69.7	16,091	8,609	59.9	682	89.0	7.6	3.4
Calhoun, IA	19025	23,758	4.8	37.8	57.5	20,748	10,613	65.9	400	97.3	2.5	0.3
Carroll, IA	19027	33,498	4.6	45.0	50.3	27,738	8,817	67.3	1,085	90.1	4.2	1.4
Cass, IA	19029	30,119	5.4	43.5	51.1	25,082	9,726	64.6	703	76.0	19.9	3.7
Cedar, IA	19031	37,931	3.4	43.5	53.0	28,932	8,507	63.9	874	89.9	7.4	1.3
Cerro Gordo, IA	19033	69,934	3.8	42.8	53.4	55,776	8,926	66.0	2,353	88.1	7.9	3.1
Cherokee, IA	19035	19,316	4.5	46.1	49.3	15,425	8,627	66.5	664	81.9	8.1	2.1
Chickasaw, IA	19037	22,935	4.6	43.6	51.9	19,044	8,756	67.6	747	85.7	9.9	2.3
Clarke, IA	19039	17,603	7.2	53.4	39.4	14,800	8,605	66.3	401	91.3	2.7	6.0
Clay, IA	19041	28,865	5.2	42.3	52.5	23,168	9,418	67.2	865	83.7	15.1	1.2
Clayton, IA	19043	31,986	24.4	38.6	37.0	39,249	18,281	32.7	887	78.0	16.5	4.7
Clinton, IA	19045	91,814	5.8	50.4	43.8	75,276	9,078	64.3	2,763	90.0	4.7	3.5
Crawford, IA	19047	36,483	8.0	49.6	42.3	30,009	9,245	65.1	1,092	81.1	9.5	9.3
Dallas, IA	19049	147,571	3.9	38.4	57.7	106,687	8,321	63.9	2,515	85.1	13.0	0.6
Davis, IA	19051	12,400	7.9	52.8	39.4	10,545	8,532	65.9	545	63.7	1.3	17.6
Decatur, IA	19053	12,635	10.9	49.5	39.6	9,978	8,692	65.0	657	83.1	15.2	0.2
Delaware, IA	19055	32,223	5.0	45.6	49.4	25,924	8,656	63.9	948	88.0	11.2	0.5
Des Moines, IA	19057	73,293	7.0	48.7	44.3	57,596	8,887	67.2	2,118	80.8	16.4	2.3
Dickinson, IA	19059	31,938	5.4	21.8	72.9	22,941	8,673	66.4	731	81.3	15.1	0.3
Dubuque, IA	19061	161,712	6.2	45.5	48.4	130,301	9,233	66.5	6,113	87.4	7.4	3.9
Emmet, IA	19063	20,658	5.9	45.5	48.6	16,445	9,572	66.9	705	88.9	11.1	0.0
Fayette, IA	19065	43,120	5.9	50.2	43.9	35,350	9,146	66.5	1,310	89.8	5.2	2.1
Floyd, IA	19067	29,031	6.5	48.2	45.3	23,482	8,949	65.4	985	78.7	8.2	11.4
Franklin, IA	19069	23,478	4.8	43.4	51.8	16,551	8,865	67.9	498	85.9	8.8	3.6
Fremont, IA	19071	11,181	6.0	42.9	51.1	8,719	9,285	61.7	385	88.6	9.9	1.6
Greene, IA	19073	19,551	6.0	43.1	51.0	15,330	9,382	64.6	531	87.2	8.9	0.4
Grundy, IA	19075	31,095	5.0	44.5	50.5	22,663	8,217	61.5	680	96.0	4.0	0.0
Guthrie, IA	19077	31,050	4.5	43.3	52.2	22,591	8,336	64.0	488	96.5	1.2	0.8
Hamilton, IA	19079	32,135	4.7	44.4	50.8	26,190	9,177	64.4	793	91.4	3.9	1.3
Hancock, IA	19081	20,352	4.5	41.0	54.5	15,919	8,834	64.4	505	88.9	6.5	2.0
Hardin, IA	19083	40,203	4.6	39.1	56.3	30,179	10,578	66.6	1,219	92.0	5.7	0.7
Harrison, IA	19085	34,570	5.3	46.5	48.2	28,035	9,256	63.4	835	84.6	12.1	2.5
Henry, IA	19087	50,015	5.6	49.1	45.3	40,411	8,702	67.8	1,020	91.7	7.4	0.6
Howard, IA	19089	16,236	5.0	46.4	48.7	13,216	9,366	61.6	509	91.4	2.2	3.9
Humboldt, IA	19091	17,016	5.0	41.5	53.5	14,395	9,571	66.2	466	86.5	13.1	0.4
Ida, IA	19093	12,721	4.4	43.6	51.9	10,301	8,314	65.6	381	82.7	16.3	0.0
Iowa, IA	19095	31,087	4.0	45.1	50.8	24,536	9,125	67.0	865	82.3	14.7	1.9
Jackson, IA	19097	36,416	6.4	48.5	45.1	30,314	9,228	65.2	1,068	76.8	15.0	7.6
Jasper, IA	19099	63,169	5.1	51.3	43.6	51,258	8,535	65.0	1,821	79.2	14.8	4.1
Jefferson, IA	19101	28,932	4.8	42.9	52.3	24,731	9,737	61.3	807	87.1	3.1	3.4
Johnson, IA	19103	182,168	4.8	37.8	57.5	139,917	9,496	65.6	9,878	95.3	2.8	1.1
Jones, IA	19105	36,812	5.4	45.9	48.8	28,039	8,904	62.4	1,122	86.3	5.5	4.2

Note. Data in columns 26 through 41 from the American Community Survey are subject to sampling error, which can be especially large in small counties and small population groups. See notes and definitions for more information.

Table C-1. Population, School, and Student Characteristics by County, Selected Years—*Continued*

County	State/ County Code	High school graduates, 2006–2010			College enrollment, 2006–2010		College graduates, 2006–2010 (percent)						
		Population 25 years and over	High school diploma or less (percent)	High school diploma or more (percent)	Number	Percent public	Bachelor's degree or more	+/- U.S. percent with Bachelor's degree or more	Non-Hispanic White	Black or African American	American Indian and Alaska Native	Asian, Hawaiian, and Pacific Islander	Hispanic or Latino[3]
		30	31	32	33	34	35	36	37	38	39	40	41
IOWA	19000	1,985,012	44.5	90.0	222,660	71.7	24.5	-3.4	24.8	16.9	12.9	47.9	10.9
Adair, IA	19001	5,446	53.5	91.4	167	72.5	13.6	-14.3	13.6	0.0	0.0	0.0	0.0
Adams, IA	19003	3,024	54.2	89.0	126	80.2	15.6	-12.3	15.5	0.0	0.0	0.0	16.1
Allamakee, IA	19005	9,889	59.5	86.9	503	75.5	13.5	-14.4	13.5	0.0	4.4	40.7	6.3
Appanoose, IA	19007	9,062	54.3	87.1	492	81.7	16.6	-11.3	16.4	0.0	0.0	83.3	0.0
Audubon, IA	19009	4,414	55.4	86.6	143	76.2	15.0	-12.9	15.2	0.0	0.0	0.0	0.0
Benton, IA	19011	17,595	48.1	92.6	1,221	70.8	17.8	-10.1	17.7	41.1	0.0	84.0	7.8
Black Hawk, IA	19013	80,476	45.2	88.8	17,161	90.7	24.7	-3.2	25.6	11.8	9.6	51.7	15.8
Boone, IA	19015	18,046	45.5	92.1	1,310	83.2	19.6	-8.3	19.8	0.0	50.0	0.0	9.1
Bremer, IA	19017	15,733	42.3	93.6	2,457	31.1	26.5	-1.4	26.8	0.0	0.0	0.0	9.2
Buchanan, IA	19019	13,705	51.5	90.5	929	86.0	18.6	-9.3	18.4	0.0	30.0	75.0	19.2
Buena Vista, IA	19021	12,523	50.6	79.5	1,606	40.0	22.6	-5.3	25.7	24.7	39.5	8.7	9.2
Butler, IA	19023	10,523	56.4	88.0	510	82.4	14.9	-13.0	14.9	32.0	0.0	13.5	0.0
Calhoun, IA	19025	7,325	50.6	90.7	344	91.3	18.0	-9.9	18.6	0.0	0.0	27.3	0.0
Carroll, IA	19027	14,184	51.2	89.6	638	77.9	20.0	-7.9	19.9	0.0	68.6	40.0	7.5
Cass, IA	19029	9,805	53.7	91.1	391	74.4	14.5	-13.4	14.8	0.0	0.0	0.0	0.0
Cedar, IA	19031	12,777	49.6	92.0	690	78.0	18.6	-9.3	18.6	100.0	14.3	50.0	24.3
Cerro Gordo, IA	19033	30,981	39.7	91.9	2,568	82.8	21.2	-6.7	21.7	0.0	7.3	33.1	6.3
Cherokee, IA	19035	8,704	49.3	92.6	327	66.7	19.2	-8.7	19.5	0.0	0.0	2.2	26.4
Chickasaw, IA	19037	8,663	59.0	88.2	374	80.7	13.5	-14.4	13.8	0.0	0.0	0.0	0.0
Clarke, IA	19039	6,174	59.7	84.8	274	97.4	12.9	-15.0	13.8	0.0	0.0	0.0	2.1
Clay, IA	19041	11,644	47.3	91.3	608	61.0	18.5	-9.4	18.8	0.0	0.0	54.4	3.3
Clayton, IA	19043	12,712	57.0	90.2	547	79.9	14.9	-13.0	15.1	0.0	0.0	26.1	5.4
Clinton, IA	19045	33,395	50.1	89.3	2,292	56.8	17.0	-10.9	17.1	12.5	14.8	53.3	11.0
Crawford, IA	19047	11,012	59.7	79.0	463	84.4	15.0	-12.9	17.1	0.0	0.0	0.0	2.1
Dallas, IA	19049	40,116	32.0	92.7	2,681	59.1	40.2	12.3	40.6	54.1	0.0	74.0	12.3
Davis, IA	19051	5,540	53.1	81.8	329	92.7	17.0	-10.9	17.1	0.0	0.0	0.0	0.0
Decatur, IA	19053	5,331	56.6	83.0	932	12.4	17.8	-10.1	17.0	0.0	0.0	40.7	43.4
Delaware, IA	19055	12,082	55.8	91.3	655	58.8	14.6	-13.3	14.8	0.0	0.0	0.0	0.0
Des Moines, IA	19057	27,635	47.2	89.7	1,839	89.9	17.6	-10.3	17.7	5.0	41.7	57.9	17.3
Dickinson, IA	19059	12,430	40.2	93.3	648	84.1	27.2	-0.7	27.2	0.0	0.0	70.0	21.1
Dubuque, IA	19061	60,526	48.1	89.4	7,434	32.7	25.3	-2.6	25.2	8.4	0.0	57.9	26.5
Emmet, IA	19063	7,071	47.2	86.9	483	82.6	18.1	-9.8	18.5	0.0	100.0	100.0	3.5
Fayette, IA	19065	14,243	54.6	88.2	1,466	40.5	16.5	-11.4	16.6	0.0	75.0	26.7	2.1
Floyd, IA	19067	11,254	52.4	91.6	589	79.8	14.9	-13.0	14.7	0.0	0.0	51.0	11.3
Franklin, IA	19069	7,426	50.2	84.3	307	88.3	14.5	-13.4	15.1	100.0	0.0	70.0	0.0
Fremont, IA	19071	5,278	53.3	91.1	209	79.4	17.4	-10.5	17.3	100.0	27.3	21.4	6.3
Greene, IA	19073	6,633	50.8	88.4	283	97.2	17.5	-10.4	17.6	0.0	0.0	100.0	0.0
Grundy, IA	19075	8,610	43.8	91.2	629	81.4	21.6	-6.3	21.6	0.0	0.0	16.7	44.2
Guthrie, IA	19077	7,798	48.4	91.2	356	60.4	18.9	-9.0	19.0	0.0	12.5	0.0	17.7
Hamilton, IA	19079	10,933	47.1	90.3	616	95.5	16.4	-11.5	16.7	0.0	0.0	5.2	8.8
Hancock, IA	19081	8,061	49.9	89.5	410	68.8	15.4	-12.5	15.6	35.7	0.0	0.0	12.3
Hardin, IA	19083	12,080	44.1	90.5	937	89.8	20.2	-7.7	20.6	27.3	0.0	30.0	9.7
Harrison, IA	19085	10,382	51.4	90.4	690	82.5	15.5	-12.4	15.4	69.2	66.7	42.9	4.8
Henry, IA	19087	13,485	48.6	89.3	1,221	68.1	19.9	-8.0	20.3	82.6	0.0	5.5	15.3
Howard, IA	19089	6,518	58.6	86.8	308	88.6	11.5	-16.4	11.6	0.0	0.0	0.0	0.0
Humboldt, IA	19091	6,857	51.6	88.8	319	83.7	15.9	-12.0	16.1	0.0	0.0	0.0	0.0
Ida, IA	19093	4,957	51.0	90.1	225	73.8	18.3	-9.6	18.2	0.0	0.0	61.5	0.0
Iowa, IA	19095	11,304	48.9	92.0	635	87.2	19.2	-8.7	18.9	100.0	0.0	0.0	10.6
Jackson, IA	19097	13,872	58.3	87.4	605	72.6	15.0	-12.9	15.0	25.0	20.0	37.5	13.1
Jasper, IA	19099	25,933	52.9	90.0	1,435	67.3	16.6	-11.3	16.8	3.5	9.6	46.2	15.8
Jefferson, IA	19101	11,949	41.3	91.5	1,201	36.0	30.1	2.2	29.5	59.4	0.0	49.6	8.6
Johnson, IA	19103	73,111	23.1	95.0	30,178	96.6	50.8	22.9	51.0	26.0	35.3	79.5	31.7
Jones, IA	19105	14,543	55.7	89.4	551	77.3	16.0	-11.9	16.2	5.4	8.5	6.9	9.5

Note. Data in columns 26 through 41 from the American Community Survey are subject to sampling error, which can be especially large in small counties and small population groups. See notes and definitions for more information.
[3]May be of any race.

Table C-1. Population, School, and Student Characteristics by County, Selected Years—*Continued*

County	State/ County Code	County Type[1]	Population, 2010		Percent of related children 5–17 years in poverty, 2010	Percent of children under 19 years with no health insurance, 2010	Number of schools and students, 2010–2011			Resident enrollment, 2006–2010 K–12 enrollment	
			Total	Percent 5–17 years			School districts	Schools	Students	Number	Percent public
			1	2	3	4	5	6	7	8	9
IOWA—*(Continued)*											
Keokuk, IA	19107	8	10,511	17.4	16.4	4.9	3	10	1,282	1,908	98.3
Kossuth, IA	19109	7	15,543	17.1	12.6	4.4	5	12	2,060	2,797	83.7
Lee, IA	19111	5	35,862	16.4	21.3	3.8	3	14	5,167	6,336	79.0
Linn, IA	19113	3	211,226	17.8	10.2	2.8	12	78	36,063	37,088	87.8
Louisa, IA	19115	8	11,387	19.9	13.8	6.7	4	10	2,836	2,478	97.6
Lucas, IA	19117	6	8,898	18.3	22.8	4.5	1	4	1,483	1,641	97.3
Lyon, IA	19119	8	11,581	19.7	11.1	5.4	3	10	2,076	2,167	83.2
Madison, IA	19121	2	15,679	20.2	9.4	3.8	3	12	3,433	3,098	93.8
Mahaska, IA	19123	7	22,381	17.5	15.9	3.8	4	10	4,020	3,932	88.7
Marion, IA	19125	6	33,309	18.4	10.3	3.5	5	18	5,741	6,036	80.2
Marshall, IA	19127	4	40,648	18.3	16.8	5.1	3	16	6,963	7,336	91.9
Mills, IA	19129	2	15,059	19.0	11.2	3.7	4	11	3,255	2,941	94.1
Mitchell, IA	19131	7	10,776	18.6	15.4	5.4	2	6	1,633	1,995	90.6
Monona, IA	19133	6	9,243	16.7	17.6	5.0	3	8	1,438	1,550	94.1
Monroe, IA	19135	7	7,970	17.6	17.2	5.3	1	5	1,270	1,383	96.0
Montgomery, IA	19137	6	10,740	17.8	19.1	4.0	3	9	1,890	2,051	96.3
Muscatine, IA	19139	4	42,745	18.9	16.2	4.1	3	17	7,719	8,171	98.3
O'Brien, IA	19141	7	14,398	17.2	13.0	5.0	3	8	2,419	2,582	88.0
Osceola, IA	19143	7	6,462	16.9	13.9	5.1	1	3	798	1,113	92.2
Page, IA	19145	7	15,932	16.2	19.6	4.2	4	12	2,455	2,910	91.3
Palo Alto, IA	19147	7	9,421	15.7	13.1	4.6	4	12	1,750	1,479	92.5
Plymouth, IA	19149	6	24,986	19.3	9.1	3.6	5	19	4,119	4,964	84.3
Pocahontas, IA	19151	9	7,310	15.6	17.3	4.7	3	6	904	1,282	92.2
Polk, IA	19153	2	430,640	17.9	12.7	3.9	10	125	71,160	74,736	91.2
Pottawattamie, IA	19155	2	93,158	17.3	16.8	3.9	9	37	16,047	16,262	92.1
Poweshiek, IA	19157	7	18,914	15.6	12.9	3.6	3	10	2,914	2,979	97.2
Ringgold, IA	19159	9	5,131	17.8	26.7	9.5	2	4	738	829	90.4
Sac, IA	19161	9	10,350	16.7	13.4	5.5	4	8	1,781	1,726	93.4
Scott, IA	19163	2	165,224	17.7	17.8	3.7	5	55	28,408	29,031	90.8
Shelby, IA	19165	6	12,167	17.9	10.6	4.0	2	6	1,777	2,246	92.5
Sioux, IA	19167	6	33,704	19.0	8.8	5.4	5	15	4,531	6,258	64.5
Story, IA	19169	3	89,542	12.5	10.1	3.6	7	27	10,843	11,037	96.0
Tama, IA	19171	6	17,767	19.3	15.8	5.6	3	7	2,489	3,451	90.8
Taylor, IA	19173	9	6,317	17.4	16.9	5.6	3	5	1,067	1,147	95.6
Union, IA	19175	6	12,534	16.8	19.6	4.1	2	7	1,980	2,074	95.5
Van Buren, IA	19177	9	7,570	17.6	23.8	7.7	2	6	1,116	1,210	84.5
Wapello, IA	19179	5	35,625	16.2	21.2	3.9	3	13	5,452	5,799	94.3
Warren, IA	19181	2	46,225	19.6	7.5	3.1	5	19	8,966	8,847	94.4
Washington, IA	19183	3	21,704	18.8	13.5	6.3	3	15	3,753	3,993	85.5
Wayne, IA	19185	9	6,403	17.2	24.3	7.6	4	7	1,121	1,027	88.2
Webster, IA	19187	5	38,013	16.2	19.1	3.9	3	17	5,209	6,909	85.0
Winnebago, IA	19189	7	10,866	16.2	14.1	3.8	3	10	2,306	1,898	94.6
Winneshiek, IA	19191	7	21,056	15.3	10.2	4.7	4	12	2,943	3,234	80.6
Woodbury, IA	19193	3	102,172	18.9	18.7	4.3	8	42	18,511	19,123	87.7
Worth, IA	19195	9	7,598	17.7	14.3	4.7	2	4	1,016	1,389	96.3
Wright, IA	19197	7	13,229	16.9	15.3	4.5	4	10	2,618	2,146	99.6
KANSAS	20000	X	2,853,118	18.3	15.9	8.1	324	1,378	483,701	516,142	89.6
Allen, KS	20001	7	13,371	17.0	24.0	8.7	4	10	2,252	2,343	95.8
Anderson, KS	20003	6	8,102	18.4	19.6	9.0	2	8	1,359	1,457	96.7
Atchison, KS	20005	6	16,924	17.6	18.2	7.2	2	6	2,417	3,023	87.7
Barber, KS	20007	9	4,861	16.1	18.5	12.0	2	4	713	783	96.7
Barton, KS	20009	7	27,674	17.3	19.4	10.1	3	14	4,366	5,041	96.4
Bourbon, KS	20011	6	15,173	18.2	24.5	8.6	2	6	2,449	2,918	91.2
Brown, KS	20013	6	9,984	18.1	23.8	9.7	3	6	1,511	1,909	96.3
Butler, KS	20015	2	65,880	20.3	10.4	6.8	9	46	15,220	13,334	93.3
Chase, KS	20017	8	2,790	16.6	16.7	16.0	1	2	400	561	98.9
Chautauqua, KS	20019	9	3,669	15.8	23.5	13.3	2	4	518	628	95.7

[1]County type codes are from the Economic Research Service of the United States Department of Agriculture. See notes and definitions for more information.

Table C-1. Population, School, and Student Characteristics by County, Selected Years—*Continued*

County	State/ County Code	Characteristics of students, 2010–2011				Number of graduates, 2008–2009	Staff and students, 2010–2011			
		Percent with IEP[2]	Percent eligible for free or reduced lunch	Percent minority	Percent English-language learners		Total staff	Number of teachers	Student/ teacher ratio	Central admin. staff
		10	11	12	13	14	15	16	17	18
IOWA—*(Continued)*										
Keokuk, IA	19107	13.3	34.5	2.1	. . .	103	202	107	11.9	14
Kossuth, IA	19109	17.6	38.1	6.2	0.1	127	331	160	12.9	12
Lee, IA	19111	18.0	44.5	13.3	0.2	309	780	366	14.1	22
Linn, IA	19113	13.5	32.2	16.8	1.8	2,288	5,542	2,478	14.6	319
Louisa, IA	19115	14.8	55.4	32.2	8.8	184	426	215	13.2	17
Lucas, IA	19117	15.5	51.4	2.4	6.4	125	190	109	13.7	9
Lyon, IA	19119	11.7	28.6	4.8	0.6	142	268	147	14.2	11
Madison, IA	19121	11.8	30.4	4.4	0.3	237	428	237	14.5	17
Mahaska, IA	19123	13.4	44.6	7.8	0.8	272	574	276	14.6	24
Marion, IA	19125	14.0	31.0	6.0	1.0	420	783	397	14.5	24
Marshall, IA	19127	15.2	55.4	38.2	22.7	427	1,001	478	14.6	34
Mills, IA	19129	14.2	37.0	6.5	0.3	247	455	213	15.3	21
Mitchell, IA	19131	11.0	28.6	2.5	0.5	193	193	105	15.6	5
Monona, IA	19133	15.0	49.3	5.8	0.4	121	229	119	12.1	10
Monroe, IA	19135	10.7	40.5	6.7	1.0	82	154	81	15.7	8
Montgomery, IA	19137	15.6	48.4	7.7	1.7	132	275	139	13.6	12
Muscatine, IA	19139	12.7	46.0	32.9	8.4	534	966	524	14.7	40
O'Brien, IA	19141	16.0	34.7	9.9	2.3	178	332	169	14.3	8
Osceola, IA	19143	11.3	33.1	12.8	6.1	82	117	61	13.1	3
Page, IA	19145	12.5	42.3	13.7	1.0	215	393	209	11.7	15
Palo Alto, IA	19147	15.1	36.0	6.1	0.1	150	290	140	12.5	13
Plymouth, IA	19149	12.3	25.5	9.3	2.0	319	525	303	13.6	21
Pocahontas, IA	19151	12.2	44.6	5.5	0.7	112	384	103	8.8	35
Polk, IA	19153	13.2	41.4	31.3	8.8	4,004	9,653	4,704	15.1	512
Pottawattamie, IA	19155	15.1	47.7	14.7	4.8	1,039	2,253	1,058	15.2	114
Poweshiek, IA	19157	14.8	35.6	9.0	1.8	217	399	199	14.7	12
Ringgold, IA	19159	16.7	44.3	2.7	0.4	60	141	69	10.8	11
Sac, IA	19161	9.7	40.2	6.0	0.7	135	236	131	13.6	9
Scott, IA	19163	11.7	42.7	28.9	1.9	1,711	3,787	1,828	15.5	231
Shelby, IA	19165	12.1	31.9	4.2	0.6	188	234	124	14.4	10
Sioux, IA	19167	11.9	34.6	21.3	10.3	298	604	326	13.9	20
Story, IA	19169	10.2	22.7	15.9	2.6	776	1,307	751	14.4	45
Tama, IA	19171	15.6	34.2	24.6	6.1	166	364	190	13.1	13
Taylor, IA	19173	15.3	52.0	14.1	4.8	70	184	89	11.9	9
Union, IA	19175	15.5	48.5	8.1	1.7	121	324	153	12.9	13
Van Buren, IA	19177	14.7	48.0	4.3	0.1	74	170	79	14.1	9
Wapello, IA	19179	14.3	51.8	24.3	8.9	342	959	398	13.7	37
Warren, IA	19181	11.8	23.1	7.7	0.4	642	1,098	580	15.5	38
Washington, IA	19183	14.5	34.6	14.3	2.6	268	523	275	13.7	17
Wayne, IA	19185	14.2	50.1	4.3	0.7	104	194	102	11.0	11
Webster, IA	19187	16.3	49.8	16.2	0.8	414	708	369	14.1	30
Winnebago, IA	19189	16.1	29.9	8.7	1.1	197	330	181	12.8	5
Winneshiek, IA	19191	11.9	26.4	5.8	1.2	258	419	212	13.9	24
Woodbury, IA	19193	13.9	50.1	33.9	13.9	1,150	2,485	1,241	14.9	92
Worth, IA	19195	13.0	36.5	5.9	. . .	121	143	74	13.7	6
Wright, IA	19197	14.5	46.5	18.9	5.9	198	368	186	14.1	15
KANSAS	20000	13.8	47.7	31.9	8.1	30,366	67,751	34,644	14.0	1,884
Allen, KS	20001	17.4	56.0	9.9	. . .	170	389	194	11.6	12
Anderson, KS	20003	14.9	53.2	7.4	. . .	104	188	121	11.2	5
Atchison, KS	20005	21.3	60.3	19.3	0.1	127	351	184	13.2	10
Barber, KS	20007	19.1	41.5	6.2	0.6	73	124	70	10.2	8
Barton, KS	20009	13.4	56.8	28.8	14.4	305	648	320	13.6	24
Bourbon, KS	20011	9.5	62.0	11.2	0.7	168	347	188	13.0	10
Brown, KS	20013	16.9	57.0	24.4	4.5	109	231	133	11.4	12
Butler, KS	20015	13.2	30.8	12.7	1.3	962	2,265	1,018	15.0	53
Chase, KS	20017	15.8	39.5	6.3	. . .	28	64	34	11.6	3
Chautauqua, KS	20019	18.9	58.1	16.0	0.2	34	76	47	11.0	6

[2]IEP=Individual Education Program. See notes and definitions for more information.
. . . = Not available.

Table C-1. Population, School, and Student Characteristics by County, Selected Years—*Continued*

County	State/ County Code	Revenues, 2008–2009				Current expenditures, 2008–2009			Resident population 16 to 19 years, 2006–2010			
		Total revenue ($1,000's)	Percentage of revenue from			Amount ($1,000's)	Amount per student	Percent for instruction	Total population 16 to 19 years	Percent enrolled in school	Percent high school graduates, not enrolled in school	Percent not enrolled, not grads, not employed, or not in labor force
			Federal government	State government	Local government							
		19	20	21	22	23	24	25	26	27	28	29
IOWA—*(Continued)*												
Keokuk, IA	19107	14,137	5.2	42.8	51.9	11,798	8,765	64.0	547	83.4	9.1	5.7
Kossuth, IA	19109	25,991	4.8	34.4	60.7	19,801	9,930	67.6	854	87.1	4.8	6.0
Lee, IA	19111	49,364	8.0	54.2	37.8	40,830	9,391	67.1	1,884	87.4	8.7	3.6
Linn, IA	19113	439,310	9.2	42.5	48.3	374,015	10,669	57.8	11,980	89.4	6.9	1.8
Louisa, IA	19115	33,410	5.9	46.1	48.1	26,229	9,500	68.2	690	89.4	7.8	2.8
Lucas, IA	19117	15,908	6.1	58.4	35.5	12,455	8,103	67.0	526	72.4	23.0	4.6
Lyon, IA	19119	19,978	4.7	46.3	49.1	15,824	8,619	66.8	572	87.6	10.3	0.0
Madison, IA	19121	34,774	4.6	49.7	45.8	27,732	8,437	65.1	781	91.4	8.1	0.5
Mahaska, IA	19123	44,793	5.0	43.7	51.3	36,135	8,883	65.2	1,235	90.8	6.7	1.6
Marion, IA	19125	61,178	4.5	49.5	45.9	49,382	8,329	64.5	2,214	95.5	3.9	0.6
Marshall, IA	19127	75,553	6.5	53.4	40.1	59,086	8,748	66.0	2,363	80.1	10.9	4.4
Mills, IA	19129	38,659	5.0	43.8	51.2	28,464	8,774	65.6	779	85.9	13.0	1.2
Mitchell, IA	19131	22,877	4.4	40.8	54.8	17,891	9,110	67.1	617	94.2	2.9	0.0
Monona, IA	19133	17,244	6.9	43.1	50.0	13,163	9,422	64.0	510	80.8	14.9	1.2
Monroe, IA	19135	12,281	6.3	51.6	42.0	10,173	8,658	65.0	355	90.1	9.9	0.0
Montgomery, IA	19137	20,894	6.5	48.8	44.6	17,851	9,660	64.5	607	89.3	7.1	1.5
Muscatine, IA	19139	77,668	5.9	53.3	40.7	65,788	8,661	66.5	2,561	80.5	12.4	5.0
O'Brien, IA	19141	25,777	4.7	47.0	48.4	21,387	8,990	65.1	841	92.5	6.4	1.1
Osceola, IA	19143	9,205	3.9	48.2	47.9	7,480	8,608	62.5	375	76.8	2.4	12.8
Page, IA	19145	28,408	7.0	45.9	47.1	23,438	8,554	65.4	888	77.9	10.9	5.1
Palo Alto, IA	19147	18,729	4.3	37.0	58.7	15,125	9,597	66.3	517	79.3	20.7	0.0
Plymouth, IA	19149	43,875	4.7	46.6	48.7	36,309	8,428	66.9	1,490	92.1	4.2	3.8
Pocahontas, IA	19151	11,604	4.6	43.3	52.2	9,429	9,721	63.3	391	96.7	3.3	0.0
Polk, IA	19153	857,639	9.2	42.0	48.8	718,164	10,644	59.6	21,522	85.5	10.2	1.7
Pottawattamie, IA	19155	191,227	9.6	44.8	45.6	166,695	10,360	58.0	5,456	81.6	10.9	5.2
Poweshiek, IA	19157	32,214	4.2	40.8	55.0	24,509	8,286	63.3	1,517	96.2	3.4	0.3
Ringgold, IA	19159	11,520	6.6	37.1	56.3	8,723	11,098	65.8	224	85.7	10.7	1.3
Sac, IA	19161	18,543	5.6	44.6	49.8	16,445	9,495	68.3	531	84.0	10.7	4.7
Scott, IA	19163	320,776	9.5	43.6	46.9	276,660	9,947	59.9	8,847	83.1	11.3	4.0
Shelby, IA	19165	19,771	4.3	49.1	46.6	17,117	8,702	66.0	725	92.8	4.4	0.0
Sioux, IA	19167	49,304	5.6	46.1	48.3	38,209	8,529	67.6	2,771	92.2	4.9	1.2
Story, IA	19169	125,939	3.9	39.0	57.1	98,592	9,068	66.4	8,612	95.6	3.3	0.1
Tama, IA	19171	28,307	8.9	49.4	41.7	22,842	8,643	64.7	1,040	85.7	7.4	2.4
Taylor, IA	19173	12,180	7.0	45.9	47.1	9,590	9,677	63.7	328	88.7	4.6	2.4
Union, IA	19175	25,336	16.5	45.1	38.4	24,710	12,281	48.5	738	83.5	16.3	0.3
Van Buren, IA	19177	13,769	10.4	44.8	44.8	11,384	9,772	57.7	349	80.5	12.0	7.5
Wapello, IA	19179	63,791	19.1	51.8	29.1	67,446	12,346	45.1	2,101	76.8	13.2	5.9
Warren, IA	19181	91,561	3.1	51.9	44.9	73,034	8,327	64.4	2,826	94.4	4.8	0.1
Washington, IA	19183	41,213	7.1	47.3	45.6	33,180	8,727	65.5	1,313	84.3	8.3	1.6
Wayne, IA	19185	15,088	10.3	43.3	46.4	11,729	9,823	64.6	350	73.1	14.3	2.3
Webster, IA	19187	73,669	16.9	43.3	39.8	73,244	13,791	44.6	2,566	89.8	7.5	2.1
Winnebago, IA	19189	27,810	4.4	45.2	50.4	22,737	9,128	64.6	698	97.4	1.2	1.4
Winneshiek, IA	19191	36,000	4.5	38.5	57.0	27,730	9,679	66.3	1,836	96.7	3.1	0.2
Woodbury, IA	19193	210,924	10.4	49.7	39.9	191,633	10,676	59.0	6,088	83.2	11.1	3.7
Worth, IA	19195	12,792	3.5	37.1	59.5	9,714	10,323	66.3	406	90.4	4.4	1.2
Wright, IA	19197	32,603	5.1	41.0	53.8	24,382	9,152	65.5	648	83.0	9.6	7.4
KANSAS	20000	5,615,208	6.7	58.6	34.6	4,678,561	9,945	61.6	166,744	85.9	9.6	2.5
Allen, KS	20001	28,367	7.6	72.7	19.8	25,215	10,968	63.2	881	89.0	10.1	0.3
Anderson, KS	20003	15,758	4.9	69.4	25.8	13,926	10,077	62.7	426	83.3	12.0	3.8
Atchison, KS	20005	28,692	7.7	67.0	25.4	24,445	10,284	58.8	1,373	87.5	11.9	0.6
Barber, KS	20007	10,626	3.5	42.7	53.8	9,043	11,594	58.7	234	85.9	8.6	3.4
Barton, KS	20009	54,239	7.0	63.2	29.7	44,115	10,181	62.5	1,674	88.3	6.9	1.1
Bourbon, KS	20011	25,701	8.2	73.6	18.3	22,409	8,900	65.6	955	90.8	6.1	2.3
Brown, KS	20013	21,198	6.1	67.4	26.5	17,961	11,521	65.0	590	77.6	12.9	2.5
Butler, KS	20015	162,145	3.0	63.3	33.7	128,250	8,776	62.4	4,303	85.9	9.5	2.5
Chase, KS	20017	6,097	3.5	53.6	42.9	5,072	11,741	61.7	241	88.8	10.4	0.0
Chautauqua, KS	20019	7,314	5.2	68.3	26.5	6,139	11,540	68.2	232	77.2	22.8	0.0

Note. Data in columns 26 through 41 from the American Community Survey are subject to sampling error, which can be especially large in small counties and small population groups. See notes and definitions for more information.

Table C-1. Population, School, and Student Characteristics by County, Selected Years—*Continued*

County	State/ County Code	High school graduates, 2006–2010			College enrollment, 2006–2010		College graduates, 2006–2010 (percent)						
		Population 25 years and over	High school diploma or less (percent)	High school diploma or more (percent)	Number	Percent public	Bachelor's degree or more	+/- U.S. percent with Bachelor's degree or more	Non-Hispanic White	Black or African American	American Indian and Alaska Native	Asian, Hawaiian, and Pacific Islander	Hispanic or Latino[3]
		30	31	32	33	34	35	36	37	38	39	40	41
IOWA—*(Continued)*													
Keokuk, IA	19107	7,324	55.8	89.7	316	80.1	13.8	-14.1	13.9	0.0	0.0	12.5	0.0
Kossuth, IA	19109	11,103	50.3	90.0	515	81.4	16.7	-11.2	16.8	15.4	0.0	0.0	0.0
Lee, IA	19111	24,989	54.6	86.3	1,448	83.8	14.8	-13.1	15.4	3.8	33.3	53.4	3.0
Linn, IA	19113	136,245	35.5	93.2	15,690	66.0	29.7	1.8	29.9	15.9	14.5	46.7	19.0
Louisa, IA	19115	7,670	60.3	81.5	476	88.7	13.1	-14.8	14.9	0.0	0.0	0.0	0.6
Lucas, IA	19117	6,265	57.9	87.4	96	59.4	10.5	-17.4	10.7	0.0	0.0	0.0	0.0
Lyon, IA	19119	7,644	53.6	85.9	314	73.9	15.9	-12.0	16.2	0.0	0.0	0.0	0.0
Madison, IA	19121	10,320	50.2	93.0	571	73.6	18.2	-9.7	18.2	0.0	0.0	100.0	0.0
Mahaska, IA	19123	14,673	54.8	88.0	1,820	32.1	17.9	-10.0	18.0	2.6	57.1	34.7	7.5
Marion, IA	19125	21,598	46.0	91.4	2,362	23.9	24.0	-3.9	23.7	61.2	13.4	32.2	23.7
Marshall, IA	19127	26,538	50.0	85.7	1,825	85.5	18.7	-9.2	20.5	7.7	9.2	30.7	4.1
Mills, IA	19129	10,354	44.6	86.7	609	84.4	22.6	-5.3	22.5	0.0	0.0	86.6	22.2
Mitchell, IA	19131	7,323	50.3	89.6	554	59.9	16.6	-11.3	16.4	100.0	100.0	18.2	25.0
Monona, IA	19133	6,694	55.5	87.6	280	90.0	14.7	-13.2	14.9	0.0	0.0	0.0	3.5
Monroe, IA	19135	5,528	54.3	88.3	277	81.2	15.1	-12.8	14.3	0.0	14.5	0.0	100.0
Montgomery, IA	19137	7,622	49.7	87.7	361	77.3	17.6	-10.3	17.9	0.0	0.0	0.0	5.4
Muscatine, IA	19139	27,870	48.3	84.3	1,916	83.6	19.9	-8.0	21.4	20.7	37.0	29.4	4.5
O'Brien, IA	19141	9,996	49.3	88.8	577	62.0	19.3	-8.6	19.4	0.0	0.0	80.0	6.8
Osceola, IA	19143	4,495	56.1	86.5	220	81.8	16.3	-11.6	16.9	0.0	0.0	0.0	0.0
Page, IA	19145	11,546	53.8	87.5	402	83.1	16.7	-11.2	17.3	17.6	0.0	7.6	0.0
Palo Alto, IA	19147	6,530	49.5	87.2	469	89.8	16.1	-11.8	16.3	0.0	0.0	0.0	0.0
Plymouth, IA	19149	16,704	47.6	91.2	914	71.6	19.8	-8.1	19.9	0.0	20.0	26.1	12.2
Pocahontas, IA	19151	5,400	48.5	91.7	247	79.4	16.4	-11.5	16.3	45.5	0.0	53.9	0.0
Polk, IA	19153	273,378	36.5	90.9	26,771	53.5	32.9	5.0	34.8	17.2	24.7	41.1	9.9
Pottawattamie, IA	19155	61,007	49.7	88.5	4,590	77.9	17.3	-10.6	17.7	11.3	4.1	20.1	8.8
Poweshiek, IA	19157	12,442	50.7	92.1	2,372	19.1	21.7	-6.2	20.7	57.4	0.0	64.7	31.3
Ringgold, IA	19159	3,613	50.8	90.3	210	77.6	20.8	-7.1	19.7	0.0	0.0	100.0	0.0
Sac, IA	19161	7,471	54.0	89.3	240	75.4	18.2	-9.7	18.2	0.0	0.0	45.5	14.5
Scott, IA	19163	107,368	38.2	90.5	11,425	63.1	29.7	1.8	31.4	14.6	10.0	33.8	16.6
Shelby, IA	19165	8,658	55.3	90.6	414	89.9	16.1	-11.8	16.1	0.0	0.0	100.0	0.0
Sioux, IA	19167	19,711	49.3	86.5	3,452	24.6	22.4	-5.5	23.6	27.7	0.0	0.0	3.6
Story, IA	19169	46,052	24.9	95.3	25,557	97.5	47.3	19.4	45.1	55.4	43.2	81.5	50.4
Tama, IA	19171	12,106	52.5	88.1	676	81.4	16.5	-11.4	17.3	0.0	14.6	25.7	0.4
Taylor, IA	19173	4,470	56.8	87.3	198	88.4	12.4	-15.5	12.4	100.0	20.0	0.0	5.8
Union, IA	19175	8,345	52.5	89.4	686	93.9	15.6	-12.3	15.6	0.0	0.0	0.0	0.0
Van Buren, IA	19177	5,371	56.6	86.1	247	92.3	13.5	-14.4	13.9	0.0	0.0	0.0	0.0
Wapello, IA	19179	23,929	55.5	83.7	1,606	80.9	14.9	-13.0	15.5	3.7	0.0	58.0	2.8
Warren, IA	19181	29,228	39.3	94.6	3,132	37.8	26.7	-1.2	26.7	19.2	20.0	54.0	24.5
Washington, IA	19183	14,744	48.8	89.1	758	79.7	19.5	-8.4	19.6	25.6	0.0	64.1	7.8
Wayne, IA	19185	4,492	62.1	84.4	236	89.0	10.8	-17.1	11.0	0.0	0.0	10.6	0.0
Webster, IA	19187	25,334	48.2	88.3	2,600	86.5	18.0	-9.9	18.4	14.0	0.0	57.0	3.6
Winnebago, IA	19189	7,537	44.3	89.9	674	33.5	19.3	-8.6	19.8	0.0	0.0	0.0	12.0
Winneshiek, IA	19191	13,150	46.7	91.2	2,888	19.4	26.3	-1.6	26.1	61.0	0.0	55.5	3.1
Woodbury, IA	19193	63,764	49.5	85.4	6,735	55.7	20.8	-7.1	23.1	18.1	1.7	10.9	5.6
Worth, IA	19195	5,357	45.1	89.8	241	72.2	16.0	-11.9	16.2	0.0	0.0	40.0	6.5
Wright, IA	19197	9,284	51.0	88.7	381	62.2	15.7	-12.2	16.5	0.0	0.0	65.4	0.0
KANSAS	20000	1,802,904	39.7	89.2	211,067	83.5	29.4	1.5	31.3	18.1	19.1	47.4	11.2
Allen, KS	20001	8,964	46.6	89.3	873	88.2	17.7	-10.2	18.4	11.4	0.0	13.8	10.3
Anderson, KS	20003	5,470	54.2	87.3	228	99.6	15.9	-12.0	15.9	0.0	0.0	0.0	0.0
Atchison, KS	20005	10,412	55.8	87.8	1,518	48.6	22.3	-5.6	23.2	9.9	10.9	0.0	19.3
Barber, KS	20007	3,480	42.1	91.8	154	93.5	18.7	-9.2	18.7	23.8	0.0	0.0	22.1
Barton, KS	20009	18,170	45.6	85.6	1,427	87.4	20.5	-7.4	21.1	27.5	30.2	100.0	11.7
Bourbon, KS	20011	9,841	43.8	86.5	908	84.1	20.4	-7.5	21.3	17.7	10.3	0.0	0.0
Brown, KS	20013	6,748	54.2	88.3	254	90.2	16.3	-11.6	17.3	9.5	8.1	36.0	5.2
Butler, KS	20015	41,328	36.7	91.9	4,119	83.1	24.8	-3.1	25.0	31.1	30.4	30.7	17.0
Chase, KS	20017	1,964	47.8	90.4	112	91.1	18.8	-9.1	19.3	0.0	0.0	100.0	0.0
Chautauqua, KS	20019	2,702	51.0	87.0	42	66.7	17.0	-10.9	16.8	0.0	17.7	0.0	7.5

Note. Data in columns 26 through 41 from the American Community Survey are subject to sampling error, which can be especially large in small counties and small population groups. See notes and definitions for more information.
[3]May be of any race.

Table C-1. Population, School, and Student Characteristics by County, Selected Years—*Continued*

County	State/ County Code	County Type[1]	Population, 2010		Percent of related children 5–17 years in poverty, 2010	Percent of children under 19 years with no health insurance, 2010	Number of schools and students, 2010–2011			Resident enrollment, 2006–2010 K–12 enrollment	
			Total	Percent 5–17 years			School districts	Schools	Students	Number	Percent public
			1	2	3	4	5	6	7	8	9
KANSAS—*(Continued)*											
Cherokee, KS	20021	6	21,603	18.5	26.6	7.7	4	15	3,784	4,123	95.9
Cheyenne, KS	20023	9	2,726	16.2	16.5	17.7	2	4	441	527	98.9
Clark, KS	20025	9	2,215	18.7	13.0	12.1	2	5	505	512	94.3
Clay, KS	20027	7	8,535	16.9	16.1	8.1	2	9	1,729	1,343	96.9
Cloud, KS	20029	7	9,533	15.9	17.4	8.6	2	7	1,392	1,541	96.3
Coffey, KS	20031	6	8,601	18.6	11.1	7.5	3	11	1,664	1,671	93.9
Comanche, KS	20033	9	1,891	17.7	11.1	12.9	1	3	335	318	98.4
Cowley, KS	20035	4	36,311	17.7	19.6	7.5	7	24	6,192	6,793	94.6
Crawford, KS	20037	4	39,134	15.9	23.3	7.9	7	18	6,077	5,993	87.3
Decatur, KS	20039	9	2,961	13.7	18.9	14.3	1	2	370	343	100.0
Dickinson, KS	20041	7	19,754	18.3	14.1	8.2	4	17	3,504	3,730	89.7
Doniphan, KS	20043	3	7,945	16.6	15.2	8.0	4	10	1,551	1,375	95.4
Douglas, KS	20045	3	110,826	13.5	12.4	8.3	4	32	14,148	14,374	87.4
Edwards, KS	20047	9	3,037	17.8	17.0	13.0	2	3	479	530	94.2
Elk, KS	20049	8	2,882	15.4	28.6	14.1	2	3	535	423	96.2
Ellis, KS	20051	5	28,452	14.5	13.2	6.8	3	12	3,789	3,922	87.5
Ellsworth, KS	20053	7	6,497	13.5	14.1	9.0	2	9	1,234	961	94.6
Finney, KS	20055	5	36,776	22.4	19.8	10.8	2	20	8,639	8,305	93.9
Ford, KS	20057	5	33,848	21.3	17.9	11.0	3	16	7,328	7,063	97.4
Franklin, KS	20059	1	25,992	18.8	15.0	6.8	4	16	4,664	4,956	95.2
Geary, KS	20061	5	34,362	19.8	15.4	6.4	1	17	7,947	6,141	98.1
Gove, KS	20063	9	2,695	15.7	18.2	18.5	3	6	456	445	99.6
Graham, KS	20065	9	2,597	13.6	15.6	13.2	1	2	402	421	98.3
Grant, KS	20067	7	7,829	22.4	15.7	12.2	2	5	1,737	1,721	90.4
Gray, KS	20069	9	6,006	21.9	11.4	16.5	5	8	1,283	1,295	83.4
Greeley, KS	20071	9	1,247	14.8	16.8	15.2	1	2	205	268	97.8
Greenwood, KS	20073	6	6,689	16.1	21.7	9.8	3	6	1,027	1,166	98.1
Hamilton, KS	20075	9	2,690	19.0	20.1	20.1	1	2	510	539	100.0
Harper, KS	20077	8	6,034	16.9	20.6	12.4	2	5	1,072	1,041	96.1
Harvey, KS	20079	2	34,684	18.7	12.1	8.1	5	20	6,134	6,582	89.3
Haskell, KS	20081	9	4,256	23.0	16.0	15.4	3	5	905	959	93.5
Hodgeman, KS	20083	9	1,916	18.1	13.6	11.9	2	3	324	412	98.8
Jackson, KS	20085	3	13,462	19.8	14.2	9.5	3	9	2,403	2,723	90.7
Jefferson, KS	20087	3	19,126	19.0	10.6	8.5	7	15	3,868	3,628	94.2
Jewell, KS	20089	9	3,077	13.9	16.8	14.4	1	3	305	490	90.2
Johnson, KS	20091	1	544,179	19.1	6.5	5.5	7	156	92,916	101,122	85.0
Kearny, KS	20093	9	3,977	22.1	16.3	16.5	2	6	957	943	98.9
Kingman, KS	20095	6	7,858	18.4	15.6	8.9	2	9	1,268	1,436	79.3
Kiowa, KS	20097	9	2,553	16.4	17.5	12.2	3	5	655	448	82.4
Labette, KS	20099	7	21,607	17.4	22.5	8.7	5	21	4,033	4,045	85.0
Lane, KS	20101	9	1,750	17.6	13.1	12.1	2	4	345	291	100.0
Leavenworth, KS	20103	1	76,227	18.3	11.4	5.2	7	28	13,175	13,841	87.0
Lincoln, KS	20105	9	3,241	17.6	16.2	14.6	2	4	625	569	93.7
Linn, KS	20107	1	9,656	17.6	19.5	10.6	3	9	1,891	1,703	97.4
Logan, KS	20109	9	2,756	17.3	13.0	12.0	3	5	539	515	88.5
Lyon, KS	20111	5	33,690	16.6	20.2	9.3	3	18	5,683	5,636	92.2
McPherson, KS	20113	6	29,180	17.3	10.3	6.4	5	19	4,761	4,895	85.5
Marion, KS	20115	6	12,660	17.3	12.3	9.5	6	11	2,069	2,205	91.7
Marshall, KS	20117	7	10,117	16.6	15.7	9.1	3	9	1,761	1,757	88.1
Meade, KS	20119	9	4,575	21.6	12.9	13.9	2	4	659	969	95.1
Miami, KS	20121	1	32,787	20.4	10.4	7.6	3	14	5,022	6,406	91.7
Mitchell, KS	20123	7	6,373	15.5	14.4	8.7	2	8	1,170	1,080	85.1
Montgomery, KS	20125	5	35,471	16.8	23.9	9.5	5	14	5,837	5,930	91.0
Morris, KS	20127	9	5,923	16.3	15.1	11.8	2	8	1,165	1,073	95.3
Morton, KS	20129	9	3,233	20.4	16.3	14.3	2	7	1,157	594	98.8
Nemaha, KS	20131	8	10,178	19.7	11.2	8.4	3	13	1,906	2,102	90.9
Neosho, KS	20133	7	16,512	17.8	21.1	7.7	2	6	2,532	2,902	93.1
Ness, KS	20135	9	3,107	17.0	13.4	12.1	2	5	504	528	83.7
Norton, KS	20137	7	5,671	15.0	16.2	10.4	2	6	958	824	95.5
Osage, KS	20139	3	16,295	18.6	14.5	8.4	6	14	2,899	3,145	94.3
Osborne, KS	20141	9	3,858	15.7	19.3	12.1	2	4	503	642	97.0
Ottawa, KS	20143	9	6,091	19.7	11.2	10.2	2	6	1,272	1,255	93.2
Pawnee, KS	20145	7	6,973	16.4	15.2	8.3	4	7	1,252	1,210	97.9

[1]County type codes are from the Economic Research Service of the United States Department of Agriculture. See notes and definitions for more information.

Table C-1. Population, School, and Student Characteristics by County, Selected Years—*Continued*

County	State/ County Code	Characteristics of students, 2010–2011				Number of graduates, 2008–2009	Staff and students, 2010–2011			
		Percent with IEP[2]	Percent eligible for free or reduced lunch	Percent minority	Percent English-language learners		Total staff	Number of teachers	Student/ teacher ratio	Central admin. staff
		10	11	12	13	14	15	16	17	18
KANSAS—*(Continued)*										
Cherokee, KS	20021	13.5	61.3	16.1	0.5	250	538	272	13.9	14
Cheyenne, KS	20023	15.6	50.8	14.3	9.1	42	87	53	8.4	3
Clark, KS	20025	13.9	45.6	20.0	4.0	36	85	47	10.7	3
Clay, KS	20027	18.0	39.9	7.4	0.4	139	324	137	12.6	9
Cloud, KS	20029	16.5	55.6	8.5	1.5	99	297	140	10.0	10
Coffey, KS	20031	19.7	44.2	7.5	0.1	128	301	149	11.2	11
Comanche, KS	20033	18.5	33.7	9.3	...	18	35	26	13.1	2
Cowley, KS	20035	20.0	59.1	28.8	5.0	447	1,009	456	13.6	24
Crawford, KS	20037	14.2	58.8	17.2	3.3	387	979	534	11.4	31
Decatur, KS	20039	15.4	44.3	6.5	...	33	62	34	11.0	3
Dickinson, KS	20041	16.8	43.9	9.5	0.8	296	520	275	12.8	21
Doniphan, KS	20043	17.3	48.2	11.0	...	52	199	110	14.1	6
Douglas, KS	20045	13.1	33.8	24.3	4.4	902	1,845	980	14.4	49
Edwards, KS	20047	19.6	56.8	34.7	17.7	29	87	43	11.1	5
Elk, KS	20049	22.8	62.4	10.3	...	34	149	51	10.4	6
Ellis, KS	20051	17.6	39.3	13.0	4.5	211	586	274	13.8	22
Ellsworth, KS	20053	17.0	48.9	11.9	0.5	71	139	54	23.1	6
Finney, KS	20055	11.3	68.8	71.1	35.6	415	1,235	689	12.5	36
Ford, KS	20057	11.5	76.7	75.4	42.1	404	1,056	471	15.6	49
Franklin, KS	20059	13.9	51.1	10.3	0.6	324	653	345	13.5	19
Geary, KS	20061	16.0	61.9	51.0	7.9	327	1,145	562	14.1	41
Gove, KS	20063	18.6	35.6	6.0	1.3	51	117	58	7.9	4
Graham, KS	20065	23.6	50.3	10.6	...	31	46	29	14.0	3
Grant, KS	20067	12.0	57.7	66.4	28.7	88	270	138	12.6	13
Gray, KS	20069	9.1	42.6	28.8	23.4	75	220	112	11.4	7
Greeley, KS	20071	14.1	46.3	28.3	18.5	23	43	25	8.3	2
Greenwood, KS	20073	16.9	58.3	10.1	0.1	64	193	103	10.0	8
Hamilton, KS	20075	11.0	61.8	49.8	38.4	28	88	45	11.3	4
Harper, KS	20077	18.2	63.3	14.7	4.4	47	162	96	11.1	6
Harvey, KS	20079	15.0	49.2	26.8	4.3	419	875	442	13.9	24
Haskell, KS	20081	7.2	65.7	42.3	39.7	63	179	85	10.6	7
Hodgeman, KS	20083	15.7	41.4	13.9	6.2	32	50	25	13.1	3
Jackson, KS	20085	13.7	41.1	19.7	0.8	173	384	184	13.0	13
Jefferson, KS	20087	15.7	39.0	6.0	...	305	574	308	12.6	22
Jewell, KS	20089	14.1	43.6	4.6	...	24	66	30	10.2	2
Johnson, KS	20091	10.5	23.0	25.3	4.4	5,984	11,373	6,023	15.4	241
Kearny, KS	20093	12.4	60.9	44.3	28.7	87	170	85	11.3	8
Kingman, KS	20095	24.4	47.8	6.5	0.5	103	179	114	11.1	6
Kiowa, KS	20097	11.3	53.9	51.4	...	67	88	47	13.9	7
Labette, KS	20099	15.4	63.0	25.4	0.1	301	584	313	12.9	13
Lane, KS	20101	18.6	42.9	15.1	2.6	22	90	40	8.7	4
Leavenworth, KS	20103	15.2	31.8	24.4	1.5	802	1,776	876	15.0	44
Lincoln, KS	20105	16.2	52.4	6.9	1.0	41	100	53	11.7	7
Linn, KS	20107	16.4	57.8	5.4	1.1	151	279	146	13.0	11
Logan, KS	20109	17.8	46.4	6.1	...	31	123	72	7.5	6
Lyon, KS	20111	12.7	62.7	46.0	26.0	372	905	440	12.9	24
McPherson, KS	20113	15.6	35.3	10.8	1.6	280	806	358	13.3	26
Marion, KS	20115	17.7	44.9	8.4	0.7	153	329	184	11.3	15
Marshall, KS	20117	17.6	40.8	7.5	0.5	176	336	147	12.0	11
Meade, KS	20119	15.0	53.4	28.2	5.5	50	112	76	8.7	4
Miami, KS	20121	15.0	38.6	8.5	0.5	331	831	325	15.5	21
Mitchell, KS	20123	18.4	43.6	4.1	0.5	94	223	103	11.4	9
Montgomery, KS	20125	12.3	60.5	30.7	1.8	365	752	436	13.4	24
Morris, KS	20127	14.3	42.8	10.2	1.8	63	189	116	10.1	5
Morton, KS	20129	7.0	61.3	29.9	15.6	59	157	81	14.4	5
Nemaha, KS	20131	13.6	29.0	5.2	0.3	125	383	192	10.0	23
Neosho, KS	20133	16.7	60.1	12.2	0.8	185	324	182	14.0	7
Ness, KS	20135	17.1	42.3	20.4	9.1	23	96	58	8.7	4
Norton, KS	20137	20.3	47.1	3.8	...	40	151	86	11.1	6
Osage, KS	20139	18.9	44.8	7.2	...	227	410	247	11.8	17
Osborne, KS	20141	18.7	54.0	5.0	...	34	99	52	9.7	3
Ottawa, KS	20143	16.5	39.3	6.5	...	87	185	107	11.9	7
Pawnee, KS	20145	24.1	57.2	20.3	1.8	80	301	111	11.3	9

[2]IEP=Individual Education Program. See notes and definitions for more information.
. . . = Not available.

Table C-1. Population, School, and Student Characteristics by County, Selected Years—*Continued*

County	State/ County Code	Revenues, 2008–2009				Current expenditures, 2008–2009			Resident population 16 to 19 years, 2006–2010			
		Total revenue ($1,000's)	Percentage of revenue from			Amount ($1,000's)	Amount per student	Percent for instruction	Total population 16 to 19 years	Percent enrolled in school	Percent high school graduates, not enrolled in school	Percent not enrolled, not grads, not employed, or not in labor force
			Federal government	State government	Local government							
		19	20	21	22	23	24	25	26	27	28	29
KANSAS—*(Continued)*												
Cherokee, KS	20021	44,883	6.0	75.0	19.0	40,562	10,468	61.8	1,217	82.2	8.5	7.8
Cheyenne, KS	20023	5,717	4.4	59.8	35.8	5,239	11,826	65.0	177	85.9	14.1	0.0
Clark, KS	20025	6,786	3.5	55.7	40.7	5,998	11,669	59.8	147	78.2	11.6	10.2
Clay, KS	20027	18,270	4.5	70.6	24.9	16,127	9,258	62.6	472	74.4	23.3	0.4
Cloud, KS	20029	16,490	4.8	71.1	24.1	14,646	10,321	62.0	816	96.3	2.0	1.4
Coffey, KS	20031	23,729	3.1	38.0	58.9	19,201	11,295	63.8	508	88.6	11.4	0.0
Comanche, KS	20033	4,281	4.6	46.3	49.2	3,832	11,577	59.8	58	94.8	5.2	0.0
Cowley, KS	20035	72,401	6.4	72.2	21.4	61,325	9,579	62.2	2,453	83.1	12.2	3.3
Crawford, KS	20037	67,679	6.7	71.0	22.3	60,266	10,065	62.8	2,827	87.0	10.6	1.2
Decatur, KS	20039	5,315	4.3	54.2	41.5	4,485	11,710	64.2	107	73.8	17.8	0.0
Dickinson, KS	20041	67,756	2.9	46.3	50.8	39,082	9,815	64.4	1,036	81.3	17.4	0.0
Doniphan, KS	20043	18,742	4.0	74.0	22.0	17,632	12,740	67.0	556	82.9	9.7	5.9
Douglas, KS	20045	159,315	6.1	47.9	46.0	129,146	9,397	61.6	9,762	94.5	4.4	0.6
Edwards, KS	20047	6,157	7.5	60.5	32.0	5,667	13,655	65.8	94	95.7	3.2	1.1
Elk, KS	20049	7,836	5.6	74.3	20.1	7,191	12,313	65.6	152	89.5	7.2	3.3
Ellis, KS	20051	42,874	7.4	49.5	43.0	38,297	10,755	66.3	2,133	85.2	11.0	1.4
Ellsworth, KS	20053	13,561	3.3	60.5	36.2	11,592	11,432	61.2	396	93.2	6.8	0.0
Finney, KS	20055	94,519	10.4	59.1	30.5	81,982	10,044	58.4	2,461	82.4	10.9	3.0
Ford, KS	20057	81,982	9.2	72.7	18.1	66,207	9,699	60.6	2,051	75.0	20.9	1.9
Franklin, KS	20059	54,675	4.7	68.6	26.7	46,766	9,875	62.0	1,578	83.1	14.5	1.9
Geary, KS	20061	87,185	25.8	58.3	15.8	71,216	10,151	56.5	1,895	69.5	19.7	6.2
Gove, KS	20063	7,534	3.3	62.4	34.2	6,937	16,208	64.5	137	95.6	4.4	0.0
Graham, KS	20065	5,215	3.7	45.6	50.8	4,488	11,391	66.0	152	89.5	4.0	4.0
Grant, KS	20067	18,986	8.7	26.5	64.8	16,106	9,294	63.7	409	90.2	0.0	6.6
Gray, KS	20069	16,895	5.5	67.4	27.1	14,486	11,962	62.6	389	79.4	9.3	0.8
Greeley, KS	20071	3,152	3.8	50.6	45.7	2,898	12,711	58.5	122	73.8	23.0	0.0
Greenwood, KS	20073	13,405	6.1	70.8	23.2	11,215	11,104	59.5	345	86.7	11.9	1.5
Hamilton, KS	20075	6,812	6.0	47.6	46.4	5,302	10,541	61.2	115	85.2	14.8	0.0
Harper, KS	20077	12,404	6.2	65.3	28.5	11,632	11,563	60.2	253	81.8	17.0	1.2
Harvey, KS	20079	67,189	4.7	70.3	24.9	55,444	9,031	62.2	1,919	91.0	5.7	0.9
Haskell, KS	20081	14,159	4.2	21.7	74.1	10,449	11,901	65.4	351	89.2	6.6	0.0
Hodgeman, KS	20083	5,370	3.0	53.1	43.9	4,569	15,976	56.4	139	97.8	2.2	0.0
Jackson, KS	20085	28,880	6.7	75.3	17.9	25,298	10,720	64.5	685	87.7	11.5	0.3
Jefferson, KS	20087	47,394	3.4	73.0	23.7	41,882	10,521	64.1	1,101	85.5	11.2	3.2
Jewell, KS	20089	4,558	3.3	69.9	26.9	3,907	13,757	56.1	81	100.0	0.0	0.0
Johnson, KS	20091	1,059,244	3.6	42.8	53.6	846,449	9,553	63.6	26,232	87.4	9.6	1.6
Kearny, KS	20093	14,128	7.3	22.9	69.9	11,052	11,335	65.5	196	86.7	5.1	4.6
Kingman, KS	20095	15,902	4.0	54.3	41.7	13,875	10,756	62.1	310	89.0	11.0	0.0
Kiowa, KS	20097	23,427	51.0	17.5	31.4	7,106	10,481	59.0	205	94.2	4.9	1.0
Labette, KS	20099	49,241	7.4	74.2	18.5	41,154	10,099	63.6	1,216	82.6	13.9	2.6
Lane, KS	20101	5,197	4.4	48.4	47.2	4,557	12,316	61.6	55	100.0	0.0	0.0
Leavenworth, KS	20103	141,325	9.6	63.1	27.3	115,123	8,869	61.3	3,919	87.8	6.7	4.7
Lincoln, KS	20105	6,857	3.5	63.1	33.4	5,907	11,382	66.8	152	85.5	6.6	2.0
Linn, KS	20107	25,790	4.1	55.4	40.5	20,952	10,789	59.1	369	76.4	11.1	11.4
Logan, KS	20109	6,818	5.0	56.9	38.2	6,168	11,054	67.9	182	91.8	8.2	0.0
Lyon, KS	20111	66,624	6.6	71.9	21.5	57,484	9,954	62.7	2,518	90.7	8.3	0.4
McPherson, KS	20113	42,165	5.8	55.9	38.3	34,815	9,471	63.4	1,700	86.7	5.8	0.0
Marion, KS	20115	27,374	3.5	70.4	26.1	23,410	10,888	61.8	779	92.9	2.7	1.5
Marshall, KS	20117	25,665	3.7	68.7	27.5	23,543	11,313	61.4	557	92.3	5.6	0.0
Meade, KS	20119	8,884	3.7	49.8	46.5	7,517	11,219	61.3	309	86.4	5.8	6.5
Miami, KS	20121	58,475	3.4	57.4	39.2	46,190	9,341	61.9	1,884	83.5	12.6	2.1
Mitchell, KS	20123	14,856	3.8	63.9	32.3	12,821	11,468	63.9	290	100.0	0.0	0.0
Montgomery, KS	20125	59,210	6.3	67.7	26.1	52,148	9,141	64.2	2,131	90.0	8.3	0.6
Morris, KS	20127	9,343	4.4	64.4	31.2	8,453	10,423	66.6	284	83.8	16.2	0.0
Morton, KS	20129	12,590	7.7	32.6	59.8	10,488	10,573	69.4	155	65.8	18.1	0.0
Nemaha, KS	20131	21,844	3.8	61.8	34.4	16,587	10,133	61.3	517	97.7	0.0	1.0
Neosho, KS	20133	31,925	6.2	72.3	21.5	24,884	9,994	65.3	1,499	96.4	1.3	0.9
Ness, KS	20135	6,024	3.6	46.4	50.0	4,937	10,617	58.5	108	86.1	0.9	0.0
Norton, KS	20137	11,812	4.1	74.3	21.6	10,359	11,187	60.6	276	76.1	23.9	0.0
Osage, KS	20139	33,642	4.4	75.8	19.8	29,102	9,929	64.2	962	80.2	10.4	3.5
Osborne, KS	20141	7,036	2.4	59.9	37.6	6,267	12,895	63.9	206	85.4	13.1	1.5
Ottawa, KS	20143	15,408	3.3	71.0	25.7	13,267	10,341	58.4	287	85.0	11.5	3.5
Pawnee, KS	20145	14,388	3.9	66.1	30.1	12,672	12,220	62.1	790	93.5	4.4	2.0

Note. Data in columns 26 through 41 from the American Community Survey are subject to sampling error, which can be especially large in small counties and small population groups. See notes and definitions for more information.

Table C-1. Population, School, and Student Characteristics by County, Selected Years—*Continued*

County	State/ County Code	High school graduates, 2006–2010			College enrollment, 2006–2010		College graduates, 2006–2010 (percent)						
		Population 25 years and over	High school diploma or less (percent)	High school diploma or more (percent)	Number	Percent public	Bachelor's degree or more	+/- U.S. percent with Bachelor's degree or more	Non-Hispanic White	Black or African American	American Indian and Alaska Native	Asian, Hawaiian, and Pacific Islander	Hispanic or Latino[3]
		30	31	32	33	34	35	36	37	38	39	40	41
KANSAS— *(Continued)*													
Cherokee, KS	20021	14,566	52.5	86.6	569	93.0	14.5	-13.4	14.5	16.4	19.4	0.0	0.0
Cheyenne, KS	20023	2,017	46.9	86.5	67	62.7	16.4	-11.5	16.8	0.0	0.0	33.3	0.0
Clark, KS	20025	1,557	45.6	91.7	50	92.0	19.7	-8.2	19.9	0.0	0.0	100.0	13.7
Clay, KS	20027	6,001	47.0	91.2	207	79.2	18.9	-9.0	19.2	0.0	0.0	22.2	9.5
Cloud, KS	20029	6,405	48.6	89.1	723	96.0	15.2	-12.7	15.4	0.0	0.0	0.0	0.0
Coffey, KS	20031	5,917	46.6	91.5	310	84.8	20.0	-7.9	20.0	23.7	57.1	27.3	20.0
Comanche, KS	20033	1,382	48.5	92.7	45	80.0	16.4	-11.5	16.2	0.0	42.9	100.0	7.1
Cowley, KS	20035	23,389	44.2	86.5	2,276	65.9	19.5	-8.4	20.6	15.2	20.7	12.1	6.5
Crawford, KS	20037	23,450	41.1	88.2	6,162	94.8	26.4	-1.5	26.6	12.6	8.2	80.2	5.9
Decatur, KS	20039	2,382	50.3	91.1	82	91.5	17.6	-10.3	16.9	0.0	0.0	0.0	0.0
Dickinson, KS	20041	13,354	47.9	90.2	608	84.2	19.9	-8.0	20.3	0.0	15.5	0.0	11.2
Doniphan, KS	20043	5,174	51.7	86.9	517	92.1	16.3	-11.6	16.6	9.1	3.0	0.0	0.0
Douglas, KS	20045	59,845	24.8	95.2	28,453	91.8	48.3	20.4	48.2	40.5	37.9	70.6	38.3
Edwards, KS	20047	2,203	46.1	82.9	97	75.3	21.1	-6.8	23.4	0.0	0.0	42.5	3.9
Elk, KS	20049	2,183	47.8	87.8	103	100.0	17.1	-10.8	17.5	0.0	0.0	43.8	4.7
Ellis, KS	20051	16,667	35.2	91.7	4,992	96.5	33.6	5.7	33.8	22.1	14.9	65.5	20.1
Ellsworth, KS	20053	4,680	50.6	90.6	225	93.8	19.8	-8.1	20.8	0.0	0.0	61.9	15.2
Finney, KS	20055	20,552	54.6	69.8	1,649	85.3	17.3	-10.6	25.5	6.4	18.1	5.0	5.7
Ford, KS	20057	19,233	56.3	69.5	1,255	81.4	17.2	-10.7	26.6	0.0	36.4	29.2	3.0
Franklin, KS	20059	16,700	49.3	90.1	1,694	59.3	18.5	-9.4	19.1	2.5	8.1	0.0	19.4
Geary, KS	20061	17,336	39.1	91.1	1,879	86.0	19.4	-8.5	21.3	12.5	7.0	33.7	12.6
Gove, KS	20063	2,002	51.2	91.0	21	81.0	16.9	-11.0	16.7	0.0	0.0	0.0	35.7
Graham, KS	20065	1,968	43.8	91.6	77	85.7	24.2	-3.7	22.5	53.8	33.3	65.0	0.0
Grant, KS	20067	4,696	52.2	77.6	228	84.2	15.9	-12.0	21.5	0.0	0.0	0.0	5.5
Gray, KS	20069	3,608	54.8	74.7	229	78.6	19.8	-8.1	21.3	0.0	0.0	0.0	5.6
Greeley, KS	20071	844	46.2	90.1	45	100.0	20.7	-7.2	22.9	0.0	0.0	0.0	0.0
Greenwood, KS	20073	4,856	54.4	90.5	175	97.1	14.6	-13.3	15.1	0.0	0.0	0.0	0.0
Hamilton, KS	20075	1,638	50.1	80.9	47	91.5	14.9	-13.0	18.1	0.0	0.0	0.0	1.9
Harper, KS	20077	4,198	48.6	86.0	116	81.9	16.3	-11.6	16.9	0.0	7.1	0.0	6.8
Harvey, KS	20079	22,278	42.3	90.4	2,125	62.4	25.5	-2.4	27.0	23.7	33.9	36.3	6.8
Haskell, KS	20081	2,492	56.0	77.2	159	78.6	14.9	-13.0	17.7	0.0	0.0	0.0	3.5
Hodgeman, KS	20083	1,325	37.0	91.1	57	93.0	22.9	-5.0	23.8	0.0	0.0	0.0	6.7
Jackson, KS	20085	8,779	51.8	92.2	565	80.4	17.7	-10.2	18.3	0.0	8.8	100.0	8.2
Jefferson, KS	20087	12,977	49.4	91.8	760	87.9	22.2	-5.7	22.0	0.0	41.7	46.7	7.0
Jewell, KS	20089	2,405	43.7	90.7	89	86.5	18.9	-9.0	19.2	100.0	0.0	0.0	0.0
Johnson, KS	20091	351,293	21.2	95.6	33,719	76.9	51.1	23.2	53.0	34.7	39.5	62.6	24.9
Kearny, KS	20093	2,365	49.5	75.9	161	100.0	12.3	-15.6	14.4	0.0	0.0	100.0	1.8
Kingman, KS	20095	5,546	43.2	88.7	218	78.9	20.2	-7.7	19.5	0.0	31.1	9.4	43.5
Kiowa, KS	20097	1,767	44.5	89.7	321	11.8	20.9	-7.0	21.3	0.0	81.8	0.0	0.0
Labette, KS	20099	14,470	43.8	86.2	1,181	91.4	17.8	-10.1	19.0	11.0	10.7	4.2	8.5
Lane, KS	20101	1,259	49.7	87.8	60	40.0	22.2	-5.7	23.2	0.0	0.0	0.0	0.0
Leavenworth, KS	20103	49,645	41.5	91.4	4,669	76.2	28.8	0.9	30.5	16.3	4.7	49.8	19.3
Lincoln, KS	20105	2,349	45.2	88.6	138	87.7	17.1	-10.8	16.4	0.0	50.0	50.0	36.4
Linn, KS	20107	6,882	54.1	86.8	175	72.0	13.5	-14.4	13.7	0.0	0.0	54.0	0.0
Logan, KS	20109	1,980	47.1	91.4	101	84.2	18.0	-9.9	18.8	0.0	0.0	0.0	30.8
Lyon, KS	20111	20,552	47.2	83.6	5,037	96.9	23.5	-4.4	27.1	8.0	17.6	35.6	5.8
McPherson, KS	20113	19,617	44.3	88.1	2,368	49.8	25.1	-2.8	25.2	42.9	22.1	50.6	11.0
Marion, KS	20115	8,597	46.8	89.8	930	23.9	19.5	-8.4	19.5	0.0	2.0	73.1	3.5
Marshall, KS	20117	7,156	57.8	88.7	211	80.1	12.7	-15.2	12.6	0.0	0.0	53.9	34.0
Meade, KS	20119	2,871	47.9	85.9	173	60.7	20.9	-7.0	22.3	0.0	0.0	0.0	2.4
Miami, KS	20121	21,257	42.4	92.4	1,143	75.8	23.0	-4.9	23.3	4.7	13.1	64.8	14.4
Mitchell, KS	20123	4,500	42.2	91.9	339	93.2	20.8	-7.1	21.1	0.0	11.8	14.3	8.7
Montgomery, KS	20125	23,646	46.1	86.4	2,110	92.9	18.6	-9.3	19.8	11.7	20.9	29.3	5.2
Morris, KS	20127	4,223	55.6	90.1	206	84.5	16.7	-11.2	16.8	0.0	9.8	0.0	11.8
Morton, KS	20129	2,091	45.8	89.0	103	87.4	19.1	-8.8	19.6	0.0	0.0	76.7	14.6
Nemaha, KS	20131	6,934	58.3	89.0	237	65.8	17.1	-10.8	17.4	0.0	0.0	0.0	7.7
Neosho, KS	20133	10,671	45.9	87.1	1,764	99.6	16.2	-11.7	17.0	0.0	18.3	8.3	9.5
Ness, KS	20135	2,289	46.4	90.8	73	91.8	18.9	-9.0	20.0	0.0	0.0	0.0	0.0
Norton, KS	20137	4,215	46.0	89.6	148	58.8	17.3	-10.6	18.0	5.7	0.0	33.3	0.0
Osage, KS	20139	11,161	49.8	91.1	624	85.7	19.4	-8.5	19.5	0.0	45.7	17.7	18.5
Osborne, KS	20141	2,817	51.1	87.3	142	81.0	18.0	-9.9	18.1	0.0	14.3	14.3	8.3
Ottawa, KS	20143	4,212	41.6	90.7	105	86.7	19.6	-8.3	19.5	0.0	0.0	0.0	12.2
Pawnee, KS	20145	4,901	46.2	88.0	244	99.2	16.9	-11.0	19.1	0.0	0.0	0.0	0.8

Note. Data in columns 26 through 41 from the American Community Survey are subject to sampling error, which can be especially large in small counties and small population groups. See notes and definitions for more information.

[3]May be of any race.

Table C-1. Population, School, and Student Characteristics by County, Selected Years—*Continued*

County	State/ County Code	County Type[1]	Population, 2010: Total	Population, 2010: Percent 5–17 years	Percent of related children 5–17 years in poverty, 2010	Percent of children under 19 years with no health insurance, 2010	Number of schools and students, 2010–2011: School districts	Number of schools and students, 2010–2011: Schools	Number of schools and students, 2010–2011: Students	Resident enrollment, 2006–2010, K-12 enrollment: Number	Resident enrollment, 2006–2010, K-12 enrollment: Percent public
			1	2	3	4	5	6	7	8	9
KANSAS—*(Continued)*											
Phillips, KS	20147	7	5,642	18.0	15.2	10.7	3	5	831	1,068	96.0
Pottawatomie, KS	20149	6	21,604	21.2	11.2	7.3	5	13	3,961	4,229	86.0
Pratt, KS	20151	7	9,656	16.2	15.7	10.3	3	7	1,468	1,668	91.5
Rawlins, KS	20153	9	2,519	13.7	17.8	15.0	1	2	316	398	100.0
Reno, KS	20155	4	64,511	17.0	18.8	7.3	8	33	10,252	10,823	90.6
Republic, KS	20157	9	4,980	14.2	15.1	13.5	2	6	784	717	95.3
Rice, KS	20159	7	10,083	17.7	15.4	10.5	4	15	1,840	1,697	96.8
Riley, KS	20161	5	71,115	11.7	17.6	7.2	3	17	7,322	7,991	91.7
Rooks, KS	20163	9	5,181	17.4	17.5	13.0	3	7	905	905	92.7
Rush, KS	20165	9	3,307	14.5	20.0	10.3	2	5	489	453	98.7
Russell, KS	20167	7	6,970	15.6	18.5	10.9	1	4	850	1,033	98.2
Saline, KS	20169	5	55,606	17.9	23.8	8.4	4	16	8,547	9,865	93.0
Scott, KS	20171	7	4,936	17.4	13.2	10.4	1	3	930	841	95.7
Sedgwick, KS	20173	2	498,365	19.3	17.5	7.6	12	155	81,908	94,446	86.9
Seward, KS	20175	7	22,952	21.9	21.2	11.5	2	15	5,563	4,748	98.8
Shawnee, KS	20177	3	177,934	17.9	21.3	8.2	8	59	28,320	31,069	90.4
Sheridan, KS	20179	9	2,556	16.9	18.2	17.0	2	5	595	446	94.0
Sherman, KS	20181	7	6,010	15.8	23.4	11.8	1	4	900	970	96.5
Smith, KS	20183	9	3,853	15.2	16.9	12.2	2	5	702	561	97.9
Stafford, KS	20185	9	4,437	17.7	18.0	15.5	3	6	900	765	95.6
Stanton, KS	20187	9	2,235	20.9	16.8	17.3	1	3	508	412	94.9
Stevens, KS	20189	7	5,724	22.1	17.4	15.7	2	6	1,348	1,169	94.7
Sumner, KS	20191	2	24,132	19.5	14.4	7.9	8	20	4,033	5,053	91.0
Thomas, KS	20193	7	7,900	16.8	10.9	9.0	2	5	1,052	1,360	94.2
Trego, KS	20195	9	3,001	15.5	14.1	12.5	1	2	406	480	92.9
Wabaunsee, KS	20197	3	7,053	18.8	11.8	10.5	2	7	995	1,306	91.9
Wallace, KS	20199	9	1,485	19.7	13.9	16.2	2	4	318	267	94.8
Washington, KS	20201	9	5,799	17.1	14.2	11.6	2	6	764	966	81.5
Wichita, KS	20203	9	2,234	19.8	20.0	18.9	1	2	458	473	100.0
Wilson, KS	20205	7	9,409	17.9	22.8	10.3	3	8	1,704	1,646	95.4
Woodson, KS	20207	9	3,309	14.5	25.6	12.3	1	2	466	455	92.3
Wyandotte, KS	20209	1	157,505	19.5	33.1	12.7	6	61	28,609	31,165	90.9
KENTUCKY	21000	X	4,339,367	17.1	23.7	6.7	194	1,554	673,128	743,465	88.7
Adair, KY	21001	7	18,656	16.3	32.7	8.2	1	6	2,580	3,039	88.7
Allen, KY	21003	6	19,956	17.7	27.0	7.2	1	5	3,055	3,689	95.9
Anderson, KY	21005	6	21,421	18.7	15.9	6.3	1	7	3,990	4,005	94.5
Ballard, KY	21007	9	8,249	16.9	19.9	8.4	1	4	1,460	1,410	92.5
Barren, KY	21009	6	42,173	17.7	26.8	7.5	3	22	7,700	7,341	95.2
Bath, KY	21011	8	11,591	17.7	35.4	7.7	1	4	2,050	2,237	91.9
Bell, KY	21013	7	28,691	16.2	39.4	6.1	3	21	4,973	4,748	93.9
Boone, KY	21015	1	118,811	20.7	10.0	5.6	2	27	20,864	23,321	85.3
Bourbon, KY	21017	2	19,985	17.9	21.6	8.8	2	10	3,645	3,695	89.0
Boyd, KY	21019	2	49,542	15.5	26.2	5.9	5	23	7,159	7,721	91.4
Boyle, KY	21021	7	28,432	16.3	21.4	7.5	3	15	4,606	4,844	93.1
Bracken, KY	21023	1	8,488	18.6	20.7	7.6	2	4	1,512	1,612	95.2
Breathitt, KY	21025	7	13,878	17.1	38.4	6.2	2	11	2,711	2,221	99.8
Breckinridge, KY	21027	8	20,059	18.1	26.6	9.5	2	10	3,090	3,671	86.1
Bullitt, KY	21029	1	74,319	19.0	13.6	6.2	1	26	12,873	14,280	88.4
Butler, KY	21031	8	12,690	16.8	27.5	8.1	1	7	2,148	2,140	96.7
Caldwell, KY	21033	6	12,984	16.2	26.8	7.3	1	5	2,023	2,284	99.8
Calloway, KY	21035	7	37,191	12.8	21.3	7.1	4	11	4,619	4,974	89.0
Campbell, KY	21037	1	90,336	16.4	15.8	5.7	8	29	11,654	15,346	79.0
Carlisle, KY	21039	9	5,104	16.3	22.4	8.8	1	3	836	797	85.6
Carroll, KY	21041	6	10,811	17.7	35.3	7.0	1	7	1,934	1,908	98.6
Carter, KY	21043	6	27,720	17.2	31.3	6.3	1	12	4,874	4,930	94.1
Casey, KY	21045	9	15,955	17.4	38.4	9.7	2	7	2,318	2,888	91.7
Christian, KY	21047	3	73,955	18.7	28.7	7.0	1	21	9,291	13,574	88.4
Clark, KY	21049	2	35,613	17.2	22.2	6.6	1	14	5,710	5,972	93.1
Clay, KY	21051	7	21,730	16.0	43.6	6.2	1	12	3,509	4,123	93.7
Clinton, KY	21053	9	10,272	17.5	34.0	7.7	1	6	1,806	1,719	99.2

[1]County type codes are from the Economic Research Service of the United States Department of Agriculture. See notes and definitions for more information.

Table C-1. Population, School, and Student Characteristics by County, Selected Years—*Continued*

County	State/ County Code	Characteristics of students, 2010–2011				Number of graduates, 2008–2009	Staff and students, 2010–2011			
		Percent with IEP[2]	Percent eligible for free or reduced lunch	Percent minority	Percent English-language learners		Total staff	Number of teachers	Student/ teacher ratio	Central admin. staff
		10	11	12	13	14	15	16	17	18
KANSAS—*(Continued)*										
Phillips, KS	20147	16.8	48.6	10.3	0.5	54	143	94	8.9	7
Pottawatomie, KS	20149	16.2	34.8	10.4	0.5	265	624	309	12.8	20
Pratt, KS	20151	17.0	45.6	15.7	4.4	102	235	151	9.7	11
Rawlins, KS	20153	17.4	50.6	6.3	1.6	30	56	25	12.5	2
Reno, KS	20155	15.1	55.2	20.9	3.9	602	1,424	716	14.3	41
Republic, KS	20157	22.8	55.0	4.8	...	67	119	74	10.6	6
Rice, KS	20159	17.7	56.6	22.3	8.6	119	336	173	10.6	11
Riley, KS	20161	15.6	37.0	30.2	3.1	536	1,056	532	13.8	29
Rooks, KS	20163	17.3	45.7	4.5	...	76	149	85	10.6	7
Rush, KS	20165	17.8	46.8	5.5	...	44	84	50	9.8	4
Russell, KS	20167	20.8	52.5	10.0	...	75	145	78	10.9	6
Saline, KS	20169	15.6	54.2	26.8	5.7	574	1,488	603	14.2	22
Scott, KS	20171	11.9	52.8	28.3	18.7	48	119	76	12.2	4
Sedgwick, KS	20173	13.3	57.2	45.2	10.2	4,690	10,059	5,216	15.7	216
Seward, KS	20175	9.0	76.4	78.8	49.6	268	824	384	14.5	23
Shawnee, KS	20177	15.7	52.3	35.1	4.3	1,649	4,065	2,109	13.4	111
Sheridan, KS	20179	20.0	38.4	10.1	5.0	45	107	53	11.3	4
Sherman, KS	20181	20.1	46.7	23.1	10.8	62	182	73	12.4	4
Smith, KS	20183	18.2	48.0	6.1	...	62	121	71	9.8	5
Stafford, KS	20185	17.9	59.3	25.1	8.3	76	156	83	10.8	7
Stanton, KS	20187	9.3	60.0	51.4	40.0	25	70	40	12.8	2
Stevens, KS	20189	7.2	58.0	47.6	28.6	80	205	109	12.4	7
Sumner, KS	20191	19.3	49.3	13.4	0.3	414	679	333	12.1	22
Thomas, KS	20193	18.3	44.2	9.8	1.6	89	161	82	12.9	7
Trego, KS	20195	21.2	31.8	7.1	...	41	78	40	10.1	4
Wabaunsee, KS	20197	19.1	38.7	9.0	0.2	82	182	90	11.1	7
Wallace, KS	20199	18.6	41.5	10.4	7.5	38	75	41	7.8	3
Washington, KS	20201	18.6	41.7	6.7	1.8	65	135	83	9.2	5
Wichita, KS	20203	10.7	58.6	40.9	25.3	26	84	39	11.9	4
Wilson, KS	20205	15.8	58.7	8.5	...	132	255	151	11.3	11
Woodson, KS	20207	17.2	54.9	13.9	...	35	78	41	11.4	3
Wyandotte, KS	20209	13.3	77.9	72.6	23.8	1,415	3,628	1,889	15.1	80
KENTUCKY	21000	15.2	56.6	18.1	2.4	41,645	99,225	42,042	16.0	3,184
Adair, KY	21001	15.3	63.0	7.8	1.2	186	403	163	15.8	17
Allen, KY	21003	11.8	56.9	4.5	1.0	234	434	184	16.6	18
Anderson, KY	21005	17.3	44.8	7.5	0.9	290	510	229	17.4	11
Ballard, KY	21007	15.5	55.0	8.2	0.1	106	216	79	18.4	8
Barren, KY	21009	16.8	57.4	10.8	1.3	424	1,114	460	16.7	52
Bath, KY	21011	11.3	73.4	3.9	0.5	152	293	130	15.8	15
Bell, KY	21013	17.7	79.7	3.6	0.1	339	749	345	14.4	26
Boone, KY	21015	13.0	31.6	12.3	4.2	1,164	2,809	1,227	17.0	53
Bourbon, KY	21017	13.0	58.7	21.5	3.8	230	552	231	15.8	20
Boyd, KY	21019	16.7	55.2	6.2	0.2	531	1,159	479	15.0	50
Boyle, KY	21021	21.1	50.3	17.7	1.3	329	695	297	15.5	22
Bracken, KY	21023	16.9	55.0	2.5	...	95	224	97	15.5	13
Breathitt, KY	21025	21.9	79.6	1.5	...	168	479	186	14.6	22
Breckinridge, KY	21027	14.8	61.3	5.7	0.5	209	486	181	17.1	25
Bullitt, KY	21029	13.4	47.2	4.3	0.6	777	1,586	726	17.7	39
Butler, KY	21031	15.3	56.5	5.0	1.2	158	317	131	16.4	8
Caldwell, KY	21033	11.6	61.7	9.7	...	139	290	112	18.1	15
Calloway, KY	21035	14.3	51.3	10.8	1.3	337	755	299	15.5	29
Campbell, KY	21037	17.4	47.9	9.7	1.1	726	1,571	728	16.0	76
Carlisle, KY	21039	15.9	56.7	4.2	...	51	137	61	13.7	5
Carroll, KY	21041	11.9	65.8	13.6	2.9	114	306	120	16.2	18
Carter, KY	21043	16.7	61.3	2.1	0.7	302	821	341	14.3	14
Casey, KY	21045	18.2	70.2	4.7	1.9	136	390	152	15.3	15
Christian, KY	21047	13.6	68.6	41.8	1.7	498	1,259	574	16.2	29
Clark, KY	21049	13.2	56.0	12.7	1.4	345	738	308	18.5	18
Clay, KY	21051	19.4	70.7	2.2	0.4	224	680	267	13.1	18
Clinton, KY	21053	15.4	69.5	4.6	1.7	99	328	118	15.3	17

[2]IEP=Individual Education Program. See notes and definitions for more information.
. . . = Not available.

Table C-1. Population, School, and Student Characteristics by County, Selected Years—*Continued*

County	State/ County Code	Revenues, 2008–2009				Current expenditures, 2008–2009			Resident population 16 to 19 years, 2006–2010			
		Total revenue ($1,000's)	Percentage of revenue from: Federal government	State government	Local government	Amount ($1,000's)	Amount per student	Percent for instruction	Total population 16 to 19 years	Percent enrolled in school	Percent high school graduates, not enrolled in school	Percent not enrolled, not grads, not employed, or not in labor force
		19	20	21	22	23	24	25	26	27	28	29
KANSAS—*(Continued)*												
Phillips, KS	20147	10,677	4.0	71.9	24.1	9,464	10,916	64.5	244	100.0	0.0	0.0
Pottawatomie, KS	20149	44,355	3.7	55.6	40.8	36,773	9,614	62.3	1,272	79.6	16.4	2.4
Pratt, KS	20151	18,287	4.8	63.8	31.5	15,956	11,365	65.7	569	96.7	2.1	0.9
Rawlins, KS	20153	4,513	3.9	59.3	36.8	3,977	12,162	66.0	133	86.5	11.3	0.0
Reno, KS	20155	116,260	8.3	63.5	28.2	97,568	9,957	60.9	3,584	88.0	8.1	1.6
Republic, KS	20157	10,183	4.0	70.9	25.1	8,620	11,166	62.0	224	86.6	12.5	0.9
Rice, KS	20159	23,573	5.1	69.8	25.1	20,919	11,759	63.3	677	92.6	7.4	0.0
Riley, KS	20161	79,235	9.1	48.7	42.3	68,134	9,636	62.9	7,927	92.2	6.7	1.1
Rooks, KS	20163	12,709	3.5	43.9	52.5	10,767	11,251	61.5	280	81.4	6.4	8.9
Rush, KS	20165	6,819	4.2	62.6	33.2	5,985	12,340	63.3	146	82.9	2.1	6.9
Russell, KS	20167	10,782	6.8	60.5	32.7	9,836	10,225	63.0	242	81.0	19.0	0.0
Saline, KS	20169	118,540	8.7	57.3	34.0	94,269	10,271	60.5	3,015	84.1	11.7	3.3
Scott, KS	20171	11,675	4.4	46.4	49.2	9,104	10,252	62.5	143	93.0	2.1	2.8
Sedgwick, KS	20173	893,718	7.8	63.9	28.3	766,687	9,945	57.9	27,638	83.5	9.9	3.7
Seward, KS	20175	55,698	8.9	67.3	23.9	48,938	9,026	62.3	1,511	70.7	17.9	6.6
Shawnee, KS	20177	311,540	9.1	61.6	29.3	264,992	9,752	61.3	9,363	83.5	11.3	3.0
Sheridan, KS	20179	6,944	3.7	62.8	33.5	6,026	10,761	61.1	116	87.9	10.3	0.0
Sherman, KS	20181	10,308	5.0	67.6	27.4	9,562	10,172	65.0	391	84.7	4.6	10.7
Smith, KS	20183	10,693	3.5	72.4	24.2	8,798	12,374	63.6	97	84.5	15.5	0.0
Stafford, KS	20185	13,557	5.0	55.5	39.5	11,486	11,915	62.0	247	75.7	6.9	13.0
Stanton, KS	20187	6,184	5.9	32.2	61.9	5,315	11,707	62.4	102	100.0	0.0	0.0
Stevens, KS	20189	16,938	7.3	11.3	81.3	13,859	10,777	63.1	163	71.2	20.9	8.0
Sumner, KS	20191	68,717	5.1	73.6	21.3	58,932	9,723	63.4	1,420	87.4	7.4	0.9
Thomas, KS	20193	12,361	3.4	68.3	28.3	10,820	10,424	59.9	700	96.3	3.7	0.0
Trego, KS	20195	6,174	7.6	54.0	38.4	5,081	11,266	64.8	114	100.0	0.0	0.0
Wabaunsee, KS	20197	14,117	4.8	60.9	34.4	11,103	11,399	59.1	426	86.2	9.9	0.0
Wallace, KS	20199	4,759	3.7	61.5	34.8	4,120	13,248	61.6	58	94.8	0.0	5.2
Washington, KS	20201	11,194	3.5	68.7	27.8	9,790	11,437	63.1	302	86.4	13.6	0.0
Wichita, KS	20203	5,932	5.1	61.3	33.6	4,935	10,545	58.6	82	80.5	9.8	0.0
Wilson, KS	20205	20,880	5.0	70.3	24.7	18,380	10,473	60.3	437	72.1	15.6	10.1
Woodson, KS	20207	5,399	6.6	73.1	20.4	5,199	11,952	59.1	150	68.0	22.7	1.3
Wyandotte, KS	20209	345,050	9.2	64.9	25.9	298,232	10,458	60.6	8,880	78.2	11.9	6.2
KENTUCKY	21000	6,706,922	10.7	57.7	31.6	5,865,030	8,756	59.1	239,572	81.6	11.2	5.3
Adair, KY	21001	25,532	14.2	68.2	17.6	23,240	9,125	62.7	1,316	78.3	9.4	7.5
Allen, KY	21003	27,759	12.6	68.6	18.8	23,857	7,855	61.3	1,167	86.6	6.3	7.0
Anderson, KY	21005	35,708	7.8	62.2	30.0	31,420	7,837	67.2	1,114	81.6	14.1	4.3
Ballard, KY	21007	13,884	9.6	66.2	24.2	12,878	9,069	58.0	411	74.9	6.3	10.0
Barren, KY	21009	74,508	12.4	61.7	25.9	65,436	8,821	63.6	2,036	79.0	12.3	7.9
Bath, KY	21011	18,989	13.7	71.5	14.8	17,276	8,510	57.3	715	84.5	9.4	6.2
Bell, KY	21013	54,490	14.7	70.5	14.8	49,557	9,450	58.6	1,682	74.4	9.9	12.4
Boone, KY	21015	188,771	5.4	43.8	50.7	157,505	7,874	59.7	5,915	81.7	12.5	2.0
Bourbon, KY	21017	35,862	16.3	58.7	25.0	31,610	8,825	60.4	1,148	82.8	11.9	3.3
Boyd, KY	21019	70,760	13.4	61.3	25.3	64,185	8,599	61.9	2,626	73.3	16.4	6.9
Boyle, KY	21021	47,323	9.1	59.1	31.8	43,398	9,572	57.7	1,675	90.9	6.5	2.0
Bracken, KY	21023	14,108	11.3	72.6	16.0	12,345	7,803	60.0	423	75.9	21.3	2.8
Breathitt, KY	21025	29,406	16.7	71.3	12.0	26,822	9,905	59.0	764	86.0	1.4	8.5
Breckinridge, KY	21027	30,938	15.7	62.8	21.5	28,420	9,515	55.3	930	72.8	13.0	11.0
Bullitt, KY	21029	110,986	8.1	59.7	32.2	96,065	7,540	62.1	4,317	80.6	14.8	3.4
Butler, KY	21031	21,037	13.2	72.0	14.9	17,710	8,218	61.5	817	84.2	0.2	7.7
Caldwell, KY	21033	18,564	11.5	69.7	18.8	17,216	8,514	58.8	767	83.8	5.7	10.4
Calloway, KY	21035	45,567	14.0	57.6	28.4	39,984	8,304	58.8	3,029	95.8	3.5	0.7
Campbell, KY	21037	118,823	8.7	49.8	41.5	105,640	9,228	56.6	5,799	92.3	4.8	1.8
Carlisle, KY	21039	7,875	9.3	70.9	19.8	7,342	8,998	59.3	327	67.9	1.8	30.3
Carroll, KY	21041	21,357	11.6	51.3	37.1	18,323	9,226	56.2	537	80.5	8.0	11.6
Carter, KY	21043	45,828	12.6	74.8	12.6	41,900	8,380	61.5	1,695	82.4	9.3	7.4
Casey, KY	21045	24,683	14.2	70.8	15.0	21,217	8,721	64.6	714	75.9	9.0	5.7
Christian, KY	21047	86,022	14.1	64.1	21.8	76,757	8,394	62.5	3,855	66.3	24.0	5.8
Clark, KY	21049	49,495	10.0	57.8	32.2	43,670	7,843	61.7	1,798	76.9	15.7	6.4
Clay, KY	21051	39,905	15.7	71.6	12.6	36,285	9,860	58.9	1,508	87.5	4.2	8.3
Clinton, KY	21053	20,242	19.4	65.3	15.4	17,371	9,848	62.3	492	80.3	19.7	0.0

Note. Data in columns 26 through 41 from the American Community Survey are subject to sampling error, which can be especially large in small counties and small population groups. See notes and definitions for more information.

Table C-1. Population, School, and Student Characteristics by County, Selected Years—*Continued*

County	State/ County Code	High school graduates, 2006–2010: Population 25 years and over	High school graduates, 2006–2010: High school diploma or less (percent)	High school graduates, 2006–2010: High school diploma or more (percent)	College enrollment, 2006–2010: Number	College enrollment, 2006–2010: Percent public	College graduates, 2006–2010 (percent): Bachelor's degree or more	+/- U.S. percent with Bachelor's degree or more	Non-Hispanic White	Black or African American	American Indian and Alaska Native	Asian, Hawaiian, and Pacific Islander	Hispanic or Latino[3]
		30	31	32	33	34	35	36	37	38	39	40	41
KANSAS— *(Continued)*													
Phillips, KS	20147	3,930	46.8	89.7	117	100.0	17.1	-10.8	17.3	0.0	0.0	0.0	63.6
Pottawatomie, KS	20149	13,173	38.3	92.7	868	91.2	28.4	0.5	28.4	40.8	7.3	83.1	14.1
Pratt, KS	20151	6,427	40.0	89.5	772	89.6	22.7	-5.2	23.1	23.0	57.1	100.0	12.1
Rawlins, KS	20153	1,940	41.6	91.7	62	95.2	19.8	-8.1	19.8	100.0	0.0	0.0	10.3
Reno, KS	20155	42,998	44.4	87.7	3,611	89.7	18.8	-9.1	19.7	2.0	12.2	15.4	11.7
Republic, KS	20157	3,827	40.6	95.0	122	91.0	18.6	-9.3	18.5	0.0	8.3	40.7	0.0
Rice, KS	20159	6,641	47.6	88.0	689	32.7	20.9	-7.0	21.8	0.0	0.0	19.0	9.1
Riley, KS	20161	32,680	27.0	94.2	21,951	97.5	42.3	14.4	41.9	36.9	36.3	71.1	23.0
Rooks, KS	20163	3,643	46.6	90.4	142	85.9	20.4	-7.5	20.9	0.0	0.0	0.0	0.0
Rush, KS	20165	2,448	47.9	87.3	88	100.0	16.2	-11.7	16.3	0.0	0.0	0.0	0.0
Russell, KS	20167	5,042	45.8	90.1	225	100.0	20.4	-7.5	21.1	0.0	0.0	0.0	0.0
Saline, KS	20169	36,148	44.3	88.3	2,804	75.5	23.6	-4.3	24.8	8.2	10.6	19.9	18.2
Scott, KS	20171	3,333	41.6	89.4	71	100.0	20.3	-7.6	23.1	0.0	0.0	0.0	0.0
Sedgwick, KS	20173	306,701	41.1	87.7	32,879	81.1	27.5	-0.4	30.8	15.1	15.0	33.0	10.6
Seward, KS	20175	12,638	63.7	67.6	817	83.8	13.5	-14.4	20.1	21.9	22.5	16.7	5.0
Shawnee, KS	20177	116,622	41.0	90.0	11,332	73.1	28.9	1.0	31.7	14.4	17.5	58.9	11.5
Sheridan, KS	20179	1,808	40.5	92.6	65	90.8	21.8	-6.1	22.1	0.0	0.0	0.0	0.0
Sherman, KS	20181	4,342	43.2	90.1	274	95.3	19.1	-8.8	19.2	55.0	0.0	75.8	0.4
Smith, KS	20183	3,050	51.9	88.0	39	100.0	14.9	-13.0	14.9	0.0	0.0	100.0	0.0
Stafford, KS	20185	3,085	44.7	87.7	96	85.4	20.8	-7.1	21.0	0.0	26.1	75.7	8.2
Stanton, KS	20187	1,469	59.4	70.5	66	74.2	14.2	-13.7	18.8	0.0	40.0	100.0	2.7
Stevens, KS	20189	3,614	49.5	79.0	83	75.9	13.9	-14.0	17.3	0.0	0.0	27.5	0.5
Sumner, KS	20191	15,892	45.4	90.7	932	85.0	18.7	-9.2	18.9	28.7	36.0	57.1	4.6
Thomas, KS	20193	4,883	39.9	86.8	851	97.2	23.4	-4.5	24.1	19.4	0.0	0.0	10.0
Trego, KS	20195	2,210	48.5	88.7	46	45.7	22.2	-5.7	22.1	0.0	0.0	0.0	50.0
Wabaunsee, KS	20197	4,742	47.4	94.2	347	86.5	21.8	-6.1	22.3	7.7	0.0	25.0	0.0
Wallace, KS	20199	1,037	45.6	87.0	21	100.0	23.4	-4.5	25.0	0.0	0.0	0.0	6.3
Washington, KS	20201	4,206	49.0	87.0	176	94.9	18.2	-9.7	18.7	0.0	0.0	22.2	0.0
Wichita, KS	20203	1,524	52.0	80.7	33	84.8	15.9	-12.0	18.7	0.0	0.0	0.0	2.8
Wilson, KS	20205	6,567	59.0	82.3	402	79.6	10.7	-17.2	10.8	100.0	17.7	0.0	0.0
Woodson, KS	20207	2,457	52.8	90.3	64	93.8	12.8	-15.1	12.9	0.0	12.5	0.0	10.0
Wyandotte, KS	20209	96,423	57.9	78.6	8,031	77.2	15.2	-12.7	19.2	14.2	14.8	28.6	4.3
KENTUCKY	21000	2,856,001	53.4	81.0	270,931	80.0	20.3	-7.6	20.6	14.0	13.8	53.9	14.5
Adair, KY	21001	12,228	66.5	68.7	1,312	39.5	14.4	-13.5	14.8	0.0	100.0	50.0	0.0
Allen, KY	21003	13,142	65.8	73.7	744	87.4	10.6	-17.3	10.5	0.0	0.0	0.0	23.5
Anderson, KY	21005	14,156	53.6	87.2	1,121	81.7	17.3	-10.6	17.6	8.3	0.0	20.0	0.0
Ballard, KY	21007	5,791	59.6	81.2	386	82.1	10.7	-17.2	11.0	1.3	0.0	81.8	0.0
Barren, KY	21009	28,523	63.5	77.0	1,696	85.6	15.0	-12.9	15.1	8.9	0.0	88.4	9.0
Bath, KY	21011	7,851	66.0	72.2	396	87.6	13.3	-14.6	13.5	7.2	0.0	0.0	0.0
Bell, KY	21013	19,716	68.6	66.0	1,480	65.5	11.3	-16.6	11.2	15.7	0.0	18.8	44.2
Boone, KY	21015	73,330	40.4	90.5	6,218	79.9	28.2	0.3	27.6	33.9	30.1	60.0	22.4
Bourbon, KY	21017	13,648	57.4	81.9	766	81.7	17.5	-10.4	18.7	14.0	0.0	0.0	0.0
Boyd, KY	21019	35,017	52.8	83.9	2,437	90.8	15.8	-12.1	16.0	7.0	0.0	46.5	24.7
Boyle, KY	21021	18,983	52.5	82.6	2,245	29.8	23.3	-4.6	24.9	8.7	0.0	45.1	11.6
Bracken, KY	21023	5,610	70.6	74.0	330	93.3	11.6	-16.3	11.8	0.0	0.0	0.0	0.0
Breathitt, KY	21025	9,749	73.0	62.6	566	79.9	10.4	-17.5	10.5	0.0	0.0	26.3	0.0
Breckinridge, KY	21027	13,560	70.0	76.1	696	78.4	7.8	-20.1	7.8	5.4	0.0	100.0	6.5
Bullitt, KY	21029	48,084	58.5	83.2	3,396	75.5	11.1	-16.8	11.1	19.5	5.4	19.2	7.4
Butler, KY	21031	8,774	68.6	72.6	399	93.7	7.8	-20.1	7.5	0.0	54.8	0.0	0.0
Caldwell, KY	21033	9,110	63.2	82.4	662	79.2	14.0	-13.9	14.2	0.0	100.0	48.7	0.0
Calloway, KY	21035	22,347	47.2	85.4	6,899	96.5	28.2	0.3	28.1	38.3	4.9	63.3	3.5
Campbell, KY	21037	58,522	47.6	86.9	8,285	88.4	26.3	-1.6	26.4	12.4	0.0	58.6	15.0
Carlisle, KY	21039	3,602	65.0	78.9	182	79.7	10.6	-17.3	10.9	0.0	0.0	0.0	0.0
Carroll, KY	21041	7,063	66.1	75.0	225	88.0	9.3	-18.6	9.4	0.0	0.0	0.0	15.2
Carter, KY	21043	18,703	67.8	72.5	1,614	52.7	10.2	-17.7	10.1	0.0	0.0	100.0	0.0
Casey, KY	21045	10,912	70.0	66.4	551	73.0	9.5	-18.4	9.5	0.0	0.0	0.0	12.4
Christian, KY	21047	41,563	53.0	84.0	3,928	84.5	13.7	-14.2	15.4	7.2	4.8	36.9	8.9
Clark, KY	21049	24,262	55.6	81.4	1,390	87.1	17.7	-10.2	18.5	3.6	100.0	3.9	4.0
Clay, KY	21051	15,049	79.8	58.9	623	65.2	7.5	-20.4	7.8	5.8	0.0	0.0	0.0
Clinton, KY	21053	6,935	75.1	57.5	501	95.8	3.7	-24.2	3.8	0.0	0.0	0.0	0.0

Note. Data in columns 26 through 41 from the American Community Survey are subject to sampling error, which can be especially large in small counties and small population groups. See notes and definitions for more information.
[3]May be of any race.

Table C-1. Population, School, and Student Characteristics by County, Selected Years—*Continued*

County	State/ County Code	County Type[1]	Population, 2010		Percent of related children 5–17 years in poverty, 2010	Percent of children under 19 years with no health insurance, 2010	Number of schools and students, 2010–2011			Resident enrollment, 2006–2010	
										K–12 enrollment	
			Total	Percent 5–17 years			School districts	Schools	Students	Number	Percent public
			1	2	3	4	5	6	7	8	9
KENTUCKY—*(Continued)*											
Crittenden, KY	21055	6	9,315	15.9	31.2	8.3	1	4	1,339	1,462	95.3
Cumberland, KY	21057	9	6,856	15.8	38.3	9.0	1	3	1,030	1,095	90.6
Daviess, KY	21059	3	96,656	17.5	22.5	5.5	3	33	15,482	17,022	87.4
Edmonson, KY	21061	3	12,161	16.4	28.1	9.1	1	6	2,072	2,051	97.0
Elliott, KY	21063	9	7,852	14.7	33.7	7.5	1	4	1,105	1,223	97.7
Estill, KY	21065	6	14,672	16.9	36.9	6.6	1	5	2,527	2,505	91.7
Fayette, KY	21067	2	295,803	14.7	22.0	7.2	3	72	37,819	41,208	85.6
Fleming, KY	21069	7	14,348	18.1	29.1	8.4	1	6	2,325	2,589	89.2
Floyd, KY	21071	7	39,451	16.2	37.4	6.6	1	19	6,050	6,298	94.4
Franklin, KY	21073	4	49,285	15.6	20.3	7.0	2	17	6,866	7,894	89.3
Fulton, KY	21075	7	6,813	14.2	40.8	6.0	2	4	949	1,075	82.1
Gallatin, KY	21077	1	8,589	19.8	22.9	8.1	1	5	1,661	1,725	97.1
Garrard, KY	21079	6	16,912	17.0	24.2	8.6	1	6	2,669	3,137	94.9
Grant, KY	21081	1	24,662	20.3	24.4	7.1	2	10	4,694	4,999	93.6
Graves, KY	21083	7	37,121	17.7	28.0	9.2	2	18	6,303	6,607	92.3
Grayson, KY	21085	6	25,746	17.6	29.1	7.8	1	7	4,320	4,695	91.9
Green, KY	21087	8	11,258	16.6	29.5	9.4	1	5	1,723	1,861	92.7
Greenup, KY	21089	2	36,910	16.8	21.7	6.4	3	18	6,250	6,340	94.3
Hancock, KY	21091	3	8,565	19.5	17.8	6.7	1	4	1,716	1,741	97.8
Hardin, KY	21093	3	105,543	18.4	20.7	6.1	3	36	17,212	18,921	93.2
Harlan, KY	21095	7	29,278	16.4	37.0	6.3	2	14	5,132	5,306	97.9
Harrison, KY	21097	6	18,846	18.2	22.3	6.9	1	8	3,068	3,441	97.0
Hart, KY	21099	8	18,199	18.5	33.8	8.1	1	6	2,396	3,487	90.3
Henderson, KY	21101	2	46,250	16.8	20.7	6.5	1	13	7,195	8,028	87.9
Henry, KY	21103	1	15,416	18.7	22.2	8.7	2	8	2,879	3,080	97.1
Hickman, KY	21105	9	4,902	15.7	27.3	8.5	1	2	810	851	95.1
Hopkins, KY	21107	4	46,920	16.7	25.7	7.3	3	20	7,768	8,000	93.8
Jackson, KY	21109	9	13,494	17.5	36.7	7.9	1	6	2,260	2,375	98.7
Jefferson, KY	21111	1	741,096	16.6	22.1	5.7	4	176	97,749	124,663	79.0
Jessamine, KY	21113	2	48,586	18.5	21.3	7.7	1	12	7,749	8,954	85.2
Johnson, KY	21115	7	23,356	16.6	29.7	6.3	2	16	4,596	3,737	94.6
Kenton, KY	21117	1	159,720	17.8	16.3	5.2	5	45	22,663	28,517	79.7
Knott, KY	21119	9	16,346	15.8	31.4	7.0	1	8	2,547	2,666	90.9
Knox, KY	21121	7	31,883	17.9	42.3	5.5	2	13	5,436	5,625	98.3
Larue, KY	21123	3	14,193	17.5	26.9	7.9	1	5	2,418	2,642	95.9
Laurel, KY	21125	7	58,849	17.8	29.8	6.8	2	22	9,942	10,235	92.3
Lawrence, KY	21127	6	15,860	16.5	29.5	6.5	1	7	2,524	2,662	96.7
Lee, KY	21129	9	7,887	14.8	46.1	6.8	1	6	1,124	1,199	95.6
Leslie, KY	21131	9	11,310	15.6	33.6	7.0	1	7	1,856	1,851	95.7
Letcher, KY	21133	9	24,519	15.9	31.1	6.7	2	11	3,941	3,886	95.7
Lewis, KY	21135	8	13,870	17.7	36.9	8.7	1	6	2,372	2,486	86.1
Lincoln, KY	21137	7	24,742	18.1	31.3	7.3	1	11	4,047	4,506	94.1
Livingston, KY	21139	9	9,519	14.9	22.6	8.4	1	4	1,279	1,491	96.5
Logan, KY	21141	6	26,835	18.2	24.7	9.4	2	10	4,756	4,610	92.6
Lyon, KY	21143	8	8,314	11.4	18.9	9.4	1	5	760	1,005	94.8
McCracken, KY	21145	5	65,565	16.4	23.2	5.4	2	22	9,905	10,962	90.8
McCreary, KY	21147	9	18,306	16.6	46.2	6.8	1	8	3,145	3,222	93.2
McLean, KY	21149	3	9,531	17.5	21.2	7.9	1	5	1,652	1,809	97.4
Madison, KY	21151	4	82,916	15.4	22.5	6.6	3	24	12,245	11,898	87.1
Magoffin, KY	21153	9	13,333	17.9	37.1	6.5	1	5	2,222	2,895	97.9
Marion, KY	21155	6	19,820	18.0	23.7	7.8	1	8	3,213	3,783	91.5
Marshall, KY	21157	7	31,448	15.5	17.9	7.3	1	12	4,857	4,961	95.3
Martin, KY	21159	8	12,929	15.7	38.2	6.4	1	8	2,164	2,113	97.7
Mason, KY	21161	6	17,490	17.5	31.4	7.8	1	5	2,860	2,876	90.3
Meade, KY	21163	1	28,602	19.6	19.5	7.2	1	14	5,158	5,958	95.0
Menifee, KY	21165	9	6,306	17.7	37.9	8.1	1	4	1,135	995	100.0
Mercer, KY	21167	6	21,331	17.6	19.9	7.4	2	11	3,586	3,723	96.5
Metcalfe, KY	21169	9	10,099	17.6	33.6	9.1	1	7	1,672	1,700	88.4
Monroe, KY	21171	9	10,963	17.4	35.6	10.8	1	6	2,007	1,893	98.9
Montgomery, KY	21173	6	26,499	17.7	25.4	6.8	1	10	4,739	4,484	95.6

[1]County type codes are from the Economic Research Service of the United States Department of Agriculture. See notes and definitions for more information.

Table C-1. Population, School, and Student Characteristics by County, Selected Years—*Continued*

County	State/ County Code	Characteristics of students, 2010–2011				Number of graduates, 2008–2009	Staff and students, 2010–2011			
		Percent with IEP[2]	Percent eligible for free or reduced lunch	Percent minority	Percent English-language learners		Total staff	Number of teachers	Student/ teacher ratio	Central admin. staff
		10	11	12	13	14	15	16	17	18
KENTUCKY—*(Continued)*										
Crittenden, KY	21055	15.0	50.6	3.4	. . .	80	189	79	16.9	11
Cumberland, KY	21057	16.7	73.4	7.6	. . .	68	160	65	15.8	7
Daviess, KY	21059	17.9	58.5	15.6	1.2	1,020	2,494	1,004	15.4	83
Edmonson, KY	21061	17.2	54.9	4.3	0.3	122	317	120	17.3	9
Elliott, KY	21063	13.4	77.6	0.8	. . .	69	177	76	14.5	7
Estill, KY	21065	12.6	68.2	0.9	. . .	152	358	154	16.5	10
Fayette, KY	21067	10.6	48.2	42.2	7.9	2,101	5,502	2,602	14.5	146
Fleming, KY	21069	13.8	60.2	5.2	0.6	139	389	155	15.0	10
Floyd, KY	21071	20.5	76.1	1.7	. . .	446	970	391	15.5	27
Franklin, KY	21073	13.9	50.1	21.3	1.9	475	1,013	452	15.2	29
Fulton, KY	21075	20.7	87.8	41.6	0.2	76	175	77	12.4	10
Gallatin, KY	21077	16.2	70.0	11.1	4.6	96	219	86	19.3	12
Garrard, KY	21079	16.5	61.8	8.8	0.6	162	382	165	16.2	11
Grant, KY	21081	13.1	56.9	4.5	1.0	281	687	273	17.2	24
Graves, KY	21083	15.6	63.0	19.1	4.6	412	899	377	16.7	26
Grayson, KY	21085	14.8	68.1	2.8	0.2	267	604	275	15.7	12
Green, KY	21087	13.3	64.4	6.3	. . .	122	288	115	15.0	6
Greenup, KY	21089	13.4	47.8	3.5	0.2	433	931	372	16.8	38
Hancock, KY	21091	15.3	51.7	4.1	0.1	122	274	104	16.5	12
Hardin, KY	21093	17.0	47.7	28.0	1.6	1,174	2,489	1,067	16.1	65
Harlan, KY	21095	19.3	70.0	4.1	0.2	314	798	324	15.9	34
Harrison, KY	21097	16.8	54.3	6.2	0.5	217	434	188	16.3	9
Hart, KY	21099	17.5	63.7	7.4	0.6	151	395	161	14.9	12
Henderson, KY	21101	15.8	55.4	15.1	1.2	484	1,129	435	16.6	32
Henry, KY	21103	14.7	56.3	11.3	1.2	183	418	182	15.8	25
Hickman, KY	21105	20.9	44.4	15.1	0.2	56	136	59	13.6	5
Hopkins, KY	21107	20.2	56.2	14.9	0.5	477	1,131	508	15.3	37
Jackson, KY	21109	24.6	83.5	0.8	. . .	141	416	157	14.4	15
Jefferson, KY	21111	13.9	63.2	47.8	5.3	5,506	14,224	6,172	15.8	439
Jessamine, KY	21113	14.8	52.1	10.2	2.4	443	1,173	494	15.7	28
Johnson, KY	21115	17.9	60.0	3.1	0.1	287	692	281	16.4	23
Kenton, KY	21117	16.9	46.4	16.5	1.6	1,340	3,033	1,318	17.2	76
Knott, KY	21119	16.6	69.7	1.7	. . .	142	433	159	16.0	11
Knox, KY	21121	17.5	70.0	2.9	0.1	334	891	387	14.1	19
Larue, KY	21123	17.6	57.7	10.9	1.8	189	349	148	16.3	7
Laurel, KY	21125	17.6	58.9	3.6	0.1	558	1,316	529	18.8	39
Lawrence, KY	21127	17.9	67.8	1.2	. . .	136	366	160	15.8	13
Lee, KY	21129	15.2	77.9	1.7	0.2	80	175	69	16.3	11
Leslie, KY	21131	21.0	64.4	1.2	. . .	109	313	120	15.5	9
Letcher, KY	21133	21.5	70.4	1.3	. . .	249	663	265	14.8	26
Lewis, KY	21135	13.0	71.6	2.5	. . .	164	379	143	16.6	9
Lincoln, KY	21137	18.9	72.3	7.8	0.5	274	669	271	14.9	17
Livingston, KY	21139	15.9	59.5	4.0	1.6	122	232	83	15.4	8
Logan, KY	21141	15.1	55.8	12.8	1.1	300	735	297	16.0	29
Lyon, KY	21143	13.0	45.7	9.5	1.2	87	141	56	13.5	5
McCracken, KY	21145	11.0	53.9	24.4	0.7	609	1,321	584	17.0	44
McCreary, KY	21147	19.8	74.3	2.4	. . .	193	515	191	16.5	12
McLean, KY	21149	18.0	55.9	3.2	1.0	105	262	112	14.7	5
Madison, KY	21151	16.2	49.5	11.2	1.4	693	1,581	722	17.0	36
Magoffin, KY	21153	21.2	92.8	1.0	0.2	167	408	167	13.3	16
Marion, KY	21155	17.0	59.0	11.1	0.5	200	464	194	16.6	13
Marshall, KY	21157	12.6	48.5	2.0	0.1	332	701	318	15.3	34
Martin, KY	21159	18.9	68.9	0.7	. . .	152	416	151	14.3	13
Mason, KY	21161	16.6	59.3	13.7	0.9	184	397	181	15.8	12
Meade, KY	21163	13.0	48.4	6.2	0.3	345	689	292	17.6	14
Menifee, KY	21165	13.4	72.2	6.6	. . .	70	202	82	13.8	16
Mercer, KY	21167	16.1	50.0	12.2	0.8	249	543	237	15.1	23
Metcalfe, KY	21169	17.2	74.5	2.6	0.4	86	255	108	15.5	11
Monroe, KY	21171	12.9	69.6	7.8	1.8	148	343	117	17.1	12
Montgomery, KY	21173	13.7	58.9	7.1	1.9	255	659	295	16.0	33

[2]IEP=Individual Education Program. See notes and definitions for more information.
. . . = Not available.

Table C-1. Population, School, and Student Characteristics by County, Selected Years—*Continued*

County	State/ County Code	Revenues, 2008–2009				Current expenditures, 2008–2009			Resident population 16 to 19 years, 2006–2010			
		Total revenue ($1,000's)	Percentage of revenue from: Federal government	State government	Local government	Amount ($1,000's)	Amount per student	Percent for instruction	Total population 16 to 19 years	Percent enrolled in school	Percent high school graduates, not enrolled in school	Percent not enrolled, not grads, not employed, or not in labor force
		19	20	21	22	23	24	25	26	27	28	29
KENTUCKY— *(Continued)*												
Crittenden, KY	21055	12,030	12.5	67.6	19.9	11,189	8,288	50.3	578	69.0	7.4	18.3
Cumberland, KY	21057	11,658	14.8	66.4	18.7	10,217	10,076	59.9	542	61.3	16.4	20.5
Daviess, KY	21059	157,849	9.7	60.4	29.9	139,743	9,062	61.2	5,165	83.2	13.4	2.9
Edmonson, KY	21061	20,349	10.7	74.3	14.9	18,166	8,784	62.2	883	64.8	22.0	12.5
Elliott, KY	21063	11,952	16.6	73.3	10.1	10,814	9,469	56.8	377	79.3	14.1	6.6
Estill, KY	21065	24,191	12.8	74.5	12.7	20,754	8,288	57.8	703	70.3	12.4	10.0
Fayette, KY	21067	395,446	7.7	37.4	55.0	336,274	9,313	61.6	17,531	86.1	7.3	4.3
Fleming, KY	21069	23,219	12.8	71.7	15.5	20,375	8,659	60.5	746	81.6	14.3	3.4
Floyd, KY	21071	65,357	13.7	67.9	18.4	56,797	8,811	58.9	2,152	70.5	13.8	12.0
Franklin, KY	21073	69,389	7.5	57.9	34.6	57,142	8,285	58.0	3,008	85.8	9.8	2.4
Fulton, KY	21075	12,996	15.7	63.7	20.6	11,135	10,495	61.6	338	86.1	9.5	4.4
Gallatin, KY	21077	16,918	9.8	63.0	27.1	14,197	8,912	53.9	588	87.9	4.1	0.0
Garrard, KY	21079	26,346	8.7	66.1	25.2	21,589	8,147	63.4	856	79.1	13.3	3.5
Grant, KY	21081	46,530	10.1	68.6	21.3	39,248	8,321	57.1	1,383	68.3	12.2	8.3
Graves, KY	21083	57,918	12.0	68.0	20.0	51,938	8,239	58.8	1,913	79.7	12.0	5.4
Grayson, KY	21085	40,304	11.9	69.8	18.2	34,026	7,961	62.0	1,285	86.2	8.6	4.4
Green, KY	21087	17,271	10.3	72.9	16.8	14,749	8,640	59.5	649	80.1	19.9	0.0
Greenup, KY	21089	59,205	10.4	66.9	22.7	54,135	8,372	56.6	1,900	82.4	10.5	7.1
Hancock, KY	21091	16,904	7.8	61.6	30.6	14,505	8,409	57.5	477	86.6	12.8	0.6
Hardin, KY	21093	151,417	9.3	63.3	27.4	132,121	8,088	59.5	5,977	75.9	20.2	2.9
Harlan, KY	21095	53,860	15.8	70.0	14.1	45,571	8,730	58.9	1,563	83.2	6.7	8.9
Harrison, KY	21097	29,112	9.4	69.5	21.1	25,276	7,879	60.1	975	76.4	16.6	6.1
Hart, KY	21099	26,112	13.6	68.9	17.5	22,696	9,476	53.8	1,152	80.5	7.0	7.2
Henderson, KY	21101	65,630	9.7	61.6	28.7	58,978	8,508	61.4	2,276	78.8	11.6	8.4
Henry, KY	21103	27,182	9.5	66.7	23.8	22,952	7,759	60.1	767	78.9	15.8	2.4
Hickman, KY	21105	8,888	11.6	65.5	23.0	7,380	9,122	55.3	274	88.0	12.0	0.0
Hopkins, KY	21107	75,997	9.6	69.5	20.8	65,564	8,340	62.8	2,352	80.1	8.9	5.6
Jackson, KY	21109	24,779	17.6	72.1	10.3	22,232	9,721	57.7	706	73.4	20.8	5.8
Jefferson, KY	21111	1,101,846	10.8	41.7	47.5	988,930	9,973	53.7	36,928	82.4	10.8	5.0
Jessamine, KY	21113	74,403	7.4	55.8	36.8	63,764	8,316	60.5	3,037	88.9	9.5	1.6
Johnson, KY	21115	46,054	11.5	72.0	16.5	41,654	9,123	65.4	1,142	66.5	20.0	12.6
Kenton, KY	21117	223,593	9.0	51.9	39.1	187,917	8,440	60.3	8,244	84.6	7.1	6.1
Knott, KY	21119	29,131	13.5	61.3	25.2	23,697	9,434	57.0	1,016	91.7	1.7	6.3
Knox, KY	21121	54,889	15.7	70.5	13.9	48,380	8,808	61.1	1,942	70.6	16.7	10.0
Larue, KY	21123	23,222	10.0	71.8	18.2	19,588	8,044	61.7	865	84.4	15.6	0.0
Laurel, KY	21125	89,974	11.6	67.6	20.8	79,662	8,116	56.2	2,862	72.0	17.1	8.9
Lawrence, KY	21127	24,954	15.1	67.8	17.2	21,816	8,879	59.6	927	72.4	15.2	8.6
Lee, KY	21129	11,399	19.5	66.4	14.1	10,874	9,539	50.2	291	76.6	6.2	10.7
Leslie, KY	21131	21,363	13.8	70.4	15.8	19,003	10,049	53.9	571	82.3	13.8	3.9
Letcher, KY	21133	41,896	12.5	68.6	18.8	36,909	9,622	57.2	1,283	83.5	9.4	6.6
Lewis, KY	21135	25,402	14.7	72.4	12.9	22,098	9,053	58.1	705	74.9	13.1	12.1
Lincoln, KY	21137	43,396	15.8	70.1	14.0	40,075	9,834	64.1	1,294	68.2	20.3	11.0
Livingston, KY	21139	13,211	11.3	59.4	29.3	12,266	9,421	63.6	463	88.3	8.4	2.6
Logan, KY	21141	46,124	11.4	67.5	21.1	39,782	8,372	60.9	1,377	75.7	21.5	2.8
Lyon, KY	21143	9,011	8.6	49.4	42.0	7,903	8,416	58.2	230	83.9	13.0	3.0
McCracken, KY	21145	101,037	11.0	53.8	35.2	86,290	8,455	60.9	3,102	81.5	10.2	6.1
McCreary, KY	21147	33,675	16.7	72.4	11.0	29,971	9,194	59.1	1,130	65.5	17.6	16.9
McLean, KY	21149	17,242	9.1	72.6	18.3	13,096	7,800	55.8	502	83.3	13.9	2.8
Madison, KY	21151	112,490	9.9	61.6	28.5	96,407	8,116	63.3	6,167	88.9	7.2	3.6
Magoffin, KY	21153	25,655	14.7	70.9	14.4	22,922	9,762	55.4	1,011	66.0	23.2	10.9
Marion, KY	21155	30,135	10.2	65.8	24.0	27,041	8,382	64.7	1,117	81.0	14.8	4.2
Marshall, KY	21157	43,679	9.5	57.7	32.8	41,475	8,573	61.3	1,516	83.3	12.7	2.8
Martin, KY	21159	23,670	15.2	64.9	19.9	21,122	9,451	55.0	616	65.4	11.5	23.1
Mason, KY	21161	25,784	10.1	60.2	29.8	24,085	8,544	63.9	878	68.6	13.0	15.2
Meade, KY	21163	45,245	7.7	73.0	19.3	38,119	7,656	62.8	1,568	82.2	15.7	1.2
Menifee, KY	21165	13,047	12.1	77.5	10.3	10,094	8,965	57.1	395	83.8	4.3	11.9
Mercer, KY	21167	36,893	9.2	63.3	27.5	31,955	8,653	64.4	998	76.6	16.7	6.2
Metcalfe, KY	21169	18,120	14.0	69.0	16.9	14,413	8,138	57.8	567	77.4	9.4	13.2
Monroe, KY	21171	21,085	13.6	71.0	15.4	18,647	9,208	58.9	604	78.6	17.9	3.5
Montgomery, KY	21173	42,868	12.3	65.5	22.3	35,377	7,548	62.6	1,132	71.7	13.3	14.3

Note. Data in columns 26 through 41 from the American Community Survey are subject to sampling error, which can be especially large in small counties and small population groups. See notes and definitions for more information.

Table C-1. Population, School, and Student Characteristics by County, Selected Years—*Continued*

County	State/ County Code	High school graduates, 2006–2010			College enrollment, 2006–2010		College graduates, 2006–2010 (percent)						
		Population 25 years and over	High school diploma or less (percent)	High school diploma or more (percent)	Number	Percent public	Bachelor's degree or more	+/- U.S. percent with Bachelor's degree or more	Non-Hispanic White	Black or African American	American Indian and Alaska Native	Asian, Hawaiian, and Pacific Islander	Hispanic or Latino[3]
		30	31	32	33	34	35	36	37	38	39	40	41
KENTUCKY— *(Continued)*													
Crittenden, KY	21055	6,374	66.5	75.3	344	100.0	9.3	-18.6	9.5	0.0	0.0	0.0	0.0
Cumberland, KY	21057	4,788	73.0	70.5	294	88.8	7.9	-20.0	8.0	3.7	0.0	0.0	0.0
Daviess, KY	21059	63,474	53.0	86.7	5,031	74.6	18.2	-9.7	18.7	7.0	0.0	39.7	10.3
Edmonson, KY	21061	8,223	70.4	76.3	356	91.6	7.2	-20.7	7.2	0.0	0.0	0.0	8.0
Elliott, KY	21063	5,151	73.2	69.6	177	89.8	7.1	-20.8	7.5	0.0	0.0	0.0	0.0
Estill, KY	21065	10,244	75.0	67.0	273	85.3	6.6	-21.3	6.8	0.0	0.0	0.0	0.0
Fayette, KY	21067	185,370	32.8	88.3	37,986	86.2	39.1	11.2	42.8	17.0	35.4	75.5	16.0
Fleming, KY	21069	9,623	60.9	74.7	651	90.0	12.7	-15.2	12.5	26.7	0.0	0.0	0.0
Floyd, KY	21071	27,592	65.8	68.9	1,420	83.8	11.7	-16.2	11.8	2.8	0.0	11.3	2.6
Franklin, KY	21073	33,519	48.0	85.5	2,979	89.4	27.2	-0.7	26.4	33.6	42.9	51.8	22.4
Fulton, KY	21075	4,892	66.2	77.6	134	86.6	10.9	-17.0	11.3	10.3	0.0	0.0	0.0
Gallatin, KY	21077	5,445	69.1	71.3	286	99.0	9.0	-18.9	8.6	0.0	0.0	100.0	26.2
Garrard, KY	21079	11,924	64.6	78.8	405	74.6	13.8	-14.1	14.2	0.0	100.0	0.0	0.0
Grant, KY	21081	15,585	61.5	79.4	1,214	79.0	10.8	-17.1	10.8	31.9	0.0	0.0	10.2
Graves, KY	21083	25,124	59.7	79.3	1,879	83.9	14.4	-13.5	15.2	5.8	0.0	19.3	2.8
Grayson, KY	21085	17,193	70.6	72.2	925	85.8	7.5	-20.4	7.5	0.0	0.0	0.0	0.0
Green, KY	21087	8,021	68.0	73.4	412	67.5	11.4	-16.5	11.1	12.3	0.0	0.0	44.3
Greenup, KY	21089	25,806	56.3	80.1	1,467	88.9	14.9	-13.0	14.6	20.8	0.0	87.6	0.0
Hancock, KY	21091	5,708	60.4	84.1	399	90.7	10.8	-17.1	10.6	36.6	31.6	0.0	0.0
Hardin, KY	21093	64,604	47.2	87.4	6,225	85.1	18.5	-9.4	18.8	14.4	15.2	31.8	14.1
Harlan, KY	21095	20,301	68.4	68.4	1,215	78.8	11.1	-16.8	11.1	12.3	15.2	0.0	0.0
Harrison, KY	21097	12,790	59.7	79.2	648	77.5	13.8	-14.1	14.1	0.0	0.0	0.0	16.3
Hart, KY	21099	12,191	70.8	67.7	648	84.9	9.2	-18.7	9.8	1.7	0.0	100.0	0.0
Henderson, KY	21101	31,323	54.6	83.5	1,613	86.5	16.1	-11.8	16.5	10.0	0.0	52.9	12.9
Henry, KY	21103	10,491	65.3	80.0	249	92.8	14.1	-13.8	14.0	20.6	26.7	0.0	7.9
Hickman, KY	21105	3,569	59.0	75.8	185	90.8	16.5	-11.4	17.1	11.8	0.0	0.0	0.0
Hopkins, KY	21107	32,328	59.1	77.8	2,097	90.0	13.2	-14.7	13.2	14.9	4.4	11.3	10.3
Jackson, KY	21109	9,245	75.8	61.8	655	85.3	6.2	-21.7	6.1	0.0	0.0	0.0	63.3
Jefferson, KY	21111	493,092	42.4	87.0	47,414	74.7	28.5	0.6	31.4	15.1	6.5	57.1	18.7
Jessamine, KY	21113	30,075	45.7	85.2	3,475	47.2	27.4	-0.5	27.8	20.1	12.3	67.6	4.2
Johnson, KY	21115	16,091	67.9	67.8	752	95.3	10.5	-17.4	10.5	0.0	0.0	32.6	0.0
Kenton, KY	21117	104,296	44.3	87.0	10,301	76.1	27.5	-0.4	28.3	13.6	23.1	38.8	16.3
Knott, KY	21119	11,299	65.8	67.1	1,188	40.9	12.4	-15.5	12.4	100.0	100.0	0.0	0.0
Knox, KY	21121	20,852	77.2	62.8	1,443	46.8	8.5	-19.4	8.4	20.1	20.5	0.0	0.0
Larue, KY	21123	9,639	63.7	76.8	584	90.4	12.1	-15.8	12.2	18.9	0.0	0.0	5.6
Laurel, KY	21125	39,043	62.7	74.2	2,591	77.7	13.6	-14.3	13.5	1.4	0.0	81.8	14.9
Lawrence, KY	21127	10,714	67.9	70.0	740	83.9	8.2	-19.7	8.1	0.0	0.0	0.0	0.0
Lee, KY	21129	5,625	75.4	65.3	299	86.6	7.8	-20.1	8.0	0.0	0.0	0.0	0.0
Leslie, KY	21131	7,850	74.5	56.8	439	78.1	8.1	-19.8	8.1	0.0	0.0	20.7	0.0
Letcher, KY	21133	17,044	64.1	71.0	1,140	80.6	11.7	-16.2	11.8	3.8	0.0	60.0	9.1
Lewis, KY	21135	9,616	74.0	66.2	445	82.9	11.6	-16.3	11.4	0.0	0.0	100.0	100.0
Lincoln, KY	21137	16,612	69.0	72.5	986	90.1	10.4	-17.5	10.4	3.0	0.0	0.0	34.4
Livingston, KY	21139	6,839	61.1	79.1	342	70.5	10.7	-17.2	10.7	0.0	0.0	16.7	0.0
Logan, KY	21141	18,300	67.5	74.2	830	84.2	10.3	-17.6	10.6	7.7	0.0	0.0	8.9
Lyon, KY	21143	6,532	57.7	81.2	186	85.5	10.8	-17.1	11.9	0.5	0.0	0.0	0.0
McCracken, KY	21145	45,586	45.3	85.3	3,176	78.1	21.0	-6.9	21.9	10.0	24.5	46.9	24.4
McCreary, KY	21147	11,958	71.3	64.7	650	83.8	8.0	-19.9	8.1	5.1	0.0	0.0	0.0
McLean, KY	21149	6,533	64.7	77.3	443	88.7	9.7	-18.2	9.8	0.0	0.0	0.0	0.0
Madison, KY	21151	49,941	45.9	83.8	13,540	83.3	27.4	-0.5	27.8	22.4	35.4	59.6	17.8
Magoffin, KY	21153	8,528	70.7	65.5	390	90.8	10.5	-17.4	10.6	0.0	0.0	0.0	0.0
Marion, KY	21155	13,135	65.6	78.5	820	73.5	11.4	-16.5	12.4	3.1	0.0	44.4	0.0
Marshall, KY	21157	22,469	58.1	83.2	1,299	90.8	14.8	-13.1	14.9	0.0	34.7	0.0	15.2
Martin, KY	21159	9,125	68.5	64.7	532	100.0	8.9	-19.0	7.4	54.0	8.3	0.0	0.0
Mason, KY	21161	11,760	60.3	77.9	711	89.2	14.3	-13.6	15.2	1.3	28.6	100.0	6.5
Meade, KY	21163	18,334	54.5	85.0	1,478	85.3	11.5	-16.4	11.3	14.1	0.0	29.2	9.9
Menifee, KY	21165	4,591	70.8	68.8	221	79.6	10.3	-17.6	10.1	0.0	0.0	0.0	100.0
Mercer, KY	21167	14,718	58.2	82.3	782	71.4	17.0	-10.9	17.7	5.0	0.0	0.0	12.5
Metcalfe, KY	21169	6,906	75.2	67.6	404	98.8	7.2	-20.7	7.3	4.1	0.0	0.0	0.0
Monroe, KY	21171	7,597	70.9	74.6	586	91.5	11.6	-16.3	11.2	0.0	0.0	0.0	49.0
Montgomery, KY	21173	17,492	62.9	75.7	988	82.0	15.1	-12.8	15.5	9.3	0.0	0.0	2.7

Note. Data in columns 26 through 41 from the American Community Survey are subject to sampling error, which can be especially large in small counties and small population groups. See notes and definitions for more information.
[3]May be of any race.

Table C-1. Population, School, and Student Characteristics by County, Selected Years—*Continued*

County	State/ County Code	County Type[1]	Population, 2010		Percent of related children 5–17 years in poverty, 2010	Percent of children under 19 years with no health insurance, 2010	Number of schools and students, 2010–2011			Resident enrollment, 2006–2010 K-12 enrollment	
			Total	Percent 5–17 years			School districts	Schools	Students	Number	Percent public
			1	2	3	4	5	6	7	8	9
KENTUCKY—*(Continued)*											
Morgan, KY	21175	7	13,923	15.2	34.2	7.2	1	9	2,090	2,449	95.4
Muhlenberg, KY	21177	6	31,499	16.0	26.9	7.0	1	12	5,238	5,208	94.6
Nelson, KY	21179	1	43,437	19.1	19.6	6.7	2	16	7,560	8,081	83.9
Nicholas, KY	21181	8	7,135	17.9	26.7	8.3	1	2	1,217	1,169	88.4
Ohio, KY	21183	6	23,842	17.7	26.9	6.7	1	9	3,966	4,142	91.6
Oldham, KY	21185	1	60,316	22.2	6.5	5.1	1	26	11,951	13,317	88.7
Owen, KY	21187	8	10,841	18.1	22.5	8.0	1	4	1,947	2,047	96.4
Owsley, KY	21189	9	4,755	16.7	49.4	6.7	1	2	811	819	97.2
Pendleton, KY	21191	1	14,877	18.5	20.3	8.2	1	4	2,646	2,917	92.6
Perry, KY	21193	7	28,712	15.9	33.6	5.8	3	16	5,262	4,955	96.8
Pike, KY	21195	7	65,024	16.1	30.2	6.5	2	28	11,175	10,767	97.2
Powell, KY	21197	6	12,613	17.8	37.6	6.4	1	5	2,467	2,225	91.6
Pulaski, KY	21199	5	63,063	16.7	27.8	7.3	3	22	10,331	10,522	93.3
Robertson, KY	21201	8	2,282	15.3	30.7	8.7	1	1	370	477	100.0
Rockcastle, KY	21203	7	17,056	17.5	31.7	6.9	1	7	3,014	3,193	92.3
Rowan, KY	21205	7	23,333	13.8	28.8	7.9	1	12	3,363	3,433	91.4
Russell, KY	21207	9	17,565	16.3	36.4	8.2	1	7	2,982	2,739	92.0
Scott, KY	21209	2	47,173	19.3	14.4	5.7	1	14	8,424	8,350	92.0
Shelby, KY	21211	1	42,074	18.2	15.6	8.3	3	15	7,051	7,622	83.6
Simpson, KY	21213	6	17,327	18.0	22.5	7.0	1	6	3,061	3,105	95.0
Spencer, KY	21215	1	17,061	19.2	11.2	7.5	1	6	2,866	3,230	89.5
Taylor, KY	21217	7	24,512	15.9	30.1	7.8	2	8	3,758	3,865	94.4
Todd, KY	21219	8	12,460	19.3	33.4	11.1	1	5	2,142	2,370	91.5
Trigg, KY	21221	3	14,339	16.8	22.1	9.6	1	4	2,106	2,397	92.8
Trimble, KY	21223	1	8,809	18.8	18.3	7.8	1	4	1,530	1,649	96.1
Union, KY	21225	6	15,007	16.8	24.2	7.0	1	9	2,224	2,595	93.7
Warren, KY	21227	3	113,792	16.4	23.4	7.7	4	44	17,787	17,732	91.9
Washington, KY	21229	8	11,717	17.2	22.6	9.0	1	4	1,669	2,150	85.2
Wayne, KY	21231	7	20,813	16.5	36.6	7.2	2	12	3,524	3,788	99.0
Webster, KY	21233	2	13,621	16.7	20.7	10.0	1	7	2,220	2,343	97.1
Whitley, KY	21235	7	35,637	17.8	34.1	6.5	4	20	8,081	6,658	97.2
Wolfe, KY	21237	9	7,355	17.5	44.7	6.8	1	5	1,273	1,181	95.2
Woodford, KY	21239	2	24,939	18.3	14.7	8.5	1	8	4,093	4,458	86.0
LOUISIANA	22000	X	4,533,372	17.7	25.0	6.4	126	1,471	696,558	807,978	82.7
Acadia, LA	22001	4	61,773	19.7	27.1	6.3	1	26	9,551	12,515	80.1
Allen, LA	22003	6	25,764	16.4	23.2	6.8	1	12	4,277	4,474	93.3
Ascension, LA	22005	2	107,215	20.9	15.3	5.7	1	27	19,953	21,749	86.3
Assumption, LA	22007	6	23,421	18.3	20.5	6.6	1	10	3,806	4,355	86.7
Avoyelles, LA	22009	6	42,073	17.7	27.9	6.2	2	12	6,728	8,100	87.4
Beauregard, LA	22011	6	35,654	19.1	19.7	6.7	1	12	6,077	6,947	92.2
Bienville, LA	22013	6	14,353	17.4	32.5	6.3	1	9	2,307	2,751	93.8
Bossier, LA	22015	2	116,979	18.3	19.8	5.9	1	35	20,656	21,170	94.8
Caddo, LA	22017	2	254,969	17.6	30.5	6.1	2	72	42,338	46,196	89.9
Calcasieu, LA	22019	3	192,768	18.3	21.9	5.4	1	60	33,063	35,064	88.2
Caldwell, LA	22021	8	10,132	17.2	29.0	7.3	1	6	1,670	1,890	93.8
Cameron, LA	22023	3	6,839	18.4	16.8	11.7	1	4	1,287	1,466	94.0
Catahoula, LA	22025	9	10,407	16.3	32.6	9.3	1	10	1,555	1,717	90.7
Claiborne, LA	22027	7	17,195	14.4	37.9	6.9	1	8	2,105	2,729	90.7
Concordia, LA	22029	7	20,822	18.2	38.1	6.1	1	11	3,876	3,968	95.1
De Soto, LA	22031	2	26,656	18.2	26.0	7.4	1	13	4,923	4,889	94.8
East Baton Rouge, LA	22033	2	440,171	16.8	24.9	5.8	14	146	58,962	75,607	74.2
East Carroll, LA	22035	7	7,759	18.4	51.0	6.7	1	4	1,229	1,424	88.8
East Feliciana, LA	22037	2	20,267	15.3	22.9	7.1	1	6	2,114	3,454	74.3
Evangeline, LA	22039	6	33,984	19.4	29.8	5.8	1	12	5,995	6,780	81.1

[1]County type codes are from the Economic Research Service of the United States Department of Agriculture. See notes and definitions for more information.

Table C-1. Population, School, and Student Characteristics by County, Selected Years—*Continued*

County	State/ County Code	Characteristics of students, 2010–2011				Number of graduates, 2008–2009	Staff and students, 2010–2011			
		Percent with IEP[2]	Percent eligible for free or reduced lunch	Percent minority	Percent English-language learners		Total staff	Number of teachers	Student/ teacher ratio	Central admin. staff
		10	11	12	13	14	15	16	17	18
KENTUCKY—*(Continued)*										
Morgan, KY	21175	16.7	70.4	2.0	0.1	145	340	133	15.7	16
Muhlenberg, KY	21177	14.3	56.1	7.7	0.1	315	867	371	14.1	24
Nelson, KY	21179	14.6	54.1	12.9	0.8	665	1,036	432	17.5	35
Nicholas, KY	21181	12.2	62.1	3.9	0.1	84	176	78	15.6	11
Ohio, KY	21183	12.3	65.2	6.2	2.5	267	670	250	15.9	17
Oldham, KY	21185	14.2	20.2	10.8	2.0	785	1,709	691	17.3	79
Owen, KY	21187	13.0	58.9	5.4	1.7	132	264	111	17.5	4
Owsley, KY	21189	18.9	82.9	1.4	. . .	47	163	64	12.7	9
Pendleton, KY	21191	18.1	55.7	2.9	0.2	183	398	170	15.5	16
Perry, KY	21193	18.1	69.5	4.0	0.2	336	851	344	15.3	23
Pike, KY	21195	14.2	60.7	2.0	0.1	695	1,705	650	17.2	42
Powell, KY	21197	19.4	72.9	1.9	0.2	148	378	158	15.6	15
Pulaski, KY	21199	14.5	65.7	6.0	1.2	665	1,556	635	16.3	54
Robertson, KY	21201	17.6	58.1	2.2	1.1	32	72	30	12.5	3
Rockcastle, KY	21203	20.6	68.0	1.6	0.1	213	487	193	15.6	15
Rowan, KY	21205	17.3	59.1	5.2	0.7	217	483	208	16.2	15
Russell, KY	21207	14.2	68.4	5.8	1.6	191	478	186	16.0	22
Scott, KY	21209	15.6	40.8	14.9	3.0	389	1,017	455	18.5	26
Shelby, KY	21211	16.7	46.1	27.3	8.9	350	908	404	17.4	37
Simpson, KY	21213	15.9	57.5	17.6	1.4	186	424	178	17.2	15
Spencer, KY	21215	13.8	40.8	7.1	0.3	. . .	351	150	19.1	16
Taylor, KY	21217	13.9	61.7	10.4	0.7	290	550	243	15.5	26
Todd, KY	21219	19.9	61.2	18.0	2.3	137	346	135	15.9	6
Trigg, KY	21221	11.2	56.6	16.6	0.3	172	321	125	16.9	16
Trimble, KY	21223	11.8	55.7	4.1	0.8	83	218	85	17.9	5
Union, KY	21225	17.7	60.1	17.0	. . .	159	409	165	13.5	16
Warren, KY	21227	12.8	40.7	25.4	8.8	1,060	2,547	1,113	16.0	68
Washington, KY	21229	19.2	59.9	16.8	3.5	142	257	107	15.6	14
Wayne, KY	21231	14.9	72.7	6.9	1.9	223	583	207	17.0	29
Webster, KY	21233	16.3	62.0	13.5	3.4	165	371	144	15.4	9
Whitley, KY	21235	16.6	70.1	2.3	0.1	494	1,297	551	14.7	42
Wolfe, KY	21237	22.1	84.1	1.6	. . .	69	238	87	14.7	9
Woodford, KY	21239	13.2	34.8	19.4	5.6	295	543	245	16.7	11
LOUISIANA	22000	11.9	66.2	51.4	1.7	35,621	100,881	48,655	14.3	3,192
Acadia, LA	22001	11.5	69.7	30.8	0.5	468	1,416	615	15.5	42
Allen, LA	22003	10.0	64.9	27.2	0.3	213	672	344	12.4	13
Ascension, LA	22005	11.4	48.3	37.3	1.6	1,083	2,745	1,356	14.7	60
Assumption, LA	22007	11.6	68.0	45.3	0.7	192	558	262	14.5	19
Avoyelles, LA	22009	8.0	77.9	46.3	0.3	359	791	401	16.8	22
Beauregard, LA	22011	16.1	51.8	21.0	0.5	310	852	416	14.6	26
Bienville, LA	22013	8.9	71.0	55.9	0.4	134	405	202	11.4	12
Bossier, LA	22015	10.6	44.7	37.8	2.7	1,041	2,850	1,357	15.2	59
Caddo, LA	22017	10.2	65.4	67.8	0.8	2,126	6,681	2,924	14.5	198
Calcasieu, LA	22019	15.0	60.2	39.1	0.7	1,785	4,856	2,381	13.9	145
Caldwell, LA	22021	13.4	70.5	20.9	0.2	109	293	137	12.2	9
Cameron, LA	22023	13.3	44.1	8.3	1.4	0	325	158	8.2	8
Catahoula, LA	22025	10.2	71.3	42.3	. . .	91	283	121	12.9	11
Claiborne, LA	22027	15.6	75.5	70.8	0.4	157	395	179	11.8	12
Concordia, LA	22029	9.8	75.2	51.2	0.2	149	573	260	14.9	28
De Soto, LA	22031	9.9	65.6	50.9	1.1	247	840	380	13.0	24
East Baton Rouge, LA	22033	11.1	73.5	76.6	2.1	2,675	8,642	4,457	13.2	271
East Carroll, LA	22035	10.7	92.2	99.8	. . .	77	231	97	12.6	10
East Feliciana, LA	22037	13.4	84.6	73.1	. . .	109	341	138	15.3	14
Evangeline, LA	22039	14.0	77.8	41.2	0.2	261	875	422	14.2	27

[2]IEP=Individual Education Program. See notes and definitions for more information.
. . . = Not available.

Table C-1. Population, School, and Student Characteristics by County, Selected Years—*Continued*

County	State/ County Code	Revenues, 2008–2009				Current expenditures, 2008–2009			Resident population 16 to 19 years, 2006–2010			
		Total revenue ($1,000's)	Percentage of revenue from: Federal government	State government	Local government	Amount ($1,000's)	Amount per student	Percent for instruction	Total population 16 to 19 years	Percent enrolled in school	Percent high school graduates, not enrolled in school	Percent not enrolled, not grads, not employed, or not in labor force
		19	20	21	22	23	24	25	26	27	28	29
KENTUCKY— *(Continued)*												
Morgan, KY	21175	21,060	13.7	71.4	14.9	19,737	9,197	55.3	647	89.5	8.0	1.1
Muhlenberg, KY	21177	55,674	9.6	60.2	30.2	47,428	9,158	64.2	1,628	80.0	12.7	5.1
Nelson, KY	21179	92,164	7.5	60.3	32.1	79,130	7,830	57.1	2,211	75.6	18.3	6.1
Nicholas, KY	21181	11,814	12.3	71.4	16.4	10,218	8,155	60.1	242	72.7	12.8	7.0
Ohio, KY	21183	39,344	10.9	70.5	18.5	33,803	8,369	58.2	1,232	83.4	10.8	4.6
Oldham, KY	21185	110,867	4.1	53.3	42.5	90,719	7,684	59.5	3,020	90.1	6.2	3.7
Owen, KY	21187	18,947	13.9	64.4	21.6	17,261	9,051	61.2	534	85.8	11.6	0.0
Owsley, KY	21189	11,027	29.9	59.9	10.2	9,656	12,238	56.9	130	74.6	25.4	0.0
Pendleton, KY	21191	26,039	8.7	71.6	19.8	22,585	8,276	58.3	926	84.5	11.8	3.8
Perry, KY	21193	53,542	12.7	67.3	20.0	48,241	9,078	60.6	1,589	90.6	4.7	4.8
Pike, KY	21195	110,234	13.8	60.1	26.0	99,143	8,821	59.5	3,320	80.5	13.1	5.9
Powell, KY	21197	24,055	13.9	74.3	11.8	21,975	8,868	61.2	646	66.3	30.5	3.3
Pulaski, KY	21199	97,782	12.0	64.2	23.8	87,345	8,596	58.0	3,216	81.6	11.7	5.1
Robertson, KY	21201	4,399	13.3	72.6	14.1	3,826	9,494	60.1	218	74.8	11.0	12.8
Rockcastle, KY	21203	28,737	12.3	75.4	12.4	26,751	8,777	63.5	846	80.9	12.2	6.3
Rowan, KY	21205	31,249	11.0	64.0	25.0	28,146	8,607	61.1	2,624	91.2	2.8	5.0
Russell, KY	21207	31,538	12.5	64.9	22.6	26,854	8,925	57.7	676	71.3	11.4	17.3
Scott, KY	21209	71,038	6.1	56.3	37.6	60,140	7,463	60.0	2,569	90.5	5.2	2.2
Shelby, KY	21211	64,066	6.4	54.7	38.9	54,148	8,336	61.6	2,145	75.4	12.3	2.3
Simpson, KY	21213	26,346	10.7	62.6	26.7	24,379	8,225	60.3	1,017	70.8	22.6	3.3
Spencer, KY	21215	...	...	...	...	...	...	...	952	83.6	8.9	6.4
Taylor, KY	21217	36,921	12.4	65.6	22.1	32,475	8,639	62.2	1,692	76.2	12.8	6.6
Todd, KY	21219	22,004	11.4	71.7	16.9	18,701	8,650	54.7	725	70.5	17.2	6.6
Trigg, KY	21221	22,757	7.4	52.4	40.2	17,767	8,353	56.2	687	85.7	8.2	4.7
Trimble, KY	21223	14,601	13.0	62.5	24.5	12,071	7,978	59.7	526	90.1	8.0	0.0
Union, KY	21225	24,399	9.5	65.3	25.2	21,270	8,826	55.1	1,249	59.2	20.3	16.6
Warren, KY	21227	158,199	10.1	56.0	33.9	131,993	7,775	65.1	8,139	88.1	8.5	2.9
Washington, KY	21229	18,104	10.6	65.1	24.3	15,678	8,995	61.9	694	84.2	9.8	6.1
Wayne, KY	21231	35,438	15.0	71.9	13.0	29,881	8,591	60.2	929	84.6	10.1	5.3
Webster, KY	21233	17,878	13.2	61.1	25.7	16,153	7,075	48.4	849	83.3	7.8	8.1
Whitley, KY	21235	80,513	13.9	72.0	14.1	71,675	8,713	62.1	2,778	84.4	13.3	0.8
Wolfe, KY	21237	14,515	16.4	73.7	9.9	13,615	10,875	59.2	415	82.7	17.4	0.0
Woodford, KY	21239	33,947	6.8	51.8	41.5	29,742	7,300	62.5	1,328	83.7	12.1	0.0
LOUISIANA	22000	8,202,325	15.7	44.7	39.6	7,191,615	10,542	57.9	266,231	79.6	10.9	6.5
Acadia, LA	22001	87,712	15.2	60.1	24.7	82,148	8,801	60.6	3,842	79.8	7.0	10.5
Allen, LA	22003	45,897	8.7	61.9	29.4	45,080	10,744	58.0	1,486	75.0	14.7	4.2
Ascension, LA	22005	218,215	7.8	44.5	47.7	190,536	9,974	59.3	6,181	83.1	7.8	4.3
Assumption, LA	22007	50,316	13.0	56.6	30.4	49,713	12,410	56.3	1,545	71.9	10.2	15.6
Avoyelles, LA	22009	60,953	17.1	65.7	17.2	57,080	8,285	59.7	2,413	74.5	13.0	11.7
Beauregard, LA	22011	60,738	8.1	60.2	31.7	54,309	9,114	58.3	1,859	78.5	14.5	4.3
Bienville, LA	22013	37,994	9.0	26.3	64.7	29,302	13,277	58.6	926	84.5	7.7	2.2
Bossier, LA	22015	210,453	8.6	48.4	43.0	187,349	9,507	58.4	6,390	72.5	16.3	7.0
Caddo, LA	22017	490,653	12.8	48.0	39.2	435,192	10,213	58.4	14,717	77.6	10.6	9.6
Calcasieu, LA	22019	410,639	15.4	40.5	44.0	352,052	10,356	56.5	10,840	81.0	11.9	4.0
Caldwell, LA	22021	19,543	11.3	62.6	26.0	17,498	10,203	59.9	656	56.9	28.7	7.8
Cameron, LA	22023	...	...	...	...	...	...	...	442	81.2	5.0	9.1
Catahoula, LA	22025	17,708	15.9	63.2	20.8	16,874	10,080	55.4	566	67.0	19.4	11.8
Claiborne, LA	22027	29,980	10.7	56.2	33.1	24,570	10,460	58.4	881	82.4	6.7	9.0
Concordia, LA	22029	42,356	15.1	59.3	25.6	36,407	9,321	57.8	1,454	82.7	9.2	6.3
De Soto, LA	22031	83,761	8.8	34.6	56.7	66,413	13,719	58.3	1,638	73.4	14.5	11.7
East Baton Rouge, LA	22033	728,700	12.1	37.2	50.7	654,856	11,400	56.7	29,375	84.4	8.3	4.9
East Carroll, LA	22035	16,685	24.8	59.9	15.2	16,761	11,887	59.6	323	76.2	3.7	16.4
East Feliciana, LA	22037	23,445	12.9	63.0	24.1	23,351	10,481	55.1	1,161	85.7	5.3	6.1
Evangeline, LA	22039	59,765	14.2	63.9	21.9	57,939	9,661	59.6	2,017	82.5	6.0	8.8

Note. Data in columns 26 through 41 from the American Community Survey are subject to sampling error, which can be especially large in small counties and small population groups. See notes and definitions for more information.
. . . = Not available.

Table C-1. Population, School, and Student Characteristics by County, Selected Years—*Continued*

County	State/ County Code	High school graduates, 2006–2010			College enrollment, 2006–2010		College graduates, 2006–2010 (percent)						
		Population 25 years and over	High school diploma or less (percent)	High school diploma or more (percent)	Number	Percent public	Bachelor's degree or more	+/- U.S. percent with Bachelor's degree or more	Non-Hispanic White	Black or African American	American Indian and Alaska Native	Asian, Hawaiian, and Pacific Islander	Hispanic or Latino[3]
		30	31	32	33	34	35	36	37	38	39	40	41
KENTUCKY—*(Continued)*													
Morgan, KY	21175	9,920	68.1	68.8	545	90.5	11.8	-16.1	12.4	0.0	0.0	0.0	25.0
Muhlenberg, KY	21177	22,054	64.5	76.5	1,371	87.4	10.2	-17.7	10.3	2.9	37.5	70.9	7.6
Nelson, KY	21179	28,143	57.4	83.8	1,655	66.7	15.4	-12.5	15.7	5.8	31.4	17.1	20.2
Nicholas, KY	21181	4,949	69.6	75.7	276	94.6	9.4	-18.5	9.7	0.0	0.0	0.0	0.0
Ohio, KY	21183	16,086	67.8	73.8	681	88.0	9.4	-18.5	9.5	11.8	0.0	11.2	0.0
Oldham, KY	21185	38,733	34.3	89.6	2,445	78.9	37.0	9.1	37.9	15.3	21.5	75.4	29.6
Owen, KY	21187	7,400	60.5	81.3	264	87.5	18.6	-9.3	18.6	26.4	0.0	0.0	0.0
Owsley, KY	21189	3,263	77.7	57.7	275	82.9	5.9	-22.0	5.9	0.0	0.0	0.0	0.0
Pendleton, KY	21191	9,761	65.7	77.9	700	70.4	10.5	-17.4	10.6	0.0	0.0	0.0	0.0
Perry, KY	21193	19,798	67.9	68.7	1,161	93.9	11.9	-16.0	11.7	13.1	59.5	76.5	0.0
Pike, KY	21195	45,445	67.3	71.2	2,832	57.3	12.0	-15.9	11.5	23.6	23.7	45.8	37.6
Powell, KY	21197	8,498	74.8	70.8	338	93.8	10.4	-17.5	10.3	16.0	0.0	0.0	0.0
Pulaski, KY	21199	43,219	60.8	76.1	2,933	86.1	14.5	-13.4	14.7	17.0	0.0	44.0	3.9
Robertson, KY	21201	1,376	73.1	69.6	133	100.0	7.4	-20.5	7.4	0.0	0.0	0.0	0.0
Rockcastle, KY	21203	11,658	69.3	68.5	594	89.7	11.6	-16.3	11.5	37.5	0.0	0.0	0.0
Rowan, KY	21205	13,421	55.9	76.5	4,240	97.7	24.7	-3.2	24.8	0.0	0.0	68.3	2.2
Russell, KY	21207	12,166	64.1	72.3	461	75.1	12.7	-15.2	12.4	0.0	0.0	100.0	23.4
Scott, KY	21209	28,688	44.9	86.5	3,586	47.4	26.3	-1.6	27.5	14.7	0.0	33.1	8.3
Shelby, KY	21211	27,262	50.6	83.1	2,034	72.1	23.2	-4.7	24.7	17.6	0.0	12.0	8.3
Simpson, KY	21213	11,504	61.6	81.1	722	84.6	15.6	-12.3	16.6	3.7	0.0	85.0	0.0
Spencer, KY	21215	11,090	51.7	83.7	547	71.8	16.7	-11.2	15.4	34.4	61.8	80.4	100.0
Taylor, KY	21217	15,967	64.2	73.7	1,733	40.5	15.0	-12.9	15.6	4.8	0.0	20.8	14.5
Todd, KY	21219	7,824	67.1	72.8	472	80.3	10.0	-17.9	10.4	6.3	0.0	0.0	13.3
Trigg, KY	21221	10,029	56.7	82.6	684	77.0	15.8	-12.1	17.2	0.8	0.0	31.0	21.7
Trimble, KY	21223	5,980	62.8	79.0	566	80.6	13.1	-14.8	12.7	0.0	30.8	0.0	9.6
Union, KY	21225	9,553	55.9	82.5	702	96.4	12.4	-15.5	12.1	13.2	0.0	10.3	31.0
Warren, KY	21227	66,578	45.8	84.7	15,053	95.9	27.5	-0.4	29.1	16.2	4.4	33.6	12.7
Washington, KY	21229	7,644	64.0	80.6	602	69.1	12.8	-15.1	13.1	6.4	0.0	0.0	10.6
Wayne, KY	21231	14,296	72.3	67.2	709	96.8	9.0	-18.9	9.2	0.0	0.0	0.0	0.0
Webster, KY	21233	9,395	67.8	74.4	568	68.8	8.5	-19.4	8.9	6.6	0.0	0.0	0.0
Whitley, KY	21235	23,273	67.7	70.2	2,253	35.5	11.9	-16.0	11.7	0.0	0.0	7.8	0.0
Wolfe, KY	21237	4,928	77.6	57.2	303	90.1	7.6	-20.3	7.5	0.0	0.0	100.0	0.0
Woodford, KY	21239	16,780	42.4	88.4	1,103	74.2	33.1	5.2	34.9	25.0	0.0	39.3	6.1
LOUISIANA	22000	2,856,356	53.8	81.0	274,598	81.7	20.9	-7.0	24.3	12.6	11.0	38.7	18.0
Acadia, LA	22001	38,553	69.9	69.5	2,269	88.2	10.9	-17.0	12.0	4.8	20.9	58.5	3.8
Allen, LA	22003	17,578	68.5	71.8	990	89.2	9.1	-18.8	11.4	3.3	5.8	1.4	5.2
Ascension, LA	22005	64,419	52.1	86.6	4,678	75.7	21.9	-6.0	23.2	17.7	18.3	48.2	13.1
Assumption, LA	22007	15,451	74.1	69.2	693	83.4	8.5	-19.4	9.1	6.0	22.6	0.0	24.5
Avoyelles, LA	22009	27,913	69.4	68.1	915	82.5	10.2	-17.7	12.4	3.5	2.0	7.2	21.4
Beauregard, LA	22011	22,790	58.9	83.6	1,282	82.1	14.8	-13.1	15.2	10.8	16.1	24.3	18.6
Bienville, LA	22013	9,778	63.5	79.2	509	91.7	12.8	-15.1	15.9	7.9	10.5	0.0	37.1
Bossier, LA	22015	72,872	47.1	86.8	5,625	86.0	21.6	-6.3	24.2	11.6	15.5	42.2	10.5
Caddo, LA	22017	164,587	50.6	84.3	16,594	83.3	22.0	-5.9	28.7	12.8	8.6	51.4	21.6
Calcasieu, LA	22019	121,550	53.6	81.6	10,625	90.2	19.2	-8.7	21.7	10.2	24.1	45.8	18.9
Caldwell, LA	22021	6,833	65.9	76.2	160	100.0	11.7	-16.2	11.3	11.4	0.0	0.0	38.2
Cameron, LA	22023	4,916	65.3	81.6	372	85.5	11.7	-16.2	12.1	0.0	0.0	0.0	0.0
Catahoula, LA	22025	7,053	71.7	67.9	251	98.4	10.5	-17.4	11.7	6.8	0.0	0.0	17.4
Claiborne, LA	22027	11,933	65.3	74.7	622	80.5	11.3	-16.6	18.0	4.0	0.0	68.6	0.0
Concordia, LA	22029	13,338	67.6	69.9	897	94.4	11.0	-16.9	13.7	5.5	0.0	19.2	30.3
De Soto, LA	22031	17,489	62.3	79.2	1,189	80.4	13.6	-14.3	16.6	8.8	20.0	27.1	6.3
East Baton Rouge, LA	22033	267,139	39.4	87.3	49,985	90.4	32.9	5.0	42.4	19.6	16.2	55.1	27.8
East Carroll, LA	22035	5,214	74.3	62.2	130	100.0	8.3	-19.6	10.8	6.9	26.1	0.0	0.0
East Feliciana, LA	22037	14,014	61.4	78.3	882	82.9	12.4	-15.5	16.4	7.4	0.0	4.3	13.7
Evangeline, LA	22039	21,687	70.9	66.2	1,161	90.7	10.7	-17.2	12.4	6.0	0.0	10.5	8.0

Note. Data in columns 26 through 41 from the American Community Survey are subject to sampling error, which can be especially large in small counties and small population groups. See notes and definitions for more information.
[3]May be of any race.

Table C-1. Population, School, and Student Characteristics by County, Selected Years—*Continued*

County	State/ County Code	County Type[1]	Population, 2010: Total	Population, 2010: Percent 5–17 years	Percent of related children 5–17 years in poverty, 2010	Percent of children under 19 years with no health insurance, 2010	Number of schools and students, 2010–2011: School districts	Number of schools and students, 2010–2011: Schools	Number of schools and students, 2010–2011: Students	Resident enrollment, 2006–2010, K–12 enrollment: Number	Resident enrollment, 2006–2010, K–12 enrollment: Percent public
			1	2	3	4	5	6	7	8	9
LOUISIANA—*(Continued)*											
Franklin, LA	22041	7	20,767	18.1	41.4	6.9	1	7	3,175	3,858	88.2
Grant, LA	22043	3	22,309	16.7	23.2	7.3	1	9	3,332	3,874	93.8
Iberia, LA	22045	4	73,240	19.6	29.7	6.4	1	29	13,652	15,079	86.1
Iberville, LA	22047	2	33,387	16.3	25.8	6.1	1	8	4,535	6,090	78.2
Jackson, LA	22049	6	16,274	16.0	26.4	6.5	1	5	2,246	2,720	90.0
Jefferson, LA	22051	1	432,552	16.0	22.6	7.5	1	90	45,230	70,121	65.5
Jefferson Davis, LA	22053	6	31,594	19.3	23.9	6.7	1	13	5,846	6,376	88.9
Lafayette, LA	22055	3	221,578	17.4	20.4	6.3	1	45	30,218	38,731	77.5
Lafourche, LA	22057	3	96,318	17.5	18.6	6.9	3	39	14,840	17,155	81.4
La Salle, LA	22059	6	14,890	17.2	19.5	7.1	1	9	2,649	2,793	92.6
Lincoln, LA	22061	4	46,735	14.5	29.0	6.5	4	20	6,663	6,865	89.9
Livingston, LA	22063	2	128,026	20.0	15.2	5.7	1	44	24,468	24,812	92.4
Madison, LA	22065	7	12,093	18.3	46.5	7.9	1	5	1,934	2,505	87.3
Morehouse, LA	22067	6	27,979	17.8	37.3	7.1	1	12	4,512	5,083	92.5
Natchitoches, LA	22069	6	39,566	17.5	29.6	6.2	2	17	7,127	7,134	88.4
Orleans, LA	22071	1	343,829	14.9	37.5	6.4	34	96	40,652	44,992	75.3
Ouachita, LA	22073	3	153,720	19.0	26.7	7.1	3	56	28,862	28,793	91.2
Plaquemines, LA	22075	1	23,042	20.6	16.7	7.3	2	9	4,722	4,690	82.4
Pointe Coupee, LA	22077	2	22,802	17.8	25.2	6.7	1	5	2,817	4,034	65.8
Rapides, LA	22079	3	131,613	18.9	26.0	5.1	2	51	24,024	24,795	88.4
Red River, LA	22081	6	9,091	18.1	30.9	8.2	1	4	1,523	1,644	80.7
Richland, LA	22083	6	20,725	18.4	35.2	8.6	2	13	3,974	3,921	91.1
Sabine, LA	22085	6	24,233	17.6	31.0	7.5	1	12	4,296	4,385	94.9
St. Bernard, LA	22087	1	35,897	17.6	28.7	9.4	1	10	5,916	4,924	89.0
St. Charles, LA	22089	1	52,780	19.9	16.2	5.8	1	17	9,780	11,092	84.9
St. Helena, LA	22091	2	11,203	17.2	37.4	8.5	1	2	809	2,230	91.9
St. James, LA	22093	6	22,102	18.9	21.7	5.8	1	10	3,825	4,413	82.4
St. John the Baptist, LA	22095	1	45,924	19.6	27.6	6.0	1	13	6,222	9,565	72.5
St. Landry, LA	22097	4	83,384	19.6	31.7	5.8	1	37	14,926	16,600	82.6
St. Martin, LA	22099	3	52,160	19.1	34.2	6.5	1	17	8,503	10,092	81.6
St. Mary, LA	22101	4	54,650	18.5	29.3	6.5	2	24	9,834	10,588	89.0
St. Tammany, LA	22103	1	233,740	19.2	11.8	6.6	1	52	36,651	44,852	77.5
Tangipahoa, LA	22105	4	121,097	17.9	27.6	6.3	1	37	19,400	21,643	85.7
Tensas, LA	22107	9	5,252	18.3	46.4	11.6	1	3	676	1,113	83.5
Terrebonne, LA	22109	3	111,860	18.8	23.1	6.5	1	41	18,722	21,719	84.5
Union, LA	22111	3	22,721	16.5	31.6	8.4	2	9	2,892	3,803	83.6
Vermilion, LA	22113	4	57,999	19.3	23.9	6.9	1	19	9,186	10,795	86.9
Vernon, LA	22115	4	52,334	18.5	20.9	6.2	1	20	9,993	9,241	95.2
Washington, LA	22117	6	47,168	18.4	32.6	6.2	2	19	7,562	8,818	83.7
Webster, LA	22119	6	41,207	17.2	29.7	6.1	1	19	7,054	7,070	93.5
West Baton Rouge, LA	22121	2	23,788	17.9	20.3	5.7	1	10	3,810	4,358	80.7
West Carroll, LA	22123	9	11,604	18.0	29.9	9.5	1	6	2,219	2,158	98.2
West Feliciana, LA	22125	2	15,625	13.4	16.6	6.9	1	5	2,243	2,666	95.2
Winn, LA	22127	6	15,313	16.1	29.1	6.4	1	8	2,566	2,543	92.0
MAINE	23000	X	1,328,361	15.4	15.8	4.4	258	631	188,945	212,670	90.7
Androscoggin, ME	23001	3	107,702	16.2	18.7	4.2	7	40	16,225	17,635	92.4
Aroostook, ME	23003	7	71,870	15.1	17.8	5.2	27	48	10,293	11,481	95.3
Cumberland, ME	23005	2	281,674	15.7	11.8	4.0	19	91	37,559	45,710	90.6
Franklin, ME	23007	6	30,768	14.7	18.9	5.2	7	17	3,895	4,787	93.1
Hancock, ME	23009	6	54,418	13.6	17.4	6.1	22	35	6,740	7,782	91.0
Kennebec, ME	23011	4	122,151	15.5	14.5	3.9	17	56	17,080	19,810	89.0
Knox, ME	23013	7	39,736	14.6	17.3	5.3	11	26	5,885	5,999	90.6
Lincoln, ME	23015	8	34,457	14.1	18.3	6.2	14	17	4,322	5,047	85.7
Oxford, ME	23017	6	57,833	16.2	20.3	4.7	9	36	9,551	9,902	88.1
Penobscot, ME	23019	3	153,923	14.5	17.3	4.0	34	82	22,224	23,024	90.6
Piscataquis, ME	23021	8	17,535	14.8	24.3	5.3	9	10	2,600	2,682	89.0
Sagadahoc, ME	23023	2	35,293	15.6	13.6	4.1	2	16	4,825	5,566	91.5
Somerset, ME	23025	6	52,228	16.2	22.9	4.3	11	30	8,371	8,482	92.8
Waldo, ME	23027	6	38,786	15.7	20.6	5.2	5	24	4,362	6,380	92.1
Washington, ME	23029	7	32,856	14.9	28.4	6.0	52	37	4,793	5,044	86.9
York, ME	23031	2	197,131	16.1	11.3	4.1	12	66	30,220	33,339	90.4

[1]County type codes are from the Economic Research Service of the United States Department of Agriculture. See notes and definitions for more information.

Table C-1. Population, School, and Student Characteristics by County, Selected Years—*Continued*

County	State/ County Code	Characteristics of students, 2010–2011				Number of graduates, 2008–2009	Staff and students, 2010–2011			
		Percent with IEP[2]	Percent eligible for free or reduced lunch	Percent minority	Percent English-language learners		Total staff	Number of teachers	Student/ teacher ratio	Central admin. staff
		10	11	12	13	14	15	16	17	18
LOUISIANA—*(Continued)*										
Franklin, LA	22041	11.1	83.9	53.2	...	143	490	213	14.9	19
Grant, LA	22043	15.5	64.8	14.6	...	199	442	228	14.6	11
Iberia, LA	22045	12.0	71.8	53.7	1.7	687	1,883	995	13.7	56
Iberville, LA	22047	10.7	83.7	71.1	0.5	193	737	363	12.5	22
Jackson, LA	22049	8.1	60.9	37.7	...	114	343	168	13.4	12
Jefferson, LA	22051	12.3	76.1	67.9	8.1	2,093	6,467	3,039	14.9	251
Jefferson Davis, LA	22053	14.5	59.1	27.2	0.2	307	857	391	15.0	25
Lafayette, LA	22055	9.6	59.9	49.5	2.3	1,652	4,264	2,040	14.8	130
Lafourche, LA	22057	8.7	59.8	32.1	0.9	823	2,248	1,010	14.7	44
La Salle, LA	22059	8.3	55.1	12.7	0.2	148	375	181	14.6	13
Lincoln, LA	22061	10.9	59.6	52.4	1.3	395	898	483	13.8	17
Livingston, LA	22063	12.6	47.2	9.8	0.9	1,203	3,319	1,647	14.9	49
Madison, LA	22065	11.4	88.6	93.3	...	83	297	120	16.1	14
Morehouse, LA	22067	15.7	83.0	67.1	0.4	206	666	342	13.2	19
Natchitoches, LA	22069	10.9	71.3	61.7	0.2	380	919	517	13.8	28
Orleans, LA	22071	9.7	83.9	93.9	1.3	2,115	5,106	2,787	14.6	304
Ouachita, LA	22073	13.0	64.0	51.4	0.6	1,426	4,489	1,976	14.6	143
Plaquemines, LA	22075	10.4	54.8	44.5	2.4	232	933	384	12.3	38
Pointe Coupee, LA	22077	15.3	83.2	65.1	1.3	80	416	198	14.2	19
Rapides, LA	22079	11.5	63.2	47.3	1.8	1,134	3,517	1,683	14.3	157
Red River, LA	22081	9.4	87.1	67.3	...	70	254	114	13.3	9
Richland, LA	22083	11.1	74.7	48.1	0.1	224	590	283	14.0	20
Sabine, LA	22085	12.5	67.9	47.3	0.5	254	701	324	13.3	22
St. Bernard, LA	22087	10.4	73.2	33.2	0.7	289	847	440	13.4	29
St. Charles, LA	22089	9.9	49.2	40.9	0.9	679	1,668	821	11.9	59
St. Helena, LA	22091	15.0	90.8	94.5	...	64	140	57	14.2	9
St. James, LA	22093	13.1	70.8	67.7	0.7	233	608	306	12.5	22
St. John the Baptist, LA	22095	12.8	88.6	84.0	1.7	302	933	468	13.3	30
St. Landry, LA	22097	12.4	82.7	59.5	0.7	738	2,180	1,041	14.3	52
St. Martin, LA	22099	11.3	72.1	49.8	1.2	437	1,124	524	16.2	30
St. Mary, LA	22101	13.6	70.7	51.8	2.9	542	1,480	721	13.6	37
St. Tammany, LA	22103	17.2	45.8	24.9	1.4	2,132	5,066	2,394	15.3	173
Tangipahoa, LA	22105	11.5	73.7	51.7	1.2	995	2,566	1,173	16.5	66
Tensas, LA	22107	17.6	93.8	93.2	1.2	28	150	56	12.0	8
Terrebonne, LA	22109	11.5	65.8	42.6	1.4	1,003	2,477	1,289	14.5	49
Union, LA	22111	13.6	79.2	57.1	5.5	142	375	177	16.3	12
Vermilion, LA	22113	12.0	58.2	27.0	1.9	452	1,224	633	14.5	35
Vernon, LA	22115	11.5	59.6	29.3	0.8	474	1,395	658	15.2	32
Washington, LA	22117	18.4	85.8	45.1	1.1	414	1,192	531	14.2	41
Webster, LA	22119	10.5	61.2	44.0	...	372	949	455	15.5	25
West Baton Rouge, LA	22121	9.9	70.3	54.9	0.5	211	586	299	12.7	13
West Carroll, LA	22123	10.4	74.3	21.0	0.7	104	319	160	13.9	10
West Feliciana, LA	22125	11.0	50.7	42.4	0.8	125	384	191	11.7	17
Winn, LA	22127	11.2	72.3	38.4	...	138	388	167	15.4	11
MAINE	23000	15.6	43.0	7.5	2.5	12,792	32,549	15,384	12.3	1,183
Androscoggin, ME	23001	15.6	50.3	14.1	7.0	1,000	2,654	1,266	12.8	92
Aroostook, ME	23003	17.0	51.1	6.5	2.7	798	1,986	887	11.6	71
Cumberland, ME	23005	13.6	30.4	12.1	6.0	2,782	6,383	3,112	12.1	230
Franklin, ME	23007	14.0	55.2	4.2	0.3	320	738	351	11.1	30
Hancock, ME	23009	15.8	42.8	5.4	1.0	468	1,329	634	10.6	56
Kennebec, ME	23011	15.1	44.6	4.8	0.8	1,134	2,708	1,282	13.3	88
Knox, ME	23013	17.7	45.4	4.0	0.7	430	1,193	563	10.5	51
Lincoln, ME	23015	18.0	49.5	4.5	0.4	125	702	304	14.2	24
Oxford, ME	23017	14.9	55.6	4.0	0.4	634	1,688	788	12.1	57
Penobscot, ME	23019	15.9	44.0	5.7	0.4	1,526	3,763	1,821	12.2	134
Piscataquis, ME	23021	16.1	56.0	6.0	0.1	154	433	184	14.1	24
Sagadahoc, ME	23023	17.0	37.6	5.4	0.7	402	847	426	11.3	32
Somerset, ME	23025	17.4	58.6	3.3	0.3	520	1,460	666	12.6	51
Waldo, ME	23027	21.4	57.4	4.4	0.5	288	864	397	11.0	32
Washington, ME	23029	16.3	63.0	8.4	5.2	249	951	425	11.3	35
York, ME	23031	15.7	34.8	5.6	1.3	1,962	4,851	2,278	13.3	176

Note. Data in columns 26 through 41 from the American Community Survey are subject to sampling error, which can be especially large in small counties and small population groups. See notes and definitions for more information.
[2]IEP=Individual Education Program. See notes and definitions for more information.

Table C-1. Population, School, and Student Characteristics by County, Selected Years—*Continued*

County	State/ County Code	Revenues, 2008–2009				Current expenditures, 2008–2009			Resident population 16 to 19 years, 2006–2010			
		Total revenue ($1,000's)	Percentage of revenue from			Amount ($1,000's)	Amount per student	Percent for instruction	Total population 16 to 19 years	Percent enrolled in school	Percent high school graduates, not enrolled in school	Percent not enrolled, not grads, not employed, or not in labor force
			Federal government	State government	Local government							
		19	20	21	22	23	24	25	26	27	28	29
LOUISIANA— *(Continued)*												
Franklin, LA	22041	33,902	23.2	56.4	20.4	31,491	9,505	56.2	1,189	75.5	12.2	11.4
Grant, LA	22043	30,982	13.4	72.3	14.4	28,629	8,282	55.2	1,308	73.7	19.7	6.6
Iberia, LA	22045	148,634	12.2	55.1	32.7	130,233	9,439	61.9	4,363	74.9	15.1	7.2
Iberville, LA	22047	79,602	10.0	24.9	65.0	63,282	14,838	50.5	2,028	77.1	19.4	3.2
Jackson, LA	22049	24,912	9.1	41.9	49.0	23,605	10,529	57.0	800	73.9	16.3	7.4
Jefferson, LA	22051	531,470	17.8	30.9	51.3	546,708	12,322	55.1	22,649	80.2	9.1	5.6
Jefferson Davis, LA	22053	64,167	9.6	60.8	29.6	59,533	10,196	58.9	1,825	80.1	11.7	3.6
Lafayette, LA	22055	326,921	12.3	39.6	48.1	288,559	9,731	61.6	13,255	84.1	9.5	3.3
Lafourche, LA	22057	160,840	11.0	50.4	38.6	143,579	9,833	56.7	6,166	75.5	13.5	6.4
La Salle, LA	22059	29,338	8.3	56.9	34.8	25,635	9,833	59.6	814	86.6	8.7	2.0
Lincoln, LA	22061	73,986	9.2	47.0	43.8	64,146	10,786	58.6	4,850	91.8	4.5	2.0
Livingston, LA	22063	220,753	7.6	67.4	25.0	204,064	8,457	64.4	7,074	77.3	12.0	7.2
Madison, LA	22065	27,004	21.9	52.6	25.6	21,699	10,544	57.4	777	77.9	9.8	11.1
Morehouse, LA	22067	52,569	16.8	58.5	24.7	48,287	10,174	58.8	1,527	68.6	18.1	9.6
Natchitoches, LA	22069	70,001	12.9	55.9	31.2	64,508	9,551	62.4	3,164	78.0	13.6	6.9
Orleans, LA	22071	776,507	38.7	22.8	38.5	492,079	14,019	47.9	18,131	81.5	10.3	6.9
Ouachita, LA	22073	310,407	12.1	54.5	33.4	282,314	9,999	58.3	9,895	79.6	11.4	7.9
Plaquemines, LA	22075	73,895	15.8	33.1	51.1	72,111	16,125	49.2	1,323	90.1	3.0	4.8
Pointe Coupee, LA	22077	33,155	15.9	40.5	43.5	29,571	11,227	52.7	1,111	72.9	13.1	9.8
Rapides, LA	22079	228,840	12.2	56.2	31.6	211,752	8,979	60.6	7,709	73.7	14.7	7.2
Red River, LA	22081	26,229	11.2	43.5	45.3	20,553	13,593	57.1	607	71.7	15.3	6.1
Richland, LA	22083	44,064	14.2	62.5	23.2	40,194	10,222	58.7	1,169	74.3	14.5	10.3
Sabine, LA	22085	46,157	14.2	60.5	25.3	42,074	9,893	61.4	1,426	76.7	16.1	6.9
St. Bernard, LA	22087	105,648	49.8	23.9	26.2	66,726	14,365	61.0	1,484	80.1	10.1	8.2
St. Charles, LA	22089	159,208	7.3	22.0	70.8	123,896	12,994	58.4	3,087	88.6	8.4	2.3
St. Helena, LA	22091	14,037	21.5	59.2	19.3	12,973	10,739	50.0	871	95.2	0.0	2.1
St. James, LA	22093	59,161	12.3	35.6	52.1	54,815	13,419	58.5	1,304	81.9	9.0	7.4
St. John the Baptist, LA	22095	96,709	12.0	38.0	50.0	83,844	13,193	64.2	3,185	79.3	11.3	3.2
St. Landry, LA	22097	146,117	14.5	59.4	26.1	137,588	9,115	62.5	5,027	78.0	11.7	7.5
St. Martin, LA	22099	81,974	11.2	62.3	26.5	74,180	8,827	58.1	3,014	80.5	12.5	5.4
St. Mary, LA	22101	109,128	11.5	52.5	36.0	104,936	10,598	57.6	3,308	74.7	14.4	8.0
St. Tammany, LA	22103	430,495	11.4	45.2	43.3	377,061	10,624	61.3	12,608	83.9	8.1	4.9
Tangipahoa, LA	22105	179,388	15.1	60.9	23.9	166,599	8,587	61.5	8,082	70.4	12.5	13.6
Tensas, LA	22107	10,475	22.5	50.2	27.3	9,599	12,885	54.5	280	77.9	2.1	18.2
Terrebonne, LA	22109	192,596	12.2	51.2	36.6	181,803	9,567	61.0	6,990	81.7	11.0	4.6
Union, LA	22111	29,815	12.9	58.1	29.0	28,768	10,180	60.3	1,141	70.3	19.9	9.2
Vermilion, LA	22113	92,046	17.5	48.5	34.0	83,201	9,310	58.5	3,196	74.5	12.0	12.0
Vernon, LA	22115	94,657	19.5	62.1	18.5	88,122	9,177	58.7	2,754	66.2	22.8	6.2
Washington, LA	22117	85,787	17.1	61.8	21.1	79,238	10,427	57.4	2,305	79.1	11.6	8.5
Webster, LA	22119	79,523	11.4	54.2	34.5	68,193	9,436	60.8	2,372	74.8	16.4	5.7
West Baton Rouge, LA	22121	48,952	11.6	36.2	52.2	44,180	11,660	60.3	1,271	79.9	7.1	9.2
West Carroll, LA	22123	21,359	12.3	68.5	19.2	20,073	8,894	59.7	608	73.7	12.3	9.7
West Feliciana, LA	22125	27,886	11.0	45.2	43.8	28,354	12,280	55.2	705	90.4	2.0	6.1
Winn, LA	22127	27,516	13.1	61.9	25.1	25,430	9,528	55.8	767	72.6	10.3	13.7
MAINE	23000	2,623,127	9.3	42.2	48.5	2,316,301	12,362	57.7	74,170	85.5	9.6	3.5
Androscoggin, ME	23001	209,354	9.7	55.0	35.3	185,545	11,240	59.0	6,365	84.6	8.8	4.2
Aroostook, ME	23003	142,577	12.2	57.5	30.3	129,024	12,283	55.7	3,859	85.9	9.3	3.5
Cumberland, ME	23005	517,904	7.3	32.1	60.7	475,573	12,665	59.5	15,631	88.5	7.7	2.4
Franklin, ME	23007	58,654	9.9	41.5	48.5	54,707	14,010	55.8	2,037	84.6	8.4	3.4
Hancock, ME	23009	111,849	7.2	21.1	71.7	92,834	14,340	57.3	2,908	85.2	9.2	3.1
Kennebec, ME	23011	220,554	9.4	51.6	39.0	191,438	11,458	57.6	7,172	86.8	9.0	3.4
Knox, ME	23013	103,744	8.0	28.3	63.7	87,366	13,901	56.2	1,838	83.1	11.8	3.0
Lincoln, ME	23015	55,522	5.9	26.8	67.2	46,556	13,964	59.4	1,661	78.8	17.1	4.2
Oxford, ME	23017	142,939	10.7	44.4	44.9	113,602	11,724	54.1	3,137	82.1	11.3	6.2
Penobscot, ME	23019	294,308	9.5	51.8	38.8	259,353	11,432	58.4	10,101	88.1	7.2	3.1
Piscataquis, ME	23021	35,697	14.1	50.7	35.2	28,816	11,032	57.4	827	74.9	21.4	2.7
Sagadahoc, ME	23023	77,155	7.4	40.0	52.7	71,640	21,233	54.8	1,809	77.4	10.7	6.6
Somerset, ME	23025	116,635	11.7	53.0	35.2	102,402	11,836	59.8	2,798	86.5	6.6	5.4
Waldo, ME	23027	67,348	9.9	47.1	43.0	56,032	13,382	57.4	2,142	82.4	11.5	4.8
Washington, ME	23029	77,783	22.0	38.8	39.3	67,448	16,584	56.0	1,708	82.0	12.6	4.6
York, ME	23031	391,104	8.2	38.2	53.6	353,965	11,479	57.1	10,177	83.8	12.7	3.0

Note. Data in columns 26 through 41 from the American Community Survey are subject to sampling error, which can be especially large in small counties and small population groups. See notes and definitions for more information.

Table C-1. Population, School, and Student Characteristics by County, Selected Years—*Continued*

County	State/ County Code	High school graduates, 2006–2010			College enrollment, 2006–2010		College graduates, 2006–2010 (percent)						
		Population 25 years and over	High school diploma or less (percent)	High school diploma or more (percent)	Number	Percent public	Bachelor's degree or more	+/- U.S. percent with Bachelor's degree or more	Non-Hispanic White	Black or African American	American Indian and Alaska Native	Asian, Hawaiian, and Pacific Islander	Hispanic or Latino[3]
		30	31	32	33	34	35	36	37	38	39	40	41
LOUISIANA— *(Continued)*													
Franklin, LA	22041	13,634	68.6	69.5	666	92.3	11.3	-16.6	13.2	6.2	0.0	0.0	0.0
Grant, LA	22043	14,574	62.9	79.8	896	69.0	11.8	-16.1	12.6	7.8	16.4	33.3	8.4
Iberia, LA	22045	46,094	66.8	74.8	2,097	88.0	13.4	-14.5	14.5	10.4	6.9	20.9	8.6
Iberville, LA	22047	22,333	69.3	72.7	1,671	84.7	11.0	-16.9	14.1	7.6	0.0	12.5	9.4
Jackson, LA	22049	10,822	59.3	82.3	824	86.8	13.5	-14.4	13.7	13.7	0.0	0.0	0.0
Jefferson, LA	22051	293,747	49.6	82.5	24,932	70.9	23.2	-4.7	27.2	13.3	11.3	31.0	16.4
Jefferson Davis, LA	22053	20,229	66.5	75.5	922	91.0	11.6	-16.3	12.6	6.1	0.0	23.3	8.6
Lafayette, LA	22055	135,555	45.7	84.2	18,918	91.2	27.6	-0.3	32.7	11.3	16.9	41.3	18.8
Lafourche, LA	22057	61,696	66.9	72.1	4,926	87.3	14.3	-13.6	15.3	8.1	7.9	40.2	7.9
La Salle, LA	22059	9,800	64.1	77.0	453	79.2	13.1	-14.8	14.4	4.0	8.0	66.7	5.0
Lincoln, LA	22061	25,026	42.2	84.5	10,659	95.7	31.8	3.9	35.4	25.3	0.0	76.3	16.8
Livingston, LA	22063	77,593	56.6	83.5	4,582	78.0	16.4	-11.5	16.5	15.6	25.3	43.8	11.7
Madison, LA	22065	7,878	71.5	72.9	196	86.2	10.9	-17.0	12.4	9.9	0.0	0.0	12.5
Morehouse, LA	22067	18,870	68.6	73.2	866	88.7	11.1	-16.8	15.2	5.6	0.0	73.9	0.0
Natchitoches, LA	22069	23,326	57.0	78.7	3,922	95.3	21.2	-6.7	28.4	10.2	17.8	18.0	20.5
Orleans, LA	22071	195,019	43.5	83.4	28,458	49.7	31.6	3.7	57.4	14.8	11.5	33.0	29.6
Ouachita, LA	22073	95,229	49.6	84.1	11,230	93.4	23.5	-4.4	28.2	13.6	6.9	42.5	8.7
Plaquemines, LA	22075	14,408	52.9	80.3	1,230	64.2	17.4	-10.5	20.7	4.8	18.2	19.8	15.9
Pointe Coupee, LA	22077	15,478	63.8	75.6	780	75.0	15.3	-12.6	17.3	12.0	10.5	33.3	14.1
Rapides, LA	22079	84,774	53.0	82.1	5,981	73.7	19.4	-8.5	22.7	10.4	12.4	35.5	31.3
Red River, LA	22081	5,942	64.3	74.5	509	91.0	12.5	-15.4	16.9	4.4	5.9	31.6	27.3
Richland, LA	22083	13,606	64.4	73.8	623	79.1	12.2	-15.7	15.3	5.9	0.0	25.7	16.8
Sabine, LA	22085	16,101	65.8	79.7	1,082	88.3	11.6	-16.3	13.6	3.2	9.8	43.6	7.7
St. Bernard, LA	22087	17,798	63.8	79.3	1,362	44.5	9.9	-18.0	10.4	6.6	54.7	27.1	4.3
St. Charles, LA	22089	33,682	52.4	84.5	2,743	71.2	19.7	-8.2	21.4	13.5	0.0	65.6	19.7
St. Helena, LA	22091	7,240	66.6	76.6	458	84.7	11.1	-16.8	11.7	10.6	0.0	0.0	9.3
St. James, LA	22093	14,217	66.0	82.2	982	89.2	12.4	-15.5	14.9	9.7	0.0	57.1	0.0
St. John the Baptist, LA	22095	29,054	55.9	81.5	2,115	81.0	15.8	-12.1	18.7	12.7	28.4	13.9	14.4
St. Landry, LA	22097	53,597	67.6	73.0	2,553	85.8	12.6	-15.3	14.4	9.5	20.9	11.5	17.9
St. Martin, LA	22099	33,169	68.5	74.1	2,085	88.6	11.6	-16.3	12.2	9.0	9.9	48.0	6.7
St. Mary, LA	22101	35,142	67.8	69.9	1,705	84.0	10.4	-17.5	12.0	7.4	11.1	12.4	4.6
St. Tammany, LA	22103	152,704	39.6	88.0	10,735	81.0	30.1	2.2	31.4	19.7	10.1	50.8	24.8
Tangipahoa, LA	22105	73,141	56.8	79.1	8,161	90.0	19.7	-8.2	23.7	8.2	30.2	40.4	13.7
Tensas, LA	22107	3,695	68.9	71.4	46	100.0	12.9	-15.0	14.9	11.4	0.0	0.0	0.0
Terrebonne, LA	22109	70,490	66.1	73.0	4,564	85.3	13.8	-14.1	14.3	12.5	4.5	39.1	18.3
Union, LA	22111	15,410	63.7	80.3	770	92.1	13.8	-14.1	16.5	5.7	19.0	100.0	3.1
Vermilion, LA	22113	36,826	70.0	76.0	1,666	87.7	11.7	-16.2	12.5	4.3	0.0	7.9	20.0
Vernon, LA	22115	29,670	54.7	84.5	2,728	83.2	15.6	-12.3	15.6	13.6	7.7	36.5	12.6
Washington, LA	22117	30,835	66.1	77.5	1,859	82.9	11.8	-16.1	14.1	6.9	0.0	16.9	3.0
Webster, LA	22119	27,744	64.0	75.5	1,302	87.2	13.5	-14.4	14.8	11.2	0.0	12.4	0.0
West Baton Rouge, LA	22121	15,007	60.3	80.9	1,389	88.5	16.5	-11.4	18.1	13.4	16.1	100.0	21.6
West Carroll, LA	22123	7,668	70.1	70.7	271	86.7	9.8	-18.1	10.6	2.4	100.0	48.0	12.7
West Feliciana, LA	22125	11,748	69.7	65.1	482	66.0	12.8	-15.1	21.8	4.3	0.0	37.5	0.0
Winn, LA	22127	10,678	70.1	72.6	370	82.7	11.2	-16.7	13.7	5.8	21.4	0.0	3.8
MAINE	23000	929,301	45.4	89.8	83,227	69.9	26.6	-1.3	26.6	21.3	13.7	42.0	20.4
Androscoggin, ME	23001	73,185	53.4	86.4	7,253	55.4	18.4	-9.5	18.6	16.5	0.0	43.7	9.7
Aroostook, ME	23003	51,788	55.1	83.9	4,239	82.9	16.2	-11.7	16.0	50.0	11.9	41.8	12.1
Cumberland, ME	23005	194,370	33.0	93.3	21,440	66.3	39.5	11.6	39.9	19.3	30.0	44.3	29.3
Franklin, ME	23007	20,822	49.0	87.7	2,199	92.9	24.5	-3.4	24.7	76.2	36.5	0.0	19.9
Hancock, ME	23009	39,585	42.6	91.0	3,057	73.0	30.1	2.2	29.7	61.5	13.6	77.6	19.9
Kennebec, ME	23011	84,934	47.1	90.3	7,233	57.6	24.1	-3.8	24.0	32.9	23.4	34.1	20.7
Knox, ME	23013	29,482	47.5	89.7	1,430	81.7	26.9	-1.0	27.0	13.5	0.0	73.0	6.3
Lincoln, ME	23015	25,817	40.2	92.4	909	64.1	31.6	3.7	31.8	14.7	33.3	43.4	12.4
Oxford, ME	23017	41,051	55.8	87.5	2,065	68.6	18.5	-9.4	18.8	0.0	3.2	0.0	18.6
Penobscot, ME	23019	102,301	47.2	89.5	16,725	80.7	23.3	-4.6	23.1	12.4	18.8	62.5	18.0
Piscataquis, ME	23021	13,063	56.7	88.3	465	65.2	15.0	-12.9	15.1	0.0	0.0	0.0	36.6
Sagadahoc, ME	23023	25,456	43.2	91.8	1,451	77.7	29.6	1.7	29.7	43.9	20.0	17.3	28.2
Somerset, ME	23025	37,153	57.2	86.6	2,201	66.4	15.3	-12.6	15.5	9.0	3.0	9.5	1.9
Waldo, ME	23027	27,414	49.7	90.1	1,559	67.7	23.1	-4.8	23.1	40.6	7.5	52.9	25.0
Washington, ME	23029	23,949	54.0	85.2	1,494	83.2	19.0	-8.9	19.4	32.3	7.0	46.7	16.5
York, ME	23031	138,931	44.1	90.1	9,507	64.5	26.7	-1.2	27.0	18.0	9.8	30.7	18.1

Note. Data in columns 26 through 41 from the American Community Survey are subject to sampling error, which can be especially large in small counties and small population groups. See notes and definitions for more information.

[3]May be of any race.

Table C-1. Population, School, and Student Characteristics by County, Selected Years—*Continued*

County	State/ County Code	County Type[1]	Population, 2010		Percent of related children 5–17 years in poverty, 2010	Percent of children under 19 years with no health insurance, 2010	Number of schools and students, 2010–2011			Resident enrollment, 2006–2010 K–12 enrollment	
			Total	Percent 5–17 years			School districts	Schools	Students	Number	Percent public
			1	2	3	4	5	6	7	8	9
MARYLAND	24000	X	5,773,552	17.1	11.8	5.4	25	1,449	852,211	991,336	84.6
Allegany, MD	24001	3	75,087	13.3	20.8	5.0	1	27	9,022	10,404	89.2
Anne Arundel, MD	24003	1	537,656	16.8	7.5	4.6	1	125	75,481	89,422	82.2
Baltimore, MD	24005	1	805,029	16.0	9.9	6.1	1	173	104,160	128,688	80.0
Calvert, MD	24009	1	88,737	20.6	6.6	4.4	1	26	16,795	18,600	92.0
Caroline, MD	24011	6	33,066	18.2	18.1	7.0	1	10	5,517	6,289	88.0
Carroll, MD	24013	1	167,134	19.3	5.7	4.1	1	49	27,334	31,507	86.9
Cecil, MD	24015	1	101,108	18.7	12.2	4.9	1	29	15,937	19,094	83.8
Charles, MD	24017	1	146,551	20.1	7.8	4.8	1	37	26,850	29,022	88.4
Dorchester, MD	24019	6	32,618	15.4	25.1	5.5	1	13	4,647	4,735	93.1
Frederick, MD	24021	1	233,385	18.9	6.8	4.7	1	65	40,188	43,036	91.9
Garrett, MD	24023	6	30,097	17.0	21.4	7.0	1	15	4,212	5,188	90.8
Harford, MD	24025	1	244,826	18.6	7.9	4.3	1	53	38,394	45,460	84.8
Howard, MD	24027	1	287,085	20.0	5.3	4.3	1	73	50,994	55,969	88.0
Kent, MD	24029	6	20,197	12.6	18.7	7.4	1	7	2,183	2,538	85.0
Montgomery, MD	24031	1	971,777	17.5	9.1	5.4	1	205	144,023	167,069	82.8
Prince George's, MD	24033	1	863,420	17.1	11.8	6.6	1	207	126,671	151,446	83.6
Queen Anne's, MD	24035	1	47,798	18.1	9.0	5.5	1	14	7,781	8,389	85.6
St. Mary's, MD	24037	4	105,151	19.0	9.9	4.9	1	27	17,271	18,613	86.8
Somerset, MD	24039	3	26,470	12.0	28.5	6.3	1	9	2,920	3,477	88.8
Talbot, MD	24041	6	37,782	14.6	13.2	6.7	1	8	4,504	5,438	77.1
Washington, MD	24043	3	147,430	16.8	14.6	5.2	1	46	22,206	25,003	89.5
Wicomico, MD	24045	3	98,733	16.2	19.8	5.7	1	25	14,382	15,878	86.8
Worcester, MD	24047	4	51,454	13.8	17.8	6.9	1	14	6,699	7,235	86.2
Baltimore city, MD	24510	1	620,961	14.9	31.0	5.1	2	192	84,040	98,836	86.2
MASSACHUSETTS	25000	X	6,547,629	16.1	12.8	1.7	403	1,829	954,648	1,067,698	88.4
Barnstable, MA	25001	3	215,888	13.2	14.5	2.4	21	54	26,573	29,738	89.7
Berkshire, MA	25003	3	131,219	14.9	16.7	2.0	19	48	17,508	20,344	88.5
Bristol, MA	25005	1	548,285	16.6	14.5	1.8	25	140	79,856	93,416	89.9
Dukes, MA	25007	7	16,535	13.9	11.1	3.3	6	7	2,230	2,590	93.7
Essex, MA	25009	1	743,159	17.3	13.2	1.9	43	219	113,667	130,868	87.3
Franklin, MA	25011	2	71,372	14.9	14.0	1.8	19	39	9,828	11,208	88.2
Hampden, MA	25013	2	463,490	17.7	21.5	1.9	20	138	74,455	84,263	91.5
Hampshire, MA	25015	2	158,080	13.0	10.2	1.9	21	51	19,610	20,286	91.2
Middlesex, MA	25017	1	1,503,085	15.6	7.5	1.5	71	371	213,286	231,792	88.7
Nantucket, MA	25019	7	10,172	14.0	9.6	3.1	1	3	1,289	1,532	80.0
Norfolk, MA	25021	1	670,850	17.1	6.0	1.5	36	189	102,275	113,469	84.7
Plymouth, MA	25023	1	494,919	18.4	9.1	1.7	34	141	86,974	92,237	90.0
Suffolk, MA	25025	1	722,023	12.0	29.2	2.0	21	172	75,638	93,585	84.7
Worcester, MA	25027	2	798,552	17.6	12.6	1.8	57	257	131,459	142,370	89.9
MICHIGAN	26000	X	9,883,640	17.7	21.2	4.5	863	3,877	1,584,768	1,823,898	90.1
Alcona, MI	26001	9	10,942	11.5	27.9	7.0	1	2	826	1,420	96.6
Alger, MI	26003	9	9,601	13.3	19.3	5.3	4	5	1,141	1,363	91.1
Allegan, MI	26005	4	111,408	19.5	15.9	4.3	12	54	18,287	21,954	86.6
Alpena, MI	26007	7	29,598	15.8	23.7	5.3	3	13	4,513	4,785	93.4
Antrim, MI	26009	9	23,580	16.2	23.9	6.8	7	13	3,946	3,783	92.1
Arenac, MI	26011	8	15,899	15.4	29.0	6.0	3	8	2,465	2,586	97.1
Baraga, MI	26013	9	8,860	15.5	20.0	5.7	3	6	1,273	1,384	92.9
Barry, MI	26015	2	59,173	18.5	14.0	5.0	4	19	7,627	11,389	92.7
Bay, MI	26017	3	107,771	16.4	20.4	4.0	7	37	15,313	18,372	87.7
Benzie, MI	26019	9	17,525	15.7	19.2	7.7	2	9	2,299	2,948	94.0
Berrien, MI	26021	3	156,813	17.3	26.2	4.5	21	86	26,387	28,383	87.2
Branch, MI	26023	6	45,248	17.4	25.9	5.6	6	23	7,191	8,326	90.4
Calhoun, MI	26025	3	136,146	17.8	23.3	4.2	15	60	21,556	25,181	92.2
Cass, MI	26027	2	52,293	17.7	22.0	5.1	5	22	7,303	9,747	92.6
Charlevoix, MI	26029	7	25,949	16.8	19.1	4.9	8	21	4,206	4,506	90.6
Cheboygan, MI	26031	7	26,152	15.7	23.1	5.3	4	13	3,299	4,225	92.0
Chippewa, MI	26033	5	38,520	15.0	21.7	6.1	10	23	5,301	6,113	93.5
Clare, MI	26035	7	30,926	15.2	37.2	5.3	4	18	4,743	4,908	94.0
Clinton, MI	26037	2	75,382	18.8	9.7	3.5	7	28	10,373	14,532	90.5
Crawford, MI	26039	7	14,074	15.1	25.8	5.1	1	6	1,798	2,324	95.0

[1]County type codes are from the Economic Research Service of the United States Department of Agriculture. See notes and definitions for more information.

Table C-1. Population, School, and Student Characteristics by County, Selected Years—*Continued*

County	State/ County Code	Characteristics of students, 2010–2011				Number of graduates, 2008–2009	Staff and students, 2010–2011			
		Percent with IEP[2]	Percent eligible for free or reduced lunch	Percent minority	Percent English-language learners		Total staff	Number of teachers	Student/ teacher ratio	Central admin. staff
		10	11	12	13	14	15	16	17	18
MARYLAND	24000	12.1	40.1	57.1	5.3	58,304	115,367	58,429	14.6	5,652
Allegany, MD	24001	14.6	48.9	9.4	0.2	693	1,357	683	13.2	81
Anne Arundel, MD	24003	10.6	27.9	38.1	3.5	4,908	9,424	5,116	14.8	479
Baltimore, MD	24005	12.8	42.3	53.8	3.2	7,299	14,338	7,455	14.0	602
Calvert, MD	24009	10.0	21.4	24.8	0.8	1,356	2,194	1,096	15.3	131
Caroline, MD	24011	10.2	52.5	30.1	3.3	368	793	413	13.4	47
Carroll, MD	24013	12.1	15.7	11.0	0.6	2,359	3,552	1,899	14.4	197
Cecil, MD	24015	13.1	37.7	18.8	0.9	1,080	2,169	1,158	13.8	93
Charles, MD	24017	8.9	28.5	65.2	0.7	2,172	3,147	1,619	16.6	142
Dorchester, MD	24019	9.4	59.5	47.9	1.4	313	685	373	12.5	42
Frederick, MD	24021	11.3	22.8	32.0	3.7	3,022	5,389	2,683	15.0	242
Garrett, MD	24023	11.7	48.9	1.9	0.1	359	634	338	12.5	33
Harford, MD	24025	14.4	27.4	31.4	1.1	2,666	5,288	2,763	13.9	212
Howard, MD	24027	9.1	16.1	51.2	3.9	3,711	7,525	3,742	13.6	285
Kent, MD	24029	14.2	49.6	34.9	2.9	161	354	184	11.9	29
Montgomery, MD	24031	12.0	30.6	65.4	11.8	10,129	19,976	9,511	15.1	1,101
Prince George's, MD	24033	11.4	54.4	95.5	11.2	8,266	17,087	8,314	15.2	793
Queen Anne's, MD	24035	12.3	22.6	14.9	1.5	596	957	525	14.8	63
St. Mary's, MD	24037	10.9	28.8	29.8	0.7	1,093	2,093	1,062	16.3	133
Somerset, MD	24039	14.2	65.6	54.1	2.7	169	453	224	13.1	24
Talbot, MD	24041	8.6	35.2	32.2	4.3	344	623	311	14.5	36
Washington, MD	24043	10.7	43.9	25.1	1.7	1,546	2,959	1,542	14.4	147
Wicomico, MD	24045	11.8	52.0	49.5	2.8	916	2,246	1,072	13.4	126
Worcester, MD	24047	11.2	40.9	31.4	2.1	493	1,124	591	11.3	47
Baltimore city, MD	24510	16.6	83.7	92.3	2.5	4,285	11,002	5,756	14.6	570
MASSACHUSETTS	25000	17.5	34.2	32.0	5.8	65,258	121,135	68,346	14.0	5,462
Barnstable, MA	25001	16.0	23.8	14.1	1.8	2,162	3,660	2,090	12.7	154
Berkshire, MA	25003	16.8	40.0	14.6	1.9	1,318	2,780	1,447	12.1	142
Bristol, MA	25005	17.5	38.4	21.5	2.3	5,864	8,441	4,934	16.2	361
Dukes, MA	25007	21.6	16.8	20.8	4.0	208	484	250	8.9	17
Essex, MA	25009	17.8	36.4	34.0	7.3	7,642	14,141	8,164	13.9	539
Franklin, MA	25011	18.5	38.8	11.6	1.4	695	1,643	797	12.3	87
Hampden, MA	25013	20.3	54.2	47.6	7.9	4,540	10,605	5,792	12.9	430
Hampshire, MA	25015	17.7	25.3	17.2	1.8	1,589	2,938	1,547	12.7	143
Middlesex, MA	25017	17.6	23.6	29.9	6.2	15,077	27,604	15,538	13.7	1,232
Nantucket, MA	25019	14.5	10.9	31.4	7.5	93	206	118	11.0	10
Norfolk, MA	25021	16.7	17.0	22.7	3.0	7,069	12,586	7,213	14.2	502
Plymouth, MA	25023	15.5	27.2	19.5	3.4	5,380	9,707	5,751	15.1	400
Suffolk, MA	25025	18.8	73.5	83.0	12.5	4,505	10,089	5,739	13.2	780
Worcester, MA	25027	17.2	33.6	26.8	6.7	9,116	16,253	8,967	14.7	667
MICHIGAN	26000	13.7	46.3	30.1	3.6	112,731	193,441	88,583	17.9	4,334
Alcona, MI	26001	13.7	53.8	4.1	...	56	85	45	18.3	5
Alger, MI	26003	15.9	46.5	19.7	...	97	156	72	15.8	9
Allegan, MI	26005	12.4	42.7	11.5	1.4	1,145	2,203	998	18.3	54
Alpena, MI	26007	12.7	49.1	2.8	...	315	578	247	18.3	17
Antrim, MI	26009	11.3	51.7	6.9	0.2	275	455	224	17.6	11
Arenac, MI	26011	13.3	60.5	4.3	...	212	281	127	19.4	10
Baraga, MI	26013	12.3	51.4	32.2	...	99	154	85	14.9	5
Barry, MI	26015	12.6	40.4	6.8	0.7	595	781	374	20.4	18
Bay, MI	26017	16.8	47.2	12.1	1.3	1,095	1,842	798	19.2	55
Benzie, MI	26019	12.5	60.7	10.1	...	43	241	116	19.8	7
Berrien, MI	26021	12.8	51.6	34.1	2.1	1,883	3,478	1,564	16.9	97
Branch, MI	26023	14.4	52.8	10.5	4.4	538	954	419	17.2	20
Calhoun, MI	26025	14.9	51.7	29.2	2.3	1,483	2,806	1,371	15.7	68
Cass, MI	26027	12.1	51.1	17.5	2.1	474	910	382	19.1	35
Charlevoix, MI	26029	15.3	47.6	8.9	...	361	655	288	14.6	20
Cheboygan, MI	26031	13.0	58.8	5.9	...	289	480	206	16.0	17
Chippewa, MI	26033	16.1	52.7	40.0	0.1	376	801	344	15.4	39
Clare, MI	26035	15.6	60.2	4.8	...	388	623	263	18.0	19
Clinton, MI	26037	10.5	26.5	10.4	0.1	906	1,229	550	18.9	32
Crawford, MI	26039	16.9	63.5	5.6	...	131	183	102	17.6	3

Note. Data in columns 26 through 41 from the American Community Survey are subject to sampling error, which can be especially large in small counties and small population groups. See notes and definitions for more information.
[2]IEP=Individual Education Program. See notes and definitions for more information.

Table C-1. Population, School, and Student Characteristics by County, Selected Years—*Continued*

County	State/ County Code	Revenues, 2008–2009				Current expenditures, 2008–2009			Resident population 16 to 19 years, 2006–2010			
		Total revenue ($1,000's)	Percentage of revenue from			Amount ($1,000's)	Amount per student	Percent for instruction	Total population 16 to 19 years	Percent enrolled in school	Percent high school graduates, not enrolled in school	Percent not enrolled, not grads, not employed, or not in labor force
			Federal government	State government	Local government							
		19	20	21	22	23	24	25	26	27	28	29
MARYLAND	24000	13,147,931	5.3	43.3	51.4	11,348,181	13,449	60.8	331,520	84.0	10.2	3.9
Allegany, MD	24001	143,507	8.4	65.6	26.0	130,045	14,086	61.8	5,261	87.7	8.2	4.1
Anne Arundel, MD	24003	1,031,083	4.4	35.1	60.5	926,942	12,585	61.9	27,659	81.3	14.5	3.0
Baltimore, MD	24005	1,482,453	5.1	42.4	52.5	1,295,213	12,553	60.4	46,363	83.1	11.2	3.9
Calvert, MD	24009	244,248	3.3	43.8	52.9	212,032	12,434	62.3	5,611	87.7	9.0	1.7
Caroline, MD	24011	71,895	7.3	70.6	22.1	62,892	11,408	60.8	2,032	81.2	14.2	3.9
Carroll, MD	24013	424,503	3.1	41.6	55.3	336,852	12,046	59.8	10,441	86.8	9.6	2.5
Cecil, MD	24015	221,998	5.0	51.2	43.7	190,183	11,733	62.4	6,176	72.9	13.7	7.5
Charles, MD	24017	361,876	4.6	50.5	44.9	329,352	12,323	57.2	8,687	80.7	14.3	4.0
Dorchester, MD	24019	78,637	7.6	55.7	36.7	59,167	12,975	59.8	1,697	64.5	20.0	13.7
Frederick, MD	24021	608,295	3.2	40.9	56.0	489,088	12,206	62.1	13,400	88.0	7.3	1.8
Garrett, MD	24023	69,569	7.5	42.3	50.2	57,188	12,924	59.6	1,587	75.2	17.7	2.4
Harford, MD	24025	603,562	3.6	41.5	54.9	467,246	12,102	60.7	13,258	83.4	12.3	2.6
Howard, MD	24027	835,108	2.5	31.0	66.5	731,066	14,649	63.2	15,239	91.6	5.3	2.6
Kent, MD	24029	36,068	8.9	35.5	55.6	32,454	14,626	55.6	1,388	75.9	16.4	2.5
Montgomery, MD	24031	2,508,088	3.7	24.0	72.3	2,151,476	15,447	64.3	46,886	89.7	6.2	2.5
Prince George's, MD	24033	1,914,801	6.2	55.5	38.3	1,760,448	13,756	56.9	56,878	84.6	9.4	3.5
Queen Anne's, MD	24035	108,615	5.0	37.6	57.4	89,521	11,391	61.3	2,411	79.1	15.6	3.8
St. Mary's, MD	24037	234,690	5.8	48.5	45.7	201,015	12,000	58.6	6,433	76.8	14.7	5.2
Somerset, MD	24039	45,443	13.6	60.3	26.2	41,710	14,324	55.7	2,652	90.0	5.8	3.2
Talbot, MD	24041	66,234	4.7	21.0	74.3	51,061	11,555	59.5	1,724	81.3	12.1	4.9
Washington, MD	24043	293,460	5.9	56.2	37.9	259,318	11,931	58.3	7,572	78.4	13.8	5.6
Wicomico, MD	24045	237,975	6.3	59.2	34.6	185,685	12,727	58.6	7,237	85.2	8.1	3.9
Worcester, MD	24047	142,842	5.5	18.8	75.7	105,293	15,784	63.6	2,156	77.7	17.1	2.8
Baltimore city, MD	24510	1,382,981	11.1	68.3	20.7	1,182,934	14,379	59.8	38,772	79.6	10.8	7.7
MASSACHUSETTS	25000	15,657,046	7.7	38.2	54.1	13,447,608	14,025	61.8	382,851	89.1	6.5	3.0
Barnstable, MA	25001	484,499	4.6	25.2	70.2	406,413	14,728	62.0	10,316	88.6	7.8	2.3
Berkshire, MA	25003	329,374	8.5	44.7	46.8	278,191	15,338	61.9	7,596	87.1	8.8	3.4
Bristol, MA	25005	1,319,499	9.3	48.9	41.8	1,117,032	12,917	62.0	31,859	83.3	9.2	4.1
Dukes, MA	25007	61,091	3.4	19.6	77.0	51,068	22,428	62.1	917	78.8	19.1	2.1
Essex, MA	25009	1,817,298	8.0	40.7	51.3	1,550,389	13,649	63.3	41,589	86.9	7.5	3.9
Franklin, MA	25011	187,381	7.9	41.2	50.9	152,135	15,575	59.2	3,901	86.4	8.3	2.2
Hampden, MA	25013	1,191,716	12.8	54.1	33.1	1,062,028	14,055	60.8	30,354	84.4	7.6	5.8
Hampshire, MA	25015	323,328	6.7	39.6	53.7	272,263	13,509	60.5	15,624	96.2	2.5	0.5
Middlesex, MA	25017	3,695,603	5.5	33.1	61.3	3,153,260	14,796	62.3	80,202	91.8	5.1	2.2
Nantucket, MA	25019	31,945	2.5	12.1	85.4	28,397	22,203	61.0	403	79.9	3.5	0.0
Norfolk, MA	25021	1,568,197	5.0	29.6	65.4	1,384,712	13,632	62.6	34,578	92.1	5.8	1.7
Plymouth, MA	25023	1,150,584	7.2	41.8	51.0	1,019,289	12,433	62.2	27,465	89.0	6.8	2.8
Suffolk, MA	25025	1,537,398	10.0	24.5	65.5	1,305,186	17,374	56.0	50,744	90.1	5.2	3.2
Worcester, MA	25027	1,959,133	9.2	46.5	44.3	1,667,245	12,614	63.7	47,303	88.9	7.4	2.7
MICHIGAN	26000	20,568,388	10.8	53.0	36.2	17,190,838	10,473	57.3	611,544	85.8	8.7	4.2
Alcona, MI	26001	9,859	10.5	22.2	67.4	9,271	9,308	63.0	521	80.2	7.7	12.1
Alger, MI	26003	13,497	8.6	52.7	38.7	12,223	10,135	58.4	356	88.5	0.8	1.4
Allegan, MI	26005	182,210	9.9	53.0	37.1	149,238	9,727	58.0	6,416	83.4	10.7	4.4
Alpena, MI	26007	52,050	13.6	54.3	32.1	48,686	10,423	53.7	1,631	84.7	8.3	3.8
Antrim, MI	26009	43,938	9.1	29.9	61.0	37,540	8,892	61.8	1,162	76.2	16.0	7.1
Arenac, MI	26011	26,091	9.7	57.6	32.7	22,693	8,952	60.4	856	82.5	11.9	5.4
Baraga, MI	26013	15,129	21.3	52.8	25.9	12,850	9,946	61.2	326	88.3	7.1	3.1
Barry, MI	26015	80,598	9.1	61.9	29.0	69,026	8,879	63.2	3,303	83.0	12.9	3.1
Bay, MI	26017	179,560	11.2	57.5	31.3	158,445	10,179	56.6	5,864	82.1	13.0	2.9
Benzie, MI	26019	23,706	8.7	30.4	61.0	21,838	9,103	62.6	860	90.4	4.4	3.7
Berrien, MI	26021	305,180	13.1	53.4	33.5	278,600	10,466	56.7	9,132	81.6	9.9	5.5
Branch, MI	26023	86,264	11.8	56.2	32.0	76,076	10,369	61.2	2,572	86.5	6.7	4.0
Calhoun, MI	26025	295,674	13.7	56.0	30.3	244,968	10,868	54.5	8,239	83.1	9.8	4.7
Cass, MI	26027	78,297	12.9	59.9	27.3	68,454	9,079	54.3	2,970	82.9	10.4	4.1
Charlevoix, MI	26029	75,345	9.3	26.0	64.8	59,877	14,199	50.7	1,365	80.8	12.0	6.5
Cheboygan, MI	26031	46,869	13.4	39.6	47.0	39,583	11,355	57.0	1,429	79.6	15.5	3.9
Chippewa, MI	26033	70,878	24.6	47.8	27.6	61,865	11,697	54.8	2,149	84.0	10.5	4.8
Clare, MI	26035	58,470	16.0	49.3	34.7	52,909	10,975	57.3	1,639	80.8	11.0	6.0
Clinton, MI	26037	122,981	9.6	58.8	31.6	97,961	9,558	57.3	4,514	91.3	5.4	3.0
Crawford, MI	26039	18,566	10.9	45.7	43.3	16,013	8,794	59.5	709	74.9	12.3	12.8

Note. Data in columns 26 through 41 from the American Community Survey are subject to sampling error, which can be especially large in small counties and small population groups. See notes and definitions for more information.

Table C-1. Population, School, and Student Characteristics by County, Selected Years—*Continued*

County	State/ County Code	High school graduates, 2006–2010			College enrollment, 2006–2010		College graduates, 2006–2010 (percent)						
		Population 25 years and over	High school diploma or less (percent)	High school diploma or more (percent)	Number	Percent public	Bachelor's degree or more	+/- U.S. percent with Bachelor's degree or more	Non-Hispanic White	Black or African American	American Indian and Alaska Native	Asian, Hawaiian, and Pacific Islander	Hispanic or Latino[3]
		30	31	32	33	34	35	36	37	38	39	40	41
MARYLAND	24000	3,789,931	38.7	87.8	461,300	72.9	35.7	7.8	40.0	24.8	20.9	61.8	20.0
Allegany, MD	24001	51,372	57.8	85.1	6,265	88.6	15.9	-12.0	16.2	7.8	8.1	44.9	14.0
Anne Arundel, MD	24003	355,148	36.2	90.0	37,469	74.3	35.7	7.8	37.9	23.9	25.2	49.0	25.9
Baltimore, MD	24005	541,674	38.8	88.8	70,353	75.1	35.2	7.3	36.3	27.7	19.5	61.5	26.3
Calvert, MD	24009	57,254	41.7	91.9	5,334	82.6	29.0	1.1	30.7	17.7	54.6	39.1	24.5
Caroline, MD	24011	21,563	58.9	81.6	1,268	74.5	15.2	-12.7	15.6	10.8	0.0	57.7	7.8
Carroll, MD	24013	110,747	41.9	89.5	11,024	56.3	31.1	3.2	30.9	30.1	52.0	55.3	21.0
Cecil, MD	24015	65,830	50.9	86.7	5,189	76.2	20.9	-7.0	20.3	21.5	13.6	55.1	28.0
Charles, MD	24017	92,602	40.7	90.4	10,166	77.5	26.1	-1.8	26.3	24.2	6.7	48.7	30.0
Dorchester, MD	24019	22,718	59.0	81.0	1,623	85.6	16.5	-11.4	19.5	7.2	20.0	40.9	13.5
Frederick, MD	24021	150,919	36.0	91.4	15,661	55.9	35.8	7.9	36.3	26.2	28.2	63.6	22.6
Garrett, MD	24023	20,892	58.0	84.3	1,011	87.9	17.5	-10.4	17.3	54.6	17.0	0.0	28.7
Harford, MD	24025	161,492	37.7	91.0	14,928	76.5	30.5	2.6	31.3	21.2	4.7	49.6	28.9
Howard, MD	24027	185,095	20.1	94.6	21,086	74.0	58.3	30.4	60.4	45.0	33.3	71.8	38.5
Kent, MD	24029	13,910	47.5	86.0	2,106	38.7	30.2	2.3	34.4	10.1	0.0	69.8	8.9
Montgomery, MD	24031	644,820	23.5	91.0	73,648	68.0	56.7	28.8	67.5	41.7	26.9	63.9	22.9
Prince George's, MD	24033	547,564	42.3	85.8	85,388	78.0	29.6	1.7	40.9	28.4	19.1	54.8	10.0
Queen Anne's, MD	24035	32,156	40.8	89.7	2,061	78.3	29.6	1.7	31.5	12.3	0.0	37.0	13.7
St. Mary's, MD	24037	64,802	43.8	89.0	7,869	80.3	27.4	-0.5	29.0	13.4	36.2	51.5	24.9
Somerset, MD	24039	16,869	64.3	80.9	4,516	95.2	14.3	-13.6	17.0	8.8	0.0	33.5	22.1
Talbot, MD	24041	27,431	39.7	88.0	1,641	68.6	32.7	4.8	36.5	10.6	27.5	38.8	17.4
Washington, MD	24043	100,186	54.1	83.4	8,223	80.4	18.7	-9.2	18.9	11.4	27.1	54.1	20.3
Wicomico, MD	24045	61,163	48.9	84.3	11,831	92.6	24.7	-3.2	27.2	14.9	15.1	50.5	14.3
Worcester, MD	24047	38,188	45.3	88.4	2,593	84.7	26.1	-1.8	28.9	8.7	0.0	38.8	12.5
Baltimore city, MD	24510	405,536	52.1	77.4	60,047	63.2	25.2	-2.7	46.2	12.9	17.5	70.9	17.8
MASSACHUSETTS	25000	4,382,378	38.1	88.7	557,207	45.0	38.3	10.4	40.3	22.3	21.7	56.9	16.1
Barnstable, MA	25001	164,152	30.4	94.7	10,997	67.3	40.5	12.6	41.3	22.1	38.1	42.3	29.5
Berkshire, MA	25003	93,038	43.1	90.2	9,104	55.9	29.6	1.7	29.9	23.6	38.9	47.8	21.5
Bristol, MA	25005	370,326	50.2	80.1	35,334	63.3	24.7	-3.2	25.2	23.0	19.1	40.9	12.9
Dukes, MA	25007	11,298	34.6	93.5	475	63.8	40.0	12.1	41.4	46.7	12.4	58.6	13.6
Essex, MA	25009	498,319	38.7	88.2	48,456	57.7	36.1	8.2	39.8	21.5	23.7	49.9	10.4
Franklin, MA	25011	51,066	39.6	91.1	4,691	74.1	32.5	4.6	32.4	35.8	21.7	46.7	27.4
Hampden, MA	25013	302,877	49.6	83.3	33,591	57.6	23.8	-4.1	27.1	15.8	8.4	33.7	8.7
Hampshire, MA	25015	96,015	33.2	92.4	34,834	68.7	41.3	13.4	41.2	41.6	19.9	57.6	27.2
Middlesex, MA	25017	1,019,083	31.0	91.6	138,239	35.5	49.3	21.4	50.1	30.8	25.0	64.8	27.9
Nantucket, MA	25019	7,303	33.7	93.4	285	55.8	40.2	12.3	44.6	25.9	0.0	46.5	3.3
Norfolk, MA	25021	456,151	29.8	93.1	48,089	35.1	47.4	19.5	47.8	31.4	24.0	56.2	35.7
Plymouth, MA	25023	330,142	39.2	91.8	27,929	64.3	32.5	4.6	34.1	17.4	16.1	50.4	17.9
Suffolk, MA	25025	454,713	42.3	83.1	106,366	25.2	38.9	11.0	53.2	18.4	16.4	47.3	14.1
Worcester, MA	25027	527,895	41.1	88.6	58,817	51.2	32.9	5.0	33.5	25.0	27.4	60.7	14.3
MICHIGAN	26000	6,561,843	43.4	88.0	782,258	82.3	25.0	-2.9	26.0	15.1	11.4	61.8	14.9
Alcona, MI	26001	8,930	57.8	84.3	309	85.1	12.4	-15.5	12.4	0.0	0.0	56.3	0.0
Alger, MI	26003	7,373	57.2	86.2	255	89.4	16.9	-11.0	18.9	0.0	16.3	40.0	0.0
Allegan, MI	26005	73,004	50.1	88.9	5,093	76.8	19.4	-8.5	20.2	8.0	16.2	49.1	4.3
Alpena, MI	26007	21,329	47.4	87.6	1,645	90.0	15.5	-12.4	15.1	12.5	0.0	56.6	13.3
Antrim, MI	26009	17,360	47.8	89.5	741	81.1	23.3	-4.6	23.6	0.0	17.4	43.8	8.6
Arenac, MI	26011	12,068	60.4	81.4	521	82.3	10.6	-17.3	11.0	0.0	5.1	0.0	4.0
Baraga, MI	26013	6,499	60.9	82.2	238	76.5	11.4	-16.5	13.5	1.2	4.6	17.8	0.0
Barry, MI	26015	40,157	49.4	90.5	3,007	85.7	16.6	-11.3	16.6	11.2	0.0	47.4	7.7
Bay, MI	26017	74,562	48.5	87.4	6,707	87.0	18.0	-9.9	18.2	6.8	8.8	56.3	9.1
Benzie, MI	26019	12,730	43.9	89.9	753	87.3	25.3	-2.6	25.4	100.0	11.7	65.3	8.3
Berrien, MI	26021	106,377	45.4	86.7	8,955	64.7	23.3	-4.6	24.9	10.9	16.1	62.4	12.9
Branch, MI	26023	31,309	54.6	86.6	2,131	74.0	14.1	-13.8	14.4	3.5	2.8	59.3	10.3
Calhoun, MI	26025	90,862	47.4	87.1	8,641	73.5	18.8	-9.1	19.4	13.5	11.3	39.2	11.1
Cass, MI	26027	36,097	53.0	85.2	2,354	82.2	15.8	-12.1	16.6	6.4	2.3	18.8	11.3
Charlevoix, MI	26029	18,551	43.3	91.1	716	88.5	24.5	-3.4	24.7	4.8	7.9	75.3	19.0
Cheboygan, MI	26031	19,285	51.7	88.2	895	85.4	17.8	-10.1	18.1	0.0	0.6	56.9	18.8
Chippewa, MI	26033	26,959	50.6	88.0	2,972	96.0	18.0	-9.9	20.8	1.6	11.8	26.3	6.7
Clare, MI	26035	22,041	58.1	82.6	1,301	85.7	10.3	-17.6	10.3	0.0	9.9	0.0	13.7
Clinton, MI	26037	47,992	38.3	93.0	5,632	90.4	27.2	-0.7	27.0	38.8	17.4	67.3	16.7
Crawford, MI	26039	10,411	54.9	84.3	568	85.0	14.2	-13.7	14.7	0.0	0.0	17.9	22.4

Note. Data in columns 26 through 41 from the American Community Survey are subject to sampling error, which can be especially large in small counties and small population groups. See notes and definitions for more information.
[3]May be of any race.

Table C-1. Population, School, and Student Characteristics by County, Selected Years—*Continued*

County	State/ County Code	County Type[1]	Population, 2010		Percent of related children 5–17 years in poverty, 2010	Percent of children under 19 years with no health insurance, 2010	Number of schools and students, 2010–2011			Resident enrollment, 2006–2010 K–12 enrollment	
			Total	Percent 5–17 years			School districts	Schools	Students	Number	Percent public
			1	2	3	4	5	6	7	8	9
MICHIGAN—*(Continued)*											
Delta, MI	26041	5	37,069	15.4	18.7	4.6	6	16	5,081	6,164	93.5
Dickinson, MI	26043	5	26,168	16.4	15.9	4.3	5	15	4,074	4,522	95.6
Eaton, MI	26045	2	107,759	17.6	13.6	3.7	12	49	18,538	20,040	89.3
Emmet, MI	26047	7	32,694	17.4	14.7	5.4	6	16	5,333	5,756	90.4
Genesee, MI	26049	2	425,790	18.6	27.2	3.8	32	159	71,780	84,476	93.4
Gladwin, MI	26051	6	25,692	15.2	27.6	5.7	3	9	3,374	4,052	91.5
Gogebic, MI	26053	7	16,427	12.2	28.2	5.0	4	8	1,841	2,160	94.0
Grand Traverse, MI	26055	5	86,986	16.4	13.8	4.9	8	31	13,231	15,032	88.1
Gratiot, MI	26057	6	42,476	16.0	22.3	4.7	7	26	7,193	7,677	94.7
Hillsdale, MI	26059	6	46,688	17.7	24.4	6.0	11	32	6,953	8,518	91.2
Houghton, MI	26061	5	36,628	14.8	20.5	4.1	10	22	5,381	5,338	96.8
Huron, MI	26063	7	33,118	15.7	19.3	6.2	16	27	4,703	5,525	92.7
Ingham, MI	26065	2	280,895	15.1	21.9	4.7	25	125	41,127	43,215	92.6
Ionia, MI	26067	2	63,905	18.1	18.2	4.1	11	34	11,207	12,690	92.8
Iosco, MI	26069	7	25,887	13.6	31.7	4.8	6	17	4,410	3,811	93.9
Iron, MI	26071	7	11,817	12.9	24.1	5.6	2	5	1,432	1,644	97.5
Isabella, MI	26073	5	70,311	12.8	19.8	4.7	5	21	6,596	9,319	88.8
Jackson, MI	26075	3	160,248	17.3	25.9	3.8	16	61	24,849	29,473	92.0
Kalamazoo, MI	26077	2	250,331	16.5	22.0	3.8	13	87	35,035	41,297	90.4
Kalkaska, MI	26079	7	17,153	16.6	28.5	5.0	3	11	2,333	2,956	95.0
Kent, MI	26081	2	602,622	18.9	20.7	4.4	40	257	104,943	116,206	84.0
Keweenaw, MI	26083	9	2,156	13.3	20.7	7.9	1	1	10	316	97.2
Lake, MI	26085	8	11,539	13.4	42.6	7.9	1	3	580	1,897	97.8
Lapeer, MI	26087	1	88,319	19.0	15.8	5.2	8	37	15,516	17,750	91.9
Leelanau, MI	26089	9	21,708	15.2	12.8	7.9	5	7	2,179	3,412	82.4
Lenawee, MI	26091	4	99,892	17.5	16.9	4.7	13	51	16,395	18,459	91.7
Livingston, MI	26093	1	180,967	20.1	7.1	3.4	8	47	29,234	37,324	92.3
Luce, MI	26095	7	6,631	13.3	26.0	5.1	1	3	774	1,147	95.1
Mackinac, MI	26097	7	11,113	14.4	20.8	7.5	7	14	1,453	1,685	92.9
Macomb, MI	26099	1	840,978	17.2	16.3	4.2	35	243	134,212	147,373	91.6
Manistee, MI	26101	7	24,733	14.7	22.8	5.5	6	14	3,215	3,783	85.9
Marquette, MI	26103	5	67,077	13.5	15.6	3.7	10	27	8,418	9,610	94.2
Mason, MI	26105	7	28,705	16.1	25.2	5.6	5	16	4,266	4,934	91.4
Mecosta, MI	26107	6	42,798	14.8	27.6	4.7	5	26	6,619	6,343	93.5
Menominee, MI	26109	7	24,029	16.1	18.8	5.3	6	16	3,915	4,174	94.4
Midland, MI	26111	4	83,629	18.1	12.8	3.7	8	31	13,260	15,626	91.5
Missaukee, MI	26113	9	14,849	18.2	24.1	6.3	2	7	2,191	2,785	89.3
Monroe, MI	26115	3	152,021	18.4	15.1	3.7	13	56	26,230	28,852	88.1
Montcalm, MI	26117	6	63,342	18.1	27.6	5.2	7	29	9,914	12,225	91.9
Montmorency, MI	26119	9	9,765	13.0	34.5	6.4	2	3	834	1,301	95.2
Muskegon, MI	26121	3	172,188	18.3	24.8	4.2	16	84	30,225	33,171	94.2
Newaygo, MI	26123	2	48,460	18.7	26.0	6.5	7	29	8,801	9,682	89.7
Oakland, MI	26125	1	1,202,362	17.8	11.9	4.5	46	367	193,109	217,215	86.5
Oceana, MI	26127	8	26,570	18.2	29.9	6.3	5	17	3,559	4,883	89.7
Ogemaw, MI	26129	9	21,699	15.6	27.9	6.1	1	6	2,322	3,488	91.2
Ontonagon, MI	26131	9	6,780	12.3	22.6	6.4	3	5	750	868	98.9
Osceola, MI	26133	7	23,528	18.6	25.2	5.9	4	16	4,393	4,405	88.5
Oscoda, MI	26135	9	8,640	15.2	34.2	7.7	2	4	980	1,274	86.4
Otsego, MI	26137	7	24,164	17.0	19.5	5.0	3	9	4,112	4,383	86.5
Ottawa, MI	26139	3	263,801	19.3	11.6	4.2	16	91	44,114	51,071	84.4
Presque Isle, MI	26141	7	13,376	13.5	24.0	6.1	4	9	1,572	1,939	88.5
Roscommon, MI	26143	7	24,449	12.1	36.3	5.3	3	12	3,240	3,252	95.2
Saginaw, MI	26145	3	200,169	17.5	23.6	4.0	20	86	31,310	37,719	89.7
St. Clair, MI	26147	1	163,040	18.0	18.6	4.2	21	75	31,098	30,542	93.0
St. Joseph, MI	26149	4	61,295	19.0	23.3	5.3	10	35	11,342	11,696	93.6
Sanilac, MI	26151	6	43,114	17.8	23.5	6.5	8	27	7,324	8,118	93.8
Schoolcraft, MI	26153	7	8,485	15.1	22.0	5.8	1	3	910	1,395	89.6
Shiawassee, MI	26155	4	70,648	18.5	18.4	4.0	9	39	13,214	13,780	94.1
Tuscola, MI	26157	6	55,729	17.9	21.6	5.0	10	33	9,879	10,529	91.7
Van Buren, MI	26159	2	76,258	19.1	21.0	6.0	13	50	17,240	15,390	93.2
Washtenaw, MI	26161	2	344,791	15.3	11.1	3.9	19	101	44,654	53,193	89.0
Wayne, MI	26163	1	1,820,584	18.9	32.7	4.8	126	635	306,566	373,021	91.2
Wexford, MI	26165	7	32,735	17.6	25.5	5.0	5	19	5,578	5,788	91.5

[1]County type codes are from the Economic Research Service of the United States Department of Agriculture. See notes and definitions for more information.

Table C-1. Population, School, and Student Characteristics by County, Selected Years—*Continued*

County	State/ County Code	Characteristics of students, 2010–2011				Number of graduates, 2008–2009	Staff and students, 2010–2011			
		Percent with IEP[2]	Percent eligible for free or reduced lunch	Percent minority	Percent English-language learners		Total staff	Number of teachers	Student/ teacher ratio	Central admin. staff
		10	11	12	13	14	15	16	17	18
MICHIGAN—*(Continued)*										
Delta, MI	26041	15.0	42.5	8.9	. . .	397	624	279	18.2	27
Dickinson, MI	26043	16.0	37.2	5.4	0.1	387	497	240	17.0	21
Eaton, MI	26045	15.0	37.7	17.6	0.4	1,394	2,268	1,069	17.3	52
Emmet, MI	26047	10.8	40.5	11.5	. . .	412	609	314	17.0	16
Genesee, MI	26049	14.2	52.4	35.3	0.7	4,855	9,910	4,030	17.8	190
Gladwin, MI	26051	17.5	56.9	4.6	. . .	246	358	175	19.3	7
Gogebic, MI	26053	14.4	56.9	7.7	. . .	166	222	129	14.2	8
Grand Traverse, MI	26055	14.5	39.9	8.5	0.9	991	1,988	827	16.0	44
Gratiot, MI	26057	15.7	48.1	9.7	0.6	635	1,065	433	16.6	29
Hillsdale, MI	26059	15.7	51.9	4.8	. . .	485	867	411	16.9	28
Houghton, MI	26061	10.5	48.7	3.5	. . .	365	612	325	16.5	20
Huron, MI	26063	16.4	51.4	5.1	. . .	448	629	282	16.7	29
Ingham, MI	26065	15.7	46.3	39.4	3.5	2,768	5,243	2,389	17.2	125
Ionia, MI	26067	17.5	49.3	9.2	1.3	833	1,483	634	17.7	46
Iosco, MI	26069	17.1	66.3	5.7	. . .	397	587	264	16.7	25
Iron, MI	26071	16.9	58.4	4.6	. . .	124	152	81	17.6	3
Isabella, MI	26073	16.9	40.2	17.5	0.1	500	719	384	17.2	24
Jackson, MI	26075	14.9	50.9	18.5	0.5	1,790	3,014	1,480	16.8	75
Kalamazoo, MI	26077	12.7	46.5	32.3	3.2	2,257	4,666	2,045	17.1	96
Kalkaska, MI	26079	14.3	58.0	4.2	. . .	174	247	131	17.8	3
Kent, MI	26081	13.4	46.9	35.9	7.6	6,859	12,567	5,809	18.1	224
Keweenaw, MI	26083	20.0	71.9	1.6	. . .	. . .	3	1	10.0	0
Lake, MI	26085	18.8	90.1	37.7	. . .	27	76	42	13.9	6
Lapeer, MI	26087	12.8	44.3	8.3	1.7	1,314	1,851	816	19.0	41
Leelanau, MI	26089	12.6	37.1	22.7	3.5	203	309	145	15.1	9
Lenawee, MI	26091	13.8	43.1	17.6	0.7	1,318	2,210	992	16.5	74
Livingston, MI	26093	13.6	20.6	5.0	0.2	2,295	3,234	1,560	18.7	55
Luce, MI	26095	19.9	48.6	14.1	. . .	73	94	52	14.9	4
Mackinac, MI	26097	13.1	48.0	45.6	. . .	116	175	95	15.2	6
Macomb, MI	26099	13.4	40.7	24.6	3.8	9,534	14,087	6,882	19.5	258
Manistee, MI	26101	14.8	55.2	10.8	. . .	278	437	184	17.4	13
Marquette, MI	26103	16.7	37.6	10.3	. . .	637	1,078	507	16.6	45
Mason, MI	26105	15.0	53.0	15.5	. . .	389	657	266	16.0	24
Mecosta, MI	26107	20.1	60.4	10.8	. . .	447	931	400	16.5	27
Menominee, MI	26109	13.0	49.6	6.5	. . .	288	478	216	18.1	16
Midland, MI	26111	16.7	30.7	8.2	0.3	1,081	1,605	742	17.9	28
Missaukee, MI	26113	9.9	56.6	5.0	. . .	166	235	116	19.0	3
Monroe, MI	26115	13.9	35.9	10.4	0.9	1,767	3,269	1,419	18.5	74
Montcalm, MI	26117	15.8	52.3	6.1	0.8	758	1,220	565	17.6	38
Montmorency, MI	26119	14.5	67.6	2.9	. . .	62	95	49	16.9	5
Muskegon, MI	26121	15.4	58.2	29.6	1.1	2,031	3,826	1,694	17.8	111
Newaygo, MI	26123	15.5	56.0	12.2	2.1	651	1,139	492	17.9	27
Oakland, MI	26125	12.0	30.3	33.8	4.7	14,426	23,327	10,700	18.0	413
Oceana, MI	26127	15.3	65.9	36.6	20.1	267	533	212	16.8	14
Ogemaw, MI	26129	14.0	60.5	3.8	. . .	184	272	124	18.7	5
Ontonagon, MI	26131	22.4	53.1	3.6	. . .	68	123	55	13.6	7
Osceola, MI	26133	15.8	59.5	5.7	. . .	395	477	245	17.9	13
Oscoda, MI	26135	18.9	65.9	2.9	. . .	67	112	55	18.0	3
Otsego, MI	26137	11.4	48.1	3.0	. . .	284	454	228	18.1	12
Ottawa, MI	26139	12.6	37.0	23.8	4.4	2,823	5,202	2,435	18.1	115
Presque Isle, MI	26141	9.4	56.0	3.1	. . .	124	176	89	17.7	4
Roscommon, MI	26143	17.8	63.0	5.5	. . .	255	438	191	16.9	14
Saginaw, MI	26145	17.3	54.9	42.1	0.1	2,201	4,142	1,834	17.1	120
St. Clair, MI	26147	13.6	41.6	10.4	0.4	2,249	3,637	1,671	18.6	94
St. Joseph, MI	26149	12.1	58.8	16.9	4.5	781	1,351	655	17.3	45
Sanilac, MI	26151	12.9	55.1	5.1	. . .	654	882	412	17.8	25
Schoolcraft, MI	26153	12.4	52.1	19.1	. . .	106	99	51	17.9	4
Shiawassee, MI	26155	14.3	44.6	4.4	. . .	1,032	1,630	728	18.1	48
Tuscola, MI	26157	15.2	52.5	8.3	. . .	822	1,389	563	17.5	39
Van Buren, MI	26159	12.0	51.2	23.9	5.4	1,118	2,429	1,017	17.0	61
Washtenaw, MI	26161	13.9	29.9	34.8	2.9	3,249	6,552	2,526	17.7	129
Wayne, MI	26163	13.3	59.9	55.5	7.1	20,565	35,275	16,914	18.1	655
Wexford, MI	26165	14.8	58.8	5.4	. . .	382	709	337	16.6	24

[2]IEP=Individual Education Program. See notes and definitions for more information.
. . . = Not available.

Table C-1. Population, School, and Student Characteristics by County, Selected Years—*Continued*

County	State/ County Code	Revenues, 2008–2009				Current expenditures, 2008–2009			Resident population 16 to 19 years, 2006–2010			
			Percentage of revenue from									
		Total revenue ($1,000's)	Federal government	State government	Local government	Amount ($1,000's)	Amount per student	Percent for instruction	Total population 16 to 19 years	Percent enrolled in school	Percent high school graduates, not enrolled in school	Percent not enrolled, not grads, not employed, or not in labor force
		19	20	21	22	23	24	25	26	27	28	29
MICHIGAN— *(Continued)*												
Delta, MI	26041	62,298	12.7	54.2	33.1	53,708	10,811	55.8	2,099	87.6	9.6	1.9
Dickinson, MI	26043	52,397	12.1	52.7	35.2	45,606	10,779	60.9	1,329	90.4	5.3	3.5
Eaton, MI	26045	229,620	8.8	55.8	35.4	188,765	9,726	58.5	6,447	89.1	7.4	3.0
Emmet, MI	26047	63,219	5.6	21.5	72.9	52,556	9,397	66.4	1,770	82.8	13.6	1.1
Genesee, MI	26049	899,875	13.8	61.0	25.2	796,375	10,292	56.4	25,455	83.8	8.7	6.4
Gladwin, MI	26051	32,037	11.7	58.3	30.0	28,678	8,238	60.8	1,255	80.9	15.1	3.4
Gogebic, MI	26053	21,167	14.6	50.6	34.8	18,945	9,597	62.9	815	81.8	10.9	6.5
Grand Traverse, MI	26055	194,637	13.3	39.9	46.8	157,883	12,033	50.4	4,513	82.7	11.5	3.8
Gratiot, MI	26057	98,375	15.9	56.7	27.4	76,420	10,557	58.3	2,725	86.1	8.1	4.5
Hillsdale, MI	26059	77,652	10.4	63.9	25.7	69,804	9,992	61.6	3,065	88.3	6.2	4.7
Houghton, MI	26061	62,218	11.8	57.9	30.3	53,620	10,049	57.5	3,282	94.8	4.3	0.6
Huron, MI	26063	63,337	9.8	45.7	44.5	53,992	11,112	58.4	1,703	89.3	8.0	1.8
Ingham, MI	26065	581,807	10.7	51.1	38.2	483,366	11,267	54.4	24,162	93.6	3.7	2.4
Ionia, MI	26067	140,798	11.8	57.8	30.4	115,993	10,166	57.0	3,411	84.9	10.5	3.3
Iosco, MI	26069	52,657	14.6	43.3	42.1	47,361	9,781	60.6	1,284	82.0	11.3	6.2
Iron, MI	26071	15,515	10.6	46.6	42.8	14,588	9,345	60.6	556	86.7	8.5	2.7
Isabella, MI	26073	72,050	7.2	55.3	37.5	60,426	9,092	60.0	8,708	94.5	4.3	0.9
Jackson, MI	26075	308,478	10.2	56.0	33.8	269,200	10,524	58.0	9,586	83.1	9.5	5.8
Kalamazoo, MI	26077	449,888	10.7	48.4	40.9	353,276	10,113	56.7	16,679	89.3	7.3	2.6
Kalkaska, MI	26079	23,250	11.9	46.4	41.7	20,815	8,486	61.9	964	78.1	13.6	7.5
Kent, MI	26081	1,475,807	9.2	49.2	41.6	1,126,422	10,221	57.0	36,100	86.1	8.7	3.7
Keweenaw, MI	26083	206	12.1	1.5	86.4	144	28,800	58.3	78	74.4	5.1	20.5
Lake, MI	26085	17,986	5.7	58.8	35.5	7,362	12,671	57.1	554	81.1	12.3	2.2
Lapeer, MI	26087	169,306	9.1	64.6	26.3	148,764	9,119	59.4	5,533	79.8	10.9	7.3
Leelanau, MI	26089	31,945	12.7	15.4	72.0	25,517	11,133	61.6	1,181	83.1	11.9	3.8
Lenawee, MI	26091	206,921	9.6	56.3	34.0	178,323	10,467	58.7	6,420	89.0	7.4	2.7
Livingston, MI	26093	345,272	7.8	54.4	37.8	272,314	9,173	59.0	10,273	86.1	9.2	3.3
Luce, MI	26095	9,238	11.1	48.3	40.6	9,068	9,772	64.9	290	70.7	17.2	12.1
Mackinac, MI	26097	17,630	10.5	27.0	62.5	15,208	10,402	61.1	581	79.2	13.1	7.2
Macomb, MI	26099	1,657,562	9.3	56.3	34.4	1,400,260	10,330	57.7	44,425	87.4	8.3	3.4
Manistee, MI	26101	40,243	10.6	42.8	46.6	34,908	10,540	56.1	1,170	75.6	17.1	5.7
Marquette, MI	26103	98,147	14.1	52.2	33.8	86,917	10,236	55.5	4,594	89.4	8.4	1.6
Mason, MI	26105	57,651	10.1	36.2	53.7	52,027	11,671	59.3	1,735	84.4	8.0	5.5
Mecosta, MI	26107	87,469	11.4	49.2	39.3	74,150	11,343	57.9	4,560	90.6	4.3	4.4
Menominee, MI	26109	44,673	13.7	60.1	26.2	39,402	9,669	60.6	1,094	87.4	6.3	1.2
Midland, MI	26111	158,205	8.4	58.9	32.7	136,531	9,967	61.0	5,350	89.7	6.2	3.2
Missaukee, MI	26113	20,665	10.6	61.6	27.7	19,253	8,595	61.0	829	81.1	12.4	2.8
Monroe, MI	26115	278,821	8.8	53.2	38.1	242,825	10,108	56.6	9,206	84.4	9.0	4.0
Montcalm, MI	26117	118,436	11.4	60.2	28.4	102,384	10,015	55.6	3,930	81.2	10.9	6.5
Montmorency, MI	26119	9,847	11.5	35.7	52.8	7,971	8,886	59.1	445	72.1	22.5	5.4
Muskegon, MI	26121	397,392	14.2	55.6	30.1	320,321	10,093	56.7	10,274	81.5	11.9	5.2
Newaygo, MI	26123	107,762	11.9	58.8	29.3	91,559	10,243	61.8	2,957	77.7	13.6	7.2
Oakland, MI	26125	2,825,100	7.4	44.5	48.1	2,250,278	11,318	57.6	64,169	89.4	6.9	2.7
Oceana, MI	26127	41,411	15.5	49.4	35.2	36,048	9,777	59.8	1,591	77.4	14.8	5.9
Ogemaw, MI	26129	23,598	11.9	49.5	38.6	21,739	8,957	60.1	1,096	83.6	9.7	4.6
Ontonagon, MI	26131	14,999	15.2	37.3	47.5	11,992	14,878	53.1	309	78.0	14.2	6.2
Osceola, MI	26133	47,302	13.5	58.6	27.9	43,703	9,297	64.2	1,484	80.2	10.2	6.2
Oscoda, MI	26135	10,635	16.8	34.8	48.4	9,408	9,417	62.3	362	56.1	18.5	17.1
Otsego, MI	26137	42,706	8.7	37.1	54.2	37,311	8,667	64.6	1,343	76.5	15.8	6.1
Ottawa, MI	26139	558,240	7.5	48.7	43.8	427,428	9,812	61.1	19,784	89.0	7.7	2.3
Presque Isle, MI	26141	16,322	11.2	45.5	43.3	15,103	9,022	63.2	552	91.7	5.1	1.3
Roscommon, MI	26143	43,384	17.4	27.6	54.9	37,045	11,078	57.4	1,100	76.6	11.8	11.2
Saginaw, MI	26145	384,074	16.0	61.3	22.7	341,700	10,198	56.8	13,088	80.6	11.8	5.9
St. Clair, MI	26147	369,569	8.7	54.3	37.0	321,847	9,964	58.8	9,758	83.1	12.5	3.0
St. Joseph, MI	26149	126,918	10.7	58.4	30.9	107,837	9,250	57.5	3,615	81.9	9.1	5.7
Sanilac, MI	26151	80,549	12.2	62.1	25.7	71,013	9,322	61.1	2,434	81.4	12.0	5.2
Schoolcraft, MI	26153	13,519	12.7	40.5	46.8	11,716	8,937	59.1	388	86.6	7.0	5.7
Shiawassee, MI	26155	147,145	9.4	66.7	23.8	132,159	9,607	59.9	4,216	77.3	14.9	6.6
Tuscola, MI	26157	121,508	11.4	66.4	22.2	108,684	10,308	59.8	3,365	82.5	12.0	4.4
Van Buren, MI	26159	204,710	10.4	56.2	33.4	185,227	10,616	57.6	4,644	83.8	11.0	3.6
Washtenaw, MI	26161	697,886	6.8	43.5	49.6	544,256	11,405	55.4	30,376	94.0	3.5	1.9
Wayne, MI	26163	4,090,895	13.8	58.3	27.9	3,524,221	10,727	56.2	118,799	82.2	10.2	6.3
Wexford, MI	26165	71,827	11.4	51.1	37.5	62,741	11,684	55.1	1,671	76.2	18.8	4.2

Note. Data in columns 26 through 41 from the American Community Survey are subject to sampling error, which can be especially large in small counties and small population groups. See notes and definitions for more information.

Table C-1. Population, School, and Student Characteristics by County, Selected Years—*Continued*

County	State/ County Code	High school graduates, 2006–2010			College enrollment, 2006–2010		College graduates, 2006–2010 (percent)						
		Population 25 years and over	High school diploma or less (percent)	High school diploma or more (percent)	Number	Percent public	Bachelor's degree or more	+/- U.S. percent with Bachelor's degree or more	Non-Hispanic White	Black or African American	American Indian and Alaska Native	Asian, Hawaiian, and Pacific Islander	Hispanic or Latino[3]
		30	31	32	33	34	35	36	37	38	39	40	41
MICHIGAN— *(Continued)*													
Delta, MI	26041	26,647	47.8	90.6	1,789	93.9	18.7	-9.2	18.8	0.0	7.3	26.4	25.2
Dickinson, MI	26043	18,888	50.1	92.2	1,060	90.3	17.9	-10.0	17.7	39.1	4.3	25.8	28.5
Eaton, MI	26045	72,338	37.8	92.4	7,667	77.0	24.3	-3.6	24.2	27.0	15.4	40.8	18.2
Emmet, MI	26047	22,667	36.4	92.8	2,054	92.2	29.5	1.6	30.7	0.0	7.3	16.9	22.2
Genesee, MI	26049	283,916	46.3	88.2	30,572	81.2	19.0	-8.9	20.2	12.9	14.4	49.9	16.4
Gladwin, MI	26051	18,902	56.4	84.3	918	83.0	11.1	-16.8	11.0	66.7	0.0	42.7	11.5
Gogebic, MI	26053	12,320	49.6	90.2	683	89.6	18.6	-9.3	19.1	7.2	6.0	68.4	0.0
Grand Traverse, MI	26055	59,492	35.2	92.8	4,358	90.3	28.9	1.0	29.7	4.2	18.5	29.1	17.5
Gratiot, MI	26057	28,033	54.9	87.0	3,166	43.6	13.5	-14.4	14.2	5.4	0.0	64.9	5.8
Hillsdale, MI	26059	30,998	56.2	86.6	2,920	46.9	14.2	-13.7	14.2	0.0	0.0	36.1	6.0
Houghton, MI	26061	21,258	46.5	89.9	6,958	92.5	26.9	-1.0	26.1	7.8	6.0	70.7	17.8
Huron, MI	26063	24,276	58.6	84.6	1,312	89.6	13.8	-14.1	13.4	0.0	0.0	79.9	17.9
Ingham, MI	26065	165,615	33.0	90.7	56,478	92.6	35.5	7.6	36.7	24.4	15.5	65.0	18.0
Ionia, MI	26067	42,315	52.3	86.7	3,112	81.3	13.1	-14.8	13.9	4.0	2.9	21.3	7.5
Iosco, MI	26069	19,838	55.0	84.4	847	80.2	13.6	-14.3	13.6	0.0	3.5	3.7	29.0
Iron, MI	26071	9,247	57.5	88.3	398	80.7	15.1	-12.8	15.4	0.0	5.3	23.1	1.4
Isabella, MI	26073	34,772	43.9	89.2	20,518	97.6	25.8	-2.1	26.4	17.0	6.9	71.3	12.1
Jackson, MI	26075	108,473	47.1	88.0	10,285	74.0	17.5	-10.4	18.1	9.8	3.5	55.2	12.2
Kalamazoo, MI	26077	152,139	34.3	91.7	34,956	90.1	33.4	5.5	34.7	19.3	8.3	67.4	23.5
Kalkaska, MI	26079	12,150	57.5	84.8	379	78.6	11.6	-16.3	11.7	0.0	0.0	60.4	8.1
Kent, MI	26081	376,421	39.0	88.3	45,201	69.3	30.0	2.1	33.2	12.7	14.1	35.9	11.0
Keweenaw, MI	26083	1,579	49.2	90.8	40	70.0	22.0	-5.9	21.6	0.0	0.0	0.0	100.0
Lake, MI	26085	8,360	64.8	79.7	247	81.0	8.5	-19.4	8.7	5.7	8.8	0.0	0.0
Lapeer, MI	26087	60,194	49.1	89.1	4,834	80.5	17.0	-10.9	17.5	9.4	9.3	22.7	3.6
Leelanau, MI	26089	16,033	29.8	92.7	898	84.2	39.4	11.5	41.4	0.0	10.2	80.0	6.4
Lenawee, MI	26091	67,420	49.1	87.9	6,016	59.0	19.2	-8.7	20.2	7.2	13.6	55.0	7.1
Livingston, MI	26093	120,816	34.1	93.6	10,354	85.0	31.2	3.3	31.0	44.2	40.0	60.8	19.0
Luce, MI	26095	5,063	62.2	82.6	152	96.7	13.5	-14.4	15.8	0.0	8.8	15.3	10.6
Mackinac, MI	26097	8,436	52.2	89.1	365	74.5	20.1	-7.8	21.0	17.7	11.9	83.3	9.4
Macomb, MI	26099	573,182	44.4	87.6	60,432	80.2	21.9	-6.0	21.3	17.4	14.8	48.9	18.4
Manistee, MI	26101	18,280	51.8	86.9	685	81.5	16.8	-11.1	17.5	4.8	5.5	17.6	9.6
Marquette, MI	26103	43,823	41.2	91.7	7,909	95.2	29.7	1.8	30.2	10.0	19.9	43.1	21.1
Mason, MI	26105	20,275	47.3	88.1	1,224	88.9	19.4	-8.5	19.6	3.4	14.7	78.4	7.1
Mecosta, MI	26107	25,103	50.8	87.7	8,305	96.5	20.1	-7.8	20.5	11.2	38.4	21.9	9.9
Menominee, MI	26109	17,474	54.6	89.3	762	89.4	13.4	-14.5	13.3	39.5	3.1	51.7	7.4
Midland, MI	26111	55,400	37.8	91.4	6,719	62.6	32.2	4.3	31.8	35.6	14.4	60.9	32.0
Missaukee, MI	26113	10,124	56.0	85.6	514	73.9	12.9	-15.0	12.9	0.0	7.7	26.3	10.7
Monroe, MI	26115	101,959	50.1	87.7	9,037	84.3	17.0	-10.9	17.0	12.9	13.3	50.8	10.0
Montcalm, MI	26117	42,183	54.6	85.0	3,124	84.5	12.7	-15.2	13.0	5.7	0.0	21.8	7.3
Montmorency, MI	26119	7,679	59.4	83.9	300	86.3	10.6	-17.3	10.6	0.0	50.0	0.0	0.0
Muskegon, MI	26121	113,390	48.2	87.7	9,333	77.3	16.5	-11.4	17.8	8.9	5.6	39.0	9.6
Newaygo, MI	26123	32,384	55.6	85.2	1,896	69.5	13.2	-14.7	13.7	4.3	1.0	27.5	2.9
Oakland, MI	26125	822,377	29.1	92.3	89,460	78.2	42.2	14.3	42.2	31.6	17.6	75.3	26.0
Oceana, MI	26127	18,053	55.2	82.7	957	85.3	14.3	-13.6	15.5	0.0	4.0	7.3	1.7
Ogemaw, MI	26129	15,817	60.7	81.3	1,120	85.2	10.7	-17.2	10.7	0.0	9.7	24.5	2.5
Ontonagon, MI	26131	5,529	51.4	90.3	267	83.9	16.5	-11.4	16.4	37.5	8.5	25.0	35.7
Osceola, MI	26133	15,921	58.2	85.2	931	82.5	11.9	-16.0	11.7	23.7	25.8	15.2	5.1
Oscoda, MI	26135	6,478	64.6	80.6	287	87.5	8.9	-19.0	9.0	0.0	1.8	0.0	10.6
Otsego, MI	26137	16,809	50.0	89.2	928	85.6	19.4	-8.5	19.5	0.0	27.3	41.7	15.7
Ottawa, MI	26139	158,898	41.2	90.5	24,758	77.2	28.8	0.9	30.2	14.1	6.6	32.7	11.6
Presque Isle, MI	26141	10,514	54.6	85.3	452	92.7	14.3	-13.6	14.4	0.0	7.9	23.1	14.5
Roscommon, MI	26143	19,315	55.1	83.7	847	82.1	13.6	-14.3	13.6	0.0	9.7	61.9	4.9
Saginaw, MI	26145	132,806	49.7	86.6	14,412	88.3	18.0	-9.9	19.7	9.8	11.4	59.0	11.9
St. Clair, MI	26147	111,899	49.5	87.8	9,838	78.7	15.0	-12.9	15.2	9.5	16.7	32.6	12.1
St. Joseph, MI	26149	40,451	56.3	84.2	2,473	87.7	14.1	-13.8	14.0	13.0	17.4	38.6	13.9
Sanilac, MI	26151	29,922	60.2	85.2	1,748	83.8	11.0	-16.9	11.2	14.5	2.6	10.9	7.5
Schoolcraft, MI	26153	6,391	59.3	86.5	217	78.3	13.2	-14.7	13.7	7.5	3.9	36.4	0.0
Shiawassee, MI	26155	47,748	49.6	89.3	3,908	66.2	14.9	-13.0	15.0	12.9	6.7	17.3	9.8
Tuscola, MI	26157	38,306	56.1	84.8	2,974	79.6	12.4	-15.5	12.5	2.3	1.4	48.3	12.4
Van Buren, MI	26159	50,670	49.5	84.8	3,370	87.4	18.3	-9.6	19.6	11.8	4.3	19.6	7.1
Washtenaw, MI	26161	210,871	23.1	93.6	67,045	93.1	50.8	22.9	52.2	25.4	18.6	82.7	39.8
Wayne, MI	26163	1,207,337	49.0	83.3	132,727	80.2	20.2	-7.7	25.1	11.9	11.5	56.2	12.7
Wexford, MI	26165	21,973	52.2	87.4	1,328	76.5	16.4	-11.5	16.6	5.8	0.0	8.7	7.0

Note. Data in columns 26 through 41 from the American Community Survey are subject to sampling error, which can be especially large in small counties and small population groups. See notes and definitions for more information.

[3]May be of any race.

Table C-1. Population, School, and Student Characteristics by County, Selected Years—*Continued*

County	State/ County Code	County Type[1]	Population, 2010		Percent of related children 5–17 years in poverty, 2010	Percent of children under 19 years with no health insurance, 2010	Number of schools and students, 2010–2011			Resident enrollment, 2006–2010 K–12 enrollment	
			Total	Percent 5–17 years			School districts	Schools	Students	Number	Percent public
			1	2	3	4	5	6	7	8	9
MINNESOTA	27000	X	5,303,925	17.5	13.6	6.7	555	2,392	838,037	928,956	89.0
Aitkin, MN	27001	8	16,202	13.2	21.1	10.6	4	10	2,046	2,121	93.5
Anoka, MN	27003	1	330,844	19.3	9.1	6.8	11	101	63,756	64,468	90.5
Becker, MN	27005	6	32,504	17.9	19.8	9.1	5	19	4,505	5,691	92.7
Beltrami, MN	27007	7	44,442	17.4	28.4	8.3	9	32	7,760	7,640	94.6
Benton, MN	27009	3	38,451	17.3	11.4	5.5	3	9	5,592	6,646	90.6
Big Stone, MN	27011	9	5,269	15.5	14.0	8.5	2	6	907	809	94.3
Blue Earth, MN	27013	5	64,013	13.4	14.6	5.9	5	29	10,125	8,629	90.1
Brown, MN	27015	7	25,893	15.9	11.0	6.1	5	13	3,514	4,298	75.3
Carlton, MN	27017	2	35,386	17.3	11.6	7.5	8	24	6,382	6,331	91.5
Carver, MN	27019	1	91,042	22.5	4.7	5.1	7	44	15,825	19,790	84.0
Cass, MN	27021	9	28,567	15.6	25.7	10.2	6	19	4,204	4,579	96.0
Chippewa, MN	27023	7	12,441	16.8	14.0	6.6	3	11	2,129	2,209	93.9
Chisago, MN	27025	1	53,887	19.6	7.9	6.3	5	19	7,950	10,552	92.9
Clay, MN	27027	3	58,999	16.4	13.5	5.4	5	21	8,961	9,363	92.1
Clearwater, MN	27029	8	8,695	18.0	23.6	11.8	2	5	1,508	1,471	94.2
Cook, MN	27031	9	5,176	12.6	13.7	9.4	4	8	618	696	94.8
Cottonwood, MN	27033	7	11,687	17.9	13.4	7.8	3	7	1,933	2,071	86.9
Crow Wing, MN	27035	5	62,500	16.6	16.8	8.1	5	20	9,625	10,419	91.8
Dakota, MN	27037	1	398,552	19.4	7.7	5.8	17	144	74,688	77,624	90.4
Dodge, MN	27039	3	20,087	21.6	8.2	6.2	3	9	4,138	4,032	97.5
Douglas, MN	27041	7	36,009	15.8	11.8	7.2	7	20	5,308	5,563	91.7
Faribault, MN	27043	7	14,553	16.3	16.6	7.6	3	9	1,945	2,592	87.9
Fillmore, MN	27045	8	20,866	17.3	18.4	10.2	5	13	2,478	3,513	90.7
Freeborn, MN	27047	7	31,255	15.8	15.1	7.4	3	14	4,044	5,135	95.9
Goodhue, MN	27049	4	46,183	17.4	10.4	7.2	7	23	6,925	8,079	93.0
Grant, MN	27051	9	6,018	15.2	15.0	8.9	3	8	1,095	922	96.0
Hennepin, MN	27053	1	1,152,425	16.1	17.7	7.1	72	424	157,670	185,892	87.5
Houston, MN	27055	3	19,027	17.2	11.3	6.2	5	15	4,338	3,463	84.9
Hubbard, MN	27057	7	20,428	15.7	18.3	8.6	3	9	2,304	3,228	94.1
Isanti, MN	27059	1	37,816	18.8	11.2	7.5	5	23	6,283	7,299	91.8
Itasca, MN	27061	6	45,058	16.4	17.6	7.9	8	28	6,515	7,463	91.0
Jackson, MN	27063	7	10,266	16.7	13.3	6.9	2	6	1,505	1,772	90.7
Kanabec, MN	27065	6	16,239	18.0	18.5	7.6	2	6	2,419	3,144	93.2
Kandiyohi, MN	27067	4	42,239	17.1	19.4	7.4	4	14	5,558	7,396	92.4
Kittson, MN	27069	9	4,552	16.7	12.5	9.7	3	7	723	784	95.0
Koochiching, MN	27071	7	13,311	16.1	18.9	7.0	3	8	1,980	2,228	86.5
Lac qui Parle, MN	27073	9	7,259	15.9	13.2	8.0	2	6	1,341	1,225	95.7
Lake, MN	27075	6	10,866	13.6	14.0	6.4	1	5	1,395	1,530	94.4
Lake of the Woods, MN	27077	9	4,045	15.0	17.7	9.8	1	2	524	690	99.4
Le Sueur, MN	27079	6	27,703	18.7	10.7	7.0	5	19	4,298	5,326	90.2
Lincoln, MN	27081	9	5,896	15.8	14.1	9.2	4	7	935	938	96.0
Lyon, MN	27083	7	25,857	17.0	13.1	5.8	6	21	4,236	4,392	85.5
McLeod, MN	27085	6	36,651	18.6	10.0	6.2	6	17	5,447	6,803	87.3
Mahnomen, MN	27087	8	5,413	20.4	33.0	10.2	3	8	1,388	1,064	94.1
Marshall, MN	27089	8	9,439	17.8	11.4	8.1	5	10	1,372	1,726	94.0
Martin, MN	27091	7	20,840	16.4	16.7	7.8	5	18	3,062	3,730	86.9
Meeker, MN	27093	6	23,300	18.4	11.4	7.6	3	13	3,507	4,296	93.8
Mille Lacs, MN	27095	6	26,097	18.2	17.0	8.6	4	14	6,497	4,839	89.7
Morrison, MN	27097	6	33,198	17.7	16.5	7.7	6	20	5,206	5,858	90.2
Mower, MN	27099	4	39,163	18.0	15.4	8.0	6	23	5,955	7,029	92.5
Murray, MN	27101	9	8,725	16.2	12.5	8.4	2	5	1,149	1,384	90.0
Nicollet, MN	27103	5	32,727	16.0	9.8	5.5	6	17	2,295	5,373	89.1
Nobles, MN	27105	7	21,378	17.7	17.6	9.1	6	13	3,581	3,627	92.4
Norman, MN	27107	8	6,852	18.3	16.1	9.4	3	7	1,121	1,244	96.2
Olmsted, MN	27109	3	144,248	17.8	10.0	5.1	10	58	22,528	24,815	86.7
Otter Tail, MN	27111	6	57,303	16.0	16.7	8.7	10	29	7,719	9,523	91.5
Pennington, MN	27113	6	13,930	17.0	14.4	5.7	3	6	2,210	2,330	91.2
Pine, MN	27115	6	29,750	16.4	20.2	8.4	5	15	3,918	5,063	92.4
Pipestone, MN	27117	6	9,596	18.0	13.9	7.5	2	7	1,481	1,730	80.3
Polk, MN	27119	3	31,600	17.2	14.0	6.2	8	21	5,027	5,473	91.6

[1]County type codes are from the Economic Research Service of the United States Department of Agriculture. See notes and definitions for more information.

Table C-1. Population, School, and Student Characteristics by County, Selected Years—*Continued*

County	State/ County Code	Characteristics of students, 2010–2011				Number of graduates, 2008–2009	Staff and students, 2010–2011			
		Percent with IEP[2]	Percent eligible for free or reduced lunch	Percent minority	Percent English-language learners		Total staff	Number of teachers	Student/ teacher ratio	Central admin. staff
		10	11	12	13	14	15	16	17	18
MINNESOTA	27000	14.7	36.5	26.2	5.8	59,680	108,993	52,672	15.9	4,368
Aitkin, MN	27001	17.0	51.4	8.5	0.1	159	299	142	14.4	16
Anoka, MN	27003	13.8	32.8	22.4	7.1	4,526	7,292	3,587	17.8	244
Becker, MN	27005	20.1	43.4	18.5	0.3	302	661	321	14.0	32
Beltrami, MN	27007	18.2	60.2	37.1	1.2	464	1,304	585	13.3	55
Benton, MN	27009	16.4	34.0	8.6	0.3	366	668	310	18.1	23
Big Stone, MN	27011	15.3	45.4	4.6	0.3	84	161	76	12.0	8
Blue Earth, MN	27013	18.1	34.9	14.7	3.0	709	1,386	652	15.5	50
Brown, MN	27015	16.6	35.1	11.2	2.2	319	507	253	13.9	24
Carlton, MN	27017	14.4	34.3	13.9	. . .	473	798	397	16.1	40
Carver, MN	27019	12.7	16.9	12.4	3.6	1,108	1,936	1,000	15.8	78
Cass, MN	27021	21.4	62.7	34.1	0.1	304	695	325	12.9	30
Chippewa, MN	27023	17.6	39.5	12.2	3.3	166	308	141	15.1	14
Chisago, MN	27025	11.2	26.1	5.1	0.8	618	876	423	18.8	56
Clay, MN	27027	14.8	32.3	13.8	5.0	532	1,088	543	16.5	37
Clearwater, MN	27029	17.7	52.3	24.5	. . .	105	204	106	14.3	12
Cook, MN	27031	17.5	39.0	21.9	. . .	45	104	47	13.2	9
Cottonwood, MN	27033	19.8	45.9	22.8	11.2	142	318	154	12.5	13
Crow Wing, MN	27035	17.0	43.2	5.3	. . .	714	1,227	566	17.0	43
Dakota, MN	27037	14.5	24.2	24.6	6.2	5,496	8,817	4,453	16.8	340
Dodge, MN	27039	11.1	25.5	10.9	4.0	265	458	252	16.4	16
Douglas, MN	27041	17.2	35.4	4.6	0.2	441	756	360	14.7	36
Faribault, MN	27043	20.0	45.6	11.8	3.3	150	296	128	15.2	16
Fillmore, MN	27045	13.4	37.0	2.3	. . .	253	371	190	13.0	20
Freeborn, MN	27047	18.3	45.8	14.8	5.6	317	579	280	14.4	25
Goodhue, MN	27049	12.4	26.2	11.1	2.0	625	880	440	15.7	35
Grant, MN	27051	14.3	38.8	5.4	. . .	95	164	83	13.1	9
Hennepin, MN	27053	13.9	40.2	44.7	12.0	10,027	21,810	10,047	15.7	895
Houston, MN	27055	8.2	24.3	7.6	. . .	403	459	247	17.6	22
Hubbard, MN	27057	19.0	53.2	11.5	. . .	152	318	161	14.3	17
Isanti, MN	27059	11.5	36.3	8.0	1.0	465	733	344	18.3	27
Itasca, MN	27061	16.1	45.5	15.1	. . .	546	874	394	16.6	43
Jackson, MN	27063	17.8	37.8	10.4	3.9	111	222	109	13.9	9
Kanabec, MN	27065	14.8	47.6	6.5	0.1	189	296	152	15.9	10
Kandiyohi, MN	27067	12.4	45.8	29.5	10.1	416	738	388	14.3	22
Kittson, MN	27069	18.8	39.9	5.7	. . .	68	139	68	10.6	9
Koochiching, MN	27071	13.7	40.5	10.6	0.3	156	289	130	15.3	11
Lac qui Parle, MN	27073	18.5	37.7	9.1	1.9	116	228	97	13.8	7
Lake, MN	27075	18.8	32.8	4.2	. . .	126	186	95	14.7	6
Lake of the Woods, MN	27077	15.5	48.9	8.8	. . .	48	80	38	14.0	4
Le Sueur, MN	27079	16.5	32.2	13.1	4.7	331	547	282	15.2	21
Lincoln, MN	27081	18.2	36.3	2.8	. . .	65	142	77	12.1	5
Lyon, MN	27083	15.1	39.7	18.8	10.4	388	763	345	12.3	61
McLeod, MN	27085	13.9	33.6	11.4	3.4	434	668	333	16.4	29
Mahnomen, MN	27087	19.5	73.2	69.8	. . .	82	217	116	12.0	9
Marshall, MN	27089	14.4	45.5	9.2	0.9	112	259	118	11.6	13
Martin, MN	27091	15.5	39.9	7.5	2.3	254	505	210	14.6	18
Meeker, MN	27093	15.3	39.9	6.3	0.9	246	460	235	15.0	19
Mille Lacs, MN	27095	14.9	40.9	9.6	0.2	464	812	409	15.9	31
Morrison, MN	27097	15.3	42.8	4.5	0.4	415	714	351	14.9	37
Mower, MN	27099	14.7	47.8	27.4	10.2	455	851	419	14.2	32
Murray, MN	27101	17.9	35.1	8.1	3.6	112	169	84	13.6	9
Nicollet, MN	27103	18.1	34.4	14.2	3.5	172	355	160	14.3	26
Nobles, MN	27105	16.3	56.7	48.2	13.0	248	561	273	13.1	18
Norman, MN	27107	17.0	45.8	13.0	1.5	99	200	92	12.2	7
Olmsted, MN	27109	11.9	31.0	25.5	10.0	1,625	2,599	1,340	16.8	101
Otter Tail, MN	27111	15.4	40.1	10.0	2.0	625	1,034	511	15.1	43
Pennington, MN	27113	17.0	39.1	13.3	1.3	157	331	156	14.2	16
Pine, MN	27115	12.0	49.7	11.1	0.6	305	559	283	13.9	25
Pipestone, MN	27117	15.9	43.1	10.8	4.1	75	218	106	13.9	8
Polk, MN	27119	15.2	37.7	14.1	1.3	404	733	353	14.3	36

[2]IEP=Individual Education Program. See notes and definitions for more information.
. . . = Not available.

Table C-1. Population, School, and Student Characteristics by County, Selected Years—*Continued*

County	State/ County Code	Revenues, 2008–2009				Current expenditures, 2008–2009			Resident population 16 to 19 years, 2006–2010			
			Percentage of revenue from									
		Total revenue ($1,000's)	Federal government	State government	Local government	Amount ($1,000's)	Amount per student	Percent for instruction	Total population 16 to 19 years	Percent enrolled in school	Percent high school graduates, not enrolled in school	Percent not enrolled, not grads, not employed, or not in labor force
		19	20	21	22	23	24	25	26	27	28	29
MINNESOTA	27000	10,735,056	5.7	64.4	29.9	9,219,479	11,061	65.1	301,424	88.5	7.9	2.2
Aitkin, MN	27001	23,709	6.9	70.5	22.6	22,236	10,986	65.4	668	75.6	23.7	0.5
Anoka, MN	27003	757,151	4.4	67.8	27.9	655,074	10,176	67.2	18,844	86.4	10.2	2.2
Becker, MN	27005	49,340	8.0	72.6	19.4	41,820	9,389	65.1	1,703	86.1	9.0	3.8
Beltrami, MN	27007	106,613	17.1	65.7	17.2	96,260	12,830	66.8	3,126	82.0	12.5	3.5
Benton, MN	27009	64,945	3.2	63.3	33.5	47,499	8,743	59.2	2,035	85.8	10.8	2.7
Big Stone, MN	27011	10,918	5.1	70.4	24.5	9,589	11,073	62.1	235	86.4	11.1	2.1
Blue Earth, MN	27013	110,648	4.4	69.1	26.5	93,295	9,355	66.8	5,351	92.8	5.7	0.8
Brown, MN	27015	43,801	7.1	67.0	25.9	37,072	10,739	68.1	1,561	94.2	3.4	0.5
Carlton, MN	27017	70,589	8.1	71.5	20.4	66,070	10,287	69.7	1,841	85.8	8.3	4.0
Carver, MN	27019	207,306	3.3	56.0	40.6	162,881	10,833	66.5	4,829	92.6	5.6	0.5
Cass, MN	27021	61,487	14.1	62.8	23.1	52,736	12,711	61.1	1,410	78.9	14.8	4.3
Chippewa, MN	27023	28,250	5.8	68.8	25.4	22,856	10,843	64.8	727	90.5	7.8	0.4
Chisago, MN	27025	91,302	4.7	69.0	26.3	74,293	8,889	63.8	2,847	84.6	11.2	0.8
Clay, MN	27027	96,890	4.7	74.4	20.9	89,590	10,129	69.1	5,289	91.7	5.8	1.6
Clearwater, MN	27029	17,817	7.8	71.4	20.8	14,654	9,915	63.1	413	76.3	17.2	5.6
Cook, MN	27031	9,282	8.0	61.7	30.3	6,582	10,236	65.5	146	98.6	0.7	0.0
Cottonwood, MN	27033	24,384	4.4	72.0	23.6	19,375	9,865	64.2	614	93.3	3.3	2.4
Crow Wing, MN	27035	115,498	6.2	68.0	25.8	116,755	12,011	70.3	3,280	83.8	12.0	3.1
Dakota, MN	27037	918,607	3.6	64.4	32.0	818,561	10,911	68.5	21,296	89.2	7.6	2.0
Dodge, MN	27039	39,805	2.5	75.1	22.4	31,941	7,834	63.9	1,155	88.8	8.8	1.7
Douglas, MN	27041	60,035	5.9	67.3	26.8	58,948	11,327	70.8	1,925	85.4	10.8	0.7
Faribault, MN	27043	24,087	8.0	71.4	20.6	21,317	10,543	70.2	855	89.0	8.7	1.9
Fillmore, MN	27045	30,713	5.3	69.8	24.9	25,595	9,710	66.7	1,138	81.2	5.5	8.3
Freeborn, MN	27047	49,103	5.0	73.5	21.5	47,690	11,674	67.7	1,593	89.1	9.2	1.4
Goodhue, MN	27049	92,640	4.4	65.1	30.5	73,801	9,032	65.8	2,496	84.7	10.7	2.2
Grant, MN	27051	12,980	4.1	72.0	23.9	11,141	9,654	61.6	282	81.6	11.7	1.8
Hennepin, MN	27053	2,269,809	6.2	60.7	33.1	1,862,827	12,069	65.7	58,806	90.2	6.4	2.1
Houston, MN	27055	42,428	2.3	78.0	19.7	37,036	9,109	65.2	1,075	82.1	14.7	0.2
Hubbard, MN	27057	28,915	6.0	65.5	28.5	23,408	9,741	66.2	994	83.6	11.3	4.1
Isanti, MN	27059	68,190	6.4	69.5	24.1	53,736	8,802	69.4	2,029	87.7	8.8	2.1
Itasca, MN	27061	80,462	7.4	67.8	24.8	104,168	15,747	77.2	2,338	90.2	8.9	0.8
Jackson, MN	27063	18,085	3.2	69.2	27.7	13,347	8,916	65.3	583	86.6	4.0	8.2
Kanabec, MN	27065	24,620	4.8	77.0	18.2	22,262	8,884	69.7	856	87.5	9.5	0.9
Kandiyohi, MN	27067	64,133	5.6	74.6	19.9	56,046	9,852	65.8	2,647	85.6	9.6	3.5
Kittson, MN	27069	10,715	3.9	72.2	23.9	9,226	12,484	62.1	213	80.3	15.0	4.2
Koochiching, MN	27071	24,422	5.6	74.9	19.6	21,391	10,642	63.3	590	82.2	14.4	1.5
Lac qui Parle, MN	27073	17,723	5.0	73.4	21.6	15,849	10,524	61.4	377	88.3	5.3	4.8
Lake, MN	27075	19,079	3.6	60.7	35.7	21,301	14,772	74.3	491	68.6	20.2	5.7
Lake of the Woods, MN	27077	7,926	3.2	62.1	34.7	5,967	11,112	58.6	227	90.8	9.3	0.0
Le Sueur, MN	27079	45,840	4.4	70.4	25.1	38,170	8,747	64.3	1,447	91.9	6.5	1.2
Lincoln, MN	27081	12,964	3.9	67.4	28.7	10,063	10,196	59.5	258	96.9	3.1	0.0
Lyon, MN	27083	162,908	7.0	23.6	69.4	150,955	35,959	26.2	1,745	92.8	6.7	0.4
McLeod, MN	27085	57,908	4.6	74.6	20.7	49,996	8,872	63.1	1,855	84.7	11.2	2.2
Mahnomen, MN	27087	19,379	20.0	67.1	12.9	16,045	11,956	62.9	314	77.1	13.1	7.0
Marshall, MN	27089	19,772	7.7	70.7	21.6	17,892	12,654	64.0	509	87.8	10.2	0.6
Martin, MN	27091	41,467	5.9	66.6	27.6	37,263	11,711	68.7	994	90.6	4.1	3.8
Meeker, MN	27093	37,177	5.2	71.9	22.8	31,189	8,942	63.3	1,175	86.0	11.3	1.0
Mille Lacs, MN	27095	69,416	6.2	72.8	21.1	60,863	9,129	65.5	1,428	79.9	13.3	1.8
Morrison, MN	27097	57,211	6.2	72.0	21.8	50,325	9,783	65.1	1,857	83.5	12.3	3.5
Mower, MN	27099	71,066	6.5	72.5	21.0	58,526	10,082	66.5	1,890	78.8	13.7	3.0
Murray, MN	27101	14,060	3.7	72.2	24.1	12,090	10,671	66.2	425	81.4	2.1	1.2
Nicollet, MN	27103	36,163	9.3	57.6	33.1	31,238	13,749	64.8	2,393	91.0	7.5	0.7
Nobles, MN	27105	45,333	6.3	75.8	17.9	36,822	9,728	64.8	1,362	80.8	5.7	8.9
Norman, MN	27107	13,980	4.5	78.5	17.0	12,349	10,351	63.4	342	81.9	11.1	5.3
Olmsted, MN	27109	248,854	5.9	68.1	26.0	202,880	9,159	63.7	7,045	89.1	6.9	2.0
Otter Tail, MN	27111	134,277	4.5	44.8	50.7	112,198	14,429	41.7	3,092	84.6	10.4	2.5
Pennington, MN	27113	78,910	2.7	24.0	73.3	72,651	33,083	17.6	780	88.0	10.5	1.3
Pine, MN	27115	44,215	5.4	70.8	23.9	36,245	9,272	65.9	1,426	82.2	12.9	3.9
Pipestone, MN	27117	14,717	3.6	72.1	24.3	11,417	9,783	60.1	445	89.7	8.8	0.9
Polk, MN	27119	59,071	7.2	73.1	19.7	51,040	9,973	66.0	1,973	89.4	6.5	3.7

Note. Data in columns 26 through 41 from the American Community Survey are subject to sampling error, which can be especially large in small counties and small population groups. See notes and definitions for more information.

Table C-1. Population, School, and Student Characteristics by County, Selected Years—*Continued*

County	State/ County Code	High school graduates, 2006–2010			College enrollment, 2006–2010		College graduates, 2006–2010 (percent)						
		Population 25 years and over	High school diploma or less (percent)	High school diploma or more (percent)	Number	Percent public	Bachelor's degree or more	+/- U.S. percent with Bachelor's degree or more	Non-Hispanic White	Black or African American	American Indian and Alaska Native	Asian, Hawaiian, and Pacific Islander	Hispanic or Latino[3]
		30	31	32	33	34	35	36	37	38	39	40	41
MINNESOTA	27000	3,450,999	36.5	91.3	372,005	71.2	31.4	3.5	32.4	19.4	11.9	41.9	15.2
Aitkin, MN	27001	12,533	51.7	88.1	341	75.1	14.4	-13.5	14.3	75.0	18.6	69.2	4.4
Anoka, MN	27003	213,702	37.7	92.8	18,490	72.5	25.8	-2.1	25.9	19.2	10.9	41.4	11.7
Becker, MN	27005	22,020	43.5	90.0	1,121	87.1	21.3	-6.6	22.1	17.4	13.0	26.5	0.0
Beltrami, MN	27007	26,354	38.8	89.0	4,714	91.9	29.1	1.2	32.5	1.7	11.0	42.2	22.6
Benton, MN	27009	24,392	44.2	90.2	2,695	84.0	19.6	-8.3	19.8	5.3	2.7	18.9	26.7
Big Stone, MN	27011	3,867	52.4	88.2	184	83.2	16.0	-11.9	15.8	0.0	50.0	0.0	0.0
Blue Earth, MN	27013	35,774	35.9	93.0	11,888	92.0	30.1	2.2	30.6	17.7	5.8	34.0	15.0
Brown, MN	27015	17,669	51.0	88.4	1,986	46.4	18.5	-9.4	18.8	0.0	0.0	22.6	6.4
Carlton, MN	27017	23,995	43.5	90.3	1,567	76.5	21.4	-6.5	22.1	25.4	7.8	61.5	5.7
Carver, MN	27019	55,940	27.3	94.8	4,182	62.4	42.7	14.8	43.1	50.0	11.5	51.1	19.9
Cass, MN	27021	20,447	46.7	89.6	715	85.5	20.2	-7.7	20.6	76.5	14.4	19.8	14.5
Chippewa, MN	27023	8,549	50.9	87.1	411	93.9	15.8	-12.1	16.1	0.0	15.1	50.0	6.2
Chisago, MN	27025	35,043	45.0	91.0	2,210	79.4	17.0	-10.9	17.4	0.0	8.6	29.6	10.3
Clay, MN	27027	33,714	36.4	92.4	7,998	66.1	31.5	3.6	32.3	13.4	0.9	52.5	11.1
Clearwater, MN	27029	5,888	52.6	84.4	230	92.6	14.5	-13.4	15.7	8.9	1.2	0.0	26.8
Cook, MN	27031	4,091	33.7	93.0	116	83.6	32.9	5.0	34.8	0.0	7.5	6.7	25.0
Cottonwood, MN	27033	8,134	53.8	84.9	263	81.0	15.7	-12.2	16.7	0.0	0.0	5.2	0.0
Crow Wing, MN	27035	42,642	39.8	91.3	2,499	88.8	22.0	-5.9	22.3	8.9	8.0	44.0	8.9
Dakota, MN	27037	256,491	28.7	94.4	22,956	68.5	38.1	10.2	39.5	23.2	14.3	44.5	16.5
Dodge, MN	27039	12,702	42.6	90.0	864	82.2	21.9	-6.0	22.1	60.0	0.0	44.0	9.6
Douglas, MN	27041	24,971	41.0	91.2	1,665	88.6	21.4	-6.5	21.6	8.5	2.9	38.5	15.3
Faribault, MN	27043	10,466	51.5	89.0	490	77.8	15.3	-12.6	15.8	0.0	0.0	6.3	4.2
Fillmore, MN	27045	14,342	50.3	86.7	690	76.1	19.3	-8.6	19.2	0.0	16.2	29.4	28.6
Freeborn, MN	27047	22,195	52.6	85.8	1,063	76.7	13.8	-14.1	14.2	0.0	27.1	24.4	3.2
Goodhue, MN	27049	31,477	42.8	90.2	1,765	73.5	22.7	-5.2	23.1	11.4	5.0	43.9	6.8
Grant, MN	27051	4,362	47.3	85.8	178	77.5	18.1	-9.8	18.4	0.0	0.0	0.0	0.0
Hennepin, MN	27053	762,723	27.7	92.1	96,366	72.2	44.0	16.1	48.4	19.8	15.7	48.1	18.6
Houston, MN	27055	13,309	45.8	91.1	722	79.2	22.0	-5.9	21.6	0.0	54.3	50.0	47.9
Hubbard, MN	27057	14,491	42.5	91.2	616	88.0	23.4	-4.5	23.0	0.0	28.9	74.1	12.8
Isanti, MN	27059	24,499	47.6	90.8	1,833	85.3	16.0	-11.9	15.9	33.9	15.8	27.4	24.7
Itasca, MN	27061	31,798	41.7	92.3	1,645	89.3	20.8	-7.1	21.1	0.0	5.9	30.7	12.5
Jackson, MN	27063	7,286	45.9	90.5	350	83.4	16.2	-11.7	15.9	50.0	0.0	35.7	9.3
Kanabec, MN	27065	11,256	55.1	87.1	623	79.1	13.9	-14.0	13.8	50.0	9.3	26.5	5.6
Kandiyohi, MN	27067	27,648	43.9	88.1	2,223	85.6	21.0	-6.9	22.4	7.7	4.6	47.4	2.5
Kittson, MN	27069	3,348	47.0	88.6	81	92.6	19.1	-8.8	19.4	0.0	0.0	0.0	0.0
Koochiching, MN	27071	9,710	50.6	89.0	333	92.2	16.3	-11.6	16.8	0.0	3.2	0.0	0.0
Lac qui Parle, MN	27073	5,358	50.4	88.4	185	90.8	16.2	-11.7	16.1	0.0	0.0	39.3	9.5
Lake, MN	27075	8,167	44.4	93.5	242	75.2	20.1	-7.8	19.8	0.0	11.9	61.4	0.0
Lake of the Woods, MN	27077	3,042	45.5	89.6	106	79.2	18.6	-9.3	18.8	0.0	0.0	21.7	0.0
Le Sueur, MN	27079	18,590	47.6	89.0	1,114	77.5	21.2	-6.7	21.5	0.0	27.6	54.7	11.6
Lincoln, MN	27081	4,275	52.4	89.8	224	95.5	17.8	-10.1	18.1	0.0	0.0	0.0	0.0
Lyon, MN	27083	15,972	43.1	88.2	2,644	95.3	25.7	-2.2	27.2	2.4	0.0	6.6	7.2
McLeod, MN	27085	24,513	46.6	89.4	1,558	76.1	18.3	-9.6	18.6	21.7	0.0	38.8	3.6
Mahnomen, MN	27087	3,368	53.7	83.6	138	87.7	13.5	-14.4	16.6	0.0	6.7	73.3	0.0
Marshall, MN	27089	6,744	52.9	85.4	263	89.0	16.0	-11.9	16.2	28.6	0.0	20.0	7.4
Martin, MN	27091	14,726	48.4	86.9	651	61.1	17.5	-10.4	17.9	0.0	0.0	34.5	2.1
Meeker, MN	27093	15,704	50.5	88.7	923	80.3	15.7	-12.2	16.1	0.0	12.5	0.0	3.0
Mille Lacs, MN	27095	17,420	51.1	87.7	993	75.1	14.9	-13.0	15.2	0.0	5.5	23.9	2.4
Morrison, MN	27097	22,231	53.1	86.6	1,030	84.2	14.5	-13.4	14.6	14.8	14.6	5.8	4.4
Mower, MN	27099	25,932	49.6	84.8	1,462	83.7	15.9	-12.0	16.6	0.0	12.5	11.8	8.8
Murray, MN	27101	6,353	50.8	87.8	249	82.7	15.0	-12.9	15.0	0.0	17.2	20.0	7.8
Nicollet, MN	27103	19,696	34.4	92.2	3,931	32.6	33.7	5.8	33.4	35.7	73.3	84.8	20.6
Nobles, MN	27105	13,679	54.7	78.5	1,120	90.9	16.0	-11.9	17.3	50.9	0.0	27.8	3.6
Norman, MN	27107	4,826	53.1	87.6	168	76.8	14.9	-13.0	15.3	0.0	9.4	42.9	5.9
Olmsted, MN	27109	93,614	29.5	94.3	8,931	75.3	39.2	11.3	39.9	19.9	12.9	49.7	23.4
Otter Tail, MN	27111	40,774	46.4	88.2	1,700	86.5	19.7	-8.2	20.1	15.4	4.0	10.9	7.4
Pennington, MN	27113	9,318	48.3	87.5	554	89.0	15.4	-12.5	15.3	4.2	5.0	62.0	10.8
Pine, MN	27115	20,587	55.7	85.9	988	78.7	12.9	-15.0	13.3	3.4	2.8	22.5	16.2
Pipestone, MN	27117	6,519	49.1	85.7	311	78.5	15.4	-12.5	15.9	85.7	0.0	25.0	0.0
Polk, MN	27119	20,646	45.2	86.8	1,930	91.3	20.6	-7.3	21.4	11.0	1.8	32.9	7.8

Note. Data in columns 26 through 41 from the American Community Survey are subject to sampling error, which can be especially large in small counties and small population groups. See notes and definitions for more information.

[3]May be of any race.

Table C-1. Population, School, and Student Characteristics by County, Selected Years—*Continued*

County	State/ County Code	County Type[1]	Population, 2010		Percent of related children 5–17 years in poverty, 2010	Percent of children under 19 years with no health insurance, 2010	Number of schools and students, 2010–2011			Resident enrollment, 2006–2010 K-12 enrollment	
			Total	Percent 5–17 years			School districts	Schools	Students	Number	Percent public
			1	2	3	4	5	6	7	8	9
MINNESOTA—*(Continued)*											
Pope, MN	27121	8	10,995	15.3	14.1	8.5	3	9	1,232	1,683	90.8
Ramsey, MN	27123	1	508,640	16.4	23.6	6.4	37	249	83,428	85,128	85.5
Red Lake, MN	27125	8	4,089	17.7	14.7	7.5	4	6	768	737	85.5
Redwood, MN	27127	7	16,059	18.3	12.7	7.4	7	15	2,688	2,967	87.5
Renville, MN	27129	9	15,730	17.5	14.9	7.8	3	6	1,843	2,890	90.8
Rice, MN	27131	4	64,142	17.3	10.4	7.2	7	24	8,331	11,022	88.5
Rock, MN	27133	6	9,687	18.8	11.0	7.5	2	7	1,589	1,656	92.9
Roseau, MN	27135	7	15,629	19.8	10.8	7.9	4	13	3,060	3,315	93.4
St. Louis, MN	27137	2	200,226	14.3	17.4	6.4	21	103	25,019	28,773	90.5
Scott, MN	27139	1	129,928	22.0	5.4	5.6	8	40	21,831	26,901	86.8
Sherburne, MN	27141	1	88,499	21.4	7.3	5.9	4	36	19,509	18,370	92.1
Sibley, MN	27143	8	15,226	18.8	12.9	8.9	5	10	2,324	2,879	88.9
Stearns, MN	27145	3	150,642	16.7	11.5	6.2	16	61	23,284	24,305	84.9
Steele, MN	27147	5	36,576	19.1	11.7	5.8	3	17	6,516	6,905	90.7
Stevens, MN	27149	7	9,726	14.8	9.5	7.3	4	7	1,397	1,384	86.9
Swift, MN	27151	7	9,783	16.6	12.1	7.9	2	7	1,522	1,756	94.5
Todd, MN	27153	6	24,895	18.2	23.6	12.3	8	18	3,651	4,410	86.4
Traverse, MN	27155	9	3,558	16.9	17.2	10.7	2	4	534	602	97.5
Wabasha, MN	27157	3	21,676	17.2	10.1	6.9	4	12	4,520	3,809	95.8
Wadena, MN	27159	7	13,843	17.4	22.8	7.5	4	8	2,845	2,381	96.2
Waseca, MN	27161	7	19,136	17.3	13.7	5.9	4	13	3,610	3,475	90.8
Washington, MN	27163	1	238,136	20.3	5.9	4.4	12	73	38,907	48,189	88.8
Watonwan, MN	27165	7	11,211	18.2	15.0	10.6	3	8	1,868	2,138	94.8
Wilkin, MN	27167	6	6,576	18.3	11.9	6.1	3	8	1,132	1,232	89.7
Winona, MN	27169	4	51,461	14.1	13.9	8.0	8	28	5,597	7,361	79.6
Wright, MN	27171	1	124,700	21.4	6.8	6.0	13	65	25,937	24,901	91.7
Yellow Medicine, MN	27173	9	10,438	17.4	16.8	6.8	5	7	1,647	1,867	93.2
MISSISSIPPI	28000	X	2,967,297	18.4	30.2	9.0	164	1,083	490,526	552,770	89.1
Adams, MS	28001	5	32,297	16.1	40.3	8.8	1	8	3,869	5,516	82.0
Alcorn, MS	28003	7	37,057	17.6	29.4	8.6	2	18	5,691	6,667	93.6
Amite, MS	28005	8	13,131	15.8	34.5	12.2	1	3	1,090	2,237	66.3
Attala, MS	28007	6	19,564	18.5	33.1	9.0	2	11	3,481	3,684	88.6
Benton, MS	28009	8	8,729	18.1	35.7	9.3	1	5	1,285	1,554	97.0
Bolivar, MS	28011	5	34,145	17.8	48.3	6.7	6	24	6,496	6,756	94.8
Calhoun, MS	28013	7	14,962	17.9	30.2	11.5	1	9	2,548	2,792	89.2
Carroll, MS	28015	9	10,597	15.5	27.4	12.2	1	3	934	1,818	72.0
Chickasaw, MS	28017	7	17,392	19.0	32.9	10.7	3	9	3,160	3,486	95.5
Choctaw, MS	28019	9	8,547	17.9	35.2	11.3	1	6	1,573	1,702	91.3
Claiborne, MS	28021	6	9,604	17.5	47.1	9.3	1	4	1,762	1,898	86.2
Clarke, MS	28023	9	16,732	18.2	37.1	10.9	2	9	2,996	3,419	89.9
Clay, MS	28025	7	20,634	18.7	37.6	8.4	2	9	3,461	3,982	87.1
Coahoma, MS	28027	5	26,151	21.2	48.6	6.6	3	17	5,170	5,789	90.0
Copiah, MS	28029	2	29,449	17.8	33.9	9.1	2	6	4,360	5,573	81.2
Covington, MS	28031	8	19,568	18.7	31.6	10.5	1	10	3,136	3,960	92.3
De Soto, MS	28033	1	161,252	21.1	13.8	9.6	1	40	31,916	32,465	87.8
Forrest, MS	28035	3	74,934	16.4	33.7	8.4	4	22	11,534	12,459	89.1
Franklin, MS	28037	9	8,118	18.4	29.5	10.6	1	5	1,507	1,660	89.2
George, MS	28039	3	22,578	19.5	23.6	10.0	1	8	4,254	4,302	96.4
Greene, MS	28041	8	14,400	16.2	24.2	12.2	1	6	2,085	2,264	94.4
Grenada, MS	28043	7	21,906	18.0	31.3	8.7	1	6	4,344	4,099	88.3
Hancock, MS	28045	3	43,929	17.6	28.1	12.9	2	12	6,256	7,848	86.9
Harrison, MS	28047	3	187,105	17.1	27.8	9.7	7	53	29,058	31,643	87.8
Hinds, MS	28049	2	245,285	19.2	32.9	7.4	6	88	41,542	49,336	87.7
Holmes, MS	28051	6	19,198	20.4	52.8	7.8	2	12	3,718	4,097	92.2
Humphreys, MS	28053	7	9,375	19.7	58.9	7.3	1	5	1,782	2,178	90.0
Issaquena, MS	28055	9	1,406	15.0	57.8	12.0	...	...	...	375	83.7
Itawamba, MS	28057	7	23,401	16.9	23.7	8.6	1	8	3,627	3,778	96.0
Jackson, MS	28059	3	139,668	18.7	21.3	9.2	4	50	24,302	25,764	94.0
Jasper, MS	28061	9	17,062	17.7	29.0	11.5	2	8	2,568	3,289	87.8
Jefferson, MS	28063	7	7,726	17.4	47.0	8.8	1	6	1,414	1,401	96.4

[1]County type codes are from the Economic Research Service of the United States Department of Agriculture. See notes and definitions for more information.

Table C-1. Population, School, and Student Characteristics by County, Selected Years—*Continued*

County	State/ County Code	Characteristics of students, 2010–2011				Number of graduates, 2008–2009	Staff and students, 2010–2011			
		Percent with IEP[2]	Percent eligible for free or reduced lunch	Percent minority	Percent English-language learners		Total staff	Number of teachers	Student/ teacher ratio	Central admin. staff
		10	11	12	13	14	15	16	17	18
MINNESOTA—*(Continued)*										
Pope, MN	27121	22.6	40.0	4.6	0.2	90	229	93	13.3	9
Ramsey, MN	27123	15.8	55.7	55.9	6.4	6,001	11,587	5,258	15.9	414
Red Lake, MN	27125	14.2	49.8	11.2	...	57	141	68	11.3	8
Redwood, MN	27127	15.9	37.9	19.0	0.7	204	400	210	12.8	20
Renville, MN	27129	17.9	42.9	19.4	9.0	175	286	138	13.4	8
Rice, MN	27131	16.0	37.4	21.2	11.2	629	1,203	553	15.1	55
Rock, MN	27133	14.4	35.6	8.9	2.0	121	220	112	14.3	6
Roseau, MN	27135	16.0	34.2	8.7	0.5	240	422	202	15.2	16
St. Louis, MN	27137	16.0	40.8	12.8	0.1	1,841	3,253	1,580	15.8	145
Scott, MN	27139	13.9	21.8	19.8	5.6	1,207	2,481	1,256	17.4	89
Sherburne, MN	27141	14.6	28.7	11.2	2.4	1,261	1,942	1,011	19.3	65
Sibley, MN	27143	15.6	41.4	21.3	7.1	170	308	165	14.1	11
Stearns, MN	27145	17.4	34.5	15.1	6.3	1,694	3,110	1,518	15.3	104
Steele, MN	27147	12.4	33.0	16.9	4.2	475	740	381	17.1	28
Stevens, MN	27149	18.3	29.1	7.7	1.6	115	215	103	13.6	12
Swift, MN	27151	14.0	39.2	8.7	1.7	133	221	105	14.5	9
Todd, MN	27153	17.0	57.3	14.6	6.5	375	635	285	12.8	52
Traverse, MN	27155	11.2	39.3	14.4	1.7	33	85	45	12.0	5
Wabasha, MN	27157	13.3	28.2	5.6	1.4	304	500	293	15.4	23
Wadena, MN	27159	16.0	56.9	4.4	...	224	393	200	14.2	18
Waseca, MN	27161	15.5	33.6	10.7	3.0	266	518	233	15.5	17
Washington, MN	27163	12.3	18.7	19.2	2.3	2,789	4,337	2,220	17.5	168
Watonwan, MN	27165	17.9	53.8	41.9	10.4	134	280	132	14.2	9
Wilkin, MN	27167	19.9	40.1	8.2	1.8	84	171	86	13.2	10
Winona, MN	27169	16.0	35.4	11.7	2.4	488	859	417	13.4	33
Wright, MN	27171	12.7	24.3	7.7	1.8	1,768	2,969	1,542	16.8	105
Yellow Medicine, MN	27173	19.4	49.5	18.1	2.4	133	270	133	12.4	10
MISSISSIPPI	28000	13.0	70.6	54.0	1.1	24,453	67,863	32,255	15.2	3,021
Adams, MS	28001	16.9	94.6	91.4	0.4	173	604	251	15.4	36
Alcorn, MS	28003	13.2	59.7	17.1	1.4	264	719	373	15.3	25
Amite, MS	28005	22.0	90.5	85.0	...	51	208	85	12.9	10
Attala, MS	28007	15.1	71.7	54.0	0.1	141	478	230	15.1	21
Benton, MS	28009	15.4	90.8	53.8	0.9	67	178	80	16.2	10
Bolivar, MS	28011	13.2	86.7	82.6	0.4	373	962	436	14.9	63
Calhoun, MS	28013	15.0	80.1	45.0	4.7	119	307	129	19.8	12
Carroll, MS	28015	16.1	90.4	67.6	...	45	127	67	14.0	5
Chickasaw, MS	28017	17.0	80.5	60.5	1.6	129	442	216	14.6	21
Choctaw, MS	28019	12.8	70.9	36.0	...	73	261	122	12.9	10
Claiborne, MS	28021	13.1	97.6	99.7	...	123	258	108	16.4	14
Clarke, MS	28023	13.3	66.3	37.2	0.2	183	427	217	13.8	28
Clay, MS	28025	11.7	87.2	82.0	0.2	132	478	202	17.1	24
Coahoma, MS	28027	13.1	95.6	96.8	0.2	229	827	355	14.6	48
Copiah, MS	28029	10.8	82.8	73.9	1.3	195	593	269	16.2	35
Covington, MS	28031	19.4	77.9	55.0	0.6	166	473	219	14.3	17
De Soto, MS	28033	13.6	49.2	38.4	2.9	1,551	3,507	1,746	18.3	95
Forrest, MS	28035	15.8	73.9	55.1	1.7	562	1,670	850	13.6	97
Franklin, MS	28037	17.5	71.7	44.8	...	65	223	111	13.6	13
George, MS	28039	13.7	69.8	11.8	0.7	185	586	268	15.9	19
Greene, MS	28041	13.1	81.2	18.3	0.1	85	308	145	14.4	13
Grenada, MS	28043	14.8	66.4	48.8	0.1	230	557	242	17.9	22
Hancock, MS	28045	15.9	69.2	15.3	0.5	285	814	394	15.9	44
Harrison, MS	28047	12.0	66.2	41.3	1.1	1,428	3,888	1,833	15.9	166
Hinds, MS	28049	10.7	80.5	90.0	0.5	1,990	5,974	2,590	16.0	252
Holmes, MS	28051	14.9	96.9	99.4	...	227	564	225	16.5	25
Humphreys, MS	28053	15.8	96.1	99.3	0.1	94	268	108	16.5	15
Issaquena, MS	28055	...	...	...	...	...	...	...	...	...
Itawamba, MS	28057	15.4	65.4	9.2	...	230	477	240	15.1	13
Jackson, MS	28059	11.7	59.9	36.2	3.0	1,388	3,763	1,744	13.9	170
Jasper, MS	28061	12.4	88.2	77.6	0.6	165	415	180	14.3	32
Jefferson, MS	28063	15.7	98.2	99.6	...	89	239	106	13.4	14

[2]IEP=Individual Education Program. See notes and definitions for more information.
. . . = Not available.

Table C-1. Population, School, and Student Characteristics by County, Selected Years—*Continued*

County	State/ County Code	Revenues, 2008–2009				Current expenditures, 2008–2009			Resident population 16 to 19 years, 2006–2010			
		Total revenue ($1,000's)	Percentage of revenue from			Amount ($1,000's)	Amount per student	Percent for instruction	Total population 16 to 19 years	Percent enrolled in school	Percent high school graduates, not enrolled in school	Percent not enrolled, not grads, not employed, or not in labor force
			Federal government	State government	Local government							
		19	20	21	22	23	24	25	26	27	28	29
MINNESOTA— *(Continued)*												
Pope, MN	27121	17,517	5.4	66.6	28.0	15,868	11,913	72.8	555	91.4	4.3	1.8
Ramsey, MN	27123	1,220,182	7.5	65.5	27.0	1,126,973	13,606	65.7	31,953	88.8	7.1	2.8
Red Lake, MN	27125	10,337	7.4	72.9	19.7	8,691	11,761	63.0	217	79.3	17.1	3.7
Redwood, MN	27127	30,507	5.2	72.7	22.1	25,766	9,445	62.6	848	85.9	6.5	6.6
Renville, MN	27129	21,780	5.6	73.7	20.6	18,458	9,004	61.7	845	89.0	7.3	1.9
Rice, MN	27131	99,607	4.9	66.6	28.5	75,117	8,949	66.8	5,097	93.1	4.1	1.3
Rock, MN	27133	16,865	3.5	75.3	21.2	13,809	8,875	65.6	525	86.1	6.9	5.7
Roseau, MN	27135	35,641	5.3	75.4	19.3	30,448	9,731	62.5	916	83.1	13.8	2.3
St. Louis, MN	27137	326,743	9.2	66.3	24.5	293,626	11,491	67.8	13,156	89.5	7.9	1.6
Scott, MN	27139	234,661	3.0	61.9	35.1	183,881	8,902	66.9	6,685	86.3	10.1	1.8
Sherburne, MN	27141	211,965	2.2	65.9	31.9	167,682	8,731	65.2	4,905	85.6	10.3	3.1
Sibley, MN	27143	24,634	4.3	75.4	20.3	21,525	9,478	68.3	818	88.1	11.4	0.5
Stearns, MN	27145	260,561	6.2	71.9	21.9	227,035	9,885	67.2	11,528	92.3	5.0	1.5
Steele, MN	27147	70,378	5.4	71.4	23.2	58,504	9,005	65.7	1,932	87.7	8.8	1.7
Stevens, MN	27149	18,647	6.4	59.9	33.7	14,526	10,611	70.6	873	88.3	10.8	0.0
Swift, MN	27151	17,081	4.9	74.9	20.2	15,037	9,880	65.6	558	69.4	28.7	1.4
Todd, MN	27153	57,729	10.7	64.2	25.1	48,743	12,770	66.3	1,523	78.8	9.9	5.7
Traverse, MN	27155	6,908	6.8	71.6	21.5	6,168	11,638	63.8	193	82.9	14.5	2.6
Wabasha, MN	27157	34,445	2.8	74.1	23.1	29,512	8,225	64.6	1,118	81.0	16.8	2.1
Wadena, MN	27159	29,895	6.0	78.9	15.1	24,353	8,545	63.7	799	88.1	9.6	1.9
Waseca, MN	27161	42,012	6.6	68.1	25.3	35,878	9,997	67.5	1,047	84.3	5.4	10.0
Washington, MN	27163	443,173	3.2	63.0	33.8	370,434	9,494	66.1	12,982	93.6	4.7	1.3
Watonwan, MN	27165	22,173	5.0	76.1	18.9	18,819	9,524	63.3	601	88.0	9.3	1.2
Wilkin, MN	27167	13,068	5.1	73.0	21.9	11,088	9,501	64.4	341	76.3	21.7	1.5
Winona, MN	27169	75,430	8.1	63.1	28.8	72,132	12,819	68.7	4,859	92.0	6.3	1.1
Wright, MN	27171	292,362	4.3	64.5	31.2	221,756	8,761	67.6	6,308	87.2	9.9	1.4
Yellow Medicine, MN	27173	21,660	7.5	68.6	23.8	19,238	11,485	68.6	602	80.1	11.6	4.0
MISSISSIPPI	28000	4,392,101	15.4	53.1	31.5	3,966,274	8,075	58.4	183,977	81.9	9.8	6.0
Adams, MS	28001	38,050	21.0	49.0	30.0	37,120	9,308	56.4	2,367	68.0	13.3	15.1
Alcorn, MS	28003	50,072	14.0	58.7	27.3	44,066	7,746	65.2	1,938	78.0	8.3	12.6
Amite, MS	28005	13,044	21.6	44.8	33.6	11,405	8,952	54.0	690	65.5	11.2	21.5
Attala, MS	28007	29,049	13.2	57.1	29.6	26,003	7,601	60.8	1,189	85.7	6.4	3.5
Benton, MS	28009	10,742	20.6	63.7	15.7	9,949	7,386	57.8	517	72.5	18.2	1.9
Bolivar, MS	28011	63,425	25.4	51.5	23.1	61,418	9,285	56.0	2,547	79.4	13.3	6.8
Calhoun, MS	28013	20,705	14.7	67.0	18.3	21,054	8,237	55.6	885	83.1	12.4	2.9
Carroll, MS	28015	9,443	18.3	51.1	30.7	8,714	9,280	57.5	798	88.2	10.8	1.0
Chickasaw, MS	28017	27,599	17.3	64.3	18.4	25,410	7,797	59.8	951	75.1	13.7	10.6
Choctaw, MS	28019	16,494	19.2	47.4	33.4	16,235	10,211	59.0	611	91.0	4.9	4.1
Claiborne, MS	28021	15,892	18.7	49.6	31.7	15,637	8,880	60.1	1,001	92.6	4.9	2.5
Clarke, MS	28023	25,690	16.0	55.2	28.8	24,714	8,420	57.5	1,016	91.9	2.0	6.1
Clay, MS	28025	31,809	21.2	54.8	24.0	29,915	8,470	54.4	1,115	87.3	8.1	3.4
Coahoma, MS	28027	48,989	23.7	55.0	21.2	45,763	8,583	54.8	1,852	82.8	6.8	7.8
Copiah, MS	28029	35,332	18.6	58.8	22.6	32,267	7,178	55.0	2,256	83.9	5.5	8.9
Covington, MS	28031	28,759	14.8	53.6	31.6	26,442	8,159	59.4	1,094	82.4	13.7	3.9
De Soto, MS	28033	240,093	7.3	56.5	36.2	201,685	6,588	57.5	8,538	83.5	12.3	2.5
Forrest, MS	28035	109,969	15.3	51.7	33.0	102,165	8,923	57.9	4,976	88.6	7.8	2.2
Franklin, MS	28037	14,947	17.7	51.2	31.1	14,114	9,569	59.6	398	85.9	10.1	3.0
George, MS	28039	31,392	13.1	68.2	18.7	28,524	6,775	63.0	1,120	74.4	19.3	3.8
Greene, MS	28041	17,089	14.5	62.2	23.4	16,443	8,076	61.0	647	71.6	16.4	7.0
Grenada, MS	28043	36,945	15.7	60.4	23.9	32,039	7,219	60.9	1,173	69.8	7.5	21.9
Hancock, MS	28045	67,957	25.5	39.2	35.3	57,775	9,621	51.7	2,472	79.7	14.2	3.0
Harrison, MS	28047	282,375	19.6	43.6	36.8	251,092	9,044	56.6	10,854	74.9	13.5	5.6
Hinds, MS	28049	374,222	13.7	50.6	35.6	337,656	7,999	57.0	16,525	85.6	7.0	4.8
Holmes, MS	28051	33,870	26.0	58.3	15.7	32,631	8,445	51.7	1,401	90.2	4.4	5.4
Humphreys, MS	28053	16,626	27.0	54.8	18.2	13,601	7,360	51.0	648	88.9	2.9	8.2
Issaquena, MS	28055	...	...	...	...	...	...	...	85	62.4	12.9	24.7
Itawamba, MS	28057	31,993	10.4	57.5	32.1	27,032	7,534	64.0	1,762	85.6	8.2	6.2
Jackson, MS	28059	237,262	16.6	46.5	37.0	216,885	8,822	56.0	8,452	79.2	11.1	6.3
Jasper, MS	28061	24,795	16.7	54.4	28.8	22,782	8,263	52.5	1,215	90.3	5.4	0.0
Jefferson, MS	28063	12,478	20.3	58.7	21.0	12,244	8,307	54.9	499	82.4	8.2	9.4

Note. Data in columns 26 through 41 from the American Community Survey are subject to sampling error, which can be especially large in small counties and small population groups. See notes and definitions for more information.

Table C-1. Population, School, and Student Characteristics by County, Selected Years—*Continued*

County	State/ County Code	High school graduates, 2006–2010			College enrollment, 2006–2010		College graduates, 2006–2010 (percent)						
		Population 25 years and over	High school diploma or less (percent)	High school diploma or more (percent)	Number	Percent public	Bachelor's degree or more	+/- U.S. percent with Bachelor's degree or more	Non-Hispanic White	Black or African American	American Indian and Alaska Native	Asian, Hawaiian, and Pacific Islander	Hispanic or Latino[3]
		30	31	32	33	34	35	36	37	38	39	40	41
MINNESOTA— *(Continued)*													
Pope, MN	27121	7,967	48.8	89.8	280	81.4	18.4	-9.5	18.2	0.0	53.9	0.0	0.0
Ramsey, MN	27123	324,224	33.9	89.9	49,575	55.6	38.9	11.0	43.9	17.3	13.7	31.5	15.8
Red Lake, MN	27125	2,857	54.3	86.7	74	98.6	13.0	-14.9	13.4	0.0	0.0	0.0	0.0
Redwood, MN	27127	10,955	51.9	86.6	533	82.2	16.5	-11.4	17.0	0.0	9.8	3.2	0.0
Renville, MN	27129	11,084	52.3	85.9	505	82.8	16.0	-11.9	16.6	0.0	45.5	0.0	1.6
Rice, MN	27131	38,539	43.0	90.2	6,920	26.2	27.1	-0.8	28.5	17.3	12.4	47.4	5.8
Rock, MN	27133	6,471	49.3	89.0	368	79.9	16.8	-11.1	16.9	19.5	0.0	0.0	18.5
Roseau, MN	27135	10,529	53.4	87.5	341	75.1	16.4	-11.5	16.7	0.0	4.0	11.7	9.5
St. Louis, MN	27137	133,796	38.4	92.1	19,860	81.9	25.6	-2.3	26.0	6.9	18.6	45.4	18.8
Scott, MN	27139	79,509	30.9	93.9	5,941	64.9	36.0	8.1	37.0	24.8	15.4	39.0	14.5
Sherburne, MN	27141	53,722	36.9	93.0	4,624	73.6	24.2	-3.7	24.6	4.0	4.8	43.5	8.1
Sibley, MN	27143	10,273	55.3	86.5	441	74.4	13.4	-14.5	13.8	0.0	13.3	22.7	4.0
Stearns, MN	27145	89,467	41.3	89.9	19,836	72.0	23.6	-4.3	23.8	14.9	13.0	36.5	10.8
Steele, MN	27147	24,202	46.2	89.5	1,473	78.4	22.0	-5.9	22.9	0.0	0.0	34.1	12.6
Stevens, MN	27149	5,839	47.6	89.7	1,408	96.9	23.6	-4.3	23.5	0.0	13.6	0.0	35.0
Swift, MN	27151	7,074	54.5	87.0	206	81.6	15.2	-12.7	15.9	1.0	0.0	36.4	3.2
Todd, MN	27153	16,606	52.2	85.8	553	88.6	12.2	-15.7	12.5	38.5	0.0	5.7	3.9
Traverse, MN	27155	2,677	52.5	88.1	91	87.9	14.7	-13.2	14.6	0.0	0.0	0.0	40.0
Wabasha, MN	27157	15,010	50.1	90.2	882	79.7	17.9	-10.0	18.1	5.8	0.0	55.0	6.2
Wadena, MN	27159	9,548	49.4	87.8	528	88.6	14.8	-13.1	15.0	0.0	6.5	86.7	2.4
Waseca, MN	27161	13,193	48.8	90.5	708	79.0	18.3	-9.6	19.2	1.6	2.2	15.8	7.2
Washington, MN	27163	151,939	27.9	95.7	14,117	70.5	40.0	12.1	40.0	38.4	6.4	51.6	29.7
Watonwan, MN	27165	7,581	57.6	79.6	400	78.0	15.0	-12.9	17.3	90.3	0.0	0.0	2.7
Wilkin, MN	27167	4,589	42.9	88.0	189	94.7	18.4	-9.5	19.1	0.0	0.0	0.0	0.0
Winona, MN	27169	30,060	41.9	88.8	9,249	75.7	25.1	-2.8	25.2	4.0	51.5	25.8	21.4
Wright, MN	27171	76,203	40.9	93.0	4,997	70.9	23.8	-4.1	24.1	21.3	22.0	26.3	12.7
Yellow Medicine, MN	27173	7,203	47.9	90.1	418	87.8	18.4	-9.5	18.6	0.0	13.1	65.0	2.1
MISSISSIPPI	28000	1,876,719	51.3	79.6	196,045	85.7	19.5	-8.4	23.2	12.4	11.7	38.4	11.6
Adams, MS	28001	21,170	53.0	79.6	2,106	82.8	19.3	-8.6	25.3	13.9	0.0	15.6	25.0
Alcorn, MS	28003	24,943	59.2	77.1	1,334	84.5	16.0	-11.9	16.5	9.5	0.0	55.8	19.6
Amite, MS	28005	9,079	65.0	74.0	274	80.3	9.2	-18.7	11.8	4.9	0.0	0.0	29.4
Attala, MS	28007	12,826	56.8	71.9	919	95.9	17.1	-10.8	20.5	11.9	0.0	60.0	0.0
Benton, MS	28009	5,843	68.8	69.1	195	35.9	9.6	-18.3	12.9	4.0	0.0	0.0	0.0
Bolivar, MS	28011	21,469	55.8	71.5	3,160	85.2	20.4	-7.5	32.6	12.9	0.0	46.3	0.0
Calhoun, MS	28013	9,998	65.7	67.4	511	95.1	10.1	-17.8	11.9	6.1	0.0	0.0	4.0
Carroll, MS	28015	7,553	56.9	76.3	397	86.1	16.4	-11.5	20.4	5.7	0.0	100.0	0.0
Chickasaw, MS	28017	11,297	64.7	71.8	1,069	92.0	11.2	-16.7	14.5	5.7	0.0	56.8	5.5
Choctaw, MS	28019	5,906	59.9	80.7	216	92.1	10.9	-17.0	14.4	1.7	0.0	100.0	0.0
Claiborne, MS	28021	5,780	52.7	83.6	1,237	97.8	17.5	-10.4	24.4	15.7	0.0	0.0	0.0
Clarke, MS	28023	11,156	63.3	75.1	747	92.4	8.3	-19.6	9.1	5.8	0.0	78.1	0.0
Clay, MS	28025	13,529	54.1	78.4	1,196	95.6	18.1	-9.8	25.3	12.0	0.0	100.0	0.0
Coahoma, MS	28027	15,810	54.8	74.2	1,891	96.9	14.3	-13.6	20.6	11.2	0.0	30.6	15.5
Copiah, MS	28029	18,737	55.1	76.5	2,101	92.6	14.1	-13.8	19.0	8.9	5.6	42.9	1.7
Covington, MS	28031	12,670	57.0	78.8	1,028	75.0	15.8	-12.1	19.6	8.0	0.0	13.3	0.0
De Soto, MS	28033	98,618	44.0	87.5	8,444	80.8	21.1	-6.8	22.4	18.0	11.7	36.5	6.9
Forrest, MS	28035	44,152	44.1	84.2	9,827	89.2	25.9	-2.0	29.7	17.2	25.3	61.2	21.7
Franklin, MS	28037	5,335	58.1	78.4	298	93.3	13.2	-14.7	16.1	5.6	0.0	62.1	0.0
George, MS	28039	14,125	61.1	83.7	609	82.6	11.0	-16.9	12.2	2.2	0.0	0.0	0.0
Greene, MS	28041	9,439	69.8	73.3	478	95.4	8.3	-19.6	10.5	2.9	0.0	0.0	3.2
Grenada, MS	28043	14,677	55.2	73.9	1,109	92.2	18.6	-9.3	23.4	9.7	0.0	100.0	0.0
Hancock, MS	28045	28,793	48.3	83.2	2,234	92.0	21.7	-6.2	21.9	16.4	20.6	28.0	19.5
Harrison, MS	28047	117,668	45.7	83.5	10,811	84.0	20.0	-7.9	22.3	13.1	3.6	21.5	15.5
Hinds, MS	28049	150,884	41.0	83.6	23,233	72.7	27.2	-0.7	41.0	19.1	30.3	54.2	17.6
Holmes, MS	28051	11,470	66.1	67.3	1,562	89.8	11.2	-16.7	18.4	9.2	0.0	74.1	0.0
Humphreys, MS	28053	5,878	66.3	62.9	509	89.6	11.5	-16.4	16.9	9.0	0.0	0.0	14.3
Issaquena, MS	28055	1,206	79.8	59.7	58	58.6	4.3	-23.6	7.3	1.6	0.0	0.0	0.0
Itawamba, MS	28057	15,218	61.0	71.4	1,712	94.9	12.4	-15.5	12.8	3.9	35.3	48.7	5.5
Jackson, MS	28059	89,576	48.9	84.6	7,121	83.9	18.4	-9.5	20.9	10.6	2.5	13.5	13.7
Jasper, MS	28061	11,450	60.0	76.9	826	91.8	11.6	-16.3	17.4	5.0	39.1	0.0	10.0
Jefferson, MS	28063	5,369	63.9	76.6	425	100.0	20.5	-7.4	27.7	18.6	0.0	100.0	0.0

Note. Data in columns 26 through 41 from the American Community Survey are subject to sampling error, which can be especially large in small counties and small population groups. See notes and definitions for more information.
[3]May be of any race.

Table C-1. Population, School, and Student Characteristics by County, Selected Years—*Continued*

County	State/ County Code	County Type[1]	Population, 2010		Percent of related children 5–17 years in poverty, 2010	Percent of children under 19 years with no health insurance, 2010	Number of schools and students, 2010–2011			Resident enrollment, 2006–2010	
										K–12 enrollment	
			Total	Percent 5–17 years			School districts	Schools	Students	Number	Percent public
			1	2	3	4	5	6	7	8	9
MISSISSIPPI— *(Continued)*											
Jefferson Davis, MS	28065	8	12,487	17.1	38.5	11.5	1	5	1,640	2,220	89.1
Jones, MS	28067	4	67,761	18.1	31.9	10.9	3	21	11,453	11,575	92.8
Kemper, MS	28069	9	10,456	16.7	34.9	11.2	1	4	1,164	1,725	87.9
Lafayette, MS	28071	6	47,351	13.1	21.2	10.4	3	13	6,108	5,961	93.0
Lamar, MS	28073	3	55,658	18.6	20.1	7.9	2	17	9,710	9,708	86.3
Lauderdale, MS	28075	5	80,261	17.9	32.1	7.5	3	25	12,965	14,858	90.8
Lawrence, MS	28077	8	12,929	17.9	26.5	11.1	1	6	2,108	2,321	95.9
Leake, MS	28079	6	23,805	23.0	37.3	10.7	1	8	3,233	5,467	87.4
Lee, MS	28081	5	82,910	19.3	30.0	7.9	4	37	16,673	14,420	94.5
Leflore, MS	28083	5	32,317	19.0	50.6	6.8	2	15	5,625	7,228	88.8
Lincoln, MS	28085	6	34,869	18.8	24.8	9.0	3	12	5,947	6,393	89.1
Lowndes, MS	28087	5	59,779	18.2	32.5	8.5	3	21	9,636	11,057	86.5
Madison, MS	28089	2	95,203	19.6	16.6	7.7	3	30	15,163	18,872	80.4
Marion, MS	28091	6	27,088	18.1	35.9	8.6	2	10	4,156	4,928	89.4
Marshall, MS	28093	1	37,144	16.8	33.4	9.8	2	15	4,734	6,503	79.3
Monroe, MS	28095	7	36,989	17.8	32.6	8.7	3	16	5,586	6,462	95.4
Montgomery, MS	28097	7	10,925	17.6	33.5	9.2	2	5	1,524	2,242	81.7
Neshoba, MS	28099	7	29,676	20.3	31.8	10.0	2	6	4,475	5,970	94.2
Newton, MS	28101	7	21,720	19.0	29.3	10.7	3	11	3,886	4,142	90.9
Noxubee, MS	28103	7	11,545	19.8	44.7	12.1	1	6	1,860	2,553	84.9
Oktibbeha, MS	28105	5	47,671	12.6	31.1	7.9	2	11	5,050	6,202	85.4
Panola, MS	28107	6	34,707	19.6	36.8	8.6	2	13	6,305	6,952	90.4
Pearl River, MS	28109	6	55,834	17.7	28.2	10.7	3	21	8,760	9,904	87.3
Perry, MS	28111	3	12,250	18.4	31.5	10.7	2	8	1,974	2,224	86.2
Pike, MS	28113	7	40,404	19.6	37.5	9.0	3	17	7,220	8,087	88.7
Pontotoc, MS	28115	7	29,957	19.7	23.2	8.8	2	12	5,737	5,781	97.2
Prentiss, MS	28117	7	25,276	16.8	28.6	9.0	2	12	3,589	4,413	97.9
Quitman, MS	28119	6	8,223	19.3	50.2	7.1	1	4	1,316	1,782	87.0
Rankin, MS	28121	2	141,617	18.1	18.5	8.4	4	34	22,809	25,316	86.1
Scott, MS	28123	6	28,264	18.9	31.0	11.0	2	11	5,275	5,153	93.4
Sharkey, MS	28125	9	4,916	18.7	55.0	9.5	1	4	1,020	999	86.9
Simpson, MS	28127	2	27,503	19.1	32.9	10.5	1	9	4,223	4,982	83.6
Smith, MS	28129	8	16,491	19.0	28.3	11.3	1	6	2,968	3,237	92.8
Stone, MS	28131	3	17,786	17.7	26.4	10.8	1	4	2,819	2,856	90.5
Sunflower, MS	28133	5	29,450	17.0	52.3	7.5	3	15	4,420	6,054	84.4
Tallahatchie, MS	28135	7	15,378	16.0	40.8	10.1	2	7	2,143	2,964	84.0
Tate, MS	28137	1	28,886	19.0	23.4	9.7	2	10	4,831	5,376	83.4
Tippah, MS	28139	7	22,232	18.3	29.9	10.5	2	10	4,089	4,021	97.5
Tishomingo, MS	28141	8	19,593	17.2	25.3	10.6	1	8	3,260	3,416	97.0
Tunica, MS	28143	1	10,778	20.9	42.4	7.2	1	7	2,196	2,150	90.7
Union, MS	28145	7	27,134	18.7	25.9	10.6	2	9	4,926	5,064	95.3
Walthall, MS	28147	9	15,443	19.3	35.9	10.7	1	7	2,437	3,246	93.8
Warren, MS	28149	4	48,773	19.0	29.9	9.3	1	16	8,835	9,337	91.4
Washington, MS	28151	5	51,137	20.4	51.4	6.6	4	26	9,898	11,747	92.8
Wayne, MS	28153	7	20,747	18.9	33.6	10.2	1	8	3,637	4,053	92.6
Webster, MS	28155	9	10,253	18.6	30.2	9.9	1	5	1,814	1,909	89.1
Wilkinson, MS	28157	8	9,878	16.4	40.2	10.0	1	5	1,365	1,674	76.5
Winston, MS	28159	7	19,198	17.7	39.7	9.2	1	7	2,718	3,529	88.2
Yalobusha, MS	28161	7	12,678	17.1	36.3	8.8	2	4	1,891	2,320	93.5
Yazoo, MS	28163	6	28,065	17.9	50.0	8.0	2	10	4,436	5,626	88.1

[1]County type codes are from the Economic Research Service of the United States Department of Agriculture. See notes and definitions for more information.

Table C-1. Population, School, and Student Characteristics by County, Selected Years—*Continued*

County	State/ County Code	Characteristics of students, 2010–2011				Number of graduates, 2008–2009	Staff and students, 2010–2011			
		Percent with IEP[2]	Percent eligible for free or reduced lunch	Percent minority	Percent English-language learners		Total staff	Number of teachers	Student/ teacher ratio	Central admin. staff
		10	11	12	13	14	15	16	17	18
MISSISSIPPI—*(Continued)*										
Jefferson Davis, MS	28065	19.5	99.3	90.8	. . .	98	276	119	13.7	16
Jones, MS	28067	13.2	72.6	44.3	2.1	552	1,580	768	14.9	57
Kemper, MS	28069	10.7	94.3	97.7	. . .	69	166	77	15.1	10
Lafayette, MS	28071	10.8	53.6	41.9	1.0	296	881	425	14.4	42
Lamar, MS	28073	14.3	52.8	29.9	1.3	520	1,292	632	15.4	54
Lauderdale, MS	28075	13.2	70.4	63.6	0.7	650	1,790	876	14.8	68
Lawrence, MS	28077	11.1	73.9	43.4	0.2	103	338	167	12.6	17
Leake, MS	28079	12.7	83.8	65.6	4.0	143	416	199	16.3	21
Lee, MS	28081	14.2	61.1	41.6	1.4	780	2,287	1,179	14.1	103
Leflore, MS	28083	11.2	96.3	95.9	1.2	250	866	366	15.4	47
Lincoln, MS	28085	13.6	63.8	38.5	0.3	237	825	375	15.9	48
Lowndes, MS	28087	13.3	68.0	66.3	0.4	594	1,403	731	13.2	57
Madison, MS	28089	10.0	47.8	56.1	1.3	799	1,758	936	16.2	74
Marion, MS	28091	18.5	82.5	46.9	0.1	203	573	264	15.7	33
Marshall, MS	28093	12.4	89.4	73.7	4.0	241	634	306	15.5	29
Monroe, MS	28095	16.4	69.0	41.3	. . .	328	790	406	13.8	34
Montgomery, MS	28097	15.6	79.3	65.4	0.2	93	240	118	12.9	15
Neshoba, MS	28099	12.3	68.6	43.2	. . .	212	612	287	15.6	29
Newton, MS	28101	14.3	66.5	43.3	0.6	187	551	274	14.2	32
Noxubee, MS	28103	10.0	99.4	99.2	0.3	103	308	130	14.4	15
Oktibbeha, MS	28105	12.9	70.3	70.0	0.1	224	757	339	14.9	40
Panola, MS	28107	15.0	83.4	67.5	0.4	288	934	418	15.1	35
Pearl River, MS	28109	13.2	70.3	22.2	0.7	494	1,347	578	15.2	68
Perry, MS	28111	14.0	75.5	29.4	. . .	122	313	156	12.7	10
Pike, MS	28113	10.2	80.2	69.2	0.2	336	980	458	15.8	53
Pontotoc, MS	28115	12.1	62.5	25.2	4.1	308	736	367	15.6	27
Prentiss, MS	28117	20.0	65.3	18.8	. . .	204	493	278	12.9	20
Quitman, MS	28119	12.7	99.3	97.9	0.1	85	225	94	14.0	12
Rankin, MS	28121	11.8	44.5	28.5	1.5	1,081	2,787	1,538	14.8	102
Scott, MS	28123	14.5	79.8	57.3	3.0	285	682	332	15.9	29
Sharkey, MS	28125	9.4	96.7	97.8	. . .	56	165	64	16.0	16
Simpson, MS	28127	14.2	81.5	52.3	0.6	174	549	278	15.2	26
Smith, MS	28129	14.0	66.8	30.9	0.2	149	403	200	14.8	17
Stone, MS	28131	11.8	62.9	26.6	0.5	134	418	195	14.5	18
Sunflower, MS	28133	13.1	93.4	97.2	0.4	237	676	322	13.7	35
Tallahatchie, MS	28135	12.3	92.5	82.2	0.1	102	353	153	14.0	18
Tate, MS	28137	12.5	70.8	44.3	1.3	248	640	309	15.7	23
Tippah, MS	28139	14.6	72.6	28.3	3.0	168	500	275	14.9	16
Tishomingo, MS	28141	11.3	67.1	7.2	0.8	166	453	215	15.2	13
Tunica, MS	28143	10.2	96.1	98.7	0.4	77	396	179	12.3	23
Union, MS	28145	12.6	63.8	24.5	2.0	252	672	325	15.2	23
Walthall, MS	28147	12.5	81.7	65.4	0.1	137	350	160	15.2	15
Warren, MS	28149	9.1	73.6	65.1	0.4	367	1,274	574	15.4	44
Washington, MS	28151	13.5	91.8	89.7	0.2	495	1,341	634	15.6	62
Wayne, MS	28153	17.7	81.7	55.8	0.5	168	499	233	15.6	18
Webster, MS	28155	13.8	64.0	31.0	. . .	102	251	122	14.9	11
Wilkinson, MS	28157	13.3	99.1	99.4	. . .	78	224	92	14.8	14
Winston, MS	28159	13.5	84.0	68.6	. . .	111	407	204	13.3	17
Yalobusha, MS	28161	12.0	77.4	57.5	. . .	100	265	131	14.5	20
Yazoo, MS	28163	11.1	90.8	80.6	. . .	210	599	258	17.2	37

[2]IEP=Individual Education Program. See notes and definitions for more information.
. . . = Not available.

Table C-1. Population, School, and Student Characteristics by County, Selected Years—*Continued*

County	State/ County Code	Revenues, 2008–2009				Current expenditures, 2008–2009			Resident population 16 to 19 years, 2006–2010			
		Total revenue ($1,000's)	Percentage of revenue from: Federal government	State government	Local government	Amount ($1,000's)	Amount per student	Percent for instruction	Total population 16 to 19 years	Percent enrolled in school	Percent high school graduates, not enrolled in school	Percent not enrolled, not grads, not employed, or not in labor force
		19	20	21	22	23	24	25	26	27	28	29
MISSISSIPPI— *(Continued)*												
Jefferson Davis, MS	28065	23,546	15.4	43.0	41.6	14,656	8,102	52.7	809	67.4	20.4	11.3
Jones, MS	28067	101,664	13.9	52.9	33.2	92,288	8,267	59.5	3,815	73.7	14.8	7.3
Kemper, MS	28069	11,111	23.8	55.8	20.4	10,472	8,521	57.1	820	96.1	1.5	2.0
Lafayette, MS	28071	58,427	8.7	46.9	44.4	51,296	8,847	62.8	4,974	94.8	2.6	2.4
Lamar, MS	28073	81,663	9.8	52.8	37.4	71,600	7,944	60.2	2,951	82.7	8.7	6.3
Lauderdale, MS	28075	111,850	14.0	55.6	30.4	105,826	7,995	61.4	5,236	83.0	11.1	4.1
Lawrence, MS	28077	18,640	13.7	54.3	31.9	18,898	8,471	61.0	662	78.4	6.2	14.1
Leake, MS	28079	25,114	18.1	63.3	18.6	24,789	7,585	56.8	1,911	78.9	9.5	8.4
Lee, MS	28081	149,745	11.4	52.6	36.0	134,833	8,182	61.7	4,778	74.4	10.8	12.2
Leflore, MS	28083	50,557	23.1	57.0	19.9	48,767	8,472	56.7	2,492	88.6	4.5	6.5
Lincoln, MS	28085	52,700	12.5	54.7	32.8	44,793	7,328	58.7	1,676	85.0	13.4	1.6
Lowndes, MS	28087	90,955	14.5	49.7	35.7	83,047	8,460	57.5	3,803	85.3	5.1	7.5
Madison, MS	28089	140,418	9.3	43.7	47.0	108,957	7,341	59.5	5,481	85.0	11.2	3.5
Marion, MS	28091	42,659	14.6	54.2	31.2	36,999	8,561	57.3	1,510	76.1	16.6	2.7
Marshall, MS	28093	40,843	18.7	60.8	20.5	36,556	7,430	58.8	2,200	79.8	8.6	8.9
Monroe, MS	28095	48,829	15.0	58.9	26.1	47,364	8,304	61.1	2,197	73.9	17.3	7.4
Montgomery, MS	28097	15,878	21.0	60.5	18.5	15,606	9,367	62.0	874	82.3	13.5	0.0
Neshoba, MS	28099	31,926	17.6	62.6	19.7	30,443	7,015	64.6	1,909	80.1	5.2	10.4
Newton, MS	28101	32,909	14.4	61.8	23.8	30,664	7,985	56.6	1,888	91.8	3.6	4.7
Noxubee, MS	28103	20,531	23.7	50.3	26.0	18,202	9,230	54.1	730	87.5	5.2	6.0
Oktibbeha, MS	28105	54,814	15.5	46.2	38.4	46,961	9,268	57.7	4,167	93.1	5.0	1.6
Panola, MS	28107	54,704	16.2	58.1	25.7	51,152	8,139	59.5	2,160	70.2	11.2	13.4
Pearl River, MS	28109	76,964	15.2	56.1	28.7	73,190	8,129	58.1	3,456	75.0	17.6	5.2
Perry, MS	28111	18,514	21.3	55.3	23.4	16,707	8,130	60.9	712	78.5	19.0	1.8
Pike, MS	28113	65,782	19.5	53.9	26.6	57,095	8,004	57.6	2,605	87.0	8.5	3.7
Pontotoc, MS	28115	44,184	10.4	67.1	22.5	41,043	7,327	66.5	1,593	76.4	16.8	1.1
Prentiss, MS	28117	31,319	14.1	61.6	24.3	29,151	8,177	65.0	1,766	88.9	4.4	5.7
Quitman, MS	28119	13,248	24.8	56.5	18.7	12,933	9,739	54.4	515	67.2	9.3	19.8
Rankin, MS	28121	190,682	8.6	49.9	41.5	169,127	7,679	60.5	7,060	86.1	8.8	3.3
Scott, MS	28123	40,112	16.3	64.5	19.2	37,950	7,142	60.5	1,821	72.1	10.0	8.7
Sharkey, MS	28125	11,314	28.1	46.6	25.3	10,280	8,970	51.1	318	81.5	11.0	7.6
Simpson, MS	28127	36,245	15.8	57.8	26.4	30,915	7,254	60.0	1,626	69.6	23.4	6.0
Smith, MS	28129	23,804	14.3	63.4	22.3	22,122	7,313	60.4	870	83.3	7.0	5.1
Stone, MS	28131	23,328	13.3	60.1	26.7	22,271	7,940	59.7	938	72.9	20.3	6.8
Sunflower, MS	28133	41,634	23.4	57.6	19.0	39,161	8,322	56.3	2,089	84.0	11.6	4.1
Tallahatchie, MS	28135	21,967	23.5	54.7	21.8	21,112	9,211	57.4	963	74.3	5.4	15.3
Tate, MS	28137	38,782	11.2	64.7	24.2	34,165	6,933	59.3	2,220	85.3	6.0	6.8
Tippah, MS	28139	31,463	13.1	68.6	18.3	30,529	7,577	62.1	1,060	89.9	5.9	4.3
Tishomingo, MS	28141	27,202	15.9	59.6	24.4	24,759	7,565	62.5	1,110	72.4	13.0	7.9
Tunica, MS	28143	25,685	13.2	38.9	47.8	24,166	10,707	51.6	591	54.3	11.8	31.8
Union, MS	28145	39,165	11.3	63.9	24.8	36,186	7,399	62.5	1,379	87.7	5.7	5.2
Walthall, MS	28147	21,494	17.0	59.1	24.0	18,820	7,456	63.5	910	94.4	5.6	0.0
Warren, MS	28149	75,132	13.5	50.8	35.7	70,761	7,812	58.3	2,902	76.7	10.0	8.2
Washington, MS	28151	93,735	22.7	55.7	21.6	87,576	8,172	57.3	3,331	87.7	7.1	4.5
Wayne, MS	28153	37,660	14.0	50.2	35.8	29,339	7,813	62.3	1,044	74.0	15.6	6.7
Webster, MS	28155	14,407	15.3	63.8	20.9	13,959	7,729	62.1	654	87.9	0.8	9.2
Wilkinson, MS	28157	12,644	22.0	56.3	21.7	12,018	8,975	55.0	445	58.0	23.2	16.6
Winston, MS	28159	24,598	15.4	57.1	27.5	22,452	8,254	58.5	981	86.1	7.8	6.1
Yalobusha, MS	28161	16,216	20.0	62.9	17.0	15,568	8,033	63.2	709	71.5	15.5	13.0
Yazoo, MS	28163	38,231	22.6	56.0	21.3	35,970	7,944	57.9	1,674	79.2	7.0	10.9

Note. Data in columns 26 through 41 from the American Community Survey are subject to sampling error, which can be especially large in small counties and small population groups. See notes and definitions for more information.

Table C-1. Population, School, and Student Characteristics by County, Selected Years—*Continued*

County	State/ County Code	High school graduates, 2006–2010			College enrollment, 2006–2010		College graduates, 2006–2010 (percent)						
		Population 25 years and over	High school diploma or less (percent)	High school diploma or more (percent)	Number	Percent public	Bachelor's degree or more	+/- U.S. percent with Bachelor's degree or more	Non-Hispanic White	Black or African American	American Indian and Alaska Native	Asian, Hawaiian, and Pacific Islander	Hispanic or Latino[3]
		30	31	32	33	34	35	36	37	38	39	40	41
MISSISSIPPI— *(Continued)*													
Jefferson Davis, MS..	28065	8,625	59.0	73.3	441	89.8	11.9	-16.0	14.7	9.9	0.0	0.0	0.0
Jones, MS.................	28067	43,225	54.0	77.1	3,581	87.3	15.8	-12.1	18.5	9.6	0.0	0.0	4.8
Kemper, MS..............	28069	6,946	68.3	67.5	730	100.0	8.9	-19.0	16.6	3.2	5.8	0.0	0.0
Lafayette, MS............	28071	24,683	35.1	85.4	12,161	96.0	39.3	11.4	47.1	13.5	76.6	72.2	24.4
Lamar, MS.................	28073	32,676	37.1	86.9	4,559	92.1	31.8	3.9	32.6	28.4	0.0	47.9	14.3
Lauderdale, MS.........	28075	51,273	48.9	81.6	4,546	94.9	18.8	-9.1	23.7	10.6	19.8	48.9	6.5
Lawrence, MS...........	28077	8,509	60.1	79.5	521	74.3	11.8	-16.1	12.4	10.9	0.0	0.0	0.0
Leake, MS................	28079	14,035	63.6	73.9	895	88.9	9.6	-18.3	11.9	5.3	5.4	0.0	12.8
Lee, MS....................	28081	52,650	47.1	81.0	4,909	89.7	20.9	-7.0	24.7	8.8	26.8	38.3	17.4
Leflore, MS..............	28083	19,946	60.2	68.8	3,130	91.9	16.6	-11.3	26.5	11.9	41.9	0.0	0.0
Lincoln, MS..............	28085	22,729	54.4	81.5	1,787	85.7	17.2	-10.7	19.7	10.5	18.1	0.0	49.0
Lowndes, MS............	28087	37,806	49.9	80.5	4,632	92.3	20.1	-7.8	27.2	9.7	25.5	21.5	9.9
Madison, MS............	28089	58,592	31.5	87.9	5,821	75.5	42.6	14.7	53.1	23.3	0.0	73.6	18.7
Marion, MS..............	28091	17,468	63.7	74.3	942	91.8	12.5	-15.4	13.4	10.7	0.0	0.0	0.0
Marshall, MS............	28093	24,346	66.7	69.3	1,478	69.2	10.2	-17.7	11.5	8.7	0.0	63.4	0.0
Monroe, MS..............	28095	24,839	61.5	75.2	1,749	90.9	13.2	-14.7	16.5	5.2	0.0	100.0	7.2
Montgomery, MS......	28097	7,246	56.0	74.6	460	92.6	16.3	-11.6	17.3	14.8	0.0	100.0	0.0
Neshoba, MS............	28099	18,458	57.9	73.8	1,445	88.8	12.4	-15.5	13.4	9.1	11.3	52.6	3.6
Newton, MS..............	28101	13,822	53.4	81.3	1,787	95.1	12.7	-15.2	15.5	4.4	20.3	0.0	15.7
Noxubee, MS............	28103	7,393	64.0	66.0	711	87.6	13.1	-14.8	23.6	8.2	0.0	0.0	15.6
Oktibbeha, MS..........	28105	23,384	36.7	84.5	13,825	98.2	39.9	12.0	51.6	18.9	100.0	79.0	69.4
Panola, MS..............	28107	22,060	60.5	72.4	1,011	89.5	12.5	-15.4	17.4	6.6	0.0	0.0	0.0
Pearl River, MS........	28109	37,085	53.8	80.4	2,561	86.3	14.6	-13.3	15.1	14.1	13.2	6.3	5.9
Perry, MS.................	28111	8,096	56.9	79.2	499	83.8	10.0	-17.9	10.7	7.4	0.0	0.0	0.0
Pike, MS...................	28113	25,873	54.0	77.5	2,020	74.1	15.7	-12.2	22.0	9.3	8.7	2.0	8.0
Pontotoc, MS............	28115	18,909	61.3	76.0	1,227	90.8	11.4	-16.5	12.2	6.8	7.5	0.0	4.1
Prentiss, MS............	28117	16,466	59.2	73.2	1,605	97.1	11.8	-16.1	11.9	8.9	0.0	35.4	0.0
Quitman, MS............	28119	5,391	63.8	63.6	296	81.4	11.0	-16.9	13.4	9.6	0.0	44.4	0.0
Rankin, MS..............	28121	91,932	39.0	87.4	7,631	73.7	28.0	0.1	29.8	18.1	32.7	59.7	18.8
Scott, MS.................	28123	17,733	66.0	70.8	1,154	96.7	10.3	-17.6	14.2	5.6	0.0	36.8	2.5
Sharkey, MS.............	28125	3,135	58.9	70.6	213	38.5	17.8	-10.1	39.3	7.6	0.0	0.0	0.0
Simpson, MS............	28127	17,906	59.2	76.0	1,077	75.2	14.3	-13.6	17.7	8.3	0.0	0.0	0.0
Smith, MS................	28129	10,712	61.3	77.3	563	86.3	14.8	-13.1	18.0	2.5	0.0	0.0	5.9
Stone, MS................	28131	10,907	52.3	79.0	971	91.1	13.5	-14.4	16.0	3.1	30.0	0.0	7.1
Sunflower, MS..........	28133	19,132	60.5	69.8	2,270	85.3	13.0	-14.9	20.8	9.6	20.0	11.1	7.5
Tallahatchie, MS.......	28135	9,796	68.6	65.5	842	79.8	9.0	-18.9	12.3	7.4	0.0	14.6	0.0
Tate, MS...................	28137	17,585	53.0	79.7	2,087	86.7	14.2	-13.7	16.9	7.4	0.0	22.6	8.2
Tippah, MS...............	28139	14,492	63.6	72.6	1,134	57.7	10.4	-17.5	11.6	3.8	0.0	0.0	8.8
Tishomingo, MS........	28141	13,522	63.4	75.7	635	88.2	10.7	-17.2	10.4	11.3	40.0	72.1	12.4
Tunica, MS...............	28143	6,569	59.1	72.5	533	67.7	14.6	-13.3	21.7	11.8	0.0	9.1	2.2
Union, MS................	28145	17,803	59.2	74.7	1,055	73.4	14.5	-13.4	15.4	8.2	8.6	27.0	8.3
Walthall, MS.............	28147	10,074	60.2	73.3	825	80.4	14.0	-13.9	19.2	6.4	0.0	100.0	14.6
Warren, MS..............	28149	31,871	43.8	83.0	2,335	87.3	24.4	-3.5	32.1	14.1	63.4	24.3	14.8
Washington, MS.......	28151	32,322	56.4	72.5	2,207	76.3	17.6	-10.3	26.2	12.5	0.0	85.5	0.0
Wayne, MS...............	28153	13,539	65.8	72.8	704	83.2	11.3	-16.6	12.8	7.2	0.0	81.0	34.2
Webster, MS............	28155	6,788	58.3	76.4	382	100.0	17.2	-10.7	20.1	4.7	0.0	0.0	18.6
Wilkinson, MS..........	28157	6,719	72.5	68.9	313	76.4	9.0	-18.9	15.2	6.0	0.0	0.0	0.0
Winston, MS............	28159	12,934	58.8	78.3	625	89.0	14.7	-13.2	18.2	10.0	0.0	0.0	0.0
Yalobusha, MS.........	28161	8,506	61.9	75.4	535	97.2	12.3	-15.6	17.1	3.4	0.0	0.0	0.0
Yazoo, MS................	28163	18,587	62.0	73.6	988	63.7	11.9	-16.0	20.5	5.6	0.0	0.0	6.4

Note. Data in columns 26 through 41 from the American Community Survey are subject to sampling error, which can be especially large in small counties and small population groups. See notes and definitions for more information.

[3]May be of any race.

Table C-1. Population, School, and Student Characteristics by County, Selected Years—*Continued*

County	State/ County Code	County Type[1]	Population, 2010		Percent of related children 5–17 years in poverty, 2010	Percent of children under 19 years with no health insurance, 2010	Number of schools and students, 2010–2011			Resident enrollment, 2006–2010 K–12 enrollment	
			Total	Percent 5–17 years			School districts	Schools	Students	Number	Percent public
			1	2	3	4	5	6	7	8	9
MISSOURI	29000	X	5,988,927	17.3	18.5	6.6	567	2,410	918,710	1,042,933	86.6
Adair, MO	29001	7	25,607	13.8	20.9	7.0	3	9	3,087	3,370	93.3
Andrew, MO	29003	3	17,291	18.3	11.8	7.2	3	10	2,889	3,213	94.1
Atchison, MO	29005	9	5,685	15.7	12.6	8.4	3	6	841	892	97.7
Audrain, MO	29007	6	25,529	18.2	25.5	7.1	3	10	3,369	5,067	87.8
Barry, MO	29009	6	35,597	17.8	26.4	10.0	7	21	6,725	6,600	94.5
Barton, MO	29011	6	12,402	19.2	22.6	7.7	3	11	2,080	2,372	93.7
Bates, MO	29013	1	17,049	18.3	21.0	8.3	6	12	2,702	3,252	93.1
Benton, MO	29015	9	19,056	13.7	31.3	10.7	3	10	2,632	2,564	94.7
Bollinger, MO	29017	9	12,363	17.4	26.2	8.4	4	9	1,883	2,285	93.5
Boone, MO	29019	3	162,642	14.8	15.4	6.5	6	50	22,710	23,058	90.5
Buchanan, MO	29021	3	89,201	16.6	19.9	5.6	3	30	12,752	15,494	88.5
Butler, MO	29023	7	42,794	16.9	28.7	6.4	3	16	6,778	6,984	85.1
Caldwell, MO	29025	1	9,424	19.2	18.1	8.6	8	14	1,657	1,787	94.4
Callaway, MO	29027	3	44,332	16.6	16.6	7.2	5	18	5,077	7,714	91.6
Camden, MO	29029	7	44,002	14.1	23.3	8.9	4	15	5,317	6,162	94.1
Cape Girardeau, MO	29031	5	75,674	15.7	16.5	5.3	5	23	9,929	11,834	82.5
Carroll, MO	29033	6	9,295	17.9	18.6	7.3	5	13	1,605	1,634	94.5
Carter, MO	29035	9	6,265	17.1	38.5	9.1	2	5	1,317	1,011	100.0
Cass, MO	29037	1	99,478	19.7	10.0	6.2	10	44	18,608	19,339	91.9
Cedar, MO	29039	6	13,982	17.7	29.8	10.6	2	6	2,304	2,397	79.0
Chariton, MO	29041	9	7,831	16.4	17.6	9.2	4	8	1,040	1,300	82.2
Christian, MO	29043	2	77,422	19.9	15.0	7.6	7	31	14,392	14,529	90.7
Clark, MO	29045	9	7,139	17.2	24.8	10.3	3	6	1,100	1,358	93.5
Clay, MO	29047	1	221,939	18.5	11.6	5.1	6	70	38,813	39,034	90.9
Clinton, MO	29049	1	20,743	18.3	13.8	7.1	4	13	4,220	3,831	94.5
Cole, MO	29051	3	75,990	17.0	13.5	5.0	7	123	13,160	13,616	76.3
Cooper, MO	29053	6	17,601	16.5	20.1	7.1	6	15	2,508	3,315	84.1
Crawford, MO	29055	6	24,696	17.6	26.0	7.2	3	9	3,352	4,650	88.5
Dade, MO	29057	8	7,883	17.5	27.4	9.6	4	9	1,140	1,403	88.2
Dallas, MO	29059	2	16,777	18.0	29.3	8.7	1	5	1,820	2,777	89.8
Daviess, MO	29061	8	8,433	19.3	26.5	14.0	5	10	1,234	1,569	91.9
De Kalb, MO	29063	3	12,892	13.3	14.3	8.0	4	8	1,107	2,286	92.9
Dent, MO	29065	7	15,657	17.2	27.2	7.8	5	8	2,182	2,626	94.3
Douglas, MO	29067	6	13,684	16.4	34.5	9.3	3	5	1,616	2,601	89.3
Dunklin, MO	29069	7	31,953	18.4	34.1	6.4	7	20	5,935	5,733	95.9
Franklin, MO	29071	1	101,492	18.3	17.3	7.0	10	43	16,449	19,013	86.1
Gasconade, MO	29073	6	15,222	16.6	17.8	8.3	2	7	2,965	2,688	92.0
Gentry, MO	29075	8	6,738	17.8	19.5	11.5	3	7	1,154	1,217	94.6
Greene, MO	29077	2	275,174	15.0	19.6	6.9	8	82	37,133	39,643	91.4
Grundy, MO	29079	7	10,261	17.1	24.4	7.8	5	8	1,599	1,687	89.6
Harrison, MO	29081	7	8,957	17.5	24.7	8.6	5	12	1,503	1,476	97.0
Henry, MO	29083	6	22,272	16.2	22.9	7.0	8	16	3,399	3,681	89.3
Hickory, MO	29085	8	9,627	12.7	37.7	11.1	4	10	1,725	1,265	94.0
Holt, MO	29087	8	4,912	14.1	20.7	9.8	3	7	607	723	97.4
Howard, MO	29089	3	10,144	15.6	18.7	8.0	3	7	1,470	1,597	92.6
Howell, MO	29091	7	40,400	17.8	30.1	7.8	7	13	5,657	7,241	94.3
Iron, MO	29093	6	10,630	16.8	28.5	7.4	4	9	1,869	1,877	94.7
Jackson, MO	29095	1	674,158	17.5	21.0	6.9	33	222	105,975	116,600	88.4
Jasper, MO	29097	3	117,404	18.2	20.3	8.7	7	50	21,233	20,870	91.8
Jefferson, MO	29099	1	218,733	18.3	13.2	5.9	12	62	36,395	40,839	90.1
Johnson, MO	29101	4	52,595	16.1	17.2	6.8	7	27	7,690	8,332	93.3
Knox, MO	29103	9	4,131	18.6	29.6	17.0	1	2	533	731	89.3
Laclede, MO	29105	6	35,571	17.9	25.9	6.8	4	13	6,147	6,404	91.5
Lafayette, MO	29107	1	33,381	18.3	15.3	7.0	6	18	5,425	6,062	87.3
Lawrence, MO	29109	6	38,634	19.4	21.7	8.6	6	19	6,178	7,293	90.9
Lewis, MO	29111	9	10,211	17.1	22.8	9.2	2	4	1,553	1,655	84.0
Lincoln, MO	29113	1	52,566	20.3	13.7	7.2	4	18	9,032	10,732	88.0
Linn, MO	29115	7	12,761	18.0	22.0	8.6	5	13	2,380	2,295	92.4
Livingston, MO	29117	6	15,195	15.9	20.9	6.6	3	10	2,213	2,348	94.4

[1]County type codes are from the Economic Research Service of the United States Department of Agriculture. See notes and definitions for more information.

Table C-1. Population, School, and Student Characteristics by County, Selected Years—*Continued*

County	State/ County Code	Characteristics of students, 2010–2011				Number of graduates, 2008–2009	Staff and students, 2010–2011			
		Percent with IEP[2]	Percent eligible for free or reduced lunch	Percent minority	Percent English-language learners		Total staff	Number of teachers	Student/ teacher ratio	Central admin. staff
		10	11	12	13	14	15	16	17	18
MISSOURI	29000	13.8	44.3	25.2	2.4	62,969	128,259	66,724	13.8	9,480
Adair, MO	29001	17.9	44.5	7.2	0.9	215	458	253	12.2	34
Andrew, MO	29003	12.6	33.0	5.3	0.3	200	364	210	13.7	26
Atchison, MO	29005	13.6	44.7	2.5	. . .	75	176	104	8.1	12
Audrain, MO	29007	13.3	50.4	16.4	1.9	306	543	257	13.1	47
Barry, MO	29009	10.9	57.6	18.9	11.6	406	891	473	14.2	64
Barton, MO	29011	16.6	54.2	5.0	0.7	141	283	166	12.5	13
Bates, MO	29013	13.1	50.6	4.1	0.2	163	348	203	13.3	29
Benton, MO	29015	16.6	59.6	4.1	. . .	202	356	186	14.1	23
Bollinger, MO	29017	12.4	53.5	1.2	0.1	137	252	142	13.3	18
Boone, MO	29019	12.4	35.6	29.7	2.9	1,555	3,011	1,627	14.0	177
Buchanan, MO	29021	14.9	54.8	16.4	2.5	861	2,072	948	13.5	95
Butler, MO	29023	15.6	58.5	12.6	. . .	377	832	460	14.7	56
Caldwell, MO	29025	16.1	51.2	4.3	. . .	74	267	164	10.1	31
Callaway, MO	29027	11.8	45.1	9.0	0.1	485	856	433	11.7	61
Camden, MO	29029	11.0	54.8	6.2	1.1	402	743	404	13.2	64
Cape Girardeau, MO	29031	12.1	43.0	20.0	0.8	702	1,378	718	13.8	101
Carroll, MO	29033	16.1	51.9	5.5	. . .	121	246	138	11.6	22
Carter, MO	29035	15.6	65.0	1.6	0.1	83	199	104	12.7	20
Cass, MO	29037	10.0	33.4	16.9	1.3	1,230	2,278	1,229	15.1	175
Cedar, MO	29039	14.5	55.3	2.8	0.2	140	329	165	13.9	21
Chariton, MO	29041	16.5	48.5	4.7	. . .	86	200	106	9.9	14
Christian, MO	29043	10.9	38.0	8.2	0.8	888	1,684	979	14.7	105
Clark, MO	29045	11.3	48.7	2.1	. . .	68	179	95	11.6	12
Clay, MO	29047	10.5	32.7	22.5	3.0	2,465	5,600	2,579	15.1	344
Clinton, MO	29049	15.5	37.0	6.8	. . .	286	547	316	13.4	43
Cole, MO	29051	25.2	41.5	23.5	1.3	1,137	2,184	1,079	12.2	187
Cooper, MO	29053	13.4	47.8	11.6	0.4	206	379	216	11.6	28
Crawford, MO	29055	15.9	56.6	3.5	0.4	252	431	227	14.8	34
Dade, MO	29057	12.2	58.0	3.5	. . .	255	185	106	10.7	17
Dallas, MO	29059	13.2	61.1	2.9	0.8	130	178	137	13.3	4
Daviess, MO	29061	16.9	50.6	2.4	. . .	157	215	127	9.7	20
De Kalb, MO	29063	11.5	41.5	2.7	. . .	78	169	107	10.4	15
Dent, MO	29065	17.3	48.5	5.9	0.1	156	345	166	13.2	22
Douglas, MO	29067	14.5	66.2	1.7	0.1	133	232	127	12.7	15
Dunklin, MO	29069	14.9	65.0	27.2	3.3	376	779	427	13.9	68
Franklin, MO	29071	17.0	41.0	4.5	0.6	1,268	2,232	1,121	14.7	169
Gasconade, MO	29073	14.1	43.8	3.6	0.1	261	407	213	13.9	35
Gentry, MO	29075	14.9	45.8	3.5	. . .	89	193	105	10.9	13
Greene, MO	29077	11.6	45.6	11.9	1.8	2,361	4,996	2,476	15.0	299
Grundy, MO	29079	17.8	50.2	4.0	0.7	101	277	138	11.6	29
Harrison, MO	29081	13.3	51.2	2.7	0.2	82	272	144	10.4	25
Henry, MO	29083	14.8	53.3	5.0	0.2	247	483	272	12.5	46
Hickory, MO	29085	9.8	60.4	4.0	0.1	70	243	136	12.7	29
Holt, MO	29087	12.9	44.2	2.3	. . .	68	110	60	10.1	11
Howard, MO	29089	17.2	43.7	13.3	0.1	97	224	120	12.2	18
Howell, MO	29091	13.9	51.5	3.5	2.0	415	795	412	13.7	64
Iron, MO	29093	16.1	64.0	3.5	. . .	104	306	164	11.4	31
Jackson, MO	29095	10.8	49.8	48.9	5.8	6,420	14,366	7,031	15.1	936
Jasper, MO	29097	12.9	51.9	16.1	4.2	1,187	2,720	1,423	14.9	160
Jefferson, MO	29099	14.2	36.0	4.2	0.3	2,558	4,337	2,286	15.9	392
Johnson, MO	29101	13.6	35.1	14.0	0.7	558	1,110	587	13.1	78
Knox, MO	29103	9.8	59.1	3.2	. . .	45	100	45	11.8	6
Laclede, MO	29105	13.3	52.4	5.5	0.6	425	876	411	15.0	61
Lafayette, MO	29107	13.9	37.7	7.8	1.0	439	711	419	12.9	56
Lawrence, MO	29109	13.3	55.5	13.6	2.2	402	766	426	14.5	65
Lewis, MO	29111	17.7	47.1	7.8	0.2	107	187	123	12.7	5
Lincoln, MO	29113	12.5	44.0	8.7	1.1	614	1,035	531	17.0	80
Linn, MO	29115	17.1	44.7	6.1	0.7	184	354	208	11.5	32
Livingston, MO	29117	19.2	45.9	4.7	. . .	172	344	176	12.6	27

[2]IEP=Individual Education Program. See notes and definitions for more information.
. . . = Not available.

Table C-1. Population, School, and Student Characteristics by County, Selected Years—*Continued*

County	State/ County Code	Revenues, 2008–2009				Current expenditures, 2008–2009			Resident population 16 to 19 years, 2006–2010			
		Total revenue ($1,000's)	Percentage of revenue from			Amount ($1,000's)	Amount per student	Percent for instruction	Total population 16 to 19 years	Percent enrolled in school	Percent high school graduates, not enrolled in school	Percent not enrolled, not grads, not employed, or not in labor force
			Federal government	State government	Local government							
		19	20	21	22	23	24	25	26	27	28	29
MISSOURI	29000	9,671,463	8.1	31.6	60.3	8,746,169	9,601	60.2	345,137	83.1	10.3	4.6
Adair, MO	29001	30,560	8.5	40.8	50.7	27,763	9,040	65.1	2,689	96.4	2.0	1.2
Andrew, MO	29003	24,921	5.6	44.8	49.6	24,537	8,490	62.2	919	87.4	8.2	1.1
Atchison, MO	29005	9,389	7.3	36.3	56.5	9,024	9,714	63.2	290	79.7	15.2	5.2
Audrain, MO	29007	32,489	12.0	35.8	52.2	27,974	8,027	61.0	1,401	81.7	6.3	9.9
Barry, MO	29009	59,306	10.7	45.6	43.8	50,962	7,998	63.0	1,791	84.3	6.8	7.7
Barton, MO	29011	17,762	9.9	39.4	50.7	17,247	8,093	63.1	542	68.8	14.8	16.4
Bates, MO	29013	20,249	8.2	44.7	47.1	19,046	8,112	62.7	887	74.4	13.6	9.4
Benton, MO	29015	22,010	11.9	38.0	50.1	20,859	7,907	62.3	809	63.4	15.3	17.1
Bollinger, MO	29017	14,890	11.1	50.4	38.5	14,345	7,345	59.5	695	79.9	10.1	8.9
Boone, MO	29019	231,692	7.2	31.4	61.4	203,763	9,091	62.5	13,143	92.2	4.9	2.4
Buchanan, MO	29021	124,564	10.2	37.1	52.6	112,380	8,769	60.6	5,104	81.8	13.9	3.4
Butler, MO	29023	53,473	15.2	41.7	43.1	50,231	7,615	62.1	2,325	81.9	6.8	9.9
Caldwell, MO	29025	10,842	8.1	46.4	45.6	9,659	9,378	60.0	548	85.2	10.0	3.8
Callaway, MO	29027	46,909	8.2	35.7	56.2	43,833	8,568	59.4	2,836	80.6	9.6	5.8
Camden, MO	29029	55,039	8.0	17.3	74.8	47,543	8,808	59.6	1,864	78.5	17.1	2.6
Cape Girardeau, MO	29031	89,547	9.0	26.5	64.5	78,511	8,128	61.8	5,136	89.2	7.7	2.7
Carroll, MO	29033	17,285	8.3	37.1	54.6	14,968	9,099	61.3	510	77.7	8.0	13.5
Carter, MO	29035	11,333	17.5	50.7	31.8	11,120	8,330	62.3	454	80.8	10.1	2.2
Cass, MO	29037	177,336	5.0	40.8	54.2	157,288	8,536	58.4	5,358	84.1	10.2	3.0
Cedar, MO	29039	20,144	11.0	42.1	46.9	18,044	7,808	62.8	672	72.2	4.6	13.1
Chariton, MO	29041	11,732	7.4	26.2	66.3	10,384	9,189	61.9	404	81.9	15.8	2.2
Christian, MO	29043	114,150	6.6	43.7	49.7	104,646	7,449	63.1	4,031	85.1	9.5	2.5
Clark, MO	29045	9,464	9.5	38.7	51.8	8,538	7,692	63.3	371	95.4	4.6	0.0
Clay, MO	29047	405,186	4.4	26.0	69.5	349,216	9,355	59.4	10,616	83.6	11.9	3.7
Clinton, MO	29049	41,711	5.4	44.5	50.1	38,065	8,957	65.3	1,110	85.1	13.1	0.5
Cole, MO	29051	97,551	8.3	20.0	71.6	87,435	8,225	63.8	4,969	90.5	6.0	2.3
Cooper, MO	29053	24,619	7.9	37.5	54.6	23,742	9,344	62.7	983	77.6	8.6	6.7
Crawford, MO	29055	33,302	9.8	39.2	51.0	30,607	7,989	62.6	1,310	77.1	16.5	3.2
Dade, MO	29057	27,223	9.9	46.8	43.3	26,067	8,774	59.6	448	72.3	16.7	4.0
Dallas, MO	29059	15,978	10.5	49.1	40.4	15,202	8,325	59.8	837	66.6	15.3	5.9
Daviess, MO	29061	19,927	8.4	45.9	45.7	19,207	9,397	62.5	477	76.1	8.0	7.6
De Kalb, MO	29063	10,869	6.9	48.6	44.5	11,262	9,836	60.5	603	82.9	12.4	4.6
Dent, MO	29065	20,490	10.3	42.7	47.0	18,173	7,803	63.5	827	73.9	18.3	3.6
Douglas, MO	29067	15,226	17.1	46.0	36.9	14,016	8,398	60.9	951	89.6	9.3	1.2
Dunklin, MO	29069	51,234	15.6	46.2	38.2	48,749	8,121	62.3	1,869	66.8	9.2	21.7
Franklin, MO	29071	163,035	6.7	30.3	63.0	140,650	8,405	61.1	5,774	83.7	8.0	6.4
Gasconade, MO	29073	26,825	7.1	34.6	58.3	24,686	8,226	61.5	808	81.6	8.8	5.2
Gentry, MO	29075	12,221	7.2	42.9	49.9	11,848	10,393	63.7	405	78.5	3.7	14.3
Greene, MO	29077	312,910	8.2	26.0	65.8	286,300	7,876	61.1	16,572	89.0	7.5	2.2
Grundy, MO	29079	15,550	8.7	41.8	49.5	13,941	9,041	63.2	594	78.1	9.9	4.2
Harrison, MO	29081	13,914	10.3	41.5	48.2	14,070	9,488	62.4	457	75.1	12.7	5.7
Henry, MO	29083	31,745	11.9	35.8	52.2	30,115	9,033	61.5	1,058	70.7	17.7	5.2
Hickory, MO	29085	10,067	13.3	38.1	48.6	9,098	9,246	58.3	355	87.6	11.8	0.0
Holt, MO	29087	6,986	7.1	27.4	65.5	6,991	10,388	58.0	208	84.6	6.3	3.9
Howard, MO	29089	12,174	8.8	41.2	50.0	11,699	7,868	62.3	896	91.9	4.0	1.3
Howell, MO	29091	69,731	12.2	40.8	47.1	55,426	8,071	65.1	2,129	78.6	13.0	4.5
Iron, MO	29093	15,373	13.0	45.8	41.2	15,240	9,922	58.7	570	87.9	8.6	3.5
Jackson, MO	29095	1,288,326	8.7	34.7	56.6	1,170,107	11,037	57.2	36,041	79.8	11.8	6.1
Jasper, MO	29097	180,058	9.8	35.9	54.3	154,494	7,479	63.8	6,557	82.1	9.8	3.7
Jefferson, MO	29099	339,137	6.0	40.6	53.3	309,665	8,720	64.2	12,114	84.9	10.5	3.0
Johnson, MO	29101	70,728	15.8	39.1	45.1	67,283	8,690	61.2	4,311	87.0	8.9	3.3
Knox, MO	29103	5,476	9.8	30.3	59.9	5,215	9,413	54.8	221	73.3	3.2	0.0
Laclede, MO	29105	48,993	10.5	45.5	44.0	46,890	7,682	64.0	2,106	68.4	18.0	11.4
Lafayette, MO	29107	52,723	7.3	42.1	50.5	50,484	9,062	63.8	1,897	76.5	18.5	5.0
Lawrence, MO	29109	51,358	10.1	47.1	42.8	49,231	8,129	63.8	2,100	78.7	13.9	5.9
Lewis, MO	29111	13,903	8.9	46.7	44.4	12,942	8,339	64.0	842	83.3	3.4	11.3
Lincoln, MO	29113	73,850	6.8	42.7	50.6	65,767	7,487	60.8	2,777	76.5	14.3	5.2
Linn, MO	29115	23,591	8.7	47.5	43.8	22,765	9,258	63.8	703	81.2	6.8	12.0
Livingston, MO	29117	22,616	9.6	41.9	48.5	21,119	9,445	66.8	826	80.3	11.9	7.9

Note. Data in columns 26 through 41 from the American Community Survey are subject to sampling error, which can be especially large in small counties and small population groups. See notes and definitions for more information.

Table C-1. Population, School, and Student Characteristics by County, Selected Years—*Continued*

County	State/ County Code	High school graduates, 2006–2010			College enrollment, 2006–2010		College graduates, 2006–2010 (percent)						
		Population 25 years and over	High school diploma or less (percent)	High school diploma or more (percent)	Number	Percent public	Bachelor's degree or more	+/- U.S. percent with Bachelor's degree or more	Non-Hispanic White	Black or African American	American Indian and Alaska Native	Asian, Hawaiian, and Pacific Islander	Hispanic or Latino[3]
		30	31	32	33	34	35	36	37	38	39	40	41
MISSOURI	29000	3,906,865	46.4	86.2	405,055	69.8	25.1	-2.8	26.0	15.4	17.8	53.4	16.9
Adair, MO	29001	13,641	49.7	88.1	6,371	91.9	25.5	-2.4	26.0	7.2	0.0	13.1	26.0
Andrew, MO	29003	11,554	51.9	89.6	728	85.0	20.5	-7.4	20.6	90.5	0.0	0.0	0.0
Atchison, MO	29005	4,175	53.3	85.9	164	86.0	21.0	-6.9	21.0	0.0	76.2	0.0	0.0
Audrain, MO	29007	17,303	63.6	81.2	851	81.3	14.0	-13.9	14.3	14.8	52.8	3.5	3.1
Barry, MO	29009	23,981	61.3	79.7	1,138	80.9	12.4	-15.5	12.9	0.0	16.0	0.0	4.1
Barton, MO	29011	8,349	60.6	84.8	272	86.8	13.2	-14.7	13.0	0.0	15.0	0.0	0.0
Bates, MO	29013	11,534	64.6	83.1	575	57.0	11.7	-16.2	11.5	18.8	31.1	100.0	13.5
Benton, MO	29015	14,344	64.7	80.5	491	87.4	12.5	-15.4	11.6	0.0	0.0	0.0	35.6
Bollinger, MO	29017	8,429	69.3	75.1	451	96.2	10.1	-17.8	10.3	0.0	0.0	0.0	0.0
Boone, MO	29019	90,698	31.4	91.9	31,948	88.5	45.2	17.3	47.2	14.6	19.2	76.2	33.3
Buchanan, MO	29021	57,978	53.8	86.2	5,649	87.9	19.4	-8.5	20.1	9.8	8.8	35.5	12.9
Butler, MO	29023	28,931	60.0	76.2	2,008	92.8	14.1	-13.8	14.2	4.7	0.0	71.5	7.3
Caldwell, MO	29025	6,324	60.2	85.8	252	76.6	11.8	-16.1	12.0	0.0	13.3	34.8	0.0
Callaway, MO	29027	28,454	53.1	85.1	2,907	38.8	20.4	-7.5	21.0	14.7	0.0	32.1	0.0
Camden, MO	29029	31,990	45.7	90.2	1,783	53.3	21.0	-6.9	21.3	0.0	4.8	63.8	5.9
Cape Girardeau, MO	29031	47,328	48.2	85.8	8,007	93.0	26.9	-1.0	27.7	11.1	19.7	52.6	9.1
Carroll, MO	29033	6,545	60.4	84.1	335	69.6	17.9	-10.0	17.2	19.5	0.0	100.0	28.6
Carter, MO	29035	4,135	62.5	75.7	424	92.5	11.1	-16.8	11.4	0.0	0.0	0.0	0.0
Cass, MO	29037	63,821	45.4	91.6	4,864	72.1	21.4	-6.5	21.3	26.6	15.2	39.9	17.0
Cedar, MO	29039	9,823	63.0	83.1	727	58.9	11.9	-16.0	12.0	0.0	12.9	9.1	7.8
Chariton, MO	29041	5,551	61.8	84.7	286	79.0	14.2	-13.7	14.3	1.6	50.0	73.3	75.0
Christian, MO	29043	48,180	39.6	91.7	4,196	74.2	26.9	-1.0	27.1	49.6	15.0	37.2	16.0
Clark, MO	29045	4,910	59.4	84.3	277	70.4	12.9	-15.0	12.3	0.0	0.0	52.2	0.0
Clay, MO	29047	141,602	37.9	91.5	12,667	64.8	30.2	2.3	30.9	27.2	33.9	27.5	22.3
Clinton, MO	29049	13,929	50.9	90.2	747	80.2	17.6	-10.3	18.0	1.7	4.4	0.0	6.8
Cole, MO	29051	48,725	42.3	88.9	6,081	84.9	30.5	2.6	30.9	24.6	10.9	55.2	18.1
Cooper, MO	29053	11,765	56.0	82.7	663	69.1	15.7	-12.2	17.0	0.0	0.0	0.0	9.2
Crawford, MO	29055	16,595	63.6	77.7	868	81.7	10.8	-17.1	10.7	0.0	22.8	32.1	6.0
Dade, MO	29057	5,608	64.3	82.0	125	65.6	9.1	-18.8	9.4	0.0	0.0	0.0	0.0
Dallas, MO	29059	11,368	67.1	79.6	419	77.1	10.7	-17.2	10.9	0.0	0.0	0.0	10.8
Daviess, MO	29061	5,511	59.7	84.0	334	65.9	14.4	-13.5	14.3	100.0	0.0	0.0	0.0
De Kalb, MO	29063	9,449	63.9	82.6	454	91.2	12.0	-15.9	13.2	1.4	14.1	32.0	0.0
Dent, MO	29065	10,703	62.3	76.0	392	72.4	11.2	-16.7	11.3	16.4	6.7	0.0	14.5
Douglas, MO	29067	9,279	65.4	79.3	550	82.0	10.2	-17.7	10.3	0.0	0.0	0.0	0.0
Dunklin, MO	29069	21,326	70.4	67.5	907	86.4	10.1	-17.8	10.9	4.9	0.0	0.0	1.8
Franklin, MO	29071	66,820	51.5	85.0	4,606	77.7	16.5	-11.4	16.5	9.1	7.6	39.2	18.0
Gasconade, MO	29073	10,819	58.7	81.9	565	72.6	14.1	-13.8	14.0	0.0	0.0	70.0	0.0
Gentry, MO	29075	4,542	62.7	82.5	192	91.1	12.0	-15.9	12.2	0.0	0.0	0.0	0.0
Greene, MO	29077	174,128	41.2	88.6	29,699	75.2	27.5	-0.4	27.7	12.4	18.4	50.7	24.3
Grundy, MO	29079	6,868	57.3	83.7	428	85.5	12.8	-15.1	12.9	0.0	0.0	0.0	56.3
Harrison, MO	29081	6,154	66.2	84.6	253	71.9	7.6	-20.3	7.5	0.0	0.0	14.6	0.0
Henry, MO	29083	15,804	58.9	83.7	657	82.0	15.1	-12.8	15.3	37.1	0.0	6.2	2.2
Hickory, MO	29085	7,403	65.9	78.9	156	51.9	8.1	-19.8	8.2	0.0	2.9	0.0	0.0
Holt, MO	29087	3,623	60.9	88.7	115	81.7	16.3	-11.6	16.1	75.0	11.1	32.1	0.0
Howard, MO	29089	6,582	56.5	85.6	974	15.5	21.6	-6.3	23.1	1.7	10.0	0.0	9.8
Howell, MO	29091	26,493	59.5	82.4	1,668	91.8	14.1	-13.8	14.2	36.8	0.0	71.4	4.1
Iron, MO	29093	7,390	66.2	75.2	250	97.2	9.1	-18.8	8.9	0.0	0.0	100.0	34.3
Jackson, MO	29095	439,574	42.8	87.3	42,338	69.7	26.9	-1.0	32.1	14.2	19.7	38.7	9.9
Jasper, MO	29097	73,429	51.9	81.3	6,212	79.5	18.6	-9.3	19.1	4.1	24.8	41.7	7.7
Jefferson, MO	29099	142,692	49.2	85.5	11,597	74.0	16.1	-11.8	16.1	16.4	15.3	28.7	15.9
Johnson, MO	29101	29,506	41.6	90.7	8,680	95.1	24.1	-3.8	23.8	26.8	37.4	27.1	19.6
Knox, MO	29103	2,822	66.3	86.3	64	84.4	13.9	-14.0	13.9	0.0	0.0	62.5	26.3
Laclede, MO	29105	23,499	60.8	81.2	1,334	80.6	13.0	-14.9	12.5	15.7	3.8	63.4	25.6
Lafayette, MO	29107	22,483	55.6	85.0	1,092	76.4	15.9	-12.0	16.2	12.9	0.0	57.9	8.7
Lawrence, MO	29109	25,380	60.6	80.5	1,033	79.2	13.3	-14.6	13.6	0.0	0.0	66.7	5.9
Lewis, MO	29111	6,550	60.0	84.4	1,077	19.8	13.0	-14.9	13.0	8.2	0.0	23.3	28.6
Lincoln, MO	29113	32,630	59.4	83.1	1,762	64.0	11.9	-16.0	11.6	15.6	0.0	39.2	16.8
Linn, MO	29115	8,746	62.7	88.0	417	88.7	14.3	-13.6	14.4	0.0	0.0	29.0	14.3
Livingston, MO	29117	10,389	59.6	85.1	717	81.9	19.0	-8.9	19.3	0.4	0.0	0.0	0.0

Note. Data in columns 26 through 41 from the American Community Survey are subject to sampling error, which can be especially large in small counties and small population groups. See notes and definitions for more information.
[3]May be of any race.

Table C-1. Population, School, and Student Characteristics by County, Selected Years—*Continued*

County	State/ County Code	County Type[1]	Population, 2010		Percent of related children 5–17 years in poverty, 2010	Percent of children under 19 years with no health insurance, 2010	Number of schools and students, 2010–2011			Resident enrollment, 2006–2010 K–12 enrollment	
			Total	Percent 5–17 years			School districts	Schools	Students	Number	Percent public
			1	2	3	4	5	6	7	8	9
MISSOURI—*(Continued)*											
McDonald, MO	29119	2	23,083	20.7	26.8	11.5	1	10	3,797	4,934	92.0
Macon, MO	29121	7	15,566	17.5	22.1	9.7	6	14	2,301	2,630	90.7
Madison, MO	29123	7	12,226	17.5	26.7	7.5	2	6	2,057	2,074	100.0
Maries, MO	29125	8	9,176	17.3	21.0	10.5	2	5	1,378	1,622	83.9
Marion, MO	29127	5	28,781	17.1	19.5	5.9	3	13	5,057	4,926	88.4
Mercer, MO	29129	9	3,785	18.5	19.6	12.4	2	4	578	677	99.4
Miller, MO	29131	6	24,748	18.3	27.4	7.1	5	15	5,122	4,580	91.8
Mississippi, MO	29133	7	14,358	16.0	35.8	6.1	2	7	2,211	2,523	92.8
Moniteau, MO	29135	3	15,607	18.2	18.2	9.2	6	10	2,401	3,002	89.1
Monroe, MO	29137	9	8,840	17.2	21.5	9.8	5	10	1,521	1,643	88.7
Montgomery, MO	29139	8	12,236	17.0	24.2	7.3	2	6	1,802	2,229	92.1
Morgan, MO	29141	8	20,565	15.9	31.3	12.2	2	7	2,092	2,906	77.9
New Madrid, MO	29143	7	18,956	17.2	31.5	6.4	4	12	2,849	3,347	97.0
Newton, MO	29145	3	58,114	18.7	20.9	9.3	6	21	8,771	10,576	87.9
Nodaway, MO	29147	6	23,370	13.0	14.0	6.5	7	17	2,725	3,223	88.2
Oregon, MO	29149	9	10,881	16.6	32.8	8.5	4	8	1,966	1,888	97.6
Osage, MO	29151	3	13,878	18.3	12.3	8.3	3	6	1,696	2,577	71.1
Ozark, MO	29153	9	9,723	15.0	36.1	11.2	5	9	1,668	1,446	98.1
Pemiscot, MO	29155	7	18,296	19.8	42.5	5.4	8	18	3,852	3,831	98.8
Perry, MO	29157	7	18,971	18.5	14.8	6.7	2	6	2,498	3,440	72.6
Pettis, MO	29159	4	42,201	18.1	22.9	9.2	7	19	6,533	7,844	89.7
Phelps, MO	29161	5	45,156	15.5	21.0	7.4	4	14	6,440	7,268	87.4
Pike, MO	29163	6	18,516	16.1	22.6	9.0	4	11	2,661	2,989	84.3
Platte, MO	29165	1	89,322	18.3	7.7	4.7	4	31	15,197	15,475	86.1
Polk, MO	29167	2	31,137	18.2	27.0	8.1	6	17	5,495	5,240	90.4
Pulaski, MO	29169	5	52,274	16.4	16.0	6.5	6	20	9,044	8,694	94.5
Putnam, MO	29171	9	4,979	17.3	24.3	11.3	1	3	768	872	90.5
Ralls, MO	29173	9	10,167	17.1	14.0	8.4	1	4	740	1,746	86.7
Randolph, MO	29175	6	25,414	16.9	21.8	6.9	5	15	3,985	4,669	89.3
Ray, MO	29177	1	23,494	18.7	13.7	6.4	5	13	3,571	4,571	94.7
Reynolds, MO	29179	9	6,696	17.0	33.0	8.0	4	8	1,114	1,131	99.7
Ripley, MO	29181	9	14,100	17.6	38.1	8.2	4	8	2,353	2,406	94.6
St. Charles, MO	29183	1	360,485	19.0	6.0	4.3	5	77	58,532	67,393	82.1
St. Clair, MO	29185	8	9,805	15.0	29.6	10.1	4	6	963	1,524	89.6
Ste. Genevieve, MO	29186	6	18,145	17.6	14.6	7.1	1	4	1,958	3,249	75.1
St. Francois, MO	29187	4	65,359	15.9	23.1	6.1	5	25	10,644	11,267	91.3
St. Louis, MO	29189	1	998,954	17.6	12.0	4.9	23	262	146,579	181,043	77.3
Saline, MO	29195	6	23,370	16.6	23.7	7.7	8	17	3,680	4,097	94.9
Schuyler, MO	29197	9	4,431	19.1	28.7	10.3	1	3	672	722	90.0
Scotland, MO	29199	9	4,843	20.2	24.7	19.7	2	3	606	716	64.1
Scott, MO	29201	5	39,191	18.1	24.6	6.4	7	22	6,853	7,567	90.0
Shannon, MO	29203	9	8,441	17.3	39.0	8.9	3	8	2,083	1,477	99.3
Shelby, MO	29205	9	6,373	18.1	22.0	10.4	2	7	1,079	1,198	96.1
Stoddard, MO	29207	7	29,968	16.8	23.4	7.4	7	20	5,122	5,339	93.4
Stone, MO	29209	8	32,202	14.3	26.6	11.4	5	18	4,367	5,059	95.2
Sullivan, MO	29211	9	6,714	17.9	20.8	12.3	3	7	1,141	1,185	96.9
Taney, MO	29213	6	51,675	16.0	25.6	9.6	7	20	8,018	8,129	92.6
Texas, MO	29215	9	26,008	15.8	29.1	8.3	7	15	4,047	4,538	94.1
Vernon, MO	29217	7	21,159	18.0	25.3	9.3	4	13	3,212	3,864	87.4
Warren, MO	29219	1	32,513	17.9	17.2	6.2	2	9	4,548	5,635	80.7
Washington, MO	29221	1	25,195	17.5	31.7	6.8	4	12	3,789	4,506	96.3
Wayne, MO	29223	9	13,521	15.5	35.2	7.8	2	7	1,835	2,089	93.0
Webster, MO	29225	2	36,202	20.3	26.5	9.2	5	18	7,091	6,971	88.9
Worth, MO	29227	9	2,171	15.9	19.9	12.5	1	2	356	355	97.5
Wright, MO	29229	6	18,815	19.0	32.2	8.6	5	14	3,592	3,560	90.3
St. Louis city, MO	29510	1	319,294	14.5	38.6	6.0	17	103	35,535	50,545	79.3

[1]County type codes are from the Economic Research Service of the United States Department of Agriculture. See notes and definitions for more information.

Table C-1. Population, School, and Student Characteristics by County, Selected Years—*Continued*

County	State/ County Code	Characteristics of students, 2010–2011				Number of graduates, 2008–2009	Staff and students, 2010–2011			
		Percent with IEP[2]	Percent eligible for free or reduced lunch	Percent minority	Percent English-language learners		Total staff	Number of teachers	Student/ teacher ratio	Central admin. staff
		10	11	12	13	14	15	16	17	18
MISSOURI—*(Continued)*										
McDonald, MO	29119	13.2	64.7	24.1	7.0	224	490	282	13.5	28
Macon, MO	29121	14.1	48.5	7.7	. . .	172	324	203	11.3	20
Madison, MO	29123	12.9	57.9	3.2	0.9	139	270	150	13.7	23
Maries, MO	29125	14.9	49.4	1.2	0.1	111	167	102	13.6	9
Marion, MO	29127	15.6	47.9	11.5	0.1	374	737	387	13.1	59
Mercer, MO	29129	16.1	46.9	1.0	. . .	39	102	57	10.1	14
Miller, MO	29131	13.4	51.7	4.7	0.4	381	730	382	13.4	56
Mississippi, MO	29133	14.0	65.4	32.6	. . .	117	297	160	13.9	24
Moniteau, MO	29135	13.7	41.3	8.9	4.3	170	347	193	12.4	24
Monroe, MO	29137	15.5	47.6	8.2	0.4	124	242	136	11.2	22
Montgomery, MO	29139	10.5	52.4	8.2	0.1	138	233	138	13.1	21
Morgan, MO	29141	13.5	59.5	5.8	0.1	163	327	173	12.1	25
New Madrid, MO	29143	16.6	60.9	26.6	. . .	220	449	241	11.8	38
Newton, MO	29145	14.3	54.5	18.4	4.4	549	1,120	599	14.7	75
Nodaway, MO	29147	14.1	35.6	3.0	0.5	223	466	259	10.5	46
Oregon, MO	29149	16.1	58.7	3.4	. . .	127	303	169	11.7	21
Osage, MO	29151	12.1	31.5	1.2	0.1	188	244	134	12.7	20
Ozark, MO	29153	14.3	62.5	1.7	. . .	119	284	151	11.1	25
Pemiscot, MO	29155	14.3	65.9	41.0	0.2	233	572	333	11.6	59
Perry, MO	29157	16.1	46.6	3.4	1.1	176	331	182	13.7	31
Pettis, MO	29159	12.2	57.9	21.5	8.2	427	889	497	13.1	55
Phelps, MO	29161	14.1	49.0	8.6	0.9	490	883	440	14.6	84
Pike, MO	29163	12.1	46.4	10.5	0.7	178	359	206	12.9	26
Platte, MO	29165	10.4	24.1	23.8	2.8	1,056	1,996	1,063	14.3	159
Polk, MO	29167	15.9	48.0	6.6	0.6	376	796	402	13.7	45
Pulaski, MO	29169	13.1	41.5	27.9	2.3	565	1,261	632	14.3	98
Putnam, MO	29171	14.1	46.9	2.7	0.1	61	102	60	12.7	7
Ralls, MO	29173	15.1	40.9	4.2	0.1	67	97	59	12.5	7
Randolph, MO	29175	16.8	52.9	11.2	. . .	282	554	323	12.3	47
Ray, MO	29177	10.6	35.8	4.4	. . .	258	447	269	13.3	35
Reynolds, MO	29179	15.9	62.0	4.7	0.1	79	211	105	10.6	18
Ripley, MO	29181	13.1	65.8	2.4	. . .	132	324	182	13.0	23
St. Charles, MO	29183	14.5	19.9	14.4	1.4	3,964	7,522	3,770	15.5	605
St. Clair, MO	29185	13.1	53.7	3.4	0.2	62	142	80	12.0	13
Ste. Genevieve, MO	29186	14.6	46.4	3.9	. . .	155	259	145	13.5	20
St. Francois, MO	29187	15.4	54.7	4.7	0.2	794	1,422	730	14.6	106
St. Louis, MO	29189	16.9	34.8	46.4	2.5	11,084	23,539	11,745	12.5	1,979
Saline, MO	29195	14.9	53.6	23.1	3.2	274	499	300	12.3	40
Schuyler, MO	29197	17.0	55.4	2.4	. . .	59	98	56	12.0	6
Scotland, MO	29199	13.7	56.1	1.3	. . .	63	119	58	10.5	7
Scott, MO	29201	11.9	56.0	23.7	0.3	477	966	511	13.4	107
Shannon, MO	29203	14.2	70.8	3.1	0.1	67	345	163	12.8	24
Shelby, MO	29205	13.1	45.7	3.5	. . .	103	155	84	12.8	13
Stoddard, MO	29207	13.4	52.6	3.3	0.1	458	721	384	13.3	54
Stone, MO	29209	15.3	54.9	4.9	0.5	314	644	332	13.1	54
Sullivan, MO	29211	10.8	62.0	25.7	13.1	83	183	104	11.0	13
Taney, MO	29213	10.7	57.3	12.0	3.1	529	1,096	522	15.4	99
Texas, MO	29215	14.5	55.4	3.3	0.1	290	554	325	12.5	37
Vernon, MO	29217	13.2	50.4	4.1	0.5	223	475	269	11.9	33
Warren, MO	29219	12.4	47.7	10.0	1.9	327	650	305	14.9	46
Washington, MO	29221	16.2	59.8	4.2	. . .	238	498	265	14.3	39
Wayne, MO	29223	15.4	64.3	2.9	0.2	132	287	148	12.4	24
Webster, MO	29225	12.5	47.7	5.9	0.4	435	930	496	14.3	68
Worth, MO	29227	16.0	51.7	0.6	. . .	30	56	34	10.5	3
Wright, MO	29229	13.6	63.6	2.9	0.1	218	528	282	12.7	41
St. Louis city, MO	29510	14.7	79.6	87.2	6.1	1,810	3,990	2,750	12.9	128

[2]IEP=Individual Education Program. See notes and definitions for more information.

. . . = Not available.

Table C-1. Population, School, and Student Characteristics by County, Selected Years—*Continued*

County	State/ County Code	Revenues, 2008–2009				Current expenditures, 2008–2009			Resident population 16 to 19 years, 2006–2010			
		Total revenue ($1,000's)	Percentage of revenue from: Federal government	State government	Local government	Amount ($1,000's)	Amount per student	Percent for instruction	Total population 16 to 19 years	Percent enrolled in school	Percent high school graduates, not enrolled in school	Percent not enrolled, not grads, not employed, or not in labor force
		19	20	21	22	23	24	25	26	27	28	29
MISSOURI— *(Continued)*												
McDonald, MO	29119	33,110	11.8	48.3	40.0	32,278	8,528	65.7	1,697	87.0	10.5	0.8
Macon, MO	29121	21,871	9.4	42.9	47.7	20,889	8,770	61.1	712	76.8	12.9	8.9
Madison, MO	29123	15,817	11.6	48.2	40.2	16,423	7,783	65.2	680	66.6	11.0	22.1
Maries, MO	29125	10,986	8.9	39.6	51.5	11,300	8,490	60.4	557	86.9	11.5	1.6
Marion, MO	29127	46,956	9.1	37.8	53.2	41,015	8,224	65.1	1,475	84.1	7.3	2.8
Mercer, MO	29129	6,181	7.4	34.5	58.1	5,875	10,235	59.9	197	76.7	6.1	13.2
Miller, MO	29131	48,740	9.9	29.2	61.0	42,663	8,308	62.0	1,396	82.4	10.1	5.8
Mississippi, MO	29133	17,582	15.7	46.4	37.9	18,662	8,283	63.2	1,023	67.3	14.3	18.5
Moniteau, MO	29135	21,706	8.5	40.4	51.1	19,643	8,161	62.6	783	81.4	5.1	3.2
Monroe, MO	29137	15,537	8.5	37.8	53.7	14,612	9,025	61.1	505	85.9	9.5	3.4
Montgomery, MO	29139	15,760	9.8	35.7	54.5	15,597	8,532	62.8	665	87.4	9.3	1.2
Morgan, MO	29141	18,836	11.9	22.7	65.4	18,559	8,360	67.3	1,028	75.6	10.4	11.1
New Madrid, MO	29143	28,300	13.3	31.0	55.7	27,838	9,398	59.0	1,007	81.2	4.1	11.8
Newton, MO	29145	66,947	11.2	49.0	39.7	63,676	7,247	63.2	3,382	79.0	14.6	4.2
Nodaway, MO	29147	30,975	6.4	30.0	63.6	28,460	10,315	61.1	2,565	93.6	5.7	0.6
Oregon, MO	29149	15,373	17.4	47.0	35.6	13,623	7,780	66.4	561	72.9	20.5	2.5
Osage, MO	29151	13,961	7.2	35.8	56.9	13,943	8,344	58.2	933	90.1	7.2	0.9
Ozark, MO	29153	15,063	12.7	43.5	43.9	14,776	8,966	61.1	481	79.8	16.0	2.5
Pemiscot, MO	29155	41,627	15.2	47.6	37.3	40,328	10,359	63.8	1,111	74.4	14.8	9.7
Perry, MO	29157	21,158	9.6	27.0	63.3	19,271	7,699	59.0	1,001	80.6	13.7	5.7
Pettis, MO	29159	56,396	11.5	38.2	50.2	50,125	7,779	63.3	2,358	82.4	12.0	2.3
Phelps, MO	29161	61,391	8.8	43.0	48.1	53,912	8,429	62.1	3,666	90.0	7.1	2.7
Pike, MO	29163	26,247	8.9	36.2	54.9	24,062	8,775	62.4	995	73.6	15.3	7.8
Platte, MO	29165	173,155	3.7	16.6	79.7	144,333	9,769	58.8	4,540	86.3	8.4	2.4
Polk, MO	29167	48,565	10.2	48.2	41.6	46,341	8,626	62.8	2,177	82.3	9.8	7.5
Pulaski, MO	29169	89,264	27.2	45.9	26.8	73,717	8,509	60.8	5,972	45.2	52.6	1.1
Putnam, MO	29171	7,529	13.8	36.8	49.5	7,450	9,371	65.1	350	54.0	28.3	7.4
Ralls, MO	29173	6,290	8.5	35.9	55.6	5,590	7,365	61.3	519	89.6	5.0	5.4
Randolph, MO	29175	38,322	9.3	34.2	56.5	34,163	8,773	62.4	1,274	73.9	10.4	13.3
Ray, MO	29177	33,319	6.7	45.5	47.7	30,685	8,264	59.7	1,361	77.2	9.0	6.3
Reynolds, MO	29179	13,978	12.0	32.2	55.9	12,298	10,675	55.5	322	69.3	13.0	14.3
Ripley, MO	29181	18,708	14.4	54.1	31.5	17,729	7,421	64.5	845	76.6	4.9	18.6
St. Charles, MO	29183	573,913	3.6	22.8	73.6	512,628	8,889	61.7	19,931	88.6	8.5	1.4
St. Clair, MO	29185	9,186	10.5	43.6	46.0	8,776	8,537	59.7	487	81.9	11.7	6.4
Ste. Genevieve, MO	29186	18,305	8.8	18.0	73.3	17,760	8,779	62.8	955	86.5	12.8	0.7
St. Francois, MO	29187	93,176	10.1	45.3	44.7	85,390	7,952	61.3	3,318	80.7	9.0	9.5
St. Louis, MO	29189	2,029,701	5.2	18.5	76.3	1,800,612	12,504	60.4	56,582	87.5	7.5	3.5
Saline, MO	29195	32,634	10.6	44.5	44.9	31,150	8,410	64.0	1,647	89.6	6.5	3.1
Schuyler, MO	29197	6,055	10.6	48.2	41.2	5,873	8,662	61.6	205	61.0	26.3	12.7
Scotland, MO	29199	6,886	8.8	36.7	54.5	6,299	8,421	65.2	257	50.6	15.6	6.6
Scott, MO	29201	57,406	12.5	43.6	43.9	55,047	7,919	63.1	2,297	82.2	10.6	4.5
Shannon, MO	29203	7,588	14.6	49.4	36.0	7,603	9,019	61.0	504	76.2	8.1	8.9
Shelby, MO	29205	10,799	8.4	40.2	51.4	10,399	9,268	64.5	311	93.6	2.6	0.0
Stoddard, MO	29207	43,172	9.6	41.2	49.2	40,678	7,719	63.7	1,765	71.8	14.8	7.9
Stone, MO	29209	43,026	9.9	32.0	58.1	37,701	8,509	59.8	1,323	76.5	10.6	12.3
Sullivan, MO	29211	11,643	10.9	48.4	40.8	10,843	9,315	62.1	311	68.5	23.8	4.2
Taney, MO	29213	71,558	8.8	24.7	66.5	60,744	7,940	59.4	2,736	91.5	6.3	0.8
Texas, MO	29215	35,201	16.9	47.8	35.3	32,493	8,150	63.0	1,385	81.9	7.2	10.8
Vernon, MO	29217	29,115	11.3	45.5	43.2	28,623	8,873	64.9	1,275	82.2	9.3	3.2
Warren, MO	29219	40,947	7.0	33.7	59.2	34,926	7,673	58.2	1,617	80.3	10.1	8.2
Washington, MO	29221	33,602	11.3	52.4	36.3	30,750	7,911	57.1	1,294	73.6	12.8	9.5
Wayne, MO	29223	16,250	14.6	47.4	38.0	15,053	8,230	58.9	605	74.6	19.7	2.2
Webster, MO	29225	56,208	9.7	43.1	47.1	53,099	7,318	65.0	2,216	75.5	10.3	10.5
Worth, MO	29227	3,429	9.8	46.0	44.2	3,397	8,823	61.4	135	71.1	28.9	0.0
Wright, MO	29229	30,980	13.5	49.9	36.6	29,674	8,077	63.4	1,082	81.0	12.9	3.3
St. Louis city, MO	29510	501,341	13.7	36.5	49.8	486,383	13,268	49.1	18,661	79.3	10.4	7.8

Note. Data in columns 26 through 41 from the American Community Survey are subject to sampling error, which can be especially large in small counties and small population groups. See notes and definitions for more information.

Table C-1. Population, School, and Student Characteristics by County, Selected Years—*Continued*

County	State/ County Code	High school graduates, 2006–2010			College enrollment, 2006–2010		College graduates, 2006–2010 (percent)						
		Population 25 years and over	High school diploma or less (percent)	High school diploma or more (percent)	Number	Percent public	Bachelor's degree or more	+/- U.S. percent with Bachelor's degree or more	Non-Hispanic White	Black or African American	American Indian and Alaska Native	Asian, Hawaiian, and Pacific Islander	Hispanic or Latino[3]
		30	31	32	33	34	35	36	37	38	39	40	41
MISSOURI— *(Continued)*													
McDonald, MO	29119	14,412	61.4	76.6	721	78.9	8.9	-19.0	9.0	34.0	5.9	11.5	4.4
Macon, MO	29121	10,688	60.5	82.1	459	78.6	15.0	-12.9	15.4	0.0	13.5	32.8	0.0
Madison, MO	29123	8,339	61.1	75.6	330	88.2	10.7	-17.2	10.9	0.0	50.0	2.7	2.2
Maries, MO	29125	6,205	63.6	79.6	362	94.2	14.2	-13.7	14.3	16.7	0.0	0.0	0.0
Marion, MO	29127	19,017	56.9	83.9	1,533	60.1	16.9	-11.0	17.6	7.6	16.4	15.3	7.2
Mercer, MO	29129	2,565	59.6	87.3	150	84.0	14.2	-13.7	14.1	0.0	0.0	72.7	0.0
Miller, MO	29131	16,737	61.4	82.6	860	84.7	11.9	-16.0	11.9	15.9	5.1	34.3	15.5
Mississippi, MO	29133	9,573	74.8	66.2	225	89.8	10.5	-17.4	13.3	1.1	0.0	0.0	0.0
Moniteau, MO	29135	10,276	58.7	80.4	542	85.2	17.1	-10.8	18.5	0.4	13.0	9.1	2.0
Monroe, MO	29137	6,224	62.7	84.6	292	62.0	11.9	-16.0	11.7	11.6	0.0	0.0	11.4
Montgomery, MO	29139	8,468	65.2	78.3	356	56.2	12.2	-15.7	12.1	17.3	0.0	0.0	17.7
Morgan, MO	29141	14,651	62.7	78.7	619	83.2	11.8	-16.1	12.1	16.9	0.0	0.0	2.3
New Madrid, MO	29143	12,807	68.0	73.2	670	83.0	12.2	-15.7	12.8	6.6	0.0	100.0	3.3
Newton, MO	29145	37,757	49.7	84.9	2,842	78.4	18.3	-9.6	18.6	17.9	19.1	19.1	4.5
Nodaway, MO	29147	12,509	50.6	88.4	5,173	95.8	23.7	-4.2	23.7	6.2	0.0	30.6	29.1
Oregon, MO	29149	7,552	65.6	76.8	371	75.5	10.2	-17.7	10.2	0.0	3.7	0.0	21.0
Osage, MO	29151	9,025	60.8	86.0	586	69.6	13.2	-14.7	13.3	6.3	0.0	0.0	20.0
Ozark, MO	29153	7,161	65.1	78.7	190	87.4	11.1	-16.8	11.0	0.0	0.0	0.0	25.5
Pemiscot, MO	29155	11,738	69.7	70.1	631	73.2	9.8	-18.1	11.8	2.5	0.0	0.0	19.7
Perry, MO	29157	12,607	66.2	80.5	698	72.3	12.2	-15.7	12.1	0.0	0.0	47.5	0.0
Pettis, MO	29159	26,970	53.6	81.3	2,208	89.0	15.8	-12.1	16.1	16.5	0.0	66.5	5.1
Phelps, MO	29161	26,750	47.4	85.9	6,980	92.0	25.3	-2.6	24.1	51.9	26.4	75.6	1.1
Pike, MO	29163	12,779	63.6	79.5	566	52.3	12.6	-15.3	13.8	2.0	0.0	31.8	2.7
Platte, MO	29165	58,211	30.7	94.1	6,238	61.1	36.9	9.0	37.5	31.5	21.0	44.9	25.9
Polk, MO	29167	19,570	58.9	79.6	2,896	32.6	16.6	-11.3	17.2	0.0	0.0	25.4	18.8
Pulaski, MO	29169	26,113	45.9	88.1	4,872	74.7	18.4	-9.5	18.6	14.1	9.1	10.3	27.4
Putnam, MO	29171	3,464	58.0	85.8	168	89.9	15.6	-12.3	16.1	0.0	0.0	0.0	0.0
Ralls, MO	29173	7,136	62.2	84.5	382	70.9	16.1	-11.8	16.3	13.3	0.0	100.0	4.1
Randolph, MO	29175	17,194	59.1	82.2	1,016	74.7	11.7	-16.2	12.3	3.3	0.0	13.5	11.0
Ray, MO	29177	15,765	58.3	86.1	917	70.3	13.5	-14.4	13.7	2.9	11.1	0.0	11.4
Reynolds, MO	29179	4,707	69.8	72.8	161	93.2	6.7	-21.2	6.7	0.0	18.0	100.0	0.0
Ripley, MO	29181	9,632	68.1	70.6	527	84.8	12.2	-15.7	12.2	0.0	0.0	0.0	21.7
St. Charles, MO	29183	228,191	35.3	92.2	22,729	60.5	33.4	5.5	32.9	31.8	49.6	61.4	27.8
St. Clair, MO	29185	7,163	64.9	82.9	184	75.0	14.1	-13.8	14.3	0.0	0.0	0.0	0.0
Ste. Genevieve, MO	29186	12,583	61.6	81.1	682	73.3	11.6	-16.3	11.8	1.5	0.0	0.0	9.0
St. Francois, MO	29187	44,083	56.3	79.2	3,185	79.2	14.8	-13.1	15.4	1.7	5.8	36.3	7.9
St. Louis, MO	29189	673,957	32.5	90.7	73,444	57.4	39.1	11.2	43.5	18.7	31.9	67.8	34.1
Saline, MO	29195	15,046	58.1	79.8	1,959	37.0	17.7	-10.2	18.5	15.3	0.0	12.2	7.7
Schuyler, MO	29197	2,930	62.4	87.0	119	89.9	9.6	-18.3	9.6	0.0	0.0	0.0	0.0
Scotland, MO	29199	3,191	59.4	81.5	85	75.3	17.8	-10.1	17.5	0.0	0.0	0.0	0.0
Scott, MO	29201	26,119	67.0	75.8	1,492	87.5	13.7	-14.2	14.9	2.8	54.2	40.9	4.5
Shannon, MO	29203	5,717	65.5	76.4	308	70.1	13.7	-14.2	13.4	0.0	40.5	0.0	0.0
Shelby, MO	29205	4,397	56.3	88.6	160	61.9	13.4	-14.5	13.5	0.0	0.0	0.0	14.8
Stoddard, MO	29207	20,624	67.7	75.1	906	81.3	11.7	-16.2	11.9	0.0	8.6	0.0	2.7
Stone, MO	29209	23,933	53.6	83.4	622	68.3	16.8	-11.1	17.1	0.0	15.8	41.6	29.9
Sullivan, MO	29211	4,640	64.2	80.9	137	97.1	9.9	-18.0	10.8	100.0	0.0	100.0	3.9
Taney, MO	29213	33,674	49.0	86.6	2,979	29.9	20.0	-7.9	20.6	6.0	16.4	15.0	7.5
Texas, MO	29215	17,654	64.9	79.4	838	66.1	11.8	-16.1	12.3	0.0	0.0	36.4	2.6
Vernon, MO	29217	13,833	61.6	84.1	857	68.1	14.4	-13.5	14.3	0.0	19.4	33.9	21.1
Warren, MO	29219	21,180	55.4	83.0	1,240	66.6	16.9	-11.0	17.2	4.8	29.1	0.0	13.2
Washington, MO	29221	16,802	71.4	70.3	799	82.1	7.7	-20.2	7.7	0.0	45.0	66.7	0.0
Wayne, MO	29223	9,607	67.4	72.9	428	89.3	8.7	-19.2	8.6	0.0	15.9	0.0	24.2
Webster, MO	29225	22,902	58.0	82.2	1,101	78.0	14.7	-13.2	14.9	0.0	6.5	0.0	22.5
Worth, MO	29227	1,536	63.4	85.6	62	62.9	12.8	-15.1	12.9	0.0	0.0	0.0	0.0
Wright, MO	29229	12,427	65.0	76.3	482	59.5	11.3	-16.6	11.2	38.5	18.2	11.8	0.0
St. Louis city, MO	29510	209,910	46.5	80.6	30,919	46.6	26.9	-1.0	39.6	12.1	24.7	53.0	21.2

Note. Data in columns 26 through 41 from the American Community Survey are subject to sampling error, which can be especially large in small counties and small population groups. See notes and definitions for more information.

[3]May be of any race.

Table C-1. Population, School, and Student Characteristics by County, Selected Years—*Continued*

County	State/ County Code	County Type[1]	Population, 2010		Percent of related children 5–17 years in poverty, 2010	Percent of children under 19 years with no health insurance, 2010	Number of schools and students, 2010–2011			Resident enrollment, 2006–2010 K–12 enrollment	
			Total	Percent 5–17 years			School districts	Schools	Students	Number	Percent public
			1	2	3	4	5	6	7	8	9
MONTANA	30000	X	989,415	16.3	18.7	12.7	505	827	141,693	160,584	91.4
Beaverhead, MT	30001	7	9,246	14.8	23.2	18.5	10	13	1,200	1,407	93.7
Big Horn, MT	30003	6	12,865	22.6	30.8	13.5	9	15	2,256	2,633	92.0
Blaine, MT	30005	9	6,491	21.2	34.9	18.8	13	17	1,213	1,374	93.2
Broadwater, MT	30007	9	5,612	16.7	15.8	18.3	2	3	686	1,224	96.8
Carbon, MT	30009	3	10,078	15.6	13.9	16.4	10	19	1,357	1,741	94.6
Carter, MT	30011	9	1,160	14.1	25.0	29.1	5	6	123	213	93.9
Cascade, MT	30013	3	81,327	16.1	19.1	11.0	16	42	11,598	13,648	89.9
Chouteau, MT	30015	8	5,813	19.5	19.4	20.3	13	15	637	1,158	94.3
Custer, MT	30017	7	11,699	16.5	18.3	11.0	10	12	1,730	1,990	94.6
Daniels, MT	30019	9	1,751	15.4	12.1	18.8	2	3	267	304	100.0
Dawson, MT	30021	7	8,966	14.7	14.0	10.4	9	10	1,223	1,226	92.4
Deer Lodge, MT	30023	7	9,298	14.4	22.9	10.7	3	4	1,106	1,168	100.0
Fallon, MT	30025	9	2,890	16.0	13.1	15.8	3	7	477	456	100.0
Fergus, MT	30027	7	11,586	14.8	18.2	16.5	16	24	1,595	1,762	100.0
Flathead, MT	30029	5	90,928	17.1	18.6	13.2	25	48	13,464	15,510	89.8
Gallatin, MT	30031	5	89,513	14.5	12.2	12.1	23	44	11,199	12,004	86.1
Garfield, MT	30033	9	1,206	16.5	25.4	40.2	9	8	189	239	100.0
Glacier, MT	30035	7	13,399	22.4	35.4	12.7	7	16	2,745	2,842	93.7
Golden Valley, MT	30037	8	884	18.7	29.9	24.6	3	6	144	141	94.3
Granite, MT	30039	8	3,079	13.3	22.6	23.0	5	7	378	439	95.9
Hill, MT	30041	7	16,096	19.0	22.8	11.9	12	17	3,064	3,074	91.5
Jefferson, MT	30043	9	11,406	18.0	10.7	13.0	10	12	1,547	1,984	87.6
Judith Basin, MT	30045	8	2,072	15.9	20.5	25.9	5	10	262	274	99.3
Lake, MT	30047	6	28,746	17.9	28.0	18.3	13	21	4,300	5,149	95.4
Lewis and Clark, MT	30049	5	63,395	16.4	13.3	9.5	16	31	9,662	10,306	91.1
Liberty, MT	30051	9	2,339	16.5	22.5	17.0	5	7	276	390	95.4
Lincoln, MT	30053	7	19,687	15.0	29.4	15.6	10	13	2,596	2,930	87.3
McCone, MT	30055	9	1,734	15.3	21.2	26.6	4	6	265	283	92.6
Madison, MT	30057	9	7,691	13.2	15.9	20.0	7	13	886	1,019	86.0
Meagher, MT	30059	9	1,891	14.6	27.9	20.5	4	4	240	332	99.1
Mineral, MT	30061	8	4,223	13.2	25.2	15.4	4	9	612	636	93.2
Missoula, MT	30063	3	109,299	14.2	16.8	10.8	16	40	13,201	15,550	91.1
Musselshell, MT	30065	8	4,538	16.1	28.3	18.6	5	6	698	603	97.2
Park, MT	30067	7	15,636	14.5	18.6	13.9	12	16	2,016	2,560	94.0
Petroleum, MT	30069	9	494	17.8	23.3	31.1	2	3	98	111	90.1
Phillips, MT	30071	9	4,253	17.6	18.2	19.3	6	14	696	862	97.3
Pondera, MT	30073	7	6,153	17.9	25.8	17.3	10	15	993	1,160	92.0
Powder River, MT	30075	9	1,743	17.0	15.1	26.9	7	6	301	335	100.0
Powell, MT	30077	7	7,027	13.0	20.2	13.8	10	9	809	980	93.6
Prairie, MT	30079	9	1,179	12.8	23.6	25.6	2	3	157	149	100.0
Ravalli, MT	30081	6	40,212	16.6	22.8	16.9	10	23	5,755	6,619	86.1
Richland, MT	30083	7	9,746	17.0	13.3	15.1	12	14	1,635	1,492	96.7
Roosevelt, MT	30085	7	10,425	22.1	36.0	12.0	14	22	2,298	2,496	100.0
Rosebud, MT	30087	9	9,233	21.5	25.2	12.7	11	15	1,702	2,086	93.0
Sanders, MT	30089	8	11,413	15.5	28.8	18.6	14	17	1,456	1,825	93.1
Sheridan, MT	30091	9	3,384	14.9	12.9	16.6	5	9	508	460	92.0
Silver Bow, MT	30093	5	34,200	15.2	19.9	9.5	7	12	4,447	5,435	91.5
Stillwater, MT	30095	8	9,117	16.9	11.7	12.7	15	18	1,413	1,585	93.8
Sweet Grass, MT	30097	9	3,651	17.6	13.7	19.4	6	6	539	697	90.4
Teton, MT	30099	8	6,073	18.0	17.7	20.2	12	18	1,173	1,042	91.6
Toole, MT	30101	7	5,324	15.4	15.8	14.6	5	10	747	872	82.0
Treasure, MT	30103	8	718	13.6	17.5	23.3	2	3	91	138	94.9
Valley, MT	30105	7	7,369	17.5	18.7	16.4	9	17	1,218	1,330	91.9
Wheatland, MT	30107	9	2,168	16.5	23.2	24.2	6	7	322	187	82.4
Wibaux, MT	30109	9	1,017	16.1	14.1	20.3	2	3	137	198	90.4
Yellowstone, MT	30111	3	147,972	16.8	14.4	9.3	22	59	21,986	23,956	92.3

[1]County type codes are from the Economic Research Service of the United States Department of Agriculture. See notes and definitions for more information.

Table C-1. Population, School, and Student Characteristics by County, Selected Years—*Continued*

County	State/ County Code	Characteristics of students, 2010–2011				Number of graduates, 2008–2009	Staff and students, 2010–2011			
		Percent with IEP[2]	Percent eligible for free or reduced lunch	Percent minority	Percent English-language learners		Total staff	Number of teachers	Student/ teacher ratio	Central admin. staff
		10	11	12	13	14	15	16	17	18
MONTANA	30000	11.8	40.8	18.3	2.3	10,077	15,151	10,361	13.7	175
Beaverhead, MT	30001	12.8	29.7	7.2	1.4	72	130	88	13.6	3
Big Horn, MT	30003	9.4	71.2	86.6	18.0	134	313	192	11.7	3
Blaine, MT	30005	13.7	74.9	64.1	14.6	75	170	117	10.4	5
Broadwater, MT	30007	9.9	42.0	13.6	. . .	41	75	52	13.2	1
Carbon, MT	30009	12.9	28.7	7.1	0.3	113	178	132	10.2	3
Carter, MT	30011	11.4	35.0	4.1	. . .	12	21	19	6.5	0
Cascade, MT	30013	10.3	37.5	18.6	3.1	867	1,223	877	13.2	8
Chouteau, MT	30015	11.5	46.6	5.2	. . .	52	99	69	9.2	2
Custer, MT	30017	13.2	29.1	8.6	. . .	135	204	124	13.9	1
Daniels, MT	30019	18.4	30.0	9.4	0.7	18	31	21	12.8	1
Dawson, MT	30021	15.5	26.3	6.4	. . .	101	159	99	12.4	3
Deer Lodge, MT	30023	13.0	45.3	7.8	. . .	97	105	71	15.6	1
Fallon, MT	30025	11.3	22.6	7.8	. . .	54	71	55	8.8	2
Fergus, MT	30027	13.8	41.8	5.9	0.3	137	220	150	10.7	4
Flathead, MT	30029	11.1	38.9	6.9	0.5	1,023	1,301	883	15.3	10
Gallatin, MT	30031	9.1	25.3	8.9	0.8	727	1,000	691	16.2	9
Garfield, MT	30033	10.6	23.8	0.5	. . .	9	26	22	8.6	0
Glacier, MT	30035	13.4	80.8	82.6	23.3	176	338	216	12.7	2
Golden Valley, MT	30037	17.4	58.3	5.6	16.7	16	30	23	6.3	1
Granite, MT	30039	19.3	23.8	5.3	. . .	39	45	39	9.8	1
Hill, MT	30041	13.5	61.9	48.0	8.2	209	352	214	14.4	6
Jefferson, MT	30043	10.8	25.7	9.1	. . .	100	157	120	12.9	4
Judith Basin, MT	30045	11.1	44.3	5.7	1.1	22	52	40	6.6	1
Lake, MT	30047	12.1	58.3	51.8	3.7	252	496	321	13.4	5
Lewis and Clark, MT	30049	11.5	31.9	10.6	0.2	666	953	624	15.5	7
Liberty, MT	30051	14.5	33.7	2.5	3.3	20	35	26	10.7	1
Lincoln, MT	30053	8.8	49.4	8.6	0.2	230	268	185	14.1	3
McCone, MT	30055	12.5	35.8	6.0	. . .	17	31	22	11.9	1
Madison, MT	30057	10.7	37.9	6.5	0.3	82	105	82	10.8	2
Meagher, MT	30059	8.8	54.6	3.8	6.3	20	34	27	9.0	1
Mineral, MT	30061	22.2	62.4	12.4	. . .	67	83	59	10.4	3
Missoula, MT	30063	13.0	41.9	10.7	1.7	912	1,274	855	15.4	9
Musselshell, MT	30065	14.3	51.7	6.7	. . .	44	82	52	13.4	2
Park, MT	30067	12.3	35.7	6.0	. . .	146	218	149	13.5	5
Petroleum, MT	30069	10.2	65.3	5.1	. . .	7	13	11	8.9	0
Phillips, MT	30071	10.6	54.5	25.7	0.3	68	106	77	9.0	3
Pondera, MT	30073	11.8	43.0	26.7	8.1	71	132	87	11.4	3
Powder River, MT	30075	12.0	33.2	12.0	. . .	35	40	29	10.4	1
Powell, MT	30077	23.1	40.4	8.3	0.2	50	110	71	11.4	3
Prairie, MT	30079	8.9	52.9	8.9	. . .	8	21	16	9.8	0
Ravalli, MT	30081	13.4	44.4	8.0	0.1	458	632	401	14.4	7
Richland, MT	30083	14.3	27.1	10.4	0.2	129	197	136	12.1	3
Roosevelt, MT	30085	15.2	84.9	77.6	15.2	147	355	231	9.9	5
Rosebud, MT	30087	16.1	54.5	51.6	8.3	126	253	165	10.3	4
Sanders, MT	30089	9.8	63.0	17.4	1.1	123	182	123	11.9	5
Sheridan, MT	30091	17.9	39.2	12.2	. . .	37	80	60	8.4	3
Silver Bow, MT	30093	10.2	42.0	11.6	. . .	298	366	277	16.1	2
Stillwater, MT	30095	11.6	20.8	6.4	. . .	109	182	122	11.6	5
Sweet Grass, MT	30097	10.9	25.2	3.3	. . .	47	66	44	12.3	1
Teton, MT	30099	9.7	33.3	7.6	2.3	76	149	108	10.9	3
Toole, MT	30101	13.0	31.6	10.0	5.9	57	95	69	10.9	2
Treasure, MT	30103	9.9	33.0	18.7	. . .	8	16	13	6.8	1
Valley, MT	30105	12.4	46.3	21.3	. . .	106	177	127	9.6	3
Wheatland, MT	30107	10.6	61.2	7.1	17.7	24	53	41	7.9	2
Wibaux, MT	30109	7.3	26.3	8.8	. . .	13	22	17	8.1	1
Yellowstone, MT	30111	11.7	35.8	17.5	0.5	1,395	2,030	1,425	15.4	13

[2]IEP=Individual Education Program. See notes and definitions for more information.
. . . = Not available.

Table C-1. Population, School, and Student Characteristics by County, Selected Years—*Continued*

County	State/ County Code	Revenues, 2008–2009				Current expenditures, 2008–2009			Resident population 16 to 19 years, 2006–2010			
		Total revenue ($1,000's)	Percentage of revenue from: Federal government	Percentage of revenue from: State government	Percentage of revenue from: Local government	Amount ($1,000's)	Amount per student	Percent for instruction	Total population 16 to 19 years	Percent enrolled in school	Percent high school graduates, not enrolled in school	Percent not enrolled, not grads, not employed, or not in labor force
		19	20	21	22	23	24	25	26	27	28	29
MONTANA	30000	1,607,935	12.2	47.6	40.2	1,424,480	10,047	60.1	56,076	80.7	10.9	4.9
Beaverhead, MT	30001	13,358	5.6	48.3	46.1	12,402	10,501	67.0	737	86.3	6.8	3.7
Big Horn, MT	30003	33,594	37.3	37.9	24.8	29,598	13,527	54.6	896	63.1	16.9	20.1
Blaine, MT	30005	20,101	34.6	45.5	19.9	18,487	16,536	53.9	356	85.7	10.4	3.9
Broadwater, MT	30007	6,770	7.7	51.8	40.5	5,855	7,966	66.5	353	78.5	8.8	2.8
Carbon, MT	30009	20,790	4.2	43.4	52.3	15,873	11,629	62.3	490	81.0	11.0	7.6
Carter, MT	30011	2,413	6.3	52.0	41.7	2,212	16,632	57.3	79	81.0	5.1	0.0
Cascade, MT	30013	108,269	12.4	49.8	37.9	105,164	8,940	61.8	4,588	75.4	17.4	5.1
Chouteau, MT	30015	10,163	7.4	40.0	52.5	9,465	14,495	54.7	351	84.9	11.1	2.6
Custer, MT	30017	15,693	9.9	55.0	35.1	15,233	8,785	61.8	630	82.2	17.1	0.6
Daniels, MT	30019	4,047	5.6	51.6	42.8	3,649	13,718	56.2	62	82.3	17.7	0.0
Dawson, MT	30021	14,872	8.8	53.5	37.7	13,797	10,605	57.2	446	80.7	15.3	3.1
Deer Lodge, MT	30023	11,817	10.6	56.3	33.1	11,300	9,956	53.9	931	46.1	2.4	14.4
Fallon, MT	30025	18,052	1.0	86.9	12.1	7,659	16,192	58.9	129	91.5	8.5	0.0
Fergus, MT	30027	22,945	8.4	44.8	46.8	20,779	12,123	55.3	727	76.1	16.1	6.5
Flathead, MT	30029	130,631	8.0	45.5	46.5	119,168	8,781	62.2	4,962	78.1	13.9	5.6
Gallatin, MT	30031	116,892	5.8	37.7	56.5	92,725	8,625	60.2	5,895	91.8	4.4	1.9
Garfield, MT	30033	2,434	7.9	47.9	44.2	2,410	14,094	54.4	66	72.7	27.3	0.0
Glacier, MT	30035	39,808	37.9	40.4	21.7	35,169	13,347	54.3	886	73.6	12.9	7.1
Golden Valley, MT	30037	2,899	5.8	43.7	50.5	2,493	15,201	60.0	36	86.1	0.0	5.6
Granite, MT	30039	5,342	7.0	40.9	52.1	4,688	11,990	61.5	130	80.0	8.5	4.6
Hill, MT	30041	41,914	30.9	43.2	25.9	37,991	12,651	53.9	1,031	87.9	5.6	3.4
Jefferson, MT	30043	16,521	4.8	52.7	42.5	14,985	9,093	63.6	645	85.9	13.8	0.0
Judith Basin, MT	30045	5,169	5.4	44.1	50.5	4,731	15,115	61.1	105	82.9	11.4	5.7
Lake, MT	30047	47,939	24.2	46.1	29.7	42,885	10,155	64.3	1,735	79.0	9.7	7.8
Lewis and Clark, MT	30049	92,151	9.3	46.8	43.8	84,671	8,886	62.8	3,437	87.3	5.9	2.6
Liberty, MT	30051	3,549	5.3	52.7	42.0	3,230	13,077	55.2	195	55.9	0.0	41.0
Lincoln, MT	30053	27,942	12.9	50.8	36.3	26,011	9,566	61.2	882	75.4	17.5	1.9
McCone, MT	30055	3,204	5.7	45.3	49.0	2,919	11,227	59.4	74	94.6	5.4	0.0
Madison, MT	30057	15,680	5.6	33.4	61.0	11,965	12,756	59.0	307	89.9	5.9	2.6
Meagher, MT	30059	3,150	7.9	41.5	50.6	2,910	11,687	59.6	84	100.0	0.0	0.0
Mineral, MT	30061	9,479	9.9	47.2	42.8	8,886	13,283	64.5	201	71.1	18.4	10.5
Missoula, MT	30063	136,153	9.1	45.3	45.6	125,029	9,536	60.9	6,761	84.4	10.3	2.4
Musselshell, MT	30065	7,993	9.3	54.9	35.8	6,848	10,376	57.8	150	92.0	6.0	2.0
Park, MT	30067	22,210	8.6	47.9	43.5	20,991	9,963	58.2	628	89.5	9.4	1.1
Petroleum, MT	30069	1,436	9.3	53.3	37.5	1,287	13,000	50.9	9	100.0	0.0	0.0
Phillips, MT	30071	12,443	8.3	60.2	31.5	10,472	14,075	58.8	256	90.2	3.9	2.3
Pondera, MT	30073	14,951	25.1	43.8	31.1	12,282	12,394	53.3	326	81.6	5.2	13.2
Powder River, MT	30075	3,864	6.2	61.4	32.4	3,850	12,145	56.1	142	95.1	2.8	2.1
Powell, MT	30077	12,463	15.4	44.9	39.7	10,557	12,177	59.6	299	71.6	14.4	10.0
Prairie, MT	30079	1,919	8.7	47.1	44.2	1,858	14,630	59.6	60	86.7	13.3	0.0
Ravalli, MT	30081	55,207	9.3	53.3	37.4	49,956	8,535	62.0	2,156	76.3	15.5	5.8
Richland, MT	30083	43,739	3.2	81.3	15.5	22,733	13,475	59.7	564	65.4	22.5	2.1
Roosevelt, MT	30085	38,212	33.2	42.9	23.9	36,444	16,321	56.1	788	76.8	10.9	11.6
Rosebud, MT	30087	29,204	26.4	39.1	34.4	26,196	14,725	52.9	594	86.5	7.7	5.7
Sanders, MT	30089	19,186	13.7	48.2	38.1	17,907	12,018	57.7	662	77.5	7.9	11.3
Sheridan, MT	30091	10,879	5.8	65.3	28.9	8,241	17,205	57.4	84	83.3	14.3	0.0
Silver Bow, MT	30093	45,049	9.7	50.0	40.3	40,502	8,865	56.5	1,951	82.7	13.4	2.1
Stillwater, MT	30095	17,736	5.6	42.5	52.0	15,359	10,870	60.1	425	85.9	6.4	3.1
Sweet Grass, MT	30097	6,334	6.3	41.9	51.8	5,878	10,065	65.9	175	72.0	17.1	0.0
Teton, MT	30099	14,747	5.9	47.8	46.3	13,034	11,364	63.7	327	63.3	7.3	20.8
Toole, MT	30101	10,633	6.3	54.2	39.5	8,833	10,655	59.3	224	90.6	0.9	8.5
Treasure, MT	30103	1,756	4.6	43.7	51.7	1,643	14,670	62.0	49	100.0	0.0	0.0
Valley, MT	30105	16,991	14.5	42.2	43.4	15,120	12,213	61.0	450	71.6	15.8	12.7
Wheatland, MT	30107	5,097	8.5	38.9	52.6	4,469	12,311	61.2	139	60.4	0.0	39.6
Wibaux, MT	30109	2,661	5.5	71.6	22.9	2,144	14,487	61.1	51	90.2	9.8	0.0
Yellowstone, MT	30111	210,502	8.1	47.6	44.3	194,325	8,982	61.7	7,360	78.8	11.3	4.9

Note. Data in columns 26 through 41 from the American Community Survey are subject to sampling error, which can be especially large in small counties and small population groups. See notes and definitions for more information.

Table C-1. Population, School, and Student Characteristics by County, Selected Years—*Continued*

County	State/ County Code	High school graduates, 2006–2010			College enrollment, 2006–2010		College graduates, 2006–2010 (percent)						
		Population 25 years and over	High school diploma or less (percent)	High school diploma or more (percent)	Number	Percent public	Bachelor's degree or more	+/- U.S. percent with Bachelor's degree or more	Non-Hispanic White	Black or African American	American Indian and Alaska Native	Asian, Hawaiian, and Pacific Islander	Hispanic or Latino[3]
		30	31	32	33	34	35	36	37	38	39	40	41
MONTANA	30000	654,124	40.3	91.0	62,193	87.8	27.9	0.0	28.9	22.5	12.8	34.9	18.8
Beaverhead, MT	30001	5,987	37.7	91.9	1,062	91.5	30.4	2.5	31.1	0.0	37.8	6.9	13.9
Big Horn, MT	30003	7,144	52.1	83.6	631	94.9	12.6	-15.3	16.3	0.0	10.4	29.4	0.0
Blaine, MT	30005	3,943	45.1	85.4	233	89.3	17.2	-10.7	21.4	0.0	11.4	0.0	31.8
Broadwater, MT	30007	3,501	56.7	89.8	93	34.4	15.2	-12.7	14.9	0.0	100.0	0.0	40.0
Carbon, MT	30009	7,347	44.7	91.3	207	80.2	28.5	0.6	28.5	0.0	34.6	54.3	7.8
Carter, MT	30011	996	46.4	91.1	10	90.0	15.2	-12.7	14.3	0.0	75.0	0.0	0.0
Cascade, MT	30013	53,534	39.6	90.8	4,707	76.3	23.9	-4.0	24.9	13.8	9.9	27.5	9.4
Chouteau, MT	30015	3,767	45.5	90.2	167	77.2	22.5	-5.4	24.8	0.0	9.3	0.0	0.0
Custer, MT	30017	7,894	45.5	91.2	493	87.6	19.2	-8.7	19.3	0.0	26.0	0.0	5.1
Daniels, MT	30019	1,232	38.6	94.6	20	95.0	19.7	-8.2	20.0	0.0	0.0	0.0	0.0
Dawson, MT	30021	6,249	41.6	89.6	559	93.4	18.4	-9.5	18.3	0.0	0.0	45.5	78.9
Deer Lodge, MT	30023	6,576	51.6	85.1	273	90.8	18.8	-9.1	19.2	0.0	0.0	0.0	26.7
Fallon, MT	30025	1,978	54.3	88.1	70	88.6	15.7	-12.2	15.9	0.0	0.0	0.0	31.6
Fergus, MT	30027	8,365	44.1	89.1	495	89.9	23.1	-4.8	23.3	0.0	21.8	100.0	0.0
Flathead, MT	30029	60,842	40.6	92.1	2,770	76.7	26.8	-1.1	27.5	23.0	9.9	16.8	12.9
Gallatin, MT	30031	54,330	25.1	96.0	13,209	96.6	45.0	17.1	45.3	71.3	27.7	55.2	29.0
Garfield, MT	30033	832	57.7	91.1	36	50.0	14.1	-13.8	14.1	0.0	0.0	0.0	0.0
Glacier, MT	30035	7,759	48.8	78.8	689	88.8	15.6	-12.3	24.4	0.0	7.3	44.8	48.5
Golden Valley, MT	30037	579	50.6	86.7	13	100.0	23.7	-4.2	23.1	0.0	100.0	0.0	0.0
Granite, MT	30039	2,338	45.8	90.9	84	84.5	23.9	-4.0	23.7	0.0	0.0	100.0	62.5
Hill, MT	30041	9,977	38.5	91.4	1,126	88.7	20.5	-7.4	22.2	0.0	11.9	19.5	8.5
Jefferson, MT	30043	7,902	40.2	92.2	304	82.6	32.0	4.1	33.1	0.0	9.1	17.5	18.8
Judith Basin, MT	30045	1,559	38.9	91.3	28	92.9	28.5	0.6	28.9	0.0	0.0	0.0	0.0
Lake, MT	30047	18,900	41.5	89.3	1,181	85.6	25.2	-2.7	27.7	100.0	15.4	20.7	7.8
Lewis and Clark, MT	30049	41,914	32.9	94.4	3,418	56.8	34.7	6.8	35.2	78.0	13.8	32.8	33.3
Liberty, MT	30051	1,539	51.7	73.0	10	100.0	17.0	-10.9	17.4	0.0	0.0	0.0	0.0
Lincoln, MT	30053	14,544	51.8	85.7	367	94.0	16.4	-11.5	16.7	0.0	7.5	57.7	10.5
McCone, MT	30055	1,200	51.3	91.0	48	79.2	18.6	-9.3	18.2	0.0	0.0	0.0	0.0
Madison, MT	30057	5,869	36.7	94.6	130	72.3	33.8	5.9	33.3	0.0	0.0	88.4	35.2
Meagher, MT	30059	1,422	57.7	82.4	52	65.4	15.8	-12.1	15.9	0.0	0.0	0.0	10.2
Mineral, MT	30061	3,038	60.5	83.0	70	92.9	13.6	-14.3	13.8	0.0	0.0	100.0	0.0
Missoula, MT	30063	68,597	32.7	92.6	15,245	94.3	38.4	10.5	38.9	7.6	24.5	46.4	38.6
Musselshell, MT	30065	3,262	54.4	86.3	148	93.2	13.4	-14.5	14.0	0.0	0.0	0.0	0.0
Park, MT	30067	11,729	40.5	89.4	762	85.0	31.4	3.5	31.8	0.0	10.5	23.1	36.8
Petroleum, MT	30069	450	52.0	92.2	11	100.0	13.8	-14.1	16.4	0.0	0.0	0.0	0.0
Phillips, MT	30071	3,054	53.4	88.2	37	100.0	15.8	-12.1	16.8	0.0	8.6	0.0	0.0
Pondera, MT	30073	4,179	44.8	86.7	206	62.6	19.3	-8.6	20.3	0.0	15.0	0.0	0.0
Powder River, MT	30075	1,162	41.3	91.9	48	79.2	16.1	-11.8	16.2	0.0	0.0	0.0	40.0
Powell, MT	30077	5,313	53.3	89.0	232	93.1	18.7	-9.2	19.9	0.0	3.2	13.6	0.0
Prairie, MT	30079	848	49.4	85.3	24	100.0	13.4	-14.5	13.6	0.0	0.0	0.0	0.0
Ravalli, MT	30081	28,378	43.6	90.7	1,037	93.2	25.0	-2.9	25.0	0.0	28.8	37.0	16.5
Richland, MT	30083	6,545	54.2	84.9	157	84.7	16.6	-11.3	17.4	0.0	3.7	0.0	3.3
Roosevelt, MT	30085	5,889	51.7	89.1	456	92.1	17.3	-10.6	20.4	0.0	15.1	0.0	0.0
Rosebud, MT	30087	5,580	47.9	88.5	313	94.9	17.6	-10.3	19.5	15.0	13.6	17.7	0.0
Sanders, MT	30089	8,374	56.9	86.6	177	72.9	15.6	-12.3	15.9	0.0	10.7	42.9	11.9
Sheridan, MT	30091	2,746	44.7	85.3	75	93.3	15.7	-12.2	16.3	0.0	5.3	0.0	20.0
Silver Bow, MT	30093	23,065	47.7	91.2	2,318	96.5	22.9	-5.0	23.6	13.9	3.5	14.5	22.6
Stillwater, MT	30095	6,386	47.1	92.0	176	86.4	22.3	-5.6	22.1	0.0	0.0	50.0	21.2
Sweet Grass, MT	30097	2,695	44.2	92.8	55	49.1	28.8	0.9	29.5	0.0	27.3	0.0	0.0
Teton, MT	30099	4,295	47.2	85.6	187	65.8	22.9	-5.0	23.0	0.0	11.2	0.0	30.4
Toole, MT	30101	3,704	47.3	87.5	188	45.7	17.4	-10.5	18.9	0.0	0.0	0.0	0.0
Treasure, MT	30103	570	49.5	87.2	28	89.3	20.9	-7.0	21.3	0.0	0.0	100.0	0.0
Valley, MT	30105	5,168	50.0	87.4	223	86.1	16.9	-11.0	17.5	0.0	10.6	0.0	20.8
Wheatland, MT	30107	1,560	59.4	81.8	11	100.0	16.4	-11.5	15.9	0.0	70.6	0.0	0.0
Wibaux, MT	30109	768	56.0	75.1	23	100.0	15.9	-12.0	16.4	0.0	0.0	0.0	0.0
Yellowstone, MT	30111	96,750	39.4	91.4	7,501	83.3	29.0	1.1	30.0	29.4	16.4	27.7	14.3

Note. Data in columns 26 through 41 from the American Community Survey are subject to sampling error, which can be especially large in small counties and small population groups. See notes and definitions for more information.

[3]May be of any race.

Table C-1. Population, School, and Student Characteristics by County, Selected Years—*Continued*

County	State/ County Code	County Type[1]	Population, 2010		Percent of related children 5–17 years in poverty, 2010	Percent of children under 19 years with no health insurance, 2010	Number of schools and students, 2010–2011			Resident enrollment, 2006–2010 K–12 enrollment	
			Total	Percent 5–17 years			School districts	Schools	Students	Number	Percent public
			1	2	3	4	5	6	7	8	9
NEBRASKA	31000	X	1,826,341	17.9	15.5	5.9	290	1,096	298,500	324,192	87.3
Adams, NE	31001	5	31,364	17.3	15.7	6.2	6	26	4,938	5,458	87.0
Antelope, NE	31003	9	6,685	17.0	20.9	7.7	4	13	1,063	1,186	85.6
Arthur, NE	31005	9	460	19.6	16.1	15.0	1	2	106	87	100.0
Banner, NE	31007	9	690	17.1	23.4	15.5	1	2	171	122	96.7
Blaine, NE	31009	9	478	19.9	32.0	23.4	1	2	113	60	100.0
Boone, NE	31011	9	5,505	17.6	11.6	7.5	3	8	880	1,002	93.5
Box Butte, NE	31013	7	11,308	18.3	17.1	5.8	2	7	1,970	2,069	90.8
Boyd, NE	31015	9	2,099	16.8	21.1	13.1	2	5	343	350	89.7
Brown, NE	31017	9	3,145	16.9	17.4	14.4	2	4	517	531	78.5
Buffalo, NE	31019	5	46,102	16.8	13.5	5.0	9	27	7,546	7,355	91.6
Burt, NE	31021	8	6,858	16.8	15.0	6.9	3	8	1,289	1,210	96.9
Butler, NE	31023	6	8,395	18.9	10.1	5.5	3	9	1,138	1,677	70.5
Cass, NE	31025	2	25,241	19.0	9.5	5.2	5	14	3,783	4,946	90.0
Cedar, NE	31027	9	8,852	18.5	13.8	11.3	5	13	1,176	1,812	75.3
Chase, NE	31029	9	3,966	16.7	14.7	10.5	2	6	780	706	99.6
Cherry, NE	31031	7	5,713	16.7	22.5	10.9	2	12	777	927	91.6
Cheyenne, NE	31033	7	9,998	17.4	13.5	6.1	3	11	1,693	1,794	91.1
Clay, NE	31035	9	6,542	19.1	14.0	7.6	3	11	1,507	1,296	94.6
Colfax, NE	31037	7	10,515	19.8	14.7	9.3	4	14	2,253	2,007	95.9
Cuming, NE	31039	7	9,139	18.7	10.9	8.8	3	9	1,613	1,844	75.2
Custer, NE	31041	7	10,939	17.4	19.6	8.1	6	16	1,755	2,027	96.6
Dakota, NE	31043	3	21,006	21.0	18.0	8.1	4	18	4,483	4,105	87.4
Dawes, NE	31045	7	9,182	13.8	16.5	7.2	3	11	1,271	1,236	97.5
Dawson, NE	31047	7	24,326	20.6	15.8	8.5	5	19	5,332	5,166	97.6
Deuel, NE	31049	9	1,941	15.2	20.6	10.1	2	5	451	294	100.0
Dixon, NE	31051	3	6,000	19.0	13.4	8.3	3	8	814	1,270	98.8
Dodge, NE	31053	4	36,691	17.1	16.4	5.7	6	23	5,945	6,399	92.8
Douglas, NE	31055	2	517,110	18.3	18.5	5.5	15	183	89,173	92,757	83.0
Dundy, NE	31057	9	2,008	17.0	16.8	14.4	1	4	379	367	100.0
Fillmore, NE	31059	9	5,890	18.2	12.1	6.4	4	10	993	1,121	94.4
Franklin, NE	31061	9	3,225	16.0	17.6	7.4	1	2	336	517	98.8
Frontier, NE	31063	9	2,756	16.2	15.6	10.4	3	6	596	480	94.6
Furnas, NE	31065	9	4,959	18.1	17.5	8.0	3	6	1,109	953	97.9
Gage, NE	31067	6	22,311	16.8	16.3	4.6	5	13	3,205	3,809	93.4
Garden, NE	31069	9	2,057	13.5	25.5	11.6	1	3	272	237	98.7
Garfield, NE	31071	9	2,049	16.7	17.0	13.0	1	3	386	436	100.0
Gosper, NE	31073	9	2,044	16.7	14.4	7.3	1	2	252	305	97.1
Grant, NE	31075	9	614	12.5	23.6	13.6	1	2	132	99	100.0
Greeley, NE	31077	9	2,538	16.6	21.8	15.8	3	8	448	519	87.9
Hall, NE	31079	5	58,607	19.2	15.6	6.8	4	31	11,417	10,885	94.6
Hamilton, NE	31081	7	9,124	19.9	9.5	5.4	3	8	1,628	1,840	96.0
Harlan, NE	31083	9	3,423	16.2	15.8	8.5	1	2	304	604	98.0
Hayes, NE	31085	9	967	18.3	24.3	24.1	1	2	141	140	97.1
Hitchcock, NE	31087	9	2,908	15.9	26.6	9.4	2	3	278	451	90.2
Holt, NE	31089	7	10,435	17.1	18.0	8.6	5	13	1,587	1,923	86.3
Hooker, NE	31091	9	736	16.6	11.3	10.6	1	2	202	138	100.0
Howard, NE	31093	9	6,274	18.3	13.6	9.2	3	7	1,290	1,200	98.3
Jefferson, NE	31095	7	7,547	15.7	17.6	5.6	2	6	1,144	1,391	94.1
Johnson, NE	31097	8	5,217	13.6	14.4	9.2	2	7	740	708	95.2
Kearney, NE	31099	7	6,489	17.4	11.9	5.6	3	11	1,285	1,199	96.0
Keith, NE	31101	7	8,368	16.0	16.9	9.4	3	7	1,181	1,300	92.5
Keya Paha, NE	31103	9	824	16.6	32.8	28.7	1	3	102	83	89.2
Kimball, NE	31105	6	3,821	16.0	19.1	8.3	1	3	542	675	98.8
Knox, NE	31107	9	8,701	18.1	19.2	9.3	6	12	1,501	1,606	92.7
Lancaster, NE	31109	2	285,407	16.0	16.1	4.8	10	86	40,888	43,707	84.1
Lincoln, NE	31111	5	36,288	18.0	15.7	4.4	6	23	5,745	6,750	91.4

[1]County type codes are from the Economic Research Service of the United States Department of Agriculture. See notes and definitions for more information.

Table C-1. Population, School, and Student Characteristics by County, Selected Years—*Continued*

County	State/ County Code	Characteristics of students, 2010–2011				Number of graduates, 2008–2009	Staff and students, 2010–2011			
		Percent with IEP[2]	Percent eligible for free or reduced lunch	Percent minority	Percent English-language learners		Total staff	Number of teachers	Student/ teacher ratio	Central admin. staff
		10	11	12	13	14	15	16	17	18
NEBRASKA	31000	14.8	42.6	29.2	6.7	19,501	45,505	22,345	13.4	1,701
Adams, NE	31001	20.5	45.6	19.6	6.3	347	854	385	12.8	47
Antelope, NE	31003	16.8	48.8	8.0	2.3	110	306	123	8.6	12
Arthur, NE	31005	15.1	0.0	4.7	...	8	24	13	8.4	2
Banner, NE	31007	9.9	53.2	19.3	1.8	19	43	20	8.4	2
Blaine, NE	31009	22.1	51.6	...	...	13	30	18	6.5	1
Boone, NE	31011	12.8	36.3	4.9	...	93	176	89	9.8	7
Box Butte, NE	31013	15.0	47.6	27.0	4.4	136	341	157	12.6	14
Boyd, NE	31015	20.4	47.8	6.4	...	22	84	38	9.1	3
Brown, NE	31017	13.3	46.0	5.8	...	46	85	43	12.0	9
Buffalo, NE	31019	13.9	36.8	18.0	5.4	465	1,167	549	13.8	95
Burt, NE	31021	16.4	35.7	8.3	...	103	224	114	11.3	7
Butler, NE	31023	18.7	41.5	7.0	2.3	97	210	108	10.6	6
Cass, NE	31025	14.2	29.8	5.8	0.4	265	614	302	12.5	20
Cedar, NE	31027	16.2	38.9	3.6	...	120	229	111	10.6	10
Chase, NE	31029	10.8	37.8	19.9	6.9	55	159	72	10.8	7
Cherry, NE	31031	13.4	47.0	18.8	0.1	62	159	86	9.0	6
Cheyenne, NE	31033	14.1	34.7	15.0	1.3	109	321	138	12.3	11
Clay, NE	31035	19.5	43.6	15.7	4.5	116	264	129	11.7	9
Colfax, NE	31037	10.7	64.0	62.1	20.9	189	365	183	12.3	10
Cuming, NE	31039	17.0	47.9	24.1	2.2	130	259	130	12.4	12
Custer, NE	31041	17.2	39.8	6.0	0.3	178	337	164	10.7	14
Dakota, NE	31043	14.0	62.4	64.6	21.0	265	674	357	12.6	23
Dawes, NE	31045	10.5	45.4	17.9	2.0	143	237	118	10.7	12
Dawson, NE	31047	14.2	62.1	52.8	19.7	351	735	389	13.7	31
Deuel, NE	31049	11.5	45.7	5.8	...	27	85	44	10.2	5
Dixon, NE	31051	14.3	33.6	7.3	0.5	87	143	74	10.9	7
Dodge, NE	31053	18.8	47.0	20.1	6.3	413	889	433	13.7	34
Douglas, NE	31055	14.9	46.0	43.9	8.9	4,873	12,228	6,153	14.5	454
Dundy, NE	31057	17.2	39.0	11.4	2.9	35	80	35	10.9	3
Fillmore, NE	31059	21.1	32.4	9.0	...	123	195	103	9.7	7
Franklin, NE	31061	17.3	46.5	2.7	...	26	62	30	11.2	1
Frontier, NE	31063	13.9	43.0	6.2	0.5	66	125	64	9.3	4
Furnas, NE	31065	17.8	44.6	5.8	0.1	96	213	102	10.8	7
Gage, NE	31067	19.4	37.7	7.2	0.3	192	493	250	12.8	21
Garden, NE	31069	10.3	61.4	14.7	...	25	52	23	11.8	2
Garfield, NE	31071	10.9	35.2	1.8	...	29	64	34	11.3	2
Gosper, NE	31073	17.5	35.3	9.9	1.2	20	52	24	10.4	2
Grant, NE	31075	12.1	44.7	0.0	...	15	30	17	7.7	2
Greeley, NE	31077	17.9	62.2	6.7	0.2	35	122	59	7.6	5
Hall, NE	31079	11.7	54.9	44.8	23.2	613	1,557	827	13.8	54
Hamilton, NE	31081	16.8	29.5	7.0	...	137	261	135	12.1	10
Harlan, NE	31083	16.8	44.1	5.6	...	19	58	30	10.3	2
Hayes, NE	31085	11.3	39.7	4.3	0.7	16	37	16	9.0	2
Hitchcock, NE	31087	14.4	65.3	5.0	...	15	67	27	10.3	7
Holt, NE	31089	17.7	47.5	10.1	4.5	153	285	161	9.9	12
Hooker, NE	31091	9.9	50.5	2.0	...	12	43	21	9.7	2
Howard, NE	31093	11.9	36.0	4.6	...	105	205	108	11.9	6
Jefferson, NE	31095	23.3	47.9	7.8	1.0	97	180	90	12.8	7
Johnson, NE	31097	16.1	38.4	17.2	4.6	74	128	68	10.9	4
Kearney, NE	31099	18.9	33.9	7.3	1.1	107	230	110	11.7	8
Keith, NE	31101	13.9	43.1	14.9	...	103	243	98	12.1	17
Keya Paha, NE	31103	8.8	48.0	2.0	...	9	32	17	6.1	2
Kimball, NE	31105	10.1	49.6	19.5	1.7	38	96	43	12.7	5
Knox, NE	31107	14.9	48.2	21.8	...	129	297	151	9.9	16
Lancaster, NE	31109	14.6	40.3	26.6	7.1	2,323	5,970	2,879	14.2	143
Lincoln, NE	31111	15.0	38.9	17.4	1.0	390	784	408	14.1	27

[2]IEP=Individual Education Program. See notes and definitions for more information.

. . . = Not available.

Table C-1. Population, School, and Student Characteristics by County, Selected Years—*Continued*

County	State/ County Code	Revenues, 2008–2009				Current expenditures, 2008–2009			Resident population 16 to 19 years, 2006–2010			
		Total revenue ($1,000's)	Percentage of revenue from			Amount ($1,000's)	Amount per student	Percent for instruction	Total population 16 to 19 years	Percent enrolled in school	Percent high school graduates, not enrolled in school	Percent not enrolled, not grads, not employed, or not in labor force
			Federal government	State government	Local government							
		19	20	21	22	23	24	25	26	27	28	29
NEBRASKA	31000	3,522,481	8.5	33.6	58.0	2,934,813	10,045	64.3	105,109	87.9	7.7	2.4
Adams, NE	31001	65,450	7.5	36.4	56.2	55,231	11,509	67.7	2,130	92.2	5.5	0.0
Antelope, NE	31003	22,855	11.8	20.2	68.1	20,609	18,855	67.7	375	85.9	7.5	3.7
Arthur, NE	31005	1,850	2.8	31.7	65.5	1,448	15,912	65.3	21	100.0	0.0	0.0
Banner, NE	31007	2,803	4.5	38.6	56.9	2,487	14,892	58.3	33	100.0	0.0	0.0
Blaine, NE	31009	2,298	9.6	9.8	80.6	1,998	16,113	59.9	21	100.0	0.0	0.0
Boone, NE	31011	13,575	4.8	10.9	84.3	10,661	11,793	68.6	274	79.9	12.0	8.0
Box Butte, NE	31013	22,736	7.7	47.9	44.4	19,283	9,828	65.7	639	85.9	11.6	0.0
Boyd, NE	31015	5,803	6.7	37.8	55.5	4,991	14,260	63.6	91	85.7	4.4	9.9
Brown, NE	31017	11,923	8.9	35.0	56.1	8,441	16,882	62.8	133	75.9	14.3	6.0
Buffalo, NE	31019	92,165	8.6	32.7	58.7	76,416	10,545	61.7	3,433	87.9	7.5	1.6
Burt, NE	31021	15,127	6.4	24.4	69.2	13,079	9,710	66.2	371	81.7	12.1	3.5
Butler, NE	31023	13,751	5.6	16.2	78.2	12,094	10,453	64.8	509	96.5	3.1	0.4
Cass, NE	31025	44,524	8.4	31.9	59.6	35,609	9,435	63.3	1,373	89.2	7.1	1.5
Cedar, NE	31027	16,898	6.9	20.4	72.7	15,214	12,678	66.9	562	93.8	3.0	0.5
Chase, NE	31029	11,170	5.8	21.5	72.7	8,910	11,786	63.5	161	80.1	11.8	0.0
Cherry, NE	31031	12,848	6.0	30.8	63.3	10,281	13,030	68.3	245	83.3	15.5	0.0
Cheyenne, NE	31033	22,416	6.7	37.0	56.3	17,463	10,272	63.9	513	90.8	9.2	0.0
Clay, NE	31035	20,184	8.9	26.5	64.6	16,835	11,306	63.8	421	94.3	4.0	1.2
Colfax, NE	31037	25,192	5.5	35.0	59.5	20,969	9,307	69.0	623	62.3	13.8	13.0
Cuming, NE	31039	19,377	7.0	17.7	75.3	15,340	9,987	66.7	501	91.2	8.0	0.6
Custer, NE	31041	24,224	5.4	28.9	65.6	20,981	11,409	65.5	605	86.5	8.4	2.8
Dakota, NE	31043	45,774	13.4	55.7	30.9	38,446	9,395	66.9	1,413	80.3	10.7	8.7
Dawes, NE	31045	14,901	10.1	43.0	47.0	12,590	10,770	64.4	1,020	92.8	3.4	3.6
Dawson, NE	31047	59,690	12.8	49.5	37.7	49,908	9,539	69.4	1,509	84.4	7.2	6.4
Deuel, NE	31049	3,963	4.4	29.7	65.9	3,447	13,518	57.8	90	98.9	1.1	0.0
Dixon, NE	31051	13,719	7.0	35.2	57.8	11,708	9,990	66.8	299	96.0	4.0	0.0
Dodge, NE	31053	70,055	8.4	34.7	56.9	58,703	9,724	64.3	1,949	86.6	8.2	3.3
Douglas, NE	31055	959,018	9.5	35.0	55.5	809,448	9,408	60.9	28,277	86.7	8.5	2.8
Dundy, NE	31057	15,244	20.4	42.7	36.9	11,840	14,248	58.4	77	96.1	3.9	0.0
Fillmore, NE	31059	18,387	5.5	19.3	75.2	14,895	11,259	65.4	404	86.4	5.7	0.0
Franklin, NE	31061	4,217	8.0	39.2	52.7	3,549	10,082	67.4	148	84.5	4.1	3.4
Frontier, NE	31063	8,926	5.8	34.8	59.4	7,570	12,985	61.6	149	100.0	0.0	0.0
Furnas, NE	31065	15,556	7.1	41.7	51.1	12,619	10,740	63.9	287	86.8	3.5	8.4
Gage, NE	31067	44,222	8.6	34.3	57.1	35,484	11,180	65.7	1,084	91.9	5.7	1.9
Garden, NE	31069	5,098	8.6	11.5	80.0	3,588	12,204	66.1	82	85.4	8.5	6.1
Garfield, NE	31071	4,063	7.5	40.8	51.8	3,909	10,480	65.8	111	100.0	0.0	0.0
Gosper, NE	31073	3,142	4.9	16.7	78.4	2,870	11,434	65.4	84	100.0	0.0	0.0
Grant, NE	31075	2,838	3.5	7.2	89.3	2,234	18,463	59.1	23	100.0	0.0	0.0
Greeley, NE	31077	7,723	9.2	27.6	63.2	6,700	13,988	62.9	98	79.6	17.4	3.1
Hall, NE	31079	133,624	8.5	40.3	51.2	114,808	10,406	73.3	2,932	81.0	13.6	2.9
Hamilton, NE	31081	19,703	5.5	27.3	67.3	16,374	9,793	68.0	493	88.6	6.3	2.2
Harlan, NE	31083	4,019	12.4	37.5	50.1	3,291	10,481	65.5	177	98.9	0.0	1.1
Hayes, NE	31085	3,260	4.4	30.2	65.4	2,448	15,396	60.7	46	100.0	0.0	0.0
Hitchcock, NE	31087	6,026	9.8	22.4	67.8	5,212	22,274	64.4	122	81.2	8.2	6.6
Holt, NE	31089	23,208	6.9	27.4	65.8	21,293	13,079	62.9	576	91.7	6.9	0.0
Hooker, NE	31091	3,480	5.9	15.5	78.6	2,517	13,754	61.8	19	100.0	0.0	0.0
Howard, NE	31093	14,699	7.1	40.1	52.8	11,563	8,767	61.8	385	95.8	4.2	0.0
Jefferson, NE	31095	13,305	6.9	28.5	64.6	11,630	10,611	66.9	501	89.0	5.4	0.0
Johnson, NE	31097	10,070	5.8	28.8	65.4	8,373	10,974	65.7	144	88.9	2.1	0.0
Kearney, NE	31099	17,007	5.6	20.3	74.1	14,121	10,617	60.8	340	79.7	13.2	7.1
Keith, NE	31101	24,338	9.7	26.1	64.2	20,958	15,343	62.7	263	88.2	9.5	1.1
Keya Paha, NE	31103	2,940	3.8	6.2	89.9	1,635	17,031	59.7	40	85.0	15.0	0.0
Kimball, NE	31105	7,025	5.9	30.7	63.5	6,302	10,663	73.4	208	87.5	12.5	0.0
Knox, NE	31107	22,738	19.3	33.5	47.2	18,399	11,809	61.5	450	86.2	13.8	0.0
Lancaster, NE	31109	451,985	6.0	28.0	66.0	357,268	9,168	65.6	17,782	90.8	6.3	1.4
Lincoln, NE	31111	62,379	7.9	37.8	54.3	52,818	9,168	64.8	1,803	88.3	6.5	1.1

Note. Data in columns 26 through 41 from the American Community Survey are subject to sampling error, which can be especially large in small counties and small population groups. See notes and definitions for more information.

Table C-1. Population, School, and Student Characteristics by County, Selected Years—*Continued*

County	State/ County Code	High school graduates, 2006–2010			College enrollment, 2006–2010		College graduates, 2006–2010 (percent)						
		Population 25 years and over	High school diploma or less (percent)	High school diploma or more (percent)	Number	Percent public	Bachelor's degree or more	+/- U.S. percent with Bachelor's degree or more	Non-Hispanic White	Black or African American	American Indian and Alaska Native	Asian, Hawaiian, and Pacific Islander	Hispanic or Latino[3]
		30	31	32	33	34	35	36	37	38	39	40	41
NEBRASKA	31000	1,160,884	39.6	90.0	137,387	76.9	27.7	-0.2	29.1	16.2	10.4	49.8	9.9
Adams, NE	31001	19,909	43.1	89.1	2,322	53.1	21.5	-6.4	22.7	10.2	15.8	12.7	3.0
Antelope, NE	31003	4,699	50.7	89.8	204	90.7	16.5	-11.4	16.6	0.0	100.0	100.0	4.9
Arthur, NE	31005	285	32.6	93.0	5	100.0	17.9	-10.0	18.1	0.0	0.0	0.0	0.0
Banner, NE	31007	494	36.8	94.1	46	93.5	25.1	-2.8	26.4	0.0	0.0	0.0	0.0
Blaine, NE	31009	414	49.5	95.7	37	100.0	19.8	-8.1	21.5	0.0	0.0	0.0	0.0
Boone, NE	31011	3,844	50.5	91.8	66	75.8	15.8	-12.1	15.8	0.0	0.0	0.0	40.0
Box Butte, NE	31013	7,594	47.5	89.1	395	92.7	19.5	-8.4	21.0	0.0	0.0	21.4	3.4
Boyd, NE	31015	1,511	51.9	89.7	29	100.0	13.2	-14.7	13.5	0.0	0.0	0.0	0.0
Brown, NE	31017	2,291	53.3	88.3	64	79.7	16.8	-11.1	17.1	0.0	0.0	0.0	0.0
Buffalo, NE	31019	26,933	37.8	92.1	5,596	93.9	32.0	4.1	33.0	37.7	0.0	31.4	13.2
Burt, NE	31021	4,987	48.4	90.4	244	71.7	18.3	-9.6	18.4	0.0	0.0	100.0	0.0
Butler, NE	31023	5,791	49.3	91.3	274	83.6	15.7	-12.2	15.7	0.0	0.0	0.0	17.4
Cass, NE	31025	17,125	39.3	93.8	1,227	71.5	23.5	-4.4	23.9	0.0	0.0	32.7	3.7
Cedar, NE	31027	6,000	55.1	89.5	346	81.2	15.1	-12.8	15.2	0.0	0.0	0.0	11.8
Chase, NE	31029	2,746	53.2	89.2	123	96.7	14.6	-13.3	15.4	0.0	60.0	0.0	0.0
Cherry, NE	31031	4,078	44.4	89.5	216	83.3	22.6	-5.3	24.0	0.0	0.0	6.1	0.0
Cheyenne, NE	31033	6,940	37.5	93.5	367	89.4	27.2	-0.7	27.1	0.0	0.0	78.0	4.7
Clay, NE	31035	4,427	49.8	89.7	240	68.3	16.4	-11.5	17.1	0.0	0.0	0.0	1.9
Colfax, NE	31037	6,393	59.4	73.2	252	91.7	12.7	-15.2	15.4	0.0	0.0	100.0	3.1
Cuming, NE	31039	6,337	52.9	86.4	242	87.6	15.7	-12.2	16.3	0.0	0.0	88.9	0.0
Custer, NE	31041	7,673	47.4	90.7	294	90.8	18.0	-9.9	17.9	0.0	66.7	0.0	21.9
Dakota, NE	31043	12,690	64.3	74.3	799	92.2	10.8	-17.1	14.3	0.0	7.6	0.0	4.2
Dawes, NE	31045	5,352	30.9	91.4	1,653	99.8	36.5	8.6	38.2	0.0	23.7	48.0	8.5
Dawson, NE	31047	15,446	59.7	75.5	607	84.2	14.7	-13.2	19.3	0.0	0.0	0.0	2.3
Deuel, NE	31049	1,471	44.7	90.4	45	100.0	18.2	-9.7	19.3	0.0	0.0	0.0	0.0
Dixon, NE	31051	4,022	55.4	85.8	163	96.3	13.0	-14.9	13.9	0.0	0.0	0.0	1.1
Dodge, NE	31053	24,686	53.1	84.8	2,051	52.2	17.3	-10.6	18.3	0.0	13.1	15.3	2.6
Douglas, NE	31055	321,302	33.7	90.0	43,070	70.0	35.8	7.9	40.2	14.9	14.5	62.6	10.7
Dundy, NE	31057	1,465	36.3	91.7	70	95.7	25.9	-2.0	24.2	0.0	0.0	0.0	65.2
Fillmore, NE	31059	4,218	46.8	91.8	156	80.1	17.6	-10.3	17.8	0.0	0.0	0.0	0.0
Franklin, NE	31061	2,356	47.3	88.2	115	83.5	16.3	-11.6	16.6	0.0	0.0	0.0	0.0
Frontier, NE	31063	1,880	41.8	93.5	117	92.3	19.8	-8.1	20.1	0.0	0.0	0.0	9.1
Furnas, NE	31065	3,499	53.6	86.5	137	65.0	16.3	-11.6	16.5	0.0	0.0	33.3	0.0
Gage, NE	31067	15,598	48.8	90.1	1,090	88.3	19.1	-8.8	19.3	0.0	8.1	12.3	8.5
Garden, NE	31069	1,631	46.0	88.8	52	48.1	20.2	-7.7	21.4	0.0	0.0	85.7	0.0
Garfield, NE	31071	1,504	49.9	89.3	22	63.6	13.8	-14.1	14.1	0.0	0.0	0.0	0.0
Gosper, NE	31073	1,506	46.4	94.4	57	89.5	16.4	-11.5	17.0	0.0	0.0	0.0	3.8
Grant, NE	31075	468	54.1	95.1	20	90.0	17.3	-10.6	17.4	0.0	0.0	0.0	0.0
Greeley, NE	31077	1,765	56.5	90.3	40	77.5	12.5	-15.4	12.6	0.0	0.0	0.0	0.0
Hall, NE	31079	36,542	50.6	82.6	2,048	88.3	16.3	-11.6	18.2	11.2	0.0	54.7	4.9
Hamilton, NE	31081	6,218	42.2	94.3	284	86.3	21.8	-6.1	21.9	0.0	0.0	100.0	0.0
Harlan, NE	31083	2,553	46.7	90.6	79	88.6	16.9	-11.0	17.2	0.0	0.0	0.0	0.0
Hayes, NE	31085	727	44.7	86.5	30	83.3	16.6	-11.3	17.5	0.0	0.0	0.0	0.0
Hitchcock, NE	31087	2,146	44.5	88.0	83	84.3	13.7	-14.2	13.9	0.0	0.0	0.0	0.0
Holt, NE	31089	7,370	49.2	88.2	255	69.0	16.1	-11.8	16.3	100.0	6.5	53.9	0.0
Hooker, NE	31091	511	36.4	94.9	26	100.0	22.1	-5.8	21.3	0.0	0.0	100.0	0.0
Howard, NE	31093	4,350	51.2	90.9	226	79.6	13.9	-14.0	14.0	0.0	44.4	14.3	0.0
Jefferson, NE	31095	5,516	51.0	89.7	201	78.6	14.7	-13.2	14.7	0.0	19.7	0.0	14.3
Johnson, NE	31097	4,013	61.2	82.3	105	86.7	11.8	-16.1	12.5	2.6	0.0	50.0	13.3
Kearney, NE	31099	4,543	39.9	92.7	184	100.0	25.1	-2.8	24.9	0.0	0.0	100.0	20.6
Keith, NE	31101	6,088	45.6	88.0	231	88.3	19.5	-8.4	20.0	0.0	13.3	47.8	5.4
Keya Paha, NE	31103	586	52.7	91.0	8	100.0	14.0	-13.9	14.1	0.0	0.0	0.0	0.0
Kimball, NE	31105	2,714	48.5	87.6	102	92.2	19.8	-8.1	20.8	0.0	0.0	81.3	0.0
Knox, NE	31107	6,202	51.6	88.2	306	84.6	17.5	-10.4	18.1	0.0	9.2	71.4	7.8
Lancaster, NE	31109	171,989	31.0	93.1	37,751	82.7	35.3	7.4	36.2	20.3	14.9	48.3	20.5
Lincoln, NE	31111	24,391	42.0	92.0	1,354	91.1	19.0	-8.9	19.6	0.0	6.7	37.0	11.5

Note. Data in columns 26 through 41 from the American Community Survey are subject to sampling error, which can be especially large in small counties and small population groups. See notes and definitions for more information.
[3]May be of any race.

Table C-1. Population, School, and Student Characteristics by County, Selected Years—*Continued*

County	State/ County Code	County Type[1]	Population, 2010		Percent of related children 5–17 years in poverty, 2010	Percent of children under 19 years with no health insurance, 2010	Number of schools and students, 2010–2011			Resident enrollment, 2006–2010 K–12 enrollment	
			Total	Percent 5–17 years			School districts	Schools	Students	Number	Percent public
			1	2	3	4	5	6	7	8	9
NEBRASKA—*(Continued)*											
Logan, NE	31113	9	763	18.1	20.6	16.1	1	2	198	96	100.0
Loup, NE	31115	9	632	16.3	22.4	14.0	1	2	89	114	89.5
McPherson, NE	31117	9	539	19.5	33.0	18.4	1	2	114	98	100.0
Madison, NE	31119	5	34,876	17.6	16.0	6.5	7	22	5,484	6,002	80.3
Merrick, NE	31121	7	7,845	18.8	13.6	6.7	2	5	1,007	1,469	93.1
Morrill, NE	31123	9	5,042	17.6	20.1	7.3	2	4	916	896	98.4
Nance, NE	31125	9	3,735	17.3	16.7	8.7	2	5	828	643	99.4
Nemaha, NE	31127	7	7,248	15.6	14.4	5.9	3	9	1,153	1,135	94.7
Nuckolls, NE	31129	9	4,500	16.0	18.5	7.8	1	3	447	745	93.4
Otoe, NE	31131	6	15,740	17.7	12.6	5.7	3	9	2,567	2,820	88.3
Pawnee, NE	31133	9	2,773	16.8	19.6	10.9	2	4	499	424	89.2
Perkins, NE	31135	9	2,970	18.2	12.7	7.8	1	3	373	604	90.4
Phelps, NE	31137	7	9,188	18.1	11.9	5.0	4	11	1,604	1,614	90.6
Pierce, NE	31139	9	7,266	19.7	11.0	8.7	3	6	1,293	1,431	90.3
Platte, NE	31141	5	32,237	19.0	10.5	6.6	4	14	4,697	6,438	73.8
Polk, NE	31143	9	5,406	18.4	10.5	6.5	4	12	1,181	1,003	92.7
Red Willow, NE	31145	7	11,055	16.9	15.9	5.6	2	7	1,762	1,837	94.6
Richardson, NE	31147	7	8,363	16.4	17.3	6.5	2	7	1,286	1,483	86.1
Rock, NE	31149	9	1,526	14.7	23.5	18.3	1	4	200	268	95.5
Saline, NE	31151	6	14,200	17.4	12.0	6.7	5	11	3,226	2,531	94.2
Sarpy, NE	31153	2	158,840	20.4	7.4	4.0	7	51	24,182	30,981	90.1
Saunders, NE	31155	2	20,780	19.1	8.7	5.1	5	13	2,732	4,017	78.7
Scotts Bluff, NE	31157	5	36,970	17.6	22.0	5.9	7	27	6,426	6,531	93.2
Seward, NE	31159	2	16,750	17.6	7.9	4.2	4	8	2,543	2,931	79.9
Sheridan, NE	31161	9	5,469	17.6	27.8	8.9	2	13	892	902	89.9
Sherman, NE	31163	9	3,152	16.7	18.3	10.3	2	4	486	540	100.0
Sioux, NE	31165	9	1,311	17.5	26.3	14.7	1	5	94	237	90.7
Stanton, NE	31167	9	6,129	19.9	13.6	7.1	1	2	467	1,270	89.2
Thayer, NE	31169	9	5,228	15.6	15.7	7.6	3	9	818	857	92.3
Thomas, NE	31171	9	647	17.8	21.6	21.1	1	2	112	134	97.0
Thurston, NE	31173	8	6,940	24.9	33.4	7.9	4	9	1,527	1,848	96.3
Valley, NE	31175	9	4,260	16.2	20.3	11.2	2	6	646	674	93.5
Washington, NE	31177	2	20,234	19.3	7.1	4.4	3	11	3,500	3,900	90.0
Wayne, NE	31179	6	9,595	14.0	13.1	6.9	4	8	1,562	1,454	98.3
Webster, NE	31181	9	3,812	16.5	15.6	8.0	2	4	667	688	95.2
Wheeler, NE	31183	9	818	18.7	30.6	23.5	1	2	110	94	96.8
York, NE	31185	7	13,665	16.0	14.3	5.4	4	9	1,849	2,347	88.7
NEVADA	32000	X	2,700,551	17.7	19.2	17.8	18	645	437,149	465,177	94.7
Churchill, NV	32001	6	24,877	18.5	16.8	17.9	1	7	4,174	4,642	92.9
Clark, NV	32003	1	1,951,269	17.9	20.1	17.5	1	364	314,059	334,264	94.8
Douglas, NV	32005	4	46,997	15.3	12.8	17.5	1	13	6,343	7,593	93.9
Elko, NV	32007	5	48,818	20.8	10.0	19.0	1	30	9,529	9,965	98.2
Esmeralda, NV	32009	9	783	11.9	16.4	33.0	1	4	64	79	94.9
Eureka, NV	32011	9	1,987	17.0	12.3	21.3	1	3	239	341	94.4
Humboldt, NV	32013	7	16,528	19.7	13.3	20.6	1	14	3,380	3,370	98.6
Lander, NV	32015	7	5,775	19.8	11.9	18.7	1	5	1,118	1,114	95.1
Lincoln, NV	32017	8	5,345	20.9	17.0	24.8	1	9	972	1,300	90.4
Lyon, NV	32019	6	51,980	18.3	15.2	19.2	1	19	8,578	10,007	92.3
Mineral, NV	32021	7	4,772	13.7	22.0	18.6	1	5	517	586	100.0
Nye, NV	32023	6	43,946	15.7	24.2	17.3	1	26	5,933	7,279	96.6
Pershing, NV	32027	8	6,753	14.5	20.9	25.5	1	4	677	1,237	99.4
Storey, NV	32029	2	4,010	13.1	12.5	24.9	1	4	427	615	100.0
Washoe, NV	32031	2	421,407	16.9	17.4	18.6	1	106	64,380	71,670	93.4
White Pine, NV	32033	7	10,030	15.3	14.0	15.6	1	9	1,433	1,767	97.0
Carson City city, NV	32510	3	55,274	15.5	19.0	17.0	2	23	15,326	9,348	96.4

[1]County type codes are from the Economic Research Service of the United States Department of Agriculture. See notes and definitions for more information.

Table C-1. Population, School, and Student Characteristics by County, Selected Years—*Continued*

County	State/ County Code	Characteristics of students, 2010–2011				Number of graduates, 2008–2009	Staff and students, 2010–2011			
		Percent with IEP[2]	Percent eligible for free or reduced lunch	Percent minority	Percent English-language learners		Total staff	Number of teachers	Student/ teacher ratio	Central admin. staff
		10	11	12	13	14	15	16	17	18
NEBRASKA—*(Continued)*										
Logan, NE	31113	12.6	33.8	6.6	0.5	23	38	20	9.9	1
Loup, NE	31115	30.3	53.9	5.6	. . .	13	28	14	6.5	2
McPherson, NE	31117	15.8	0.0	8.8	. . .	. . .	23	13	8.5	1
Madison, NE	31119	16.1	45.2	32.3	4.4	412	818	409	13.4	35
Merrick, NE	31121	14.4	42.8	6.5	. . .	66	152	78	13.0	6
Morrill, NE	31123	11.0	55.6	21.7	6.2	60	165	76	12.1	8
Nance, NE	31125	13.5	34.0	5.8	. . .	71	138	65	12.8	5
Nemaha, NE	31127	16.0	39.8	6.5	0.2	78	248	97	11.9	15
Nuckolls, NE	31129	21.7	39.8	4.0	. . .	31	78	36	12.6	2
Otoe, NE	31131	16.0	36.9	12.5	2.6	203	387	200	12.8	14
Pawnee, NE	31133	14.0	53.4	5.5	1.0	41	95	50	9.9	3
Perkins, NE	31135	15.0	31.1	7.5	2.9	28	81	39	9.6	2
Phelps, NE	31137	18.3	33.4	9.9	2.4	123	269	129	12.4	20
Pierce, NE	31139	15.5	26.0	3.8	0.2	134	215	107	12.1	6
Platte, NE	31141	15.5	46.6	34.0	13.4	364	736	322	14.6	33
Polk, NE	31143	15.0	31.5	6.0	1.1	97	216	110	10.8	8
Red Willow, NE	31145	17.9	41.0	8.6	1.6	148	269	131	13.4	8
Richardson, NE	31147	18.6	52.1	10.2	. . .	100	230	109	11.8	7
Rock, NE	31149	12.5	37.0	4.5	. . .	17	47	24	8.2	3
Saline, NE	31151	12.9	41.1	32.9	14.3	201	493	236	13.6	16
Sarpy, NE	31153	13.1	30.8	24.7	1.5	1,682	3,488	1,646	14.7	118
Saunders, NE	31155	15.0	30.2	6.2	0.3	190	401	207	13.2	17
Scotts Bluff, NE	31157	10.9	51.3	40.6	4.2	405	1,011	469	13.7	32
Seward, NE	31159	13.3	22.1	6.1	0.3	202	439	189	13.5	23
Sheridan, NE	31161	15.4	51.9	34.3	0.1	62	181	88	10.1	7
Sherman, NE	31163	15.6	53.3	5.3	0.2	28	90	46	10.5	3
Sioux, NE	31165	8.5	28.4	5.7	. . .	8	28	18	5.4	2
Stanton, NE	31167	16.3	41.4	12.3	. . .	33	65	37	12.6	2
Thayer, NE	31169	18.1	31.9	7.1	. . .	77	156	85	9.7	5
Thomas, NE	31171	11.6	38.0	1.2	. . .	9	34	14	7.8	2
Thurston, NE	31173	21.6	71.3	71.9	5.0	64	328	168	9.1	13
Valley, NE	31175	11.8	38.9	4.9	1.5	50	137	62	10.5	5
Washington, NE	31177	13.8	20.6	5.3	1.1	286	515	244	14.3	15
Wayne, NE	31179	11.1	38.7	20.7	5.3	122	284	122	12.8	10
Webster, NE	31181	16.0	44.0	8.4	0.1	49	92	50	13.3	3
Wheeler, NE	31183	14.5	55.5	0.9	. . .	11	25	16	6.8	3
York, NE	31185	19.7	37.8	13.0	1.5	169	310	151	12.2	8
NEVADA	32000	11.0	50.3	61.3	19.1	. . .	25,267	21,840	20.0	30
Churchill, NV	32001	14.4	43.6	33.9	5.7	. . .	238	217	19.2	0
Clark, NV	32003	10.3	52.8	67.6	21.6	. . .	17,811	15,269	20.6	8
Douglas, NV	32005	11.5	34.2	29.7	4.4	. . .	388	340	18.7	0
Elko, NV	32007	11.2	34.6	37.8	10.4	. . .	640	554	17.2	0
Esmeralda, NV	32009	10.9	64.1	51.6	26.6	. . .	6	6	10.7	0
Eureka, NV	32011	9.2	25.5	17.6	0.4	. . .	30	26	9.3	0
Humboldt, NV	32013	14.1	39.5	42.3	11.1	. . .	221	201	16.8	1
Lander, NV	32015	11.4	26.0	37.5	8.7	. . .	73	68	16.4	0
Lincoln, NV	32017	8.8	49.1	19.5	. . .	. . .	77	69	14.1	0
Lyon, NV	32019	13.8	45.5	34.8	6.7	. . .	592	505	17.0	1
Mineral, NV	32021	15.3	46.6	43.3	. . .	. . .	54	48	10.8	0
Nye, NV	32023	16.9	54.8	32.0	7.1	. . .	353	323	18.4	0
Pershing, NV	32027	15.5	64.8	47.4	7.7	. . .	60	52	13.0	1
Storey, NV	32029	19.7	5.2	18.7	. . .	. . .	36	30	14.2	0
Washoe, NV	32031	13.0	45.3	50.3	17.4	. . .	3,811	3,364	19.1	6
White Pine, NV	32033	13.8	31.5	25.3	2.2	. . .	99	87	16.5	1
Carson City city, NV	32510	10.3	43.3	45.8	7.7	. . .	781	682	22.5	12

[2]IEP=Individual Education Program. See notes and definitions for more information.
. . . = Not available.

Table C-1. Population, School, and Student Characteristics by County, Selected Years—*Continued*

County	State/ County Code	Revenues, 2008–2009				Current expenditures, 2008–2009			Resident population 16 to 19 years, 2006–2010			
		Total revenue ($1,000's)	Percentage of revenue from			Amount ($1,000's)	Amount per student	Percent for instruction	Total population 16 to 19 years	Percent enrolled in school	Percent high school graduates, not enrolled in school	Percent not enrolled, not grads, not employed, or not in labor force
			Federal government	State government	Local government							
		19	20	21	22	23	24	25	26	27	28	29
NEBRASKA— *(Continued)*												
Logan, NE	31113	4,515	4.5	29.5	66.0	3,676	14,883	65.9	3	100.0	0.0	0.0
Loup, NE	31115	1,731	8.3	15.0	76.8	1,468	11,935	55.8	59	100.0	0.0	0.0
McPherson, NE	31117	...	...	...	...	...	...	...	33	100.0	0.0	0.0
Madison, NE	31119	65,417	9.3	28.6	62.2	52,635	9,560	67.5	2,118	90.5	4.6	1.7
Merrick, NE	31121	12,884	6.6	29.9	63.4	9,679	9,406	63.8	407	86.5	0.7	6.6
Morrill, NE	31123	14,353	8.5	50.8	40.7	10,945	11,461	62.9	249	87.6	3.2	9.2
Nance, NE	31125	10,434	6.9	26.6	66.5	8,174	9,439	59.1	186	91.9	5.9	2.2
Nemaha, NE	31127	19,644	6.2	40.6	53.2	16,158	14,075	52.6	569	93.7	5.5	0.9
Nuckolls, NE	31129	6,128	10.3	44.1	45.6	4,836	10,652	66.9	256	87.9	12.1	0.0
Otoe, NE	31131	28,842	5.4	30.3	64.3	24,470	9,304	67.6	764	89.9	3.8	1.2
Pawnee, NE	31133	6,652	7.3	33.7	58.9	5,905	12,277	66.3	121	90.9	2.5	5.0
Perkins, NE	31135	7,414	4.6	30.3	65.0	5,328	14,133	66.5	161	88.8	11.2	0.0
Phelps, NE	31137	22,740	7.1	23.6	69.3	19,685	12,055	67.3	456	84.9	14.5	0.0
Pierce, NE	31139	16,818	5.3	28.2	66.5	13,858	10,676	66.4	390	93.1	2.3	4.1
Platte, NE	31141	57,535	9.2	30.1	60.7	48,378	10,054	68.4	1,954	89.2	5.7	5.1
Polk, NE	31143	15,997	4.4	12.5	83.1	13,063	10,351	63.7	264	86.4	11.7	0.8
Red Willow, NE	31145	21,752	7.4	42.3	50.3	19,366	10,682	67.1	768	84.0	11.3	1.2
Richardson, NE	31147	18,339	7.4	32.0	60.6	15,028	11,132	64.5	413	85.2	12.1	0.0
Rock, NE	31149	3,481	6.7	9.7	83.6	3,021	15,900	68.7	52	100.0	0.0	0.0
Saline, NE	31151	33,085	7.2	32.6	60.1	27,098	9,491	64.3	1,396	90.3	5.1	2.4
Sarpy, NE	31153	257,674	8.6	38.8	52.6	219,389	9,523	66.1	8,081	85.3	10.5	2.0
Saunders, NE	31155	34,484	8.3	28.8	62.9	28,174	10,019	66.5	1,034	87.8	8.9	3.1
Scotts Bluff, NE	31157	74,827	11.0	45.2	43.8	66,293	10,461	64.0	2,102	81.3	8.9	4.4
Seward, NE	31159	36,549	6.2	22.9	70.9	31,844	12,309	61.4	1,355	93.0	4.7	1.9
Sheridan, NE	31161	13,389	11.1	42.3	46.6	11,710	12,198	65.9	233	88.4	3.4	3.9
Sherman, NE	31163	6,680	11.3	28.9	59.8	5,516	11,280	62.2	179	83.8	8.4	6.7
Sioux, NE	31165	2,380	3.5	10.4	86.1	2,151	21,088	67.6	78	96.2	0.0	3.9
Stanton, NE	31167	5,545	8.6	34.6	56.8	4,375	9,744	64.0	366	80.1	16.9	1.6
Thayer, NE	31169	12,636	4.1	19.5	76.5	11,390	14,238	64.8	284	91.6	2.8	2.1
Thomas, NE	31171	2,148	5.9	18.9	75.2	1,756	15,820	61.2	39	100.0	0.0	0.0
Thurston, NE	31173	19,093	31.6	42.6	25.7	13,844	12,472	63.8	551	80.9	12.2	4.4
Valley, NE	31175	9,512	5.3	34.9	59.8	7,994	12,471	61.6	163	88.3	6.1	5.5
Washington, NE	31177	36,246	4.4	31.3	64.3	30,873	8,689	62.7	1,351	94.1	5.4	0.0
Wayne, NE	31179	25,821	7.8	27.2	65.0	22,159	14,704	65.4	1,182	99.2	0.9	0.0
Webster, NE	31181	8,503	5.1	45.1	49.8	6,163	9,721	65.7	151	76.2	21.9	0.0
Wheeler, NE	31183	2,241	5.4	9.4	85.2	2,030	18,796	57.9	36	86.1	13.9	0.0
York, NE	31185	23,481	6.6	31.4	62.0	19,523	10,870	65.3	886	87.4	8.5	2.8
NEVADA	32000	4,442,101	9.6	30.7	59.8	3,629,764	8,422	59.1	141,293	75.3	14.0	6.6
Churchill, NV	32001	45,962	15.2	46.3	38.6	40,270	9,253	56.7	1,310	78.8	13.8	7.4
Clark, NV	32003	3,179,037	9.0	27.4	63.6	2,539,486	8,120	59.3	100,034	73.5	14.7	7.3
Douglas, NV	32005	68,895	7.9	31.8	60.3	62,773	9,560	56.7	2,548	82.5	10.2	3.3
Elko, NV	32007	110,520	10.0	42.3	47.7	102,083	10,644	57.5	3,046	74.2	15.0	8.3
Esmeralda, NV	32009	2,254	26.8	36.6	36.6	2,017	30,105	53.8	24	58.3	41.7	0.0
Eureka, NV	32011	20,372	2.3	1.5	96.2	8,589	33,815	39.8	66	92.4	7.6	0.0
Humboldt, NV	32013	35,653	8.3	37.2	54.5	33,013	9,914	61.9	910	86.6	5.3	4.4
Lander, NV	32015	13,890	14.6	35.8	49.6	11,307	9,478	55.7	345	80.9	18.0	1.2
Lincoln, NV	32017	15,263	13.1	61.6	25.4	16,050	16,196	61.8	379	78.6	20.1	1.3
Lyon, NV	32019	91,513	10.6	56.5	32.9	80,272	9,000	57.8	2,945	80.8	13.6	3.0
Mineral, NV	32021	9,563	24.1	56.0	19.9	8,173	14,569	54.1	163	67.5	32.5	0.0
Nye, NV	32023	77,066	12.8	42.7	44.5	67,448	10,618	56.9	1,975	75.4	12.9	8.9
Pershing, NV	32027	10,864	14.1	58.1	27.8	9,624	13,517	61.2	271	88.6	5.9	4.1
Storey, NV	32029	6,800	10.5	20.1	69.4	6,449	14,825	56.4	272	88.6	5.2	6.3
Washoe, NV	32031	647,707	11.0	35.2	53.9	552,403	8,444	59.9	23,522	81.0	11.0	4.5
White Pine, NV	32033	19,175	10.9	43.1	46.0	16,393	11,569	53.1	779	49.9	35.2	9.2
Carson City city, NV	32510	87,567	11.4	45.6	43.0	73,414	9,105	59.5	2,704	82.3	13.5	2.9

Note. Data in columns 26 through 41 from the American Community Survey are subject to sampling error, which can be especially large in small counties and small population groups. See notes and definitions for more information.

Table C-1. Population, School, and Student Characteristics by County, Selected Years—*Continued*

County	State/ County Code	High school graduates, 2006–2010			College enrollment, 2006–2010		College graduates, 2006–2010 (percent)						
		Population 25 years and over	High school diploma or less (percent)	High school diploma or more (percent)	Number	Percent public	Bachelor's degree or more	+/- U.S. percent with Bachelor's degree or more	Non-Hispanic White	Black or African American	American Indian and Alaska Native	Asian, Hawaiian, and Pacific Islander	Hispanic or Latino[3]
		30	31	32	33	34	35	36	37	38	39	40	41
NEBRASKA— *(Continued)*													
Logan, NE	31113	495	45.3	97.0	10	100.0	18.8	-9.1	19.8	0.0	0.0	0.0	0.0
Loup, NE	31115	431	58.7	92.6	33	0.0	10.0	-17.9	10.1	0.0	0.0	0.0	0.0
McPherson, NE	31117	345	34.8	86.7	14	100.0	24.4	-3.5	25.2	0.0	0.0	0.0	0.0
Madison, NE	31119	22,175	43.7	86.1	2,360	92.7	20.0	-7.9	21.6	14.6	1.6	32.1	5.1
Merrick, NE	31121	5,298	50.5	90.3	314	90.1	13.5	-14.4	13.7	0.0	0.0	0.0	0.0
Morrill, NE	31123	3,452	50.6	86.1	205	74.1	21.0	-6.9	22.7	0.0	0.0	15.8	5.6
Nance, NE	31125	2,620	53.4	85.2	78	94.9	11.6	-16.3	11.9	0.0	0.0	0.0	0.0
Nemaha, NE	31127	4,718	45.0	89.6	750	97.7	23.0	-4.9	23.3	0.0	0.0	57.1	0.0
Nuckolls, NE	31129	3,343	56.8	90.5	175	91.4	12.4	-15.5	12.5	0.0	0.0	0.0	50.0
Otoe, NE	31131	10,820	48.2	87.8	618	82.7	21.5	-6.4	21.9	0.0	0.0	0.0	14.4
Pawnee, NE	31133	2,059	61.2	88.0	39	79.5	14.8	-13.1	15.1	0.0	0.0	0.0	0.0
Perkins, NE	31135	2,044	37.3	91.9	84	81.0	18.4	-9.5	18.5	0.0	0.0	0.0	14.3
Phelps, NE	31137	6,445	40.7	92.3	359	84.7	22.7	-5.2	23.6	0.0	0.0	9.7	2.2
Pierce, NE	31139	4,919	50.6	89.8	203	88.7	14.3	-13.6	14.4	0.0	0.0	25.0	0.0
Platte, NE	31141	20,451	44.7	89.7	1,463	87.6	18.9	-9.0	19.7	0.0	0.0	32.8	9.0
Polk, NE	31143	3,825	47.8	92.9	182	91.2	16.1	-11.8	16.3	0.0	0.0	100.0	7.7
Red Willow, NE	31145	7,506	43.3	91.7	380	90.3	21.6	-6.3	21.6	100.0	0.0	100.0	0.0
Richardson, NE	31147	6,100	58.3	86.3	229	75.5	15.2	-12.7	15.5	0.0	0.0	33.3	33.7
Rock, NE	31149	1,246	46.2	92.1	30	100.0	23.3	-4.6	23.4	0.0	0.0	0.0	0.0
Saline, NE	31151	8,685	54.8	82.7	1,412	30.2	15.3	-12.6	16.7	0.0	35.9	9.8	7.4
Sarpy, NE	31153	94,145	28.7	94.6	12,194	76.9	36.1	8.2	37.2	31.7	23.3	32.3	21.5
Saunders, NE	31155	13,838	43.8	92.8	830	68.0	23.7	-4.2	23.9	0.0	0.0	23.7	6.7
Scotts Bluff, NE	31157	24,259	46.3	86.1	1,815	79.8	19.5	-8.4	22.5	20.0	16.7	23.2	3.2
Seward, NE	31159	10,396	38.3	93.2	1,910	38.8	27.3	-0.6	27.2	0.0	0.0	100.0	36.8
Sheridan, NE	31161	3,935	47.0	90.3	190	78.9	22.6	-5.3	23.7	0.0	8.7	54.2	5.5
Sherman, NE	31163	2,261	56.3	87.8	39	87.2	15.7	-12.2	15.8	0.0	0.0	0.0	0.0
Sioux, NE	31165	1,014	37.9	94.3	36	100.0	26.0	-1.9	25.6	0.0	0.0	48.0	0.0
Stanton, NE	31167	4,024	44.7	91.6	188	75.5	12.0	-15.9	12.2	0.0	0.0	0.0	9.9
Thayer, NE	31169	3,866	50.7	88.1	94	74.5	16.1	-11.8	16.3	0.0	0.0	50.0	0.0
Thomas, NE	31171	554	38.6	93.3	17	100.0	16.3	-11.6	16.9	0.0	0.0	0.0	0.0
Thurston, NE	31173	3,738	50.0	84.6	312	89.4	13.2	-14.7	18.6	0.0	7.4	0.0	14.7
Valley, NE	31175	3,085	51.8	91.2	168	84.5	17.1	-10.8	17.3	0.0	0.0	0.0	0.0
Washington, NE	31177	13,180	40.3	93.6	1,512	45.9	29.1	1.2	29.1	0.0	0.0	60.7	12.4
Wayne, NE	31179	5,094	39.6	91.6	2,189	98.4	28.0	0.1	27.8	100.0	0.0	61.8	0.0
Webster, NE	31181	2,743	55.4	86.9	43	90.7	12.7	-15.2	13.0	0.0	0.0	8.7	15.4
Wheeler, NE	31183	544	37.3	97.6	19	73.7	23.5	-4.4	23.1	0.0	0.0	0.0	0.0
York, NE	31185	9,442	45.5	90.6	767	48.0	21.5	-6.4	22.0	0.0	6.0	35.9	9.3
NEVADA	32000	1,733,764	45.4	84.3	148,397	81.1	21.9	-6.0	25.1	16.0	10.1	36.1	8.4
Churchill, NV	32001	16,407	48.1	87.7	1,386	90.6	18.2	-9.7	18.6	8.2	3.9	25.2	17.9
Clark, NV	32003	1,242,450	46.4	83.5	102,710	78.5	21.7	-6.2	25.5	15.8	11.2	35.7	8.3
Douglas, NV	32005	34,150	34.8	91.2	2,088	78.5	25.9	-2.0	27.0	0.0	21.1	33.4	8.5
Elko, NV	32007	29,139	48.6	84.5	2,111	90.1	15.8	-12.1	17.7	30.1	7.8	42.1	8.0
Esmeralda, NV	32009	759	53.1	84.1	51	100.0	21.1	-6.8	22.2	0.0	0.0	0.0	0.0
Eureka, NV	32011	1,191	48.5	88.2	31	87.1	17.8	-10.1	19.1	0.0	0.0	0.0	9.2
Humboldt, NV	32013	10,163	54.8	80.9	529	84.3	13.4	-14.5	15.7	18.8	1.1	3.6	5.2
Lander, NV	32015	3,497	56.8	75.0	81	100.0	12.9	-15.0	15.5	0.0	0.0	0.0	3.9
Lincoln, NV	32017	3,069	46.3	83.0	72	54.2	15.8	-12.1	17.1	0.0	18.1	9.0	0.0
Lyon, NV	32019	34,574	51.0	85.8	2,253	73.4	12.7	-15.2	13.2	0.0	5.3	26.9	9.3
Mineral, NV	32021	3,793	61.5	86.3	147	81.0	8.2	-19.7	8.5	0.0	7.1	43.0	0.0
Nye, NV	32023	31,686	56.7	81.7	848	80.5	10.5	-17.4	10.6	28.6	5.0	34.3	3.3
Pershing, NV	32027	5,109	56.0	79.4	149	93.3	12.4	-15.5	15.0	8.4	0.0	65.0	3.2
Storey, NV	32029	3,021	36.4	91.8	157	78.3	13.9	-14.0	13.6	0.0	0.0	59.5	0.0
Washoe, NV	32031	270,427	38.6	86.4	31,727	88.9	26.7	-1.2	30.0	20.6	12.0	40.7	9.1
White Pine, NV	32033	6,317	53.2	83.8	610	73.8	13.4	-14.5	13.7	8.0	20.9	0.0	11.2
Carson City city, NV	32510	38,012	44.1	88.0	3,447	86.9	21.6	-6.3	24.0	15.2	6.1	28.0	10.5

Note. Data in columns 26 through 41 from the American Community Survey are subject to sampling error, which can be especially large in small counties and small population groups. See notes and definitions for more information.
[3]May be of any race.

Table C-1. Population, School, and Student Characteristics by County, Selected Years—*Continued*

County	State/ County Code	County Type[1]	Population, 2010		Percent of related children 5–17 years in poverty, 2010	Percent of children under 19 years with no health insurance, 2010	Number of schools and students, 2010–2011			Resident enrollment, 2006–2010 K–12 enrollment	
			Total	Percent 5–17 years			School districts	Schools	Students	Number	Percent public
			1	2	3	4	5	6	7	8	9
NEW HAMPSHIRE	33000	X	1,316,470	16.5	9.0	5.2	277	480	194,711	224,834	89.1
Belknap, NH	33001	4	60,088	15.7	11.2	6.5	19	26	9,706	10,135	91.1
Carroll, NH	33003	8	47,818	14.5	14.0	7.6	18	21	6,016	7,429	90.5
Cheshire, NH	33005	4	77,117	14.8	11.3	5.9	16	31	9,032	11,692	90.5
Coos, NH	33007	7	33,055	14.5	18.7	7.5	21	25	4,557	5,043	91.6
Grafton, NH	33009	5	89,118	13.8	10.9	6.0	41	51	11,683	12,884	92.2
Hillsborough, NH	33011	2	400,721	17.5	8.8	4.8	39	107	60,221	72,043	88.5
Merrimack, NH	33013	4	146,445	16.7	8.8	5.1	33	60	22,574	25,029	89.2
Rockingham, NH	33015	1	295,223	17.8	5.6	4.6	55	94	48,500	54,368	88.2
Strafford, NH	33017	1	123,143	15.1	10.1	5.4	18	35	16,273	19,001	87.9
Sullivan, NH	33019	7	43,742	15.7	12.7	5.6	17	30	6,149	7,210	90.2
NEW JERSEY	34000	X	8,791,894	17.3	13.1	6.3	698	2,607	1,398,878	1,540,561	87.7
Atlantic, NJ	34001	2	274,549	17.3	16.4	6.2	30	78	45,408	46,737	90.0
Bergen, NJ	34003	1	905,116	17.0	7.3	6.9	80	280	135,133	153,582	86.8
Burlington, NJ	34005	1	448,734	17.4	7.1	5.0	42	136	72,802	81,344	89.1
Camden, NJ	34007	1	513,657	17.9	17.1	5.8	46	164	86,537	95,146	87.7
Cape May, NJ	34009	3	97,265	14.2	16.6	6.8	19	32	13,364	14,278	87.1
Cumberland, NJ	34011	3	156,898	17.1	24.1	7.9	16	50	28,828	27,802	91.3
Essex, NJ	34013	1	783,969	18.0	20.8	7.3	40	242	125,010	142,230	88.0
Gloucester, NJ	34015	1	288,288	18.3	7.9	4.7	30	86	49,207	53,223	88.9
Hudson, NJ	34017	1	634,266	14.0	25.3	8.2	24	119	87,921	91,679	89.6
Hunterdon, NJ	34019	1	128,349	18.9	3.5	3.9	30	50	22,043	25,033	90.6
Mercer, NJ	34021	2	366,513	16.8	14.3	6.3	24	221	59,335	63,867	88.2
Middlesex, NJ	34023	1	809,858	16.7	9.4	6.9	28	172	113,849	134,024	90.1
Monmouth, NJ	34025	1	630,380	18.3	7.3	4.7	60	204	116,127	118,763	86.7
Morris, NJ	34027	1	492,276	18.4	4.9	4.3	42	154	79,762	89,348	87.2
Ocean, NJ	34029	1	576,567	16.7	17.2	5.8	29	111	75,761	94,838	77.2
Passaic, NJ	34031	1	501,226	18.0	23.1	7.8	24	140	86,759	91,096	86.6
Salem, NJ	34033	1	66,083	17.6	14.7	5.4	16	31	11,648	12,225	90.2
Somerset, NJ	34035	1	323,444	19.0	5.6	4.4	19	76	55,551	60,599	88.7
Sussex, NJ	34037	1	149,265	18.6	6.2	5.3	27	47	24,598	29,619	89.3
Union, NJ	34039	1	536,499	17.8	14.0	8.1	27	170	91,169	95,328	89.1
Warren, NJ	34041	2	108,692	18.0	8.2	5.8	25	44	18,066	19,800	92.8
NEW MEXICO	35000	X	2,059,179	18.1	26.7	11.0	130	862	338,122	371,897	91.7
Bernalillo, NM	35001	2	662,564	17.2	22.5	10.5	26	189	100,718	111,411	87.3
Catron, NM	35003	9	3,725	11.7	42.0	23.8	2	6	336	332	91.9
Chaves, NM	35005	5	65,645	20.0	31.6	11.3	4	31	11,864	12,769	91.5
Cibola, NM	35006	6	27,213	18.2	37.6	10.3	1	11	3,676	5,783	91.1
Colfax, NM	35007	7	13,750	15.4	25.9	11.2	4	18	2,025	2,254	97.0
Curry, NM	35009	5	48,376	19.5	27.9	9.7	4	27	9,723	9,254	97.4
De Baca, NM	35011	9	2,022	16.7	30.0	15.7	1	3	314	235	92.8
Dona Ana, NM	35013	3	209,233	19.3	31.7	10.7	5	68	41,184	39,431	96.6
Eddy, NM	35015	5	53,829	19.0	21.9	7.9	3	27	10,251	10,345	94.9
Grant, NM	35017	7	29,514	15.9	27.7	10.5	3	16	4,499	4,642	92.4
Guadalupe, NM	35019	7	4,687	16.1	28.3	10.0	2	7	741	785	93.6
Harding, NM	35021	9	695	9.2	18.5	25.4	2	4	89	218	100.0
Hidalgo, NM	35023	7	4,894	19.0	35.9	14.0	2	8	828	870	99.1
Lea, NM	35025	5	64,727	20.3	23.2	12.7	5	36	13,119	12,808	96.8
Lincoln, NM	35027	7	20,497	14.2	30.5	14.3	5	15	3,149	3,257	96.1
Los Alamos, NM	35028	6	17,950	18.9	2.7	3.1	1	7	3,455	3,465	94.6
Luna, NM	35029	6	25,095	19.2	48.4	12.1	1	11	5,529	5,053	97.4
McKinley, NM	35031	4	71,492	22.7	42.0	13.5	2	42	13,667	17,491	95.5
Mora, NM	35033	8	4,881	16.2	29.4	13.6	2	6	584	857	95.1
Otero, NM	35035	4	63,797	17.5	30.7	10.8	4	24	7,811	11,100	95.7

[1]County type codes are from the Economic Research Service of the United States Department of Agriculture. See notes and definitions for more information.

Table C-1. Population, School, and Student Characteristics by County, Selected Years—*Continued*

County	State/ County Code	Characteristics of students, 2010–2011				Number of graduates, 2008–2009	Staff and students, 2010–2011			
		Percent with IEP[2]	Percent eligible for free or reduced lunch	Percent minority	Percent English-language learners		Total staff	Number of teachers	Student/ teacher ratio	Central admin. staff
		10	11	12	13	14	15	16	17	18
NEW HAMPSHIRE	33000	15.3	25.2	10.3	2.0	14,757	32,951	15,365	12.7	1,459
Belknap, NH	33001	13.5	33.5	6.0	1.0	749	1,799	830	11.7	71
Carroll, NH	33003	14.7	32.8	3.5	0.5	534	1,220	548	11.0	71
Cheshire, NH	33005	19.8	33.8	5.9	0.4	708	1,860	808	11.2	93
Coos, NH	33007	16.7	43.0	4.7	0.3	375	940	404	11.3	44
Grafton, NH	33009	13.7	27.4	7.7	1.2	1,017	2,302	1,099	10.6	116
Hillsborough, NH	33011	14.2	26.2	16.9	4.3	4,587	8,729	4,271	14.1	475
Merrimack, NH	33013	15.8	25.2	7.7	1.7	1,536	4,103	1,767	12.8	176
Rockingham, NH	33015	15.2	14.1	6.8	0.9	3,691	8,098	3,864	12.6	250
Strafford, NH	33017	17.1	31.5	9.7	1.6	1,160	2,654	1,216	13.4	101
Sullivan, NH	33019	18.4	35.4	5.4	0.4	400	1,247	559	11.0	62
NEW JERSEY	34000	16.1	32.8	48.0	3.8	95,083	202,329	110,202	12.7	6,996
Atlantic, NJ	34001	16.4	46.0	53.1	5.3	3,115	7,422	3,978	11.4	265
Bergen, NJ	34003	16.7	17.1	41.9	3.5	9,878	19,312	10,690	12.6	723
Burlington, NJ	34005	17.6	21.4	34.2	1.0	5,616	11,234	5,757	12.6	422
Camden, NJ	34007	17.4	40.5	51.5	2.3	5,500	11,107	6,540	13.2	296
Cape May, NJ	34009	20.4	34.5	20.6	2.0	1,133	2,352	1,227	10.9	115
Cumberland, NJ	34011	16.5	65.8	63.8	5.1	1,634	4,675	2,274	12.7	157
Essex, NJ	34013	14.6	49.4	70.9	3.8	8,059	18,893	9,574	13.1	628
Gloucester, NJ	34015	17.6	22.7	24.8	0.6	3,559	7,830	3,974	12.4	312
Hudson, NJ	34017	12.4	67.5	82.3	8.3	4,682	12,648	6,712	13.1	447
Hunterdon, NJ	34019	16.6	5.8	12.4	0.5	1,647	3,563	1,949	11.3	136
Mercer, NJ	34021	16.6	29.8	56.2	3.8	4,014	9,317	5,094	11.6	317
Middlesex, NJ	34023	13.8	28.1	62.1	4.3	7,659	15,017	8,629	13.2	463
Monmouth, NJ	34025	16.8	19.2	27.3	2.2	8,413	16,654	9,089	12.8	601
Morris, NJ	34027	17.1	10.5	27.2	2.0	5,696	11,787	6,364	12.5	436
Ocean, NJ	34029	21.7	26.0	21.5	1.6	5,515	10,466	5,785	13.1	328
Passaic, NJ	34031	14.6	55.7	66.9	10.0	4,997	11,496	6,405	13.5	346
Salem, NJ	34033	16.0	39.0	34.0	1.1	760	1,860	999	11.7	77
Somerset, NJ	34035	16.2	16.1	42.8	2.5	3,957	7,358	4,464	12.4	223
Sussex, NJ	34037	17.6	12.9	11.3	0.4	2,220	3,544	1,961	12.5	143
Union, NJ	34039	14.1	45.0	62.4	6.1	5,665	13,224	7,258	12.6	439
Warren, NJ	34041	16.3	20.5	17.6	1.3	1,364	2,571	1,480	12.2	124
NEW MEXICO	35000	13.8	67.6	74.0	15.5	17,930	46,519	22,437	15.1	984
Bernalillo, NM	35001	13.9	61.5	76.8	16.2	4,784	13,143	6,709	15.0	323
Catron, NM	35003	17.6	75.1	33.6	...	29	77	40	8.4	2
Chaves, NM	35005	14.8	82.0	71.4	10.2	643	1,433	734	16.2	27
Cibola, NM	35006	14.3	71.9	83.0	13.2	225	566	265	13.9	9
Colfax, NM	35007	13.5	63.4	59.5	6.0	135	328	170	11.9	8
Curry, NM	35009	12.4	70.3	62.5	8.3	494	1,226	563	17.3	29
De Baca, NM	35011	19.4	55.4	52.2	...	34	64	30	10.5	2
Dona Ana, NM	35013	13.2	75.2	84.5	24.3	2,276	5,483	2,662	15.5	136
Eddy, NM	35015	14.5	57.6	57.5	4.0	611	1,274	658	15.6	20
Grant, NM	35017	11.4	70.5	70.8	3.7	300	649	312	14.4	16
Guadalupe, NM	35019	12.0	97.1	93.3	13.4	15	156	72	10.3	8
Harding, NM	35021	13.5	60.7	40.4	...	6	33	16	5.5	3
Hidalgo, NM	35023	15.5	67.1	76.3	3.5	60	161	65	12.8	8
Lea, NM	35025	12.4	62.0	70.1	16.8	597	1,538	789	16.6	16
Lincoln, NM	35027	10.9	65.0	60.6	8.4	207	423	215	14.7	9
Los Alamos, NM	35028	17.3	0.0	31.3	3.8	270	618	247	14.0	18
Luna, NM	35029	11.6	99.4	84.2	33.5	310	800	335	16.5	12
McKinley, NM	35031	11.8	83.1	95.2	30.9	902	2,453	1,040	13.1	40
Mora, NM	35033	13.5	96.9	95.3	9.9	69	108	48	12.2	4
Otero, NM	35035	15.6	62.3	51.6	2.3	485	1,255	521	15.0	25

[2]IEP=Individual Education Program. See notes and definitions for more information.
. . . = Not available.

Table C-1. Population, School, and Student Characteristics by County, Selected Years—*Continued*

County	State/ County Code	Revenues, 2008–2009				Current expenditures, 2008–2009			Resident population 16 to 19 years, 2006–2010			
			Percentage of revenue from									
		Total revenue ($1,000's)	Federal government	State government	Local government	Amount ($1,000's)	Amount per student	Percent for instruction	Total population 16 to 19 years	Percent enrolled in school	Percent high school graduates, not enrolled in school	Percent not enrolled, not grads, not employed, or not in labor force
		19	20	21	22	23	24	25	26	27	28	29
NEW HAMPSHIRE	33000	2,816,162	5.2	35.6	59.2	2,361,813	11,987	62.3	78,250	89.0	7.7	2.1
Belknap, NH	33001	149,599	5.6	34.9	59.4	125,533	12,423	60.7	3,195	87.6	7.4	2.5
Carroll, NH	33003	132,861	4.7	35.7	59.7	101,854	14,072	62.2	2,248	85.1	10.1	3.9
Cheshire, NH	33005	157,267	5.0	36.5	58.5	128,530	14,166	59.3	6,477	91.0	6.1	1.4
Coos, NH	33007	73,344	9.2	46.5	44.4	61,851	13,797	57.4	1,693	80.0	14.4	2.1
Grafton, NH	33009	210,616	4.4	31.3	64.3	179,822	15,435	62.8	6,383	91.6	6.7	1.0
Hillsborough, NH	33011	756,655	6.5	36.7	56.8	667,106	11,154	64.0	22,012	88.1	8.2	2.4
Merrimack, NH	33013	343,546	4.2	36.5	59.3	281,720	11,564	61.4	8,558	88.1	8.2	2.1
Rockingham, NH	33015	683,262	3.4	32.6	64.0	554,915	11,290	62.0	16,041	89.9	7.1	2.5
Strafford, NH	33017	206,681	6.7	36.6	56.7	174,215	11,902	63.5	9,459	91.8	6.1	1.1
Sullivan, NH	33019	102,331	7.2	42.8	50.0	86,267	13,237	61.4	2,184	81.7	13.6	2.9
NEW JERSEY	34000	26,802,459	3.9	39.4	56.8	22,396,563	16,297	57.4	477,310	87.6	8.1	2.9
Atlantic, NJ	34001	963,090	4.5	37.9	57.6	756,274	16,212	57.7	16,609	86.9	8.1	2.6
Bergen, NJ	34003	2,613,276	2.5	16.8	80.6	2,209,859	16,501	57.8	45,286	92.4	5.1	1.9
Burlington, NJ	34005	1,366,941	3.9	36.7	59.4	1,181,207	16,101	57.2	23,902	89.6	6.8	2.6
Camden, NJ	34007	1,690,173	5.1	52.0	42.9	1,365,968	16,271	58.0	29,485	85.4	9.0	3.7
Cape May, NJ	34009	304,084	4.5	29.4	66.2	247,020	18,073	58.2	4,957	81.7	15.1	1.6
Cumberland, NJ	34011	512,036	6.3	75.8	17.9	437,999	16,383	58.0	9,124	78.9	12.1	6.6
Essex, NJ	34013	2,934,477	4.7	56.6	38.7	2,320,624	18,567	54.3	44,507	83.3	10.1	5.5
Gloucester, NJ	34015	850,409	3.5	40.5	56.0	710,353	14,270	57.0	16,327	90.7	6.6	2.2
Hudson, NJ	34017	1,652,612	6.4	65.5	28.1	1,403,554	17,615	61.0	30,971	84.4	11.4	2.9
Hunterdon, NJ	34019	454,582	1.7	17.9	80.4	400,575	17,482	53.8	6,761	90.6	6.3	2.2
Mercer, NJ	34021	1,249,949	3.7	40.9	55.4	1,000,040	16,686	57.2	22,981	90.8	5.5	2.2
Middlesex, NJ	34023	1,966,007	3.5	32.9	63.6	1,676,412	15,358	58.2	47,057	90.5	6.8	1.7
Monmouth, NJ	34025	2,116,511	2.9	31.5	65.6	1,819,379	15,602	57.2	34,494	89.9	7.0	2.3
Morris, NJ	34027	1,477,917	2.0	18.2	79.8	1,287,589	16,065	56.3	25,168	89.7	7.5	1.8
Ocean, NJ	34029	1,224,574	4.0	34.5	61.6	1,071,042	14,068	57.6	27,205	84.8	9.5	3.1
Passaic, NJ	34031	1,699,782	5.0	53.3	41.6	1,323,663	16,651	58.4	30,206	83.3	10.5	4.9
Salem, NJ	34033	215,023	5.4	49.3	45.3	184,941	15,407	55.9	3,847	85.5	11.8	1.2
Somerset, NJ	34035	993,681	2.1	19.1	78.8	854,045	15,593	56.9	15,668	91.2	6.2	2.1
Sussex, NJ	34037	477,686	2.4	32.4	65.2	431,934	16,732	55.8	8,676	91.5	5.8	1.6
Union, NJ	34039	1,704,753	4.2	41.6	54.2	1,434,010	16,671	58.9	28,168	85.0	9.3	3.5
Warren, NJ	34041	334,896	3.0	40.1	56.9	280,075	15,119	58.9	5,911	90.2	7.6	2.0
NEW MEXICO	35000	3,714,092	14.0	70.7	15.3	3,112,643	9,437	58.2	121,304	80.4	10.4	6.1
Bernalillo, NM	35001	1,040,603	10.1	72.4	17.5	852,489	8,785	59.9	35,796	81.7	9.2	5.5
Catron, NM	35003	6,857	50.3	42.0	7.7	6,101	17,382	50.0	146	83.6	12.3	4.1
Chaves, NM	35005	131,418	12.8	79.4	7.8	102,687	8,987	57.4	4,522	78.4	12.1	4.9
Cibola, NM	35006	41,457	26.3	65.0	8.6	39,144	10,849	57.6	1,737	80.7	12.4	5.2
Colfax, NM	35007	32,220	7.2	79.2	13.7	24,547	11,338	57.4	781	79.5	7.7	3.8
Curry, NM	35009	85,279	14.0	78.2	7.8	77,717	8,502	59.1	2,807	82.0	13.8	1.9
De Baca, NM	35011	5,780	6.1	78.2	15.7	4,992	15,082	53.2	50	60.0	0.0	40.0
Dona Ana, NM	35013	426,362	14.4	74.3	11.3	366,331	9,255	59.9	14,379	83.8	7.0	7.4
Eddy, NM	35015	124,784	8.7	69.8	21.4	101,101	9,855	59.7	3,006	82.6	8.5	6.1
Grant, NM	35017	56,064	13.0	76.9	10.1	48,718	10,370	56.3	1,582	80.0	9.9	7.0
Guadalupe, NM	35019	12,288	11.4	75.1	13.5	10,755	14,593	47.7	209	68.4	16.3	15.3
Harding, NM	35021	3,858	2.5	84.6	13.0	3,289	34,989	50.6	120	96.7	3.3	0.0
Hidalgo, NM	35023	15,548	12.2	76.9	10.9	13,143	13,997	51.4	295	50.2	49.8	0.0
Lea, NM	35025	134,775	9.0	70.3	20.7	107,102	8,508	60.8	3,814	77.1	9.1	9.1
Lincoln, NM	35027	43,036	10.2	73.7	16.1	35,752	11,110	57.4	1,012	95.4	2.3	2.0
Los Alamos, NM	35028	43,319	21.9	64.0	14.1	39,322	11,610	57.2	875	93.3	5.6	1.1
Luna, NM	35029	56,720	15.6	77.4	7.0	51,250	9,421	57.5	1,443	83.7	9.6	6.0
McKinley, NM	35031	169,914	44.3	48.1	7.7	148,477	10,551	55.9	6,102	75.5	13.5	8.1
Mora, NM	35033	13,156	19.2	73.9	6.9	11,407	16,825	47.3	270	78.2	21.9	0.0
Otero, NM	35035	81,158	13.8	74.6	11.6	71,994	9,441	56.8	3,976	81.3	14.9	2.4

Note. Data in columns 26 through 41 from the American Community Survey are subject to sampling error, which can be especially large in small counties and small population groups. See notes and definitions for more information.

Table C-1. Population, School, and Student Characteristics by County, Selected Years—*Continued*

County	State/ County Code	High school graduates, 2006–2010			College enrollment, 2006–2010		College graduates, 2006–2010 (percent)						
		Population 25 years and over	High school diploma or less (percent)	High school diploma or more (percent)	Number	Percent public	Bachelor's degree or more	+/- U.S. percent with Bachelor's degree or more	Non-Hispanic White	Black or African American	American Indian and Alaska Native	Asian, Hawaiian, and Pacific Islander	Hispanic or Latino[3]
		30	31	32	33	34	35	36	37	38	39	40	41
NEW HAMPSHIRE	33000	895,399	38.8	91.0	90,346	60.2	32.9	5.0	32.6	28.7	22.5	58.4	25.5
Belknap, NH	33001	43,122	42.6	89.5	2,136	69.8	26.9	-1.0	26.8	26.9	40.8	27.9	33.6
Carroll, NH	33003	35,587	40.5	90.6	1,638	68.1	30.3	2.4	30.6	23.1	0.0	20.7	17.8
Cheshire, NH	33005	51,160	43.7	89.8	8,791	73.4	29.8	1.9	29.7	19.2	28.8	60.8	28.0
Coos, NH	33007	24,698	56.5	84.8	1,086	85.5	16.1	-11.8	16.0	0.0	17.7	97.1	11.7
Grafton, NH	33009	59,014	40.1	90.9	10,572	43.7	35.3	7.4	34.7	24.3	2.9	70.4	39.7
Hillsborough, NH	33011	269,258	37.4	90.5	24,694	46.4	34.6	6.7	34.2	28.1	18.2	63.7	21.7
Merrimack, NH	33013	100,432	37.9	91.3	9,923	47.1	32.7	4.8	32.8	20.3	12.8	55.1	24.1
Rockingham, NH	33015	203,356	34.2	93.5	14,475	62.9	36.6	8.7	36.4	38.9	26.5	50.8	34.1
Strafford, NH	33017	77,593	40.3	89.5	15,287	87.6	30.0	2.1	29.7	26.2	28.0	50.5	29.0
Sullivan, NH	33019	31,179	48.7	89.9	1,744	64.9	25.9	-2.0	25.6	65.6	66.7	42.7	24.1
NEW JERSEY	34000	5,889,519	42.5	87.3	563,961	66.7	34.6	6.7	37.5	20.5	16.6	67.2	15.6
Atlantic, NJ	34001	183,469	50.8	84.7	21,081	84.6	23.6	-4.3	27.1	14.4	11.6	33.3	9.9
Bergen, NJ	34003	625,632	34.5	90.9	55,536	57.8	44.5	16.6	44.4	33.7	16.9	66.2	25.8
Burlington, NJ	34005	304,778	39.4	90.9	28,754	69.8	33.5	5.6	34.6	25.0	24.4	57.4	21.3
Camden, NJ	34007	339,797	47.1	85.4	31,958	71.7	27.9	0.0	31.1	18.0	16.3	52.5	10.5
Cape May, NJ	34009	71,205	48.4	88.2	3,713	77.6	26.4	-1.5	27.3	14.4	24.7	36.6	17.5
Cumberland, NJ	34011	103,033	64.0	75.8	6,817	83.1	13.3	-14.6	18.0	6.3	6.7	31.9	5.6
Essex, NJ	34013	511,207	47.0	82.0	53,268	66.2	31.6	3.7	49.2	18.5	5.9	67.0	13.1
Gloucester, NJ	34015	188,051	46.0	89.5	20,957	76.5	26.9	-1.0	26.4	26.1	23.4	58.0	21.2
Hudson, NJ	34017	428,810	46.7	80.3	44,693	59.3	34.6	6.7	45.0	22.0	18.9	67.4	16.8
Hunterdon, NJ	34019	88,130	29.3	94.0	6,368	63.9	47.5	19.6	47.8	23.5	26.7	79.9	27.7
Mercer, NJ	34021	241,243	39.4	86.5	32,139	56.9	38.2	10.3	44.9	15.4	27.2	76.8	12.8
Middlesex, NJ	34023	534,021	40.1	88.0	65,714	81.2	38.4	10.5	33.8	29.6	19.0	72.6	14.8
Monmouth, NJ	34025	425,642	36.1	91.3	36,785	58.5	39.2	11.3	41.2	20.1	9.0	66.5	17.2
Morris, NJ	34027	336,089	30.6	93.1	29,373	53.5	48.4	20.5	49.4	31.0	22.8	74.0	22.5
Ocean, NJ	34029	394,735	48.9	89.1	29,168	54.8	24.3	-3.6	24.6	18.2	23.2	53.3	14.0
Passaic, NJ	34031	321,436	53.6	81.5	32,034	71.6	25.2	-2.7	32.4	12.1	26.4	61.0	11.9
Salem, NJ	34033	44,751	53.5	85.6	3,859	78.1	18.3	-9.6	20.0	8.0	9.2	49.7	7.0
Somerset, NJ	34035	217,831	29.5	92.7	17,109	65.0	49.8	21.9	50.9	33.4	38.2	78.2	19.9
Sussex, NJ	34037	101,352	40.2	93.0	8,198	69.5	31.4	3.5	31.3	28.4	51.0	49.8	27.4
Union, NJ	34039	354,191	47.2	84.3	30,481	71.1	31.2	3.3	41.2	20.9	8.1	64.5	11.6
Warren, NJ	34041	74,116	45.8	89.3	5,956	58.9	28.6	0.7	27.5	40.6	32.6	66.8	23.6
NEW MEXICO	35000	1,296,627	44.3	82.7	146,741	86.9	25.5	-2.4	37.5	25.1	9.4	47.9	12.9
Bernalillo, NM	35001	423,230	38.1	86.2	58,945	86.6	31.5	3.6	45.1	27.6	16.5	46.2	15.5
Catron, NM	35003	3,157	46.9	86.0	115	75.7	21.3	-6.6	26.0	100.0	0.0	100.0	4.5
Chaves, NM	35005	39,742	53.0	76.3	3,808	83.5	15.7	-12.2	22.0	0.0	2.3	39.9	7.7
Cibola, NM	35006	17,529	61.3	76.4	931	89.6	11.5	-16.4	20.6	0.0	7.0	67.7	8.6
Colfax, NM	35007	9,907	48.9	86.0	425	92.2	19.9	-8.0	28.2	0.0	7.6	100.0	7.9
Curry, NM	35009	28,386	46.4	81.5	3,346	85.0	18.2	-9.7	23.9	17.9	27.0	23.1	6.3
De Baca, NM	35011	1,312	50.2	79.0	37	100.0	19.7	-8.2	25.5	100.0	0.0	0.0	3.1
Dona Ana, NM	35013	120,632	46.7	75.5	22,351	94.5	25.4	-2.5	43.2	26.1	31.7	61.8	12.7
Eddy, NM	35015	34,100	53.3	80.2	2,425	90.5	15.1	-12.8	18.7	9.9	13.6	62.2	8.9
Grant, NM	35017	20,749	42.3	85.4	2,312	90.6	24.1	-3.8	32.6	0.0	17.8	25.5	12.3
Guadalupe, NM	35019	3,389	61.0	80.0	321	91.3	7.4	-20.5	15.9	0.0	0.0	0.0	5.0
Harding, NM	35021	567	50.4	89.8	55	100.0	18.2	-9.7	27.7	0.0	0.0	0.0	6.7
Hidalgo, NM	35023	3,182	54.9	77.7	247	84.2	15.6	-12.3	25.5	45.9	0.0	0.0	5.0
Lea, NM	35025	37,689	57.1	72.7	2,879	73.5	12.9	-15.0	19.1	9.1	11.1	0.0	5.2
Lincoln, NM	35027	15,070	40.4	86.5	767	97.1	23.9	-4.0	30.1	15.0	4.6	46.0	5.2
Los Alamos, NM	35028	12,830	10.7	99.3	1,072	81.9	64.0	36.1	66.8	100.0	48.7	90.4	34.2
Luna, NM	35029	16,055	61.3	69.5	819	98.4	13.5	-14.4	19.3	0.0	9.7	47.2	7.8
McKinley, NM	35031	39,339	65.3	69.6	3,571	89.7	10.9	-17.0	39.2	54.6	4.4	51.8	9.1
Mora, NM	35033	3,486	55.7	85.1	528	93.4	15.4	-12.5	36.4	0.0	0.0	0.0	10.8
Otero, NM	35035	40,187	43.8	85.0	4,552	91.3	17.7	-10.2	22.9	20.2	12.1	33.0	6.8

Note. Data in columns 26 through 41 from the American Community Survey are subject to sampling error, which can be especially large in small counties and small population groups. See notes and definitions for more information.
[3]May be of any race.

Table C-1. Population, School, and Student Characteristics by County, Selected Years—*Continued*

County	State/ County Code	County Type[1]	Population, 2010		Percent of related children 5–17 years in poverty, 2010	Percent of children under 19 years with no health insurance, 2010	Number of schools and students, 2010–2011			Resident enrollment, 2006–2010: K–12 enrollment	
			Total	Percent 5–17 years			School districts	Schools	Students	Number	Percent public
			1	2	3	4	5	6	7	8	9
NEW MEXICO— *(Continued)*											
Quay, NM	35037	7	9,041	16.0	34.6	11.5	4	12	1,576	1,669	98.0
Rio Arriba, NM	35039	6	40,246	17.9	25.5	10.4	5	32	6,205	6,960	84.7
Roosevelt, NM	35041	7	19,846	18.6	28.2	10.4	4	13	3,727	3,611	94.7
Sandoval, NM	35043	2	131,561	19.8	15.3	9.0	6	39	21,259	24,537	91.2
San Juan, NM	35045	3	130,044	20.6	31.2	14.2	4	49	23,846	26,177	95.4
San Miguel, NM	35047	6	29,393	16.5	31.9	10.6	3	21	4,335	4,990	93.1
Santa Fe, NM	35049	3	144,170	15.3	23.2	11.9	9	51	16,822	22,498	83.3
Sierra, NM	35051	6	11,988	11.3	39.2	12.3	1	5	1,423	1,941	96.8
Socorro, NM	35053	6	17,866	17.2	36.7	12.3	2	10	2,420	3,253	96.8
Taos, NM	35055	7	32,937	15.1	28.1	11.7	5	22	4,238	4,815	94.0
Torrance, NM	35057	2	16,383	18.4	30.2	13.1	3	17	4,571	3,362	91.5
Union, NM	35059	9	4,549	14.8	25.8	15.5	2	6	634	886	95.6
Valencia, NM	35061	2	76,569	19.5	31.1	9.6	3	29	13,504	14,838	93.8
NEW YORK	36000	X	19,378,102	16.4	20.0	5.1	952	4,757	2,734,955	3,282,981	86.0
Albany, NY	36001	2	304,204	14.9	15.1	4.7	26	71	35,275	46,396	87.8
Allegany, NY	36003	7	48,946	16.2	21.0	6.2	12	20	7,355	8,102	91.9
Bronx, NY	36005	1	1,385,108	19.1	41.0	4.8	38	386	213,259	281,607	87.1
Broome, NY	36007	2	200,600	15.0	21.2	5.6	12	54	28,054	31,345	93.4
Cattaraugus, NY	36009	4	80,317	17.1	20.0	7.5	14	37	14,224	14,164	90.8
Cayuga, NY	36011	4	80,026	16.3	17.3	5.3	8	24	9,894	13,824	90.7
Chautauqua, NY	36013	4	134,905	16.2	23.6	5.0	19	52	20,775	22,943	94.4
Chemung, NY	36015	3	88,830	16.4	20.4	4.4	3	23	12,404	14,715	91.6
Chenango, NY	36017	6	50,477	17.3	21.5	5.1	9	25	8,367	9,407	95.5
Clinton, NY	36019	5	82,128	14.4	16.0	5.0	9	30	11,462	12,699	94.8
Columbia, NY	36021	6	63,096	15.5	14.2	6.0	7	18	7,847	9,570	88.1
Cortland, NY	36023	4	49,336	15.6	18.1	4.2	6	18	6,850	7,877	94.5
Delaware, NY	36025	6	47,980	14.6	19.7	5.9	14	22	6,512	7,519	92.5
Dutchess, NY	36027	2	297,488	17.1	9.2	4.7	14	77	44,898	53,442	89.7
Erie, NY	36029	1	919,040	16.3	18.3	4.4	48	222	131,194	156,830	87.0
Essex, NY	36031	6	39,370	14.6	17.5	6.4	11	15	4,171	6,288	89.9
Franklin, NY	36033	5	51,599	15.3	20.3	8.3	8	21	7,948	8,249	94.0
Fulton, NY	36035	4	55,531	16.7	22.5	5.5	7	21	8,867	9,648	97.8
Genesee, NY	36037	4	60,079	16.4	15.4	4.6	10	23	9,097	10,252	94.5
Greene, NY	36039	6	49,221	14.6	18.8	6.0	6	17	6,771	7,052	89.7
Hamilton, NY	36041	8	4,836	13.0	14.1	9.4	7	6	546	615	96.6
Herkimer, NY	36043	2	64,519	16.6	20.1	5.5	13	27	10,156	11,053	95.4
Jefferson, NY	36045	4	116,229	17.2	21.4	6.4	12	39	19,074	20,507	92.5
Kings, NY	36047	1	2,504,700	16.7	32.8	5.2	60	512	307,149	439,102	77.6
Lewis, NY	36049	6	27,087	18.2	20.6	6.7	5	14	4,365	5,068	90.6
Livingston, NY	36051	1	65,393	15.3	13.9	4.7	9	23	8,563	10,378	92.9
Madison, NY	36053	2	73,442	16.5	13.7	5.8	10	28	10,843	12,239	93.9
Monroe, NY	36055	1	744,344	16.8	18.3	4.5	27	193	113,168	130,608	90.3
Montgomery, NY	36057	4	50,219	17.4	25.5	6.0	6	17	7,560	8,904	92.1
Nassau, NY	36059	1	1,339,532	17.7	7.0	5.3	60	320	206,507	240,128	86.5
New York, NY	36061	1	1,585,873	10.0	25.0	4.5	40	386	181,702	168,095	75.0
Niagara, NY	36063	1	216,469	16.1	18.8	4.8	11	56	31,667	36,340	90.4
Oneida, NY	36065	2	234,878	16.2	21.3	4.9	18	73	34,549	39,748	94.0
Onondaga, NY	36067	2	467,026	17.1	17.6	4.6	21	123	73,483	81,785	92.2
Ontario, NY	36069	1	107,931	17.1	13.0	4.9	10	31	17,149	18,778	93.5
Orange, NY	36071	2	372,813	20.1	15.2	5.6	18	85	63,266	76,880	84.4
Orleans, NY	36073	1	42,883	16.9	18.9	5.8	6	14	6,829	8,225	95.3
Oswego, NY	36075	2	122,109	17.3	21.0	4.7	11	43	21,907	22,418	96.1
Otsego, NY	36077	6	62,259	14.3	17.0	6.2	13	24	7,962	9,516	97.4
Putnam, NY	36079	1	99,710	18.6	5.2	4.2	6	22	15,922	19,478	90.0

[1]County type codes are from the Economic Research Service of the United States Department of Agriculture. See notes and definitions for more information.

Table C-1. Population, School, and Student Characteristics by County, Selected Years—*Continued*

County	State/ County Code	Characteristics of students, 2010–2011				Number of graduates, 2008–2009	Staff and students, 2010–2011			
		Percent with IEP[2]	Percent eligible for free or reduced lunch	Percent minority	Percent English-language learners		Total staff	Number of teachers	Student/ teacher ratio	Central admin. staff
		10	11	12	13	14	15	16	17	18
NEW MEXICO—*(Continued)*										
Quay, NM	35037	18.3	87.1	56.3	1.6	102	267	128	12.4	8
Rio Arriba, NM	35039	12.0	86.2	95.9	26.2	249	947	433	14.3	17
Roosevelt, NM	35041	17.7	66.2	55.8	7.2	180	504	257	14.5	11
Sandoval, NM	35043	12.9	56.9	62.7	10.3	1,175	2,901	1,424	14.9	34
San Juan, NM	35045	14.7	66.9	67.8	13.8	1,189	3,235	1,515	15.7	52
San Miguel, NM	35047	13.1	81.3	92.5	21.0	230	677	305	14.2	16
Santa Fe, NM	35049	14.6	66.5	75.7	22.0	766	2,235	1,137	14.8	44
Sierra, NM	35051	14.8	75.3	51.8	6.6	80	232	92	15.4	6
Socorro, NM	35053	15.7	66.1	76.0	3.6	143	425	187	12.9	12
Taos, NM	35055	17.5	84.5	81.0	12.0	294	640	302	14.0	22
Torrance, NM	35057	14.9	62.8	52.7	4.5	319	706	315	14.5	11
Union, NM	35059	10.6	67.8	53.9	...	43	122	56	11.4	3
Valencia, NM	35061	14.4	77.9	75.9	7.8	708	1,844	796	17.0	36
NEW YORK	36000	16.5	48.1	50.7	7.6	180,913	412,931	211,165	13.0	25,037
Albany, NY	36001	17.8	35.8	37.9	2.5	2,905	5,899	2,891	12.2	429
Allegany, NY	36003	15.3	47.7	4.1	0.1	591	1,388	644	11.4	89
Bronx, NY	36005	21.5	84.2	96.0	17.7	10,328	17,985	14,846	14.4	117
Broome, NY	36007	16.5	39.6	18.0	1.5	2,152	5,454	2,585	10.9	353
Cattaraugus, NY	36009	16.1	43.5	12.2	0.1	899	2,709	1,369	10.4	174
Cayuga, NY	36011	13.9	34.9	11.4	0.2	755	1,674	894	11.1	104
Chautauqua, NY	36013	13.3	46.4	17.4	2.3	1,598	3,589	1,835	11.3	237
Chemung, NY	36015	14.6	44.0	16.3	0.3	815	2,090	929	13.4	137
Chenango, NY	36017	15.9	49.8	4.0	0.1	689	1,754	853	9.8	99
Clinton, NY	36019	19.0	37.6	6.1	0.1	917	2,353	1,183	9.7	133
Columbia, NY	36021	18.5	36.6	18.9	2.4	626	1,532	673	11.7	122
Cortland, NY	36023	16.1	39.7	6.1	0.1	476	1,251	582	11.8	84
Delaware, NY	36025	16.6	48.9	6.2	0.9	526	1,477	715	9.1	107
Dutchess, NY	36027	16.9	26.2	28.7	2.3	3,318	7,150	3,322	13.5	483
Erie, NY	36029	17.0	41.7	31.9	3.4	9,125	20,209	10,745	12.2	1,363
Essex, NY	36031	16.4	41.0	3.4	...	341	896	422	9.9	69
Franklin, NY	36033	15.8	47.8	15.4	0.2	531	1,596	735	10.8	93
Fulton, NY	36035	15.7	44.2	6.5	0.2	619	1,345	635	14.0	92
Genesee, NY	36037	13.3	35.7	9.9	0.8	718	1,780	880	10.3	115
Greene, NY	36039	16.1	33.3	12.8	0.7	553	1,243	593	11.4	81
Hamilton, NY	36041	12.1	27.8	3.1	...	40	180	88	6.2	17
Herkimer, NY	36043	14.8	43.2	4.3	0.2	786	1,745	911	11.2	113
Jefferson, NY	36045	14.6	45.8	16.6	1.2	1,158	3,027	1,471	13.0	186
Kings, NY	36047	18.5	75.6	85.3	13.1	15,826	24,272	20,410	15.0	87
Lewis, NY	36049	15.1	43.1	3.4	...	344	732	343	12.7	47
Livingston, NY	36051	12.4	30.2	6.3	0.9	677	1,563	775	11.1	105
Madison, NY	36053	14.1	35.4	5.1	...	813	1,780	864	12.6	119
Monroe, NY	36055	15.2	41.1	39.2	3.6	8,003	20,372	9,685	11.7	1,399
Montgomery, NY	36057	17.2	40.4	22.8	2.0	450	1,220	668	11.3	79
Nassau, NY	36059	14.5	19.1	42.6	5.5	15,669	34,730	17,594	11.7	2,974
New York, NY	36061	14.8	69.1	86.0	12.5	12,408	63,580	15,542	11.7	4,023
Niagara, NY	36063	15.4	39.7	19.4	0.7	2,396	4,727	2,363	13.4	329
Oneida, NY	36065	15.6	44.3	20.5	4.4	2,531	5,732	2,960	11.7	377
Onondaga, NY	36067	16.7	38.2	30.2	3.9	4,903	12,333	5,837	12.6	793
Ontario, NY	36069	13.7	26.6	11.0	1.0	1,303	3,019	1,399	12.3	183
Orange, NY	36071	15.7	35.0	38.9	5.0	4,627	9,596	4,906	12.9	757
Orleans, NY	36073	14.0	42.9	15.3	1.1	540	1,357	717	9.5	89
Oswego, NY	36075	15.2	44.4	4.4	0.2	1,608	3,909	1,748	12.5	250
Otsego, NY	36077	17.1	38.5	7.7	0.3	628	1,555	716	11.1	91
Putnam, NY	36079	16.1	9.9	18.8	2.1	1,319	2,651	1,156	13.8	194

[2]IEP=Individual Education Program. See notes and definitions for more information.

Table C-1. Population, School, and Student Characteristics by County, Selected Years—*Continued*

County	State/ County Code	Revenues, 2008–2009				Current expenditures, 2008–2009			Resident population 16 to 19 years, 2006–2010			
			Percentage of revenue from									
		Total revenue ($1,000's)	Federal government	State government	Local government	Amount ($1,000's)	Amount per student	Percent for instruction	Total population 16 to 19 years	Percent enrolled in school	Percent high school graduates, not enrolled in school	Percent not enrolled, not grads, not employed, or not in labor force
		19	20	21	22	23	24	25	26	27	28	29
NEW MEXICO— *(Continued)*												
Quay, NM	35037	21,067	11.8	80.0	8.2	18,728	12,083	56.1	653	91.0	6.7	0.0
Rio Arriba, NM	35039	96,785	17.0	62.0	21.0	78,657	12,475	51.1	2,309	71.1	16.3	9.6
Roosevelt, NM	35041	40,735	11.8	77.5	10.7	35,717	10,502	58.9	1,487	86.8	11.5	1.7
Sandoval, NM	35043	216,457	11.0	70.5	18.5	181,221	8,781	60.6	7,022	82.5	12.0	2.9
San Juan, NM	35045	260,506	20.2	62.9	16.9	219,466	9,285	59.0	8,122	75.0	15.0	7.9
San Miguel, NM	35047	60,542	16.6	74.1	9.2	53,371	12,048	52.7	2,178	86.9	9.2	0.9
Santa Fe, NM	35049	187,623	9.6	63.4	27.0	143,555	9,118	56.7	6,986	77.0	11.1	5.4
Sierra, NM	35051	17,067	15.0	72.0	13.0	14,599	9,726	58.0	593	53.8	12.1	34.1
Socorro, NM	35053	30,173	18.9	68.4	12.7	26,567	11,262	56.9	1,576	81.6	8.9	7.4
Taos, NM	35055	52,179	12.4	74.9	12.7	46,537	11,274	55.3	1,556	68.8	8.2	17.4
Torrance, NM	35057	54,913	8.9	78.7	12.4	46,519	9,883	55.8	1,000	87.9	9.1	1.8
Union, NM	35059	9,630	6.7	84.0	9.3	9,245	13,536	48.5	153	74.5	14.4	11.1
Valencia, NM	35061	141,819	10.8	75.4	13.8	122,143	9,130	55.0	4,747	78.7	7.1	9.4
NEW YORK	36000	56,024,652	5.7	46.0	48.3	49,011,590	18,156	69.1	1,113,417	87.0	7.5	3.9
Albany, NY	36001	677,543	4.2	43.1	52.7	547,637	16,326	64.1	20,538	90.8	5.9	2.3
Allegany, NY	36003	154,902	6.5	73.5	20.0	126,344	16,581	64.1	4,599	95.1	2.4	2.2
Bronx, NY	36005	([6])	([6])	([6])	([6])	([6])	([6])	([6])	91,493	80.4	8.4	8.8
Broome, NY	36007	520,616	5.1	58.2	36.7	448,759	15,281	65.6	13,771	90.4	4.3	3.5
Cattaraugus, NY	36009	280,484	5.3	70.8	23.9	227,800	15,519	64.2	5,127	83.6	9.4	4.1
Cayuga, NY	36011	181,571	4.8	63.7	31.5	154,256	14,972	66.4	4,364	79.3	11.4	5.6
Chautauqua, NY	36013	383,221	6.5	66.0	27.5	320,994	14,922	66.1	9,256	83.9	8.8	4.5
Chemung, NY	36015	215,151	5.6	66.6	27.8	186,360	14,942	63.8	5,128	86.3	9.8	1.3
Chenango, NY	36017	174,975	5.1	73.4	21.5	144,030	16,442	61.9	3,066	84.0	9.1	4.7
Clinton, NY	36019	232,692	4.6	59.8	35.6	204,381	17,067	67.9	5,772	88.6	6.4	3.3
Columbia, NY	36021	178,310	5.3	40.1	54.6	153,492	18,598	63.4	4,276	85.1	6.7	7.1
Cortland, NY	36023	122,024	5.2	66.8	27.9	107,292	15,325	65.4	4,337	91.4	5.4	1.4
Delaware, NY	36025	155,332	4.4	55.4	40.2	128,268	18,684	62.0	3,171	78.2	13.8	5.7
Dutchess, NY	36027	832,327	2.9	40.7	56.4	735,042	15,880	63.7	19,927	92.4	4.8	2.0
Erie, NY	36029	2,359,769	5.8	58.7	35.5	1,850,873	14,510	63.3	53,433	87.7	7.9	2.9
Essex, NY	36031	97,417	5.3	41.5	53.2	84,161	20,000	64.9	2,037	86.6	8.8	3.2
Franklin, NY	36033	160,333	5.6	65.5	28.9	138,015	16,699	65.1	2,915	86.4	6.0	6.2
Fulton, NY	36035	154,910	5.8	67.5	26.7	127,088	13,674	67.2	3,047	85.4	9.4	5.0
Genesee, NY	36037	168,603	4.2	64.4	31.3	145,294	15,362	63.5	3,515	81.8	12.6	4.7
Greene, NY	36039	140,852	4.3	44.2	51.5	120,587	17,071	61.6	2,740	66.7	12.1	17.6
Hamilton, NY	36041	19,527	2.1	20.0	77.9	17,149	31,067	59.5	140	78.6	2.9	0.0
Herkimer, NY	36043	178,719	4.8	67.3	27.8	149,618	14,211	65.7	3,707	82.7	8.2	6.1
Jefferson, NY	36045	293,397	11.6	64.7	23.6	246,703	13,208	64.5	6,372	77.0	16.6	4.5
Kings, NY	36047	([6])	([6])	([6])	([6])	([6])	([6])	([6])	139,111	83.9	9.1	5.1
Lewis, NY	36049	83,971	4.2	68.2	27.6	67,614	15,232	63.2	1,527	81.1	7.9	6.5
Livingston, NY	36051	161,901	3.7	64.0	32.3	129,325	14,615	62.9	5,078	92.9	5.7	1.3
Madison, NY	36053	188,427	4.1	61.5	34.4	163,481	14,717	63.2	5,901	92.0	5.6	1.8
Monroe, NY	36055	2,113,058	5.7	53.9	40.4	1,799,896	15,716	61.1	48,731	89.6	6.7	3.1
Montgomery, NY	36057	130,099	5.9	67.1	27.0	111,809	14,536	66.6	2,863	78.0	8.5	9.0
Nassau, NY	36059	4,949,777	2.1	26.2	71.7	4,448,930	21,547	65.4	73,541	91.9	5.0	2.3
New York, NY	36061	21,165,693[6]	8.6[6]	47.4[6]	44.0[6]	18,795,097[6]	19,146[6]	75.8[6]	66,516	87.5	6.0	5.2
Niagara, NY	36063	548,552	5.3	62.2	32.4	465,418	14,540	65.6	12,563	84.4	11.6	2.6
Oneida, NY	36065	601,886	5.9	64.6	29.5	520,986	14,858	64.9	13,795	88.7	7.7	2.7
Onondaga, NY	36067	1,302,340	5.3	56.2	38.5	1,131,939	15,315	65.5	30,063	89.5	5.7	3.2
Ontario, NY	36069	305,609	4.4	52.7	42.9	257,289	14,574	65.2	6,226	90.0	6.8	1.7
Orange, NY	36071	1,275,749	4.6	47.0	48.4	1,118,988	17,248	66.4	23,783	86.7	7.6	3.2
Orleans, NY	36073	121,888	5.8	69.6	24.6	100,251	14,011	67.0	2,708	85.2	8.1	4.4
Oswego, NY	36075	393,516	5.5	61.4	33.1	344,126	15,189	64.7	9,022	88.6	7.3	2.9
Otsego, NY	36077	159,549	4.8	61.3	33.9	135,463	16,173	63.5	5,415	88.5	5.4	4.7
Putnam, NY	36079	371,728	1.5	32.0	66.5	331,444	20,216	66.4	5,638	91.8	5.7	0.9

Note. Data in columns 26 through 41 from the American Community Survey are subject to sampling error, which can be especially large in small counties and small population groups. See notes and definitions for more information.

[6]Bronx, Kings, Queens, and Richmond counties are included with New York county.

Table C-1. Population, School, and Student Characteristics by County, Selected Years—*Continued*

County	State/ County Code	High school graduates, 2006–2010			College enrollment, 2006–2010		College graduates, 2006–2010 (percent)						
		Population 25 years and over	High school diploma or less (percent)	High school diploma or more (percent)	Number	Percent public	Bachelor's degree or more	+/- U.S. percent with Bachelor's degree or more	Non-Hispanic White	Black or African American	American Indian and Alaska Native	Asian, Hawaiian, and Pacific Islander	Hispanic or Latino[3]
		30	31	32	33	34	35	36	37	38	39	40	41
NEW MEXICO— *(Continued)*													
Quay, NM	35037	6,306	59.5	77.3	378	98.1	14.8	-13.1	21.1	30.6	1.9	55.8	3.2
Rio Arriba, NM	35039	26,481	53.7	78.7	1,820	83.5	16.1	-11.8	35.0	0.0	10.5	87.2	12.0
Roosevelt, NM	35041	11,109	52.2	77.8	2,371	95.7	21.2	-6.7	27.2	27.4	36.1	23.6	7.8
Sandoval, NM	35043	80,864	37.5	90.3	7,372	82.9	28.4	0.5	37.3	35.6	12.7	35.0	16.8
San Juan, NM	35045	77,149	52.1	80.9	5,479	85.3	15.0	-12.9	21.0	43.9	7.3	54.7	9.2
San Miguel, NM	35047	19,458	48.4	81.9	3,059	90.3	23.3	-4.6	45.0	23.8	26.1	45.8	16.2
Santa Fe, NM	35049	100,215	34.9	86.3	8,313	70.5	40.0	12.1	60.2	26.2	15.0	54.8	17.0
Sierra, NM	35051	8,488	53.4	83.9	125	92.8	16.9	-11.0	19.1	29.4	2.7	0.0	4.6
Socorro, NM	35053	11,063	53.1	79.7	1,686	85.8	22.3	-5.6	41.1	90.6	2.0	52.4	6.3
Taos, NM	35055	23,437	38.7	88.3	1,712	87.1	30.1	2.2	52.3	58.8	9.9	48.8	13.5
Torrance, NM	35057	11,023	55.0	77.2	462	82.0	14.0	-13.9	16.9	0.0	38.1	54.2	4.5
Union, NM	35059	2,880	54.3	84.1	53	75.5	17.8	-10.1	22.1	0.0	0.0	0.0	7.4
Valencia, NM	35061	47,616	49.9	80.1	4,405	84.4	16.8	-11.1	23.7	19.7	7.5	31.8	10.9
NEW YORK	36000	12,914,436	43.8	84.5	1,475,400	57.4	32.1	4.2	37.1	20.3	16.0	45.5	15.8
Albany, NY	36001	201,036	36.3	90.7	34,336	67.6	37.6	9.7	39.1	16.5	13.4	71.9	26.9
Allegany, NY	36003	30,577	51.8	88.3	5,964	43.0	18.6	-9.3	18.1	18.7	2.8	66.8	23.4
Bronx, NY	36005	840,009	59.4	68.8	95,491	60.1	17.7	-10.2	32.1	17.9	13.0	38.9	11.4
Broome, NY	36007	133,739	44.9	88.3	20,528	91.1	25.1	-2.8	24.6	17.7	35.5	55.4	24.1
Cattaraugus, NY	36009	53,557	53.9	87.4	5,114	45.4	18.1	-9.8	18.1	24.2	7.3	46.9	18.2
Cayuga, NY	36011	55,354	51.7	84.9	3,770	57.1	18.4	-9.5	19.1	1.7	21.1	50.2	7.9
Chautauqua, NY	36013	89,926	50.7	86.2	9,312	88.3	20.3	-7.6	20.9	11.4	16.9	50.8	6.2
Chemung, NY	36015	60,491	49.0	87.6	5,629	45.6	20.9	-7.0	21.3	12.1	3.7	61.7	13.9
Chenango, NY	36017	35,113	54.6	85.1	2,008	79.3	17.0	-10.9	17.1	9.7	16.0	41.1	8.8
Clinton, NY	36019	55,210	52.8	84.2	7,980	90.1	21.7	-6.2	22.7	5.1	11.0	30.7	10.2
Columbia, NY	36021	45,089	45.1	87.0	4,021	71.4	28.2	0.3	29.1	13.2	10.6	40.1	15.4
Cortland, NY	36023	30,088	47.2	89.1	6,994	91.0	24.3	-3.6	24.1	22.3	18.8	36.9	34.8
Delaware, NY	36025	33,831	52.1	87.0	2,406	89.4	19.1	-8.8	18.8	15.7	21.8	68.9	13.3
Dutchess, NY	36027	196,715	40.4	89.1	26,168	42.1	32.0	4.1	33.5	19.8	17.5	61.2	18.9
Erie, NY	36029	622,588	41.7	88.4	76,210	73.1	29.1	1.2	30.9	14.2	10.7	62.0	18.1
Essex, NY	36031	28,503	45.8	88.7	1,765	75.6	25.5	-2.4	26.7	1.8	12.2	33.9	8.3
Franklin, NY	36033	35,561	57.0	83.3	2,211	43.2	17.3	-10.6	18.4	1.5	18.2	60.6	3.6
Fulton, NY	36035	38,702	56.5	83.2	1,809	75.0	14.3	-13.6	14.4	8.3	0.0	5.3	16.2
Genesee, NY	36037	40,945	47.3	90.4	3,039	80.9	20.2	-7.7	19.7	21.9	12.7	46.5	36.9
Greene, NY	36039	34,621	54.0	85.7	1,803	67.4	19.2	-8.7	20.0	2.8	0.0	38.7	10.5
Hamilton, NY	36041	3,828	46.6	88.6	101	88.1	25.9	-2.0	26.1	0.0	0.0	37.5	52.2
Herkimer, NY	36043	44,207	50.5	86.4	3,419	78.6	18.2	-9.7	18.2	22.2	28.3	40.8	11.2
Jefferson, NY	36045	71,402	48.8	87.8	6,363	80.2	20.2	-7.7	20.4	17.4	23.0	39.9	14.5
Kings, NY	36047	1,613,215	51.1	77.8	189,214	59.0	28.8	0.9	44.2	19.3	19.3	28.2	12.7
Lewis, NY	36049	17,994	61.5	86.0	812	73.4	14.4	-13.5	14.3	13.6	43.1	66.7	0.0
Livingston, NY	36051	42,311	46.9	88.7	7,583	85.3	23.4	-4.5	24.0	10.9	17.7	42.4	14.3
Madison, NY	36053	46,639	46.4	88.5	7,489	50.0	23.7	-4.2	23.5	13.4	15.1	66.9	24.7
Monroe, NY	36055	487,246	37.3	88.4	67,855	46.6	34.8	6.9	38.5	14.1	27.9	52.1	16.1
Montgomery, NY	36057	34,034	55.2	82.7	2,268	76.9	15.9	-12.0	16.2	20.5	0.0	32.6	11.2
Nassau, NY	36059	904,445	35.8	89.7	94,983	51.9	40.9	13.0	44.0	30.5	19.1	61.5	18.9
New York, NY	36061	1,166,760	28.7	84.6	149,734	35.6	57.0	29.1	79.9	25.4	17.4	57.3	21.0
Niagara, NY	36063	148,173	49.0	88.4	13,645	61.9	19.6	-8.3	20.4	8.2	12.8	38.3	13.6
Oneida, NY	36065	159,341	48.1	86.0	15,640	56.4	21.5	-6.4	22.2	8.8	14.8	40.6	10.2
Onondaga, NY	36067	304,320	38.6	89.3	41,787	44.1	32.0	4.1	33.6	15.1	14.3	51.1	21.8
Ontario, NY	36069	72,132	37.1	91.5	6,814	48.6	31.0	3.1	31.8	6.3	22.1	48.2	13.6
Orange, NY	36071	232,097	44.0	86.7	25,853	70.7	27.7	-0.2	29.6	22.6	17.7	54.6	17.1
Orleans, NY	36073	29,133	57.0	84.2	2,019	80.2	15.1	-12.8	16.2	3.0	0.0	3.9	9.3
Oswego, NY	36075	78,127	56.3	86.3	11,392	86.5	15.7	-12.2	15.7	18.0	9.4	35.0	14.8
Otsego, NY	36077	39,938	47.3	88.3	7,862	71.2	25.5	-2.4	25.4	42.4	10.8	42.8	16.8
Putnam, NY	36079	68,000	35.4	93.7	4,980	55.0	38.0	10.1	39.3	28.7	0.0	61.4	24.7

Note. Data in columns 26 through 41 from the American Community Survey are subject to sampling error, which can be especially large in small counties and small population groups. See notes and definitions for more information.
[3]May be of any race.

Table C-1. Population, School, and Student Characteristics by County, Selected Years—*Continued*

County	State/ County Code	County Type[1]	Population, 2010		Percent of related children 5–17 years in poverty, 2010	Percent of children under 19 years with no health insurance, 2010	Number of schools and students, 2010–2011			Resident enrollment, 2006–2010 K-12 enrollment	
			Total	Percent 5–17 years			School districts	Schools	Students	Number	Percent public
			1	2	3	4	5	6	7	8	9
NEW YORK—*(Continued)*											
Queens, NY	36081	1	2,230,722	14.8	21.4	6.1	16	323	272,135	339,193	83.5
Rensselaer, NY	36083	2	159,429	15.8	16.6	4.3	16	45	21,515	26,103	91.8
Richmond, NY	36085	1	468,730	17.3	15.8	4.1	4	69	59,705	82,266	77.1
Rockland, NY	36087	1	311,687	20.5	16.5	5.6	9	67	41,140	63,375	67.2
St. Lawrence, NY	36089	5	111,944	15.4	22.4	7.4	19	42	15,968	17,854	90.4
Saratoga, NY	36091	2	219,607	17.2	7.5	4.1	11	48	31,709	38,429	92.6
Schenectady, NY	36093	2	154,727	17.0	16.5	5.0	7	50	25,842	26,525	94.0
Schoharie, NY	36095	2	32,749	15.4	14.8	5.2	6	12	4,784	5,358	93.5
Schuyler, NY	36097	6	18,343	16.4	20.7	5.7	3	7	2,310	3,396	88.9
Seneca, NY	36099	6	35,251	15.7	20.3	7.9	4	13	4,354	5,682	89.0
Steuben, NY	36101	4	98,990	17.6	19.2	7.3	13	40	16,214	18,405	94.4
Suffolk, NY	36103	1	1,493,350	18.2	7.3	4.9	74	350	254,764	276,204	93.3
Sullivan, NY	36105	4	77,547	16.7	25.4	6.8	9	20	10,101	13,952	89.8
Tioga, NY	36107	2	51,125	17.6	13.9	5.2	6	21	7,969	9,629	94.8
Tompkins, NY	36109	3	101,564	12.1	13.7	6.2	9	32	11,526	12,305	91.9
Ulster, NY	36111	3	182,493	15.2	13.9	5.7	12	53	25,108	29,428	91.4
Warren, NY	36113	3	65,707	15.7	15.3	4.9	9	21	9,926	10,588	95.0
Washington, NY	36115	3	63,216	15.8	17.1	5.4	12	23	9,280	11,165	92.1
Wayne, NY	36117	1	93,772	17.9	13.9	6.1	12	39	15,210	17,326	92.5
Westchester, NY	36119	1	949,113	18.0	10.6	4.6	50	252	150,620	172,625	85.7
Wyoming, NY	36121	6	42,155	15.7	13.9	5.7	5	13	4,637	7,059	93.1
Yates, NY	36123	6	25,348	18.3	26.5	8.8	2	5	2,547	4,320	75.3
NORTH CAROLINA	37000	X	9,535,483	17.3	22.6	8.3	236	2,567	1,490,605	1,627,528	91.2
Alamance, NC	37001	3	151,131	17.2	23.8	8.6	4	38	24,016	25,773	92.1
Alexander, NC	37003	2	37,198	16.8	23.3	7.8	1	10	5,532	6,431	91.9
Alleghany, NC	37005	9	11,155	14.8	30.4	15.7	1	4	1,558	1,520	98.4
Anson, NC	37007	1	26,948	16.3	30.0	6.9	1	11	3,845	4,733	97.9
Ashe, NC	37009	9	27,281	14.1	27.1	9.4	2	5	3,297	3,880	93.3
Avery, NC	37011	8	17,797	12.8	28.7	11.9	2	9	2,324	2,568	91.2
Beaufort, NC	37013	6	47,759	16.2	29.5	8.4	2	15	7,493	7,712	93.8
Bertie, NC	37015	9	21,282	15.3	34.9	6.9	1	9	2,900	3,492	88.6
Bladen, NC	37017	6	35,190	17.0	29.4	8.9	1	14	5,360	6,295	95.5
Brunswick, NC	37019	2	107,431	13.3	24.8	8.6	3	20	13,175	14,242	93.9
Buncombe, NC	37021	2	238,318	14.8	22.6	8.5	5	53	30,388	34,605	86.9
Burke, NC	37023	2	90,912	16.6	24.6	7.9	2	28	13,968	16,443	95.0
Cabarrus, NC	37025	1	178,011	20.1	14.8	8.0	3	46	34,699	33,648	91.7
Caldwell, NC	37027	2	83,029	17.0	23.9	7.1	1	26	12,811	14,415	93.3
Camden, NC	37029	8	9,980	19.7	11.6	8.2	1	5	1,958	2,108	94.8
Carteret, NC	37031	4	66,469	14.0	22.3	8.8	3	18	8,890	9,257	93.7
Caswell, NC	37033	8	23,719	15.6	26.7	8.0	1	6	3,012	3,947	89.0
Catawba, NC	37035	2	154,358	17.6	21.6	8.2	3	45	24,767	26,978	92.3
Chatham, NC	37037	2	63,505	15.6	20.6	10.3	3	19	8,825	9,609	90.2
Cherokee, NC	37039	9	27,444	14.2	30.9	10.3	2	15	3,752	4,026	89.3
Chowan, NC	37041	7	14,793	16.5	29.3	8.3	1	4	2,393	2,657	95.0
Clay, NC	37043	9	10,587	14.0	28.2	10.7	1	3	1,421	1,686	99.7
Cleveland, NC	37045	4	98,078	17.5	28.4	5.9	2	29	16,417	17,731	95.5
Columbus, NC	37047	6	58,098	17.2	38.5	9.1	3	25	9,605	10,112	94.5
Craven, NC	37049	5	103,505	16.0	25.3	6.8	1	25	15,048	16,622	90.9
Cumberland, NC	37051	2	319,431	18.5	24.9	7.5	3	91	53,568	59,872	92.3
Currituck, NC	37053	1	23,547	18.1	16.3	9.4	1	10	3,979	4,309	92.5
Dare, NC	37055	5	33,920	14.6	20.7	11.3	1	11	4,994	5,134	95.9
Davidson, NC	37057	4	162,878	17.7	23.8	8.4	3	44	26,261	29,051	92.6
Davie, NC	37059	2	41,240	17.9	19.1	8.8	1	12	6,786	7,466	93.1

[1]County type codes are from the Economic Research Service of the United States Department of Agriculture. See notes and definitions for more information.

Table C-1. Population, School, and Student Characteristics by County, Selected Years—*Continued*

County	State/ County Code	Characteristics of students, 2010–2011				Number of graduates, 2008–2009	Staff and students, 2010–2011			
		Percent with IEP[2]	Percent eligible for free or reduced lunch	Percent minority	Percent English-language learners		Total staff	Number of teachers	Student/ teacher ratio	Central admin. staff
		10	11	12	13	14	15	16	17	18
NEW YORK—*(Continued)*										
Queens, NY	36081	16.3	70.4	86.4	15.5	14,762	19,807	16,706	16.3	72
Rensselaer, NY	36083	18.8	33.0	19.4	0.9	1,493	3,272	1,626	13.2	191
Richmond, NY	36085	23.2	53.1	47.7	5.8	3,536	4,450	3,741	16.0	8
Rockland, NY	36087	16.9	25.9	46.9	7.0	2,997	6,680	3,337	12.3	497
St. Lawrence, NY	36089	15.0	45.5	5.9	0.1	1,141	2,736	1,399	11.4	166
Saratoga, NY	36091	12.9	16.4	7.8	0.4	2,116	4,941	2,398	13.2	348
Schenectady, NY	36093	16.2	37.6	33.4	1.4	1,813	4,080	1,943	13.3	231
Schoharie, NY	36095	13.4	36.7	4.0	0.1	353	969	432	11.1	60
Schuyler, NY	36097	13.7	33.9	5.0	...	182	407	209	11.1	33
Seneca, NY	36099	16.8	37.5	7.6	0.1	353	830	386	11.3	51
Steuben, NY	36101	15.3	46.9	7.7	0.1	1,329	3,164	1,546	10.5	176
Suffolk, NY	36103	15.1	24.3	32.5	5.6	18,997	39,196	19,674	12.9	3,454
Sullivan, NY	36105	15.0	44.8	27.9	3.2	728	1,898	943	10.7	150
Tioga, NY	36107	15.4	40.7	4.0	0.2	598	1,348	612	13.0	80
Tompkins, NY	36109	19.2	34.5	18.6	2.1	840	2,429	1,118	10.3	153
Ulster, NY	36111	18.4	33.7	23.1	1.7	1,947	4,146	2,058	12.2	346
Warren, NY	36113	15.5	29.5	5.9	0.3	773	1,746	840	11.8	141
Washington, NY	36115	16.6	38.3	3.3	0.2	682	1,900	915	10.1	115
Wayne, NY	36117	14.6	37.7	12.0	1.1	1,236	3,437	1,563	9.7	239
Westchester, NY	36119	15.0	31.1	48.6	7.0	9,963	22,729	11,596	13.0	1,739
Wyoming, NY	36121	13.7	32.8	3.2	0.3	389	801	427	10.9	63
Yates, NY	36123	17.4	44.4	5.0	0.4	174	515	219	11.6	37
NORTH CAROLINA	37000	12.4	50.3	46.8	6.9	86,712	193,039	98,358	15.2	6,500
Alamance, NC	37001	12.0	50.4	45.7	11.4	1,421	2,906	1,566	15.3	78
Alexander, NC	37003	14.3	50.8	15.9	4.2	342	741	344	16.1	26
Alleghany, NC	37005	13.2	65.3	16.7	5.4	87	242	124	12.6	15
Anson, NC	37007	16.4	0.0	68.0	2.5	239	515	249	15.5	25
Ashe, NC	37009	15.5	41.9	11.1	4.0	218	513	244	13.5	18
Avery, NC	37011	13.0	58.9	9.9	5.2	152	369	177	13.2	20
Beaufort, NC	37013	14.5	59.4	48.5	6.1	445	982	527	14.2	35
Bertie, NC	37015	14.6	77.0	86.4	0.6	170	419	192	15.1	24
Bladen, NC	37017	10.6	68.7	59.0	5.2	331	777	360	14.9	32
Brunswick, NC	37019	10.9	55.3	31.3	4.1	684	1,674	847	15.5	65
Buncombe, NC	37021	13.2	49.2	26.0	6.4	1,881	4,411	2,058	14.8	155
Burke, NC	37023	15.7	56.8	25.6	7.0	990	1,790	927	15.1	56
Cabarrus, NC	37025	13.4	42.0	39.0	7.5	1,824	4,369	2,322	14.9	131
Caldwell, NC	37027	11.2	56.3	18.4	3.2	769	1,717	872	14.7	49
Camden, NC	37029	12.8	30.2	20.3	0.5	120	259	126	15.5	13
Carteret, NC	37031	14.3	38.6	20.4	2.0	591	1,179	661	13.5	33
Caswell, NC	37033	13.7	62.6	46.7	1.4	189	440	215	14.0	23
Catawba, NC	37035	12.1	51.0	35.2	9.6	1,621	3,040	1,588	15.6	114
Chatham, NC	37037	14.2	43.7	42.5	14.4	497	1,261	629	14.0	51
Cherokee, NC	37039	13.5	62.8	9.1	0.4	255	536	264	14.2	20
Chowan, NC	37041	13.3	58.3	50.0	1.7	166	370	171	14.0	24
Clay, NC	37043	12.5	54.3	5.6	1.4	91	189	100	14.3	9
Cleveland, NC	37045	12.8	55.7	36.4	1.8	1,027	2,234	1,131	14.5	85
Columbus, NC	37047	10.4	67.2	47.9	3.5	596	1,238	611	15.7	51
Craven, NC	37049	10.7	52.6	45.5	4.4	867	1,802	958	15.7	57
Cumberland, NC	37051	13.5	54.3	65.8	2.2	3,327	7,467	3,716	14.4	218
Currituck, NC	37053	8.5	31.4	22.3	0.7	282	587	250	15.9	33
Dare, NC	37055	10.6	34.8	17.4	5.2	352	765	399	12.5	35
Davidson, NC	37057	11.6	50.2	25.2	5.3	1,585	3,273	1,637	16.0	115
Davie, NC	37059	11.5	41.8	21.4	4.3	375	904	442	15.3	32

[2]IEP=Individual Education Program. See notes and definitions for more information.

Table C-1. Population, School, and Student Characteristics by County, Selected Years—*Continued*

County	State/ County Code	Revenues, 2008–2009				Current expenditures, 2008–2009			Resident population 16 to 19 years, 2006–2010			
		Total revenue ($1,000's)	Percentage of revenue from			Amount ($1,000's)	Amount per student	Percent for instruction	Total population 16 to 19 years	Percent enrolled in school	Percent high school graduates, not enrolled in school	Percent not enrolled, not grads, not employed, or not in labor force
			Federal government	State government	Local government							
		19	20	21	22	23	24	25	26	27	28	29
NEW YORK— *(Continued)*												
Queens, NY	36081	([6])	([6])	([6])	([6])	([6])	([6])	([6])	110,202	86.0	8.4	3.4
Rensselaer, NY	36083	390,321	4.8	54.2	41.0	330,318	15,953	63.8	9,951	87.0	7.2	2.9
Richmond, NY	36085	([6])	([6])	([6])	([6])	([6])	([6])	([6])	26,588	88.0	7.5	3.3
Rockland, NY	36087	967,639	3.5	29.1	67.3	871,796	21,050	65.6	18,391	90.1	6.0	2.8
St. Lawrence, NY	36089	307,110	5.3	69.6	25.2	256,453	15,882	64.9	9,541	93.4	3.5	2.3
Saratoga, NY	36091	522,774	3.0	44.7	52.4	448,187	13,922	64.0	11,776	87.2	9.7	1.9
Schenectady, NY	36093	446,793	5.1	52.1	42.7	385,986	14,439	68.0	8,751	87.1	7.8	2.8
Schoharie, NY	36095	102,162	3.8	59.9	36.3	85,736	16,981	63.4	2,569	95.9	2.6	0.9
Schuyler, NY	36097	47,679	4.3	68.1	27.7	38,722	16,161	62.7	1,058	86.8	6.3	3.7
Seneca, NY	36099	94,196	4.3	63.6	32.1	73,644	15,800	63.2	1,958	74.9	10.2	9.7
Steuben, NY	36101	307,127	5.4	65.1	29.4	260,625	15,520	64.7	5,548	84.9	8.9	3.2
Suffolk, NY	36103	5,591,234	2.5	39.2	58.3	4,969,214	19,341	66.0	84,817	88.8	7.2	2.4
Sullivan, NY	36105	259,201	4.2	45.9	49.9	223,000	21,484	65.1	4,309	84.5	10.4	4.4
Tioga, NY	36107	140,563	4.6	67.3	28.1	120,711	14,685	63.4	2,874	85.9	9.7	2.8
Tompkins, NY	36109	229,066	3.8	43.7	52.5	200,961	16,716	64.6	11,787	97.5	2.2	0.2
Ulster, NY	36111	556,035	5.4	40.8	53.8	492,226	18,768	67.0	10,865	86.5	8.6	3.2
Warren, NY	36113	189,669	4.3	44.0	51.7	161,970	15,912	66.4	3,503	89.1	8.6	0.9
Washington, NY	36115	179,299	4.6	63.4	32.0	150,261	15,568	66.3	3,623	79.8	16.1	3.4
Wayne, NY	36117	297,292	5.0	61.1	33.9	246,882	15,517	62.9	5,261	83.4	9.8	3.9
Westchester, NY	36119	3,701,397	3.2	28.3	68.5	3,294,231	22,092	64.7	50,944	89.6	6.6	2.7
Wyoming, NY	36121	89,152	4.3	68.8	26.9	72,394	14,667	62.1	2,149	81.2	12.1	4.6
Yates, NY	36123	49,525	6.9	54.4	38.7	42,074	15,711	64.3	1,740	81.2	5.0	7.3
NORTH CAROLINA	37000	15,699,836	8.9	53.6	37.5	12,732,543	8,556	63.7	525,554	82.7	9.9	4.9
Alamance, NC	37001	203,955	9.4	63.6	27.0	184,061	7,782	65.9	8,756	85.5	8.0	4.2
Alexander, NC	37003	47,780	10.6	68.3	21.1	44,146	7,847	63.8	1,793	78.3	14.8	4.2
Alleghany, NC	37005	19,032	11.3	64.0	24.7	17,108	10,574	61.9	505	77.6	5.4	3.4
Anson, NC	37007	43,067	14.1	68.8	17.1	39,929	9,869	58.1	1,517	84.5	6.2	9.3
Ashe, NC	37009	37,375	10.9	63.5	25.7	31,925	9,036	62.8	1,155	81.5	10.2	3.3
Avery, NC	37011	26,898	9.3	61.9	28.8	24,495	10,060	58.7	663	92.0	6.0	0.0
Beaufort, NC	37013	74,690	11.5	61.2	27.3	67,567	8,470	63.1	2,131	86.1	7.0	6.2
Bertie, NC	37015	37,067	19.6	63.1	17.2	33,642	10,807	58.2	953	85.0	11.2	3.4
Bladen, NC	37017	54,670	17.1	64.2	18.7	51,075	9,494	61.2	2,066	80.8	10.8	5.7
Brunswick, NC	37019	135,891	8.5	51.0	40.5	113,806	8,954	61.3	4,002	81.0	13.3	1.5
Buncombe, NC	37021	303,941	9.6	55.6	34.7	274,355	9,007	62.4	11,637	82.1	9.8	4.6
Burke, NC	37023	129,634	11.8	65.2	23.0	120,524	7,702	63.7	5,753	81.0	7.0	8.9
Cabarrus, NC	37025	315,149	7.4	55.5	37.1	266,538	7,933	65.6	9,006	81.0	14.0	2.8
Caldwell, NC	37027	112,811	10.4	66.2	23.4	104,128	7,954	66.9	4,467	84.4	7.6	7.0
Camden, NC	37029	18,679	5.0	73.9	21.0	17,085	8,959	58.9	641	89.1	6.7	0.0
Carteret, NC	37031	105,888	6.1	46.0	47.9	81,017	9,265	64.5	3,028	85.6	8.1	3.9
Caswell, NC	37033	32,161	9.7	72.2	18.1	29,662	8,613	63.7	1,130	76.4	7.7	15.1
Catawba, NC	37035	257,312	7.7	54.1	38.2	206,095	8,118	65.6	8,006	82.8	10.8	4.8
Chatham, NC	37037	98,837	7.7	49.2	43.1	84,309	9,904	63.5	2,576	76.3	11.3	2.8
Cherokee, NC	37039	39,994	12.4	63.6	24.0	36,933	9,497	57.9	1,208	82.2	14.1	0.4
Chowan, NC	37041	27,243	9.1	68.7	22.2	25,822	10,548	56.0	1,156	85.6	11.8	0.0
Clay, NC	37043	14,167	7.4	76.3	16.3	13,724	9,336	66.9	608	91.6	7.1	1.3
Cleveland, NC	37045	155,403	11.9	66.4	21.7	146,757	8,633	65.7	5,907	81.7	10.7	5.8
Columbus, NC	37047	89,580	15.3	70.1	14.6	86,273	8,650	62.1	2,983	83.5	10.4	5.9
Craven, NC	37049	130,132	12.4	63.1	24.5	119,837	8,092	64.1	5,441	73.8	18.3	3.7
Cumberland, NC	37051	475,769	13.7	61.1	25.2	455,883	8,365	64.6	18,934	81.7	11.1	5.3
Currituck, NC	37053	42,195	5.9	58.1	36.0	38,358	9,462	58.2	1,182	78.2	14.8	0.0
Dare, NC	37055	71,797	3.7	40.1	56.2	55,066	11,167	61.1	1,483	80.5	12.1	2.8
Davidson, NC	37057	226,116	10.4	65.2	24.4	204,369	7,626	64.4	8,440	78.3	14.5	4.2
Davie, NC	37059	60,557	7.0	62.8	30.2	53,055	7,972	65.7	2,087	82.5	10.6	4.7

Note. Data in columns 26 through 41 from the American Community Survey are subject to sampling error, which can be especially large in small counties and small population groups. See notes and definitions for more information.

Table C-1. Population, School, and Student Characteristics by County, Selected Years—*Continued*

County	State/ County Code	High school graduates, 2006–2010			College enrollment, 2006–2010		College graduates, 2006–2010 (percent)						
		Population 25 years and over	High school diploma or less (percent)	High school diploma or more (percent)	Number	Percent public	Bachelor's degree or more	+/- U.S. percent with Bachelor's degree or more	Non-Hispanic White	Black or African American	American Indian and Alaska Native	Asian, Hawaiian, and Pacific Islander	Hispanic or Latino[3]
		30	31	32	33	34	35	36	37	38	39	40	41
NEW YORK— *(Continued)*													
Queens, NY	36081	1,527,856	48.6	80.0	172,053	63.9	29.5	1.6	36.4	22.0	16.7	40.2	16.0
Rensselaer, NY	36083	106,304	43.1	89.2	13,043	43.9	26.7	-1.2	27.1	17.2	10.9	61.9	15.5
Richmond, NY	36085	311,146	46.2	87.5	32,774	60.8	28.5	0.6	29.4	22.7	11.1	43.8	18.2
Rockland, NY	36087	192,620	35.9	87.9	21,373	44.0	40.7	12.8	44.4	27.7	29.0	63.8	21.3
St. Lawrence, NY	36089	70,150	52.9	85.8	14,102	47.5	18.7	-9.2	18.9	6.5	19.7	47.2	14.8
Saratoga, NY	36091	149,410	36.8	91.8	11,579	56.1	34.6	6.7	34.5	22.5	16.0	59.3	31.5
Schenectady, NY	36093	103,555	41.6	90.0	10,460	49.6	28.7	0.8	30.3	11.1	24.0	50.2	13.4
Schoharie, NY	36095	22,096	52.6	86.5	2,915	90.8	21.0	-6.9	21.1	14.0	29.1	15.5	15.0
Schuyler, NY	36097	12,977	52.2	87.4	862	69.1	17.4	-10.5	17.5	0.0	0.0	0.0	17.0
Seneca, NY	36099	24,267	51.9	83.7	1,592	49.4	18.1	-9.8	18.9	2.7	24.6	48.9	6.4
Steuben, NY	36101	67,276	49.4	87.5	4,058	69.0	19.9	-8.0	19.2	17.2	6.0	75.4	27.3
Suffolk, NY	36103	993,716	41.2	89.4	94,989	66.8	31.9	4.0	34.5	21.5	12.4	57.8	15.6
Sullivan, NY	36105	53,448	50.5	83.9	3,074	68.5	20.3	-7.6	22.1	10.5	12.2	37.9	10.0
Tioga, NY	36107	35,124	48.3	89.1	2,243	77.6	22.7	-5.2	22.4	28.4	18.8	56.0	31.2
Tompkins, NY	36109	56,968	28.4	92.4	28,627	25.3	49.7	21.8	48.7	30.1	63.3	75.3	51.8
Ulster, NY	36111	126,669	41.9	87.5	13,478	81.6	29.5	1.6	31.2	12.5	17.7	53.4	15.3
Warren, NY	36113	46,676	43.4	89.6	3,057	58.1	27.3	-0.6	27.3	17.3	0.0	49.3	23.1
Washington, NY	36115	43,839	56.0	85.9	2,361	80.3	16.8	-11.1	17.2	2.4	17.5	32.2	7.8
Wayne, NY	36117	63,678	47.6	86.7	3,926	71.8	21.5	-6.4	22.4	2.2	2.7	29.9	13.2
Westchester, NY	36119	635,503	35.6	87.4	59,273	48.3	44.5	16.6	53.4	25.9	13.8	70.6	18.8
Wyoming, NY	36121	29,888	55.4	85.5	1,384	75.1	14.8	-13.1	15.9	3.2	21.1	62.6	2.6
Yates, NY	36123	16,273	54.7	83.9	1,806	25.2	22.1	-5.8	22.2	7.5	22.8	37.0	16.2
NORTH CAROLINA	37000	6,121,611	44.7	83.6	653,923	78.7	26.1	-1.8	29.4	16.7	11.5	50.5	11.9
Alamance, NC	37001	97,250	48.6	81.4	10,315	57.0	21.4	-6.5	25.2	12.6	1.1	36.8	3.0
Alexander, NC	37003	25,536	63.0	75.7	1,478	80.7	11.8	-16.1	12.7	1.0	9.3	2.1	5.3
Alleghany, NC	37005	8,061	58.7	71.4	425	88.0	16.1	-11.8	17.6	0.0	0.0	3.5	1.5
Anson, NC	37007	18,424	68.0	77.6	923	91.9	8.4	-19.5	11.7	5.0	0.0	18.5	0.0
Ashe, NC	37009	19,761	56.0	76.8	1,068	90.6	17.2	-10.7	17.6	0.0	0.0	36.0	3.6
Avery, NC	37011	13,043	49.4	81.4	1,323	47.8	20.3	-7.6	22.0	2.0	0.0	49.5	4.7
Beaufort, NC	37013	33,210	54.4	81.5	2,245	88.2	19.0	-8.9	23.5	6.1	35.9	46.0	10.5
Bertie, NC	37015	14,564	65.8	72.3	617	85.3	10.1	-17.8	12.5	7.6	44.0	49.2	0.0
Bladen, NC	37017	23,393	59.1	74.0	1,901	87.0	9.8	-18.1	12.9	5.7	4.3	0.0	0.4
Brunswick, NC	37019	76,063	46.2	84.7	3,461	83.3	23.4	-4.5	25.7	8.5	13.3	17.9	13.7
Buncombe, NC	37021	164,764	39.5	87.2	14,340	76.5	31.2	3.3	33.3	11.6	9.7	37.4	12.6
Burke, NC	37023	61,880	56.8	74.9	4,509	87.0	15.1	-12.8	15.7	11.3	12.4	16.2	6.1
Cabarrus, NC	37025	110,674	42.8	85.0	8,840	82.7	23.5	-4.4	24.6	20.0	31.4	40.2	10.7
Caldwell, NC	37027	56,957	59.4	74.6	4,967	85.8	12.3	-15.6	13.0	2.9	35.0	18.1	5.3
Camden, NC	37029	6,247	43.6	88.4	550	74.2	19.0	-8.9	17.8	21.6	0.0	100.0	24.4
Carteret, NC	37031	47,857	41.4	87.6	3,230	89.0	23.8	-4.1	25.1	9.1	0.0	34.6	9.2
Caswell, NC	37033	17,082	62.6	75.0	1,292	80.4	11.1	-16.8	13.5	7.4	9.4	30.8	2.8
Catawba, NC	37035	103,625	50.6	81.4	8,114	77.3	19.4	-8.5	21.3	10.2	20.7	12.8	8.0
Chatham, NC	37037	44,104	41.7	83.8	2,643	83.8	35.1	7.2	41.5	12.6	4.4	69.8	9.5
Cherokee, NC	37039	20,310	50.5	81.5	1,066	84.5	15.9	-12.0	16.4	0.0	0.0	32.9	0.0
Chowan, NC	37041	10,032	54.9	77.4	929	53.2	15.7	-12.2	18.8	8.9	0.0	89.7	0.0
Clay, NC	37043	7,851	50.8	83.0	482	76.6	18.6	-9.3	18.9	0.0	0.0	0.0	20.9
Cleveland, NC	37045	65,648	54.3	79.5	6,589	74.0	15.7	-12.2	17.3	8.8	34.0	37.8	6.0
Columbus, NC	37047	38,348	54.8	77.5	2,371	88.8	12.0	-15.9	14.4	7.0	12.4	42.4	3.6
Craven, NC	37049	64,280	40.9	87.5	6,189	86.6	21.3	-6.6	25.3	9.2	13.3	23.3	12.7
Cumberland, NC	37051	187,269	39.7	88.3	29,336	79.6	21.9	-6.0	24.2	19.4	11.3	27.7	16.4
Currituck, NC	37053	15,949	49.1	84.7	1,059	74.4	17.3	-10.6	17.8	8.7	0.0	20.9	16.5
Dare, NC	37055	24,643	35.4	91.8	1,076	67.8	32.1	4.2	33.2	22.6	0.0	4.8	19.7
Davidson, NC	37057	109,764	56.1	79.1	6,914	82.3	16.3	-11.6	17.4	11.1	14.8	15.0	5.6
Davie, NC	37059	28,179	48.3	84.4	1,770	71.5	23.6	-4.3	24.8	19.6	13.8	29.3	4.3

Note. Data in columns 26 through 41 from the American Community Survey are subject to sampling error, which can be especially large in small counties and small population groups. See notes and definitions for more information.
[3]May be of any race.

Table C-1. Population, School, and Student Characteristics by County, Selected Years—*Continued*

County	State/ County Code	County Type[1]	Population, 2010: Total	Population, 2010: Percent 5–17 years	Percent of related children 5–17 years in poverty, 2010	Percent of children under 19 years with no health insurance, 2010	Number of schools and students, 2010–2011: School districts	Number of schools and students, 2010–2011: Schools	Number of schools and students, 2010–2011: Students	Resident enrollment, 2006–2010, K–12 enrollment: Number	Resident enrollment, 2006–2010, K–12 enrollment: Percent public
			1	2	3	4	5	6	7	8	9
NORTH CAROLINA— *(Continued)*											
Duplin, NC	37061	6	58,505	18.1	31.9	10.6	1	16	9,145	10,150	94.9
Durham, NC	37063	2	267,587	15.1	22.6	8.6	13	61	35,537	39,571	89.1
Edgecombe, NC	37065	3	56,552	18.0	34.0	7.1	1	15	7,477	10,876	95.6
Forsyth, NC	37067	2	350,670	17.5	22.8	8.7	7	86	55,232	59,408	91.1
Franklin, NC	37069	2	60,619	17.9	20.2	9.0	2	16	8,715	10,545	88.9
Gaston, NC	37071	1	206,086	17.5	24.8	9.0	4	58	34,154	36,209	91.5
Gates, NC	37073	8	12,197	18.1	20.9	7.8	1	5	1,872	2,272	94.7
Graham, NC	37075	9	8,861	15.9	32.0	10.5	1	3	1,252	1,344	91.5
Granville, NC	37077	6	59,916	16.6	17.5	7.8	1	19	8,825	10,704	93.1
Greene, NC	37079	3	21,362	16.7	33.7	10.6	1	5	3,348	3,585	95.9
Guilford, NC	37081	2	488,406	17.2	24.2	8.6	6	125	75,108	82,024	90.5
Halifax, NC	37083	4	54,691	17.1	33.9	7.0	4	20	8,386	10,354	90.6
Harnett, NC	37085	4	114,678	19.6	24.4	9.0	2	27	19,704	21,439	94.2
Haywood, NC	37087	2	59,036	14.6	23.0	8.5	1	16	7,813	8,743	89.6
Henderson, NC	37089	2	106,740	14.9	21.6	10.0	2	24	13,652	15,140	91.0
Hertford, NC	37091	7	24,669	15.3	33.2	6.5	1	7	3,302	4,387	88.2
Hoke, NC	37093	2	46,952	20.5	27.0	8.2	1	13	8,298	8,875	90.9
Hyde, NC	37095	9	5,810	13.5	28.6	13.2	1	5	609	962	70.5
Iredell, NC	37097	4	159,437	19.2	16.6	8.9	6	47	29,042	29,623	91.2
Jackson, NC	37099	6	40,271	12.6	24.7	10.2	2	10	3,830	4,862	96.2
Johnston, NC	37101	2	168,878	20.2	20.5	9.2	2	45	32,840	32,057	95.3
Jones, NC	37103	8	10,153	15.7	30.8	9.6	1	6	1,251	1,674	94.3
Lee, NC	37105	4	57,866	18.4	25.5	9.0	1	16	9,834	10,601	93.0
Lenoir, NC	37107	4	59,495	17.7	31.0	7.1	3	19	9,890	10,920	94.9
Lincoln, NC	37109	4	78,265	17.7	20.0	10.0	2	25	13,295	13,909	95.1
McDowell, NC	37111	6	44,996	16.0	27.2	7.5	1	12	6,706	7,180	94.9
Macon, NC	37113	7	33,922	14.1	27.9	12.3	1	11	4,339	4,392	88.2
Madison, NC	37115	2	20,764	15.2	25.1	8.2	1	7	2,576	3,115	89.3
Martin, NC	37117	6	24,505	16.5	35.4	6.8	1	11	3,896	4,235	95.6
Mecklenburg, NC	37119	1	919,628	17.9	19.6	7.9	13	184	142,318	158,642	86.9
Mitchell, NC	37121	9	15,579	14.5	26.3	8.4	1	9	2,088	2,335	96.2
Montgomery, NC	37123	6	27,798	18.0	30.4	10.0	1	11	4,325	4,801	91.5
Moore, NC	37125	4	88,247	16.0	23.4	8.7	3	26	13,219	14,033	90.1
Nash, NC	37127	3	95,840	17.8	22.8	8.7	2	28	18,441	17,638	91.7
New Hanover, NC	37129	2	202,667	14.2	21.9	7.0	3	43	25,261	28,579	91.3
Northampton, NC	37131	9	22,099	15.4	33.2	7.1	2	10	3,206	3,849	86.8
Onslow, NC	37133	3	177,772	15.7	23.0	6.7	1	35	23,890	27,512	90.5
Orange, NC	37135	2	133,801	15.8	14.9	7.6	4	34	19,248	19,910	88.5
Pamlico, NC	37137	9	13,144	13.4	28.2	10.0	2	5	1,826	1,805	92.8
Pasquotank, NC	37139	7	40,661	16.0	28.7	7.5	1	12	6,212	6,960	93.2
Pender, NC	37141	2	52,217	16.9	22.8	10.9	1	16	8,450	8,845	95.4
Perquimans, NC	37143	9	13,453	15.0	27.8	8.8	1	4	1,832	2,099	91.4
Person, NC	37145	2	39,464	17.1	21.9	7.6	3	12	6,176	7,076	90.9
Pitt, NC	37147	3	168,148	15.8	25.7	7.3	1	36	23,630	26,454	89.2
Polk, NC	37149	8	20,510	14.7	22.9	12.0	1	7	2,506	2,918	93.9
Randolph, NC	37151	2	141,752	18.1	24.5	8.5	2	39	23,775	25,767	93.0
Richmond, NC	37153	4	46,639	17.8	35.2	8.4	1	17	7,875	8,840	91.6
Robeson, NC	37155	4	134,168	19.2	41.1	9.4	2	43	24,046	26,944	97.2
Rockingham, NC	37157	2	93,643	16.6	24.8	7.6	2	27	14,152	16,183	96.8
Rowan, NC	37159	4	138,428	17.3	26.7	9.2	1	35	20,460	23,746	93.3
Rutherford, NC	37161	4	67,810	16.7	31.1	7.6	3	20	10,474	11,482	93.2
Sampson, NC	37163	6	63,431	18.7	28.9	10.0	2	23	11,680	11,861	96.4
Scotland, NC	37165	6	36,157	18.2	36.3	7.0	1	19	6,517	7,314	96.7
Stanly, NC	37167	6	60,585	16.7	21.2	8.5	2	24	9,597	10,533	92.0
Stokes, NC	37169	2	47,401	16.9	19.9	7.4	1	19	7,084	8,180	91.6
Surry, NC	37171	4	73,673	17.4	28.3	9.2	4	27	12,072	12,682	93.4
Swain, NC	37173	8	13,981	17.1	25.2	10.1	3	6	2,225	2,299	93.3
Transylvania, NC	37175	6	33,090	13.0	27.1	9.3	3	10	3,752	4,155	86.5
Tyrrell, NC	37177	9	4,407	12.8	42.5	12.0	1	3	607	576	97.7

[1]County type codes are from the Economic Research Service of the United States Department of Agriculture. See notes and definitions for more information.

Table C-1. Population, School, and Student Characteristics by County, Selected Years—*Continued*

County	State/ County Code	Characteristics of students, 2010–2011				Number of graduates, 2008–2009	Staff and students, 2010–2011			
		Percent with IEP[2]	Percent eligible for free or reduced lunch	Percent minority	Percent English-language learners		Total staff	Number of teachers	Student/ teacher ratio	Central admin. staff
		10	11	12	13	14	15	16	17	18
NORTH CAROLINA— *(Continued)*										
Duplin, NC	37061	9.6	67.7	62.3	19.7	468	1,263	609	15.0	42
Durham, NC	37063	13.2	56.2	77.5	13.0	1,832	4,466	2,332	15.2	168
Edgecombe, NC	37065	10.8	77.4	71.6	4.5	446	958	455	16.4	37
Forsyth, NC	37067	11.9	52.3	56.3	12.2	3,165	7,279	3,948	14.0	175
Franklin, NC	37069	10.5	56.9	47.6	5.6	500	1,079	581	15.0	34
Gaston, NC	37071	11.3	53.4	33.5	4.4	2,052	4,039	2,026	16.9	126
Gates, NC	37073	17.8	52.1	41.4	0.4	123	308	148	12.6	18
Graham, NC	37075	12.1	59.5	16.2	0.6	57	200	87	14.4	12
Granville, NC	37077	10.2	51.0	49.0	5.9	490	1,047	561	15.7	46
Greene, NC	37079	11.7	70.8	67.6	16.2	182	481	231	14.5	26
Guilford, NC	37081	13.5	51.9	60.0	8.0	4,616	10,247	5,052	14.9	335
Halifax, NC	37083	12.8	51.2	71.4	1.6	543	1,212	571	14.7	69
Harnett, NC	37085	12.2	53.9	46.7	6.9	1,108	2,302	1,235	16.0	54
Haywood, NC	37087	15.3	51.6	9.9	1.9	476	1,072	546	14.3	40
Henderson, NC	37089	12.7	50.8	27.3	9.8	825	1,752	925	14.8	80
Hertford, NC	37091	14.5	36.0	84.6	1.5	236	521	224	14.8	25
Hoke, NC	37093	12.6	51.4	72.5	7.2	334	1,069	566	14.7	48
Hyde, NC	37095	16.1	59.6	48.1	7.1	55	153	73	8.4	14
Iredell, NC	37097	11.2	38.1	28.5	4.4	1,749	3,406	1,764	16.5	100
Jackson, NC	37099	15.7	53.1	21.6	3.9	201	545	264	14.5	23
Johnston, NC	37101	14.2	42.8	37.8	8.9	1,625	4,029	2,232	14.7	101
Jones, NC	37103	14.5	74.8	56.3	1.8	75	218	103	12.2	15
Lee, NC	37105	10.6	60.3	55.5	14.6	604	1,213	604	16.3	50
Lenoir, NC	37107	13.9	67.7	61.5	5.3	608	1,193	629	15.7	45
Lincoln, NC	37109	12.8	42.5	18.9	3.2	891	1,651	879	15.1	56
McDowell, NC	37111	13.9	57.7	19.0	5.4	384	932	453	14.8	35
Macon, NC	37113	17.1	60.5	16.3	7.4	273	651	335	13.0	29
Madison, NC	37115	13.3	57.4	5.1	1.5	140	374	189	13.6	19
Martin, NC	37117	14.3	63.2	56.8	1.5	242	598	297	13.1	21
Mecklenburg, NC	37119	10.0	51.5	66.1	10.2	7,245	17,934	8,965	15.9	613
Mitchell, NC	37121	17.1	60.7	9.3	4.6	128	363	161	13.0	17
Montgomery, NC	37123	13.1	73.6	54.5	15.6	271	622	299	14.4	21
Moore, NC	37125	10.8	42.1	34.1	4.3	714	1,728	855	15.5	57
Nash, NC	37127	12.0	62.6	62.6	5.0	1,084	2,417	1,176	15.7	59
New Hanover, NC	37129	11.6	41.8	36.1	3.6	1,462	3,431	1,626	15.5	118
Northampton, NC	37131	10.4	75.5	83.3	1.4	190	504	240	13.4	24
Onslow, NC	37133	11.1	41.4	38.0	1.4	1,472	3,101	1,503	15.9	85
Orange, NC	37135	11.6	28.5	42.0	9.4	1,325	2,961	1,470	13.1	121
Pamlico, NC	37137	16.2	58.7	31.2	2.0	141	278	141	13.0	20
Pasquotank, NC	37139	14.3	55.7	52.3	1.7	354	878	446	13.9	35
Pender, NC	37141	11.7	55.0	32.8	4.5	541	988	537	15.7	39
Perquimans, NC	37143	14.7	57.8	36.8	0.6	102	276	117	15.7	19
Person, NC	37145	14.0	48.8	41.1	2.7	343	771	424	14.6	23
Pitt, NC	37147	11.8	54.4	61.2	4.3	1,298	3,092	1,604	14.7	83
Polk, NC	37149	15.0	53.4	20.6	3.8	168	374	177	14.2	26
Randolph, NC	37151	11.2	54.0	28.6	9.5	1,279	3,022	1,542	15.4	98
Richmond, NC	37153	10.2	70.1	55.6	4.9	470	1,080	500	15.8	33
Robeson, NC	37155	16.6	80.3	84.0	6.6	1,389	3,233	1,562	15.4	79
Rockingham, NC	37157	14.1	55.3	36.2	4.9	898	1,806	942	15.0	63
Rowan, NC	37159	12.6	59.5	35.6	7.4	1,352	2,749	1,401	14.6	87
Rutherford, NC	37161	12.7	55.5	25.0	2.2	664	1,467	678	15.5	45
Sampson, NC	37163	10.3	69.4	60.2	14.8	575	1,501	774	15.1	47
Scotland, NC	37165	14.5	73.6	67.2	0.9	389	1,021	505	12.9	47
Stanly, NC	37167	16.0	51.2	25.6	4.1	678	1,265	686	14.0	33
Stokes, NC	37169	18.0	46.3	13.2	1.6	492	954	492	14.4	27
Surry, NC	37171	13.1	53.5	24.0	8.8	677	1,623	815	14.8	59
Swain, NC	37173	16.4	53.2	31.3	1.6	130	315	148	15.0	16
Transylvania, NC	37175	13.2	52.8	15.4	1.7	251	542	271	13.8	26
Tyrrell, NC	37177	17.0	68.5	59.1	9.1	40	133	55	11.1	13

[2]IEP=Individual Education Program. See notes and definitions for more information.

Table C-1. Population, School, and Student Characteristics by County, Selected Years—*Continued*

County	State/ County Code	Revenues, 2008–2009				Current expenditures, 2008–2009			Resident population 16 to 19 years, 2006–2010			
		Total revenue ($1,000's)	Percentage of revenue from			Amount ($1,000's)	Amount per student	Percent for instruction	Total population 16 to 19 years	Percent enrolled in school	Percent high school graduates, not enrolled in school	Percent not enrolled, not grads, not employed, or not in labor force
			Federal government	State government	Local government							
		19	20	21	22	23	24	25	26	27	28	29
NORTH CAROLINA— *(Continued)*												
Duplin, NC	37061	84,016	13.5	67.0	19.5	77,998	8,698	63.3	2,996	70.3	13.9	6.7
Durham, NC	37063	402,679	8.8	48.4	42.9	342,618	9,628	61.3	15,749	86.0	5.7	5.8
Edgecombe, NC	37065	68,051	13.4	70.1	16.4	65,843	8,162	62.3	3,150	79.6	13.4	5.1
Forsyth, NC	37067	590,451	8.7	52.2	39.1	485,831	8,852	67.1	19,866	84.4	7.3	5.3
Franklin, NC	37069	97,798	8.1	50.0	41.8	70,320	8,144	61.8	3,402	83.1	8.5	3.9
Gaston, NC	37071	281,360	10.6	63.0	26.5	254,928	7,570	65.0	11,512	78.4	10.1	7.1
Gates, NC	37073	21,566	8.0	67.4	24.5	19,578	9,770	59.4	609	82.9	14.5	2.6
Graham, NC	37075	14,180	12.3	72.4	15.3	12,889	10,470	55.8	397	82.1	6.1	11.8
Granville, NC	37077	84,902	10.0	60.7	29.3	73,531	7,911	63.3	3,161	77.6	9.9	11.3
Greene, NC	37079	35,135	13.2	72.2	14.6	33,122	9,908	62.0	1,335	72.4	10.5	8.6
Guilford, NC	37081	759,213	12.0	52.7	35.3	672,367	9,010	61.2	30,003	85.6	7.9	5.3
Halifax, NC	37083	93,792	18.1	63.6	18.3	88,358	9,870	62.5	3,382	77.4	11.4	10.4
Harnett, NC	37085	191,122	9.4	59.3	31.3	143,211	7,553	66.7	7,551	88.6	5.8	3.9
Haywood, NC	37087	76,456	9.7	60.2	30.1	69,116	8,681	62.2	2,436	77.5	13.1	5.0
Henderson, NC	37089	125,756	9.5	57.9	32.6	108,095	7,992	66.7	4,530	78.1	7.1	10.1
Hertford, NC	37091	37,107	13.2	68.6	18.2	35,050	10,460	59.7	1,400	77.1	11.1	7.9
Hoke, NC	37093	73,708	14.7	69.1	16.2	69,107	8,703	62.8	2,150	68.8	14.9	9.4
Hyde, NC	37095	11,623	9.9	70.4	19.7	10,882	16,563	54.6	162	75.3	11.7	0.0
Iredell, NC	37097	301,663	6.2	49.8	44.1	230,126	7,991	63.3	8,450	81.9	13.3	4.2
Jackson, NC	37099	41,138	9.6	57.7	32.7	34,785	8,924	62.6	3,147	84.9	7.9	6.0
Johnston, NC	37101	366,329	6.7	49.9	43.4	262,307	8,269	65.5	8,507	79.7	9.5	6.5
Jones, NC	37103	16,131	12.1	71.1	16.8	15,838	11,029	56.9	397	80.1	9.8	9.6
Lee, NC	37105	94,321	10.1	61.6	28.2	82,941	8,338	65.0	3,132	77.8	12.3	5.6
Lenoir, NC	37107	90,297	11.4	67.1	21.5	82,862	8,389	62.0	3,352	80.8	13.4	4.4
Lincoln, NC	37109	109,682	8.0	65.0	27.0	103,558	7,739	61.6	4,018	86.6	8.0	2.3
McDowell, NC	37111	55,617	7.7	73.1	19.2	54,669	8,305	67.9	2,124	78.7	5.1	13.5
Macon, NC	37113	43,413	10.2	60.1	29.7	39,282	8,857	61.2	1,765	73.5	9.4	7.8
Madison, NC	37115	30,461	9.2	63.4	27.4	24,255	9,205	59.4	1,365	90.0	8.1	1.0
Martin, NC	37117	42,867	13.2	66.9	19.9	39,979	10,012	61.9	1,369	94.2	2.7	2.9
Mecklenburg, NC	37119	1,738,785	6.7	42.9	50.4	1,206,862	8,629	63.7	46,387	84.5	9.0	4.0
Mitchell, NC	37121	22,574	9.7	75.0	15.3	21,855	10,146	61.9	699	81.7	15.7	2.6
Montgomery, NC	37123	45,506	14.0	62.5	23.4	42,886	9,436	64.4	1,569	65.1	25.8	7.8
Moore, NC	37125	141,970	6.1	51.2	42.7	108,762	8,491	63.1	3,994	83.1	9.2	4.1
Nash, NC	37127	163,810	13.5	67.0	19.5	159,240	8,374	63.0	5,288	84.3	8.6	5.3
New Hanover, NC	37129	260,038	8.4	50.6	41.1	229,519	9,337	59.7	11,353	87.6	5.8	4.6
Northampton, NC	37131	38,750	14.1	67.3	18.6	35,791	8,955	62.0	1,156	84.8	9.3	5.5
Onslow, NC	37133	214,281	12.0	60.1	27.9	193,524	8,057	63.8	12,173	46.4	48.0	4.1
Orange, NC	37135	239,363	5.4	43.1	51.4	203,920	10,698	64.9	10,909	94.6	3.5	1.5
Pamlico, NC	37137	23,537	11.4	63.0	25.6	19,458	10,621	60.0	573	80.5	11.7	6.8
Pasquotank, NC	37139	60,976	11.7	61.8	26.4	56,328	8,825	62.8	2,612	85.1	7.6	4.3
Pender, NC	37141	80,913	12.5	56.2	31.3	70,309	8,516	61.9	2,395	83.6	9.7	4.2
Perquimans, NC	37143	32,239	11.1	43.0	45.9	19,908	11,260	60.2	737	91.5	8.6	0.0
Person, NC	37145	61,649	9.6	60.9	29.4	53,823	8,823	66.4	1,986	84.0	6.1	6.0
Pitt, NC	37147	220,217	9.9	64.4	25.7	195,080	8,306	65.4	13,130	90.2	4.2	2.8
Polk, NC	37149	30,258	8.9	56.6	34.6	27,259	10,404	61.5	980	83.2	16.4	0.0
Randolph, NC	37151	208,720	10.5	62.9	26.6	187,750	7,846	65.1	7,091	77.2	13.0	7.9
Richmond, NC	37153	75,556	14.3	68.1	17.6	71,278	9,028	64.3	2,726	75.1	14.4	8.0
Robeson, NC	37155	228,285	17.2	67.3	15.5	218,698	8,846	63.5	8,733	78.1	10.1	9.1
Rockingham, NC	37157	130,350	10.4	66.7	22.9	123,986	8,533	62.1	4,803	78.9	9.8	5.9
Rowan, NC	37159	199,289	9.6	60.8	29.7	174,324	8,252	63.9	7,654	80.6	10.4	5.4
Rutherford, NC	37161	100,683	11.6	65.1	23.3	92,718	8,838	63.5	3,592	81.4	9.3	8.3
Sampson, NC	37163	116,026	12.1	57.9	30.0	97,626	8,327	63.1	3,439	79.4	14.4	3.9
Scotland, NC	37165	83,488	13.4	56.4	30.3	70,567	10,108	63.3	2,413	87.8	4.8	6.4
Stanly, NC	37167	89,836	11.4	65.8	22.8	83,826	8,452	65.8	3,327	87.2	9.3	2.5
Stokes, NC	37169	63,083	9.3	69.1	21.6	60,659	8,163	61.3	2,197	82.2	10.7	5.6
Surry, NC	37171	105,881	10.0	64.1	26.0	91,848	8,321	64.4	3,722	80.9	10.4	7.3
Swain, NC	37173	22,770	19.3	67.3	13.4	20,453	9,549	60.6	762	78.0	20.1	2.0
Transylvania, NC	37175	41,271	9.0	55.5	35.5	36,751	9,337	62.9	1,608	72.8	15.2	9.3
Tyrrell, NC	37177	9,574	11.0	75.5	13.4	9,237	14,803	53.2	208	85.6	0.5	9.1

Note. Data in columns 26 through 41 from the American Community Survey are subject to sampling error, which can be especially large in small counties and small population groups. See notes and definitions for more information.

Table C-1. Population, School, and Student Characteristics by County, Selected Years—*Continued*

County	State/ County Code	High school graduates, 2006–2010			College enrollment, 2006–2010		College graduates, 2006–2010 (percent)						
		Population 25 years and over	High school diploma or less (percent)	High school diploma or more (percent)	Number	Percent public	Bachelor's degree or more	+/- U.S. percent with Bachelor's degree or more	Non-Hispanic White	Black or African American	American Indian and Alaska Native	Asian, Hawaiian, and Pacific Islander	Hispanic or Latino[3]
		30	31	32	33	34	35	36	37	38	39	40	41
NORTH CAROLINA— *(Continued)*													
Duplin, NC	37061	37,252	61.8	69.7	2,728	80.6	10.1	-17.8	13.6	5.5	28.6	0.0	3.8
Durham, NC	37063	169,113	32.6	86.3	31,164	52.2	44.1	16.2	57.0	30.0	18.4	79.0	14.6
Edgecombe, NC	37065	37,002	61.8	76.7	2,945	91.9	10.1	-17.8	14.3	6.7	48.4	23.8	10.1
Forsyth, NC	37067	225,318	41.3	86.9	25,555	58.9	31.2	3.3	36.1	22.4	26.8	57.3	10.6
Franklin, NC	37069	39,241	54.9	80.1	3,003	64.3	15.2	-12.7	18.0	9.4	6.0	37.5	7.0
Gaston, NC	37071	136,654	51.2	78.9	10,768	78.8	18.1	-9.8	18.8	13.3	13.8	45.6	9.0
Gates, NC	37073	8,177	56.2	82.6	429	77.6	10.5	-17.4	11.5	8.7	0.0	35.7	0.0
Graham, NC	37075	6,031	55.3	79.4	186	93.5	13.1	-14.8	12.5	100.0	18.7	26.5	0.0
Granville, NC	37077	39,670	54.7	79.9	2,852	88.4	13.8	-14.1	16.6	9.3	18.2	43.2	7.2
Greene, NC	37079	14,449	61.4	73.9	1,320	91.7	9.2	-18.7	14.5	3.4	0.0	0.0	3.8
Guilford, NC	37081	309,065	39.7	86.9	44,100	83.2	32.4	4.5	38.6	21.9	7.7	36.4	14.4
Halifax, NC	37083	37,436	61.9	73.3	2,343	81.4	11.4	-16.5	15.0	8.3	4.6	68.6	7.2
Harnett, NC	37085	68,026	50.0	81.0	9,957	51.7	16.0	-11.9	17.5	11.8	7.9	20.6	12.0
Haywood, NC	37087	42,828	47.1	84.2	2,150	84.9	20.6	-7.3	21.3	7.7	10.5	0.0	6.4
Henderson, NC	37089	75,775	40.3	87.2	4,035	83.7	27.3	-0.6	28.8	17.4	10.6	41.4	10.0
Hertford, NC	37091	16,521	58.6	73.5	1,470	64.5	15.7	-12.2	18.8	12.2	21.7	75.7	4.7
Hoke, NC	37093	26,735	48.3	79.9	3,318	80.2	15.1	-12.8	17.5	16.5	2.4	38.9	12.3
Hyde, NC	37095	4,198	60.4	76.7	328	71.3	11.7	-16.2	18.5	3.0	0.0	40.0	0.0
Iredell, NC	37097	103,048	47.2	84.5	7,216	78.9	21.6	-6.3	23.3	8.4	4.6	38.5	18.5
Jackson, NC	37099	24,654	45.9	81.4	6,496	95.3	27.0	-0.9	30.1	18.4	7.6	35.0	7.2
Johnston, NC	37101	104,350	48.2	81.2	7,760	79.2	19.3	-8.6	21.9	13.8	9.2	33.7	5.3
Jones, NC	37103	7,066	59.5	78.2	356	97.5	10.7	-17.2	13.7	5.6	40.0	0.0	0.6
Lee, NC	37105	36,558	49.6	80.7	2,505	89.0	18.0	-9.9	22.5	9.4	13.6	39.4	4.6
Lenoir, NC	37107	40,291	54.7	76.2	3,482	91.0	14.5	-13.4	18.9	8.4	18.6	86.1	6.3
Lincoln, NC	37109	52,228	51.0	79.5	3,585	82.3	17.8	-10.1	19.0	6.1	8.3	33.3	8.4
McDowell, NC	37111	31,364	57.7	79.0	2,080	91.2	14.0	-13.9	14.3	9.6	0.0	54.2	11.7
Macon, NC	37113	24,532	48.8	83.0	1,104	89.9	19.5	-8.4	20.2	0.0	0.0	34.6	7.8
Madison, NC	37115	14,375	57.0	77.3	1,684	37.6	19.2	-8.7	19.5	15.3	0.0	0.0	17.9
Martin, NC	37117	16,971	57.6	78.6	1,373	86.8	12.2	-15.7	13.7	10.0	0.0	0.0	11.6
Mecklenburg, NC	37119	572,959	32.0	88.3	64,331	74.2	40.0	12.1	50.7	24.2	20.8	52.1	16.0
Mitchell, NC	37121	11,528	60.9	76.5	579	81.7	14.4	-13.5	13.6	0.0	0.0	67.9	31.3
Montgomery, NC	37123	18,622	59.0	72.1	1,305	88.1	14.8	-13.1	17.6	10.4	22.1	10.0	1.1
Moore, NC	37125	61,549	38.8	88.4	4,206	84.6	29.8	1.9	33.2	12.3	17.5	31.6	14.6
Nash, NC	37127	63,511	51.8	81.8	5,473	75.6	19.1	-8.8	24.8	10.1	28.1	39.8	8.7
New Hanover, NC	37129	131,944	33.0	89.5	20,492	90.1	36.1	8.2	41.4	11.8	14.5	36.5	17.0
Northampton, NC	37131	15,549	66.6	69.1	1,035	81.2	12.0	-15.9	14.9	9.7	0.0	0.0	0.0
Onslow, NC	37133	86,750	42.6	88.1	10,802	86.9	17.7	-10.2	19.1	12.9	5.7	24.7	12.8
Orange, NC	37135	78,273	27.0	89.9	25,375	93.4	54.4	26.5	59.9	26.7	47.6	75.3	21.1
Pamlico, NC	37137	9,833	51.0	82.7	616	86.4	17.5	-10.4	20.6	8.1	0.0	53.6	1.6
Pasquotank, NC	37139	25,742	47.0	81.9	3,704	89.8	18.7	-9.2	20.4	15.3	0.0	36.7	10.4
Pender, NC	37141	35,187	51.9	83.8	2,257	78.5	17.8	-10.1	20.6	8.1	7.4	27.9	9.5
Perquimans, NC	37143	9,392	53.8	85.3	857	85.3	18.1	-9.8	20.9	9.7	0.0	0.0	14.0
Person, NC	37145	26,753	57.4	82.0	2,344	88.0	13.8	-14.1	14.2	11.5	49.1	100.0	13.9
Pitt, NC	37147	94,503	41.1	85.1	28,776	94.5	28.2	0.3	37.4	11.4	35.3	68.9	12.6
Polk, NC	37149	15,288	44.7	86.1	781	78.7	27.2	-0.7	28.8	8.4	0.0	0.0	15.3
Randolph, NC	37151	94,347	59.4	75.6	5,792	86.2	13.0	-14.9	13.6	13.9	3.1	24.2	3.9
Richmond, NC	37153	30,707	62.0	74.9	2,302	92.3	10.0	-17.9	11.7	6.9	11.1	15.2	0.4
Robeson, NC	37155	81,721	64.2	68.7	8,201	95.0	12.1	-15.8	18.0	8.2	10.5	26.1	2.9
Rockingham, NC	37157	65,263	58.9	76.6	4,040	85.3	12.5	-15.4	14.0	7.5	13.1	44.2	6.5
Rowan, NC	37159	91,558	54.3	80.0	7,456	63.8	17.0	-10.9	18.1	14.3	10.1	14.3	8.3
Rutherford, NC	37161	46,835	53.6	79.6	3,573	87.7	14.6	-13.3	15.5	4.9	22.4	43.1	11.7
Sampson, NC	37163	41,616	60.1	75.2	3,364	83.9	12.4	-15.5	16.5	7.4	8.1	31.2	2.4
Scotland, NC	37165	23,492	60.1	75.2	1,975	61.4	14.0	-13.9	20.0	7.6	5.3	51.1	0.0
Stanly, NC	37167	40,563	55.9	80.5	3,812	66.5	15.3	-12.6	16.1	10.0	14.0	28.0	2.4
Stokes, NC	37169	33,083	63.4	79.2	1,858	79.2	10.9	-17.0	10.9	15.5	0.0	22.4	6.3
Surry, NC	37171	50,816	56.1	74.5	3,030	88.9	14.9	-13.0	15.8	10.8	0.0	26.0	3.8
Swain, NC	37173	9,531	53.5	79.4	755	72.2	18.6	-9.3	20.9	6.9	5.7	34.5	21.7
Transylvania, NC	37175	24,182	43.5	86.1	1,662	70.3	27.0	-0.9	28.8	3.4	0.0	13.3	4.4
Tyrrell, NC	37177	3,424	67.2	73.9	117	82.1	8.4	-19.5	11.9	3.3	0.0	0.0	0.0

Note. Data in columns 26 through 41 from the American Community Survey are subject to sampling error, which can be especially large in small counties and small population groups. See notes and definitions for more information.
[3]May be of any race.

Table C-1. Population, School, and Student Characteristics by County, Selected Years—*Continued*

County	State/ County Code	County Type[1]	Population, 2010		Percent of related children 5–17 years in poverty, 2010	Percent of children under 19 years with no health insurance, 2010	Number of schools and students, 2010–2011			Resident enrollment, 2006–2010 K–12 enrollment	
			Total	Percent 5–17 years			School districts	Schools	Students	Number	Percent public
			1	2	3	4	5	6	7	8	9
NORTH CAROLINA— *(Continued)*											
Union, NC	37179	1	201,292	23.0	11.7	8.1	2	53	41,253	42,690	88.6
Vance, NC	37181	4	45,422	18.6	33.3	7.6	3	18	7,961	8,925	90.4
Wake, NC	37183	2	900,993	18.8	13.9	7.9	18	202	150,753	157,464	88.0
Warren, NC	37185	8	20,972	14.6	34.3	9.0	1	8	2,620	3,490	93.2
Washington, NC	37187	7	13,228	16.5	36.5	7.6	1	5	1,913	2,499	83.9
Watauga, NC	37189	6	51,079	10.0	20.2	8.5	3	10	4,526	5,049	90.3
Wayne, NC	37191	3	122,623	17.7	28.0	7.4	2	32	19,631	21,833	92.7
Wilkes, NC	37193	6	69,340	16.7	24.2	8.9	2	23	10,525	11,326	92.3
Wilson, NC	37195	4	81,234	18.0	28.8	9.0	3	26	13,084	15,119	94.2
Yadkin, NC	37197	2	38,406	17.3	20.4	9.6	1	14	6,064	6,677	96.4
Yancey, NC	37199	8	17,818	15.2	28.7	11.7	1	9	2,361	2,960	93.3
NORTH DAKOTA	38000	X	672,591	15.7	13.7	6.1	223	516	94,273	104,443	92.2
Adams, ND	38001	9	2,343	14.0	11.8	11.8	1	2	263	304	100.0
Barnes, ND	38003	6	11,066	15.3	11.6	6.8	4	11	1,429	1,612	96.3
Benson, ND	38005	9	6,660	23.8	37.5	7.9	6	10	845	1,505	96.9
Billings, ND	38007	9	783	12.4	16.2	14.3	1	2	39	117	94.0
Bottineau, ND	38009	9	6,429	13.6	12.6	8.9	4	7	792	906	93.9
Bowman, ND	38011	9	3,151	14.9	9.0	9.6	2	5	532	504	100.0
Burke, ND	38013	9	1,968	14.9	11.7	7.8	3	6	253	256	95.3
Burleigh, ND	38015	3	81,308	15.9	9.8	4.4	12	35	11,281	12,877	88.7
Cass, ND	38017	3	149,778	14.9	10.9	4.4	11	53	20,194	21,280	90.7
Cavalier, ND	38019	9	3,993	15.1	13.7	8.3	2	5	452	613	89.4
Dickey, ND	38021	9	5,289	16.4	12.6	8.2	2	5	855	893	92.8
Divide, ND	38023	9	2,071	12.4	15.5	10.0	2	3	226	252	87.3
Dunn, ND	38025	9	3,536	16.0	15.2	15.2	2	4	395	604	93.2
Eddy, ND	38027	9	2,385	15.6	14.3	9.7	2	3	344	483	100.0
Emmons, ND	38029	8	3,550	16.6	17.9	14.9	5	8	571	665	99.3
Foster, ND	38031	9	3,343	16.5	9.6	6.6	1	2	530	542	99.5
Golden Valley, ND	38033	9	1,680	19.0	18.1	12.9	2	3	309	288	94.1
Grand Forks, ND	38035	3	66,861	13.6	13.2	4.2	10	31	8,526	9,135	92.2
Grant, ND	38037	8	2,394	14.2	25.7	24.0	2	3	252	420	98.8
Griggs, ND	38039	9	2,420	13.9	13.6	7.8	2	4	378	296	100.0
Hettinger, ND	38041	9	2,477	14.0	14.6	12.2	3	5	398	375	100.0
Kidder, ND	38043	8	2,435	16.1	23.5	18.3	2	5	402	356	100.0
La Moure, ND	38045	9	4,139	15.8	11.9	9.6	4	10	786	650	99.5
Logan, ND	38047	9	1,990	16.4	16.7	19.2	3	5	345	349	100.0
McHenry, ND	38049	9	5,395	16.5	16.1	13.7	4	8	871	933	87.9
McIntosh, ND	38051	9	2,809	12.9	18.1	15.2	3	6	396	336	100.0
McKenzie, ND	38053	9	6,360	18.5	16.3	10.3	4	6	672	1,198	97.8
McLean, ND	38055	8	8,962	14.7	12.4	8.7	6	12	1,310	1,348	99.1
Mercer, ND	38057	6	8,424	15.8	8.7	5.6	3	7	1,269	1,455	99.0
Morton, ND	38059	3	27,471	16.9	14.0	6.0	10	21	4,244	4,709	86.7
Mountrail, ND	38061	9	7,673	17.2	18.3	8.8	3	7	1,525	1,381	99.4
Nelson, ND	38063	8	3,126	13.6	11.6	9.1	2	4	446	540	96.5
Oliver, ND	38065	8	1,846	16.5	18.2	12.6	1	2	196	348	88.5
Pembina, ND	38067	9	7,413	16.0	11.4	8.1	5	12	1,110	1,213	97.4
Pierce, ND	38069	7	4,357	16.1	15.0	8.4	3	5	615	700	89.9
Ramsey, ND	38071	7	11,451	15.6	17.9	6.1	6	11	1,865	1,907	91.6
Ransom, ND	38073	8	5,457	17.9	10.1	7.3	3	6	938	1,018	95.3
Renville, ND	38075	9	2,470	16.3	9.3	7.3	2	5	587	384	93.0
Richland, ND	38077	6	16,321	16.1	11.2	5.7	9	17	2,333	2,648	92.6
Rolette, ND	38079	9	13,937	23.3	32.6	9.1	6	11	1,353	2,296	100.0
Sargent, ND	38081	9	3,829	17.4	9.9	7.5	3	7	673	730	99.2
Sheridan, ND	38083	9	1,321	12.6	25.6	18.6	2	4	106	163	100.0
Sioux, ND	38085	8	4,153	25.1	49.5	7.5	4	6	412	1,002	92.7
Slope, ND	38087	9	727	14.6	16.1	19.6	2	2	19	110	95.5
Stark, ND	38089	7	24,199	15.2	12.2	5.9	7	18	3,336	3,925	85.9
Steele, ND	38091	8	1,975	16.2	10.2	8.8	2	3	242	419	100.0
Stutsman, ND	38093	7	21,100	14.9	12.3	5.2	8	20	2,613	3,156	87.6
Towner, ND	38095	9	2,246	14.5	13.4	12.2	2	4	296	455	100.0

Note. Data in columns 26 through 41 from the American Community Survey are subject to sampling error, which can be especially large in small counties and small population groups. See notes and definitions for more information.

Table C-1. Population, School, and Student Characteristics by County, Selected Years—*Continued*

County	State/ County Code	Characteristics of students, 2010–2011				Number of graduates, 2008–2009	Staff and students, 2010–2011			
		Percent with IEP[2]	Percent eligible for free or reduced lunch	Percent minority	Percent English-language learners		Total staff	Number of teachers	Student/ teacher ratio	Central admin. staff
		10	11	12	13	14	15	16	17	18
NORTH CAROLINA— *(Continued)*										
Union, NC	37179	9.2	32.5	30.9	5.3	2,171	4,995	2,533	16.3	137
Vance, NC	37181	13.3	75.9	73.7	6.5	477	1,125	582	13.7	49
Wake, NC	37183	13.1	32.2	49.8	8.0	8,460	17,177	9,516	15.8	505
Warren, NC	37185	14.0	78.2	82.6	3.2	179	414	178	14.8	28
Washington, NC	37187	13.0	79.3	77.8	2.8	129	305	144	13.3	15
Watauga, NC	37189	15.7	35.0	11.9	3.0	347	632	345	13.1	27
Wayne, NC	37191	14.1	59.7	58.1	7.4	1,170	2,561	1,297	15.1	64
Wilkes, NC	37193	12.1	60.3	18.7	5.2	652	1,347	647	16.3	54
Wilson, NC	37195	9.0	65.1	64.8	7.1	629	1,605	820	16.0	63
Yadkin, NC	37197	13.9	49.4	23.6	8.2	397	801	389	15.6	22
Yancey, NC	37199	15.5	58.1	12.4	6.7	185	426	177	13.4	20
NORTH DAKOTA	38000	13.9	31.7	14.5	3.0	7,232	15,691	8,160	11.6	677
Adams, ND	38001	10.3	28.1	7.2	. . .	23	53	28	9.3	4
Barnes, ND	38003	13.8	34.9	5.1	0.1	109	288	165	8.7	11
Benson, ND	38005	19.6	69.1	67.0	7.5	55	188	91	9.3	11
Billings, ND	38007	23.1	23.1	0.0	. . .	. . .	24	12	3.3	3
Bottineau, ND	38009	14.1	32.2	11.4	. . .	104	180	86	9.2	10
Bowman, ND	38011	12.0	25.6	5.8	1.7	61	98	57	9.3	5
Burke, ND	38013	19.4	17.0	5.1	1.2	32	75	45	5.6	4
Burleigh, ND	38015	11.9	21.9	11.8	1.2	773	1,530	812	13.9	52
Cass, ND	38017	11.9	27.1	14.3	6.8	1,369	2,849	1,511	13.4	105
Cavalier, ND	38019	14.4	35.6	5.1	. . .	62	84	47	9.6	3
Dickey, ND	38021	11.9	29.5	8.3	5.0	62	115	66	13.0	7
Divide, ND	38023	8.4	36.3	3.1	. . .	30	50	26	8.8	3
Dunn, ND	38025	10.1	24.1	14.9	. . .	42	84	46	8.6	4
Eddy, ND	38027	15.7	45.6	10.8	. . .	37	68	31	11.1	5
Emmons, ND	38029	11.6	44.7	2.1	. . .	67	110	57	10.0	7
Foster, ND	38031	14.0	25.9	2.7	. . .	61	68	39	13.6	3
Golden Valley, ND	38033	14.2	40.8	9.1	. . .	29	85	39	7.9	3
Grand Forks, ND	38035	14.6	36.6	15.8	3.0	647	1,461	736	11.6	54
Grant, ND	38037	19.8	44.8	8.3	. . .	23	61	31	8.1	3
Griggs, ND	38039	13.0	45.1	2.8	. . .	48	64	37	10.3	4
Hettinger, ND	38041	13.1	33.9	5.5	. . .	30	84	42	9.5	4
Kidder, ND	38043	12.4	44.5	8.5	1.2	29	82	43	9.3	4
La Moure, ND	38045	10.7	43.4	4.8	2.4	63	145	80	9.9	8
Logan, ND	38047	10.4	33.0	2.6	. . .	25	62	34	10.0	5
McHenry, ND	38049	13.2	42.6	3.3	0.2	74	169	88	9.9	8
McIntosh, ND	38051	8.8	38.4	5.3	1.3	25	79	46	8.6	4
McKenzie, ND	38053	13.7	20.7	6.5	. . .	57	106	53	12.7	7
McLean, ND	38055	13.6	30.7	7.9	. . .	114	255	139	9.4	12
Mercer, ND	38057	13.2	22.7	6.7	0.4	142	213	101	12.6	9
Morton, ND	38059	14.0	33.0	11.6	0.1	271	710	347	12.2	35
Mountrail, ND	38061	15.9	44.3	62.1	0.9	77	246	126	12.1	11
Nelson, ND	38063	16.1	39.0	7.2	0.2	38	97	53	8.4	3
Oliver, ND	38065	11.7	28.1	9.7	. . .	25	42	24	8.3	3
Pembina, ND	38067	18.8	36.8	13.8	7.1	90	228	127	8.7	9
Pierce, ND	38069	11.9	32.4	6.2	0.2	53	109	67	9.2	5
Ramsey, ND	38071	19.7	42.7	26.6	0.2	152	406	182	10.2	29
Ransom, ND	38073	16.4	32.7	4.3	0.5	85	137	80	11.8	7
Renville, ND	38075	14.1	34.1	8.7	. . .	55	102	57	10.3	5
Richland, ND	38077	18.4	34.1	10.1	1.6	234	490	242	9.7	19
Rolette, ND	38079	14.0	68.7	72.2	10.8	200	258	141	9.6	14
Sargent, ND	38081	18.1	28.9	2.4	5.3	51	120	72	9.3	8
Sheridan, ND	38083	16.0	55.7	4.7	. . .	18	48	26	4.1	3
Sioux, ND	38085	17.0	84.2	98.5	47.3	5	144	75	5.5	9
Slope, ND	38087	21.1	0.0	0.0	. . .	. . .	11	3	5.9	1
Stark, ND	38089	14.9	29.7	6.7	0.4	307	508	265	12.6	24
Steele, ND	38091	12.0	23.1	2.1	. . .	32	49	30	8.0	2
Stutsman, ND	38093	14.8	38.2	7.5	1.1	228	476	265	9.9	20
Towner, ND	38095	13.9	29.7	9.8	0.7	21	59	31	9.7	6

[2]IEP=Individual Education Program. See notes and definitions for more information.
. . . = Not available.

Table C-1. Population, School, and Student Characteristics by County, Selected Years—*Continued*

County	State/ County Code	Revenues, 2008–2009				Current expenditures, 2008–2009			Resident population 16 to 19 years, 2006–2010			
		Total revenue ($1,000's)	Percentage of revenue from			Amount ($1,000's)	Amount per student	Percent for instruction	Total population 16 to 19 years	Percent enrolled in school	Percent high school graduates, not enrolled in school	Percent not enrolled, not grads, not employed, or not in labor force
			Federal government	State government	Local government							
		19	20	21	22	23	24	25	26	27	28	29
NORTH CAROLINA— *(Continued)*												
Union, NC	37179	549,286	3.7	36.7	59.6	321,268	8,148	63.9	11,256	83.7	9.5	4.9
Vance, NC	37181	76,938	13.0	69.1	17.9	71,947	8,474	65.1	2,826	71.3	11.6	16.3
Wake, NC	37183	1,989,480	4.0	38.1	58.0	1,177,307	8,166	64.8	47,164	90.3	4.9	3.1
Warren, NC	37185	30,682	15.6	66.5	17.9	29,035	10,551	60.2	1,354	80.6	14.6	2.7
Washington, NC	37187	25,313	18.5	68.9	12.7	24,478	11,695	64.1	836	86.6	8.0	5.4
Watauga, NC	37189	55,018	6.1	52.0	41.9	45,554	9,769	63.4	5,878	96.5	2.4	0.3
Wayne, NC	37191	167,416	12.7	71.0	16.3	163,516	8,267	68.3	6,690	82.6	11.6	3.9
Wilkes, NC	37193	108,020	8.9	63.6	27.4	100,476	8,511	61.9	3,215	70.1	15.2	8.5
Wilson, NC	37195	120,469	11.9	62.4	25.7	109,098	8,096	63.0	4,504	85.0	5.8	6.4
Yadkin, NC	37197	72,904	6.2	51.7	42.1	50,861	8,201	63.7	2,018	79.6	16.0	1.7
Yancey, NC	37199	26,008	10.7	69.9	19.4	23,768	9,615	59.9	966	80.4	12.9	6.2
NORTH DAKOTA	38000	1,152,034	14.0	35.4	50.6	961,323	10,156	60.3	40,579	85.6	10.0	2.8
Adams, ND	38001	3,286	5.1	40.1	54.8	2,813	10,011	55.2	104	78.9	14.4	0.0
Barnes, ND	38003	18,400	10.0	36.7	53.3	16,019	11,483	65.4	596	90.8	7.4	1.9
Benson, ND	38005	13,198	45.7	34.5	19.9	11,487	13,823	64.9	506	76.3	7.3	13.8
Billings, ND	38007	2,753	13.7	4.2	82.1	1,714	40,810	43.2	32	100.0	0.0	0.0
Bottineau, ND	38009	12,237	15.5	29.7	54.8	10,884	12,482	55.9	422	92.7	7.4	0.0
Bowman, ND	38011	7,865	5.4	32.2	62.5	6,007	10,502	60.9	183	91.3	6.6	0.0
Burke, ND	38013	4,286	5.3	25.8	68.9	3,735	14,940	61.0	56	100.0	0.0	0.0
Burleigh, ND	38015	114,315	10.3	37.2	52.6	98,044	8,807	64.9	4,636	88.9	9.1	0.9
Cass, ND	38017	222,204	7.0	32.2	60.8	186,777	9,535	62.9	9,179	87.7	10.6	1.2
Cavalier, ND	38019	6,550	6.1	28.4	65.5	5,709	11,723	49.9	204	100.0	0.0	0.0
Dickey, ND	38021	8,504	5.4	37.9	56.7	6,461	7,610	52.0	293	87.7	6.5	0.0
Divide, ND	38023	3,952	9.9	31.9	58.2	3,316	14,480	53.8	67	82.1	17.9	0.0
Dunn, ND	38025	8,941	33.2	21.6	45.2	6,567	14,891	56.4	206	85.0	1.0	9.7
Eddy, ND	38027	4,787	13.2	37.6	49.2	4,191	11,740	54.9	124	100.0	0.0	0.0
Emmons, ND	38029	6,976	8.9	41.6	49.5	6,257	9,948	53.9	179	95.0	5.0	0.0
Foster, ND	38031	5,707	5.5	42.9	51.6	4,619	8,019	60.8	201	90.1	10.0	0.0
Golden Valley, ND	38033	5,278	13.8	37.8	48.3	4,863	15,840	48.7	113	100.0	0.0	0.0
Grand Forks, ND	38035	101,857	14.7	33.3	52.0	83,363	9,692	61.9	5,647	86.4	10.4	1.5
Grant, ND	38037	3,735	9.7	37.1	53.2	3,471	13,148	50.9	201	100.0	0.0	0.0
Griggs, ND	38039	5,281	6.9	33.9	59.2	4,644	11,847	53.5	78	93.6	3.9	2.6
Hettinger, ND	38041	6,349	7.2	34.7	58.2	4,603	12,646	52.4	96	86.5	11.5	2.1
Kidder, ND	38043	4,436	4.5	44.1	51.4	4,090	10,174	59.2	90	94.4	5.6	0.0
La Moure, ND	38045	10,859	8.6	31.7	59.7	9,377	12,420	54.0	202	82.7	14.4	3.0
Logan, ND	38047	4,585	12.1	40.6	47.3	3,914	12,231	56.4	78	96.2	3.9	0.0
McHenry, ND	38049	10,853	9.8	35.5	54.7	9,967	11,224	58.2	267	90.3	9.7	0.0
McIntosh, ND	38051	4,796	6.5	37.9	55.6	4,517	11,981	55.0	95	91.6	8.4	0.0
McKenzie, ND	38053	12,803	36.9	25.3	37.8	11,570	14,872	54.4	310	72.9	11.9	5.8
McLean, ND	38055	16,727	7.7	39.7	52.6	14,863	10,077	55.4	309	93.9	3.2	0.0
Mercer, ND	38057	15,090	5.8	39.3	54.9	13,375	9,871	52.1	397	84.6	12.3	1.8
Morton, ND	38059	46,132	10.9	43.8	45.4	38,024	9,414	58.2	1,339	81.6	12.9	5.1
Mountrail, ND	38061	26,683	50.6	23.2	26.1	14,112	10,109	54.4	503	82.1	10.7	5.4
Nelson, ND	38063	5,847	5.3	35.6	59.1	5,176	11,013	53.6	116	100.0	0.0	0.0
Oliver, ND	38065	3,214	4.4	35.8	59.8	2,815	13,405	57.3	88	93.2	6.8	0.0
Pembina, ND	38067	14,650	8.6	32.9	58.5	12,066	10,880	58.3	294	91.5	7.1	1.4
Pierce, ND	38069	6,394	7.2	42.3	50.5	5,512	8,992	57.4	164	97.6	1.8	0.6
Ramsey, ND	38071	23,958	13.1	46.4	40.5	20,344	11,087	56.8	686	89.8	5.8	1.9
Ransom, ND	38073	9,934	5.2	44.5	50.3	7,958	8,096	55.4	323	83.3	5.6	3.7
Renville, ND	38075	7,601	9.3	36.3	54.4	6,186	10,629	58.8	130	82.3	17.7	0.0
Richland, ND	38077	29,624	8.7	37.0	54.3	25,606	10,782	61.4	1,343	93.0	6.0	0.8
Rolette, ND	38079	38,353	49.0	38.9	12.1	35,314	12,127	61.0	986	49.1	17.3	31.7
Sargent, ND	38081	7,957	6.0	45.8	48.2	6,732	9,061	52.5	214	96.7	3.3	0.0
Sheridan, ND	38083	1,915	5.2	35.0	59.7	1,859	13,471	59.4	48	95.8	0.0	0.0
Sioux, ND	38085	8,703	55.7	28.3	16.0	7,281	20,338	63.2	350	68.0	19.7	12.3
Slope, ND	38087	425	12.9	4.0	83.1	263	18,786	62.7	16	100.0	0.0	0.0
Stark, ND	38089	35,072	11.2	43.0	45.8	29,838	9,295	60.6	1,499	90.1	8.3	0.5
Steele, ND	38091	3,698	2.6	32.2	65.2	2,944	10,590	52.3	114	93.0	3.5	3.5
Stutsman, ND	38093	32,610	8.8	39.0	52.2	26,225	9,900	60.8	1,279	91.6	4.1	1.9
Towner, ND	38095	4,424	5.7	32.6	61.7	3,573	11,638	59.4	136	100.0	0.0	0.0

Note. Data in columns 26 through 41 from the American Community Survey are subject to sampling error, which can be especially large in small counties and small population groups. See notes and definitions for more information.

Table C-1. Population, School, and Student Characteristics by County, Selected Years—*Continued*

County	State/ County Code	High school graduates, 2006–2010			College enrollment, 2006–2010		College graduates, 2006–2010 (percent)						
		Population 25 years and over	High school diploma or less (percent)	High school diploma or more (percent)	Number	Percent public	Bachelor's degree or more	+/- U.S. percent with Bachelor's degree or more	Non-Hispanic White	Black or African American	American Indian and Alaska Native	Asian, Hawaiian, and Pacific Islander	Hispanic or Latino[3]
		30	31	32	33	34	35	36	37	38	39	40	41
NORTH CAROLINA— *(Continued)*													
Union, NC	37179	119,001	41.6	86.4	8,330	74.0	29.1	1.2	30.4	21.3	21.8	60.0	20.9
Vance, NC	37181	29,172	62.8	72.6	2,216	88.3	10.7	-17.2	16.3	5.6	0.0	42.0	0.8
Wake, NC	37183	546,652	26.0	91.6	71,869	77.4	47.5	19.6	54.3	29.6	34.0	67.6	17.1
Warren, NC	37185	14,628	59.9	73.1	1,129	89.9	13.9	-14.0	21.9	6.3	18.6	0.0	18.4
Washington, NC	37187	9,086	59.5	76.0	631	98.7	11.8	-16.1	15.5	8.0	0.0	0.0	0.0
Watauga, NC	37189	26,812	36.0	86.9	14,898	98.2	37.1	9.2	37.4	32.0	7.8	75.8	19.2
Wayne, NC	37191	77,961	49.8	81.2	8,452	72.7	16.2	-11.7	18.9	11.9	5.4	32.9	7.3
Wilkes, NC	37193	48,285	60.0	72.6	2,395	86.1	12.3	-15.6	12.7	4.1	25.8	40.8	5.9
Wilson, NC	37195	52,665	55.9	77.3	4,793	66.5	17.5	-10.4	23.4	9.2	0.0	61.8	8.3
Yadkin, NC	37197	26,142	61.1	76.9	1,497	89.5	11.2	-16.7	11.9	4.1	9.3	50.0	4.2
Yancey, NC	37199	12,990	58.1	77.9	529	77.7	15.2	-12.7	14.6	6.2	0.0	93.9	17.4
NORTH DAKOTA	38000	429,333	38.7	89.4	57,481	87.4	26.3	-1.6	26.8	23.8	15.3	46.2	16.1
Adams, ND	38001	1,760	54.8	85.3	33	100.0	18.4	-9.5	19.0	0.0	0.0	0.0	0.0
Barnes, ND	38003	7,755	45.1	88.5	747	97.6	25.8	-2.1	24.8	0.0	0.0	100.0	26.9
Benson, ND	38005	3,820	55.4	80.2	165	78.8	9.8	-18.1	13.5	0.0	4.0	0.0	21.9
Billings, ND	38007	653	48.7	89.1	30	93.3	16.9	-11.0	17.6	0.0	0.0	0.0	0.0
Bottineau, ND	38009	4,655	40.3	85.9	351	93.7	21.6	-6.3	21.6	50.0	14.1	0.0	55.0
Bowman, ND	38011	2,262	46.5	88.4	36	100.0	19.7	-8.2	19.8	0.0	0.0	0.0	17.5
Burke, ND	38013	1,523	48.7	89.0	15	100.0	17.6	-10.3	16.4	0.0	0.0	100.0	92.9
Burleigh, ND	38015	52,342	31.8	92.0	5,976	63.7	32.3	4.4	32.6	8.2	21.3	68.1	14.4
Cass, ND	38017	88,460	28.7	94.0	19,536	91.9	36.4	8.5	36.8	17.8	24.3	47.7	20.3
Cavalier, ND	38019	3,035	45.7	87.4	128	73.4	17.8	-10.1	18.0	0.0	0.0	0.0	0.0
Dickey, ND	38021	3,586	44.3	86.4	317	57.7	19.1	-8.8	18.9	20.0	0.0	0.0	0.0
Divide, ND	38023	1,613	41.6	90.9	12	100.0	19.2	-8.7	19.0	0.0	0.0	100.0	0.0
Dunn, ND	38025	2,424	52.1	84.0	89	95.5	15.1	-12.8	15.7	0.0	14.5	0.0	0.0
Eddy, ND	38027	1,756	47.0	82.4	77	94.8	17.8	-10.1	18.2	0.0	6.3	0.0	0.0
Emmons, ND	38029	2,695	57.0	79.1	73	89.0	13.7	-14.2	13.8	0.0	0.0	0.0	0.0
Foster, ND	38031	2,454	46.8	87.7	134	74.6	18.2	-9.7	18.4	0.0	0.0	0.0	0.0
Golden Valley, ND	38033	1,095	41.8	91.7	66	86.4	19.5	-8.4	20.1	0.0	0.0	0.0	0.0
Grand Forks, ND	38035	37,927	31.7	92.4	13,385	95.2	33.3	5.4	33.8	34.6	25.9	58.1	11.4
Grant, ND	38037	1,869	51.4	87.1	70	97.1	16.4	-11.5	16.0	0.0	41.7	100.0	0.0
Griggs, ND	38039	1,880	50.6	86.0	50	74.0	19.0	-8.9	19.1	0.0	0.0	0.0	0.0
Hettinger, ND	38041	1,891	48.2	86.3	30	76.7	19.7	-8.2	19.8	0.0	0.0	0.0	0.0
Kidder, ND	38043	1,822	52.5	78.5	150	85.3	16.0	-11.9	17.1	0.0	0.0	0.0	0.0
La Moure, ND	38045	3,130	47.3	86.4	88	76.1	20.0	-7.9	20.3	0.0	0.0	0.0	0.0
Logan, ND	38047	1,502	59.1	69.7	24	91.7	12.5	-15.4	12.6	0.0	0.0	0.0	0.0
McHenry, ND	38049	3,904	52.3	85.5	144	88.9	14.3	-13.6	14.1	0.0	50.0	20.0	19.5
McIntosh, ND	38051	2,295	59.9	71.1	74	87.8	16.1	-11.8	16.5	0.0	62.5	0.0	0.0
McKenzie, ND	38053	3,918	40.1	88.4	144	86.8	21.2	-6.7	23.2	100.0	10.5	32.6	0.0
McLean, ND	38055	6,695	45.6	85.8	240	90.4	17.4	-10.5	17.7	0.0	12.2	22.2	13.5
Mercer, ND	38057	5,952	42.3	85.0	211	98.1	16.7	-11.2	17.0	0.0	0.0	0.0	75.0
Morton, ND	38059	18,269	45.1	87.8	1,383	64.0	22.3	-5.6	22.2	100.0	13.0	100.0	17.8
Mountrail, ND	38061	4,768	41.5	88.5	238	86.6	20.0	-7.9	20.5	0.0	21.3	0.0	13.5
Nelson, ND	38063	2,366	43.6	88.8	112	84.8	21.4	-6.5	21.2	0.0	0.0	100.0	0.0
Oliver, ND	38065	1,304	45.6	86.4	25	64.0	19.4	-8.5	19.8	0.0	0.0	100.0	0.0
Pembina, ND	38067	5,439	47.1	85.9	197	80.2	16.7	-11.2	17.2	0.0	7.8	0.0	9.3
Pierce, ND	38069	3,222	53.2	81.9	121	79.3	11.1	-16.8	11.6	100.0	0.0	0.0	28.1
Ramsey, ND	38071	7,819	42.1	86.4	466	97.9	21.0	-6.9	20.7	70.6	10.1	68.8	0.0
Ransom, ND	38073	3,959	51.1	87.3	96	89.6	17.7	-10.2	17.7	0.0	9.1	0.0	12.9
Renville, ND	38075	1,746	37.5	88.1	36	72.2	20.3	-7.6	18.9	0.0	63.6	0.0	0.0
Richland, ND	38077	10,514	39.3	87.1	1,628	97.6	22.4	-5.5	22.7	0.0	27.6	10.5	9.2
Rolette, ND	38079	7,751	45.1	82.1	465	87.5	16.5	-11.4	23.5	0.0	13.7	0.0	28.9
Sargent, ND	38081	2,812	52.3	88.4	123	95.1	15.0	-12.9	14.9	0.0	0.0	23.1	0.0
Sheridan, ND	38083	1,035	59.2	80.1	24	45.8	14.7	-13.2	14.6	0.0	33.3	0.0	0.0
Sioux, ND	38085	2,157	50.1	80.2	272	86.0	12.3	-15.6	16.2	0.0	10.8	0.0	62.5
Slope, ND	38087	523	38.1	91.4	18	100.0	28.1	0.2	28.4	0.0	0.0	0.0	0.0
Stark, ND	38089	15,451	44.0	87.3	1,915	92.6	23.1	-4.8	22.9	60.0	60.0	20.8	15.6
Steele, ND	38091	1,394	42.3	88.7	66	92.4	18.4	-9.5	18.3	0.0	0.0	0.0	0.0
Stutsman, ND	38093	14,360	49.4	85.7	1,517	39.9	22.7	-5.2	22.4	42.6	16.3	66.7	46.7
Towner, ND	38095	1,650	42.4	88.6	58	91.4	20.2	-7.7	20.1	100.0	0.0	100.0	0.0

Note. Data in columns 26 through 41 from the American Community Survey are subject to sampling error, which can be especially large in small counties and small population groups. See notes and definitions for more information.
[3]May be of any race.

Table C-1. Population, School, and Student Characteristics by County, Selected Years—*Continued*

County	State/ County Code	County Type[1]	Population, 2010		Percent of related children 5–17 years in poverty, 2010	Percent of children under 19 years with no health insurance, 2010	Number of schools and students, 2010–2011			Resident enrollment, 2006–2010 K–12 enrollment	
			Total	Percent 5–17 years			School districts	Schools	Students	Number	Percent public
			1	2	3	4	5	6	7	8	9
NORTH DAKOTA— *(Continued)*											
Traill, ND	38097	8	8,121	16.0	8.4	6.6	5	10	1,321	1,394	99.8
Walsh, ND	38099	6	11,119	16.1	14.0	7.3	8	15	1,804	1,878	97.2
Ward, ND	38101	5	61,675	15.7	14.4	5.3	10	34	9,234	9,484	91.3
Wells, ND	38103	9	4,207	13.2	11.9	8.1	4	6	576	523	96.9
Williams, ND	38105	7	22,398	16.2	10.8	5.2	7	19	3,462	3,508	91.5
OHIO	39000	X	11,536,504	17.4	20.8	6.3	1,091	3,758	1,754,191	2,048,897	87.0
Adams, OH	39001	6	28,550	18.3	30.9	8.0	2	9	4,971	5,158	93.3
Allen, OH	39003	3	106,331	17.6	27.2	6.4	14	38	15,341	18,893	87.0
Ashland, OH	39005	4	53,139	17.7	19.6	9.4	9	25	9,201	8,967	81.3
Ashtabula, OH	39007	4	101,497	17.4	24.2	7.0	9	34	15,094	18,667	91.7
Athens, OH	39009	4	64,757	11.7	24.6	7.8	7	21	7,443	7,738	97.8
Auglaize, OH	39011	4	45,949	18.7	11.7	7.2	7	18	7,907	8,851	94.6
Belmont, OH	39013	3	70,400	14.6	23.4	6.3	8	23	8,661	10,829	91.3
Brown, OH	39015	1	44,846	18.3	19.5	7.9	7	17	7,558	8,328	94.8
Butler, OH	39017	1	368,130	18.3	16.6	6.2	17	87	59,119	65,778	89.8
Carroll, OH	39019	2	28,836	17.3	23.2	8.6	3	11	3,583	5,031	91.1
Champaign, OH	39021	6	40,097	18.8	16.9	7.0	9	19	7,739	7,893	92.1
Clark, OH	39023	3	138,333	17.3	25.9	6.5	12	48	21,402	24,950	90.6
Clermont, OH	39025	1	197,363	18.8	13.2	5.9	11	46	27,683	36,912	85.3
Clinton, OH	39027	6	42,040	18.1	18.6	5.8	5	16	8,086	7,505	93.9
Columbiana, OH	39029	4	107,841	16.3	25.8	6.0	16	39	16,277	18,690	94.1
Coshocton, OH	39031	6	36,901	17.9	26.4	10.0	5	15	5,119	6,694	89.1
Crawford, OH	39033	4	43,784	17.3	23.0	6.9	6	19	6,834	8,077	89.8
Cuyahoga, OH	39035	1	1,280,122	16.8	25.9	5.3	103	363	179,993	228,342	80.3
Darke, OH	39037	6	52,959	18.3	15.9	8.3	9	22	8,613	9,791	91.8
Defiance, OH	39039	4	39,037	18.2	16.5	7.2	5	14	6,451	7,241	92.4
Delaware, OH	39041	1	174,214	21.5	5.8	4.1	6	41	26,159	34,123	84.8
Erie, OH	39043	3	77,079	16.8	20.3	7.0	9	27	12,244	13,380	91.1
Fairfield, OH	39045	1	146,156	19.9	13.6	5.9	12	49	24,977	28,322	88.0
Fayette, OH	39047	6	29,030	17.6	21.9	7.5	2	7	4,795	5,276	92.9
Franklin, OH	39049	1	1,163,414	16.8	23.1	5.8	99	387	192,848	195,230	89.1
Fulton, OH	39051	2	42,698	19.3	14.7	7.9	8	21	7,877	8,725	95.1
Gallia, OH	39053	6	30,934	17.4	28.3	7.4	4	14	4,528	5,546	96.1
Geauga, OH	39055	1	93,389	20.4	10.6	8.3	8	26	12,028	18,346	80.6
Greene, OH	39057	2	161,573	16.1	14.0	6.5	12	38	22,539	25,828	84.0
Guernsey, OH	39059	6	40,087	17.8	30.4	6.4	4	13	5,136	7,264	92.5
Hamilton, OH	39061	1	802,374	17.0	25.3	5.7	49	206	112,938	141,699	77.9
Hancock, OH	39063	4	74,782	17.2	15.4	6.8	12	41	14,178	12,933	90.7
Hardin, OH	39065	6	32,058	17.2	18.0	7.2	7	16	4,467	5,504	94.2
Harrison, OH	39067	6	15,864	16.0	24.7	7.8	1	3	1,575	2,552	93.4
Henry, OH	39069	6	28,215	18.7	15.7	7.4	5	15	4,523	5,411	87.7
Highland, OH	39071	6	43,589	18.8	25.2	9.5	5	19	7,647	8,319	94.5
Hocking, OH	39073	6	29,380	17.9	23.1	7.7	1	7	3,973	5,355	94.8
Holmes, OH	39075	7	42,366	24.7	25.9	16.8	2	16	4,362	8,445	66.6
Huron, OH	39077	4	59,626	19.5	19.4	8.2	8	33	11,557	11,843	91.4
Jackson, OH	39079	7	33,225	18.0	33.6	7.4	4	12	5,345	5,751	94.7
Jefferson, OH	39081	3	69,709	15.1	26.1	6.4	7	26	9,412	10,397	87.4
Knox, OH	39083	4	60,921	17.9	21.2	10.6	7	21	8,050	10,540	91.0
Lake, OH	39085	1	230,041	16.7	12.7	7.3	12	60	33,844	39,137	86.2
Lawrence, OH	39087	2	62,450	17.3	29.8	6.1	9	23	10,010	11,138	95.5
Licking, OH	39089	1	166,492	18.3	14.3	7.0	16	54	26,582	30,057	89.7
Logan, OH	39091	4	45,858	18.8	24.8	8.1	6	15	6,833	8,687	94.5
Lorain, OH	39093	1	301,356	17.9	20.1	5.8	28	98	46,149	54,604	86.2
Lucas, OH	39095	2	441,815	17.3	26.7	6.1	46	143	73,263	80,319	83.4
Madison, OH	39097	1	43,435	16.7	17.4	7.1	7	18	7,101	7,829	90.4
Mahoning, OH	39099	2	238,823	16.1	23.6	6.2	31	84	34,681	40,845	88.6

[1]County type codes are from the Economic Research Service of the United States Department of Agriculture. See notes and definitions for more information.

Table C-1. Population, School, and Student Characteristics by County, Selected Years—*Continued*

County	State/ County Code	Characteristics of students, 2010–2011				Number of graduates, 2008–2009	Staff and students, 2010–2011			
		Percent with IEP[2]	Percent eligible for free or reduced lunch	Percent minority	Percent English-language learners		Total staff	Number of teachers	Student/ teacher ratio	Central admin. staff
		10	11	12	13	14	15	16	17	18
NORTH DAKOTA— *(Continued)*										
Traill, ND	38097	13.0	26.7	8.9	2.3	128	223	125	10.6	9
Walsh, ND	38099	16.1	40.1	22.9	12.3	161	364	197	9.1	19
Ward, ND	38101	14.7	29.4	13.5	0.2	540	1,458	700	13.2	42
Wells, ND	38103	15.3	31.4	2.8	. . .	64	105	51	11.3	8
Williams, ND	38105	17.2	27.0	13.9	1.0	204	554	283	12.2	24
OHIO	39000	14.8	42.6	25.7	2.1	122,140	241,208	109,282	16.1	15,627
Adams, OH	39001	16.6	56.5	2.1	. . .	348	642	307	16.2	24
Allen, OH	39003	14.1	51.2	26.9	0.3	1,116	2,237	1,092	14.1	157
Ashland, OH	39005	15.0	41.4	4.7	0.2	720	1,230	623	14.8	54
Ashtabula, OH	39007	16.9	54.9	13.8	2.1	1,118	2,123	950	15.9	89
Athens, OH	39009	19.7	47.1	7.2	0.7	553	1,469	587	12.7	168
Auglaize, OH	39011	15.2	31.1	3.4	0.3	658	1,049	503	15.7	66
Belmont, OH	39013	15.3	45.4	6.8	0.1	651	1,163	593	14.6	66
Brown, OH	39015	14.9	51.5	3.3	. . .	547	1,025	451	16.8	55
Butler, OH	39017	13.2	37.8	22.1	3.7	3,856	6,845	3,250	18.2	306
Carroll, OH	39019	19.2	50.8	2.5	0.1	292	454	208	17.2	33
Champaign, OH	39021	16.5	39.9	7.2	0.1	468	1,062	503	15.4	86
Clark, OH	39023	13.4	50.8	20.4	1.3	1,546	2,844	1,312	16.3	154
Clermont, OH	39025	15.4	35.8	6.3	0.7	2,001	3,386	1,617	17.1	165
Clinton, OH	39027	13.6	45.1	8.5	0.3	530	1,046	457	17.7	97
Columbiana, OH	39029	16.1	48.6	6.2	0.1	1,258	2,083	1,048	15.5	143
Coshocton, OH	39031	20.8	51.6	4.5	0.2	449	739	347	14.7	53
Crawford, OH	39033	20.5	53.3	5.5	0.4	546	899	440	15.5	45
Cuyahoga, OH	39035	15.9	50.4	53.4	2.9	11,505	27,440	11,378	15.8	1,963
Darke, OH	39037	13.4	32.8	4.4	0.3	685	1,197	592	14.6	64
Defiance, OH	39039	17.7	41.7	17.5	0.2	512	918	461	14.0	63
Delaware, OH	39041	11.6	16.7	18.2	1.6	1,433	2,960	1,483	17.6	126
Erie, OH	39043	16.0	46.8	21.8	0.6	922	2,005	911	13.4	132
Fairfield, OH	39045	12.6	33.1	16.3	1.4	1,760	2,867	1,393	17.9	149
Fayette, OH	39047	16.4	50.1	7.8	0.4	305	562	276	17.4	27
Franklin, OH	39049	13.9	45.9	45.3	7.3	12,377	24,983	11,323	17.0	1,932
Fulton, OH	39051	14.0	36.5	14.0	0.9	683	1,728	588	13.4	96
Gallia, OH	39053	20.0	54.4	6.3	. . .	236	656	332	13.6	39
Geauga, OH	39055	13.6	18.7	4.9	0.7	1,013	1,754	735	16.4	114
Greene, OH	39057	14.0	30.3	18.6	1.4	1,685	2,954	1,408	16.0	159
Guernsey, OH	39059	20.1	57.8	6.6	0.1	364	930	387	13.3	68
Hamilton, OH	39061	16.2	43.3	47.5	2.6	7,212	15,204	6,493	17.4	1,059
Hancock, OH	39063	15.3	31.7	11.7	1.0	1,024	1,968	932	15.2	121
Hardin, OH	39065	14.7	42.4	4.5	0.8	306	684	317	14.1	43
Harrison, OH	39067	23.2	53.5	5.9	. . .	148	202	89	17.8	10
Henry, OH	39069	17.6	39.2	9.7	0.6	442	898	433	10.4	24
Highland, OH	39071	12.8	43.1	5.8	0.1	572	934	443	17.3	47
Hocking, OH	39073	16.7	58.6	2.7	. . .	303	525	226	17.6	37
Holmes, OH	39075	15.2	43.8	1.8	17.5	249	585	263	16.6	17
Huron, OH	39077	15.1	45.8	11.7	1.6	859	1,447	720	16.0	72
Jackson, OH	39079	16.4	60.8	2.6	. . .	384	695	343	15.6	32
Jefferson, OH	39081	16.5	57.5	14.2	. . .	706	1,592	828	11.4	78
Knox, OH	39083	16.0	43.5	6.3	0.4	594	1,261	610	13.2	69
Lake, OH	39085	12.6	31.0	14.4	4.3	2,626	4,469	2,043	16.6	253
Lawrence, OH	39087	16.2	48.1	5.5	. . .	690	1,455	686	14.6	60
Licking, OH	39089	14.1	37.0	12.4	1.5	1,758	3,386	1,641	16.2	209
Logan, OH	39091	16.5	42.6	10.5	0.5	548	1,164	584	11.7	80
Lorain, OH	39093	14.4	44.0	29.6	1.2	3,132	6,119	2,838	16.3	392
Lucas, OH	39095	13.0	43.9	36.5	1.0	4,028	8,950	4,141	17.7	743
Madison, OH	39097	13.4	35.2	6.4	1.0	513	1,030	457	15.5	54
Mahoning, OH	39099	16.0	49.1	31.8	1.2	2,468	5,087	2,320	14.9	374

[2]IEP=Individual Education Program. See notes and definitions for more information.
. . . = Not available.

Table C-1. Population, School, and Student Characteristics by County, Selected Years—*Continued*

County	State/ County Code	Revenues, 2008–2009				Current expenditures, 2008–2009			Resident population 16 to 19 years, 2006–2010			
			Percentage of revenue from									
		Total revenue ($1,000's)	Federal government	State government	Local government	Amount ($1,000's)	Amount per student	Percent for instruction	Total population 16 to 19 years	Percent enrolled in school	Percent high school graduates, not enrolled in school	Percent not enrolled, not grads, not employed, or not in labor force
		19	20	21	22	23	24	25	26	27	28	29
NORTH DAKOTA— *(Continued)*												
Traill, ND	38097	16,689	7.0	35.2	57.8	14,446	10,311	58.2	472	93.4	5.7	0.9
Walsh, ND	38099	25,380	13.4	41.6	45.0	22,121	11,420	60.4	492	79.7	12.0	1.8
Ward, ND	38101	105,832	18.8	33.4	47.8	83,884	9,806	60.8	3,766	74.5	16.5	4.2
Wells, ND	38103	7,832	12.5	32.6	54.9	6,726	11,759	54.2	227	84.6	11.5	3.1
Williams, ND	38105	41,479	14.7	36.6	48.7	34,313	11,001	62.1	1,123	83.2	10.7	4.3
OHIO	39000	23,550,502	6.9	46.2	46.9	19,031,702	10,490	56.2	669,425	86.1	8.6	3.6
Adams, OH	39001	82,999	6.2	67.8	26.0	49,608	9,870	58.3	1,495	73.9	18.7	2.5
Allen, OH	39003	198,576	7.6	47.6	44.8	155,983	9,608	56.7	7,136	87.4	8.7	2.7
Ashland, OH	39005	109,133	6.5	47.2	46.2	91,726	9,018	60.1	3,667	83.0	6.1	10.8
Ashtabula, OH	39007	223,224	6.9	60.9	32.3	158,411	9,741	57.7	5,465	83.4	11.1	4.2
Athens, OH	39009	120,439	10.7	49.2	40.2	96,052	11,831	52.8	9,280	93.7	5.1	0.9
Auglaize, OH	39011	129,701	3.6	60.7	35.7	79,374	9,497	60.5	2,794	87.2	12.5	0.3
Belmont, OH	39013	100,312	9.0	56.3	34.7	88,500	9,803	59.4	3,436	81.8	12.8	5.4
Brown, OH	39015	98,754	6.6	63.3	30.0	76,305	9,295	56.2	2,593	80.3	11.4	5.6
Butler, OH	39017	751,473	5.8	49.2	45.0	589,920	9,781	54.6	22,847	89.9	6.3	2.8
Carroll, OH	39019	35,889	8.4	53.5	38.1	31,411	8,013	56.9	1,415	77.1	18.1	2.9
Champaign, OH	39021	100,463	4.5	53.9	41.6	78,947	9,749	55.1	2,357	82.8	9.5	7.6
Clark, OH	39023	254,383	8.8	52.9	38.3	216,124	9,456	56.6	7,867	84.9	10.0	3.7
Clermont, OH	39025	308,888	5.0	42.1	52.9	264,108	9,197	56.1	10,441	83.6	11.2	3.4
Clinton, OH	39027	91,768	6.3	54.8	38.9	71,697	8,441	53.4	2,718	85.3	9.8	3.5
Columbiana, OH	39029	203,751	7.5	59.3	33.2	154,539	9,098	58.3	5,794	84.5	9.3	4.0
Coshocton, OH	39031	57,020	7.6	55.0	37.4	50,581	9,142	58.8	2,131	81.7	9.2	5.5
Crawford, OH	39033	95,546	6.5	59.0	34.4	66,315	8,824	57.6	2,461	86.0	9.5	2.7
Cuyahoga, OH	39035	2,865,060	7.9	42.0	50.1	2,361,984	12,722	56.5	73,705	86.0	7.6	5.0
Darke, OH	39037	117,506	5.0	57.3	37.8	79,705	8,708	58.5	3,005	84.6	10.8	3.9
Defiance, OH	39039	71,041	5.0	49.0	46.0	56,390	8,259	60.5	2,416	87.2	7.0	5.1
Delaware, OH	39041	297,577	2.7	22.0	75.4	247,317	10,077	57.9	8,526	91.5	6.3	1.1
Erie, OH	39043	194,436	6.5	35.7	57.8	167,953	12,936	54.7	4,283	82.4	12.2	3.8
Fairfield, OH	39045	302,680	3.8	46.8	49.4	222,943	8,834	57.0	8,276	84.0	11.5	2.1
Fayette, OH	39047	68,283	4.6	63.7	31.8	42,844	8,883	57.5	1,665	79.8	16.3	0.2
Franklin, OH	39049	2,584,480	8.0	39.0	53.0	2,145,624	11,262	55.0	64,778	86.9	8.3	3.1
Fulton, OH	39051	133,719	6.2	42.4	51.4	100,315	11,727	55.0	2,383	88.4	5.3	4.4
Gallia, OH	39053	92,205	7.9	60.6	31.5	55,015	11,371	57.6	1,712	91.9	6.5	1.6
Geauga, OH	39055	161,443	3.5	28.7	67.8	136,920	10,862	53.8	5,547	81.5	4.5	4.5
Greene, OH	39057	279,676	5.2	35.1	59.7	238,972	10,278	56.8	11,624	92.2	4.9	2.5
Guernsey, OH	39059	65,491	9.6	53.0	37.4	58,051	10,019	53.4	2,107	85.4	7.8	4.5
Hamilton, OH	39061	1,672,618	8.0	39.5	52.5	1,335,092	11,565	54.3	48,634	85.5	9.1	3.9
Hancock, OH	39063	165,071	6.0	44.9	49.2	141,198	9,573	58.1	4,474	90.8	7.3	0.5
Hardin, OH	39065	53,604	6.3	56.0	37.7	42,874	9,082	58.9	3,076	92.1	4.3	3.2
Harrison, OH	39067	19,241	8.6	64.3	27.1	17,561	9,447	57.7	759	81.2	9.1	4.4
Henry, OH	39069	74,246	4.2	50.2	45.6	58,212	11,659	59.1	1,498	90.7	9.0	0.0
Highland, OH	39071	85,936	5.7	64.1	30.2	65,612	8,160	57.8	2,585	82.5	8.8	4.9
Hocking, OH	39073	60,835	5.6	68.0	26.4	36,337	8,826	54.0	1,639	80.7	15.3	4.0
Holmes, OH	39075	44,091	9.5	43.7	46.8	39,005	8,693	60.8	2,822	48.9	9.1	9.3
Huron, OH	39077	118,311	6.6	54.0	39.4	106,913	8,582	59.3	3,275	79.2	13.2	6.2
Jackson, OH	39079	58,766	8.5	61.7	29.8	50,993	9,093	57.8	1,769	73.3	20.9	5.5
Jefferson, OH	39081	123,654	8.5	48.4	43.1	103,086	10,158	51.3	4,138	90.6	5.0	3.4
Knox, OH	39083	97,944	7.2	49.4	43.4	88,082	10,170	59.5	4,271	88.7	4.7	3.9
Lake, OH	39085	432,808	4.6	36.1	59.3	369,063	10,748	56.0	11,948	89.4	7.8	1.1
Lawrence, OH	39087	143,333	7.9	67.6	24.5	109,938	10,318	57.0	3,347	84.2	10.5	3.7
Licking, OH	39089	316,529	5.2	41.7	53.1	257,422	9,412	54.7	9,244	86.5	9.9	2.5
Logan, OH	39091	94,880	6.0	44.3	49.6	78,949	10,774	57.6	2,572	81.8	13.5	3.0
Lorain, OH	39093	581,576	7.1	48.7	44.2	459,716	9,520	57.1	16,645	87.2	8.6	3.2
Lucas, OH	39095	988,803	8.6	53.9	37.5	791,326	10,778	54.1	27,281	85.1	8.3	5.3
Madison, OH	39097	93,922	4.3	40.7	55.0	73,234	10,007	55.7	2,417	83.3	11.9	4.5
Mahoning, OH	39099	485,300	9.8	53.1	37.1	382,017	10,386	54.0	13,148	87.0	8.4	3.8

Note. Data in columns 26 through 41 from the American Community Survey are subject to sampling error, which can be especially large in small counties and small population groups. See notes and definitions for more information.

Table C-1. Population, School, and Student Characteristics by County, Selected Years—*Continued*

County	State/ County Code	High school graduates, 2006–2010			College enrollment, 2006–2010		College graduates, 2006–2010 (percent)						
		Population 25 years and over	High school diploma or less (percent)	High school diploma or more (percent)	Number	Percent public	Bachelor's degree or more	+/- U.S. percent with Bachelor's degree or more	Non-Hispanic White	Black or African American	American Indian and Alaska Native	Asian, Hawaiian, and Pacific Islander	Hispanic or Latino[3]
		30	31	32	33	34	35	36	37	38	39	40	41
NORTH DAKOTA— *(Continued)*													
Traill, ND	38097	5,547	41.5	88.0	568	97.5	26.3	-1.6	26.5	25.0	30.9	53.3	4.7
Walsh, ND	38099	7,993	51.4	81.4	219	78.1	15.8	-12.1	16.1	0.0	40.9	0.0	3.3
Ward, ND	38101	36,926	36.5	92.3	4,741	92.7	25.8	-2.1	25.8	19.3	23.5	25.9	21.5
Wells, ND	38103	3,292	50.5	83.1	103	59.2	19.6	-8.3	19.4	0.0	31.4	0.0	0.0
Williams, ND	38105	14,363	42.7	87.9	695	90.6	19.3	-8.6	19.7	0.0	10.1	20.9	23.6
OHIO	39000	7,655,994	48.4	87.4	810,275	74.5	24.1	-3.8	24.9	14.6	16.2	61.4	16.8
Adams, OH	39001	19,088	71.5	74.7	918	87.7	10.7	-17.2	10.4	24.6	0.0	0.0	32.4
Allen, OH	39003	69,224	54.9	87.2	8,082	68.9	15.8	-12.1	16.6	9.3	0.7	44.6	12.1
Ashland, OH	39005	34,775	58.4	85.6	3,956	33.2	17.5	-10.4	17.1	28.7	0.0	55.6	43.1
Ashtabula, OH	39007	69,327	61.8	84.2	4,816	76.5	13.0	-14.9	13.0	7.0	6.5	72.3	7.8
Athens, OH	39009	33,138	47.7	86.8	20,589	97.4	27.3	-0.6	25.1	44.0	0.0	89.5	56.7
Auglaize, OH	39011	30,640	56.8	90.4	1,754	79.9	15.5	-12.4	15.4	9.6	5.7	70.5	1.4
Belmont, OH	39013	50,549	58.1	86.8	3,051	80.5	14.1	-13.8	14.4	4.9	21.9	29.4	15.2
Brown, OH	39015	29,912	67.8	80.0	2,070	79.0	9.8	-18.1	9.8	10.8	0.0	0.0	7.1
Butler, OH	39017	230,847	48.0	86.8	31,570	88.5	25.9	-2.0	25.6	22.7	14.1	50.4	24.3
Carroll, OH	39019	20,164	66.1	83.3	949	64.5	12.1	-15.8	11.8	25.9	0.0	51.1	29.8
Champaign, OH	39021	26,542	59.7	88.4	1,883	60.9	15.3	-12.6	15.1	13.8	0.0	39.8	13.0
Clark, OH	39023	93,541	54.3	84.8	8,140	57.8	16.2	-11.7	16.5	12.3	16.2	55.4	11.0
Clermont, OH	39025	128,470	48.6	87.2	9,565	82.1	24.8	-3.1	24.5	28.4	33.5	49.2	24.9
Clinton, OH	39027	27,651	58.4	86.3	2,455	54.3	14.7	-13.2	14.7	11.4	25.0	40.5	3.5
Columbiana, OH	39029	75,907	61.8	85.3	4,547	83.5	12.4	-15.5	12.6	4.9	0.0	44.9	3.2
Coshocton, OH	39031	24,883	64.8	85.0	1,310	75.0	11.6	-16.3	11.7	11.1	0.0	0.0	13.2
Crawford, OH	39033	30,606	63.1	85.8	1,792	79.1	10.5	-17.4	10.2	25.5	31.3	38.8	16.1
Cuyahoga, OH	39035	881,312	43.8	86.4	88,284	63.6	28.2	0.3	33.5	13.2	21.0	64.0	15.4
Darke, OH	39037	35,588	62.2	85.6	2,029	75.4	11.3	-16.6	11.2	7.0	35.3	58.2	7.2
Defiance, OH	39039	25,893	57.4	87.8	2,399	61.3	16.3	-11.6	16.6	11.8	9.9	24.2	13.4
Delaware, OH	39041	107,421	25.1	95.6	9,644	52.3	49.5	21.6	48.9	46.6	5.7	76.1	32.1
Erie, OH	39043	54,004	51.9	89.0	3,251	74.9	20.1	-7.8	20.7	11.1	1.9	38.7	19.8
Fairfield, OH	39045	94,413	46.0	91.6	7,402	79.0	24.4	-3.5	23.6	34.0	16.3	53.0	29.2
Fayette, OH	39047	19,374	65.4	82.2	961	79.5	13.1	-14.8	13.3	5.8	0.0	25.0	5.2
Franklin, OH	39049	732,714	38.2	88.9	111,977	79.3	35.1	7.2	38.8	17.8	14.0	64.7	17.4
Fulton, OH	39051	28,265	55.1	88.3	2,101	83.1	14.9	-13.0	15.1	56.6	15.7	61.5	7.8
Gallia, OH	39053	20,687	62.8	80.8	1,920	66.7	14.3	-13.6	14.7	1.5	0.0	38.1	0.0
Geauga, OH	39055	62,437	38.0	89.8	3,893	70.4	34.0	6.1	33.9	27.1	44.1	65.8	27.0
Greene, OH	39057	101,427	36.4	91.7	22,793	73.1	34.6	6.7	32.9	38.5	68.1	73.6	32.9
Guernsey, OH	39059	27,242	62.7	84.3	1,412	71.9	11.2	-16.7	11.1	3.0	42.4	48.9	20.5
Hamilton, OH	39061	526,827	40.5	87.7	65,148	71.2	32.5	4.6	37.3	14.5	21.9	68.4	27.1
Hancock, OH	39063	49,182	47.1	90.7	5,452	52.6	24.4	-3.5	24.9	8.1	20.8	36.2	12.2
Hardin, OH	39065	19,450	64.8	86.2	4,186	21.2	15.2	-12.7	15.0	0.0	25.9	48.0	12.9
Harrison, OH	39067	11,207	67.4	83.6	661	87.9	9.1	-18.8	9.4	0.0	0.0	0.0	0.0
Henry, OH	39069	19,040	58.2	87.6	1,494	77.2	13.1	-14.8	13.5	3.3	34.4	27.8	4.1
Highland, OH	39071	28,839	65.4	80.0	1,494	87.3	9.7	-18.2	9.5	2.3	3.9	100.0	100.0
Hocking, OH	39073	19,907	62.7	84.0	1,339	86.7	10.2	-17.7	10.1	6.4	0.0	76.9	0.0
Holmes, OH	39075	23,393	77.4	56.3	814	72.5	9.4	-18.5	9.4	0.0	0.0	13.6	20.8
Huron, OH	39077	39,177	63.5	86.4	2,387	77.8	12.1	-15.8	12.3	8.7	18.3	38.0	4.1
Jackson, OH	39079	22,209	63.5	79.4	1,224	82.3	12.0	-15.9	12.1	0.0	0.0	58.8	0.0
Jefferson, OH	39081	49,348	57.4	87.3	4,611	49.5	14.1	-13.8	13.9	10.6	0.0	37.6	33.8
Knox, OH	39083	38,342	56.0	87.5	4,932	31.9	19.0	-8.9	19.0	23.2	0.0	27.2	7.5
Lake, OH	39085	160,406	44.6	90.7	13,307	73.1	24.3	-3.6	24.5	13.0	7.4	56.3	9.6
Lawrence, OH	39087	42,872	61.0	82.0	2,791	92.4	12.9	-15.0	13.0	6.8	0.0	45.0	31.8
Licking, OH	39089	108,213	50.5	88.2	10,935	60.0	22.1	-5.8	21.9	27.6	15.1	40.2	21.5
Logan, OH	39091	30,679	60.8	85.9	1,647	74.5	14.3	-13.6	14.3	7.5	2.2	26.5	41.8
Lorain, OH	39093	201,559	48.2	88.5	18,782	70.6	20.6	-7.3	22.1	9.2	14.5	44.5	11.0
Lucas, OH	39095	288,265	46.0	87.1	36,853	83.8	23.1	-4.8	25.4	11.2	7.4	62.4	11.3
Madison, OH	39097	29,362	58.1	84.4	1,732	71.3	15.7	-12.2	16.4	3.7	0.0	42.1	13.2
Mahoning, OH	39099	168,490	53.3	87.4	14,638	84.4	20.4	-7.5	22.4	8.1	10.0	65.0	8.9

Note. Data in columns 26 through 41 from the American Community Survey are subject to sampling error, which can be especially large in small counties and small population groups. See notes and definitions for more information.

[3]May be of any race.

Table C-1. Population, School, and Student Characteristics by County, Selected Years—*Continued*

County	State/ County Code	County Type[1]	Population, 2010		Percent of related children 5–17 years in poverty, 2010	Percent of children under 19 years with no health insurance, 2010	Number of schools and students, 2010–2011			Resident enrollment, 2006–2010 K–12 enrollment	
			Total	Percent 5–17 years			School districts	Schools	Students	Number	Percent public
			1	2	3	4	5	6	7	8	9
OHIO—*(Continued)*											
Marion, OH	39101	4	66,501	16.3	22.1	6.4	13	29	11,795	11,475	93.5
Medina, OH	39103	1	172,332	19.4	9.1	6.2	8	45	28,143	33,800	87.6
Meigs, OH	39105	6	23,770	17.0	30.0	7.4	3	8	3,500	3,952	92.4
Mercer, OH	39107	7	40,814	19.3	11.9	7.6	7	21	8,281	8,028	92.1
Miami, OH	39109	2	102,506	18.0	16.8	6.7	10	38	15,476	18,572	88.6
Monroe, OH	39111	8	14,642	16.0	26.3	7.4	1	10	2,561	2,370	93.8
Montgomery, OH	39113	2	535,153	16.8	24.5	5.8	48	166	78,072	92,945	85.7
Morgan, OH	39115	6	15,054	17.5	27.1	7.8	1	5	2,136	2,809	95.9
Morrow, OH	39117	1	34,827	19.5	20.0	8.2	6	17	5,327	6,693	85.8
Muskingum, OH	39119	4	86,074	17.9	24.9	6.8	11	36	15,101	15,444	94.7
Noble, OH	39121	6	14,645	14.0	21.5	7.4	2	4	1,736	1,690	99.5
Ottawa, OH	39123	2	41,428	15.8	14.7	7.0	7	19	5,503	6,777	92.0
Paulding, OH	39125	6	19,614	18.2	18.4	7.3	5	13	3,575	3,619	94.8
Perry, OH	39127	6	36,058	19.5	27.7	7.4	6	15	6,272	6,791	90.4
Pickaway, OH	39129	1	55,698	17.8	17.1	6.3	5	22	9,560	10,588	93.3
Pike, OH	39131	7	28,709	18.3	33.3	6.6	5	14	4,850	5,508	96.3
Portage, OH	39133	2	161,419	15.8	14.7	5.7	16	58	23,550	26,125	92.7
Preble, OH	39135	2	42,270	18.1	17.8	7.4	7	17	6,608	7,752	94.4
Putnam, OH	39137	6	34,499	19.2	10.6	6.6	9	21	5,591	6,921	88.1
Richland, OH	39139	3	124,475	16.5	21.9	7.3	19	46	16,374	22,163	86.2
Ross, OH	39141	4	78,064	16.6	24.9	7.2	9	27	11,413	13,524	96.8
Sandusky, OH	39143	4	60,944	18.1	16.3	6.7	6	22	8,667	11,197	87.6
Scioto, OH	39145	4	79,499	16.6	29.1	6.5	14	32	12,482	13,540	92.5
Seneca, OH	39147	4	56,745	17.3	19.7	6.6	10	21	5,937	10,302	89.1
Shelby, OH	39149	4	49,423	20.2	15.6	7.1	9	22	8,817	10,239	90.6
Stark, OH	39151	2	375,586	17.1	20.7	6.1	25	113	58,907	66,246	89.5
Summit, OH	39153	2	541,781	17.0	19.4	5.8	35	155	77,660	96,112	84.6
Trumbull, OH	39155	2	210,312	16.6	28.8	6.1	28	74	30,805	36,365	91.9
Tuscarawas, OH	39157	4	92,582	17.6	20.6	7.7	12	43	15,916	16,416	91.8
Union, OH	39159	1	52,300	20.3	8.7	6.2	3	14	7,717	10,511	93.7
Van Wert, OH	39161	6	28,744	18.3	17.3	7.6	6	16	4,890	5,466	88.7
Vinton, OH	39163	9	13,435	18.8	33.2	7.5	1	5	2,386	2,636	100.0
Warren, OH	39165	1	212,693	20.8	6.4	4.7	11	48	36,069	42,586	86.3
Washington, OH	39167	3	61,778	15.7	20.2	7.2	7	24	8,516	10,064	91.9
Wayne, OH	39169	4	114,520	18.6	18.8	9.6	13	46	15,953	20,536	83.8
Williams, OH	39171	7	37,642	17.7	17.5	7.5	7	18	5,941	7,025	92.7
Wood, OH	39173	2	125,488	16.3	12.8	5.2	12	48	17,888	20,232	89.3
Wyandot, OH	39175	7	22,615	18.0	13.2	7.5	3	9	3,520	4,138	96.3
OKLAHOMA	40000	X	3,751,351	17.7	22.5	10.5	578	1,785	659,828	659,071	92.5
Adair, OK	40001	6	22,683	20.8	35.7	9.6	11	17	4,781	4,736	97.2
Alfalfa, OK	40003	9	5,642	13.0	20.8	16.5	4	8	837	776	97.4
Atoka, OK	40005	7	14,182	17.1	30.9	14.2	8	12	2,375	2,525	95.6
Beaver, OK	40007	9	5,636	19.3	16.2	18.1	4	8	1,104	1,022	98.5
Beckham, OK	40009	7	22,119	16.5	24.1	11.5	5	13	3,774	3,825	93.9
Blaine, OK	40011	6	11,943	14.7	24.2	10.9	4	11	1,893	2,248	98.1
Bryan, OK	40013	6	42,416	16.7	24.9	11.5	9	23	7,334	6,898	94.1
Caddo, OK	40015	6	29,600	18.4	27.3	14.5	12	30	6,102	5,364	96.6
Canadian, OK	40017	1	115,541	19.5	12.7	8.4	10	37	20,143	21,357	94.5
Carter, OK	40019	5	47,557	18.7	25.1	10.7	10	28	9,251	8,990	92.7
Cherokee, OK	40021	6	46,987	17.5	28.2	12.3	12	18	7,603	7,668	94.6
Choctaw, OK	40023	7	15,205	17.2	36.7	10.8	7	13	2,718	2,831	98.5
Cimarron, OK	40025	9	2,475	17.7	26.4	23.9	3	6	433	436	94.3
Cleveland, OK	40027	1	255,755	16.6	15.6	7.8	7	68	42,370	41,015	91.8
Coal, OK	40029	9	5,925	18.9	29.3	13.9	3	6	1,242	1,069	93.9
Comanche, OK	40031	3	124,098	17.5	24.0	9.9	11	55	22,300	21,740	95.0
Cotton, OK	40033	6	6,193	18.1	21.6	12.0	3	7	1,156	1,082	89.8
Craig, OK	40035	6	15,029	17.0	22.6	12.5	5	14	3,982	2,523	97.4
Creek, OK	40037	2	69,967	18.6	21.0	10.9	16	40	13,174	13,105	94.6
Custer, OK	40039	7	27,469	16.3	20.3	12.5	4	15	4,807	4,460	92.9

[1]County type codes are from the Economic Research Service of the United States Department of Agriculture. See notes and definitions for more information.

Table C-1. Population, School, and Student Characteristics by County, Selected Years—*Continued*

County	State/ County Code	Characteristics of students, 2010–2011				Number of graduates, 2008–2009	Staff and students, 2010–2011			
		Percent with IEP[2]	Percent eligible for free or reduced lunch	Percent minority	Percent English-language learners		Total staff	Number of teachers	Student/ teacher ratio	Central admin. staff
		10	11	12	13	14	15	16	17	18
OHIO—*(Continued)*										
Marion, OH	39101	17.7	42.6	12.9	0.6	821	1,512	749	15.8	89
Medina, OH	39103	12.3	20.8	6.0	0.4	2,113	3,457	1,550	18.2	179
Meigs, OH	39105	14.6	55.0	3.1	0.1	261	471	225	15.6	24
Mercer, OH	39107	14.4	24.2	3.4	0.3	737	1,138	548	15.1	68
Miami, OH	39109	13.1	35.4	9.5	0.9	1,237	2,189	1,032	15.0	129
Monroe, OH	39111	21.5	53.4	2.0	. . .	195	354	188	13.6	19
Montgomery, OH	39113	15.1	48.6	37.6	1.8	5,149	10,889	4,841	16.1	691
Morgan, OH	39115	13.8	57.0	10.7	. . .	161	278	140	15.2	11
Morrow, OH	39117	16.7	41.7	4.1	0.2	407	685	342	15.6	34
Muskingum, OH	39119	16.9	53.3	11.0	0.1	1,176	2,145	948	15.9	157
Noble, OH	39121	15.7	47.7	0.5	0.2	160	254	113	15.4	17
Ottawa, OH	39123	16.2	36.1	10.7	0.1	466	897	357	15.4	44
Paulding, OH	39125	19.0	44.9	6.6	0.1	269	569	265	13.5	38
Perry, OH	39127	16.2	51.9	1.8	. . .	458	1,115	426	14.7	79
Pickaway, OH	39129	14.0	42.5	4.9	0.2	722	1,244	565	16.9	50
Pike, OH	39131	14.9	57.2	3.8	. . .	357	723	314	15.5	53
Portage, OH	39133	14.2	35.3	10.4	0.3	1,857	3,480	1,544	15.3	231
Preble, OH	39135	11.4	40.3	2.9	0.3	481	908	423	15.6	64
Putnam, OH	39137	14.2	24.6	10.7	1.2	542	786	397	14.1	57
Richland, OH	39139	15.8	53.6	17.5	0.3	1,174	2,545	1,209	13.5	149
Ross, OH	39141	12.5	46.4	8.7	. . .	784	1,656	821	13.9	109
Sandusky, OH	39143	15.3	49.2	21.4	3.1	632	1,138	578	15.0	61
Scioto, OH	39145	15.5	59.9	5.5	. . .	872	1,738	858	14.5	100
Seneca, OH	39147	16.3	39.5	10.0	0.2	450	1,060	442	13.4	110
Shelby, OH	39149	15.9	36.4	8.0	1.1	660	1,180	512	17.2	86
Stark, OH	39151	14.4	45.1	18.4	0.7	4,588	7,866	3,437	17.1	491
Summit, OH	39153	14.7	41.2	29.5	1.8	5,603	11,547	4,919	15.8	810
Trumbull, OH	39155	14.1	50.4	17.5	0.3	2,306	4,340	2,004	15.4	248
Tuscarawas, OH	39157	17.2	42.9	5.4	0.8	1,095	2,233	1,050	15.2	191
Union, OH	39159	15.5	24.5	9.0	0.2	570	960	448	17.2	49
Van Wert, OH	39161	17.8	38.0	6.8	0.2	381	721	374	13.1	35
Vinton, OH	39163	17.6	68.2	1.0	. . .	168	319	166	14.4	15
Warren, OH	39165	12.0	16.1	13.5	1.6	2,372	4,449	1,997	18.1	241
Washington, OH	39167	16.9	46.5	3.5	. . .	682	1,097	542	15.7	64
Wayne, OH	39169	14.2	40.7	7.3	2.1	1,237	2,289	1,095	14.6	110
Williams, OH	39171	16.4	30.7	6.9	0.7	495	816	411	14.5	61
Wood, OH	39173	13.2	35.0	14.5	0.5	1,499	2,843	1,278	14.0	179
Wyandot, OH	39175	15.7	34.5	7.2	0.9	304	419	214	16.5	24
OKLAHOMA	40000	14.7	60.5	45.4	6.3	37,219	82,260	41,277	16.0	3,612
Adair, OK	40001	18.5	77.2	75.9	17.0	263	719	342	14.0	26
Alfalfa, OK	40003	19.7	58.5	11.4	. . .	65	150	73	11.5	9
Atoka, OK	40005	19.1	73.9	51.3	. . .	168	349	171	13.9	17
Beaver, OK	40007	13.2	58.2	33.2	14.9	79	186	96	11.5	11
Beckham, OK	40009	12.7	53.9	24.7	3.7	188	432	245	15.4	20
Blaine, OK	40011	16.3	73.5	42.1	4.7	141	264	131	14.5	16
Bryan, OK	40013	18.0	69.9	44.5	2.3	416	966	474	15.5	41
Caddo, OK	40015	15.6	74.4	55.9	1.6	337	845	414	14.7	45
Canadian, OK	40017	12.9	39.6	27.4	3.9	1,292	2,237	1,140	17.7	89
Carter, OK	40019	15.9	66.0	42.1	4.1	523	1,158	578	16.0	61
Cherokee, OK	40021	16.4	74.5	72.8	6.9	418	976	487	15.6	35
Choctaw, OK	40023	20.9	78.5	51.8	0.1	187	381	174	15.6	25
Cimarron, OK	40025	14.1	65.3	34.4	12.9	31	86	42	10.3	4
Cleveland, OK	40027	15.1	46.4	34.2	3.4	2,366	4,783	2,542	16.7	225
Coal, OK	40029	27.0	73.2	51.4	0.2	77	195	97	12.9	8
Comanche, OK	40031	15.4	56.8	50.1	3.4	1,319	3,081	1,462	15.3	132
Cotton, OK	40033	16.8	56.3	30.1	0.3	85	162	87	13.3	7
Craig, OK	40035	14.5	58.4	48.1	. . .	225	417	207	19.2	23
Creek, OK	40037	15.8	63.3	34.6	1.3	732	1,571	802	16.4	72
Custer, OK	40039	11.9	62.0	40.6	11.0	262	650	316	15.2	28

[2]IEP=Individual Education Program. See notes and definitions for more information.
. . . = Not available.

Table C-1. Population, School, and Student Characteristics by County, Selected Years—*Continued*

County	State/ County Code	Revenues, 2008–2009				Current expenditures, 2008–2009			Resident population 16 to 19 years, 2006–2010			
		Total revenue ($1,000's)	Percentage of revenue from			Amount ($1,000's)	Amount per student	Percent for instruction	Total population 16 to 19 years	Percent enrolled in school	Percent high school graduates, not enrolled in school	Percent not enrolled, not grads, not employed, or not in labor force
			Federal government	State government	Local government							
		19	20	21	22	23	24	25	26	27	28	29
OHIO—*(Continued)*												
Marion, OH	39101	135,443	8.4	56.7	35.0	112,311	9,111	60.5	3,654	74.3	14.7	9.6
Medina, OH	39103	320,693	3.4	37.3	59.2	272,844	9,345	58.1	9,118	89.0	8.5	2.1
Meigs, OH	39105	39,191	13.5	63.7	22.9	34,243	9,465	55.9	1,239	78.4	9.4	12.2
Mercer, OH	39107	96,134	6.4	47.6	46.0	85,627	9,790	64.2	2,510	86.7	8.8	2.5
Miami, OH	39109	207,391	4.9	42.6	52.6	169,821	10,262	59.7	5,732	84.9	13.4	1.0
Monroe, OH	39111	27,102	10.6	57.2	32.2	24,537	9,316	58.5	773	83.4	10.0	3.1
Montgomery, OH	39113	1,117,847	7.3	49.0	43.7	880,619	10,987	55.5	30,169	85.5	7.8	5.2
Morgan, OH	39115	38,229	6.4	77.3	16.3	20,296	9,370	57.4	816	88.7	7.0	3.8
Morrow, OH	39117	76,070	5.1	63.9	30.9	49,598	8,636	58.2	2,010	74.0	18.9	4.7
Muskingum, OH	39119	213,332	7.9	59.4	32.8	159,892	10,028	54.4	4,836	83.8	11.8	2.6
Noble, OH	39121	18,754	7.9	57.8	34.3	16,319	7,914	54.6	543	70.9	9.8	19.3
Ottawa, OH	39123	72,406	4.2	37.6	58.1	63,346	10,663	58.2	1,960	88.6	8.9	0.5
Paulding, OH	39125	49,984	7.1	48.1	44.8	42,447	10,994	54.1	1,001	84.8	12.2	0.2
Perry, OH	39127	72,134	9.7	62.0	28.3	66,612	10,081	53.4	1,950	80.2	11.9	5.3
Pickaway, OH	39129	133,397	5.1	58.8	36.1	92,495	9,172	56.4	3,337	91.0	5.8	2.6
Pike, OH	39131	69,029	11.0	61.7	27.2	61,011	11,232	50.3	1,658	83.5	11.5	3.9
Portage, OH	39133	290,202	4.6	43.7	51.7	244,610	9,744	58.2	11,923	91.4	6.7	1.9
Preble, OH	39135	77,214	4.7	44.2	51.1	64,696	9,195	55.0	2,264	86.9	8.0	2.8
Putnam, OH	39137	79,585	4.9	54.3	40.8	56,047	9,346	59.8	1,998	91.6	7.6	0.8
Richland, OH	39139	243,476	7.6	49.7	42.7	200,269	11,543	53.8	6,949	80.6	9.9	5.5
Ross, OH	39141	148,286	8.0	55.5	36.5	128,074	10,632	60.1	3,769	75.0	17.5	6.6
Sandusky, OH	39143	121,429	5.7	56.8	37.5	86,783	9,601	62.0	3,380	83.4	14.1	1.8
Scioto, OH	39145	167,538	10.6	62.5	26.9	132,736	10,183	53.8	4,624	89.2	7.8	2.6
Seneca, OH	39147	77,796	6.5	42.2	51.3	63,125	10,449	53.7	3,719	90.4	8.0	1.2
Shelby, OH	39149	111,362	4.5	53.3	42.2	83,920	9,129	55.7	2,731	87.4	6.3	4.1
Stark, OH	39151	689,986	7.0	49.9	43.1	580,512	9,454	57.6	21,944	86.8	8.8	3.2
Summit, OH	39153	1,021,594	7.1	44.4	48.4	858,049	10,705	58.1	29,700	87.9	8.3	3.0
Trumbull, OH	39155	446,187	6.4	56.5	37.1	334,673	10,161	54.9	11,235	83.1	10.5	4.8
Tuscarawas, OH	39157	183,411	6.5	51.1	42.4	149,916	9,112	57.4	4,821	80.3	11.2	5.1
Union, OH	39159	93,476	3.6	44.2	52.2	72,102	9,253	57.1	2,444	86.0	11.5	0.9
Van Wert, OH	39161	71,213	4.5	48.5	47.0	51,387	9,907	62.4	1,726	91.3	7.4	1.0
Vinton, OH	39163	26,813	12.3	68.1	19.5	24,186	9,651	49.6	846	83.5	8.4	6.2
Warren, OH	39165	411,162	2.7	37.2	60.1	347,321	9,487	55.2	10,689	85.3	9.2	3.0
Washington, OH	39167	99,050	8.3	47.3	44.3	84,453	8,983	56.7	3,321	88.6	7.1	1.8
Wayne, OH	39169	218,010	5.8	46.8	47.4	171,843	10,025	57.0	6,996	77.0	9.7	6.2
Williams, OH	39171	73,952	4.6	49.5	45.9	55,889	8,592	61.2	1,913	83.1	12.0	3.8
Wood, OH	39173	267,854	4.0	37.5	58.5	219,402	11,396	58.9	10,460	96.3	3.3	0.4
Wyandot, OH	39175	36,386	5.2	46.5	48.3	29,427	8,152	58.8	1,201	84.2	14.0	1.5
OKLAHOMA	40000	6,029,807	12.8	50.0	37.2	5,082,185	7,885	55.8	214,973	81.7	10.6	4.6
Adair, OK	40001	45,741	24.0	62.6	13.4	42,314	8,691	55.7	1,421	70.4	18.9	8.9
Alfalfa, OK	40003	9,375	7.8	47.2	45.1	8,623	10,364	57.4	186	74.2	4.8	1.6
Atoka, OK	40005	50,549	10.4	46.2	43.4	28,882	12,343	50.4	768	77.5	21.1	1.4
Beaver, OK	40007	13,068	7.0	45.6	47.4	12,472	11,267	52.7	334	71.6	20.4	3.6
Beckham, OK	40009	39,517	9.5	47.7	42.8	30,875	8,053	56.3	1,459	74.3	8.3	9.9
Blaine, OK	40011	20,258	18.6	52.9	28.5	18,674	10,040	56.0	655	92.7	2.6	3.4
Bryan, OK	40013	64,197	17.0	59.7	23.3	59,008	8,340	56.2	2,366	84.5	4.4	6.4
Caddo, OK	40015	66,127	20.6	53.5	25.9	55,098	9,369	55.7	1,862	86.9	5.4	5.0
Canadian, OK	40017	191,091	8.8	48.1	43.1	153,481	7,094	56.2	5,977	85.4	8.7	2.4
Carter, OK	40019	84,549	13.1	53.2	33.8	74,777	8,151	56.0	2,598	76.8	13.4	6.3
Cherokee, OK	40021	70,215	22.2	58.8	18.9	63,293	8,392	57.0	3,721	82.6	7.7	7.3
Choctaw, OK	40023	25,273	21.2	62.1	16.6	22,690	8,460	55.8	776	74.7	3.7	16.4
Cimarron, OK	40025	5,747	8.3	49.4	42.3	5,465	12,421	53.8	122	56.6	24.6	0.0
Cleveland, OK	40027	349,504	7.6	48.6	43.8	290,720	7,146	59.0	16,541	87.5	7.6	2.7
Coal, OK	40029	14,279	17.7	52.2	30.2	12,949	10,196	53.9	249	76.3	14.9	8.8
Comanche, OK	40031	184,479	18.5	58.7	22.9	169,264	7,750	55.6	8,132	69.2	25.3	3.0
Cotton, OK	40033	10,523	17.0	61.8	21.2	9,812	8,049	58.7	280	85.4	3.6	0.0
Craig, OK	40035	27,166	13.9	57.2	28.9	25,616	8,358	59.1	783	80.0	11.0	8.8
Creek, OK	40037	127,771	11.2	54.5	34.3	102,690	7,858	55.9	3,903	85.8	9.5	3.1
Custer, OK	40039	41,420	11.3	54.2	34.5	36,291	7,615	56.3	1,891	89.7	9.1	1.2

Note. Data in columns 26 through 41 from the American Community Survey are subject to sampling error, which can be especially large in small counties and small population groups. See notes and definitions for more information.

Table C-1. Population, School, and Student Characteristics by County, Selected Years—*Continued*

County	State/ County Code	High school graduates, 2006–2010			College enrollment, 2006–2010		College graduates, 2006–2010 (percent)						
		Population 25 years and over	High school diploma or less (percent)	High school diploma or more (percent)	Number	Percent public	Bachelor's degree or more	+/- U.S. percent with Bachelor's degree or more	Non-Hispanic White	Black or African American	American Indian and Alaska Native	Asian, Hawaiian, and Pacific Islander	Hispanic or Latino[3]
		30	31	32	33	34	35	36	37	38	39	40	41
OHIO—*(Continued)*													
Marion, OH	39101	45,697	61.6	83.0	2,709	80.1	12.0	-15.9	12.5	2.7	1.6	68.7	4.1
Medina, OH	39103	114,384	40.9	92.5	9,063	75.7	29.5	1.6	29.6	22.7	9.9	53.6	21.8
Meigs, OH	39105	16,408	65.4	82.2	881	70.0	10.3	-17.6	10.2	14.3	0.0	33.3	9.6
Mercer, OH	39107	26,828	58.6	88.3	1,860	76.2	15.4	-12.5	15.6	0.0	12.8	6.8	10.7
Miami, OH	39109	69,543	51.6	87.5	4,496	76.5	20.0	-7.9	19.7	14.2	57.1	43.5	23.9
Monroe, OH	39111	10,546	65.9	85.5	656	92.5	9.2	-18.7	9.4	0.0	0.0	0.0	0.0
Montgomery, OH	39113	361,642	42.6	87.7	46,237	67.1	24.3	-3.6	25.4	16.7	26.8	54.6	28.0
Morgan, OH	39115	10,383	63.3	83.0	628	75.6	8.7	-19.2	9.1	0.0	0.0	0.0	0.0
Morrow, OH	39117	23,153	60.4	86.3	1,249	81.2	13.6	-14.3	14.1	15.9	11.6	16.1	0.0
Muskingum, OH	39119	57,225	59.1	86.5	5,332	66.7	14.2	-13.7	14.3	10.0	36.3	27.1	10.8
Noble, OH	39121	10,905	69.2	80.3	583	85.6	9.1	-18.8	9.9	0.0	0.0	0.0	0.0
Ottawa, OH	39123	29,989	46.7	89.8	1,749	71.7	18.9	-9.0	19.4	13.7	0.0	38.8	3.9
Paulding, OH	39125	13,184	63.1	86.1	800	76.4	10.7	-17.2	10.5	12.0	0.0	46.0	18.3
Perry, OH	39127	23,472	67.4	84.2	1,551	82.1	8.9	-19.0	8.6	10.6	0.0	95.2	9.8
Pickaway, OH	39129	37,248	63.7	82.9	2,096	76.8	13.5	-14.4	13.8	6.8	0.0	8.8	8.0
Pike, OH	39131	18,972	66.7	77.4	1,236	87.5	12.6	-15.3	12.4	10.8	15.1	100.0	0.0
Portage, OH	39133	100,830	49.2	90.4	20,828	89.5	24.9	-3.0	24.2	24.9	3.1	70.6	30.1
Preble, OH	39135	28,755	60.1	85.6	1,895	76.6	12.0	-15.9	11.9	0.0	15.2	64.9	12.9
Putnam, OH	39137	22,496	55.4	90.9	1,615	74.6	18.1	-9.8	18.7	0.0	18.4	71.4	1.3
Richland, OH	39139	86,399	57.6	84.3	5,981	72.4	14.9	-13.0	15.5	6.8	2.5	52.8	11.7
Ross, OH	39141	53,806	62.6	82.4	3,861	83.5	13.1	-14.8	13.3	7.2	6.2	56.8	18.3
Sandusky, OH	39143	41,362	56.3	87.4	2,840	75.1	13.1	-14.8	13.8	5.2	0.0	55.1	6.5
Scioto, OH	39145	53,292	59.1	81.2	4,449	90.6	12.7	-15.2	12.8	4.5	31.6	26.5	20.9
Seneca, OH	39147	37,411	56.3	87.5	4,364	40.6	16.1	-11.8	16.7	1.1	9.1	33.6	6.1
Shelby, OH	39149	31,910	60.8	85.5	2,359	78.6	14.0	-13.9	13.9	4.6	0.0	47.2	9.0
Stark, OH	39151	255,874	52.8	87.8	24,218	67.4	20.4	-7.5	20.8	10.7	20.6	64.5	16.3
Summit, OH	39153	368,126	43.2	89.5	36,281	85.3	29.2	1.3	30.8	15.4	8.8	49.1	27.5
Trumbull, OH	39155	147,798	58.9	86.5	9,691	83.4	16.3	-11.6	16.7	8.5	28.9	54.0	15.0
Tuscarawas, OH	39157	63,191	64.9	84.5	3,778	78.5	14.3	-13.6	14.1	12.3	0.0	64.1	17.9
Union, OH	39159	33,134	47.3	90.3	2,230	79.6	27.4	-0.5	26.8	19.6	64.6	65.1	5.8
Van Wert, OH	39161	19,539	60.3	89.9	1,056	75.3	14.1	-13.8	14.0	0.0	42.9	30.8	15.0
Vinton, OH	39163	9,030	69.7	76.3	528	86.6	9.2	-18.7	9.3	0.0	0.0	6.9	0.0
Warren, OH	39165	136,044	37.4	90.8	9,862	76.6	35.9	8.0	34.7	24.2	58.4	76.9	36.1
Washington, OH	39167	43,186	56.4	88.0	4,159	66.3	16.0	-11.9	16.1	0.0	0.0	25.2	22.5
Wayne, OH	39169	73,642	58.7	84.7	6,244	57.1	19.1	-8.8	19.1	8.1	0.0	60.3	16.1
Williams, OH	39171	25,896	59.9	88.7	1,396	79.4	12.9	-15.0	12.5	0.0	11.8	72.3	15.0
Wood, OH	39173	76,468	42.0	92.2	20,486	92.5	29.3	1.4	29.1	33.8	28.4	65.7	18.2
Wyandot, OH	39175	15,418	59.9	87.6	1,088	67.3	13.4	-14.5	13.5	0.0	0.0	9.6	11.2
OKLAHOMA	40000	2,380,819	47.2	85.4	241,981	81.9	22.6	-5.3	24.6	16.7	15.1	40.2	9.5
Adair, OK	40001	14,055	65.0	76.5	765	80.7	10.6	-17.3	13.1	0.0	6.4	19.1	2.7
Alfalfa, OK	40003	4,296	54.0	81.7	111	79.3	17.9	-10.0	20.5	0.0	2.6	0.0	0.0
Atoka, OK	40005	9,694	64.6	77.3	426	84.3	14.5	-13.4	16.2	4.1	11.4	29.8	8.1
Beaver, OK	40007	3,814	53.5	83.6	117	81.2	17.9	-10.0	20.0	0.0	5.6	100.0	2.9
Beckham, OK	40009	13,707	56.0	80.3	678	92.2	14.7	-13.2	16.3	7.0	3.9	35.1	3.8
Blaine, OK	40011	8,310	56.0	81.1	400	75.0	15.9	-12.0	19.5	15.1	3.9	8.5	4.4
Bryan, OK	40013	26,723	50.7	84.1	3,536	74.6	20.3	-7.6	20.3	30.7	23.7	17.7	13.4
Caddo, OK	40015	18,814	59.5	81.0	1,394	65.9	13.8	-14.1	15.4	6.0	12.5	20.2	4.6
Canadian, OK	40017	71,643	38.5	90.8	6,091	86.7	25.3	-2.6	26.5	13.2	16.0	31.7	7.3
Carter, OK	40019	31,139	59.0	83.2	1,603	68.9	16.4	-11.5	17.4	8.9	14.3	39.5	4.8
Cherokee, OK	40021	28,143	47.1	83.9	5,253	85.3	23.8	-4.1	26.5	37.9	19.3	13.8	16.8
Choctaw, OK	40023	10,163	64.7	76.5	409	87.0	11.5	-16.4	12.7	4.8	11.7	84.2	0.0
Cimarron, OK	40025	1,694	57.4	79.3	71	66.2	16.9	-11.0	19.7	0.0	0.0	0.0	0.0
Cleveland, OK	40027	152,417	36.0	90.4	33,240	92.9	31.2	3.3	31.2	36.2	23.5	48.1	21.9
Coal, OK	40029	3,845	68.7	78.5	103	92.2	9.1	-18.8	9.3	0.0	13.6	0.0	0.0
Comanche, OK	40031	72,905	47.1	88.5	8,377	88.2	19.8	-8.1	22.1	15.9	12.7	17.7	16.2
Cotton, OK	40033	4,253	57.2	82.5	277	89.9	18.6	-9.3	21.0	0.0	10.4	0.0	2.4
Craig, OK	40035	10,338	59.0	80.5	589	87.9	13.5	-14.4	14.2	5.5	14.0	8.6	13.6
Creek, OK	40037	46,115	56.3	83.5	3,145	81.5	14.9	-13.0	15.6	12.1	12.2	11.0	8.5
Custer, OK	40039	15,704	45.8	84.4	3,480	97.1	25.0	-2.9	29.2	2.1	17.1	25.0	5.1

Note. Data in columns 26 through 41 from the American Community Survey are subject to sampling error, which can be especially large in small counties and small population groups. See notes and definitions for more information.
[3]May be of any race.

Table C-1. Population, School, and Student Characteristics by County, Selected Years—*Continued*

County	State/ County Code	County Type[1]	Population, 2010		Percent of related children 5–17 years in poverty, 2010	Percent of children under 19 years with no health insurance, 2010	Number of schools and students, 2010–2011			Resident enrollment, 2006–2010 K–12 enrollment	
			Total	Percent 5–17 years			School districts	Schools	Students	Number	Percent public
			1	2	3	4	5	6	7	8	9
OKLAHOMA—*(Continued)*											
Delaware, OK	40041	6	41,487	16.7	31.5	12.5	10	19	6,798	7,148	95.6
Dewey, OK	40043	9	4,810	19.1	18.5	20.0	4	9	1,023	830	100.0
Ellis, OK	40045	9	4,151	18.5	19.2	14.8	4	8	845	745	96.8
Garfield, OK	40047	5	60,580	17.1	23.8	10.9	10	32	10,388	10,333	90.0
Garvin, OK	40049	6	27,576	17.7	22.5	13.4	8	21	5,354	5,195	98.6
Grady, OK	40051	1	52,431	18.3	20.4	9.5	13	33	9,167	9,923	94.0
Grant, OK	40053	9	4,527	16.9	17.2	15.9	4	8	764	829	95.8
Greer, OK	40055	7	6,239	14.6	26.4	11.8	3	6	975	810	98.9
Harmon, OK	40057	9	2,922	17.7	36.5	18.5	1	3	547	443	99.3
Harper, OK	40059	9	3,685	17.2	17.4	20.0	2	4	752	676	100.0
Haskell, OK	40061	6	12,769	18.4	27.9	13.2	6	10	2,397	2,205	98.4
Hughes, OK	40063	7	14,003	16.5	28.0	13.5	7	13	2,358	2,266	98.9
Jackson, OK	40065	5	26,446	18.5	23.3	10.1	7	19	5,179	4,982	95.6
Jefferson, OK	40067	8	6,472	17.3	30.6	17.1	4	9	1,197	1,136	93.1
Johnston, OK	40069	7	10,957	17.3	32.6	13.4	8	19	4,648	1,812	99.5
Kay, OK	40071	5	46,562	18.1	24.5	10.1	8	23	8,376	8,656	91.7
Kingfisher, OK	40073	6	15,034	19.1	15.3	14.3	7	15	3,328	2,981	95.2
Kiowa, OK	40075	6	9,446	17.6	29.5	11.7	4	10	1,676	1,671	96.5
Latimer, OK	40077	7	11,154	17.9	24.1	11.7	4	7	1,505	1,997	92.8
Le Flore, OK	40079	2	50,384	17.9	28.0	13.3	19	40	10,129	9,219	97.0
Lincoln, OK	40081	1	34,273	18.9	20.8	11.7	8	22	5,687	6,681	95.2
Logan, OK	40083	1	41,848	18.4	17.0	11.4	4	13	4,528	7,821	89.6
Love, OK	40085	9	9,423	17.8	21.5	14.0	4	8	1,705	1,648	98.3
McClain, OK	40087	1	34,506	19.6	14.4	12.4	8	22	7,092	6,541	96.1
McCurtain, OK	40089	7	33,151	19.0	31.8	11.3	14	30	6,938	6,470	95.3
McIntosh, OK	40091	6	20,252	15.7	28.6	13.3	5	11	3,582	3,192	96.1
Major, OK	40093	9	7,527	16.7	16.9	17.8	3	5	997	1,253	92.3
Marshall, OK	40095	6	15,840	17.2	26.1	17.3	2	6	2,972	2,654	98.3
Mayes, OK	40097	6	41,259	18.5	24.8	12.4	9	24	7,475	7,421	98.3
Murray, OK	40099	7	13,488	17.0	20.7	11.6	3	9	2,606	2,401	95.3
Muskogee, OK	40101	4	70,990	17.8	28.7	10.5	16	41	13,887	13,006	96.6
Noble, OK	40103	6	11,561	17.6	19.9	10.3	4	10	2,185	1,952	98.8
Nowata, OK	40105	6	10,536	18.3	21.5	11.8	3	8	1,972	2,088	98.4
Okfuskee, OK	40107	6	12,191	17.0	29.8	12.3	6	14	2,235	2,158	97.1
Oklahoma, OK	40109	1	718,633	17.5	25.2	9.7	20	211	119,980	123,336	90.4
Okmulgee, OK	40111	2	40,069	18.0	25.5	10.1	10	23	7,129	7,124	97.6
Osage, OK	40113	2	47,472	18.2	19.6	11.4	11	22	3,659	9,148	92.6
Ottawa, OK	40115	6	31,848	17.6	29.4	11.7	8	21	6,080	5,708	95.0
Pawnee, OK	40117	2	16,577	18.3	21.4	13.6	4	11	3,173	3,152	92.6
Payne, OK	40119	4	77,350	13.1	19.6	10.7	8	28	10,474	9,959	92.8
Pittsburg, OK	40121	5	45,837	15.8	23.1	11.7	15	33	8,140	7,551	90.3
Pontotoc, OK	40123	7	37,492	16.5	21.7	10.3	9	24	7,011	5,851	97.9
Pottawatomie, OK	40125	4	69,442	18.1	24.5	9.0	16	37	13,155	12,510	94.5
Pushmataha, OK	40127	9	11,572	16.2	35.2	13.3	7	13	2,248	2,001	94.8
Roger Mills, OK	40129	9	3,647	18.1	18.5	18.5	4	8	787	610	98.7
Rogers, OK	40131	2	86,905	19.8	11.8	9.8	10	32	14,179	17,478	90.2
Seminole, OK	40133	7	25,482	19.1	32.0	11.5	10	23	5,048	4,841	95.8
Sequoyah, OK	40135	2	42,391	19.1	28.2	10.5	11	25	8,634	8,242	96.5
Stephens, OK	40137	4	45,048	17.5	22.3	10.5	9	24	8,321	7,572	93.0
Texas, OK	40139	7	20,640	20.0	16.4	15.0	10	24	4,423	3,974	94.6
Tillman, OK	40141	6	7,992	18.5	32.1	12.0	5	11	1,624	1,453	98.1
Tulsa, OK	40143	2	603,403	18.2	21.8	10.1	18	188	115,202	106,759	88.0
Wagoner, OK	40145	2	73,085	19.6	15.5	11.1	4	18	6,738	13,838	92.2
Washington, OK	40147	4	50,976	17.0	19.0	10.1	5	19	8,188	8,627	94.3
Washita, OK	40149	7	11,629	18.9	21.7	11.3	5	9	2,148	2,136	95.3
Woods, OK	40151	7	8,878	12.8	20.9	10.6	4	9	1,204	1,050	96.9
Woodward, OK	40153	7	20,081	17.0	20.0	13.7	5	12	3,637	3,338	91.0

[1]County type codes are from the Economic Research Service of the United States Department of Agriculture. See notes and definitions for more information.

Table C-1. Population, School, and Student Characteristics by County, Selected Years—*Continued*

County	State/ County Code	Characteristics of students, 2010–2011				Number of graduates, 2008–2009	Staff and students, 2010–2011			
		Percent with IEP[2]	Percent eligible for free or reduced lunch	Percent minority	Percent English-language learners		Total staff	Number of teachers	Student/ teacher ratio	Central admin. staff
		10	11	12	13	14	15	16	17	18
OKLAHOMA—*(Continued)*										
Delaware, OK	40041	16.8	72.0	57.5	3.6	451	908	448	15.2	40
Dewey, OK	40043	15.6	50.6	17.7	2.1	69	183	93	11.0	15
Ellis, OK	40045	13.4	58.7	13.5	0.4	50	136	70	12.0	10
Garfield, OK	40047	13.1	66.2	31.5	8.1	571	1,308	660	15.7	61
Garvin, OK	40049	18.2	63.1	35.3	3.5	307	675	356	15.1	26
Grady, OK	40051	14.2	51.0	22.2	1.4	453	1,073	556	16.5	48
Grant, OK	40053	15.2	52.6	16.5	. . .	69	148	78	9.7	10
Greer, OK	40055	15.6	62.3	24.9	4.2	62	126	71	13.7	8
Harmon, OK	40057	19.9	83.0	47.9	15.0	48	80	43	12.7	3
Harper, OK	40059	14.0	59.2	30.1	10.1	46	109	55	13.7	6
Haskell, OK	40061	22.6	74.6	39.8	1.0	127	302	155	15.5	14
Hughes, OK	40063	20.4	75.4	45.7	. . .	160	357	177	13.3	22
Jackson, OK	40065	11.5	58.6	47.1	6.2	291	662	365	14.2	29
Jefferson, OK	40067	20.1	72.6	31.5	. . .	81	185	95	12.6	14
Johnston, OK	40069	13.6	72.1	42.0	1.2	125	576	299	15.6	25
Kay, OK	40071	17.0	67.9	35.6	3.8	470	1,141	528	15.9	57
Kingfisher, OK	40073	13.9	60.9	34.0	6.3	229	421	232	14.4	15
Kiowa, OK	40075	14.9	69.2	33.9	1.3	124	255	126	13.4	16
Latimer, OK	40077	18.3	65.9	41.3	0.6	93	221	112	13.4	11
Le Flore, OK	40079	15.9	73.4	45.8	5.7	645	1,273	688	14.7	63
Lincoln, OK	40081	14.6	61.0	27.2	. . .	357	664	365	15.6	39
Logan, OK	40083	14.3	64.8	29.9	3.1	294	517	289	15.7	27
Love, OK	40085	15.6	70.6	41.1	12.1	95	229	108	15.8	16
McClain, OK	40087	13.6	44.1	30.0	4.5	481	770	421	16.8	26
McCurtain, OK	40089	15.4	77.7	48.3	2.3	468	978	499	13.9	43
McIntosh, OK	40091	16.4	77.9	45.1	0.1	201	413	207	17.3	19
Major, OK	40093	18.4	60.0	20.3	10.2	84	143	73	13.6	9
Marshall, OK	40095	14.4	80.3	57.7	12.8	141	347	181	16.4	17
Mayes, OK	40097	16.3	68.8	55.5	1.6	461	935	490	15.3	32
Murray, OK	40099	17.0	53.1	35.5	. . .	141	262	154	16.9	11
Muskogee, OK	40101	16.3	67.4	59.5	2.4	792	1,734	864	16.1	81
Noble, OK	40103	15.9	60.5	31.4	0.7	146	337	161	13.6	19
Nowata, OK	40105	12.8	64.7	47.7	. . .	142	268	139	14.2	13
Okfuskee, OK	40107	20.0	72.0	53.1	0.9	111	293	148	15.1	16
Oklahoma, OK	40109	13.0	62.5	56.7	13.7	6,100	13,645	7,111	16.9	445
Okmulgee, OK	40111	16.9	71.7	52.7	0.5	442	932	460	15.5	45
Osage, OK	40113	17.8	59.4	50.2	2.6	180	528	257	14.2	29
Ottawa, OK	40115	15.1	72.1	48.7	5.0	352	748	381	16.0	35
Pawnee, OK	40117	16.8	69.4	33.3	0.8	200	397	206	15.4	19
Payne, OK	40119	15.7	50.3	28.5	2.7	637	1,399	654	16.0	71
Pittsburg, OK	40121	17.4	68.3	47.5	0.7	487	1,075	535	15.2	55
Pontotoc, OK	40123	17.0	62.5	47.7	2.1	410	993	491	14.3	41
Pottawatomie, OK	40125	14.4	64.3	38.1	1.9	801	1,615	852	15.4	69
Pushmataha, OK	40127	21.3	77.6	40.8	. . .	129	333	170	13.3	20
Roger Mills, OK	40129	12.1	49.5	18.8	0.6	33	162	82	9.6	13
Rogers, OK	40131	16.0	47.1	41.6	2.2	861	1,730	887	16.0	73
Seminole, OK	40133	16.9	75.3	48.1	0.6	298	689	345	14.7	36
Sequoyah, OK	40135	19.1	75.0	53.5	3.0	499	1,081	580	14.9	39
Stephens, OK	40137	13.2	54.4	25.9	3.1	533	1,008	496	16.8	46
Texas, OK	40139	12.5	68.5	62.8	30.5	190	619	312	14.2	33
Tillman, OK	40141	17.1	78.7	50.9	11.2	114	246	126	12.9	13
Tulsa, OK	40143	13.4	56.5	49.6	8.7	6,048	14,499	6,702	17.2	651
Wagoner, OK	40145	17.4	53.5	44.4	1.2	407	863	431	15.6	34
Washington, OK	40147	13.2	51.7	34.3	4.2	560	1,103	528	15.5	48
Washita, OK	40149	14.6	68.9	26.2	2.6	126	283	154	13.9	10
Woods, OK	40151	14.8	46.3	15.0	0.2	80	217	104	11.6	13
Woodward, OK	40153	12.9	59.3	21.0	7.8	173	464	231	15.7	19

[2]IEP=Individual Education Program. See notes and definitions for more information.
. . . = Not available.

Table C-1. Population, School, and Student Characteristics by County, Selected Years—*Continued*

County	State/ County Code	Revenues, 2008–2009				Current expenditures, 2008–2009			Resident population 16 to 19 years, 2006–2010			
		Total revenue ($1,000's)	Percentage of revenue from			Amount ($1,000's)	Amount per student	Percent for instruction	Total population 16 to 19 years	Percent enrolled in school	Percent high school graduates, not enrolled in school	Percent not enrolled, not grads, not employed, or not in labor force
			Federal government	State government	Local government							
		19	20	21	22	23	24	25	26	27	28	29
OKLAHOMA— *(Continued)*												
Delaware, OK	40041	78,565	14.4	46.0	39.6	61,304	8,883	54.8	2,236	78.6	11.8	6.3
Dewey, OK	40043	11,640	8.4	56.1	35.5	11,323	11,578	54.1	207	98.6	1.5	0.0
Ellis, OK	40045	9,495	7.9	55.4	36.7	8,347	10,460	50.2	205	91.7	4.9	0.0
Garfield, OK	40047	92,225	10.1	53.3	36.6	76,424	7,618	57.7	3,444	78.1	7.1	6.9
Garvin, OK	40049	46,880	15.4	56.6	28.0	42,474	7,999	58.2	1,506	85.7	8.2	5.2
Grady, OK	40051	60,489	11.2	59.1	29.7	55,413	7,147	58.9	3,095	80.3	12.3	4.9
Grant, OK	40053	10,375	10.1	40.2	49.7	9,653	11,588	57.2	257	86.8	3.1	3.1
Greer, OK	40055	8,819	12.1	66.3	21.6	8,666	9,084	58.2	148	77.7	2.7	19.6
Harmon, OK	40057	5,172	12.3	67.7	20.0	5,060	9,370	63.8	143	92.3	0.0	7.7
Harper, OK	40059	7,503	8.6	45.7	45.7	6,873	9,428	54.9	240	99.6	0.4	0.0
Haskell, OK	40061	20,217	15.9	63.7	20.4	18,511	7,958	59.6	623	80.7	7.4	3.5
Hughes, OK	40063	26,411	17.5	49.8	32.7	21,545	9,053	54.4	710	74.9	9.7	11.0
Jackson, OK	40065	45,675	15.8	62.5	21.7	41,297	7,919	60.1	1,533	73.9	13.8	10.4
Jefferson, OK	40067	11,792	12.3	67.3	20.5	11,398	9,578	58.0	332	75.9	13.0	7.2
Johnston, OK	40069	17,533	18.4	57.5	24.1	16,642	8,764	57.6	667	93.6	3.5	3.0
Kay, OK	40071	81,836	11.7	49.2	39.1	71,005	8,270	52.3	2,825	86.6	7.9	2.8
Kingfisher, OK	40073	32,132	11.2	46.6	42.2	27,366	8,366	55.6	877	81.3	14.9	3.3
Kiowa, OK	40075	15,705	13.7	58.5	27.8	15,191	8,968	56.3	613	72.8	8.8	17.6
Latimer, OK	40077	16,686	15.6	59.6	24.8	16,227	9,358	51.2	864	85.1	10.9	2.8
Le Flore, OK	40079	86,095	18.1	62.2	19.7	79,097	7,889	59.5	2,938	78.7	15.2	4.4
Lincoln, OK	40081	46,374	14.9	59.4	25.8	43,672	7,768	56.5	2,170	77.4	16.8	5.5
Logan, OK	40083	37,192	12.5	55.8	31.7	33,993	7,489	56.3	2,607	87.1	7.1	4.3
Love, OK	40085	14,509	14.8	59.0	26.3	12,665	7,775	55.8	482	95.0	5.0	0.0
McClain, OK	40087	69,605	8.2	55.0	36.8	57,067	7,086	59.9	1,610	80.8	15.1	1.3
McCurtain, OK	40089	64,372	18.1	62.3	19.7	60,769	8,515	55.3	1,887	79.8	12.0	4.6
McIntosh, OK	40091	27,500	20.3	54.7	25.0	24,173	8,018	56.4	1,133	76.9	10.3	11.8
Major, OK	40093	15,339	9.1	49.7	41.2	10,757	10,434	55.8	355	74.9	12.7	1.4
Marshall, OK	40095	24,111	16.8	55.1	28.2	21,511	7,564	57.0	909	76.7	18.5	3.5
Mayes, OK	40097	61,834	15.4	58.0	26.7	56,470	7,625	57.6	2,421	78.5	11.8	6.9
Murray, OK	40099	17,488	14.1	62.5	23.4	16,106	6,960	58.9	562	74.6	24.6	0.9
Muskogee, OK	40101	133,277	13.9	51.6	34.5	113,984	8,132	55.4	3,600	79.6	13.9	3.6
Noble, OK	40103	20,720	11.7	43.0	45.2	18,673	8,523	55.4	602	85.4	5.3	4.3
Nowata, OK	40105	17,478	12.2	62.9	25.0	15,694	7,644	59.0	505	84.6	4.6	0.0
Okfuskee, OK	40107	19,646	18.7	61.3	20.0	18,892	8,920	55.7	543	77.4	12.7	7.7
Oklahoma, OK	40109	1,116,497	12.3	41.7	46.0	885,558	7,705	54.9	38,106	81.3	9.5	5.2
Okmulgee, OK	40111	66,024	16.9	61.5	21.5	57,542	8,046	56.5	2,275	80.5	15.1	1.4
Osage, OK	40113	34,173	14.6	59.0	26.4	31,458	8,851	56.3	2,843	85.0	11.7	1.8
Ottawa, OK	40115	50,775	16.4	62.5	21.1	46,850	7,793	59.2	2,166	79.2	13.7	4.3
Pawnee, OK	40117	27,105	14.4	61.3	24.3	24,893	8,064	56.2	860	79.4	17.1	3.5
Payne, OK	40119	100,458	9.3	46.5	44.2	79,823	7,800	55.8	6,957	91.5	4.1	1.3
Pittsburg, OK	40121	69,577	16.6	55.7	27.8	65,446	8,104	56.6	2,430	84.3	6.4	5.7
Pontotoc, OK	40123	68,558	15.2	57.3	27.4	59,947	8,704	59.5	2,277	85.0	9.5	4.9
Pottawatomie, OK	40125	117,614	15.3	58.9	25.8	102,918	7,767	57.3	4,232	80.9	12.9	3.7
Pushmataha, OK	40127	21,869	18.8	65.9	15.3	20,527	9,131	57.1	602	81.4	6.3	10.1
Roger Mills, OK	40129	15,997	9.1	40.2	50.7	12,028	16,123	45.8	194	79.9	11.3	8.8
Rogers, OK	40131	113,781	10.2	52.3	37.5	100,423	6,969	57.5	5,189	85.4	10.4	2.4
Seminole, OK	40133	45,178	17.4	60.1	22.5	41,901	8,166	55.9	1,540	82.5	5.8	8.5
Sequoyah, OK	40135	73,430	17.8	64.8	17.4	68,114	7,631	57.3	2,416	80.8	16.0	2.6
Stephens, OK	40137	74,058	11.0	54.4	34.5	63,603	7,773	55.8	2,315	82.1	12.3	1.9
Texas, OK	40139	36,569	12.1	55.3	32.6	35,169	8,716	54.0	1,213	86.9	2.6	9.5
Tillman, OK	40141	36,960	9.3	52.7	37.9	22,361	14,090	50.9	549	74.9	14.0	10.0
Tulsa, OK	40143	1,067,234	11.1	41.9	47.0	863,559	7,727	53.5	32,882	80.4	10.7	5.6
Wagoner, OK	40145	52,836	13.5	60.9	25.6	46,328	6,868	59.5	4,075	82.1	11.5	3.9
Washington, OK	40147	76,639	9.6	51.8	38.6	63,479	7,758	57.0	2,822	82.0	10.4	1.7
Washita, OK	40149	19,719	11.5	58.7	29.8	18,181	8,230	55.8	597	73.7	13.9	4.0
Woods, OK	40151	13,115	7.9	44.1	48.0	12,366	9,729	53.1	665	80.8	16.2	3.0
Woodward, OK	40153	36,102	8.1	48.7	43.2	28,475	7,851	54.2	895	72.7	17.8	7.2

Note. Data in columns 26 through 41 from the American Community Survey are subject to sampling error, which can be especially large in small counties and small population groups. See notes and definitions for more information.

Table C-1. Population, School, and Student Characteristics by County, Selected Years—*Continued*

County	State/County Code	High school graduates, 2006–2010			College enrollment, 2006–2010		College graduates, 2006–2010 (percent)						
		Population 25 years and over	High school diploma or less (percent)	High school diploma or more (percent)	Number	Percent public	Bachelor's degree or more	+/- U.S. percent with Bachelor's degree or more	Non-Hispanic White	Black or African American	American Indian and Alaska Native	Asian, Hawaiian, and Pacific Islander	Hispanic or Latino[3]
		30	31	32	33	34	35	36	37	38	39	40	41
OKLAHOMA— *(Continued)*													
Delaware, OK	40041	28,695	60.5	82.1	804	75.6	14.3	-13.6	15.7	0.0	10.7	5.1	3.5
Dewey, OK	40043	3,333	60.3	84.8	120	87.5	19.2	-8.7	20.2	22.6	16.3	0.0	0.0
Ellis, OK	40045	2,881	50.6	87.8	78	96.2	23.3	-4.6	23.7	0.0	0.0	0.0	19.8
Garfield, OK	40047	38,865	51.1	85.6	2,618	80.3	21.8	-6.1	22.9	16.7	18.4	26.7	7.8
Garvin, OK	40049	18,723	64.6	80.5	756	47.0	15.4	-12.5	15.1	14.4	22.6	100.0	0.0
Grady, OK	40051	33,677	52.8	85.3	2,512	88.8	16.8	-11.1	17.3	5.2	17.9	11.9	9.8
Grant, OK	40053	3,212	47.0	90.0	215	90.2	20.8	-7.1	21.6	0.0	6.5	0.0	4.8
Greer, OK	40055	4,395	63.7	77.2	102	89.2	13.0	-14.9	16.9	0.0	2.7	0.0	0.3
Harmon, OK	40057	1,990	57.4	71.6	48	60.4	15.5	-12.4	20.8	0.0	5.1	0.0	2.1
Harper, OK	40059	2,467	57.8	84.1	136	64.7	17.2	-10.7	18.1	0.0	0.0	50.0	0.0
Haskell, OK	40061	8,439	61.7	75.9	437	89.0	13.4	-14.5	13.8	10.9	11.2	15.3	25.2
Hughes, OK	40063	9,468	62.5	75.8	408	92.6	11.8	-16.1	13.6	0.0	7.4	0.0	0.4
Jackson, OK	40065	16,448	45.7	82.0	1,432	86.5	21.2	-6.7	25.2	6.9	32.9	26.1	8.2
Jefferson, OK	40067	4,425	67.5	75.8	104	90.4	11.2	-16.7	11.1	0.0	17.4	100.0	3.3
Johnston, OK	40069	6,840	49.8	81.2	1,561	90.8	19.0	-8.9	18.5	31.3	23.3	0.0	4.3
Kay, OK	40071	30,650	50.5	85.7	2,113	94.5	19.9	-8.0	21.6	7.2	10.7	35.7	7.1
Kingfisher, OK	40073	9,662	50.7	83.2	635	84.6	17.1	-10.8	18.5	0.0	6.2	32.3	8.9
Kiowa, OK	40075	6,492	57.4	84.4	277	68.6	16.4	-11.5	17.8	1.0	20.7	32.0	0.5
Latimer, OK	40077	7,101	53.6	81.3	730	98.2	13.8	-14.1	14.8	0.0	13.4	0.0	0.0
Le Flore, OK	40079	32,777	59.3	79.1	1,844	93.1	11.5	-16.4	12.2	12.7	10.1	19.6	4.0
Lincoln, OK	40081	22,304	57.7	85.3	972	84.3	13.7	-14.2	14.1	5.0	14.8	41.8	1.0
Logan, OK	40083	25,978	45.5	87.2	2,639	89.9	23.2	-4.7	23.2	26.0	21.0	44.3	19.1
Love, OK	40085	6,371	65.5	78.3	237	64.6	13.9	-14.0	13.4	22.5	21.7	100.0	0.0
McClain, OK	40087	22,014	49.3	87.8	1,373	90.3	17.9	-10.0	18.2	0.0	20.7	11.1	7.6
McCurtain, OK	40089	21,731	62.4	78.9	949	86.0	12.4	-15.5	13.5	8.9	8.0	64.7	6.0
McIntosh, OK	40091	14,341	62.4	77.1	746	77.2	11.1	-16.8	12.2	11.8	8.1	0.0	0.0
Major, OK	40093	5,254	56.3	85.9	144	100.0	16.4	-11.5	17.7	0.0	0.0	0.0	2.9
Marshall, OK	40095	10,649	61.9	79.6	456	96.9	15.9	-12.0	17.0	0.0	8.6	0.0	7.2
Mayes, OK	40097	27,071	57.5	83.4	1,248	87.9	11.9	-16.0	12.8	2.3	8.9	40.5	11.0
Murray, OK	40099	9,142	57.6	79.8	372	73.1	13.4	-14.5	13.9	6.3	10.0	0.0	10.6
Muskogee, OK	40101	46,204	50.7	83.0	3,424	77.5	17.5	-10.4	18.4	15.5	21.7	22.7	2.8
Noble, OK	40103	7,839	51.3	88.5	617	97.9	17.5	-10.4	18.3	0.0	9.5	10.5	0.9
Nowata, OK	40105	7,153	60.4	83.5	300	87.0	12.6	-15.3	13.4	0.0	15.5	0.0	0.0
Okfuskee, OK	40107	8,261	62.2	78.8	508	84.3	10.9	-17.0	11.5	10.9	5.4	0.0	0.0
Oklahoma, OK	40109	452,383	40.8	85.4	50,185	77.3	28.2	0.3	33.1	18.0	17.8	43.0	8.1
Okmulgee, OK	40111	26,009	55.7	82.4	2,180	90.4	13.5	-14.4	14.7	9.3	12.4	24.4	14.5
Osage, OK	40113	31,963	51.7	87.3	1,922	76.2	17.8	-10.1	18.4	21.4	14.4	55.4	6.9
Ottawa, OK	40115	21,119	54.7	82.5	1,632	93.1	13.1	-14.8	13.5	17.2	13.8	6.5	5.7
Pawnee, OK	40117	11,224	56.9	86.3	443	89.4	16.1	-11.8	16.8	18.9	13.7	0.0	18.4
Payne, OK	40119	40,732	37.9	89.2	20,271	96.4	34.0	6.1	34.0	14.4	23.5	76.4	24.5
Pittsburg, OK	40121	31,824	56.5	81.8	1,321	83.3	15.1	-12.8	15.7	14.5	14.5	22.9	8.2
Pontotoc, OK	40123	23,453	46.8	84.4	3,417	84.7	26.2	-1.7	27.2	27.3	22.6	17.7	14.2
Pottawatomie, OK	40125	44,386	53.6	83.5	4,672	53.2	16.6	-11.3	17.6	14.0	12.5	40.4	7.1
Pushmataha, OK	40127	7,944	61.2	80.4	208	94.2	11.6	-16.3	11.3	15.4	7.7	81.3	15.8
Roger Mills, OK	40129	2,449	49.1	88.6	113	96.5	20.1	-7.8	20.7	0.0	19.0	0.0	0.0
Rogers, OK	40131	55,144	45.9	89.1	4,678	85.3	21.2	-6.7	22.6	23.1	14.1	33.4	8.8
Seminole, OK	40133	16,293	59.6	79.6	1,288	81.5	13.3	-14.6	15.5	6.8	4.5	4.6	8.2
Sequoyah, OK	40135	27,601	60.8	80.0	1,673	94.0	12.3	-15.6	13.5	0.0	9.8	33.1	2.5
Stephens, OK	40137	30,290	57.2	85.1	1,519	93.2	16.5	-11.4	17.0	7.9	17.2	35.6	6.0
Texas, OK	40139	11,889	55.7	73.1	968	76.5	20.3	-7.6	26.9	0.0	26.8	83.9	5.4
Tillman, OK	40141	5,380	62.3	74.3	302	94.7	14.6	-13.3	17.8	1.6	18.3	0.0	4.8
Tulsa, OK	40143	381,369	39.3	88.0	36,990	66.3	28.8	0.9	32.5	16.2	20.9	41.6	10.8
Wagoner, OK	40145	46,096	44.4	87.9	3,543	80.6	20.8	-7.1	22.3	19.7	10.2	21.0	14.6
Washington, OK	40147	34,145	46.2	88.1	1,974	65.5	26.1	-1.8	27.8	15.1	13.3	70.4	3.8
Washita, OK	40149	7,644	59.5	84.3	247	93.1	16.4	-11.5	17.3	0.0	14.7	5.3	1.8
Woods, OK	40151	5,628	44.2	88.2	1,221	90.6	28.5	0.6	29.3	0.0	25.6	100.0	33.6
Woodward, OK	40153	13,230	55.3	83.3	234	92.7	17.4	-10.5	17.8	0.0	0.0	92.9	6.0

Note. Data in columns 26 through 41 from the American Community Survey are subject to sampling error, which can be especially large in small counties and small population groups. See notes and definitions for more information.

[3]May be of any race.

Table C-1. Population, School, and Student Characteristics by County, Selected Years—*Continued*

County	State/ County Code	County Type[1]	Population, 2010: Total	Population, 2010: Percent 5–17 years	Percent of related children 5–17 years in poverty, 2010	Percent of children under 19 years with no health insurance, 2010	Number of schools and students, 2010–2011: School districts	Number of schools and students, 2010–2011: Schools	Number of schools and students, 2010–2011: Students	Resident enrollment, 2006–2010, K–12 enrollment: Number	Resident enrollment, 2006–2010, K–12 enrollment: Percent public
			1	2	3	4	5	6	7	8	9
OREGON	41000	X	3,831,074	16.4	19.5	9.2	221	1,296	560,983	625,794	90.6
Baker, OR	41001	7	16,134	15.0	29.3	10.2	4	12	2,361	2,527	92.2
Benton, OR	41003	3	85,579	13.4	13.5	8.1	4	23	8,799	11,539	88.8
Clackamas, OR	41005	1	375,992	18.0	11.8	8.1	11	121	58,220	67,885	89.5
Clatsop, OR	41007	4	37,039	14.9	22.0	9.6	5	14	4,901	5,902	96.7
Columbia, OR	41009	1	49,351	17.9	14.7	7.7	5	23	8,250	9,609	95.7
Coos, OR	41011	5	63,043	13.8	25.4	8.3	7	26	8,424	9,283	93.0
Crook, OR	41013	6	20,978	16.5	25.6	10.9	1	8	2,933	3,678	88.7
Curry, OR	41015	7	22,364	11.9	22.5	10.4	3	7	2,468	2,836	93.2
Deschutes, OR	41017	3	157,733	16.9	20.4	10.5	4	42	24,464	24,957	89.9
Douglas, OR	41019	4	107,667	15.3	27.4	8.9	15	48	14,709	17,059	90.4
Gilliam, OR	41021	9	1,871	13.8	17.5	13.0	3	4	247	210	97.6
Grant, OR	41023	9	7,445	14.7	21.8	13.4	6	9	966	1,167	93.7
Harney, OR	41025	7	7,422	17.0	26.3	12.3	11	14	1,157	1,340	99.7
Hood River, OR	41027	6	22,346	19.3	19.1	12.5	1	10	3,989	4,230	95.6
Jackson, OR	41029	3	203,206	15.9	21.0	11.2	10	63	28,358	32,214	90.9
Jefferson, OR	41031	6	21,720	18.1	30.3	13.7	5	12	3,470	3,871	94.0
Josephine, OR	41033	4	82,713	15.3	28.6	8.3	2	24	10,882	12,957	92.3
Klamath, OR	41035	5	66,380	16.3	24.7	11.5	2	31	9,713	11,404	92.4
Lake, OR	41037	7	7,895	14.7	25.6	12.9	6	8	1,046	1,218	96.2
Lane, OR	41039	2	351,715	14.6	20.8	8.8	17	123	45,446	52,134	91.9
Lincoln, OR	41041	4	46,034	12.4	28.3	11.4	1	16	5,188	5,812	92.3
Linn, OR	41043	4	116,672	17.6	25.0	9.6	8	52	21,207	20,429	91.3
Malheur, OR	41045	6	31,313	18.2	33.0	12.1	11	23	5,025	6,531	92.5
Marion, OR	41047	2	315,335	19.0	23.8	10.6	15	134	60,382	58,692	90.8
Morrow, OR	41049	6	11,173	21.4	20.5	13.4	2	9	2,371	2,441	95.9
Multnomah, OR	41051	1	735,334	14.2	23.0	8.3	9	173	91,839	102,547	88.4
Polk, OR	41053	2	75,403	17.8	18.9	8.7	5	18	7,537	13,255	91.6
Sherman, OR	41055	9	1,765	14.5	18.1	12.1	1	2	236	309	90.3
Tillamook, OR	41057	6	25,250	14.4	21.9	11.6	3	11	3,242	3,714	95.0
Umatilla, OR	41059	5	75,889	19.2	19.5	10.6	11	37	13,757	14,669	96.5
Union, OR	41061	7	25,748	16.2	19.8	10.0	7	14	3,844	4,273	88.7
Wallowa, OR	41063	9	7,008	13.5	25.3	14.5	5	8	876	912	93.2
Wasco, OR	41065	6	25,213	16.7	22.4	12.8	4	9	3,517	3,819	94.0
Washington, OR	41067	1	529,710	18.4	11.4	7.4	8	131	85,259	94,075	89.0
Wheeler, OR	41069	9	1,441	13.2	31.8	17.8	3	3	219	208	86.5
Yamhill, OR	41071	1	99,193	18.5	16.3	11.5	6	34	15,681	18,088	90.4
PENNSYLVANIA	42000	X	12,702,379	16.2	17.5	5.4	773	3,233	1,793,284	2,084,682	85.6
Adams, PA	42001	4	101,407	16.6	13.6	6.8	9	28	16,457	17,039	86.8
Allegheny, PA	42003	1	1,223,348	14.6	14.6	3.7	66	296	149,281	182,096	85.7
Armstrong, PA	42005	1	68,941	15.4	19.3	5.3	3	15	6,794	10,981	93.6
Beaver, PA	42007	1	170,539	15.2	19.4	4.4	19	53	33,698	26,967	92.6
Bedford, PA	42009	6	49,762	16.3	18.7	6.8	6	22	7,612	8,214	92.4
Berks, PA	42011	2	411,442	17.7	20.4	6.2	21	111	70,453	72,063	91.0
Blair, PA	42013	3	127,089	15.5	18.7	5.3	10	35	18,417	19,510	89.4
Bradford, PA	42015	6	62,622	16.7	15.9	6.7	8	28	9,904	10,927	93.1
Bucks, PA	42017	1	625,249	17.5	7.4	4.3	20	137	91,484	111,806	82.3
Butler, PA	42019	1	183,862	17.0	10.1	4.5	10	55	32,676	32,200	88.8
Cambria, PA	42021	3	143,679	14.6	20.5	4.6	16	41	18,960	21,411	88.9
Cameron, PA	42023	7	5,085	15.1	20.2	5.9	1	2	731	793	98.2
Carbon, PA	42025	2	65,249	15.4	16.2	5.4	7	22	9,273	10,107	92.3
Centre, PA	42027	3	153,990	11.5	13.2	6.0	9	31	13,519	17,939	92.1
Chester, PA	42029	1	498,886	18.6	7.5	5.2	24	107	85,045	90,556	81.0
Clarion, PA	42031	6	39,988	14.3	25.8	6.5	8	16	5,723	5,550	92.1
Clearfield, PA	42033	4	81,642	15.0	20.9	5.3	11	32	12,102	12,579	91.7
Clinton, PA	42035	6	39,238	15.1	22.5	6.3	3	14	4,655	5,644	89.2
Columbia, PA	42037	4	67,295	13.9	16.1	5.3	7	17	7,268	9,492	95.6
Crawford, PA	42039	4	88,765	16.7	28.8	8.1	5	28	11,964	15,057	86.9

[1]County type codes are from the Economic Research Service of the United States Department of Agriculture. See notes and definitions for more information.

Table C-1. Population, School, and Student Characteristics by County, Selected Years—*Continued*

County	State/ County Code	Characteristics of students, 2010–2011				Number of graduates, 2008–2009	Staff and students, 2010–2011			
		Percent with IEP[2]	Percent eligible for free or reduced lunch	Percent minority	Percent English-language learners		Total staff	Number of teachers	Student/ teacher ratio	Central admin. staff
		10	11	12	13	14	15	16	17	18
OREGON	41000	14.3	50.6	33.7	10.5	35,137	63,211	28,034	20.0	3,626
Baker, OR	41001	14.5	51.6	14.2	1.4	164	292	127	18.6	12
Benton, OR	41003	11.7	36.0	22.4	6.0	664	964	422	20.8	36
Clackamas, OR	41005	13.8	35.6	24.1	8.0	3,946	5,884	2,645	22.0	167
Clatsop, OR	41007	16.8	51.0	20.3	5.7	331	632	279	17.5	26
Columbia, OR	41009	14.6	43.0	15.6	1.6	585	874	401	20.6	34
Coos, OR	41011	15.2	54.7	26.4	1.5	557	999	408	20.6	40
Crook, OR	41013	15.5	60.8	25.2	4.9	200	296	127	23.1	10
Curry, OR	41015	12.9	59.8	29.9	1.5	186	287	126	19.6	14
Deschutes, OR	41017	14.7	51.9	16.2	3.9	1,680	2,556	1,130	21.7	99
Douglas, OR	41019	13.7	59.7	16.9	1.0	953	1,830	791	18.6	85
Gilliam, OR	41021	17.0	48.2	11.7	. . .	19	66	26	9.5	11
Grant, OR	41023	17.0	51.3	8.2	0.3	97	187	84	11.5	22
Harney, OR	41025	18.6	49.4	13.2	1.0	91	207	87	13.3	18
Hood River, OR	41027	15.9	58.7	50.8	23.3	280	504	232	17.2	15
Jackson, OR	41029	12.9	54.6	25.8	7.5	1,811	3,016	1,303	21.8	142
Jefferson, OR	41031	14.4	79.6	62.7	30.9	206	481	196	17.7	20
Josephine, OR	41033	12.0	60.4	16.0	1.3	705	1,123	479	22.7	37
Klamath, OR	41035	15.5	66.6	29.5	6.2	616	1,140	495	19.6	76
Lake, OR	41037	14.4	42.5	21.6	5.4	70	163	69	15.3	19
Lane, OR	41039	17.0	51.6	27.1	3.5	3,075	5,158	2,142	21.2	323
Lincoln, OR	41041	14.2	63.0	30.2	6.3	410	522	231	22.5	29
Linn, OR	41043	12.9	48.4	18.6	3.1	1,125	2,381	1,005	21.1	92
Malheur, OR	41045	13.8	66.2	55.4	21.0	316	746	309	16.2	37
Marion, OR	41047	14.9	62.2	48.4	19.6	3,649	7,236	3,163	19.1	1,094
Morrow, OR	41049	13.4	69.4	50.2	19.6	166	338	145	16.4	8
Multnomah, OR	41051	14.9	54.4	45.7	15.1	4,774	10,524	4,732	19.4	222
Polk, OR	41053	14.8	46.4	30.5	9.1	441	808	369	20.4	35
Sherman, OR	41055	22.5	54.7	14.1	5.5	24	51	23	10.3	1
Tillamook, OR	41057	13.8	60.6	28.3	10.1	232	438	184	17.6	23
Umatilla, OR	41059	12.6	63.6	43.5	15.3	830	1,675	711	19.3	77
Union, OR	41061	16.7	50.4	13.2	2.0	263	435	216	17.8	29
Wallowa, OR	41063	16.8	46.2	6.5	0.1	71	135	65	13.5	12
Wasco, OR	41065	16.5	57.4	34.0	14.5	199	477	193	18.2	31
Washington, OR	41067	13.2	38.8	42.6	13.8	5,374	9,041	4,306	19.8	668
Wheeler, OR	41069	11.0	61.0	13.9	3.2	16	52	24	9.3	3
Yamhill, OR	41071	13.5	51.4	29.5	11.2	1,011	1,694	791	19.8	62
PENNSYLVANIA	42000	16.5	38.9	28.5	2.6	130,658	266,796	129,911	13.8	10,129
Adams, PA	42001	11.8	32.9	14.4	2.5	1,089	3,554	1,441	11.4	143
Allegheny, PA	42003	16.6	36.5	29.3	0.9	11,617	23,345	11,632	12.8	843
Armstrong, PA	42005	19.0	40.4	2.4	. . .	614	947	549	12.4	37
Beaver, PA	42007	14.2	27.8	14.6	0.2	2,889	3,909	1,911	17.6	153
Bedford, PA	42009	16.1	44.0	2.6	0.2	596	1,060	543	14.0	55
Berks, PA	42011	18.0	40.5	34.7	5.8	4,784	11,375	4,932	14.3	537
Blair, PA	42013	17.7	44.5	5.3	0.2	1,343	3,181	1,418	13.0	172
Bradford, PA	42015	17.1	40.9	3.5	0.2	686	1,436	735	13.5	69
Bucks, PA	42017	17.4	17.5	16.3	1.7	7,384	13,730	6,517	14.0	439
Butler, PA	42019	14.1	21.3	3.8	0.3	2,474	4,009	2,247	14.5	134
Cambria, PA	42021	16.5	44.0	9.1	0.2	1,539	2,490	1,367	13.9	99
Cameron, PA	42023	23.3	21.6	2.7	0.1	63	139	55	13.3	5
Carbon, PA	42025	17.7	41.5	8.8	0.4	706	1,316	662	14.0	62
Centre, PA	42027	15.0	24.6	9.0	1.6	1,136	2,428	1,081	12.5	81
Chester, PA	42029	17.1	20.7	23.6	2.9	5,929	12,262	6,005	14.2	533
Clarion, PA	42031	17.5	37.9	2.6	. . .	442	1,123	519	11.0	35
Clearfield, PA	42033	19.6	46.6	2.4	0.1	944	1,953	936	12.9	85
Clinton, PA	42035	20.4	47.0	4.1	0.2	370	668	370	12.6	20
Columbia, PA	42037	17.0	35.6	5.3	0.4	671	1,117	568	12.8	50
Crawford, PA	42039	17.9	44.7	7.8	0.3	971	1,763	929	12.9	76

[2]IEP=Individual Education Program. See notes and definitions for more information.

Table C-1. Population, School, and Student Characteristics by County, Selected Years—*Continued*

County	State/ County Code	Revenues, 2008–2009				Current expenditures, 2008–2009			Resident population 16 to 19 years, 2006–2010			
		Total revenue ($1,000's)	Percentage of revenue from: Federal government	State government	Local government	Amount ($1,000's)	Amount per student	Percent for instruction	Total population 16 to 19 years	Percent enrolled in school	Percent high school graduates, not enrolled in school	Percent not enrolled, not grads, not employed, or not in labor force
		19	20	21	22	23	24	25	26	27	28	29
OREGON	41000	6,158,756	10.7	50.6	38.7	5,510,193	9,827	58.0	205,598	81.2	11.9	4.3
Baker, OR	41001	22,908	12.2	57.0	30.8	23,761	10,761	54.5	1,050	76.9	3.4	10.6
Benton, OR	41003	94,780	7.3	44.8	47.9	81,547	9,031	58.1	7,583	91.5	5.4	1.8
Clackamas, OR	41005	626,855	7.1	48.6	44.3	531,757	9,059	57.9	20,195	81.3	11.5	3.6
Clatsop, OR	41007	53,410	7.7	39.6	52.7	52,618	10,482	59.6	2,364	91.9	5.8	0.9
Columbia, OR	41009	79,947	8.1	46.4	45.5	72,580	8,460	58.7	2,786	86.1	11.0	2.9
Coos, OR	41011	96,068	10.9	51.5	37.6	91,353	10,803	54.1	3,125	81.5	10.7	2.8
Crook, OR	41013	30,601	10.0	49.6	40.5	27,506	8,574	59.4	1,136	80.4	12.0	4.1
Curry, OR	41015	26,956	13.9	42.7	43.3	25,393	9,919	59.3	894	72.8	20.9	6.3
Deschutes, OR	41017	270,501	9.2	42.0	48.8	230,049	9,319	58.3	7,515	75.9	16.9	4.8
Douglas, OR	41019	174,616	13.6	52.9	33.5	156,517	10,330	52.9	5,495	82.8	10.5	5.6
Gilliam, OR	41021	6,866	4.8	36.3	58.9	6,227	26,725	51.6	33	87.9	12.1	0.0
Grant, OR	41023	16,734	19.8	51.3	28.9	15,622	15,123	55.6	370	75.1	18.1	0.0
Harney, OR	41025	18,457	13.8	62.2	23.9	15,544	13,095	50.0	442	84.6	7.0	0.2
Hood River, OR	41027	45,552	11.7	53.1	35.2	41,221	10,375	63.3	1,184	76.8	18.2	0.8
Jackson, OR	41029	310,504	10.1	51.1	38.8	274,417	9,674	58.2	10,854	76.4	15.4	5.6
Jefferson, OR	41031	46,192	17.6	57.1	25.3	39,358	10,692	53.6	1,327	69.3	9.0	15.7
Josephine, OR	41033	108,518	11.8	54.6	33.6	102,687	9,221	60.1	4,380	77.0	14.0	6.9
Klamath, OR	41035	108,319	15.8	58.0	26.1	98,218	9,755	56.0	3,508	72.7	12.5	5.0
Lake, OR	41037	14,839	16.5	56.9	26.6	13,596	12,326	50.0	271	87.1	12.2	0.7
Lane, OR	41039	520,698	12.0	48.6	39.4	470,528	10,084	59.3	21,645	81.7	13.1	3.7
Lincoln, OR	41041	57,945	14.7	26.4	58.9	50,190	9,341	58.6	2,163	78.1	11.2	6.6
Linn, OR	41043	218,724	11.1	59.1	29.8	178,956	8,414	56.4	6,118	83.3	9.7	4.7
Malheur, OR	41045	60,655	14.0	69.6	16.4	57,648	11,099	58.4	1,677	81.3	10.0	4.5
Marion, OR	41047	650,219	11.1	60.4	28.4	591,493	10,094	59.8	18,748	76.3	14.9	5.1
Morrow, OR	41049	25,134	9.2	58.5	32.3	23,747	9,845	61.0	748	87.3	12.7	0.0
Multnomah, OR	41051	1,034,209	12.4	44.9	42.7	960,710	10,596	57.6	33,926	84.0	9.5	3.7
Polk, OR	41053	75,619	10.3	61.9	27.8	69,093	8,960	60.4	4,670	86.5	10.6	2.0
Sherman, OR	41055	4,312	7.9	60.3	31.7	4,383	15,938	52.6	73	86.3	11.0	2.7
Tillamook, OR	41057	42,015	10.3	32.4	57.2	37,513	11,364	57.2	1,297	79.0	18.0	1.9
Umatilla, OR	41059	158,937	11.7	58.4	29.9	151,904	11,216	55.6	4,510	77.3	15.4	5.5
Union, OR	41061	40,697	9.3	61.5	29.2	39,530	10,397	57.9	1,617	80.5	13.9	3.3
Wallowa, OR	41063	15,262	12.2	47.4	40.3	13,016	14,944	57.9	296	77.7	17.6	3.7
Wasco, OR	41065	41,774	13.0	54.3	32.7	40,256	11,668	55.9	1,283	70.1	14.2	14.5
Washington, OR	41067	899,509	8.7	49.0	42.4	782,324	9,388	58.1	26,237	81.3	11.6	5.0
Wheeler, OR	41069	4,076	16.9	63.9	19.2	3,945	19,924	53.2	61	100.0	0.0	0.0
Yamhill, OR	41071	156,348	9.4	56.4	34.1	134,986	8,605	61.9	6,017	86.6	10.1	1.8
PENNSYLVANIA	42000	27,597,348	6.8	35.9	57.4	21,984,821	12,493	60.0	745,237	86.6	8.3	3.3
Adams, PA	42001	280,971	10.7	32.7	56.6	251,228	17,552	60.8	6,297	90.5	6.8	1.2
Allegheny, PA	42003	2,624,706	7.2	32.8	60.0	2,069,721	13,742	59.1	66,798	88.6	7.8	2.5
Armstrong, PA	42005	105,309	4.3	51.5	44.2	87,343	13,380	59.9	3,424	83.7	10.1	3.0
Beaver, PA	42007	427,375	5.8	41.1	53.1	356,187	11,139	61.0	9,086	85.6	10.0	3.5
Bedford, PA	42009	95,141	6.2	57.0	36.8	78,708	10,055	59.0	2,603	81.9	11.9	3.0
Berks, PA	42011	1,079,336	7.8	36.7	55.5	841,687	11,997	57.3	25,708	86.8	7.9	2.9
Blair, PA	42013	266,088	12.1	49.9	38.0	214,347	11,687	58.5	7,383	84.6	10.1	3.1
Bradford, PA	42015	120,735	5.2	57.7	37.1	100,529	11,625	61.9	3,262	83.1	12.0	3.9
Bucks, PA	42017	1,569,544	3.1	21.4	75.5	1,273,184	14,122	63.5	32,973	89.2	6.3	3.6
Butler, PA	42019	395,251	2.5	38.8	58.6	328,999	9,922	62.7	10,770	89.9	7.1	1.9
Cambria, PA	42021	247,421	5.9	58.4	35.8	201,708	10,534	60.6	8,014	90.5	7.2	1.7
Cameron, PA	42023	11,297	2.3	67.3	30.4	8,641	10,980	58.4	266	85.7	11.7	2.6
Carbon, PA	42025	130,979	4.3	34.2	61.5	100,428	10,920	61.6	3,143	82.3	8.6	6.8
Centre, PA	42027	207,793	2.9	26.5	70.6	166,986	12,174	61.4	19,716	92.4	5.4	1.0
Chester, PA	42029	1,411,678	4.0	18.6	77.4	1,119,528	14,145	57.8	28,768	90.5	5.9	2.2
Clarion, PA	42031	106,374	11.1	56.4	32.4	83,332	14,184	60.6	3,178	90.2	4.5	3.2
Clearfield, PA	42033	186,211	9.8	53.2	37.0	150,832	12,082	58.7	4,164	74.4	17.0	7.4
Clinton, PA	42035	65,963	5.6	51.7	42.8	55,648	14,365	64.7	2,917	90.2	7.2	1.0
Columbia, PA	42037	94,933	3.6	40.9	55.4	76,573	11,309	60.6	5,681	93.4	3.8	1.2
Crawford, PA	42039	166,784	2.9	55.2	41.8	137,228	10,899	60.0	5,523	85.0	7.5	4.7

Note. Data in columns 26 through 41 from the American Community Survey are subject to sampling error, which can be especially large in small counties and small population groups. See notes and definitions for more information.

Table C-1. Population, School, and Student Characteristics by County, Selected Years—*Continued*

County	State/ County Code	High school graduates, 2006–2010			College enrollment, 2006–2010		College graduates, 2006–2010 (percent)						
		Population 25 years and over	High school diploma or less (percent)	High school diploma or more (percent)	Number	Percent public	Bachelor's degree or more	+/- U.S. percent with Bachelor's degree or more	Non-Hispanic White	Black or African American	American Indian and Alaska Native	Asian, Hawaiian, and Pacific Islander	Hispanic or Latino[3]
		30	31	32	33	34	35	36	37	38	39	40	41
OREGON	41000	2,543,151	37.0	88.6	256,045	79.1	28.6	0.7	30.0	22.3	10.5	44.6	10.9
Baker, OR	41001	11,637	45.0	88.7	516	88.4	20.5	-7.4	21.2	0.0	0.0	100.0	2.8
Benton, OR	41003	49,192	22.9	94.2	19,066	97.4	47.9	20.0	48.2	16.2	23.3	73.4	27.1
Clackamas, OR	41005	252,044	32.7	91.5	19,856	76.7	31.4	3.5	31.9	29.8	13.2	45.3	16.2
Clatsop, OR	41007	25,647	38.0	91.1	2,391	91.0	21.6	-6.3	21.8	41.5	13.0	56.0	7.6
Columbia, OR	41009	33,250	45.6	88.5	1,830	76.1	16.8	-11.1	16.3	37.7	36.0	37.5	17.0
Coos, OR	41011	46,316	45.1	85.8	2,425	84.6	18.3	-9.6	18.7	59.4	11.4	30.9	5.3
Crook, OR	41013	15,283	50.6	85.7	477	91.8	15.4	-12.5	15.2	0.0	14.9	24.5	13.6
Curry, OR	41015	17,499	43.8	91.6	504	96.6	18.5	-9.4	19.1	0.0	14.0	39.5	6.9
Deschutes, OR	41017	106,786	32.3	92.9	6,547	83.1	29.1	1.2	29.9	24.5	5.8	49.4	11.5
Douglas, OR	41019	76,540	48.0	86.4	4,702	90.0	15.5	-12.4	15.7	25.6	6.1	40.1	7.0
Gilliam, OR	41021	1,339	40.5	84.8	62	82.3	18.8	-9.1	20.9	0.0	0.0	0.0	3.6
Grant, OR	41023	5,433	48.1	90.1	184	78.8	17.3	-10.6	17.7	35.7	0.0	20.0	5.7
Harney, OR	41025	5,172	53.1	90.2	77	68.8	16.2	-11.7	16.1	21.4	14.3	28.6	18.8
Hood River, OR	41027	14,418	43.4	83.7	812	80.4	25.9	-2.0	31.7	34.8	3.9	29.0	5.9
Jackson, OR	41029	138,879	39.7	88.9	10,267	90.1	24.4	-3.5	25.3	27.6	13.3	48.9	10.0
Jefferson, OR	41031	14,021	54.1	82.6	653	81.9	15.9	-12.0	18.1	21.1	8.9	0.0	10.8
Josephine, OR	41033	59,335	46.1	86.2	2,835	87.5	16.5	-11.4	16.9	15.2	10.2	27.5	4.9
Klamath, OR	41035	45,136	46.3	86.5	3,928	93.6	18.1	-9.8	19.1	13.8	11.5	41.1	7.2
Lake, OR	41037	5,823	49.5	88.2	137	100.0	16.4	-11.5	16.8	0.0	12.6	18.2	11.8
Lane, OR	41039	231,878	35.6	89.9	36,305	85.3	27.7	-0.2	27.9	43.0	8.6	52.7	17.6
Lincoln, OR	41041	34,622	38.5	90.0	1,914	85.9	23.8	-4.1	25.2	68.8	15.5	32.8	3.3
Linn, OR	41043	76,769	45.7	86.9	5,471	93.4	16.3	-11.6	16.8	21.7	8.7	16.4	12.2
Malheur, OR	41045	20,314	54.1	79.0	1,566	85.9	13.8	-14.1	17.3	0.0	5.3	5.5	4.6
Marion, OR	41047	197,234	44.5	82.2	16,956	70.4	20.9	-7.0	24.1	13.7	9.4	27.8	6.0
Morrow, OR	41049	7,043	55.3	78.5	331	98.8	11.5	-16.4	14.7	0.0	0.0	26.5	1.4
Multnomah, OR	41051	494,930	32.0	89.0	62,495	70.1	37.5	9.6	41.5	17.7	14.4	34.7	15.4
Polk, OR	41053	46,939	37.1	88.8	6,312	89.1	28.1	0.2	29.8	30.2	1.5	37.7	11.3
Sherman, OR	41055	1,284	39.5	90.0	34	88.2	15.4	-12.5	15.5	0.0	0.0	0.0	0.0
Tillamook, OR	41057	18,406	44.7	89.0	828	83.9	20.0	-7.9	20.9	47.4	0.0	4.0	5.3
Umatilla, OR	41059	47,883	49.6	81.2	3,315	89.6	14.6	-13.3	16.9	20.6	4.9	20.9	5.1
Union, OR	41061	16,733	47.4	88.5	1,996	90.9	20.3	-7.6	20.6	60.0	8.2	24.1	13.3
Wallowa, OR	41063	5,198	42.4	92.8	219	58.9	21.1	-6.8	21.3	0.0	0.0	35.3	4.1
Wasco, OR	41065	17,080	45.8	84.3	853	85.5	21.5	-6.4	24.1	7.7	11.3	10.9	4.1
Washington, OR	41067	339,652	28.7	90.4	33,320	75.1	38.9	11.0	40.7	35.6	8.7	57.3	11.2
Wheeler, OR	41069	1,151	54.0	88.2	35	57.1	18.2	-9.7	18.7	0.0	0.0	0.0	0.0
Yamhill, OR	41071	62,285	43.1	86.8	6,826	41.9	23.0	-4.9	25.3	30.1	5.3	30.9	5.4
PENNSYLVANIA	42000	8,558,693	50.4	87.4	894,685	58.3	26.4	-1.5	27.4	14.9	17.8	52.8	13.6
Adams, PA	42001	67,971	58.6	84.7	7,056	41.6	18.5	-9.4	18.9	19.1	0.0	35.2	6.3
Allegheny, PA	42003	856,341	40.7	91.6	102,861	58.5	34.1	6.2	35.2	17.1	32.3	72.2	39.4
Armstrong, PA	42005	49,894	64.3	87.7	2,399	83.7	13.9	-14.0	13.8	17.3	2.9	67.1	25.1
Beaver, PA	42007	122,510	53.2	89.6	8,576	62.1	19.2	-8.7	19.7	9.2	16.8	46.5	15.9
Bedford, PA	42009	35,391	67.4	83.9	1,499	82.3	12.5	-15.4	12.5	0.0	0.0	30.8	6.7
Berks, PA	42011	269,301	55.8	83.1	27,660	71.1	21.7	-6.2	23.5	15.1	19.0	41.9	7.4
Blair, PA	42013	88,355	59.0	89.7	6,558	78.5	17.3	-10.6	17.2	13.6	0.0	35.1	14.9
Bradford, PA	42015	43,312	63.0	85.4	2,135	72.0	15.7	-12.2	15.5	16.1	2.4	45.8	23.6
Bucks, PA	42017	429,091	39.8	91.9	33,018	58.7	34.5	6.6	34.5	20.1	22.6	60.4	20.3
Butler, PA	42019	124,152	45.9	91.9	12,113	80.6	28.8	0.9	28.5	27.6	11.9	71.7	20.5
Cambria, PA	42021	102,479	60.4	87.6	9,262	67.4	17.5	-10.4	17.7	9.5	12.9	46.9	13.0
Cameron, PA	42023	3,810	64.0	85.2	148	71.6	14.9	-13.0	14.7	0.0	0.0	35.7	0.0
Carbon, PA	42025	46,367	59.9	86.7	2,781	66.0	14.6	-13.3	13.9	25.5	68.1	47.4	28.6
Centre, PA	42027	82,659	40.1	92.6	41,714	94.8	40.0	12.1	38.4	22.8	26.9	86.0	33.3
Chester, PA	42029	323,963	31.7	92.5	33,695	61.7	47.8	19.9	49.6	24.9	39.4	78.0	17.1
Clarion, PA	42031	25,931	63.5	87.2	4,626	89.9	17.2	-10.7	17.0	13.9	31.8	53.6	16.5
Clearfield, PA	42033	58,311	65.7	86.0	2,746	68.5	12.3	-15.6	12.4	2.4	0.0	52.0	9.6
Clinton, PA	42035	25,139	61.9	85.6	4,865	91.1	16.7	-11.2	16.7	7.5	0.0	26.0	16.5
Columbia, PA	42037	43,372	60.3	86.7	9,259	94.5	18.3	-9.6	17.9	20.1	14.3	57.6	10.3
Crawford, PA	42039	60,455	61.0	85.8	4,862	49.5	18.3	-9.6	18.4	2.2	15.1	44.7	30.2

Note. Data in columns 26 through 41 from the American Community Survey are subject to sampling error, which can be especially large in small counties and small population groups. See notes and definitions for more information.

[3]May be of any race.

Table C-1. Population, School, and Student Characteristics by County, Selected Years—*Continued*

County	State/ County Code	County Type[1]	Population, 2010		Percent of related children 5–17 years in poverty, 2010	Percent of children under 19 years with no health insurance, 2010	Number of schools and students, 2010–2011			Resident enrollment, 2006–2010 K–12 enrollment	
			Total	Percent 5–17 years			School districts	Schools	Students	Number	Percent public
			1	2	3	4	5	6	7	8	9
PENNSYLVANIA— *(Continued)*											
Cumberland, PA	42041	2	235,406	15.3	9.6	4.5	11	48	29,976	34,987	88.9
Dauphin, PA	42043	2	268,100	16.9	22.2	5.4	13	69	37,193	45,504	88.2
Delaware, PA	42045	1	558,979	17.3	12.5	4.9	19	111	74,066	97,933	78.1
Elk, PA	42047	7	31,946	16.0	15.2	5.0	3	10	3,898	5,471	76.0
Erie, PA	42049	2	280,566	16.8	21.8	5.2	19	82	41,016	47,327	85.4
Fayette, PA	42051	1	136,606	15.3	29.3	5.4	8	46	18,348	21,717	93.9
Forest, PA	42053	9	7,716	10.0	24.8	7.2	3	6	1,172	909	93.3
Franklin, PA	42055	4	149,618	17.2	13.7	7.6	11	45	22,357	24,774	85.3
Fulton, PA	42057	8	14,845	16.9	17.2	6.6	4	8	2,353	2,639	89.5
Greene, PA	42059	6	38,686	14.8	22.5	4.7	6	15	5,387	6,125	96.4
Huntingdon, PA	42061	6	45,913	14.7	18.3	5.8	7	21	5,843	6,583	90.5
Indiana, PA	42063	4	88,880	13.9	21.0	5.7	11	27	11,769	12,200	91.4
Jefferson, PA	42065	7	45,200	15.8	22.5	6.5	4	15	5,444	7,260	91.1
Juniata, PA	42067	6	24,636	17.7	16.9	8.2	1	12	3,092	4,213	80.4
Lackawanna, PA	42069	2	214,437	15.1	18.1	5.6	14	51	28,410	32,740	83.5
Lancaster, PA	42071	2	519,445	18.0	14.9	9.8	21	121	69,063	89,249	79.6
Lawrence, PA	42073	4	91,108	15.9	23.8	5.6	10	30	13,382	14,882	94.6
Lebanon, PA	42075	3	133,568	16.7	15.5	6.3	7	33	18,884	22,222	87.5
Lehigh, PA	42077	2	349,497	17.5	18.7	6.3	15	76	53,920	60,753	88.5
Luzerne, PA	42079	2	320,918	15.0	21.9	5.9	17	74	45,974	49,059	87.1
Lycoming, PA	42081	3	116,111	15.3	22.0	6.0	11	36	16,834	18,252	93.0
McKean, PA	42083	7	43,450	15.6	22.3	5.6	7	14	7,188	7,342	92.2
Mercer, PA	42085	2	116,638	16.5	23.9	6.5	15	42	17,140	18,813	88.8
Mifflin, PA	42087	4	46,682	16.8	25.0	7.7	3	14	5,472	7,325	81.8
Monroe, PA	42089	4	169,842	18.8	14.9	6.4	7	41	30,310	33,632	91.4
Montgomery, PA	42091	1	799,874	17.0	6.5	3.9	31	161	109,414	135,267	79.5
Montour, PA	42093	6	18,267	15.5	17.2	5.7	3	8	2,537	2,861	87.9
Northampton, PA	42095	2	297,735	16.4	12.8	5.5	14	65	46,715	48,595	88.5
Northumberland, PA	42097	4	94,528	15.0	20.2	5.0	9	27	12,546	14,550	88.2
Perry, PA	42099	2	45,969	17.3	14.5	7.8	5	15	6,658	7,859	90.9
Philadelphia, PA	42101	1	1,526,006	15.9	36.4	5.6	78	340	206,555	253,105	79.5
Pike, PA	42103	1	57,369	18.4	11.9	7.1	2	12	8,913	11,217	95.0
Potter, PA	42105	9	17,457	16.8	22.5	8.1	5	10	2,573	2,966	93.8
Schuylkill, PA	42107	4	148,289	14.9	17.4	5.1	14	37	19,083	22,583	90.4
Snyder, PA	42109	7	39,702	16.3	17.5	7.1	2	11	4,919	6,178	86.8
Somerset, PA	42111	4	77,742	14.7	21.0	6.6	13	33	10,151	12,135	88.9
Sullivan, PA	42113	8	6,428	12.0	22.0	8.9	1	3	630	903	96.1
Susquehanna, PA	42115	6	43,356	16.1	17.7	6.2	7	15	7,023	7,441	93.0
Tioga, PA	42117	6	41,981	15.2	22.4	7.0	3	16	5,671	6,638	93.5
Union, PA	42119	4	44,947	13.8	15.1	6.7	3	12	4,061	6,284	80.9
Venango, PA	42121	4	54,984	15.9	24.7	5.2	5	21	6,389	9,323	90.7
Warren, PA	42123	6	41,815	15.9	19.5	6.0	3	14	5,207	6,801	87.4
Washington, PA	42125	1	207,820	15.5	13.0	4.1	17	57	29,576	33,104	90.8
Wayne, PA	42127	6	52,822	14.9	16.2	7.0	2	11	5,234	8,319	91.6
Westmoreland, PA	42129	1	365,169	15.0	13.6	4.2	22	99	51,722	56,667	91.6
Wyoming, PA	42131	2	28,276	16.4	17.9	5.4	2	8	3,991	4,780	94.2
York, PA	42133	2	434,972	17.3	11.8	4.8	22	121	69,209	74,264	89.8
RHODE ISLAND	44000	X	1,052,567	15.8	17.7	6.0	54	317	143,793	169,702	86.8
Bristol, RI	44001	1	49,875	16.0	7.0	4.6	2	12	6,972	8,158	81.0
Kent, RI	44003	1	166,158	15.7	10.5	5.0	6	49	23,376	26,453	88.5
Newport, RI	44005	1	82,888	14.9	10.5	4.9	6	24	9,947	12,658	83.4
Providence, RI	44007	1	626,667	16.0	23.2	6.9	32	195	86,997	101,541	87.1
Washington, RI	44009	1	126,979	15.6	8.3	4.1	8	37	16,501	20,892	87.7

[1]County type codes are from the Economic Research Service of the United States Department of Agriculture. See notes and definitions for more information.

Table C-1. Population, School, and Student Characteristics by County, Selected Years—*Continued*

County	State/ County Code	Characteristics of students, 2010–2011: Percent with IEP[2]	Percent eligible for free or reduced lunch	Percent minority	Percent English-language learners	Number of graduates, 2008–2009	Staff and students, 2010–2011: Total staff	Number of teachers	Student/ teacher ratio	Central admin. staff
		10	11	12	13	14	15	16	17	18
PENNSYLVANIA—*(Continued)*										
Cumberland, PA	42041	15.3	21.3	15.3	1.4	2,035	4,428	2,245	13.4	184
Dauphin, PA	42043	16.6	41.3	43.4	3.3	2,900	5,126	2,783	13.4	190
Delaware, PA	42045	18.9	34.5	39.9	2.5	5,505	12,407	5,434	13.6	518
Elk, PA	42047	18.0	37.4	3.9	0.1	346	537	281	13.9	18
Erie, PA	42049	18.3	47.9	21.4	2.6	2,968	5,993	3,133	13.1	230
Fayette, PA	42051	18.2	53.6	9.4	0.1	1,351	2,362	1,316	13.9	84
Forest, PA	42053	23.6	45.1	2.1	. . .	102	180	96	12.3	11
Franklin, PA	42055	15.0	33.9	15.4	2.0	1,607	2,841	1,413	15.8	82
Fulton, PA	42057	15.6	43.8	3.2	0.3	159	334	187	12.6	12
Greene, PA	42059	21.4	45.7	2.5	0.1	389	790	460	11.7	30
Huntingdon, PA	42061	20.2	44.0	4.4	0.3	517	879	483	12.1	45
Indiana, PA	42063	19.3	44.0	4.6	0.4	894	1,923	950	12.4	106
Jefferson, PA	42065	18.3	46.7	2.0	0.1	522	866	420	13.0	39
Juniata, PA	42067	13.9	39.9	6.8	1.5	239	484	215	14.4	15
Lackawanna, PA	42069	17.0	40.9	17.2	2.7	2,151	3,777	2,070	13.7	123
Lancaster, PA	42071	16.0	34.5	26.6	4.9	5,222	10,709	5,077	13.6	484
Lawrence, PA	42073	15.1	39.9	12.1	0.3	1,056	1,863	956	14.0	88
Lebanon, PA	42075	16.6	33.1	23.4	4.2	1,308	2,449	1,268	14.9	99
Lehigh, PA	42077	15.3	44.3	43.6	5.1	3,729	8,362	3,649	14.8	291
Luzerne, PA	42079	16.0	49.3	20.2	3.5	3,437	6,186	3,168	14.5	199
Lycoming, PA	42081	16.7	38.9	12.9	0.2	1,215	2,690	1,345	12.5	153
McKean, PA	42083	14.0	42.8	3.5	0.1	594	1,161	573	12.5	71
Mercer, PA	42085	15.4	44.6	14.3	0.4	1,403	2,890	1,355	12.6	125
Mifflin, PA	42087	16.8	45.7	5.4	0.5	433	806	457	12.0	27
Monroe, PA	42089	18.0	39.8	40.3	2.5	2,468	5,004	2,512	12.1	140
Montgomery, PA	42091	16.5	18.9	27.9	2.4	8,195	16,884	8,129	13.5	667
Montour, PA	42093	15.3	25.3	12.0	0.5	202	391	223	11.4	11
Northampton, PA	42095	14.9	33.0	29.2	3.5	3,518	7,330	3,434	13.6	263
Northumberland, PA	42097	16.2	44.2	7.6	1.3	923	2,468	1,002	12.5	85
Perry, PA	42099	19.3	34.2	5.1	0.2	479	967	507	13.1	63
Philadelphia, PA	42101	14.8	78.3	85.9	6.7	10,363	28,398	13,089	15.8	823
Pike, PA	42103	16.3	38.7	22.0	0.2	768	1,267	583	15.3	20
Potter, PA	42105	15.8	46.9	3.3	. . .	223	392	210	12.3	20
Schuylkill, PA	42107	20.4	41.0	7.2	0.8	1,457	3,118	1,498	12.7	125
Snyder, PA	42109	14.5	35.8	6.8	0.9	364	730	367	13.4	22
Somerset, PA	42111	17.0	40.8	2.2	0.3	887	1,592	796	12.8	68
Sullivan, PA	42113	18.1	34.3	2.9	. . .	64	115	48	13.0	5
Susquehanna, PA	42115	17.6	36.1	4.3	0.4	592	1,122	585	12.0	59
Tioga, PA	42117	17.2	42.1	3.5	0.2	448	877	482	11.8	27
Union, PA	42119	15.4	27.6	9.0	1.2	290	654	330	12.3	29
Venango, PA	42121	25.9	47.6	5.0	0.2	541	984	498	12.8	35
Warren, PA	42123	19.7	42.5	2.7	0.1	449	862	456	11.4	35
Washington, PA	42125	16.1	30.1	8.5	0.2	2,170	4,449	2,280	13.0	149
Wayne, PA	42127	16.4	41.9	4.9	0.4	369	735	389	13.5	26
Westmoreland, PA	42129	14.2	29.4	7.7	0.2	4,180	6,512	3,560	14.5	260
Wyoming, PA	42131	17.5	39.4	3.3	0.3	408	623	332	12.0	24
York, PA	42133	16.0	28.2	21.4	3.2	4,971	9,480	4,852	14.3	327
RHODE ISLAND	44000	17.6	42.9	34.9	5.3	10,028	18,615	11,197	12.8	571
Bristol, RI	44001	12.7	18.7	8.2	1.6	544	818	525	13.3	24
Kent, RI	44003	18.1	27.9	11.4	0.9	1,691	3,139	1,937	12.1	107
Newport, RI	44005	18.5	26.6	19.2	1.7	636	1,211	815	12.2	36
Providence, RI	44007	18.4	55.0	49.9	8.1	5,842	11,029	6,542	13.3	345
Washington, RI	44009	14.6	20.8	10.0	0.9	1,315	2,418	1,377	12.0	59

[2]IEP=Individual Education Program. See notes and definitions for more information.
. . . = Not available.

Table C-1. Population, School, and Student Characteristics by County, Selected Years—*Continued*

County	State/ County Code	Revenues, 2008–2009				Current expenditures, 2008–2009			Resident population 16 to 19 years, 2006–2010			
		Total revenue ($1,000's)	Percentage of revenue from			Amount ($1,000's)	Amount per student	Percent for instruction	Total population 16 to 19 years	Percent enrolled in school	Percent high school graduates, not enrolled in school	Percent not enrolled, not grads, not employed, or not in labor force
			Federal government	State government	Local government							
		19	20	21	22	23	24	25	26	27	28	29
PENNSYLVANIA— *(Continued)*												
Cumberland, PA	42041	446,724	7.1	28.3	64.7	361,233	12,887	55.6	14,250	91.9	5.0	1.2
Dauphin, PA	42043	560,483	5.7	34.5	59.8	436,734	11,823	61.8	14,010	82.8	10.5	4.0
Delaware, PA	42045	1,248,670	5.7	27.9	66.5	1,022,673	14,030	61.0	36,806	90.7	5.7	2.9
Elk, PA	42047	47,541	2.7	51.9	45.4	41,650	10,249	60.8	1,614	92.7	4.9	2.0
Erie, PA	42049	567,691	10.6	46.7	42.7	463,992	11,276	60.0	18,035	87.1	9.6	2.6
Fayette, PA	42051	238,253	7.5	63.6	28.9	199,299	10,789	60.2	6,669	78.8	10.1	7.5
Forest, PA	42053	18,869	9.6	52.6	37.8	15,713	12,796	56.7	306	80.7	16.7	2.6
Franklin, PA	42055	267,459	3.8	36.0	60.2	216,335	9,662	63.8	7,731	78.0	12.2	3.9
Fulton, PA	42057	33,115	6.5	57.9	35.6	26,753	11,317	60.2	754	87.1	11.4	1.5
Greene, PA	42059	89,791	6.6	49.1	44.3	68,069	12,138	57.9	2,372	88.6	7.5	3.9
Huntingdon, PA	42061	73,260	5.9	56.8	37.3	60,591	9,941	58.9	2,602	88.5	8.3	1.3
Indiana, PA	42063	205,602	7.6	51.5	40.8	170,241	14,112	58.5	7,818	84.8	7.9	5.8
Jefferson, PA	42065	79,661	5.3	58.0	36.7	64,092	12,309	58.2	2,476	82.0	10.4	5.1
Juniata, PA	42067	30,876	5.2	52.2	42.6	27,593	8,898	58.8	1,236	70.8	18.2	5.4
Lackawanna, PA	42069	375,517	8.1	39.3	52.6	320,418	11,298	60.2	12,268	90.0	6.3	2.6
Lancaster, PA	42071	1,049,764	8.6	28.8	62.6	846,962	12,313	60.1	31,099	80.4	8.1	4.0
Lawrence, PA	42073	174,123	4.6	57.5	38.0	138,655	10,293	63.8	5,112	85.7	8.0	4.5
Lebanon, PA	42075	230,813	4.6	38.3	57.2	187,859	9,943	62.1	6,891	80.8	11.2	5.4
Lehigh, PA	42077	761,176	6.1	30.8	63.1	594,972	11,800	59.3	19,112	86.2	8.4	3.7
Luzerne, PA	42079	578,936	7.2	42.7	50.1	477,996	10,622	62.2	17,707	88.3	7.3	3.0
Lycoming, PA	42081	239,074	8.4	46.2	45.4	195,922	11,729	61.8	7,135	87.4	7.1	3.3
McKean, PA	42083	114,332	10.4	55.6	34.0	91,546	13,615	59.9	2,566	86.4	11.3	2.0
Mercer, PA	42085	287,467	13.1	45.0	41.9	229,685	13,240	63.2	7,316	91.4	3.4	3.9
Mifflin, PA	42087	96,230	19.8	47.2	33.1	91,261	16,135	48.9	2,259	59.0	15.1	15.1
Monroe, PA	42089	501,411	2.8	28.9	68.3	406,115	12,620	61.5	11,708	88.7	7.5	1.6
Montgomery, PA	42091	1,943,683	3.6	18.1	78.3	1,618,709	15,066	61.4	41,489	91.6	5.7	1.9
Montour, PA	42093	32,212	6.1	38.0	55.9	27,405	11,607	65.5	967	83.5	12.0	1.8
Northampton, PA	42095	699,562	5.7	25.9	68.4	542,896	11,912	58.7	17,961	88.9	7.6	2.6
Northumberland, PA	42097	207,417	15.0	44.9	40.1	179,146	14,556	55.8	4,859	79.6	10.4	6.0
Perry, PA	42099	90,496	3.0	48.4	48.6	71,252	10,689	58.6	2,590	75.6	15.4	4.1
Philadelphia, PA	42101	3,414,265	11.9	46.8	41.3	2,444,238	12,772	57.0	98,067	82.3	11.3	5.5
Pike, PA	42103	129,215	3.7	28.3	68.1	107,964	11,211	66.2	3,464	85.9	9.6	3.9
Potter, PA	42105	39,861	3.9	58.0	38.1	30,588	11,851	58.4	1,006	82.4	11.0	4.0
Schuylkill, PA	42107	273,875	7.0	45.3	47.7	220,585	11,517	58.4	6,768	84.6	8.9	3.8
Snyder, PA	42109	61,131	3.9	42.3	53.8	50,549	10,198	62.3	2,893	85.8	6.9	2.2
Somerset, PA	42111	144,332	5.0	57.0	38.0	112,881	10,713	59.9	3,655	84.2	10.3	2.4
Sullivan, PA	42113	12,174	3.9	36.5	59.7	10,303	15,424	57.7	388	63.1	19.6	17.3
Susquehanna, PA	42115	104,934	5.8	55.9	38.4	90,476	12,573	60.5	2,453	84.7	9.7	3.9
Tioga, PA	42117	79,920	6.5	53.4	40.0	67,693	11,512	62.0	2,850	88.7	8.5	1.8
Union, PA	42119	55,332	3.2	34.2	62.6	46,665	11,466	62.8	3,685	93.5	2.7	2.0
Venango, PA	42121	95,095	6.0	58.6	35.3	78,170	11,769	60.4	2,745	79.6	12.5	4.3
Warren, PA	42123	73,701	6.1	57.9	36.1	62,306	11,364	62.7	2,306	80.2	14.0	3.9
Washington, PA	42125	427,607	7.6	42.0	50.3	346,925	11,907	59.4	11,343	88.8	7.7	2.6
Wayne, PA	42127	79,299	5.6	34.1	60.3	67,822	12,525	62.6	2,558	83.6	11.2	2.7
Westmoreland, PA	42129	694,877	4.9	41.7	53.4	552,990	10,702	60.5	19,184	88.5	8.7	2.2
Wyoming, PA	42131	77,897	5.3	50.4	44.2	66,427	12,062	63.0	1,676	84.1	12.5	2.5
York, PA	42133	949,736	3.4	31.6	65.0	729,635	10,871	63.0	22,804	82.4	12.2	3.2
RHODE ISLAND	44000	2,213,933	9.5	35.5	55.1	2,009,449	13,997	58.6	66,832	87.9	6.2	3.6
Bristol, RI	44001	103,014	5.1	26.3	68.6	87,693	12,720	57.9	3,759	93.0	4.4	2.0
Kent, RI	44003	374,571	6.1	25.8	68.1	349,063	14,479	61.3	8,177	84.8	10.1	3.6
Newport, RI	44005	167,659	8.2	23.5	68.3	139,516	13,700	61.4	4,651	88.7	6.0	0.8
Providence, RI	44007	1,285,985	11.9	44.0	44.1	1,174,397	13,742	57.4	40,945	86.2	6.5	4.7
Washington, RI	44009	282,704	5.0	19.8	75.2	258,780	15,292	58.8	9,300	96.0	2.2	1.1

Note. Data in columns 26 through 41 from the American Community Survey are subject to sampling error, which can be especially large in small counties and small population groups. See notes and definitions for more information.

Table C-1. Population, School, and Student Characteristics by County, Selected Years—*Continued*

County	State/ County Code	High school graduates, 2006–2010			College enrollment, 2006–2010		College graduates, 2006–2010 (percent)						
		Population 25 years and over	High school diploma or less (percent)	High school diploma or more (percent)	Number	Percent public	Bachelor's degree or more	+/- U.S. percent with Bachelor's degree or more	Non-Hispanic White	Black or African American	American Indian and Alaska Native	Asian, Hawaiian, and Pacific Islander	Hispanic or Latino[3]
		30	31	32	33	34	35	36	37	38	39	40	41
PENNSYLVANIA— *(Continued)*													
Cumberland, PA	42041	157,430	44.6	90.4	21,017	57.2	32.3	4.4	32.0	17.0	10.8	62.3	26.8
Dauphin, PA	42043	180,510	48.5	88.5	14,702	75.5	27.1	-0.8	29.8	12.4	44.4	52.8	13.8
Delaware, PA	42045	367,139	41.7	90.5	47,718	43.0	34.7	6.8	37.2	19.1	16.5	52.0	27.8
Elk, PA	42047	23,435	61.7	89.8	1,149	74.8	16.2	-11.7	16.1	0.0	0.0	32.9	1.8
Erie, PA	42049	182,858	53.5	89.0	23,334	52.7	23.3	-4.6	24.2	9.3	6.3	46.5	15.9
Fayette, PA	42051	99,517	65.9	82.9	4,980	78.6	13.9	-14.0	14.0	9.8	5.9	45.1	10.6
Forest, PA	42053	5,633	70.1	80.7	173	48.0	9.6	-18.3	10.6	6.9	0.0	0.0	0.0
Franklin, PA	42055	99,646	59.4	83.8	6,358	67.2	18.3	-9.6	18.4	18.7	43.9	33.8	10.0
Fulton, PA	42057	10,221	70.0	83.4	441	87.3	9.9	-18.0	9.8	8.8	9.5	100.0	12.0
Greene, PA	42059	27,244	64.1	83.9	1,854	44.5	14.6	-13.3	15.1	4.4	38.0	10.5	16.0
Huntingdon, PA	42061	32,059	66.5	85.5	2,675	33.9	13.8	-14.1	14.4	4.8	25.0	51.9	12.5
Indiana, PA	42063	55,798	59.7	86.7	11,309	91.3	19.2	-8.7	19.1	13.3	14.6	34.7	17.0
Jefferson, PA	42065	31,674	67.5	86.9	1,572	77.0	12.0	-15.9	11.9	0.0	0.0	58.3	34.9
Juniata, PA	42067	16,609	71.2	80.1	706	68.8	10.8	-17.1	10.9	13.2	0.0	21.5	3.0
Lackawanna, PA	42069	148,559	51.8	87.5	15,838	31.9	23.7	-4.2	23.8	13.9	16.2	58.9	9.4
Lancaster, PA	42071	333,043	56.5	82.3	29,327	64.5	23.3	-4.6	24.1	17.4	19.9	29.9	8.7
Lawrence, PA	42073	64,062	58.4	86.5	4,847	48.0	18.6	-9.3	18.9	8.7	12.2	2.7	35.6
Lebanon, PA	42075	89,924	61.1	84.4	6,417	49.8	18.3	-9.6	19.0	9.8	8.6	48.4	5.6
Lehigh, PA	42077	232,033	48.1	85.9	21,376	51.0	27.0	-0.9	29.4	13.2	8.9	59.3	8.8
Luzerne, PA	42079	225,294	54.4	87.0	19,937	54.8	20.2	-7.7	20.6	9.1	16.6	57.3	7.9
Lycoming, PA	42081	79,106	54.9	85.9	8,116	74.7	18.8	-9.1	18.9	16.0	0.0	38.3	18.8
McKean, PA	42083	30,480	61.3	88.3	1,971	78.6	15.7	-12.2	16.1	3.5	6.0	40.7	8.9
Mercer, PA	42085	80,405	58.0	87.1	7,837	39.1	19.0	-8.9	19.5	9.3	2.0	36.3	13.3
Mifflin, PA	42087	32,106	72.0	80.8	1,208	78.3	11.1	-16.8	10.8	28.5	0.0	41.6	42.8
Monroe, PA	42089	109,921	49.4	88.7	11,772	78.4	23.8	-4.1	24.2	20.8	23.4	48.6	17.1
Montgomery, PA	42091	545,630	33.7	92.6	54,432	48.2	44.2	16.3	44.8	30.3	43.0	62.9	26.8
Montour, PA	42093	12,845	53.7	87.5	749	65.8	25.0	-2.9	24.3	59.8	0.0	59.5	22.2
Northampton, PA	42095	200,204	48.7	87.0	23,098	40.6	26.3	-1.6	27.0	19.1	3.9	52.8	14.0
Northumberland, PA	42097	67,281	66.9	84.2	3,121	68.0	13.5	-14.4	13.5	11.0	0.0	43.6	12.3
Perry, PA	42099	31,250	65.0	85.4	1,371	80.0	14.0	-13.9	14.1	21.4	6.4	19.4	6.2
Philadelphia, PA	42101	965,571	56.3	79.4	144,975	43.9	22.2	-5.7	32.5	12.1	14.9	35.0	10.6
Pike, PA	42103	39,243	46.5	91.5	2,283	73.1	23.3	-4.6	23.3	31.4	20.6	60.9	15.6
Potter, PA	42105	12,284	64.4	85.5	485	72.8	12.4	-15.5	12.4	11.1	12.5	44.8	6.3
Schuylkill, PA	42107	107,374	65.0	83.6	5,605	74.5	13.6	-14.3	13.8	6.0	33.7	29.2	9.2
Snyder, PA	42109	25,477	65.5	81.6	3,236	23.6	15.3	-12.6	15.3	11.7	0.0	39.1	11.3
Somerset, PA	42111	56,779	66.3	82.9	2,662	77.9	14.3	-13.6	14.4	11.5	0.0	40.6	4.2
Sullivan, PA	42113	4,721	65.3	86.1	137	65.7	11.4	-16.5	11.4	0.0	0.0	0.0	0.0
Susquehanna, PA	42115	30,656	60.3	86.8	1,402	57.8	15.4	-12.5	15.4	8.5	12.8	35.4	11.9
Tioga, PA	42117	28,291	56.2	87.1	3,004	81.4	17.7	-10.2	17.6	35.6	0.0	40.5	21.3
Union, PA	42119	30,194	57.0	83.1	5,260	15.3	22.2	-5.7	24.8	3.0	0.0	54.6	11.2
Venango, PA	42121	39,082	61.8	87.3	1,812	74.7	14.1	-13.8	14.1	5.2	13.2	57.0	5.0
Warren, PA	42123	29,927	58.4	88.9	1,274	63.4	16.9	-11.0	16.8	35.7	26.4	46.5	8.1
Washington, PA	42125	145,518	51.7	89.0	11,983	71.1	24.2	-3.7	24.5	8.7	29.3	55.6	25.3
Wayne, PA	42127	38,289	57.2	86.7	2,169	47.4	17.9	-10.0	18.2	13.7	10.0	45.4	7.1
Westmoreland, PA	42129	263,845	49.6	91.4	18,550	64.0	24.0	-3.9	23.9	14.0	4.8	70.6	25.0
Wyoming, PA	42131	19,444	58.9	89.1	1,468	43.9	16.8	-11.1	16.8	29.6	0.0	41.0	9.2
York, PA	42133	291,278	54.8	86.8	21,142	60.0	21.5	-6.4	22.1	16.0	17.2	32.7	10.7
RHODE ISLAND	44000	708,598	44.6	83.7	99,378	54.6	30.3	2.4	32.7	18.6	10.6	44.3	12.3
Bristol, RI	44001	33,830	36.3	86.2	5,399	35.8	41.1	13.2	40.5	46.0	0.0	86.6	36.8
Kent, RI	44003	119,341	42.0	89.5	10,132	71.2	29.2	1.3	29.0	26.3	13.1	49.2	22.8
Newport, RI	44005	58,973	32.5	91.1	7,289	51.3	43.4	15.5	44.6	19.2	9.8	52.0	37.6
Providence, RI	44007	412,477	50.2	79.0	62,005	46.9	25.6	-2.3	28.7	18.1	12.7	39.9	10.2
Washington, RI	44009	83,977	32.4	91.9	14,553	84.5	41.7	13.8	42.1	16.8	5.4	57.8	40.4

Note. Data in columns 26 through 41 from the American Community Survey are subject to sampling error, which can be especially large in small counties and small population groups. See notes and definitions for more information.
[3]May be of any race.

Table C-1. Population, School, and Student Characteristics by County, Selected Years—*Continued*

County	State/ County Code	County Type[1]	Population, 2010		Percent of related children 5–17 years in poverty, 2010	Percent of children under 19 years with no health insurance, 2010	Number of schools and students, 2010–2011			Resident enrollment, 2006–2010	
										K–12 enrollment	
			Total	Percent 5–17 years			School districts	Schools	Students	Number	Percent public
			1	2	3	4	5	6	7	8	9
SOUTH CAROLINA	45000	X	4,625,364	16.8	23.6	9.8	105	1,214	725,838	788,807	90.0
Abbeville, SC	45001	6	25,417	16.8	24.7	10.0	1	9	3,123	4,556	92.1
Aiken, SC	45003	2	160,099	16.7	22.1	9.7	1	40	24,632	27,849	90.6
Allendale, SC	45005	6	10,419	16.4	44.0	9.6	1	4	1,539	1,940	95.8
Anderson, SC	45007	3	187,126	17.5	24.0	9.2	6	49	30,875	32,974	92.4
Bamberg, SC	45009	7	15,987	16.5	36.3	8.0	2	7	2,370	2,867	88.5
Barnwell, SC	45011	6	22,621	19.0	34.5	8.0	4	11	4,295	4,228	94.9
Beaufort, SC	45013	5	162,233	14.4	21.8	13.5	1	33	19,648	23,457	84.4
Berkeley, SC	45015	2	177,843	17.8	20.0	10.1	1	39	29,400	31,951	89.1
Calhoun, SC	45017	2	15,175	15.7	25.2	11.1	1	3	1,731	2,650	81.1
Charleston, SC	45019	2	350,209	14.2	22.5	9.0	1	78	43,654	51,268	85.7
Cherokee, SC	45021	4	55,342	17.9	26.9	9.1	1	19	9,014	10,116	95.9
Chester, SC	45023	6	33,140	17.3	27.7	9.5	1	13	5,550	6,244	92.8
Chesterfield, SC	45025	6	46,734	18.3	32.7	9.1	1	16	7,720	8,919	91.5
Clarendon, SC	45027	6	34,971	16.5	35.3	9.7	4	13	5,241	6,514	85.0
Colleton, SC	45029	6	38,892	17.8	34.1	9.8	1	12	6,245	7,502	88.7
Darlington, SC	45031	3	68,681	17.9	31.9	8.5	1	23	10,693	13,335	88.1
Dillon, SC	45033	6	32,062	19.3	34.6	7.8	4	14	6,058	6,131	94.9
Dorchester, SC	45035	2	136,555	20.0	16.4	9.1	3	26	25,025	26,883	84.6
Edgefield, SC	45037	2	26,985	16.2	24.1	9.5	1	9	4,011	4,743	89.3
Fairfield, SC	45039	2	23,956	16.7	29.3	8.4	1	8	3,172	4,537	89.1
Florence, SC	45041	3	136,885	17.9	27.7	8.3	5	39	23,010	25,515	89.7
Georgetown, SC	45043	4	60,158	16.1	28.0	11.1	1	18	9,789	10,137	93.0
Greenville, SC	45045	2	451,225	17.3	18.9	10.5	1	95	71,930	76,451	86.3
Greenwood, SC	45047	4	69,661	16.9	30.4	10.0	4	22	11,798	11,694	94.1
Hampton, SC	45049	6	21,090	17.8	31.5	9.4	2	10	3,629	3,948	91.3
Horry, SC	45051	3	269,291	14.5	31.1	14.7	1	50	38,534	37,279	94.1
Jasper, SC	45053	6	24,777	17.3	34.9	13.9	2	6	3,255	4,456	80.6
Kershaw, SC	45055	2	61,697	17.9	23.2	10.4	1	19	10,359	11,358	93.6
Lancaster, SC	45057	4	76,652	16.5	25.5	8.7	1	20	11,696	12,857	95.3
Laurens, SC	45059	2	66,537	16.7	28.5	9.8	2	17	8,974	11,821	91.9
Lee, SC	45061	6	19,220	16.4	34.7	8.7	1	7	2,291	3,644	88.6
Lexington, SC	45063	2	262,391	17.8	17.4	8.3	4	53	37,129	45,740	94.0
McCormick, SC	45065	8	10,233	10.3	34.0	10.0	2	4	869	1,142	88.6
Marion, SC	45067	6	33,062	17.6	36.8	8.2	4	11	5,252	6,196	94.5
Marlboro, SC	45069	6	28,933	16.1	40.8	7.8	1	9	4,471	5,335	92.9
Newberry, SC	45071	6	37,508	16.3	27.8	10.7	1	14	5,833	6,225	92.1
Oconee, SC	45073	6	74,273	15.5	21.0	10.8	1	19	10,606	11,834	91.6
Orangeburg, SC	45075	4	92,501	16.5	34.5	8.2	5	29	13,841	15,787	85.6
Pickens, SC	45077	2	119,224	15.0	18.5	9.6	1	25	16,319	18,363	89.6
Richland, SC	45079	2	384,504	16.4	18.3	7.4	6	129	77,416	64,094	89.4
Saluda, SC	45081	2	19,875	16.2	28.2	12.3	1	5	2,133	3,470	93.6
Spartanburg, SC	45083	2	284,307	17.8	23.5	12.1	11	81	46,832	50,242	92.1
Sumter, SC	45085	3	107,456	18.1	29.4	8.5	4	27	17,060	19,835	87.0
Union, SC	45087	6	28,961	17.0	27.4	8.3	1	8	4,437	4,889	96.7
Williamsburg, SC	45089	6	34,423	17.6	40.1	10.9	1	14	4,975	7,083	89.8
York, SC	45091	1	226,073	18.7	16.0	9.5	4	57	39,404	40,748	92.5
SOUTH DAKOTA	46000	X	814,180	17.6	17.1	8.0	172	710	125,883	141,505	91.2
Aurora, SD	46003	9	2,710	19.6	15.5	18.0	3	11	573	519	92.7
Beadle, SD	46005	7	17,398	16.8	18.1	8.4	2	13	2,457	2,676	86.1
Bennett, SD	46007	9	3,431	24.6	42.6	10.0	1	3	535	693	90.8
Bon Homme, SD	46009	9	7,070	14.5	16.2	11.2	4	13	1,113	1,057	99.2
Brookings, SD	46011	7	31,965	12.9	10.3	7.0	5	20	4,141	3,829	96.2
Brown, SD	46013	5	36,531	16.3	11.5	5.5	7	22	5,084	5,920	89.9
Brule, SD	46015	9	5,255	18.8	16.5	11.6	2	8	1,158	1,221	76.0
Buffalo, SD	46017	9	1,912	27.4	43.6	8.6	...	...	...	548	85.2
Butte, SD	46019	6	10,110	17.5	20.4	9.8	2	8	1,709	1,688	91.7
Campbell, SD	46021	9	1,466	15.1	12.6	15.5	1	3	121	238	95.8

[1]County type codes are from the Economic Research Service of the United States Department of Agriculture. See notes and definitions for more information.

Table C-1. Population, School, and Student Characteristics by County, Selected Years—*Continued*

County	State/ County Code	Characteristics of students, 2010–2011				Number of graduates, 2008–2009	Staff and students, 2010–2011			
		Percent with IEP[2]	Percent eligible for free or reduced lunch	Percent minority	Percent English-language learners		Total staff	Number of teachers	Student/ teacher ratio	Central admin. staff
		10	11	12	13	14	15	16	17	18
SOUTH CAROLINA	45000	13.8	54.5	46.6	5.0	39,114	65,508	45,210	16.1	1,478
Abbeville, SC	45001	16.8	60.5	39.9	1.7	173	345	222	14.1	11
Aiken, SC	45003	11.3	55.8	42.3	5.2	1,276	2,293	1,472	16.7	19
Allendale, SC	45005	12.2	93.1	96.9	2.0	77	191	117	13.1	7
Anderson, SC	45007	15.0	50.1	27.7	2.7	1,692	2,586	1,872	16.5	68
Bamberg, SC	45009	15.9	66.7	71.9	0.8	145	228	144	16.5	11
Barnwell, SC	45011	15.8	64.8	58.7	0.9	239	460	302	14.2	14
Beaufort, SC	45013	11.3	51.4	55.8	15.6	995	1,615	1,256	15.6	29
Berkeley, SC	45015	14.2	56.3	46.9	5.6	1,422	2,582	1,777	16.5	56
Calhoun, SC	45017	14.7	84.3	72.2	2.5	81	186	115	15.1	3
Charleston, SC	45019	10.1	49.2	55.2	4.3	2,158	4,118	2,997	14.6	62
Cherokee, SC	45021	10.9	68.5	32.6	4.5	498	816	580	15.6	9
Chester, SC	45023	12.5	66.8	51.0	1.1	366	510	354	15.7	8
Chesterfield, SC	45025	10.5	63.4	45.6	2.8	423	626	465	16.6	10
Clarendon, SC	45027	18.0	69.4	66.6	2.3	352	442	277	18.9	14
Colleton, SC	45029	16.7	77.1	55.8	2.6	246	596	369	16.9	7
Darlington, SC	45031	15.4	71.4	58.6	1.4	569	1,010	626	17.1	16
Dillon, SC	45033	11.3	77.7	63.7	4.3	327	493	339	17.9	14
Dorchester, SC	45035	12.0	41.4	43.6	2.6	1,262	1,973	1,437	17.4	21
Edgefield, SC	45037	17.7	61.9	52.5	1.3	239	394	265	15.2	11
Fairfield, SC	45039	16.9	74.1	88.7	1.3	205	395	244	13.0	16
Florence, SC	45041	17.1	62.4	58.0	1.8	1,267	2,355	1,474	15.6	75
Georgetown, SC	45043	11.8	62.5	49.7	2.5	636	883	669	14.6	22
Greenville, SC	45045	14.0	46.1	40.6	9.4	3,805	6,264	4,155	17.3	202
Greenwood, SC	45047	13.3	57.0	47.1	7.6	729	1,163	690	17.1	66
Hampton, SC	45049	14.3	74.9	68.4	1.7	230	422	233	15.6	32
Horry, SC	45051	15.8	62.2	34.1	6.5	2,091	3,719	2,447	15.7	57
Jasper, SC	45053	12.8	69.6	87.1	21.7	158	363	243	13.4	8
Kershaw, SC	45055	12.5	54.6	34.7	2.6	609	888	616	16.8	10
Lancaster, SC	45057	13.7	55.0	37.7	4.9	747	1,062	703	16.6	16
Laurens, SC	45059	19.2	68.9	40.4	5.1	459	879	511	17.6	53
Lee, SC	45061	14.5	87.9	95.5	1.6	125	233	155	14.8	7
Lexington, SC	45063	13.5	44.1	31.1	5.2	1,980	3,543	2,355	15.8	114
McCormick, SC	45065	11.5	67.7	81.2	...	61	110	56	15.5	9
Marion, SC	45067	17.7	82.7	77.5	1.4	303	516	314	16.7	13
Marlboro, SC	45069	18.5	79.0	69.4	0.5	220	417	279	16.0	7
Newberry, SC	45071	16.0	63.8	51.7	8.8	365	620	420	13.9	16
Oconee, SC	45073	16.5	55.1	20.8	5.6	599	1,104	757	14.0	22
Orangeburg, SC	45075	15.4	70.5	79.7	1.3	795	1,284	880	15.7	21
Pickens, SC	45077	12.7	44.6	16.3	3.4	855	1,356	982	16.6	25
Richland, SC	45079	13.6	47.5	65.3	3.1	3,838	6,210	4,805	16.1	100
Saluda, SC	45081	15.7	68.7	55.8	19.5	111	234	145	14.7	20
Spartanburg, SC	45083	14.2	51.7	37.9	8.8	2,648	4,149	3,121	15.0	70
Sumter, SC	45085	14.0	68.5	66.9	1.1	1,010	1,669	996	17.1	49
Union, SC	45087	17.9	65.8	39.9	0.6	248	398	277	16.0	8
Williamsburg, SC	45089	17.9	89.5	93.3	0.1	309	465	278	17.9	5
York, SC	45091	12.3	40.4	32.5	3.6	2,171	3,343	2,422	16.3	50
SOUTH DAKOTA	46000	14.3	37.1	20.2	3.5	8,122	19,545	9,512	13.2	1,167
Aurora, SD	46003	12.0	33.2	14.1	2.4	40	107	50	11.5	8
Beadle, SD	46005	14.3	47.1	24.4	13.6	157	358	160	15.3	22
Bennett, SD	46007	15.9	61.5	74.4	0.9	37	107	49	11.0	10
Bon Homme, SD	46009	15.4	35.9	4.3	3.0	88	225	94	11.8	20
Brookings, SD	46011	12.5	23.5	9.6	1.7	256	543	295	14.0	31
Brown, SD	46013	15.0	29.9	9.9	0.5	329	800	377	13.5	40
Brule, SD	46015	15.1	47.5	33.4	1.1	71	183	104	11.1	14
Buffalo, SD	46017	0.0	0.0	0.0	...	...	...	...	...	...
Butte, SD	46019	15.4	46.5	10.9	0.4	134	264	121	14.1	15
Campbell, SD	46021	13.2	31.8	0.8	...	11	29	15	8.2	3

[2]IEP=Individual Education Program. See notes and definitions for more information.
. . . = Not available.

Table C-1. Population, School, and Student Characteristics by County, Selected Years—*Continued*

County	State/ County Code	Revenues, 2008–2009				Current expenditures, 2008–2009			Resident population 16 to 19 years, 2006–2010			
		Total revenue ($1,000's)	Percentage of revenue from			Amount ($1,000's)	Amount per student	Percent for instruction	Total population 16 to 19 years	Percent enrolled in school	Percent high school graduates, not enrolled in school	Percent not enrolled, not grads, not employed, or not in labor force
			Federal government	State government	Local government							
		19	20	21	22	23	24	25	26	27	28	29
SOUTH CAROLINA	45000	7,688,810	9.6	47.7	42.7	6,637,688	9,261	57.5	266,213	81.3	11.5	4.8
Abbeville, SC	45001	33,411	11.4	60.7	27.9	31,981	9,700	58.1	1,521	88.6	8.6	2.6
Aiken, SC	45003	216,341	10.4	55.5	34.1	198,014	8,021	60.8	8,847	83.7	8.7	5.9
Allendale, SC	45005	22,908	14.7	56.3	28.9	19,027	12,065	51.7	701	68.1	12.4	18.3
Anderson, SC	45007	294,936	9.8	52.9	37.3	264,262	8,489	59.2	9,865	78.4	10.8	6.6
Bamberg, SC	45009	28,474	15.3	58.2	26.4	25,186	10,455	54.5	1,276	86.8	0.2	12.3
Barnwell, SC	45011	47,801	12.5	55.7	31.8	43,797	10,064	56.1	1,258	86.8	2.9	7.2
Beaufort, SC	45013	261,728	7.0	27.6	65.4	200,801	10,376	57.9	8,269	68.2	26.4	3.0
Berkeley, SC	45015	282,791	9.8	51.5	38.7	242,841	8,386	55.8	9,984	72.9	19.8	2.3
Calhoun, SC	45017	23,903	11.4	46.0	42.6	20,339	11,999	52.8	824	76.7	10.1	13.2
Charleston, SC	45019	538,429	8.8	32.0	59.2	414,710	9,803	56.8	19,052	83.8	9.6	3.0
Cherokee, SC	45021	92,829	10.3	49.5	40.2	81,820	8,742	57.0	2,968	82.0	11.1	6.9
Chester, SC	45023	61,801	10.3	52.6	37.1	55,406	9,643	54.4	1,912	78.9	15.2	5.1
Chesterfield, SC	45025	75,597	11.7	56.9	31.4	68,112	8,526	58.1	2,826	77.2	11.2	10.2
Clarendon, SC	45027	53,464	16.0	55.1	28.9	49,767	9,262	54.5	2,134	77.1	8.8	13.4
Colleton, SC	45029	71,239	14.7	45.0	40.4	58,964	9,395	55.2	2,348	77.4	6.7	13.7
Darlington, SC	45031	119,099	12.6	50.3	37.2	102,353	9,272	55.7	4,164	82.7	10.8	6.5
Dillon, SC	45033	52,994	17.7	61.6	20.7	53,146	8,744	52.3	1,982	77.9	13.9	7.9
Dorchester, SC	45035	225,230	7.6	57.3	35.2	205,460	8,525	59.8	7,753	83.6	9.9	3.1
Edgefield, SC	45037	42,496	11.0	53.8	35.2	36,440	8,995	60.9	1,387	69.1	19.7	9.4
Fairfield, SC	45039	44,899	11.0	39.3	49.7	44,139	13,051	51.1	1,156	86.4	8.9	4.7
Florence, SC	45041	227,245	14.0	55.7	30.3	215,289	9,315	57.0	7,470	87.8	6.3	5.0
Georgetown, SC	45043	113,502	10.2	37.6	52.2	98,240	9,752	56.3	2,897	87.1	8.0	4.9
Greenville, SC	45045	687,992	9.2	49.6	41.2	556,811	7,905	57.9	24,591	85.7	7.6	3.4
Greenwood, SC	45047	126,942	8.6	48.0	43.3	106,319	8,816	56.7	4,173	71.3	12.2	11.7
Hampton, SC	45049	42,707	14.3	58.4	27.3	42,333	10,797	53.3	1,275	74.8	15.8	6.4
Horry, SC	45051	444,243	8.4	33.2	58.4	373,594	9,845	59.4	12,847	74.6	17.3	4.5
Jasper, SC	45053	41,693	12.2	42.7	45.1	38,638	11,472	53.9	1,363	69.3	21.7	5.4
Kershaw, SC	45055	105,393	9.5	47.9	42.6	92,945	8,848	57.7	3,215	80.7	11.9	6.1
Lancaster, SC	45057	114,576	12.6	53.1	34.3	103,233	8,743	59.1	3,647	85.2	7.6	3.2
Laurens, SC	45059	88,174	14.0	55.6	30.4	83,283	8,995	54.8	4,024	78.4	10.0	8.6
Lee, SC	45061	33,246	15.8	60.3	23.9	25,749	10,194	52.0	1,089	74.7	12.2	9.9
Lexington, SC	45063	383,882	7.0	54.1	39.0	337,998	9,306	57.5	13,449	82.4	12.5	3.3
McCormick, SC	45065	14,935	14.7	48.6	36.7	10,863	12,151	48.2	304	76.3	6.3	9.2
Marion, SC	45067	58,855	17.8	57.2	25.0	55,219	9,891	56.2	2,091	79.2	12.2	4.2
Marlboro, SC	45069	49,170	18.9	53.6	27.5	46,972	10,218	51.0	1,501	74.9	8.6	14.3
Newberry, SC	45071	68,945	11.5	49.6	38.8	61,236	10,235	55.0	2,023	83.6	7.5	1.8
Oconee, SC	45073	120,805	7.9	40.0	52.1	103,802	9,751	56.9	3,749	78.2	14.9	4.4
Orangeburg, SC	45075	165,576	13.2	49.3	37.6	153,697	10,718	53.3	6,553	89.4	4.2	5.4
Pickens, SC	45077	172,082	7.1	47.7	45.2	129,824	7,799	59.6	10,774	90.2	5.5	2.8
Richland, SC	45079	846,418	7.3	45.7	47.0	737,804	10,841	57.7	28,448	81.2	14.5	3.0
Saluda, SC	45081	19,738	11.2	59.6	29.1	19,003	9,049	52.5	1,024	86.4	12.2	1.4
Spartanburg, SC	45083	490,188	8.6	51.4	40.0	431,942	9,200	59.1	16,754	83.4	9.7	4.9
Sumter, SC	45085	164,699	13.5	55.7	30.8	146,205	8,323	56.7	6,610	78.7	15.5	4.8
Union, SC	45087	43,972	11.8	62.4	25.9	41,600	8,987	58.7	1,537	75.3	16.7	6.4
Williamsburg, SC	45089	59,429	18.4	54.1	27.5	56,728	10,488	52.7	2,058	82.3	14.8	2.9
York, SC	45091	414,033	6.0	49.8	44.2	351,796	9,058	59.4	12,520	82.1	9.1	5.9
SOUTH DAKOTA	46000	1,236,104	16.1	32.7	51.2	1,058,358	8,358	59.9	47,617	85.1	8.6	4.0
Aurora, SD	46003	6,611	12.6	40.2	47.2	6,136	10,957	66.9	121	92.6	3.3	4.1
Beadle, SD	46005	22,773	13.1	36.6	50.3	19,643	7,937	57.8	812	65.6	25.7	6.2
Bennett, SD	46007	6,217	38.2	37.0	24.8	5,480	9,856	60.9	224	51.8	29.9	9.4
Bon Homme, SD	46009	10,994	14.2	40.1	45.7	9,955	9,116	55.7	304	91.1	8.9	0.0
Brookings, SD	46011	41,350	7.1	30.7	62.1	33,127	7,994	61.8	3,274	96.3	1.7	1.3
Brown, SD	46013	46,962	8.8	32.6	58.5	38,952	7,701	59.1	2,187	90.8	8.7	0.5
Brule, SD	46015	13,462	23.7	34.5	41.9	11,326	9,823	63.0	316	89.2	7.3	0.3
Buffalo, SD	46017	. . .	. . .	. . .	. . .	. . .	. . .	. . .	197	88.3	6.1	5.6
Butte, SD	46019	14,900	16.1	45.2	38.7	12,871	7,410	60.6	472	83.9	5.9	10.2
Campbell, SD	46021	1,462	7.9	42.5	49.5	1,433	10,774	57.6	73	93.2	6.9	0.0

Note. Data in columns 26 through 41 from the American Community Survey are subject to sampling error, which can be especially large in small counties and small population groups. See notes and definitions for more information.
. . . = Not available.

Table C-1. Population, School, and Student Characteristics by County, Selected Years—*Continued*

County	State/ County Code	High school graduates, 2006–2010			College enrollment, 2006–2010		College graduates, 2006–2010 (percent)						
		Population 25 years and over	High school diploma or less (percent)	High school diploma or more (percent)	Number	Percent public	Bachelor's degree or more	+/- U.S. percent with Bachelor's degree or more	Non-Hispanic White	Black or African American	American Indian and Alaska Native	Asian, Hawaiian, and Pacific Islander	Hispanic or Latino[3]
		30	31	32	33	34	35	36	37	38	39	40	41
SOUTH CAROLINA	45000	2,981,382	48.2	83.0	292,736	76.9	24.0	-3.9	28.4	12.9	10.2	45.8	12.4
Abbeville, SC	45001	17,270	57.1	76.8	1,567	46.2	15.3	-12.6	16.4	10.6	0.0	54.8	39.9
Aiken, SC	45003	105,906	48.1	83.7	9,037	87.7	23.5	-4.4	27.2	12.3	9.0	62.5	9.2
Allendale, SC	45005	7,176	65.9	73.2	476	81.9	13.2	-14.7	22.4	9.2	0.0	0.0	0.0
Anderson, SC	45007	123,927	52.8	80.6	9,693	68.1	18.0	-9.9	19.6	8.6	13.6	28.4	13.2
Bamberg, SC	45009	10,306	55.6	76.4	1,742	52.1	17.4	-10.5	17.4	17.0	0.0	37.8	0.0
Barnwell, SC	45011	14,997	63.5	78.2	1,172	79.5	11.5	-16.4	15.5	6.7	0.0	0.0	0.0
Beaufort, SC	45013	105,953	33.6	90.6	7,064	80.3	37.4	9.5	45.6	15.1	9.7	48.9	11.8
Berkeley, SC	45015	108,359	49.9	86.4	10,196	77.2	18.3	-9.6	19.7	14.0	2.7	28.7	16.1
Calhoun, SC	45017	10,575	54.1	81.6	789	83.8	20.3	-7.6	26.3	11.1	0.0	100.0	33.7
Charleston, SC	45019	227,578	36.1	87.4	31,028	81.4	37.5	9.6	48.6	14.2	20.0	49.3	13.0
Cherokee, SC	45021	36,304	65.5	74.3	2,906	74.0	11.7	-16.2	12.6	7.3	0.0	39.2	4.1
Chester, SC	45023	22,223	63.7	74.3	1,229	83.2	11.2	-16.7	12.7	8.0	0.0	70.2	12.9
Chesterfield, SC	45025	30,541	66.0	73.4	1,692	79.1	11.1	-16.8	13.1	6.9	0.0	69.8	0.7
Clarendon, SC	45027	23,075	65.4	75.4	1,197	71.8	13.2	-14.7	18.0	8.4	0.0	100.0	1.2
Colleton, SC	45029	25,798	63.8	75.3	1,761	82.2	13.6	-14.3	18.8	6.1	0.0	0.0	2.8
Darlington, SC	45031	45,670	60.4	76.9	3,057	64.2	15.9	-12.0	20.1	8.9	36.1	79.1	5.9
Dillon, SC	45033	20,171	71.6	65.8	1,021	86.7	9.2	-18.7	11.7	5.9	1.1	36.0	0.0
Dorchester, SC	45035	83,422	41.6	88.9	7,571	71.0	24.1	-3.8	27.4	15.6	14.5	31.6	11.5
Edgefield, SC	45037	18,628	58.3	78.3	1,200	86.9	16.3	-11.6	21.9	8.3	0.0	0.0	13.0
Fairfield, SC	45039	16,337	60.6	78.5	1,012	64.3	15.9	-12.0	23.1	10.1	36.4	0.0	63.0
Florence, SC	45041	88,587	53.4	80.8	7,855	84.5	20.8	-7.1	25.6	12.3	5.3	55.7	20.3
Georgetown, SC	45043	42,620	49.2	83.4	2,345	87.6	21.8	-6.1	28.4	7.7	0.0	12.6	10.4
Greenville, SC	45045	289,136	43.3	84.0	26,662	57.9	30.0	2.1	34.4	14.3	20.4	52.5	11.1
Greenwood, SC	45047	45,222	52.3	79.5	4,593	90.3	22.0	-5.9	26.8	11.0	3.7	50.8	12.9
Hampton, SC	45049	14,047	65.1	75.9	904	87.4	11.0	-16.9	15.2	6.8	0.0	15.7	21.6
Horry, SC	45051	180,994	47.3	86.9	12,837	88.6	21.8	-6.1	24.0	10.5	8.4	30.3	9.8
Jasper, SC	45053	14,899	64.8	74.9	627	90.4	9.4	-18.5	15.3	4.1	0.0	70.0	6.4
Kershaw, SC	45055	40,449	53.2	82.6	2,387	77.2	18.5	-9.4	20.3	13.2	0.0	41.0	10.8
Lancaster, SC	45057	49,463	57.9	77.8	2,464	81.5	15.4	-12.5	18.0	6.8	0.0	21.1	13.4
Laurens, SC	45059	44,849	60.4	74.7	3,811	53.5	14.5	-13.4	16.9	8.2	0.0	19.9	5.2
Lee, SC	45061	13,003	71.3	67.7	533	67.4	8.5	-19.4	13.7	5.2	0.0	100.0	0.0
Lexington, SC	45063	168,213	41.5	88.1	14,204	80.8	27.6	-0.3	29.3	18.0	10.1	52.1	15.6
McCormick, SC	45065	8,029	54.3	78.1	381	89.2	16.0	-11.9	25.7	4.8	0.0	66.7	0.0
Marion, SC	45067	22,307	65.4	78.7	1,352	83.8	12.9	-15.0	18.6	7.9	12.9	100.0	11.3
Marlboro, SC	45069	20,084	72.0	67.5	946	91.9	8.6	-19.3	11.8	6.3	0.7	26.7	11.1
Newberry, SC	45071	25,006	56.9	75.1	2,022	67.1	19.3	-8.6	24.6	9.6	27.0	20.5	3.0
Oconee, SC	45073	51,524	51.5	81.2	3,725	88.1	21.4	-6.5	22.3	12.2	17.5	83.1	9.6
Orangeburg, SC	45075	59,136	60.1	77.2	8,150	73.8	16.7	-11.2	18.8	14.9	14.2	81.0	3.7
Pickens, SC	45077	71,984	49.4	81.4	19,585	93.9	23.6	-4.3	22.6	22.5	20.0	77.4	16.5
Richland, SC	45079	230,300	34.4	88.4	43,888	75.4	36.5	8.6	49.5	21.9	21.4	61.0	20.2
Saluda, SC	45081	13,407	64.1	75.1	716	75.1	12.6	-15.3	18.1	3.1	0.0	0.0	1.4
Spartanburg, SC	45083	183,336	51.4	79.9	16,233	63.9	19.9	-8.0	22.6	11.1	17.7	24.8	9.2
Sumter, SC	45085	67,416	51.6	81.8	6,259	76.2	17.4	-10.5	23.1	10.5	13.5	38.2	10.5
Union, SC	45087	20,117	59.5	75.6	1,298	84.1	12.9	-15.0	14.4	9.1	0.0	41.3	22.0
Williamsburg, SC	45089	22,930	67.4	78.3	1,166	81.0	11.3	-16.6	16.5	8.3	0.0	0.0	3.0
York, SC	45091	140,108	42.8	85.9	12,383	84.9	27.0	-0.9	29.7	14.5	5.7	40.0	23.5
SOUTH DAKOTA	46000	518,285	43.5	89.3	53,122	80.2	25.3	-2.6	26.4	18.1	11.6	41.4	14.8
Aurora, SD	46003	1,892	59.4	85.3	63	84.1	12.2	-15.7	13.3	0.0	0.0	0.0	0.0
Beadle, SD	46005	11,495	51.9	82.3	355	64.8	19.7	-8.2	20.2	0.0	0.0	21.9	11.6
Bennett, SD	46007	1,943	54.8	73.1	91	95.6	15.8	-12.1	17.6	0.0	14.5	100.0	0.0
Bon Homme, SD	46009	5,189	53.9	87.7	99	76.8	15.4	-12.5	16.1	9.7	5.0	100.0	0.0
Brookings, SD	46011	16,168	37.7	92.0	8,602	98.2	37.7	9.8	36.2	100.0	21.7	82.6	17.3
Brown, SD	46013	23,803	44.0	89.8	2,628	85.9	24.1	-3.8	23.9	0.0	21.7	63.9	35.8
Brule, SD	46015	3,244	46.5	87.7	193	72.0	25.2	-2.7	25.6	0.0	9.6	0.0	0.0
Buffalo, SD	46017	932	62.2	76.5	16	100.0	8.3	-19.6	25.5	100.0	4.5	100.0	0.0
Butte, SD	46019	6,708	49.5	87.5	404	93.6	19.3	-8.6	20.0	0.0	0.0	0.0	13.6
Campbell, SD	46021	1,074	50.8	86.0	34	91.2	17.0	-10.9	17.1	0.0	0.0	0.0	0.0

Note. Data in columns 26 through 41 from the American Community Survey are subject to sampling error, which can be especially large in small counties and small population groups. See notes and definitions for more information.
[3]May be of any race.

Table C-1. Population, School, and Student Characteristics by County, Selected Years—*Continued*

County	State/ County Code	County Type[1]	Population, 2010: Total	Population, 2010: Percent 5–17 years	Percent of related children 5–17 years in poverty, 2010	Percent of children under 19 years with no health insurance, 2010	Number of schools and students, 2010–2011: School districts	Number of schools and students, 2010–2011: Schools	Number of schools and students, 2010–2011: Students	Resident enrollment, 2006–2010, K–12 enrollment: Number	Resident enrollment, 2006–2010, K–12 enrollment: Percent public
			1	2	3	4	5	6	7	8	9
SOUTH DAKOTA— *(Continued)*											
Charles Mix, SD	46023	9	9,129	21.2	34.2	11.8	4	13	1,625	1,922	83.5
Clark, SD	46025	9	3,691	17.1	22.2	13.7	2	11	588	674	97.5
Clay, SD	46027	6	13,864	12.3	16.9	7.8	1	4	1,286	1,789	92.1
Codington, SD	46029	7	27,227	17.3	12.3	6.6	5	19	4,370	4,901	89.4
Corson, SD	46031	9	4,050	24.2	50.3	11.7	3	8	849	974	98.5
Custer, SD	46033	8	8,216	15.0	17.2	11.1	3	10	1,036	1,134	92.7
Davison, SD	46035	7	19,504	16.4	15.8	6.2	4	14	2,944	3,187	90.8
Day, SD	46037	9	5,710	16.0	21.3	14.2	2	6	723	925	90.3
Deuel, SD	46039	9	4,364	17.4	12.5	13.9	1	3	571	790	96.5
Dewey, SD	46041	9	5,301	24.5	36.2	10.6	3	10	648	1,454	97.7
Douglas, SD	46043	9	3,002	17.4	17.2	14.2	2	6	340	484	71.3
Edmunds, SD	46045	9	4,071	18.4	14.4	11.2	3	12	631	650	91.5
Fall River, SD	46047	7	7,094	14.1	21.6	9.5	3	8	1,113	981	82.8
Faulk, SD	46049	9	2,364	17.4	22.5	13.7	1	7	322	397	93.5
Grant, SD	46051	7	7,356	17.2	13.5	9.4	3	9	1,131	1,287	95.7
Gregory, SD	46053	9	4,271	16.7	29.4	14.4	3	9	728	705	96.2
Haakon, SD	46055	8	1,937	16.2	17.3	21.4	2	5	292	249	98.8
Hamlin, SD	46057	9	5,903	21.2	17.9	12.1	4	11	1,282	1,175	93.8
Hand, SD	46059	9	3,431	15.4	13.1	15.1	1	4	440	583	92.6
Hanson, SD	46061	8	3,331	23.0	16.1	12.5	1	6	414	718	77.2
Harding, SD	46063	9	1,255	18.1	25.8	23.6	1	5	195	272	94.5
Hughes, SD	46065	7	17,022	16.9	11.9	6.4	3	6	2,578	3,005	91.8
Hutchinson, SD	46067	8	7,343	18.0	15.5	11.3	4	22	1,464	1,394	91.5
Hyde, SD	46069	9	1,420	17.3	18.4	15.6	1	3	294	275	94.6
Jackson, SD	46071	8	3,031	23.9	44.8	13.0	1	5	350	857	97.1
Jerauld, SD	46073	9	2,071	14.1	24.0	14.1	1	5	295	230	100.0
Jones, SD	46075	9	1,006	15.3	26.0	19.8	1	3	174	205	76.6
Kingsbury, SD	46077	9	5,148	16.1	13.1	10.5	4	13	1,051	787	96.4
Lake, SD	46079	6	11,200	15.9	13.2	7.0	5	17	2,066	1,692	96.3
Lawrence, SD	46081	6	24,097	13.9	15.8	7.1	2	9	2,869	3,973	96.2
Lincoln, SD	46083	3	44,828	19.8	5.4	4.7	4	16	5,650	7,940	90.8
Lyman, SD	46085	9	3,755	21.9	29.0	13.4	1	4	368	778	97.3
McCook, SD	46087	3	5,618	18.6	11.9	9.6	4	15	1,150	1,064	96.6
McPherson, SD	46089	9	2,459	16.7	23.7	17.6	2	9	407	416	96.9
Marshall, SD	46091	9	4,656	16.3	20.3	13.6	2	9	726	896	100.0
Meade, SD	46093	3	25,434	17.1	15.2	8.3	3	18	2,717	4,619	91.9
Mellette, SD	46095	9	2,048	22.8	42.4	11.9	1	5	394	483	100.0
Miner, SD	46097	8	2,389	17.6	16.3	10.6	1	4	377	422	100.0
Minnehaha, SD	46099	3	169,468	17.5	11.8	6.8	9	74	28,729	28,571	89.4
Moody, SD	46101	8	6,486	18.5	14.0	10.6	2	7	907	1,223	95.7
Pennington, SD	46103	3	100,948	17.3	18.7	6.7	5	44	17,030	17,341	89.3
Perkins, SD	46105	9	2,982	16.1	23.2	24.0	2	6	432	446	86.3
Potter, SD	46107	9	2,329	14.1	15.4	12.3	2	6	364	359	88.0
Roberts, SD	46109	9	10,149	20.2	25.7	11.8	4	13	1,584	2,018	97.0
Sanborn, SD	46111	9	2,355	16.7	17.7	16.0	2	6	396	422	87.4
Shannon, SD	46113	7	13,586	27.5	43.2	8.9	1	8	1,395	3,509	96.8
Spink, SD	46115	7	6,415	18.9	11.7	8.9	4	20	1,358	1,241	88.1
Stanley, SD	46117	9	2,966	18.3	12.2	10.6	1	4	451	508	88.4
Sully, SD	46119	9	1,373	16.9	10.4	11.9	1	4	293	232	89.2
Todd, SD	46121	9	9,612	27.5	51.6	6.7	1	12	1,976	2,701	95.8
Tripp, SD	46123	7	5,644	17.3	24.9	14.4	2	9	967	1,011	98.2
Turner, SD	46125	3	8,347	17.4	10.2	9.9	6	19	1,535	1,599	93.6
Union, SD	46127	3	14,399	19.4	7.1	5.0	5	14	2,790	2,658	91.6
Walworth, SD	46129	7	5,438	15.8	22.1	9.1	3	8	866	766	90.7
Yankton, SD	46135	7	22,438	16.3	13.0	6.8	2	9	3,127	3,511	88.7
Ziebach, SD	46137	9	2,801	26.5	49.5	10.4	1	3	334	713	87.1

[1]County type codes are from the Economic Research Service of the United States Department of Agriculture. See notes and definitions for more information.

Table C-1. Population, School, and Student Characteristics by County, Selected Years—*Continued*

County	State/ County Code	Characteristics of students, 2010–2011				Number of graduates, 2008–2009	Staff and students, 2010–2011			
		Percent with IEP[2]	Percent eligible for free or reduced lunch	Percent minority	Percent English-language learners		Total staff	Number of teachers	Student/ teacher ratio	Central admin. staff
		10	11	12	13	14	15	16	17	18
SOUTH DAKOTA— *(Continued)*										
Charles Mix, SD	46023	15.8	55.3	48.2	3.8	86	458	158	10.3	39
Clark, SD	46025	10.2	48.8	4.8	10.4	37	127	54	11.0	7
Clay, SD	46027	14.9	32.5	18.0	0.9	91	176	98	13.1	9
Codington, SD	46029	13.3	30.4	7.6	0.8	317	643	315	13.9	43
Corson, SD	46031	15.0	97.2	82.9	4.8	45	210	91	9.3	17
Custer, SD	46033	16.0	43.3	21.0	0.5	71	185	94	11.1	16
Davison, SD	46035	14.6	29.6	9.6	1.3	215	454	218	13.5	29
Day, SD	46037	15.2	41.9	13.4	0.1	60	159	62	11.7	7
Deuel, SD	46039	10.5	15.0	3.4	. . .	34	76	37	15.6	8
Dewey, SD	46041	42.1	71.8	75.5	1.1	112	220	95	6.8	20
Douglas, SD	46043	9.7	41.3	5.0	. . .	23	69	38	9.0	3
Edmunds, SD	46045	11.1	30.3	6.6	7.1	46	112	61	10.3	7
Fall River, SD	46047	14.6	51.7	26.7	0.4	86	195	98	11.3	14
Faulk, SD	46049	12.1	27.6	1.9	14.0	30	50	29	11.3	3
Grant, SD	46051	15.8	34.0	5.0	0.5	117	177	88	12.8	14
Gregory, SD	46053	12.8	59.5	18.4	0.5	52	149	63	11.5	9
Haakon, SD	46055	9.9	36.7	11.5	. . .	24	64	25	11.8	9
Hamlin, SD	46057	11.2	38.5	4.1	0.8	77	237	95	13.5	19
Hand, SD	46059	13.0	32.5	1.4	1.4	43	83	42	10.4	4
Hanson, SD	46061	11.6	22.7	2.4	8.5	48	58	32	13.1	3
Harding, SD	46063	11.3	23.9	4.4	. . .	16	43	25	7.8	6
Hughes, SD	46065	20.5	26.3	21.4	0.3	188	351	161	16.0	21
Hutchinson, SD	46067	13.9	33.9	5.6	6.3	97	239	136	10.7	18
Hyde, SD	46069	10.9	30.3	18.0	. . .	23	51	26	11.5	5
Jackson, SD	46071	14.6	52.6	52.6	. . .	20	77	43	8.2	5
Jerauld, SD	46073	9.5	44.1	3.7	9.5	26	64	29	10.1	8
Jones, SD	46075	13.8	52.9	22.4	0.6	14	41	22	7.9	4
Kingsbury, SD	46077	11.1	31.7	4.8	1.6	85	173	91	11.5	18
Lake, SD	46079	10.2	27.8	5.8	2.4	134	291	155	13.3	24
Lawrence, SD	46081	13.8	33.7	13.4	0.6	211	426	227	12.7	20
Lincoln, SD	46083	13.1	19.6	5.2	0.7	246	767	392	14.4	42
Lyman, SD	46085	16.8	51.1	34.8	. . .	26	88	40	9.3	3
McCook, SD	46087	14.9	34.4	3.1	1.7	84	200	105	11.0	16
McPherson, SD	46089	10.8	53.8	2.8	11.8	33	79	46	8.8	8
Marshall, SD	46091	12.7	42.0	7.3	4.5	52	111	56	12.9	9
Meade, SD	46093	14.1	39.4	10.1	0.1	175	532	213	12.8	64
Mellette, SD	46095	21.3	92.1	83.8	2.8	23	88	41	9.7	4
Miner, SD	46097	15.6	36.1	5.0	1.9	27	71	34	11.0	5
Minnehaha, SD	46099	14.2	34.0	20.8	6.2	1,735	3,735	1,921	15.0	125
Moody, SD	46101	14.8	40.0	34.6	6.4	51	144	77	11.8	9
Pennington, SD	46103	13.6	35.7	26.7	0.6	1,036	2,232	1,155	14.7	91
Perkins, SD	46105	13.0	37.5	3.7	. . .	20	87	42	10.2	6
Potter, SD	46107	14.6	28.6	6.0	. . .	39	84	37	9.8	6
Roberts, SD	46109	16.9	50.8	41.2	1.3	93	314	140	11.3	31
Sanborn, SD	46111	8.8	53.3	6.6	5.6	22	88	41	9.6	6
Shannon, SD	46113	19.4	98.4	99.3	15.6	. . .	371	105	13.3	23
Spink, SD	46115	17.2	34.0	4.1	5.8	89	241	121	11.2	12
Stanley, SD	46117	17.1	36.4	20.0	0.2	34	77	40	11.4	5
Sully, SD	46119	13.7	21.6	5.9	0.3	27	50	28	10.5	6
Todd, SD	46121	17.4	98.3	97.4	38.2	70	458	171	11.5	33
Tripp, SD	46123	10.9	49.3	24.4	0.6	81	131	72	13.5	9
Turner, SD	46125	15.1	30.9	5.3	0.3	133	257	140	11.0	22
Union, SD	46127	13.7	21.5	7.5	0.2	182	425	210	13.3	30
Walworth, SD	46129	13.4	42.0	25.9	. . .	53	147	76	11.3	14
Yankton, SD	46135	15.2	34.4	11.1	0.5	227	423	205	15.3	18
Ziebach, SD	46137	10.8	96.9	85.2	1.2	13	72	35	9.6	5

[2]IEP=Individual Education Program. See notes and definitions for more information.
. . . = Not available.

Table C-1. Population, School, and Student Characteristics by County, Selected Years—*Continued*

County	State/ County Code	Revenues, 2008–2009				Current expenditures, 2008–2009			Resident population 16 to 19 years, 2006–2010			
		Total revenue ($1,000's)	Percentage of revenue from			Amount ($1,000's)	Amount per student	Percent for instruction	Total population 16 to 19 years	Percent enrolled in school	Percent high school graduates, not enrolled in school	Percent not enrolled, not grads, not employed, or not in labor force
			Federal government	State government	Local government							
		19	20	21	22	23	24	25	26	27	28	29
SOUTH DAKOTA— *(Continued)*												
Charles Mix, SD	46023	24,199	46.9	26.5	26.6	16,934	10,086	59.2	504	80.8	9.3	4.0
Clark, SD	46025	5,889	10.9	31.7	57.4	5,470	9,209	62.0	208	81.7	12.5	1.9
Clay, SD	46027	11,848	10.4	35.9	53.7	10,053	7,866	58.4	2,071	99.4	0.6	0.0
Codington, SD	46029	38,742	9.5	39.8	50.7	32,488	7,158	62.1	1,573	82.6	8.2	4.1
Corson, SD	46031	13,778	56.2	33.9	9.9	11,728	12,557	60.0	348	57.5	31.3	11.2
Custer, SD	46033	10,415	14.8	14.3	70.9	9,338	9,301	59.8	265	97.4	2.6	0.0
Davison, SD	46035	26,544	12.0	37.4	50.6	23,224	7,846	60.2	1,162	83.8	12.1	1.8
Day, SD	46037	8,122	16.6	33.9	49.5	7,166	9,037	55.3	256	91.8	2.0	4.7
Deuel, SD	46039	4,827	8.0	36.0	56.0	3,990	7,586	55.0	220	89.6	8.6	0.0
Dewey, SD	46041	11,090	51.3	31.3	17.4	10,804	16,934	62.3	471	75.4	15.7	8.9
Douglas, SD	46043	3,768	10.9	36.9	52.2	3,301	9,738	53.5	166	85.5	9.6	4.8
Edmunds, SD	46045	6,788	9.7	25.1	65.2	5,898	8,738	58.7	156	84.0	10.3	1.9
Fall River, SD	46047	11,244	19.8	33.2	47.0	10,567	8,748	57.7	250	94.4	0.4	0.0
Faulk, SD	46049	3,224	10.3	30.0	59.7	2,865	8,735	57.1	129	81.4	3.1	15.5
Grant, SD	46051	11,637	9.4	30.8	59.9	9,861	8,273	57.8	403	85.9	12.7	1.5
Gregory, SD	46053	7,914	18.3	36.8	45.0	7,494	10,365	58.6	145	89.0	7.6	3.5
Haakon, SD	46055	2,803	12.5	30.4	57.2	2,557	8,697	62.4	53	98.1	1.9	0.0
Hamlin, SD	46057	12,010	8.8	37.9	53.3	9,680	7,909	55.7	360	83.3	8.1	8.6
Hand, SD	46059	4,458	6.9	23.6	69.5	3,765	7,943	58.8	170	89.4	10.6	0.0
Hanson, SD	46061	5,538	9.0	43.0	48.0	5,246	9,060	59.7	161	77.0	1.9	11.8
Harding, SD	46063	3,220	13.8	19.2	67.0	2,846	12,593	58.4	98	100.0	0.0	0.0
Hughes, SD	46065	22,772	10.2	40.0	49.8	18,783	7,006	62.3	787	88.6	3.2	0.1
Hutchinson, SD	46067	16,019	11.9	37.1	51.1	14,096	9,255	62.0	369	84.3	7.1	8.7
Hyde, SD	46069	4,085	15.0	24.2	60.8	2,799	9,000	60.6	61	100.0	0.0	0.0
Jackson, SD	46071	4,655	32.7	36.9	30.3	4,271	10,546	58.8	244	71.3	9.4	19.3
Jerauld, SD	46073	3,293	10.3	19.5	70.2	3,092	10,105	61.5	109	84.4	4.6	8.3
Jones, SD	46075	2,052	14.5	26.2	59.4	1,876	10,599	55.7	44	100.0	0.0	0.0
Kingsbury, SD	46077	10,612	9.0	33.4	57.6	9,591	9,939	56.3	201	89.1	6.5	2.5
Lake, SD	46079	18,117	8.9	34.4	56.7	16,124	7,538	57.8	885	96.2	1.2	0.0
Lawrence, SD	46081	27,607	9.6	18.0	72.3	22,849	7,939	61.7	1,879	87.1	8.9	2.8
Lincoln, SD	46083	46,311	6.1	30.0	63.9	37,265	7,469	59.1	1,709	90.5	6.9	0.5
Lyman, SD	46085	5,183	27.4	22.5	50.1	4,527	10,830	52.0	246	74.0	6.5	18.3
McCook, SD	46087	11,300	8.9	36.5	54.6	9,731	9,721	58.8	290	97.2	1.0	1.7
McPherson, SD	46089	4,937	10.6	29.4	60.0	4,180	9,522	59.3	163	78.5	8.6	11.0
Marshall, SD	46091	6,542	10.2	32.1	57.7	5,772	8,141	58.2	284	94.4	5.6	0.0
Meade, SD	46093	24,590	11.2	33.2	55.6	21,146	7,681	61.3	1,521	75.1	21.4	3.6
Mellette, SD	46095	5,712	46.5	31.5	22.0	5,064	12,086	59.7	127	87.4	3.9	8.7
Miner, SD	46097	3,938	8.5	28.9	62.6	3,520	9,049	54.7	97	91.8	3.1	5.2
Minnehaha, SD	46099	260,642	10.8	33.2	56.0	215,888	7,442	61.9	9,436	86.3	9.1	2.3
Moody, SD	46101	9,068	14.3	37.2	48.5	7,663	8,144	55.4	425	80.0	11.1	2.8
Pennington, SD	46103	152,121	15.9	29.6	54.5	137,276	8,096	61.2	5,253	79.2	12.9	4.4
Perkins, SD	46105	4,939	14.9	37.6	47.5	4,822	11,481	53.0	127	80.3	18.1	0.0
Potter, SD	46107	4,086	8.7	31.3	60.0	4,082	11,003	64.1	121	77.7	12.4	0.0
Roberts, SD	46109	18,400	27.9	33.4	38.7	15,471	9,621	57.8	484	79.8	13.8	2.9
Sanborn, SD	46111	4,819	13.2	26.9	59.9	3,742	9,426	61.3	132	77.3	1.5	11.4
Shannon, SD	46113	23,124	62.7	30.6	6.7	20,300	14,256	53.8	1,152	63.0	5.1	28.7
Spink, SD	46115	12,784	14.8	35.7	49.5	11,852	8,779	60.5	320	92.8	5.6	1.6
Stanley, SD	46117	4,728	17.4	23.6	59.0	4,492	9,339	56.8	195	98.0	0.0	2.1
Sully, SD	46119	3,167	6.3	13.6	80.0	3,169	10,323	56.2	81	100.0	0.0	0.0
Todd, SD	46121	32,010	59.8	32.6	7.6	27,065	13,951	51.1	824	76.6	1.9	19.4
Tripp, SD	46123	9,627	16.3	34.5	49.2	8,375	8,284	58.4	236	78.8	14.8	6.4
Turner, SD	46125	16,877	8.9	35.4	55.7	14,125	8,873	56.1	446	90.6	7.2	0.0
Union, SD	46127	26,473	7.7	27.6	64.7	24,283	8,569	57.4	686	88.2	7.1	2.2
Walworth, SD	46129	8,333	13.5	41.1	45.4	8,061	9,384	60.8	120	85.0	5.0	10.0
Yankton, SD	46135	28,885	9.9	40.5	49.7	24,820	7,845	62.0	1,223	79.6	6.1	5.9
Ziebach, SD	46137	4,925	55.2	35.3	9.6	3,906	11,455	56.1	191	71.2	11.5	15.2

Note. Data in columns 26 through 41 from the American Community Survey are subject to sampling error, which can be especially large in small counties and small population groups. See notes and definitions for more information.

Table C-1. Population, School, and Student Characteristics by County, Selected Years—*Continued*

County	State/ County Code	High school graduates, 2006–2010			College enrollment, 2006–2010		College graduates, 2006–2010 (percent)						
		Population 25 years and over	High school diploma or less (percent)	High school diploma or more (percent)	Number	Percent public	Bachelor's degree or more	+/- U.S. percent with Bachelor's degree or more	Non-Hispanic White	Black or African American	American Indian and Alaska Native	Asian, Hawaiian, and Pacific Islander	Hispanic or Latino[3]
		30	31	32	33	34	35	36	37	38	39	40	41
SOUTH DAKOTA— *(Continued)*													
Charles Mix, SD	46023	5,754	56.3	80.7	160	65.0	15.5	-12.4	18.3	11.1	7.6	0.0	0.0
Clark, SD	46025	2,593	58.7	85.2	63	95.2	12.5	-15.4	12.6	0.0	0.0	0.0	5.9
Clay, SD	46027	6,909	32.8	90.6	5,056	98.2	40.4	12.5	40.6	0.0	30.9	79.1	0.0
Codington, SD	46029	17,824	48.6	88.5	1,458	79.2	22.7	-5.2	23.0	0.0	0.0	52.2	39.2
Corson, SD	46031	2,230	52.9	83.6	163	85.9	14.3	-13.6	17.1	0.0	11.7	28.6	0.0
Custer, SD	46033	6,177	39.8	92.0	132	74.2	28.6	0.7	27.8	0.0	43.6	0.0	29.6
Davison, SD	46035	12,685	43.7	87.8	1,240	49.6	21.5	-6.4	21.7	100.0	0.0	0.0	0.0
Day, SD	46037	4,102	54.2	88.6	146	60.3	17.7	-10.2	17.7	100.0	15.9	0.0	50.0
Deuel, SD	46039	3,062	52.9	86.9	131	67.2	17.8	-10.1	18.1	0.0	40.0	0.0	0.0
Dewey, SD	46041	2,995	58.3	79.7	184	83.7	12.6	-15.3	17.2	0.0	10.3	0.0	0.0
Douglas, SD	46043	2,162	57.1	74.1	70	82.9	16.0	-11.9	16.2	0.0	9.1	0.0	0.0
Edmunds, SD	46045	2,921	54.5	83.7	76	64.5	20.5	-7.4	19.7	0.0	0.0	52.9	51.6
Fall River, SD	46047	5,255	46.7	86.8	201	48.3	20.2	-7.7	20.2	17.7	14.5	7.4	42.9
Faulk, SD	46049	1,685	56.2	82.1	38	86.8	15.5	-12.4	15.4	0.0	0.0	0.0	0.0
Grant, SD	46051	5,265	57.7	84.0	101	85.1	15.5	-12.4	16.0	0.0	0.0	100.0	0.0
Gregory, SD	46053	3,130	52.8	85.7	74	71.6	14.7	-13.2	14.5	0.0	31.5	0.0	0.0
Haakon, SD	46055	1,457	49.4	88.0	15	100.0	20.0	-7.9	20.0	100.0	0.0	50.0	0.0
Hamlin, SD	46057	3,640	54.8	87.3	204	88.7	16.7	-11.2	16.8	0.0	0.0	0.0	11.3
Hand, SD	46059	2,540	50.9	88.4	60	73.3	17.1	-10.8	17.0	0.0	100.0	0.0	0.0
Hanson, SD	46061	2,119	57.0	84.0	59	83.1	18.9	-9.0	18.9	0.0	0.0	0.0	0.0
Harding, SD	46063	875	35.7	90.3	16	87.5	34.3	6.4	34.6	0.0	0.0	0.0	0.0
Hughes, SD	46065	11,509	35.3	93.3	526	82.7	33.3	5.4	34.9	70.7	5.9	73.0	40.7
Hutchinson, SD	46067	5,244	52.2	80.5	156	80.1	21.7	-6.2	21.9	100.0	0.0	100.0	9.3
Hyde, SD	46069	1,066	58.4	86.0	6	100.0	16.8	-11.1	15.6	0.0	17.7	100.0	0.0
Jackson, SD	46071	1,597	47.7	88.4	94	95.7	19.4	-8.5	19.9	0.0	19.8	0.0	75.0
Jerauld, SD	46073	1,559	61.2	82.6	28	100.0	11.0	-16.9	10.3	0.0	0.0	87.5	0.0
Jones, SD	46075	712	45.4	92.4	15	100.0	15.6	-12.3	15.5	0.0	0.0	100.0	0.0
Kingsbury, SD	46077	3,801	52.8	87.1	116	83.6	20.3	-7.6	20.5	0.0	44.4	45.5	0.0
Lake, SD	46079	7,086	47.2	91.3	1,300	93.1	22.1	-5.8	21.8	0.0	0.0	94.0	23.2
Lawrence, SD	46081	15,384	39.6	92.6	2,299	95.3	31.8	3.9	31.9	0.0	40.8	10.0	27.6
Lincoln, SD	46083	26,136	30.5	95.6	1,849	68.3	36.9	9.0	36.6	45.9	40.3	45.8	49.4
Lyman, SD	46085	2,303	55.6	85.5	98	84.7	19.8	-8.1	26.5	0.0	3.3	0.0	0.0
McCook, SD	46087	3,903	47.8	90.2	186	61.8	20.4	-7.5	20.5	0.0	0.0	27.3	0.0
McPherson, SD	46089	1,767	63.4	67.9	45	88.9	14.8	-13.1	15.0	0.0	0.0	0.0	0.0
Marshall, SD	46091	3,109	50.2	85.3	145	93.8	16.7	-11.2	17.5	0.0	17.0	0.0	0.0
Meade, SD	46093	16,142	43.2	92.6	1,125	85.3	21.0	-6.9	21.3	0.0	8.0	32.0	24.0
Mellette, SD	46095	1,198	53.6	85.6	80	83.8	14.9	-13.0	19.7	0.0	7.8	0.0	0.0
Miner, SD	46097	1,813	54.3	85.6	50	78.0	17.5	-10.4	17.5	0.0	37.5	0.0	0.0
Minnehaha, SD	46099	107,348	38.8	90.9	11,274	58.3	28.9	1.0	30.5	10.9	7.6	38.4	4.3
Moody, SD	46101	4,365	46.0	90.6	233	84.5	21.7	-6.2	23.6	0.0	6.4	48.8	0.0
Pennington, SD	46103	64,038	36.9	91.4	6,451	85.7	27.8	-0.1	29.1	29.8	15.3	22.8	17.6
Perkins, SD	46105	2,161	51.9	82.7	70	87.1	17.8	-10.1	17.9	0.0	0.0	0.0	0.0
Potter, SD	46107	1,758	51.7	87.0	64	54.7	19.9	-8.0	19.9	0.0	100.0	0.0	0.0
Roberts, SD	46109	6,386	52.4	86.0	318	88.1	15.0	-12.9	16.2	0.0	8.6	100.0	0.0
Sanborn, SD	46111	1,598	61.6	84.6	35	94.3	15.3	-12.6	15.4	0.0	0.0	0.0	20.0
Shannon, SD	46113	6,197	53.0	81.3	930	100.0	16.1	-11.8	66.5	0.0	11.4	0.0	22.0
Spink, SD	46115	4,485	55.3	83.5	137	84.7	15.9	-12.0	16.3	0.0	7.6	0.0	0.0
Stanley, SD	46117	2,025	49.2	91.1	47	51.1	27.7	-0.2	29.4	100.0	5.3	0.0	17.7
Sully, SD	46119	950	44.3	92.0	43	100.0	25.1	-2.8	23.7	0.0	100.0	0.0	75.0
Todd, SD	46121	4,574	48.5	83.0	580	86.4	18.1	-9.8	44.0	100.0	11.7	80.0	33.9
Tripp, SD	46123	4,092	51.8	88.3	138	60.9	16.0	-11.9	14.6	0.0	41.0	0.0	0.0
Turner, SD	46125	5,852	49.6	90.1	273	74.4	21.6	-6.3	21.7	0.0	6.3	100.0	7.0
Union, SD	46127	9,465	41.6	92.3	598	74.4	29.1	1.2	29.3	71.9	20.3	0.0	41.2
Walworth, SD	46129	4,022	48.8	82.9	131	96.9	21.3	-6.6	23.0	0.0	9.0	0.0	0.0
Yankton, SD	46135	15,390	45.3	88.5	1,393	39.8	26.8	-1.1	27.8	15.1	10.5	21.6	11.3
Ziebach, SD	46137	1,422	55.8	76.9	157	87.3	12.0	-15.9	20.5	0.0	6.6	0.0	75.0

Note. Data in columns 26 through 41 from the American Community Survey are subject to sampling error, which can be especially large in small counties and small population groups. See notes and definitions for more information.
[3]May be of any race.

Table C-1. Population, School, and Student Characteristics by County, Selected Years—*Continued*

County	State/ County Code	County Type[1]	Population, 2010: Total	Population, 2010: Percent 5–17 years	Percent of related children 5–17 years in poverty, 2010	Percent of children under 19 years with no health insurance, 2010	Number of schools and students, 2010–2011: School districts	Number of schools and students, 2010–2011: Schools	Number of schools and students, 2010–2011: Students	Resident enrollment, 2006–2010, K–12 enrollment: Number	Resident enrollment, 2006–2010, K–12 enrollment: Percent public
			1	2	3	4	5	6	7	8	9
TENNESSEE	47000	X	6,346,105	17.1	23.9	5.6	140	1,784	987,422	1,086,730	88.4
Anderson, TN	47001	2	75,129	16.3	23.2	4.6	3	28	12,757	12,395	91.1
Bedford, TN	47003	6	45,058	19.1	29.4	8.3	1	13	7,951	8,627	93.7
Benton, TN	47005	7	16,489	15.4	31.1	5.8	1	8	2,311	2,610	93.9
Bledsoe, TN	47007	8	12,876	16.5	30.7	6.7	1	6	1,975	2,304	90.6
Blount, TN	47009	2	123,010	16.7	18.6	5.1	3	30	18,577	20,523	92.7
Bradley, TN	47011	3	98,963	16.9	24.6	5.3	2	26	15,606	16,189	91.2
Campbell, TN	47013	6	40,716	16.3	33.1	4.8	1	13	6,151	6,687	93.5
Cannon, TN	47015	1	13,801	16.7	23.9	6.1	1	7	2,201	2,248	92.2
Carroll, TN	47017	6	28,522	16.1	27.6	5.5	6	15	4,778	4,610	97.1
Carter, TN	47019	3	57,424	14.8	34.4	4.9	2	22	8,161	8,681	95.2
Cheatham, TN	47021	1	39,105	18.7	16.8	6.4	1	13	6,815	7,659	89.6
Chester, TN	47023	3	17,131	17.6	24.6	5.0	1	6	2,754	2,915	93.1
Claiborne, TN	47025	6	32,213	15.9	32.2	5.0	1	13	4,889	5,231	96.7
Clay, TN	47027	8	7,861	14.8	36.6	6.3	1	5	1,102	1,063	98.8
Cocke, TN	47029	6	35,662	15.8	45.6	4.8	2	13	5,625	5,333	98.3
Coffee, TN	47031	4	52,796	17.7	30.9	5.1	3	19	9,341	9,683	94.2
Crockett, TN	47033	8	14,586	17.9	27.3	7.0	3	7	2,938	2,628	97.0
Cumberland, TN	47035	7	56,053	14.1	28.6	6.6	1	12	7,659	7,879	92.3
Davidson, TN	47037	1	626,681	14.6	29.1	6.8	2	139	78,923	91,468	81.8
Decatur, TN	47039	9	11,757	15.8	27.9	6.5	1	4	1,701	1,844	92.7
De Kalb, TN	47041	6	18,723	16.8	30.4	7.1	1	6	3,019	3,120	93.6
Dickson, TN	47043	1	49,666	18.4	20.9	5.4	1	16	8,595	9,082	93.3
Dyer, TN	47045	5	38,335	18.5	28.6	4.6	2	12	6,942	6,930	96.9
Fayette, TN	47047	1	38,413	16.6	18.7	6.6	1	10	3,809	6,501	62.4
Fentress, TN	47049	9	17,959	17.4	35.2	6.2	2	7	3,166	2,716	96.9
Franklin, TN	47051	6	41,052	16.6	22.1	5.9	1	11	6,106	6,767	93.4
Gibson, TN	47053	4	49,683	18.5	26.2	5.3	5	21	9,393	8,997	91.7
Giles, TN	47055	6	29,485	16.3	24.5	6.0	1	8	4,177	5,255	92.0
Grainger, TN	47057	3	22,657	16.4	28.7	6.2	1	9	3,626	3,492	95.8
Greene, TN	47059	6	68,831	15.9	27.4	5.5	2	25	10,351	10,065	96.1
Grundy, TN	47061	8	13,703	17.3	39.2	5.5	1	8	2,357	2,396	95.3
Hamblen, TN	47063	3	62,544	17.1	28.3	6.6	1	18	9,966	10,713	93.8
Hamilton, TN	47065	2	336,463	15.5	24.1	5.4	1	76	42,589	52,201	79.2
Hancock, TN	47067	8	6,819	16.3	41.7	5.1	1	3	1,120	1,113	98.2
Hardeman, TN	47069	6	27,253	15.7	30.0	5.0	1	9	4,154	4,766	86.5
Hardin, TN	47071	6	26,026	16.2	31.7	5.9	1	7	3,724	4,533	94.1
Hawkins, TN	47073	3	56,833	16.8	27.1	5.2	2	19	8,330	9,491	93.3
Haywood, TN	47075	6	18,787	19.1	30.0	4.7	1	6	3,506	3,615	93.2
Henderson, TN	47077	6	27,769	17.8	23.2	5.3	2	12	4,935	4,841	92.7
Henry, TN	47079	7	32,330	15.8	29.9	5.8	2	9	4,926	4,970	94.9
Hickman, TN	47081	1	24,690	16.9	28.1	6.0	1	8	3,853	4,547	94.1
Houston, TN	47083	8	8,426	18.0	26.5	6.8	1	5	1,483	1,602	99.3
Humphreys, TN	47085	6	18,538	17.5	24.7	5.8	1	7	3,225	3,530	94.6
Jackson, TN	47087	8	11,638	15.6	30.2	6.1	1	4	1,588	1,569	96.9
Jefferson, TN	47089	3	51,407	16.3	23.8	5.9	1	12	7,645	8,419	95.0
Johnson, TN	47091	6	18,244	13.5	35.0	5.3	1	7	2,325	2,494	95.0
Knox, TN	47093	2	432,226	15.8	15.1	5.3	2	90	58,168	66,036	84.8
Lake, TN	47095	9	7,832	12.2	41.3	4.8	1	3	975	1,045	83.3
Lauderdale, TN	47097	6	27,815	17.6	30.5	4.4	1	8	4,688	5,165	97.4
Lawrence, TN	47099	6	41,869	18.4	26.3	5.6	1	13	7,036	7,653	91.4
Lewis, TN	47101	6	12,161	17.9	30.0	5.4	1	4	1,973	2,232	93.2
Lincoln, TN	47103	6	33,361	16.9	23.7	5.2	2	11	5,342	5,979	86.6
Loudon, TN	47105	2	48,556	15.1	21.8	6.2	2	12	7,459	7,273	91.9
McMinn, TN	47107	4	52,266	16.9	26.1	5.4	3	16	8,182	9,085	93.3
McNairy, TN	47109	6	26,075	17.6	27.6	5.6	1	8	4,531	4,629	88.0
Macon, TN	47111	1	22,248	18.2	34.4	6.6	1	8	3,822	4,117	97.9
Madison, TN	47113	3	98,294	17.3	26.8	4.9	2	29	13,146	17,939	82.5
Marion, TN	47115	2	28,237	16.3	30.2	5.2	2	11	4,705	4,702	81.4
Marshall, TN	47117	6	30,617	18.2	21.8	7.1	1	9	5,334	5,450	98.3
Maury, TN	47119	4	80,956	17.1	19.8	5.5	1	20	11,713	14,038	81.9

[1]County type codes are from the Economic Research Service of the United States Department of Agriculture. See notes and definitions for more information.

Table C-1. Population, School, and Student Characteristics by County, Selected Years—*Continued*

County	State/ County Code	Characteristics of students, 2010–2011				Number of graduates, 2008–2009	Staff and students, 2010–2011			
		Percent with IEP[2]	Percent eligible for free or reduced lunch	Percent minority	Percent English-language learners		Total staff	Number of teachers	Student/ teacher ratio	Central admin. staff
		10	11	12	13	14	15	16	17	18
TENNESSEE	47000	12.1	55.0	32.7	3.0	60,368	128,197	66,558	14.8	984
Anderson, TN	47001	14.8	48.9	13.0	1.2	905	1,833	970	13.2	21
Bedford, TN	47003	10.8	59.4	28.8	6.7	444	1,056	525	15.2	8
Benton, TN	47005	16.6	69.7	7.1	0.5	187	372	177	13.1	2
Bledsoe, TN	47007	19.3	74.1	7.2	0.6	117	314	133	14.8	3
Blount, TN	47009	12.0	43.8	8.6	1.3	1,231	2,360	1,167	15.9	11
Bradley, TN	47011	10.0	56.2	10.3	2.0	929	1,783	1,000	15.6	12
Campbell, TN	47013	10.9	73.9	1.6	0.4	343	796	386	15.9	1
Cannon, TN	47015	13.6	61.9	4.5	0.5	134	329	161	13.7	3
Carroll, TN	47017	13.8	58.4	15.3	0.2	369	667	339	14.1	16
Carter, TN	47019	14.0	62.9	4.4	0.3	553	1,395	613	13.3	23
Cheatham, TN	47021	11.3	46.3	5.0	0.6	474	935	440	15.5	21
Chester, TN	47023	8.4	53.4	17.5	0.5	162	387	167	16.5	2
Claiborne, TN	47025	11.4	69.5	2.7	0.3	292	806	371	13.2	5
Clay, TN	47027	12.3	49.9	3.9	0.3	85	188	83	13.3	2
Cocke, TN	47029	13.7	74.6	6.6	0.6	411	813	410	13.7	4
Coffee, TN	47031	14.8	53.4	12.8	1.9	638	1,327	660	14.2	15
Crockett, TN	47033	9.8	65.7	30.1	4.9	192	400	197	14.9	5
Cumberland, TN	47035	11.3	63.6	13.6	1.0	514	1,036	489	15.7	28
Davidson, TN	47037	10.9	64.5	67.4	10.7	3,978	10,428	5,595	14.1	36
Decatur, TN	47039	21.1	57.1	8.4	1.2	96	250	126	13.5	1
De Kalb, TN	47041	13.9	65.0	10.8	3.8	173	418	206	14.7	4
Dickson, TN	47043	14.7	52.0	11.7	0.9	538	1,176	587	14.6	5
Dyer, TN	47045	10.1	65.1	25.3	0.7	464	891	421	16.5	6
Fayette, TN	47047	10.2	77.3	62.7	1.3	221	619	264	14.4	7
Fentress, TN	47049	13.6	75.6	1.5	0.3	233	413	209	15.1	4
Franklin, TN	47051	14.6	58.3	10.8	0.5	388	789	403	15.2	5
Gibson, TN	47053	12.6	57.1	27.6	0.7	563	1,214	602	15.6	33
Giles, TN	47055	9.9	59.4	18.1	0.2	322	639	313	13.3	4
Grainger, TN	47057	12.7	65.3	4.6	1.2	230	449	232	15.7	9
Greene, TN	47059	14.6	56.2	7.2	1.0	784	1,376	681	15.2	12
Grundy, TN	47061	18.8	79.6	1.0	0.1	167	377	180	13.1	1
Hamblen, TN	47063	11.2	59.2	22.8	7.0	576	1,185	648	15.4	6
Hamilton, TN	47065	11.6	54.2	40.3	3.0	2,367	5,034	2,969	14.3	26
Hancock, TN	47067	18.8	82.0	0.8	. . .	76	225	95	11.9	3
Hardeman, TN	47069	13.5	82.4	57.2	0.4	259	652	308	13.5	7
Hardin, TN	47071	13.6	66.0	8.8	0.2	271	605	285	13.1	4
Hawkins, TN	47073	13.6	60.4	4.5	0.6	502	1,280	589	14.1	11
Haywood, TN	47075	10.8	77.5	68.2	1.6	179	573	240	14.6	5
Henderson, TN	47077	12.3	59.9	14.3	0.6	277	641	330	15.0	8
Henry, TN	47079	13.9	64.0	15.2	0.3	273	715	338	14.6	10
Hickman, TN	47081	15.4	64.9	5.5	0.4	272	526	280	13.8	5
Houston, TN	47083	15.6	59.9	8.2	0.1	101	279	99	15.0	1
Humphreys, TN	47085	14.2	49.8	6.3	0.3	255	520	215	15.0	4
Jackson, TN	47087	13.0	72.6	2.4	0.3	108	264	116	13.7	1
Jefferson, TN	47089	11.0	57.9	8.5	2.6	483	1,013	483	15.8	13
Johnson, TN	47091	15.7	70.2	2.7	0.5	182	377	166	14.0	5
Knox, TN	47093	11.2	44.0	22.7	2.5	3,500	7,203	3,986	14.6	24
Lake, TN	47095	19.0	72.7	30.9	0.2	50	158	79	12.3	1
Lauderdale, TN	47097	15.1	78.4	44.6	0.6	255	658	328	14.3	7
Lawrence, TN	47099	14.6	58.7	5.4	0.2	446	982	461	15.3	4
Lewis, TN	47101	11.4	65.7	7.0	0.1	134	272	137	14.4	13
Lincoln, TN	47103	11.4	50.0	14.1	1.0	322	761	352	15.2	4
Loudon, TN	47105	11.1	55.4	14.3	4.4	475	887	482	15.5	9
McMinn, TN	47107	10.7	60.7	12.8	0.9	497	997	503	16.3	12
McNairy, TN	47109	11.1	59.5	10.3	0.3	283	693	354	12.8	3
Macon, TN	47111	13.7	58.6	6.4	1.8	236	559	249	15.3	14
Madison, TN	47113	14.3	73.9	66.1	2.6	881	2,041	985	13.4	11
Marion, TN	47115	11.7	64.6	6.5	0.6	252	637	322	14.6	14
Marshall, TN	47117	9.2	52.7	15.5	2.0	343	742	378	14.1	6
Maury, TN	47119	14.8	51.2	27.6	2.3	699	1,572	805	14.5	7

[2]IEP=Individual Education Program. See notes and definitions for more information.
. . . = Not available.

Table C-1. Population, School, and Student Characteristics by County, Selected Years—*Continued*

County	State/ County Code	Revenues, 2008–2009				Current expenditures, 2008–2009			Resident population 16 to 19 years, 2006–2010			
		Total revenue ($1,000's)	Percentage of revenue from			Amount ($1,000's)	Amount per student	Percent for instruction	Total population 16 to 19 years	Percent enrolled in school	Percent high school graduates, not enrolled in school	Percent not enrolled, not grads, not employed, or not in labor force
			Federal government	State government	Local government							
		19	20	21	22	23	24	25	26	27	28	29
TENNESSEE	47000	8,112,895	10.7	46.8	42.4	7,667,511	7,893	62.7	347,966	82.3	11.9	3.8
Anderson, TN	47001	124,141	9.2	44.1	46.7	114,576	9,190	61.1	3,655	79.7	12.6	6.5
Bedford, TN	47003	54,509	11.1	63.1	25.8	49,890	6,367	65.6	2,373	79.0	10.8	4.8
Benton, TN	47005	21,579	13.2	55.9	30.9	19,521	7,862	62.8	774	75.6	22.2	0.0
Bledsoe, TN	47007	16,992	15.2	66.7	18.0	14,961	7,680	60.9	600	81.0	11.0	8.0
Blount, TN	47009	154,766	8.0	46.3	45.7	150,276	8,089	66.5	6,570	84.9	8.8	4.6
Bradley, TN	47011	114,767	10.1	51.8	38.1	110,043	7,174	66.4	5,544	83.5	10.2	3.6
Campbell, TN	47013	44,562	17.1	62.1	20.8	40,836	6,791	60.9	2,152	75.9	14.6	7.8
Cannon, TN	47015	17,393	10.5	67.4	22.0	16,621	7,158	64.9	704	69.0	23.4	3.1
Carroll, TN	47017	42,560	11.4	60.3	28.3	35,437	7,200	62.2	1,713	84.7	8.4	6.7
Carter, TN	47019	67,616	13.9	58.7	27.4	63,092	7,816	65.1	2,947	79.3	14.8	1.4
Cheatham, TN	47021	49,164	8.4	61.7	29.9	48,877	7,116	64.0	2,105	82.0	15.0	1.4
Chester, TN	47023	19,002	11.6	69.2	19.2	17,186	6,222	61.9	1,441	80.2	15.9	4.0
Claiborne, TN	47025	42,929	14.3	58.7	26.9	35,216	7,261	67.7	1,915	78.9	21.1	0.0
Clay, TN	47027	10,407	12.4	64.2	23.4	9,269	8,496	56.4	376	77.7	9.6	8.2
Cocke, TN	47029	45,228	15.1	59.3	25.6	41,760	7,254	62.4	1,713	77.1	13.0	3.7
Coffee, TN	47031	82,188	9.9	47.0	43.1	75,412	8,087	64.8	2,888	85.0	11.3	2.9
Crockett, TN	47033	21,699	13.3	70.6	16.0	20,242	7,090	63.1	787	79.0	20.2	0.8
Cumberland, TN	47035	52,878	12.7	54.2	33.1	50,953	6,769	63.6	2,465	79.5	16.0	3.7
Davidson, TN	47037	740,320	11.6	27.8	60.6	719,741	9,685	58.2	32,226	83.2	10.2	4.4
Decatur, TN	47039	13,700	13.5	61.8	24.7	11,068	6,612	68.5	474	71.7	13.3	13.3
De Kalb, TN	47041	21,079	13.8	62.0	24.3	20,086	6,774	64.1	812	68.6	28.3	1.0
Dickson, TN	47043	64,983	9.1	54.2	36.7	60,949	7,154	64.5	2,862	77.3	15.7	3.2
Dyer, TN	47045	58,274	11.1	52.1	36.8	54,232	7,760	61.3	2,218	81.8	14.0	3.3
Fayette, TN	47047	33,269	21.5	49.6	28.9	30,852	8,070	58.6	1,860	78.6	16.1	3.3
Fentress, TN	47049	19,942	15.0	64.2	20.8	17,896	7,225	64.9	810	84.1	14.2	1.0
Franklin, TN	47051	48,749	10.5	55.2	34.3	46,249	7,531	62.2	2,376	85.3	8.8	4.1
Gibson, TN	47053	73,401	11.6	57.1	31.3	63,740	7,031	62.9	2,517	80.9	14.3	1.7
Giles, TN	47055	35,655	10.4	56.3	33.3	34,288	7,712	61.8	1,909	81.8	10.9	7.0
Grainger, TN	47057	28,377	14.7	65.9	19.3	24,502	7,851	66.1	1,239	75.8	21.8	1.1
Greene, TN	47059	81,549	11.4	53.0	35.6	75,596	7,207	63.3	3,433	69.5	22.3	5.6
Grundy, TN	47061	20,515	17.5	66.0	16.4	18,195	7,802	65.8	707	76.4	15.3	6.2
Hamblen, TN	47063	74,991	10.6	49.5	39.8	70,066	6,937	68.5	3,101	81.6	11.7	4.5
Hamilton, TN	47065	360,795	11.6	32.8	55.7	357,851	8,613	62.8	18,943	84.1	9.2	4.7
Hancock, TN	47067	10,159	16.8	68.2	15.0	9,032	8,189	64.7	307	91.5	7.2	0.0
Hardeman, TN	47069	35,564	13.8	62.7	23.4	33,109	7,617	62.7	1,349	82.1	10.7	6.7
Hardin, TN	47071	31,803	14.5	52.0	33.5	29,898	7,692	61.2	1,409	81.8	11.2	5.5
Hawkins, TN	47073	66,035	10.6	60.6	28.9	60,939	7,180	63.8	2,789	78.5	16.0	3.8
Haywood, TN	47075	27,714	13.2	61.2	25.6	26,343	7,930	61.0	1,031	78.0	17.4	2.2
Henderson, TN	47077	36,654	10.7	61.0	28.2	32,838	6,884	67.1	1,281	80.4	11.4	2.0
Henry, TN	47079	41,872	10.6	54.3	35.0	36,458	7,496	62.5	1,413	70.7	20.3	6.9
Hickman, TN	47081	32,074	10.4	65.1	24.4	30,081	7,594	64.0	1,387	81.6	13.6	3.6
Houston, TN	47083	12,081	9.6	71.1	19.3	10,743	7,101	59.9	462	84.2	11.3	4.6
Humphreys, TN	47085	24,241	10.0	60.7	29.3	23,051	7,132	66.2	974	85.4	10.4	2.1
Jackson, TN	47087	15,262	16.1	59.1	24.8	12,810	7,966	61.6	565	64.8	34.2	1.1
Jefferson, TN	47089	55,053	10.8	59.9	29.3	53,018	6,986	63.8	3,495	81.7	13.4	2.4
Johnson, TN	47091	21,210	16.3	58.6	25.1	19,191	8,333	59.4	838	65.8	25.1	6.6
Knox, TN	47093	465,157	9.4	33.3	57.2	440,078	7,924	61.6	24,535	86.9	8.7	2.7
Lake, TN	47095	8,708	18.2	63.0	18.8	7,967	8,334	69.0	281	70.8	9.3	19.9
Lauderdale, TN	47097	37,040	14.1	65.4	20.5	34,055	7,194	66.7	1,498	72.4	14.8	6.5
Lawrence, TN	47099	54,656	11.0	58.4	30.5	50,853	7,355	67.3	2,178	79.8	10.8	2.4
Lewis, TN	47101	14,548	12.3	68.5	19.2	12,829	6,357	62.7	639	78.1	14.2	7.7
Lincoln, TN	47103	41,313	10.3	58.4	31.3	37,186	7,075	64.1	1,607	81.7	10.2	5.5
Loudon, TN	47105	63,771	8.9	47.2	43.9	55,295	7,418	70.7	2,507	77.7	16.0	1.8
McMinn, TN	47107	62,308	12.2	55.1	32.7	59,498	7,057	63.4	2,667	72.5	19.1	7.8
McNairy, TN	47109	35,097	13.3	61.2	25.5	31,551	7,036	70.7	1,368	79.0	13.7	4.9
Macon, TN	47111	27,249	10.8	66.6	22.6	23,270	6,069	68.2	1,394	75.6	9.6	0.5
Madison, TN	47113	114,099	11.1	42.9	46.0	112,157	8,204	63.2	6,311	87.3	9.9	2.4
Marion, TN	47115	35,781	11.2	58.9	30.0	33,620	7,296	61.4	1,389	79.1	17.2	3.7
Marshall, TN	47117	39,553	9.2	57.0	33.8	39,145	7,343	63.1	1,561	80.3	17.6	1.7
Maury, TN	47119	91,246	10.3	50.3	39.4	88,973	7,547	62.4	4,250	81.3	12.1	3.9

Note. Data in columns 26 through 41 from the American Community Survey are subject to sampling error, which can be especially large in small counties and small population groups. See notes and definitions for more information.

Table C-1. Population, School, and Student Characteristics by County, Selected Years—*Continued*

County	State/County Code	High school graduates, 2006–2010			College enrollment, 2006–2010		College graduates, 2006–2010 (percent)						
		Population 25 years and over	High school diploma or less (percent)	High school diploma or more (percent)	Number	Percent public	Bachelor's degree or more	+/- U.S. percent with Bachelor's degree or more	Non-Hispanic White	Black or African American	American Indian and Alaska Native	Asian, Hawaiian, and Pacific Islander	Hispanic or Latino[3]
		30	31	32	33	34	35	36	37	38	39	40	41
TENNESSEE	47000	4,156,132	50.9	82.5	378,617	73.5	22.7	-5.2	23.9	15.9	15.4	50.2	12.0
Anderson, TN	47001	51,932	52.0	83.7	2,716	79.4	22.1	-5.8	21.6	20.7	11.5	74.0	23.0
Bedford, TN	47003	28,696	67.4	74.2	1,141	80.4	12.8	-15.1	14.9	3.6	19.6	26.8	1.0
Benton, TN	47005	12,013	65.1	76.6	286	84.6	12.6	-15.3	13.0	3.8	0.0	0.0	0.0
Bledsoe, TN	47007	9,371	71.5	71.5	508	94.9	8.8	-19.1	9.5	0.9	0.0	0.0	0.0
Blount, TN	47009	84,160	50.2	85.5	5,501	65.0	20.6	-7.3	21.0	12.8	12.9	27.0	13.1
Bradley, TN	47011	64,690	52.0	80.0	7,429	45.4	19.2	-8.7	19.4	9.2	4.3	68.6	12.6
Campbell, TN	47013	28,486	72.0	69.0	1,352	61.5	9.2	-18.7	9.1	32.3	0.0	23.2	9.6
Cannon, TN	47015	9,405	70.8	77.7	341	90.3	11.1	-16.8	10.8	52.7	26.1	0.0	0.0
Carroll, TN	47017	19,583	63.9	77.4	1,354	54.3	15.5	-12.4	15.7	13.8	0.0	19.5	22.5
Carter, TN	47019	40,387	62.3	76.9	3,611	63.7	14.9	-13.0	14.6	25.8	0.0	58.8	27.3
Cheatham, TN	47021	25,952	55.7	81.6	1,240	68.8	17.9	-10.0	17.6	25.6	41.2	58.9	12.8
Chester, TN	47023	10,626	61.8	77.0	1,606	17.0	13.8	-14.1	13.8	12.2	90.9	0.0	11.3
Claiborne, TN	47025	22,047	69.7	69.2	1,698	36.8	11.1	-16.8	10.8	0.0	0.0	47.1	12.7
Clay, TN	47027	5,881	71.2	71.8	154	100.0	11.0	-16.9	11.3	0.0	0.0	0.0	0.0
Cocke, TN	47029	25,118	71.4	71.4	1,182	70.6	7.8	-20.1	7.9	11.2	0.0	0.0	3.4
Coffee, TN	47031	35,268	56.6	81.4	2,261	81.8	19.0	-8.9	19.2	18.5	0.0	37.8	11.7
Crockett, TN	47033	9,765	66.8	76.8	450	83.8	12.2	-15.7	14.4	0.9	78.6	0.0	4.2
Cumberland, TN	47035	40,666	59.5	80.0	1,355	83.1	15.6	-12.3	15.5	30.9	0.0	48.8	22.8
Davidson, TN	47037	407,124	40.0	85.1	53,550	49.2	34.0	6.1	40.2	23.5	26.4	45.9	9.1
Decatur, TN	47039	8,324	68.2	71.9	383	59.8	10.4	-17.5	10.6	1.6	0.0	71.4	8.4
De Kalb, TN	47041	12,811	71.7	68.9	951	86.8	11.7	-16.2	12.3	0.0	0.0	47.1	2.7
Dickson, TN	47043	32,378	61.4	80.6	1,738	79.1	14.9	-13.0	15.4	1.9	68.8	64.9	13.3
Dyer, TN	47045	25,474	63.4	78.6	1,457	86.9	14.5	-13.4	15.1	11.6	0.0	0.0	0.0
Fayette, TN	47047	25,845	53.3	82.8	1,512	77.8	18.9	-9.0	22.3	9.9	0.0	45.0	7.5
Fentress, TN	47049	12,365	73.4	71.6	363	93.7	10.1	-17.8	9.8	0.0	22.0	68.4	52.6
Franklin, TN	47051	27,830	58.7	79.7	2,574	40.4	16.5	-11.4	17.1	6.6	0.0	52.4	4.1
Gibson, TN	47053	33,038	59.1	79.8	1,878	80.9	14.8	-13.1	16.4	7.8	13.9	74.3	0.0
Giles, TN	47055	20,277	64.9	78.0	1,266	68.7	12.1	-15.8	12.4	9.9	0.0	61.5	7.9
Grainger, TN	47057	15,780	74.8	67.9	737	84.9	7.3	-20.6	7.4	0.0	0.0	0.0	4.2
Greene, TN	47059	48,165	65.0	76.6	2,219	67.7	14.0	-13.9	14.0	13.4	6.5	59.0	5.8
Grundy, TN	47061	9,566	77.0	64.3	392	91.8	8.0	-19.9	8.6	0.0	15.9	0.0	17.1
Hamblen, TN	47063	42,091	58.1	78.4	2,295	77.7	15.6	-12.3	16.5	5.7	11.7	52.5	7.6
Hamilton, TN	47065	224,351	43.4	85.4	22,864	77.3	27.0	-0.9	30.3	13.6	8.8	52.6	11.7
Hancock, TN	47067	4,834	79.0	68.3	139	82.7	7.4	-20.5	7.1	21.4	0.0	59.3	0.0
Hardeman, TN	47069	19,126	68.2	70.4	760	71.7	10.7	-17.2	11.8	8.3	25.7	37.1	26.8
Hardin, TN	47071	18,235	70.6	72.7	878	81.2	9.4	-18.5	9.3	11.3	0.0	0.0	20.7
Hawkins, TN	47073	39,741	62.4	78.1	1,923	90.6	12.4	-15.5	12.4	9.4	0.0	38.9	15.2
Haywood, TN	47075	12,386	66.3	74.8	553	77.9	12.9	-15.0	17.4	7.5	0.0	74.7	9.9
Henderson, TN	47077	18,881	64.3	78.8	1,093	88.0	11.8	-16.1	12.6	5.3	0.0	0.0	11.3
Henry, TN	47079	22,701	62.4	81.2	1,049	81.4	14.8	-13.1	14.8	10.8	37.9	0.0	37.3
Hickman, TN	47081	16,883	66.5	74.5	865	79.2	10.6	-17.3	10.8	3.9	0.0	59.3	15.2
Houston, TN	47083	5,651	70.6	79.6	225	77.3	7.5	-20.4	7.5	0.0	0.0	0.0	48.9
Humphreys, TN	47085	12,729	61.8	81.9	483	88.0	13.2	-14.7	13.2	20.8	9.7	25.0	1.1
Jackson, TN	47087	8,253	73.6	69.1	425	81.4	9.4	-18.5	9.0	0.0	0.0	0.0	0.0
Jefferson, TN	47089	34,224	57.9	77.8	3,296	38.1	13.5	-14.4	13.6	10.4	17.0	0.0	12.5
Johnson, TN	47091	13,583	70.3	69.1	270	71.1	10.1	-17.8	10.1	2.5	0.0	28.6	22.9
Knox, TN	47093	280,049	38.6	88.3	40,149	85.0	33.8	5.9	34.8	19.5	18.9	66.6	21.4
Lake, TN	47095	5,769	77.0	66.1	205	96.1	5.2	-22.7	6.6	1.5	0.0	38.9	0.0
Lauderdale, TN	47097	18,292	72.0	73.2	978	85.5	9.9	-18.0	12.1	5.0	15.4	88.3	0.0
Lawrence, TN	47099	27,453	66.7	75.2	1,679	82.5	11.0	-16.9	11.0	9.7	0.0	24.6	5.1
Lewis, TN	47101	8,056	65.1	77.9	236	89.0	11.2	-16.7	11.3	0.0	0.0	0.0	0.0
Lincoln, TN	47103	22,507	60.6	79.4	1,041	86.5	15.8	-12.1	16.9	4.5	0.0	0.0	3.5
Loudon, TN	47105	34,061	49.6	84.3	1,220	80.9	22.6	-5.3	23.3	7.9	13.8	63.6	3.1
McMinn, TN	47107	36,026	62.6	78.3	1,786	62.1	13.9	-14.0	13.5	19.1	34.0	29.4	14.4
McNairy, TN	47109	17,784	68.3	75.1	929	73.3	10.9	-17.0	11.1	7.2	0.0	67.8	8.6
Macon, TN	47111	14,363	73.6	72.6	803	75.5	7.6	-20.3	7.7	0.0	0.0	0.0	10.2
Madison, TN	47113	62,820	47.6	84.7	6,766	56.6	24.5	-3.4	29.2	13.9	14.0	66.1	16.1
Marion, TN	47115	19,667	62.0	73.7	1,124	82.2	13.3	-14.6	13.6	7.6	16.7	15.2	13.2
Marshall, TN	47117	20,058	63.4	79.1	956	78.5	11.5	-16.4	12.1	8.9	50.0	11.4	1.3
Maury, TN	47119	53,118	53.8	83.4	3,314	78.7	16.1	-11.8	17.4	8.6	62.5	35.4	9.3

Note. Data in columns 26 through 41 from the American Community Survey are subject to sampling error, which can be especially large in small counties and small population groups. See notes and definitions for more information.

[3]May be of any race.

Table C-1. Population, School, and Student Characteristics by County, Selected Years—*Continued*

County	State/ County Code	County Type[1]	Population, 2010: Total	Population, 2010: Percent 5–17 years	Percent of related children 5–17 years in poverty, 2010	Percent of children under 19 years with no health insurance, 2010	Number of schools and students, 2010–2011: School districts	Number of schools and students, 2010–2011: Schools	Number of schools and students, 2010–2011: Students	Resident enrollment, 2006–2010, K–12 enrollment: Number	Resident enrollment, 2006–2010, K–12 enrollment: Percent public
			1	2	3	4	5	6	7	8	9
TENNESSEE—*(Continued)*											
Meigs, TN	47121	8	11,753	16.4	33.0	5.8	1	4	1,827	1,848	94.5
Monroe, TN	47123	6	44,519	16.9	29.7	5.5	2	17	7,223	7,624	94.6
Montgomery, TN	47125	3	172,331	19.1	20.2	4.5	1	36	29,780	31,393	91.1
Moore, TN	47127	9	6,362	17.4	19.1	6.6	1	2	977	1,269	96.3
Morgan, TN	47129	6	21,987	15.9	25.2	5.8	1	8	3,313	3,470	92.3
Obion, TN	47131	7	31,807	17.3	23.5	5.8	2	11	5,423	5,467	95.9
Overton, TN	47133	7	22,083	17.3	28.4	5.4	1	9	3,567	3,579	96.9
Perry, TN	47135	8	7,915	16.7	31.1	7.3	1	4	1,192	1,327	95.4
Pickett, TN	47137	9	5,077	14.6	29.6	7.6	1	2	724	731	99.5
Polk, TN	47139	3	16,825	16.8	28.1	5.9	1	6	2,771	2,798	91.4
Putnam, TN	47141	4	72,321	15.5	24.7	6.2	1	21	10,955	10,239	94.2
Rhea, TN	47143	6	31,809	17.2	30.9	5.4	2	7	5,080	5,492	92.2
Roane, TN	47145	4	54,181	15.8	22.5	4.7	1	18	7,385	8,314	94.3
Robertson, TN	47147	1	66,283	18.7	19.0	6.6	1	19	11,288	12,318	90.8
Rutherford, TN	47149	1	262,604	18.8	15.8	5.7	2	58	46,107	47,466	92.2
Scott, TN	47151	6	22,228	18.7	34.2	5.4	2	10	4,261	4,260	99.6
Sequatchie, TN	47153	2	14,112	17.4	31.1	5.3	1	3	2,361	2,474	92.5
Sevier, TN	47155	4	89,889	16.3	25.1	6.5	1	28	14,581	14,269	93.2
Shelby, TN	47157	1	927,644	19.2	27.3	5.8	2	264	159,540	184,488	85.4
Smith, TN	47159	1	19,166	18.1	25.2	5.7	1	10	3,351	3,649	92.9
Stewart, TN	47161	3	13,324	17.7	22.0	6.8	1	6	2,162	2,452	89.2
Sullivan, TN	47163	3	156,823	15.3	26.3	4.9	3	46	22,282	24,649	91.3
Sumner, TN	47165	1	160,645	18.8	15.9	5.9	1	46	27,907	29,796	89.7
Tipton, TN	47167	1	61,081	20.5	17.9	4.9	1	14	12,153	12,569	88.4
Trousdale, TN	47169	1	7,870	18.3	23.7	6.1	1	3	1,293	1,638	91.3
Unicoi, TN	47171	3	18,313	15.1	25.0	5.3	1	8	2,697	2,927	94.2
Union, TN	47173	2	19,109	17.2	40.4	5.9	1	7	3,009	3,451	93.5
Van Buren, TN	47175	9	5,548	15.7	30.5	6.4	1	2	783	866	81.3
Warren, TN	47177	6	39,839	17.8	32.7	6.8	1	11	6,618	6,809	92.3
Washington, TN	47179	3	122,979	14.8	22.1	5.4	2	27	16,705	18,227	92.0
Wayne, TN	47181	8	17,021	14.6	29.2	6.3	1	8	2,552	2,752	94.4
Weakley, TN	47183	7	35,021	14.7	26.5	5.9	1	11	4,588	5,201	95.8
White, TN	47185	7	25,841	16.6	28.3	5.6	1	9	4,142	4,302	95.4
Williamson, TN	47187	1	183,182	22.5	6.5	3.9	2	48	35,520	38,623	81.7
Wilson, TN	47189	1	113,993	18.6	13.0	5.0	2	25	19,106	20,348	86.0
TEXAS	48000	X	25,145,561	19.6	24.2	15.3	1,277	8,732	4,934,366	4,806,074	93.4
Anderson, TX	48001	5	58,458	14.3	24.7	14.4	7	23	8,476	9,609	95.2
Andrews, TX	48003	6	14,786	20.9	18.1	18.5	1	6	3,250	3,004	94.9
Angelina, TX	48005	5	86,771	19.2	25.6	14.8	7	43	17,461	16,667	96.2
Aransas, TX	48007	2	23,158	14.4	35.7	15.3	1	5	3,093	3,716	91.4
Archer, TX	48009	3	9,054	18.9	13.3	19.8	3	8	1,868	1,756	98.4
Armstrong, TX	48011	3	1,901	16.6	11.3	17.6	1	2	349	374	100.0
Atascosa, TX	48013	1	44,911	21.2	28.4	14.3	5	28	8,802	9,091	95.9
Austin, TX	48015	1	28,417	18.6	16.4	16.8	3	13	5,614	5,314	86.0
Bailey, TX	48017	7	7,165	21.4	30.0	19.5	1	5	1,502	1,601	98.6
Bandera, TX	48019	1	20,485	15.1	23.4	18.2	2	6	2,772	3,183	94.5
Bastrop, TX	48021	1	74,171	19.5	22.5	16.9	4	27	14,973	14,038	91.7
Baylor, TX	48023	6	3,726	14.5	29.3	21.0	1	3	579	710	100.0
Bee, TX	48025	4	31,861	15.9	32.8	10.6	5	14	5,306	5,353	93.2
Bell, TX	48027	2	310,235	19.3	18.0	12.7	12	107	64,511	55,459	95.8
Bexar, TX	48029	1	1,714,773	19.5	23.2	11.9	41	511	328,550	325,777	92.3
Blanco, TX	48031	8	10,497	16.6	18.3	21.9	2	6	1,677	1,667	95.0
Borden, TX	48033	9	641	17.2	14.8	17.8	1	1	227	120	96.7
Bosque, TX	48035	6	18,212	17.3	24.8	18.5	8	13	3,114	3,234	99.5
Bowie, TX	48037	3	92,565	17.9	25.2	12.2	13	48	17,902	17,012	96.3
Brazoria, TX	48039	1	313,166	19.9	15.1	13.7	8	92	61,341	60,776	93.5

[1]County type codes are from the Economic Research Service of the United States Department of Agriculture. See notes and definitions for more information.

Table C-1. Population, School, and Student Characteristics by County, Selected Years—*Continued*

County	State/ County Code	Characteristics of students, 2010–2011				Number of graduates, 2008–2009	Staff and students, 2010–2011			
		Percent with IEP[2]	Percent eligible for free or reduced lunch	Percent minority	Percent English-language learners		Total staff	Number of teachers	Student/ teacher ratio	Central admin. staff
		10	11	12	13	14	15	16	17	18
TENNESSEE—*(Continued)*										
Meigs, TN	47121	14.4	70.5	3.0	0.2	120	267	127	14.4	6
Monroe, TN	47123	12.4	72.7	9.0	1.7	512	876	436	16.6	6
Montgomery, TN	47125	11.7	45.3	42.0	2.0	1,826	3,799	1,989	15.0	29
Moore, TN	47127	16.0	48.7	3.8	0.3	71	152	71	13.7	1
Morgan, TN	47129	14.8	62.3	1.2	0.1	360	500	248	13.3	4
Obion, TN	47131	12.9	57.1	19.9	2.0	327	757	379	14.3	3
Overton, TN	47133	13.0	65.0	2.3	0.1	200	507	232	15.4	1
Perry, TN	47135	16.7	69.5	6.8	0.2	79	193	90	13.3	2
Pickett, TN	47137	11.7	66.0	2.6	. . .	44	109	56	12.9	1
Polk, TN	47139	11.5	64.6	2.5	0.2	183	332	181	15.3	2
Putnam, TN	47141	13.2	53.8	14.0	4.1	630	1,379	666	16.4	10
Rhea, TN	47143	11.4	67.4	9.7	2.4	298	697	350	14.5	3
Roane, TN	47145	13.4	52.8	7.6	0.2	438	959	475	15.6	6
Robertson, TN	47147	12.7	46.1	19.2	3.9	703	1,490	743	15.2	4
Rutherford, TN	47149	10.1	41.2	32.5	4.0	2,649	5,275	3,074	15.0	48
Scott, TN	47151	10.6	77.4	1.0	. . .	278	635	303	14.1	9
Sequatchie, TN	47153	16.1	65.8	6.3	1.1	141	315	151	15.7	2
Sevier, TN	47155	11.5	55.5	8.8	2.3	845	2,055	996	14.6	4
Shelby, TN	47157	11.2	63.1	79.5	4.4	9,286	17,934	10,274	15.5	187
Smith, TN	47159	12.8	57.1	7.7	0.5	245	486	229	14.6	3
Stewart, TN	47161	12.9	56.6	5.5	0.2	176	355	145	15.0	3
Sullivan, TN	47163	15.4	50.1	6.9	0.6	1,404	3,252	1,539	14.5	15
Sumner, TN	47165	13.5	37.5	16.4	1.5	1,689	3,691	1,914	14.6	4
Tipton, TN	47167	11.9	53.1	27.3	0.2	824	1,504	767	15.8	4
Trousdale, TN	47169	18.3	53.8	14.8	1.0	101	184	95	13.6	4
Unicoi, TN	47171	17.1	61.4	8.5	3.2	171	361	177	15.2	5
Union, TN	47173	13.1	72.9	1.9	0.4	202	443	228	13.2	3
Van Buren, TN	47175	11.9	62.7	1.5	. . .	54	135	60	13.1	2
Warren, TN	47177	16.9	62.7	18.5	5.2	380	994	465	14.2	3
Washington, TN	47179	12.1	46.8	12.6	1.6	1,194	2,188	1,088	15.4	14
Wayne, TN	47181	15.9	65.5	2.9	. . .	203	447	203	12.6	1
Weakley, TN	47183	14.5	56.5	12.5	0.3	293	645	328	14.0	4
White, TN	47185	15.9	61.2	5.6	. . .	276	583	273	15.1	2
Williamson, TN	47187	8.9	13.8	13.7	2.2	2,300	4,307	2,283	15.6	23
Wilson, TN	47189	12.0	34.3	15.6	2.2	1,175	2,507	1,239	15.4	23
TEXAS	48000	9.0	50.1	68.8	15.0	264,237	665,349	334,973	14.7	28,893
Anderson, TX	48001	8.5	60.4	42.8	5.5	494	1,289	676	12.5	55
Andrews, TX	48003	8.5	26.8	67.5	7.7	172	461	236	13.8	19
Angelina, TX	48005	10.6	66.8	50.5	10.6	1,052	2,288	1,254	13.9	97
Aransas, TX	48007	9.1	65.1	47.6	4.1	205	500	246	12.6	22
Archer, TX	48009	9.3	35.3	15.0	3.2	139	277	156	12.0	10
Armstrong, TX	48011	11.2	40.4	12.9	1.1	29	67	37	9.4	4
Atascosa, TX	48013	7.6	69.4	75.3	3.6	480	1,370	639	13.8	83
Austin, TX	48015	9.2	50.3	50.2	9.0	403	835	431	13.0	43
Bailey, TX	48017	10.7	83.7	81.9	14.6	69	229	121	12.4	7
Bandera, TX	48019	13.1	49.1	30.3	4.0	180	440	227	12.2	18
Bastrop, TX	48021	10.9	65.1	59.0	14.3	841	2,024	1,017	14.7	88
Baylor, TX	48023	9.5	52.2	27.5	0.3	43	92	53	10.9	4
Bee, TX	48025	9.9	71.7	80.5	2.1	302	783	368	14.4	35
Bell, TX	48027	10.3	52.4	63.2	6.5	3,094	9,380	4,510	14.3	352
Bexar, TX	48029	10.4	46.0	82.5	9.2	16,543	44,387	21,382	15.4	2,084
Blanco, TX	48031	9.8	46.7	34.5	5.2	123	282	152	11.1	14
Borden, TX	48033	4.4	0.0	27.3	2.2	9	50	19	11.9	2
Bosque, TX	48035	11.8	61.4	35.6	6.6	206	542	287	10.9	22
Bowie, TX	48037	11.4	56.4	43.2	2.0	1,056	2,635	1,437	12.5	116
Brazoria, TX	48039	9.8	45.7	58.2	8.1	3,378	7,945	3,858	15.9	308

[2]IEP=Individual Education Program. See notes and definitions for more information.
. . . = Not available.

Table C-1. Population, School, and Student Characteristics by County, Selected Years—*Continued*

County	State/ County Code	Revenues, 2008–2009				Current expenditures, 2008–2009			Resident population 16 to 19 years, 2006–2010			
			Percentage of revenue from									
		Total revenue ($1,000's)	Federal government	State government	Local government	Amount ($1,000's)	Amount per student	Percent for instruction	Total population 16 to 19 years	Percent enrolled in school	Percent high school graduates, not enrolled in school	Percent not enrolled, not grads, not employed, or not in labor force
		19	20	21	22	23	24	25	26	27	28	29
TENNESSEE— *(Continued)*												
Meigs, TN	47121	15,157	13.4	66.1	20.5	13,341	7,146	66.5	505	65.7	29.7	1.4
Monroe, TN	47123	67,155	9.6	49.1	41.3	49,958	6,957	63.9	2,252	79.4	17.9	. . .
Montgomery, TN	47125	216,251	11.5	54.3	34.3	203,491	7,081	59.0	9,556	79.1	16.3	2.5
Moore, TN	47127	8,340	7.4	57.1	35.5	7,991	7,967	59.1	368	83.2	16.9	0.0
Morgan, TN	47129	26,875	12.9	69.3	17.8	26,042	7,619	66.2	891	66.1	28.0	6.0
Obion, TN	47131	43,658	10.4	55.5	34.1	40,983	7,450	61.7	1,395	77.5	18.6	2.5
Overton, TN	47133	26,532	12.5	66.1	21.5	23,483	6,811	62.0	1,122	81.1	13.4	5.5
Perry, TN	47135	9,736	12.8	64.4	22.8	9,385	7,974	59.7	353	89.5	8.2	2.3
Pickett, TN	47137	6,267	12.2	63.7	24.1	5,655	8,268	63.7	217	59.5	40.6	0.0
Polk, TN	47139	21,368	11.8	63.4	24.8	20,236	7,316	64.0	839	86.5	9.2	2.0
Putnam, TN	47141	86,345	11.3	46.3	42.4	75,502	6,927	61.9	5,083	82.0	10.5	6.9
Rhea, TN	47143	38,883	12.5	61.7	25.8	34,966	6,893	65.3	1,770	91.0	6.3	2.4
Roane, TN	47145	61,681	10.5	52.1	37.4	59,941	7,933	63.2	2,613	71.6	22.1	4.1
Robertson, TN	47147	81,448	8.7	56.6	34.7	75,666	6,824	69.7	3,541	79.1	15.7	3.5
Rutherford, TN	47149	331,645	6.9	51.2	41.8	321,397	7,252	64.6	15,405	87.5	8.5	2.7
Scott, TN	47151	32,569	13.2	67.2	19.7	32,241	7,431	68.2	1,066	79.0	13.3	5.1
Sequatchie, TN	47153	19,772	14.6	57.6	27.8	15,081	6,626	65.6	565	71.3	21.8	6.9
Sevier, TN	47155	120,354	8.7	32.6	58.7	115,009	7,961	61.6	4,786	80.1	11.4	2.7
Shelby, TN	47157	1,426,742	12.3	43.5	44.2	1,388,120	8,708	60.8	56,616	81.5	11.6	5.2
Smith, TN	47159	24,432	9.7	64.3	26.0	22,701	6,840	63.6	1,061	88.9	11.1	0.0
Stewart, TN	47161	18,227	10.7	74.1	15.2	17,549	7,532	57.5	658	80.6	19.5	0.0
Sullivan, TN	47163	207,422	9.2	38.8	52.0	190,294	8,431	62.8	7,909	81.8	11.6	4.0
Sumner, TN	47165	204,301	7.4	52.5	40.1	202,158	7,561	65.6	7,868	84.8	11.1	2.4
Tipton, TN	47167	87,244	10.4	65.5	24.1	83,686	6,942	67.1	4,046	79.6	13.0	4.5
Trousdale, TN	47169	10,778	10.4	69.4	20.2	9,118	7,365	65.2	625	77.1	3.0	1.8
Unicoi, TN	47171	35,249	7.5	35.2	57.3	19,007	7,189	61.0	833	90.5	8.4	1.1
Union, TN	47173	25,308	13.8	66.6	19.6	24,542	8,026	63.3	1,188	84.0	13.3	0.0
Van Buren, TN	47175	7,645	10.8	66.3	22.9	6,284	7,729	59.8	374	67.4	27.5	5.1
Warren, TN	47177	49,826	13.3	57.3	29.4	46,707	7,070	62.3	1,932	78.1	17.0	4.9
Washington, TN	47179	131,610	10.1	42.8	47.1	123,477	7,409	66.0	6,558	88.2	7.8	2.6
Wayne, TN	47181	21,901	15.4	65.9	18.8	20,887	8,130	68.2	1,007	84.6	13.2	2.2
Weakley, TN	47183	36,928	10.9	61.4	27.7	34,918	7,225	64.4	2,774	88.1	8.9	2.7
White, TN	47185	30,509	12.2	63.3	24.5	26,836	6,599	68.2	1,296	69.2	19.4	3.2
Williamson, TN	47187	280,990	4.2	38.3	57.5	269,396	8,000	65.1	9,333	91.4	6.3	1.8
Wilson, TN	47189	141,520	6.8	46.9	46.3	127,996	7,072	63.3	5,867	85.7	10.5	1.5
TEXAS	48000	49,075,266	10.2	41.8	48.0	40,538,183	8,537	60.1	1,479,164	81.5	11.1	4.5
Anderson, TX	48001	80,562	9.8	50.1	40.0	70,982	8,342	61.9	2,856	73.0	19.6	5.4
Andrews, TX	48003	58,914	3.9	14.2	81.9	31,431	10,074	60.9	1,045	78.7	7.2	6.1
Angelina, TX	48005	149,406	11.4	60.4	28.2	134,407	7,878	59.7	5,056	79.6	9.9	6.9
Aransas, TX	48007	42,752	8.8	25.5	65.7	30,237	9,950	59.9	1,228	80.5	11.7	0.0
Archer, TX	48009	18,305	4.3	61.2	34.5	15,299	8,467	65.4	514	83.7	14.6	0.0
Armstrong, TX	48011	4,227	4.3	62.3	33.4	3,719	11,443	59.4	65	78.5	21.5	0.0
Atascosa, TX	48013	81,959	12.8	61.9	25.3	76,169	8,795	58.5	2,571	78.5	16.6	3.7
Austin, TX	48015	56,386	7.2	37.2	55.6	49,233	8,763	60.6	1,608	83.0	11.4	5.5
Bailey, TX	48017	16,611	13.3	57.7	28.9	13,281	9,053	63.2	666	71.8	23.0	0.0
Bandera, TX	48019	30,603	7.4	37.4	55.3	27,086	9,474	62.1	871	77.2	6.2	13.3
Bastrop, TX	48021	143,742	9.5	45.3	45.2	118,666	8,133	59.6	3,703	78.5	17.8	2.8
Baylor, TX	48023	6,573	6.6	61.9	31.5	5,736	10,335	64.8	302	85.8	12.3	2.0
Bee, TX	48025	51,560	12.4	57.9	29.6	43,402	8,479	60.1	1,907	73.9	10.1	13.7
Bell, TX	48027	582,187	17.0	55.3	27.7	500,281	8,113	61.6	17,756	74.0	17.6	4.9
Bexar, TX	48029	3,157,601	11.8	46.1	42.0	2,654,864	8,444	59.6	102,817	79.0	14.0	4.4
Blanco, TX	48031	20,672	4.1	29.6	66.3	17,248	10,466	62.7	562	75.1	14.8	8.4
Borden, TX	48033	13,023	1.6	11.3	87.0	4,015	20,912	47.5	29	100.0	0.0	0.0
Bosque, TX	48035	26,961	9.5	45.9	44.6	23,589	9,372	61.1	956	93.3	2.5	1.6
Bowie, TX	48037	181,476	9.6	55.3	35.1	152,025	8,609	64.3	5,258	83.6	11.9	3.6
Brazoria, TX	48039	566,354	7.7	39.3	53.0	447,564	7,576	59.6	16,950	84.4	9.7	4.6

Note. Data in columns 26 through 41 from the American Community Survey are subject to sampling error, which can be especially large in small counties and small population groups. See notes and definitions for more information.

Table C-1. Population, School, and Student Characteristics by County, Selected Years—*Continued*

County	State/ County Code	High school graduates, 2006–2010			College enrollment, 2006–2010		College graduates, 2006–2010 (percent)						
		Population 25 years and over	High school diploma or less (percent)	High school diploma or more (percent)	Number	Percent public	Bachelor's degree or more	+/- U.S. percent with Bachelor's degree or more	Non-Hispanic White	Black or African American	American Indian and Alaska Native	Asian, Hawaiian, and Pacific Islander	Hispanic or Latino[3]
		30	31	32	33	34	35	36	37	38	39	40	41
TENNESSEE— *(Continued)*													
Meigs, TN	47121	8,171	67.9	73.0	416	76.7	9.0	-18.9	8.7	42.4	7.7	0.0	0.0
Monroe, TN	47123	30,301	67.7	72.7	1,472	65.8	10.4	-17.5	10.2	11.9	0.0	23.0	7.0
Montgomery, TN	47125	97,784	41.9	90.0	14,076	85.2	22.3	-5.6	23.9	16.6	11.1	26.1	18.2
Moore, TN	47127	4,295	63.6	80.0	165	77.0	12.6	-15.3	13.1	0.0	0.0	100.0	0.0
Morgan, TN	47129	15,194	73.2	75.6	443	79.0	6.3	-21.6	6.3	0.0	0.0	33.6	11.3
Obion, TN	47131	22,203	64.8	79.9	1,252	89.9	11.9	-16.0	13.1	2.1	0.0	0.0	9.4
Overton, TN	47133	15,114	69.7	71.4	836	94.9	10.5	-17.4	10.6	0.0	0.0	0.0	64.5
Perry, TN	47135	5,457	69.1	76.6	275	74.2	10.6	-17.3	10.0	20.1	0.0	0.0	0.0
Pickett, TN	47137	3,589	70.3	74.1	106	83.0	12.0	-15.9	11.7	0.0	0.0	0.0	33.3
Polk, TN	47139	11,802	67.6	70.8	575	77.2	10.1	-17.8	10.2	0.0	0.0	0.0	21.1
Putnam, TN	47141	44,442	54.5	80.8	8,190	96.1	21.7	-6.2	21.5	27.3	0.0	72.8	9.6
Rhea, TN	47143	20,918	63.0	74.3	1,331	46.5	11.2	-16.7	11.0	18.7	47.4	48.5	0.0
Roane, TN	47145	39,024	54.6	81.3	1,650	85.7	16.7	-11.2	16.7	5.6	21.1	47.7	30.2
Robertson, TN	47147	42,359	59.7	81.1	2,219	69.0	14.2	-13.7	15.4	3.9	11.5	0.0	4.8
Rutherford, TN	47149	154,397	43.4	88.0	23,960	89.4	26.3	-1.6	27.9	21.1	13.3	28.2	11.4
Scott, TN	47151	14,750	70.0	73.5	669	86.1	9.9	-18.0	9.5	0.0	24.6	70.6	0.0
Sequatchie, TN	47153	9,446	68.6	74.1	724	92.3	13.3	-14.6	14.3	0.0	0.0	0.0	0.0
Sevier, TN	47155	60,764	57.7	80.9	3,070	75.0	15.2	-12.7	14.7	20.1	0.0	50.8	12.9
Shelby, TN	47157	581,947	43.2	84.9	63,934	76.1	27.8	-0.1	40.9	15.0	17.8	59.6	12.7
Smith, TN	47159	12,906	65.2	78.3	664	83.3	12.8	-15.1	13.3	0.0	25.7	0.0	0.0
Stewart, TN	47161	9,060	60.2	80.9	535	83.2	11.5	-16.4	11.7	0.0	16.5	2.1	33.3
Sullivan, TN	47163	111,615	51.9	82.1	7,593	78.2	20.0	-7.9	20.1	13.9	9.6	42.5	14.2
Sumner, TN	47165	103,914	47.2	85.4	7,044	76.7	23.0	-4.9	23.1	24.0	4.2	41.7	12.2
Tipton, TN	47167	38,124	55.2	83.2	2,635	80.8	13.8	-14.1	14.8	8.0	14.8	30.9	17.3
Trousdale, TN	47169	5,174	69.3	75.2	195	90.3	10.0	-17.9	11.4	0.0	0.0	0.0	0.0
Unicoi, TN	47171	13,285	63.5	74.7	754	92.7	12.2	-15.7	12.3	27.9	0.0	0.0	9.0
Union, TN	47173	12,931	75.7	66.1	470	70.0	6.3	-21.6	5.9	0.0	0.0	35.0	0.0
Van Buren, TN	47175	3,829	79.9	74.8	200	82.0	9.0	-18.9	8.8	0.0	0.0	0.0	0.0
Warren, TN	47177	26,715	68.3	75.3	1,493	85.7	11.0	-16.9	11.6	5.6	15.4	0.7	3.3
Washington, TN	47179	81,837	45.4	84.4	11,269	90.3	27.9	0.0	28.1	18.9	32.0	46.5	21.1
Wayne, TN	47181	12,181	72.0	75.0	595	82.9	8.7	-19.2	9.4	1.6	0.0	0.0	0.0
Weakley, TN	47183	21,722	58.1	82.0	4,672	96.2	18.4	-9.5	18.0	13.4	75.2	56.8	19.6
White, TN	47185	17,590	71.3	74.3	810	91.7	11.0	-16.9	11.1	13.8	0.0	7.9	5.8
Williamson, TN	47187	112,798	23.0	94.9	7,609	66.2	51.8	23.9	52.9	37.4	32.6	72.4	25.4
Wilson, TN	47189	73,779	47.3	87.7	5,207	61.7	24.0	-3.9	24.8	13.8	9.8	43.7	11.4
TEXAS	48000	15,116,371	46.0	80.0	1,595,990	82.3	25.8	-2.1	33.7	18.9	17.4	53.2	11.2
Anderson, TX	48001	41,118	61.6	74.8	2,749	94.7	11.4	-16.5	15.2	4.0	8.9	27.3	4.5
Andrews, TX	48003	8,552	58.0	72.7	349	89.1	12.4	-15.5	18.0	14.5	8.3	33.3	3.9
Angelina, TX	48005	54,308	52.3	78.0	3,616	90.7	15.9	-12.0	19.3	9.4	0.0	43.0	3.8
Aransas, TX	48007	16,773	46.5	85.2	839	84.3	23.9	-4.0	28.7	0.0	0.0	12.6	6.7
Archer, TX	48009	6,069	53.6	84.0	260	94.2	18.8	-9.1	19.4	26.7	0.0	48.4	3.1
Armstrong, TX	48011	1,374	35.4	91.5	76	85.5	25.9	-2.0	25.1	0.0	25.0	0.0	40.0
Atascosa, TX	48013	27,445	63.4	73.8	1,512	86.2	11.0	-16.9	18.4	1.7	13.0	0.0	5.5
Austin, TX	48015	18,420	53.7	81.2	804	76.6	17.9	-10.0	23.1	3.1	0.0	20.0	3.1
Bailey, TX	48017	3,974	57.7	73.4	189	100.0	18.5	-9.4	27.0	21.1	0.0	0.0	0.9
Bandera, TX	48019	14,986	41.8	89.0	612	63.1	24.0	-3.9	24.6	0.0	59.6	10.6	19.9
Bastrop, TX	48021	47,673	52.4	80.6	2,301	70.8	17.9	-10.0	21.3	14.3	18.5	64.1	8.2
Baylor, TX	48023	2,709	48.9	84.7	118	89.0	24.5	-3.4	26.3	10.0	0.0	0.0	6.3
Bee, TX	48025	21,374	60.9	69.5	1,516	82.1	9.2	-18.7	18.4	1.7	0.0	39.1	3.6
Bell, TX	48027	172,225	40.7	88.6	22,190	77.2	21.2	-6.7	25.9	14.0	15.8	30.8	11.1
Bexar, TX	48029	1,015,746	44.3	81.4	128,497	77.1	25.3	-2.6	40.8	22.8	18.3	49.3	13.8
Blanco, TX	48031	7,200	45.2	88.3	274	96.0	25.4	-2.5	28.6	0.0	0.0	0.0	10.7
Borden, TX	48033	388	64.4	85.1	7	71.4	19.1	-8.8	22.0	0.0	0.0	0.0	0.0
Bosque, TX	48035	12,744	56.1	80.1	581	95.5	14.8	-13.1	16.5	6.3	0.0	0.0	3.8
Bowie, TX	48037	60,644	49.6	83.5	4,993	91.2	18.1	-9.8	21.1	9.6	15.3	41.5	11.1
Brazoria, TX	48039	191,856	41.3	84.3	16,920	87.1	26.1	-1.8	27.3	30.9	18.2	61.6	12.5

Note. Data in columns 26 through 41 from the American Community Survey are subject to sampling error, which can be especially large in small counties and small population groups. See notes and definitions for more information.
[3]May be of any race.

Table C-1. Population, School, and Student Characteristics by County, Selected Years—*Continued*

County	State/ County Code	County Type[1]	Population, 2010		Percent of related children 5–17 years in poverty, 2010	Percent of children under 19 years with no health insurance, 2010	Number of schools and students, 2010–2011			Resident enrollment, 2006–2010	
										K–12 enrollment	
			Total	Percent 5–17 years			School districts	Schools	Students	Number	Percent public
			1	2	3	4	5	6	7	8	9
TEXAS—*(Continued)*											
Brazos, TX	48041	3	194,851	14.0	23.4	13.6	4	45	26,780	26,156	92.5
Brewster, TX	48043	7	9,232	14.5	22.1	15.6	4	7	1,285	1,349	92.1
Briscoe, TX	48045	9	1,637	15.8	27.1	30.8	2	2	402	297	100.0
Brooks, TX	48047	6	7,223	19.2	48.9	11.4	3	6	1,642	1,757	95.1
Brown, TX	48049	5	38,106	17.7	24.8	16.7	10	30	7,085	6,991	96.1
Burleson, TX	48051	3	17,187	17.3	23.4	18.1	3	12	2,887	3,117	93.9
Burnet, TX	48053	6	42,750	17.4	22.3	19.8	2	14	7,423	7,542	95.0
Caldwell, TX	48055	1	38,066	19.6	25.1	16.0	3	13	6,409	7,447	94.9
Calhoun, TX	48057	3	21,381	19.4	26.4	13.8	1	9	4,227	4,103	95.1
Callahan, TX	48059	3	13,544	18.1	22.0	15.2	4	12	2,522	2,359	97.2
Cameron, TX	48061	2	406,220	24.2	44.9	17.6	11	159	101,629	94,891	96.5
Camp, TX	48063	6	12,401	19.8	31.2	16.9	1	5	2,505	2,427	96.8
Carson, TX	48065	3	6,182	19.8	9.2	14.2	4	7	1,298	1,282	96.7
Cass, TX	48067	6	30,464	17.3	28.2	12.2	7	20	5,639	5,329	94.4
Castro, TX	48069	6	8,062	22.6	27.7	22.9	3	6	1,747	1,837	96.0
Chambers, TX	48071	1	35,096	21.6	12.9	13.5	3	18	6,782	7,094	97.6
Cherokee, TX	48073	6	50,845	18.8	32.7	19.3	6	25	10,727	9,768	97.0
Childress, TX	48075	7	7,041	15.4	30.6	15.8	1	3	1,095	1,059	100.0
Clay, TX	48077	3	10,752	17.1	16.7	16.2	5	9	1,775	1,902	95.9
Cochran, TX	48079	9	3,127	21.4	31.6	20.8	2	7	756	668	98.5
Coke, TX	48081	8	3,320	16.1	20.0	25.4	2	9	553	655	99.4
Coleman, TX	48083	6	8,895	16.6	33.2	17.6	3	8	1,339	1,446	99.3
Collin, TX	48085	1	782,341	21.2	8.2	10.3	14	253	169,023	152,392	90.3
Collingsworth, TX	48087	9	3,057	19.3	30.1	27.3	2	4	617	589	98.8
Colorado, TX	48089	6	20,874	17.4	24.6	19.2	3	12	3,445	3,658	87.2
Comal, TX	48091	1	108,472	18.0	14.2	13.4	3	41	25,307	19,000	87.8
Comanche, TX	48093	7	13,974	17.5	28.2	22.7	4	10	2,216	2,571	94.6
Concho, TX	48095	8	4,087	10.2	30.6	20.6	2	10	411	441	100.0
Cooke, TX	48097	6	38,437	18.6	22.5	18.7	9	22	6,391	7,359	91.8
Coryell, TX	48099	2	75,388	19.0	15.1	11.7	4	17	11,495	14,524	96.4
Cottle, TX	48101	9	1,505	18.1	28.2	27.0	1	1	239	337	96.4
Crane, TX	48103	6	4,375	21.8	14.3	18.2	1	3	1,014	914	100.0
Crockett, TX	48105	7	3,719	18.7	23.2	20.3	1	3	756	593	100.0
Crosby, TX	48107	3	6,059	20.5	38.1	15.2	3	10	1,289	1,312	98.3
Culberson, TX	48109	9	2,398	20.4	35.7	20.8	1	3	465	670	100.0
Dallam, TX	48111	7	6,703	20.6	21.8	21.1	2	6	1,866	1,482	77.7
Dallas, TX	48113	1	2,368,139	19.5	28.7	18.0	53	469	304,629	453,644	91.8
Dawson, TX	48115	7	13,833	17.1	35.9	14.8	4	8	2,538	2,671	98.1
Deaf Smith, TX	48117	6	19,372	22.7	29.6	19.6	2	9	4,510	4,356	95.5
Delta, TX	48119	1	5,231	16.7	26.1	19.0	1	3	831	970	95.8
Denton, TX	48121	1	662,614	20.0	8.9	11.4	15	213	119,986	123,298	92.1
De Witt, TX	48123	6	20,097	16.2	30.6	15.1	6	17	4,337	3,281	95.1
Dickens, TX	48125	8	2,444	14.7	27.7	22.2	2	2	403	309	99.0
Dimmit, TX	48127	6	9,996	21.8	41.3	13.6	1	6	2,400	2,057	96.1
Donley, TX	48129	8	3,677	15.1	25.1	25.1	2	4	650	634	96.2
Duval, TX	48131	7	11,782	18.9	35.9	13.5	4	9	2,640	2,433	98.9
Eastland, TX	48133	6	18,583	16.4	30.1	17.7	5	16	3,040	3,055	95.6
Ector, TX	48135	3	137,130	20.2	26.0	18.5	3	41	28,601	26,900	94.8
Edwards, TX	48137	9	2,002	15.1	38.3	23.4	2	4	590	349	98.0
Ellis, TX	48139	1	149,610	21.6	15.6	12.7	10	55	32,085	30,955	91.8
El Paso, TX	48141	2	800,647	22.0	33.1	16.2	17	253	181,347	176,040	95.6
Erath, TX	48143	7	37,890	16.0	22.4	19.7	9	18	5,953	6,114	99.2
Falls, TX	48145	6	17,866	15.7	31.6	15.8	4	14	2,537	3,338	95.5
Fannin, TX	48147	6	33,915	16.3	22.2	16.5	9	25	5,524	5,904	90.8
Fayette, TX	48149	6	24,554	16.3	18.1	18.5	5	11	3,678	4,100	95.7
Fisher, TX	48151	8	3,974	17.1	21.8	21.9	2	6	621	816	98.7
Floyd, TX	48153	6	6,446	21.2	32.2	16.7	2	9	1,435	1,475	96.6
Foard, TX	48155	9	1,336	16.5	25.8	22.0	1	2	240	212	100.0
Fort Bend, TX	48157	1	585,375	22.2	11.2	13.0	6	180	160,838	121,563	92.5
Franklin, TX	48159	8	10,605	17.9	23.5	17.6	1	4	1,570	1,828	97.3
Freestone, TX	48161	7	19,816	17.2	21.8	15.8	4	13	3,708	3,413	98.4
Frio, TX	48163	6	17,217	17.7	40.1	11.6	2	8	3,229	3,867	96.0
Gaines, TX	48165	7	17,526	24.5	26.5	23.2	3	10	3,181	3,456	84.1

[1]County type codes are from the Economic Research Service of the United States Department of Agriculture. See notes and definitions for more information.

Table C-1. Population, School, and Student Characteristics by County, Selected Years—*Continued*

County	State/ County Code	Characteristics of students, 2010–2011				Number of graduates, 2008–2009	Staff and students, 2010–2011			
		Percent with IEP[2]	Percent eligible for free or reduced lunch	Percent minority	Percent English-language learners		Total staff	Number of teachers	Student/ teacher ratio	Central admin. staff
		10	11	12	13	14	15	16	17	18
TEXAS—*(Continued)*										
Brazos, TX	48041	7.5	50.2	61.5	12.3	1,369	3,790	1,844	14.5	148
Brewster, TX	48043	10.8	51.4	68.1	10.1	88	235	123	10.5	14
Briscoe, TX	48045	7.7	54.7	42.3	7.0	39	81	45	9.0	3
Brooks, TX	48047	9.9	13.3	98.2	2.8	84	262	124	13.3	17
Brown, TX	48049	10.6	59.4	37.6	1.5	403	1,046	545	13.0	32
Burleson, TX	48051	9.9	59.0	48.6	7.9	168	491	239	12.1	30
Burnet, TX	48053	11.5	59.0	36.8	7.3	514	1,110	522	14.2	30
Caldwell, TX	48055	11.2	66.2	69.3	8.8	418	877	453	14.1	37
Calhoun, TX	48057	12.1	63.6	68.0	9.5	309	607	294	14.4	12
Callahan, TX	48059	10.2	52.2	15.8	0.7	184	425	232	10.9	15
Cameron, TX	48061	8.9	18.6	97.1	24.5	5,162	15,268	6,780	15.0	642
Camp, TX	48063	12.6	75.5	58.2	13.5	140	436	213	11.8	15
Carson, TX	48065	9.7	33.0	12.1	0.5	94	236	126	10.3	12
Cass, TX	48067	10.5	59.5	30.0	1.4	383	960	473	11.9	42
Castro, TX	48069	6.6	58.4	78.3	11.7	97	308	148	11.8	14
Chambers, TX	48071	7.4	34.0	33.5	3.2	405	973	495	13.7	39
Cherokee, TX	48073	10.0	68.1	48.7	13.6	488	1,654	818	13.1	60
Childress, TX	48075	10.8	54.9	45.7	2.6	78	203	96	11.4	7
Clay, TX	48077	10.5	47.1	12.0	0.5	129	318	165	10.8	14
Cochran, TX	48079	11.0	74.8	69.2	10.6	60	174	91	8.3	8
Coke, TX	48081	10.7	53.2	32.8	4.0	43	107	60	9.3	6
Coleman, TX	48083	9.6	64.6	33.2	2.9	117	253	128	10.5	19
Collin, TX	48085	9.7	23.6	46.2	7.2	8,628	20,863	11,845	14.3	767
Collingsworth, TX	48087	13.3	64.2	48.5	8.9	45	114	63	9.8	5
Colorado, TX	48089	10.7	62.6	60.9	9.3	228	531	298	11.6	18
Comal, TX	48091	9.0	37.1	43.3	5.2	1,489	3,337	1,614	15.7	126
Comanche, TX	48093	8.1	65.8	44.9	7.3	144	393	204	10.9	11
Concho, TX	48095	8.8	63.1	58.1	2.9	33	77	39	10.6	6
Cooke, TX	48097	10.4	55.5	37.3	8.8	391	915	493	13.0	38
Coryell, TX	48099	9.7	52.6	46.5	1.8	627	1,697	826	13.9	50
Cottle, TX	48101	12.6	68.2	54.8	...	17	39	24	10.1	3
Crane, TX	48103	7.2	24.5	69.6	8.7	58	169	96	10.6	11
Crockett, TX	48105	8.1	59.4	78.6	13.4	43	164	80	9.4	4
Crosby, TX	48107	12.5	62.5	77.3	2.9	75	299	137	9.4	12
Culberson, TX	48109	5.8	74.0	92.5	8.0	37	86	45	10.3	5
Dallam, TX	48111	10.6	61.9	49.3	6.8	110	324	168	11.1	11
Dallas, TX	48113	9.5	71.0	84.9	17.5	23,966	37,460	19,886	15.3	2,001
Dawson, TX	48115	9.0	31.4	74.0	7.9	138	453	218	11.7	14
Deaf Smith, TX	48117	8.4	78.8	86.8	15.6	219	701	323	14.0	24
Delta, TX	48119	10.2	62.7	25.0	1.9	68	134	72	11.5	4
Denton, TX	48121	9.8	31.2	44.8	11.3	6,882	14,975	8,555	14.0	649
De Witt, TX	48123	9.9	61.8	58.2	5.3	289	813	363	12.0	26
Dickens, TX	48125	11.7	42.2	43.9	...	27	93	44	9.2	6
Dimmit, TX	48127	8.7	76.9	94.0	6.2	125	370	156	15.4	19
Donley, TX	48129	10.9	57.7	28.9	1.2	45	122	69	9.4	8
Duval, TX	48131	7.2	54.3	94.2	5.3	152	443	208	12.7	23
Eastland, TX	48133	11.5	64.5	26.1	4.4	214	579	295	10.3	23
Ector, TX	48135	8.9	59.5	74.9	10.4	1,424	3,447	1,758	16.3	139
Edwards, TX	48137	13.2	71.8	69.1	3.1	46	124	64	9.2	4
Ellis, TX	48139	11.0	47.6	47.9	7.4	2,027	4,328	2,149	14.9	154
El Paso, TX	48141	8.6	68.8	93.4	22.5	10,170	23,649	11,729	15.5	1,115
Erath, TX	48143	8.1	54.5	38.7	10.1	399	833	436	13.7	33
Falls, TX	48145	15.6	76.8	71.4	8.4	156	533	239	10.6	22
Fannin, TX	48147	12.0	56.7	23.1	3.9	396	913	457	12.1	36
Fayette, TX	48149	9.1	52.4	46.8	10.1	204	598	302	12.2	27
Fisher, TX	48151	10.8	56.8	46.4	1.8	41	129	63	9.9	6
Floyd, TX	48153	10.0	71.8	78.7	6.3	91	270	136	10.6	9
Foard, TX	48155	15.4	63.8	28.8	...	24	43	22	11.0	2
Fort Bend, TX	48157	7.4	32.5	70.3	11.3	9,740	19,996	9,957	16.2	699
Franklin, TX	48159	10.6	56.3	31.9	7.9	114	231	125	12.5	10
Freestone, TX	48161	8.7	49.8	38.1	5.4	231	659	324	11.4	22
Frio, TX	48163	8.4	66.2	92.4	4.2	174	556	260	12.4	26
Gaines, TX	48165	10.2	56.7	52.0	8.2	211	600	278	11.5	19

[2]IEP=Individual Education Program. See notes and definitions for more information.
. . . = Not available.

Table C-1. Population, School, and Student Characteristics by County, Selected Years—*Continued*

County	State/ County Code	Revenues, 2008–2009				Current expenditures, 2008–2009			Resident population 16 to 19 years, 2006–2010			
		Total revenue ($1,000's)	Percentage of revenue from: Federal government	State government	Local government	Amount ($1,000's)	Amount per student	Percent for instruction	Total population 16 to 19 years	Percent enrolled in school	Percent high school graduates, not enrolled in school	Percent not enrolled, not grads, not employed, or not in labor force
		19	20	21	22	23	24	25	26	27	28	29
TEXAS—*(Continued)*												
Brazos, TX	48041	251,110	10.0	37.1	52.9	209,908	8,170	60.8	20,961	94.2	3.3	1.2
Brewster, TX	48043	17,720	13.5	49.4	37.0	14,771	11,989	59.3	471	95.8	0.0	4.3
Briscoe, TX	48045	4,907	8.9	67.3	23.8	4,362	11,071	65.4	90	87.8	12.2	0.0
Brooks, TX	48047	22,027	13.6	36.5	49.9	19,691	12,088	57.7	641	82.1	10.8	4.5
Brown, TX	48049	69,566	11.3	51.8	36.9	59,208	8,796	62.4	2,510	79.2	16.9	3.9
Burleson, TX	48051	30,624	13.1	41.9	45.0	28,134	10,044	56.6	932	86.3	9.7	4.1
Burnet, TX	48053	82,630	6.8	25.5	67.7	67,506	9,207	57.1	2,278	76.9	12.3	5.4
Caldwell, TX	48055	61,177	10.6	61.9	27.5	52,072	8,340	60.2	2,726	65.3	23.8	9.2
Calhoun, TX	48057	60,586	5.6	18.3	76.1	38,868	8,846	59.2	1,085	85.2	12.5	0.5
Callahan, TX	48059	59,935	37.9	33.7	28.4	35,605	13,870	41.5	751	78.3	9.7	11.3
Cameron, TX	48061	984,185	16.5	65.3	18.2	872,683	8,877	59.5	27,099	81.6	9.8	6.5
Camp, TX	48063	24,125	12.1	54.9	33.0	21,992	9,335	66.6	730	81.4	13.3	4.1
Carson, TX	48065	18,333	3.9	25.7	70.4	13,356	10,172	59.8	380	90.5	7.1	2.4
Cass, TX	48067	58,298	12.1	57.7	30.2	49,661	8,794	62.7	1,646	85.2	10.9	3.8
Castro, TX	48069	18,258	15.1	62.0	22.8	14,923	8,968	61.1	612	83.2	5.6	0.0
Chambers, TX	48071	100,801	6.6	28.9	64.5	72,730	11,162	47.3	1,900	86.8	8.1	4.0
Cherokee, TX	48073	98,942	11.3	56.8	31.9	83,311	8,144	61.9	2,887	68.1	16.6	11.5
Childress, TX	48075	12,551	6.6	65.9	27.5	11,520	10,407	58.2	409	46.7	29.6	19.6
Clay, TX	48077	20,378	9.4	53.2	37.5	17,751	9,791	62.7	602	78.2	19.3	2.5
Cochran, TX	48079	26,765	7.6	42.1	50.3	19,360	14,835	56.6	302	84.8	15.2	0.0
Coke, TX	48081	8,960	4.8	46.5	48.7	6,394	11,500	60.0	280	78.2	18.2	3.6
Coleman, TX	48083	17,431	9.6	67.9	22.5	15,208	9,920	59.8	478	79.9	12.3	7.7
Collin, TX	48085	1,668,545	3.3	28.5	68.2	1,261,583	8,134	63.5	38,648	88.1	8.4	1.9
Collingsworth, TX	48087	8,583	6.0	71.3	22.7	6,530	10,171	64.1	162	95.7	1.9	0.0
Colorado, TX	48089	37,208	8.7	33.7	57.6	31,054	9,131	63.4	1,015	76.0	12.7	5.7
Comal, TX	48091	249,681	6.4	24.5	69.1	186,629	7,872	59.8	5,088	80.5	10.4	5.3
Comanche, TX	48093	23,175	11.7	63.2	25.1	21,401	9,470	63.8	826	73.9	24.2	1.9
Concho, TX	48095	5,373	6.2	43.4	50.4	4,682	11,309	56.6	127	69.3	30.7	0.0
Cooke, TX	48097	64,385	9.2	42.3	48.5	54,500	8,845	61.5	2,397	74.6	17.5	7.6
Coryell, TX	48099	106,896	17.8	57.1	25.1	89,771	8,121	61.3	4,910	63.3	31.9	2.2
Cottle, TX	48101	3,287	10.0	41.2	48.8	2,628	10,266	67.4	132	96.2	0.0	3.8
Crane, TX	48103	30,111	2.4	20.9	76.8	13,233	12,910	65.4	362	89.8	0.0	3.0
Crockett, TX	48105	33,160	1.6	10.8	87.5	9,962	13,195	59.8	268	47.4	39.9	5.2
Crosby, TX	48107	20,073	18.4	59.0	22.5	16,000	12,831	63.0	372	85.0	14.5	0.5
Culberson, TX	48109	6,827	10.1	37.3	52.6	6,176	12,427	58.3	408	94.9	0.0	5.2
Dallam, TX	48111	17,725	11.3	42.7	46.0	15,928	9,019	60.1	586	60.4	18.1	0.5
Dallas, TX	48113	4,608,644	10.8	37.8	51.5	3,809,975	8,480	60.9	132,515	79.4	11.1	5.1
Dawson, TX	48115	37,562	10.1	41.0	48.9	25,480	10,119	62.3	761	76.1	12.6	10.8
Deaf Smith, TX	48117	40,187	14.3	55.9	29.8	36,632	8,470	61.9	1,494	64.3	22.8	5.9
Delta, TX	48119	9,439	9.9	63.1	27.0	7,322	8,594	61.1	325	85.5	4.0	10.5
Denton, TX	48121	1,184,025	4.5	30.0	65.5	938,792	8,521	62.6	36,216	89.1	6.8	1.9
De Witt, TX	48123	47,919	12.7	52.4	34.9	40,758	9,383	61.0	1,114	78.3	7.6	5.0
Dickens, TX	48125	7,699	6.7	30.7	62.6	5,752	14,979	53.5	129	51.9	6.2	27.9
Dimmit, TX	48127	24,891	19.3	59.6	21.0	23,498	9,865	61.3	897	60.8	2.2	26.6
Donley, TX	48129	7,938	6.9	68.5	24.6	7,529	11,171	62.4	497	97.6	0.8	0.8
Duval, TX	48131	35,512	15.1	37.7	47.1	28,078	10,588	56.2	794	78.7	14.7	3.9
Eastland, TX	48133	33,070	10.9	56.5	32.6	31,019	9,866	63.2	1,663	87.3	8.5	3.0
Ector, TX	48135	234,098	11.0	41.9	47.1	212,304	7,584	60.1	8,520	77.4	10.1	6.7
Edwards, TX	48137	9,194	8.5	34.9	56.6	8,298	13,671	56.5	173	38.2	61.9	0.0
Ellis, TX	48139	327,615	6.4	48.7	44.9	264,390	7,809	59.6	9,120	84.0	9.3	3.7
El Paso, TX	48141	1,691,392	16.1	59.9	24.0	1,505,762	8,636	60.0	53,143	84.0	10.3	4.2
Erath, TX	48143	54,238	9.1	45.5	45.4	47,864	8,204	60.8	3,158	89.3	6.6	2.4
Falls, TX	48145	31,945	13.2	67.2	19.6	25,883	9,906	58.6	1,488	65.6	21.9	6.3
Fannin, TX	48147	60,142	9.2	62.6	28.1	50,857	8,993	61.8	1,794	81.8	11.9	5.7
Fayette, TX	48149	40,752	5.7	33.5	60.8	32,782	9,058	61.0	905	85.5	5.9	3.1
Fisher, TX	48151	7,421	8.9	65.3	25.8	6,709	10,306	61.6	207	92.3	0.0	0.0
Floyd, TX	48153	17,234	11.7	57.9	30.3	16,184	11,200	59.6	395	76.5	15.2	0.0
Foard, TX	48155	3,427	8.4	61.5	30.1	2,959	12,381	57.5	87	92.0	8.1	0.0
Fort Bend, TX	48157	1,415,083	5.6	38.3	56.1	1,188,713	7,691	63.5	33,676	86.5	9.2	2.5
Franklin, TX	48159	14,715	8.9	30.0	61.1	12,668	8,406	62.2	781	79.6	18.7	1.7
Freestone, TX	48161	78,363	4.4	16.2	79.4	37,907	10,320	60.0	1,040	83.0	11.2	1.0
Frio, TX	48163	39,508	14.4	63.4	22.2	32,570	10,359	57.3	1,123	79.5	8.6	8.4
Gaines, TX	48165	88,273	4.3	13.5	82.3	38,250	12,343	60.4	1,313	58.3	25.3	6.5

Note. Data in columns 26 through 41 from the American Community Survey are subject to sampling error, which can be especially large in small counties and small population groups. See notes and definitions for more information.

Table C-1. Population, School, and Student Characteristics by County, Selected Years—*Continued*

County	State/ County Code	High school graduates, 2006–2010			College enrollment, 2006–2010		College graduates, 2006–2010 (percent)						
		Population 25 years and over	High school diploma or less (percent)	High school diploma or more (percent)	Number	Percent public	Bachelor's degree or more	+/- U.S. percent with Bachelor's degree or more	Non-Hispanic White	Black or African American	American Indian and Alaska Native	Asian, Hawaiian, and Pacific Islander	Hispanic or Latino[3]
		30	31	32	33	34	35	36	37	38	39	40	41
TEXAS—*(Continued)*													
Brazos, TX	48041	88,193	38.1	84.5	54,251	96.8	39.3	11.4	49.0	16.3	14.2	75.8	12.2
Brewster, TX	48043	6,045	43.3	80.3	946	98.5	30.4	2.5	43.9	13.3	18.2	0.0	9.7
Briscoe, TX	48045	1,203	54.1	81.0	15	100.0	15.0	-12.9	17.7	14.3	0.0	66.7	1.0
Brooks, TX	48047	4,477	74.1	53.7	101	100.0	12.5	-15.4	38.9	0.0	0.0	0.0	10.1
Brown, TX	48049	25,086	58.4	81.7	1,546	44.2	15.0	-12.9	17.2	4.3	0.0	48.2	4.2
Burleson, TX	48051	11,756	63.9	76.8	492	78.5	10.5	-17.4	12.6	3.6	0.0	14.7	1.8
Burnet, TX	48053	29,358	46.9	83.5	985	76.5	21.4	-6.5	24.3	5.2	18.1	0.0	6.7
Caldwell, TX	48055	23,245	62.7	75.6	1,448	88.7	14.3	-13.6	21.6	6.4	1.6	37.4	5.4
Calhoun, TX	48057	13,737	55.8	78.2	638	88.7	14.7	-13.2	17.6	2.3	0.0	73.6	5.0
Callahan, TX	48059	9,224	49.4	86.3	711	52.5	17.1	-10.8	17.3	70.5	13.0	41.9	13.0
Cameron, TX	48061	223,309	62.0	62.3	20,840	92.5	14.6	-13.3	31.9	20.1	38.5	54.9	10.8
Camp, TX	48063	8,033	58.2	74.7	454	89.9	14.9	-13.0	19.2	8.1	18.8	63.3	1.6
Carson, TX	48065	4,266	44.9	87.9	247	89.5	23.6	-4.3	24.2	61.4	0.0	23.5	11.3
Cass, TX	48067	20,980	57.4	82.3	1,153	89.1	12.9	-15.0	14.2	8.0	0.0	40.9	2.0
Castro, TX	48069	4,723	63.1	68.1	237	98.7	14.9	-13.0	27.2	0.0	0.0	0.0	2.9
Chambers, TX	48071	20,522	45.2	84.8	1,635	87.0	16.2	-11.7	17.2	13.2	12.6	35.9	11.1
Cherokee, TX	48073	32,139	63.0	74.2	1,637	79.0	11.8	-16.1	15.0	4.8	8.3	12.6	3.3
Childress, TX	48075	4,798	59.5	82.1	233	65.7	15.7	-12.2	22.4	0.0	0.0	0.0	2.0
Clay, TX	48077	7,634	49.7	89.2	340	94.4	19.3	-8.6	19.4	75.8	24.0	15.2	17.3
Cochran, TX	48079	1,939	64.7	66.5	108	89.8	11.7	-16.2	17.0	13.5	0.0	0.0	5.0
Coke, TX	48081	2,306	53.1	86.3	72	54.2	11.8	-16.1	13.9	0.0	0.0	0.0	0.0
Coleman, TX	48083	6,029	60.7	77.8	217	78.8	13.7	-14.2	13.7	13.2	47.8	56.7	9.9
Collin, TX	48085	472,393	23.0	92.8	45,242	82.7	48.3	20.4	49.6	41.5	39.1	71.8	23.8
Collingsworth, TX	48087	1,876	56.7	74.2	113	95.6	18.3	-9.6	26.3	0.0	0.0	0.0	4.4
Colorado, TX	48089	14,101	60.1	79.6	568	77.6	15.4	-12.5	20.1	6.9	40.5	5.6	4.4
Comal, TX	48091	70,763	36.5	88.6	3,769	77.3	32.6	4.7	37.6	45.8	4.6	37.2	12.5
Comanche, TX	48093	9,439	57.8	74.7	271	93.7	18.1	-9.8	19.6	17.7	0.0	58.2	8.9
Concho, TX	48095	3,252	67.1	71.7	48	68.8	10.5	-17.4	20.0	13.9	0.0	0.0	1.8
Cooke, TX	48097	24,940	49.2	81.8	1,463	91.3	19.5	-8.4	21.5	3.4	14.5	19.6	6.8
Coryell, TX	48099	42,927	44.8	87.6	4,444	86.7	15.4	-12.5	17.3	9.8	4.9	16.8	12.6
Cottle, TX	48101	1,117	59.2	79.1	56	94.6	15.9	-12.0	18.8	0.0	0.0	0.0	4.6
Crane, TX	48103	2,589	58.1	72.2	193	100.0	13.1	-14.8	23.7	0.0	0.0	0.0	3.3
Crockett, TX	48105	2,293	60.2	61.9	65	40.0	9.1	-18.8	14.7	0.0	0.0	0.0	3.2
Crosby, TX	48107	3,906	63.3	75.2	144	84.7	13.3	-14.6	22.0	10.9	28.6	43.5	1.9
Culberson, TX	48109	1,447	72.0	61.8	97	100.0	13.8	-14.1	35.8	0.0	0.0	0.0	4.0
Dallam, TX	48111	3,763	64.2	71.8	126	73.8	8.4	-19.5	10.6	0.0	8.8	100.0	4.4
Dallas, TX	48113	1,442,630	46.8	76.5	131,837	74.0	28.0	0.1	43.3	19.0	17.5	52.6	8.4
Dawson, TX	48115	9,035	67.4	67.0	510	77.3	8.7	-19.2	17.8	0.0	0.0	0.0	1.3
Deaf Smith, TX	48117	10,984	64.8	66.3	439	90.0	13.2	-14.7	24.3	0.0	52.4	38.1	4.5
Delta, TX	48119	3,586	54.8	84.2	179	100.0	15.0	-12.9	14.9	4.3	57.8	0.0	5.3
Denton, TX	48121	388,383	28.4	91.2	57,041	89.8	39.5	11.6	42.4	38.3	35.0	56.2	18.4
De Witt, TX	48123	14,033	61.1	75.5	626	89.8	12.1	-15.8	17.4	2.2	0.0	48.4	3.2
Dickens, TX	48125	1,762	61.3	72.9	40	92.5	12.7	-15.2	16.9	0.0	0.0	100.0	0.0
Dimmit, TX	48127	6,051	71.1	61.0	312	80.8	12.6	-15.3	14.8	0.0	0.0	78.3	10.4
Donley, TX	48129	2,374	52.7	82.2	470	94.7	16.6	-11.3	17.7	0.0	0.0	0.0	2.7
Duval, TX	48131	7,487	68.7	64.9	448	89.5	8.5	-19.4	12.0	0.0	0.0	0.0	8.2
Eastland, TX	48133	12,335	56.6	77.7	1,313	93.5	15.5	-12.4	17.1	0.0	0.0	57.1	3.3
Ector, TX	48135	79,023	57.2	72.9	7,665	90.7	13.1	-14.8	17.8	16.1	11.3	63.6	6.1
Edwards, TX	48137	1,369	57.7	67.7	18	77.8	22.1	-5.8	32.0	0.0	0.0	0.0	9.2
Ellis, TX	48139	88,522	47.7	82.9	7,728	71.6	21.0	-6.9	24.6	18.8	11.2	41.0	6.6
El Paso, TX	48141	451,053	53.1	71.0	64,784	88.8	19.3	-8.6	37.7	25.2	15.5	48.4	14.7
Erath, TX	48143	21,584	47.5	79.5	5,575	98.4	24.0	-3.9	26.8	46.6	0.0	39.8	7.9
Falls, TX	48145	11,678	62.4	73.5	755	93.9	9.8	-18.1	13.3	4.0	20.0	16.2	2.2
Fannin, TX	48147	23,242	57.9	82.4	1,187	86.4	14.7	-13.2	16.2	1.0	0.0	41.0	10.7
Fayette, TX	48149	17,293	56.4	79.0	579	88.4	17.6	-10.3	20.9	1.5	0.0	0.0	3.2
Fisher, TX	48151	2,861	60.9	81.0	92	71.7	15.2	-12.7	18.3	0.0	48.6	0.0	3.6
Floyd, TX	48153	4,216	57.2	74.6	154	93.5	17.1	-10.8	27.8	4.8	0.0	0.0	4.2
Foard, TX	48155	963	60.0	75.8	6	100.0	15.6	-12.3	18.5	0.0	0.0	0.0	2.8
Fort Bend, TX	48157	335,452	31.7	88.6	34,782	76.5	40.4	12.5	47.6	35.5	16.2	57.7	16.1
Franklin, TX	48159	6,881	49.1	82.7	739	93.2	23.6	-4.3	26.3	0.0	0.0	100.0	0.0
Freestone, TX	48161	13,563	56.2	78.7	813	97.3	14.0	-13.9	17.2	6.4	0.0	0.0	3.6
Frio, TX	48163	10,620	72.9	64.3	592	76.9	8.1	-19.8	19.4	0.0	0.0	67.7	4.1
Gaines, TX	48165	9,268	69.0	58.2	405	79.3	12.9	-15.0	15.8	22.7	38.8	79.1	4.6

Note. Data in columns 26 through 41 from the American Community Survey are subject to sampling error, which can be especially large in small counties and small population groups. See notes and definitions for more information.
[3]May be of any race.

Table C-1. Population, School, and Student Characteristics by County, Selected Years—*Continued*

County	State/ County Code	County Type[1]	Population, 2010		Percent of related children 5–17 years in poverty, 2010	Percent of children under 19 years with no health insurance, 2010	Number of schools and students, 2010–2011			Resident enrollment, 2006–2010 K–12 enrollment	
			Total	Percent 5–17 years			School districts	Schools	Students	Number	Percent public
			1	2	3	4	5	6	7	8	9
TEXAS—*(Continued)*											
Galveston, TX	48167	1	291,309	18.6	18.4	12.9	14	121	76,668	54,152	92.9
Garza, TX	48169	6	6,461	13.8	28.6	15.4	2	4	931	1,158	99.7
Gillespie, TX	48171	7	24,837	15.3	17.9	20.3	3	10	3,588	3,744	86.4
Glasscock, TX	48173	8	1,226	22.3	16.1	20.5	1	2	283	368	89.1
Goliad, TX	48175	3	7,210	17.5	22.5	15.0	1	5	1,385	1,285	93.2
Gonzales, TX	48177	6	19,807	19.4	30.2	18.7	3	12	3,936	3,831	90.5
Gray, TX	48179	6	22,535	17.5	20.9	15.5	4	10	3,892	3,919	94.1
Grayson, TX	48181	3	120,877	17.6	19.8	17.4	13	58	21,022	21,117	95.0
Gregg, TX	48183	3	121,730	18.0	28.1	15.9	9	49	24,044	21,774	93.7
Grimes, TX	48185	6	26,604	16.8	25.5	17.4	4	11	4,318	4,874	95.8
Guadalupe, TX	48187	1	131,533	20.7	16.1	14.5	4	38	22,902	25,819	94.1
Hale, TX	48189	4	36,273	20.5	27.9	14.0	5	23	7,707	7,676	93.6
Hall, TX	48191	9	3,353	19.4	37.4	25.8	1	4	553	718	99.3
Hamilton, TX	48193	6	8,517	15.8	25.8	20.5	3	8	1,665	1,373	97.1
Hansford, TX	48195	7	5,613	22.0	18.9	20.2	3	7	1,373	1,286	99.1
Hardeman, TX	48197	7	4,139	18.1	31.0	19.4	2	5	735	689	95.5
Hardin, TX	48199	2	54,635	19.1	16.0	11.3	5	24	10,848	10,419	92.7
Harris, TX	48201	1	4,092,459	19.8	25.6	18.1	67	995	761,743	793,722	93.6
Harrison, TX	48203	4	65,631	18.7	24.1	16.3	6	30	12,938	11,950	95.6
Hartley, TX	48205	9	6,062	16.8	11.9	17.9	2	2	338	1,079	78.0
Haskell, TX	48207	6	5,899	15.5	35.8	18.0	3	5	963	843	96.9
Hays, TX	48209	1	157,107	17.9	13.7	11.7	6	44	29,517	25,418	90.4
Hemphill, TX	48211	9	3,807	20.8	12.8	17.6	1	4	848	668	90.7
Henderson, TX	48213	4	78,532	16.8	26.7	16.0	9	37	12,018	13,336	95.7
Hidalgo, TX	48215	2	774,769	25.0	44.6	16.3	23	332	213,987	184,131	97.7
Hill, TX	48217	6	35,089	17.8	25.0	15.9	12	28	6,506	6,281	93.9
Hockley, TX	48219	6	22,935	19.5	25.1	14.1	6	19	4,749	4,355	96.5
Hood, TX	48221	4	51,182	15.6	19.1	14.7	3	16	7,527	7,876	92.6
Hopkins, TX	48223	6	35,161	18.7	26.9	19.7	7	17	6,575	6,431	96.2
Houston, TX	48225	7	23,732	15.0	31.2	19.0	6	15	3,401	4,251	93.8
Howard, TX	48227	5	35,012	16.0	28.5	12.7	3	14	5,391	5,868	97.9
Hudspeth, TX	48229	8	3,476	23.2	37.6	29.6	3	5	786	902	100.0
Hunt, TX	48231	1	86,129	18.2	25.6	15.0	11	47	14,541	15,598	94.5
Hutchinson, TX	48233	6	22,150	19.1	17.8	17.8	3	13	4,227	4,263	98.1
Irion, TX	48235	3	1,599	18.8	12.2	19.2	1	2	329	302	94.0
Jack, TX	48237	6	9,044	16.7	17.9	19.1	3	7	1,526	1,734	90.6
Jackson, TX	48239	6	14,075	18.1	25.3	15.8	3	11	3,180	2,713	96.8
Jasper, TX	48241	6	35,710	18.1	27.1	14.4	4	15	6,264	6,552	90.5
Jeff Davis, TX	48243	9	2,342	16.0	16.5	24.2	2	4	359	428	68.2
Jefferson, TX	48245	2	252,273	17.1	29.3	15.9	11	84	41,805	44,085	92.1
Jim Hogg, TX	48247	6	5,300	20.3	36.2	15.9	1	3	1,153	986	100.0
Jim Wells, TX	48249	4	40,838	20.6	31.3	12.5	4	21	8,484	8,930	96.1
Johnson, TX	48251	1	150,934	20.1	17.4	15.5	9	63	31,567	29,877	92.0
Jones, TX	48253	3	20,202	13.8	28.1	14.5	5	14	2,707	3,082	93.9
Karnes, TX	48255	6	14,824	14.4	31.4	12.4	4	17	2,286	1,207	94.7
Kaufman, TX	48257	1	103,350	21.3	15.7	14.5	6	46	23,056	20,125	93.4
Kendall, TX	48259	1	33,410	19.0	12.3	13.2	3	15	7,856	6,139	82.8
Kenedy, TX	48261	9	416	18.0	16.0	17.2	1	1	80	33	100.0
Kent, TX	48263	9	808	18.2	14.7	20.8	1	1	153	142	100.0
Kerr, TX	48265	4	49,625	15.0	26.3	18.5	5	21	6,761	7,469	86.1
Kimble, TX	48267	7	4,607	15.3	31.1	22.7	1	3	695	737	100.0
King, TX	48269	9	286	19.9	14.8	14.0	1	1	116	24	100.0
Kinney, TX	48271	9	3,598	14.8	33.9	16.3	1	4	614	532	92.1
Kleberg, TX	48273	4	32,061	17.4	32.8	13.4	4	14	5,505	5,481	95.4
Knox, TX	48275	9	3,719	17.9	35.0	21.1	3	6	713	611	99.5
Lamar, TX	48277	4	49,793	17.9	25.6	15.1	5	23	8,866	9,165	96.1
Lamb, TX	48279	6	13,977	21.1	29.8	19.6	5	15	3,179	2,999	95.1
Lampasas, TX	48281	2	19,677	18.5	24.9	19.1	2	6	3,724	3,828	96.2
La Salle, TX	48283	6	6,886	15.7	43.0	14.1	1	5	1,192	1,252	97.2
Lavaca, TX	48285	6	19,263	16.7	20.1	16.1	6	13	2,098	3,290	87.0

[1]County type codes are from the Economic Research Service of the United States Department of Agriculture. See notes and definitions for more information.

Table C-1. Population, School, and Student Characteristics by County, Selected Years—*Continued*

County	State/ County Code	Characteristics of students, 2010–2011				Number of graduates, 2008–2009	Staff and students, 2010–2011			
		Percent with IEP[2]	Percent eligible for free or reduced lunch	Percent minority	Percent English-language learners		Total staff	Number of teachers	Student/ teacher ratio	Central admin. staff
		10	11	12	13	14	15	16	17	18
TEXAS—*(Continued)*										
Galveston, TX	48167	8.8	44.0	49.8	6.5	4,710	10,080	5,122	15.0	478
Garza, TX	48169	10.3	66.5	64.5	6.6	46	207	113	8.3	8
Gillespie, TX	48171	9.5	49.5	42.2	8.6	265	551	268	13.4	19
Glasscock, TX	48173	9.2	33.9	46.3	9.2	17	47	23	12.3	3
Goliad, TX	48175	10.5	52.3	56.0	3.0	100	239	119	11.7	20
Gonzales, TX	48177	8.8	74.5	74.6	12.2	253	621	299	13.2	20
Gray, TX	48179	9.5	60.0	43.1	10.5	225	610	315	12.4	27
Grayson, TX	48181	12.3	51.8	30.8	4.3	1,390	2,962	1,631	12.9	115
Gregg, TX	48183	9.1	56.9	54.2	9.7	1,431	3,410	1,671	14.4	148
Grimes, TX	48185	7.4	68.2	56.1	11.2	241	654	345	12.5	35
Guadalupe, TX	48187	9.5	43.1	59.3	4.7	1,474	3,063	1,515	15.1	134
Hale, TX	48189	12.0	71.0	78.4	6.6	410	1,045	577	13.4	34
Hall, TX	48191	13.4	69.4	65.6	12.1	34	116	51	10.8	6
Hamilton, TX	48193	11.0	43.9	21.3	5.2	136	267	154	10.8	12
Hansford, TX	48195	7.4	59.0	59.0	20.3	91	244	138	10.0	10
Hardeman, TX	48197	12.8	72.8	40.8	2.9	47	157	75	9.8	11
Hardin, TX	48199	10.1	40.5	16.0	1.4	697	1,700	782	13.9	49
Harris, TX	48201	7.8	53.5	80.1	21.0	36,340	97,213	47,911	15.9	4,813
Harrison, TX	48203	10.0	56.9	43.7	5.9	829	2,047	1,019	12.7	70
Hartley, TX	48205	8.0	55.5	49.2	19.5	19	61	37	9.1	4
Haskell, TX	48207	11.5	61.6	42.8	2.2	67	182	97	9.9	6
Hays, TX	48209	9.3	47.0	59.8	10.1	1,555	4,277	2,045	14.4	174
Hemphill, TX	48211	6.0	35.4	42.0	14.4	51	152	82	10.4	7
Henderson, TX	48213	10.8	63.3	32.2	7.4	719	1,793	881	13.6	79
Hidalgo, TX	48215	6.8	11.4	98.3	34.1	9,997	29,269	13,756	15.6	1,059
Hill, TX	48217	11.5	66.1	41.4	7.5	400	1,088	527	12.3	53
Hockley, TX	48219	11.6	59.8	64.7	3.9	302	769	419	11.3	33
Hood, TX	48221	11.0	45.3	21.7	4.8	497	1,127	578	13.0	39
Hopkins, TX	48223	9.3	60.9	35.5	7.6	411	1,024	528	12.4	40
Houston, TX	48225	10.4	65.9	48.4	5.1	194	589	298	11.4	29
Howard, TX	48227	10.1	55.9	59.9	1.4	319	828	382	14.1	27
Hudspeth, TX	48229	6.2	84.1	88.8	35.5	40	146	74	10.6	10
Hunt, TX	48231	10.5	58.6	36.3	8.1	824	2,167	1,119	13.0	87
Hutchinson, TX	48233	11.1	48.3	38.0	6.2	263	620	351	12.0	21
Irion, TX	48235	6.4	37.7	32.5	...	32	61	32	10.3	3
Jack, TX	48237	11.0	51.2	24.6	7.4	111	273	154	9.9	13
Jackson, TX	48239	10.3	52.4	47.0	5.9	217	490	254	12.5	14
Jasper, TX	48241	10.9	58.4	33.5	3.0	385	1,044	497	12.6	34
Jeff Davis, TX	48243	13.9	48.7	51.3	13.4	64	87	53	6.8	10
Jefferson, TX	48245	8.4	62.3	70.2	6.4	2,300	5,813	2,953	14.2	215
Jim Hogg, TX	48247	7.3	41.8	96.4	16.4	70	162	81	14.2	8
Jim Wells, TX	48249	9.7	71.9	86.3	3.7	438	1,236	599	14.2	41
Johnson, TX	48251	9.3	51.1	33.5	7.6	1,734	4,373	2,201	14.3	156
Jones, TX	48253	10.9	63.9	43.0	3.3	189	506	256	10.6	16
Karnes, TX	48255	8.8	65.5	70.1	0.9	137	397	195	11.8	30
Kaufman, TX	48257	8.4	49.0	39.2	7.4	1,178	3,060	1,583	14.6	129
Kendall, TX	48259	8.3	29.1	35.3	4.7	569	1,071	558	14.1	35
Kenedy, TX	48261	7.5	51.1	70.0	3.8	...	21	10	8.1	3
Kent, TX	48263	11.8	45.1	27.5	...	10	43	21	7.5	4
Kerr, TX	48265	9.1	24.7	49.1	6.8	453	1,037	486	13.9	42
Kimble, TX	48267	10.4	56.1	40.3	2.3	45	99	56	12.4	6
King, TX	48269	12.1	29.3	19.0	6.0	7	38	20	5.8	2
Kinney, TX	48271	11.7	68.7	71.7	5.2	47	109	55	11.2	4
Kleberg, TX	48273	7.6	70.7	85.9	3.3	314	831	392	14.0	44
Knox, TX	48275	12.5	66.7	55.2	7.6	53	154	87	8.2	7
Lamar, TX	48277	11.9	57.4	32.8	3.3	589	1,435	753	11.8	50
Lamb, TX	48279	11.6	64.9	71.9	7.6	177	510	257	12.4	18
Lampasas, TX	48281	10.5	54.6	35.0	3.9	273	561	251	14.8	17
La Salle, TX	48283	8.1	82.4	94.1	8.8	66	213	96	12.4	15
Lavaca, TX	48285	11.6	39.2	29.3	2.1	144	340	180	11.7	15

[2]IEP=Individual Education Program. See notes and definitions for more information.
. . . = Not available.

Table C-1. Population, School, and Student Characteristics by County, Selected Years—*Continued*

County	State/ County Code	Revenues, 2008–2009				Current expenditures, 2008–2009			Resident population 16 to 19 years, 2006–2010			
		Total revenue ($1,000's)	Percentage of revenue from: Federal government	State government	Local government	Amount ($1,000's)	Amount per student	Percent for instruction	Total population 16 to 19 years	Percent enrolled in school	Percent high school graduates, not enrolled in school	Percent not enrolled, not grads, not employed, or not in labor force
		19	20	21	22	23	24	25	26	27	28	29
TEXAS—*(Continued)*												
Galveston, TX	48167	797,031	8.1	33.3	58.6	637,262	8,577	60.3	16,853	83.8	8.8	4.8
Garza, TX	48169	14,973	12.2	23.4	64.4	12,080	12,068	64.1	397	77.8	16.9	5.3
Gillespie, TX	48171	45,068	5.9	26.1	68.0	32,122	9,319	61.2	1,024	82.2	9.4	2.2
Glasscock, TX	48173	13,038	1.5	4.8	93.7	4,647	17,737	62.0	88	78.4	6.8	14.8
Goliad, TX	48175	21,461	5.0	28.0	67.0	13,482	10,253	59.9	370	91.1	5.4	2.7
Gonzales, TX	48177	38,708	11.9	61.6	26.6	33,040	8,677	60.8	1,260	70.5	15.6	8.1
Gray, TX	48179	41,824	7.1	36.2	56.7	30,848	8,078	62.4	942	75.9	15.2	6.5
Grayson, TX	48181	210,326	8.1	47.6	44.3	182,057	8,665	62.1	6,991	81.9	10.4	7.0
Gregg, TX	48183	249,692	14.6	34.6	50.9	206,193	8,756	57.0	6,965	80.6	8.7	4.7
Grimes, TX	48185	44,170	10.0	34.0	56.0	38,242	9,045	57.5	1,211	77.6	15.3	4.1
Guadalupe, TX	48187	194,278	7.0	43.9	49.1	163,250	7,572	62.3	7,725	83.5	11.1	4.4
Hale, TX	48189	71,247	13.8	57.9	28.3	61,597	8,185	62.5	2,308	77.0	11.6	6.7
Hall, TX	48191	7,098	10.6	68.4	21.1	5,791	10,323	61.7	254	85.4	14.6	0.0
Hamilton, TX	48193	18,848	6.2	61.8	32.0	16,266	8,992	64.0	411	89.1	8.8	2.2
Hansford, TX	48195	21,491	3.6	32.2	64.2	15,268	11,411	63.7	434	82.3	1.6	9.9
Hardeman, TX	48197	9,827	15.4	43.4	41.2	9,586	12,954	61.6	205	79.5	19.5	0.0
Hardin, TX	48199	110,419	7.4	45.4	47.2	95,670	8,804	56.6	2,919	78.0	15.5	5.7
Harris, TX	48201	7,258,004	10.3	38.4	51.2	6,219,664	8,507	59.1	233,618	80.8	10.8	4.8
Harrison, TX	48203	128,866	9.4	26.0	64.7	110,882	8,765	59.4	3,688	81.5	15.2	1.7
Hartley, TX	48205	4,744	5.3	34.6	60.1	3,752	10,659	57.2	251	86.9	11.6	1.6
Haskell, TX	48207	11,660	9.8	65.2	25.0	10,610	11,881	58.0	297	56.9	28.6	14.5
Hays, TX	48209	292,442	6.3	39.1	54.6	226,066	8,178	59.1	11,570	86.2	6.6	5.6
Hemphill, TX	48211	24,209	2.0	13.1	84.8	9,106	11,256	62.8	216	89.8	6.5	0.0
Henderson, TX	48213	121,263	10.3	44.4	45.3	101,754	8,552	60.7	4,071	78.7	12.5	4.0
Hidalgo, TX	48215	2,054,387	16.7	63.7	19.7	1,826,414	9,082	59.4	52,370	82.0	8.8	6.0
Hill, TX	48217	68,782	9.5	54.8	35.6	59,969	9,302	58.9	1,897	93.3	5.2	0.3
Hockley, TX	48219	67,624	8.8	28.9	62.3	49,599	10,250	63.9	2,105	85.9	12.4	1.8
Hood, TX	48221	86,152	7.4	24.6	68.0	72,019	9,213	59.9	2,731	69.8	16.3	11.8
Hopkins, TX	48223	64,504	13.3	56.1	30.6	56,256	8,548	61.5	2,008	78.0	15.9	3.0
Houston, TX	48225	37,008	11.2	47.5	41.3	32,292	9,529	58.4	1,509	66.7	20.1	11.8
Howard, TX	48227	54,645	9.5	41.3	49.2	43,816	8,150	58.5	1,573	74.3	10.2	5.2
Hudspeth, TX	48229	11,442	12.0	62.6	25.4	9,307	12,376	58.9	385	78.2	20.3	1.6
Hunt, TX	48231	139,070	10.8	53.7	35.5	123,795	8,572	58.6	4,938	78.9	11.6	5.3
Hutchinson, TX	48233	53,039	8.6	41.4	50.0	37,546	8,797	63.3	1,386	84.3	10.4	4.6
Irion, TX	48235	10,114	1.9	10.7	87.4	4,102	12,208	59.5	48	100.0	0.0	0.0
Jack, TX	48237	21,407	4.1	24.3	71.6	16,713	10,433	63.8	660	79.6	16.8	1.7
Jackson, TX	48239	36,301	10.0	41.6	48.3	28,181	8,671	59.7	826	69.9	21.6	8.6
Jasper, TX	48241	61,429	11.2	54.3	34.5	54,609	8,818	59.2	1,905	76.1	17.0	4.4
Jeff Davis, TX	48243	5,543	5.9	54.7	39.5	6,252	15,788	64.3	241	85.9	2.9	1.7
Jefferson, TX	48245	516,728	11.6	30.1	58.4	410,220	9,842	53.7	14,857	80.8	10.7	6.1
Jim Hogg, TX	48247	12,290	13.5	43.3	43.2	11,955	10,589	62.8	231	92.6	3.5	0.0
Jim Wells, TX	48249	81,975	12.1	62.3	25.6	70,531	8,380	60.0	2,707	74.8	9.8	8.9
Johnson, TX	48251	311,602	6.8	36.5	56.8	251,469	8,218	61.4	8,538	79.7	14.0	3.8
Jones, TX	48253	31,042	12.3	64.4	23.3	27,945	10,096	60.2	913	88.4	3.2	7.3
Karnes, TX	48255	25,540	17.2	58.1	24.6	22,587	9,955	60.4	329	76.3	5.5	18.2
Kaufman, TX	48257	209,867	7.3	47.0	45.7	175,373	7,893	58.7	6,019	83.3	10.0	4.6
Kendall, TX	48259	94,445	3.7	26.1	70.2	69,130	9,193	61.8	1,684	87.9	6.6	0.5
Kenedy, TX	48261	7,419	0.0	5.3	94.7	1,369	15,557	48.4	11	54.6	45.5	0.0
Kent, TX	48263	8,898	1.0	9.2	89.8	2,821	19,727	49.2	41	100.0	0.0	0.0
Kerr, TX	48265	68,993	9.9	35.1	55.0	60,206	8,718	61.2	2,488	79.6	13.9	6.5
Kimble, TX	48267	6,515	9.0	50.0	41.1	6,185	9,231	65.0	175	72.6	25.1	2.3
King, TX	48269	5,117	0.7	23.2	76.1	3,000	31,579	51.2	3	100.0	0.0	0.0
Kinney, TX	48271	6,832	9.1	65.8	25.1	5,846	9,842	63.1	224	61.6	30.4	6.3
Kleberg, TX	48273	58,977	12.2	53.2	34.6	51,756	9,421	58.2	2,793	88.7	4.8	4.8
Knox, TX	48275	9,301	13.4	64.5	22.1	8,668	11,360	62.0	98	95.9	2.0	2.0
Lamar, TX	48277	87,011	11.6	51.3	37.1	74,892	8,290	62.6	3,071	78.0	14.6	6.5
Lamb, TX	48279	34,490	13.7	59.4	26.9	29,833	9,480	62.9	871	73.1	18.4	2.8
Lampasas, TX	48281	38,546	9.5	47.2	43.2	30,008	8,190	59.4	1,180	82.6	12.8	2.8
La Salle, TX	48283	15,694	9.6	48.4	42.0	13,289	11,102	51.4	212	76.9	23.1	0.0
Lavaca, TX	48285	25,166	3.9	35.7	60.3	18,385	9,003	63.2	864	86.8	7.2	2.3

Note. Data in columns 26 through 41 from the American Community Survey are subject to sampling error, which can be especially large in small counties and small population groups. See notes and definitions for more information.

Table C-1. Population, School, and Student Characteristics by County, Selected Years—*Continued*

County	State/ County Code	High school graduates, 2006–2010			College enrollment, 2006–2010		College graduates, 2006–2010 (percent)						
		Population 25 years and over	High school diploma or less (percent)	High school diploma or more (percent)	Number	Percent public	Bachelor's degree or more	+/- U.S. percent with Bachelor's degree or more	Non-Hispanic White	Black or African American	American Indian and Alaska Native	Asian, Hawaiian, and Pacific Islander	Hispanic or Latino[3]
		30	31	32	33	34	35	36	37	38	39	40	41
TEXAS—*(Continued)*													
Galveston, TX	48167	187,867	41.2	85.9	18,804	89.7	26.4	-1.5	30.5	14.7	26.7	56.6	14.1
Garza, TX	48169	4,412	68.0	62.9	230	83.9	8.6	-19.3	16.0	5.1	0.0	100.0	2.2
Gillespie, TX	48171	17,820	43.0	86.4	359	72.4	26.8	-1.1	29.4	0.0	0.0	100.0	9.1
Glasscock, TX	48173	769	48.4	78.0	42	100.0	16.4	-11.5	19.7	0.0	0.0	0.0	5.8
Goliad, TX	48175	5,203	52.3	83.8	107	95.3	18.0	-9.9	23.7	9.8	0.0	0.0	4.9
Gonzales, TX	48177	12,625	65.5	67.6	315	89.5	13.9	-14.0	21.2	5.6	0.0	62.5	4.4
Gray, TX	48179	15,202	55.6	79.3	707	84.3	12.2	-15.7	13.8	1.7	6.8	14.0	8.1
Grayson, TX	48181	79,204	47.7	85.2	6,690	73.2	19.2	-8.7	20.5	14.6	19.5	27.7	7.0
Gregg, TX	48183	76,167	46.9	82.4	6,616	72.2	20.3	-7.6	25.1	10.1	17.8	29.3	6.4
Grimes, TX	48185	18,050	63.7	77.2	661	86.2	11.3	-16.6	15.1	3.0	0.0	11.1	3.2
Guadalupe, TX	48187	78,269	44.2	85.1	7,438	70.6	24.0	-3.9	30.0	27.0	47.5	34.9	10.3
Hale, TX	48189	21,616	62.0	70.0	1,982	47.4	14.1	-13.8	26.1	7.0	20.0	41.8	2.9
Hall, TX	48191	2,309	60.6	72.2	68	85.3	15.2	-12.7	20.7	2.0	0.0	23.8	2.0
Hamilton, TX	48193	6,018	49.1	82.6	243	93.0	23.4	-4.5	24.9	0.0	0.0	50.0	0.8
Hansford, TX	48195	3,373	56.5	76.1	139	86.3	20.3	-7.6	29.6	0.0	0.0	9.1	1.7
Hardeman, TX	48197	2,949	59.6	79.4	124	65.3	14.7	-13.2	17.0	0.0	100.0	0.0	4.9
Hardin, TX	48199	34,787	54.6	85.1	1,964	90.6	15.4	-12.5	16.0	3.9	0.0	29.1	13.2
Harris, TX	48201	2,434,606	46.5	77.6	239,619	81.1	27.7	-0.2	42.6	19.3	17.5	50.1	9.8
Harrison, TX	48203	41,785	52.6	83.7	4,348	53.0	16.2	-11.7	17.9	12.4	0.0	24.1	9.2
Hartley, TX	48205	4,465	57.8	78.4	175	73.7	19.8	-8.1	27.7	3.1	31.0	0.0	2.0
Haskell, TX	48207	4,205	65.9	77.9	118	94.1	11.7	-16.2	15.3	0.0	0.0	0.0	1.1
Hays, TX	48209	83,247	35.0	88.1	22,496	95.8	35.0	7.1	44.7	24.1	16.2	69.1	13.3
Hemphill, TX	48211	2,484	48.4	80.7	119	70.6	16.3	-11.6	19.0	0.0	0.0	0.0	5.1
Henderson, TX	48213	53,980	55.6	79.0	3,827	88.7	14.2	-13.7	15.4	10.1	7.7	6.5	2.8
Hidalgo, TX	48215	400,905	64.3	60.2	41,944	91.1	15.1	-12.8	30.5	25.6	14.2	64.4	12.3
Hill, TX	48217	23,309	51.8	78.2	1,770	82.6	15.3	-12.6	16.4	19.3	1.0	35.9	7.4
Hockley, TX	48219	13,809	52.8	74.1	2,102	91.0	18.0	-9.9	25.7	3.5	0.0	47.5	5.5
Hood, TX	48221	35,619	42.4	86.2	1,549	84.7	23.9	-4.0	25.2	21.6	25.3	55.4	8.0
Hopkins, TX	48223	22,737	54.4	78.7	1,348	89.5	16.7	-11.2	19.0	7.4	0.0	47.2	4.9
Houston, TX	48225	16,066	62.7	78.5	708	73.3	13.4	-14.5	17.6	3.3	9.1	0.0	5.7
Howard, TX	48227	23,701	57.1	70.8	1,110	90.5	10.1	-17.8	15.3	2.5	6.6	18.2	2.5
Hudspeth, TX	48229	2,006	72.6	50.5	160	91.3	10.5	-17.4	29.2	0.0	0.0	17.7	4.5
Hunt, TX	48231	54,979	54.6	80.0	5,325	90.5	17.0	-10.9	18.8	8.6	15.5	37.8	6.7
Hutchinson, TX	48233	14,312	52.6	83.5	1,091	85.7	13.0	-14.9	14.4	9.6	3.8	33.3	5.3
Irion, TX	48235	1,250	57.7	81.6	29	100.0	12.3	-15.6	15.0	0.0	0.0	100.0	2.7
Jack, TX	48237	6,112	61.8	78.9	184	93.5	10.5	-17.4	11.2	0.0	0.0	13.0	11.4
Jackson, TX	48239	9,217	55.5	77.2	339	86.1	16.9	-11.0	21.7	9.1	0.0	0.0	4.5
Jasper, TX	48241	23,809	59.6	81.6	1,016	79.5	14.0	-13.9	15.5	5.4	10.5	67.6	9.6
Jeff Davis, TX	48243	1,598	38.3	83.9	35	68.6	34.3	6.4	43.4	0.0	0.0	0.0	14.3
Jefferson, TX	48245	162,605	51.3	81.4	15,811	91.0	17.8	-10.1	24.5	9.2	10.3	34.9	7.8
Jim Hogg, TX	48247	3,051	73.4	68.9	221	97.3	12.4	-15.5	10.1	0.0	0.0	0.0	12.7
Jim Wells, TX	48249	24,689	63.2	70.6	1,294	86.6	10.6	-17.3	21.3	0.0	0.0	24.6	7.4
Johnson, TX	48251	94,257	53.3	81.7	5,781	77.5	16.1	-11.8	17.2	13.6	29.1	41.4	7.8
Jones, TX	48253	14,661	65.4	69.6	565	52.9	9.3	-18.6	13.5	2.5	26.1	21.1	0.8
Karnes, TX	48255	11,819	68.0	65.6	398	78.6	8.4	-19.5	15.3	3.1	0.0	49.2	3.5
Kaufman, TX	48257	62,284	51.0	82.7	4,879	74.0	17.2	-10.7	18.3	15.3	28.8	47.7	9.0
Kendall, TX	48259	21,718	31.5	91.1	1,271	79.9	35.5	7.6	39.7	14.4	0.0	60.1	12.8
Kenedy, TX	48261	184	48.4	59.8	5	100.0	17.9	-10.0	61.5	0.0	0.0	0.0	0.8
Kent, TX	48263	563	48.0	90.6	26	92.3	19.4	-8.5	19.6	100.0	0.0	0.0	13.7
Kerr, TX	48265	34,796	42.6	86.2	1,920	46.1	27.0	-0.9	31.8	0.0	0.0	44.3	5.9
Kimble, TX	48267	3,444	51.2	76.5	86	46.5	20.3	-7.6	23.8	0.0	0.0	44.3	3.8
King, TX	48269	174	29.3	90.8	4	100.0	36.8	8.9	38.9	0.0	0.0	100.0	0.0
Kinney, TX	48271	2,491	58.0	75.4	62	91.9	14.5	-13.4	25.7	0.0	0.0	100.0	0.9
Kleberg, TX	48273	17,807	50.5	76.1	5,399	96.9	20.4	-7.5	30.2	10.0	0.0	70.9	15.3
Knox, TX	48275	2,724	62.7	75.5	107	80.4	12.9	-15.0	18.1	0.0	0.0	0.0	2.7
Lamar, TX	48277	32,752	52.2	82.4	2,363	90.2	17.4	-10.5	18.5	10.4	15.1	36.5	13.5
Lamb, TX	48279	8,709	61.2	71.9	450	85.8	13.8	-14.1	20.3	7.0	0.0	0.0	5.9
Lampasas, TX	48281	13,165	49.3	82.6	802	87.8	17.3	-10.6	18.2	36.7	7.0	0.0	7.2
La Salle, TX	48283	4,314	69.1	59.9	223	77.1	8.1	-19.8	19.3	0.0	0.0	100.0	3.1
Lavaca, TX	48285	13,511	62.0	76.3	445	82.2	14.0	-13.9	16.8	0.0	0.0	68.4	0.0

Note. Data in columns 26 through 41 from the American Community Survey are subject to sampling error, which can be especially large in small counties and small population groups. See notes and definitions for more information.
[3]May be of any race.

Table C-1. Population, School, and Student Characteristics by County, Selected Years—*Continued*

County	State/ County Code	County Type[1]	Population, 2010		Percent of related children 5–17 years in poverty, 2010	Percent of children under 19 years with no health insurance, 2010	Number of schools and students, 2010–2011			Resident enrollment, 2006–2010 K–12 enrollment	
			Total	Percent 5–17 years			School districts	Schools	Students	Number	Percent public
			1	2	3	4	5	6	7	8	9
TEXAS—*(Continued)*											
Lee, TX	48287	6	16,612	19.7	16.7	21.0	4	9	3,274	3,448	90.0
Leon, TX	48289	8	16,801	16.2	24.3	19.4	5	13	3,155	2,704	96.0
Liberty, TX	48291	1	75,643	18.7	23.9	15.9	7	37	14,782	14,926	96.1
Limestone, TX	48293	6	23,384	17.1	27.3	15.8	3	13	4,018	3,621	97.5
Lipscomb, TX	48295	9	3,302	19.9	19.7	24.9	4	5	829	632	100.0
Live Oak, TX	48297	6	11,531	15.4	25.5	16.6	2	7	1,704	2,074	96.4
Llano, TX	48299	7	19,301	11.7	27.6	16.4	1	4	1,910	2,343	92.2
Loving, TX	48301	9	82	7.3	75.0	22.3	...	...	...	2	100.0
Lubbock, TX	48303	3	278,831	17.1	24.5	12.6	12	100	47,153	45,936	94.2
Lynn, TX	48305	6	5,915	20.4	28.7	18.3	4	7	1,244	1,285	94.9
McCulloch, TX	48307	7	8,283	18.1	34.4	17.7	3	7	1,574	1,601	93.1
McLennan, TX	48309	3	234,906	18.3	26.9	12.4	24	129	45,117	42,028	93.5
McMullen, TX	48311	8	707	12.9	17.4	17.4	1	2	178	97	100.0
Madison, TX	48313	6	13,664	16.0	29.0	19.6	2	6	2,605	2,667	92.3
Marion, TX	48315	8	10,546	13.9	33.2	17.2	1	4	1,225	1,448	88.4
Martin, TX	48317	6	4,799	22.2	22.3	17.4	2	4	999	895	95.5
Mason, TX	48319	9	4,012	16.2	28.0	25.3	1	3	677	800	88.4
Matagorda, TX	48321	4	36,702	19.3	25.8	17.1	5	24	7,159	7,319	98.0
Maverick, TX	48323	5	54,258	25.0	48.9	15.3	1	24	14,850	13,892	98.9
Medina, TX	48325	1	46,006	19.3	24.6	15.7	5	21	9,111	9,251	93.2
Menard, TX	48327	8	2,242	13.9	40.9	28.2	1	4	330	312	100.0
Midland, TX	48329	3	136,872	19.4	21.6	15.0	4	42	23,954	26,265	88.6
Milam, TX	48331	6	24,757	19.6	27.7	15.9	6	16	4,587	4,987	95.2
Mills, TX	48333	9	4,936	18.2	26.8	25.6	4	7	885	767	97.7
Mitchell, TX	48335	7	9,403	14.1	26.6	13.6	3	7	1,456	1,569	100.0
Montague, TX	48337	6	19,719	16.7	22.9	17.3	7	15	3,379	3,390	90.9
Montgomery, TX	48339	1	455,746	20.4	14.0	14.2	6	114	90,000	87,394	91.6
Moore, TX	48341	6	21,904	22.7	21.5	16.7	2	12	5,113	4,919	99.2
Morris, TX	48343	6	12,934	16.8	29.4	13.9	2	7	2,284	2,274	94.6
Motley, TX	48345	8	1,210	16.6	23.4	21.3	1	1	183	185	81.1
Nacogdoches, TX	48347	5	64,524	16.5	30.2	14.1	10	27	10,931	10,111	95.8
Navarro, TX	48349	4	47,735	19.8	29.9	17.2	8	23	9,666	9,328	95.9
Newton, TX	48351	8	14,445	17.4	28.7	14.6	3	9	2,124	2,785	96.7
Nolan, TX	48353	6	15,216	18.4	29.7	14.2	4	12	3,076	2,771	98.8
Nueces, TX	48355	2	340,223	18.9	28.2	11.3	19	114	61,794	63,768	94.0
Ochiltree, TX	48357	7	10,223	22.3	18.4	20.8	1	6	2,289	2,339	96.9
Oldham, TX	48359	8	2,052	29.1	19.0	17.9	4	8	909	533	95.3
Orange, TX	48361	2	81,837	18.5	21.3	11.7	5	26	15,392	15,472	94.3
Palo Pinto, TX	48363	6	28,111	18.2	25.9	17.1	6	13	4,900	5,198	97.6
Panola, TX	48365	6	23,796	18.2	19.4	14.5	4	11	4,111	4,475	95.0
Parker, TX	48367	1	116,927	19.3	15.9	14.1	9	39	19,388	22,209	91.6
Parmer, TX	48369	7	10,269	22.4	20.8	20.4	4	11	2,465	2,254	95.4
Pecos, TX	48371	7	15,507	17.1	27.9	17.8	3	10	2,962	2,766	99.1
Polk, TX	48373	6	45,413	15.3	29.8	17.5	6	17	6,944	6,878	95.3
Potter, TX	48375	3	121,073	19.3	34.8	15.5	4	64	36,473	23,483	94.9
Presidio, TX	48377	7	7,818	21.7	34.5	21.4	2	5	1,837	1,769	100.0
Rains, TX	48379	8	10,914	16.4	25.7	18.3	1	4	1,623	1,763	96.4
Randall, TX	48381	3	120,725	18.1	10.4	14.2	3	17	9,064	21,028	92.2
Reagan, TX	48383	6	3,367	21.8	15.0	22.6	1	3	794	775	99.5
Real, TX	48385	9	3,309	15.0	43.6	22.3	2	3	398	596	91.8
Red River, TX	48387	6	12,860	15.7	30.1	13.5	4	12	2,335	2,233	94.7
Reeves, TX	48389	7	13,783	16.2	34.7	15.3	2	6	2,324	2,591	99.6
Refugio, TX	48391	6	7,383	18.1	23.9	14.8	3	6	1,388	1,407	100.0
Roberts, TX	48393	9	929	17.5	9.2	17.3	1	1	193	152	97.4
Robertson, TX	48395	3	16,622	18.4	31.7	17.1	5	12	3,303	3,316	88.5
Rockwall, TX	48397	1	78,337	22.7	8.2	12.5	2	27	18,628	16,480	92.7
Runnels, TX	48399	6	10,501	18.4	32.8	16.5	3	11	2,008	1,857	97.9
Rusk, TX	48401	3	53,330	16.8	22.4	16.3	8	21	7,890	9,246	93.5
Sabine, TX	48403	9	10,834	14.6	28.5	16.6	3	7	2,012	1,613	99.6
San Augustine, TX	48405	9	8,865	15.7	32.2	17.1	2	5	1,311	1,539	97.4

[1]County type codes are from the Economic Research Service of the United States Department of Agriculture. See notes and definitions for more information.
. . . = Not available.

Table C-1. Population, School, and Student Characteristics by County, Selected Years—*Continued*

County	State/ County Code	Characteristics of students, 2010–2011: Percent with IEP[2]	Percent eligible for free or reduced lunch	Percent minority	Percent English-language learners	Number of graduates, 2008–2009	Staff and students, 2010–2011: Total staff	Number of teachers	Student/ teacher ratio	Central admin. staff
		10	11	12	13	14	15	16	17	18
TEXAS—*(Continued)*										
Lee, TX	48287	9.8	62.7	54.2	7.9	195	456	251	13.0	19
Leon, TX	48289	9.3	55.3	33.6	9.5	186	558	284	11.1	31
Liberty, TX	48291	7.7	62.4	37.9	10.5	830	2,181	1,054	14.0	88
Limestone, TX	48293	12.9	68.6	58.0	7.9	244	632	285	14.1	24
Lipscomb, TX	48295	8.7	65.0	47.4	11.0	31	172	97	8.6	9
Live Oak, TX	48297	9.7	53.5	57.1	2.9	123	309	151	11.3	24
Llano, TX	48299	10.3	58.7	22.7	3.4	111	304	147	13.0	15
Loving, TX	48301	0.0	0.0	0.0	. . .	. . .	. . .	. . .	. . .	. . .
Lubbock, TX	48303	10.8	55.7	62.2	2.4	2,474	5,966	3,347	14.1	267
Lynn, TX	48305	9.1	56.6	63.1	5.4	86	252	135	9.2	10
McCulloch, TX	48307	12.3	64.0	45.6	2.5	109	298	149	10.6	14
McLennan, TX	48309	9.7	61.2	57.1	7.1	2,347	6,386	3,257	13.9	233
McMullen, TX	48311	6.7	41.0	50.6	0.6	10	42	19	9.4	4
Madison, TX	48313	7.8	68.9	47.7	9.9	131	357	191	13.7	18
Marion, TX	48315	12.0	38.6	46.5	1.6	83	233	106	11.5	8
Martin, TX	48317	7.5	36.3	59.2	5.5	65	180	94	10.7	8
Mason, TX	48319	9.7	59.5	36.3	5.5	44	133	61	11.1	7
Matagorda, TX	48321	8.9	64.0	68.7	7.2	472	1,206	580	12.3	44
Maverick, TX	48323	7.5	1.0	98.8	32.7	797	2,058	897	16.6	71
Medina, TX	48325	9.2	50.1	65.6	3.5	572	1,337	631	14.4	47
Menard, TX	48327	9.7	73.3	57.3	3.3	30	74	34	9.7	3
Midland, TX	48329	6.7	50.7	65.6	7.4	1,315	3,004	1,585	15.1	137
Milam, TX	48331	10.4	65.5	51.0	5.8	295	706	370	12.4	33
Mills, TX	48333	11.2	61.9	30.8	4.2	67	197	96	9.2	11
Mitchell, TX	48335	9.5	59.5	55.6	1.9	89	286	141	10.3	7
Montague, TX	48337	11.5	50.8	21.0	5.2	174	589	284	11.9	23
Montgomery, TX	48339	8.4	41.8	40.4	9.9	4,795	11,385	5,790	15.5	359
Moore, TX	48341	8.7	66.5	77.1	27.8	274	758	400	12.8	25
Morris, TX	48343	12.0	68.1	45.8	4.0	131	414	200	11.4	17
Motley, TX	48345	5.5	78.1	27.3	1.1	8	42	19	9.6	4
Nacogdoches, TX	48347	7.9	64.1	53.4	13.7	584	1,609	821	13.3	57
Navarro, TX	48349	9.2	67.8	56.2	12.9	529	1,405	730	13.2	53
Newton, TX	48351	11.0	67.6	30.5	0.1	144	394	187	11.4	18
Nolan, TX	48353	13.4	63.6	52.7	3.2	206	542	252	12.2	24
Nueces, TX	48355	10.3	59.6	79.9	4.0	3,592	8,396	4,024	15.4	381
Ochiltree, TX	48357	6.3	62.6	66.7	25.3	156	329	174	13.1	12
Oldham, TX	48359	10.7	26.6	25.2	0.3	73	202	129	7.0	10
Orange, TX	48361	12.9	51.6	24.1	2.0	948	2,317	1,084	14.2	73
Palo Pinto, TX	48363	10.2	56.8	34.2	6.8	319	736	385	12.7	31
Panola, TX	48365	9.6	44.8	34.4	5.7	262	653	323	12.7	28
Parker, TX	48367	8.6	36.7	20.2	3.7	1,271	2,481	1,320	14.7	100
Parmer, TX	48369	6.7	36.6	74.8	18.4	142	479	232	10.6	18
Pecos, TX	48371	6.6	63.8	83.0	11.6	194	509	255	11.6	21
Polk, TX	48373	12.1	65.6	36.6	5.3	427	1,138	536	13.0	40
Potter, TX	48375	9.1	71.6	64.7	10.7	1,918	4,596	2,510	14.5	147
Presidio, TX	48377	6.2	54.5	96.0	40.2	106	363	170	10.8	18
Rains, TX	48379	11.0	55.1	20.3	4.4	160	271	128	12.7	7
Randall, TX	48381	9.5	38.9	35.0	0.8	606	1,150	585	15.5	65
Reagan, TX	48383	5.9	55.2	79.2	9.7	53	143	73	10.9	9
Real, TX	48385	27.6	65.5	39.8	4.5	26	117	57	6.9	20
Red River, TX	48387	12.3	63.5	36.4	3.4	171	462	217	10.8	23
Reeves, TX	48389	9.3	72.6	92.8	6.5	146	408	198	11.7	18
Refugio, TX	48391	12.2	57.6	68.5	1.9	107	292	142	9.8	13
Roberts, TX	48393	5.2	25.4	10.9	. . .	7	38	21	9.2	4
Robertson, TX	48395	11.3	66.2	55.6	5.5	211	600	283	11.7	27
Rockwall, TX	48397	8.3	27.8	34.1	6.2	1,095	2,481	1,245	15.0	89
Runnels, TX	48399	9.3	54.3	49.6	2.9	139	350	182	11.0	19
Rusk, TX	48401	8.9	61.4	45.6	7.4	493	1,258	627	12.6	41
Sabine, TX	48403	9.8	50.0	17.5	1.2	131	335	177	11.4	17
San Augustine, TX	48405	11.8	88.1	52.4	5.0	74	218	109	12.0	9

[2]IEP=Individual Education Program. See notes and definitions for more information.
. . . = Not available.

Table C-1. Population, School, and Student Characteristics by County, Selected Years—*Continued*

County	State/ County Code	Revenues, 2008–2009				Current expenditures, 2008–2009			Resident population 16 to 19 years, 2006–2010			
		Total revenue ($1,000's)	Percentage of revenue from			Amount ($1,000's)	Amount per student	Percent for instruction	Total population 16 to 19 years	Percent enrolled in school	Percent high school graduates, not enrolled in school	Percent not enrolled, not grads, not employed, or not in labor force
			Federal government	State government	Local government							
		19	20	21	22	23	24	25	26	27	28	29
TEXAS—*(Continued)*												
Lee, TX	48287	34,083	9.4	37.7	52.9	27,593	9,122	62.3	1,107	87.9	4.7	0.7
Leon, TX	48289	48,228	5.8	28.8	65.5	30,276	10,025	61.2	996	79.6	15.8	0.2
Liberty, TX	48291	145,361	9.5	49.4	41.1	124,076	8,554	57.0	4,404	75.5	15.6	6.8
Limestone, TX	48293	54,617	8.6	39.5	51.8	40,721	10,067	58.6	1,323	72.2	5.2	21.8
Lipscomb, TX	48295	16,568	3.5	22.8	73.7	10,739	13,340	61.5	173	87.3	6.9	2.9
Live Oak, TX	48297	20,661	5.5	34.4	60.1	17,044	9,886	61.6	442	77.8	14.0	3.2
Llano, TX	48299	39,192	4.5	11.9	83.6	18,057	9,208	59.0	855	75.6	3.4	20.1
Loving, TX	48301	...	...	...	...	...	...	...	...	...	...	...
Lubbock, TX	48303	435,609	13.3	43.5	43.2	378,174	8,278	59.6	19,850	85.1	9.3	3.7
Lynn, TX	48305	15,372	12.6	61.5	25.9	14,237	11,002	61.1	373	85.5	11.3	3.2
McCulloch, TX	48307	20,425	12.1	58.0	29.8	16,701	10,116	60.4	435	68.7	22.8	8.5
McLennan, TX	48309	426,436	11.5	49.7	38.8	362,758	8,702	57.1	16,943	87.2	6.8	4.1
McMullen, TX	48311	6,771	0.9	17.6	81.5	2,894	17,539	50.2	58	100.0	0.0	0.0
Madison, TX	48313	24,472	9.3	58.2	32.5	21,050	8,200	58.9	829	73.9	19.4	6.6
Marion, TX	48315	14,427	14.3	37.7	48.0	12,606	10,207	56.9	449	80.0	12.5	7.6
Martin, TX	48317	17,768	4.3	19.7	76.0	12,157	12,906	61.2	403	77.2	7.7	15.1
Mason, TX	48319	8,141	9.6	53.2	37.2	6,597	10,405	55.7	172	100.0	0.0	0.0
Matagorda, TX	48321	89,258	8.6	37.1	54.3	70,865	9,726	60.4	2,405	77.1	15.7	4.3
Maverick, TX	48323	135,400	16.2	67.8	16.0	123,996	8,776	60.1	3,865	84.5	8.1	5.4
Medina, TX	48325	86,560	10.7	57.0	32.3	74,967	8,400	60.2	2,868	86.3	5.7	5.5
Menard, TX	48327	4,952	25.9	45.9	28.2	4,970	14,364	49.6	151	88.1	6.6	5.3
Midland, TX	48329	217,877	12.0	29.6	58.4	191,188	8,099	58.2	8,050	78.8	11.2	6.2
Milam, TX	48331	47,982	7.6	48.9	43.5	38,560	8,262	64.5	1,380	87.3	9.6	1.5
Mills, TX	48333	11,367	17.2	56.6	26.2	11,112	13,213	61.2	172	91.3	8.7	0.0
Mitchell, TX	48335	19,909	7.9	43.1	49.0	14,826	10,361	61.6	276	62.0	16.3	21.7
Montague, TX	48337	34,809	9.2	46.2	44.5	31,175	9,467	62.8	1,065	83.4	10.8	3.5
Montgomery, TX	48339	776,887	6.4	40.4	53.2	634,554	7,508	61.1	24,593	81.7	11.4	3.4
Moore, TX	48341	50,782	8.5	31.6	59.9	39,381	8,118	63.8	1,318	84.5	5.8	4.0
Morris, TX	48343	24,191	10.3	42.5	47.2	22,492	9,835	59.7	708	77.5	18.6	3.0
Motley, TX	48345	2,805	20.7	45.3	34.0	2,531	14,299	64.6	78	42.3	26.9	0.0
Nacogdoches, TX	48347	104,311	10.3	49.7	40.0	85,282	8,260	60.2	5,820	84.1	8.4	4.4
Navarro, TX	48349	89,999	9.4	55.5	35.1	78,218	8,240	60.2	3,115	87.3	8.9	2.0
Newton, TX	48351	26,239	10.8	44.5	44.7	22,854	10,460	56.3	995	81.1	14.8	4.1
Nolan, TX	48353	47,423	9.7	33.2	57.0	31,060	10,137	58.3	926	93.4	6.6	0.0
Nueces, TX	48355	603,280	13.7	44.6	41.7	514,595	8,400	57.1	20,223	81.5	11.4	4.7
Ochiltree, TX	48357	20,023	13.7	36.2	50.1	18,109	8,088	64.1	632	85.4	11.9	2.7
Oldham, TX	48359	13,983	7.8	40.8	51.4	12,492	15,124	67.6	227	100.0	0.0	0.0
Orange, TX	48361	158,473	14.3	48.9	36.9	132,164	8,723	57.9	4,644	79.5	13.0	5.8
Palo Pinto, TX	48363	60,429	8.2	42.1	49.7	44,705	9,075	60.1	1,467	80.2	10.7	6.5
Panola, TX	48365	76,479	4.1	18.9	77.0	37,837	9,692	58.7	1,421	77.4	10.4	10.3
Parker, TX	48367	192,489	4.8	32.2	62.9	158,515	8,238	61.6	6,781	82.3	10.8	5.4
Parmer, TX	48369	26,379	11.7	64.4	23.9	22,614	9,490	66.6	670	79.3	16.1	3.6
Pecos, TX	48371	62,108	6.4	14.4	79.1	33,881	11,156	58.6	894	71.5	18.5	4.7
Polk, TX	48373	72,359	11.2	45.9	42.9	61,060	8,793	58.5	2,162	75.3	21.2	1.7
Potter, TX	48375	306,711	12.0	49.2	38.8	275,227	7,966	63.6	6,546	75.5	13.2	6.9
Presidio, TX	48377	24,198	12.2	70.1	17.6	18,411	10,710	61.5	609	68.6	3.8	12.2
Rains, TX	48379	23,139	7.2	53.2	39.6	21,974	8,904	62.4	637	71.3	27.5	0.5
Randall, TX	48381	102,494	25.3	31.0	43.7	78,383	8,887	50.9	7,329	84.9	12.8	1.7
Reagan, TX	48383	22,667	4.0	14.1	81.9	9,696	12,015	61.9	211	77.7	20.4	1.9
Real, TX	48385	7,172	5.7	62.0	32.3	6,588	18,000	60.6	135	68.2	16.3	15.6
Red River, TX	48387	29,227	12.7	65.1	22.1	26,182	10,566	60.7	569	86.6	5.8	5.6
Reeves, TX	48389	27,100	12.2	20.8	67.0	24,712	10,361	61.5	1,215	64.6	13.2	19.2
Refugio, TX	48391	23,315	11.9	31.6	56.5	18,598	12,558	57.4	386	82.1	14.5	0.0
Roberts, TX	48393	10,311	0.7	9.4	89.9	2,414	14,901	56.3	81	84.0	16.1	0.0
Robertson, TX	48395	75,473	5.7	20.7	73.6	36,784	11,198	58.7	800	82.0	8.3	7.5
Rockwall, TX	48397	180,619	3.8	36.6	59.7	145,958	8,191	60.7	4,035	87.0	7.5	3.7
Runnels, TX	48399	25,505	11.8	63.3	24.9	20,524	9,690	62.2	532	85.9	5.8	4.9
Rusk, TX	48401	92,750	7.3	30.2	62.5	68,980	8,963	61.3	3,019	74.1	17.9	4.5
Sabine, TX	48403	22,929	16.0	52.3	31.7	19,269	9,202	61.1	549	87.4	12.6	0.0
San Augustine, TX	48405	13,648	13.1	62.9	23.9	12,038	9,078	58.2	673	79.6	0.5	19.9

Note. Data in columns 26 through 41 from the American Community Survey are subject to sampling error, which can be especially large in small counties and small population groups. See notes and definitions for more information.
. . . = Not available.

Table C-1. Population, School, and Student Characteristics by County, Selected Years—*Continued*

County	State/ County Code	High school graduates, 2006–2010			College enrollment, 2006–2010		College graduates, 2006–2010 (percent)						
		Population 25 years and over	High school diploma or less (percent)	High school diploma or more (percent)	Number	Percent public	Bachelor's degree or more	+/- U.S. percent with Bachelor's degree or more	Non-Hispanic White	Black or African American	American Indian and Alaska Native	Asian, Hawaiian, and Pacific Islander	Hispanic or Latino[3]
		30	31	32	33	34	35	36	37	38	39	40	41
TEXAS—*(Continued)*													
Lee, TX	48287	10,784	57.3	79.1	444	70.7	14.5	-13.4	17.3	14.3	3.0	0.0	0.4
Leon, TX	48289	11,805	59.2	78.7	377	82.5	12.6	-15.3	14.4	6.5	14.9	91.7	0.6
Liberty, TX	48291	48,349	63.0	73.2	2,391	84.8	8.8	-19.1	10.4	6.0	5.5	19.8	1.5
Limestone, TX	48293	15,825	60.8	74.6	706	99.6	12.0	-15.9	15.9	5.9	0.0	100.0	0.1
Lipscomb, TX	48295	2,046	48.5	81.5	90	84.4	22.5	-5.4	24.7	0.0	7.4	77.8	12.5
Live Oak, TX	48297	8,237	55.7	77.1	329	73.9	14.0	-13.9	20.1	0.0	0.0	54.6	3.0
Llano, TX	48299	14,809	42.4	88.0	241	80.5	26.0	-1.9	26.9	100.0	36.6	49.2	4.3
Loving, TX	48301	39	82.1	92.3	0	0.0	18.0	-9.9	23.3	0.0	0.0	0.0	0.0
Lubbock, TX	48303	157,203	43.5	83.4	38,135	90.1	27.5	-0.4	35.6	12.1	19.8	59.5	9.6
Lynn, TX	48305	3,851	63.1	74.2	100	73.0	15.9	-12.0	25.4	0.0	0.0	44.4	2.1
McCulloch, TX	48307	5,651	58.0	74.8	97	90.7	20.4	-7.5	25.8	0.0	0.0	70.2	3.2
McLennan, TX	48309	137,142	48.5	80.3	25,635	46.1	20.6	-7.3	26.0	10.6	11.4	41.5	6.8
McMullen, TX	48311	648	59.3	78.7	73	68.5	10.5	-17.4	16.9	0.0	0.0	0.0	2.5
Madison, TX	48313	8,873	64.4	78.2	600	84.5	11.5	-16.4	16.4	1.6	5.3	100.0	3.0
Marion, TX	48315	8,063	60.2	76.9	266	91.7	11.2	-16.7	13.1	3.8	0.0	28.4	14.5
Martin, TX	48317	2,852	62.5	70.9	223	95.1	12.6	-15.3	19.6	0.0	0.0	100.0	1.6
Mason, TX	48319	2,747	52.4	79.9	77	100.0	28.9	1.0	31.0	0.0	100.0	0.0	13.6
Matagorda, TX	48321	23,533	58.1	76.6	942	81.0	14.1	-13.8	20.9	9.9	17.3	9.9	3.3
Maverick, TX	48323	29,215	67.1	55.2	2,742	93.9	13.7	-14.2	38.7	0.0	21.6	86.7	12.4
Medina, TX	48325	28,979	50.7	78.3	2,486	80.4	19.3	-8.6	27.1	18.7	11.9	18.8	10.2
Menard, TX	48327	1,646	58.3	80.1	40	95.0	13.9	-14.0	17.3	0.0	0.0	0.0	1.9
Midland, TX	48329	81,841	44.2	81.2	6,841	93.6	23.9	-4.0	32.5	12.1	17.9	66.6	6.4
Milam, TX	48331	16,526	60.3	81.5	629	83.6	13.5	-14.4	17.6	2.7	6.2	0.0	1.8
Mills, TX	48333	3,553	58.6	77.2	81	59.3	18.7	-9.2	22.4	0.0	0.0	0.0	0.0
Mitchell, TX	48335	6,520	60.2	73.4	227	97.8	9.4	-18.5	16.2	0.0	0.0	0.0	0.9
Montague, TX	48337	13,762	53.7	81.2	491	96.9	16.7	-11.2	17.6	0.0	0.0	23.1	5.9
Montgomery, TX	48339	273,731	39.7	85.9	18,544	84.0	29.7	1.8	32.1	20.7	21.0	59.6	15.7
Moore, TX	48341	12,244	60.7	69.5	1,095	83.5	13.7	-14.2	19.1	0.0	9.4	34.5	5.8
Morris, TX	48343	8,967	52.2	82.3	469	97.9	17.3	-10.6	20.3	10.9	0.0	22.2	2.0
Motley, TX	48345	784	52.6	84.7	0	0.0	18.5	-9.4	19.1	0.0	0.0	0.0	13.2
Nacogdoches, TX	48347	35,551	49.6	80.5	10,009	94.8	24.0	-3.9	29.5	8.5	35.0	71.3	6.8
Navarro, TX	48349	30,196	55.8	76.5	2,861	94.7	15.7	-12.2	19.9	9.5	11.5	42.0	2.6
Newton, TX	48351	9,887	68.7	77.7	449	75.5	8.6	-19.3	9.4	3.9	0.0	50.9	0.0
Nolan, TX	48353	9,867	55.9	77.4	697	91.5	17.1	-10.8	20.8	14.5	0.0	0.0	8.1
Nueces, TX	48355	211,489	48.8	78.3	22,777	91.9	19.9	-8.0	31.4	15.2	21.3	46.2	11.2
Ochiltree, TX	48357	5,864	63.8	70.7	220	86.4	17.9	-10.0	25.0	0.0	0.0	100.0	4.6
Oldham, TX	48359	1,247	42.7	82.3	106	88.7	29.8	1.9	31.4	100.0	0.0	100.0	9.5
Orange, TX	48361	54,138	56.6	85.9	3,201	93.7	12.5	-15.4	13.3	6.0	29.1	16.6	7.5
Palo Pinto, TX	48363	18,615	57.8	76.8	763	88.9	13.7	-14.2	15.5	1.8	0.0	18.6	4.1
Panola, TX	48365	15,544	55.9	81.5	926	89.0	11.4	-16.5	12.6	6.5	0.0	6.0	2.2
Parker, TX	48367	73,335	43.6	85.4	4,961	85.0	22.4	-5.5	23.5	9.8	24.4	44.2	10.4
Parmer, TX	48369	6,017	59.7	65.0	402	84.1	15.7	-12.2	25.3	0.0	0.0	0.0	5.5
Pecos, TX	48371	10,143	66.7	65.1	245	86.9	11.3	-16.6	25.6	5.7	0.0	0.0	4.5
Polk, TX	48373	32,493	62.8	74.9	1,302	72.6	10.6	-17.3	12.1	2.8	26.3	40.7	3.2
Potter, TX	48375	74,629	52.7	75.4	6,400	88.1	15.0	-12.9	20.5	12.6	7.4	13.8	3.9
Presidio, TX	48377	4,771	68.5	53.7	126	81.7	17.8	-10.1	38.9	0.0	0.0	0.0	13.9
Rains, TX	48379	7,667	59.5	80.8	302	75.2	12.1	-15.8	12.4	29.2	0.0	0.0	2.6
Randall, TX	48381	74,274	33.2	91.3	10,507	93.0	30.1	2.2	32.5	21.6	37.6	35.3	12.3
Reagan, TX	48383	1,918	66.2	68.5	44	81.8	10.0	-17.9	21.1	0.0	0.0	0.0	0.5
Real, TX	48385	2,311	49.4	77.6	82	85.4	19.4	-8.5	22.5	0.0	0.0	100.0	4.3
Red River, TX	48387	9,234	64.7	72.5	527	93.0	8.6	-19.3	9.7	4.3	0.0	4.3	4.6
Reeves, TX	48389	7,996	76.3	52.8	434	100.0	7.6	-20.3	32.0	0.0	2.4	0.0	3.6
Refugio, TX	48391	5,044	60.2	72.7	185	98.9	11.2	-16.7	15.3	21.9	0.0	83.8	3.6
Roberts, TX	48393	616	33.8	91.9	9	100.0	34.1	6.2	34.4	0.0	0.0	100.0	0.0
Robertson, TX	48395	11,037	60.0	76.6	414	96.6	15.8	-12.1	20.8	5.8	0.0	42.6	3.9
Rockwall, TX	48397	46,366	32.2	91.3	3,681	72.6	35.6	7.7	38.9	34.9	3.6	33.2	14.9
Runnels, TX	48399	7,232	61.6	77.1	246	97.6	16.4	-11.5	19.3	0.0	0.0	100.0	7.5
Rusk, TX	48401	35,118	55.1	79.4	2,016	87.7	14.8	-13.1	17.3	8.4	37.0	51.7	4.6
Sabine, TX	48403	7,854	61.7	77.5	277	98.2	12.2	-15.7	12.7	7.6	100.0	0.0	0.0
San Augustine, TX	48405	6,180	69.4	71.4	364	84.1	11.9	-16.0	13.8	6.9	0.0	0.0	0.0

Note. Data in columns 26 through 41 from the American Community Survey are subject to sampling error, which can be especially large in small counties and small population groups. See notes and definitions for more information.

[3]May be of any race.

Table C-1. Population, School, and Student Characteristics by County, Selected Years—*Continued*

County	State/ County Code	County Type[1]	Population, 2010		Percent of related children 5–17 years in poverty, 2010	Percent of children under 19 years with no health insurance, 2010	Number of schools and students, 2010–2011			Resident enrollment, 2006–2010 K–12 enrollment	
			Total	Percent 5–17 years			School districts	Schools	Students	Number	Percent public
			1	2	3	4	5	6	7	8	9
TEXAS—*(Continued)*											
San Jacinto, TX	48407	1	26,384	17.9	28.8	19.8	2	8	3,579	4,497	97.8
San Patricio, TX	48409	2	64,804	20.9	29.2	11.2	7	33	14,437	14,161	97.6
San Saba, TX	48411	7	6,131	15.2	32.8	19.3	3	5	961	961	95.8
Schleicher, TX	48413	8	3,461	21.9	24.7	23.6	1	3	595	737	98.5
Scurry, TX	48415	7	16,921	17.5	23.3	15.8	3	7	3,273	3,107	100.0
Shackelford, TX	48417	8	3,378	18.1	19.3	22.0	2	3	666	601	97.2
Shelby, TX	48419	6	25,448	18.9	28.8	18.5	6	14	5,464	4,330	97.0
Sherman, TX	48421	9	3,034	23.1	15.5	30.0	2	4	958	706	89.8
Smith, TX	48423	3	209,714	18.5	20.3	17.7	9	61	33,792	37,432	88.2
Somervell, TX	48425	8	8,490	20.6	15.5	19.1	2	5	1,773	1,739	97.1
Starr, TX	48427	4	60,968	24.9	54.7	16.4	3	26	17,679	14,867	98.7
Stephens, TX	48429	7	9,630	17.4	29.1	18.7	1	5	1,561	1,701	99.1
Sterling, TX	48431	8	1,143	16.7	18.9	22.4	1	4	217	209	98.1
Stonewall, TX	48433	8	1,490	17.2	24.5	23.7	1	2	240	261	100.0
Sutton, TX	48435	7	4,128	20.0	20.8	19.8	1	4	918	1,079	96.0
Swisher, TX	48437	6	7,854	18.3	29.1	16.7	3	8	1,546	1,507	98.7
Tarrant, TX	48439	1	1,809,034	20.1	19.4	14.4	32	739	499,531	348,336	91.5
Taylor, TX	48441	3	131,506	17.0	21.9	12.8	6	53	22,869	21,486	95.3
Terrell, TX	48443	9	984	15.5	22.6	25.3	1	2	138	161	100.0
Terry, TX	48445	6	12,651	18.0	34.4	17.1	3	8	2,331	2,421	99.1
Throckmorton, TX	48447	9	1,641	16.6	23.2	26.4	2	3	315	274	100.0
Titus, TX	48449	7	32,334	21.5	27.7	17.9	5	15	6,948	6,588	96.6
Tom Green, TX	48451	3	110,224	16.5	25.8	13.4	9	61	18,679	18,095	95.6
Travis, TX	48453	1	1,024,266	16.5	22.9	12.8	24	238	149,894	159,252	91.8
Trinity, TX	48455	8	14,585	15.2	30.4	17.5	4	10	2,288	2,160	99.4
Tyler, TX	48457	6	21,766	14.8	26.0	14.7	5	14	3,552	3,328	96.2
Upshur, TX	48459	3	39,309	18.3	23.0	15.3	7	24	7,147	6,998	90.6
Upton, TX	48461	8	3,355	19.9	22.1	23.6	2	5	713	483	99.0
Uvalde, TX	48463	7	26,405	21.2	36.7	14.0	5	16	6,121	5,917	96.0
Val Verde, TX	48465	5	48,879	21.5	36.4	15.7	2	15	10,634	10,496	95.6
Van Zandt, TX	48467	6	52,579	18.1	21.5	18.0	8	31	9,981	9,478	93.7
Victoria, TX	48469	3	86,793	19.2	25.8	13.1	5	34	15,096	16,534	88.6
Walker, TX	48471	4	67,861	11.9	24.4	16.0	4	14	7,169	8,889	93.3
Waller, TX	48473	1	43,205	17.4	26.4	20.4	3	17	9,030	7,138	92.0
Ward, TX	48475	6	10,658	19.8	24.9	16.9	2	7	2,083	2,329	98.0
Washington, TX	48477	6	33,718	16.1	22.1	16.0	2	10	5,260	5,182	84.5
Webb, TX	48479	3	250,304	25.5	38.9	18.7	5	78	68,055	61,614	96.7
Wharton, TX	48481	4	41,280	19.5	23.9	16.7	5	18	8,164	8,130	93.7
Wheeler, TX	48483	9	5,410	18.1	20.1	24.9	4	6	1,066	949	98.5
Wichita, TX	48485	3	131,500	16.3	23.4	12.9	7	49	21,361	22,210	95.3
Wilbarger, TX	48487	6	13,535	18.5	24.1	12.3	4	8	2,541	2,543	99.2
Willacy, TX	48489	6	22,134	19.7	45.4	14.0	4	14	4,560	4,850	97.6
Williamson, TX	48491	1	422,679	20.8	9.8	11.1	13	152	102,190	80,500	93.5
Wilson, TX	48493	1	42,918	20.3	15.4	14.3	4	26	8,409	8,506	93.9
Winkler, TX	48495	6	7,110	20.8	22.1	16.5	2	5	1,586	1,433	99.0
Wise, TX	48497	1	59,127	19.3	16.0	17.2	7	25	9,069	11,613	94.6
Wood, TX	48499	6	41,964	15.1	28.8	17.1	6	20	6,164	6,149	96.9
Yoakum, TX	48501	7	7,879	22.5	20.8	21.5	2	6	2,038	1,690	97.8
Young, TX	48503	6	18,550	17.5	24.2	16.5	3	10	3,453	3,284	96.5
Zapata, TX	48505	6	14,018	23.8	44.9	19.9	1	6	3,767	3,002	100.0
Zavala, TX	48507	7	11,677	22.4	48.3	12.0	2	7	2,556	2,681	99.3
UTAH	49000	X	2,763,885	22.0	14.9	10.9	127	1,016	585,552	571,818	95.0
Beaver, UT	49001	9	6,629	24.6	15.3	15.0	1	7	1,581	1,654	99.6
Box Elder, UT	49003	4	49,975	24.0	11.6	10.4	1	27	11,310	11,731	97.4
Cache, UT	49005	3	112,656	21.4	15.4	10.1	8	43	23,833	21,766	97.3
Carbon, UT	49007	7	21,403	18.7	17.6	8.6	3	11	4,086	3,764	94.8
Daggett, UT	49009	8	1,059	16.6	5.1	14.1	1	4	210	76	100.0
Davis, UT	49011	2	306,479	24.1	9.6	7.9	9	107	72,144	70,254	97.1
Duchesne, UT	49013	6	18,607	23.2	14.8	13.0	1	14	4,541	4,004	98.4
Emery, UT	49015	9	10,976	22.4	15.4	11.3	1	10	2,425	2,344	98.5
Garfield, UT	49017	9	5,172	19.4	18.5	14.2	1	9	982	901	100.0
Grand, UT	49019	7	9,225	16.5	23.7	13.3	2	6	1,607	1,271	89.9

[1]County type codes are from the Economic Research Service of the United States Department of Agriculture. See notes and definitions for more information.

Table C-1. Population, School, and Student Characteristics by County, Selected Years—*Continued*

County	State/ County Code	Characteristics of students, 2010–2011				Number of graduates, 2008–2009	Staff and students, 2010–2011			
		Percent with IEP[2]	Percent eligible for free or reduced lunch	Percent minority	Percent English-language learners		Total staff	Number of teachers	Student/ teacher ratio	Central admin. staff
		10	11	12	13	14	15	16	17	18
TEXAS—*(Continued)*										
San Jacinto, TX	48407	9.8	67.7	31.8	4.4	199	569	270	13.3	23
San Patricio, TX	48409	9.9	63.0	72.1	3.0	983	2,172	984	14.7	112
San Saba, TX	48411	11.2	65.3	43.9	9.8	72	182	101	9.5	9
Schleicher, TX	48413	4.9	28.2	67.6	7.4	42	111	61	9.7	4
Scurry, TX	48415	12.3	53.1	56.5	5.5	178	473	246	13.3	26
Shackelford, TX	48417	11.7	49.2	18.2	2.3	49	114	62	10.7	4
Shelby, TX	48419	10.6	70.1	48.2	15.0	285	854	428	12.8	31
Sherman, TX	48421	7.9	48.6	56.4	15.7	64	132	74	13.0	7
Smith, TX	48423	8.3	59.0	55.6	12.7	1,805	4,811	2,461	13.7	224
Somervell, TX	48425	8.9	46.0	31.8	8.9	163	292	152	11.7	16
Starr, TX	48427	8.8	36.0	99.8	59.9	933	3,021	1,250	14.1	110
Stephens, TX	48429	9.0	63.8	38.9	8.1	88	281	140	11.1	9
Sterling, TX	48431	12.0	50.9	52.8	6.9	21	50	25	8.8	4
Stonewall, TX	48433	7.5	50.4	32.1	2.5	10	48	26	9.4	1
Sutton, TX	48435	8.2	52.4	72.2	10.2	57	179	95	9.7	8
Swisher, TX	48437	10.7	71.2	60.0	3.9	99	276	146	10.6	12
Tarrant, TX	48439	8.1	51.6	63.1	20.4	17,845	61,239	32,358	15.4	2,777
Taylor, TX	48441	12.8	54.3	48.7	2.1	1,246	3,207	1,636	14.0	83
Terrell, TX	48443	7.2	34.8	57.2	0.7	9	44	21	6.7	4
Terry, TX	48445	8.0	69.9	74.1	5.8	136	419	198	11.8	23
Throckmorton, TX	48447	8.3	58.4	20.0	0.3	17	67	39	8.1	4
Titus, TX	48449	10.4	76.3	70.5	26.6	357	1,179	554	12.5	36
Tom Green, TX	48451	10.8	55.1	58.3	4.0	1,170	2,644	1,334	14.0	102
Travis, TX	48453	9.8	54.6	69.6	21.3	7,046	20,247	10,631	14.1	992
Trinity, TX	48455	12.1	54.2	31.4	5.4	128	408	196	11.7	14
Tyler, TX	48457	11.9	55.5	19.5	1.1	238	636	307	11.6	33
Upshur, TX	48459	9.1	48.8	25.5	3.9	461	1,165	593	12.1	53
Upton, TX	48461	6.7	34.9	62.3	3.2	45	152	68	10.5	7
Uvalde, TX	48463	10.3	75.3	84.6	5.1	359	913	451	13.6	29
Val Verde, TX	48465	9.8	69.8	92.9	14.7	549	1,431	674	15.8	58
Van Zandt, TX	48467	11.0	53.0	21.4	4.1	656	1,473	762	13.1	52
Victoria, TX	48469	10.8	65.5	71.2	2.3	691	2,302	1,053	14.3	84
Walker, TX	48471	9.6	40.1	54.4	9.2	433	1,023	511	14.0	46
Waller, TX	48473	8.3	72.1	74.9	18.9	458	1,218	633	14.3	49
Ward, TX	48475	10.7	54.2	64.5	4.7	120	344	165	12.7	8
Washington, TX	48477	12.7	54.9	51.4	9.1	370	734	400	13.2	32
Webb, TX	48479	7.9	48.3	99.1	47.9	3,460	10,169	4,256	16.0	387
Wharton, TX	48481	7.6	59.9	68.4	8.5	520	1,272	616	13.3	51
Wheeler, TX	48483	8.3	51.6	43.4	12.3	59	223	128	8.4	12
Wichita, TX	48485	12.8	56.1	45.1	3.9	1,346	2,986	1,623	13.2	141
Wilbarger, TX	48487	9.4	65.1	51.5	5.1	143	388	204	12.5	15
Willacy, TX	48489	7.6	10.9	97.7	9.4	212	773	329	13.9	44
Williamson, TX	48491	8.4	34.2	47.8	6.2	5,408	13,596	7,143	14.3	598
Wilson, TX	48493	11.1	44.6	50.0	2.8	530	1,181	593	14.2	43
Winkler, TX	48495	9.5	34.4	67.2	10.2	104	320	145	10.9	11
Wise, TX	48497	10.0	44.0	30.3	9.8	592	1,390	707	12.8	48
Wood, TX	48499	9.8	55.4	24.5	5.4	366	965	509	12.1	46
Yoakum, TX	48501	7.6	57.8	71.9	16.5	107	318	169	12.0	13
Young, TX	48503	10.7	55.7	29.2	7.0	214	538	289	11.9	20
Zapata, TX	48505	6.1	77.7	99.3	27.2	187	566	251	15.0	28
Zavala, TX	48507	7.7	84.0	98.1	7.2	145	439	171	14.9	19
UTAH	49000	12.0	38.2	22.0	7.3	30,461	52,341	25,677	22.8	1,098
Beaver, UT	49001	15.7	51.0	13.7	4.7	96	158	78	20.4	5
Box Elder, UT	49003	11.5	41.8	12.2	2.9	704	1,444	488	23.2	21
Cache, UT	49005	12.6	37.7	17.4	5.2	1,368	2,304	1,008	23.7	43
Carbon, UT	49007	17.8	54.5	15.0	1.0	308	488	210	19.5	13
Daggett, UT	49009	11.4	32.9	6.7	0.5	14	39	14	14.7	3
Davis, UT	49011	10.7	27.2	14.0	4.2	3,904	6,169	3,040	23.7	104
Duchesne, UT	49013	16.0	45.4	12.5	1.3	228	475	225	20.2	13
Emery, UT	49015	19.8	50.2	9.7	3.9	155	265	126	19.2	8
Garfield, UT	49017	11.8	53.1	9.0	3.3	54	130	61	16.0	6
Grand, UT	49019	12.8	48.5	22.7	9.9	108	192	84	19.2	7

[2]IEP=Individual Education Program. See notes and definitions for more information.

Table C-1. Population, School, and Student Characteristics by County, Selected Years—*Continued*

County	State/ County Code	Revenues, 2008–2009				Current expenditures, 2008–2009			Resident population 16 to 19 years, 2006–2010			
		Total revenue ($1,000's)	Percentage of revenue from			Amount ($1,000's)	Amount per student	Percent for instruction	Total population 16 to 19 years	Percent enrolled in school	Percent high school graduates, not enrolled in school	Percent not enrolled, not grads, not employed, or not in labor force
			Federal government	State government	Local government							
		19	20	21	22	23	24	25	26	27	28	29
TEXAS—*(Continued)*												
San Jacinto, TX	48407	34,064	12.0	47.2	40.8	31,289	9,072	57.2	1,321	76.4	12.2	8.3
San Patricio, TX	48409	145,018	13.5	49.8	36.7	125,559	8,444	59.0	4,213	75.9	17.5	2.7
San Saba, TX	48411	11,910	8.2	64.0	27.8	10,702	10,932	62.7	398	72.6	18.8	5.0
Schleicher, TX	48413	7,632	6.0	21.6	72.5	6,194	9,910	65.3	137	65.7	15.3	7.3
Scurry, TX	48415	51,828	6.2	22.3	71.5	28,300	9,010	59.4	1,161	86.5	7.8	5.8
Shackelford, TX	48417	8,380	7.2	45.9	46.9	7,148	10,496	62.6	209	78.5	7.7	6.2
Shelby, TX	48419	57,012	11.8	56.1	32.1	48,541	9,347	60.0	1,368	74.3	11.8	10.1
Sherman, TX	48421	10,580	7.8	24.7	67.5	7,982	9,060	67.0	191	72.8	26.2	0.0
Smith, TX	48423	311,287	11.4	38.3	50.3	271,252	8,301	61.2	12,415	81.6	9.5	5.3
Somervell, TX	48425	38,255	3.5	15.5	81.0	20,659	11,107	62.4	490	82.9	17.1	0.0
Starr, TX	48427	191,703	18.1	66.0	15.9	163,021	9,772	60.6	4,225	70.1	15.9	7.8
Stephens, TX	48429	15,032	8.6	31.5	59.8	14,847	9,641	59.5	471	68.4	19.1	12.5
Sterling, TX	48431	17,105	0.9	1.5	97.7	3,124	15,542	56.9	98	72.5	27.6	0.0
Stonewall, TX	48433	3,049	5.6	29.2	65.2	2,964	12,831	62.5	57	87.7	12.3	0.0
Sutton, TX	48435	24,695	3.2	18.0	78.8	11,499	11,385	60.8	324	89.2	10.8	0.0
Swisher, TX	48437	15,814	10.4	67.5	22.2	14,095	9,628	61.0	472	72.3	22.7	5.1
Tarrant, TX	48439	3,158,712	8.6	37.1	54.4	2,635,547	8,015	61.2	99,554	82.0	11.0	4.0
Taylor, TX	48441	201,958	12.4	50.5	37.1	177,942	8,082	62.5	9,449	86.2	8.0	3.9
Terrell, TX	48443	12,109	1.5	8.4	90.2	3,368	20,048	52.4	90	100.0	0.0	0.0
Terry, TX	48445	26,261	17.0	36.3	46.7	23,326	10,376	61.9	791	66.6	20.4	11.0
Throckmorton, TX	48447	4,408	6.3	49.8	43.9	4,119	12,150	64.2	116	72.4	16.4	0.0
Titus, TX	48449	82,025	18.1	35.5	46.4	69,540	10,276	56.5	2,139	84.5	8.3	2.8
Tom Green, TX	48451	169,764	14.6	54.7	30.7	154,418	8,544	57.7	7,748	75.6	18.8	2.8
Travis, TX	48453	1,819,376	8.3	26.2	65.5	1,310,187	9,327	57.5	54,546	83.5	9.2	3.7
Trinity, TX	48455	25,725	16.3	60.3	23.5	22,287	9,775	59.2	872	75.2	4.1	1.7
Tyler, TX	48457	43,023	8.9	46.5	44.6	34,609	9,566	57.0	1,127	73.4	19.2	7.1
Upshur, TX	48459	69,974	9.5	50.7	39.8	61,010	8,620	62.2	1,955	75.5	16.7	5.3
Upton, TX	48461	42,202	2.1	9.1	88.9	11,825	17,014	55.0	143	98.6	0.0	1.4
Uvalde, TX	48463	61,781	15.3	60.0	24.6	55,237	9,051	60.1	1,878	82.9	12.1	3.9
Val Verde, TX	48465	93,337	16.4	62.6	21.0	81,099	7,834	64.2	3,071	78.5	14.1	5.5
Van Zandt, TX	48467	97,673	8.4	57.3	34.3	82,285	8,293	60.5	3,080	84.0	6.4	5.5
Victoria, TX	48469	150,061	13.1	39.1	47.9	122,814	8,214	58.5	4,894	76.4	16.6	2.5
Walker, TX	48471	81,791	15.2	40.6	44.2	64,468	9,353	51.6	5,365	87.4	8.4	4.1
Waller, TX	48473	86,001	9.6	44.7	45.7	74,166	8,648	60.3	2,630	80.2	14.2	3.7
Ward, TX	48475	27,822	6.1	22.6	71.3	19,674	9,245	61.5	734	75.5	21.9	2.3
Washington, TX	48477	51,627	7.7	34.3	58.0	44,408	8,404	60.0	3,032	86.8	9.2	4.0
Webb, TX	48479	693,662	13.4	62.0	24.6	566,736	8,558	58.8	16,993	83.3	8.7	5.3
Wharton, TX	48481	81,767	9.7	48.7	41.6	74,510	9,302	62.1	2,355	79.2	14.1	5.8
Wheeler, TX	48483	32,651	4.0	16.7	79.2	13,525	13,195	60.9	292	73.0	13.0	3.4
Wichita, TX	48485	207,019	15.2	46.5	38.3	183,550	8,488	59.3	9,488	70.7	26.0	1.3
Wilbarger, TX	48487	25,458	9.5	50.6	39.9	22,077	8,852	64.7	1,076	80.9	5.3	11.4
Willacy, TX	48489	56,587	18.3	62.6	19.1	45,601	10,170	57.7	1,746	80.1	15.6	4.2
Williamson, TX	48491	948,749	4.6	29.5	65.9	773,708	8,208	59.9	20,300	84.3	10.8	2.3
Wilson, TX	48493	78,082	8.1	55.9	36.0	66,998	8,153	60.9	2,516	81.4	9.4	4.6
Winkler, TX	48495	39,341	5.3	16.6	78.1	20,274	12,600	56.5	446	71.8	17.7	10.5
Wise, TX	48497	112,898	5.1	30.6	64.4	81,623	9,118	62.0	3,597	78.7	15.4	3.0
Wood, TX	48499	56,162	9.0	39.8	51.2	47,600	9,075	62.6	2,444	84.0	8.1	5.7
Yoakum, TX	48501	54,321	3.1	13.4	83.5	21,653	10,897	61.7	427	64.6	34.2	0.0
Young, TX	48503	34,977	9.7	53.9	36.4	28,569	8,264	66.4	902	76.4	11.6	9.1
Zapata, TX	48505	58,730	9.7	25.2	65.1	35,246	9,549	60.1	758	79.0	21.0	0.0
Zavala, TX	48507	30,646	20.0	64.1	16.0	28,754	11,483	58.9	938	70.4	13.0	16.6
UTAH	49000	4,591,053	12.5	54.9	32.6	3,540,428	6,327	64.0	174,312	80.7	13.5	3.0
Beaver, UT	49001	14,316	11.4	56.0	32.5	10,522	6,660	63.3	435	67.1	26.0	3.0
Box Elder, UT	49003	89,391	13.4	56.7	29.9	70,296	6,241	63.6	3,200	77.8	17.5	1.1
Cache, UT	49005	166,622	13.2	61.3	25.5	145,646	6,521	67.0	8,458	87.8	8.8	1.2
Carbon, UT	49007	41,905	14.7	47.0	38.3	32,668	7,950	62.1	1,243	86.7	6.8	6.0
Daggett, UT	49009	3,880	14.3	46.3	39.4	2,757	15,317	52.7	20	100.0	0.0	0.0
Davis, UT	49011	513,031	11.7	58.2	30.2	424,974	6,126	63.4	18,838	83.3	12.5	1.9
Duchesne, UT	49013	42,350	13.1	54.4	32.5	30,790	6,928	59.5	1,155	67.7	29.7	2.4
Emery, UT	49015	23,876	11.2	44.7	44.1	20,204	8,739	62.2	804	67.7	25.6	2.5
Garfield, UT	49017	14,203	13.3	52.8	33.9	11,310	11,893	61.4	215	62.3	34.0	0.0
Grand, UT	49019	16,923	14.3	38.0	47.7	12,310	7,963	61.3	549	70.7	20.4	4.7

Note. Data in columns 26 through 41 from the American Community Survey are subject to sampling error, which can be especially large in small counties and small population groups. See notes and definitions for more information.
. . . = Not available.

Table C-1. Population, School, and Student Characteristics by County, Selected Years—*Continued*

County	State/ County Code	High school graduates, 2006–2010			College enrollment, 2006–2010		College graduates, 2006–2010 (percent)						
		Population 25 years and over	High school diploma or less (percent)	High school diploma or more (percent)	Number	Percent public	Bachelor's degree or more	+/- U.S. percent with Bachelor's degree or more	Non-Hispanic White	Black or African American	American Indian and Alaska Native	Asian, Hawaiian, and Pacific Islander	Hispanic or Latino[3]
		30	31	32	33	34	35	36	37	38	39	40	41
TEXAS—*(Continued)*													
San Jacinto, TX	48407	17,623	61.9	77.0	590	63.7	9.6	-18.3	10.9	5.6	35.7	0.0	2.1
San Patricio, TX	48409	41,003	54.7	76.3	2,595	86.4	15.1	-12.8	23.3	13.1	2.5	29.3	6.5
San Saba, TX	48411	4,038	54.9	81.4	200	92.5	18.1	-9.8	21.3	0.0	13.5	0.0	6.1
Schleicher, TX	48413	2,095	60.6	78.5	127	82.7	17.4	-10.5	28.1	0.0	0.0	0.0	2.3
Scurry, TX	48415	10,689	55.9	74.2	1,092	95.8	16.3	-11.6	22.1	1.8	19.2	62.0	4.5
Shackelford, TX	48417	2,002	44.8	86.8	107	63.6	27.6	-0.3	30.7	0.0	0.0	0.0	0.0
Shelby, TX	48419	16,735	63.9	75.4	791	92.4	13.5	-14.4	16.5	4.7	0.0	100.0	7.9
Sherman, TX	48421	1,858	54.6	74.4	63	100.0	19.1	-8.8	24.5	0.0	0.0	0.0	5.7
Smith, TX	48423	129,159	42.4	84.2	14,736	88.5	24.5	-3.4	30.2	13.4	6.8	43.6	4.9
Somervell, TX	48425	5,314	42.0	87.4	318	86.5	28.4	0.5	32.2	0.0	0.0	0.0	6.3
Starr, TX	48427	32,826	74.0	47.9	2,865	88.1	9.8	-18.1	40.1	0.0	0.0	39.7	9.2
Stephens, TX	48429	6,363	55.2	82.2	123	75.6	12.2	-15.7	13.6	0.0	0.0	0.0	6.4
Sterling, TX	48431	750	54.3	77.5	49	100.0	22.7	-5.2	27.6	0.0	0.0	0.0	6.9
Stonewall, TX	48433	1,027	47.6	85.5	37	29.7	22.4	-5.5	25.4	0.0	0.0	0.0	0.0
Sutton, TX	48435	2,603	64.3	69.4	160	75.6	11.8	-16.1	21.9	0.0	0.0	0.0	3.9
Swisher, TX	48437	5,019	59.4	75.9	224	93.3	14.6	-13.3	21.3	4.5	63.6	0.0	1.7
Tarrant, TX	48439	1,085,929	40.8	83.8	111,320	73.3	28.8	0.9	35.4	21.7	17.8	42.5	10.7
Taylor, TX	48441	78,960	43.6	84.1	13,586	37.0	24.2	-3.7	28.4	17.1	5.1	38.2	8.0
Terrell, TX	48443	632	60.1	80.4	4	100.0	20.7	-7.2	32.0	0.0	0.0	7.3	11.2
Terry, TX	48445	7,882	66.0	68.1	448	88.8	14.3	-13.6	24.8	1.7	0.0	36.1	1.2
Throckmorton, TX	48447	1,311	57.2	78.4	42	69.0	16.7	-11.2	17.7	0.0	0.0	0.0	0.0
Titus, TX	48449	18,520	58.1	72.9	1,727	91.7	13.7	-14.2	19.8	7.3	0.0	1.9	3.8
Tom Green, TX	48451	67,208	48.6	81.2	8,659	88.3	21.6	-6.3	28.0	16.9	12.4	17.7	8.2
Travis, TX	48453	621,227	31.3	86.3	99,611	86.0	43.5	15.6	56.3	22.7	23.5	65.1	17.8
Trinity, TX	48455	10,153	65.6	80.9	384	85.2	11.2	-16.7	11.5	7.1	0.0	30.4	4.9
Tyler, TX	48457	15,260	57.5	83.0	497	87.1	12.2	-15.7	14.0	3.6	0.0	100.0	0.0
Upshur, TX	48459	26,067	51.7	83.4	1,342	83.1	15.1	-12.8	15.6	10.2	11.7	23.2	9.2
Upton, TX	48461	2,331	62.6	75.5	57	100.0	12.7	-15.2	19.5	15.8	0.0	0.0	2.5
Uvalde, TX	48463	16,159	54.7	69.9	1,526	88.7	16.1	-11.8	28.0	0.0	0.0	82.1	7.8
Val Verde, TX	48465	28,626	61.6	64.0	2,126	86.3	15.9	-12.0	33.0	21.1	10.7	24.3	10.8
Van Zandt, TX	48467	35,745	58.2	78.8	1,768	86.6	12.1	-15.8	12.3	11.3	10.9	52.2	4.9
Victoria, TX	48469	54,847	50.2	80.1	3,563	91.6	17.0	-10.9	24.6	9.2	0.0	54.6	5.7
Walker, TX	48471	41,872	53.7	80.3	11,624	98.0	17.1	-10.8	22.9	6.6	21.4	49.1	4.9
Waller, TX	48473	23,580	57.1	79.6	4,483	75.1	19.6	-8.3	23.4	25.5	20.2	13.7	6.4
Ward, TX	48475	6,722	63.2	70.4	142	93.0	10.0	-17.9	15.2	26.2	3.9	0.0	2.1
Washington, TX	48477	21,713	50.7	79.2	2,630	93.6	25.9	-2.0	30.7	7.1	0.0	22.5	17.2
Webb, TX	48479	128,485	58.8	62.7	16,188	92.5	16.7	-11.2	36.6	51.3	9.9	44.5	15.5
Wharton, TX	48481	26,319	58.5	75.1	1,965	95.2	15.5	-12.4	23.5	5.7	46.2	88.1	3.3
Wheeler, TX	48483	3,499	58.2	79.4	110	95.5	15.1	-12.8	16.6	0.0	0.0	58.8	3.2
Wichita, TX	48485	81,757	50.9	82.8	9,496	90.5	20.1	-7.8	23.2	12.2	16.4	23.0	7.4
Wilbarger, TX	48487	8,365	59.8	73.6	548	91.1	15.9	-12.0	20.6	3.9	0.0	66.7	1.4
Willacy, TX	48489	13,068	71.9	57.4	883	96.3	8.6	-19.3	27.1	0.0	36.0	100.0	5.4
Williamson, TX	48491	248,488	29.3	91.6	20,404	80.7	37.3	9.4	40.6	25.3	17.0	67.5	20.4
Wilson, TX	48493	27,015	51.6	84.5	1,697	84.6	18.2	-9.7	23.1	22.0	11.9	0.0	8.4
Winkler, TX	48495	4,273	65.3	62.9	196	61.7	9.8	-18.1	15.1	0.0	0.0	0.0	4.5
Wise, TX	48497	37,568	54.1	81.5	1,948	86.8	15.6	-12.3	17.0	3.1	10.8	14.4	6.6
Wood, TX	48499	29,402	54.8	80.8	2,345	47.2	16.5	-11.4	16.8	25.5	7.6	21.7	6.1
Yoakum, TX	48501	4,677	57.8	71.4	99	68.7	15.0	-12.9	26.9	0.0	0.0	0.0	3.3
Young, TX	48503	12,557	56.8	76.6	424	77.4	13.6	-14.3	15.8	0.0	0.0	0.0	0.5
Zapata, TX	48505	7,529	72.4	56.7	427	86.7	9.6	-18.3	19.6	0.0	0.0	0.0	8.1
Zavala, TX	48507	6,470	61.5	57.7	330	96.4	7.7	-20.2	16.3	0.0	0.0	0.0	6.8
UTAH	49000	1,503,241	34.2	90.6	234,412	70.9	29.4	1.5	31.7	24.5	10.3	34.4	11.2
Beaver, UT	49001	3,776	52.7	90.3	102	89.2	10.4	-17.5	11.2	0.0	0.0	0.0	1.2
Box Elder, UT	49003	27,548	41.5	91.4	2,515	81.3	22.7	-5.2	24.1	72.2	9.2	7.5	7.5
Cache, UT	49005	53,913	29.6	92.4	18,005	93.2	35.1	7.2	37.1	44.1	14.8	53.4	9.6
Carbon, UT	49007	13,085	44.8	85.7	1,782	93.5	14.2	-13.7	15.0	23.1	9.1	68.2	5.3
Daggett, UT	49009	640	51.7	84.5	21	66.7	18.8	-9.1	20.0	0.0	0.0	0.0	0.0
Davis, UT	49011	164,053	27.7	95.0	21,535	84.2	33.8	5.9	35.5	30.9	12.1	36.2	13.4
Duchesne, UT	49013	9,955	52.1	84.9	459	86.7	16.0	-11.9	16.2	0.0	19.8	51.5	4.0
Emery, UT	49015	6,344	48.9	90.4	315	88.9	13.2	-14.7	13.4	0.0	39.0	8.8	0.0
Garfield, UT	49017	3,306	40.1	91.9	191	93.7	19.6	-8.3	21.1	0.0	0.0	18.2	0.0
Grand, UT	49019	6,184	44.0	83.9	220	100.0	24.3	-3.6	26.3	100.0	3.2	34.6	2.4

Note. Data in columns 26 through 41 from the American Community Survey are subject to sampling error, which can be especially large in small counties and small population groups. See notes and definitions for more information.
[3]May be of any race.

Table C-1. Population, School, and Student Characteristics by County, Selected Years—*Continued*

County	State/ County Code	County Type[1]	Population, 2010: Total	Population, 2010: Percent 5–17 years	Percent of related children 5–17 years in poverty, 2010	Percent of children under 19 years with no health insurance, 2010	Number of schools and students, 2010–2011: School districts	Schools	Students	Resident enrollment, 2006–2010, K–12 enrollment: Number	Percent public
			1	2	3	4	5	6	7	8	9
UTAH—*(Continued)*											
Iron, UT	49021	4	46,163	20.9	27.0	12.5	4	19	9,500	9,238	93.8
Juab, UT	49023	2	10,246	27.1	16.5	13.7	2	12	2,545	2,676	93.9
Kane, UT	49025	6	7,125	17.3	19.5	12.5	1	10	1,200	1,103	99.0
Millard, UT	49027	7	12,503	23.6	18.6	17.7	1	11	3,007	2,934	99.2
Morgan, UT	49029	2	9,469	25.8	6.3	11.1	1	5	2,487	2,341	99.6
Piute, UT	49031	9	1,556	23.0	30.0	21.0	1	5	341	474	64.6
Rich, UT	49033	8	2,264	21.5	16.4	19.7	1	5	493	440	97.5
Salt Lake, UT	49035	2	1,029,655	20.4	16.3	11.1	35	299	198,981	202,993	93.0
San Juan, UT	49037	7	14,746	24.9	25.3	13.3	1	12	2,997	3,692	98.3
Sanpete, UT	49039	6	27,822	22.0	20.7	16.0	2	14	5,573	6,035	95.4
Sevier, UT	49041	7	20,802	23.0	18.4	11.6	2	13	4,740	4,804	95.9
Summit, UT	49043	2	36,324	20.9	10.7	12.1	4	19	7,366	7,224	95.7
Tooele, UT	49045	2	58,218	25.9	10.6	9.9	2	31	14,250	13,451	98.2
Uintah, UT	49047	7	32,588	22.7	17.0	14.0	2	14	6,709	6,675	96.5
Utah, UT	49049	2	516,564	23.9	12.5	10.2	23	161	121,876	110,873	95.2
Wasatch, UT	49051	6	23,530	24.0	12.4	16.8	3	9	5,435	5,210	98.1
Washington, UT	49053	3	138,115	21.2	21.6	13.5	4	49	27,917	27,401	93.6
Wayne, UT	49055	9	2,778	23.0	19.4	18.2	1	4	603	531	98.3
Weber, UT	49057	2	231,236	21.0	16.6	11.6	9	86	46,813	45,958	96.6
VERMONT	50000	X	625,741	15.5	13.6	2.1	360	320	91,939	99,990	90.6
Addison, VT	50001	6	36,821	15.6	12.0	2.3	29	22	4,921	6,127	92.2
Bennington, VT	50003	6	37,125	15.4	16.9	2.5	22	17	5,085	5,849	84.7
Caledonia, VT	50005	7	31,227	16.2	19.0	2.2	19	13	4,486	5,205	76.0
Chittenden, VT	50007	3	156,545	15.0	10.0	1.6	33	51	22,343	23,816	92.8
Essex, VT	50009	9	6,306	15.0	22.3	3.0	21	6	897	983	91.3
Franklin, VT	50011	3	47,746	18.4	13.7	2.1	21	22	8,760	9,111	94.2
Grand Isle, VT	50013	3	6,970	15.8	12.9	2.9	6	5	1,035	1,155	93.5
Lamoille, VT	50015	8	24,475	16.2	15.1	2.7	13	15	3,762	3,871	92.0
Orange, VT	50017	9	28,936	15.8	14.9	2.4	21	22	4,699	4,804	84.2
Orleans, VT	50019	7	27,231	16.1	21.6	2.7	28	22	4,181	4,377	92.3
Rutland, VT	50021	5	61,642	14.7	15.2	2.0	39	33	8,587	9,554	93.8
Washington, VT	50023	4	59,534	15.5	11.5	2.0	31	27	8,603	9,368	95.0
Windham, VT	50025	6	44,513	15.0	15.6	2.3	35	30	6,248	6,905	87.6
Windsor, VT	50027	7	56,670	15.1	12.3	2.2	41	35	8,332	8,865	87.6
VIRGINIA	51000	X	8,001,024	16.8	13.1	7.0	225	2,175	1,251,440	1,336,494	90.0
Accomack, VA	51001	7	33,164	15.0	25.4	9.3	1	13	5,088	5,462	90.1
Albemarle, VA	51003	3	98,970	15.9	9.0	7.4	3	3	(7)	15,907	81.5
Alleghany, VA	51005	6	16,250	16.4	17.3	7.1	3	9	2,669	2,860	93.7
Amelia, VA	51007	1	12,690	16.4	15.2	11.2	3	5	1,778	2,056	91.1
Amherst, VA	51009	3	32,353	16.0	16.5	8.3	3	11	4,599	5,210	83.7
Appomattox, VA	51011	3	14,973	16.8	18.9	8.3	1	4	2,300	2,582	87.9
Arlington, VA	51013	1	207,627	10.0	10.6	5.3	1	33	21,485	19,608	90.8
Augusta, VA	51015	4	73,750	16.2	11.0	7.3	6	26	10,769	11,692	89.9
Bath, VA	51017	9	4,731	13.7	12.7	9.9	1	3	658	624	86.4
Bedford, VA	51019	3	68,676	17.4	10.6	7.4	(8)	(8)	(8)	12,060	87.1
Bland, VA	51021	8	6,824	13.7	15.4	9.4	1	4	897	919	93.3
Botetourt, VA	51023	2	33,148	17.5	7.6	7.3	2	13	5,009	5,551	86.6
Brunswick, VA	51025	6	17,434	14.6	24.0	7.6	2	6	2,097	2,413	86.7
Buchanan, VA	51027	9	24,098	14.1	32.6	7.6	1	11	3,333	3,623	89.1
Buckingham, VA	51029	8	17,146	13.8	23.8	9.0	1	6	2,035	1,253	68.4
Campbell, VA	51031	3	54,842	16.5	16.2	7.9	1	15	8,528	9,369	86.7
Caroline, VA	51033	1	28,545	16.9	15.6	8.1	1	6	4,257	4,814	90.1
Carroll, VA	51035	6	30,042	15.4	21.9	8.8	3	13	4,471	4,668	95.0
Charles City County, VA	51036	1	7,256	13.7	16.2	11.2	1	3	844	1,138	91.5
Charlotte, VA	51037	8	12,586	17.5	25.1	9.7	2	8	2,125	2,349	94.1
Chesterfield, VA	51041	1	316,236	19.8	7.7	7.3	1	63	59,243	61,765	92.7
Clarke, VA	51043	1	14,034	17.7	8.4	8.1	1	4	2,082	2,499	80.0
Craig, VA	51045	2	5,190	16.4	15.8	9.6	1	2	718	826	82.6
Culpeper, VA	51047	6	46,689	18.9	13.8	8.4	1	11	7,710	8,490	85.6

[1]County type codes are from the Economic Research Service of the United States Department of Agriculture. See notes and definitions for more information.
[7]Albermarle county is included with Charlottesville city.
[8]Bedford county is included with Bedford city.

Table C-1. Population, School, and Student Characteristics by County, Selected Years—*Continued*

County	State/ County Code	Characteristics of students, 2010–2011				Number of graduates, 2008–2009	Staff and students, 2010–2011			
		Percent with IEP[2]	Percent eligible for free or reduced lunch	Percent minority	Percent English-language learners		Total staff	Number of teachers	Student/ teacher ratio	Central admin. staff
		10	11	12	13	14	15	16	17	18
UTAH—*(Continued)*										
Iron, UT	49021	14.6	50.3	15.1	2.8	570	955	441	21.5	19
Juab, UT	49023	12.9	40.9	5.6	. . .	152	259	124	20.5	7
Kane, UT	49025	14.8	48.6	6.7	0.8	80	151	70	17.2	5
Millard, UT	49027	16.8	50.5	20.5	7.9	240	328	149	20.2	8
Morgan, UT	49029	8.2	19.4	3.9	0.2	166	211	112	22.1	7
Piute, UT	49031	16.4	73.9	10.0	1.8	18	59	26	13.1	3
Rich, UT	49033	12.4	60.4	3.4	1.2	33	57	32	15.4	3
Salt Lake, UT	49035	11.4	41.0	32.1	11.9	10,421	16,821	8,559	23.2	401
San Juan, UT	49037	12.2	69.5	57.2	24.9	211	413	171	17.5	12
Sanpete, UT	49039	15.5	53.1	15.0	4.9	349	662	288	19.3	14
Sevier, UT	49041	13.7	52.4	9.5	1.7	282	451	229	20.7	10
Summit, UT	49043	9.1	21.3	18.5	5.9	479	799	398	18.5	20
Tooele, UT	49045	12.4	42.7	15.1	3.6	589	1,313	676	21.1	18
Uintah, UT	49047	13.1	46.3	16.6	1.6	298	578	278	24.1	13
Utah, UT	49049	12.2	32.2	15.7	4.7	5,605	10,456	5,204	23.4	218
Wasatch, UT	49051	14.5	37.4	16.7	8.3	269	542	269	20.2	11
Washington, UT	49053	11.5	40.0	17.0	6.3	1,331	2,479	1,242	22.5	37
Wayne, UT	49055	11.4	48.1	6.0	1.2	29	71	35	17.2	3
Weber, UT	49057	13.2	45.7	26.9	7.5	2,400	4,076	2,040	22.9	69
VERMONT	50000	14.8	36.8	7.4	1.6	. . .	18,485	8,382	11.0	579
Addison, VT	50001	12.5	33.0	4.1	0.8	. . .	1,058	486	10.1	44
Bennington, VT	50003	13.1	46.4	3.7	0.2	. . .	929	447	11.4	34
Caledonia, VT	50005	16.2	50.3	3.7	0.4	. . .	725	321	14.0	32
Chittenden, VT	50007	12.4	26.1	12.7	4.9	. . .	4,375	1,875	11.9	139
Essex, VT	50009	13.2	52.2	2.7	0.7	. . .	168	82	11.0	6
Franklin, VT	50011	16.3	38.9	10.7	0.4	. . .	1,705	806	10.9	40
Grand Isle, VT	50013	15.2	55.1	4.9	0.3	. . .	145	67	15.4	6
Lamoille, VT	50015	14.1	39.7	5.3	0.7	. . .	716	326	11.5	26
Orange, VT	50017	14.5	44.7	3.0	0.2	. . .	974	444	10.6	27
Orleans, VT	50019	18.7	54.7	4.9	0.2	. . .	975	439	9.5	23
Rutland, VT	50021	14.9	41.9	4.2	0.4	. . .	1,947	864	9.9	57
Washington, VT	50023	14.5	33.0	5.8	1.2	. . .	1,685	820	10.5	49
Windham, VT	50025	18.5	41.4	7.4	1.0	. . .	1,312	610	10.3	36
Windsor, VT	50027	16.5	34.5	4.6	0.7	. . .	1,773	797	10.5	61
VIRGINIA	51000	13.0	36.7	45.9	7.0	79,651	201,047	70,947	17.6	5,710
Accomack, VA	51001	11.4	64.9	57.3	11.0	319	830	299	17.0	20
Albemarle, VA	51003	(7)	25.1	29.6	(7)	(7)	(7)	(7)	(7)	(7)
Alleghany, VA	51005	16.6	46.4	10.3	0.6	175	491	175	15.2	10
Amelia, VA	51007	12.3	49.0	33.7	0.8	127	288	98	18.1	8
Amherst, VA	51009	11.8	45.6	31.0	0.4	342	781	298	15.5	24
Appomattox, VA	51011	11.6	46.0	33.3	. . .	137	336	141	16.3	13
Arlington, VA	51013	14.2	31.1	55.6	22.8	1,124	3,489	1,179	18.2	203
Augusta, VA	51015	9.4	35.7	7.7	1.3	747	1,582	695	15.5	43
Bath, VA	51017	13.7	41.5	7.1	1.5	50	118	46	14.5	3
Bedford, VA	51019	(8)	34.3	12.8	(8)	(8)	(8)	(8)	(8)	(8)
Bland, VA	51021	14.5	41.9	1.4	. . .	72	156	60	15.0	4
Botetourt, VA	51023	16.3	20.5	4.7	0.3	324	781	265	18.9	14
Brunswick, VA	51025	11.5	80.8	81.8	0.7	109	434	141	14.9	16
Buchanan, VA	51027	18.0	64.4	0.7	. . .	187	481	200	16.6	4
Buckingham, VA	51029	11.1	60.7	45.1	0.0	126	410	132	15.4	14
Campbell, VA	51031	10.8	36.4	22.6	1.0	544	717	477	17.9	4
Caroline, VA	51033	15.1	47.8	44.7	1.3	224	788	224	19.0	23
Carroll, VA	51035	13.1	49.7	11.3	2.7	250	728	253	17.7	18
Charles City County, VA	51036	14.9	63.3	69.2	1.7	58	118	57	14.9	4
Charlotte, VA	51037	14.7	54.1	38.5	0.6	137	333	126	16.9	8
Chesterfield, VA	51041	12.4	20.2	43.9	4.4	4,103	7,920	3,116	19.0	124
Clarke, VA	51043	9.1	19.3	16.6	1.1	182	348	129	16.1	7
Craig, VA	51045	17.1	38.9	1.7	0.1	46	106	50	14.3	3
Culpeper, VA	51047	9.5	38.0	36.2	4.0	413	1,252	444	17.4	34

[2]IEP=Individual Education Program. See notes and definitions for more information.
[7]Albermarle county is included with Charlottesville city.
[8]Bedford county is included with Bedford city.
. . . = Not available.

Table C-1. Population, School, and Student Characteristics by County, Selected Years—*Continued*

County	State/ County Code	Revenues, 2008–2009				Current expenditures, 2008–2009			Resident population 16 to 19 years, 2006–2010			
		Total revenue ($1,000's)	Percentage of revenue from			Amount ($1,000's)	Amount per student	Percent for instruction	Total population 16 to 19 years	Percent enrolled in school	Percent high school graduates, not enrolled in school	Percent not enrolled, not grads, not employed, or not in labor force
			Federal government	State government	Local government							
		19	20	21	22	23	24	25	26	27	28	29
UTAH—*(Continued)*												
Iron, UT	49021	73,450	13.0	52.9	34.1	57,907	6,162	64.7	4,026	85.8	12.5	1.0
Juab, UT	49023	22,085	12.0	57.7	30.3	17,232	6,965	65.0	613	77.8	15.0	2.0
Kane, UT	49025	14,756	10.9	44.8	44.4	11,749	9,783	62.8	378	85.5	7.9	4.8
Millard, UT	49027	30,502	12.7	44.2	43.0	25,041	8,248	63.0	968	76.3	8.7	13.8
Morgan, UT	49029	16,509	8.6	55.8	35.6	13,822	5,976	63.7	655	87.0	9.6	1.7
Piute, UT	49031	4,858	14.0	70.5	15.5	4,130	11,440	63.1	123	87.0	13.0	0.0
Rich, UT	49033	6,333	9.1	44.8	46.1	5,309	11,668	58.8	149	96.0	4.0	0.0
Salt Lake, UT	49035	1,659,126	12.2	54.9	33.0	1,203,697	6,285	63.6	59,001	77.9	14.2	3.9
San Juan, UT	49037	44,513	27.1	42.4	30.5	36,122	12,142	52.1	1,071	78.6	16.0	3.7
Sanpete, UT	49039	50,287	14.6	64.8	20.6	40,423	7,507	66.7	2,923	89.3	6.8	2.5
Sevier, UT	49041	38,396	16.7	58.2	25.1	29,722	6,281	66.7	1,488	83.5	12.2	2.0
Summit, UT	49043	89,605	5.9	16.6	77.5	62,054	8,913	62.6	2,136	79.9	15.7	3.7
Tooele, UT	49045	103,659	11.5	59.3	29.2	79,958	5,921	64.8	3,069	79.5	15.6	3.1
Uintah, UT	49047	63,689	12.6	40.6	46.8	41,894	6,535	62.2	1,751	68.7	15.8	8.2
Utah, UT	49049	834,830	12.6	58.8	28.6	655,125	5,770	66.9	38,389	84.5	12.3	1.9
Wasatch, UT	49051	49,010	10.5	36.6	52.9	34,454	6,887	68.6	1,295	80.2	15.9	1.4
Washington, UT	49053	214,220	10.9	48.4	40.6	170,523	6,369	62.5	8,013	76.2	15.2	5.5
Wayne, UT	49055	6,172	14.0	65.4	20.5	5,313	9,176	61.3	155	74.2	18.7	7.1
Weber, UT	49057	342,556	14.9	58.9	26.3	284,476	6,344	60.9	13,192	78.7	15.7	3.0
VERMONT	50000	1,698,930	6.0	79.2	14.7	1,350,880	15,449	60.6	38,879	86.5	10.3	2.1
Addison, VT	50001	100,019	4.6	78.1	17.3	79,638	16,121	60.0	2,905	84.8	11.3	1.7
Bennington, VT	50003	104,166	7.8	73.5	18.7	70,310	16,661	55.0	2,352	79.9	14.4	4.4
Caledonia, VT	50005	74,612	8.8	83.2	8.0	51,140	16,189	58.3	1,972	91.1	6.8	1.4
Chittenden, VT	50007	381,040	5.2	80.8	14.0	322,856	14,807	62.0	11,571	92.3	6.5	0.8
Essex, VT	50009	16,733	6.9	79.3	13.8	11,526	15,682	56.4	339	73.5	25.7	0.9
Franklin, VT	50011	142,172	6.9	78.6	14.6	113,492	13,495	62.0	2,534	76.8	20.3	1.1
Grand Isle, VT	50013	17,241	6.3	87.2	6.5	11,379	17,863	58.3	333	85.0	10.2	2.7
Lamoille, VT	50015	66,858	5.5	81.8	12.8	52,687	14,514	58.7	1,457	85.2	8.7	2.7
Orange, VT	50017	88,738	4.8	80.3	14.8	71,668	16,729	58.3	1,766	89.1	8.4	1.1
Orleans, VT	50019	79,023	8.2	76.7	15.1	64,808	15,811	60.5	1,431	72.7	18.5	5.5
Rutland, VT	50021	170,684	5.8	76.6	17.6	138,609	15,539	64.5	3,557	88.4	9.4	1.3
Washington, VT	50023	142,650	5.6	84.1	10.4	126,232	14,281	60.6	3,528	84.0	9.9	3.8
Windham, VT	50025	144,632	7.3	75.4	17.3	103,361	17,357	62.3	2,519	86.7	10.8	1.8
Windsor, VT	50027	170,362	5.0	79.5	15.5	133,174	17,056	57.0	2,615	83.4	11.6	4.4
VIRGINIA	51000	15,251,481	6.0	41.4	52.6	13,499,037	10,930	60.7	451,221	84.9	11.0	2.7
Accomack, VA	51001	53,540	11.6	57.7	30.7	50,122	9,652	60.3	1,633	77.9	15.4	4.4
Albemarle, VA	51003	(7)	(7)	(7)	(7)	(7)	(7)	(7)	7,687	92.1	6.7	1.1
Alleghany, VA	51005	33,063	7.4	58.2	34.4	29,343	10,132	59.5	819	88.2	8.3	3.1
Amelia, VA	51007	18,666	9.8	59.5	30.7	17,554	9,494	60.9	627	76.4	20.3	3.4
Amherst, VA	51009	51,498	7.9	59.7	32.3	45,695	9,578	64.0	2,235	87.6	7.0	5.5
Appomattox, VA	51011	23,730	7.4	64.1	28.5	21,024	9,357	60.2	796	82.2	17.6	0.0
Arlington, VA	51013	424,432	3.0	12.0	85.0	361,647	18,452	60.0	5,526	89.0	7.9	1.7
Augusta, VA	51015	123,659	6.5	51.8	41.7	103,983	9,454	63.0	3,578	78.6	16.2	4.2
Bath, VA	51017	9,971	7.7	21.0	71.3	9,388	12,825	52.4	147	59.2	30.6	10.2
Bedford, VA	51019	(8)	(8)	(8)	(8)	(8)	(8)	(8)	3,473	82.3	14.3	0.8
Bland, VA	51021	9,438	8.5	68.2	23.3	8,462	9,099	62.1	245	85.3	14.7	0.0
Botetourt, VA	51023	53,640	4.6	51.0	44.4	48,739	9,852	62.2	1,750	80.8	12.3	5.5
Brunswick, VA	51025	25,732	12.8	62.1	25.1	24,463	11,289	51.2	1,036	88.5	8.3	1.8
Buchanan, VA	51027	39,618	11.8	60.0	28.2	37,086	10,911	59.9	1,135	82.9	9.3	5.3
Buckingham, VA	51029	24,155	10.2	62.0	27.8	22,053	10,664	59.5	418	69.1	2.2	28.7
Campbell, VA	51031	81,224	6.1	68.5	25.4	78,455	8,983	60.5	2,738	82.4	14.8	0.6
Caroline, VA	51033	46,560	6.5	50.2	43.3	38,162	8,992	62.5	1,522	69.8	23.4	5.9
Carroll, VA	51035	45,181	12.0	58.5	29.6	39,504	9,692	57.8	1,236	82.9	11.7	2.9
Charles City County, VA.	51036	12,762	6.0	43.4	50.6	11,103	12,926	52.1	437	79.2	16.9	1.8
Charlotte, VA	51037	22,969	8.1	70.7	21.2	21,777	9,980	57.0	680	80.9	19.1	0.0
Chesterfield, VA	51041	638,573	4.1	49.1	46.8	546,995	9,259	62.5	19,454	88.6	7.5	2.7
Clarke, VA	51043	24,347	4.6	35.3	60.1	20,592	9,494	59.9	496	94.0	6.1	0.0
Craig, VA	51045	8,158	8.5	61.0	30.4	6,834	9,735	59.5	305	63.6	30.8	3.6
Culpeper, VA	51047	81,415	5.3	44.1	50.5	71,244	9,635	62.5	2,422	72.8	21.0	4.1

Note. Data in columns 26 through 41 from the American Community Survey are subject to sampling error, which can be especially large in small counties and small population groups. See notes and definitions for more information.
[7]Albermarle county is included with Charlottesville city.
[8]Bedford county is included with Bedford city.

Table C-1. Population, School, and Student Characteristics by County, Selected Years—*Continued*

County	State/ County Code	High school graduates, 2006–2010			College enrollment, 2006–2010		College graduates, 2006–2010 (percent)						
		Population 25 years and over	High school diploma or less (percent)	High school diploma or more (percent)	Number	Percent public	Bachelor's degree or more	+/- U.S. percent with Bachelor's degree or more	Non-Hispanic White	Black or African American	American Indian and Alaska Native	Asian, Hawaiian, and Pacific Islander	Hispanic or Latino[3]
		30	31	32	33	34	35	36	37	38	39	40	41
UTAH—*(Continued)*													
Iron, UT	49021	22,930	36.0	91.0	5,757	79.9	28.2	0.3	29.4	0.0	0.9	100.0	9.1
Juab, UT	49023	5,443	48.2	91.5	352	88.9	13.1	-14.8	13.7	0.0	0.0	0.0	5.1
Kane, UT	49025	4,769	38.5	89.5	219	76.7	23.7	-4.2	22.8	0.0	0.9	52.6	52.4
Millard, UT	49027	7,263	44.2	86.4	313	85.6	19.3	-8.6	20.8	46.9	4.7	0.0	9.1
Morgan, UT	49029	5,104	32.9	96.9	404	83.2	27.1	-0.8	26.7	0.0	0.0	0.0	66.7
Piute, UT	49031	1,014	50.3	88.7	45	100.0	16.2	-11.7	16.6	0.0	0.0	0.0	0.0
Rich, UT	49033	1,395	39.4	94.9	98	90.8	22.2	-5.7	22.3	100.0	0.0	0.0	0.0
Salt Lake, UT	49035	599,749	35.6	88.9	78,546	80.9	30.1	2.2	33.4	22.2	11.8	33.4	10.8
San Juan, UT	49037	8,162	51.1	81.8	577	70.7	17.2	-10.7	31.3	0.0	3.4	13.6	0.0
Sanpete, UT	49039	14,350	42.7	88.2	3,128	79.5	18.7	-9.2	20.7	0.0	0.0	0.0	4.6
Sevier, UT	49041	12,088	44.1	90.0	897	94.0	16.9	-11.0	17.3	0.0	6.7	12.0	4.7
Summit, UT	49043	22,867	24.7	93.7	1,145	71.1	50.8	22.9	54.7	50.6	42.9	63.2	11.0
Tooele, UT	49045	30,996	39.1	91.8	2,662	79.0	18.6	-9.3	19.6	19.3	37.0	11.3	6.6
Uintah, UT	49047	17,663	52.6	84.5	1,121	84.8	14.8	-13.1	16.6	0.0	4.3	1.3	6.5
Utah, UT	49049	233,978	24.8	93.3	69,369	41.6	35.5	7.6	37.3	27.3	18.0	41.9	17.8
Wasatch, UT	49051	12,755	31.7	91.0	1,054	70.3	31.1	3.2	33.4	0.0	28.3	50.0	5.9
Washington, UT	49053	80,011	37.7	90.7	8,231	86.4	24.0	-3.9	25.5	29.5	12.7	25.5	6.2
Wayne, UT	49055	1,750	41.0	90.0	70	84.3	22.7	-5.2	24.7	0.0	0.0	0.0	0.0
Weber, UT	49057	132,150	40.7	89.1	15,279	82.5	22.5	-5.4	24.3	24.7	14.5	30.7	9.1
VERMONT	50000	426,409	41.5	90.6	47,991	61.8	33.3	5.4	33.2	35.2	14.7	48.6	36.9
Addison, VT	50001	24,213	44.5	89.8	3,529	26.2	32.6	4.7	32.4	27.1	16.3	64.8	38.1
Bennington, VT	50003	26,087	43.2	89.8	2,187	51.6	31.1	3.2	31.2	33.3	0.0	33.6	31.9
Caledonia, VT	50005	21,325	46.5	88.5	2,042	79.8	27.5	-0.4	27.5	33.9	31.2	22.7	34.5
Chittenden, VT	50007	99,254	29.9	92.7	19,909	69.8	44.8	16.9	44.8	35.4	16.5	53.0	46.1
Essex, VT	50009	4,686	61.6	82.8	186	65.6	15.9	-12.0	15.3	53.3	50.0	28.6	50.0
Franklin, VT	50011	31,963	52.7	87.8	1,899	79.9	21.2	-6.7	21.4	13.1	4.4	20.2	11.2
Grand Isle, VT	50013	5,176	43.3	92.1	310	72.3	28.6	0.7	28.7	100.0	22.2	100.0	57.9
Lamoille, VT	50015	16,306	38.9	92.2	1,725	89.4	34.6	6.7	34.7	0.0	42.5	4.4	65.5
Orange, VT	50017	20,331	44.8	90.3	1,841	77.6	29.2	1.3	29.0	35.9	0.0	58.4	43.5
Orleans, VT	50019	19,207	56.4	85.0	906	78.9	19.9	-8.0	20.1	37.9	0.0	12.5	11.1
Rutland, VT	50021	43,640	48.5	89.1	4,317	66.1	26.3	-1.6	26.3	51.2	10.0	32.2	22.7
Washington, VT	50023	41,179	37.8	92.4	4,093	32.1	37.4	9.5	37.5	22.6	11.0	68.7	23.9
Windham, VT	50025	31,535	40.8	91.3	2,669	42.3	33.8	5.9	33.8	56.1	3.3	28.6	50.4
Windsor, VT	50027	41,507	42.0	91.6	2,378	53.1	32.8	4.9	32.7	40.6	29.1	64.4	29.8
VIRGINIA	51000	5,208,536	39.9	86.1	607,582	75.7	33.8	5.9	37.0	18.5	19.4	56.0	22.7
Accomack, VA	51001	24,217	59.1	78.9	1,212	88.9	18.0	-9.9	21.8	7.9	25.0	20.3	21.2
Albemarle, VA	51003	63,226	28.0	90.9	11,797	91.2	51.6	23.7	55.1	15.8	71.4	79.4	27.6
Alleghany, VA	51005	11,741	56.5	81.8	739	84.8	14.9	-13.0	15.0	11.4	0.0	53.3	0.0
Amelia, VA	51007	8,617	62.0	78.0	328	84.5	13.1	-14.8	13.7	11.2	100.0	100.0	4.6
Amherst, VA	51009	21,925	56.7	78.3	2,432	45.0	15.6	-12.3	17.9	6.1	15.0	21.4	6.4
Appomattox, VA	51011	10,218	62.1	79.8	595	73.9	11.8	-16.1	12.9	7.9	0.0	0.0	0.0
Arlington, VA	51013	146,410	17.0	92.5	18,116	53.7	70.1	42.2	80.8	38.3	35.5	71.0	35.3
Augusta, VA	51015	52,058	58.4	83.7	2,720	73.9	19.1	-8.8	19.9	4.5	18.1	50.0	5.8
Bath, VA	51017	3,657	68.2	79.2	169	72.8	11.5	-16.4	10.6	32.5	0.0	0.0	0.0
Bedford, VA	51019	47,831	47.8	85.0	2,967	57.6	24.2	-3.7	24.4	14.2	37.8	56.1	26.6
Bland, VA	51021	5,163	57.5	83.0	80	76.3	12.0	-15.9	12.2	0.0	0.0	31.9	0.0
Botetourt, VA	51023	23,387	46.7	89.2	1,377	73.5	22.9	-5.0	22.9	26.9	37.5	17.5	36.6
Brunswick, VA	51025	12,403	65.1	67.3	1,306	41.3	11.9	-16.0	14.5	9.5	0.0	75.0	0.0
Buchanan, VA	51027	18,082	67.8	63.7	996	81.1	8.9	-19.0	8.7	3.4	0.0	42.3	22.6
Buckingham, VA	51029	13,773	74.0	61.6	228	71.9	12.4	-15.5	15.9	7.9	0.0	0.0	0.0
Campbell, VA	51031	36,943	53.2	82.6	3,254	46.6	16.3	-11.6	17.8	5.0	14.2	52.2	27.1
Caroline, VA	51033	18,818	57.7	81.8	1,069	81.7	15.5	-12.4	18.0	9.4	4.9	44.1	16.9
Carroll, VA	51035	22,107	63.1	72.4	1,276	81.8	11.7	-16.2	12.1	0.0	0.0	0.0	6.9
Charles City County, VA	51036	5,256	66.1	74.9	252	81.3	10.9	-17.0	16.2	7.2	2.3	69.2	6.9
Charlotte, VA	51037	8,657	58.5	71.6	772	85.6	15.1	-12.8	20.0	4.1	0.0	0.0	46.7
Chesterfield, VA	51041	200,663	35.4	89.4	21,802	81.0	35.7	7.8	38.4	29.2	8.2	45.3	16.3
Clarke, VA	51043	9,949	43.8	87.5	419	70.6	29.2	1.3	29.8	13.9	43.8	93.8	11.3
Craig, VA	51045	3,660	56.3	83.4	196	89.3	13.6	-14.3	13.6	0.0	0.0	0.0	0.0
Culpeper, VA	51047	30,319	51.5	82.6	1,973	76.6	21.6	-6.3	24.0	11.1	0.0	38.0	16.3

Note. Data in columns 26 through 41 from the American Community Survey are subject to sampling error, which can be especially large in small counties and small population groups. See notes and definitions for more information.
[3]May be of any race.

Table C-1. Population, School, and Student Characteristics by County, Selected Years—*Continued*

County	State/ County Code	County Type[1]	Population, 2010: Total	Population, 2010: Percent 5–17 years	Percent of related children 5–17 years in poverty, 2010	Percent of children under 19 years with no health insurance, 2010	Number of schools and students, 2010–2011: School districts	Number of schools and students, 2010–2011: Schools	Number of schools and students, 2010–2011: Students	Resident enrollment, 2006–2010, K–12 enrollment: Number	Resident enrollment, 2006–2010, K–12 enrollment: Percent public
			1	2	3	4	5	6	7	8	9
VIRGINIA—*(Continued)*											
Cumberland, VA	51049	1	10,052	16.5	23.1	9.2	1	3	1,503	1,771	86.5
Dickenson, VA	51051	9	15,903	15.4	23.8	7.9	1	9	2,521	2,352	99.0
Dinwiddie, VA	51053	1	28,001	17.1	14.6	8.6	3	10	4,570	4,877	95.8
Essex, VA	51057	8	11,151	16.2	22.5	7.1	2	4	1,634	1,705	87.0
Fairfax, VA	51059	1	1,081,726	17.5	6.7	7.0	4	213[10]	174,479[10]	185,323	86.8
Fauquier, VA	51061	1	65,203	19.4	7.4	7.2	3	22	11,286	12,677	86.0
Floyd, VA	51063	8	15,279	16.4	17.6	9.8	1	5	2,071	2,394	80.5
Fluvanna, VA	51065	3	25,691	16.8	8.2	7.5	3	7	3,773	4,189	92.0
Franklin, VA	51067	2	56,159	15.2	20.7	9.1	1	16	7,408	8,705	93.1
Frederick, VA	51069	3	78,305	18.8	9.4	8.3	1	1	([13])	14,643	89.2
Giles, VA	51071	3	17,286	16.4	16.4	7.4	1	6	2,507	2,839	87.1
Gloucester, VA	51073	1	36,858	17.1	12.0	7.9	2	10	6,015	6,330	93.9
Goochland, VA	51075	1	21,717	15.6	8.4	6.8	1	5	2,481	3,124	74.5
Grayson, VA	51077	9	15,533	14.5	24.9	8.8	1	8	1,950	2,265	99.4
Greene, VA	51079	3	18,403	17.8	12.2	9.2	1	7	2,882	3,311	87.2
Greensville, VA	51081	6	12,243	12.3	22.5	6.5	([9])	([9])	([9])	1,468	93.1
Halifax, VA	51083	6	36,241	16.5	23.0	7.6	1	12	5,910	6,229	96.2
Hanover, VA	51085	1	99,863	19.6	5.5	5.5	1	26	18,628	19,402	92.5
Henrico, VA	51087	1	306,935	17.6	11.4	7.0	1	78	49,405	53,273	90.3
Henry, VA	51089	4	54,151	15.1	24.3	9.6	4	17	7,491	8,652	93.9
Highland, VA	51091	9	2,321	12.1	18.9	15.7	1	2	238	271	94.1
Isle of Wight, VA	51093	1	35,270	17.5	10.3	6.5	1	9	5,515	6,363	82.2
James City County, VA	51095	1	67,009	16.3	8.9	6.2	3[12]	16[12]	10,857[12]	10,746	90.0
King and Queen, VA	51097	1	6,945	15.6	17.2	9.8	1	3	781	898	84.3
King George, VA	51099	8	23,584	20.1	8.0	5.7	1	5	4,138	4,464	87.1
King William, VA	51101	1	15,935	18.4	9.6	7.4	3	8	3,010	3,020	87.1
Lancaster, VA	51103	9	11,391	12.1	24.0	10.1	1	3	1,321	1,433	90.7
Lee, VA	51105	8	25,587	15.1	28.3	7.4	1	14	3,597	4,030	94.6
Loudoun, VA	51107	1	312,311	21.7	3.8	4.7	1	79	63,142	60,800	89.0
Louisa, VA	51109	1	33,153	16.0	14.6	8.2	1	6	4,731	5,154	89.5
Lunenburg, VA	51111	9	12,914	14.0	25.5	8.9	1	4	1,653	1,882	85.0
Madison, VA	51113	8	13,308	16.6	14.9	10.7	1	4	1,849	2,136	95.7
Mathews, VA	51115	1	8,978	14.3	14.4	9.9	1	3	1,212	1,269	96.7
Mecklenburg, VA	51117	7	32,727	14.7	25.3	8.0	1	10	4,816	4,800	96.0
Middlesex, VA	51119	8	10,959	12.1	19.7	10.4	1	3	1,191	1,576	81.3
Montgomery, VA	51121	3	94,392	11.4	15.3	7.5	2	21	9,553	10,335	92.1
Nelson, VA	51125	3	15,020	14.4	18.8	10.2	1	4	1,966	2,175	95.8
New Kent, VA	51127	1	18,429	17.0	7.3	8.6	1	4	2,888	3,073	96.4
Northampton, VA	51131	9	12,389	14.2	29.0	10.4	2	5	1,800	1,762	85.2
Northumberland, VA	51133	9	12,330	12.1	25.1	11.6	2	4	1,474	1,545	91.4
Nottoway, VA	51135	6	15,853	15.0	26.4	9.0	2	6	2,347	2,450	91.6
Orange, VA	51137	6	33,481	16.9	13.1	8.3	1	10	5,237	5,790	91.0
Page, VA	51139	6	24,042	16.1	20.1	8.2	1	9	3,697	3,952	92.6
Patrick, VA	51141	8	18,490	14.3	25.4	8.6	1	7	2,507	2,865	92.3
Pittsylvania, VA	51143	3	63,506	16.1	19.1	8.1	2	20	9,258	10,615	89.8
Powhatan, VA	51145	1	28,046	18.0	7.7	8.5	2	8	4,476	4,706	88.7
Prince Edward, VA	51147	6	23,368	13.0	24.9	7.2	1	3	2,551	3,443	85.1
Prince George, VA	51149	1	35,725	17.0	11.6	6.6	2	9	6,357	6,545	97.3
Prince William, VA	51153	1	402,002	20.6	8.0	7.8	3	87	79,358	77,652	91.1
Pulaski, VA	51155	3	34,872	14.6	20.1	6.8	2	9	4,685	5,051	97.6
Rappahannock, VA	51157	8	7,373	15.4	13.8	11.6	1	2	928	1,158	76.3
Richmond, VA	51159	9	9,254	12.9	21.1	10.1	3	5	1,214	1,261	93.0
Roanoke, VA	51161	2	92,376	16.8	7.9	6.3	1	27	14,622	15,864	91.8
Rockbridge, VA	51163	6	22,307	14.4	14.9	8.1	1	7	2,798	3,284	94.8
Rockingham, VA	51165	3	76,314	17.6	13.2	11.2	([14])	([14])	([14])	12,681	86.7

[1]County type codes are from the Economic Research Service of the United States Department of Agriculture. See notes and definitions for more information.
[9]Fairfax city is included with Fairfax county.
[10]Falls Church city is included with Fairfax county.
[12]Greensville county is included with Emporia city.
[13]Williamsburg city is included with James City county.
[14]Rockingham county is included with Harrisonburg city.

Table C-1. Population, School, and Student Characteristics by County, Selected Years—*Continued*

County	State/ County Code	Characteristics of students, 2010–2011				Number of graduates, 2008–2009	Staff and students, 2010–2011			
		Percent with IEP[2]	Percent eligible for free or reduced lunch	Percent minority	Percent English-language learners		Total staff	Number of teachers	Student/ teacher ratio	Central admin. staff
		10	11	12	13	14	15	16	17	18
VIRGINIA—*(Continued)*										
Cumberland, VA	51049	10.5	63.3	49.2	1.7	113	241	74	20.3	8
Dickenson, VA	51051	16.3	52.9	1.5	. . .	161	448	132	19.1	9
Dinwiddie, VA	51053	12.4	54.4	45.9	0.8	303	757	219	20.9	17
Essex, VA	51057	14.0	66.2	60.5	0.7	110	279	94	17.4	7
Fairfax, VA	51059	13.9[10]	24.8	55.5	20.5[10]	12,003[10]	32,890[10]	9,761[10]	17.9[10]	1,339[10]
Fauquier, VA	51061	11.0	23.5	25.1	3.6	807	2,148	713	15.8	57
Floyd, VA	51063	14.6	44.9	8.1	1.6	132	391	129	16.1	17
Fluvanna, VA	51065	13.4	24.9	25.3	0.8	243	590	143	26.4	8
Franklin, VA	51067	15.8	49.0	16.8	1.4	425	1,338	449	16.5	28
Frederick, VA	51069	([13])	30.2	19.2	([13])	([13])	([13])	([13])	([13])	([13])
Giles, VA	51071	15.7	42.2	5.5	0.1	135	417	158	15.8	10
Gloucester, VA	51073	11.7	32.7	17.5	0.2	389	959	345	17.4	20
Goochland, VA	51075	13.0	23.5	28.5	1.3	154	407	139	17.8	10
Grayson, VA	51077	14.9	55.0	7.6	1.0	152	413	116	16.8	13
Greene, VA	51079	13.4	34.2	21.8	3.2	201	526	176	16.4	10
Greensville, VA	51081	([9])	72.5	74.4	([9])	([9])	([9])	([9])	([9])	([9])
Halifax, VA	51083	18.5	61.4	49.6	0.6	389	1,372	361	16.4	33
Hanover, VA	51085	13.5	11.5	16.3	0.6	1,446	2,933	1,000	18.6	55
Henrico, VA	51087	12.7	37.0	55.2	4.4	3,090	5,166	2,619	18.9	89
Henry, VA	51089	13.9	56.0	37.6	5.3	496	1,193	388	19.3	25
Highland, VA	51091	17.6	66.0	4.6	0.8	27	69	18	13.3	3
Isle of Wight, VA	51093	12.1	33.4	37.8	0.5	390	858	322	17.1	21
James City County, VA	51095	14.2[12]	27.0	32.8	2.1[12]	679[12]	2,269[12]	654[12]	16.6[12]	26[12]
King and Queen, VA	51097	14.0	72.0	48.1	1.7	52	98	56	14.0	6
King George, VA	51099	12.3	26.4	30.7	0.3	268	737	205	20.2	17
King William, VA	51101	11.5	33.6	26.5	0.6	170	535	176	17.1	18
Lancaster, VA	51103	13.3	69.8	55.0	0.2	98	208	65	20.3	7
Lee, VA	51105	19.8	57.4	2.2	0.2	183	767	205	17.5	12
Loudoun, VA	51107	10.5	16.0	42.1	7.5	3,389	10,545	3,378	18.7	281
Louisa, VA	51109	15.6	44.3	27.8	0.4	328	834	287	16.5	20
Lunenburg, VA	51111	13.8	65.6	48.8	1.7	95	335	89	18.5	12
Madison, VA	51113	10.2	34.2	18.2	0.8	141	294	118	15.7	10
Mathews, VA	51115	14.4	34.2	17.3	0.8	109	276	66	18.3	5
Mecklenburg, VA	51117	12.7	58.0	50.6	0.6	309	767	323	14.9	27
Middlesex, VA	51119	12.8	47.5	27.9	0.7	107	234	88	13.5	6
Montgomery, VA	51121	9.9	36.7	14.9	1.4	580	1,711	633	15.1	48
Nelson, VA	51125	12.7	47.1	26.4	2.0	108	354	126	15.6	10
New Kent, VA	51127	12.5	21.7	22.0	0.2	173	476	166	17.4	9
Northampton, VA	51131	15.4	75.0	67.1	9.5	112	274	128	14.1	22
Northumberland, VA	51133	12.6	50.8	46.2	0.9	99	245	86	17.2	7
Nottoway, VA	51135	11.0	58.5	52.1	3.7	148	358	133	17.7	11
Orange, VA	51137	9.3	38.1	29.1	1.7	338	721	271	19.3	23
Page, VA	51139	11.5	50.6	7.2	0.8	253	653	232	15.9	14
Patrick, VA	51141	17.4	56.0	13.2	2.8	188	426	150	16.7	14
Pittsylvania, VA	51143	14.5	53.3	29.9	1.5	601	1,488	581	15.9	41
Powhatan, VA	51145	12.6	17.2	16.8	0.3	288	751	245	18.3	21
Prince Edward, VA	51147	14.4	63.2	62.1	0.4	132	471	159	16.0	16
Prince George, VA	51149	11.6	36.7	48.1	1.1	383	897	383	16.6	22
Prince William, VA	51153	11.5	35.3	63.7	16.9	4,590	9,723	4,141	19.2	329
Pulaski, VA	51155	17.3	49.6	12.0	0.5	318	939	295	15.9	19
Rappahannock, VA	51157	14.1	34.1	11.7	. . .	80	126	60	15.5	3
Richmond, VA	51159	13.2	50.2	42.8	6.3	87	180	76	15.9	8
Roanoke, VA	51161	14.6	24.1	17.0	2.0	1,140	2,435	783	18.7	44
Rockbridge, VA	51163	12.6	40.6	11.3	0.9	211	509	188	14.9	22
Rockingham, VA	51165	([14])	36.8	15.8	([14])	([14])	([14])	([14])	([14])	([14])

[2]IEP=Individual Education Program. See notes and definitions for more information.
[9]Fairfax city is included with Fairfax county.
[10]Falls Church city is included with Fairfax county.
[12]Greensville county is included with Emporia city.
[13]Williamsburg city is included with James City county.
[14]Rockingham county is included with Harrisonburg city.
. . . = Not available.

Table C-1. Population, School, and Student Characteristics by County, Selected Years—*Continued*

County	State/ County Code	Revenues, 2008–2009				Current expenditures, 2008–2009			Resident population 16 to 19 years, 2006–2010			
		Total revenue ($1,000's)	Percentage of revenue from			Amount ($1,000's)	Amount per student	Percent for instruction	Total population 16 to 19 years	Percent enrolled in school	Percent high school graduates, not enrolled in school	Percent not enrolled, not grads, not employed, or not in labor force
			Federal government	State government	Local government							
		19	20	21	22	23	24	25	26	27	28	29
VIRGINIA—*(Continued)*												
Cumberland, VA	51049	17,786	13.0	60.3	26.7	16,535	10,668	57.7	557	84.4	4.0	2.7
Dickenson, VA	51051	29,426	10.2	62.6	27.3	26,868	10,607	59.8	754	67.0	26.4	3.9
Dinwiddie, VA	51053	53,744	5.4	57.9	36.7	44,461	9,510	56.3	1,615	77.2	18.0	4.3
Essex, VA	51057	20,168	9.2	49.2	41.5	16,849	10,343	62.9	589	83.7	10.7	5.6
Fairfax, VA	51059	2,371,152	4.0	19.4	76.6	2,233,687[10]	13,210[10]	60.9[10]	52,768	93.3	4.8	1.2
Fauquier, VA	51061	147,361	3.2	25.7	71.1	125,326	11,126	64.9	3,580	83.0	14.1	2.5
Floyd, VA	51063	21,333	6.7	60.8	32.4	19,356	9,383	61.9	685	88.8	7.0	0.4
Fluvanna, VA	51065	40,195	4.4	52.5	43.1	37,496	10,120	67.7	1,003	80.6	12.8	6.2
Franklin, VA	51067	84,380	7.8	51.2	41.0	72,233	9,723	58.8	2,991	79.1	19.4	0.0
Frederick, VA	51069	([13])	([13])	([13])	([13])	([13])	([13])	([13])	3,940	82.8	13.8	1.8
Giles, VA	51071	27,936	5.8	61.5	32.7	23,264	9,014	63.0	856	85.9	9.9	2.8
Gloucester, VA	51073	66,823	5.6	51.3	43.2	59,140	9,803	58.0	2,090	77.9	14.5	3.9
Goochland, VA	51075	28,744	3.9	21.0	75.1	26,632	10,996	59.8	530	95.9	2.6	1.5
Grayson, VA	51077	28,381	8.4	54.3	37.2	22,381	10,875	62.4	838	87.4	7.5	5.1
Greene, VA	51079	32,267	5.9	55.0	39.1	28,291	9,920	67.1	839	69.0	30.4	0.6
Greensville, VA	51081	([9])	([9])	([9])	([9])	([9])	([9])	([9])	698	56.6	27.1	8.9
Halifax, VA	51083	63,671	8.9	65.8	25.3	61,145	10,152	58.9	1,763	84.3	10.6	3.5
Hanover, VA	51085	206,157	3.6	44.7	51.7	179,181	9,446	68.0	6,094	90.3	7.8	0.5
Henrico, VA	51087	510,259	6.0	48.2	45.8	444,889	9,081	60.3	14,872	87.6	9.3	2.2
Henry, VA	51089	82,038	10.1	64.9	24.9	70,181	9,280	60.6	2,750	77.9	10.3	8.2
Highland, VA	51091	4,466	7.0	42.6	50.4	3,650	13,370	61.2	103	81.6	18.5	0.0
Isle of Wight, VA	51093	66,779	5.6	45.7	48.7	56,276	10,241	62.9	1,711	88.5	7.7	1.9
James City County, VA	51095	143,941[12]	3.4[12]	30.3[12]	66.3[12]	120,070[12]	11,393[12]	61.6[12]	3,143	88.0	9.9	2.0
King and Queen, VA	51097	11,853	11.9	46.2	41.8	10,682	13,319	56.0	447	63.5	36.5	0.0
King George, VA	51099	40,860	4.4	50.5	45.1	33,998	8,366	61.3	1,344	68.8	28.3	0.9
King William, VA	51101	35,874	3.7	54.0	42.3	30,369	10,174	62.1	758	74.3	22.2	3.6
Lancaster, VA	51103	16,945	7.8	21.9	70.3	14,893	10,792	56.6	513	79.0	19.3	1.8
Lee, VA	51105	42,884	15.1	71.2	13.7	39,853	10,789	61.3	1,380	89.1	7.3	3.6
Loudoun, VA	51107	799,102	2.2	23.5	74.3	740,357	13,013	63.5	13,050	93.5	5.2	0.5
Louisa, VA	51109	51,622	5.6	39.0	55.5	46,703	9,861	60.0	1,465	78.6	15.6	2.7
Lunenburg, VA	51111	18,913	11.5	64.6	23.9	17,092	10,138	60.9	639	85.9	10.3	0.3
Madison, VA	51113	18,996	5.5	48.9	45.6	17,359	9,283	60.4	669	86.6	13.5	0.0
Mathews, VA	51115	13,589	5.5	42.4	52.1	12,188	9,673	60.8	430	81.6	14.4	4.0
Mecklenburg, VA	51117	47,904	9.1	64.7	26.2	43,788	9,053	64.2	1,313	78.1	12.8	7.5
Middlesex, VA	51119	14,272	7.1	30.5	62.4	12,507	9,726	54.4	494	90.3	8.5	0.0
Montgomery, VA	51121	112,057	5.9	51.2	42.9	98,314	10,112	61.0	13,126	96.7	2.3	0.5
Nelson, VA	51125	24,126	7.8	37.4	54.8	22,504	11,630	53.6	685	82.5	17.1	0.4
New Kent, VA	51127	26,754	4.0	52.8	43.2	25,527	9,169	58.6	877	78.3	13.0	8.7
Northampton, VA	51131	22,513	11.5	40.9	47.7	20,538	11,150	58.9	572	64.5	22.6	4.9
Northumberland, VA	51133	17,360	8.8	27.0	64.2	14,831	10,035	63.0	526	65.4	15.6	17.9
Nottoway, VA	51135	24,790	12.9	66.7	20.4	22,953	9,454	61.8	784	70.4	18.1	8.8
Orange, VA	51137	49,513	7.7	52.3	40.0	46,855	8,809	59.7	1,475	83.5	10.7	5.8
Page, VA	51139	42,102	6.9	51.8	41.3	35,135	9,529	64.7	1,233	83.5	13.1	2.7
Patrick, VA	51141	27,180	7.1	65.5	27.4	24,166	9,147	62.4	971	70.7	24.5	4.8
Pittsylvania, VA	51143	89,591	8.9	69.5	21.6	83,517	9,027	59.7	3,174	88.6	6.8	1.7
Powhatan, VA	51145	47,424	3.8	48.6	47.5	44,835	10,019	57.6	1,190	78.7	8.2	11.3
Prince Edward, VA	51147	29,127	9.6	61.4	29.0	27,427	10,488	62.5	2,987	93.5	2.5	2.5
Prince George, VA	51149	68,420	10.2	60.4	29.5	59,093	9,420	61.5	2,914	58.3	34.3	6.0
Prince William, VA	51153	934,669	4.3	41.3	54.5	773,119	10,459	57.6	21,078	83.3	11.6	2.5
Pulaski, VA	51155	48,164	8.8	63.5	27.7	46,468	9,583	57.1	1,662	77.7	15.8	6.4
Rappahannock, VA	51157	12,215	3.9	21.7	74.4	11,144	12,100	59.6	347	98.3	1.7	0.0
Richmond, VA	51159	14,414	5.9	53.3	40.9	12,907	10,641	58.4	291	85.2	14.8	0.0
Roanoke, VA	51161	169,418	4.1	49.3	46.6	140,562	9,410	65.1	4,836	91.4	6.9	1.5
Rockbridge, VA	51163	32,614	8.3	40.1	51.6	28,858	9,992	62.2	1,070	81.9	15.8	0.0
Rockingham, VA	51165	([14])	([14])	([14])	([14])	([14])	([14])	([14])	4,284	79.9	13.0	3.3

Note. Data in columns 26 through 41 from the American Community Survey are subject to sampling error, which can be especially large in small counties and small population groups. See notes and definitions for more information.
[9]Fairfax city is included with Fairfax county.
[10]Falls Church city is included with Fairfax county.
[12]Greensville county is included with Emporia city.
[13]Williamsburg city is included with James City county.
[14]Rockingham county is included with Harrisonburg city.

Table C-1. Population, School, and Student Characteristics by County, Selected Years—*Continued*

County	State/ County Code	High school graduates, 2006–2010			College enrollment, 2006–2010		College graduates, 2006–2010 (percent)						
		Population 25 years and over	High school diploma or less (percent)	High school diploma or more (percent)	Number	Percent public	Bachelor's degree or more	+/- U.S. percent with Bachelor's degree or more	Non-Hispanic White	Black or African American	American Indian and Alaska Native	Asian, Hawaiian, and Pacific Islander	Hispanic or Latino[3]
		30	31	32	33	34	35	36	37	38	39	40	41
VIRGINIA— *(Continued)*													
Cumberland, VA	51049	6,714	64.0	72.5	375	74.9	12.5	-15.4	14.0	9.6	100.0	0.0	5.3
Dickenson, VA	51051	11,204	72.4	64.2	601	96.0	8.6	-19.3	8.7	3.9	0.0	0.0	27.3
Dinwiddie, VA	51053	18,615	62.4	77.1	1,033	72.5	13.1	-14.8	13.3	11.5	25.6	37.3	30.7
Essex, VA	51057	7,620	56.4	80.1	299	71.2	16.6	-11.3	20.0	12.0	0.0	48.8	4.4
Fairfax, VA	51059	709,589	22.0	91.9	82,157	74.7	58.0	30.1	66.8	39.5	25.9	59.7	27.6
Fauquier, VA	51061	43,280	39.4	89.7	3,547	80.5	30.8	2.9	33.8	8.1	0.0	40.8	14.6
Floyd, VA	51063	10,768	55.0	79.5	469	78.7	19.3	-8.6	19.8	1.7	32.5	10.8	18.1
Fluvanna, VA	51065	17,906	44.5	85.5	911	78.8	25.8	-2.1	29.5	8.3	14.0	38.5	17.4
Franklin, VA	51067	38,779	57.0	79.9	2,589	51.1	15.2	-12.7	16.3	3.4	0.0	0.0	6.7
Frederick, VA	51069	50,725	50.2	83.0	3,392	77.7	23.1	-4.8	23.3	17.1	0.0	33.9	18.2
Giles, VA	51071	12,201	57.1	80.3	872	87.3	16.1	-11.8	15.8	17.8	0.0	0.0	48.6
Gloucester, VA	51073	25,420	48.0	85.3	1,784	77.4	19.2	-8.7	20.1	8.4	36.0	25.7	24.1
Goochland, VA	51075	16,292	47.3	79.3	277	55.2	30.7	2.8	41.9	4.3	0.0	46.9	63.9
Grayson, VA	51077	11,733	62.0	73.4	454	94.3	10.3	-17.6	10.4	0.0	0.0	84.2	15.9
Greene, VA	51079	12,216	55.9	79.5	362	85.9	20.0	-7.9	20.8	17.0	0.0	33.6	5.1
Greensville, VA	51081	8,708	75.6	69.7	364	90.9	5.5	-22.4	7.5	3.6	29.7	42.4	0.0
Halifax, VA	51083	25,544	61.5	72.9	1,619	77.3	13.2	-14.7	15.3	8.7	52.0	20.3	23.2
Hanover, VA	51085	65,816	37.6	91.2	5,874	64.4	33.0	5.1	33.8	22.8	10.4	63.8	33.8
Henrico, VA	51087	201,889	34.1	89.1	18,900	77.0	38.9	11.0	45.1	22.0	4.0	59.2	21.1
Henry, VA	51089	39,369	61.2	72.3	2,253	90.5	10.9	-17.0	12.0	7.5	0.0	27.0	1.1
Highland, VA	51091	1,965	63.2	73.7	36	58.3	21.4	-6.5	21.8	0.0	0.0	0.0	0.0
Isle of Wight, VA	51093	24,290	44.7	86.2	2,010	75.1	25.1	-2.8	29.0	13.3	0.0	47.9	28.6
James City County, VA	51095	45,744	28.0	93.3	3,351	81.6	45.0	17.1	50.8	9.9	0.0	52.5	24.5
King and Queen, VA	51097	4,778	66.8	75.8	182	78.6	9.9	-18.0	12.9	3.8	0.0	0.0	0.0
King George, VA	51099	14,651	40.2	90.2	904	83.1	30.5	2.6	34.2	14.3	34.1	36.6	23.4
King William, VA	51101	10,411	53.2	87.0	579	90.8	19.8	-8.1	22.8	7.2	23.7	30.8	10.0
Lancaster, VA	51103	9,033	45.3	82.3	267	85.0	27.7	-0.2	35.1	5.0	0.0	58.3	32.8
Lee, VA	51105	18,033	60.7	71.5	1,090	86.4	12.0	-15.9	12.5	2.1	0.0	9.3	9.1
Loudoun, VA	51107	185,191	21.0	93.5	18,160	72.5	57.2	29.3	61.1	45.6	36.2	64.8	29.2
Louisa, VA	51109	22,804	57.3	80.6	1,226	78.3	17.9	-10.0	19.8	8.3	21.4	10.9	36.2
Lunenburg, VA	51111	9,258	67.3	71.5	692	94.9	10.0	-17.9	13.1	4.9	0.0	0.0	10.7
Madison, VA	51113	9,396	54.5	80.4	674	82.3	20.7	-7.2	21.1	11.9	0.0	0.0	10.5
Mathews, VA	51115	6,695	53.1	84.5	285	81.4	20.6	-7.3	22.5	8.4	0.0	0.0	0.0
Mecklenburg, VA	51117	23,871	61.5	75.2	1,351	73.4	13.4	-14.5	17.2	5.9	0.0	58.1	10.3
Middlesex, VA	51119	8,400	46.0	87.6	224	95.1	27.5	-0.4	31.8	9.7	0.0	0.0	32.7
Montgomery, VA	51121	48,009	36.1	88.1	30,227	97.4	39.4	11.5	37.5	34.8	41.7	77.6	36.4
Nelson, VA	51125	11,197	54.8	77.7	426	53.3	22.9	-5.0	24.5	11.0	0.0	54.2	31.9
New Kent, VA	51127	12,561	49.0	86.3	721	88.1	22.6	-5.3	24.4	14.5	10.5	15.4	15.7
Northampton, VA	51131	9,063	58.0	78.0	311	78.1	18.8	-9.1	27.4	4.9	0.0	35.4	18.6
Northumberland, VA	51133	9,702	46.9	84.1	169	78.7	22.3	-5.6	26.4	7.5	0.0	100.0	20.8
Nottoway, VA	51135	11,175	65.1	72.8	735	78.5	11.6	-16.3	15.2	7.6	0.0	0.0	2.1
Orange, VA	51137	23,007	50.7	83.5	1,002	84.5	21.5	-6.4	23.1	11.1	0.0	38.9	8.9
Page, VA	51139	16,968	69.6	72.5	682	87.1	11.1	-16.8	11.1	0.7	0.0	18.8	39.6
Patrick, VA	51141	13,542	62.7	74.1	935	86.0	9.5	-18.4	9.8	2.1	0.0	0.0	30.7
Pittsylvania, VA	51143	44,887	59.9	76.0	2,893	72.6	12.8	-15.1	14.6	7.1	0.0	26.9	1.6
Powhatan, VA	51145	20,443	52.2	79.3	611	85.1	21.9	-6.0	26.7	4.5	0.0	24.6	21.6
Prince Edward, VA	51147	12,569	62.2	81.2	4,767	80.0	18.5	-9.4	25.9	7.2	0.0	78.6	18.6
Prince George, VA	51149	22,984	51.0	86.1	1,682	77.9	17.2	-10.7	18.8	14.2	8.9	39.0	5.7
Prince William, VA	51153	235,845	33.8	88.4	25,936	76.4	37.5	9.6	43.7	33.0	29.3	49.1	16.4
Pulaski, VA	51155	25,578	54.6	79.1	1,554	89.5	13.9	-14.0	13.7	7.7	0.0	100.0	27.0
Rappahannock, VA	51157	5,355	43.0	79.8	397	75.1	37.4	9.5	38.6	5.8	0.0	100.0	89.5
Richmond, VA	51159	6,833	66.6	74.6	279	98.9	9.8	-18.1	13.3	2.5	0.0	0.0	0.0
Roanoke, VA	51161	64,583	36.3	89.7	4,817	64.9	32.6	4.7	32.7	20.5	0.0	55.6	33.3
Rockbridge, VA	51163	16,132	55.5	79.6	1,351	58.5	21.8	-6.1	22.2	5.3	0.0	0.0	18.5
Rockingham, VA	51165	50,489	58.7	77.9	4,017	54.9	21.9	-6.0	22.2	8.7	15.7	69.6	13.7

Note. Data in columns 26 through 41 from the American Community Survey are subject to sampling error, which can be especially large in small counties and small population groups. See notes and definitions for more information.

[3]May be of any race.

Table C-1. Population, School, and Student Characteristics by County, Selected Years—*Continued*

County	State/ County Code	County Type[1]	Population, 2010		Percent of related children 5–17 years in poverty, 2010	Percent of children under 19 years with no health insurance, 2010	Number of schools and students, 2010–2011			Resident enrollment, 2006–2010 K–12 enrollment	
			Total	Percent 5–17 years			School districts	Schools	Students	Number	Percent public
			1	2	3	4	5	6	7	8	9
VIRGINIA—*(Continued)*											
Russell, VA	51167	6	28,897	15.1	22.6	7.4	2	15	4,333	4,486	96.4
Scott, VA	51169	3	23,177	14.3	22.2	6.8	2	15	3,712	3,371	97.6
Shenandoah, VA	51171	6	41,993	16.1	16.1	8.9	2	11	6,201	7,127	92.8
Smyth, VA	51173	6	32,208	15.4	23.8	6.9	2	15	4,855	5,110	98.1
Southampton, VA	51175	6	18,570	16.0	17.2	7.2	1	7	2,887	3,143	90.5
Spotsylvania, VA	51177	1	122,397	21.1	8.9	7.5	2	35	23,585	26,120	92.2
Stafford, VA	51179	1	128,961	22.1	5.6	5.6	2	31	27,257	28,157	92.1
Surry, VA	51181	1	7,058	15.8	17.6	8.4	1	3	977	1,238	75.4
Sussex, VA	51183	1	12,087	12.4	22.1	9.7	1	4	1,190	1,891	90.1
Tazewell, VA	51185	7	45,078	15.2	21.3	7.5	1	16	6,623	6,923	92.1
Warren, VA	51187	1	37,575	17.7	12.7	8.4	1	8	5,340	6,596	86.4
Washington, VA	51191	3	54,876	14.6	17.0	7.4	2	18	7,411	7,915	90.1
Westmoreland, VA	51193	7	17,454	14.7	23.8	9.2	2	6	2,307	2,796	92.1
Wise, VA	51195	7	41,452	15.2	25.0	6.6	2	18	6,655	6,567	96.1
Wythe, VA	51197	6	29,235	15.5	20.7	7.5	2	14	4,369	4,681	95.8
York, VA	51199	1	65,464	20.6	5.6	5.7	2	20	12,619	13,636	93.9
Alexandria City, VA	51510	1	139,966	10.0	15.9	6.7	1	19	11,999	12,518	84.6
Bedford City, VA	51515	3	6,222	14.1	26.6	6.3	2[8]	22[8]	10,592[8]	1,019	91.5
Bristol City, VA	51520	3	17,835	14.6	30.6	5.3	2	8	2,397	2,766	94.2
Buena Vista City, VA	51530	6	6,650	15.2	20.8	6.8	2	5	1,118	1,105	96.7
Charlottesville City, VA	51540	3	43,475	9.6	22.4	7.5	2	36	17242[7]	4,422	90.6
Chesapeake City, VA	51550	1	222,209	19.4	10.0	6.1	2	48	39,748	43,709	89.1
Colonial Heights City, VA	51570	1	17,411	16.9	13.5	7.1	1	5	2,909	2,955	97.7
Covington City, VA	51580	6	5,961	15.5	21.3	5.9	1	3	980	941	98.9
Danville City, VA	51590	3	43,055	15.2	36.8	5.7	1	17	6,416	7,055	88.3
Emporia City, VA	51595	6	5,927	18.9	30.0	6.0	2[9]	4[9]	2,669[9]	790	90.0
Fairfax City, VA	51600	1	22,565	14.7	7.2	7.0	1	([10])	([10])	3,231	86.6
Falls Church City, VA	51610	1	12,332	18.4	2.2	3.8	1	4	2,084	2,099	89.3
Franklin City, VA	51620	6	8,582	16.5	32.0	5.6	1	3	1,283	1,478	95.1
Fredericksburg City, VA	51630	1	24,286	13.1	23.5	6.9	1	5	3,220	2,870	90.1
Galax City, VA	51640	6	7,042	16.0	33.0	7.9	2	4	1,273	1,022	100.0
Hampton City, VA	51650	1	137,436	16.3	18.6	6.2	4	37	21,568	23,356	93.7
Harrisonburg City, VA	51660	3	48,914	10.1	20.7	8.3	3[14]	32[14]	16,542[14]	4,861	93.0
Hopewell City, VA	51670	1	22,591	17.4	25.4	6.5	1	8	4,235	4,161	97.6
Lexington City, VA	51678	6	7,042	7.5	11.9	7.9	1	2	488	444	96.2
Lynchburg City, VA	51680	3	75,568	13.5	26.1	6.5	4	20	8,646	10,358	83.3
Manassas City, VA	51683	1	37,821	20.0	16.2	9.4	1	9	6,986	7,123	93.2
Manassas Park City, VA	51685	1	14,273	19.4	12.5	10.5	2	5	2,957	2,719	92.5
Martinsville City, VA	51690	4	13,821	15.2	34.1	6.1	1	5	2,379	2,197	92.3
Newport News City, VA	51700	1	180,719	16.9	21.2	6.4	2	46	30,488	31,575	91.2
Norfolk City, VA	51710	1	242,803	14.1	24.5	6.5	5	65	33,787	36,517	88.9
Norton City, VA	51720	7	3,958	15.7	29.0	4.8	1	2	876	670	100.0
Petersburg City, VA	51730	1	32,420	14.2	34.8	5.4	3	11	4,557	5,164	97.4
Poquoson City, VA	51735	1	12,150	20.0	5.3	6.2	1	4	2,324	2,595	96.1
Portsmouth City, VA	51740	1	95,535	16.3	26.1	5.2	1	26	15,126	16,174	88.9
Radford City, VA	51750	3	16,408	9.4	16.9	6.5	1	4	1,567	1,494	96.9
Richmond City, VA	51760	1	204,214	12.3	33.8	6.3	7	151	23,931	26,586	87.1
Roanoke City, VA	51770	2	97,032	14.6	31.7	6.1	3	28	13,039	14,417	93.7
Salem City, VA	51775	2	24,802	15.1	11.9	6.3	1	6	3,932	3,492	96.5
Staunton City, VA	51790	4	23,746	13.8	22.1	6.2	4	10	2,776	3,243	88.8
Suffolk City, VA	51800	1	84,585	19.1	15.4	5.8	2	23	14,507	15,918	87.3
Virginia Beach City, VA	51810	1	437,994	17.4	10.2	6.2	1	85	71,185	78,880	90.3
Waynesboro City, VA	51820	4	21,006	16.0	27.9	6.3	1	6	3,298	3,503	94.9
Williamsburg City, VA	51830	1	14,068	6.9	21.5	7.0	([12])	([12])	([12])	1,117	91.6
Winchester City, VA	51840	3	26,203	15.4	22.6	8.7	2	24	17,019[13]	3,877	97.1

[1]County type codes are from the Economic Research Service of the United States Department of Agriculture. See notes and definitions for more information.
[8]Bedford county is included with Bedford city.
[9]Fairfax city is included with Fairfax county.
[10]Falls Church city is included with Fairfax county.
[12]Greensville county is included with Emporia city.
[14]Rockingham county is included with Harrisonburg city.

Table C-1. Population, School, and Student Characteristics by County, Selected Years—*Continued*

County	State/ County Code	Characteristics of students, 2010–2011				Number of graduates, 2008–2009	Staff and students, 2010–2011			
		Percent with IEP[2]	Percent eligible for free or reduced lunch	Percent minority	Percent English-language learners		Total staff	Number of teachers	Student/ teacher ratio	Central admin. staff
		10	11	12	13	14	15	16	17	18
VIRGINIA—*(Continued)*										
Russell, VA	51167	18.5	52.4	2.7	0.8	281	609	223	19.5	11
Scott, VA	51169	16.2	56.2	3.9	0.5	263	597	225	16.5	10
Shenandoah, VA	51171	11.9	39.4	17.3	4.9	416	1,256	368	16.8	20
Smyth, VA	51173	15.7	55.6	5.2	0.4	357	841	224	21.7	10
Southampton, VA	51175	13.0	43.4	44.8	...	169	514	153	18.9	14
Spotsylvania, VA	51177	11.3	29.1	35.3	3.5	1,669	2,531	1,306	18.1	74
Stafford, VA	51179	8.8	21.3	40.5	4.1	1,960	4,066	1,495	18.2	70
Surry, VA	51181	12.4	57.3	65.5	0.1	60	254	74	13.3	11
Sussex, VA	51183	16.3	80.2	76.5	1.4	81	276	88	13.5	8
Tazewell, VA	51185	14.7	48.6	4.8	0.3	378	1,050	389	17.0	22
Warren, VA	51187	11.3	35.7	17.2	2.2	417	888	320	16.7	23
Washington, VA	51191	15.4	42.9	6.5	0.6	515	1,073	456	16.3	28
Westmoreland, VA	51193	11.7	63.7	54.1	5.3	147	368	149	15.5	15
Wise, VA	51195	13.1	52.8	3.5	0.7	418	876	423	15.7	17
Wythe, VA	51197	9.6	46.7	7.8	0.2	286	583	234	18.7	19
York, VA	51199	9.5	18.6	34.3	1.4	991	2,165	718	17.6	24
Alexandria City, VA	51510	13.7	51.1	75.0	21.5	585	2,260	828	14.5	114
Bedford City, VA	51515	10.0[8]	58.8	26.1	1.0[8]	817[8]	1,761[8]	618[8]	17.1[8]	29[8]
Bristol City, VA	51520	16.4	61.8	15.9	0.3	138	431	153	15.6	20
Buena Vista City, VA	51530	14.4	41.7	10.6	...	65	207	74	15.2	5
Charlottesville City, VA	51540	12.0[7]	50.6	54.9	6.7[7]	1135[7]	2981[7]	1082[7]	15.9[7]	49[7]
Chesapeake City, VA	51550	17.1	31.1	48.5	1.3	2,871	6,071	2,068	19.2	218
Colonial Heights City, VA	51570	15.4	34.5	27.3	2.1	199	483	161	18.1	15
Covington City, VA	51580	17.1	54.1	24.3	0.3	51	147	64	15.3	6
Danville City, VA	51590	15.4	72.7	75.1	2.8	406	1,160	436	14.7	43
Emporia City, VA	51595	13.6[9]	59.3	76.4	1.9[9]	147[9]	390[9]	150[9]	17.8[9]	14[9]
Fairfax City, VA	51600	([10])	25.9	58.7	([10])	([10])	([10])	([10])	([10])	([10])
Falls Church City, VA	51610	11.7	8.7	23.5	6.5	152	404	142	14.7	14
Franklin City, VA	51620	14.7	76.7	81.8	0.1	91	241	86	14.9	9
Fredericksburg City, VA	51630	9.7	52.7	65.5	7.1	196	522	176	18.3	27
Galax City, VA	51640	11.7	61.1	35.4	14.8	64	186	64	20.0	9
Hampton City, VA	51650	13.6	49.1	72.1	1.3	1,357	3,627	1,244	17.3	90
Harrisonburg City, VA	51660	10.0[14]	67.1	52.1	14.1[14]	1,046[14]	2,735[14]	1,080[14]	15.3[14]	66[14]
Hopewell City, VA	51670	15.1	64.7	65.7	1.5	192	626	235	18.0	19
Lexington City, VA	51678	10.5	30.5	11.8	2.7	...	62	34	14.4	4
Lynchburg City, VA	51680	13.3	58.3	61.6	1.7	476	1,212	539	16.1	29
Manassas City, VA	51683	13.6	45.5	69.9	34.3	345	990	392	17.8	29
Manassas Park City, VA	51685	11.9	53.1	68.8	25.9	113	370	156	19.0	15
Martinsville City, VA	51690	11.4	68.9	67.0	4.2	178	404	136	17.5	10
Newport News City, VA	51700	12.7	52.7	71.0	2.3	1,852	5,368	1,726	17.7	67
Norfolk City, VA	51710	13.6	63.4	77.6	1.9	1,560	6,031	2,081	16.2	168
Norton City, VA	51720	12.0	53.1	17.0	0.9	57	134	40	22.1	5
Petersburg City, VA	51730	10.0	69.5	93.4	2.9	235	722	287	15.9	31
Poquoson City, VA	51735	10.9	12.6	6.1	0.2	217	345	137	17.0	11
Portsmouth City, VA	51740	12.8	58.2	77.5	0.3	826	2,320	768	19.7	77
Radford City, VA	51750	14.5	39.6	19.3	0.3	98	228	102	15.4	8
Richmond City, VA	51760	20.0	69.9	91.0	4.3	1,026	4,452	1,407	17.0	80
Roanoke City, VA	51770	13.1	59.8	56.2	6.8	630	2,211	814	16.0	79
Salem City, VA	51775	12.8	29.8	18.6	1.7	279	572	231	17.0	18
Staunton City, VA	51790	19.3	51.5	31.7	1.0	163	685	135	20.6	27
Suffolk City, VA	51800	11.9	41.3	64.8	0.3	868	2,265	787	18.4	44
Virginia Beach City, VA	51810	12.6	29.8	47.1	1.2	4,789	10,667	3,935	18.1	256
Waynesboro City, VA	51820	9.8	55.4	29.4	4.6	179	549	205	16.1	16
Williamsburg City, VA	51830	([12])	37.5	41.4	([12])	([12])	([12])	([12])	([12])	([12])
Winchester City, VA	51840	11.8[13]	47.0	39.0	6.5[13]	1,121[13]	2,774[13]	1,031[13]	16.5[13]	110[13]

[2]IEP=Individual Education Program. See notes and definitions for more information.
[7]Albermarle county is included with Charlottesville city.
[8]Bedford county is included with Bedford city.
[9]Fairfax city is included with Fairfax county.
[10]Falls Church city is included with Fairfax county.
[12]Greensville county is included with Emporia city.
[13]Williamsburg city is included with James City county.
[14]Rockingham county is included with Harrisonburg city.
. . . = Not available.

Table C-1. Population, School, and Student Characteristics by County, Selected Years—*Continued*

County	State/ County Code	Revenues, 2008–2009				Current expenditures, 2008–2009			Resident population 16 to 19 years, 2006–2010			
		Total revenue ($1,000's)	Percentage of revenue from: Federal government	State government	Local government	Amount ($1,000's)	Amount per student	Percent for instruction	Total population 16 to 19 years	Percent enrolled in school	Percent high school graduates, not enrolled in school	Percent not enrolled, not grads, not employed, or not in labor force
		19	20	21	22	23	24	25	26	27	28	29
VIRGINIA—*(Continued)*												
Russell, VA	51167	46,163	12.9	66.5	20.6	41,093	9,499	60.6	1,399	76.6	23.2	0.2
Scott, VA	51169	39,692	9.0	73.3	17.7	37,823	9,544	59.8	1,154	76.8	21.1	2.2
Shenandoah, VA	51171	69,398	4.6	47.4	48.0	63,335	10,012	67.8	2,133	84.2	11.6	1.4
Smyth, VA	51173	51,842	9.8	70.2	20.0	47,467	9,414	65.8	1,567	78.8	13.0	4.8
Southampton, VA	51175	34,364	7.0	57.5	35.4	29,557	10,371	56.1	936	87.9	9.2	2.9
Spotsylvania, VA	51177	272,186	4.3	48.6	47.1	232,226	9,630	59.9	7,023	85.7	9.3	1.6
Stafford, VA	51179	266,330	4.6	52.1	43.3	253,166	9,429	60.7	7,869	87.8	9.3	2.2
Surry, VA	51181	16,901	6.5	25.0	68.5	15,175	14,577	56.0	422	74.9	12.8	5.9
Sussex, VA	51183	20,301	8.8	46.8	44.4	19,375	15,947	51.8	637	87.3	6.4	3.0
Tazewell, VA	51185	64,712	8.4	69.5	22.1	57,910	8,447	62.4	1,925	82.4	11.2	3.6
Warren, VA	51187	50,500	5.2	52.6	42.2	47,431	8,729	57.5	2,157	83.5	13.3	1.7
Washington, VA	51191	76,680	7.9	56.2	35.9	70,017	9,318	61.8	2,657	89.3	10.4	0.1
Westmoreland, VA	51193	27,229	11.5	45.6	42.9	24,473	10,227	57.3	897	81.5	12.5	6.0
Wise, VA	51195	72,727	11.5	64.3	24.2	66,073	9,742	63.9	2,360	79.8	13.9	5.9
Wythe, VA	51197	47,715	8.4	56.1	35.5	39,968	9,045	64.1	1,199	78.1	17.9	2.8
York, VA	51199	131,343	9.6	50.2	40.2	118,893	9,222	60.2	4,420	83.6	15.2	1.2
Alexandria City, VA	51510	218,269	4.9	14.7	80.4	203,045	18,092	58.9	3,788	82.1	11.3	5.9
Bedford City, VA	51515	125,066[8]	5.0[8]	47.7[8]	47.4[8]	95,398[8]	8,731[8]	59.0[8]	299	47.8	48.5	3.7
Bristol City, VA	51520	25,791	10.3	57.6	32.1	23,581	9,768	65.8	707	86.7	10.2	3.1
Buena Vista City, VA	51530	11,843	5.0	68.3	26.6	11,395	9,900	60.2	462	84.6	10.6	4.8
Charlottesville City, VA	51540	254104[7]	5.4[7]	26.5[7]	68.0[7]	216943[7]	12860[7]	57.8[7]	4,135	92.5	3.3	4.0
Chesapeake City, VA	51550	505,165	4.5	47.5	48.0	432,958	10,851	62.0	13,759	80.5	15.6	2.8
Colonial Heights City, VA	51570	36,883	3.6	39.2	57.2	32,708	11,271	66.3	949	68.1	26.2	2.5
Covington City, VA	51580	11,406	8.6	49.4	42.0	10,422	11,365	65.4	397	78.3	8.8	4.0
Danville City, VA	51590	75,805	11.6	62.3	26.1	69,989	10,676	62.1	2,544	88.0	9.0	1.2
Emporia City, VA	51595	34,126[9]	9.3[9]	55.9[9]	34.7[9]	27,182[9]	9,971[9]	59.1[9]	250	77.2	5.2	17.6
Fairfax City, VA	51600	48,133	0.0	14.5	85.5	([10])	([10])	([10])	957	83.0	15.8	1.3
Falls Church City, VA	51610	38,270	1.6	13.4	85.0	35,582	18,090	59.3	485	94.2	3.3	2.5
Franklin City, VA	51620	18,220	10.6	51.8	37.6	15,867	12,215	59.4	651	60.2	25.2	3.2
Fredericksburg City, VA	51630	37,132	9.2	19.6	71.2	36,190	12,734	59.9	2,643	83.8	9.9	0.9
Galax City, VA	51640	15,107	8.4	59.8	31.9	12,502	9,186	62.1	267	88.8	11.2	0.0
Hampton City, VA	51650	245,858	8.5	59.0	32.5	231,305	10,607	58.2	8,731	85.1	10.0	3.5
Harrisonburg City, VA	51660	221,078[14]	5.4[14]	42.5[14]	52.1[14]	170,209[14]	10,343[14]	62.4[14]	8,387	98.6	0.9	0.3
Hopewell City, VA	51670	45,867	11.2	58.0	30.8	42,175	10,070	63.0	1,269	83.5	12.7	1.9
Lexington City, VA	51678	6,501	4.1	49.2	46.7	4,581	9,330	63.0	1,537	98.4	1.6	0.0
Lynchburg City, VA	51680	101,764	10.3	51.7	37.9	93,777	10,861	61.6	7,461	92.8	3.8	2.4
Manassas City, VA	51683	95,309	4.8	36.6	58.6	83,433	12,707	62.8	2,132	80.8	16.2	0.9
Manassas Park City, VA	51685	35,601	3.7	41.4	55.0	28,740	11,664	56.8	538	90.9	0.0	9.1
Martinsville City, VA	51690	28,880	11.8	59.8	28.4	27,151	10,673	55.5	781	86.3	12.6	1.2
Newport News City, VA	51700	371,904	10.8	53.1	36.1	321,653	10,277	56.3	13,229	71.7	24.2	3.1
Norfolk City, VA	51710	393,928	11.7	56.0	32.3	359,689	10,447	63.3	15,950	72.5	19.9	4.4
Norton City, VA	51720	13,349	8.1	36.6	55.3	7,151	8,883	66.3	225	99.6	0.4	0.0
Petersburg City, VA	51730	59,320	13.2	57.6	29.2	50,085	10,713	55.4	1,685	77.1	13.6	5.6
Poquoson City, VA	51735	23,902	4.1	56.4	39.5	22,479	9,024	60.4	709	89.7	7.3	3.0
Portsmouth City, VA	51740	189,864	10.3	56.0	33.7	159,561	10,413	57.2	5,420	69.4	21.9	7.3
Radford City, VA	51750	26,709	3.6	76.0	20.5	14,580	9,740	62.0	3,909	97.2	0.5	1.1
Richmond City, VA	51760	337,998	12.8	43.2	44.0	311,097	13,423	58.2	14,612	85.3	8.6	4.6
Roanoke City, VA	51770	180,268	7.7	44.8	47.5	147,856	11,189	57.8	4,369	73.3	17.8	5.6
Salem City, VA	51775	43,685	4.3	47.2	48.5	39,829	10,135	64.6	2,095	89.5	7.6	1.2
Staunton City, VA	51790	35,942	6.6	49.7	43.7	32,093	11,739	64.5	1,290	76.2	20.5	3.3
Suffolk City, VA	51800	171,803	6.9	50.2	42.8	139,315	9,885	63.8	4,178	83.0	7.5	5.1
Virginia Beach City, VA	51810	830,709	6.6	46.6	46.7	755,533	10,559	59.0	24,703	79.9	15.9	2.9
Waynesboro City, VA	51820	36,229	8.2	47.5	44.3	31,028	9,733	62.6	986	70.5	18.5	9.4
Williamsburg City, VA	51830	([12])	([12])	([12])	([12])	([12])	([12])	([12])	2,853	97.7	1.5	0.0
Winchester City, VA	51840	207,007[13]	4.0[13]	41.0[13]	55.0[13]	177,281	10,526	59.5	1,376	76.0	12.9	8.5

Note. Data in columns 26 through 41 from the American Community Survey are subject to sampling error, which can be especially large in small counties and small population groups. See notes and definitions for more information.
[7]Albermarle county is included with Charlottesville city.
[8]Bedford county is included with Bedford city.
[9]Fairfax city is included with Fairfax county.
[10]Falls Church city is included with Fairfax county.
[12]Greensville county is included with Emporia city.
[14]Rockingham county is included with Harrisonburg city.

Table C-1. Population, School, and Student Characteristics by County, Selected Years—*Continued*

County	State/ County Code	High school graduates, 2006–2010			College enrollment, 2006–2010		College graduates, 2006–2010 (percent)						
		Population 25 years and over	High school diploma or less (percent)	High school diploma or more (percent)	Number	Percent public	Bachelor's degree or more	+/- U.S. percent with Bachelor's degree or more	Non-Hispanic White	Black or African American	American Indian and Alaska Native	Asian, Hawaiian, and Pacific Islander	Hispanic or Latino[3]
		30	31	32	33	34	35	36	37	38	39	40	41
VIRGINIA— *(Continued)*													
Russell, VA	51167	20,681	64.0	71.4	1,272	93.6	10.7	-17.2	10.5	7.7	0.0	63.8	100.0
Scott, VA	51169	16,807	65.8	73.6	916	92.1	10.3	-17.6	10.1	31.3	0.0	0.0	8.0
Shenandoah, VA	51171	29,234	57.3	82.7	1,465	77.2	17.5	-10.4	17.7	24.0	24.3	63.9	2.8
Smyth, VA	51173	22,907	60.7	75.7	1,578	77.6	14.6	-13.3	14.9	0.0	0.0	0.0	27.0
Southampton, VA	51175	13,077	58.7	73.4	739	83.5	12.6	-15.3	16.1	7.0	8.3	0.0	0.0
Spotsylvania, VA	51177	75,976	41.0	88.5	7,109	85.3	29.9	2.0	31.4	23.3	9.2	44.4	21.2
Stafford, VA	51179	76,116	35.1	91.5	8,135	75.9	35.4	7.5	36.5	33.3	36.5	44.1	25.5
Surry, VA	51181	4,784	60.6	78.8	345	58.0	13.6	-14.3	17.5	8.8	0.0	0.0	8.3
Sussex, VA	51183	8,373	70.7	67.8	798	92.6	10.0	-17.9	14.0	7.3	10.5	0.0	0.0
Tazewell, VA	51185	32,115	57.6	75.6	2,114	83.7	14.4	-13.5	13.8	23.5	0.0	49.6	46.7
Warren, VA	51187	24,876	53.4	83.3	1,884	63.8	21.4	-6.5	21.2	13.2	31.7	55.1	28.6
Washington, VA	51191	39,200	52.2	80.4	2,937	43.8	20.6	-7.3	20.7	5.0	0.0	51.7	17.2
Westmoreland, VA	51193	12,494	58.7	76.5	624	88.3	15.9	-12.0	19.1	9.0	0.0	38.3	1.8
Wise, VA	51195	28,720	64.1	70.3	1,844	90.6	11.3	-16.6	11.9	0.9	0.0	55.7	0.0
Wythe, VA	51197	20,699	56.2	77.0	1,083	84.8	14.0	-13.9	13.9	12.9	0.0	32.7	46.4
York, VA	51199	42,288	25.5	94.5	4,813	86.3	41.5	13.6	44.1	25.5	50.9	44.0	43.9
Alexandria City, VA	51510	101,028	21.8	90.9	11,162	59.7	60.4	32.5	75.8	31.2	16.9	67.1	30.5
Bedford City, VA	51515	4,160	47.8	84.5	300	80.3	20.8	-7.1	25.3	5.7	0.0	100.0	0.0
Bristol City, VA	51520	12,456	50.1	79.8	1,155	62.6	19.7	-8.2	21.1	1.7	64.0	0.0	32.0
Buena Vista City, VA	51530	4,268	61.6	72.8	562	50.7	16.5	-11.4	17.3	7.3	0.0	0.0	100.0
Charlottesville City, VA	51540	23,696	34.7	85.2	12,510	96.5	46.7	18.8	57.6	8.1	0.0	73.1	25.6
Chesapeake City, VA	51550	141,347	38.1	89.3	14,738	75.3	27.9	0.0	30.0	22.2	15.5	42.9	22.7
Colonial Heights City, VA	51570	12,075	50.0	88.1	792	80.6	20.0	-7.9	20.6	15.4	0.0	27.8	6.1
Covington City, VA	51580	4,145	58.3	80.9	268	100.0	10.4	-17.5	10.2	12.6	0.0	15.1	0.0
Danville City, VA	51590	30,072	54.0	75.9	2,910	71.7	16.2	-11.7	21.0	9.7	41.3	47.6	8.6
Emporia City, VA	51595	3,947	65.3	71.7	193	87.6	15.4	-12.5	28.0	7.0	0.0	61.8	0.0
Fairfax City, VA	51600	15,503	22.1	93.1	1,926	79.1	53.2	25.3	57.7	42.0	33.7	56.6	30.4
Falls Church City, VA	51610	7,737	15.7	95.7	993	70.7	71.0	43.1	74.7	36.3	0.0	64.5	55.9
Franklin City, VA	51620	5,674	53.3	76.1	490	85.1	19.0	-8.9	32.6	5.6	0.0	19.7	0.0
Fredericksburg City, VA	51630	13,277	43.6	86.6	4,090	92.1	31.9	4.0	40.6	15.6	0.0	19.1	13.0
Galax City, VA	51640	5,281	56.6	73.6	272	71.3	12.7	-15.2	13.9	11.4	32.1	0.0	0.0
Hampton City, VA	51650	89,047	42.1	88.6	13,826	59.2	21.8	-6.1	23.7	19.2	5.8	27.9	25.7
Harrisonburg City, VA	51660	20,360	46.8	77.5	17,938	90.1	33.3	5.4	38.3	16.3	100.0	43.6	12.6
Hopewell City, VA	51670	14,739	62.7	76.1	807	84.3	10.9	-17.0	13.8	5.3	0.0	39.0	6.3
Lexington City, VA	51678	2,987	39.7	81.3	3,172	45.4	44.4	16.5	46.2	30.1	0.0	75.3	13.5
Lynchburg City, VA	51680	42,759	45.6	83.1	14,147	19.5	28.3	0.4	35.6	10.3	13.7	60.4	18.8
Manassas City, VA	51683	22,290	44.7	80.6	2,019	61.1	28.3	0.4	36.0	21.5	44.4	49.6	8.5
Manassas Park City, VA	51685	8,090	52.5	78.5	711	71.4	21.9	-6.0	23.7	28.7	0.0	42.1	9.3
Martinsville City, VA	51690	9,875	52.1	78.3	822	77.6	20.4	-7.5	31.5	5.8	0.0	46.0	0.0
Newport News City, VA	51700	112,043	40.4	88.9	17,542	81.4	23.5	-4.4	28.8	16.9	13.6	30.8	16.2
Norfolk City, VA	51710	142,294	45.9	83.9	25,943	83.1	23.7	-4.2	32.5	11.8	31.9	39.4	20.7
Norton City, VA	51720	2,558	46.1	77.6	236	85.6	20.6	-7.3	20.1	11.8	0.0	100.0	0.0
Petersburg City, VA	51730	21,562	61.6	72.0	1,317	93.2	15.2	-12.7	23.1	13.5	10.3	26.7	5.1
Poquoson City, VA	51735	8,204	31.1	93.9	633	80.9	36.0	8.1	36.0	91.7	0.0	34.1	28.5
Portsmouth City, VA	51740	62,635	49.1	81.7	6,566	77.8	18.7	-9.2	24.2	13.5	4.8	35.7	10.3
Radford City, VA	51750	6,496	35.9	88.9	7,407	98.9	35.1	7.2	36.5	18.7	0.0	35.6	41.4
Richmond City, VA	51760	127,463	44.1	80.2	28,135	75.8	32.7	4.8	58.9	12.1	20.7	56.7	10.3
Roanoke City, VA	51770	66,618	49.6	80.9	5,785	78.7	21.9	-6.0	27.1	9.5	21.2	23.0	8.1
Salem City, VA	51775	16,349	43.8	87.5	3,072	29.2	29.1	1.2	30.1	20.6	0.0	30.1	0.0
Staunton City, VA	51790	16,897	49.4	82.7	1,633	52.6	28.5	0.6	30.3	12.0	41.4	41.1	34.6
Suffolk City, VA	51800	54,205	44.4	84.7	4,816	73.3	25.1	-2.8	30.0	17.4	0.0	49.5	14.2
Virginia Beach City, VA	51810	281,624	32.1	92.5	34,083	75.6	31.9	4.0	34.8	20.8	16.1	40.1	18.9
Waynesboro City, VA	51820	14,241	56.8	81.2	819	75.1	21.8	-6.1	22.6	16.9	17.2	41.9	15.1
Williamsburg City, VA	51830	6,229	28.3	93.6	5,664	99.3	43.3	15.4	52.7	13.6	0.0	50.8	7.3
Winchester City, VA	51840	17,048	48.2	79.7	1,722	54.4	29.7	1.8	34.9	13.4	14.4	44.7	3.7

Note. Data in columns 26 through 41 from the American Community Survey are subject to sampling error, which can be especially large in small counties and small population groups. See notes and definitions for more information.

[3]May be of any race.

Table C-1. Population, School, and Student Characteristics by County, Selected Years—*Continued*

County	State/ County Code	County Type[1]	Population, 2010		Percent of related children 5–17 years in poverty, 2010	Percent of children under 19 years with no health insurance, 2010	Number of schools and students, 2010–2011			Resident enrollment, 2006–2010 K–12 enrollment	
			Total	Percent 5–17 years			School districts	Schools	Students	Number	Percent public
			1	2	3	4	5	6	7	8	9
WASHINGTON	53000	X	6,724,540	17.0	16.1	6.8	314	2,338	1,043,640	1,135,142	90.6
Adams, WA	53001	6	18,728	24.0	27.9	8.8	5	11	4,429	3,904	94.2
Asotin, WA	53003	3	21,623	15.9	22.4	5.8	2	11	3,399	3,443	89.1
Benton, WA	53005	3	175,177	19.7	15.6	6.5	6	59	33,269	33,841	93.9
Chelan, WA	53007	3	72,453	18.1	19.8	9.1	8	37	12,779	13,457	93.5
Clallam, WA	53009	5	71,404	13.5	19.3	8.0	5	28	11,660	9,973	90.5
Clark, WA	53011	1	425,363	19.5	15.5	6.9	12	131	76,755	81,776	92.8
Columbia, WA	53013	6	4,078	14.9	18.6	8.0	2	4	492	666	97.0
Cowlitz, WA	53015	3	102,410	17.7	22.3	6.9	6	43	17,324	18,366	92.9
Douglas, WA	53017	3	38,431	20.0	18.9	8.6	6	21	7,025	7,430	96.1
Ferry, WA	53019	9	7,551	14.7	24.7	10.7	5	12	979	1,358	99.7
Franklin, WA	53021	3	78,163	23.6	24.1	8.9	5	30	17,267	16,740	91.5
Garfield, WA	53023	8	2,266	15.8	16.3	10.4	1	2	329	377	100.0
Grant, WA	53025	4	89,120	21.5	25.4	9.6	10	53	18,928	18,794	96.3
Grays Harbor, WA	53027	4	72,797	15.7	25.6	7.7	13	42	10,780	12,142	94.4
Island, WA	53029	4	78,506	15.0	12.3	7.4	3	23	8,444	12,071	91.2
Jefferson, WA	53031	6	29,872	11.3	19.6	8.1	5	13	2,787	3,691	92.0
King, WA	53033	1	1,931,249	15.2	13.3	5.8	20	472	243,549	287,642	87.1
Kitsap, WA	53035	3	251,133	16.6	13.2	6.2	6	80	37,109	42,592	90.9
Kittitas, WA	53037	6	40,915	13.3	16.9	7.3	7	20	4,907	5,598	95.4
Klickitat, WA	53039	6	20,318	16.6	25.5	8.6	10	21	3,191	3,411	93.5
Lewis, WA	53041	4	75,455	17.1	19.2	7.2	14	43	11,948	13,575	92.3
Lincoln, WA	53043	8	10,570	17.5	16.3	8.6	8	16	2,087	1,853	91.2
Mason, WA	53045	6	60,699	15.0	19.1	7.8	7	21	8,050	9,320	94.4
Okanogan, WA	53047	6	41,120	16.7	30.1	10.6	8	30	7,231	7,055	92.9
Pacific, WA	53049	7	20,920	13.2	24.2	8.9	6	17	3,144	2,802	96.3
Pend Oreille, WA	53051	8	13,001	16.2	26.4	7.4	3	9	1,663	2,228	91.3
Pierce, WA	53053	1	795,225	17.9	15.7	6.2	17	267	127,495	143,288	91.5
San Juan, WA	53055	9	15,769	12.4	17.5	11.6	4	14	1,820	1,850	90.4
Skagit, WA	53057	3	116,901	17.2	18.9	7.4	8	50	19,014	19,848	93.1
Skamania, WA	53059	1	11,066	16.8	17.2	7.3	4	9	1,537	1,955	98.2
Snohomish, WA	53061	1	713,335	17.8	11.3	6.1	15	242	127,750	126,562	90.4
Spokane, WA	53063	2	471,221	16.8	15.9	5.5	18	161	75,917	79,012	89.4
Stevens, WA	53065	6	43,531	18.8	23.0	8.8	12	40	8,015	8,375	89.4
Thurston, WA	53067	3	252,264	16.9	12.1	5.7	9	78	40,549	41,927	92.1
Wahkiakum, WA	53069	8	3,978	14.5	22.5	9.6	1	2	470	624	93.1
Walla Walla, WA	53071	4	58,781	16.5	19.5	9.2	7	27	8,692	10,232	88.7
Whatcom, WA	53073	3	201,140	15.3	14.3	6.9	7	68	27,064	31,026	87.0
Whitman, WA	53075	4	44,776	10.6	13.9	6.9	13	26	4,516	4,713	92.9
Yakima, WA	53077	3	243,231	21.6	32.4	11.9	16	105	51,276	51,625	94.9
WEST VIRGINIA	54000	X	1,852,994	15.3	23.4	5.0	57	757	282,879	285,777	93.1
Barbour, WV	54001	7	16,589	16.0	27.6	6.0	1	9	2,499	2,597	97.2
Berkeley, WV	54003	3	104,169	18.2	16.1	5.3	1	29	17,720	18,550	90.5
Boone, WV	54005	2	24,629	16.6	23.3	4.3	1	16	4,545	4,133	99.4
Braxton, WV	54007	8	14,523	15.3	31.4	6.0	1	8	2,220	2,171	98.4
Brooke, WV	54009	3	24,069	14.4	18.8	4.6	1	10	3,363	3,583	91.3
Cabell, WV	54011	2	96,319	13.9	32.9	4.2	1	28	12,700	13,545	90.1
Calhoun, WV	54013	8	7,627	14.4	33.3	6.5	1	4	1,122	1,128	97.6
Clay, WV	54015	2	9,386	17.6	34.1	5.8	1	6	2,071	1,793	97.0
Doddridge, WV	54017	9	8,202	15.7	25.9	5.9	1	3	1,169	1,537	96.6
Fayette, WV	54019	6	46,039	14.8	29.3	5.2	1	21	6,827	7,237	90.2
Gilmer, WV	54021	9	8,693	10.3	29.3	5.3	1	5	943	1,113	90.7
Grant, WV	54023	6	11,937	16.1	22.9	5.6	1	6	1,887	1,976	96.0
Greenbrier, WV	54025	7	35,480	14.9	25.3	6.0	1	13	5,247	5,261	91.1
Hampshire, WV	54027	3	23,964	17.1	23.4	6.6	2	13	3,732	4,199	91.9
Hancock, WV	54029	3	30,676	15.1	18.3	4.5	1	10	4,308	4,530	89.4
Hardy, WV	54031	8	14,025	15.8	22.4	5.6	1	6	2,297	2,946	97.7
Harrison, WV	54033	5	69,099	16.1	22.1	4.4	1	26	11,128	11,043	95.1
Jackson, WV	54035	6	29,211	16.8	28.2	5.1	1	13	5,046	4,833	98.3
Jefferson, WV	54037	1	53,498	17.4	13.8	4.8	1	16	8,845	9,277	90.3
Kanawha, WV	54039	2	193,063	15.0	20.4	4.4	2	94	29,065	29,159	89.7

[1]County type codes are from the Economic Research Service of the United States Department of Agriculture. See notes and definitions for more information.

Table C-1. Population, School, and Student Characteristics by County, Selected Years—*Continued*

County	State/ County Code	Characteristics of students, 2010–2011				Number of graduates, 2008–2009	Staff and students, 2010–2011			
		Percent with IEP[2]	Percent eligible for free or reduced lunch	Percent minority	Percent English-language learners		Total staff	Number of teachers	Student/ teacher ratio	Central admin. staff
		10	11	12	13	14	15	16	17	18
WASHINGTON	53000	12.3	40.1	37.1	8.7	62,764	103,682	53,934	19.4	4,331
Adams, WA	53001	9.6	76.2	76.2	31.8	214	474	249	17.8	26
Asotin, WA	53003	17.7	52.8	11.5	0.5	199	353	176	19.3	15
Benton, WA	53005	10.9	45.1	34.2	9.6	2,017	3,140	1,627	20.4	115
Chelan, WA	53007	9.6	56.6	48.5	19.9	878	1,360	687	18.6	61
Clallam, WA	53009	11.3	40.0	27.6	1.6	536	1,034	583	20.0	44
Clark, WA	53011	12.4	41.2	25.6	6.7	4,426	7,467	3,940	19.5	254
Columbia, WA	53013	12.0	50.2	17.7	. . .	43	58	32	15.2	5
Cowlitz, WA	53015	13.0	48.7	23.2	4.0	1,109	1,678	840	20.6	71
Douglas, WA	53017	11.4	54.8	48.6	20.5	417	692	375	18.7	25
Ferry, WA	53019	10.6	53.1	28.4	. . .	52	140	73	13.5	15
Franklin, WA	53021	12.2	70.8	44.2	35.2	752	1,813	913	18.9	75
Garfield, WA	53023	17.6	47.4	9.1	0.6	32	42	22	15.2	3
Grant, WA	53025	11.5	70.2	58.3	21.9	1,064	2,003	1,019	18.6	83
Grays Harbor, WA	53027	13.7	59.4	27.6	4.8	683	1,247	634	17.0	70
Island, WA	53029	12.6	35.1	26.9	1.8	609	771	401	21.1	35
Jefferson, WA	53031	13.4	44.2	16.0	1.1	252	316	155	18.0	23
King, WA	53033	11.6	30.1	46.6	10.8	14,567	23,981	12,611	19.3	879
Kitsap, WA	53035	14.0	28.5	31.7	1.8	2,736	3,946	1,958	19.0	158
Kittitas, WA	53037	11.8	34.2	18.5	6.0	288	501	266	18.5	38
Klickitat, WA	53039	15.5	50.4	28.9	7.7	205	382	200	16.0	27
Lewis, WA	53041	13.8	54.9	21.7	4.4	791	1,227	652	18.3	61
Lincoln, WA	53043	11.0	42.4	9.6	. . .	120	292	151	13.8	28
Mason, WA	53045	16.4	56.7	28.9	5.2	518	893	460	17.5	51
Okanogan, WA	53047	12.3	52.2	44.6	12.1	387	767	399	18.1	42
Pacific, WA	53049	14.7	50.1	27.9	5.6	221	361	184	17.1	23
Pend Oreille, WA	53051	13.7	58.3	15.0	. . .	104	197	101	16.5	13
Pierce, WA	53053	12.6	38.2	38.4	4.6	7,206	12,759	6,590	19.3	567
San Juan, WA	53055	12.5	33.0	15.3	3.7	104	207	110	16.6	17
Skagit, WA	53057	12.9	50.1	36.7	13.4	1,145	2,012	988	19.2	87
Skamania, WA	53059	10.8	39.6	17.7	1.8	65	152	80	19.1	10
Snohomish, WA	53061	12.2	31.2	33.3	7.2	8,012	11,233	6,029	21.2	453
Spokane, WA	53063	13.4	44.9	17.1	2.6	4,841	7,794	4,040	18.8	308
Stevens, WA	53065	9.3	40.6	15.1	0.7	437	811	390	20.5	60
Thurston, WA	53067	12.2	30.4	28.8	2.5	2,532	4,181	2,122	19.1	171
Wahkiakum, WA	53069	19.8	54.7	11.7	4.5	38	45	24	19.3	3
Walla Walla, WA	53071	11.4	45.8	39.4	12.9	601	949	498	17.5	39
Whatcom, WA	53073	13.0	34.8	25.9	5.9	1,643	2,606	1,367	19.8	104
Whitman, WA	53075	10.5	31.5	20.2	2.0	330	555	289	15.6	40
Yakima, WA	53077	11.8	70.0	70.9	22.7	2,590	5,242	2,702	19.0	231
WEST VIRGINIA	54000	15.9	51.5	8.0	0.6	17,690	38,954	20,339	13.9	1,907
Barbour, WV	54001	15.8	57.9	6.5	. . .	157	327	169	14.8	14
Berkeley, WV	54003	15.8	48.5	19.9	1.9	1,018	2,565	1,344	13.2	127
Boone, WV	54005	18.8	50.9	1.3	0.1	256	739	423	10.7	40
Braxton, WV	54007	16.4	61.1	1.6	. . .	158	335	178	12.5	21
Brooke, WV	54009	22.2	49.0	4.0	0.1	259	466	247	13.6	30
Cabell, WV	54011	14.4	47.6	11.2	1.1	680	1,629	884	14.4	79
Calhoun, WV	54013	12.6	61.5	1.4	. . .	70	163	86	13.0	15
Clay, WV	54015	16.1	67.2	0.8	. . .	128	283	149	13.9	16
Doddridge, WV	54017	19.8	58.6	1.4	. . .	84	193	95	12.3	11
Fayette, WV	54019	12.8	62.8	7.8	0.1	433	955	512	13.3	49
Gilmer, WV	54021	16.4	56.1	4.2	. . .	75	141	72	13.1	12
Grant, WV	54023	19.3	50.6	2.3	0.5	139	267	139	13.5	15
Greenbrier, WV	54025	18.6	57.2	6.2	0.6	325	798	391	13.4	47
Hampshire, WV	54027	19.3	58.2	3.6	0.1	268	578	301	12.4	28
Hancock, WV	54029	19.7	49.0	5.5	0.2	327	564	301	14.3	31
Hardy, WV	54031	13.1	51.4	7.9	3.0	144	286	146	15.8	12
Harrison, WV	54033	17.3	46.0	5.2	0.8	700	1,559	785	14.2	74
Jackson, WV	54035	16.8	47.7	1.7	0.4	323	683	368	13.7	39
Jefferson, WV	54037	13.8	31.9	17.6	3.1	556	1,175	597	14.8	49
Kanawha, WV	54039	14.8	50.3	16.0	0.8	1,656	3,855	1,969	14.8	185

[2]IEP=Individual Education Program. See notes and definitions for more information.

. . . = Not available.

Table C-1. Population, School, and Student Characteristics by County, Selected Years—*Continued*

County	State/ County Code	Revenues, 2008–2009				Current expenditures, 2008–2009			Resident population 16 to 19 years, 2006–2010			
		Total revenue ($1,000's)	Percentage of revenue from			Amount ($1,000's)	Amount per student	Percent for instruction	Total population 16 to 19 years	Percent enrolled in school	Percent high school graduates, not enrolled in school	Percent not enrolled, not grads, not employed, or not in labor force
			Federal government	State government	Local government							
		19	20	21	22	23	24	25	26	27	28	29
WASHINGTON	53000	12,025,012	11.5	59.4	29.0	9,894,819	9,552	60.5	370,519	82.8	11.0	3.9
Adams, WA	53001	57,206	12.2	74.4	13.4	40,454	9,720	62.3	1,134	65.9	7.7	13.5
Asotin, WA	53003	35,724	15.5	65.1	19.5	33,177	10,048	62.0	1,101	87.9	7.6	2.8
Benton, WA	53005	324,042	11.4	66.8	21.8	284,321	9,028	61.1	9,852	83.9	11.2	3.4
Chelan, WA	53007	150,776	16.1	60.1	23.8	127,124	9,879	58.7	4,295	83.2	12.6	1.6
Clallam, WA	53009	105,685	14.9	66.8	18.3	94,932	8,937	65.2	3,402	79.0	13.6	3.9
Clark, WA	53011	841,934	11.1	59.8	29.2	718,762	9,381	58.7	23,394	82.8	10.5	4.6
Columbia, WA	53013	6,352	14.2	65.3	20.5	5,977	11,048	58.5	230	87.8	5.7	6.5
Cowlitz, WA	53015	177,029	12.3	64.9	22.7	161,051	9,091	59.0	5,381	81.1	14.3	2.1
Douglas, WA	53017	76,361	13.0	67.8	19.1	67,094	9,773	62.3	2,295	83.4	10.9	2.8
Ferry, WA	53019	13,546	25.9	67.2	6.9	12,420	11,806	56.5	541	72.5	17.7	8.0
Franklin, WA	53021	193,563	13.0	69.1	18.0	148,833	9,382	60.5	4,587	77.2	12.3	5.3
Garfield, WA	53023	4,794	15.0	62.5	22.5	4,175	12,613	59.6	113	92.9	7.1	0.0
Grant, WA	53025	200,366	14.7	68.2	17.0	175,238	9,593	61.8	5,879	76.7	14.5	6.5
Grays Harbor, WA	53027	130,220	15.7	62.5	21.8	114,208	10,159	61.6	3,954	81.8	11.0	4.2
Island, WA	53029	94,267	16.0	59.1	24.9	76,073	8,732	61.4	3,557	74.3	19.2	4.1
Jefferson, WA	53031	35,118	15.2	55.0	29.8	30,344	10,353	57.6	1,097	73.6	19.6	3.7
King, WA	53033	2,958,903	9.7	52.0	38.3	2,331,068	9,759	60.6	92,892	86.5	8.8	2.7
Kitsap, WA	53035	431,396	13.9	60.0	26.1	369,613	9,716	60.1	14,420	78.1	16.4	3.8
Kittitas, WA	53037	52,483	12.1	62.8	25.2	48,417	9,003	60.2	3,302	90.7	6.9	1.6
Klickitat, WA	53039	41,543	14.4	66.4	19.2	35,199	10,804	61.8	891	79.4	5.6	12.2
Lewis, WA	53041	130,420	13.9	65.2	20.9	115,269	9,418	61.2	4,679	82.2	14.3	3.2
Lincoln, WA	53043	30,655	10.3	70.9	18.8	28,215	13,117	56.8	564	82.3	15.6	1.6
Mason, WA	53045	88,055	13.4	62.9	23.6	79,240	9,620	58.9	2,922	78.3	12.6	7.6
Okanogan, WA	53047	72,985	18.7	65.1	16.3	66,756	10,731	60.7	2,416	69.7	16.8	11.7
Pacific, WA	53049	44,932	10.9	66.8	22.3	33,208	11,681	60.7	955	85.2	8.9	2.1
Pend Oreille, WA	53051	19,825	16.8	68.0	15.3	18,902	10,661	60.3	661	79.9	4.2	14.4
Pierce, WA	53053	1,515,049	11.3	60.6	28.0	1,231,214	9,417	59.5	45,937	80.2	12.0	5.5
San Juan, WA	53055	23,178	9.6	51.3	39.1	18,918	11,564	58.6	556	68.2	13.3	10.6
Skagit, WA	53057	235,114	14.0	55.4	30.6	196,568	10,187	60.8	6,534	79.6	10.9	4.5
Skamania, WA	53059	14,594	42.9	50.3	6.8	14,473	11,185	61.8	580	86.7	8.3	5.0
Snohomish, WA	53061	1,443,612	8.6	57.6	33.8	1,158,779	9,085	61.7	39,097	81.4	12.1	3.5
Spokane, WA	53063	851,052	12.0	63.5	24.6	721,081	9,542	60.3	28,053	83.7	11.2	3.5
Stevens, WA	53065	77,250	17.2	68.0	14.9	70,873	10,331	60.7	2,612	83.3	13.7	2.5
Thurston, WA	53067	502,704	10.4	60.0	29.6	379,573	9,201	61.5	13,272	86.1	10.4	2.6
Wahkiakum, WA	53069	5,405	12.3	66.4	21.2	4,424	9,373	57.3	265	72.8	5.3	15.1
Walla Walla, WA	53071	105,028	13.4	63.0	23.6	87,755	9,990	61.0	4,110	90.9	3.5	3.8
Whatcom, WA	53073	285,653	11.0	59.6	29.4	247,546	9,358	61.3	13,433	85.5	9.6	2.3
Whitman, WA	53075	59,064	9.2	65.9	24.9	52,643	11,580	57.2	5,915	97.6	1.8	0.5
Yakima, WA	53077	589,129	17.1	68.9	14.1	490,902	9,844	60.2	15,641	73.2	13.8	8.1
WEST VIRGINIA	54000	3,097,212	11.5	57.9	30.6	2,922,539	10,367	60.2	98,922	81.6	10.9	5.6
Barbour, WV	54001	25,580	12.5	72.4	15.1	24,321	9,744	62.0	899	93.7	5.3	0.7
Berkeley, WV	54003	181,207	7.8	54.2	38.0	172,032	9,994	60.5	4,773	75.2	14.9	6.3
Boone, WV	54005	56,225	11.7	45.5	42.8	53,155	11,500	55.8	1,169	72.7	16.3	9.6
Braxton, WV	54007	23,150	17.0	65.9	17.1	24,000	10,485	59.8	758	65.2	20.2	11.7
Brooke, WV	54009	39,663	9.0	59.1	31.9	36,884	10,775	60.8	1,374	83.4	11.5	1.2
Cabell, WV	54011	144,184	11.3	54.3	34.3	129,255	10,322	61.0	5,374	81.3	6.6	8.8
Calhoun, WV	54013	11,982	22.3	62.7	15.0	11,209	9,955	56.5	426	74.7	12.7	12.7
Clay, WV	54015	20,114	16.1	66.7	17.2	20,977	10,354	55.9	385	84.4	15.6	0.0
Doddridge, WV	54017	16,538	11.3	48.5	40.3	14,326	11,879	53.6	630	81.4	18.6	0.0
Fayette, WV	54019	66,832	11.6	63.1	25.3	71,047	10,433	61.2	2,395	84.4	10.2	3.8
Gilmer, WV	54021	11,014	17.6	51.1	31.3	10,928	11,613	54.4	588	92.9	0.9	3.1
Grant, WV	54023	18,542	13.3	59.5	27.1	18,141	9,185	61.1	496	74.2	16.7	9.1
Greenbrier, WV	54025	58,554	13.6	59.7	26.7	55,733	10,620	63.5	1,652	80.4	14.2	4.4
Hampshire, WV	54027	34,785	12.9	62.9	24.2	33,643	9,027	58.8	1,104	85.4	10.7	3.9
Hancock, WV	54029	45,050	8.8	62.3	29.0	43,783	10,119	60.6	1,519	81.5	7.1	10.3
Hardy, WV	54031	21,342	13.1	65.3	21.6	20,495	8,710	58.8	812	80.2	14.9	0.0
Harrison, WV	54033	120,623	11.0	57.2	31.7	117,431	10,492	57.2	3,135	77.9	12.0	4.8
Jackson, WV	54035	53,080	8.6	59.7	31.7	51,406	10,145	58.0	1,520	80.3	9.9	7.0
Jefferson, WV	54037	102,163	5.4	41.3	53.2	89,706	10,682	61.8	3,294	91.2	4.6	2.9
Kanawha, WV	54039	319,705	11.9	53.6	34.5	290,094	10,191	61.0	9,363	83.4	9.7	4.4

Note. Data in columns 26 through 41 from the American Community Survey are subject to sampling error, which can be especially large in small counties and small population groups. See notes and definitions for more information.

Table C-1. Population, School, and Student Characteristics by County, Selected Years—*Continued*

County	State/ County Code	High school graduates, 2006–2010: Population 25 years and over	High school graduates, 2006–2010: High school diploma or less (percent)	High school graduates, 2006–2010: High school diploma or more (percent)	College enrollment, 2006–2010: Number	College enrollment, 2006–2010: Percent public	College graduates, 2006–2010 (percent): Bachelor's degree or more	+/- U.S. percent with Bachelor's degree or more	Non-Hispanic White	Black or African American	American Indian and Alaska Native	Asian, Hawaiian, and Pacific Islander	Hispanic or Latino[3]
		30	31	32	33	34	35	36	37	38	39	40	41
WASHINGTON	53000	4,360,316	34.7	89.6	430,935	79.6	31.0	3.1	32.4	20.4	13.2	43.5	12.4
Adams, WA	53001	10,003	61.2	67.6	351	83.2	13.4	-14.5	21.3	0.0	0.0	59.6	3.8
Asotin, WA	53003	14,924	46.4	88.9	904	95.7	18.2	-9.7	18.7	0.0	11.1	18.7	12.0
Benton, WA	53005	106,378	37.6	88.0	7,971	87.7	27.6	-0.3	30.2	20.9	24.7	41.7	8.1
Chelan, WA	53007	46,916	45.0	83.1	2,257	83.3	23.2	-4.7	26.2	55.2	15.6	26.9	7.1
Clallam, WA	53009	52,473	37.1	91.1	2,863	86.8	23.3	-4.6	24.3	0.0	10.7	41.5	4.4
Clark, WA	53011	268,818	35.8	90.8	21,999	82.3	25.7	-2.2	25.9	19.1	16.4	40.7	13.8
Columbia, WA	53013	2,904	39.7	89.4	132	83.3	20.0	-7.9	20.3	0.0	0.0	100.0	14.0
Cowlitz, WA	53015	68,232	44.7	86.1	5,179	81.8	14.7	-13.2	14.9	0.0	11.7	27.3	6.9
Douglas, WA	53017	23,820	47.2	79.3	1,663	87.3	17.3	-10.6	21.0	0.0	7.5	43.0	2.2
Ferry, WA	53019	5,102	50.7	88.6	229	98.7	16.7	-11.2	16.7	100.0	14.0	65.1	0.0
Franklin, WA	53021	39,514	58.0	67.6	3,367	88.2	14.6	-13.3	22.2	12.8	5.2	19.4	4.1
Garfield, WA	53023	1,621	42.9	91.7	44	100.0	17.7	-10.2	17.9	0.0	0.0	25.0	30.4
Grant, WA	53025	50,568	54.6	75.0	3,165	91.0	14.4	-13.5	18.6	15.1	7.7	19.9	4.2
Grays Harbor, WA	53027	49,829	48.5	84.4	2,890	90.0	14.5	-13.4	14.9	27.3	11.4	16.8	8.0
Island, WA	53029	54,588	29.9	94.8	3,824	78.5	29.8	1.9	31.1	8.7	8.7	27.5	17.6
Jefferson, WA	53031	23,462	30.7	94.2	877	78.2	34.8	6.9	35.5	28.5	18.0	36.6	35.8
King, WA	53033	1,299,736	25.8	91.9	142,781	76.3	45.2	17.3	48.6	21.6	17.1	50.0	21.8
Kitsap, WA	53035	165,105	31.4	92.7	12,943	79.8	28.0	0.1	29.6	11.4	17.7	26.9	14.9
Kittitas, WA	53037	23,102	39.1	89.8	8,249	98.3	32.0	4.1	32.1	83.6	24.4	65.7	9.3
Klickitat, WA	53039	14,360	48.1	87.3	701	88.3	17.9	-10.0	19.7	0.0	2.8	11.3	4.4
Lewis, WA	53041	50,746	47.9	84.9	2,672	83.1	15.0	-12.9	15.3	8.2	7.4	60.9	6.8
Lincoln, WA	53043	7,488	39.9	91.4	217	69.6	20.3	-7.6	20.3	0.0	10.0	100.0	18.9
Mason, WA	53045	42,462	45.2	86.6	2,860	83.5	17.9	-10.0	18.7	28.2	6.5	26.1	5.3
Okanogan, WA	53047	27,596	48.7	83.8	1,133	87.6	17.7	-10.2	20.1	0.0	10.2	31.5	6.5
Pacific, WA	53049	15,938	46.3	86.2	608	80.1	16.8	-11.1	17.9	8.5	3.6	8.9	2.5
Pend Oreille, WA	53051	9,266	46.2	87.7	262	91.2	17.9	-10.0	18.6	63.2	6.3	5.3	11.2
Pierce, WA	53053	506,145	39.7	89.8	47,291	70.3	23.4	-4.5	25.1	16.7	11.7	24.1	11.9
San Juan, WA	53055	12,343	24.3	94.3	284	71.5	44.9	17.0	46.3	24.2	21.6	52.8	16.5
Skagit, WA	53057	77,925	37.7	87.7	4,821	90.8	23.2	-4.7	25.6	21.4	10.0	29.7	4.6
Skamania, WA	53059	7,639	43.7	90.2	367	88.8	19.7	-8.2	20.6	0.0	0.0	55.1	0.0
Snohomish, WA	53061	459,785	34.9	90.8	37,970	81.1	28.2	0.3	27.9	27.7	11.1	43.8	13.8
Spokane, WA	53063	299,842	33.3	92.0	37,338	74.2	27.9	0.0	28.4	17.6	15.2	36.0	17.2
Stevens, WA	53065	29,752	42.9	90.2	1,225	88.2	19.2	-8.7	19.4	70.9	9.9	44.4	22.2
Thurston, WA	53067	164,498	31.6	92.6	16,298	84.7	31.6	3.7	32.6	25.9	26.3	31.9	19.2
Wahkiakum, WA	53069	3,016	40.3	92.4	85	83.5	15.3	-12.6	14.9	0.0	28.6	0.0	0.0
Walla Walla, WA	53071	37,145	38.7	86.6	5,801	48.9	24.2	-3.7	28.1	14.5	10.7	35.9	4.7
Whatcom, WA	53073	125,073	33.8	90.7	22,880	92.1	31.7	3.8	33.2	36.9	11.4	34.8	13.5
Whitman, WA	53075	21,163	23.5	95.7	17,285	98.3	47.4	19.5	45.8	29.0	27.8	76.0	41.1
Yakima, WA	53077	141,039	56.7	70.8	9,149	79.9	15.6	-12.3	21.3	14.7	8.8	30.8	4.7
WEST VIRGINIA	54000	1,282,621	59.4	81.9	113,245	83.2	17.3	-10.6	17.1	14.0	7.9	61.6	19.3
Barbour, WV	54001	11,209	68.5	80.4	961	35.8	13.3	-14.6	13.6	22.5	0.0	15.0	0.0
Berkeley, WV	54003	67,518	54.6	84.9	5,017	74.7	19.7	-8.2	19.8	19.4	5.9	30.1	19.9
Boone, WV	54005	17,385	73.4	71.5	568	69.7	8.2	-19.7	8.2	9.9	0.0	0.0	0.0
Braxton, WV	54007	10,380	72.5	73.9	335	67.5	9.5	-18.4	9.6	2.1	0.0	21.2	0.0
Brooke, WV	54009	17,382	58.2	87.9	1,286	65.6	15.6	-12.3	15.7	0.0	0.0	100.0	0.0
Cabell, WV	54011	64,645	49.4	85.7	10,215	89.6	23.0	-4.9	22.7	19.5	0.0	75.0	34.7
Calhoun, WV	54013	5,498	72.6	71.7	261	85.1	8.0	-19.9	7.9	0.0	0.0	0.0	0.0
Clay, WV	54015	6,581	73.5	73.0	206	100.0	8.3	-19.6	8.2	48.2	0.0	0.0	0.0
Doddridge, WV	54017	5,604	72.1	73.9	206	73.3	8.0	-19.9	7.7	0.0	0.0	0.0	17.1
Fayette, WV	54019	32,771	68.5	76.7	2,283	86.6	10.7	-17.2	11.0	7.0	0.0	0.0	0.0
Gilmer, WV	54021	5,869	65.9	74.9	1,275	87.5	12.2	-15.7	14.5	5.7	0.0	36.7	2.8
Grant, WV	54023	8,514	71.6	79.4	338	86.1	11.5	-16.4	11.7	0.0	0.0	0.0	0.0
Greenbrier, WV	54025	25,568	61.0	77.8	1,631	81.7	17.2	-10.7	17.3	8.9	100.0	0.0	50.9
Hampshire, WV	54027	16,506	74.6	78.4	843	91.9	9.4	-18.5	9.2	0.0	0.0	34.4	0.0
Hancock, WV	54029	22,638	57.2	87.5	1,281	87.7	15.3	-12.6	14.8	29.5	0.0	77.7	7.8
Hardy, WV	54031	8,925	70.6	80.9	388	84.3	9.5	-18.4	9.5	15.8	0.0	0.0	0.0
Harrison, WV	54033	48,222	55.9	84.1	2,757	75.4	17.6	-10.3	17.6	12.1	13.0	37.2	22.7
Jackson, WV	54035	20,352	58.6	82.2	1,277	92.7	14.5	-13.4	14.5	0.0	0.0	52.4	0.0
Jefferson, WV	54037	34,480	47.9	85.2	4,590	85.1	27.7	-0.2	28.7	13.7	25.8	47.7	24.3
Kanawha, WV	54039	137,904	52.2	85.9	9,974	81.7	23.4	-4.5	23.3	20.0	17.0	65.5	23.6

Note. Data in columns 26 through 41 from the American Community Survey are subject to sampling error, which can be especially large in small counties and small population groups. See notes and definitions for more information.

[3]May be of any race.

Table C-1. Population, School, and Student Characteristics by County, Selected Years—*Continued*

County	State/ County Code	County Type[1]	Population, 2010		Percent of related children 5–17 years in poverty, 2010	Percent of children under 19 years with no health insurance, 2010	Number of schools and students, 2010–2011			Resident enrollment, 2006–2010 K-12 enrollment	
			Total	Percent 5–17 years			School districts	Schools	Students	Number	Percent public
			1	2	3	4	5	6	7	8	9
WEST VIRGINIA— *(Continued)*											
Lewis, WV	54041	7	16,372	15.0	25.8	5.5	1	6	2,605	2,353	93.6
Lincoln, WV	54043	2	21,720	16.7	29.7	5.4	1	9	3,679	3,591	96.8
Logan, WV	54045	6	36,743	15.3	26.0	5.9	1	18	6,449	5,606	98.4
McDowell, WV	54047	7	22,113	14.5	42.6	4.5	1	11	3,559	3,190	94.0
Marion, WV	54049	4	56,418	14.3	23.1	4.6	1	21	8,104	7,920	94.6
Marshall, WV	54051	3	33,107	15.6	22.8	4.4	1	13	4,778	5,299	91.8
Mason, WV	54053	6	27,324	16.0	24.9	5.1	1	11	4,381	4,309	96.1
Mercer, WV	54055	5	62,264	14.8	30.3	4.5	1	25	9,611	8,941	96.3
Mineral, WV	54057	3	28,212	15.4	21.8	4.9	1	14	4,373	4,730	92.2
Mingo, WV	54059	6	26,839	16.0	28.5	4.9	1	15	4,573	4,335	96.6
Monongalia, WV	54061	3	96,189	11.2	15.8	5.0	1	20	10,731	10,524	91.4
Monroe, WV	54063	8	13,502	15.4	23.4	6.8	1	5	1,921	2,110	90.1
Morgan, WV	54065	3	17,541	15.7	18.2	6.5	1	8	2,617	2,918	95.0
Nicholas, WV	54067	6	26,233	15.2	26.5	5.4	1	16	4,076	4,106	97.4
Ohio, WV	54069	3	44,443	14.0	22.2	4.5	1	13	5,370	6,619	75.3
Pendleton, WV	54071	8	7,695	14.0	21.7	7.9	1	4	1,065	1,013	97.4
Pleasants, WV	54073	3	7,605	15.7	17.3	5.0	1	5	1,278	1,345	98.6
Pocahontas, WV	54075	9	8,719	13.4	27.7	7.0	1	5	1,183	1,309	98.9
Preston, WV	54077	3	33,520	14.2	21.9	6.2	1	12	4,600	5,022	95.8
Putnam, WV	54079	2	55,486	17.7	12.2	4.6	1	23	9,631	9,012	94.1
Raleigh, WV	54081	4	78,859	14.7	25.3	5.0	1	30	12,372	11,626	92.1
Randolph, WV	54083	7	29,405	14.3	26.8	5.2	1	16	4,294	4,274	95.7
Ritchie, WV	54085	8	10,449	15.7	25.6	6.1	1	6	1,578	1,689	99.1
Roane, WV	54087	6	14,926	16.2	29.8	5.5	1	6	2,505	2,422	99.8
Summers, WV	54089	7	13,927	13.6	31.6	5.5	1	5	1,551	2,087	94.7
Taylor, WV	54091	6	16,895	15.1	25.5	5.7	1	6	2,395	2,812	93.9
Tucker, WV	54093	9	7,141	14.5	22.2	6.9	1	3	1,053	1,076	95.9
Tyler, WV	54095	6	9,208	15.8	23.1	5.6	1	4	1,419	1,509	99.5
Upshur, WV	54097	7	24,254	14.8	26.3	5.5	1	10	3,867	3,411	97.3
Wayne, WV	54099	2	42,481	16.7	25.5	5.0	1	21	7,448	7,405	96.0
Webster, WV	54101	9	9,154	15.6	37.7	6.2	1	6	1,534	1,413	98.3
Wetzel, WV	54103	6	16,583	15.8	24.3	5.2	1	9	2,844	2,668	98.6
Wirt, WV	54105	3	5,717	15.7	31.1	6.9	1	3	1,010	1,052	93.9
Wood, WV	54107	3	86,956	16.0	22.4	4.4	1	28	13,462	13,693	93.9
Wyoming, WV	54109	7	23,796	15.9	27.0	5.6	1	14	4,229	3,777	96.1
WISCONSIN	55000	X	5,686,986	17.3	17.0	5.3	461	2,238	872,286	1,000,109	87.0
Adams, WI	55001	8	20,875	12.3	27.3	7.4	1	5	1,820	2,812	94.6
Ashland, WI	55003	7	16,157	17.0	25.7	5.7	4	11	2,671	2,707	94.1
Barron, WI	55005	6	45,870	16.2	20.4	7.2	9	36	7,924	7,469	91.8
Bayfield, WI	55007	8	15,014	14.6	21.7	8.1	4	12	1,523	2,238	89.3
Brown, WI	55009	2	248,007	18.0	13.0	4.5	10	79	42,755	44,767	88.5
Buffalo, WI	55011	8	13,587	16.5	14.9	7.5	4	10	2,161	2,341	94.3
Burnett, WI	55013	8	15,457	14.8	24.9	8.3	3	10	2,717	2,315	88.8
Calumet, WI	55015	3	48,971	20.1	6.9	4.2	6	15	3,959	9,852	86.9
Chippewa, WI	55017	3	62,415	17.0	17.0	5.5	7	23	8,874	10,880	87.6
Clark, WI	55019	8	34,690	20.7	22.9	16.0	8	21	5,005	6,634	77.6
Columbia, WI	55021	2	56,833	17.3	12.1	4.8	9	35	8,929	9,680	90.9
Crawford, WI	55023	7	16,644	16.7	19.6	7.0	4	13	2,278	3,016	82.5
Dane, WI	55025	2	488,073	15.5	11.3	4.0	18	186	69,798	74,720	91.6
Dodge, WI	55027	4	88,759	16.4	10.8	4.5	11	33	10,843	14,882	83.3
Door, WI	55029	6	27,785	13.7	15.0	6.4	5	17	3,589	3,724	91.0
Douglas, WI	55031	2	44,159	15.6	17.4	5.4	3	14	6,658	7,015	91.2
Dunn, WI	55033	6	43,857	15.1	18.5	5.2	4	15	6,069	6,563	90.5
Eau Claire, WI	55035	3	98,736	15.2	15.6	4.7	4	33	13,905	15,042	90.7
Florence, WI	55037	9	4,423	13.3	19.0	8.1	1	3	481	680	93.1
Fond du Lac, WI	55039	3	101,633	16.8	13.6	5.1	6	35	13,377	17,491	86.7

[1]County type codes are from the Economic Research Service of the United States Department of Agriculture. See notes and definitions for more information.

Table C-1. Population, School, and Student Characteristics by County, Selected Years—*Continued*

County	State/ County Code	Characteristics of students, 2010–2011				Number of graduates, 2008–2009	Staff and students, 2010–2011			
		Percent with IEP[2]	Percent eligible for free or reduced lunch	Percent minority	Percent English-language learners		Total staff	Number of teachers	Student/ teacher ratio	Central admin. staff
		10	11	12	13	14	15	16	17	18
WEST VIRGINIA— *(Continued)*										
Lewis, WV	54041	16.2	55.2	2.0	0.3	161	378	188	13.9	21
Lincoln, WV	54043	20.7	67.8	1.2	...	186	528	270	13.6	24
Logan, WV	54045	11.4	57.2	3.8	0.1	416	852	438	14.7	40
McDowell, WV	54047	17.5	78.5	11.5	...	222	549	275	12.9	35
Marion, WV	54049	14.4	50.8	8.5	0.1	517	1,084	567	14.3	43
Marshall, WV	54051	15.4	49.1	2.6	...	362	690	350	13.7	34
Mason, WV	54053	17.7	60.0	2.5	0.2	267	590	295	14.8	30
Mercer, WV	54055	14.2	62.4	12.2	0.1	499	1,238	663	14.5	56
Mineral, WV	54057	16.8	42.9	5.3	...	333	614	309	14.1	24
Mingo, WV	54059	15.1	70.3	3.4	...	310	699	356	12.8	38
Monongalia, WV	54061	14.0	39.6	12.2	3.0	676	1,405	722	14.9	64
Monroe, WV	54063	15.9	59.0	2.6	...	118	298	138	14.0	15
Morgan, WV	54065	12.8	54.6	3.1	0.6	175	353	185	14.2	21
Nicholas, WV	54067	18.8	54.8	1.5	0.2	289	588	299	13.7	25
Ohio, WV	54069	16.3	45.9	11.7	0.1	390	750	384	14.0	48
Pendleton, WV	54071	18.9	55.9	5.4	0.2	61	169	88	12.0	12
Pleasants, WV	54073	17.8	47.3	3.3	...	99	201	102	12.6	12
Pocahontas, WV	54075	16.7	59.9	0.9	0.1	80	186	93	12.7	7
Preston, WV	54077	20.4	48.2	1.0	...	274	622	336	13.7	30
Putnam, WV	54079	17.6	34.4	4.2	0.4	598	1,217	665	14.5	66
Raleigh, WV	54081	12.7	50.1	12.7	0.3	739	1,612	868	14.3	63
Randolph, WV	54083	17.2	56.7	3.3	0.1	271	600	330	13.0	23
Ritchie, WV	54085	18.4	46.0	1.7	...	87	233	116	13.6	10
Roane, WV	54087	17.6	56.5	2.5	...	163	346	178	14.1	15
Summers, WV	54089	13.3	65.4	5.1	...	91	210	108	14.4	11
Taylor, WV	54091	16.3	48.5	1.7	...	134	316	162	14.7	17
Tucker, WV	54093	15.2	59.4	1.9	...	108	157	83	12.7	10
Tyler, WV	54095	17.4	52.8	0.8	...	96	217	113	12.6	14
Upshur, WV	54097	17.9	52.3	1.9	...	220	524	278	13.9	24
Wayne, WV	54099	17.9	57.0	1.6	0.3	505	1,040	557	13.4	42
Webster, WV	54101	13.5	64.0	2.0	0.1	96	231	124	12.4	9
Wetzel, WV	54103	19.1	51.7	1.6	...	243	405	218	13.1	18
Wirt, WV	54105	14.8	55.6	2.0	...	77	145	78	12.9	6
Wood, WV	54107	14.0	49.1	5.1	0.4	839	1,775	931	14.5	85
Wyoming, WV	54109	18.4	59.1	1.6	...	232	580	321	13.2	30
WISCONSIN	55000	14.3	39.3	25.6	5.0	65,408	103,901	57,625	15.1	3,606
Adams, WI	55001	20.9	68.6	7.7	0.1	144	265	140	13.0	9
Ashland, WI	55003	17.0	58.4	20.4	...	242	366	208	12.9	28
Barron, WI	55005	13.0	46.2	8.5	1.9	652	1,015	556	14.3	59
Bayfield, WI	55007	18.8	57.0	30.1	0.3	153	259	140	10.8	14
Brown, WI	55009	13.8	38.0	26.2	10.0	3,083	4,973	2,870	14.9	168
Buffalo, WI	55011	14.2	35.6	3.9	0.3	188	279	158	13.7	15
Burnett, WI	55013	15.1	51.2	16.8	0.9	190	307	176	15.5	20
Calumet, WI	55015	14.7	26.0	12.2	2.6	334	513	295	13.4	18
Chippewa, WI	55017	13.4	39.3	5.1	...	644	1,074	590	15.0	63
Clark, WI	55019	12.2	49.9	11.1	5.2	422	656	385	13.0	28
Columbia, WI	55021	13.2	28.6	9.8	1.7	704	1,249	660	13.5	66
Crawford, WI	55023	16.5	56.0	4.8	...	190	314	179	12.7	16
Dane, WI	55025	13.9	30.5	29.9	8.6	4,923	9,368	5,014	13.9	277
Dodge, WI	55027	15.0	37.2	12.0	3.4	880	1,332	755	14.4	52
Door, WI	55029	12.8	33.8	8.9	2.2	359	502	283	12.7	20
Douglas, WI	55031	14.6	46.1	9.9	0.1	491	833	442	15.1	27
Dunn, WI	55033	14.0	39.4	11.4	4.0	459	679	397	15.3	29
Eau Claire, WI	55035	12.8	40.2	16.0	3.2	1,084	1,519	882	15.8	45
Florence, WI	55037	15.6	45.9	5.4	...	49	68	37	13.0	4
Fond du Lac, WI	55039	13.9	36.3	13.9	3.2	1,088	1,467	875	15.3	38

[2]IEP=Individual Education Program. See notes and definitions for more information.
. . . = Not available.

Table C-1. Population, School, and Student Characteristics by County, Selected Years—*Continued*

County	State/ County Code	Revenues, 2008–2009				Current expenditures, 2008–2009			Resident population 16 to 19 years, 2006–2010			
		Total revenue ($1,000's)	Percentage of revenue from			Amount ($1,000's)	Amount per student	Percent for instruction	Total population 16 to 19 years	Percent enrolled in school	Percent high school graduates, not enrolled in school	Percent not enrolled, not grads, not employed, or not in labor force
			Federal government	State government	Local government							
		19	20	21	22	23	24	25	26	27	28	29
WEST VIRGINIA— *(Continued)*												
Lewis, WV	54041	29,709	11.3	54.9	33.8	29,851	11,114	56.3	782	78.8	8.6	12.7
Lincoln, WV	54043	41,766	17.3	64.0	18.7	39,627	10,989	57.1	1,161	64.1	14.0	15.8
Logan, WV	54045	71,398	11.5	57.2	31.4	63,850	9,814	60.8	1,624	78.5	14.6	7.0
McDowell, WV	54047	46,631	20.5	52.2	27.3	42,874	11,666	57.8	1,186	72.1	17.5	10.1
Marion, WV	54049	86,442	10.5	59.2	30.2	86,258	10,620	63.4	3,299	81.8	12.6	5.1
Marshall, WV	54051	67,655	11.0	50.8	38.2	57,597	11,788	59.4	1,631	80.1	9.6	9.9
Mason, WV	54053	51,175	11.8	54.9	33.3	47,390	11,024	60.6	1,337	78.2	10.6	10.0
Mercer, WV	54055	98,046	13.8	66.1	20.1	97,114	10,182	60.0	3,103	73.6	17.4	7.9
Mineral, WV	54057	49,075	12.4	66.3	21.3	48,026	10,553	58.4	1,818	85.0	11.7	2.5
Mingo, WV	54059	54,354	14.5	55.2	30.3	51,202	10,922	59.4	1,398	78.4	13.5	6.3
Monongalia, WV	54061	122,804	9.5	48.8	41.7	107,989	10,491	58.4	9,318	94.0	4.0	1.9
Monroe, WV	54063	21,083	15.4	67.6	17.1	20,333	10,401	60.0	658	80.1	13.4	1.7
Morgan, WV	54065	27,436	7.8	54.5	37.7	27,099	10,067	57.6	935	81.8	10.8	3.3
Nicholas, WV	54067	44,035	16.1	63.5	20.4	42,917	10,511	61.1	1,376	78.9	13.4	6.8
Ohio, WV	54069	60,015	10.9	58.7	30.4	59,084	11,192	59.7	2,731	86.8	7.8	5.3
Pendleton, WV	54071	12,376	9.4	72.2	18.5	12,161	11,045	58.7	318	66.0	18.6	15.4
Pleasants, WV	54073	17,133	7.9	43.3	48.9	16,611	12,341	56.1	427	90.2	2.3	1.9
Pocahontas, WV	54075	13,744	19.6	50.1	30.3	13,498	11,165	57.7	253	79.1	11.5	9.5
Preston, WV	54077	45,612	13.8	67.6	18.6	45,730	10,031	66.0	1,637	74.4	16.1	8.4
Putnam, WV	54079	98,181	6.6	58.3	35.1	94,784	10,147	61.2	2,609	79.8	12.7	5.4
Raleigh, WV	54081	131,587	11.3	57.8	30.8	120,125	9,754	58.3	3,628	74.6	14.5	7.3
Randolph, WV	54083	44,273	16.3	70.5	13.2	42,460	9,596	63.3	1,446	80.2	15.6	1.6
Ritchie, WV	54085	18,944	12.0	62.1	25.9	17,490	11,007	57.4	503	89.1	4.4	6.6
Roane, WV	54087	24,495	14.5	72.9	12.7	24,107	9,498	60.2	705	73.1	11.2	8.4
Summers, WV	54089	15,300	14.6	69.8	15.6	16,040	10,470	58.0	760	80.5	7.9	8.0
Taylor, WV	54091	25,357	11.0	66.1	22.9	23,768	9,797	59.4	773	78.9	16.6	3.4
Tucker, WV	54093	11,997	13.9	57.2	28.9	12,265	10,883	58.2	329	71.1	24.6	4.3
Tyler, WV	54095	18,597	11.3	59.4	29.3	17,198	11,628	58.1	550	83.5	2.9	13.6
Upshur, WV	54097	40,034	13.4	66.2	20.4	38,288	9,914	61.0	1,589	88.8	7.2	3.4
Wayne, WV	54099	78,689	12.1	66.0	21.9	75,098	9,720	61.8	2,242	83.1	12.0	3.8
Webster, WV	54101	20,768	13.0	76.9	10.1	15,730	10,148	62.1	446	75.8	11.2	3.4
Wetzel, WV	54103	33,502	11.6	62.5	25.9	32,790	11,230	59.5	966	84.3	9.1	5.3
Wirt, WV	54105	10,075	15.3	70.2	14.5	10,044	10,528	56.8	386	81.1	18.9	0.0
Wood, WV	54107	143,817	10.2	60.8	29.0	138,506	10,274	63.8	4,107	78.0	14.7	5.3
Wyoming, WV	54109	50,774	10.8	56.5	32.7	46,069	11,128	61.2	1,225	76.3	13.2	9.6
WISCONSIN	55000	10,991,081	11.5	43.5	45.0	9,605,409	11,079	61.0	327,328	86.3	9.5	2.6
Adams, WI	55001	25,094	13.9	34.2	51.9	21,363	11,655	62.6	895	67.4	30.4	1.6
Ashland, WI	55003	37,218	15.7	55.0	29.3	33,883	11,822	59.5	982	80.7	14.0	0.9
Barron, WI	55005	102,080	10.0	43.0	47.0	85,178	10,770	60.5	2,344	78.8	14.1	3.5
Bayfield, WI	55007	26,543	14.2	21.2	64.6	21,907	14,115	59.4	661	87.6	8.8	2.0
Brown, WI	55009	502,358	11.7	50.3	38.1	433,077	10,294	61.9	14,164	87.8	7.5	3.1
Buffalo, WI	55011	28,754	10.6	51.1	38.3	23,367	10,464	61.9	745	85.0	10.7	3.5
Burnett, WI	55013	31,824	8.1	28.7	63.2	25,839	9,892	62.4	746	82.7	14.5	2.6
Calumet, WI	55015	50,822	8.1	47.8	44.1	38,257	9,519	57.8	2,512	87.6	10.0	0.8
Chippewa, WI	55017	107,442	10.4	50.6	39.0	91,569	10,362	61.6	3,279	84.1	13.3	1.6
Clark, WI	55019	67,740	12.0	54.0	34.0	54,243	10,476	58.2	2,061	67.2	9.8	11.5
Columbia, WI	55021	108,971	9.2	44.0	46.8	94,874	10,633	62.5	2,934	81.7	9.5	4.4
Crawford, WI	55023	30,372	13.1	53.3	33.6	26,707	11,612	60.2	957	88.9	6.2	1.8
Dane, WI	55025	895,870	7.8	31.7	60.5	765,592	11,517	60.7	28,044	91.6	6.6	1.1
Dodge, WI	55027	136,055	9.9	49.6	40.5	118,115	10,804	63.4	4,596	81.7	14.0	3.5
Door, WI	55029	51,787	6.5	20.8	72.7	44,948	12,080	61.8	1,278	72.5	25.0	1.4
Douglas, WI	55031	82,925	12.1	50.5	37.4	70,092	10,446	59.9	2,239	86.6	11.3	1.5
Dunn, WI	55033	71,644	10.9	49.9	39.1	61,345	10,253	63.1	4,205	94.7	4.0	1.0
Eau Claire, WI	55035	172,801	10.5	47.7	41.7	147,594	10,741	60.4	7,114	87.5	9.0	2.4
Florence, WI	55037	8,586	6.9	22.1	71.0	6,496	12,589	51.2	212	76.9	21.2	1.9
Fond du Lac, WI	55039	165,543	11.1	50.7	38.2	140,061	10,284	63.1	5,642	89.6	8.5	1.2

Note. Data in columns 26 through 41 from the American Community Survey are subject to sampling error, which can be especially large in small counties and small population groups. See notes and definitions for more information.

Table C-1. Population, School, and Student Characteristics by County, Selected Years—*Continued*

County	State/ County Code	High school graduates, 2006–2010			College enrollment, 2006–2010		College graduates, 2006–2010 (percent)						
		Population 25 years and over	High school diploma or less (percent)	High school diploma or more (percent)	Number	Percent public	Bachelor's degree or more	+/- U.S. percent with Bachelor's degree or more	Non-Hispanic White	Black or African American	American Indian and Alaska Native	Asian, Hawaiian, and Pacific Islander	Hispanic or Latino[3]
		30	31	32	33	34	35	36	37	38	39	40	41
WEST VIRGINIA— *(Continued)*													
Lewis, WV	54041	11,833	68.6	79.4	520	77.7	12.0	-15.9	11.8	29.5	0.0	69.1	0.0
Lincoln, WV	54043	15,237	73.9	66.4	493	83.0	7.7	-20.2	7.6	100.0	0.0	0.0	0.0
Logan, WV	54045	26,264	69.7	74.9	1,217	90.5	8.9	-19.0	8.6	10.0	0.0	75.6	0.0
McDowell, WV	54047	16,177	78.5	59.7	735	82.9	6.3	-21.6	6.0	8.5	0.0	0.0	0.0
Marion, WV	54049	39,085	55.4	86.4	4,674	83.1	19.2	-8.7	19.3	13.5	0.0	61.4	5.3
Marshall, WV	54051	23,901	61.1	85.2	1,609	85.0	12.2	-15.7	11.9	0.0	0.0	60.4	14.2
Mason, WV	54053	19,238	65.5	79.0	1,139	77.3	10.3	-17.6	10.5	0.0	16.7	100.0	0.0
Mercer, WV	54055	43,748	62.1	79.1	3,612	78.1	16.4	-11.5	16.4	13.8	0.0	32.2	20.2
Mineral, WV	54057	19,302	62.7	86.4	1,533	91.2	13.0	-14.9	13.0	1.7	0.0	0.0	46.2
Mingo, WV	54059	18,793	70.4	69.5	815	85.9	9.0	-18.9	8.8	10.0	0.0	58.7	0.0
Monongalia, WV	54061	52,709	44.3	87.2	23,629	98.1	35.8	7.9	34.4	27.8	0.0	87.1	49.0
Monroe, WV	54063	9,729	66.5	75.7	243	74.5	13.3	-14.6	13.1	0.0	35.8	0.0	47.2
Morgan, WV	54065	12,554	66.8	84.1	448	82.6	12.7	-15.2	12.4	11.2	48.7	60.0	4.7
Nicholas, WV	54067	18,691	67.7	79.9	897	90.7	13.0	-14.9	13.0	0.0	0.0	0.0	0.0
Ohio, WV	54069	31,116	47.9	89.1	3,432	82.6	25.9	-2.0	26.2	8.8	21.3	59.1	42.1
Pendleton, WV	54071	5,777	64.7	79.9	203	95.1	13.1	-14.8	13.5	0.5	0.0	0.0	0.0
Pleasants, WV	54073	5,479	61.0	87.1	418	98.6	10.4	-17.5	10.6	0.0	60.0	0.0	0.0
Pocahontas, WV	54075	6,595	67.0	79.0	188	85.1	13.5	-14.4	13.7	0.0	0.0	0.0	0.0
Preston, WV	54077	23,780	67.8	82.5	924	84.5	11.6	-16.3	12.1	3.2	0.0	0.0	6.5
Putnam, WV	54079	38,322	48.9	88.9	2,092	83.6	23.8	-4.1	23.8	7.8	0.0	58.9	16.6
Raleigh, WV	54081	55,909	61.3	78.4	4,106	49.9	15.4	-12.5	16.0	6.2	0.0	61.5	0.0
Randolph, WV	54083	20,936	65.4	81.1	1,583	47.9	17.6	-10.3	17.6	0.0	17.3	59.7	45.0
Ritchie, WV	54085	7,540	61.7	79.5	321	74.1	10.3	-17.6	10.3	100.0	0.0	0.0	12.8
Roane, WV	54087	10,762	74.1	76.6	436	86.2	9.1	-18.8	9.3	0.0	10.2	0.0	4.6
Summers, WV	54089	10,430	67.7	75.7	628	79.8	11.2	-16.7	11.3	13.1	0.0	0.0	0.0
Taylor, WV	54091	11,968	64.3	83.5	554	75.6	14.5	-13.4	14.3	12.6	0.0	84.0	0.0
Tucker, WV	54093	5,253	66.2	81.5	161	57.1	13.7	-14.2	13.7	0.0	0.0	0.0	0.0
Tyler, WV	54095	6,661	70.9	82.8	209	100.0	8.4	-19.5	8.2	0.0	63.0	0.0	0.0
Upshur, WV	54097	16,276	67.0	79.6	2,376	37.8	15.2	-12.7	15.1	0.0	0.0	19.4	18.5
Wayne, WV	54099	29,805	62.0	78.1	2,035	81.9	12.7	-15.2	12.5	0.0	0.0	60.2	5.6
Webster, WV	54101	6,637	76.6	69.1	49	95.9	8.0	-19.9	8.1	0.0	0.0	0.0	0.0
Wetzel, WV	54103	11,893	64.7	82.5	643	82.6	12.6	-15.3	12.8	0.0	0.0	0.0	0.0
Wirt, WV	54105	4,159	68.5	84.0	106	100.0	11.0	-16.9	11.1	0.0	0.0	0.0	0.0
Wood, WV	54107	61,144	49.3	86.6	4,694	80.6	19.1	-8.8	18.8	20.4	12.7	79.9	22.8
Wyoming, WV	54109	16,967	73.1	72.7	831	84.2	9.4	-18.5	9.2	32.4	0.0	40.3	0.0
WISCONSIN	55000	3,739,243	44.6	89.4	401,113	77.1	25.8	-2.1	26.9	13.1	11.5	45.6	10.9
Adams, WI	55001	16,187	58.7	84.0	611	81.8	10.8	-17.1	11.2	3.4	0.0	13.1	6.9
Ashland, WI	55003	10,804	46.6	89.5	1,194	48.5	20.7	-7.2	21.2	0.0	12.3	56.5	26.1
Barron, WI	55005	32,008	53.4	86.1	1,842	89.9	17.6	-10.3	17.7	0.0	12.8	13.5	11.8
Bayfield, WI	55007	11,392	40.3	91.8	475	79.8	26.8	-1.1	28.5	0.0	9.3	28.9	48.9
Brown, WI	55009	157,917	44.5	90.0	17,809	69.9	25.6	-2.3	27.0	13.2	15.3	29.2	6.8
Buffalo, WI	55011	9,635	55.6	87.7	506	85.6	15.5	-12.4	15.7	0.0	4.4	0.0	9.3
Burnett, WI	55013	11,806	52.4	88.0	465	86.9	16.0	-11.9	16.8	0.0	4.2	0.0	31.0
Calumet, WI	55015	31,706	45.7	92.0	1,921	79.1	25.3	-2.6	25.6	7.7	0.0	46.9	1.8
Chippewa, WI	55017	41,948	50.4	88.4	2,407	88.3	17.6	-10.3	17.7	17.8	6.0	18.2	18.7
Clark, WI	55019	21,800	63.3	80.7	911	83.0	11.3	-16.6	11.4	25.0	15.7	21.6	2.2
Columbia, WI	55021	39,088	48.1	90.6	2,261	78.9	19.9	-8.0	20.4	1.3	7.9	24.6	8.8
Crawford, WI	55023	11,723	56.7	88.7	813	82.8	15.9	-12.0	16.1	5.7	16.0	0.0	0.0
Dane, WI	55025	308,170	26.6	94.3	60,978	88.3	45.4	17.5	46.8	20.2	40.6	65.2	22.0
Dodge, WI	55027	61,794	55.2	86.1	3,495	78.2	15.2	-12.7	15.9	2.3	3.2	29.4	6.1
Door, WI	55029	21,323	44.3	92.6	793	74.9	27.6	-0.3	27.2	66.7	0.0	61.6	9.0
Douglas, WI	55031	29,966	42.9	90.5	3,055	86.2	22.0	-5.9	22.1	16.4	9.2	33.7	31.1
Dunn, WI	55033	25,597	46.3	90.8	7,483	94.2	24.9	-3.0	24.8	36.6	10.6	37.7	19.8
Eau Claire, WI	55035	58,925	38.0	91.9	13,652	92.4	30.2	2.3	30.8	10.1	19.7	18.9	11.5
Florence, WI	55037	3,425	57.5	87.4	221	79.6	12.1	-15.8	12.3	0.0	4.0	0.0	28.6
Fond du Lac, WI	55039	68,474	51.6	88.5	6,492	63.7	18.0	-9.9	18.1	0.0	5.5	70.4	10.2

Note. Data in columns 26 through 41 from the American Community Survey are subject to sampling error, which can be especially large in small counties and small population groups. See notes and definitions for more information.

[3]May be of any race.

Table C-1. Population, School, and Student Characteristics by County, Selected Years—*Continued*

County	State/ County Code	County Type[1]	Population, 2010		Percent of related children 5–17 years in poverty, 2010	Percent of children under 19 years with no health insurance, 2010	Number of schools and students, 2010–2011			Resident enrollment, 2006–2010 K–12 enrollment	
			Total	Percent 5–17 years			School districts	Schools	Students	Number	Percent public
			1	2	3	4	5	6	7	8	9
WISCONSIN—*(Continued)*											
Forest, WI	55041	9	9,304	16.6	24.9	7.7	3	8	1,652	1,635	95.5
Grant, WI	55043	6	51,208	15.4	19.5	7.1	11	27	7,120	7,757	86.2
Green, WI	55045	6	36,842	17.9	13.1	5.3	6	21	5,859	6,648	94.0
Green Lake, WI	55047	6	19,051	17.2	21.2	7.5	4	12	3,167	3,309	87.7
Iowa, WI	55049	2	23,687	18.1	12.4	5.8	5	14	3,611	4,264	89.3
Iron, WI	55051	9	5,916	13.0	22.6	6.7	2	4	791	771	98.7
Jackson, WI	55053	6	20,449	16.5	23.5	7.4	3	12	3,164	3,433	94.2
Jefferson, WI	55055	4	83,686	17.5	13.7	5.1	8	37	13,754	14,630	82.3
Juneau, WI	55057	7	26,664	15.8	23.9	7.0	5	16	3,878	4,652	90.9
Kenosha, WI	55059	1	166,426	19.1	17.2	5.8	12	56	30,174	32,505	91.5
Kewaunee, WI	55061	2	20,574	17.9	11.0	5.9	3	11	3,526	3,789	83.5
La Crosse, WI	55063	3	114,638	15.5	12.7	4.1	6	39	16,098	17,657	87.3
Lafayette, WI	55065	8	16,836	18.8	19.2	10.7	7	16	2,903	3,217	92.3
Langlade, WI	55067	6	19,977	15.9	20.0	5.8	3	13	3,120	3,318	83.3
Lincoln, WI	55069	6	28,743	16.8	14.7	5.7	3	12	4,468	4,876	87.0
Manitowoc, WI	55071	4	81,442	16.8	14.8	5.0	6	31	11,249	14,377	83.2
Marathon, WI	55073	3	134,063	18.0	16.1	5.4	9	48	19,842	24,580	89.6
Marinette, WI	55075	6	41,749	15.5	19.6	5.5	8	23	6,227	6,470	90.8
Marquette, WI	55077	8	15,404	14.8	19.5	7.4	2	8	1,832	2,312	91.0
Menominee, WI	55078	8	4,232	22.9	47.7	5.5	1	3	822	980	94.0
Milwaukee, WI	55079	1	947,735	17.6	32.5	5.8	35	307	140,704	177,037	82.5
Monroe, WI	55081	6	44,673	18.9	21.4	8.4	4	26	7,046	8,041	84.9
Oconto, WI	55083	2	37,660	16.8	16.3	6.0	6	20	4,510	6,607	95.8
Oneida, WI	55085	7	35,998	13.8	15.9	5.8	4	14	4,589	5,302	90.8
Outagamie, WI	55087	3	176,695	18.5	10.8	4.7	8	71	33,751	32,909	88.6
Ozaukee, WI	55089	1	86,395	18.3	5.1	3.6	5	26	13,123	16,193	80.5
Pepin, WI	55091	8	7,469	16.5	19.4	7.9	2	4	1,227	1,272	86.9
Pierce, WI	55093	1	41,019	16.4	9.3	4.4	6	24	7,435	6,599	90.8
Polk, WI	55095	6	44,205	17.6	16.1	6.1	8	26	7,831	7,853	95.3
Portage, WI	55097	4	70,019	15.2	12.1	4.6	4	27	9,464	10,846	83.7
Price, WI	55099	9	14,159	14.7	18.9	6.2	3	12	2,089	2,242	87.3
Racine, WI	55101	3	195,408	18.3	18.6	4.8	13	56	30,883	36,986	83.7
Richland, WI	55103	6	18,021	16.8	22.9	6.9	2	8	1,750	3,148	84.0
Rock, WI	55105	3	160,331	18.5	18.5	6.0	9	69	27,701	30,285	92.8
Rusk, WI	55107	6	14,755	17.0	27.4	7.4	3	12	2,104	2,476	94.0
St. Croix, WI	55109	1	84,345	19.8	7.3	4.4	6	27	14,036	16,183	90.0
Sauk, WI	55111	4	61,976	17.4	15.1	6.4	6	37	11,906	10,513	91.6
Sawyer, WI	55113	9	16,557	15.0	29.9	8.8	2	12	2,206	2,399	81.2
Shawano, WI	55115	6	41,949	17.0	17.1	7.4	6	16	5,580	7,252	91.9
Sheboygan, WI	55117	3	115,507	17.7	12.2	5.0	9	48	19,358	21,237	87.8
Taylor, WI	55119	6	20,689	18.0	20.0	7.1	3	10	3,056	3,618	90.3
Trempealeau, WI	55121	8	28,816	17.7	16.5	7.6	7	23	5,832	5,146	92.8
Vernon, WI	55123	6	29,773	19.3	24.5	12.3	6	20	4,129	5,368	78.0
Vilas, WI	55125	9	21,430	13.3	22.2	8.7	5	10	2,739	3,056	93.6
Walworth, WI	55127	4	102,228	17.4	14.5	6.8	16	38	16,252	18,014	91.7
Washburn, WI	55129	6	15,911	14.8	24.4	6.6	4	13	2,619	2,419	94.1
Washington, WI	55131	1	131,887	18.3	7.0	4.0	9	36	20,215	24,484	81.4
Waukesha, WI	55133	1	389,891	18.6	6.0	2.9	20	107	63,698	73,221	83.1
Waupaca, WI	55135	6	52,410	17.1	15.5	5.3	7	26	9,259	9,270	88.5
Waushara, WI	55137	8	24,496	15.0	20.3	7.8	3	10	2,811	3,965	86.4
Winnebago, WI	55139	3	166,994	15.7	11.4	4.0	6	53	22,949	27,143	89.1
Wood, WI	55141	4	74,749	16.8	15.9	4.5	6	33	12,841	13,017	90.0

[1]County type codes are from the Economic Research Service of the United States Department of Agriculture. See notes and definitions for more information.

Table C-1. Population, School, and Student Characteristics by County, Selected Years—*Continued*

County	State/ County Code	Characteristics of students, 2010–2011				Number of graduates, 2008–2009	Staff and students, 2010–2011			
		Percent with IEP[2]	Percent eligible for free or reduced lunch	Percent minority	Percent English-language learners		Total staff	Number of teachers	Student/ teacher ratio	Central admin. staff
		10	11	12	13	14	15	16	17	18
WISCONSIN—*(Continued)*										
Forest, WI	55041	16.7	40.4	27.5	0.1	130	243	129	12.8	10
Grant, WI	55043	16.8	41.7	5.2	0.3	629	969	547	13.0	46
Green, WI	55045	13.1	33.2	7.9	1.4	494	747	433	13.5	32
Green Lake, WI	55047	11.4	38.2	11.2	4.9	261	421	236	13.4	14
Iowa, WI	55049	14.5	30.8	4.2	0.8	306	477	275	13.1	19
Iron, WI	55051	15.2	53.1	3.7	0.6	63	109	62	12.7	7
Jackson, WI	55053	12.3	46.5	18.7	0.9	260	444	243	13.0	14
Jefferson, WI	55055	14.5	32.7	15.5	4.4	977	1,685	908	15.1	56
Juneau, WI	55057	15.3	52.8	7.4	0.4	307	544	312	12.4	20
Kenosha, WI	55059	13.2	43.5	34.5	5.9	1,997	3,438	1,972	15.3	88
Kewaunee, WI	55061	15.0	21.3	7.2	2.3	295	440	258	13.7	14
La Crosse, WI	55063	12.9	34.4	16.8	4.4	1,223	2,081	1,193	13.5	76
Lafayette, WI	55065	14.8	33.0	6.6	1.4	268	413	240	12.1	15
Langlade, WI	55067	18.0	54.3	7.4	1.1	274	407	233	13.4	16
Lincoln, WI	55069	14.5	43.9	4.8	0.5	389	526	293	15.3	25
Manitowoc, WI	55071	15.9	32.1	15.8	2.6	928	1,395	791	14.2	48
Marathon, WI	55073	13.0	35.9	19.2	9.2	1,656	2,294	1,336	14.9	66
Marinette, WI	55075	14.8	48.1	4.6	0.3	478	753	448	13.9	40
Marquette, WI	55077	10.6	48.7	7.6	0.8	133	257	147	12.4	7
Menominee, WI	55078	22.9	85.3	99.4	. . .	76	191	102	8.1	8
Milwaukee, WI	55079	16.6	59.2	64.5	7.4	8,966	16,133	7,892	17.8	398
Monroe, WI	55081	15.5	45.1	11.9	2.4	516	895	515	13.7	30
Oconto, WI	55083	17.3	40.9	7.4	0.9	385	630	350	12.9	37
Oneida, WI	55085	14.4	40.3	9.7	0.1	492	556	299	15.3	24
Outagamie, WI	55087	12.8	28.5	15.7	5.4	2,506	3,316	2,071	16.3	85
Ozaukee, WI	55089	13.6	14.9	11.3	1.8	1,153	1,409	796	16.5	55
Pepin, WI	55091	17.1	37.5	4.0	0.7	111	177	86	14.3	10
Pierce, WI	55093	12.1	23.9	5.9	0.6	637	896	477	15.6	29
Polk, WI	55095	12.4	40.7	5.9	0.1	602	965	524	15.0	34
Portage, WI	55097	13.0	34.7	13.5	4.5	734	1,049	566	16.7	42
Price, WI	55099	15.3	46.2	5.0	0.3	184	316	168	12.4	13
Racine, WI	55101	15.8	47.8	40.9	7.5	1,973	3,629	2,037	15.2	221
Richland, WI	55103	18.6	49.1	5.9	1.3	164	230	136	12.8	10
Rock, WI	55105	14.2	46.5	26.4	6.7	2,001	3,562	1,937	14.3	125
Rusk, WI	55107	15.8	60.5	5.9	. . .	176	261	159	13.2	13
St. Croix, WI	55109	13.0	22.9	8.2	0.9	992	1,521	878	16.0	51
Sauk, WI	55111	15.1	39.3	11.6	2.9	929	1,508	822	14.5	54
Sawyer, WI	55113	14.6	59.0	27.3	0.1	160	293	164	13.4	9
Shawano, WI	55115	14.8	48.4	19.3	1.0	477	696	403	13.8	31
Sheboygan, WI	55117	15.0	35.7	22.7	10.2	1,542	2,290	1,310	14.8	70
Taylor, WI	55119	13.3	47.0	4.3	0.8	257	349	208	14.7	12
Trempealeau, WI	55121	14.3	39.4	9.9	0.7	421	777	440	13.2	32
Vernon, WI	55123	15.2	43.3	4.6	0.3	335	564	327	12.6	25
Vilas, WI	55125	14.9	44.5	22.8	0.2	148	424	245	11.2	19
Walworth, WI	55127	13.1	40.3	24.4	9.8	1,208	1,905	1,141	14.2	54
Washburn, WI	55129	14.8	53.5	8.6	0.2	211	330	198	13.2	16
Washington, WI	55131	12.7	23.5	9.8	1.6	1,680	2,099	1,243	16.3	78
Waukesha, WI	55133	12.0	16.2	15.5	2.6	5,182	6,693	3,847	16.6	222
Waupaca, WI	55135	13.3	38.9	7.8	1.9	785	1,137	611	15.1	38
Waushara, WI	55137	11.4	58.0	20.9	6.7	208	369	213	13.2	12
Winnebago, WI	55139	15.1	36.3	16.1	4.8	1,786	2,624	1,506	15.2	97
Wood, WI	55141	13.3	36.1	10.5	2.4	1,064	1,430	858	15.0	52

[2]IEP=Individual Education Program. See notes and definitions for more information.
. . . = Not available.

Table C-1. Population, School, and Student Characteristics by County, Selected Years—*Continued*

County	State/ County Code	Revenues, 2008–2009				Current expenditures, 2008–2009			Resident population 16 to 19 years, 2006–2010			
		Total revenue ($1,000's)	Percentage of revenue from: Federal government	State government	Local government	Amount ($1,000's)	Amount per student	Percent for instruction	Total population 16 to 19 years	Percent enrolled in school	Percent high school graduates, not enrolled in school	Percent not enrolled, not grads, not employed, or not in labor force
		19	20	21	22	23	24	25	26	27	28	29
WISCONSIN— *(Continued)*												
Forest, WI	55041	22,417	13.1	26.0	60.9	20,520	11,814	59.1	642	66.2	23.8	6.5
Grant, WI	55043	90,314	11.9	53.1	35.0	82,241	11,502	62.3	4,164	92.4	3.5	3.0
Green, WI	55045	75,971	10.6	49.7	39.7	63,674	10,542	61.4	1,917	84.8	10.6	3.7
Green Lake, WI	55047	41,543	7.3	36.5	56.2	34,098	11,224	60.8	921	86.8	9.2	2.7
Iowa, WI	55049	46,962	9.7	51.0	39.3	41,038	11,182	61.5	1,097	81.3	10.1	7.9
Iron, WI	55051	11,142	12.1	33.9	54.0	9,838	12,012	56.3	295	66.4	33.6	0.0
Jackson, WI	55053	37,736	12.1	55.2	32.6	33,446	10,352	60.7	1,004	75.3	10.5	5.5
Jefferson, WI	55055	166,004	9.7	44.1	46.2	144,210	10,634	59.8	5,340	88.4	8.9	1.6
Juneau, WI	55057	54,815	9.7	44.2	46.1	43,649	11,101	59.6	1,425	83.9	11.0	1.5
Kenosha, WI	55059	364,730	11.9	48.8	39.3	333,389	11,127	63.5	10,075	88.7	8.9	0.9
Kewaunee, WI	55061	40,753	11.0	54.4	34.7	36,056	10,137	60.8	1,057	90.6	7.4	1.2
La Crosse, WI	55063	206,088	11.0	47.8	41.2	186,547	11,676	60.8	8,346	92.3	6.7	0.7
Lafayette, WI	55065	40,816	11.0	53.1	35.9	34,024	11,577	61.1	933	83.3	9.0	5.0
Langlade, WI	55067	41,359	12.2	47.8	39.9	36,766	11,724	59.2	1,011	77.4	19.5	3.0
Lincoln, WI	55069	54,133	10.9	46.7	42.4	47,933	10,539	61.3	1,564	77.2	18.7	3.4
Manitowoc, WI	55071	137,318	11.5	54.5	34.0	120,968	10,347	62.1	4,558	86.7	8.7	2.7
Marathon, WI	55073	247,378	11.1	52.6	36.4	221,946	11,110	61.1	7,575	85.2	11.9	1.4
Marinette, WI	55075	79,289	9.6	42.2	48.2	67,265	10,474	61.1	2,241	76.2	16.4	5.1
Marquette, WI	55077	26,666	10.7	32.9	56.4	22,089	11,363	59.6	703	77.7	19.9	0.0
Menominee, WI	55078	19,384	41.2	39.7	19.1	15,593	19,274	50.9	300	63.3	30.3	2.3
Milwaukee, WI	55079	1,884,197	18.1	44.7	37.2	1,707,353	12,463	57.9	56,970	85.7	8.9	4.3
Monroe, WI	55081	84,744	14.4	57.4	28.2	73,225	10,622	61.3	2,505	70.9	15.8	8.2
Oconto, WI	55083	59,890	10.7	50.2	39.1	49,372	10,381	61.0	1,977	85.4	9.3	1.5
Oneida, WI	55085	68,523	9.2	15.7	75.2	59,223	12,471	58.3	1,799	70.7	19.2	1.6
Outagamie, WI	55087	379,395	10.8	52.6	36.6	336,360	10,082	63.2	9,998	88.8	8.2	1.4
Ozaukee, WI	55089	161,072	5.8	25.1	69.1	143,786	10,590	60.6	4,947	91.6	5.5	2.3
Pepin, WI	55091	18,689	9.5	44.0	46.5	15,725	12,392	57.7	376	83.0	12.5	2.9
Pierce, WI	55093	91,304	8.9	43.3	47.8	76,295	10,238	62.7	3,418	94.0	4.5	1.2
Polk, WI	55095	101,257	8.2	41.1	50.7	83,086	10,491	62.5	2,325	83.1	12.7	1.9
Portage, WI	55097	114,684	10.2	49.6	40.2	99,947	10,427	62.7	5,227	90.7	8.1	0.3
Price, WI	55099	25,910	11.8	36.2	52.0	23,245	10,975	59.2	654	92.1	6.3	1.2
Racine, WI	55101	374,961	12.9	49.5	37.5	337,959	11,081	63.0	10,675	82.5	11.0	3.9
Richland, WI	55103	24,361	12.0	51.2	36.8	20,191	11,472	59.1	1,048	80.6	10.9	3.4
Rock, WI	55105	334,787	13.1	56.9	29.9	303,112	10,686	61.7	9,097	82.2	13.8	2.8
Rusk, WI	55107	34,774	11.2	47.1	41.7	28,164	12,166	58.7	732	67.1	8.3	16.5
St. Croix, WI	55109	159,987	8.4	45.4	46.2	133,224	9,870	60.2	4,200	91.4	6.9	0.7
Sauk, WI	55111	140,330	9.7	39.6	50.6	123,843	10,690	62.1	3,152	81.0	12.5	3.1
Sawyer, WI	55113	30,764	10.7	11.8	77.5	25,900	11,315	58.2	794	53.5	15.2	30.9
Shawano, WI	55115	75,751	12.2	50.4	37.4	62,610	10,961	59.6	2,188	82.7	11.6	2.4
Sheboygan, WI	55117	240,864	10.7	50.4	39.0	215,825	10,938	65.4	6,155	84.9	11.5	2.1
Taylor, WI	55119	35,255	11.9	55.1	33.1	32,692	10,542	59.8	1,100	78.9	16.5	4.2
Trempealeau, WI	55121	76,383	11.2	55.2	33.6	62,737	10,596	60.2	1,404	86.1	9.7	1.9
Vernon, WI	55123	54,057	12.9	50.5	36.6	45,356	10,856	58.8	1,591	70.0	14.2	11.4
Vilas, WI	55125	48,487	10.3	8.1	81.6	39,022	14,144	58.0	994	75.9	21.7	0.1
Walworth, WI	55127	217,841	7.4	29.0	63.6	178,380	10,880	62.7	6,290	85.8	12.0	1.6
Washburn, WI	55129	38,953	8.1	17.5	74.4	30,561	11,585	60.6	538	75.8	1.9	0.6
Washington, WI	55131	234,540	7.7	38.0	54.4	207,355	10,292	61.9	6,996	88.7	9.0	1.7
Waukesha, WI	55133	787,868	6.2	25.7	68.1	677,445	10,822	62.0	21,622	91.2	6.5	1.2
Waupaca, WI	55135	117,055	10.7	50.6	38.8	100,545	10,589	61.1	2,754	80.3	15.1	3.4
Waushara, WI	55137	36,706	11.7	36.7	51.6	31,649	10,861	60.2	1,190	83.5	10.8	3.7
Winnebago, WI	55139	267,329	10.9	51.2	37.9	240,602	10,382	63.4	10,093	87.6	8.5	2.6
Wood, WI	55141	161,116	11.1	50.7	38.2	140,823	10,752	61.8	3,741	83.3	15.2	0.9

Note. Data in columns 26 through 41 from the American Community Survey are subject to sampling error, which can be especially large in small counties and small population groups. See notes and definitions for more information.

Table C-1. Population, School, and Student Characteristics by County, Selected Years—*Continued*

County	State/ County Code	High school graduates, 2006–2010			College enrollment, 2006–2010		College graduates, 2006–2010 (percent)						
		Population 25 years and over	High school diploma or less (percent)	High school diploma or more (percent)	Number	Percent public	Bachelor's degree or more	+/- U.S. percent with Bachelor's degree or more	Non-Hispanic White	Black or African American	American Indian and Alaska Native	Asian, Hawaiian, and Pacific Islander	Hispanic or Latino[3]
		30	31	32	33	34	35	36	37	38	39	40	41
WISCONSIN— *(Continued)*													
Forest, WI	55041	6,617	58.4	85.6	335	82.4	12.0	-15.9	13.0	0.0	4.4	0.0	1.6
Grant, WI	55043	31,159	51.6	88.8	6,443	95.0	19.3	-8.6	19.2	6.5	4.8	74.8	3.9
Green, WI	55045	25,020	49.1	90.1	1,491	85.0	18.8	-9.1	18.7	42.9	8.3	36.5	18.5
Green Lake, WI	55047	13,445	55.2	87.0	649	80.6	16.5	-11.4	16.9	20.0	0.0	0.0	6.3
Iowa, WI	55049	16,179	44.7	91.9	725	80.7	22.3	-5.6	22.3	7.8	0.0	31.3	11.1
Iron, WI	55051	4,742	49.3	88.8	106	87.7	17.9	-10.0	17.8	0.0	24.1	0.0	0.0
Jackson, WI	55053	14,085	56.6	86.0	606	80.5	14.8	-13.1	15.5	6.0	8.1	23.9	3.5
Jefferson, WI	55055	54,421	47.4	89.1	6,685	82.1	22.7	-5.2	23.4	18.7	9.9	64.7	6.0
Juneau, WI	55057	18,701	58.3	84.7	864	85.6	12.1	-15.8	12.2	10.9	6.2	27.6	2.7
Kenosha, WI	55059	105,351	46.6	87.7	12,591	68.9	22.5	-5.4	23.5	18.8	13.9	56.1	9.4
Kewaunee, WI	55061	14,231	56.9	89.8	902	83.5	13.6	-14.3	13.5	0.0	53.8	0.0	4.9
La Crosse, WI	55063	70,494	37.2	92.9	14,439	86.1	28.8	0.9	29.4	16.0	12.6	19.7	27.1
Lafayette, WI	55065	11,127	56.8	88.1	522	83.1	15.9	-12.0	16.1	0.0	57.1	0.0	9.5
Langlade, WI	55067	14,480	60.4	87.3	702	77.5	12.9	-15.0	13.1	0.0	0.0	16.0	8.5
Lincoln, WI	55069	20,739	55.1	87.3	787	89.2	14.7	-13.2	14.5	7.8	3.1	67.8	0.0
Manitowoc, WI	55071	56,570	52.4	89.7	3,796	76.6	17.5	-10.4	17.6	28.6	10.3	14.5	15.2
Marathon, WI	55073	88,786	49.4	88.4	7,010	86.8	20.8	-7.1	21.0	39.5	13.7	16.7	14.2
Marinette, WI	55075	29,997	56.0	87.6	1,921	59.3	14.2	-13.7	13.9	52.8	6.8	60.0	24.0
Marquette, WI	55077	11,284	60.3	85.6	377	76.1	12.8	-15.1	13.0	100.0	0.0	33.3	3.2
Menominee, WI	55078	2,480	54.7	82.0	158	79.1	10.5	-17.4	16.6	0.0	9.9	0.0	0.0
Milwaukee, WI	55079	597,175	45.5	84.9	78,714	62.5	26.7	-1.2	34.0	11.9	10.5	41.7	9.2
Monroe, WI	55081	29,028	52.7	87.7	1,215	75.4	16.4	-11.5	16.4	51.9	6.8	18.0	5.3
Oconto, WI	55083	26,677	56.6	87.2	1,315	75.4	13.2	-14.7	13.0	39.2	8.8	22.9	10.4
Oneida, WI	55085	27,098	42.4	91.9	1,316	81.0	22.4	-5.5	22.4	0.0	26.7	79.3	17.7
Outagamie, WI	55087	114,198	43.9	92.3	10,038	71.9	25.8	-2.1	26.2	12.8	14.4	39.7	9.0
Ozaukee, WI	55089	58,540	27.3	95.1	5,664	52.1	43.1	15.2	43.0	44.6	32.1	72.7	23.7
Pepin, WI	55091	5,214	53.1	88.5	291	93.8	17.2	-10.7	17.3	75.0	11.1	33.3	3.3
Pierce, WI	55093	24,448	40.7	92.3	5,880	94.2	25.4	-2.5	25.6	12.2	17.4	60.3	5.8
Polk, WI	55095	30,702	49.0	91.4	1,836	79.6	18.4	-9.5	18.5	34.9	14.6	19.8	7.4
Portage, WI	55097	43,015	45.5	90.4	10,049	94.8	27.1	-0.8	27.6	57.1	3.0	27.6	6.8
Price, WI	55099	10,792	55.5	89.4	478	85.6	15.3	-12.6	15.3	0.0	0.0	48.3	8.9
Racine, WI	55101	129,568	46.8	87.3	10,716	79.1	23.1	-4.8	25.3	11.6	12.0	51.8	9.6
Richland, WI	55103	12,559	57.8	86.6	656	83.4	14.4	-13.5	14.6	100.0	0.0	14.5	7.3
Rock, WI	55105	105,158	50.9	87.4	8,693	67.3	19.8	-8.1	20.7	13.0	13.9	37.4	7.1
Rusk, WI	55107	10,545	59.7	85.3	299	88.6	14.8	-13.1	14.2	76.7	47.1	48.2	10.8
St. Croix, WI	55109	54,308	34.6	94.6	4,296	78.7	32.5	4.6	32.8	17.5	29.1	32.0	15.6
Sauk, WI	55111	41,613	50.6	88.9	2,330	89.2	20.0	-7.9	20.5	8.8	3.7	17.1	10.4
Sawyer, WI	55113	12,079	48.5	87.7	455	88.6	20.5	-7.4	22.3	0.0	9.0	8.5	30.7
Shawano, WI	55115	29,047	59.9	86.5	1,586	81.8	14.4	-13.5	14.8	0.0	8.5	28.1	11.7
Sheboygan, WI	55117	77,975	49.2	89.5	6,104	65.4	20.6	-7.3	21.2	9.0	14.3	19.9	7.0
Taylor, WI	55119	14,026	61.1	84.6	672	76.3	13.6	-14.3	13.7	0.0	0.0	40.0	3.5
Trempealeau, WI	55121	19,648	55.3	85.7	971	83.3	17.1	-10.8	17.7	0.0	15.5	11.8	4.4
Vernon, WI	55123	19,673	51.4	85.5	897	70.5	18.8	-9.1	19.1	20.0	9.5	4.9	3.7
Vilas, WI	55125	16,814	43.6	91.7	580	69.5	25.0	-2.9	26.8	0.0	4.9	14.6	20.4
Walworth, WI	55127	65,441	45.6	89.2	8,338	88.2	25.1	-2.8	26.7	17.6	24.1	51.1	3.5
Washburn, WI	55129	11,764	49.6	89.7	420	81.0	18.7	-9.2	18.9	0.0	1.4	57.5	7.1
Washington, WI	55131	88,723	41.9	92.2	6,052	72.1	26.0	-1.9	25.9	25.3	0.0	76.0	14.1
Waukesha, WI	55133	263,971	31.4	95.0	21,720	62.9	39.2	11.3	38.9	38.7	21.8	71.5	21.1
Waupaca, WI	55135	36,767	57.6	88.2	1,978	84.4	16.1	-11.8	16.3	26.4	1.5	15.8	6.8
Waushara, WI	55137	18,125	59.8	84.4	802	77.9	13.3	-14.6	13.9	2.3	19.5	6.7	4.8
Winnebago, WI	55139	109,253	46.3	89.8	15,180	90.5	23.7	-4.2	24.1	5.1	6.2	35.2	13.7
Wood, WI	55141	51,703	49.1	89.2	3,079	86.9	19.2	-8.7	19.2	18.3	4.8	31.5	8.9

Note. Data in columns 26 through 41 from the American Community Survey are subject to sampling error, which can be especially large in small counties and small population groups. See notes and definitions for more information.

[3]May be of any race.

Table C-1. Population, School, and Student Characteristics by County, Selected Years—*Continued*

County	State/ County Code	County Type[1]	Population, 2010		Percent of related children 5–17 years in poverty, 2010	Percent of children under 19 years with no health insurance, 2010	Number of schools and students, 2010–2011			Resident enrollment, 2006–2010 K–12 enrollment	
			Total	Percent 5–17 years			School districts	Schools	Students	Number	Percent public
			1	2	3	4	5	6	7	8	9
WYOMING	56000	X	563,626	16.9	12.8	8.3	61	360	88,993	92,276	94.9
Albany, WY	56001	4	36,299	11.0	14.2	7.8	2	17	3,682	3,763	95.7
Big Horn, WY	56003	9	11,668	19.1	15.0	12.6	4	16	2,178	2,285	95.1
Campbell, WY	56005	5	46,133	19.3	7.9	6.9	3	22	8,330	8,401	97.5
Carbon, WY	56007	7	15,885	16.5	13.8	9.5	2	16	2,462	2,392	97.6
Converse, WY	56009	6	13,833	18.4	11.8	7.4	2	12	2,360	2,378	91.0
Crook, WY	56011	9	7,083	16.8	10.4	12.8	1	6	1,101	1,221	91.9
Fremont, WY	56013	7	40,123	17.6	18.8	10.3	8	30	6,572	6,828	94.2
Goshen, WY	56015	7	13,249	15.1	19.3	10.4	2	12	1,831	1,947	90.3
Hot Springs, WY	56017	7	4,812	14.8	13.2	10.5	2	4	657	556	100.0
Johnson, WY	56019	7	8,569	15.4	12.1	11.3	1	5	1,247	1,274	97.3
Laramie, WY	56021	3	91,738	17.1	13.2	6.5	6	44	14,178	15,744	94.2
Lincoln, WY	56023	7	18,106	20.2	11.7	9.9	2	13	3,192	3,548	94.8
Natrona, WY	56025	3	75,450	16.8	13.1	6.9	2	35	12,153	12,416	94.5
Niobrara, WY	56027	9	2,484	15.1	15.4	15.6	1	4	728	485	92.0
Park, WY	56029	7	28,205	15.1	14.7	8.5	3	15	3,973	4,244	94.6
Platte, WY	56031	7	8,667	15.4	14.7	10.0	2	13	1,255	1,449	94.1
Sheridan, WY	56033	7	29,116	15.9	12.4	8.1	4	22	4,245	4,293	94.5
Sublette, WY	56035	9	10,247	16.7	7.1	8.9	2	8	1,692	1,539	94.8
Sweetwater, WY	56037	5	43,806	18.7	11.1	8.4	2	27	7,794	7,343	96.5
Teton, WY	56039	7	21,294	13.1	11.6	11.5	3	11	2,456	2,863	86.5
Uinta, WY	56041	7	21,118	21.7	11.7	8.3	3	15	4,404	4,669	99.6
Washakie, WY	56043	7	8,533	18.4	13.7	9.6	2	6	1,460	1,548	92.9
Weston, WY	56045	7	7,208	16.1	10.4	8.7	2	7	1,043	1,090	98.3

[1]County type codes are from the Economic Research Service of the United States Department of Agriculture. See notes and definitions for more information.

Table C-1. Population, School, and Student Characteristics by County, Selected Years—*Continued*

County	State/ County Code	Characteristics of students, 2010–2011				Number of graduates, 2008–2009	Staff and students, 2010–2011			
		Percent with IEP[2]	Percent eligible for free or reduced lunch	Percent minority	Percent English-language learners		Total staff	Number of teachers	Student/ teacher ratio	Central admin. staff
		10	11	12	13	14	15	16	17	18
WYOMING	56000	17.1	37.1	19.1	2.9	5,493	...	...	...	...
Albany, WY	56001	16.3	28.9	24.0	2.7	205	...	...	...	...
Big Horn, WY	56003	23.5	43.3	15.7	3.1	166	...	...	...	...
Campbell, WY	56005	14.8	31.0	11.8	2.4	511	...	...	...	...
Carbon, WY	56007	19.6	38.7	27.3	4.0	151	...	...	...	...
Converse, WY	56009	19.8	31.5	9.8	1.4	165	...	...	...	...
Crook, WY	56011	20.6	31.4	6.0	0.4	83	...	...	...	...
Fremont, WY	56013	18.5	50.6	41.4	5.4	383	...	...	...	...
Goshen, WY	56015	17.6	52.9	20.8	1.3	134	...	...	...	...
Hot Springs, WY	56017	17.2	45.1	6.8	...	41	...	...	...	...
Johnson, WY	56019	14.6	32.5	10.4	0.6	96	...	...	...	...
							...	...	...	...
Laramie, WY	56021	16.7	40.9	26.8	1.5	782	...	...	...	...
Lincoln, WY	56023	17.2	38.0	7.9	1.0	219	...	...	...	...
Natrona, WY	56025	15.2	38.2	13.2	2.0	705	...	...	...	...
Niobrara, WY	56027	13.3	29.4	6.3	0.1	34	...	...	...	...
Park, WY	56029	19.8	36.9	10.0	0.9	301	...	...	...	...
Platte, WY	56031	17.1	30.5	12.7	1.0	95	...	...	...	...
Sheridan, WY	56033	16.0	37.3	8.8	0.6	266	...	...	...	...
Sublette, WY	56035	16.4	15.7	13.8	4.1	91	...	...	...	...
Sweetwater, WY	56037	18.3	33.3	23.9	5.6	450	...	...	...	...
Teton, WY	56039	12.2	18.3	30.9	15.2	160	...	...	...	...
							...	...	...	...
Uinta, WY	56041	17.1	39.9	12.1	4.4	267	...	...	...	...
Washakie, WY	56043	22.6	49.0	26.6	4.7	102	...	...	...	...
Weston, WY	56045	23.3	30.8	7.2	0.3	86	...	...	...	...

[2]IEP=Individual Education Program. See notes and definitions for more information.

. . . = Not available.

Table C-1. Population, School, and Student Characteristics by County, Selected Years—*Continued*

County	State/ County Code	Revenues, 2008–2009				Current expenditures, 2008–2009			Resident population 16 to 19 years, 2006–2010			
		Total revenue ($1,000's)	Percentage of revenue from: Federal government	State government	Local government	Amount ($1,000's)	Amount per student	Percent for instruction	Total population 16 to 19 years	Percent enrolled in school	Percent high school graduates, not enrolled in school	Percent not enrolled, not grads, not employed, or not in labor force
		19	20	21	22	23	24	25	26	27	28	29
WYOMING	56000	1,675,761	6.5	56.4	37.1	1,267,400	14,573	58.8	31,073	81.6	11.6	4.0
Albany, WY	56001	53,693	7.5	65.7	26.8	49,943	13,873	62.7	3,720	88.4	10.3	0.2
Big Horn, WY	56003	43,444	7.3	68.8	23.9	34,935	16,668	57.5	632	91.0	5.9	3.2
Campbell, WY	56005	145,510	4.1	20.9	75.0	104,736	13,117	55.2	2,302	76.9	16.1	2.0
Carbon, WY	56007	48,504	6.0	30.2	63.8	38,828	15,933	56.8	658	80.6	11.6	4.0
Converse, WY	56009	42,783	5.3	42.5	52.2	34,554	14,512	65.5	836	76.8	15.7	5.1
Crook, WY	56011	21,019	5.0	62.9	32.2	16,882	15,559	57.9	414	85.0	11.8	3.1
Fremont, WY	56013	150,442	17.0	62.9	20.0	120,521	18,858	59.1	2,174	70.7	12.9	8.0
Goshen, WY	56015	35,081	8.2	75.7	16.1	28,735	15,823	57.3	755	89.5	8.3	0.3
Hot Springs, WY	56017	12,701	7.0	26.8	66.2	10,544	16,098	54.3	160	59.4	10.6	18.1
Johnson, WY	56019	24,418	4.2	8.8	87.0	19,736	16,151	53.7	366	92.6	3.8	3.6
Laramie, WY	56021	289,414	4.7	81.5	13.9	191,533	13,905	59.2	4,570	76.8	15.7	5.6
Lincoln, WY	56023	57,055	4.3	51.3	44.4	44,690	13,629	61.7	920	78.0	9.9	5.2
Natrona, WY	56025	210,031	7.2	71.3	21.5	165,564	13,810	60.4	4,218	82.5	11.2	4.8
Niobrara, WY	56027	7,503	3.6	59.6	36.9	6,379	16,965	54.3	175	89.1	10.9	0.0
Park, WY	56029	73,600	5.4	55.0	39.7	55,100	13,942	61.4	1,676	96.1	2.9	1.0
Platte, WY	56031	26,558	6.2	69.6	24.1	22,681	17,528	60.6	522	78.7	19.9	1.3
Sheridan, WY	56033	98,096	4.3	70.6	25.1	60,239	14,512	59.4	1,459	81.1	11.7	6.2
Sublette, WY	56035	36,508	2.2	15.4	82.4	25,582	15,227	52.9	455	71.0	19.1	6.4
Sweetwater, WY	56037	127,589	5.6	29.0	65.4	100,795	13,214	54.8	2,431	83.3	9.7	2.0
Teton, WY	56039	55,000	3.8	29.7	66.5	36,024	15,704	62.0	757	74.0	14.5	4.5
Uinta, WY	56041	69,142	6.3	55.9	37.8	60,042	13,724	57.7	1,174	81.2	10.7	6.3
Washakie, WY	56043	25,910	6.9	70.5	22.6	22,065	15,761	62.9	468	83.3	2.6	9.8
Weston, WY	56045	21,760	5.2	64.6	30.1	17,292	15,564	55.7	231	94.4	0.0	5.6

Note. Data in columns 26 through 41 from the American Community Survey are subject to sampling error, which can be especially large in small counties and small population groups. See notes and definitions for more information.

Table C-1. Population, School, and Student Characteristics by County, Selected Years—*Continued*

County	State/ County Code	High school graduates, 2006–2010			College enrollment, 2006–2010		College graduates, 2006–2010 (percent)						
		Population 25 years and over	High school diploma or less (percent)	High school diploma or more (percent)	Number	Percent public	Bachelor's degree or more	+/- U.S. percent with Bachelor's degree or more	Non-Hispanic White	Black or African American	American Indian and Alaska Native	Asian, Hawaiian, and Pacific Islander	Hispanic or Latino[3]
		30	31	32	33	34	35	36	37	38	39	40	41
WYOMING	56000	357,859	39.9	91.3	36,192	88.5	23.6	-4.3	24.8	18.4	10.0	41.9	9.6
Albany, WY	56001	18,540	23.6	93.3	10,645	91.7	47.4	19.5	48.6	51.1	71.4	80.0	15.3
Big Horn, WY	56003	7,736	41.3	89.4	352	90.1	20.3	-7.6	21.9	0.0	2.2	0.0	1.1
Campbell, WY	56005	26,762	44.8	91.0	1,647	93.4	17.6	-10.3	18.1	0.0	24.2	18.6	11.6
Carbon, WY	56007	10,902	48.4	90.9	566	82.7	17.9	-10.0	20.3	0.0	0.0	41.4	6.2
Converse, WY	56009	9,024	45.1	92.0	518	82.2	17.6	-10.3	17.2	100.0	48.0	0.0	14.5
Crook, WY	56011	4,545	46.2	91.9	167	72.5	22.8	-5.1	22.7	0.0	27.3	0.0	43.3
Fremont, WY	56013	25,715	39.6	88.8	1,975	89.4	22.8	-5.1	26.7	3.9	7.5	32.9	8.8
Goshen, WY	56015	8,886	45.1	90.0	1,014	65.1	19.6	-8.3	20.8	0.0	0.0	47.4	5.0
Hot Springs, WY	56017	3,498	45.9	88.1	5	100.0	19.3	-8.6	19.6	0.0	0.0	0.0	0.0
Johnson, WY	56019	5,964	40.5	94.6	302	87.1	25.3	-2.6	26.0	0.0	0.0	0.0	11.5
Laramie, WY	56021	58,230	37.6	91.7	5,999	83.4	22.9	-5.0	24.7	13.8	7.2	10.4	12.4
Lincoln, WY	56023	11,378	46.1	91.1	538	82.0	19.3	-8.6	19.9	0.0	0.0	61.5	3.5
Natrona, WY	56025	48,548	39.4	91.9	4,496	89.5	20.9	-7.0	21.7	18.7	2.4	55.2	7.3
Niobrara, WY	56027	1,752	41.7	91.1	59	94.9	19.8	-8.1	19.4	0.0	0.0	0.0	54.1
Park, WY	56029	19,277	36.3	92.6	1,925	96.7	27.7	-0.2	28.7	0.0	11.6	38.4	12.7
Platte, WY	56031	6,209	48.0	89.0	356	66.6	17.3	-10.6	17.7	0.0	0.0	0.0	9.5
Sheridan, WY	56033	19,843	38.5	92.7	1,476	91.7	23.1	-4.8	23.7	0.0	17.9	69.9	0.0
Sublette, WY	56035	6,462	38.7	92.4	303	93.4	22.8	-5.1	26.0	0.0	0.0	60.6	5.2
Sweetwater, WY	56037	26,435	44.9	89.9	2,408	90.7	17.1	-10.8	19.0	6.1	7.6	54.9	2.0
Teton, WY	56039	14,901	26.9	95.1	329	80.2	49.7	21.8	52.7	100.0	100.0	0.0	19.1
Uinta, WY	56041	12,742	45.3	88.3	669	87.9	17.4	-10.5	17.8	0.0	7.9	69.6	15.8
Washakie, WY	56043	5,546	44.7	89.6	225	89.8	24.5	-3.4	25.1	0.0	0.0	65.0	7.2
Weston, WY	56045	4,964	49.7	91.1	218	95.4	17.9	-10.0	17.6	0.0	0.0	72.0	6.5

Note. Data in columns 26 through 41 from the American Community Survey are subject to sampling error, which can be especially large in small counties and small population groups. See notes and definitions for more information.
[3]May be of any race.

NOTES AND DEFINITIONS: COUNTY EDUCATION STATISTICS

Part C presents 41 data items for each county, county equivalent, and independent city. The counties are presented in alphabetical order within states, which are also in alphabetical order. Independent cities, found in Maryland, Missouri, Nevada, and Virginia, are placed in alphabetical order at the end of the list of counties for those states. The District of Columbia is included as both a county and a state.

COMMON CORE OF DATA

For Items 5–7 and 10–25, National Center for Education Statistics, U.S. Department of Education. *Common Core of Data: 2010–2011 and 2008–2009.* http://nces.ed.gov/ccd/ .

NCES uses the Common Core of Data (CCD) system to acquire and maintain statistical data from each of the 50 states, the District of Columbia, and the outlying areas. Information about staff and students is collected annually at the school, local education agency (LEA), or school district, and state levels. Information about revenues and expenditures is also collected at the state level. In addition, information about revenues and expenditures at the school district level is assembled from the Census Bureau's annual surveys of government finances.

Data are collected for a particular school year (July 1 through June 30) via survey instruments sent to the state education agencies during the subsequent school year. States have one year to modify the data originally submitted. This edition uses the data from the 2010–2011 school year, except for the revenue and expenditure data for counties, which is for school year 2008–2009 (fiscal year 2009). The high school graduates data also come from earlier years.

Since the CCD is a universe survey, the CCD information is not subject to sampling error. However, nonsampling errors could come from two sources—nonreturn and inaccurate reporting. Almost all of the states submit the six CCD survey instruments each year, but submissions are sometimes incomplete or made too late for publication.

Understandably, when 51 education agencies compile and submit data for more than 98,000 public schools and 18,000 local school districts, misreporting can occur. This typically results from varying interpretation of NCES definitions and differences in record keeping systems. NCES attempts to minimize these errors by working closely with the Council of Chief State School Officers (CCSSO) and its Committee on Evaluation and Information Systems (CEIS).

The state education agencies report data to NCES from data collected and edited during their regular reporting cycles. NCES encourages the agencies to incorporate the NCES items they do not already collect into their own survey systems so that those items will be available for the subsequent CCD survey. Over time, this has meant fewer missing data cells in each state's response and a reduction in the need to impute data.

Data from the education agencies is subjected to a comprehensive edit by NCES. Where data are determined to be inconsistent, missing, or out of range, NCES contacts the education agencies for verification. NCES-prepared state summary forms are returned to the state education agencies for verification. States are also given an opportunity to revise their state-level aggregates from the previous survey cycle. The county-level data in this edition have not been adjusted,

The CCD data are collected at three levels—the school, the school district, and the state. In Part C, selected school and school district data items have been aggregated to the county level because the county is a widely used statistical area. School districts, and even some schools, can serve populations in different counties. In this volume, schools and school districts are assigned to the county where the school district office is located, as coded by NCES in their files. Consequently, the numbers do not necessarily represent the population of a given county. NCES has begun to include the county code in the schools data file. A few items thus represent the county of the individual schools, rather than the school district office.

The structure of school districts ranges from that of states like West Virginia and Nevada, where most counties have a single school district, to Maricopa County, Arizona, which includes 310 separate school districts. Some counties have no school districts. Hawaii has a single statewide school district whose offices are located in Honolulu County. New York City has a single school system for all five boroughs (counties). It is now divided into geographic districts within the city, allowing most of the CCD data to be tallied by county, but the fiscal data for New York County represent the entire city school system. A few other counties report no school districts. These are usually counties with very small populations or independent cities in Virginia whose school systems are run by the neighboring or surrounding county.

The CCD data files now include charter schools. Charter schools are often managed independently from the local school district. When this is the case, each charter school is considered a single district. This affects the county aggregations and should be considered in interpreting these data. Additional attention should be given to the fiscal data because some states include revenues and expenditures for charter schools, while others do not.

AMERICAN COMMUNITY SURVEY, 2006–2010

Items 8, 9, and 26–41 are from the American Community Survey, the sample survey that has replaced the long form of the decennial census. The sample data are estimates of the actual figures that would have been obtained from a complete count. Estimates derived from a sample are expected to be different from the 100-percent figures because they are subject to sampling and nonsampling errors. Sampling error in data arises from the selection of people and housing units included in the sample. Nonsampling error affects both sample and 100-percent data. It is introduced as a result of errors that may occur during the data collection and processing phases of the census.

The American Community Survey is ongoing and data are released on an annual basis. Single-year data are available for geographic areas with populations of 65,000 or more. Three-year data are available for areas with populations of 20,000 or more, and five-year data are available for all geographic areas. This book uses the 2006-2010 five-year data for the county table.

ACS data are subject to sampling error which can be especially large in small geographic areas or small population groups. Margins of error can be found on the Census Bureau website.

For additional information about the American Community Survey, see www.census.gov/acs/www/ .

GEOGRAPHIC IDENTIFICATION

Data are presented for 3,143 counties and county equivalents. A five-digit state and county code is given for each entity. The first two digits indicate the state; the remaining three identify the county. Within each state, the counties are numbered in alphabetical order, beginning with 001, with even numbers usually omitted. Independent cities follow the counties and begin with the number 510.

These codes have been established by the U.S. government as Federal Information

Processing Standards and are often referred to as "FIPS codes." They are used by U.S. government agencies and many other organizations for data presentation. They are provided in this volume for use in matching the data given here with other data sources in which counties may be identified by FIPS codes.

County equivalents. In Louisiana, the primary divisions of the state are known as parishes rather than counties. In Alaska, the county equivalents are the organized boroughs, together with the census areas that were developed for general statistical purposes by the state of Alaska and the U.S. Census Bureau. Several recent changes have occurred in Alaska's county equivalents.

The old Skagway–Hoonah–Angoon Census Area has been divided into the Skagway Municipality and the Hoonah–Angoon Census Area.

A new Prince of Wales–Hyder Census Area was created after part of the old Prince of Wales–Outer Ketchikan Census Area was annexed by the Ketchikan Gateway Borough.

The old Wrangell–Petersburg Census Area was divided into the Wrangell City and Borough and the Petersburg Census Area.

Independent cities. Independent cities are not included in any county; data are presented separately in this edition where available.

Maryland
Baltimore (separate from Baltimore County)

Missouri
St. Louis (separate from St. Louis County)

Nevada
Carson City

Virginia
Alexandria
Bedford
Bristol
Buena Vista
Charlottesville
Chesapeake
Colonial Heights
Covington
Danville
Emporia
Fairfax
Falls Church
Franklin
Fredericksburg
Galax
Hampton
Harrisonburg
Hopewell
Lexington
Lynchburg
Manassas
Manassas Park
Martinsville
Newport News
Norfolk
Norton
Petersburg
Poquoson
Portsmouth
Radford
Richmond
Roanoke
Salem
Staunton
Suffolk
Virginia Beach
Waynesboro
Williamsburg
Winchester

County type. Table C-1's third column provides a county type code that identifies each county by its metropolitan/nonmetropolitan status and size. These are the "rural-urban continuum codes" developed by the Economic Research Service of the U.S. Department of Agriculture.

The 2003 Rural-Urban Continuum Codes form a classification scheme to distinguish metropolitan counties by size and nonmetropolitan counties by degree of urbanization and proximity to metro areas. The standard Office of Management and Budget (OMB) metro and nonmetro categories have been subdivided into three metro and six nonmetro categories, resulting in a nine-part county codification. This scheme was originally developed in 1974. The codes were updated in 1983, 1993, and slightly revised in 1988. The 1988 revision was first published in 1990. This scheme allows researchers to break county data into residential groups beyond metro and nonmetro; this is particularly helpful in analyzing trends in nonmetro areas related to population density and metro influence. The 2003 Rural-Urban Continuum Codes are not directly comparable with the codes from previous years because of the new methodology used in developing the 2003 metropolitan areas.

Metropolitan counties:

1 Counties in metro areas with population of 1 million or more.

2 Counties in metro areas with population of 250,000 to 1 million.

3 Counties in metro areas with population fewer than 250,000.

Nonmetropolitan counties:

4 Urban population of 20,000 or more, adjacent to a metro area.

5 Urban population of 20,000 or more, not adjacent to a metro area.

6 Urban population of 2,500 to 19,999, adjacent to a metro area.

7 Urban population of 2,500 to 19,999, not adjacent to a metro area.

8 Completely rural or less than 2,500 urban population, adjacent to a metro area.

9 Completely rural or less than 2,500 urban population, not adjacent to a metro area.

DATA SOURCES AND EXPLANATIONS

The schools and students data in Table C have been developed by Bernan from the individual school and school district data from the CCD or generated through the "Build a Table" feature on the CCD website. The files used were:

Local Education Agency Universe Survey: School Year 2010–2011, version 1a
Public Elementary/Secondary School Universe Survey: School Year 2010–2011, version 1b
School District Finance Survey (F-33), School Year 2008–2009 (Fiscal Year 2009), version 1a

The population, characteristics, enrollment, and attainment data in Table C-1 have been compiled from the detailed tables of the American Community Survey (2006–2010) and can be found on the Census Bureau's website in the "American FactFinder" section.

ACS data are subject to sampling error, which can be especially large in small geographic areas or small population groups. Margins of error can be found on the Census Bureau website.

TABLE C-1

POPULATION, ITEMS 1–2

Source: U.S. Bureau of the Census. 2010 *Decennial Census*.
www.census.gov/2010census/ .

The population data for 2010 are from the decennial census and represent the resident population as of April 1, 2010.

Age is defined as age at last birthday (that is, number of completed years from birth to April 1, 2010).

CHILDREN IN POVERTY, ITEM 3

Source: U.S. Bureau of the Census, Small Area Income and Poverty Estimates Program. www.census.gov/did/www/saipe/ .

The U.S. Census Bureau, with support from other federal agencies, created the Small Area Income and Poverty Estimates (SAIPE) program to provide more current estimates of selected income and poverty statistics than those from the most recent decennial census.

Estimates are created for school districts, counties, and states. The main objective of this program is to provide updated estimates of income and poverty statistics for the administration of federal programs and the allocation of federal funds to local jurisdictions. These estimates combine data from administrative records, intercensal population estimates, and the decennial census with direct estimates from the American Community Survey to provide consistent and reliable single-year estimates. These model-based single-year estimates are more reflective of current conditions than multiyear survey estimates.

The estimate in column 3 is the percentage of related children age 5 to 17 in families who are in poverty. Poverty status is determined by comparing total annual income to a set of dollar values called thresholds that vary by family size, number of related children, and age of householder. If a family's before tax money income is less than the dollar value of their thresholds, then that family and every individual in it are considered to be in poverty.

CHILDREN WITH NO HEALTH INSURANCE, ITEM 4

Source: U.S. Bureau of the Census, Small Area Health Insurance Estimates for Counties and States. www.census.gov/did/www/sahie/ .

The Small Area Health Insurance Estimates (SAHIE) program was created to develop model-based estimates of health insurance coverage for counties and states. This developmental program builds on the work of the Small Area Income and Poverty Estimates (SAIPE) program. The American Community Survey provides health insurance estimates, but only five-year estimates for counties with populations of less than 20,000.

SCHOOL DISTRICTS, ITEM 5

Source: National Center for Education Statistics, U.S. Department of Education. *Common Core of Data, 2010–2011.* http://nces.ed.gov/ccd/pubagency.asp .

A school district or Local Education Agency (LEA) is a local-level education agency that exists primarily to operate public schools or to contract for public school services. A public school is controlled and operated by publicly elected or appointed officials. It derives its primary support from public funds.

The county totals in this edition include 18,045 regular and special school districts. Special districts typically offer research, administrative or other support services to client agencies. Charter schools are often included as one agency for each school.

NUMBER OF SCHOOLS AND STUDENTS, ITEMS 6–7

Source: National Center for Education Statistics, U.S. Department of Education. *Common Core of Data, 2010–2011.* http://nces.ed.gov/ccd/pubagency.asp .

The county table shows the number of schools and students as reported by the LEAs in the school file.

RESIDENT ENROLLMENT AND TYPE OF SCHOOL, ITEMS 8–9 AND 33–34

Source: U.S. Bureau of the Census. American Community Survey, 2006–2010. http://factfinder2.census.gov .

Data on school enrollment of county residents are from the 2006–2010 American

Community Survey (ACS). The ACS gathers demographic, social, economic, housing, and financial information about the nation's people and communities on a continuous basis, providing the detailed characteristics that have previously come from the sample long form of the decennial census. This book uses the five-year estimates data from 2006–2010, available for all geographic areas.

People were classified as enrolled in school if they reported attending a "regular" public or private school or college during the three months prior to the interview. The question included instructions to "include only nursery school or preschool, kindergarten, elementary school, and schooling which leads to a high school diploma or a college degree" as regular school or college. Respondents who did not answer the enrollment question were assigned the enrollment status and type of school of a person with the same age, sex, and race/Hispanic or Latino origin whose residence was in the same or a nearby area. All persons 3 years old and over are included.

Public and private schools. Public and private schools include people who attended school during the reference period and who indicated they were enrolled by marking one of the questionnaire categories for either "public school, public college" or "private school, private college." Schools primarily supported and controlled by a federal, state, or local government are defined as public (including tribal schools). Those primarily supported and controlled by religious organizations or other private groups are considered private, as are home schools.

ACS data are subject to sampling error, which can be especially large in small geographic areas or small population groups. Margins of error can be found on the Census Bureau website.

STUDENTS WITH INDIVIDUAL EDUCATION PROGRAMS, ITEM 10

Source: National Center for Education Statistics, U.S. Department of Education. *Common Core of Data, 2010–2011.* http://nces.ed.gov/ccd// .

An Individualized Education Program (IEP) is a written instructional plan for students with disabilities designated as special education students under IDEA (Individuals with Disabilities Education Act). This includes a statement of the child's present levels of educational performance; a statement of annual goals, including short-term instructional objectives; a statement of the specific educational services to be provided and the extent to which the child will be able to participate in regular educational programs; a projected date for initiation and the anticipated duration of services; appropriate objectives, criteria and evaluation procedures; and schedules for determining, on at least an annual basis, whether instructional objectives are being achieved.

IEP counts for counties are from the agency universe through the Build-a-Table data tool. Some agencies did not report this information.

STUDENTS WHO ARE ELIGIBLE FOR FREE OR REDUCED-PRICE LUNCH, ITEM 11

Source: National Center for Education Statistics, U.S. Department of Education. *Common Core of Data, 2010–2011.* http://nces.ed.gov/ccd// .

The Free and Reduced-Price Lunch Program is a program under the National School Lunch Act that provides cash subsidies for free or reduced-price meals to students based on family size and income criteria. Participation in the Free and Reduced-Price Lunch Program depends on income, and eligibility is often used to estimate student needs.

The number of students eligible for free or reduced-price meals was aggregated from the school universe data file for 2010–2011, using the Build-a-Table data tool.

MINORITY STUDENTS, ITEM 12
National Center for Education Statistics, U.S. Department of Education. *Common Core of Data, 2010–2011.*
http://nces.ed.gov/ccd// .

The percentage of a county's students belonging to a minority group was tallied from the CCD school universe. Individual schools reported the number of students who were American Indian/Alaskan Native, Asian/Pacific Islander, Hispanic, Black non-Hispanic, and White non-Hispanic. "Minority" includes all categories except White non-Hispanic.

The number of students by race and Hispanic origin is from the school universe data file, using the Build-a-Table data tool.

ENGLISH LANGUAGE LEARNERS, ITEM 13
Source: National Center for Education Statistics, U.S. Department of Education. *Common Core of Data, 2010–2011.*
http://nces.ed.gov/ccd// .

This category contains the number of students served in appropriate programs of language assistance (for example, English as a Second Language, High Intensity Language Training, and bilingual education). The name of this field changed from Limited-English Proficient (LEP) to English Language Learners (ELL) in the 2001–2002 school year.

ELL counts for counties are from the agency universe through the Build-a-Table data tool. Some agencies did not report this information.

GRADUATES, ITEM 14
Source: National Center for Education Statistics, U.S. Department of Education. *Common Core of Data (CCD), "Local Education Agency (School District) Universe Dropout and Completion Data," 2008–2009, v.1a.*
http://nces.ed.gov/ccd// .

The county data are from the CCD agency universe. The number of graduates includes those who received a regular diploma, those who received a diploma from a program different from the regular school program, and those who received a certificate of attendance or other certificate of completion in lieu of a diploma during the previous school year and subsequent summer school session. Recipients of high school equivalency certificates are not included.

The counts of diploma recipients and other high school completers are from the agency universe through the Build-a-Table data tool.

STAFF AND TEACHERS, ITEMS 15–18
Source: National Center for Education Statistics, U.S. Department of Education. *Common Core of Data (CCD), "Local Education Agency Universe Survey," 2010–2011, v.1a.*
http://nces.ed.gov/ccd// .

The total staff of the school systems in each county is aggregated from the CCD agency universe. The number of teachers in each county is aggregated from the full-time-equivalent numbers in the CCD agency universe. The student–teacher ratio is calculated from this agency-based number and the total number of students reported by the school districts in the county.

The county data for the central administrative staff are aggregated from the CCD agency universe. Central administration staff and support include the LEA superintendents, deputies, assistant superintendents, all persons with district-wide responsibilities, and their support staffs, as well as all staff, such as curriculum coordinators, supervising instructional programs at the district or sub-district level.

The counts of staff and teachers are from the agency universe through the Build-a-Table data tool. The state totals in this section were aggregated from the counties and often will differ from the numbers in Table B-3, which come from the state file.

REVENUES, ITEMS 19–22
Source: National Center for Education Statistics, U.S. Department of Education. *Common Core of Data, School District Finance Survey, Fiscal Year 2009.*
http://nces.ed.gov/ccd// .

The county data are aggregated from the agencies in the Public School District Financial Survey data file for fiscal year 2009 (school year 2008–2009), using the Build-a-Table data tool. Some of these school districts have no students in membership. However, the districts have revenues and expenditures, usually because of financial arrangements with neighboring counties or regional agencies. These revenue and expenditure data are obtained by the U.S. Census Bureau through its annual surveys of government finances and are supplied to NCES by the Census Bureau. The state totals in Table C-1 are also aggregated from the agencies in this file, sometimes resulting in different numbers from the state data in Table B-3.

Charter school systems' reporting requirements vary from state to state, and data are currently not reported uniformly to the State Education Agencies (SEAs). Note that some charter school data may be missing from this edition, since some charter schools are not required to submit finance data to the SEA. Only those charter schools that submit data to the SEA and whose data are maintained by the SEA are included in the CCD fiscal files.

Revenues from federal sources include direct grants-in-aid from the federal government, federal grants-in-aid through the state or an intermediate agency, and other revenue in lieu of taxes to compensate a school district for nontaxable federal institutions within a district's boundaries.

State revenues include those that can be used without restriction; those for categorical purposes; and revenues in lieu of taxation. Included are revenues from payments made by a state for the benefit of the LEA or contributions of equipment or supplies. Such revenues include the payment of a pension fund by the state on behalf of an LEA employee for services rendered and contributions of fixed assets (property, plant, and equipment), such as school buses and textbooks.

Revenues from local sources include local property and nonproperty tax revenues, taxes levied or assessed by an LEA, revenues from a local government to the LEA, tuition received, transportation fees, earnings on investments from LEA holdings, net revenues from food services (gross receipts less gross expenditures), net revenues from student activities (gross receipts less gross expenditures), and other revenues (textbook sales, donations, or property rentals). Intermediate revenues are included in local revenue totals. Intermediate revenues come from sources that are not local or state education agencies, but operate at an intermediate level between local and state education agencies and possess independent fundraising capability (such as county or municipal agencies).

EXPENDITURES, ITEMS 23–25
Source: National Center for Education Statistics, U.S. Department of Education. *Common Core of Data, School District Finance Survey, Fiscal Year 2009.*
http://nces.ed.gov/ccd// .

The county data are aggregated from the agencies in the Public School District Financial Survey data file for fiscal year 2009 (school year 2008–2009). Some of these school districts have no students in membership but they have revenues and expenditures, usually because of financial arrangements with neighboring counties or regional agencies. These revenue and expenditure data are obtained by the U.S. Census Bureau through its annual surveys of government finances and are supplied to NCES by the Census Bureau. The state totals in Table C-1 are also aggregated from the agencies in this file, sometimes resulting in different numbers from the state data in Table B-3.

Current expenditures are defined as expenditures for the categories of instruction, support services, and non-instructional services for salaries, employee benefits, purchased services and supplies, and state-level payments made for or on behalf of school systems. This does not include expenditures for debt service, capital outlay, and property (for example, equipment), direct costs (for example, Head Start, adult education, community colleges, and so on), or community services expenditures.

Current expenditures per student for counties are calculated by dividing current expenditures by the number of students in fall membership. Student membership is the count of students enrolled on or about October 1 and is comparable across all counties. However, comparisons should be made with caution because counties vary greatly in type of school districts as well as contractual arrangements with regional administrative school agencies or neighboring counties. For example, a county with a small population may have a school district that operates an elementary school and pays an intergovernmental fee to a neighboring county's school district for educational services to children in middle and high school. This hypothetical county would have artificially high per student expenditures because only the elementary school children would be included in its membership count.

Current expenditures for instruction are expenditures for activities dealing directly with the interaction between students and teachers (salaries, including sabbatical leave; employee benefits; instructional staff support such as librarians and instructional specialists; and purchased instructional services).

POPULATION 16 TO 19 YEARS, BY SCHOOL ENROLLMENT AND EMPLOYMENT STATUS, ITEMS 26–29

Source: U.S. Bureau of the Census. American Community Survey, 2006–2010. http://factfinder2.census.gov .

American Community Survey data on school enrollment, educational attainment, and employment status for the population 16 to 19 years old allows for calculating the proportion of people 16 to 19 years old who are not enrolled in school and not high school graduates ("dropouts") and an unemployment rate for the "dropout" population. Data are from the 2006–2010 ACS. The ACS gathers demographic, social, economic, housing and financial information about the nation's people and communities on a continuous basis, providing the detailed characteristics that have previously come from the sample long form of the decennial census. This book uses the five-year estimates data from 2006–2010, available for all geographic areas.

ACS data are subject to sampling error, which can be especially large in small geographic areas or small population groups. Margins of error can be found on the Census Bureau website.

EDUCATIONAL ATTAINMENT, ITEMS 30–32 AND 35–41

Source: U.S. Bureau of the Census. American Community Survey, 2006–2010. http://factfinder2.census.gov .

Data are from the 2006–2010 ACS. The ACS gathers demographic, social, economic, housing and financial information about the nation's people and communities on a continuous basis, providing the detailed characteristics that have previously come from the sample long form of the decennial census. This edition uses the five-year estimates data from 2006–2010, available for all geographic areas.

Data on attainment are tabulated for the population age 25 years old and over. People are classified according to the highest degree or level of school completed. The order in which degrees were listed on the questionnaire suggested that doctorate degrees were "higher" than professional school degrees, which were "higher" than master's degrees. The question included instructions for people currently enrolled in school to report the level of the previous grade attended or the highest degree received. Respondents who did not report educational attainment or enrollment level were assigned the attainment of a person of the same age, race, Hispanic or Latino origin, occupation, and sex, where possible, who resided in the same area or nearby. Respondents who filled in more than one box were edited to the highest level or degree reported. The question included a response category that allowed respondents to report completing the 12th grade without receiving a high school diploma. It allowed people who received either a high school diploma or the equivalent, such as those who passed the Test of General Educational Development (G.E.D.) and did not attend college, to be reported as "high school graduate(s)."

High school diploma or less. This category includes all persons who have not received a high school diploma, as well as those high school graduates who never attended college.

High school diploma or more. This category includes people whose highest degree was a high school diploma or its equivalent, people who attended college but did not receive a degree, and people who received a college, university, or professional degree. People who reported completing the 12th grade but not receiving a diploma are not high school graduates.

Bachelor's degree or more. This category includes people whose highest degree was a bachelor's, master's, professional, or doctoral degree. Master's degree includes the traditional M.A. and M.S. degrees and field-specific degrees. Some examples of professional degrees include medicine, dentistry, chiropractic, optometry, osteopathic medicine, pharmacy, podiatry, veterinary medicine, law, and theology. Vocational and technical training, such as barber school training; business, trade, technical, and vocational schools; or other training for a specific trade are specifically excluded.

ACS data are subject to sampling error, which can be especially large in small geographic areas or small population groups. Margins of error can be found on the Census Bureau website.

APPENDIX

GUIDE TO EDUCATIONAL RESOURCES ON THE INTERNET

APPENDIX—GUIDE TO EDUCATIONAL RESOURCES ON THE INTERNET

The Department of Education is naturally the leader in publishing federal government education information on the Internet. This chapter includes many of the online resources made available by the Education Department, but also includes information about military education activities, federally sponsored scholarships, and some education-related social service programs. The Kids' Pages section of this chapter includes more than 40 websites designed for a younger audience and it covers a wide variety of subject areas. Subsections in this chapter are Adult Education, Curriculum, Early Childhood Education, Education Funding, Education Policy, Education Research and Statistics, Educational Technology, Elementary and Secondary Education, Higher Education, International Education, Kids' Pages, and Teaching.

Site Name: Determining the site name of an Internet source is not as easy as finding the title of a book. For the purposes of this work, several sources may have been used to identify the site name, including agency press releases referring to the site, the name given to the site in the HTML <title> tag, or the initial heading or graphic.
URL: The web address or URL indicates the location that should be entered into your web browser to retrieve the website.
Sponsors: This section identifies the lead organizations that produce the site. Sponsors are most often federal government agencies, but commercial, educational, and nonprofit organizations will be listed here as well when they host or sponsor a specific resource.
Description: The resource description explains a site's organization, principal features, menu items, and significant links. For many agencies, a brief description of the agency's mission is included to help explain the site's subject coverage. The description may mention significant publications available on the site or which sections of the site include online documents. If the site content is available in languages other than English, this is noted. The utility of the site, its ease of use, and the potential audience may be evaluated as well, usually in the last paragraph of the description.

ADULT EDUCATION

DANTES—Defense Activity for Non-Traditional Education Support

www.dantes.doded.mil/
Sponsor: Defense Department
Description: DANTES provides support for the Department of Defense's off-duty, voluntary education programs. Its website has information about certification programs, counselor support, distance learning, and tuition assistance. It also has a section about the Troops-to-Teachers program, which assists military personnel interested in beginning a second career as public school teacher.

Graduate School USA

http://graduateschool.edu/
Sponsor: Graduate School USA
Description: Graduate School USA, formerly referred to as the Graduate School, USDA, is an independent educational institution headquartered in Washington, DC, with regional campuses around the United States. In 2009, Graduate School USA acquired most of the assets of Southeastern University and the merged programs offer career-related courses to federal workers

and the public. The website has the current course catalog and information on faculty and certification programs.

National Commission on Adult Literacy
www.nationalcommissiononadultliteracy.org/
Sponsor: National Commission on Adult Literacy
Description: The National Commission on Adult Literacy was formed in June 2006 and spent the next two years examining adult education and literacy services in America. The Commission's report, *Reach Higher, AMERICA: Overcoming Crisis in the U.S. Workforce*, calls for a dramatically revamped service system with the capacity to effectively serve 20 million adults annually by the year 2020.

Literacy Information and Communication System (LINCS)
lincs.ed.gov/
Sponsor: U.S. Department of Education's Office of Vocational and Adult Education
Description: LINCS is an initiative of the U.S. Department of Education, Office of Vocational and Adult Education (OVAE) to expand evidence-based practice in the field of adult literacy. The LINCS initiative features on-demand, web-based professional development opportunities; targeted face-to-face training, high-quality resources; and an interactive online learning community. The National Institute for Literacy established the LINCS discussion lists in 1995 to increase access to electronic information for adult educators, provide a forum for discussion of adult literacy-related policy, and connect the work of NIFL with the field. It was transferred to the Department of Education in 2010.

National Audiovisual Center (NAC)
www.ntis.gov/products/nac.aspx
Sponsor(s): Commerce Department—Technology Administration (TA)—National Technical Information Service (NTIS)
Description: NAC manages a catalog of more than 9,000 training and education materials on video, audiocassette, CD-ROM, and other types of media. The products are available for sale. The website features an online "screening room," with clips from the most popular videos available for purchase. Major topics covered by the collection include occupational safety and health, fire services, law enforcement, and foreign languages. Information and educational materials include areas such as history, health, agriculture, and natural resources.

Office of Vocational and Adult Education, Department of Education
www.ed.gov/about/offices/list/ovae/index.html
Sponsor(s): Education Department—Vocational and Adult Education Office
Description: This site provides information about the Office of Vocational and Adult Education programs, grants, events, legislation, and resources concerning the fields of adult education and vocational education. Key sections are Career and Technical Education, Community Colleges, and Adult Literacy and Education.

CURRICULUM

Agriculture in the Classroom
www.agclassroom.org/
Sponsor(s): Agriculture Department (USDA)—National Institute of Food and Agriculture (NIFA)
Description: The USDA's Agriculture in the Classroom program coordinates state education programs designed to teach children about the role of agriculture in the economy and in society. The site includes a directory of state programs, a National Resource Directory of educational materials about agriculture, information on the national Agriculture in the Classroom conference, and the online magazine *AgroWorld* for high school educators and students.

ArtsEdge: The National Arts and Education Information Network
artsedge.kennedy-center.org/

Sponsor(s): Kennedy Center for the Performing Arts; National Endowment for the Arts (NEA)
Description: ArtsEdge, from the Kennedy Center, is a major arts resource for educators and students. The site includes lesson plans and content standards for grades K–12. It also highlights articles, reports, and organizations related to arts education and features an arts education advocacy section. This well-designed site should be a primary starting point for people involved in arts education.

The Kennedy Center is a federal government building, but its programs are privately funded. ArtsEdge and the John F. Kennedy Center for the Performing Arts hold the copyright to all of the content on the site.

BLM Learning Landscapes
www.blm.gov/wo/st/en/res/Education_in_BLM/Learning_Landscapes.html
Sponsor(s): Interior Department—Bureau of Land Management (BLM)
Description: This BLM website has information and activities for students and teachers. The Teachers section has information about field programs (mostly in western states), websites, resources, and classroom activities. The site's Curriculum Connections correlates BLM classroom activities to National Science Education Standards and National Geography Standards. Online resources for teachers and learners cover such areas as archeology, geology, paleontology, American history, wildlife, and energy.

Census in Schools
www.census.gov/dmd/www/teachers.html
Sponsor(s): Commerce Department—Economics and Statistics Administration (ESA)—Census Bureau
Description: The Census in Schools program provides K–12 teaching materials, workshops for educators, and other outreach activities. Its website includes teaching kits and reference materials (primarily about the decennial census).

EDSITEment
edsitement.neh.gov/
Sponsor: National Endowment for the Humanities (NEH)
Description: The EDSITEment website's tag line is "the best of the humanities on the web." It provides a cataloged selection of lesson plans built around high-quality, freely accessible material available on the Internet. The lesson plans are organized into sections including Art and Culture, Literature and Language Arts, Foreign Language, and History and Social Studies. Each detailed lesson plan is labeled with the appropriate grade level, subject area, time required, and skills taught. The site is sponsored by a partnership between the National Endowment for the Humanities and the Verizon Foundation.

EDSITEment provides quality resources on a well-designed and attractive website.

Energy Education and Workforce Development
www.eere.energy.gov/education/
Sponsor(s): Energy Department—Energy Efficiency and Renewable Energy Office
Description: The Energy Education site links to numerous resources, including more than 350 lesson plans and activities on energy efficiency and renewable energy for grades K–12. It also features science projects, science contests, and links to other energy education resources. The site also links to information on education opportunities for teachers, higher education students, and energy professionals.

For Educators and Students
www.archives.gov/education/
Sponsor: National Archives and Records Administration (NARA)
Description: The "Teachers's Resources" section of the National Archives site features history lesson plans and teaching activities correlated to the National History Standards and the National Standards for Civics and Government. It focuses on teaching, with primary documents available on the

Archives site. The site also links to information on teacher training, videoconferences, workshops, and other educational services from the National Archives.

GLOBE Program
www.globe.gov/
Sponsor(s): National Aeronautics and Space Administration (NASA); National Oceanic and Atmospheric Administration (NOAA); National Science Foundation (NSF)
Description: The GLOBE (Global Learning and Observations to Benefit the Environment) program is designed to promote science education at the primary and secondary school levels. GLOBE is funded by NASA and the National Science Foundation, supported by the Department of State, and implemented through a cooperative agreement between NASA; the University Corporation for Atmospheric Research in Boulder, Colorado; and Colorado State University in Fort Collins, Colorado. The GLOBE program's primary objective is to involve students in taking environmental measurements. Schools in more than 100 countries are participating. The data they collect is accessible to anyone and there is information on how new schools can register to be included in the program. The site also has a teacher's guide and schedule of teacher workshops. Much of the content is available in Spanish and other non-English languages.

With participating schools from all over the world, this kind of collaborative project demonstrates how the Internet can be used in a K–12 environment. In addition, this website is well designed and makes navigation easy even for users who are unfamiliar with the program.

Learning Page of the Library of Congress
www.loc.gov/teachers/
Sponsor: Library of Congress
Description: Designed for the educational community, this website helps students and teachers find relevant materials within the National Digital Library collection on the Library of Congress web pages, with particular emphasis on the American Memory project. For educators, the site has guides and information on workshops about teaching with primary sources.

NASA Education
www.nasa.gov/offices/education/about/index.html
Sponsor(s): National Aeronautics and Space Administration (NASA)—Education Office
Description: The NASA Education website provides information about the education programs that NASA offers to K–12 educators and students, as well as those offered to undergraduate and graduate students and faculty at universities. News and resources are divided into sections including Elementary and Secondary Education, Higher Education, and Informal Education. The section on Elementary and Secondary School programs has information on Educator Astronauts and the NASA Explorer Schools program. Under the NASA Education Offices heading, the site links to the individual websites of NASA education programs, NASA Flight and Research Centers, and each of NASA's directorates.

National Marine Sanctuaries Education
sanctuaries.noaa.gov/education/
Sponsor(s): Commerce Department—National Oceanic and Atmospheric Administration (NOAA)
Description: The National Marine Sanctuaries Education website features lesson plans, free materials, information on workshops, and other items of interest to science or environment teachers. The site has a section specifically for teachers, but resources can also be found in other sections, such as the sections for events and references.

NIH Office of Science Education
science-education.nih.gov/
Sponsor: National Institutes of Health (NIH)
Description: The NIH Office of Science Education (OSE) develops curriculum

supplements, model programs, and other resources focusing on medicine, biology, and research to promote public science education. This website serves as a portal to resources from NIH. The site features the *NIH Curriculum Supplement Series* for grades K–12, a LifeWorks site about health careers, information on science education funding programs, and many other online resources.

NOAA Education Resources
www.education.noaa.gov/
Sponsor(s): Commerce Department—National Oceanic and Atmospheric Administration (NOAA)
Description: The NOAA Education site has teacher training opportunity announcements and materials for teachers that cover weather and atmosphere, climate, oceans and coasts, marine life, freshwater, and special topics. News, Resource Collections, and Data Visualizations are also provided.

NSF Classroom Resources
www.nsf.gov/news/classroom/
Sponsor: National Science Foundation (NSF)
Description: The NSF provides organized links to classroom resources on the Internet. The website describes its intended audience as "classroom teachers, their students, and students' families." Links are organized into science topics such as biology, computing, environment, mathematics, and physics. The linked sites are from a variety of educational organizations and institutions.

Office of English Language Acquisition
www.ed.gov/about/offices/list/oela/
Sponsor(s): Education Department—English Language Acquisition Office
Description: The full title of this office is the Office of English Language Acquisition, Language Enhancement, and Academic Achievement for Limited English Proficient Students (OELA). OELA administers Title III of the No Child Left Behind Act (Public Law 107-110) on Language Instruction for Limited English Proficient and Immigrant Students. It also administers a state formula grant program. The site has program information and technical assistance for those applying for Title III grants, and also links to the National Clearinghouse for English Language Acquisition and Language Instruction Educational Programs (NCELA), which is funded by the Department of Education.

USGS and Science Education
education.usgs.gov/
Sponsor(s): Interior Department—U.S. Geological Survey (USGS)
Description: The USGS education website covers topics of concern to USGS scientists, including geography, geology, biology, and water resources. Educational resources are organized for grades K–6, grades 7–12, and undergraduate education. The site also covers USGS careers, internships, and postdoctoral fellowships.

EARLY CHILDHOOD EDUCATION

Early Childhood Learning and Knowledge Center
eclkc.ohs.acf.hhs.gov/hslc/
Sponsor(s): Health and Human Services Department—Administration for Children and Families (ACF)—Office of Head Start (OHS)
Description: The Early Childhood Learning and Knowledge Center (ECLKC) website states that it is designed to provide "relevant, timely information, knowledge and learning to Head Start programs and the early childhood community in an easy-to-use format." The site has information on the Head Start Program and on topics such as early education, child health, supporting your child in Head Start, and professional development for program grantees. It includes an online directory of Head Start programs. ECLKC also provides information on Head Start regulations and policy, performance standards, and program monitoring. Some information is provided in Spanish.

This website duplicates some information provided on the Office of Head Start website, but also offers unique resources—particularly for the support of program grantees.

Head Start
www.acf.hhs.gov/programs/ohs/
Sponsor(s): Health and Human Services Department—Administration for Children and Families (ACF)—Office of Head Start (OHS)
Description: The Office of Head Start administers grants for local public and private non-profit and for-profit agencies that provide child development services for low-income children and their families. The website has information on the program and relevant laws and regulations. The site also links to research on outcomes for the Head Start (preschool) and Early Head Start (infant to three years) programs.

EDUCATION FUNDING

FAFSA4caster
www.fafsa4caster.ed.gov/
Sponsor(s): Education Department—Federal Student Aid Office
Description: The FAFSA4caster website is for those planning for higher education but not yet ready to apply for financial aid. The site provides an orientation to the financial aid process and an estimate of eligibility for aid. FAFSA4caster is available in English and Spanish.

Federal Cyber Service: Scholarship for Service
www.sfs.opm.gov/
Sponsor: Office of Personnel Management (OPM)
Description: OPM's Scholarship for Service program funds the education expenses of graduate and undergraduate students in information assurance fields in exchange for an obligation to work for the federal government for an agreed-upon term. The program is designed to strengthen the federal government's expertise in information assurance (the security of computer and communication networks and the information they carry). This website has further details about the program and a list of participating higher education institutions.

Federal School Code Search Page
fafsa.ed.gov/FAFSA/app/schoolSearch
Sponsor(s): Education Department—Federal Student Aid Office
Description: This site provides searchable access to the federal Title IV School Codes required on many financial aid forms.

Federal Student Aid Gateway
federalstudentaid.ed.gov/
Sponsor(s): Education Department—Federal Student Aid Office
Description: This site provides information, referrals, and web links for students, parents, financial aid professionals, those repaying student loans, and those doing business with the Federal Student Aid Office. The site also has press releases and general information about the office.

The Federal Student Aid Gateway serves a broad audience. Other financial aid websites listed in this section are more specialized.

Free Application for Federal Student Aid (FAFSA)
www.fafsa.ed.gov/
Sponsor(s): Education Department—Federal Student Aid Office
Description: FAFSA on the web makes it possible to apply online for federal financial aid for college. The site provides guidance on applying for aid, the application process, and deadlines.

GI Bill Website
www.gibill.va.gov/
Sponsor: Department of Veterans Affairs
Description: The GI Bill site provides information on the range of education benefits for active duty and reserve servicemembers,

veterans, survivors, and dependents. Information on the programs is available in the Education Benefits, Information for Benefit Recipients, and Questions and Answers sections. The site includes a database of approved programs at colleges, non-college degree granting institutions, licensing and certification granting providers, and national testing providers.

The site has a history of the original GI Bill—the Servicemembers' Readjustment Act of 1944—which preceded the current program.

Information for Financial Aid Professionals (IFAP)
ifap.ed.gov/
Sponsor(s): Education Department—Federal Student Aid Office
Description: IFAP is an electronic library for financial aid professionals that contains publications, regulations, and guidance regarding the administration of the Title IV Federal Student Aid (FSA) Programs. This site features technical documentation, online tools, worksheets, and schedules related to the programs. The site also has an RSS feed of program news.

Student Aid on the Web
studentaid.ed.gov/
Sponsor(s): Education Department—Federal Student Aid Office
Description: This website is a portal and service center for federal student aid information and programs, designed for students and their parents or advisers. It begins with information about preparing for, choosing, applying to, and attending a college. Other sections contain facts about funding a college education and repaying student loans. The site links to the Free Application for Federal Student Aid (FAFSA) online.

Tax Benefits for Education
www.irs.gov/publications/p970/
Sponsor(s): Treasury Department—Internal Revenue Service (IRS)
Description: This web page has the full text of Publication 970, *Tax Benefits for Education.* The publication outlines the tax deductions and benefits available to those saving for or paying education costs.

EDUCATION POLICY

The Center for the Book
read.gov
Sponsor: Library of Congress
Description: This website is a companion to an advertising campaign to encourage young people to read. The site links to resources from the Library of Congress and elsewhere that promote reading, books, poetry, Braille literacy, and libraries.

Directorate for Education and Human Resources—NSF
www.nsf.gov/dir/index.jsp?org=ehr
Sponsor: National Science Foundation (NSF)
Description: The Directorate for Education and Human Resources (EHR) provides leadership in the effort to improve science, mathematics, engineering, and technology education in the United States. Its website includes links to descriptions of the EHR divisions—the Division of Graduate Education (DGE); the Division of Undergraduate Education (DUE); Research on Learning in Formal and Informal Settings (DRL); and Human Resource Development (HRD)—and the types of projects they sponsor. The Publications category includes selected full-text documents.

This site will be of assistance to science and engineering students and educators at all levels who are interested in pursuing grants or scholarships.

ED.gov—U.S. Department of Education
www.ed.gov
Sponsor: Education Department
Description: The Department of Education website features current news and links to information on student loans, the No Child

Left Behind program, and other high-profile initiatives. The site organizes its content into several information centers, including Funding, Research, Policy, and News. In addition, it has a site map and side bars with sections for Teachers, Parents and Families, Education Reform, and College Completion.

The About ED section has a directory of offices, budget and appropriations information, and press releases. Publications are available through the linked ED Pubs website and the ERIC (Education Resources Information Center) database. Some information is available in Spanish.

Elementary and Secondary Education Act (No Child Left Behind)
www.ed.gov/esea
Sponsor: Education Department
Description: This Department of Education website is dedicated to information about the No Child Left Behind Act of 2001 (the current reauthorization of the Elementary and Secondary Education Act). The law concerns educational standards and testing, teacher training and recruitment, English language instruction, school safety, and other matters.

Office of Innovation and Improvement (OII)
www.ed.gov/about/offices/list/oii/
Sponsor(s): Education Department—Innovation and Improvement Office
Description: OII makes strategic investments in innovative educational programs and practices, and administers more than 25 discretionary grant programs managed by five program offices: Charter Schools Program, Improvement Programs, Parental Options and Information, Teacher Quality Programs, and the Investing in Innovation Programs. OII also serves as the Department's liaison and resource to the nonpublic education community through the Office of Non-Public Education.

White House Initiative on Educational Excellence for Hispanic Americans
www2.ed.gov/about/inits/list/hispanic-initiative/index.html
Sponsor: President's Advisory Commission on Educational Excellence for Hispanic Americans
Description: The White House Initiative on Educational Excellence for Hispanic Americans and the President's Advisory Commission on Educational Excellence for Hispanic Americans were established by executive order in 2001. The Education Department provides the primary support for the initiative. The website has information on the commission and also features a series of toolkits, or online guides, with educational tips relevant to early childhood, elementary and secondary schooling, and postsecondary education.

EDUCATION RESEARCH AND STATISTICS

ERIC—Educational Resources Information Center
www.eric.ed.gov/
Sponsor(s): Education Department—Institute of Education Sciences
Description: ERIC is a database and information system funded by the Department of Education to provide organized access to a wide array of published and unpublished material about education. It references education literature from 1966 to the present. The website describes ERIC as "the world's largest digital library of education literature."

The ERIC search interface has basic and advanced versions. Searchable fields include title, author, ERIC number, identifier, ISBN, ISSN, journal name, source institution, sponsoring agency, thesaurus descriptor, and date range. Searches can be limited by type of material cited (for example, journal article, nonprint media, or dissertation) and full-text availability. The ERIC Thesaurus is linked to the search interface; users can also browse and search the thesaurus separately. An interface called My ERIC allows for some customization once users register for a My ERIC account.

ERIC is a key resource for research in education and related fields. Although the database was previously handled by a network of academic and nonprofit clearinghouses, the Department of Education established centralized control in late 2004. Since then, new features and content have been phased in. ERIC users should check the ERIC online news for regular updates; however, there is no e-mail or RSS feed subscription for the news.

Institute of Education Sciences (IES)
www.ed.gov/about/offices/list/ies/
Sponsor(s): Education Department—Institute of Education Sciences
Description: IES was established in 2002 to focus on education research. It includes the National Center for Education Research (NCER), the National Center for Education Statistics (NCES), the National Center for Education Evaluation and Regional Assistance (NCEE), and the National Center for Special Education Research (NCSER). The website has information on IES and its grants and component programs.

International Activities Program
nces.ed.gov/surveys/international/
Sponsor(s): Education Department—Institute of Education Sciences—National Center for Education Statistics (NCES)
Description: NCES provides a central page for linking to the international education statistics that the agency collects. The site links to information on the Trends in International Mathematics and Science Study (TIMSS) and Program for International Student Assessment (PISA) assessments, as well as the Progress in International Reading Literacy Study (PIRLS) and Adult Literacy and Lifeskills (ALL) international comparative studies.

National Center for Education Statistics
nces.ed.gov/
Sponsor(s): Education Department—Institute of Education Sciences—National Center for Education Statistics (NCES)
Description: NCES collects and analyzes data concerning education in the United States and other nations. Its website is a primary source for education statistics for all educational levels and for data on educational assessment, libraries, and international educational outcomes. Most data on the site are from surveys and data collection programs that NCES conducts, and results are published in major NCES statistical publications, such as *Education Statistics Quarterly*, *The Condition of Education*, and the *Digest of Education Statistics*. The site provides a variety of tools to search and report the data. The Fast Facts section highlights frequently requested information, such as data on high school dropout rates or the effects of reading to children. The site also includes a searchable directory of private and public schools, colleges, and public libraries.

For users searching for statistics related to any form of education, this site should be the first place to visit.

Research on Learning in Formal and Informal Settings
www.nsf.gov/div/index.jsp?div=DRL
Sponsor: National Science Foundation (NSF)
Description: The NSF Division of Research on Learning in Formal and Informal Settings (DRL) is concerned with teaching and learning in science, technology, engineering, and mathematics at all age levels. The division's website has information on funding opportunities for research in this area, along with division news and events.

EDUCATIONAL TECHNOLOGY

Computers for Learning
computersforlearning.gov/
Sponsor: General Services Administration (GSA)
Description: The Computers for Learning website is designed for public, private, parochial, and home schools serving the K–12 student population, as well as other nonprofit educational organizations. The service allows these groups of students and nonprofit organizations to request donations of surplus federal computer equipment. The site

includes program and eligibility information and sections on how to give and receive computers.

Minority University Space Interdisciplinary Network (MU-SPIN)
muspin.gsfc.nasa.gov/
Sponsor(s): National Aeronautics and Space Administration (NASA)—Goddard Space Flight Center (GSFC)
Description: MU-SPIN is designed for Historically Black Colleges and Universities (HBCUs), Hispanic Serving Institutions (HSIs), and Tribal Colleges. The program focuses on training the next generation of minority scientists and engineers through technology, research, and education programs. The website has information about the program and its associated events, conferences, and resources.

For minority colleges and universities, this is an important resource for high technology and computer networking information and training.

Office of Educational Technology (OET), Department of Education
www.ed.gov/about/offices/list/os/technology/
Sponsor(s): Education Department—Educational Technology Office
Description: OET develops national educational technology policy and works with the educational community and the Department of Education to promote national goals for educational technology. Major sections of the site are Grants Programs, Reports and Research, and Internet Safety. The site also has a directory of state government contacts for educational technology.

ELEMENTARY AND SECONDARY EDUCATION

Education Resource Organizations Directory (EROD)
wdcrobcolp01.ed.gov/Programs/EROD/
Sponsor(s): Education Department—Elementary and Secondary Education Office
Description: EROD is a database of approximately 3,000 state and regional organizations that provide education-related information. It includes organizations such as state literary resource centers and regional education laboratories. Each organization's entry has complete contact information and a description of its services.

Emergency Planning
www.ed.gov/emergencyplan/
Sponsor(s): Education Department—Office of Safe and Drug-Free Schools
Description: The Emergency Planning website, launched in March 2003, provides school leaders with information to plan for emergencies such as natural disasters or violent incidents. The site includes instructional webcasts, a crisis planning guide, information on pandemic flu preparedness, and links to related assistance programs from the Education Department.

The Nation's Report Card
nces.ed.gov/nationsreportcard/
Sponsor(s): Education Department—Institute of Education Sciences—National Center for Education Statistics (NCES)
Description: This is the online home of the National Assessment of Educational Progress (NAEP), an ongoing national assessment for student achievement in grades 4, 8, and 12. It provides background information on the history and current operations of the NAEP. Current results are available in the form of state profiles. Users can also construct custom data tables and get reports at the national level or by state, region, or major urban district. The Subject Areas section provides background and reports on assessments in mathematics, reading, science, civics, and other specific subjects.

Office of Elementary and Secondary Education (OESE)
www.ed.gov/about/offices/list/oese/
Sponsor(s): Education Department—Elementary and Secondary Education Office

Description: The OESE website has information on its programs, office contacts, and reports. The Laws, Regulations, and Guidance section is largely concerned with the No Child Left Behind Act. The Standards, Assessment, and Accountability and the Flexibility and Waivers sections also cover areas of No Child Left Behind. The Consolidated State Info section has information on the No Child Left Behind Consolidated State Performance Report for states reporting accomplishments and data. The site is searchable through an A to Z index.

The alphabetical index is useful in uncovering all of the information at this site. Much of the information on the site is intended for elementary and secondary education professionals and officials who need to comply with the No Child Left Behind Act or who are interested in its documents.

Office of Safe and Healthy Students
www2.ed.gov/about/offices/list/oese/oshs/index.html
Sponsor(s): Education Department—Office of Elementary and Secondary Education—Office of Safe and Healthy Students
Description: Formerly the Office of Safe and Drug-Free Schools, the OSHS's major programs come under the categories of Safe and Supportive Schools; Health, Mental Health, Environmental Health, and Physical Education; Drug-Violence Prevention; Character and Civic Education; and Homeland Security, Emergency Management, and school preparedness. Many of the programs are for the elementary and secondary level, although some programs also apply to higher education. The website has information on the grants that fall under these program categories and offers news, publications; it also links to related resources on the Internet.

Office of Special Education Programs (OSEP)
www.ed.gov/about/offices/list/osers/osep/
Sponsor(s): Education Department—Special Education and Rehabilitative Services Office—Office of Special Education Programs (OSEP)
Description: OSEP has the primary responsibility of administering programs and projects relating to the education of all children, youth, and adults with disabilities, from birth through age 21. Sections describe OSEP's Programs and Projects, Grants and Funding, Legislation and Policy, Publications and Products, and Research and Statistics. It includes extensive information on the Individuals with Disabilities Education Act (IDEA), which authorizes OSEP programs.

School District Demographics System
nces.ed.gov/surveys/sdds/
Sponsor(s): Education Department—Institute of Education Sciences—National Center for Education Statistics (NCES)
Description: This site presents demographic, social, economic, and geographic data for school districts from the decennial census and the American Community Survey. The Map Viewer application allows users to view state or individual school district maps. The School District Profiles section can be used to compare demographic information between any of the nation's school districts. Users can also download school district data from the American Community Survey in spreadsheet file format. Documentation for the data and the system can be found in the Library section.

The data from this special census tabulation can be helpful for studying school districts and for examining general demographics of children and families with children.

U.S. Presidential Scholars Program
www.ed.gov/programs/psp/
Sponsor: Education Department
Description: The U.S. Presidential Scholars Program recognizes up to 141 outstanding high school graduates each year. The website has information on eligibility, the application process, and the current year's presidential scholars.

HIGHER EDUCATION

Air Force Institute of Technology
www.afit.edu/
Sponsor(s): Air Force—Air Force Institute of Technology (AFIT)
Description: A component of Air University, AFIT is the Air Force's graduate school of engineering and management and its institute for technical professional continuing education. The website provides information on each of AFIT's schools and centers.

Air University
www.au.af.mil/au/
Sponsor(s): Air Force—Air University
Description: Air University (AU), located at Maxwell Air Force Base, conducts professional military education, graduate education, and professional continuing education for officers, enlisted personnel, and civilians. This site links to each of the component schools that make up AU and to its research centers, including the USAF Counterproliferation Center, National Space Studies Center, and Cyberspace and Information Operations Study Center. It also provides information on the university's history and mission. The Other AU Links section links to the university's course catalogs and publications, Air University Press, and the Air University Library.

Army Logistics University
www.almc.army.mil/
Sponsor(s): Army—Army Logistics University (ALU)
Description: The Army Logistics University site features a course catalog, course schedule, online version of *Army Logistician*, and a link to the Army Logistics Library website.

Barry M. Goldwater Scholarships
www.act.org/goldwater/
Sponsor(s): Goldwater Scholarship and Excellence in Education Foundation
Description: Goldwater Scholarships are awarded for undergraduate education in the fields of mathematics, science, and engineering. The Goldwater Foundation was established by Congress to encourage study in these fields. The website has scholarship application information and lists of past awardees.

Carlisle Barracks and the U.S. Army War College
carlisle-www.army.mil/
Sponsor(s): Army—Carlisle Barracks
Description: Carlisle Barracks is the home of the U.S. Army War College, the Center for Strategic Leadership, the Strategic Studies Institute, the Peacekeeping and Stability Operations Institute, the Army Physical Fitness Research Institute, the Army Heritage and Education Center, and the Military History Institute. This site features information on the barracks and the resident institutions. The website's home page features summaries of timely studies in national defense. The site also carries the quarterly *Parameters*, the Army's senior professional journal; issues are archived online from 1996 onward.

College Navigator
nces.ed.gov/collegenavigator/
Sponsor(s): Education Department—Institute of Education Sciences—National Center for Education Statistics (NCES)
Description: College Navigator is a database of information on colleges, universities, community colleges, technical colleges, and similar institutions. Prior to September 2007, it was known as the College Opportunities Online (COOL) database. The database can be searched by institution name or by location, type of school, programs offered, tuition and enrollment ranges, and other criteria. For each institution, the database typically supplies phone numbers, a URL, average costs, and basic background information. Colleges can also be compared side-by-side for such factors as estimated student expenses and graduation rates.

College Navigator is a useful reference for college-bound students as well as for those simply looking for a college's phone number or URL. Note that the site states that an institution's inclusion in the database does not constitute a recommendation by the Department of Education.

Command and General Staff College
www.cgsc.edu/
Sponsor(s): Army—Army Command and General Staff College
Description: The U.S. Army Command and General Staff College is focused on leadership development within the Army. This site offers information on the college, its training programs, and its organizations.

Defense Language Institute Foreign Language Center (DLIFLC)
www.dliflc.edu/
Sponsor(s): Defense Department—Defense Language Institute (DLI)
Description: DLIFLC is the primary foreign-language training institution within the Department of Defense. Programs are for U.S. military personnel and select agency staff. The website has information on the history of the center and its current language programs. The center's journal, *Applied Language Learning*, is online dating back to 1996.

The site is primarily of interest to those eligible for and interested in DLI language training.

Harry S. Truman Scholarship Foundation
www.truman.gov/
Sponsor: Truman Scholarship Foundation
Description: Truman Scholarships are awarded to outstanding undergraduate students who wish to pursue graduate study and careers in government or public service. This website has information about the Truman Foundation and its scholarship program, with sections for candidates, faculty, and current Truman scholars.

Marine Corps University Foundation
www.mcuf.og/about_mcu.html
Sponsor(s): Marine Corps University Foundation
Description: The Marine Corps University's website provides information about its schools, including the Expeditionary Warfare School, the Command and Staff College, the School of Advanced Warfighting, the Marine Corps War College, and the Lejeune Leadership Institute.

NASA Academy
www.nasa.gov/offices/education/programs/descriptions/NASA_Academy.html
Sponsor(s): National Aeronautics and Space Administration (NASA)—Goddard Space Flight Center (GSFC)
Description: This is the central page for NASA Academy summer programs for college students in science, math, engineering, or computer science. The site has application forms and detailed program information.

The information on these pages will be of interest to college students interested in careers or further study with NASA and to the advisers of students in relevant fields of study.

NASA Office of Higher Education at Goddard Space Flight Center
university.gsfc.nasa.gov/
Sponsor(s): National Aeronautics and Space Administration (NASA)—Goddard Space Flight Center (GSFC)
Description: This office manages fellowships, grants, and other higher education programs at NASA's Goddard Space Flight Center in Maryland. The programs target colleges and universities along the eastern seaboard and aerospace-oriented institutions nationwide with programs of mutual interest to Goddard. The site has information about these and other NASA-wide higher education programs.

National Defense University (NDU)
www.ndu.edu/
Sponsor(s): Defense Department—National Defense University (NDU)
Description: The NDU website provides an online course catalog and links to the university's component colleges and schools: the Joint Forces Staff College, the National

War College, the Industrial College of the Armed Forces, the Information Resources Management College, and the School for National Security Executive Education. NDU Research Centers online include the Institute for National Strategic Studies and the Center for the Study of Weapons of Mass Destruction. A Professional Military Reading List section presents bibliographies of recommended reading from the chiefs of the armed services and others.

Naval Postgraduate School
www.nps.edu/
Sponsor(s): Navy—Naval Postgraduate School (NPS)
Description: NPS emphasizes education and research programs relevant to the Navy, defense, and national and international security interests. The website links to information from each of the NPS component schools: Business and Public Policy, Engineering and Applied Sciences, Operational and Information Sciences, and International Graduate Studies. The Research section includes archives of technical reports and abstracts from theses.

Naval War College
www.nwc.navy.mil/
Sponsor(s): Navy—Naval War College (NWC)
Description: The Naval War College in Newport, Rhode Island, is open to selected midgrade and senior military officers of the U.S. armed services and civilian government officials. Naval officers from other countries attend international programs by invitation. The website has information on the component colleges, the Center for Naval Warfare Studies, and the Naval War College Press. The Press section includes the full texts of studies in the Newport Papers series and the *Naval War College Review*.

NSF Division of Graduate Education
www.nsf.gov/div/index.jsp?div=DGE
Sponsor: National Science Foundation (NSF)
Description: The programs of the NSF's Division of Graduate Education promote the early career development of scientists and engineers by offering support at critical junctures of their careers. This website describes the division's research and teaching fellowships for graduate students in the sciences. The Publications section includes program guidelines. There is also a page to search for awards.

NSF Division of Undergraduate Education
www.nsf.gov/div/index.jsp?div=DUE
Sponsor: National Science Foundation (NSF)
Description: The NSF's Division of Undergraduate Education (DUE) focuses on improving undergraduate education in science, technology, mathematics, and engineering. The division awards funds to scholarship programs at educational institutions; they do not award scholarships directly to students. The division also funds programs for teacher education and curriculum development. The website has information on the programs, deadlines, and awards.

Office of Postsecondary Education (OPE)
www.ed.gov/about/offices/list/ope/
Sponsor(s): Education Department—Postsecondary Education Office
Description: In the Programs/Initiatives section, this website provides a guide to the more than 40 postsecondary-related education programs administered by the OPE. Initiatives include programs for improving educational institutions, supporting international education, funding teacher training, and reaching out to students from disadvantaged backgrounds. The Reports and Resources section of the site includes the *Federal Campus-Based Programs Data Book*. The Accreditation section of the site explains the accreditation of educational institutions and has a directory of the numerous accrediting agencies.

This is a useful site with a substantial body of information sources of interest to students, educators, and financial aid offices.

Smithsonian Office of Fellowships and Internships
www.si.edu/ofg/
Sponsor: Smithsonian Institution
Description: The Office of Fellowships and Internships has applications, lists of fellowship and internship opportunities, and announcements of current recipients. The publication *Smithsonian Opportunities for Research and Study* is available online in an HTML format.

U.S. Merchant Marine Academy
www.usmma.edu/
Sponsor(s): Transportation Department—Maritime Administration (MARAD)
Description: The Merchant Marine Academy website has information about admissions, academics, and other activities. The site also links to the Global Maritime and Transportation School (GMATS) for maritime and transportation industry professionals.

United States Air Force Academy
www.usafa.af.mil/
Sponsor(s): Air Force—Air Force Academy
Description: The United States Air Force Academy website provides information for cadets, staff, and faculty. It includes visitor information and sections on admissions, academics, and cadet life. The academy's libraries are listed in the USAFA Organizations section.

United States Military Academy at West Point
www.usma.edu/
Sponsor(s): Army—United States Military Academy (USMA)
Description: The West Point website has information for prospective and current students, alumni, visitors, and the West Point community. Sections include Admissions, Community, and the Academic, Athletic, and Military Programs. A brief section on USMA history, found in the About the Academy section, includes a timeline and list of notable graduates.

United States Naval Academy
www.usna.edu
Sponsor(s): Navy—United States Naval Academy (USNA)
Description: This site contains information on the Naval Academy, mainly for students, prospective students, and midshipmen. The About USNA section links to information about the academy's history and notable graduates.

White House Initiative on Historically Black Colleges and Universities
www.ed.gov/edblogs/whhbcu/
Sponsor(s): Education Department—White House Initiative on Historically Black Colleges and Universities
Description: The White House Initiative on Historically Black Colleges and Universities was established by executive order in 1981. This website has information on the initiative's work, board of advisers and staff, and budget. It also has a list of Historically Black Colleges and Universities by state and type of institution, with URLs provided for each institution.

White House Initiative on Tribal Colleges and Universities
www.ed.gov/about/inits/list/whtc/edlite-index.html
Sponsor(s): Education Department—White House Initiative on Tribal Colleges and Universities
Description: The President's Board of Advisors on Tribal Colleges and Universities and the White House Initiative on Tribal Colleges and Universities were established by executive order in 2002. In addition to information on the board and its activities, this site has a directory of tribal colleges and universities.

INTERNATIONAL EDUCATION

Bureau of Educational and Cultural Affairs
exchanges.state.gov/
Sponsor(s): State Department—Educational and Cultural Affairs Bureau

Description: The Bureau of Educational and Cultural Affairs website has information about its many international exchange and education programs. For U.S. citizens, the site has information on Fulbright Scholarships, English-language teaching abroad, study abroad, and other opportunities. For the audience abroad, the site has information about studying in the United States, the Fulbright Program, and a range of programs from the high school level up to the scholar and professional level. The site covers a range of other initiatives, such as the National Security Language Initiative, the Global Cultural Initiative, and the Edward R. Murrow Journalism Initiative.

EducationUSA
www.educationusa.info/
Sponsor(s): State Department—Educational and Cultural Affairs Bureau
Description: EducationUSA is a global network of hundreds of advising and information centers around the world, supported by the Department of State's Bureau of Educational and Cultural Affairs. The website provides contact information for individual centers worldwide. Other sections of the site provide information about finding a school, student visas, and living in the United States. Information is available for all levels of higher education and specialized professional study. Booklets from the department's "If You Want to Study in the United States" series are available online in Arabic, Chinese, French, Russian, Spanish, and English.

Fulbright Scholar Program
www.cies.org/
Alternate URL: www.iie.org/en/Fulbright/
Sponsor(s): State Department—Educational and Cultural Affairs Bureau; Institute of International Education (IIE)
Description: The Fulbright Program, sponsored by the United States, is an international education program that provides grants for graduate students, scholars, professionals, teachers, and administrators from the United States and other countries. This site, geared toward U.S. and non-U.S. applicants, describes the program and links to the Fulbright Commissions around the world.

Much of the program is administered for the Department of State by the Institute of International Education (IIE), an independent nonprofit organization. The alternate URL for this entry leads to the IIE Fulbright website. For applicants from the United States, the relevant applications are available online.

International Affairs Office
www.ed.gov/about/inits/ed/internationaled/
Sponsor: Education Department
Description: The International Affairs Office coordinates the Education Department's international programs and works with international agencies such as the United Nations Educational, Scientific, and Cultural Organization (UNESCO). The website provides a directory to Education Department programs that have an international aspect. It also describes the office's activities, such as International Education Week and the United States Network for Education Information (USNEI) program.

National Security Education Program
www.nsep.gov/
Sponsor: National Security Education Program
Description: The National Security Education Program (NSEP) works to strengthen national security by helping educate U.S. citizens about world cultures and languages. NSEP awards the David L. Boren Scholarships and Fellowships for study relating to global security at the graduate and undergraduate levels. The site provides information on the Boren grants and features accounts of student experiences while studying abroad.

State Department—Youth and Education
www.state.gov/youthandeducation/
Sponsor: State Department

Description: This section of the State Department's website includes information and materials for students and teachers. The site explains the work of the department, international education opportunities available to students, and the nature of careers within the Department of State.

U.S. Network for Education Information (USNEI)
http://www.ed.gov/about/offices/list/ous/international/usnei/edlite-index.html
Sponsor: Education Department
Description: USNEI is an interagency and public-private partnership set up to provide official information for anyone researching U.S. education. It also provides U.S. citizens with authoritative information about education in other countries. The site covers all levels of education, with topics including visas, accreditation, professional licensure, and teaching abroad (or in the United States). The site's Foreign Country Database links to websites for individual countries' official education agencies and organizations.

KIDS' PAGES

America's Story from America's Library
www.americaslibrary.gov/
Sponsor: Library of Congress
Description: This Library of Congress website is designed for children and their families. It uses digitized images from the library's collection, accompanied by text and graphics, to create educational pages about American history and culture. Sections include Explore the States, Jump Back in Time, and Meet Amazing Americans.

ATF Kids' Page
www.atf.gov/kids/
Sponsor(s): Justice Department—Bureau of Alcohol, Tobacco, Firearms, and Explosives
Description: Several sections of the site are designed specifically for children, such as those about Elliot Ness and ATF canines. Other menu items link to content on the main ATF website, such as those about ATF history and ATF special agents killed in the line of duty.

BAM! Body and Mind
www.bam.gov/
Sponsor(s): Health and Human Services Department—Centers for Disease Control and Prevention (CDC)
Description: BAM!, designed for children age 9 to 13, has tips on fighting stress and adopting healthy lifestyles. It contains information about fitness, nutrition, safety, and handling peer pressure.

Ben's Guide to U.S. Government for Kids
bensguide.gpo.gov/
Sponsor(s): Government Printing Office (GPO)—Superintendent of Documents
Description: With a cartoon version of Benjamin Franklin as a guide, this GPO site for children covers topics such as the U.S. Constitution, how laws are made, the branches of the federal government, and citizenship. It features sections for specific age groups, plus a special section for parents and educators. The major sections are About Ben, K–2, 3–5, 6–8, 9–12, and Parents and Teachers.

Ben's Guide has received numerous accolades. It is useful as a grade school or high school student's homework helper, but may also help older students refresh their basic knowledge of U.S. government and history.

BLS Career Information
www.bls.gov/k12/
Sponsor(s): Labor Department—Bureau of Labor Statistics (BLS)
Description: The BLS Career Information page for youth uses a graphical interface to match kids' interests with potential careers. A Teachers' Guide refers teachers to additional information available from the BLS.

The site is easy and fun to use. It is most appropriate for upper elementary grades and high school students.

CIA Kids' Page
www.cia.gov/kids-page/index.html
Sponsor(s): Central Intelligence Agency (CIA)
Description: The CIA Kids' Page has sections for students in grades K–5 and 6–12 and for parents and teachers. It also has a separate games section and links to the kids' pages at other intelligence agency websites. Kids' activities include learning about the CIA seal, CIA history, and working for the CIA. Parent and teacher materials include lesson plans and guidance on topics such as Internet safety and helping children avoid drug abuse.

CryptoKids™
www.nsa.gov/kids/
Sponsor(s): Defense Department—National Security Agency (NSA)
Description: This site has games, activities, and background information about NSA's specialty, cryptography. The Student Resources section has NSA career information for high school and college students. The site has both a Flash and text version.

DOI Just For Kids
www.doi.gov/public/teachandlearn_kids.cfm
Sponsor: Interior Department
Description: This Department of the Interior site is a portal to the various kids' pages hosted by the department's agencies and bureaus. Linked sites include Endangered Species, Astrogeology for Kids, Earthquakes for Kids, Web Rangers, and Careers in Science. The target audience age varies with the sites. Many sites include sections for teachers and field trip information.

EIA Energy Kid's Page
www.eia.doe.gov/kids/
Sponsor(s): Energy Department—Energy Information Administration (EIA)
Description: The Department of Energy's Information Administration provides this educational page. Sections include: Energy Facts, Fun and Games, Energy History, Classroom Activities, and Glossary. The Classroom Activities section includes materials for teachers and parents to use in working with learners from grades K–12.

Energy Department—Science Education
energy.gov/science-innovation/science-education
Sponsor: Energy Department
Description: This site centralizes access to Energy Department websites for kids and students, including energy glossaries and agency-sponsored contests and competitions. Linked sites cover a range of topics, including links to various student science competitions, Kids' Pages in the Energy Department, and information about internships.

EPA Climate Change Kids Site
www.epa.gov/climatechange/kids/
Sponsor: Environmental Protection Agency (EPA)
Description: This site provides explanations of climate, weather, and the greenhouse effect. It also has games and a section for teachers. Due to the amount of text and the complicated nature of the subject, this site is best for students in the upper grades.

EPA Student Center
www.epa.gov/students/
Sponsor: Environmental Protection Agency (EPA)
Description: The EPA Student Center website serves as a portal to information at a variety of educational levels and offers links to a Kids' Page, a site for high school students, and a site for teachers. Sections include Environmental Club Projects, Environmental Youth Awards, Fun Activities, and Environmental Basics.

FBI Kids' Page
www.fbi.gov/fbikids.htm
Sponsor(s): Justice Department—Federal Bureau of Investigation (FBI)
Description: The FBI website provides pages for kids in kindergarten through fifth grade,

such as the About Our Dogs section, and pages for those in grades 6–12, such as the How We Investigate section.

FCC Kids Zone
www.fcc.gov/cgb/kidszone/
Sponsor(s): Federal Communications Commission (FCC)—Consumer and Governmental Affairs Bureau
Description: The FCC Kids Zone has information on the history of communications technology, online games, and a section about satellites. It also has answers to questions kids ask, such as "What is 911?" and "What is the difference between AM radio and FM radio?"

FDA Kids' Site
www.fda.gov/ForConsumers/ByAudience/ForKids/default.htm
Sponsor(s): Health and Human Services Department—Food and Drug Administration (FDA)
Description: The FDA website for children presents health and safety information through several links, including Food Safety Information, the Center for Veterinary Medicine, and the National Agricultural Library.

Federal Reserve Education Page
www.federalreserveeducation.org/
Sponsor: Federal Reserve
Description: The Federal Reserve education site has resources for teachers, for the public, and news and general information about the Federal Reserve System. The page includes lesson plans for grades K–4, 5–8, and 9–12 that include activities and academic competitions to educate students about the history of the Federal Reserve, money and banking, credit, and consumer resources.

FEMA for Kids
www.fema.gov/kids/
Sponsor: Federal Emergency Management Agency (FEMA)
Description: This FEMA site provides information and resources to help children prepare for and prevent disasters. Children can go through a series of activities and receive a Disaster Action Kid certificate. A section called the Disaster Area explains threats like floods and hurricanes. The site includes a section for parents and teachers with curriculum resources and links to further information.

Because of the sensitive nature of disaster threats, parents and teachers will probably want to review this site before sharing sections of it with young children.

FSAKids
www.fsa.usda.gov/FSA/kidsapp?area=home&subject=landing&topic=landing
Sponsor(s): Agriculture Department (USDA)—Farm Service Agency (FSA)
Description: The Farm Service Agency provides coloring books and games with an agricultural theme, along with recipes for kids to try. The site also has online games in Spanish. Each section of the site also has information for parents and educators.

GirlsHealth.gov
Girlshealth.gov/
Sponsor: Health and Human Services Department
Description: GirlsHealth.gov is designed to help adolescent girls (ages 10 to 16) learn about the health issues and social situations that they will encounter during the teen years. Sections provide information about fitness, nutrition, the mind, relationships, and other related topics. The site also has sections for parents, caregivers, and teachers.

Inside the Courtroom
www.usdoj.gov/usao/eousa/kidspage/
Sponsor(s): Justice Department—United States Attorneys
Description: This kids' page describes a typical courtroom and the jobs of the people who work in a courthouse. It also presents a fictional account of an FBI case and how it moved from investigation to prosecution.

Kidd Safety
www.cpsc.gov/kids/kidsafety/
Sponsor: Consumer Product Safety Commission (CPSC)
Description: The Kidd Safety page uses a cartoon goat named Kidd to guide users through games and information about safety. The site covers topics such as bicycle helmets, riding a scooter, and safety around the house.

Kids and Families—Social Security
www.ssa.gov/kids/
Sponsor: Social Security Administration (SSA)
Description: This SSA website includes a Kids' Place and a Parents' Place. The Kids' Place offers tales about saving for the future and an introduction to the Social Security card. On the main page there is also a link to information for the families of youth with disabilities.

Kids in the House
kids.clerk.house.gov/young-learners/
Sponsor(s): The Congress—House of Representatives—Office of the Clerk
Description: The House Clerk's website for kids includes material on House procedures and history. It also discusses how bills are made into law. Features include a cartoon field trip to Capitol Hill, games, and a resource section for parents and teachers.

Kids Next Door
www.hud.gov/kids/kids.html
Sponsor: Housing and Urban Development (HUD)
Description: HUD's website for children is subtitled "Where kids can learn more about being good citizens." The page features sections including Meet Cool People, See Neat Things, and Visit Awesome Places. Within each of these sections are activities and pages such as Help the Homeless, Kids Volunteer, Safe Places to Play, and Build A Community. A section called Franklin's Fair Housing Corner provides educational materials on fair housing law that will be of interest to teachers and schools.

Kids Saving Energy
www.eere.energy.gov/kids/
Sponsor(s): Energy Department—Energy Efficiency and Renewable Energy Office
Description: This Department of Energy page for children includes home energy saving tips, an introduction to renewable energy technologies, games, and an energy quiz. A section for parents and teachers includes lesson plans for grades K–4, 5–8, and 9–12.

Kids.gov
www.kids.gov/
Sponsor: General Services Administration (GSA)
Description: Kids.gov is a portal to U.S. federal and state government web pages designed for children. The site groups links by age group, grades K–5 and grades 6–8. Links are then organized by topic, such as careers, computers, and "fun stuff." A section for educators provides links organized in the same categories, supplemented with parent and teacher resource sites.

Kids.gov provides an easy way for children (as well as teachers and parents) to find kid-friendly information on the Web.

Letsmove.gov
www.hhs.gov/kids/
Sponsor: Health and Human Services Department
Description: Let's Move is a website of the Department of Health and Human Services devoted to helping children learn to eat right and stay active. The site includes sections for parents, schools, community leaders, and chefs.

NASA Kids
www.nasa.gov/audience/forkids/home/
Alternate URL(s): http://www.nasa.gov/audience/forkids/kidsclub/flash/index.html and www.nasa.gov/audience/forstudents/
Sponsor(s): National Aeronautics and Space Administration (NASA)—Education Office
Description: The NASA Kids page features games, stories, and activities related to space

and science. It also has information on current NASA missions.

The alternate URL above links to the NASA For Students page, which has sections for students in grades K–4, 5–8, 9–12, and postsecondary levels. Both the Kids page and the For Students page are part of a comprehensive NASA Education website at http://education.nasa.gov/home/ .

This site and the central NASA education site are rich sources of material for students and teachers.

NIEHS Kids' Pages
www.niehs.nih.gov/kids/home.htm
Sponsor(s): National Institutes of Health (NIH)—National Institute of Environmental Health Sciences (NIEHS)
Description: This Kids page from the NIEHS includes sections such as Games and Activities, Color Our World, and Sing-Along Songs. It also has a large glossary (What's that Word?) and a collection of stories.

NLS Kids Zone
www.loc.gov/nls/children/
Sponsor(s): Library of Congress—National Library Services for the Blind and Physically Handicapped (NLS)
Description: This website for kids is designed to be used with text-based browsers, such as Lynx, frequently used by blind readers. It recommends audio, Braille, and print/Braille books for children.

NRC: Students' Corner
www.nrc.gov/reading-rm/basic-ref/students.html
Sponsor: Nuclear Regulatory Commission (NRC)
Description: The NRC student's website explains everything from what nuclear energy is, to emergency planning, to radioactive waste. It also has a section for teachers' lesson plans.

NROjr.GOV
www.nrojr.gov/
Sponsor(s): Defense Department—National Reconnaissance Office (NRO)
Description: The NRO kids' page features games and activities with a satellite and space theme. With content including simple online coloring pages, stories, and music, it is aimed at the younger set.

Patent and Trademark Office Kids' Page
www.uspto.gov/go/kids/
Sponsor(s): Commerce Department—Patent and Trademark Office (PTO)
Description: The PTO website offers children's contests, games, and puzzles having to do with creativity, invention, and the operations of the PTO. The site has sections designed for students in grades K–6 and 6–12, as well as information for parents, teachers, and coaches.

Peace Corps Kids' World
www.peacecorps.gov/kids/
Sponsor: Peace Corps
Description: The Peace Corps offers this kids' page, with sections including: What is the Peace Corps?; Make a Difference; Explore the World; Tell Me a Story; and Food, Friends, and Fun. This site mainly provides information about the Peace Corps program. Some resources on foreign countries are listed in the Explore the World and Food, Friends, and Fun sections.

Sci4Kids
www.ars.usda.gov/is/kids/
Alternate URL:
www.ars.usda.gov/is/espanol/kids/
Sponsor(s): Agriculture Department (USDA)—Agricultural Research Service (ARS)
Description: Sci4Kids is designed for children between the ages of 8 and 13. With a colorful all-graphics menu, it shows how scientific research affects many areas of life. The site includes information about careers in science. The alternate URL links to the Spanish-language version of the site.

ScienceLab
www.osti.gov/sciencelab/

Sponsor(s): Energy Department—Scientific and Technical Information Office
Description: ScienceLab links to student resources at government and other websites. Major sections for students include Elementary Lab, Middle School Lab, High School Lab, and Experiments. The site also has a Teachers' Lab section and sections about science careers, competitions, and summer camps.

Smithsonian Education
www.smithsonianeducation.org/students/
Sponsor: Smithsonian Institution
Description: The Smithsonian website for kids and students features themed IdeaLabs called Sizing up the Universe, Walking on the Moon, and Digging for Answers. The At the Smithsonian section links to pages of interest to kids from many Smithsonian websites. More activities are organized under the topics of art, science and nature, history and culture, and people and places.

Much of the content will be of interest to students in the upper grades through high school and their parents. The site will be particularly useful for kids preparing to visit Smithsonian museums.

Space Place
spaceplace.jpl.nasa.gov/spacepl.htm
Alternate URL: spaceplace.jpl.nasa.gov/sp/kids/index.shtml
Sponsor(s): National Aeronautics and Space Administration (NASA)—Jet Propulsion Laboratory (JPL)
Description: Space Place is full of games, projects, and animations relating to earth and space science. The Teachers' Corner has classroom activity articles. The site has a Spanish-language version available; this can be linked from the top of the home page or directly accessed at the alternate URL listed above.

State Facts for Children
www.census.gov/schools/facts/
Sponsor(s): Commerce Department—Economics and Statistics Administration (ESA)—Census Bureau
Description: A map of the United States serves as a menu for basic Census statistics, history, and trivia concerning each of the states, Puerto Rico, and the District of Columbia.

Stop Bullying Now
www.stopbullying.gov/
Sponsor(s): Health and Human Services Department—Health Resources and Services Administration (HRSA)
Description: This site has extensive information and a variety of activities for kids about dealing with bullying behavior. This site has information on preventing bullying and responding to bullying. There is a collection of videos and a section on cyberbullying.

ToxMystery
toxmystery.nlm.nih.gov/
Sponsor(s): National Institutes of Health (NIH)—National Library of Medicine (NLM)
Description: ToxMystery is an interactive game designed to teach kids about dangerous household substances. The site includes sections for parents and teachers, and has a version in Spanish and a text version.

United States Mint's Site for Kids
www.usmint.gov/kids/
Sponsor(s): Treasury Department—United States Mint
Description: This site is alternatively called H.I.P. (History in Your Pocket)/Pocket Change. It features games and activities to teach children about the history of coins, coins around the world, and coin collecting. It also includes a section for teachers.

United We Serve
www.serve.gov/
Sponsor: Corporation for National and Community Service
Description: This United We Serve page has information for kids, youth, parents, and teachers—all focused on volunteering. The Toolkits section includes resources for teachers.

USFA Kidswww.usfa.fema.gov/kids/flash.shtm
Sponsor(s): Homeland Security Department—Federal Emergency Management Agency (FEMA)—U.S. Fire Administration
Description: USFA Kids has information on home fire safety, smoke alarms, and escaping from fire. It includes coloring pages and a Hazard House game. The section for parents and teachers includes lesson plans and downloadable activity sheets.

VA KIDS
www.va.gov/kids/
Sponsor: Veterans Affairs Department
Description: VA KIDS has sections for teachers and for grades K–5 and 6–12. The grades 6–12 section includes information about volunteer and scholarship opportunities. The teacher section has resource guides and contacts for finding classroom speakers.

TEACHING

Federal Resources for Educational Excellence (FREE)
www.free.ed.gov/
Sponsor: Education Department
Description: FREE is a central finding aid for roughly 1,500 web-based teaching and learning resources on government and government-supported sites. Resources are organized by broad topics, such as Arts and Music, History and Social Studies, and Math. The Subject Map provides a detailed breakdown of the topics. Announcements of newly added resources are available via RSS feed.

This is one of the most comprehensive finding aids for education-related U.S. government websites. Its primary focus is on K–12 resources.

For Teachers
www.loc.gov/teachers/
Sponsor: Library of Congress
Description: This site focuses on using the digital collections of the Library of Congress in classroom education. It serves as a portal to relevant resources on the library site and also links to professional development tools for teachers.

James Madison Graduate Fellowships
www.jamesmadison.com/
Sponsor: James Madison Memorial Fellowship Foundation
Description: James Madison Graduate Fellowships are for teachers at the secondary school level who wish to enhance their knowledge of the U.S. Constitution. The fellowships are for graduate study leading to a master's degree. This website has more about the program and about the James Madison Memorial Fellowship Foundation, an independent agency within the executive branch.

NCELA—National Clearinghouse for English Language Acquisition
www.ncela.gwu.edu/
Sponsor(s): Education Department—English Language Acquisition Office
Description: NCELA, known in full as the National Clearinghouse for English Language Acquisition and Language Instruction Educational Programs and funded by the Department of Education, is concerned with the effective education of linguistically and culturally diverse learners in the United States. The NCELA website provides direct access to a wealth of information on research, resources, statistics, funding, and programs to assist those working with English-language learners.

What Works Clearinghouse (WWC)
www.whatworks.ed.gov/
Sponsor(s): Education Department—Institute of Education Sciences
Description: WWC collects and reviews studies of the effectiveness of educational programs and practices. It is intended to be a "central and trusted source of scientific evidence of what works in education" (from the website). In addition to the reports and guides, the site provides a database of education program evaluators and technical information on evaluating education programs.

INDEX

INDEX